Kerala
Development Report

सत्यमेव जयते

PLANNING COMMISSION
GOVERNMENT OF INDIA
NEW DELHI

Published by

ACADEMIC FOUNDATION
NEW DELHI

First Published in 2008 by

Academic Foundation

4772-73 / 23 Bharat Ram Road, (23 Ansari Road), Darya Ganj, New Delhi - 110 002 (India).
Phones : 23245001 / 02 / 03 / 04. Fax : +91-11-23245005. E-mail : academic@vsnl.com
www.academicfoundation.com

Published under arrangement with :

Planning Commission,
Government of India,
New Delhi.

Cataloging in Publication Data--DK
Courtesy: D.K. Agencies (P) Ltd. <docinfo@dkagencies.com>

Kerala development report / Planning Commission, Government of India.
p. cm.
Includes bibliographical references.
ISBN 13: 9788171885947
ISBN 10: 8171885942

1. Kerala (India)--Economic conditions. 2. Kerala (India)--Economic policy. 3. Kerala (India)--Social policy. 4. Human services--India--Kerala. 5. Infrastructure (Economics)--India--Kerala. 6. Local government--India--Kerala. I. India. Planning Commission.

DDC 338.954 83 22

Designed and typeset by Italics India, New Delhi
Printed and bound in India.

Core Committee

Dr. Bhalchandra Mungekar
Member,
Planning Commission,
Government of India

Mr. B.C. Munda
State Plans Division,
Planning Commission

Mr. S.M. Vijayanand
Principal Secretary,
Government of Kerala

Dr. P. Rameshan
Professor,
Indian Institute of Management,
Kozhikode

Dr. M. Sivaraman
Director,
Centre for Management Development,
Thiruvananthapuram

Dr. K.N. Nair
Director,
Centre for Development Studies,
Thiruvananthapuram

Dr. P.R. Gopinathan Nair
Honorary Professor,
Centre for Development Studies,
Thiruvananthapuram

Dr. S. Irudaya Rajan
Professor and Coordinator,
Centre for Development Studies,
Thiruvananthapuram

V.S. ACHUTHANANDAN

CHIEF MINISTER OF KERALA

PHONE : 2333812
: 2333682
FAX : 0471-2333489

MESSAGE

It gives me great pleasure to note that the Planning Commission of India is bringing out the Kerala Development Report in this Golden Jubilee year of the formation of the State.

The report prepared by the Centre for Development Studies with support from the Centre for Management Development, Thiruvananthapuram and the Indian Institute of Management, Kozhikode has succinctly brought out the unique features of the State and traced its course of sociopolitical development. I have also highlighted the problem that the State faces on different economic fronts, particularly agriculture and industry. It has outlined, on the basis of detailed analysis of the prevailing situation, the socioeconomic and political scenario that is fast unfolding. I am sure that this document would be of immense help to planners, policy-makers and development managers.

(V.S. Achuthanandan)

डॉ. भालचंद्र मुणगेकर
Dr. Bhalchandra Mungekar

सदस्य
योजना आयोग
योजना भवन
नई दिल्ली–110 001
MEMBER
PLANNING COMMISSION
YOJANA BHAWAN
NEW DELHI-110 001

MESSAGE

The Kerala State Development Report has been prepared by the Planning Commission with the support of the State Government.

The Planning Commission has initiated the preparation of State Development Reports (SDRs) in coordination with the State Governments. Over the Tenth Plan period, it is proposed to cover a majority of the States in the country. The main purpose for preparing the SDRs is to provide a quality reference document on the development profile of individual States and the policy alternatives and strategies available for accelerating growth with distributive justice.

The present report takes stock of the resources available in Kerala and provides a road map for achieving a higher level of growth. It is intended to be an analytical report to serve as a policy advocacy document at the State level. The Report is expected to get integrated into the planning process of the State. As an official report of the Planning Commission, it will be widely disseminated as a public document.

I hope the Report will be useful for the State Government, non-governmental organisations and others concerned with the formulation and implementation of the plans and policies oriented towards achieving a better quality of life for the people of the State.

I would like to place on record my deep appreciation of the significant contribution to this report made by the Director and staff of the Centre for Development Studies, Thiruvananthapuram.

(Dr. Bhalchandra Mungekar)

Contents

...CONTD. ...

List of Tables, Figures and Boxes

Tables

Figures

Boxes

Preface and Acknowledgements

The request of the Planning Commission for the preparation of the State Development Report was received by the State Planning Board of Kerala as early as in 2002. The Planning Board thereupon convened a meeting in which representatives of the Centre for Development Studies (CDS); the Centre for Management Development (CMD), Thiruvananthapuram and the Indian Institute of Management (IIM), Kozhikode; attended. It was decided at that meeting that CDS would be the nodal agency in the preparation of the Report and that CMD and IIM would participate and collaborate in the preparation of reports on the various topics selected. The important areas on which the Report should pay specific attention were also discussed and decided upon at that meeting. The Director of CDS was requested to act as the coordinator of the task of preparation of the Consolidated Report on the basis of write-ups received from the faculties of CDS, CMD, IIM as well as from external experts invited for the purpose.

Owing to change of personnel of the CDS at its helm of affairs the process of preparation of the write-ups and consolidation of the Report was delayed. Though preliminary versions of various chapters were done earlier, the real task of consolidation of the write-ups received from the various agencies was begun only in 2005. As a first step towards this effort, a meeting of various stakeholders was convened at which the authors of the various chapters presented their contributions for detailed comments. Besides this, the reports were sent for critical comments to external experts, the Member-Secretary of the State Planning Board and the Union Planning Commission. On receipt of detailed comments from all these sources, the authors of chapters were requested to recast their drafts in the light of the comments. The revised versions were received by September 2005. The process of preparing the consolidated Report was earnestly taken up in the CDS in September 2005 itself.

The physical features, the historical background and the sociopolitical processes at work in Kerala are unique, which distinguish the state from its counterparts in the rest of India. The major effort that has gone into the preparation of this Report is therefore the explanation of the path that the state has taken in the past 50 years (since its coming into existence in 1956) with particular reference to its redistribution and welfare policies, agrarian reforms, expansion of its educational and health sector activities, food distribution systems and social security policies. One of the major developments that happened during the 1970s was the beginning of massive emigration flows to the Gulf region. The emphasis of the Report has been particularly on the past two decades during which tremendous changes have taken place in Kerala in its approach to productive sectors, social development processes, infrastructure development and gender attitudes. A prognosis of the development path that the state envisages is also presented.

During the past three decades or so, Kerala witnessed a slowdown of its population growth rates, significant changes in its age structure, decline in the primary producing sectors particularly agriculture, stagnation of its industrial sector and tremendous expansion of its social service activities, importantly trade, commerce, transportation and other services. The chapters that deal with these topics have tried to examine the causative factors for these observed changes and their repercussions on the state economy.

As has been already indicated, this Report is the joint product of a large number of academic experts belonging to the regular and honorary faculties of CDS,

CMD and IIM. The task of coordination of the consolidation efforts was vested with Dr. S. Irudaya Rajan, Fellow, CDS under the overall supervision of the Director, CDS. Dr. P.R. Gopinathan Nair, Honorary Fellow, undertook the task of editing, processing, integrating the individual contributions of the authors of the several topics and preparing the Report. The preparation of the write-ups for the chapters entrusted with IIM was carried under the leadership of Dr. P. Rameshan, Professor, under the overall guidance of Dr. Krishna Kumar, Director and Dr. A.H. Kalro, former Director. The other members of the IIM team included Dr. R. Radhakrishna Pillai, Dr. M. Harisankar, Dr. Santhosh G. Thampi, Dr. P. Syamala, Dr. Uday Damodaran, Dr. S.S.S. Kumar, Dr. P. Nandakumar, Dr. Tapan K. Panda, Dr. Suma, Dr. Saji Gopinath, Dr. Sunil Sahadev, Dr. Suma Damodran and Dr. V.P. Raghavan. The responsibility of preparing the write-up by the faculty of CMD, was with professor G. Suresh under the overall guidance of Dr. M. Sivaraman, Director. He was assisted in the task by Dr. M. Sivaraman, P. Pradeep Kumar, M.N. Pradeep Kumar, R.L. Sabu, K. Padmakumar and Biju S. Narayan. The CDS team comprised Dr. K.C. Zachariah, Dr. P.R. Gopinathan Nair, Dr. P.S. George, Dr. Mridul Eapen, Dr. K.N. Nair, Dr. John Kurien, Dr. M. Kabir, Dr. D. Narayana, Dr. K.N. Harilal, Dr. S. Irudaya Rajan, Dr. Chinappan Gasper, Dr. K.J. Joseph, Dr. V. Santhakumar, Dr. K. Raviraman, Dr. U.S. Mishra, Dr. Praveena Kodoth, Dr. Raghavan Nair, Dr. V. Ramankutty and Dr. Sabu Aliyar. Their contributions are gratefully acknowledged. Shri S.M. Vijayanand, formerly Secretary, State Planning Board has closely kept watch on the progress of this work and evinced keen interest in its preparation and successful completion.

I am indebted to my predecessors Dr. Chandan Mukherjee and Dr. K.P. Kannan, who initiated the work and assigned the task of preparing the individual chapters to IIM, CMD and CDS. My thanks are also due to Dr. John Kurien for coordinating the SDR during the initial stages of its preparation. Let me also express my deep sense of gratitude to all the members of the Committee constituted for reviewing the progress of SDR under the Chairmanship of Shri V. Ramachandran, the then Vice-Chairman, State Planning Board who has always been a great source of counsel and encouragement. A word of special thanks goes to Shri Som Pal, Member and Dr. Renuka Viswanathan, Principal Adviser, Central Planning Commission who were in charge of overseeing the preparation of the SDR of Kerala. The Planning Commission and the State Planning Board gave detailed chapter-wise comments on the earlier drafts, which have immensely benefited the authors in their efforts at revision of the respective chapters. Let me express my deep sense of gratitude to these agencies. I am also extremely thankful to the Administrative Wing of the CDS community under the stewardship of Shri Soman Nair and particularly to Shri K. Muraleedharan, Shri M. Krishan Kutty and Smt. D. Girija for their sincere efforts and cooperation at every stage of the preparation of the report.

Dr. K.N. Nair

Director

Centre for Development Studies

Executive Summary

Introduction

Kerala which lies on the south-western tip of India is one of the small states of India, accounting for nearly 1.18 per cent of its territory and 3.1 per cent of its population. The state came into existence on November 1, 1956 consequent on the reorganisation of states on linguistic basis.

Kerala forms a narrow strip of land along the Arabian seacoast with the Western Ghats on its eastern border, sliding towards the west from the mountain ranges and having three distinct layers of land—the highlands, the midlands and the lowlands. It has a total geographical area of nearly 3900000 hectares. Nearly 28 per cent of the land area is reportedly covered by forests; land used for non-agricultural uses comes to about 10 per cent. The net area sown is around 56 per cent. Forests and dense tree growth in the midland and lowland areas give Kerala an affable climate and protect the region from soil erosion. Forests form the resource base for a variety of industries. Kerala receives copious rainfall of about 3000 mm a year, from the two monsoons which extend from June to November. There exist 41 westward flowing and three eastward flowing rivers, which originate in the Western Ghats. A large number of lakes, backwaters, lagoons and estuaries along with the numerous rivers and their tributaries make Kerala a land rich in water resources and a great tourist destination. Groundwater resources are also rich and bountiful. However, the quality of groundwater is poor due to pollution caused by chemicals and other industrial and agricultural effluents.

Kerala is the leading fish-producing state in India, which employs 12 lakh persons and produces on the average 7.5 lakh tonnes of fish. Kerala's mineral endowments are poor except for China clay, silica sand, lignite and lime shell. The Kerala power system heavily depends on hydel resources. It had a total installed capacity of 2616 MW in March 2004. Kerala has been declared a totally electrified state.

The Malabar region which had been under direct British rule till 1947 and the princely states of Travancore and Cochin had undergone distinctly different courses of development during the British era. The differences were conspicuous in land distribution, land use patterns, education, health, demography and levels of living. In all these respects, the Travancore and the Cochin states had forged much ahead of Malabar region.

Since the formation of the state in 1956, Kerala has striven consistently to bring down the interregional disparities, gone ahead with progressive legislations on land tenures and agrarian relations, brought down mortality and fertility rates and arrested population growth rate, promoted educational growth with significant support to private sector initiatives and expanded and modernised the healthcare sector. In the materially productive sectors of agriculture and industry, Kerala's performance has not been remarkable. It is the process of large scale emigration that began in the early 1970s that has kept the Kerala economy on an even keel and promoted near-revolutionary changes in consumption patterns, housing conditions, educational levels and health status.

Demographic Transition

The growth rate of population has been steadily declining since 1971. At present it is the lowest in India. In terms of the density of population Kerala is one among the top, with 819 per sq. km in 2001. Kerala's sex ratio is unique among the states of India, being the only state which has a population of females in excess of the population of males, with 1058 females per 1000 males in 2001. Kerala achieved universal literacy as early as in 1991. However, its worker participation rates for both men and women are lower than those of all-India.

The vital rates of Kerala such as mortality and fertility are the lowest in India, the crude birth rate (CBR) and crude death rate (CDR) being 16.9 and 6.4 in 2002. All the different components of infant mortality rates are also the lowest in this state. The infant mortality rate stood at 10 in 2002. The child-woman ratios are also the lowest in Kerala among all the states in India. Kerala achieved the replacement level of fertility as early as at the beginning of the 1990s. The total fertility rate (TFR) has declined steeply too reaching the level of 1.7 by 1993. According to the 2001 Census, Malappuram was the only district with TFR above the replacement level.

Health conditions in Kerala have always remained better than in the rest of India, with a widespread network of hospitals and dispensaries in all parts of the state. But the levels of reported morbidity remain high for various reasons including climatic factors, high level of awareness on the part of the population, improvements in living standards and changes in life styles.

By the development of a system of education in which the state government and private agencies have played active roles, education has spread far and wide in Kerala through schools, colleges, professional institutions and 'parallel' colleges. High levels of literacy and higher levels of education among the women of Kerala and the predominance of the educated in the unemployed population have been special reasons for acceleration of demographic transition in recent decades.

Over-politicisation of the population, entry in large numbers of persons from the weaker sections of society in government services, land reforms and other redistributive policies, and wage increases on the one hand and specific programmes such as universal immunisation, universal literacy campaign, the India Population Project III and Gulf migration on the other, have accelerated the pace of progress of the demographic transition process which had set in Kerala several decades ago. The interaction between fertility and mortality declines has become strong in the past few years and led to the quickening of the pace of demographic transition in the state. Official policies of the state in education, family planning and healthcare as well as the socioeconomic changes brought about through redistributive policies such as land reforms also have played a significant role in the process.

The projections of population growth in Kerala indicate that the population size would not exceed 37.0 million by 2051 and that significant changes are likely to come about in age structure, a factor which has significant implications for educational planning, employment opportunities, labour force composition, marriage prospects for women and the problem of the elderly population. The school-age population would decrease, the proportion of the labour force would come down after two decades from 2001, the proportion of unemployed persons in the higher age groups of the labour force would rise, the number of males in the age group 25-29 years would become smaller than the number of females in the age group 20-24 years (who would marry males in the 25-29 years) thus creating an atmosphere favourable for marriageable females, and the problem of the elderly in general and the elderly in the oldest-old age group in particular, would become acute.

Growth and Employment

Economic Growth and Structural Change

In the Kerala economy, backwardness has coexisted with high quality of life, for quite some time. The paradox persists. Growth has in fact taken place, but with serious structural changes along with it. In relative terms, the primary and the secondary sectors have languished and even registered negative growth rates and the tertiary sector has been leaping.

The remittances boom, which began in the mid-1970s, has compensated for the deficiency in domestic production, but has done little to revive and drive the goods producing sectors. Unequal centre-state relations, the type of links with the external world, the high-wage syndrome, labour militancy and the narrow industrial base have been pointed out by scholars as the important causative factors for stagnation or low growth. Another explanation has been the 'Dutch disease effect', according to which, a booming sector would have adverse impact on domestic production, through rising wage cost and drain of workers in other industries to the booming sector. In the case of Kerala, the migration-remittances boom has an adverse effect on sectors producing tradable commodities. Remittances pushed the prices of non-tradables to levels higher than those of tradables making production of the latter uneconomical. In this context, investment would be attracted to sectors of non-tradables. Liberalisation and globalisation have not had the expected advantage in Kerala due to the high cost of non-tradable inputs.

During the 1990s, growth rates were higher in the rest of the states in South India and at the all-India level, than in Kerala. This is true not only for the overall growth rate, but growth rates in the primary and secondary sectors taken separately also. In terms of the human development index, Kerala's performance has been, nevertheless, remarkable.

After recording relatively high growth rates during the 1990s, the Kerala economy has entered a period of stagnation or even decline in recent years. The relative shares of the primary and the secondary sectors have drastically come down. An overall improvement has taken place only in the tertiary sector.

Within agriculture, there has taken place a movement away from labour-intensive annual crops to less labour-intensive commercial crops, whose products are exposed to international competition. Since the beginning of the WTO regime, which began in the mid-1990s, bilateral trade agreements and comprehensive economic cooperation agreement with ASEAN countries have done damage to the Kerala economy, even though their net impact on the national economy could have been positive.

The industrial sector of the state is hamstrung and lopsided with limited capital investment available for modernisation, technological improvements and product diversification necessary to keep up with requirements of the global market. The tertiary sector, which produces mainly non-tradables, is less exposed to international competition. Therefore, a structural shift has taken place towards such activities. This shift has adversely affected the revenue-earning capacity of the Kerala economy. The situation calls for activities that would harness the high human development gains of the state to knowledge-intensive economic sectors.

Employment and Unemployment

Unemployment rates have remained high and work participation rate low in Kerala for the past several decades. Kerala is one among the few states in India in which work participation rates have declined. Structural changes in employment caused by decline or disappearance of several labour-intensive activities such as rice cultivation and traditional cottage industries have led to decline in the work participation rate, particularly of women. Work participation rates of men and women in Kerala were 50.6 per cent and 15.3 per cent respectively in 2001. Wide significant differences do not exist in work participation rates as between urban and rural areas. It was the agricultural sector that was the main source of rural employment while it was the tertiary sector that created the most employment opportunities in urban areas. Unemployment in the state constituted 22 per cent of the labour force at the end of the 20th century, 20 per cent for males and 26 per cent for females.

Educated unemployment is the core of the unemployment problem in Kerala. It was observed that while 18 per cent of the educated men remained unemployed, the corresponding figure for women was 71 per cent, in 2003. About one-half the labour force comprising the educated, belonging to the age group 15-29 years, remained unemployed. Unemployment rates were higher among SSLC and HSE certificate holders than among the professionally qualified, the postgraduates and the higher degree holders. Unemployment rate among the educated was more than two-and-a-half times higher among women than among men. The average period of waiting for a job for the educated was found to be 5.6 years in 2003. The period was longer for persons in the higher age group of 45-49 years. It was lower for the relatively poor and the relatively rich and higher for the middle income groups.

About three-fifths of the educated employed, were in regular employment. Women in employment had a clear preference for public sector jobs. The range of choice of employment for men was much wider than for women. Women had much less spatial mobility than men. Unemployed persons received financial support from their households and their job preference and withholding power remain strong.

Financial Services and Fiscal Reforms

Financial Profile

The fiscal crisis that Kerala has been facing since the early 1980s has attracted serious research attention. Inadequacy of resource mobilisation, failure of public enterprises to generate adequate savings, financial losses caused by tax evasion through several devious methods such as undervaluation of property and proliferation of welfare schemes were some of the causes identified. The methods adopted for financing revenue deficits were also aggravating the problem. The declaration of Kerala as a state ineligible for support for its social services expenditures, by successive Finance Commissions was another reason.

By the 1990s, the fiscal problems of the state worsened. The recommendations of the Resources

Commission, which went into the causes of the problem, recommended the introduction of a value-added sales tax, computerisation of tax administration and prevention of stamp-duty evasion. The Task Force on Tax and Non-Tax Revenue recommended revision of the rate structure of sales tax, professionalisation of the management of public enterprises, increase of the user charges of various government services and introduction of value-added tax.

The major fiscal problems that confront the Kerala government are growing interest burden, increasing salaries and pensions, rising administrative costs, mounting losses of public sector enterprises, poorly targeted subsidies, declining central transfers, non-buoyancy of revenue receipts, etc. Kerala's own revenue constituted only three-fourths of its total revenues in 2003-04.

Kerala has inherent disadvantages of location and population density; it has also acquired notoriety as an investor-unfriendly destination. Kerala has therefore failed to attract industrial investment in sizeable measure in the liberalisation regime. The credit-deposit ratio of the banking sector has witnessed a nose-dive since 1991; in recent years after 2004, the rate has, however, registered a reversal of the trend. Infrastructural bottlenecks have acted as a deterrent to investments. Kerala's share in Central investments has been decreasing during the 1970s, the 1980s and the 1990s.

While the share of tax revenue in total revenues of the state has been increasing that of non-tax revenue has been declining during the past quarter of a century. Excessive dependence on tax revenue has reduced the degree of fiscal manoeuvrability of Kerala. The movements in the relative shares of the different taxes have been divergent: the share of taxes on income fell; that on property and capital transactions increased, and that of commodities and services also increased. The share of non-tax revenue has however declined steeply.

In Kerala, budgetary deficits have been a characteristic feature for a long period and the magnitude of the deficits is much larger than in other states. The gross fiscal deficit (GFD), which constituted 3.57 per cent of the gross domestic product (GDP) of the state in 1980-81, has come down in later years. The GFD-GDP ratio in 2000-01 was 5.62 as against 10.56 per cent in Bihar and 9.14 per cent in Orissa. The proportion of borrowed funds used for financing revenue expenditure went up from 5.28 per cent in 1995-96 to 8.6 per cent in 2003-04.

The predominance of social and community services over economic services is the major cause of revenue deficits and fiscal strains in Kerala. The fiscal situation of Kerala calls for urgent reform and restructuring.

Financial Services

The supply side of the financial system in Kerala comprises banking and non-banking financial institutions, post offices, chit funds, moneylenders, stock exchanges and insurance institutions. Banking institutions comprise mainly scheduled commercial banks and cooperative banks. The demand for credit emanates from business firms, households, government, cultivators and service sector operators.

Kerala has, even traditionally, been a well-banked region. In 2004, Kerala accounted for 5.1 per cent of the total number of commercial bank branches in India, with 11000 persons per bank, as against 16000 persons at all-India. In that year, the state accounted for 4.3 per cent of the total deposits in all the scheduled commercial banks in the country. The per capita commercial bank deposits in Kerala in 2001 were Rs. 13892, as against the all-India per capita deposits of Rs. 9244. Commercial bank deposits formed about 70 per cent of the SDP in 2001.

There are 60 branches of urban cooperative banks (UCBs), 24 branches of scheduled commercial banks (SCBs), 495 branches of district cooperative banks (DCBs) and 1961 primary agricultural cooperative societies (PACS) in Kerala. While the state's share of the number of PACS in all-India came to 1.75 per cent, in terms of deposits the share came to 37.45 per cent in 2003.

In terms of the mobilisation of savings done by post offices, the relative contribution of Kerala cannot be considered spectacular.

A conspicuous feature of the commercial banking sector in Kerala has been the relatively low credit-deposit ratio, it has been maintaining in recent years. The ratio stood at about 48 per cent in 2004, though indications are there that it has gone up since then. Wide interdistrict variations are observed in the ratio. The average amount of credit per account is also much lower in Kerala than at the all-India level. Kerala fares better, however, in the matter of agricultural and personal loans and retail loans. It is in the case of industrial loans that Kerala's position is one of the lowest among the states of India.

The various cooperative credit institutions have remained the important institutional agency for agricultural and non-agricultural rural credit in Kerala. They have performed remarkably well in this function. The recovery rate of loans has been quite high too. It is seen, however, that the commercial banks have met the credit needs of the agricultural sector, more than the cooperative sector has.

The all-India and the state financial institutions, which together cater to the credit requirements of the industrial sector, have evinced a steep decline in their credit disbursals in Kerala in recent years. Kerala Financial Corporation (KFC) and Kerala State Industrial Development Corporation (KSIDC) are the state-level financial institutions that have been quite active in the area of industrial finance in the state. But the disbursals of KSIDC have also come down in the recent past.

In Kerala, as many as 171 non-banking financial institutions are at work mainly in hire-purchase lending. The other constituents of the financial services sector include chit funds and moneylenders. Among chit funds, Kerala State Financial Enterprises (KSFE) is a leading institution in the public sector. Money lending by private agencies is also a flourishing business in the state, the major purposes of their lending being marriages, house construction and healthcare, particularly of the poor stratum of society. Insurance is another financial institution that helps people to cope with unanticipated exigencies and adversities. Insurance penetration in Kerala is one of the highest, among the states of India. It is however a cause for worry that the level of credit creation is low in the state, a factor which may hamper its long-term prospects for growth.

Fiscal Reforms

Sales tax has been the most important source of revenue from state taxes in Kerala. The share of sales tax increased from less than one-half of total tax receipts in 1980-81 to about two-thirds in 2002-03. With the introduction of the value-added tax (VAT) system, some teething problems have arisen such as narrow tax base, multiplicity of tax categories, and exemptions and concessions. To exploit the full potential of VAT, Kerala has to modernise its tax administration through introduction of ICT-based tax administration, motivating tax administrators, plugging loopholes of tax evasion, enforcing efficient monitoring of commodity movements and incentives to staff and to tax payers. Other tax sources than sales tax have to be explored too, such as agricultural income tax, motor vehicle tax and state excise tax.

Non-tax revenue sources, which account for about 10 per cent of the state's own revenue receipts, have some scope for improvement by appropriate policy measures such as taking steps to raise receipts from interest, dividends and profits from public sector corporations and from economic services by raising user fees on social and community services.

Expenditure management has also to be made more efficient, through appropriate arrangements for redeployment staff, introduction of VRS palatable to bureaucracy, and implementation of contributory pension schemes.

Budgeting procedures and practices have to be revamped to enforce the duties and responsibilities of controlling officers, introducing zero-based budgeting and practising outsourcing and leasing out of work in appropriate cases.

It should be possible for the government also to hand over public work schemes to private agencies through build-operate-transfer (BOT) and build-own-lease and transfer (BOLT) schemes. The state government should limit its issue of guarantee on behalf of public sector enterprises with due regard to its financial position and constraints.

Substitution to some extent is possible to convert a sizeable proportion of the state's high-cost loans to low-cost loans. The government should also explore possibilities of attracting private investments into the state. It is also high time that the government thought of creating a debt redemption fund.

The government has also to see that its projections of receipts and expenditures are made on a realistic basis, both in the revenue and the capital accounts. The overall scenario strongly indicates the need for bold innovations in resource mobilisation and expenditure management on the part of the state government.

Agriculture

The agricultural sector of Kerala is dominated by production of tradable commodities dependent on world markets. In recent decades, land utilisation has increasingly tended towards perennial and commercial crops. The average size of operational holdings is small and declining.

While the lowlands of the state are used extensively for cultivation of coconut and rice, midlands have in them a large variety of crops ranging from rice and coconut to pepper, cashew, tapioca and rubber. In the highlands, the important crops are tea, cardamom, coffee and rubber. Kerala receives copious rainfall in most of its territory, even though rainfall is scantier in the southern districts.

The overall cropped area as also the area put to non-agricultural uses have been rising in recent decades. The intensity of land use in the state is extremely high. The size of operational holdings declined from 0.74 hectare in 1966-67 to 0.33 hectare in 1990-91. There have taken place significant changes in the area cultivated, production levels and productivity measures in most crops. It is rice, tapioca and cashew nut that experienced the highest rates of decline in terms of the area cultivated and the production levels attained. The major crops which increased both in area and production have been coffee, coconut, rubber, pepper and ginger.

Farm prices and price parity ratios have gone in general, against farmers, particularly for cultivators of food crops. The relative share of agriculture in the state domestic product has gone down from 56 per cent in 1960-61 to 13 per cent in 2003-04.

Inadequate supply of irrigation water and under-utilisation of irrigation potential have accounted to a significant extent for the decline of cultivation of seasonal crops. Commercial crops such as coconut, rubber and pepper have undergone severe crises due to fall in prices. While coconut and rubber have recovered and are passing through a phase of rising prices, pepper is still in the throes of a worsening price trend, largely due to the advent of globalisation and the relaxation of import restrictions.

The livestock economy of Kerala has made substantial gains in terms of the quality of the breed, output and productivity. However, owing to scarcity of fodder, non-availability of family labour and uneconomic levels of output prices as well as the inflow of livestock products at lower prices from neighbouring states, the livestock economy of the state is facing steady decline. Urgent measures are needed to revive this sector through appropriate policies such as encouragement of organic farming, improvement of services of veterinary institutions and establishment of large commercial cattle farms.

Kerala is a state with abundant water resources, marine and inland. Kerala's share of exports of fish consists mainly of the marine fish sector, which has been continuously on the decline during the past two decades. In the context of the rising mechanised fishing sector, the plight of the traditional fishing community has become deplorable. There is however scope for expansion of inland fisheries, culture fisheries and ornamental fisheries. Enhancement of the productivity levels of aqua-culture and measures for maintaining quality standards are also urgently needed.

The cooperative movement began in India nearly 100 years ago. In Kerala also, it began in the early years of the 20th century. It began as a credit movement, but has diversified into several other activities. At present, there are more than 20,000 cooperatives in the state. The cooperative sector functions under the provisions of the Kerala Cooperative Societies Act passed in 1969, which has undergone modifications due to several amendments passed in later years. The cooperative credit structure in Kerala has two broad sectors: the agricultural credit sector and the non-agricultural credit sector. The former has the Kerala State Cooperative Bank formed in 1956, at the apex level. The share capital of this bank stood at Rs. 2269 lakh, reserves at Rs. 6994 lakh, deposits at Rs. 23676 lakh, working capital at Rs. 84887 lakh and outstanding loans and advances at Rs. 123713 lakh in the year 2003.

Primary agricultural credit societies exist in all the *panchayats* in Kerala, having a total membership of 2.26 crore. Only 46 per cent of PACS made profits in 2002-2003. For meeting the long-term credit needs of farmers, cooperative agricultural and rural development banks have been established. The Kerala Central Land Mortgage Bank which came into existence in 1956 gives loans for minor irrigation, farm mechanisation, land development, soil conservation and rural housing. Non-credit societies functioning in areas such as marketing, consumption, housing, literary endeavours and transport have also come into existence in large numbers.

Cooperatives are organised with particular focus on the welfare of the weaker sections of society including Scheduled Castes and Scheduled Tribes. Cooperatives have established hospitals, dispensaries, transport enterprises, educational institutions, labour contract agencies, women's establishments, and organisations of various types of workers, and provided employment to large numbers.

Cooperatives have not yet become effective autonomous and vibrant institutions. They remain government-dependent and swayed by economic and political vested interests and influence groups.

Industry

The industrial sector of Kerala is relatively underdeveloped. At present it is in a state of stagnation too. In order to reach levels of industrialisation comparable to those of the more advanced states of Maharashtra, Gujarat or Tamil Nadu, within the next decade or so, Kerala's industrial sector has to grow at more than 10 per cent per annum.

In recent years, Kerala's industrial sector has been showing a declining growth rate. During the past 40 years, the number of factories and the volume of industrial output increased substantially; however, capital-intensity of output and the ratio of value-added to productive capital have been on the decline. The industrial sector of Kerala manifests a lopsided structure with its base consisting of a large set of resource-based units; there is a clear dearth of capital goods industries.

It is the traditional industries, comprising coir-making, cashew-processing, handloom-weaving, rubber-processing, tea and coffee-processing, file-making and handicrafts that account for the bulk of the employment generation in the industrial sector of the state. Technological stagnation, rising costs of production, labour militancy and fierce competition have led to the decline in importance of the traditional sector. Changing consumer tastes, and emergence of cheaper varieties of substitute products also have contributed to the decline.

Kerala's public sector performance has also remained unimpressive. Overall employment in this sector has declined. The central sector of Kerala received only less than two per cent of total central sector investment in the country. The numbers of loss-making public sector enterprises have been going up.

Bulk of the industrial exports from the state come from agro-processing industry such as coir, cashew nuts, coffee and tea as well as fish and other marine products. The exports of textiles and software and hardware products face strong competition in the period since WTO regime began.

Since the Fifth Five Year Plan period, plan expenditures under industry and mining were in the range of 9 to 12 per cent. Kerala has remained one of the least attractive investment destinations in the country. The proportion of the employment proposed and FDI approved for Kerala during the period 1991-2002 to the total for India was a mere 1 per cent. The few FDI commitments in Kerala are in IT and textiles.

The district shares of the secondary sector varied widely from 7.2 per cent to 23.6 per cent in 2003-04. In terms of the number of factories and of employment, the districts of Thiruvananthapuram, Pathanamthitta, Wayanad, Kasargod and Idukki remained at the bottom.

Small-scale industrial units are concentrated in the districts of Ernakulam, Thiruvananthapuram, Trichur, Kollam, Alappuzha and Kottayam. Wide disparities existed among districts in the number of medium and large scale industrial units. About 35 per cent of the units existed in the Ernakulam district alone.

A large number of small-scale industrial units exist in the cooperative sector. However, more than four-fifths are in the private sector. A large number of handloom and coir units function in the cooperative sector. The other major sources of support than cooperatives are KSIDC, KFC, KINFRA (Kerala Industrial Infrastructure Development Corporation), HANVEEV (Kerala State Handloom Development Corporation), KITCO (Kerala Industrial & Technical Consultancy Organisation Limited), SIDCO (Small Industries Development Corporation), SISI (Small Industries Service Institute) and Techno Park. The multiplicity of supporting agencies creates confusion and duplication in activities.

The public sector institutions have in general been suffering from several major weaknesses and failed to play a leadership role in the industrial development efforts of the state. Financial institutions have been indifferent to the credit requirements of industrial units in the state. Except for SIDBI and NABARD, the share of financial assistance rendered remained at less than two per cent.

The industrial backwardness of Kerala has continued despite consistent efforts made in the state under the Five Year Plans. The new industrial policies launched under the Tenth Five Year Plan are aimed at infrastructure development, changing of Kerala's labour image, development of traditional industries and the sunrise industries of IT, biotechnology and food processing. The cluster approach is also one of the major new initiatives.

The industrial environment in the country as a whole has undergone significant change since 1991, after the emergence of the WTO system. Liberalisation, globalisation and privatisation have become the reigning dogma. Lowering of tariff barriers on imports, and sanitary and phytosanitary articles, and anti-dumping measures have altered the scene thoroughly. Political factors and labour attitudes are undergoing rapid change. However, a pestering handicap in recent years has been the deteriorating fiscal situation of the state. Kerala's fiscal deficit and public liabilities have reached unmanageable proportions.

Being a state with high population density and acute scarcity of land, Kerala cannot go in for land-intensive industrialisation. Inadequate power supply and frequent power fluctuations pose a great problem.

Infrastructure

Transport

Kerala has a relatively well-developed transport system consisting of a wide network of roads, long railway routes, fair inland waterways and developed air traffic. However, the condition of roads in general and rural roads in particular is poor. The roads are narrow, traffic congestion is intensive and passenger amenities in public transport vehicles quite inadequate. Kochi is one of the most prominent ports on the West Coast of India and Thiruvananthapuram, Nedumbassery in Kochi and Kozhikode have international airports. Narrow roadways and high density of vehicles lead to rising incidence of deaths and traffic accidents year by year.

A sizeable share of the passenger traffic along roadways is handled by the Kerala State Road Transport Corporation (KSRTC). The deteriorating quality of public transport and rising levels of the standard of living have led to a gigantic increase in the number of private vehicles such as motor cars, motor bicycles and bicycles. Pedestrian traffic along roads is also prohibitively high. Public transport may be made more efficient through greater privatisation of motor transport with necessary checks and controls over private operators.

The Road Development Policy of the Kerala government announced in 1999 pays particular attention to alleviating network deficiencies and improving road sector financing, enhancing institutional capacities, reducing accident rates and minimising adverse environmental and social impacts. The components of the Kerala State Transport Project assisted by the World Bank contain construction and non-construction components, road safety plan, institution strengthening plan, road information and road management systems and road-user satisfaction survey.

Inland water transport and shipping are also significant modes of transport in the state. Of this, inland water transport has great potential for development in Kerala, but it has remained in relative neglect in recent years. Railways are on the other hand relatively well-developed in the state. Air transport is a rapidly developing sector, though it has not received its full due in the past in terms of capital investment. Shipping and port services have great possibilities of development in Kerala and the ports at Kochi and Vizhinjam are awaiting massive improvements in the context of development of these regions as Smart Cities and Trans-shipment hubs.

The future of transport facilities would depend on the strengthening and expanding of the existing modes of transport and development of roads and railways and feeder connectivity including north-south corridors.

Power

Kerala has vast hydel resources; only about one-third of these resources have been brought into power-generation. Besides the Kerala State Electricity Board, there exist a few other agencies to facilitate development of non-conventional sources of energy. In order to meet the rising demand for energy, mostly for domestic consumption, the state has turned in recent years towards thermal energy. The state also purchases power from Central generating agencies. Kerala is at present a net importer of electricity. Exclusive dependence on hydro power has led to slow growth of installed capacity.

In recent decades there has taken place an enormous increase in the demand for power in the state mainly due to improvements in the standard of living of its population, a booming construction sector and a thriving market for electrical and electronic goods and appliances. For the past two decades, Kerala has been experiencing frequent power cuts and load-shedding. Electricity is in demand for end uses as well as for use as inputs in production. The demand for power for end uses refers primarily to household use. The demand from the household sector, which had shown quinquennial rates of increase of 75 per cent, has subsided in recent years. Commercial connected load had increased at a compound rate of annual growth of 7.8 per cent till the end of the 1980s. Since then it has fallen.

Kerala has the highest share of household consumption of power among the states of India. The commercial sector in the state is also in the forefront of the states. In terms of energy consumption, the agricultural sector of Kerala is way behind that in the other states. Industrial consumption is one of the highest. The household sector is heavily subsidised. While nearly four-fifths of the consumers are in the household sector, it contributes only about one-fourth of the total revenues from the power sales. Agriculture is also heavily subsidised.

The transmission and distribution system in the state is inadequate, inefficient and wasteful. Even though it is claimed that all the villages in the state are electrified, 40 per cent of the households remain un-electrified. Time and cost overruns have been excessively high in the case of most power projects in the state. Power losses are occasioned by several factors, technical and non-technical. Transmission and distribution losses are on the increase and stand at about 30 per cent. About 70 per cent of the loss has been due to technical reasons and 30 per cent to non-technical reasons.

The wide gap between the cost of production and the selling price of power has led to heavy financial loss. The distribution system in Kerala is characterised by high energy loss, low reliability of supply and frequent interruptions in supply. The financial situation of Kerala State Electricity Board (KSEB) is likely to worsen unless tariffs are increased and KSEB's operations made more efficient.

The power sector reforms lie unfinished in the state. With the objective of bringing additional resources for the capacity addition programmes in the power sector, private enterprises would have to be invited and encouraged to undertake power projects. And KSEB has to be revamped to make it a public limited company to make it efficient, accountable and profitable.

Water Supply

Kerala has been experiencing water shortages annually in recent years for several reasons, environmental, demographic and economic. The potential for groundwater recharge is limited in the state. Salinity intrusion accentuates the problem due to proximity to the sea, along its coastal belt. Over-exploitation of groundwater, indiscriminate sand mining and large-scale conversion of paddy-fields, have intensified the problem of water-shortage in the highland and midland areas of the state.

Though nearly four-fifths of the urban population and about three-fifths of the rural population are supposed to be receiving pipe-water, actual consumption levels are low. Dependence of the population on open wells, ponds and natural streams for drinking water needs is quite high.

The Kerala Water Authority (KWA) is the leading player in the water supply scenario of Kerala. The planning and execution of projects as well as their maintenance rest with KWA. Owing to several technical and organisational handicaps, the efficiency of the KWA has been poor in terms of material and financial management. Owing to continuous increase in capital and recurring cost, decline in allotment of government funds and accumulation of dues to funding agencies such as KSEB and HUDCO, the financial position of KWA has been steadily deteriorating. Several schemes– the Accelerated Rural Water Supply Programme (ARSWP), Accelerated Urban Water Supply Programme (AUWSP), Technology Mission Schemes, Swajaladhara and LIC-aided, HUDCO-aided, and NABARD-aided Water-Harvesting Schemes have been a few schemes under Japan Bank of International Cooperation Scheme, and some World Bank schemes implemented in Kerala in the recent decades. KWA has also transferred a few water-supply schemes to local bodies apart from giving them the responsibility of carrying out and managing new schemes at the local level. The Jalanidhi scheme is designed to give water-supply and sanitation services to below poverty line households in a few selected districts. In this scheme, Beneficiary Committees with at least 50 per cent of its members women were set up to function under Beneficiary Groups (BGs). Some water-supply schemes are owned and operated by non-governmental organisations and voluntary agencies.

Owing to human neglect and wanton misuse, traditional water sources have been polluted; people are increasingly turning to piped water supply even in rural areas. The present water supply capacity is found to be too inadequate to meet the projected demand in the coming decades.

The pricing policy followed in the case of water supply has proved to be inadequate, indiscriminate and iniquitous. Through the schemes operated by BGs have several strong points such as minimum wastage of water, effective source protection, expediency in management, and commitment of consumers, its drawbacks are also several. They include absence of purification of water, non-uniformity in water-charges across schemes, non-repair of declining supply levels and lack of adequate representation in BGs of women and other vulnerable groups.

The challenges that Kerala faces on its water supply front are the reaching out to the uncovered sections of the population and the improving the quality and quantity of the existing schemes. The financial status of KWA is precarious, the consuming public is 'water illiterate' and the pricing mechanism is irrational.

In fine, careful planning, efficient execution, proper maintenance and rational and equitable pricing are the urgent requirements in the water supply sector.

Telecommunications

Telecommunications began in Kerala in 1864 when their first sets of telegraphic offices were begun in Thiruvananthapuram, Quilon and Alleppey. By 1947, all the different parts of the present-day Kerala had posts and telegraph offices. Voice communication came to Kerala in 1923. The Kerala Telecommunications Circle established in 1974 serves Kerala, Lakshadweep islands and Pondicherry. Kerala is the first state in India to automatise all telephone exchanges, to link all exchanges through STD, to provide telephone facilities to all *panchayat* headquarters and to provide public telephones in every village.

The growth rate of telephone connections in Kerala has been steadily increasing, particularly since 2003. Both rural and urban areas are targeted for telephone connections. Teledensity is one of the highest in Kerala among the states of India.

The revenue from the telecommunications sector is one of the lowest in Kerala among the states due to the fact that a major portion of telephone connections in the state is in rural areas in which tariffs are lower. Kerala has a long waiting list for connections, mostly for connections in rural areas. New communications such as Internet, and integrated digital services have been gaining importance in recent years.

The Kerala Postal Circle had 5059 post offices in 2001 with 4183 of them in rural areas. Kerala has significant advantages in international communications, Kochi being an important landing point for major under sea cables carrying internet and international telephone traffic.

The major challenge for Kerala is the provision of cost-effective connectivity to rural areas and accommodating its rapidly rising traffic growth. The Kerala government has declared a Right of Way Policy, permitting private and public infrastructure providers to have the right of way over public properties. The telecommunication infrastructure and services should become capable of playing a key role in balancing the developments through e-education, telemedicine and e-governance.

Education

School Education

Kerala has successfully solved the first generation problems of illiteracy and inadequate school enrolment. School education is widespread between sexes, across regions and among all social groups. Compulsory and free school education, basic education, direct payment of salaries of private school teachers directly by government, reduction of intercommunity and interregional differences in school access, promotion of female education, school-feeding programme, promotion policies and travel concessions to students have been the policy measures through which the state achieved total literacy as early as by 1991.

There exist however interdistrict variations in literacy rates for both the sexes and for the different communities and socioeconomic groups. The literacy rates of Scheduled Castes and Scheduled Tribes remain lower than those of the general population.

The pre-primary stage of schooling is underdeveloped in Kerala. It is the unaided sector that attracts children to pre-primary school more than the government or the private aided sector.

Kerala follows a pattern of four years of lower primary, three years of upper primary, three years of secondary and two years of higher secondary schooling. In terms of infrastructural facilities, Kerala is much ahead of most other states in India.

Enrolment in absolute terms is declining in Kerala thanks to the impact of declining fertility. The decline is observed more in government and private aided schools; in the unaided schools, enrolment has been rising. The rate of decline has been higher at the lower stages of schools and in the southern districts of Kerala. Decline in enrolment has led to the problem of 'uneconomic' schools.

In consequence, the number of teachers has also been declining. It is the number of male teachers that has declined more than of female teachers and in government schools than in private aided schools.

The average size of schools is larger in Kerala than in the rest of the country at all the stages of school. The student-class room and the student-teacher ratios are more favourable in Kerala than in most other states. In recent years, the introduction of computer education in school has received generous governmental support.

The quality of education in Kerala is higher in terms of teacher qualifications, drop out and grade repetition rates and examination results than in several other states. But the examination results conceal the poor academic performance of students, camouflaged through the practice of 'moderation'.

Vocational higher education is well-developed and it offers a variety of subjects of study. However, the performance level of these schools has been poor. Vocational education has to be thoroughly revamped. Education of the weaker sections (e.g. Scheduled Castes) and of disabled children, and science and environmental education also need to be encouraged. Teacher education has to be streamlined further and government expenditure on technical courses and vocational education has to be increased.

Though school education is considered free, costs of education on stationery, reading materials, uniforms, travel, donations, etc. take a heavy toll on the households' resources. The private costs are the highest in unaided schools.

Higher Education

Kerala had remained a relatively under-developed region among the states of India in respect of higher education till about the beginning of the 1990s. The progress made by the state during the past decade and a half has been phenomenal, a period during which the portals of higher education were thrown wide open to private commercial agencies. The growth was marked by the opening up of self-financing institutions in the areas of engineering, information technology, and also medicine. The growth of governmental and private-aided (virtually government institutions in so far as recurring expenditure is concerned) institutions during the period has been low. In 2004-05, there were 7 regular universities and 2 deemed universities in Kerala, with 290 colleges (38 government colleges, 148 private-aided colleges, and 104 unaided self-financing colleges). The total intake was a little more than 6200 students in arts and science colleges, 18400 in engineering colleges and nearly 1200 in paramedical courses. While the overall expenditure per student had increased progressively, the proportion spent on regular tuition fees has remained fairly low, at about 10 per cent. It is seen that in terms of the quality-indicators of the faculty, universities and government institutions stand way ahead of private self-financing institutions. It is observed that while the overall expenditure on education incurred by the government has been declining, the proportion on higher and technical education has been steadily on the increase.

There has been a perceptible decline in the quality of education in recent years. The job prospects of the highly educated persons have also been decreasing in the state. The links between the institutions of higher learning and the world of work and industry have to be strengthened.

Science and Technology

Kerala stands ahead of most other states in India in the supply of technical manpower and science and technology (S&T) institutions including universities. The major areas of activity of the science and technology institutions in the state comprise water management, earth science studies, non-conventional energy research, forest research, biotechnology research, transportation research, Agricultural Research and Mathematical Studies. Several quasi-governmental and non-governmental institutions also are engaged in scientific and technological pursuits. The government institutions come under the Kerala State Council of Science, Technology and Environment (KSCSTE). Most of these institutions have been engaged in Kerala-based research; some of them have diversified their activities to topics of commercial interest also and engaged in consulting and training pursuits.

The government of Kerala included science and technology and environment in its Five Year Plans only from 1974. In absolute terms, the budget outlays on science and technology have kept on increasing; however its relative share has been negligible, which itself has been steadily on the decline. Four institutions in the state–Tropical Botanical Garden and Research Institute (TBGRI), Centre for Earth Science Studies (CESS), Centre for Water Resources Development and Management (CWRDM) and Kerala Forest Research Institute (KFRI)–have been depending substantially on government funds for more than 15 years and consuming three-fifths of the government budget on science and technology. It is high time for these and other S&T institutions to become self-reliant after an initial period of incubation. Besides, it is also necessary for the Kerala government to enhance its allocation to not less than two per cent of the budget.

Kerala has to adopt a two-pronged strategy of increased S&T spending and strengthening research institutions to do applied research and training activities with a view to strengthening the quality of manpower and reducing dependence on government support. In the years to come, Kerala would have to enter new and upcoming fields of research such as nanotechnology and communications technology and develop holistic attitudes to research. Basic research and documentation of research are also areas that cry for greater funding support

Healthcare

Kerala has achieved significant success in reducing fertility and mortality rates and in improving the general health status of its population. The reductions in infant mortality rates particularly neonatal mortality rates are remarkable. The declines have been rendered possible by large scale vaccination programmes against smallpox and other immunisation programmes and expansion of healthcare facilities, institutionalisation of child birth, to mention only a few of the more important factors. The disease profile of Kerala has undergone significant change with the prevalence of communicable diseases falling drastically and diseases relating to life style changes such as hypertension, diabetes, neoplasm and cardio-vascular ailments increasing rapidly. In fact, Kerala now occupies an unenviable position of a state with low mortality and high morbidity levels.

The state has been devoting the major part of its funds for healthcare on developing medical infrastructure (mostly in Allopathy), promoting medical education and encouraging traditional medical systems of Ayurveda, Sidha and Unani. These systems, particularly Ayurveda, have made significant progress in Kerala.

In course of time, the quality of healthcare dispensed by the public sector tended to decline and the public became increasingly disenchanted with it. Thereupon, the private sector entered the scene in a big way. The overall share of the private sector in Kerala is one of the largest, among the states of India. One of the distinct characteristics of the private sector in Kerala is its rural orientation; 80 per cent of the hospitals and 50 per cent of the hospital beds in the private sector are in rural areas.

The health infrastructure under the government has more than 6000 institutions, with medical colleges at the top, general hospitals at the district and *taluk* levels, and numerous public health centres and their sub-centres under them. There are specialist institutions for treatment of diseases such as tuberculosis and leprosy, and for ailments of women and children.

Both the public and the public sectors have medical care institutions and facilities under Allopathy, Ayurveda and Homeopathy. There are however wide interdistrict variations in such facilities.

Medical facilities are utilised by the population widely in all parts of Kerala irrespective of location of residence, income levels, or religious, community or occupational differences.

The cost of healthcare is prohibitively high for the weaker sections of the population. It is found that sizeable sections of the relatively poor sections get pushed down to below the poverty line due to healthcare expenditure. The plight of the poor is all the more helpless since there does not exist any health insurance coverage system in the state.

Food Security

Kerala has long remained a deficient state in food production. It is through imports that the state overcame food shortage. Kerala introduced informal rationing during the Second World War period and the formal system in 1965.

Kerala has stood at the lowest rung of the states of India in respect of food consumption measured in terms of calorie intake, even though some later-day calculations have assigned Kerala a higher position.

Besides foodgrains, other items such as tubers and stems, vegetables, sugar, milk, fish, meat, eggs and oil also constitute important components of the food pattern of the Keralite. Rice is the staple foodgrain in use, while tapioca used to be a major starch substitute. In the past three decades, the area under and the production of food production have drastically declined. By 2001, the per capita production of rice and tapioca fell to one-third and one-fourth respectively of their levels in 1971. The shortfall in domestic production was made good by rising imports with the result of an overall improvement in cereal intake registered since the early 1970s. The practice of consuming wheat products has also increased, even though they account only for less than 10 per cent of the cereal intake in Kerala.

The increasing trend of substituting cereals and cereal substitutes with other items is explained by rising per capita income levels, and changes in consumption preferences and tastes. The magnitude of changes in the food consumption patterns shows significant differences across income groups and between rural and urban areas. Despite decline in the intake of starchy foods, the calorie intake levels have been steadily increasing in the past among all income groups. Though there exist wide differences between the consumption levels of the rich and the poor, the differences have tended to come down. With the diversification of food intake, food expenditure has also gone up due to increase in price levels. Items such as milk, meat, eggs, fish, fruits and vegetables and fatty oils have occupied an increasing proportion in the diet of all sections of the population.

The public distribution system in Kerala comprises school meals programmes, maternal care and care of pre-school children and the general population. The school feeding programmes and the mother and child programmes together account for only less than15 per cent of the consumption of cereals and pulses in the state.

The Civil Supplies Corporation which is in charge of food distribution operates through fair price shops, spread throughout the state. The food distribution system underwent changes in 1997; since then, it works as a targeted system. Subsidised food supply is thereafter limited to households below the poverty line (BPL). The dependence of the BPL households on the public distribution system has increased, while that of the others has declined. The partial withdrawal of the public distribution has tended to generate inflationary pressures in the economy. Private trade in foodgrains has increased too. The state has become, in consequence, increasingly vulnerable to fluctuations in market conditions and to food insecurity.

Ageing and Social Security

The ageing scenario of Kerala is unique among the states of India. Kerala had 10.5 per cent of its population in the age group of 60 years and above as against only 7.5 per cent in all-India. Among the elderly in Kerala, there are 1028 females per 1000 males. The size of the elderly population in the state is expected to increase from 33 lakh in 2001 to 57 lakh in 2021 and to 120 lakh in 2061. In 2061, the proportion of the elderly would constitute 40 per cent of the total population: 6.7 per cent in the age group 60-70 years; 23.8 per cent in the age group 70-80 years and 9.1 per cent in the age group of 80 years and above. While the young dependency ratio (the number of persons aged 0-14 years per 100 persons of the working age group of 15 to 59 years) has been declining, the old age dependency ratio (the number of persons above 60 years of age per 100 persons in the working age group of 15 to 49 years) has been increasing. During the period 2001-2061, the young dependency ratio is expected to decline from 41 to 16; the aged dependency ratio would, on the other hand, increase from 17 to 76. In the old age group, women would be more than men. The cost of the dependency burden of households would be rising quite rapidly in the future.

Migration surveys indicate that the proportion of households which do not have old age persons has been decreasing. The elderly who live in households of their sons or daughters are almost entirely widows or widowers. Interdistrict variations are observed in the proportion of the elderly to total population, with Pathanamthitta, Alappuzha, Kottayam, Ernakulam and Thiruvananthapuram in the lead.

The practice of the elderly living with strangers or non-relatives or in institutions is not common in Kerala.

Kerala is the state that has introduced the largest number of social security and welfare schemes among the states in India. It spends almost three per cent of its annual budget on these schemes. Among the schemes for the elderly, the ones which have the largest number of beneficiaries are Agricultural Workers Pension Scheme, Widow/Destitute Pension Scheme, Pension Schemes for Persons with Disabilities and the National Old Age Pension Scheme. Nearly 12 lakh elderly persons in the state receive financial assistance from the government.

Kerala may be able to meet the financial requirements for running its social security schemes by diversion of some proportion of funds from Education in which primary schools are closed down due to fall in student strength consequent on declining fertility levels and from Family Planning which has nearly fulfilled its major objectives. It is also necessary to increase the rates of pensions appropriately.

Outlier Communities

The two main vulnerable groups in the state are *Adivasis* and fisherfolk. The discussion in this chapter is focused on these two groups. In the first part, the vulnerability of *Adivasis* is discussed in the context of their alienation from tribal land. The second part is devoted to the socioeconomic problems confronted by fisherfolk of Kerala, particularly marine fishing households. It is pointed out that the problems of this socioeconomic group in matters of income levels, educational status, housing conditions and health status are acute and that remedial measures are urgently called for.

Adivasis

Adivasis constitute only 1.14 per cent of the Kerala population. As many as 37 per cent of this number is accounted for by Wayanad, Palakkad and Idukki districts have 14 per cent, 11 per cent and 12 per cent respectively. *Adivasis* consist of several communities and are composed of hunters and gatherers, agricultural workers, shifting cultivators and settled cultivators. Paniyans constitute the single largest ST community in Kerala and come to 21 per cent of the total ST population. The sex ratio among STs is clearly biased against females. Access to land resources remains a concern for them.

Literacy among *Adivasis* is the highest in Kerala, 57.22 per cent in 2001, among the states of India. In terms of the quality of housing and the access to basic education also, the tribals of Kerala are much ahead of their counterparts elsewhere in the country.

The levels of poverty among *Adivasis* have declined among STs in the state, to only about half the percentage for all-India, thanks to agrarian reforms and numerous anti-poverty programmes. But in comparison with the rest of the state population, the poverty level among *Adivasis* is about two-and-a-half times higher. Access for them to medical facilities is also poor. Starvation deaths and diseases such as tuberculosis, leprosy, scabies and sickle-cell anaemia are rampant among them. Though work participation rates are high among *Adivasis*, the incidence of poverty is also paradoxically higher. They do unskilled work and are lowly paid.

Adivasis lands are alienated through lease, mortgage and downright unauthorised occupation by non-tribals. The average extent of land cultivated per tribal household came down heavily from 0.8 hectares in 1987-88 to 0.2 hectares in 1992-1994. All the promises made by successive governments in Kerala about restoration of tribal land have gone unfulfilled. Efforts made by *Adivasis* to assert their land rights have inevitably been crushed and defeated. In the new dispensation of neo-liberal agenda of globalisation, the travails of the tribals have increased manifold.

The funds under Tribal Sub Plan (TSP) have gone unutilised or misutilised and the extent of loss involved is unknown to *Adivasis* or public authorities. The numerous development programmes for advancement of education among STs, have not yielded much positive results; the *Adivasis* continue to get marginalised and deprived. The draft Scheduled Tribes (Recognition of Forest Rights) Bill of 2005 has several positive aspects, but has left a few questions unaddressed regarding the powers to be vested with *grama sabhas*, protection of *Adivasis* against maltreatment by forest officials and the need for obtaining prior consent to undertaking of development projects. Unless the society at large is seriously concerned with questions of redistributive justice, the marginalised sections are unlikely to empower themselves for a struggle for identity.

Marine Fishing Communities

The socioeconomic conditions of the fishing communities in Kerala have passed through vicissitudes—an improving phase during 1956 to 1975, fisheries development without fisherfolk development from 1975 to the mid-1990s and positive changes in economic conditions of fisherfolk thereafter. UNRISD studies conducted during 1979 to 1984, pointed out that poverty in fishing communities could be alleviated through a combined operation of public and private interventions. It was also proved that poverty alleviation was possible through motorisation of fishing crafts, generation of employment, improvement in drinking water supply, improvement in housing conditions and promotion of loan assistance. Large-scale emigration to Gulf countries also helped.

Though per capita income of fisherfolk increased, it always lay behind the state per capita income of the general population. The widening of the difference during the 1990s was due mainly to rising fixed capital costs caused by mechanisation and automation of fishing crafts and gears and the use of non-renewable sources such as kerosene or petrol, for propulsion. While costs were rising, the economic outcomes were dismal.

Literacy rates have in general improved among fisherfolk; but there exist wide interdistrict differentials. While the literacy status of fisherfolk among Christians (in Thrissur) and Muslims (in Malappuram) improved, it remained near-stagnant among Hindus (in Thiruvananthapuram) largely due to the use of *Kattumaram* as a fishing craft in the latter area. Land ownership is widespread. However, among the ownership of households, two-thirds of them owned less then 10 cents of land. The proportion of households without land ownership is the highest in Thiruvananthapuram district.

The poverty of land ownership is the highest in Thiruvananthapuram district. Housing conditions are poor for the fisherfolk. Density of population is the highest in areas in which fisherfolk live, the coastal tract along the Arabian Sea, near to the high-tide line. Housing conditions have marginally improved for the fisherfolk since the1980s. The number of households living in huts declined from 48 per cent in 1980 to 27 per cent in 1990. Health conditions of fisher households remain quite poor. Cases of cholera, malaria, dengue fever and tuberculosis outbreaks are reported from coastal areas. Porous soils and lack of land make construction of sanitary toilets difficult; supply of potable drinking water is also problematic. The levels of food intake of the fishing population are also found extremely low, deficient and unbalanced.

In order to raise the quality of life of the fishing communities it is essential to set limits to access to the fishing resources (an action which has necessarily to be taken by the state) and to lower the costs of fishing by setting ceilings to the outboard HP used by a fishing unit, granting subsidies to encourage use of diesel-run inboard engines and supporting the use of information-enhancing devices.

The following measures are also suggested for improvement of the quality of life of the fisherfolk: (i) priority access to land; (ii) drinking water, sanitation and hygiene education, and (iii) literacy and empowerment. If the real incomes of the fisherfolk were to improve significantly, radical institutional and organisational changes are required. For this purpose, strong political will and collective action are called for.

Migration and Development

Two surveys conducted in Kerala in recent years—in 1999 and in 2004—using the same type of questionnaire, using the same data-collecting agency, employing the same method of enquiry and covering the same sample size of households covering the entire state, have thrown up data that shed light not only on the magnitude of emigration, return-emigration and remittance flows but also on the rates of change that have happened in these and relative magnitudes during the intervening period.

It has been observed that the volume of emigrants increased from 13.6 lakh persons in 1999 to 18.4 lakh persons in 2004 and that the volume of return-emigrants from 7.4 lakh persons to 27.3 lakh persons during the same period. Taking these two sets of figures together it is found that in 2004 there were 26 per cent of the households in the state that directly benefited from emigration and 40 NRKs (emigrants plus returned-emigrants) per 100 households. The proportion of married female emigrants has also increased.

The destinations of emigration have expanded and diversified to encompass North America, Europe and South East Asia. In the Gulf countries, the relative importance of UAE increased while that of Saudi Arabia decreased. Emigration takes place from all the districts of Kerala, though there exist wide interdistrict differences, with Thrissur, Malappuram, Kollam and Thiruvananthapuram at the top and Idukki and Wayanad at the bottom.

In 2004, an amount of Rs. 18.5 crore was received by way of remittances registering an increase of 35 per cent over 1999. Remittances accounted for 22 per cent of the net domestic product of the state and raised per capita income by Rs. 5678, in 2004. Remittances received varied across districts in proportion with the number of emigrants from them. Remittances per emigrant increased substantially in 2004 over their levels on 1999 due to increase in the number of emigrants, increase in their average level of education and diversification of destinations to more prospectful countries. Emigrants brought goods of various kinds in addition to cash. Remittances were used by households for subsistence, acquisition or renovation of buildings, purchase of land and vehicles, education and healthcare of members of the household, marriage of daughters, education of children and acquisition of household accessories, amenities and gadgets. Interreligious and interlocational as well as intereducational differences are also observed in the amounts of remittances received and the patterns of their utilisation.

Emigration has led to vast improvements in the educational levels of the population and significant proportions of their family incomes are spent for this purpose. Healthcare also claims a substantial and rising proportion of household incomes.

Paradoxically, the proportion of gainfully employed persons in the labour force registered a decline. In fact, the rate of unemployment doubled itself during 1999-2004. Increase in the educational levels of the labour force has been a causative factor, the educated and the well-to-do refraining from unskilled, low-paid and hard physical labour. The demand for such categories of workers is met by in-migrant labour from other states extending from Tamil Nadu to West Bengal and Assam.

Migration has improved the household management efficiency of more than a million housewives, led to widening of income disparities, empowered some strong minority sections economically and politically, revolutionalised consumption patterns and rendered the educated indolent. Replacement migration is gaining strength by the day.

Gender and Development

The popular understanding of the high status of women in the Kerala society is founded on conventional indicators of well-being such as education, health and employment. The less examined questions are the mental health of women, crime against women, and political and property rights of women. Recent evidence shows rising rates of crimes against women, growing practice of dowry, and declining property rights of women.

In the educational sector, women lag behind men in professional and technical streams except nursing. The preponderance of women is observed in stenography, dress-making, cutting and tailoring, secretarial practice and data preparation. Work participation rates of women in Kerala are the lowest in India, particularly in the rural areas. Educated unemployment of women is also quite high and it is rapidly rising. Nearly three-fourths of the educated unemployed women have failed to find jobs of their preference. The younger generation among them is withdrawing from work in agriculture and other low status occupations. More than three-fourths of the women workers in manufacturing are found in the informal sector. Women in Kerala have secured a higher share of employment in the organised sector than their counterparts elsewhere in the country. But the worker-sex ratio for women is higher in the private sector. The proportion in the public sector has been declining. The majority of women at work in the formal sector are located at the lower rungs of the employment hierarchy, as teachers, nurses and other paramedical personnel. In the service occupations, they are found as housekeepers, maids, cooks and beauticians. They seldom occupy decisionmaking positions. Occupational mobility is extremely low among women workers. Women are engaged also in unpaid work in household premises, such as tutoring children, kitchen gardening and poultry-farming. Work participation rates of women among the poor including SCs and STs are higher, but are engaged in poorly paid and low status occupations.

Male migration has intensified women unemployment. Health achievements of women consequent on demographic transition are significant. But contraception has remained an exclusively women's domain. The incidence of mental stress is quite high among women. Dowry-related issues are a major cause among the mentally stressed women.

Violence against women, an atrocity rooted in patriarchal structures, is rapidly on the rise in Kerala. Ownership of property and employment status are factors for violence against women. Women's ownership of land is progressively on the decline. The growth of the practice of dowry has also led to the decline of the women's status in the household and in the society. Women's voices are not adequately heard and acted upon even in the new dispensation of decentralised planning.

Ageing has added a new dimension to the travails of women particularly since women live longer than men; there are more widows among the aged than widowers; and women lack, more than men, own sources of income. In this context, educational practices, work norms, employment opportunities, social security practices, property rights, marriage practices and behavioural patterns have to be duly modified to give respect and recognition to women's rights, responsibilities and legitimate status in society.

Tourism

Kerala is recognised as the world's fastest growing tourist destination after Turkey. The proportion of tourist arrivals in Kerala to total tourist arrivals in India increased from 2.7 per cent in 1980 to nearly 10 per cent in 2002. The amount of publicity that the state received from various quarters including the *National Geographic*, the high praise of tourists who visited Kerala and from the marketing efforts of the state government underlie this achievement. Kerala is expected to achieve an annual growth rate of 11.4 per cent and to earn Rs. 569.3 billion by 2013. Tourism receipts account for 14 per cent of the value of exports of the state. Foreign tourists to Kerala form only less than 8 per cent of the total number of tourists to the state. Foreign tourists come mainly from Europe, particularly UK. Foreign tourists spend on the average about two and a half times the amount that a domestic tourist spends (namely Rs. 1764 as against Rs. 682). The foreign tourist stays in Kerala for more than a fortnight while a domestic tourist stays for about five days. Foreign tourists arrive in large numbers during October-March.

The state is found wanting in several infrastructural facilities such as accommodation, transportation, power and water supply. However, Kerala has declared tourism as an industry, set up tourism development agencies, patented slogans and formulated a tourism policy as early as in 1986, the first state to do so in the country. In respect of organisational efficiency and worker efficiency, Kerala now stands ahead of several other states. The state tourism department is the nodal agency for tourism planning, publicity and marketing. It is also involved in human resources development, investment promotion and enactment of legislative measures for tourism promotion. The major agencies involved in tourism promotion in Kerala are Kerala Tourism Development Corporation, Bekal Resorts Development Corporation and Tourist Resorts (Kerala) Ltd., besides tourism promotion councils in all the districts.

A self-employment scheme for tourism promotion has been launched in collaboration with Kerala Financial Corporation. Kerala Institute of Tourism and Travel Studies and Institute of Hotel Management and Catering Technology are two pioneer institutes engaged in training tourism personnel. There exist several private institutes as well. Marketing of tourism is done with a view to promoting tourism and increasing the period of stay of tourists in the state. Marketing promotion is done through travel fairs, advertisements in the electronic media, international seminars and hospitality to writers and tour operators. An action plan for achieving the Tourism Vision for 2025 has been prepared which envisages a 10 per cent growth rate annually in tourism earnings, employment creation, expansion of hotel facilities and development of new tourism products every year.

Ecotourism initiatives have been developed to market the Western Ghats zone as a tourism product consisting of mountaineering, trekking and bird-watching programmes. In the endeavour to promote tourism, the private sector has been assigned a key role. The key constituents of the ABC *mantra* of tourism promotion in Kerala are Ayurveda, Backwaters, and Culture and Cuisine.

With all these programmes in operation, the Kerala and the Central governments together spend only a mere one per cent of GDP on tourism promotion. The allocation needs to be substantially enhanced. Air connectivity to Kerala also needs to be substantially increased. Prohibitive tax rates need to be reduced and taxation rationalised too.

Decentralisation and Local Self-government

The Kerala government launched the people's campaign of decentralised planning in 1996 in its attempt at deepening democracy in the state by augmenting public participation in governance and development planning. It devolved on local level self-government institutions 35 to 40 per cent of the plan funds by way of grants-in-aid. Local self-governments were able to evolve a fairly elaborate methodology for participatory plan formulation and implementation.

Local planning has had to encounter problems of lack of reliable data at the local level and local technical expertise for planning. The Constitutional Amendments (No.73 and 74), the Kerala Municipality Act of 1994, the Sen Committee Report of 1996 and the Amendment Acts of 1999 have been the bases on which local level democratisation was rendered possible in the state. The power of the state to interfere and regulate local level governments was curtailed; the State Election Commission was granted autonomy and powers to delimit wards, and *grama sabhas* were assigned well-defined powers.

The plan grants from the state government constituted about twice the amount of own resources of local self-governments (LSGs). For the vertical and horizontal integration of plans and projects of (LSGs), district-level expert committees and district planning committees were formed.

The preparation of local plans involved identification of problems, search for solutions, prioritisation of projects and project integration. The problems of technical counsel, implementation, maintenance and auditing also had to be encountered.

The methodology of planning has been evolved, field-tested and stabilised. People's participation in the process has been active. Participation of the weaker sections of society such as SCs and STs has also been strong. Participation of women has however tended to decline over time.

Plan funds allotted to LSGs have tended to decline since 1997. As a consequence, disbursements have also been steadily falling. There has crept some degree of laxity into collection of local taxes. The major part of local plan expenditure has been on crop cultivation, animal husbandry, minor irrigation, education, healthcare, sanitation, housing and transport. Field surveys have shown that the quality of all these services improved significantly after the introduction of local level planning by local self-government institutions (LSGIs).

It is however in the productive services sectors that the gains have been the lowest. In consequence, employment generation has been lacklustre and market integration has also been poor. Many development issues lie beyond the scope of LSGIs, such as removal of poverty and unemployment. The architecture of decentralised planning has therefore to be revamped. The global changes and the economic reforms introduced at the national level in recent years have had severe detrimental effects on the regional economy and the state's efforts at decentralisation of governance. Obviously, there are limits to local level participatory democracy and planning.

Governance

Kerala stands ahead of many other states of India in terms of the advances made in e-governance and in developing the ICT infrastructure and IT-enabled services. It has established numerous e-governance agencies like FRIENDS, Akshaya, KISSAN and Click, apart from introduction of computerisation and citizen-friendly electronics in almost all the government departments. However, in terms of efficiency and expediency, the state still remains backward. Kerala has also in place an elaborate grievance-redressal machinery, both administrative and legal as well as financial, consisting of a variety of high-powered institutions such as Ombudsman, Women's Commission, Lokayukta, C and AG audit, and numerous committees of the legislature. Kerala being a highly politicised state, employee organisations and political parties act hand-in-glove with each other; but the situation cannot be described as one that favours individual integrity, work ethics, commitment and dedication. Delays in all aspects of the governance system have been defeating the goals of accountability, transparency, efficiency and honesty in government. Effective mechanisms have to be introduced to improve access to information, to increase transparency of government actions, to ensure accountability and control malfeasance in government and to identify corrupt and inefficient officials. Efforts are also required to take government employees into confidence.

Chapter 1

Geographical and Historical Features

Location

Kerala is a narrow coastal strip on the south-western tip of India lying between 8° 47' and 30" and 12°47' and 40" North latitude and between 74°24' and 47" and 74°51' East Longitude. It has Karnataka state on the north, Tamil Nadu state on the east and south and the Arabian Sea on the west. The state has an area of 39,863 square kilometres constituting about 1.18 per cent of the total area of the Indian union. Kerala is the 17th state in area in the country. The population of the state in 2001 formed 3.1 per cent of the total population of the Indian union. The present state of Kerala came into existence on November 1, 1956 consequent on the reorganisation of states in India on linguistic basis, according to the State Reorganisation Act of 1956.

Geography and Physical Features

Kerala has an extensive coastline of 190 kilometres in length and has only a maximum width of 124 kilometres. It is as narrow as 11 kilometres of width at the southern and northern extremes. The state has the Western Ghats as its eastern border which peaks up to 1800 metres above mean sea level (msl) in places. Its topography slides towards the west from the mountain ranges to highlands just below them up to a level of 600 metres above msl, to midlands up to a level from 600 metres to 300 metres above msl and then on to the low lands which lie between 300 metres and 10 metres above msl. In the lowlands lie scattered numerous backwaters and lagoons. Highlands constitute more than one-fifth, midlands less than 10 per cent and lowlands almost 54 per cent of the land area. The coastal plains and lagoons together account for more than 16 per cent.

Land Use Pattern

The land use pattern of Kerala for the past few decades is given in percentage terms in Table 1.1. The total geographical area is given as 3885 thousand hectares.

TABLE 1.1

Land Use Pattern in Kerala

(in percentage)

Category	*1975-76*	*1980-81*	*1990-91*	*2000-01*	*2003-04*
Total geographical area	100.00	100.00	100.00	100.0	100.00
Forests	27.84	27.84	27.83	27.83	27.83
Land put to non-agricultural use	6.67	6.94	7.65	9.70	9.98
Barren and uncultivated land	2.02	2.21	1.50	0.77	0.76
Permanent pastures and other grazing land	0.51	0.14	0.05	0.01	0.01
Land under miscellaneous tree crops	2.17	1.64	0.89	0.13	0.31
Cultivable coast	2.92	3.32	2.43	1.93	1.82
Fallow other than current fallow	0.59	0.69	0.68	1.07	1.01
Current fallow	0.94	1.12	1.14	1.81	1.82
Net area sown	56.34	56.10	57.83	56.74	56.45
Area sown more than once	20.38	18.15	19.90	21.19	20.15
Total cropped area	76.72	74.25	77.72	77.94	76.60
Cropping intensity	136	132	134	137	136

The net area sown is seen to have been hovering around 56 per cent during the past three decades. Forests are seen to occupy about 28 per cent. Land utilised for non-agricultural uses had been hovering around 7 per cent till the end of the 1980s; however since then, it has steadily risen to nearly 10 per cent. The intensity of cropping does not seem to have risen during the past three decades even though some fluctuations were observed in the decades in between.

Forests

Forests constitute an important natural resource base of Kerala. The proportion of forests to the total land area of Kerala (28 per cent) is higher than that for the country (19.5 per cent) as a whole. Forests and the dense tree growth in the midland and lowland areas together exercise a highly moderating influence on the climate and vegetal cover and give great protection against soil erosion. The importance of forests as the major source of raw materials for several industries and of timber for construction and other uses, is obvious. The important forest products in Kerala include timber, fuelwood, poles, bamboo, ivory, sandalwood and honey. The yield per acre of forests in the state is more than three times the rate for the country as a whole.

Favourable climatic conditions and topographical features have contributed to the luxuriant growth of natural forests and a wide variety of commercial crops grown in the state. Kerala receives copious rainfall from both the monsoons—the south-west and the north-east, which together come annually to about 3000 mm.

The wide variety of climatic and topographical conditions have resulted in the growth of numerous types of forests in the state ranging from the tropical wet evergreen to the tropical dry deciduous. These two categories together account for nearly four-fifths of the forests in the state. Most of the rest of the forest lands are under plantations, all the other categories together accounting for only about two per cent.

Water Resources

Kerala is rich in water resources, both surface water and groundwater. Despite the fact that the state receives copious rainfall, its distribution over the different seasons of the year varies widely and the rainfall itself varies over years. In certain years, rainfall takes a heavy toll in terms of flood havocs and landslides and even human lives. The precipitation of water that falls on the earth is the source of both surface water and ground water resources.

In the matter of surface water, Kerala is endowed richly with 41 westward flowing and three east-ward flowing rivers that originate in the Western Ghats. Among the important rivers which run westwards are Bharathapuzha, Periyar, Pamba and Chaliyar. The east-flowing rivers are Kabani, Bhavani and Pambar.

The fresh water availability of Kerala is 77.35 billion cubic metres (BCM). Nearly 40 per cent of available water resources are lost as run off. The supply of utilisable resources is around 42 BCM as against a total requirement of 49.70 BCM (GoK, 2005).

The ultimate irrigation potential of the state is estimated to be about 25 lakh hectares (gross), 16 lakh hectares through major and medium irrigation projects and 9 lakh hectares through minor irrigation projects. Until the end of 2001, only 4.27 lakh hectares (gross) could however be brought under irrigation. The minor irrigation schemes accounted for about 51 per cent of the total irrigated area.

At the beginning of the Tenth Five Year Plan, there were 18 completed irrigation projects and 7 ongoing projects, which stood at different stages of implementation. The net area irrigated in the state as in March 2004, was 3.81 lakh hectares (gross area irrigated was 4.27 lakh hectares). The major sources of irrigation are wells (29 per cent), government canals (25 per cent), tanks (12.5 per cent) and private canals (1.5 per cent). The contribution made by private wells is significant. Rice continues to be the major crop to be irrigated. Rice is followed by coconut, arecanut, banana and vegetables.

Groundwater resources of the state are rich and numerous, except around the backwaters and the congested coastal areas. The groundwater resources of Kerala are concentrated mainly in the sedimentary aquifers of the coastal regions. The state has roughly a total availability of 6229 million cubic metres of groundwater, of which the gross water draft is 2693 million cubic metres.

Factors like overexploitation of groundwater, deep infiltration of surface water from irrigated fields using chemical fertilisers and pesticides, infiltration of saline soils and effluents from industries affect the quality of groundwater. Paradoxically, Kerala has the lowest surface run off and groundwater recharge of all the states in India (Menon, 2000).

Kerala experiences major flood disasters only rarely, unlike in the rest of India. Yet, the state faced major flood problems on several times in the past few decades:

1968, 1974, 1981, 1986, 1989, 1992, 1994 and 2002. In 2002, 776 villages and 2335 houses were affected by heavy rains and floods. Twenty-one persons were killed by the floods and eight persons went missing that year.

Compared to the national average, Kerala receives 2.78 times more of rainfall; it receives 5 times as much rainfall as Rajasthan and 3 times as much as Tamil Nadu. But owing to its steep and undulating topography, the retentivity of the land is low, resulting in the loss of advantages of having heavy rainfall. With about 3 metres of rainfall annually and with chains of backwater bodies, estuaries, tanks, ponds, springs and wells, Kerala still experiences severe droughts and drinking water scarcity.

Fisheries

Kerala is the leading fish-producing state in India. In all, nearly 11 lakh persons were employed in the fishing sector of Kerala in marine and inland fishing activities during 2003-04, 77 per cent of them was engaged in marine fishing; of the total production in 2003-04, more than 87 per cent was also accounted for by the marine sector.

The state has an extensive coastal belt of nearly 590 kilometres and an inland water spread of around 4 lakh hectares. The exclusive economic zone lying adjacent to the Kerala coast is spread over an area of 36 thousand square kilometres, which almost works out to the total land area of the state. In 2003-04 there were 2.20 lakh active fishermen, of which 81 per cent was in the marine sector.

The number of fishing crafts in the state increased enormously during the period since 1988-89 to 2003-2004, from 34007 to 55501, bulk of the increase being in motorised crafts (from 9914 to 29395 during the same period). The enormous increase in the number of crafts does not seem to have helped in boosting marine fish production proportionately. The potential marine fishery resource is estimated to be 7.50 lakh tonnes as against which the total actual production in 2003-04 stood at 6.08 lakh tonnes.

Minerals

Kerala is little endowed with mineral resources despite the fact that the state has deposits of China clay, iron ore, graphite, bauxite, silica sand, lignite, lime shell and granite. China clay and heavy minerals account for 90 per cent of the total value of mineral production in the state. The reserves of iron ore, graphite and mica may be far too inadequate to form the basis of industrial exploitation on a sustainable basis.

Energy

The Kerala power system includes 18 hydel stations, two captive power plants, two thermal stations, three IPPs (Independent Power Projects), five major inter-state transmission lines, one 400 KV substation and 220 KV substations with inter-connecting grid. The largest proportion (more than two-thirds) of the power generated is from hydel resources, which in turn depend for their supply on rainfall. Thermal power is costlier in the state than hydel power. The total installed capacity in Kerala as on March 2004 was 2616 MW. The Kerala State Electricity Board is the sole distributor of electrical energy in the state, except for Thrissur Corporation and Munnar, where distribution is done by licencees. Programmes for producing energy from wind power, solar energy and bioenergy are also under various stages of implementation. Besides, a few micro-hydel projects are also in operation.

Even though Kerala has been declared a fully electrified state, about 30 per cent of the households still are not electrified. Kerala's per capita energy consumption of about 390 kWh (in March 2004) is the lowest among the states in India. It is one of the indicators of the low levels at which the material producing sectors of the economy, particularly its industrial sector, remains at present for a variety of social, economic and political reasons.

HISTORICAL MOVEMENTS AND ECONOMIC PROCESSES

During the British period, the Kerala State consisted of three administrative units—the Malabar region as a district of the Madras Presidency directly under British rule, Travancore and Cochin as tribute-paying princely states under the imperial control of the colonial government. During the pre-British period, all these three regions had partaken of the same traditions, culture, land tenures and agricultural and non-agricultural productive and service sector practices. But with the advent of the British period, Malabar began to develop land tenures, agricultural systems, trade patterns and social movements quite different from those of Travancore and Cochin. These differences had their impacts on the level of living, inequalities in income and asset distribution, population growth rates and social sector development such as infrastructure, education and healthcare. The traditional cultural and social institutions such as matriliny underwent transformation during and under the influence of the British rule in all the three regions.

The divergent paths of development that these regions pursued had been however the result of the same policies prescribed by the colonial powers, the differences being caused by difference in the administrative setup and in socioeconomic and institutional differences that came to manifest themselves in the course of the 19th and the first half of the 20th centuries.

By the time of India's Independence (1947) and the formation of the present state of Kerala (in 1956), the Malabar region on the one hand and the Travancore and Cochin regions on the other, had reached distinctly different stages of development in education, health status, demographic transition and levels of living.

However, since the formation of the present State, the governments which came into power have pursued policies aimed at bringing a convergence of the levels of development across all the regions through a series of progressive legislations such as the one on agrarian reforms and on education, healthcare and social security. Differences in land tenure have come down, vital rates have become comparable across districts, school and college enrolment has become high in all areas and across all communities (except the outliers) and healthcare and infrastructural facilities have become widespread. The emergence and growth of the emigration flows of Keralites to the countries in South-West Asia have transformed thousands of indigent homes into prosperous families in all parts of Kerala. Under the influence of a progressive political ideology, the successive governments, which came into power in Kerala, have conferred respectability to the toiling masses of yesteryears by continuous increase in their real wage rates and protection of their rights. Technological changes of the past few decades have wrought incredible changes in all walks of life of the average Keralite whether it be in consumption items, dressing styles, communication and transport facilities or the working of the educational, healthcare or official systems. The problem for which Kerala has yet to find solutions are unemployment, industrial backwardness, environmental degradation and general apathy to hard work.

In the sections which follow we present first, the cultural ethos of Kerala epitomised in several writings as the matriliny system and its degeneration in Kerala, the divergent paths which the constituent regions of Kerala had followed during the British period in land tenures, commercialisation of agriculture, educational and healthcare developments, population growth and demographic transition. The role that social reform movements and community organisations played will also be touched upon. In the third part, a brief review of the developmental trends which Kerala followed since 1956 is attempted.

Matriliny

In common parlance, *Marumakkathayam* (Matriliny) is a system under which inheritance is traced through the mother's side. It is believed by many that this system was confined to Nair families. Recent researchers have emphasised, however, that *Marumakkathayam* was a system prevalent among all communities and religions—Nairs, Muslims, Christians and Pulayas. But it was universal among Nairs. Matriliny is supposed to have offered security, identity, and independence to women in Kerala to an extent unknown to their counterparts elsewhere in India. It has been argued that girls, old women and widows did not have problems of non-acceptance or non-protection, under matriliny. After the British rule began in Malabar, the institution of matriliny underwent significant transformation. The custom of the eldest male member becoming the *Karanavan* is, for, instance, an institutional change that the British introduced. The *Karanavan* happened to be the seniormost male on the mother's side. The British also redefined the institution of matriliny on the basis of the English legal conventions: they identified an hierarchy of property rights and legal definitions of tenurial status; they defined the *taravad* as an impartible and corporate unit with inalienable rights on land; and they chose the eldest male member as *Karanavan* on the ground of age and gender, as the individual responsible for managing its economy and making revenue payments.

Though the institution of matriliny underwent changes in its institutional characteristics and lost its hold on society over the late 19th and the early 20th centuries in the face of socioeconomic changes and reform movements, it has continued to mould the habits of thinking of several generations and conferred on Kerala women a unique sense of identity and freedom. It is widely claimed that matriliny has served to create a demand for educational upliftment and social mobility from among the women of Kerala during periods much earlier than the emergence of such developments elsewhere in India and on a much larger scale too (Saradamoni, 1999).

Land Tenures

Till the middle of the 20th century, all the areas of Kerala—Malabar, Cochin and Travancore—had similar land tenures and similar cultivation practices and cropping patterns. But since then, differences began to emerge due to several reasons such as invasion of Malabar by the Sultans of Mysore (1766-1792), the defeat of Tipu Sultan at the hands of the East India Company (1792) and the beginning of the British rule in that region. In Travancore and Cochin also, political changes appeared in the form of British paramountcy and the reduction of the rulers of these two states into tribute-paying princes of the British Empire. Since the developments that followed in the 19th and the 20th centuries till the attainment of Independence of India (1947) were almost entirely on comparable lines in Travancore and Cochin and were distinct from those of Malabar, the discussion of the changes during the colonial period that follows, is confined to Travancore and Malabar (Kabir, 2002).

Malabar

During the Mysorean rule (1788-1792), the Malabar government reached settlements with cultivators disregarding the claims of the *janmis* who had fled to neighbouring countries. And a system of land revenue was introduced for the first time in the history of the region. The British who took over also followed the policies of the Sultanate, but they reached settlements with *janmis* who had by then returned. The British superimposed on the *janmi-kana-maryada* several Anglo-Roman juridical concepts such as that of absolute property rights, till then unknown to the region. All land was thus made the private property of *janmis* in whose hands the ownership of land was concentrated. The British were guided by the motive to squeeze out as much land revenue as possible from land owners.

There also existed a large number of small *janmis* who used to lease in land from big *janmis* The bulk of 'janmom' lands were cultivated by tenants: the bigger tenants known as *Kanomdars* sub-leased lands to tenants-at-will (*verumpattakkars)* who could be hired and fired at will, and who constituted the real cultivators.

The rise in produce prices during the 1830s gave added incentives to *janmis* to resort to rack-renting, eviction of tenants and lengthening of the chain of infeudation. The *moplah* tenants rose in revolt. No legislative measures were adopted till 1887 to improve tenurial conditions except the appointment of a few commissions. The first land reform measure was the Malabar Compensation for Tenants' Improvement Act of 1887, which provided for compensation to tenants in the event of eviction, for improvements they had made on the land during their tenancy. The Act benefited *Kanom* tenants, not tenants-at-will. The Act became a dead letter because of the circumvention of the law by the *janmis*, through the device of *melcharths*. Rents became prohibitively high, as much as 75 to 80 per cent of the net produce, a large part of which was appropriated by intermediary *kanom* tenants. The actual tenant cultivator at the lowest level was most of the times 'left only with straw'.

The Malabar Tenancy Act of 1929 bestowed security of tenure to the powerful *Kanakkars*. The *Verumpattakkars* were left untouched by the Act. During the Great Depression of the 1930s, several *Kanomdars* surrendered their tenancy in lieu of the arrears of rent. The landlords leased out these lands to *Verumpattakkars* who flocked to them in increasing numbers attracted by increasing produce prices, famine conditions during the II World War and the higher demand for land following the influx of peasants from Travancore. Thus, the tenurial situation in Malabar was one of concentration of ownership rights and long chains of subinfeudation during the entire colonial period.

Travancore

In order to raise fiscal resources for payment of tribute to the British, Travancore introduced land revenue and brought about changes in land tenure. By 1757, a large part of the territory which had been the property of chieftains had come under State ownership. In 1812, the state government took over vast tracts of land of 378 major temples and 1178 minor temples. By the second half of the 19th century 80 per cent of the uncultivated land came under government ownership.

A royal proclamation was issued in 1818, promoting cultivation of wastelands and conferring possession rights on the occupants of such lands. By the royal proclamation of 1865, the government declared all government lands under *Pandaravaka pattom* private, heritable, saleable and otherwise transferable property of the cultivators concerned. This proclamation strengthened the revenue base of the state government and created a large number of small proprietors who played an important role in agricultural development. Subsequent pieces of land legislation were enacted in 1867 and 1896, which conferred security of tenure to cultivators of private *janmom* lands. The 1896 Act was amended in 1932 converting all *kanom* tenants of *janmom* lands into proprietors of those lands. The economic status of tenants below the level of *Kanakkars* was improved and made secure. The state also allowed to cultivate uncultivated lands under state ownership, by conferring on cultivators ownership rights. The government forestlands were also thus opened up for cultivation of garden crops and plantations. Besides, the Nair, Ezhava and Vellala regulations of 1925 made *taravads* partitionable and the shares of members saleable or otherwise alienable.

In Malabar, rack-renting and concentration of land ownership killed incentives to improve lands and cultivation. Tenant cultivators at the lowest rung of the land-tenancy ladder groaned under vexatious rents and insecurity of tenure. In Travancore on the other hand land reforms improved tenurial conditions, brought about widespread distribution of land ownership and favoured development of land and agriculture

Agriculture

In Travnacore, land reforms induced peasants to adopt high-valued crops meant for the world market. State policies also favoured commercialisation

In Malabar, the tenurial system discouraged peasants from turning to crops that had long gestation periods or involved heavy capital investment, even though their prices were favourable. Whatever commercialisation happened in Malabar was therefore of the 'forced type' for payment of land revenue, and peasants had to depend on traders and moneylenders and to bring the bulk of their produce for sale in the market. It would appear that the crops exported from Malabar were mostly of 'wild growth' rather than the produce of cultivation.

In Travancore, the state had the monopoly of trade in pepper, the cultivation of which was encouraged by the state. Even the production and marketing of rice without harassment of duties and other levies was encouraged and farmers were allowed cultivation of wastelands without the obligation of tax payment for several initial years. The area under cultivation kept on increasing by reclaiming even forest lands and land under backwaters. In the second half of the 20th century, Travancore, realising the revenue potential of the growth of plantation products, caused by prosperity in Europe, took to provision of land for plantation crops at low and concessional prices for infrastructural facilities such as road and waterways. The land prices fixed for such uses were much lower in Travancore than in the Madras Presidency. In consequence, the area under plantations registered a sharp increase in Travancore. The expansion of the cultivation of cash crops such as coconut, pepper, turmeric, ginger, and lemongrass, was phenomenal. Even the area under rice and tapioca showed large expansion. But in the case of rice, Travancore found that imports were necessary and even profitable rather than production though the state continued to offer several incentives to cultivators of rice.

The momentum of plantation cultivation could not be sustained in Malabar due to 'badness and uncertainity' of the titles that European planters were able to obtain from private individuals. Such unfavourable conditions existed for a long time till the early 1930s when peasant in-migrants from Travancore into the jungles of Malabar began, attracted by the lower prices of land in the Malabar region. However, even by the end of the colonial era, the proportion of area under cash crops in Malabar (38.7 per cent) was lower than in Travancore (43.6 per cent).

The production of cash crops made the two regions oriented towards the external market. Industries that grew in close linkage with agricultural activities (e.g: processing of coconut fibre, producing coconut oil), flourished. While the principal agricultural produce in Malabar continued to be rice, the majority of the labour force who found employment in the production and processing of rice led miserable lives. Travancore had a much more diversified agriculture and a widespread prosperous small-scale peasantry. Employment opportunities outside agriculture were also greater in Travancore (Kabir, 2002).

Population Growth and Demographic Transition

Kerala has remained a region with a density of population much higher than in the rest of the country from very early times. Kerala's population density of 165 persons per sq. km in 1901 was 2.14 times that for the whole of India, namely 77 persons per sq.km. The population growth rate was also much higher in Kerala during the first half of the 20th century than the all-India average. While the population of Kerala increased by 112.5 per cent from 6.39 million in 1901 to 13.55 million in 1951, the corresponding increase at the all-India level was only by 51.5 per cent, from 238.39 million to 361.09 million during the same period. It is interesting to note that while the total population of India underwent an absolute decline during the decade 1911-1921 (i.e. from 252.09 million to 251.32 million) due to epidemics mainly influenza and famine conditions during and after the First World War, population growth rates were relatively high and positive in Kerala during the period. Another unique feature of Kerala was the sex ratio in favour of females. In 1901, the sex ratio of Kerala was 1004 females per 1000 males as against the corresponding all-India ratio of 972. Paradoxically, while the sex ratio in Kerala was getting increasingly favourable to females from decade to decade, the opposite was the case with all-India, as may be seen from Table 1.2 below.

was 43.8 years for males and 44.6 years females as against 29.5 years for males and 32.7 years for females for all-Kerala and 26.9 years and 26.6 years respectively for all-India.

Birth rates must have fallen particularly in Travancore and Cochin, but only marginally, under the influence of the expansion of mass education and rising age at marriage. Falling death rates and high birth rates had been raising population growth rates in Kerala (particularly in Travancore and Cochin) till about the end of the 1950s.

TABLE 1.2

Population Size, Decadal Growth Rates, Sex Ratio and Density: 1901-1951, Kerala and India

Year	*Population (in Million)*		*Decadel Growth Rate (%)*		*Sex Ratio (Female-Male Ratio)*		*Density (per sq.km)*	
	Kerala	*India*	*Kerala*	*India*	*Kerala*	*India*	*Kerala*	*India*
1901	6.39	238.39	-	-	1004	972	165	77
1911	7.15	252.09	11.75	5.75	1008	964	184	82
1921	7.80	251.32	9.16	(-) 0.31	1011	955	201	81
1931	9.51	272.98	21.85	11.00	1022	950	245	90
1941	11.03	318.66	16.04	14.22	1027	945	284	103
1951	13.55	361.09	22.82	13.31	1028	946	349	117

Source: (1) Govt. of Kerala (2004). *Economic Review*, State Planning Board, Thiruvananthapuram, p. 30.

(2) Rajan S., Irudaya (2002). *Kerala's Population into the 21st Century*, CDS, Thiruvananthapuram (Unpublished).

The growth rates of population were higher in Travancore and Cochin than in Malabar, reflecting presumably the relative widespread conditions of penury and ill-health of the masses in the latter; see Table 1.3.

TABLE 1.3

Region-wise Population Growth Rates in Kerala, 1901-1951

Period	*Travancore*	*Cochin*	*Malabar*	*Kerala*
1901-1911	1.48	1.25	0.72	1.11
1911-1921	2.19	1.44	0.81	1.44
1921-1951	2.03	1.82	1.53	1.79

Source: Centre for Development Studies (1975). *Poverty, Unemployment and Development Policy.* New York: United Nations.

The data suggests that the decline in death rate must have been the main cause for the observed higher growth rates in population in Travancore (and Cochin) and that the infant mortality rate during the period was much lower in this part of Kerala than in Malabar. Infant mortality rate was reportedly about 120 (per 1000 live births) in Travancore during the decade 1920-1930 as against the corresponding figure of 210 for Malabar. The expectation of life in Travancore during the decade

The rapid rates of decline of death rates in Travancore and Cochin came about largely under the influence also of expansion public health and medical care facilities together with development of mass education.

Education

The emergence of mass demand for education appeared towards the closing decades of the 19th century primarily in Travancore and to about a comparable extent in Cochin too; but it was limited in the Malabar region.

Commercialisation of agriculture had led to a near-revolution in wage rates and income levels of several communities in Travancore which had in earlier times spent their lives in relative stagnancy and indigence, eking out their paltry existence from conventional and caste-determined avocations in agriculture, artisanal occupations and domestic services. In fact there had existed in Travancore up to the 1860s several obligatory services to be performed by certain communities to landlords, temples and the royal families. In Malabar, where commercialisation was not spontaneous but 'forced' upon the peasantry, the cultivators remained poor and deprived of social and political rights for long periods. In Travancore, where commercialization of agriculture was a 'normal' outcome of the trends of the times, peasants and artisans benefited and social reform movements emerged from within several caste groups. Commercialisation of agriculture also led to greater mobility of people, development of roads and water ways, increase in trade in plantation products (e.g: coffee, tea, and, at a later stage, rubber) and coir, coir mats, copra, etc. Bulk of the benefits from the expansion of export trade accrued to owners of plantations and to the Ezhava community which traditionally specialised in coconut climbing, toddy tapping, processing of coconut and coconut products and trading in them all.

Improvement in income levels, abolition of obligatory services, and increased mobility due to developments in transportation facilities enabled the communities, which had remained for ages socially and economically suppressed, to realise for the first time, the need for fighting for their rights and social freedom. In this fight, the Ezhavas stood ahead of all other communities, being numerically and economically the strongest among the backward communities.

In the meantime, lands were passing from Nairs who had formed the traditional land-owning class in Travancore to other Hindu castes, mainly Ezhavas, and to non-Hindu communities such as Syrian Christians either by way of outright sales or by leasing out. The alienation of land made the maintenance of attached agricultural labourers uneconomical. Instead they began to employ hired labourers. The institution of attached labour began to wane and that of wage labour, expand.

These developments led to the decline of the rigidities of the caste system in Travancore. But in Malabar, the caste system remained entrenched in the prevailing agrarian system. The benefits of the commercialisation of agriculture in that region were appropriated by the big landholders, the majority of whom were Namboothiris, leaving the rest of the population of poor tenant cultivators and agricultural labourers in dire poverty and illiteracy. There were a few *Thiyyas* who were an exception; they had already risen to the status of *Kanomdars* or small landholders and reaped the benefits of administrative favour from colonial officials.

The differential processes of educational expansion that began in Malabar and Travancore have to be examined against this background. As was mentioned earlier, the economic base of the caste system was eroded significantly in Travancore since the 1860s. Yet, caste rigidities and practices were slow to change. The low castes remained deprived of access to public services and public places. Denial of admission to them to public schools continued.

From the 1860s, the government launched an ambitious education programme, following directions contained in the Woods Despatch of 1854 to promote mass education. Commercialisation of the economy also made the modernisation of state administration essential, for which an increasing supply of educational manpower was required. The Travancore state simultaneously supported private initiatives for education also, by introducing a system of grants-in-aid. Large number of indigenous schools were brought under the inspection and control of government in the process of turning them into grants-in-aid institutions.

Since none of the government schools gave admission to children belonging to low castes, it was private schools particularly those run by Christian managements, that entertained them. Ezhavas constituted the major low caste community among Hindus, which made the maximum use of the educational opportunities that schools under Christian managements offered.

Economic development, occupational diversification and educational expansion emboldened Ezhavas to clamour for admission of their children in educational institutions of the government and recruitment of the educationally qualified among them in state government service. This is known as the Ezhava Memorial of 1896. The Sree Narayana Dharma Paripalana Sangham (SNDP) was established in 1903. Sree Narayana Guru's effects were instrumental in transforming the Ezhavas further along the road of development and modernisation. The thrust of the Guru's proposals was 'liberation' through education and strengthening through organisation.

In tandem with the struggle for liberation launched by the Ezhavas, Pulayas, an agrestic slave caste of earlier times, also began agitation for access to education, public services and civil liberties. Ayyankali who spearheaded the agitation, formed the Sadhu Jana Paripalana Sangham (SJPS) in 1907. He began also a school of his own.

Amidst these developments raging among the backward and depressed communities, the power and privileges of the Nair community were steadily getting eroded. Their *taravads* declined and their representation in government services dwindled. And they were losing out in their struggle for entry into state service, to Tamil Brahmins who were specially favoured by the Rao *Dewans* of those days. Nairs realised that their hold on public services could be sustained only by improving their educational qualifications. They formed the Malayali Sabha, in 1884 and opened about 25 schools. In 1913 the Malayali Sabha was expanded to the Nair Service Society as the central organisation of Nairs in Kerala for promoting education, moral values, industrial habits and unity among them.

Christians and Muslims were in the fray of educational expansion. Muslims, who were the latest to join the campaign, remained also the weakest. The Muslim community opened a school in Alleppey in 1915; in 1921, under the banner of the Travancore Muslim Mahajana Sabha, attempts were made for the spread of religious and non-religious education among the Muslims of Travancore.

In Malabar, in the aftermath of the Woods Despatch of 1854, the Madras government drew its attention to education, but the result was only its withdrawal from the scene leaving the initiative completely in the hands of private institutions. Indigenous schools were brought under a system of grants-in-aid. In the process a few Thiyyas managed to get educated, join the professions, enter government service and improve their economic position. Some of them became in course of time *Kanom* tenants as well. But the masses of Thiyyas and *Moplahs* remained tenants-at-will or agricultural labourers or domestic workers, steeped in poverty and illiteracy. Owing to indigence, they had little educational demand either. These conditions remained almost unchanged in Malabar till the end of the colonial period. No mass movement for education came up. Even among upper castes, educational demand remained confined to a few *Kanomdar* and *janmi* families.

In Travancore, government schools remained, by and large, inaccessible to Ezhavas and other 'backward' communities till about the end of the 19th century despite the rising tide of demand from among them. It was after the enactment of the grant-in-aid code of 1894, which provided for grants to special schools for low caste children, that the number of schools began to multiply rapidly. Within a decade, the number of children belonging to such communities rose to nearly 44000 from about 20000 in 1894-95. In 1906-07, the government declared its willingness to admit Ezhava students to government schools. All restrictions on caste basis to admission of children in schools were removed by 1914. In the years since then, the admission of low caste children increased by leaps and bounds. By 1928-29, all community-based restrictions on admission, even to government schools, were removed.

The government of Travancore also introduced several incentive schemes for children belonging low castes. Instruction was made free for all children in classes I to IV from 1908. Muslim students were also exempted from payment of fees from 1907. Girl students of backward communities were given liberal fee concessions.

The number of schools were continually on the increase. Private schools dominated in terms of enrolment. Community organisations such as SNDP and NSS and a very large number of individuals opened schools during the period since 1915. All communities mobilised funds through innovative ways of fund collection from households. Schools became a status symbol to every community. Inter-community competition led to increase in enrolment, mass educational levels, employment opportunities and positions of power. The competition for starting schools developed into a competition for starting colleges and other institutes of higher learning by the end of the 1940s.

The focus of the educational policy in Malabar during the British rule was the promotion of private institutions. Development of primary education, which was in the hands of Local Funds Boards, was poor due to paucity of funds. The number of private schools proliferated however under the lure of grants-in-aid but only from the closing decades of the 19th century. The transfer of the responsibility of developing primary education from Local Boards to the Provincial government in 1904, gave some temporary spurt to the opening of schools.

Proliferation of grant-in-aid schools did not lead to substantial increase in the number of students. The average number of students per school was as low as 91 in 1917-18, still lower in *Moplah* schools (only 60). Only 37 per cent of the children in the school going age were in school in 1924; for *Moplahs*, the corresponding proportion was as low as 19 per cent.

Following the *Moplah* uprising of 1921, the government introduced a system of stipends to *Moplah* children in school; but it was not implemented, on financial grounds. *Moplah* schools however increased in number, but the bulk of them were single-teacher schools or incomplete schools, run by unqualified teachers, see Table 1.4.

TABLE 1.4

Literacy Rates, 1901 and 1951

(in percentage)

	Men		*Women*	
	1901	*1951*	*1901*	*1951*
Malabar Region				
Kannur	20	53	3	28
Kozhikode	19	48	4	20
Palakkad	17	40	3	22
Travancore-Cochin Region				
Trichur	22	59	5	39
Ernakulam	24	65	5	43
Kottayam	32	71	5	55
Alleppey	30	73	4	51
Quilon	19	64	2	43
Trivandrum	23	46	4	34
Kerala	**22**	**57**	**4**	**38**

Source: Nair, P.R. Gopinathan (1981). *Primary Education, Population Growth and Socioeconomic Change: A Comparative Study with Particular Reference to Kerala.* New Delhi: Allied Publishers Private Ltd.

Demand for mass education began to manifest itself only from the 1930s due to some social reform movements among *Moplahs* and the land-owing community of Namboodirs. The new leadership, which emerged from among the Muslims began to realise that the principal means to improve their socioeconomic conditions lay in education. The *Mujahideen* (reformist) movement which began in the 1930s recommended the spread of modern education and a few English high schools and elementary schools were established during the 1930s and the 1940s. The Farook College was established in 1947.

One of the principal aims of the Yoga Kshema Sabha of the Namboodiri youth was the spread of modern education. The legislation of 1930 that permitted partition of *taravad* families of *Moplahs*, Muslims, and Nairs, gave young members of these communities greater freedom to pursue education and defray educational expenses.

From the 1930s onwards, radical political parties and activists also began to foster education among the masses, by setting up of reading rooms, night schools and study classes. In 1937, the government decided to restrict grants-in-aid to complete schools. Universal primary education was decided upon in 1944 for children in the age group of 6-14 years, as part of the all-India policy of post-war reconstruction. The policy declaration did not however bring about substantial changes in enrolment or teacher quality, though the government made bold to declare in 1950-51 that 70 per cent of the children in the school going age of 6 to 12 years had been by then brought to schools.

Thus, we find that the proportion of the government schools was low in Malabar. The state expenditure in education in per capita terms was higher in Malabar than in Travancore, due to the vast increase in the number of small and incomplete grants-in-aid schools in the former. In fact, Travancore was all the time much ahead of Malabar in terms of enrolment and territorial coverage of schools. In Travancore, the government proceeded in tandem with private schools, to open schools in places in which private schools did not exist. The role of social reform movements in educational expansion was great in Travancore while it was small and confined to the Muslim community in the Malabar region. Travancore experienced a rising tide of mass demand for education while demand remained low and incipient in Malabar, due to the widespread poverty of the masses. The gap between Travancore and Malabar in respect of literacy level widened during the first half of the 20th century.

Healthcare

As in the case of education, the State of Kerala had made great strides in the matter of establishing healthcare institutions also, during the first half of the 20th century. But the expansion of healthcare institutions was much more rapid in the Travancore area than in the Malabar region which had remained in a state of stupor due to its land tenures—which were inhospitable to the majority of its population—'forced' commercialisation of agriculture, rack-renting of cultivators and indifferent governance by the district administration.

In Travancore, though the basic conditions for progress were present such as redistribution of land among all categories of the population, reduction in economic inequalities, 'normal' commercialisation of agriculture, development of traditional industries, development of infrastructure, and a wage revolution that raised the income status of the majority of the working population, severe caste discrimination prevailed. These discriminations had deprived the so-called backward communities of their civic rights to go to school, get access to hospitals and clinics, enter government service, go near to places of worship of the Hindus, walk on roads and highways and even to go near, 'higher caste' Hindus. In such circumstances, the 'backward' castes had to wage relentless fights to get access to healthcare facilities, as they had to do in the case of access to education.

Nevertheless, healthcare facilities expanded in Travancore both under the aegis of the state and the initiatives of private individuals and institutions.

Public Health

Public health activities begun under the auspices of the state government had succeeded even by the late 19th century to bring substantial changes in the people's minds towards social and behavioural attitudes to healthcare, particularly towards control and prevention of epidemics, and infectious diseases and promotion of maternal and child healthcare. The Travancore government sanctioned funds for sinking wells for ensuring safe drinking water supply in rural areas, began inoculation against cholera in as early as 1921-22 and launched programmes for chlorination of water in 1934-35. Cholera was brought under control, however, only by 1947.

Smallpox occurred on a large scale in the early decades of the 20th century, in spite of the eradication efforts of the Travancore government which began in the early 19th century through vaccination among school children and government officials. In 1933-34, vaccination was made compulsory for all persons. The state claimed by the end of the 1930s to have brought smallpox under control through 'properly organised public health activities'.

With the first outbreak of plague in 1927-28, the government took prompt preventive action through mass inoculations, rat-hole fumigations and house disinfections. This disease was also brought under control by 1945.

Filariasis was another disease that had been fought against by the government from the early 1920s. Disease control measures were intensified from 1933-1934.

Malaria came to the serious attention of the government only from the early 1930s. Steps were taken for destruction of the malaria-causing mosquito from 1936. Mortality due to malaria was claimed to have been completely eliminated by 1947. Malaria morbidity continued, however, to exist to a small extent even thereafter.

A disease against which the government had fought incessantly from the 1920s, but with only limited success, was hookworm infestation.

The healthcare of women had attracted government attention as early as 1865 when a lying-in hospital was attached to the general hospital in Thiruvananthapuram. Women's hospitals were established in other parts of the state in the 1880s. Educational courses were started by the government towards the end of the 19th century in midwifery, gynaecology, management of children, practical pharmacy and sick nursing, and scholarships were instituted for women students. Yet, even by 1947, only 10 per cent of births were attended to by qualified medical personnel.

Health Education

Public health education programmes began in the early 20th century, through sanitary circle officers. The programmes were conducted through public lectures, with film shows and distribution of pamphlets.

By 1920, there had come into position a large number of government hospitals and dispensaries, in all *taluks*. By 1947, the state had 140 government and 20 private, government-aided medical institutions.

As against the experience of Travancore, Malabar performed poorly in the promotion of public health. The only public health activity in this region undertaken by the government was vaccination against smallpox, in which the progress remained poor due to opposition from the people and the paucity of vaccinators. The preventive measures taken by the government against cholera and other epidemics were poor and ineffective and the agencies functioned indifferently for some period before winding up by the end of the 1930s. The progress of public health activities was stalled by the narrow financial sources of the colonial government.

In Travancore, free access to medical care was confined to only high castes of Hindus and non-Hindus till about the second decade of the 20th century. It was missionary activities that had introduced the western system of medicine in the state in the year 1852. In mission hospitals, access was permitted to all caste groups. Several denominations of Christianity—the London Mission Society, the Zenana Mission, the Roman Catholics and the Salvation Army—took part in the endeavour of starting hospitals in different parts of Travancore. Social reform movements of the various communities were instrumental in building up mass demand for healthcare facilities. Even government doctors raised their voice in favour of providing these facilities to low castes. Government resistance waned slowly and all the caste-based restrictions were removed by the end of the 1920s.

The experience of Malabar was different not due to caste taboos; in fact, the rigours of the caste system had declined in this area much earlier. Strangely, it was the upper castes (typically represented by Namboothiris) that refused to avail the healthcare facilities established under the aegis of the government. In contrast to Travancore, there was little mass demand in Malabar for healthcare facilities.

By 1951, while Malabar had 53 allopathic hospitals and dispensaries, the corresponding figures for Travancore were 158. Besides, the Travancore government also followed a policy of encouraging the indigenous medical system of Ayurveda through grants-in-aid and establishment of Ayurveda schools. In 1913, the British administrators had declared that it was not the policy of the government to recognise the Indian *hakkims* as qualified physicians. The indigenous system of medical care slowly decayed in Malabar (Kabir, 2002).

Political Activity

Political activity on an organised scale began in Travancore only by the 1930s. By the early 1930s radical strains were evident among students and in popular consciousness. The central political question raised was the democratic control of the administration; owing to the rampant communalism of the times, the issue transformed itself into one of communal control of the executive. After the Vaikom *Satyagraha* of 1924—the only political agitation that Travancore encountered prior to the 1930s—a joint political congress was launched under the leadership of the Ezhavas and Christians in 1931-32, the two communities which constituted the main contenders for economic and political power in the Travancore state, along with Nairs. Muslims also jointed the joint political congress. Consequent on the threat of Ezhavas to join Christianity if social discriminations against them were not removed, the government of Travancore granted temple entry in 1937; they were also given communal representation in the legislature in the same year. The Travancore State Congress (TSC) was formed to demand resignation of the *Dewan* and for introduction of responsible government. About 40,000 coir workers struck work in 1938 to protest against the deteriorating conditions in the industry. Agricultural labourers in Kuttanadu also rose in revolt against the introduction of capital-intensive technology, which was reducing their labour opportunities. In 1946, the Punapra-Vayalar uprising broke out against the government, which was brutally supressed.

In Malabar, the Tenancy Act of 1929 produced a compromise between the *de jure* rights of landlords and the *de facto* power of *Kanom* tenants. It was the Guruvayoor confrontation (in the context of the Guruvayoor *Satyagraha* of 1931) that changed the nature of political activity in Malabar. Young activists became disenchanted with Gandhian ideology and methods of struggle. In 1939, the entire Congress socialist leadership with their followers joined the Communist Party of India (CPI), when it was formed. The CPI was the first to begin attempts to break the barriers of casteism and communalism and forge mass organisations of working class. The backward Hindu community became the bulwark of the Communist Party. The Muslims preferred to remain with the Muslim League. (Nossiter, 1988; Pillai, 1999).

From 1888, Travancore had begun to experiment with popular assemblies, which became increasingly democratic by the 1920s and the 1930s. Intensive mobilisation and agitation for communal and caste organisations led to an arrangement of proportional representation or quota in the legislative assembly. While rationalist movements for responsible government became strong in Travancore, Malabar organised a strong peasant movement.

The foregoing discussion has clearly shown that the paths and the rates of development that the district of Malabar under direct British administration and the Travancore and the Cochin states under princely rule followed, had been distinctly different and that they had landed at different levels of socioeconomic conditions by the time the colonial rule ended. In Malabar, the land tenures remained feudalistic, inegalitarian and inequitable and the bulk of the population comprising the Muslims and the suppressed communities remained landless. The large number of simple tenants (*verumpattakkars*) remained poor and highly exploited by rack-renting. The agricultural sector remained stagnant and the agricultural labour classes were steeped in misery. Malabar experienced recurring onslaughts of epidemics such as cholera and smallpox till about the end of the colonial period. Mortality rates were high, expectation of life short and population growth small. Owing to the infiltration of left wing radical political ideas, the people of the area except for a few of the elite and the landowning classes, had become conscious of their civil and political rights and begun their mass agitations against the State's oppression and injustice, which on occasion, turned violent too.

In the Travancore and Cochin states, social economic and political conditions were vastly different. The decline of the matrilineal family system, the land reforms—which resulted in the widespread distribution of cultivable land among all communities and regions—vast developments in agriculture particularly commercial cultivation and plantations, extensive educational development at the school level for both boys and girls and rapid decline in mortality rates were some of the important characteristics that had distinguished these states from Malabar. However, as in the case of Malabar, political awareness of rights and privileges of all citizens irrespective of caste or economic status had reached high levels in these states as well. In fact, the Temple Entry Proclamation of Travancore in 1937 and the mass agitations which began from the 1930s for the establishment of Responsible Government in Travancore, reflected the awakening of the political scene. The *Punnapra Vayalar* agitation of 1946 waged by agricultural labourers and factory workers marked the culmination of the agitations, which were being launched by the leftist political parties for ascertaining the rights of workers.

Thus, the whole region was on the throes of a struggle for change, the most important areas of change being land distribution, educational development, healthcare, population control and improvement of the socioeconomic conditions of the working class. The Malabar area which had been lagging far behind in these respects had to be brought on a par with Travancore and Cochin. The dawn of Independence and the ushering in of democracy based on adult franchise gave wings to the people's ambitions and aspirations. It was along these lines that Kerala State therefore has proceeded all through the period since its formation. Some of these processes of change are roughly outlined in the discussion which follows.

DEVELOPMENTS SINCE 1951

Political Development

Since Independence, the three administrative units of Travancore, Cochin and Malabar were brought into the single state of Kerala in 1956, consequent on the 'Reorganization of States in India on Linguistic Basis'. But there was an interregnum during 1949-1956 when the two princely states of Travancore and Cochin were integrated into a single political unit. During this period, Nairs and Ezhavas sought to unify themselves politically under the banner of Hindu *Mandalam*. This was a period of intense communal rivalry when seven governments were brought down. In 1951, the then Minister of Education, Panampilly Govinda Menon, passed a legislation declaring direct payment of salary to all teachers of private aided schools directly by the government, on a par with the rates of remuneration for government school teachers.

One of the major developments in the political front in Kerala during the period since Independence, has been the emergence of coalition politics. Coalition politics consists of alliances formed among political parties based on expediency, to put aside political differences. The coalition partners agree upon a minimum programme, acceptable to all of them. During the pre-Independence period, Travancore and Cochin had political groupings based on caste or community identification. The majority party system of democracy has not worked in the sociopolitical milieu of Kerala.

With the proliferation of political parties formed on the basis of caste and community, coalition politics has come to stay in Kerala. During the period since the formation of Kerala in 1956, coalition politics have most of the time ruled the roost. For instance, it was as early as in 1960 that the Congress Party, the Praja Socialist Party and the Muslim League formed a coalition and ruled Kerala for about two years after which it broke up. In the 1967 elections, a coalition of Communist and Socialist Parties along with the Muslim League swept the polls. In consequence, a Ministry was formed under the Chief Ministership of E.M.S Namboothiripad. The Ministry was quite short-lived and fell in 1969 due to internal bickerings among the coalition partners. The CPI-Congress alliance formed in 1970 remained in power for about six years. The period 1977-1980 witnessed four different coalitions. In 1980 the Left Democratic Front under the leadership of the Communist Party (Marxist) assumed office under the Chief Ministerhip of E.K. Nayanar.

In 1982, the Congress-led United Democratic Front came to power, under a coalition of the Congress, the Muslim League, the Kerala Congress (M), the Janata Party and the National Democratic Party. The coalition rule has continued in Kerala ever since. As was anticipated by political scientists, coalition politics has transgressed the borders of Kerala. Today, it is a coalition of several parties under the leadership of the

Indian National Congress that is in power in the Government of India. In short, Kerala has remained the political laboratory of democratic governance not only for Kerala, but for all the units of the federation of India.

As a result of coalition politics, it is the small splinter groups that have benefited the most. Since coalitions are broken on petty issues, political instability has remained a lingering menace and the economic development of the state continues to be at stake (Pillai, 1999).

Land Tenure

The demand for redistribution of land on equitable basis had been gathering strength in Malabar and also in Travancore and Cochin ever since the beginning of the Great Depression in the 1930s. Mass movements were witnessed in all the three regions calling for radical agrarian change. When the Communist Party of India was elected to power in the general elections which followed the formation of the State of Kerala in 1956, land reform became the centre-piece of the programme for socioeconomic progress in the state.

The Kerala government issued a stay on all evictions of tenants in early 1957 to stall the rising tide of eviction witnessed all over the state, effected in anticipation of radical land tenure reforms on the anvil. Hutment-dwellers, who did not have the legal status of tenants, were also included in the category of tenants, for the purpose of the order. The Agrarian Relations Bill introduced in that year was a comprehensive piece of legislation that sought to confer fixity of tenure to all tenants, hutment-dwellers, crop-sharers and fugitive cultivators. Fair rents were fixed and tenants were given the right to purchase ownership rights by paying an amount equal to not more than 16 times of the fair rent. Ceilings were fixed for the total area of land to be held by family units. Land in excess of the ceiling was to be taken over and distributed among agricultural labourers and others on payment of compensation to the owners concerned on a graduated scale. However, land held by plantations or cashew estates and by religious and charitable institutions were exempted from the ceiling provisions.

Since the proposal aroused great opposition from landowners, a period of political turbulence ensued and the Communist government was removed from office in 1959. The coalition government which came to power in 1960 toned down the provisions and passed the Kerala Agrarian Relations Act. Even this Act could not come into force due to the verdict of the Kerala High court declaring it *ulta vires* of the Constitution of India. The implementation of the Act was delayed even thereafter due to the political instability, which prevailed in the state during 1964-1967.

Though security of tenure for land had been ensured to a great extent in the Travancore region, tenancy continued to be widespread in the Malabar and the Cochin regions. It was only by 1969, after the return to power of a Communist-led coalition, that the amending Bill was finally passed by the legislature and approved by the President of India.

The most important effect of the Agrarian Reform Act is considered to have been the abolition of tenancy and the conferment of ownership rights to hutment–dwellers (CDS, 1975).

Population Growth and Demographic Change

The demographic trends in Kerala since Independence have taken dramatic twists and turns. The state had been experiencing high rates of population growth till the end of the 1950s, particularly in its southern parts of Cochin and Travancore, as has been shown already. It was felt by planners and demographers in Kerala during the 1950s that population growth rates would rise further in the ensuing decades and lead to a population explosion causing irreparable damage to its economy and society. Most researchers were at that time unaware of the various forces at work in the state for bringing down fertility rates along with mortality rates. These forces were triggered by the steady expansion of women's educational status, drastic decline in infant mortality rates and lastly by the introduction of the family planning programmes. In fact, the changes that were taking place in the vital rates affecting population growth attracted public attention only by the 1970s. (Nair, 1974). The consequences of the declining birth rate were already visible in 1974 in the steady fall in the number of children entering the first standard of school each year.

Despite the falling birth rate, the overall population growth rate kept on increasing till the end of the 1960s due to rising proportions of the population in the reproductive age groups, thanks to the high rates of birth during the earlier decades. Population growth rates began on a course of rapid decline since the end of the 1960s, and reached the low figure of 9.42 per cent during 1991-2001 (Table 1.5)

TABLE 1.5

Population Size and Decadal Growth Rates in Kerala and India, 1951-2001

Census Year	*Population (million)*		*Decadal Growth Rate (per cent)*	
	Kerala	*India*	*Kerala*	*India*
1951	13.55	361.09		
1961	16.90	439.23	24.76	21.64
1971	21.35	548.16	26.69	24.80
1981	25.45	683.33	19.24	24.66
1991	29.09	843.39	14.32	23.86
2001	31.84	1027.02	9.42	21.34

Source: Government of Kerala (2004); Rajan Irudaya (2002).

During the half century since 1951, Kerala's population increased by 135 per cent as against the all-India growth of 184 per cent. The sex ratio in Kerala kept on increasing while that at the all-India level was on a course of steady deterioration (Table 1.6).

TABLE 1.6

Sex Ratio and Density of Population in Kerala and India, 1951-2000

Census Year	*Sex Ratio (female per 1000 males)*		*Density of Population (per sq. km)*	
	Kerala	*India*	*Kerala*	*India*
1951	1028	946	349	117
1961	1022	941	435	142
1971	1016	930	549	177
1981	1032	934	655	216
1991	1036	927	749	267
2001	1058	933	819	324

Source: Government of Kerala (2004); Rajan Irudaya (2002).

Population growth rates, sex ratios and population densities have not been widely different across the three regions in Kerala during the latest decade 1991-2001. In Malabar, the growth rates are in general higher than those in Travancore and Cochin regions, a legacy of the pre-Independence period, which has not completely disappeared. The rates of growth of population during 1991-2000 in the three regions were 11.86 per cent in Malabar as against 9.35 per cent in Cochin and 6.87 per cent in Travancore.

It is observed that mortality and fertility rates have declined to very low levels in Kerala, comparable even to rates prevailing in advanced countries. For instance, while the birth rate in Kerala in 2001 was 17.8 the corresponding rate for the USA (for 2000) was 14.3 as against 25.4 for India. Similarly, the death rate of Kerala in 2001, namely 6.4 was even lower than that of the USA, namely 8.5. The corresponding rate for India for the year 2001 was 8.4. Kerala has also reached an extremely low infant mortality rate of 11 by 2001 as against the all-India rate of 66 for the same year.

These changes have been brought about by control of several communicable and chronic diseases to levels far lower than those of the other states of India. The state succeeded to bring under control several respiratory and diarrhoeal disorders, skin infections and gastroenteritis by the 1960s excepting in its coastal villages whose problems of environmental sanitation are still chronic. However, all through Kerala, cancer, hypertension, cardiovascular disorders and diabetes have emerged as major chronic diseases since the 1960s. Kerala has thus come to hold the status of a state with low overall mortality in the midst of high overall morbidity, caused mostly by diseases linked with both development and modernization.

It is likely that in the years to come, the proportion of the younger age group (0-14 years of age) which had already reached a relatively low figure of 26.7 per cent in 2001, would keep on declining to about 21 per cent in 2011, 19 per cent in 2021, 16 per cent in 2031 and 15 per cent in 2041. Simultaneously, there would be a steep decline in the proportion of persons in the working age group of 15 to 59 years from 62.81 per cent in 2001 to 50 per cent in 2051. The most dramatic effect of the changes in the age structure will be reflected in the proportion of the persons above 60 years of age, which would rise from about 10.5 per cent in 2001 to 36 per cent by the end of the first half of the twenty first century.

Education

Educational development in Kerala since Independence has been quite impressive not only in the growth of schools and colleges, but also in their diversification in terms of subjects of study and methods of instruction and evaluation. A most important change that has come about is the wiping out of difference in service conditions and salary scales between the government educational institutions and institutions under the private aided sector. In recent decades, Kerala has witnessed the emergence of a powerful and dynamic private unaided sector, which runs self-financing educational institutions. In the course of these developments, the gap that had been widening between Malabar on the one hand and the erstwhile princely states of Travancore and Cochin on the other, throughout the British period, has been getting progressively narrowed, as a result of a deliberate policy of all the governments, which came to power in the state since 1957. Some of the highlights of the policy interventions of the government are indicated below.

The primary attention of the government during the early years after Independence was bestowed on the rendering of school education compulsory and free. The Kerala education Act of 1959 insisted that the government should provide free and compulsory education for all children of the state within a period of 10 years from the commencement of the Act. It was also stipulated in the Act that the government shall supply noon-day meal, clothing and books and other writing materials to pupils free of cost. The abolition of tuition fees in school was implemented in a series of steps. The Travancore–Cochin state had abolished tuition fees in Standards V to VII even before the formation of the Kerala State. Thus by 1960-61, the tuition at the lower and the upper primary school became free throughout the state. The abolition of fees in the secondary school, which began in 1960-61, was completed by 1969-70. The government made education at the higher secondary stage (Standard XI and XII) free of tuition fees from the year 1991. Interestingly, tuition fees being charged in the government and the private aided institutions at the tertiary stage of education are also kept at extremely moderate levels throughout the state, through a policy of cross-subsidisation.

Efforts made by the government during the 1950s and the 1960s to develop a system of basic education in schools proved to be a disaster because it failed in achieving its goals of diversification, vocationalisation and imparting of work experience to pupils. The scheme was therefore terminated in 1967-68.

The Private Secondary School (PSS) Scheme was introduced in Travancore and Cochin in 1950 for strengthening the private school system. It laid down that the salaries of private school teachers would be paid by the government while the management had to remit 80 per cent of their fee collections to government. Almost all private middle and high schools jointed the scheme by the end of 1955.

The Kerala Education Bill received the assent of the President of India in 1959, but only after a very turbulent period of controversies and agitations. The Bill was introduced primarily to improve the service conditions of private school teachers throughout Kerala. The provisions of the Act underwent some changes in the aftermath of the liberation struggle of 1957-1959; the most important provision that was removed from the Act being the one relating to the obligation for the management to elect teachers from lists supplied by the Public Service Commission.

The educational disparities that had existed between Malabar and the rest of the regions in Kerala prior to 1956 were progressively brought down during the past five decades. One of the basic indicators of educational status is literacy level. Table 1.7 gives the literacy levels in the various districts of Kerala in 2001. It is seen that the interdistrict variations in literacy level remain within narrow ranges.

TABLE 1.7

Literacy Levels by Districts in Kerala, 2001

(in percentage)

District	*Literacy Level*		
	Persons	*Male*	*Female*
Malabar Region			
Kasargod	85.17	90.84	79.80
Kannur	92.80	96.38	89.57
Wayanad	85.52	90.28	80.80
Kozhikode	92.45	9.30	88.86
Malappuram	88.61	91.46	85.96
Palakkad	84.31	89.73	79.31
Travancore-Cochin Region			
Thrissur	92.56	95.47	89.94
Ernakulam	93.42	95.95	90.96
Idukki	88.58	92.11	85.04
Kottayam	95.90	97.41	94.45
Alappuzha	93.66	96.42	91.14
Pathanamthitta	95.09	96.62	93.71
Kollam	91.49	94.63	88.60
Thiruvananthapuram	89.36	92.68	86.26
Kerala	**90.92**	**94.20**	**87.86**

Source: GoK (2005): Table 11.1, Page S-199.

The Kerala government has also followed policies for promoting the educational levels of backward communities and other vulnerable sections of the society through seat reservations, fee concessions, subsidies, lump sum grants, special coaching programmes and reservations for appointment in government services. While male literacy increased by more than 44 percentage points (from 49.8 in 1951 to 94.2 in 2001), the corresponding increase in female literacy was by more than 56 points (from 31.4 to 87.9) during the same period.

In the higher education sector, substantial expansion was achieved only after independence. The development of higher education in Kerala took place in a rapid rate only after the expansion of the school education sector achieved significant progress, unlike in many other states in India. The efforts at expanding higher education comprised opening of colleges, starting of universities, introducing of new courses of study, permitting private appearance of students for university examinations, etc.

The Travancore-Cochin government sanctioned the starting of 17 private colleges during the period 1949-1955. During 1965-1968, the Kerala University, the only general university which existed during that period in the state, established 76 colleges. The majority of the colleges were private, in fact 72 out of 76. In 2004, there were 290 colleges in the state—38 in the government sector, 148 of the private aided category and 104 private unaided category. The unaided category of colleges has been of relatively recent origin, mostly of the 1990s and later since the advent of the liberalisation era. The number of general universities also has increased to four, one each in Thiruvananthapuram, Calicut, Kottayam and Kannur. Apart from these, there now exist a very large number of technical educational institutions including technical universities and research institutes—the Cochin University of Science and Technology, Kochi; 83 engineering colleges, 375 vocational higher secondary schools, 470 industrial training institutes, 59 polytechnics and several commercial institutes, fine arts colleges and food craft institutes (GoK, 2004; 2005).

The University Act of 1969 was aimed at increasing the control of government over the universities and private colleges in Kerala. The Direct Payment Act 1972 provided for direct payment of salaries of teachers and the non-teaching staff of colleges, by the government and unification fees, reservation of seats for backward communities, remittance of fees collected by private colleges directly into state treasury and constitution of selection committees for appointment of teachers in private colleges. The introduction of the private registration system for appearance in university examination was an innovation of the mid-1960s (Salim, and Nair, 2002).

The Kerala Education Commission under the Chairmanship of Ashok Mitra reported in 1999 that general education in Kerala was facing a serious crisis in content, organisation and management. It was urgently in need of a system of people's education that combined equality and experience. According to the Commission, Kerala was promoting two cultures of education, one for the affluent and the other for the poor. The Commission also emphasised the need for a system that dovetails the supply of education and the development of human resources with the needs of the society. The existing conflicts between the government and the unaided private agencies have to be resolved on the basis of the overall objectives and priorities of the society as expressed through the will of the people. The administrative decentralisation process can and should be used for further secularisation and democratisation of education. For achieving these goals, the Commission recommended suitable changes in curriculum, evaluation methods, teacher training, language teaching and inculcation of values (Mitra *et al.*, 1999).

Healthcare

The healthcare sector in Kerala has recorded, as has been the case with the education sector, tremendous progress during the past half a century . The healthcare infrastructure has grown under the three systems of medicine: Allopathy, Ayurveda and Homeopathy. In Kerala there exists at present at least one healthcare institution in each *gram panchayat* (GoK, 2004; 2005). Eighty-one per cent of the institutions are situated in rural areas. The growth of the private sector institutions in the healthcare sector has been enormous during the 1990s and thereafter. The cooperative sector also has a visible presence in the healthcare sector of Kerala. The number of medical institutions, beds and the number of patients treated under the three major systems are shown in the Table 1.8.

TABLE 1.8

Medical Institutions, Beds and Patients Treated, 2003

(Number in lakhs)

System	*Institutions Number*	*Beds Number*	*Patients Treated IP*	*Patients Treated OP*
Allopathy	1278	43619	18.12	401.21
Ayurveda	857	3920	0.47	187.89
Homeopathy	561	1295	0.25	167.50
Total	2696	48834	18.84	756.60

Source: GoK (2005): Table 12.2, Page 298.

Kerala today occupies a status much ahead of those of the rest of the states in India in respect of health of its population. This is reflected in its high expectancy of life at birth, low mortality (including infant mortality) rate, and low morbidity rate caused by water-borne and other infectious diseases. However, morbidity caused by life-style-related diseases is high and on the increase.

Though the demand for healthcare was steadily on the increase, the state government found, after a period of rapid expansion of healthcare facilities in the public sector during the 1960s and the 1980s, that it is impossible to increase spending on healthcare, due to fiscal constraints. Capital spending on public healthcare stagnated since the early 1980s and revenue spending since the beginning of the 1990s. The impact of this resource crunch was a severe deterioration of the quality of the services rendered by government medical care institutions. It is in this context that private medical care institutions began to proliferate. At present, they by far outstrip government institutions at all levels. During the decade 1986-1996, while private medical care institutions grew at the rate of 40 per cent per annum, the corresponding rate in the public sector was hardly by 5.5 per cent. Since 1996, the growth rate of private sector medical institutions has been still higher, though statistics for this period are not readily available (GoK, 2004; 2005).

Agriculture

The agricultural sector of Kerala since Independence has undergone several phases of change: during the 1950s and the 1960s, the major emphasis of public policy in the state was the expansion of rice cultivation; the area under, and the productivity of, rice had been increasing quite rapidly during these two decades; this was rendered possible by the acute shortage of rice in the state, its steadily rising prices and the inadequacy of the performance of the public distribution system. Increase in the area under rice was rendered possible and profitable even though wage rates of agricultural labour were increasing quite rapidly under the wage-bargaining pressures exerted by highly politicised trade unions.

From the beginning of the 1970s, the area under rice production began to decline steadily for several reasons. With the advent of the Green Revolution during the late 1960s, rice supply in the country as a whole increased at a steep rate and the scarcity situation in Kerala quickly disappeared. Zonal restrictions on rice trade were removed and private trade in rice flourished. Ever since then, the price level of rice has remained almost stable. But, the steady increase in wage rates kept on, despite the falling demand for workers in rice cultivation and in the agricultural sector as a whole. The sudden emergence of a situation in which workers and employees of all educational levels and age groups found employment chances abroad (due mainly to the opening up of the Gulf region consequent on the oil price hike in 1973-74), led to a withdrawal of labour despite increase in wage rates. Agriculture began to experience shortage in labour supply particularly for traditional items of work such as tilling, ploughing, weeding and harvesting. There took place an increasing process of shift of land from cultivation of annual and seasonal crops to perennial tree crops such as coconut and rubber and also from agriculture to non-agriculture for utilisation of land for construction of residential buildings, shopping complexes and public roads, etc. The extent of shift that has taken place in agricultural uses is shown in Table 1.9.

TABLE 1.9

Change in Area under Different Crops in Kerala, 1957-58 to 2003-2004

(Area in '000 hectare)

Crop	*1957-58*	*2003-2004*
Rice	766.76	287.34
Pulses	45.10	5.60
Sugarcane	8.73	3.44
Pepper	90.92	206.98
Cardamom	28.19	41.78
Banana and Other Plantain	40.57	107.15
Cashew nut	44.04	88.44
Arecanut	49.71	93.38
Tapioca	213.96	111.44
Coconut	463.27	906.21
Tea	39.92	36.94
Coffee	16.64	84.68
Rubber	99.87	487.40

Source: (1) Dept. of Economics and Statistics (1998). *Statistics since Independence*. Thiruvananthapuram.

(2) State Planning Board (2005). *Economic Review 2004*. Thiruvananthapuram.

The major problems that confront Kerala's agriculture include declining profitability of crops, uneconomic size of operational holdings, shortage of farm labourers, high price of land and large-scale conversion of cultivable lands for other uses (P.M. Thomas in Prakash (ed.), 2004).

Industry

Kerala has remained a non-industrial economy since Independence, thanks to the creation of an anti-investment climate in the state due primarily to militant anti-capitalist propaganda and limitation of investible resources with the public sector. It is seen that though Kerala accounts for 3.75 per cent of the total industrial employment in the country, its share in total fixed capital is as low as 1.69 per cent and its value of gross output a mere 2.19 per cent (GoK, 2004; 2005). It may be borne in mind that Kerala's share in total population is nearly 3.1 per cent. It is noted that the percentage share of the registered manufacturing sector marginally declined during the 1990s. The growth rate in the factory sector is seen to have been however, slightly more positive during the 1990s—the post-liberation decade—than during the earlier decade. The industrial sector is dominated by food processing, rubber, plastic and petroleum products and also chemical products. The other industrial groups are machinery and equipment and paper and paper products. The industrial structure is mainly natural resources dependent. Kerala's share in private industrial investment including foreign direct investment has been extremely low even during the post-liberalisation period, which began in 1991.

The small-scale sector industries including women-led units has been showing impressive rates of growth, since 1980. It is seen that Kerala has great potential in the development of such units.

Emigration

Emigration to the Gulf countries has proved to be godsend to Kerala. It began by the early 1970s when huge amounts of petro-dollars accruing to the countries in the South-West Gulf region began to be devoted to construction activities in infrastructure building and industrialisation. Pakistan was the pioneer country in South Asia to send their nationals in large numbers for taking up work in Gulf countries, to capitalise on the job opportunities, which suddenly appeared. India was not far behind. In fact, India soon far outstripped Pakistan in terms of the total number of expatriate workers in the Gulf region. Within India, it was Kerala that formed the principal supplier of workers to this region and it accounted for 40 to 50 per cent of such workers. The inward remittances received by households in Kerala began as a trickle in the early 1970s of less than Rs. 300 crores; but annual remittances from this area have risen to more than Rs. 18,000 crores by the early 2000s (Zachariah and Rajan, 2004). In the process of sending emigrants for contract work for temporary periods in the Gulf countries, all the districts in Kerala have actually participated even though in terms of absolute numbers—Malappuram, Kannur, Thrissur, Palakkad and Thiruvananthapuram now stand ahead of the others. The emigrants from Kerala have been mostly of the unskilled and semi-skilled categories, the proportion of the highly educated being less than one-fifth of the total. Since emigration to the Gulf region is of a temporary nature of two or three years, a large proportion of the earlier emigrants have returned. The total number of the returned emigrants is likely to be of the order of about a million persons by now as against a total stock of expatriate workers of nearly two million. As a consequence of the inflow of large amounts of remittances, the Kerala economy has witnessed a near-revolution in consumer preferences and consumption levels, economic conditions including housing conditions, and educational levels and health status of its population. The unemployment levels in the state have also been substantially brought down due to massive emigration flows.

The developments outlined in the foregoing discussion have generated several possibilities of further growth and diversification of the economy and society and also thrown up challenges and problems to overcome in the years ahead. Declining agriculture, stagnating industry, growing unemployment particularly of the educated, mounting fiscal deficits, changing global environment and rapidly changing technologies are some of the challenges that the state has to cope with. The nature of these challenges and the state of the economy in these respects are discussed in some details in discussions, which follow.

The Development Vision

The Government of Kerala is developing a medium-term vision of development for the state for the period 2006-2010. The priority areas identified for development are: (1) tourism; (2) inland-waterways; (3) marketing infrastructure; (4) pharmaceutical products; (5) training of paramedical personnel, (6) establishment of exclusive economic zones for NRIs and other investors; (7) fishing, fish-processing and marketing; (8) processing of and value addition to agricultural products; (9) utilisation of space technology for connectivity improvement; (10) enrichment of small scale industries and skill training; (11) watershed development, organic farming and credit marketing and provision of technological facilities for promotion of agriculture; (12) encouragement of traditional industries; and (13) measures for poverty reduction in general. The vision also includes the objectives of revitatlisation of the public sector; strengthening of the process of decentralisation of development and conservation of the environment. This development initiative is known as Kerala Vision 2010.

The Tenth Five Year Plan of Kerala

The Tenth Five Year Plan has a size of Rs. 24,000 crore for the five years 2002-03 to 2006-07 (Table 1.10). The Plan highlights are the following:

Schemes are structured in such a way as to conduct detailed studies of sub-sectors and development areas and introduce correctives.

Instead of incremental allocations, priorities have been fixed on the importance of sectors. More allocations have been made for Information Technology, Tourism Infrastructure, Poverty Reduction and Health.

The Plan gives great importance to employment generation. Strategies and programmes have been incorporated with a view to enhancing skills and creating job opportunities. Substantial employment creation is expected from Kudumbashree, Information Technology and Tourism. Local production potential will be fully exploited through proper watershed management programmes.

Besides the government directly creating jobs, much emphasis is laid on creating incentives and favourable environment for private investment in all sectors of the economy. Higher education, traditional industries and public infrastructure are some of the areas expected to attract large private investment.

Poverty reduction is given the pride of place in the Tenth Plan. Owing to low availability of land to the poor and high incidence of highly educated poor, the state will put in position anti-poverty sub-plans based on planning from below with focus on women's groups who would be networked into organisations at the level of the local government. Linkages will be effected, through a participatory planning process, with departmental and local government schemes, which have a bearing on poverty reduction. Special priority will be given to vulnerable sectors such as Scheduled Tribes, within the anti-poverty sub-plan.

Special attention will be given to the care of the disabled.

Gender issues will be tackled particularly at the local level.

Decentralisation will be strengthened and institutionalised with focus on improving the planning process and strengthening implementation capabilities and role of local governments in economic development.

Information technology will be given importance.

The government will plan and develop infrastructure for tourism promotion. Ecotourism, health tourism and backwater tourism would receive special attention.

Village and small industries will be vitalised to gain for them advantage in national and international markets.

Private participation would be increased in higher education. Only new courses will be started in the Plan. The universities will be requested to introduce reforms and become vibrant centres of study and research with a vision. Autonomous colleges would be established. Quality will be upgraded in school education through local governments.

Standardisation of facilities and fixation of standards for services will be taken up in a big way in partnership between the state and the local governments.

TABLE 1.10

Sectoral Outlays of the Tenth Five Year Plan

Sector	*Percentage*
Agriculture and Allied Activities	4.62
Rural Development	2.09
Special Area Programmes	0.42
Irrigation and Flood Control	3.87
Energy	14.58
Industry and Minerals	5.47
Transportation and Communications	11.08
Science, Technology & Environment	0.50
General Economic Services	5.58
Social Services	17.88
General Services	0.57
Forestry and Wildlife Assistance to Local Bodies	33.33
Total	100.00

Source: GoK (2002).

The main objective of the Tenth Plan is to take steps to increase investment, efficiency of resource use and employment and to adopt special measures for the uplift of the weaker sections of society. The Tenth Plan is as much a Reform Plan as it is a Programme Plan. Fiscal reforms will be an important part of the reforms.

References

Appleyard, Reginald (ed.) (1998). *Emigration Dynamics in Developing Countries,* Vol. II. South Asia, UNFPA and IOM. Aldershot, England.

Centre for Devlopment Studies (1975). *Poverty Unemployment and Development Policy.* New York: United Nations.

Dept. of Economics and Statistics (1998). *Statistics since Independence.* Thiruvananthapuram.

Government of Kerala (1998). *Statistics since Independence.* Thiruvananthapuram: Department of Economics and Statistics.

———. (2002). *Draft Tenth Five Year Plan, 2002-2007.* Thiruvananthapuram: State Planning Board. pp.19-20.

———. (2004). *Economic Review.* Thiruvananthapuram: State Planning Board. p.30.

———. (2005). *Economic Review, 2004.* Thiruvananthapuram: State Planning Board.

Irudaya, Rajan S. (2002). *Kerala's Population into the 21st Century.* Thiruvananthapuram: Centre for Development Studies (CDS). (Unpublished).

Kabir, M. (1997). *Public Health Activities and Health Transition: Lessons from Kerala.* Thiruvananthapuram: Centre for Development Studies (CDS). (Unpublished).

———. (2002). *Growth of Service Sector in Kerala.* Ph.D. thesis. Thiruvananthapuram: University of Kerala. (Unpublished).

Krishnan, T.N. (1995). *The Route to Social Development in Kerala,* UNICEF, New York.

Menon, T. Madhava (ed). (2000). *A Hand Book of Kerala.* Thiruvananthapuram: The International School of Dravidian Linguistics.

Mitra, Ashok, *et al.* (1999). *Report of the Kerala Education Commission.* Kochi: Kerala Sastra Sahitya Parishad.

Nair, P.R. Gopinathan (1974). "Decline in Birth Rate: A Hypothesis about the Inter-relationship between Demographic Variables, Health Services and Education", *Economic and Political Weekly,* Volume 9(6-8).

———. (1981). *Primary Education, Population Growth and Socio-Economic Change.* New Delhi: Allied Publishers Pvt Ltd.

National Council of Applied Economic Research (1962). *Techno-economic Survey of Kerala.* New Delhi: NCAER.

Nossiter, T.F. (1998). *Marxist State Governments in India: Politics, Economics and Society.* London: Printer Publishers.

Oommen, M.A. (ed.) (1999). *Rethinking Development,* Vol II. New Delhi: Concept Publishing Co.

Panikar, P.G.K., T.N. Krishanan and N. Krishnaji (1977). *Population Growth and Agricultural Development.* Thiruvananthapuram: Centre for Development Studies. (Unpublished).

Pillai, K. Raman (1999). Coalition Politics: The Kerala Experience. In Oommen, M A (ed). Rethinking Development, Volume I. New Delhi: Concept Publishing House.

Prakash, B.A. (ed.) (1999). *Kerala's Economic Development.* New Delhi: Sage Publications India Pvt Ltd.

Rajasenan, D. and Gerard de Groot (eds.) (2005). *Kerala Economy: Trajectories, Challenges and Implications.* Cochin: Cochin Universities of Science and Technology.

Salim, A. Abdul and P.R. Gopinathan Nair (2002). *Educational Development in India; the Kerala Experience since 1800.* New Delhi: Anmol Publications Pvt. Ltd.

Saradamoni, K. (1999). *Matriliny Transformed.* New Delhi: Sage Publications Pvt. Ltd.

State Planning Board (2005). *Economic Review 2004.* Thiruvananthapuram.

Thomas, P.M. (1999). "Agricultural Performance in Kerala", in B.A. Prakash (ed)., *Kerala's Economic Development: Issues and Problems.* Chapter 9, pp.168-185. New Delhi: Sage Publications.

Zachariah, K.C. and S. Irudaya Rajan (2004). "Gulf Revisited", *Working Paper,* No. 363. Thiruvananthapuram : Centre for Development Studies. *www.cds.edu*

Chapter 2

Demographic Transition

Introduction

The population of Kerala was around 32 million in 2001, living in around 7 million households. The average household size in Kerala is 4.7 persons. Kerala has 14 districts, 63 *taluks*, 159 census towns, 999 *panchayats* and 1364 villages. It also had a population of 3.1 million of Scheduled Castes and of 0.4 million of Scheduled Tribes.

The 2001 Census ranked Kerala as the 19th (out of 35 states and union territories) with regard to female work participation rate. The male and the female work participation rates in 2001 were 50.4 and 15.3 respectively. The rates for both males and females in Kerala are lower than those for the country as a whole.

The per capita income (per capita net national product at factor cost) is estimated as Rs. 10709 for 2001-02 (at 1993-94 prices). The net state domestic product at constant prices (1993-94) is estimated at Rs. 34509 crore in 2001-02. At current prices, the state income is estimated at Rs. 63817 crore during 2001-02. The calculation of state income does not include remittances arising out of migration. Remittances would have constituted more than 20 per cent of the state domestic product (State Planning Board, 2005).

A glaring manifestation of the unemployment problem in Kerala is the large number of migrants. Firm figures are not available but according to an earlier estimate, there were about 6.18 lakh migrants in 1991 (Zachariah *et al.*, 1994). The estimate of the number of emigrants in Kerala in the second half of 1998 was 1.36 million (Zachariah, *et al.*, 2003). By 2004, the number of emigrants increased to 1.84 million persons, roughly 27 emigrants per 100 households and the flow of remittances to Kerala in that year was estimated at Rs. 18465 crore (Zachariah and Rajan, 2004). The rate of net migration from Kerala stood at -0.16 per cent during decade 1961-1971, -0.22 per cent during 1971-1981, -0.31 per cent during 1981-1991 and -0.27 per cent during 1991-2001 (Bhat and Rajan, 1990; Rajan and Aliyar, 2005).

Against this background, the demographic transition in Kerala is reviewed and the trends, patterns and determinants of demographic transition (mortality and fertility) discussed at length in the following section.

Population Size and Growth

Kerala registered a growth rate of above 2 per cent during 1941-1971; the same pattern was true for India for the later period of 1961-1991. Until 1971, Kerala's growth rate remained always higher than India's. India overtook Kerala during 1971-1981. Over the last century, Kerala's population doubled itself five times (it increased from 6 million in 1901 to 32 million in 2001) whereas India's population grew only by slightly more than three times during the century (238 million in 1901 to 1027 million in 2001). However the growth rate of population during the past decade 1991-2001 was a mere 0.91 per cent, the lowest rate experienced since the formation of the state of Kerala (Figure 2.1). The growth rate during 1991-2001 in Kerala was the lowest in India, with Tamil Nadu closely following. The growth patterns of Kerala and India during the 20th century were almost similar.

Kerala is one of the most densely populated regions in India. Among the major states, Kerala had the highest density until 1981; but in 1991 West Bengal took the lead. However, the difference between Kerala and West Bengal was only 17 persons in 1991 and 85 persons per square kilometre in 2001. Even at the beginning of this century, the density in Kerala was higher than that of all-India (Figure 2.2). However, the density of 819 persons per square kilometre of 2001 census was nearly thrice the all-India average, much higher than that of the adjoining state of Tamil Nadu (478 persons per square kilometre). During the past 100 years, the population pressure on land has grown much higher in Kerala than in all-India, a fact which is almost ignored in discussions on the demographic transition in Kerala.

FIGURE 2.1

Population Growth Rates for Kerala and India, 1901-2001

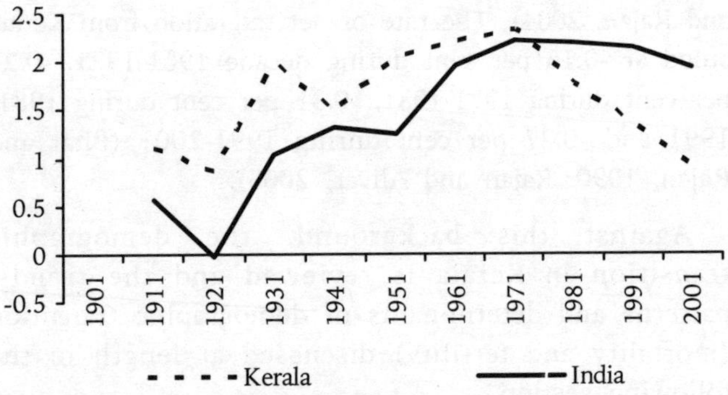

Source: Irudaya Rajan and Aliyar, 2005.

FIGURE 2.2

Human Density in Kerala and India, 1901-2001

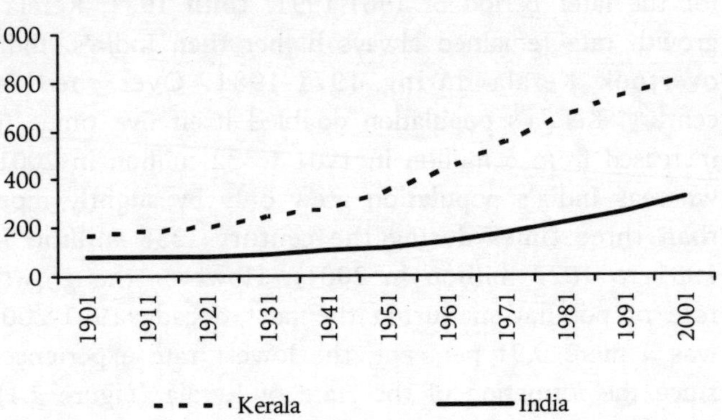

Source: Same as Figure 2.1.

Kerala's sex ratio is unique among the Indian states; it is the only state with an excess of females over males and the only state in which the excess has been growing during the entire 20th century (Table 2.1 and Figure 2.3). Since the beginning of the 20th century, Kerala has grown from a situation of 4 excess females per 1000 males in 1901 to 58 excess females for 1000 males in 2001.

FIGURE 2.3

Sex Ratio (Females per 1000 Males) for Kerala and India, 1901-2001

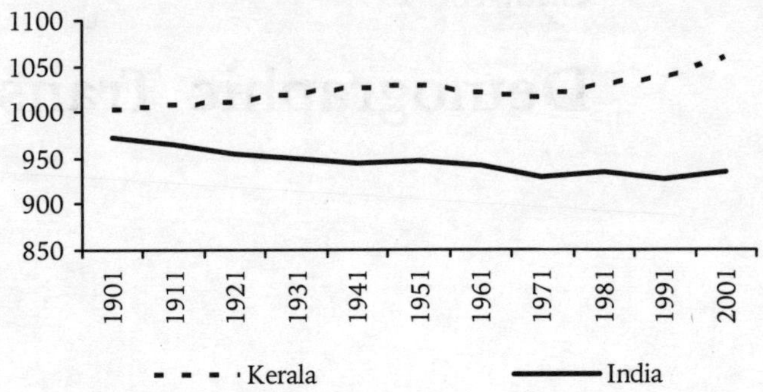

Source: Same as Figure 2.1.

Half the number of districts in Kerala registered growth rates higher than the state average. The lowest growth rate was observed in Pathanamthitta whereas the highest growth rate was registered in Malappuram. Overall, it is the northern districts of Kerala which show higher growth rates (Table 2.1). Among the 14 districts, the density of 6 districts was lower than the state average. The highest density is found in Alappuzha and the lowest in Idukki. Population density has played a major role in determining accessibility to social facilities, such as schools and hospitals and indirectly contributed to the pace of the process of demographic transition. The districts of Idukki and Wayanad have shown sex ratios with excess of males over females in 1991 and in 2001. In 2001, the highest sex ratios in the state were found in Thrissur, and Pathanamthitta with 1092 and 1094 females respectively per 1000 males.

Kottayam district ranks first, both in male and female literacy rates, while the lowest ratio is found in Palakkad district for both the sexes. Idukki leads the districts in respect of work participation rates of both males and females while Malappuram lags behind in respect of work participation rate for both the sexes.

Mortality and Life Expectancy

Although a civil registration system has been in existence in Kerala for long, its performance was highly unsatisfactory until recently. As a result, not much confidence can be placed on either the level or the trend in vital rates calculated from this source. Recent data published by the civil registration system in Kerala are of importance as they provide information for preparing district-level estimates of fertility and mortality. However, a systematic attempt is not made either by demographers or by the government to

TABLE 2.1

District Profile of Kerala as of 2001 Census

Districts	*Population*	*Growth Rate (1991-2001)*	*Sex Ratio*		*Population Density*	*Per Cent Urban*	*Literacy (%)*		*WPR (%)*	
			Total	*0-6*			*Male*	*Female*	*Male*	*Female*
Kasaragod	1203342	1.16	1047	984	604	19.42	90.84	79.8	49.3	20.8
Kannur	2412365	0.69	1090	956	813	50.46	96.38	89.57	50.0	15.2
Wayanad	786627	1.57	1000	954	369	3.76	90.28	80.80	55.7	22.8
Kozhikode	2878498	0.94	1058	966	1228	38.25	96.30	88.86	48.8	8.1
Malappuram	3629640	1.59	1063	979	1022	9.81	91.46	85.96	42.8	6.6
Palakkad	2617072	0.94	1068	963	584	13.62	89.73	79.31	52.2	21.1
Thrissur	2975440	0.83	1092	953	981	28.21	95.47	89.94	50.8	15.1
Ernakulam	3098378	0.87	1017	948	1050	47.65	95.95	90.96	55.4	17.1
Idukki	1128605	0.67	999	970	252	5.07	92.11	85.04	58.4	28.1
Kottayam	1952901	0.65	1025	957	884	15.35	97.41	94.45	52.4	13.9
Alappuzha	2105349	0.51	1079	962	1489	29.36	96.42	91.14	49.7	20.2
Pathanamthitta	1231577	0.36	1094	968	467	10.03	96.62	93.71	47.6	13.2
Kollam	2584118	0.71	1070	961	1038	18.03	94.63	88.60	48.5	16.7
Thiruvananthapuram	3234707	0.93	1058	955	1476	33.78	92.68	86.26	51.5	14.4
Kerala	**31838619**	**0.9**	**1058**	**963**	**819**	**25.97**	**94.20**	**87.86**	**50.4**	**15.3**

Notes: Sex ratio is defined as number of females per 1000 males. WPR: Work Participation Rate.

Source: All information is compiled from the Census of India 2001 reports.

produce below-district level data estimates of fertility and mortality on a regular basis using information from the civil registration system. In this context, we have to depend upon the Sample Registration System (SRS) as it offers data of more acceptable quality. According to the SRS, the crude death rate (CDR) in Kerala hovered around 6 during the past 10 years and the infant mortality rate (IMR) has marginally declined from 16 per thousand live births in 1991 to 10 per thousand live births in 2002 (see Figure 2.4 for CDR for Kerala and India).

Over the past 10 years, IMR has shown wide fluctuations. IMR has two components: neonatal mortality and post-neonatal mortality. The contribution of post-neonatal mortality (28 to 365 days) is the lowest compared to the neo-natal morality rate (0-28 days). Again, one-month mortality has two components 0-7 days and 7-28 days. In 1997, out of every seven children who died within one month after birth, six died in the first week of life (Table 2.2). This is also true for perinatal morality (still birth plus one week mortality rate) and still birth rates. The current

FIGURE 2.4

Crude Death Rates for Kerala and India, 1971-2002

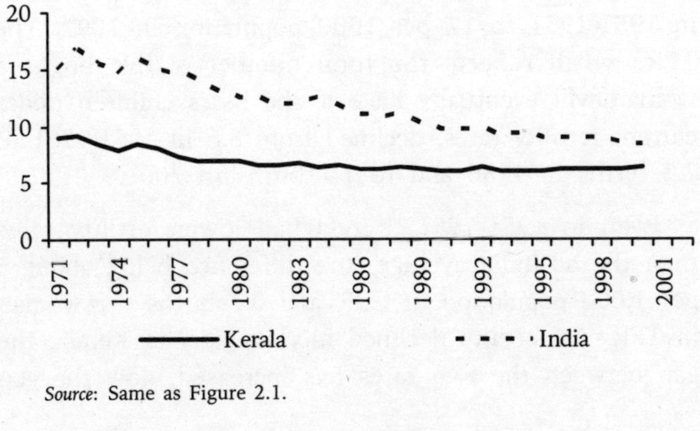

Source: Same as Figure 2.1.

FIGURE 2.5

Infant Mortality Rates for Kerala and India, 1971-2002

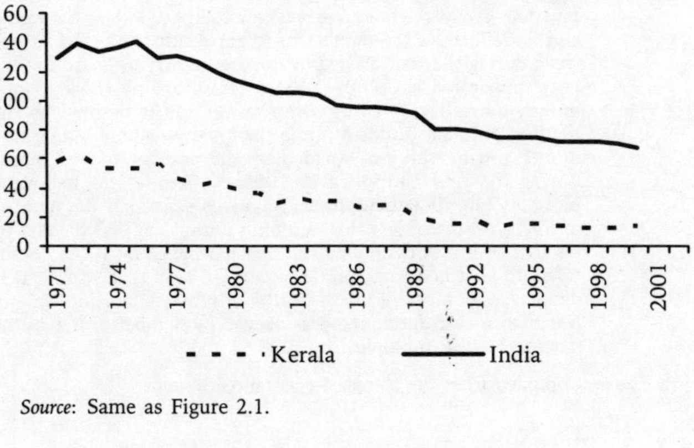

Source: Same as Figure 2.1.

TABLE 2.2

Different Components of Infant Mortality Rates, 1971-2003

Year	*PMR*	*SBR*	*OWM*	*OWOM*	*NMR*	*PNMR*	*IMR*
1971	41.5	17.5	24.0	13.5	37.5	20.5	58
1972	49.3	26.4	22.9	13.8	36.7	26.3	63
1973	43.6	24.7	18.9	11.6	30.5	26.5	58
1974	37.2	18.1	19.1	12.4	31.5	22.5	54
1975	42.5	18.6	23.9	10.1	34.0	20.0	54
1976	39.0	17.9	21.1	12.8	33.9	22.1	56
1977	27.1	12.3	14.8	13.3	28.1	18.9	47
1978	34.0	16.7	17.3	9.5	26.8	15.2	42
1979	22.5	2.4	20.1	9.7	29.8	12.9	43
1980	22.7	7.6	15.1	14.6	29.7	10.5	40
1981	28.6	11.3	17.3	8.4	25.7	11.7	37
1982	22.1	5.7	16.4	5.3	25.7	8.7	30
1983	20.6	3.4	17.2	5.8	23.0	10.0	33
1984	22.9	8.1	14.8	6.2	21.0	7.7	29
1985	24.3	8.4	15.9	6.2	22.1	9.2	31
1986	23.0	10.3	12.7	6.4	19.1	8.3	27
1987	24.9	11.1	13.8	5.5	19.3	8.6	28
1988	25.4	11.8	13.6	4.4	18.0	9.7	28
1989	25.3	14.3	10.0	4.0	14.0	7.0	21
1990	25.7	16.6	9.1	2.9	12.0	3.3	15
1991	18.0	9.2	8.8	2.5	11.3	5.1	16
1992	18.9	10.1	8.8	2.1	10.9	5.8	17
1993	16.8	8.2	8.6	1.4	10.0	3.3	13
1994	20.5	9.8	10.7	1.9	12.6	3.2	16
1995	16.0	9.0	7.0	4.0	11.0	4.0	15
1996	17.0	10.0	7.0	4.0	11.0	3.0	14
1997	17.5	11.3	6.2	1.3	7.5	4.5	12
1998	16.8	8.2	8.6	1.4	10.0	3.0	13
1999	18.0	10.0	8.0	5.0	13.0	3.0	16
2000	10.0	6.0	4.0	5.0	9.0	5.0	14
2001	13.0	7.8	6.0	3.0	9.0	2.0	11
2002	12.0	8.0	4.0	3.0	7.0	3.0	10
2003	11.0	6.0	5.0	2.0	7.0	4.0	11
2004	16.0	9.0	7.0	2.0	9.0	3.0	12
2005	10.0	6.0	4.0	5.0	9.0	5.0	14

Note: PMR refers to perinatal mortality and is defined as the number of still births and infant deaths of less than seven days during the year divided by number of live births and still births during the year multiplied by 1000; SBR refers to still birth rate and is defined as the number of still births during the year divided by number of live births and still births during the year multiplied by 1000; OWM refers to one week mortality (0-7 days mortality) and is defined as the number of infant deaths of less than one week during the year divided by number of live births during the year multiplied by 1000; OWOM refers to one week to one month mortality (7-28 days mortality) and is defined as the number of infant deaths of more than one week and less than a month during the year divided by the number of live births during the year multiplied by 1000; NMR refers to neo-natal mortality rate (0-28 days mortality) and is defined as the number of infant deaths of less than a month during the year divided by number of live births during the year multiplied by 1000; PNMR refers to post neo-natal mortality rate (28 days to 1 year) and is defined as number of infant deaths of more than a month and less than a year during the year divided by number of live births during the year multiplied by 1000.

Source: Compiled from the Sample Registration System.

perinatal mortality rate is 18 for Kerala and still birth rate 11 for Kerala. Both are extremely high given the low level of IMR (Rajan and Mohanachandran, 1999). The life expectancy at birth in Kerala is 70 years for males and 73.6 years for females with a gender gap nearly four years.

Fertility

Reliable data on fertility trends of Kerala are available only for the period since the introduction of the Sample Registration System (SRS). However, estimates made by several authors using the census data are available for some earlier periods also. The census-based estimates shown here are taken from Bhat (1987). Table 2.3 presents estimates of some fertility measures for Kerala and India from 1951-1981.

TABLE 2.3

Estimates of CBR and TFR, Kerala and India

Decade	*Crude Birth Rate*		*Total Fertility Rate*	
	Kerala	*India*	*Kerala*	*India*
1951-1961	43.9	47.1	5.6	6.3
1961-1971	37.1	43.0	5.0	6.0
1971-1981	28.1	37.2	3.4	5.2

Source: Bhat, 1987.

The inter-censal estimates of fertility shown in the Table 2.4 are somewhat higher than the official estimates. This is because any census-based estimate of the CBR is derived either explicitly or implicitly assuming a level of infant and child mortality. Since the official estimates of infant and child mortality are biased downward, so are the birth rate estimates. It should also be noted that the estimates of fertility measures from the SRS for 1971-1981 are marginally lower than the census-based estimates.

According to the figures presented in Table 2.3, CBR in Kerala has come down from 44 per 1,000 population in 1951-1961 to 17 per 1000 population in 2002. The TFR, which reflects the total number of live births a woman will eventually have if she bears children under current fertility rates, declined from 5.6 in 1951-1961 to 2.3 births in 1986 and to 1.7 births in 2001.

Even in 1951-1961, Kerala had lower fertility rates than the all-India average, the difference being about 3 per 1,000 population in CBR and 0.7 births per woman in TFR. As fertility declined more rapidly in Kerala, the gap between the two rates has increased; now the gap

TABLE 2.4

SRS Estimates of CBR and TFR, Kerala and India

Year	*Crude Birth Rate*			*Total Fertility Rate*		
	Rural	*Urban*	*Total*	*Rural*	*Urban*	*Total*
			Kerala			
1971-1975	30.0	28.4	29.3	3.8	3.2	3.4
1976-1980	26.6	25.0	26.3	3.2	2.7	3.1
1981-1985	24.6	24.3	24.6	2.7	2.4	2.6
1986-1990	20.7	21.4	20.9	2.1	2.0	2.1
1991-1995	17.8	17.9	17.8	1.8	1.7	1.7
1996-2000	17.7	18.0	17.9	1.8	1.8	1.8
			India			
1971-1975	37.2	29.3	35.6	5.3	3.8	4.8
1976-1980	34.7	28.1	33.4	4.8	3.4	4.5
1981-1985	35.2	28.1	33.6	4.8	3.4	4.5
1986-1990	33.0	26.1	31.4	4.3	3.0	4.0
1991-1995	30.5	23.4	28.9	3.9	2.7	3.5
1996-2000	28.2	21.1	26.5	3.5	2.3	3.2
2001-2005	26.3	19.6	24.5	3.3	2.2	3.0

Source: Compiled from various issues of the Sample Registration System.

TABLE 2.5

Changes in Child-Woman Ratios in Kerala, 1951-2001

Year	*Southern Kerala**		*Northern Kerala***		*Kerala*	
	CWR	*Per Cent Change*	*CWR*	*Per Cent Change*	*CWR*	*Per Cent Change*
			Child-Women Ratio, 0-4			
1951	559		590		501	
1961	638	14	647	10	622	24
1971	550	-14	526	-19	591	-5
1981	406	-26	360	-32	482	-18
1991	293	-16	384	3	329	-19
2001	281	-2	333	-7	303	-4
			Child-Women Ratio, 5-9			
1951	544		576		481	
1961	698	28	722	25	657	37
1971	666	-5	656	-9	682	4
1981	524	-21	475	-28	605	-11
1991	423	-11	599	12	493	-10
2001	346	-10	432	-16	382	-13

Notes: * Comprising Thiruvananthapuram, Kollam, Alappuzha, Kottayam, Idukki, Ernakulam, and Thrissur districts in 1981 and these districts and Pathanamthitta in 1991 (roughly, the old Travancore-Cochin state) and 2001.

** Comprising Kannur, Wayanad, Kozhikode, Malappuram, and Palakkad districts in 1981 (roughly the old Malabar) and these districts and Kasargode in 1991 and 2001.

is as much as 8 per 1,000 population in the CBR and one and half births per woman in TFR. The small difference in the 1951-1961 fertility levels between Kerala and all-India is certainly to some extent due to the higher age of marriage among Kerala women. However, the large differences in fertility levels that we see now arose mainly from the greater use of contraceptive services in Kerala. Reliable estimates of fertility levels are not available for periods before 1951; however, it is unlikely that the levels had been much higher than that of 1951-1961. There was some decline in fertility in Kerala between 1951-1961 and 1961-1971, and the rate has been falling very rapidly after 1961-1971. However, the average decadal estimates presented in the Table 2.4 do not give enough information on the actual date of onset of the rapid decline in fertility.

Table 2.5 shows the child-woman ratios calculated from the past six censuses for Kerala as a whole and for its southern and northern parts separately. Two kinds of ratios are presented, one obtained by dividing the population of ages 0-4 years by the number of women in the age interval 15-49 years (CWR1), and the other by dividing the population of 5-9 years by the number of women in the age interval 20-54 years (CWR2). The former ratio provides information on the level of fertility in the past five years preceding the census, while the latter ratio gives the same information for the 5-9 years in the past five years preceding the census. It should be noted that these ratios are also influenced by changes in the mortality rate, though by a lower degree.

Table 2.5 shows that both the CWRs had increased between 1951 and 1961, more so in the Malabar region (northern Kerala) than in the Travancore-Cochin region (southern Kerala). The increase was either due to fall in infant and child mortality rates or due to a rise in the fertility rate. A temporary increase in fertility just before its secular fall has been observed in a large number of populations (Dyson and Murphy, 1985). However, the fact that the rise in CWRs is larger in the Malabar region than in the Travancore-Cochin region suggests that the increase was due to improvements in mortality. Between 1961 and 1971, a reduction is observed in both the child-woman ratios in Kerala, more so in CWR1 than in CWR2. Given that the effect of mortality decline tends to offset the impact of declines in fertility, even a small reduction in CWR2 observed in 1971 is significant. It suggests that the level of fertility during 1961-1965 had been lower than during 1951-55. This finding supports the conclusion reached by Nair (1974) based on the trend in school enrolment rates that the fertility rate had begun to fall in Kerala even before the intensification of the family planning programme in 1965.

The trends in CWRs also suggest that the fertility decline began first in the Travancore-Cochin region about five years before it occurred in the Malabar region. It is quite possible that fertility had begun to fall in the Travancore-Cochin region even before 1961 because the increase in the child-woman ratios observed during 1951-1961 was relatively small. However, to be certain, better information of the trend in infant and child mortality during this period is required. Interestingly, there is a striking similarity in the pattern of change in the CWRs of the Malabar region and that of the nine districts lying adjacent to this region in the neighbouring Tamil Nadu. Both ratios have shown an impressive decline in the 1991 and 2001 censuses both for Kerala and for the southern region; however, the percentage of decline was much higher for CWR2 than CWR1 indicating accelerated fertility decline in Kerala during 1976-1981, especially in the southern parts of Kerala. The same phenomenon was observed in the northern Kerala around 1986-1991. During 1991-2001, the percentage decline was much higher for the northern region indicating that the differences in fertility decline are almost nil in recent decades.

FIGURE 2.6

Crude Birth Rates for Kerala and India, 1971-2002

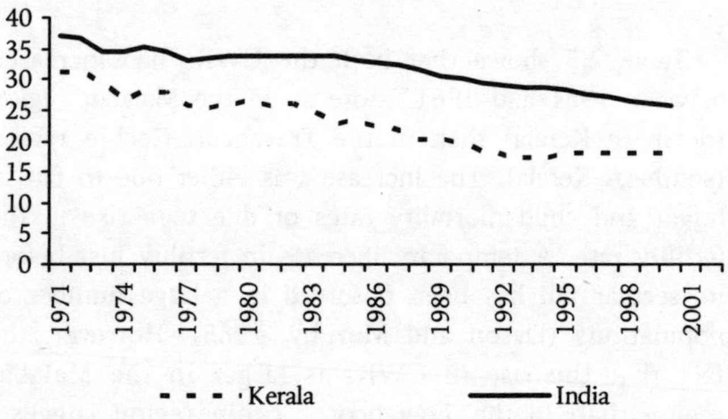

Source: Same as Figure 2.1.

Fertility indicators derived from the Sample Registration System data are provided in Table 2.6. According to the SRS, CBD declined from 31.1 in 1971 to 25.6 in 1981 (5.5 points) and to 17.4 in 1993 (8.2 points). The 2005 CBR for Kerala is 15.0 as per the latest SRS bulletin indicating smaller but further decline of 2.4 points between 1993 and 2005. (see Figure 2.6 for Kerala and India). The TFR has also registered decline throughout the period since 1971. For instance, the TFR was 4.1 children per woman in 1971, 3.1 children in 1980, 2.1 children in 1990 and 1.7 children in 2000.

Kerala achieved the replacement level of fertility by the beginning of the 1990s. At that stage, many demographers in India and abroad thought that further decline would be unlikely. Against their predictions, Kerala's TFR declined further to 1.7 by the year 1993 and has been hovering around that figure for the past 10 years. The impact of fertility decline in Kerala is

TABLE 2.6

Crude Birth Rates, Crude Death Rates and Infant Mortality Rates, SRS Estimates, Kerala and India, 1971-2002

Year	*Crude Birth Rate*		*Crude Death Rate*		*Infant Mortality Rate*	
	Kerala	*India*	*Kerala*	*India*	*Kerala*	*India*
1971	31.1	36.9	9.0	14.9	58	129
1972	31.2	36.6	9.2	16.9	63	139
1973	29.2	34.6	8.5	15.5	54	134
1974	26.8	34.5	7.8	14.5	54	136
1975	28.0	35.2	8.4	15.9	54	140
1976	27.8	34.4	8.1	15.0	56	129
1977	25.8	33.0	7.3	14.7	47	130
1978	25.2	33.3	7.0	14.2	42	127
1979	25.8	33.7	6.9	13.0	43	120
1980	26.7	33.7	7.0	12.6	40	113
1981	25.6	33.9	6.6	12.5	37	110
1982	26.2	33.8	6.6	11.9	30	105
1983	24.9	33.7	6.7	11.9	33	105
1984	22.9	33.9	6.4	12.6	29	104
1985	23.3	32.9	6.5	11.8	31	97
1986	22.5	32.6	6.1	11.1	27	96
1987	21.7	32.2	6.1	10.9	28	95
1988	20.3	31.5	6.4	11.0	28	94
1989	20.3	30.6	6.1	10.3	21	91
1990	19.6	30.2	6.0	9.7	17	80
1991	18.3	29.3	6.0	9.8	16	80
1992	17.7	29.0	6.3	10.0	17	79
1993	17.4	28.5	6.0	9.2	13	74
1994	17.4	28.7	6.0	9.3	16	74
1995	18.0	28.3	6.0	9.0	15	74
1996	18.0	27.5	6.2	9.0	14	72
1997	17.9	27.2	6.2	8.9	12	71
1998	17.9	26.5	6.2	9.0	13	72
1999	17.9	26.0	6.2	8.6	13	70
2000	17.9	25.8	6.4	8.5	14	68
2001	17.3	25.4	6.6	8.4	11	66
2002	16.9	25.0	6.4	8.1	10	63
2003	16.7	24.8	6.3	8.0	11	60
2004	15.2	24.1	6.1	7.5	12	58
2005	15.0	23.8	6.4	7.6	14	58

Note: CBR refers to the number of live births during a year divided by the population in that year multiplied by 1000; CDR refers to number of deaths during a year divided by the population in that year multiplied by 1000. IMR refers to Infant Mortality Rate and is defined as the number of infant deaths during a year divided by the number of live births during that year multiplied by 1000.

Source: Compiled from Sample Registration System data.

better appreciated by looking at the age pyramids for the periods 1961 and 2001.

District Level Differentials

Birth rate varied considerably from region to region and from district to district. According to unofficial tabulations of the SRS data, in 1988 the birth rate varied from 14.8 in Alappuzha to 28.4 in Malappuram. The average birth rate for the period 1983-1988 showed a variation from 17.7 in Alappuzha to 33.5 in Malappuram. While the birth rates in some districts in south Kerala such as Alappuzha, Ernakulam, Kottayam, and Pathanamthitta seemed to have definitely come below the replacement level, the birth rate in some of the northern districts such as Malappuram and Kasaragod was reported to be above the replacement level and near the all-India average. The existence of large inter-district variations in the birth rate in Kerala was confirmed by a more recent analysis by Bhat who has estimated fertility rates for all districts of Kerala using the 1981 and the 1991 censuses (Bhat, 1996). According to these estimates, TFR varied from 1.6 in Ernakulam to 3.4 in Malappuram during 1984-90. In 1990, only five districts (Palakkad, Malappuram, Wayanad, Kannur and Kasaragod) had registered TFRs above the replacement level. The remaining districts had already achieved fertility rates below replacement level (for details, see Table 2.7).

TABLE 2.7

Crude Birth Rate by Districts of Kerala, 1971-2001

	Crude Birth Rate			*Total Fertility Rate*		
	1974-1980	*1984-1990*	*1994-2000*	*1974-1980*	*1984-1990*	*1994-2000*
Trivandrum	22.8	19.6	16.4	2.3	1.8	1.6
Kollam	23.3	18.5	16.2	2.7	1.8	1.6
Alappuzha	21.0	16.7	15.2	2.3	1.6	1.5
Pathanamthitta	n.a	17.2	14.5	—	1.7	1.5
Kottayam	20.1	16.6	15.6	2.4	1.7	1.6
Idukki	26.7	19.8	17.0	2.9	1.8	1.6
Ernakulam	21.4	16.9	15.7	2.4	1.6	1.5
Thrissur	22.2	18.7	16.1	2.5	1.9	1.6
Palakkad	22.5	18.8	17.3	3.4	2.4	1.8
Malappuram	33.6	29.5	22.4	4.3	3.4	2.4
Kozhikode	26.3	20.5	17.4	3.0	2.0	1.7
Wayanad	31.4	23.4	19.5	3.8	2.3	2.0
Kannur	28.8	20.5	16.6	3.5	2.1	1.7
Kasaragod	n.a	24.4	18.9	2.5	—	1.9
Kerala	**25.0**	**20.3**	**17.1**	**2.9**	**2.0**	**1.7**

Sources: Bhat, 1996; Guilmoto and Rajan, 2002.

According to the latest estimates based on the 2001 Census, Malappuram is the only district in Kerala with a TFR above the replacement level (Guilmoto and Rajan, 2002). The lowest TFR of 1.5 is reported for several districts including Alappuzha, Pathanamthitta and Ernakulam. More detailed spatial studies on fertility rates in the districts of India indicate that Alappuzha in Kerala is the forerunner of the process of fertility decline which began even as early as the 1960s (Guilmoto and Rajan, 2001).

Socioeconomic Determinants of Demographic Transition

Historical Aspects

In 1980, it was argued that the fertility decline that took place in Kerala in recent years was caused as much by historical developments as by policy interventions. This is true not only with respect to fertility decline, but also with respect to mortality decline.

Even from ancient times, Kerala had extensive contacts with other cultures and countries. These connections have played a significant role in the socio-economic development of the state. From the other side of the Ghats came the caste and the land tenure systems; from West Asia came Christianity, Islam and Judaism; from Europe came Christianity as well as the modern administrative system, the plantation industry and modern education and public health systems. Foreign influences have left some permanent marks on the population of Kerala. The state has a mosaic of religions and castes that includes Hindus and their numerous castes, Christians and Muslims.

Population density in Kerala was more than twice that of all-India even in 1901. Despite significant out-migration and fall in fertility, Kerala's population grew much more rapidly than all-India population. During 1901-1991, the density of population of Kerala grew by three times the all-India average. The high population density and the peculiar settlement pattern in the state have made land reforms and other socioeconomic reforms highly relevant and helpful for fertility decline.

The modern formal educational system in the state owes its origin largely to the British rule in India and to the Christian missionaries who, finding a sizeable Christian population in Travancore-Cochin, concentrated their efforts on education and health. Fortunately, the indigenous tradition favoured education and the local rulers were supportive; by the end of the 19th century every village in the states of Travancore and Cochin had a primary school.

The influence of Europeans on health was similar. They provided the initial impetus for the development of a modern healthcare system with support from the indigenous tradition of scientific medicine and the local rulers.

It is against this historical background that the discussion on recent socioeconomic developments and policy interventions in Kerala is presented.

Health

The physical environment in most parts of Kerala is healthy and has always been so, except for malaria tracts in the hills (malaria has now been eradicated). Kerala also has a long tradition of indigenous healthcare (the Ayurvedic system). The rulers of the state in the pre-independence era had taken interest in the promotion of public health and healthcare facilities and committed sufficient funds to both curative and preventive healthcare. In addition, foreign missionaries established private hospitals with health personnel trained in the modern (Allopathic) medical system.

Health conditions in Kerala have always been better than those in other parts of India, and recent developments have evidenced the differential. For instance, IMR in 1990 was about 17 in Kerala as against 80 in India. The chance of an infant dying during the first 12 months of life in India today is more than four times higher in all-India than in Kerala. The continued improvement in health conditions of the population is to a very large extent due to their educational status and health policies of the state, which determine the availability and quality of medical facilities in position.

The hospitals in Kerala are evenly distributed throughout the state. The easy access to medical facilities (due to relatively small service area and good transport facilities), the relatively low cost and the high demand for medical services (due to more educated population) have been the important reasons for the comparatively good health conditions in Kerala.

Kerala is not advanced with respect to reported morbidity. The reported morbidity rates in the state are several times higher than in other states of India. One reason for the higher rate of morbidity in Kerala could be its climatic conditions, high humidity and the lengthy rainy season. However, an important factor is also the much higher levels of awareness of ill-health conditions and the high demand for medical treatment even for small ailments. Still another reason is the rapidly changing standards of living, which lead to the increase in the life-style related diseases such as cardio-vascular diseases, diabeties, hypertension and cancer.

Education

The contrast between Kerala and India is equally striking with respect to educational status. In 1991, more than 90 per cent of the people in Kerala were literate compared to only 52 per cent in all-India. Among women, the literacy rates were 87 per cent in Kerala and 39 per cent in all-India. These differences are not merely a carry-over from the past. The improvements in the literacy levels during the decade 1981-1991 were greater in Kerala than in all-India (21 percentage points in Kerala compared to 16 percentage points for all-India).

The improvement in the literacy levels alone or by themselves does not give the full picture of the educational 'explosion' taking place in Kerala consistently since 1950. Information on the number of students at all levels, and on the number of schools and colleges of all types, is necessary to present a full picture.

Formal channels of education i.e, the schools and colleges managed by different agencies—government, private agencies and voluntary organisations and NGOs, present only part of the picture. In addition, there exist several other educational institutions as well, including tutorial colleges and 'parallel' colleges. The parallel colleges in Kerala are a unique institution. While the tutorial colleges take students who fail in public examination and give coaching classes to regular students in colleges, during extra-college hours, the parallel colleges take students who fail to gain admission to recognised institutions. Such students take examinations in the capacity of private students. Thus through the system of parallel colleges, higher levels of education, especially in liberal arts are made accessible to large number of young persons belonging to various strata of society.

Although the average population served per school is greater in Kerala than in other parts of India, the state spends a much higher proportion of its revenue for education than elsewhere in the country. Perhaps, Kerala is the only state which finances the entire recurring institutional costs of private schools known as private aided schools. Kerala also spends proportionately more on elementary education than on higher education unlike in most other states of India.

Two aspects of these educational developments are particularly relevant to the demographic transition.

First, education is widespread that there are hardly any illiterate women or illiterate men in the prime reproductive age groups. Second, the supply of educated personnel has remained far in excess of demand, thus leading to the growing problem of the educated unemployed.

Political Awareness

Every aspect of life in Kerala is politicised. Newspaper reading and political discussions are a principal pastime of the average Keralite. Protest marches, general strikes, *bandhs*, hunger strikes and other public demonstrations have been almost a daily routine. For some people, participation in processions and protest meetings has become full-time vocation.

Such a pattern of politicisation has many disruptive consequences, but not without beneficial effects. It has had the effect of making public services much more readily available for the poor in Kerala. Political awareness and the politicisation of all issues, even those affecting only a small minority of the population, may be responsible for better delivery of government services than would otherwise be the case. What the people are eligible for, they obtain, by application, appeal or agitation.

Land Reform and Other Distributive Policies

Undoubtedly, the most significant development in the recent political economy of the state is the shift of the reins of political power from the hands of the rich to the hands of the poor. In consequence, there has taken place considerable transfer of wealth and income to the lower strata of the society. These changes have been brought about through land reforms, job reservation in public services, enforcement of minimum wages, social security benefits to agricultural labourers and other deprived sections of the population, and reservation in educational institutions and in several public bodies for the economically and socially backward groups.

Agrarian reforms were the principal means used to bring about a major redistribution of landed property. This legislative measure was introduced in 1957. It sought to assure permanent tenure rights to all tenants, to give tenants the right to purchase land and to impose a ceiling on the total area a primary family unit could own and possess. The ceiling provisions had exempted certain categories such as planatations and coconut groves. The Reforms Act was finally passed in 1963, although its actual implementation was delayed by several more years. By 1969, tenancy was altogether eliminated. The 1968 amendments to the Land Reform Act lowered the ceiling on landholding to 10 acres, removed some of the exemptions from the ceiling provisions and gave 'hutment dwellers' the right to purchase about one-tenth of an acre of land per household at nominal prices.

The impact of these land reforms on the distribution of wealth has not been fully evaluated. It is likely to have been greater on the Malabar area than on the former Travancore-Cochin area. Eviction of hutment dwellers had in fact been banned in much of Kerala some years before the Land Reform Act (in as early as 1949 in Travancore) came into force.

The Land Reform Act created a large middle class of owner-cultivators. Agrarian reforms simultaneously raised the wages and other benefits of farm workers. Since Kerala's middle-class farmers are accustomed to using hired labour for all their agricultural work, rising wage rates increased cost of cultivation. At the same time, the prices of many agricultural products are either controlled by the government or are keeping steady due to the increase in their supply following the Green Revolution in several parts of India. It is therefore doubtful whether land reforms have actually increased the income of the middle-class farming families. In fact, a large part of paddy lands has been shifted away to garden crops or plantations or to non-agricultural uses.

Agricultural laborers constitute nearly one-fourth of the total number of workers in Kerala. They have benefited from land reforms in two aspects. Most of them had used to live in houses located on land owned by other people; they now have a permanent right over their house sites and to the pieces of land immediately adjacent to their house plots (10 cents in rural areas but much less in towns). These workers have also benefited from the Minimum Wages Acts and other agrarian reforms that fix wages and working conditions for agricultural operations. The gains from higher daily wages have been partly offset, however, by losses due to reduction in the number of days of work and declining employment opportunities for other members of their households.

THE 1980s

Universal Immunisation Programme

One of the very significant achievements of Kerala in the field of health in the 1980s is the great progress made in immunising children and pregnant women. This was done under the umbrella of what is commonly known as the Universal Immunisation Programme (UIP), an international project supported by the World Health Organization (WHO). Although immunisation was a part of the MCH programmes from the early 1970s, the UIP was launched only in 1985. The programme was introduced in a phased manner beginning with just 30 districts in India. By 1989, all the districts in Kerala were brought under it.

Under UIP, every child in the country was to be given three doses each of DPT and OPV, one dose of BCG, one dose of measles vaccine, before the first birthday of the child. Pregnant women were to be given two doses of tetanus toxoid early in their pregnancy. The programme was so successful that in just one year (1989), the all-India IMR declined from 91 to 80 and Kerala's IMR declined by 11 points during 1988-1990.

Universal (Total) Literacy Campaign

The impact of the total literacy campaign in Kerala's education progress is like the impact of UIP on Kerala's health progress. This campaign was aimed at eradicating illiteracy from the entire state. It began in Ernakulum district in 1989 and spread to Kottayam town first and later to the entire state. It was supposed to have made every person between ages 5 and 60 years literate. The initial programme was completed in 1990 and a follow-up programme was implemented catering to special groups such as Scheduled Castes and Tribes.

The state claimed 100 per cent literacy by the end of 1990, but the change in the literacy rate in the state as a whole was relatively small as the level of literacy had already reached high levels; the change came to about 2 percentage points. But the programme was able to achieve much more in changing people's attitudes regarding the need to become literate.

World Bank Population Project (IPP-III), Kerala

The India Population Project III (IPP III) was started in Kerala in April 1984 and concluded in March 1990. It covered the four backward districts of Wayanad, Malappuram, Idukki and Palakkad. The main objectives of the project were to reduce fertility and mortality rates by improving maternal and child health (MCH) services in the project districts, and improving the coverage and quality of health and family welfare services through better facilities, training and management. The inputs included physical facilities such as buildings, equipments, and other supplies, vehicles, additional staff, training facilities and support for information, education and communication (IEC) and the management information and evaluation system (MIES).

The final evaluation of the project indicated that a significant decline in birth rate took place during the project period in Wayanad and Idukki districts and moderate decline in Palakkad and Malappuram. Most of the married women availed themselves of ante-natal care services, and about 60 per cent of children were fully immunised. The majority of the births took place in hospitals either by doctors or qualified nurses.

Gulf Migration

The 1980s saw Keralites becoming part of the activities of countries of the Gulf region. Practically, every household in Kerala is affected directly or indirectly by the emigration of workers to the Gulf countries. A significant proportion of the households are directly affected in the sense that one or more of their members have emigrated to the Gulf region and contributed to the household income. Others are affected indirectly thorough socioeconomic changes taking place in the state, changes which can be traced to emigration. These are discernible in female education, prices, housing, employment, wages, transportation and status of women.

Around 1975, the estimated number of migrants to the Gulf region from India was about 1.54 lakh and the majority of them were from Kerala. A study conducted by the Department of Economics and Statistics, Government of Kerala, in 1987, placed the total number of out-migrants from Kerala at 680000, of whom 301000 were Gulf emigrants (Government of Kerala, Department of Economics and Statistics, 1994). An earlier study found that nearly 10 per cent of the households from Ernakulum, Palakkad and Malappuram districts had at least one emigrant who had been living in the Gulf countries at least for six months, the largest being in Malappuram with 15 per. cent (Zachariah *et al.*, 1994). A rough estimate of the number of emigrants from Kerala in 1991 (based on the Kerala Fertility Survey) was about 6 lakh. The Bureau of Economics and Statistics of the Government of Kerala indicated that the estimated number of emigrants in the Gulf region and other foreign countries numbered around 6.69 lakh. This trend has continued till now with 1.84 million in 2004, up from 1.36 million in 1999 (Zachariah *et al.*, 2003; Zachariah and Rajan, 2004).

Emigration had a very significant impact on the status of women in Kerala, especially Muslim women. Since the man of the house was away in a Gulf country, women were forced to take the responsibilities usually borne by men—responsibilities related to education of children, banking, investments and other financial responsibilities, social obligations, etc. One important aspect of this responsibility that befell on women has been the tremendous improvement in the education of girls in Muslim households who benefited more than boys, as boys tend to emigrate on attending adulthood. A large proportion of the emigration was from among the Muslim community residing in the backward, coastal lowland areas of the state. Emigration has opened up this community to modern ways of life and ideas about the importance of female education, maternal and child healthcare and family planning (Zachariah and Rajan, 2001).

Increase in the income of households occasioned by receipt of remittances and transfer of goods from abroad has enabled large numbers of households to improve their housing conditions, to consume nutritious food, to acquire modern consumer items, to educate their children and to utilise the services of doctors and hospital facilities for healthcare. In these and several other ways, emigration has played a significant role in the demographic transition in Kerala since the 1980s.

Other Determinants of the Demographic Transition

Fertility and mortality registered significant declines during the 1980s. The extent of the decline was larger than predicated at the beginning of the decade. What were the factors associated with this accelerated decline during this decade? The immediate (or proximate) causes for the decline in fertility were the increase in the age of marriage of women and the increased use of family planning practices, especially sterilisation.

Family planning was also a proximate determinant of mortality decline. However, the more important proximate determinant of mortality decline was UIP, especially antenatal care. This programme gave immunisation to mothers and children; more importantly, it brought the population closer to the health system and thereby indirectly increased the utilisation of health facilities in child birth, in treatment of the sick and in family planning. The IPP-III, which covered the four backward districts of Kerala, was also a factor for the decline.

Whatever be the immediate means of the fertility and the mortality declines of the 1980s, the basic underlying factors were a series of socioeconomic changes which made it an economic imperative for parents to improve the quality of their children—quality in terms of health, nutrition and education. The socioeconomic changes were described in detail in the study made by Zachariah (1984). The additional factors in the 1980s, were the steady acceleration in the volume of emigration to countries in the Gulf region—a process which has continued ever since—the UIP which was introduced in 1985, the World Bank project which was executed during 1985-1990, and the Saksharata programme (the universal literacy programme) which begun in Ernakulum in 1980.

In the World Bank study (1984), prime importance was given to education for generating socioeconomic changes, and for bringing about, among other things and quickening the pace of demographic transition. The introduction of formal education as a criterion for entry into public services brought about a basic change in society after centuries of fundamental stability. The society became, so to say, unhinged, ushering in a movement away from inherited status and towards achieved status, from a complete interdependent community network to competition of individuals, and from traditional authority to modern bureaucracy.

In the changed economic perspective, quality of children has become not only merely crucial; good quality is considered essential for upward social mobility and even for sheer economic survival, both for the well-to-do and for the poor. Formerly, the rich could fall back on the family's landed property or to familial connections to make a decent living and maintain status in society. This became no longer possible. Without adequate education (and good health), a person could not make a living on the basis of caste, religion or land alone. For the poor and persons of lower castes, education offered the only hope of breaking the shackles of illiteracy, poor health and poverty. With radical political changes and social and economic reforms favouring them, the poor also perceived an opportunity to improve their lives through education and good health.

Education and healthcare are getting more and more expensive by the day. Even without any changes in the cost per child, the total cost of a family to educate and to provide good health to children would have increased because of the decline in infant and child mortality and the consequent increase in the number of surviving children.

On the positive side, though the short-term economic benefits of children have shrunk as the tight employment situation has reduced their changes to obtain paid work outside home, there is reason to believe that the long-term benefits might have increased. But these benefits would come only if the necessary initial investment is made in a child's education. With the increase in both the cost per child and the number of surviving children, most families in Kerala find it difficult even to make the initial investment. They have, therefore, reduced their family size, opting for well-endowed small homes over ill-endowed large ones.

It is, however, unclear whether the recent sharp decline in marital fertility and infant mortality, which has embraced all socioeconomic groups, was caused solely by such changes in attitudes concerning the quality of children. More likely, it was precipitated by more recent policy interventions too (land and agrarian reforms, UIP, TLC, the family planning programme and the accelerating emigration flows to the Gulf region).

Land reforms and other re-distributive policies kept on accelerating the need for healthy and well-educated children; increasing emigration flows opened up some of large conservative populations to modern ideas about the importance of small family size, education and healthcare and provided the wherewithal to realise their goals; UIP, the World Bank project and the family planning programme helped translate the manifest and the latent desire for fewer and healthier children into actual fertility and mortality reductions; and the universal literacy campaign helped not only the creation of additional demand, but also better utilisation of the government's policies and programmes in healthcare and family planning.

Not all families have emigrants in them, but almost all families in Kerala are now directly or indirectly affected by it in terms of increase in income and exposure to modern ideas about education, nutrition, health, family planning and family size. Emigration not only helped the creation of additional demand for health, education and family planning services, but also provided the additional incomes to achieve these objectives.

The official family planning programme is not merely a means for providing contraceptive services; it has also been an independent causal factor in changing family size norms, and in creating and strengthening the demand for family planning. In Kerala, it went even further. As a result of the economic incentives offered to officials and acceptors, the programme was able to create demand even where it did not exist previously. Thus the programme provided services in places where demand existed, strengthened demand where it was weak, and created demand especially among the poor where no demand had existed previously.

The role of the UIP in creating demand for antenatal care and child immunisation has been even larger than that of family planning. The programme by its very effective communication strategy played a major role in creating demand for higher levels of nutritional intake among pregnant women and children and a host of other health-related practices.

The interaction between fertility and mortality declines which has become strong lately has been another additional factor. The universal literacy programme has worked in the background to strengthen this interaction. The MCH programme had an impact not only on mortality but also on fertility. It brought people closer to the healthcare system, which also delivered family planning services. Similarly, the accelerated fertility decline resulted in fewer unwanted births, and births at older ages of mothers, thus reducing the incidence of infant mortality rates.

A good deal of credit should go the official policies in education, family planning and healthcare in providing the essential services; they were also instrumental in generating additional demand for these and related services. The socioeconomic changes that were on, created the necessary milieu in which family planning and MCH programmes became acceptable and essential. The family planning and the MCH programmes created the additional demand for their services, and provided the means by which fertility and mortality rates proceeded on a path of steady decline.

Population Growth in the 21st Century

The Kerala population for the next 50 years has been projected using the 2001 census figures and various assumptions for the trends in fertility, mortality and migration. Three projections have been made. Mortality assumptions are the same for all the three sets. The expectation of life at birth of males is projected to increase from 75.20 years during the period 2001-2006 to 77.2 years during the period 2021-2026 and to 78.9 years during the period 2046-2051. The corresponding changes in the female expectation of life at birth are 81.2 years, 83.2 years and 84.9 years respectively (Table 2.8).

Currently, Kerala's TFR is 1.7; we have examined the implications of three different courses of the fertility trends. The first is a continuation of the recent fertility decline. The TFR is assumed to decline further

TABLE 2.8

Expectation of Life at Birth, Assumed in the Projections of Kerala

Period	Expectation of Life at Birth		Total Fertility Rate		
	Males	Females	Projection I (Low)	Projection II (Medium)	Projection III (High)
2001-2006	75.20	81.20	1.5	1.7	1.7
2006-2011	75.78	81.78	1.4	1.7	1.7
2011-2016	76.29	82.29	1.4	1.7	1.8
2016-2021	76.74	82.74	1.4	1.7	1.8
2021-2026	77.15	83.15	1.4	1.7	1.9
2026-2031	77.53	83.53	1.4	1.7	1.9
2031-2036	77.89	83.89	1.4	1.7	2.0
2036-2041	78.23	84.23	1.4	1.7	2.0
2041-2046	78.55	84.55	1.4	1.7	2.0
2046-2051	78.85	84.85	1.4	1.7	2.0

Source: Based on the Population projections made by S. Irudaya Rajan, K.C. Zachariah and Sabu Aliyar exclusively for the State Development Report.

to about 1.4 during the next 10 years and to remain at this rate indefinitely thereafter (Projection I). As the second probability, it is assumed that fertility will remain constant at a TFR of 1.7 for the entire projection period (Projection II). The third assumption is one of declining fertility to a TFR of 1.7 as in projection I, followed by an increase in fertility after the period 2011-2016 (Table 2.8). In deciding on these fertility assumptions, the basic considerations have been the trend in fertility in Kerala in recent years, the social and economic progress that the state has been making and the international experience in fertility decline. According to the United Nations sources, there were nearly 40 countries with a TFR of less than 2.0 during the period 1990-1995, including the larger countries such as China, the Russian Federation, United Kingdom, Japan and Italy; nearly one-fourth of these 40 countries have a TFR of 1.5 or less.

In all the three projections, it is assumed that Kerala will continue to experience a moderate level of net out-migration. The assumed rate is -0.25 per cent, less than the observed rate of -0.27 per cent for the period 1991-2001 (Zachariah *et al.*, 2003). The assumed migration rate of -0.25 per cent is kept constant throughout the projection period. Much of the discussion in this section is based on projection II. The PEOPLE software package has been used for making the projections.

Population Stabilisation and Zero Population Growth

The population of Kerala in 2001 was 31.8 million and the decadal growth in population during the period 1991-2001 has been estimated to be around 2.8 million. It is unlikely that future decades will see growth rates compared to those of the past few decades. Population growth in Kerala during the period 2001-2051 and the projected growth according tc the three alternative set of assumptions are shown in Table 2.9.

TABLE 2.9

Population Projections for Kerala, 2001-2051

Year	Projection I ('000)	Growth Rate(%)	Projection II ('000)	Growth Rate(%)	Projection III ('000)	Growth Rate(%)
2001	31838	—	31838	—	31838	—
2006	32641	0.63	33076	0.81	33076	0.81
2011	33343	0.43	34202	0.67	34202	0.67
2016	33817	0.28	35074	0.50	35207	0.58
2021	33995	0.11	35633	0.32	35888	0.38
2026	33871	-0.07	35913	0.16	36398	0.28
2031	32459	-0.24	35965	0.03	36678	0.15
2036	32745	-0.43	35778	-0.10	36837	0.09
2041	31727	-0.63	35319	-0.26	36750	-0.05
2046	30390	-0.86	34536	-0.45	36369	-0.21
2051	28760	-1.10	33449	-0.64	35717	-0.36

Source: Same as Table 2.8.

These figures indicate that Kerala's population growth has lost much of its momentum. The current indications are that the total population of the state is unlikely to exceed ultimately the figure of 37.0 million by 2051. Also, Kerala is likely to achieve zero population growth (ZPG) in 25 to 30 years. Moreover, it is possible that Kerala would have decades of negative growth rates in another two or three decades. Thus, the demographic situation of the state in the first of half of the 21st century will be significantly different from that of the previous half century. The socioeconomic impacts of population growth in the future will be vastly different from that in the past as is discussed below.

Changing Age Structure

One of the ways through which demographic trends affect socioeconomic conditions are changes in age composition of the population. Trends in fertility rate, mortality rate and migration rate have repercussions on the age structure of the population. Likely changes in the proportion of children in Kerala's population, in the proportion of working age population, and in the proportion of the elderly are clearly brought out in these projections. Over the next 50 years, negative growth rate among children and positive growth rate among the elderly are observed (Table 2.10).

TABLE 2.10

Demographic Scenario for Kerala: Past and Future

Year	Total Population ('000)	Growth Rate (%)	Children <15 Years ('000)	Growth Rate (%)	Elderly 60+ ('000)	Growth Rate (%)
1961	16904	-	7205	-	986	-
1971	21347	2.33	8595	1.76	1328	2.98
1981	25451	1.76	8901	0.35	1910	3.63
1991	29074	1.33	8617	-0.32	2573	2.98
2001	31838	0.91	7429	-1.48	3442	2.91
2011	34201	0.74	7230	-0.27	4642	2.99
2021	35633	0.41	6624	-0.88	6624	3.56
2031	35965	0.09	5785	-1.35	9169	3.25
2041	35319	-0.18	5419	-0.65	11080	1.89
2051	33449	-0.54	4921	-0.96	11732	0.57

Source: Same as Table 2.8.

TABLE 2.11

Decomposition of Number of Children Under 15 Years of Age

Year	Children Under 15 Years ('000)	Proportion of Children to Total Population (Per cent)	Children 5-9 Years (Primary School)	Children 10-14 Years (Secondary School)
1961	7205	42.62	2443	2253
1971	8595	40.26	2876	2864
1981	8901	34.97	2922	3258
1991	8617	29.64	2847	3108
2001	7429	23.40	2256	2726
2011	7230	21.10	2343	2402
2021	6624	18.60	2219	2349
2031	5875	16.10	1896	2012
2041	5419	15.30	1814	1834
2051	4921	14.70	1638	1729

Source: Same as Table 2.8.

Educational Planning

The changes in the number and proportion of children in Kerala are analysed first. These numbers are directly relevant for the state's educational planning. In this discussion, children are defined as persons under 15 years of age. The number of children in a population is mostly contributed by the number of births and to a lesser extent by migration. As the birth rate has declined considerably (from about 40 per 1000 in the 1950s to about 17 per 1000 in the late 1990s), dramatic declines in the number of children should be expected. However, part of the expected change in the number of children is cancelled by the increase in the number of mothers and decline in the death rate among children. Table 2.11 gives the number of children according to the various censuses since the formation of Kerala (1 November 1956) and the projections up to 2051.

Between 1961 and 1981 there was an increase of about 1.7 million children; but since then the number has been declining. By 2001, the number of children is almost closer to the figures for 1961. In 1961, 4 in 10 Keralites were children and the proportion has come to 2 in 10 in 2001.

Decomposition of the number of children by five-year age groups indicates that the decline will be the largest in the youngest age group. The school age population will shrink considerably in the coming decades. Children in the lower primary school ages (taken as 5-9 years) will decline from 2847000 in 1991 to 1638000 in 2051. The expected decline is projected also for upper primary and secondary school age group (10-14 years).

The implications of a drastic decline in the school age population have been evident for quite some time in Kerala. A decline of 32 per cent in the school age population may necessitate a corresponding decline in the number of primary schools, classrooms and teachers, etc. Implementation of policies and programmes in response to these major demographic shifts might take some time, but are inevitable (see Government of Kerala, 1994; James, 1995; Rajan and Mishra, 1996; 1997a; 1997b).

An uneconomic school is defined as one which does not satisfy the requirement of Para I of Rule 22 (4) of Kerala Education Rules according to which the minimum strength per standard at the Lower Primary or the Upper Primary or the Secondary stages shall be 25. There were 2622 uneconomic schools in 2003 in Kerala of which 1284 schools were in the government sector and 1338 schools were in private aided sector. While 80.5 per cent of the uneconomic schools were lower primary schools, 16.3 per cent were upper primary schools and 3.2 per cent were secondary schools. These schools would be closed down in a phased manner.

The decline in the population of children will have repercussions on many other areas of economic activity as well, such as the children's clothing industry, toy manufacturing industry and heathcare services for children. Economic activities catering to children and pregnant women are bound to shrink and will require considerable adjustment in the coming years. Any increase in the proportion of children using such services would partly compensate for the decrease in their number. The quality of life and the care for children are likely to improve in the coming years.

Labour Force

As already mentioned, unemployment especially among the educated, is one of the major economic and social problems of Kerala. Several factors are involved in the emergence of unemployment as a very serious problem; rapid population growth since the 1950s is one of them. Efforts to find solutions to the unemployment problem were hampered by the demographic explosion in the state.

In 1961, there were only 7640000 persons in the working age group of 20-64 years in Kerala. This number more than doubled to about 15,660 thousand in 1991. The number of persons in this working age group would increase further to about 22071000 by 2021 (a 41 per cent increase), and then decline (by 22 per cent) to about 17313000 by 2051. (It may be noted that most of the persons who will be older than 20 years of age in 2021 were already born before the 2001 Census; therefore the projections of the working age population for 2021 are quite realistic.) Thus, the accentuation of the unemployment problem in the state is partly due certainly to demographic pressure. In spite of the very rapid decline in the birth rate in the state during the past two decades, the demographic pressure on the labour force would not disappear for quite some time. It is only after 2021 that a real decline is likely in the number of persons in the working age group.

However, there would be a significant decline in the growth rate of the labour force beginning with the first decade of the present century and some absolute decline after 2021. Equally important would be the change in the structure of the working age population. In 1961 and 1991, the proportion of the working age population in the young working ages (20-34 years) was nearly half of total; 49.7 per cent in 1961 and 50.3 per cent in 1991; however, after 1991, the proportion of the young has been undergoing a dramatic decline to less than 30 per cent. Between 1991 and 2021, the actual number of such workers would decrease by 1.1 million. Thus, the problem of unemployment among the young would greatly ease itself in the coming years. Thus the state could promote employment of the youth; even if migration of the youth from Kerala to other states of India and other parts of the world were to decline in the near future (Table 2.12).

Just the opposite is the case of the older workers i.e., those above 50 years of age. The proportion of the population in the 50-64 year bracket would increase from 18.6 per cent in 1991 to 35.5 per cent by 2021. The actual number would also increase considerably i.e., from 2911000 to 7164000 by 2021. Finding suitable employment for persons in the older working ages would be a major challenge in the early part of the present century.

TABLE 2.12

Working Age Population in Kerala, 1961 to 2051

Year	*Numbers*			
	20-64 Years	*20-34 Years*	*35-49 Years*	*50-64 Years*
1961	7639624	3789636	2474651	1336337
1971	9568105	4586988	3234650	1746467
1981	12312589	6290800	3709377	2312412
1991	15660910	7878650	4871010	2911250
2001	18950664	8665863	6565096	3719705
2011	22905308	8078800	8459581	6366927
2021	22070831	6695974	8210795	7164062
2031	21524558	6504858	7045439	7974261
2041	19510631	5905723	6156965	7447943
2051	17313001	5075630	6075687	6161684
Year	*Growth Rate (per cent)*			
	20-64 Years	*20-34 Years*	*35-49 Years*	*50-64 Years*
1961-1971	2.25	1.89	2.68	2.45
1971-1981	2.52	3.16	1.37	2.81
1981-1991	2.41	2.25	2.72	2.30
1991-2001	1.91	0.95	2.98	2.45
2001-2011	1.90	-0.70	2.54	5.37
2011-2021	-0.37	-1.88	-0.03	1.18
2021-2031	-0.25	-0.29	-1.53	1.07
2031-2041	-0.98	-0.97	-1.35	-0.68
2041-2051	-1.20	-1.51	-0.13	-1.90

Source: Same as Table 2.8.

TABLE 2.13

Population of Marriageable Age, Kerala 1961 to 2001

Year	*Women in Ages 20-24 Years*	*Men in Ages 25-29 Years*	*Difference*	
			Excess Number of Women	*Excess Percentage*
1961	755227	604244	150983	19.99
1971	1012032	664365	347667	34.35
1981	1364026	1005881	358145	26.26
1991	1634240	1263540	370700	22.68
2001	1448101	1377910	70191	4.85

Source: Same as Table 2.8.

The population in the middle ages (35-49 years) has also increased considerably in absolute terms (3,439 thousand) during the period 1991-2001; but in relative terms their share changed only a little, from 31 per cent to only 35 per cent.

Marriage Squeeze

A significant consequence of a rapidly declining fertility rate is its effect on the parity between the number of females and the number of males in the marriage-age groups. As females marry at relatively younger ages than those of males, the number of females in the marriage market usually exceeds the number of eligible males. However, the situation changes considerably if fertility falls rapidly as has occurred in Kerala during the past three decades. The effect of such a fertility decline is felt initially in the number of females in the usual marriage ages. The effect of a fertility decline on the size of the age group of males of marriageable ages is felt only 5-6 years later.

In Kerala, most females get married when they are in the age group 20-24 years and most males get married when they are in the 25-29 age group. The difference between the number of females and males in these age groups is a measure of the marriage squeeze in the state. These numbers are given in Table 2.13 for the years 1961 to 2001.

Women in the age group 20-24 years outnumbered men in the age group 25-29 years throughout the period. The excess was as much as 20 per cent in 1961, and 34 per cent in 1971, greatly increasing the marriage squeeze. Since then it has been on the decline. In the coming years, females in Kerala will have a much wider choice in finding a suitable groom than they had in the past four decades. The number of women in the 20-24 age group was approximately the same as the number of men in the 25-29 year age group in 2001. This is a welcome consequence of the fertility decline during the past two decades.

The Elderly

One of the inevitable consequences of the demographic transition is population ageing. Being ahead of the rest of the states in India in the process, Kerala is expected to see an increase in the number of elderly persons and their proportion in the total population of the state, during the years to come (Rajan, 1989; 1999a; 1999b; 2000; 2001; Rajan and Mishra, 1997a; 1997b; Rajan and Zachariah, 1998). Defining the elderly population as persons above 60 years of age, the number of elderly was nearly 1.0 million in 1961. By 1991, their number increased to 2.6 million. The number is expected to exceed 6.6 million by 2021 and 11.7 million by 2051. The change in the proportion of the elderly is even more dramatic; from around 9 per cent in 1991, 19 per cent in 2021 and 35 per cent in 2051.

The decomposition of the elderly population by age and their categorisation as 'young old' (60-74 years of age) and 'old old' (75 years and older) provide additional information on issues concerning the elderly in the state. Among all the age groups of the state population, the group growing most rapidly is the 'old old'; see Table 2.14.

Conclusions

Kerala's demographic trends in the first half of the 21st century would be dramatically different from those of the second half of the 20th century. Whereas the total population of the state has increased by 135 per cent during the second half of the 20th century (from 13549000 in 1951 to 31838000 in 2001), the growth, if at all, in the population during the next half century

TABLE 2.14

Composition of Young-old (60-74) and Old-old (75+) in Kerala's Elderly (60+) Population, 1961-2051

Year	Number ('000)		Proportion (Per Cent)		Growth Rate (Per Cent)		Proportion of Total Population (Per Cent)	
	60-74 Years	75 and Older	60-74 Years	75 and Older	60-74 Years	75 and Older	60-74 Years	75 and Older
1961	793	193	80.40	19.56	-	-	5.83	1.14
1971	1060	267	79.87	20.13	2.90	3.25	6.22	1.25
1981	1519	391	79.52	20.48	3.59	3.81	7.50	1.54
1991	2005	568	77.92	22.08	2.78	3.74	8.85	1.95
2001	2571	871	74.69	25.31	2.48	4.27	10.83	2.74
2011	3355	1287	72.27	27.73	2.66	3.90	13.57	3.76
2021	4889	1735	73.81	26.19	3.77	2.98	18.59	4.87
2031	6604	2565	72.02	27.98	3.01	3.61	25.49	7.13
2041	7408	3700	66.69	33.31	1.15	3.36	31.45	10.48
2051	6932	4800	59.08	40.92	-0.66	2.60	35.07	14.36

Source: Same as Table 2.8.

would be negligible. The crude death rate declined from about 20 per 1000 to about 6 per 1000 in the past half century, but it is likely to increase to 13 per 1000 during the first half of 21st century. The crude birth rate decreased from 40 per 1000 to about 16 per 1000 in the last half of the 20th century, but it is likely to remain more or less stable in the next half century. While Kerala experienced varying degrees of net out-migration and net emigration in the second half of the 20th century, the migration trends in the first half of the 21st century remain uncertain. However, they would depend more on socioeconomic developments in the country and abroad than on demographic trends.

The socioeconomic implications of the reversal of the demographic trends would be far-reaching. Mainly, the pressure on schools and colleges for admission of students would become a thing of the past, giving ample opportunities for the educational system to concentrate on the quality of education rather than on increasing numbers of students. This feature holds good also for hospitals and healthcare personnel catering to the health needs of children. It would be easier in the years ahead to bring about needed improvements in the quality of such services. In the transitional period, parity between the number of females and males in their respective marriage groups ages would be maintained, but this interregnum would offer only a temporary respite.

Other things being equal on the economic front, unemployment among Kerala's young working age population would decline in the coming decades. Educated young workers will be able virtually to pick and choose the jobs they want. But this will not be the case with older workers. The older working age population is expected to almost double in number in the 20 years during 2001 to 2021.

During the past half century, the major socioeconomic problems faced by Kerala were related to schooling places, maintenance of health and nutrition, and employment for the young. During the first half of the 21st century, the major socioeconomic problems would be of finding gainful employment for the relatively old working age population, maintenance of health and nutrition of the elderly, and providing the elderly with subsistence through social security measures, pensions and other support programmes.

References

Bhat, P.N. Mari (1987). "Mortality in India: Levels, Trends and Patterns". *Ph.D Dissertation.* USA: University of Pennsylvania.

Bhat, P.N. Mari, and S. Irudaya Rajan (1990). "Demographic Transition in Kerala Revisited", *Economic and Political Weekly.* Vol. 25(35-36): 957-80.

Bhat, P.N. Mari (1996). "Contours of Fertility Decline in India: A District Level Study Based on the 1991 Census", in K Srinivasan (ed.), *Population Policy and Reproductive Health.* Chapter 4. New Delhi: Hindustan Publishing Corporation. pp.96-177.

Department of Economics and Statistics (1994). *Report on Migration Survey, 1992-93.* Thiruvananthapuram: Government of Kerala.

Dyson T. and M. Murphy (1985). "The Onset of Fertility Transition", *Population and Development Review,* Volume 11(3): 399-440.`

Government of Kerala (1994). *Report on the Expert Committee on School Age Group Population in 2000 A.D and its Implications on Educational Policy and Planning.* Thiruvananthapuram: State Planning Board.

Guilmoto, C.Z. and S. Irudaya Rajan (2001). "Spatial Patterns of Fertility Transition in Indian Districts", *Population and Development Review,* Vol. 27(4).

———. (2002) "District Level Estimates of Fertility from India's 2001 Census", *Economic and Political Weekly* Volume 37(7): 665-72.

———. (eds.) (2005). *Fertility Transition in South India.* New Delhi: Sage Publications.

International Institute for Population Sciences (2000). *National Family Health Survey (NFHS-2), 1998-99.* Mumbai.

Irudaya Rajan, S. and U.S. Mishra (1996). "Fertility Transition in Kerala: Implications for Educational Planning", *Productivity,* Vol. 37(3): 386-96. October-December.

———. (1997a). "Kerala: Restructuring Welfare Programs-Emerging Trends", *Economic and Political Weekly,* Vol. 32(6): 261-63.

———. (1997b). "Population Ageing: Causes and Consequences", in K.C. Zachariah and S. Irudaya Rajan (eds.), *Kerala's Demographic Transition: Determinants and Consequences.* Chapter 12. New Delhi: Sage Publications. pp. 222-236.

Irudaya Rajan, S. and K.C. Zachariah (1998). "Long Term Implications of Low Fertility in Kerala, India", *Asia Pacific Population Journal,* Vol. 13(3): 41-65

Irudaya Rajan, S. and P. Mohanachandran (1999). "Estimating Infant Mortality in Kerala", *Economic and Political Weekly,* Vol. 34(12): 713-17.

Irudaya Rajan, S. (2005). "Emerging Demographic Change in South India", in C.Z. Guilmoto and Irudaya Rajan (eds.), *Fertility Transition in South India.* New Delhi: Sage Publications. pp. 23-52 .

Irudaya Rajan, S. and Sabu Aliyar (2005). "Fertility Change in Kerala", in Guilmoto and Irudaya Rajan Ibid. Chapter 5. pp.167-190.

James, K.S. (1995). "Demographic transition and education in Kerala", *Economic and Political Weekly,* Vol. 30(51): 3274-76.

Krishnamoorthy, S., P.M. Kulkarni and N. Audinaryana (2005). "Causes of Fertility Transition in Tamil Nadu", in Guilmoto and Irudaya Rajan *op. cit.* Chapter 7. pp. 227-247.

Nair, P.R. Gopinathan (1974). "Decline in Birth Rate: A Hypothesis about the Interrelationship betweem Demographic Variables, Health Services and Education", *Economic and Political Weekly,* Annual Number.

Rajna, P.N., P.M. Kulkarni and N. Thenmozhi (2005). "Fertility in Tamil Nadu: Level and Recent Trends", in Guilmoto and Irudaya Rajan *op. cit.* Chapter 6. pp.191-226.

State Planning Board (2005). *Economic Review 2004.* Thiruvananthapuram: Government of Kerala.

Vella Stephane (2005). "Low Fertility and Female Discrimination in South India: The Puzzle of Salem District in Tamil Nadu", in Guilmoto and Irudaya Rajan *op. cit.* pp.248-281.

Zachariah, K.C. (1984). "The Anomaly of the Fertility Decline in India's Kerala State: A Field Investigation", *Staff Working Paper* No. 700. Washington DC: World Bank.

Zachariah, K.C., S. Irudaya Rajan, P.S. Sarma, K. Navaneetham, P.S. Gopinathan Nair and U.S. Mishra (1994). "Demographic Transition in Kerala in the 1980s". *Centre for Development Studies Monograph Series.* Thiruvananthapuram. Reprinted in 1999.

Zachariah, K.C. and S. Irudaya Rajan (eds.). (1997). *Kerala's Demographic Transition: Determinants and Consequences.* New Delhi: Sage Publications.

Zachariah, K.C. and S. Irudaya Rajan (2001). "Gender Dimensions of Migration in Kerala: Macro and Micro Evidences", *Asia Pacific Population Journal,* Volume 16(3): 47-70,

Zachariah, K.C., E.T. Mathew and S Irudaya Rajan (2003). *Dynamics of Migration in Kerala: Dimensions, Differentials and Consequences.* Hyderabad: Orient Longman Private Limited.

Zachariah, K.C. and S. Irudaya Rajan (2004). *"Gulf Revisited", Centre for Development Studies Working Paper* No. 363. September. Thiruvananthapuram .

Chapter 3

Growth and Employment

Economic Growth and Structural Change

The landmark CDS study (CDS, 1975) on Kerala's development experience caught the attention of scholars not only within the country but the world over, mainly for the uncommon coexistence in the region of economic backwardness on the one hand and high quality of life of the people on the other. These two features are not normally expected to exist together because they are mutually antagonistic; their existence is therefore considered unstable too. In other words, it was apprehended that either the development deficit might end up pulling down the quality of life or at the other extreme, the high quality of life and the human development that goes with it would push up the economy onto higher trajectories of growth. Therefore, the literature on the region's development experience, right from the times of this first study has remained sceptical of the sustainability of human development achievements of the region. The long-drawn-out stagnation in economic growth experienced in the state since the early 1970s, and which lasted till the late 1980s, the fiscal crisis of the state government that steadily worsened and the progressive deterioration of the quality of public services over the period, have prompted scholars to ponder over the question of sustainability of the Kerala model and articulate on the topic in extension (Kannan, 1998; George, 1999). But the discussion on the limits to the Kerala model of development did not remain in currency for long. By the late 1980s, some clear signs of recovery began to emerge. The development dialogue in the state took a sharp U-turn in the early years of the present century when some scholars even claimed that the state had aiready moved on to a virtuous cycle of development (Chakravarthy, 2005; Kannan, 2005). The present analysis is intended to trace briefly the cause of economic growth and the structural changes that have taken place in the state economy. It also seeks to show that the riddle that the Kerala model had posed, remains unsolved even today.

Some sustained improvement in the growth performance of the economy did in fact take place during the past 10 to 15 years. But, a comparison of the growth rates with those of the neighbouring states and the national averages as well as of structural changes suggests that the state economy is yet to reach a stage that could be confidently referred to as the dawn of a virtuous cycle of development. The signs of unsustainability and the burden of development deficit are clearly visible at present in the crucial goods-producing sectors. But the riddle of an unenviable growth performance coexisting with high and rising quality of life of its people continuous to exist; but the economy and the society have been eminently sustained over the years. The state has maintained its lead position among the Indian states in respect of human development indicators over the past several decades. An important preoccupation of studies on Kerala's development experience has been the expatiation of the riddle and the exploration of the possibilities of its resolution. The introduction of the idea of public action by Sen is quite useful in summarising this literature because it is a catchall concept, which takes into its fold most of the explanatory hypotheses advanced. It for instance, encompasses all redistributive policies, initiated either from below by the people through their mobilisation or from above by the state itself. Another important piece of explanation, which became more relevant in the post-1970 period, ran in terms of the huge inflow of remittances into Kerala. The lingering gap in the literature is however reflected in the inability to problematise the low growth—high quality syndrome, which happens to be the two defining features of the Kerala model of development.

The question of weak growth performance, especially of the goods-producing sectors, assumes special importance when considered against the phenomenon of the migration-remittances boom experienced since the early 1970s. The remittances boom has been instrumental in maintaining—and even improving—the quality of life of the people, for it helped compensate the deficiency experienced in domestic production. But, the question as to why in spite of such huge inflow of remittances, and the remarkable human development achievements, the domestic production structures failed to respond and gain higher growth momentum remains unsolved. There were some isolated efforts to trace the historical roots of economic backwardness, focusing particularly on the Travancore region (Isaac and Tharakan 1986; Ram Mohan, 1991), which highlighted structural weaknesses inherited from the past, either on account of the specific mode of incorporation of the region with the metropolitan centres or because of the unequal centre-state relations that prevailed ever since Independence. Important explanatory hypotheses put forth in the context of the long drawn-out stagnation in industrial growth since the early 1970s are also worth mentioning. Many versions of the high-wage hypothesis, originally put forth to explain the poor industrial growth since the early 1970s, in terms of labour militancy and high wage cost, are in circulation even today. The same is the case of the explanation advanced in terms of the 'narrow industrial structure and poor agglomeration economies' (Subrahmanian and Pillai, 1987). According to another group of studies, (Balakrishnan, 1999; Harilal and Joseph, 2003) the migration-remittances boom, notwithstanding its favourable impact on income and quality of life indicators, had a clear adverse impact on domestic production, especially on sectors producing tradable commodities. The analytical distinction between tradable and non-tradable commodities that these studies make is important in understanding the process of structural change in the regional economy. The huge and sustained inflow of remittances pushed the prices of non-tradables higher than the growth of tradable commodities in the regional economy, making production of tradable commodities a much less viable proposition for the regional producers. It is only intuitive wisdom therefore to expect that investment in Kerala would be sensitive to the high cost regime of non-tradable inputs prevailing in the state, and that only the lines of production, which eminently suit to such a structure of prices, would have an edge in Kerala in the context of the ongoing process of structural change.

The recent policy shift towards liberalisation and globalisation that has come about at the national level is expected to become advantageous to regions such as Kerala, characterised by high degrees of external integration. In the new regime, the producers and regions are likely to pursue their comparative advantages unfettered by policy barriers. Nevertheless, the burden of the high cost of non-tradable inputs, an unrelenting problem caused primarily by the inflow of remittances, may prove to be a debilitating factor for the regional producers who are exposed to increasing intensive competition in the domestic as well as the external markets in the new policy environment. One of the primary challenges encountering individual investors as well as the state in general, therefore, is that of overcoming the disadvantage of high cost of non-tradable inputs in the region.

The Chapter is organised into four sections. In Section I we undertake a broad comparative analysis of the growth performance of the state economy. In Section II, we attempt an in-depth analysis of the recent growth trends. Section III presents a discussion on structural changes observed in recent decades. The important conclusions of the analysis are drawn in the final section.

Growth and Structural Change in Kerala: A Comparative Perspective

Against the background of economic reforms undertaken since the 1990s, regional development experience in India has attracted the attention of a number of scholars (Ahluwalia, 2000; Kurien, 2000). The findings of these studies have been contrary to the predictions of the neoclassical growth theory that interstate disparities in income level are likely to come down as the states tend to approach a steady state equilibrium. The observed divergences in the growth pattern have been attributed *inter-alia* to interstate variations in the allocation of private investment and in the levels of human capital base, interstate transfers and several other factors. In this section, an analysis is presented of the growth and structural change in Kerala in comparison with those of neighbouring states to highlight differences.

Table 3.1 presents the estimated trend growth rates in NSDP as a whole and on the three sectors *viz.* primary, secondary and tertiary, during the past two

TABLE 3.1

Growth Performance of Kerala, Karnataka, Tamil Nadu and All-India

Sectors	*Kerala*			*Karnataka*			*Tamil Nadu*			*India*		
	1975-76 to 1989-90	*1980-81 to 1990-91*	*1991-92 to 2000-01*	*1975-76 to 1989-90*	*1980-81 to 1990-91*	*1991-92 to 2000-01*	*1975-76 to 1989-90*	*1980-81 to 1990-91*	*1991-92 to 2000-01*	*1975-76 to 1989-90*	*1980-81 to 1990-91*	*1991-92 to 2000-01*
Primary	0.11	2.1	1.72	2.18	2.25	4.31	0.7	3.66	2.1	2.63	3.24	3.2
Secondary	2.78	2.82	5.89	5.52	6.65	6.75	3.62	4.67	5.9	5.29	6.56	6.04
Tertiary	3.89	4.15	7.9	6.4	7.26	9.69	4.62	6.39	8.85	5.86	6.78	8.06
Agriculture within the Primary	0.89	2.81	1.91	2.51	2.47	4.45	0.6	3.43	2.16	2.8	3.27	3.18
Manufacture within the Secondary	3.03	3.32	4.91	6.54	7.86	5.26	4.11	3.9	4.27	6.04	7.38	6.29
NSDP	2.11	3.08	5.65	4.35	5.05	7.15	3.11	5.14	6.37	4.38	5.31	6.06
Per Capita NSDP	0.66	1.69	4.49	2.16	3.09	5.6	1.65	3.7	5.34	2.21	3.18	4.19

Source: Domestic Product of States of India 1960-61 to 2000-01 and Government of Kerala, *Economic Review*, different years.

decades for Kerala and its neighbouring states of Karnataka, Tamil Nadu and for India. It is evident that the observed growth rates in the NSDP at the all-India level and in the three states during the 1990s were higher than those of the 1980s. Among the states, Kerala's growth during the 1990s had attracted special attention of researchers (e.g. Ahluwalia, 2000) on account of the near-doubling of the rate over that of the 1980s. While Kerala's performance was remarkable in the absolute sense, in a comparative sense, the observed growth is found to be lower than that of all-India and the other two states mentioned in the Table during all the three periods. Thanks to the low population growth rate, the growth in per capita NSDP of Kerala during the 1990s recorded high acceleration and turned out to be higher than the national average. Yet, when compared to other states, due to its lower growth in NSDP, its performance of Kerala turns out to be lacklustre.

The differential performance of the three states becomes all the more striking when their growth rates in the different sectors are examined. While the primary sector at the national level maintained more or less the same growth rate during the 1980s and the 1990s, Karnataka recorded growth acceleration during the 1990s whereas Kerala and Tamil Nadu registered decline in growth rate during the 1990s. Thus similar to the trend observed in NSDP, the growth rate in the primary sector of Kerala in general and the agricultural sector that accounted for bulk of the primary sector in particular lagged behind that of the neighbouring sates. In the secondary sector, Kerala experienced a doubling of the growth rate in the 1990s over the 1980s making it comparable to that of Tamil Nadu. Yet, the rate was lower than those of all-India and Karnataka. Studies have noted the vibrancy of the tertiary sector in Kerala resulting in a service sector-led growth of the regional economy (Pillai and Shanta, 2005). But if the data presented in Table 3.1 are any indication, such a phenomenon is not specific to Kerala alone. While the recorded growth in the service sector of Kerala almost doubled in the 1990s, it remained lower than those of other two states and all-India.

The foregoing discussion suggests that Kerala is yet to catch up with its neighbouring states of South India and all-India in terms of overall growth of NSDP and growth in the major sectors. Nevertheless, the Kerala economy has been improving its performance in terms of human development, the regional index having recorded a sustained increase from 0.685 in 1991 to 0.773 in 2001. More importantly, while the *National Human Development Report 2001* noted widening of interstate and intrastate disparities, Kerala's experience emerged unique with negligible rural-urban and interdistrict disparities (Government of Kerala, 2005). Yet, the riddle of high human development in association with lower economic growth remains. The improvement in growth performance observed during the 1990s needs, however, closer analysis at disaggregated levels for ascertaining the factors for and the nature of revival and its sustainability. Before undertaking such an exercise, the observed pattern of the structural change in the state economy *vis-à-vis* those of the neighbouring states, is attempted below.

TABLE 3.2

Structural Change in Kerala and Neighbouring States

Year	*Kerala*			*Karnataka*			*Tamil Nadu*			*India*		
	Primary	*Secondary*	*Tertiary*	*Primary*	*Secondary*	*Tertiary*	*Primary*	*Secondary*	*Tertiary*	*Primary*	*Secondary*	*Tertiary*
1975-1980	44.06	18.81	37.12	44.4	28.46	27.15	32.45	30.88	36.67	42.57	20.94	36.61
1980-1985	38.08	24.22	37.7	44.51	20.81	34.68	25.73	33.08	41.19	41.23	21.17	37.60
1985-1990	33.93	25.27	40.8	39.14	22.51	38.35	23.1	32.06	44.84	36.73	22.37	40.90
1990-1995	34.12	22.99	42.89	37.88	23.69	38.43	23.92	32.2	43.88	35.04	22.29	42.67
1995-2000	28.56	21.4	50.04	32.43	24.1	43.47	20.4	30.28	49.32	31.69	22.31	46.00

Source: Same as Table 3.1.

The estimates of the shares of the different sectors in the NSDP for five year periods since 1975 are presented in Table 3.2. It is observed that structural transformation has taken place in all the three states albeit with notable interstate variations. During 1980-1985, the primary sector held the leading position in Kerala (38%) and Karnataka (44%) whereas in Tamil Nadu it was the tertiary sector that occupied the leading position, accounting for more than 41 per cent of the NSDP. While in the Kerala and the Tamil Nadu economies, the share of both the primary and the secondary sector declined, in Karnataka the decline in the primary sector was accounted for by an increase in the secondary and the tertiary sectors. Perhaps the most distinguishing characteristic of the Kerala economy has been the growing importance of the tertiary sector. In fact, the increase in the share of the services sector in Kerala has been much higher than in the other two south Indian states and all-India. Thus, the regional economy of Kerala that used to be dominated by the primary sector in the initial period has turned out to be predominantly service-sector-oriented by the early years of the new century. While Karnataka maintained a nearly balanced sectoral composition, Tamil Nadu has retained the distinction of having the largest secondary sector among the three states along with a growing service sector.

Recent Growth Trends

The estimates of the annual growth rates in NSDP and its major sectoral components show that while there has taken place lately a deceleration in the growth rate of NSDP, the agriculture and the manufacturing sectors recorded negative growth rates after the second half of the 1990s (Figure 3.1). While the point of inflection seems to have been different for the different sectors, on the basis of the overall trend, the year 1997-1998 is found to represent the beginning of a new phase in the growth trajectory of Kerala. The trends seem to have had three phases: the first phase beginning with stagnation and lasting up to the late eighties (1975-1987), the second phase of revival (1987-1996) and the third phase, which marked re-emergence of a slow growth rate (post 1997); the third phase coincided with the entry into the WTO regime and the heightening of international competition.[1] It is thus observed that the general approach of estimating decadal growth rates, while useful to some extent in making interregional comparison, tends to conceal the actual growth trends and the turning points of the economy.

Table 3.3 presents the estimated trend growth rates using the Boyce (1986) procedure for the three sub-periods. Though there is a general consensus on the existence of a period of stagnation since the mid-seventies, the estimated growth rates of that period are presented with a view to comparing the performance of the economy with that of the crisis period. The Table indicates that there had taken place a more than threefold increase in the growth rate of NSDP in the second period compared to the first phase and that it became higher than even the all-India growth rate. During the third period, while the growth rate at the national level showed a marginal decline, that at the state level declined by more than two percentage points. What is more striking has been the intersectoral variation. In case of the primary sector, the recorded growth rate during the last period (-5.6%) was the lowest, even much lower than of the first period (0.04%). In the case of the secondary sector also the growth rate during the third period, though marginally

1. For a study on the endogenous identification of growth phases see Pushpangadan and Parameswarn (2005). According to this study, the second break in NSDP was in 1987-88 and that of the secondary sector was in 1985-86. The second break in the case of primary sector was found earlier i.e. 1982-83. The third break was found around 1993-94; it needs to be noted that the estimates covered the period only up to 2001-02.

FIGURE 3.1

Annual Growth Rate in NSDP and Leading Sectors of Kerala

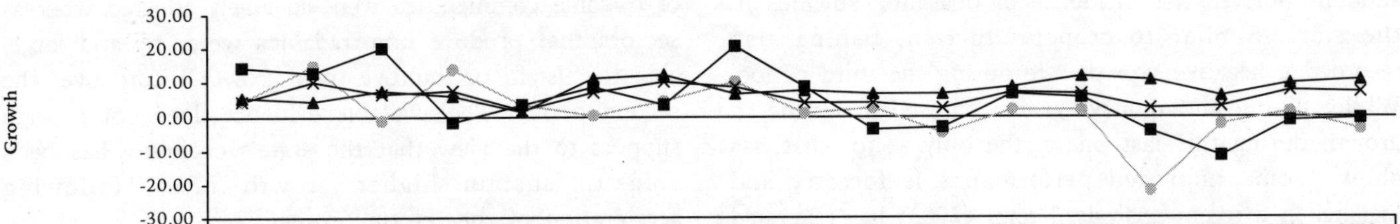

	1987-88	1988-89	1989-90	1990-91	1991-92	1992-93	1993-94	1994-95	1995-96	1996-97	1997-98	1998-99	1999-00	2000-01	2001-02	2002-03 P	2003-04 Q
Agriculture	4.32	14.86	-1.38	13.83	3.23	0.43	4.24	10.25	0.72	2.42	-4.75	1.81	1.70	-22.36	-2.51	1.30	-4.01
Manufacturing	14.41	12.83	20.27	-1.72	3.22	8.41	3.62	20.77	8.55	-3.73	-3.39	6.52	5.49	-4.48	-11.60	-1.07	-0.68
Tertiary	5.60	4.29	7.31	5.80	1.05	11.25	12.18	6.31	7.34	6.56	6.66	8.73	11.72	10.48	5.74	9.71	10.57
NSDP	4.32	10.05	6.72	7.56	1.94	7.21	10.35	8.62	4.01	4.00	2.16	7.02	6.76	2.60	2.81	7.32	7.29

Year

Source: Same as Table 3.1.

higher than of the first period, lagged much behind that of the second period and of the all-India growth rate. In contrast to the observed trend in the primary and the secondary sectors, the tertiary sector recorded growth rates higher than those of all-India and showed steady improvement over the three sub-periods. In general, the economy managed to maintain a growth rate of more than five per cent during the last phase mainly on account of the excellent performance of the tertiary sector, thus truly depicting a service-sector-driven growth phase.

It may be noted that after recording a turnaround during the second period, the goods-producing sectors entered a period of crisis in the third phase. For example, the recorded growth rate in agriculture (-7.1%) that accounted for bulk of the primary sector, during the last phase was an all-time low, even lower

TABLE 3.3

Sub-sectoral Trend Growth Rates of Net State Domestic Product in Kerala and India

Industries	*Kerala*			*India*		
	1975-76 to 1986-87	*1987-88 to 1996-97*	*1997-98 to 2003-04*	*1975-76 to 1986-87*	*1987-88 to 1996-97*	*1997-98 to 2003-04*
Agriculture	0.80	4.96	-7.14	2.69	3.68	1.14
Forestry and Logging	-14.41	1.80	2.41	-1.94	0.86	2.03
Fishing	-2.57	4.44	-1.16	3.79	6.35	2.63
Mining & Quarrying	7.27	7.12	5.50	5.50	5.49	5.09
Primary Sector	**0.04**	**4.72**	**-5.64**	**2.52**	**3.74**	**1.54**
Manufacturing	2.64	7.07	-3.37	5.87	6.36	4.18
Registered	4.14	5.97	0.74	6.94	6.77	3.50
Unregistered	0.59	8.77	-8.59	4.40	5.62	5.37
Construction	3.41	7.41	5.60	3.25	5.29	6.30
Electricity, Gas and Water Supply	-4.90	18.38	25.09	6.97	8.41	3.83
Secondary Sector	**2.36**	**7.51**	**2.97**	**5.16**	**6.22**	**4.67**
Transport, Storage and Communication	7.00	13.05	16.39	5.04	6.77	13.30
Trade, Hotels and Restaurants	1.33	5.40	6.66	4.73	6.97	7.78
Banking & Insurance	10.00	11.64	13.14	9.10	11.93	6.52
Real Estate, Ownership of Dwellings & Business Services	-9.19	-29.77	14.83	8.30	8.24	5.19
Public Administration	10.19	4.81	7.80	6.27	5.21	7.31
Other Services	1.21	4.48	8.28	4.36	6.39	8.29
Tertiary Sector	**3.56**	**6.83**	**9.11**	**5.63**	**7.34**	**8.19**
NSDP	**1.83**	**6.35**	**4.28**	**4.18**	**5.84**	**5.54**

Source: Same as Table 3.1.

than that recorded during the first phase. The negative growth phase was perhaps the background for the sudden spurt in the incidence of peasants' suicides in the state. Similar to crop production, fishing also recorded a negative growth rate during the third period. While mining and quarrying also showed a decline in growth during this last phase, the only sector that has shown some improved performance is forestry and logging. In a recent analysis, Jeromi (2003) has reiterated the fact of continuance of the decline in the performance of the agricultural sector ever since 2001-02.

After recording an all-time high growth rate of over 7 per cent per annum during second period, the manufacturing sector in the state nose-dived into a phase of negative growth rate. The decline was evident both in the organised and the unorganised sectors. The performance of the unorganised sector during the third period has been a dismal negative average rate of 8.5 per cent. In contrast to the rapid expansion in the number of small-scale industrial units during the Seventh Five Year Plan period (1985-1990), especially during the triennium ending 1989-90,[2] by 2001, Kerala accounted for more than 15 per cent of the sick units, according to the third All-India Census of Small-Scale Industries.

Unprecedented decline in the growth rate of agriculture and manufacturing notwithstanding, there took place overall improvement in the tertiary sector. In fact, such an improvement over the years has been noted by Pillai and Shanta (2005) who argued that tertiary sector was the sector propelling the growth of the economy since the 1980s and more so during the 1990s. Within the tertiary sector, while two sub-sectors (*viz.*, transport[3] storage and communication and banking and insurance), sustained two digit growth rates in the second and the third sub-periods, real estate, ownership of dwelling and business services recorded marked improvement during the third phase after recording negative growth rates during the second sub-period. Trade, hotels and restaurants and other services, which are related to the tourism sector, and other services, also improved their growth rates in the third period over their rates in the second period.

From the above discussion, it is seen that during the third phase the sectors engaged in the production of tradable commodities were adversely affected whereas sectors that produce non-tradables were, by and large, able to sustain or improve their growth record over the second period. The available evidence does not provide support to the view that the state's economy has been able to sustain higher growth rates, following acceleration of the reform process.

What explains the observed divide between poor performance of tradable sectors and the boom in sectors producing non-tradables? According to some recent studies this pattern of structural change has a lot to do with the migration-remittances boom that the state experienced since the early 1970s (Balakrishnan, 1999; Harilal and Joseph, 2003). The existing literature holds that migration-remittances phenomenon has tended to moderate the impact of stagnation in domestic production. In sharp contrast to this view, the studies mentioned here attribute the stagnation in growth, especially of the goods producing sectors, to the migration-remittances boom. According to this line of reasoning, the effects of the boom identified in the Dutch disease literature, *viz.*, the 'resource movement' and the 'spending' effects, have had a dampening impact on the goods-producing sectors of the regional economy. The huge and sustained inflow of remittances has tended to keep the prices of non-tradables high and increasing *vis-à-vis* prices of tradable commodities in the regional economy, making production of tradable commodities an unenviable proposition for the regional producers. Added to this has been the 'resource movement effect', which pushed up the wage level in the state. Under such conditions the economy had to adapt its product structure in such a way as to make it immune to the Dutch disease environment. Such an adaptation could *inter alia* involve making the commodity-producing sectors more competitive, moving towards high-value-adding products or by shifting towards products/services that are less exposed to international competition. How has the regional economy adapted itself to the new environment? To seek an answer to this issue, the structural change observed in the regional economy has to be explained in depth.

---

2. Out of the total number of 63698 small-scale units registered till the end of the Seventh Plan, 32199 units constituting more than 50 per cent of the total number of units were registered during the Seventh Plan. Of these, 23356 (36.7%) units were registered during 1987-90 "which is an all-time record" (*Economic Review 1990*, p.62).

3. Pushpangadan (2003) reported significant increase in the number of motor vehicles registered in the state during the 1990s. The trend continued after 2001 with an annual average growth rate of nearly 10 per cent. As a result, the share of Kerala in the in total number of vehicles registered in India turned out to be 3.93 per cent in 2002, much higher than its share in population (3.2%) and geographical area (1.2%). Also the density of motor vehicles per square kilometre of geographical area of the state increased from 25.9 in 1994-95 to 71.8 in 2003-04. High vehicle population in the state has generated more economic activities associated with repair, maintenance, sale of petroleum products and insurance business (Jeromi, 2003).

Structural Adaptation

Table 3.4 presents data on the share of different sub-sectors during the period under consideration. It is evident that during the past 30 years, the Kerala economy has undergone major structural changes in terms of the composition of its output. The broad direction of change has been in terms of drastic reduction in the share of the primary sector and corresponding increase in the share of tertiary sector. More importantly, the highest decline was recorded in case of agriculture with its share in NSDP declining from over 41 per cent in 1975-76 to a little over 13 per cent in 2003-04. In case of manufacturing, the share almost halved from about 13 per cent in 1975-76 to 7.5 per cent in 2003-04. But, we observe a different picture when it comes to the tertiary sector; its share in Kerala and India remained at 36 per cent in the initial year and by the terminal year it increased to over 60 per cent in Kerala and 52 per cent at the national level. Thus viewed, the broad pattern of structural change indicates that the share of tradable goods in general recorded sharp decline and the rate of decline was much higher than observed at the national level. As against this, the share of services and non-tradables showed a corresponding increase. For example, the construction activity in which tradability is limited, the share increased by more than threefold in Kerala as compared to one and a half times at the national level.

Within agriculture, the structural adaptation has been in terms of a movement away from labour-intensive annual crops like rice and cassava to less labour-intensive crops like natural rubber and other plantation crops. As a result, the commercial crops today account for nearly 85 per cent of the net sown area in the state. Since the commercial crops are exposed to international competition, their performance is governed by their competitiveness on the one hand and regime changes at the global and the national levels, on the other. This in turn called for sympathetic changes in state policy, improved productivity, greater value-addition at the farm gate level and initiatives to move up the value chain. But, policy initiatives and institutional interventions in this direction have been generally missing.[4]

The period since the mid-1990s, which coincided with the WTO regime, witnessed significant import liberalisation on account of reductions in tariff and non-tariff barriers. In addition to general reduction in tariff barriers there have been bilateral trade agreements like India-Sri Lanka Free Trade Agreement in the late 1990s. While these agreements have had the effect of providing a boost to trade as in the case of India-Sri Lanka trade and led to efficiency-induced investment restructuring, it is naïve to assume that, such free trade agreements benefit all the regions in the national economy. In fact, studies (Harilal and Joseph, 1999) have shown that the regional economy of Kerala, given the similarity in its crop structure to that of Sri Lanka, had to bear a greater burden. Further, the provision of special tariff concessions to new ASEAN member countries, under the Comprehensive Economic Cooperation Agreement between India and the ASEAN, has led to large-scale imports of black pepper from Vietnam in recent years.[5] Therefore, while entering into free trade agreements in the national interest, there has to be an appropriate provision to compensate the losers, a provision which is currently missing. As discussed at length in the chapter on Agriculture, increasing import competition, the resultant reduction in domestic prices, limited attempts towards value addition at the farm gate level through post-harvest operations and upward movement along the value chain seem to have had an adverse impact on the agricultural sector leading to a drastic reduction in its share in NSDP.

It should also be noted that the new policy regime, characterised as it has been by multilateral and regional agreements for establishing freer trade, has made the agricultural sector increasingly vulnerable to external shocks. An instance worth citing in the Kerala context is the adverse impact that the East Asian currency crisis had on the state economy. As the exchange rates of the East Asian currencies plummeted during the closing years of the previous century, prices of commodities exported from the region such as rubber, palm oil, coconut oil, etc., experienced unprecedented decline. Interestingly, the burden of the East-Asian crisis was soon transferred to the Kerala shores and onto the farming community here in the form of fall in prices of agricultural produce. The new policy regime has in general been indifferent to the adverse consequences of such external shocks.

---

4. In this context the recommendations of the Commission on WTO concerns in agriculture like launching a productivity, quality and value addition movement in all agricultural crops, launching a quality, literacy movement both for products intended for domestic consumption as well as for exports, introducing an appropriate aquarian reforms to safeguard the livelihoods of fishermen communities, preventing the abuse of the provision for concessional imports for re-exports, promoting organic farming, establishing a herbal bio-valley, setting up a consortium of innovative farmers, establishing a virtual university for agricultural trade etc. appear timely (see for details Government of Kerala, 2003). But concrete actions on these recommendations are yet to be made.
5. It is found that the second largest item of export from Vietnam to India during 2003-04 was black pepper, which in turn appears to have aggravated the crisis of the pepper growers in Kerala.

TABLE 3.4

Changes in Sectoral Composition of NSDP in Kerala and India

Industry	*Kerala*				*India*			
	1975-76	*1987-88*	*1997-98*	*2003-04*	*1975-76*	*1987-88*	*1997-98*	*2003-04*
Agriculture	41.07	31.69	23.81	13.15	40.35	30.60	27.11	21.81
Forestry & Logging	1.42	0.87	2.18	1.40	2.33	2.28	1.27	1.14
Fishing	2.97	1.29	2.32	1.86	0.77	0.92	1.26	1.03
Mining & Quarrying	0.09	0.14	0.16	0.29	1.30	2.32	2.01	2.31
Primary	**45.55**	**33.99**	**28.47**	**16.71**	**44.74**	**36.11**	**31.66**	**26.29**
Manufacturing	13.30	13.66	10.99	7.51	14.09	15.51	15.00	13.76
Registered	6.48	9.11	5.58	4.44	7.49	9.41	9.34	8.84
Unregistered	6.83	4.56	5.41	3.06	6.60	6.09	5.67	4.92
Construction	3.23	10.01	9.64	11.83	4.60	5.90	6.02	6.63
Electricity, Gas & Water Supply	1.04	0.41	0.97	3.30	0.54	0.99	1.43	1.12
Secondary	**17.57**	**24.08**	**21.60**	**22.63**	**19.23**	**22.39**	**22.45**	**21.51**
Transport, Storage and Communication	6.17	6.87	6.22	8.86	3.33	4.71	5.99	7.37
Trade, Hotels and Restaurants	12.57	15.14	22.08	23.33	11.51	13.58	15.34	16.28
Banking & Insurance	2.30	4.77	4.93	6.33	2.89	3.99	6.44	7.20
Real Estate, Ownership of Dwellings & Business Services	1.33	0.92	4.71	6.68	6.68	5.87	4.82	6.41
Public Administration	3.27	5.38	4.25	5.25	5.35	6.29	5.81	6.20
Other Services	11.24	8.86	7.74	10.21	6.45	7.06	7.49	8.74
Tertiary	**36.88**	**41.93**	**49.93**	**60.66**	**36.21**	**41.49**	**45.89**	**52.20**
Net State Domestic Product	100.00	100.00	100.00	100.00	100.00	100.00	100.00	100.00

Source: Same as Table 3.1.

There existed a tendency in the regional economy, particularly towards the end of the 1980s, when signs of recovery became visible, towards restructuring the industrial sector with focus on product lines and specialisations that are more immune to the Dutch disease environment (Harilal and Joseph, 2003). This was perhaps also facilitated by nominal and real depreciation of the currency during the early 1990s, which by favouring the tradable commodities, made some revival in growth possible. But, in spite of such signs of change, the industrial sector of the state even today remains handicapped and lopsided with limited capital investment available for introducing modernisation, technological changes and product diversification in keeping with the changing conditions in the global market. Subrahmanian (2006) shows that, relatively low growth during the post-reform period has been the net outcome of the remarkably high growth rates in a few traditional and local resource-based industries and depressingly low growth rates in large number of capital goods and modern manufacturing industries. Thus, it appears that the industries more exposed to competition have recorded low growth rates leading to the observed reduction in the growth of manufacturing sector as a whole. No wonder, in the absence of any conscious attempt towards promoting an industrial sector immune to the Dutch disease environment, the less diversified industrial structure in position which has been established mostly under the import substitution regime, has been weakly positioned to withstand increased international competition. The phenomenon of the observed low growth rate and the marked reduction in the share of the manufacturing sector in NSDP need to be viewed from this point.

The tertiary sector, on the other hand, which produces mainly non-tradables that are by their very nature, less exposed to international competition has been able to improve its growth rate as well as its share in the NSDP. Thus in the context of increased international competition, there appears to have taken place a structural shift in favour of those sectors that are relatively less exposed to international competition. Such a service sector driven growth has not been devoid of problems. Studies have shown that growth in the service sector was driven by producer services with limited linkages to the production sector within the state economy (Pillai and Shanata, 2005). Also, the structural shift in favour of the service sector is shown to have adversely affected the revenue earning capacity of the state, thus contributing towards revenue deficits and undermining the state's capability to undertake developmental expenditure (Mohan and Shyjan, 2005).

Concluding Observations

It is naïve to assume that in an economy like that of India, with size and regional diversities of a continent, all the different regions will be uniformly impacted upon by intensification of reforms, globalisation and increasing integration with the world economy. In fact, if the evidence presented in this chapter is any indication, with the intensification of reforms and increased integration with the world market on account of the WTO agreements, regional trading agreements like India-Sri Lanka Free Trade Agreement and special tariff concessions for ASEAN newcomers like Vietnam under the Comprehensive Economic Cooperation between India and ASEAN, the Kerala economy has entered a phase of deceleration in overall growth and an unprecedented crisis in its commodity-producing sectors. Such a scenario calls for appropriate policy initiatives to compensate regions unduly affected by the opening up of the economy, even when the process of opening up may be justifiable in the national interest. This is also a pointer towards the weakness of the regional economy *vis-à-vis* the rest of the economy to face the unprecedented international competition. Hence, there is need for enhancing the competitiveness of the regional economy. The available empirical evidence does not lend support to the view that the economy has entered a phase of virtuous growth with high achievements in human development. Instead the riddle of high human development with low growth of the economy remains pronounced even today like it was ever before.

The basic structural weakness of the regional economy has to be seen in the context of the migration-remittances boom and the associated resource movement and spending effects, which had a clear dampening effect on the competitiveness of the tradable commodities produced in the state. While some of the policy initiatives, undertaken at the national level during the early 1990s like high doses of devaluation of the rupee, seem to have given short-term dividends, the positive outcomes were rather short-lived in the absence of institutional arrangements at the regional level to equip its tradabales to meet the emerging challenges of globalisation. Even though there have taken place certain structural adaptations as manifested in the move towards less labour-intensive plantation crops in the agricultural sector, the agenda of adaptation has remained incomplete. It is noted that the industrial sector even today remains lopsided with limited capital investment for introducing modernisation, technological changes and product diversification in keeping with the changing conditions in the global market. More pronounced changes have taken place with greater focus on sectors less susceptible to international competition such as the non-tradables leading to structural shifts in favour of the service sector. Such shifts, however, need not be sustainable because many of the non-tradables today are likely to become tradable in the near future; further, policy reforms underway are sure indication of the opening up some of these areas for foreign direct investment. Moreover, the service sector driven growth is unlikely to contribute towards mitigating the revenue deficit of the state and might undermine its ability to make productive investment. Under such conditions there appears to be no easy policy options for the state other than to promote production of such tradables that are immune to the high cost environment currently prevailing in the region. They include, industries that are capable of sustaining their competitiveness in spite of high wages to less educated and unskilled workers and relatively high costs of non-tradables. Low wages in traditional industries and low cost of non-tradables cannot any more be sources of comparative advantage on which the state can hope to develop its domestic production sectors. Such a situation would call for activities that harness the high human development in the state and promote knowledge-intensive sectors by creating a more vibrant regional innovation system.

Employment and Unemployment of the Educated

Unemployment has remained a characteristic feature of the Kerala economy right from the days of its inception 50 years ago. Workforce participation rates in Kerala have remained far lower than in all-India and even in the neighbouring countries of South India during all the years from 1951 onwards. While at the all-India level, work participation rates hovered around two-fifths of the population, and in the South Indian states of Andhra Pradesh, Karnataka and Tamil Nadu remained in the range of 40 to 45 per cent, the rates in Kerala remained at lower than one-third during the period. Work participation rate of women falls far short of that for men. As against 51.6 per cent for males and 22.7 per cent for females in 2001 at the all-India level, the corresponding work participation rates in Kerala were 50.6 per cent and 15.3 per cent respectively. While the rate was not far lower in Kerala than an all-Indian for males, it was very much so in the case of females. Perhaps, Kerala is one among the major states in India in which the work participation rate declined; in some states, such as Punjab, Haryana and West Bengal, the rates were substantially increasing all along.

The factors that led to the decline in female work participation rate include the structural changes of employment in the state. For instance, several of the labour-intensive activities such as rice cultivation and traditional cottage industries have been declining or languishing in Kerala during more than the past three decades. These had been the two areas in which most of the women workers had found employment. The conversion of agricultural land to non-agricultural uses and of paddy fields to cultivation of commercial crops had reduced women workforce in the agricultural sector from 43.6 per cent in 1981 to 36.1 per cent in 1991. The crisis in the cottage industries led to a fall in women's workforce in them from 7.7 per cent to 5.9 per cent during the same period (Martin, 2005).

There does not exist significant differences in work participation rates as between the urban and the rural areas in Kerala. In 2001, the respective rates according to the Census, were around 32 to 33 per cent in both the areas. While it was agriculture that predominated in providing employment in rural areas, it was the tertiary sector which was predominant in the urban areas. The majority of the rural workers (accounting for about 84 per cent) were employed as casual labourers or were self-employed persons. It has been reported that 87 per cent of men workers and 85 per cent of women workers belonged to this category during 1999-2000. The proportion of the self-employed was higher among women, both in the rural and in the urban areas.

According to National Sample Survey Organisation, Kerala had in 1999-2000, 22 per cent of its labour force unemployed, 20 per cent for males and 26 per cent for females. During the 1990s unemployed, reckoned in terms of current daily status, increased from 14.7 per cent in 1993-94 to 21.7 per cent in 1999-2000.

Unemployment is a multidimensional concept involving time, income and output dimensions. The concept of 'disguised' unemployment used to signify employment that is not associated with commensurate output or income. Tertiary sector employment such as those of government officials, does not ordinarily yield tangible results in terms of physical output or productivity. There may be also persons who have jobs and work to do, but who consider themselves unemployed, an aspect referred to as the recognition aspect.

One of the widely used measures is the time dimension of unemployment. This dimension is sought to be captured through country-wide sample surveys by National Sample Survey Organisation (NSSO). Owing to complex diversities existing in the intensity of employment among different sectors and over time periods, NSSO makes multiple measures of the time dimension of employment: usual principal status (UPS), current daily status (CDS) and current weekly status (CWS). UPS is the most widely used measure of unemployment, namely the number of days spent in non-work. If the number of days of non-work come to more than 180 days in a year, the person is considered unemployed. According to this measure, the proportion of unemployed persons in the labour force was 11.4 per cent in Kerala in 1999-2000 as against 2.7 per cent for all-India. Unemployment of women (21.5 per cent) was about three times the unemployment of men (7.4 per cent). Unemployment was higher in urban areas (12.5 per cent) than in rural areas (10.9 per cent). The difference in the unemployment rates between women and men was also the highest in urban areas: 12.1 percentage points in rural areas and 19.5 percentage points in urban areas (Table 3.5).

Information on the state of unemployment for the years since 2000 is obtained from surveys conducted under the auspices of Centre for Development Studies. During October-December 2003, a survey on the phenomenon of educated unemployed in Kerala was conducted in three districts of Kerala—Thiruvananthapuram, Ernakulam and Kannur. The respondents were persons with educational qualifications of secondary school leaving certificate (SSLC) or above and belonging to the age group of 15 to 59 years. The specific objectives of the survey included an assessment of the magnitude and structure of human capital, the mismatch between education and nature of work of the employed (including the self-employed) and the waiting period for work.

The survey shows a significant increase in the supply of educated manpower in the state. The increase was mainly due to increase in the number of educated women.

It was also observed that while around 82 per cent of the educated men were employed, the corresponding proportion among women was only 71 per cent. The labour force participation rates were higher (88 per

TABLE 3.5

Incidence of Unemployment (Unemployed as Proportion of Labour Force)

Period	Rural			Urban			All		
	Male	Female	Persons	Male	Female	Persons	Male	Female	Persons
1987-88									
Kerala	**13.6**	**29.2**	**19.2**	**16.2**	**39.5**	**23.5**	**14**	**30.6**	**19.8**
India	2.2	5.5	3.8	6.5	17.8	11.9	3.1	8	5.5
1993-94									
Kerala	**12.5**	**25.9**	**16.6**	**14.2**	**34**	**19.6**	**12.8**	**26.3**	**17.1**
India	2.8	3.5	3.1	6.1	8.5	7.2	3.6	4.7	4.2
1999-2000									
Kerala	**7.6**	**19.7**	**10.9**	**6.9**	**26.4**	**12.5**	**7.4**	**21.5**	**11.4**
India	2.1	1.5	1.9	4.8	7.1	5.2	2.8	2.4	2.7

Sources: *Sarvekshana*, Various Issues; NSS Reports No.341/3, No.109, No.458.

cent) for the less educated among men, but were far lower (20 per cent) for the less educated women.

About one-half the labour force of the age group 15 to 29 years, 42 per cent for men and 54 per cent for women, was unemployed. A significant proportion (3.7 per cent) of the educated labour force was of the secondary education level; persons who had the higher secondary level accounted for 19 per cent. Technically and professionally qualified persons came to about one-fifth of the educated manpower in Kerala. Nearly 24 per cent were degree (or postgraduate degree) holders.

Unemployment rates seem to have increased significantly among the educated during the early years of the new millennium. The proportion of the work-seekers among the educated constituted 45 per cent according to this survey. The educated unemployment rate was two and a half times higher among females than among males. Unemployment rate was the highest among the younger age group of 15 to 19 years for both men and women. For women the unemployment rate remained high till they reached the age of about 40 years, after which they seem to withdraw from the labour force.

Among the educated, the unemployment rate was the lowest for technically and professionally trained persons (such as diploma holders and professionals). It was much higher for females than for males for all categories of education and very high among unmarried females; about three-fourths of the unmarried females remained unemployed, according to the present survey. The rate was high among widows and divorced or separated women too.

Naturally, it is the less well-off sections of society that bear the brunt of the problem of educated unemployment. While 54 per cent of the poor sections (judged in terms of their housing conditions) among the educated remained unemployed, the corresponding proportion was only about 37 per cent among the better-off.

The period of waiting for taking up the first job after completion of studies, is an indication of the duration of unemployment. It is estimated that an educated person in Kerala spent, on the average, about 5.6 years waiting for his/her first job. The United Nations study by CDS made in 1975 had calculated the waiting period for all categories of the unemployed as 2.9 years in 1972. Though this estimate is not strictly comparable to the results of the present survey which has been confined to SSLC holders and persons with higher qualifications and of the age group 15-59 years, the indications are that the unemployed among the educated have to wait for much longer periods than earlier to secure their first jobs.

But the waiting time for the educated seems to have been different for the different age groups. Persons in the age group 45-49 years are seen to have waited for much longer periods for their first jobs than persons in the age groups 30-44 years and 15-29 years. While on the average, a person in the age group 45-49 years had waited for 7.5 years, the corresponding figures for the age group of 30-44 years was 6.5 years and that for those in the 15-29 years age group was only 3.3 years. The indications are that employment opportunities were much higher during the 1990s than had been the case earlier. Obviously these results do not necessarily and specifically reflect the situation in the early years of 2000. During the 1990s, the waiting period for the younger age groups itself varied among persons with different types of qualifications. For postgraduates and professionals, it was the lowest, at about 1.8 years as against more than 4 years for SSLC and HSC holders.

The waiting period varied also with the economic status of the persons concerned. It was lower for the relatively poor and the relatively rich, but longer for the middle-income groups. The low-income group obviously would not have the ability to wait till appropriate job opportunities presented themselves. Persons of this category accept the job that comes first, irrespective of whether it is commensurate with the person's qualifications and expectations about conditions of work, terms of remuneration, etc. The relatively rich would have advantages of possessing educational qualifications in ready demand and of influence and contact with purveyors of jobs. It is the middle-income groups who are more punctilious about jobs, but who find themselves wanting in terms of influence or power. It is therefore this last group which stays the longest waiting for jobs.

About 90 per cent of the employment seekers comes under the age group of 15 to 34 years. Except persons who do not have specialised skills but have only general education, such as SSLC and HSC employment seekers look for security of jobs and jobs commensurate with their educational qualifications. This is true both for males and females, irrespective of economic status.

Among the educated employed, only about three-fifths were in regular or permanent employment. About one-sixth were casual labourers and one-fifth self-employed persons. Women in employment had a clear preference for public sector jobs: nearly 45 per cent of them were employed in the public sector as against only 34 per cent of men.

Men sought employment in a much wider range of occupations than women did. While men were found employed in manufacturing, construction, transport, trade, education, and community and social services activities, women found employment in education, healthcare, trade, and community and social services occupations. Persons with higher levels of education (e.g. postgraduates, professionals, diploma holders) were concentrated in education, healthcare and community and social services. Education does not seem to confer any significant advantage in earnings for persons having qualifications up to and including the higher secondary level. In fact, the salaries earned by these categories happen in most cases to be lower than the wage earnings of agricultural labourers. The difference between the two categories of jobs lies not in the earning levels, but in the nature of work, the former being white-collar, indoor and 'prestigious'. 'Jobs' are thus seen to carry a premium over 'labour'.

For the self-employed, who account for about 13.5 per cent of the labour force, trade and commerce appear to be the preferred areas for men (in which 37 per cent of the males in self-employment are engaged) and agriculture and livestock-rearing are the activities for nearly 35 per cent of the self-employed women. More than four-fifths of the employed persons among the educated, found their employment through the agency of their friends and relations.

High rates of unemployment prevailing in the economy have not significantly affected the pursuit of employment opportunities, either for men or for women. About 10 per cent of the total labour force must have turned away from job search; but curiously enough, about 90 per cent of this group comprised women. One of the major reasons for the withdrawal of women must have been their relative lack of spatial mobility. Both men and women were, in general, reluctant to leave the places of their origin; but the reluctance was much greater in the case of women. Only about 5 per cent of the women job-seekers were willing to take jobs in places inconvenient to them.

An interesting question to ask is about the financial support that the educated unemployed receive, a condition that enables them to live a life of unemployment. According to neoclassical economic theory, the labour market would find equilibrium at a price that clears the market of all excess supply and meets the total demand for labour in that market. If unemployment prevails, it implies that the market is in disequilibrium. Wage changes would continue to take place till the equilibrium wage is established.

In the Kerala context, it is known that unemployment exists on a large scale, wage rates remain rigid, and employment opportunities remain unfilled. The existence of widespread unemployment in the face of unfilled vacancies and unsatiated labour demand in general has produced a seemingly paradoxical situation. The explanation for the existence of this phenomenon has to be sought in the redoubled withholding power or staying power of the unemployed. It was noted earlier that the majority of the educated unemployed comprised young and unmarried persons. Most of them were not themselves the breadwinners of the households to which they belonged. They have found that their subsistence was being taken care of by their households, which had the required economic power. Zachariah and Irudaya Rajan (2005) have termed this type of unemployment phenomenon in Kerala a 'social' rather than an 'economic' problem.

The simultaneous existence of large-scale unemployment and of numerous unfilled job opportunities has led to a curious result in Kerala in recent years—the steady influx of labour from across the state borders, even from states as far away as Bihar, Assam and West Bengal, a phenomenon known as 'Replacement Migration'. These inmigrants work mainly in the household, agricultural and construction sectors, at wages much lower than the prevailing rates. These inmigrant workers are not given any legal rights on wages, working conditions, and terms of service and are highly exploited. These hapless workers consider their Kerala conditions much better than those at home and prefer to slog it away in Kerala. The pall of calm that covered this unsavoury practice has recently broken with the starvation deaths of a couple of these workers, allegedly suffering from 'malaria'. The stories of their ruthless exploitation have now begun to receive the attention of labour leaders, bureaucracy and political activists.

About 2.3 million persons were reportedly unemployed in Kerala in 2004 (Zachariah and Irudaya Rajan, 2005). This number worked to about 19.2 per cent of the labour force—41 per cent in the case of women. The unemployed have a waiting period of more than 5 years. Chronic unemployment involving much longer periods of waiting is experienced only by about one-fourth of the unemployed. The unemployment rate gets very small, of nearly 6 per cent, among persons in the age groups above 30 years. Many of the unemployed persons are dependent members of well-to-do householders possessing strong withholding power.

One of the serious problems encountered in eradicating the unemployment problem in the state, particularly employment of the educated unemployed, is poor employability. As was shown earlier, employability is high among the technically and professionally qualified categories and among very highly qualified persons (e.g. postgraduate degree holders). However, the majority of the educated unemployed come from the general education stream—SSLC and HSC and first degree holders. The effective solution to the problem of educated unemployment in Kerala therefore lies in the promotion of technical and professional education programmes and retraining of the unemployed through appropriate vocational courses. Of course, a lasting solution is possible only if more investment opportunities are created within the state in agriculture and industry, overcoming the resistance of a variety of sociopolitical and economic interest groups.

References

Ahluwalia, S.M. (2000). "Economic Performance of States in Post-Reforms Period, *Economic and Political Weekly*, Vol. 35(19), May 6.

Balakrishnan, Pulapre (1999). "Trends in Agricultural Wages in Kerala", *Economic and Political Weekly*, May 22.

Centre for Development Studies (1975). *Poverty, Unemployment and Development Policy: A Case Study of Selected Issues with Reference to Kerala.* New York: United Nations.

Centre for Development Studies (1975). *Poverty Unemployment and Development Policy: A Case Study of Selected Issue With Reference to Kerala.* Thiruvananthapuram : CDS and New York: United Nations.

Chakravarty, Achin (2005). "Kerala's Changing Development Narratives", *Economic and Political Weekly*, February 5.

Dreaze, Jean and Sen Amartya (1989). *Hunger and Public Action.* Oxford: Clarendon Press.

———. (ed.) (1996). *Indian Development: Selected Regional Perspectives*, Oxford University Press, New Delhi.

Franke, W. Rechard and Chasin H. Barbara (1992). *Kerala: Development Through Radical Reform.* New Delhi: Promilla Publishers.

George, K.K. (1993). *Limits to Kerala Model of Development: An Analysis of Fiscal; Crisis and its Implications.* Thiruvananthapuram: Centre for Development Studies.

Government of Kerala (2001). *White Paper on State Finances.* Thiruvananthapuram

———. (2003). *Report of the Commission on WTO Concerns in Agriculture: Building a Sustainable Agricultural Trade System for Kerala.* Thrivananthapuram.

———. (2005). *Economic Review, 2004.* Thiruvananthapuram: State Planning Board.

Harilal K.N. and K.J. Joseph (1999). "India-Srilanka Free Trade Accord", *Economic and Political Weekly*, Vol. 34, No. 13. March 27, pp 750-754.

———. (2003). "Stagnation and Revival of Kerala Economy—An Open Economy Perspective", *Economic and Political Weekly*, Vol 38(23): 2286-95.

Jeromi, P.D. (2003). "What Ails Kerala's Economy: A Sectoral Exploration", *Economic and Political Weekly*, Vol. 38(16): 1584-1600, April 19-25.

Joseph, Brigit and K.J. Joseph (2005). "Commercial Agriculture in Kerala after the WTO", *South Asia Economic Journal*, Vol 6(1): 23-37.

Kannan, K.P. (2005). "Kerala's Turnaround in Growth: Role of Social Development Remittances and Reform" *Economic and Political Weekly*, February 5.

———. (1998). 'Political Economy of Labour and Development in Kerala, in *Economic and Political Weekly*, December 26.

Kannan K.P. and Pushpangadan K. (1990). 'Dissecting Agricultural Stagnation in Kerala: An Analysis Across Crops', *Economic and Political Weekly*, September.

Kurien N.J. (2000). "Widening Regional Disparities in India: Some Implications", *Economic and Political Weekly*, Vol. 35(7), February 12.

Martin, Patrick Labour Market and Employment in Rajasenana D. and Gerard de Groot (eds.) (2005). *Kerala Economy.* Cochin: Dept. of Applied Economics, CUSAT.

Mohan R. and Shyjan D. (2005). *Taxing Powers and Developmental Role of the Indian States: A Study with Reference to Kerala, Working Paper* No. 375. Thiruvananthapuram: Centre for Development Studies.

Navaneetham, K. (2005). "Educated Unemployment in Kerala". Thiruvananthapuram : Centre for Development Studies. (*mimeo*).

Pillai, Mohanan P. and Shanta N. (2005). *Long Terms Trends in the Growth and Structure of the Net State Domestic Product in Kerala, Working Paper No. 376*, Centre for Development Studies, Thiruvananthapuram.

Prakash, B.A. and M.P. Abraham (2004). "Employment and Unemnployment in Kerala", in B.A. Prakash (ed.), *Kerala's Economic Development.* New Delhi: Sage Publications.

Pushpangadan, K. (2003). "Remittances Consumption and Economic Growth in Kerala: 1982-2000", *Working Paper* No.343. Thiruvananthapuram: Centre for Development Studies.

Pushpangadan, K. and Parameswaran (2005). *Endogenous Identification of Growth Phase: An Application to Kerala Economy*, Unpublished Document.

Ram Mohan, K.T. (1991). 'Understanding Keralam: The Tragedy of Radical Scholarship, *Monthly Review*, Vol. 43(7), December.

Ramachandran, V.K. (1996). "On Kerala's Development Achievements", in Dreaze, Jean and Amartya Sen (eds.) *Indian Development: Selected Regional Perspectives*, Oxford University Press, New Delhi.

Ranis, Gustaze and Stewart Frances (2000). "Economic Growth and Human Development". *World Development*, Vol. 28(2): 197-219, February. Elsevier.

———. (2001). "Growth and Human Development: Comparative Latin American Experience", *Centre Discussion Paper* No.826. Economic Growth Centre, Yale University.

Subrahmanian, K.K. (2006). "Economic Growth in the Regime of Reforms: Kerala's Experience", *Economic and Political Weekly*, Vol 41(10): 897-904.

Subrahmanian, K.K. and P.M. Pillai (1987). "Kerala's Industrial Backwardness: Exploration of Alternative Hypothesis", *Economic and Political Weekly*, April.

Tharamangalam, J. (1998). "The Perils of Social Development without Economic Growth: The Development Debacle of Kerala, India", *Bulletin of Concerned Asian Scholars*, Vol. 30(1).

Zachariah, K.C. and S. Irudaya Rajan (2005). "Unemployment in Kerala at the Turn of the Century", *Working Paper* 374. Thiruvananthapuram : Centre for Development Studies. (*mimeo*).

Chapter 4

Financial Services and Fiscal Reforms

This chapter consists of three parts: the first part presents the financial profile of the state; the financial system including the state of the banking and the financial services as well as their functioning in Kerala is discussed in part two; in part three, the trends of the fiscal reforms of the state and the lines on which future fiscal reforms may be formulated are examined in detail.

I. FINANCIAL PROFILE

Literature on Kerala Finances: A Brief Overview

The deepening fiscal crisis of Indian states from the early 1980s has been engaging the attention of academic economists and policy makers for quite some time. In Kerala also several studies have been undertaken on state finances both by individual scholars and expert committees formed by Government of Kerala from time to time. A brief review of these studies is attempted below.

An early attempt at analysing the fiscal problems of Kerala was made by Gopalakrishnan (1986). He analysed the causes of the state's inability to find enough resources for plan financing and came to the broad conclusion that the major factor was the state's failure in tapping the fiscal potential of sales tax.

In 1987, a study team was appointed by the state government to look into the factors for failure of the state to mobilise sufficient resources for financing the Sixth Five Year Plan. The report prepared by two experts from the National Institute of Public Finance and Policy was the first attempt to go in-depth into the finances of Kerala on scientific lines (see Bagchi and Rao, 1987). The study team came to the broad conclusion that the fiscal situation could be improved if necessary corrective actions were taken. The team took note of the failure of public enterprises of the state to generate adequate public savings for reinvestment purposes. A major untapped area was stamp duties and registration fee. The team suggested a method for preventing the rampant practice of under-valuation of property, which had caused heavy financial loss to the exchequer. The team was also critical of the proliferation of welfare schemes and the laxity in expenditure control. Government of Kerala subsequently implemented some of the recommendations of the study team.

The study by George (1990) was the first systematic analysis of the causes and consequences of the fiscal crisis of Kerala. Tracing the root causes of the fiscal crisis in Kerala, George observed that the financing of revenue deficits through capital funds would have grave consequences for development of the state. While it reduced the volume of capital expenditure on the one hand, it aggravated the debt-servicing problem on the other. The study also analysed the structure of public expenditure in Kerala. Compared to other Indian states, non-plan revenue expenditure of Kerala was higher mainly due to the predominance of social and community services particularly education, in the total revenue expenditure. The study identified the system of devolution of resources between the centre and the states as one of the factors contributing to the fiscal crisis of Kerala. By investing in the social sectors, the state had achieved several of the social goals set by the national planners. These were also the goals enshrined in the Constitution of the Country. However, successive Finance Commissions and the Planning Commission had taken note of these achievements only to categorise Kerala as a state ineligible for funds earmarked for states lagging behind in achievements on these fronts.

The author also argued that some of the problems that plagued the state like unemployment and higher pension payments were the inevitable consequences of the success of the development path that the state had chosen to follow. The author came to the conclusion that the state's fiscal and development crises were reinforcing each other and that therefore corrective steps needed to be taken on all fronts. George has repeated almost the same line of arguments in his later writings as well (George, 1993; 1994).

The recommendations of study teams and the findings of scholars did not salvage, however, the state from fiscal problems. By the early 1990s the fiscal problems worsened further, forcing the government of Kerala to appoint a Commission widely known as the Resources Commission (1991). The Commission had as its members some of the leading bureaucrats of the state who had firsthand experience in the intricacies of government's receipts and expenditures. The Commission went in-depth into the potential for additional resource mobilisation and the scope for rationalising and streamlining expenditures. In its interim report the Commission made a series of recommendations, which had to be implemented within a time frame. These recommendations were intended to tide over the immediate fiscal problems of the state. A comprehensive study of the finances of the state was undertaken at the instance of the Commission by National Institute of Public Finance and Policy. Some of the major recommendations of this study were the introduction of value-added sales tax, computerisation of sales tax administration, and administrative and procedural measures to prevent stamp duty evasion. The easing of fiscal crisis during the years immediately following the Commission report owes to a large extent to the implementation of some of its recommendations.

Another notable initiative at identifying additional resources was the formation of the Task Force on Tax and Non-tax Sources of Revenue as part of the formulation of Ninth Five Year Plan (Government of Kerala, 1997). The Task Force prepared a comprehensive report covering tax and non-tax resources. Some of its major recommendations were rationalisation of the rate structure of sales tax, introduction of Value-Added Tax, increasing of user charges of various services provided by government departments and professionalisation of management of public sector undertakings.

Aiyar and Kurup (1992) attempted an overview of the finances of Kerala in the eighties. The authors analysed the trends in revenue and expenditure and indicated the areas which needed fiscal correction. Broadly their findings conformed to the prescriptions put forward by other Committees and Commissions and study teams. Jacob (1997) made an attempt to identify the factors contributing to the fiscal crisis of Kerala. He argued that the fiscal crisis was partly due to the sluggish growth of the state's resources despite the vast potential which existed for additional resource mobilisation. He did not, however, offer any policy suggestions different from the ones already made by other Committees and Commissions.

The state of Kerala's finances continued to attract the attention of academicians and policy makers in the late 1990s and the early 2000. Srivastava *et al.*, (1999) attempted a fresh look at the issues relating to state finances in the light of major developments on the fiscal front during the initial years of economic liberalisation. The major concern of their study was the suggestion of measures for the state to tide over the fiscal crisis during the Ninth Five Year Plan. Besides making suggestions for shoring up the finances of the state, they also prepared a fiscal framework for the period 1997-98 to 2001-02 aimed at keeping the Fiscal Deficit-GSDP ratio and Debt-GSDP ratio in check, at not more than 4.79 per cent and 39 per cent respectively by the end of the period. A recent attempt has been made by George and Krishnakumar (2003). Essentially this paper is an updation of the earlier work of George referred to earlier. Concentrating more on the post-liberalisation period, they analysed the recent trends in revenue and expenditure and arrived at the broad conclusion that "fiscal reforms must target both expenditure management and resource mobilisation simultaneously." According to the authors, the role of the state needs to be redefined and expenditure priorities determined afresh. Instead of drastically reducing expenditure across the board, more attention needed to be bestowed on increasing the productivity of expenditure.

Fiscal Scenario of All States

The fiscal position of State Governments in India has been under severe stress from the mid-1990s. The Gross Fiscal Deficit (GFD)—Gross Domestic Product (GDP) ratio of All States, which was 2.6 per cent in 1995-96, went up to 5.1 per cent in 2003-04. Revenue deficit, which was 0.70 per cent in 1995-96, went upto 2.6 per cent in 2003-04 (Table 4.1).

The major problems that confront the State Governments are growing interest burden, increasing liabilities on salaries and pensions, rising administrative cost, mounting losses in public sector undertakings, poorly targeted subsidies, inappropriate and inadequate user charges and declining Central transfers coupled with inadequate buoyancy in revenue receipts (GoK, 2006).

TABLE 4.1

Key Fiscal Indicators of All States

(Rs. in Crore)

Year	*Gross Fiscal Deficit*	*Revenue Deficit*	*Primary Deficit*
1995-96	31426 (2.6)	8201 (0.70)	9494 (0.80)
1996-97	37251 (2.7)	16114 (1.2)	11675 (0.90)
1997-98	44200 (2.9)	16333 (1.1)	14087 (0.91)
1998-99	74254 (4.2)	43642 (2.5)	38381 (2.2)
1999-00	91480 (4.7)	53797 (2.7)	46309 (2.4)
2000-01	89532 (4.3)	53569 (2.5)	37830 (1.8)
2001-02	95994 (4.2)	59188 (2.6)	33488 (1.5)
2002-03	102123 (4.1)	55111 (2.2)	31981 (1.3)
2003-04 (RE)	141010 (5.1)	72126 (2.6)	57042 (2.1)

Note: Figures in brackets are per cent to GDP at Current Market Prices.

Source: *Economic Review 2004*, State Planning Board, Kerala.

State governments have initiated measures to arrest these trends through revenue augmentations, containment of non-essential expenditures, enactment of Fiscal Responsibility and Budget Management legislation and public sector reforms.

Structure of Kerala's Revenue

Like in most Indian states, the revenue structure of Kerala is also composed of tax and non-tax resources. The share of tax revenue in the total own revenue of Kerala increased from 77.08 per cent in 1980-81 to 91.88 per cent in 2003-04 whereas the corresponding figures for All States are 66.95 per cent and 79.84 per cent respectively. Among tax revenue sources, taxes on commodities and services contributed 84.58 per cent in 2003-04. Of this sales tax alone contributed 67.9 per cent. The proportion of own revenue in the total revenue of Kerala has been consistently higher than of all-India. In 2003-04, it was 74.43 per cent for Kerala as against only 61.89 per cent for All States. Table 4.2 presents the salient features of Kerala's revenue structure.

Structure of Public Expenditure

The 'Kerala model of development', accounts to a large extent for the pattern of its public expenditure with great emphasis on social and community services like health, education and social welfare at rates much higher than in most of the states. The fiscal crisis that the state has been undergoing for the past few years owes a great deal to this pattern of public expenditure (see George, 1993). Salient features of the state's budget expenditures are presented in Table 4.3.

TABLE 4.2

Salient Features of Kerala's Revenue Structure

Particulars	*Unit*	*1990-91*	*2001-02*	*2002-03**	*2003-04#*
State's Total Revenue	Rs. in Lakhs	240293	905639	1145133	1269961
State's Own Total Revenue	Rs. in Lakhs	154916	646680	814059	945179
State's Own Tax Revenue	Rs. in Lakhs	134035	592342	740363	868392
State's Own Non-Tax Revenue	Rs. in Lakhs	20881	54338	73696	76787
Central Transfers	Rs. in Lakhs	85377	258959	331074	324782
Total Revenue-GSDP Ratio**	Per cent	17.04	11.40	12.58	N.A@
Own Revenue-GSDP Ratio	Per cent	10.99	8.14	8.95	N.A
Own Tax-GSDP Ratio	Per cent	9.51	7.45	8.14	N.A
Own Non-Tax GSDP Ratio	Per cent	1.48	0.68	0.81	N.A
Per Capita Total Revenue	Rupees	829	2810.27	3553.44	3870.06
Per Capita Own Revenue	Rupees	534	2006.70	2503.33	2880.33
Per Capita Own Tax Revenue	Rupees	462	1838.09	2276.71	2646.33
Per Capita Own Non-Tax Revenue	Rupees	72	165.51	226.62	234.00

Note: *: Revised estimates; #: Budget estimates; **: The GSDP figures for 2001-02 and 2002-03 are provisional and quick estimates respectively; @: As GSDP figures are not available for 2003-04.

Source: Worked out using the data from (1) *Reserve Bank of India Bulletin*, relevant issues; (2) *Economic Review 2003*, Kerala State Planning Board, January 2004.

Fiscal Health of the State

The revenue mobilisation efforts of Kerala have not been adequate to meet the growing expenditure needs of the state. From the mid-1970s onwards, Kerala has been experiencing fiscal constraints due to budgetary deficits both in its revenue and capital accounts. Revenue deficits became almost a permanent feature of Kerala finances from 1983-84 onwards. The state has been using an increasing portion of the interest-bearing borrowed funds to finance revenue deficits. Consequently, capital expenditure has been consistently coming down causing a shrinking of the stock of capital assets and inadequate maintenance of existing capital assets. Table 4.4 presents the major indicators of the fiscal health of the state.

Debt Outstanding and Interest Obligations

A major fallout of the mounting revenue deficits and their financing through borrowed funds at high rates of interest has been growing debts and debt-servicing obligations. Table 4.5 presents details regarding debt and interest obligations for recent years.

TABLE 4.3

Salient Features of Kerala's Public Expenditure

(Rs. in Lakh)

Particulars	*Unit*	*1990-91*	*2001-02*	*2002-03@*	*2003-04#*
Aggregate Expenditure	Rs. Lakhs	337645	1313191	1544085	1731614
Revenue Expenditure	Rs. Lakhs	282495	1166203	1335000	1536465
Capital Expenditure	Rs. Lakhs	55150	146988	209085	195149
Ratio of Revenue Expen. to Capital Expenditure	Per Cent	84:16	89:11	86:14	89:11
Developmental Expenditure**	Rs. Lakhs	18770	667280	825630	956150
Non-Development Expenditure$	Rs. Lakhs	99900	564130	607000	644960
Ratio of Developmental Expenditure to Non-developmental Expenditure	Per Cent Rs. Lakhs	69:31 75960	54:46 237050	58:42 399790	60:40 430790
Plan Expenditure	Per Cent	4.60	2.98	4.39	1300830
Plan Expenditure as a % of GSDP	Rs. Lakhs	262510	1076140	1144290	
Non-Plan Expenditure	Per Cent	15.90	13.55	12.57	
Non-Plan Expenditure as a % of GSDP*					

Note: @ Denotes Revised Estimates; # Denotes Budget Estimates.

* The GSDP figures for 2002-03 are quick estimates. ** Comprise expenditure on Revenue and Capital Accounts and Loans and Advances extended by States for developmental purposes. $ Comprise expenditure on Revenue and Capital Accounts and Loans and Advances extended by States for non-developmental purposes.

Source: Worked out using the data from (1) *Reserve Bank of India Bulletin*, relevant issues; (2) *Economic Review 2003*, Kerala State Planning Board, January 2004.

TABLE 4.4

Major Indicators of the Fiscal Health of Kerala

Particulars	*Unit*	*1990-91*	*2001-02*	*2002-03@*	*2003-04#*
Revenue Deficit	Rs. Lakh	42210	260560	189870	266500
Revenue Deficit as a % of Revenue Expenditure	Per Cent	14.90	22.30	14.20	17.30
Revenue Deficit as a % of GSDP*	Per Cent	2.56	3.28	2.09	—
Gross Fiscal Deficit	Rs. Lakh	79900	326940	284500	330690
Gross Fiscal Deficit as a % of GSDP	Per Cent	4.85	4.11	3.12	—
Revenue Deficit as a % of Gross Fiscal Deficit	Per Cent	52.80	79.70	66.70	80.60

Note: @ Denotes Revised Estimates; # Denotes Budget Estimates

* The GSDP figures for 2002-03 are quick estimates.

Source: Worked out using the data from (1) *Reserve Bank of India Bulletin*, relevant issues; (2) *Economic Review 2003*, Kerala State Planning Board, January 2004.

Investment Activity Including Credit Flow

From the point of view of attracting industrial investment, Kerala has certain inherent disadvantages. The location of the state in the southernmost part of the subcontinent and the high density of its population are major handicaps. Besides, over the years, the state has acquired some degree of notoriety as an investor-hostile destination, though concerted efforts have been made in the recent past to refurbish its image. Because of these and a host of other factors, Kerala could not attract considerable industrial investment in the post-liberalisation period. (Table 4.6).

Kerala is the fourth lowest among the major states of India in attracting industrial investment during August 1991 to March 2004. It may be noted that the other southern states are way ahead of Kerala both in proposed investment and employment.

The industrial backwardness of Kerala cannot be explained in terms of one or two factors. A constellation of factors has contributed to it. Though

TABLE 4.5

Debt and Net Interest Payments of Kerala

(Rs. in Crore)

	Debt Outstanding as at end of March		*Net Interest Payments*		
Year	*Amount (Rs. crore)*	*As a % to GSDP**	*Year (Rs. crore)*	*Amount*	*As a % of Revenue Receipts*
1996	10114	26.1	1995-96	823.9	15.2
1997	11421	25.7	1996-97	1047.7	17.0
1998	12868	28.9	1997-98	1232.6	17.3
1999	15700	27.9	1998-99	1375.3	19.1
2000	20176	32.3	1999-00	1915.0	24.1
2001	23919	34.6	2000-01	2220.8	25.4
2002	26951	33.9	2001-02	2458.4	27.1
2003#	29987	37.09	2002-03#	2628.7	23.0
2004@	33708	37.38	2003-04@	2702.8	21.3

Note: # Revised Estimates; @ Budget Estimates

* The GSDP figures for 2002-03 and 2003-04 are provisional and quick estimates respectively.

Source: Worked out using the data from (1) *Reserve Bank of India Bulletin*, relevant issues; (2) *Economic Review 2004*, Kerala State Planning Board, February 2005.

TABLE 4.6

State-wise Industrial Investment Proposals (August 1991-March 2004)

(Rs. in Crore)

State	*Letter of Intents + Direct Industrial Licences*					
	Numbers Granted	*Per Cent*	*Proposed Investment (Rs. Crores)*	*Per Cent*	*Proposed Employment (Numbers)*	*Per Cent*
Andhra Pradesh	434	11.08	10715	9.64	79775	9.42
Assam	12	0.13	2433	2.19	4538	0.54
Bihar	33	0.84	1462	1.32	13674	1.61
Gujarat	438	11.18	21028	18.92	71700	8.46
Haryana	233	5.95	4318	3.89	63120	7.45
Karnataka	183	4.67	4887	4.40	54035	6.38
Kerala	**67**	**1.71**	**2782**	**2.50**	**14326**	**1.69**
Madhya Pradesh	141	3.60	3160	2.84	30163	3.56
Maharashtra	558	14.24	14567	13.11	129482	15.28
Orissa	7	0.94	5444	4.90	11882	1.40
Punjab	183	4.67	4887	4.40	54035	6.38
Rajastan	97	2.48	1626	1.46	15455	1.82
Tamil Nadu	736	18.79	11273	10.14	129056	15.23
Uttar Pradesh	353	9.01	9752	8.77	97750	11.54
West Bengal	90	2.30	4047	3.64	19132	2.26

Source: "SIA Statistics April 2004", Ministry of Commerce and Industry, Government of India, as reported in *Economic and Political Weekly*, July 10, 2004, p.3079.

the state is ahead of several Indian states in some of the factors that immediately matter for attracting industrial investment, it seems that the state is lagging behind in some of the critical factors. This is evident from the study undertaken by the Confederation of Indian Industry (CII) across 18 states in India on the attractiveness of states in industrial investment (Table 4.7).

TABLE 4.7

Kerala's Ranking in Investment Attractiveness

Attributes	*Kerala's Rank Among 18 Indian States*
Law and Order	1
Education and Health Expenditure	1
Social Sector	2
Affluence	3
Infrastructure Penetration	5
Investment Attractiveness	5
General Achievement	6
Finance	6
Labour	8
Investment Climate	13
Overall Composite Rank	3

Source: CII sponsored study on Investment Attractiveness as reported in Government of Kerala; Note on Investor Friendly Climate (presented to the Twelfth Finance Commission, December 2003, p.25).

Though Kerala has been rated as the third best in the country in overall ranking, her rank in respect of investment climate and labour are 13 and 8 respectively. This suggests that the negative perceptions, real or imaginary, will have to be removed to attract private domestic and foreign direct investments.

A major factor determining the level of investment activity in a region is the cost and availability of credit. An often used indicator of the level of credit deployment in an economy is the credit-deposit (CD) ratio. The assumed credit-deposit ratios of Kerala during this period 1991-2003 as reported by the State Level Bankers' Committee are stated in Table 4.8.

The CD ratio registered a steep fall from 59 per cent in 1991 to 41.28 per cent in 2000 (Table 4.8). A marginal recovery was visible from 2001 onwards. It is known that the ratio has got back to its 1991 level by the beginning of 2005. The CD ratio by itself may be an inadequate indicator of the investment climate in the case of states like Kerala, which receive substantial foreign remittances. Since economic growth is the major objective of credit deployment, a better yardstick

TABLE 4.8

Credit-Deposit Ratio of Kerala as at March end

Year	*Credit-Deposit Ratio in Per Cent*
1991	59.00
1992	51.00
1993	48.00
1994	43.10
1995	44.70
1996	44.40
1997	45.50
1998	44.88
1999	43.06
2000	41.28
2001	42.77
2002	42.71
2003	45.47
2004	48.31

Source: *Economic Review 2003*, State Planning Board, January, 2004, p.355.

would be the level of deployment of bank credit to the growth of the state economy. The level of advances as a proportion of Net State Domestic Product (NSDP) is therefore taken as an alternative indicator of the extent of credit support for the growth of the economy. A comparative picture of Kerala and India in terms of this indicator is given in Table 4.9.

The bank advances as a percentage of NSDP has been higher in Kerala than at the all-India levels throughout the period 1985-2002. However, the fall in the ratio from 37.7 per cent during 1985-90 to 27.9 per cent during 1996-2002 is a cause of concern from the point of view of aggregate credit deployment in the state (Table 4.9).

Another limiting factor for Kerala from the point of view of attracting industrial investment is the Infrastructural bottlenecks. In terms of power infrastructure, the state is way behind some of the industrially developed states in the country (Table 4.10).

Among the 15 major states, Kerala is the second lowest in installed capacity for power generation. It appears that the state has to invest heavily in power and infrastructure, if it is to attract massive industrial investment.

Government of India Investment

Central investment plays a major role in correcting regional disparities in industrial development in most federations. In India also, the industrially backward

TABLE 4.9

Advances as a Percentage of State Income

Year	Kerala	India
1985	35.5	24.4
1986	36.5	25.2
1987	37.7	25.5
1988	37.7	25.0
1989	40.3	25.5
1990	38.6	25.9
1991	38.1	25.4
1992	33.1	23.9
1993	33.9	25.4
1994	27.0	23.6
1995	26.9	25.8
1996	25.4	26.6
1997	25.8	25.1
1998	27.3	26.2
1999	26.6	25.4
2000	28.0	27.7
2001	30.4	30.1
2002	31.7	31.8
Average for		
1985-1990	37.7	25.2
1991-1995	31.8	24.8
1996-2002	27.9	27.6
1985-2002	32.2	26.0

Source: *Economic Review 2003*, State Planning Board of Kerala, January 2004, p.354.

TABLE 4.10

Installed Capacity (in MW) of Power in the States as on 31-1-2003

State	State Owned	Centre Owned	Private Owned	Total	% to Total
Andhra Pradesh	6328.80	2001.00	1137.40	9467.20	9.91
Assam	597.20	497.80	24.50	1119.50	1.17
Bihar	598.40	2460.80	—	3059.20	3.20
Gujarat	4683.70	1538.30	2639.80	8861.80	9.28
Haryana	1990.30	1137.00	—	3127.30	3.27
Karnataka	4508.10	674.00	683.70	5865.80	6.14
Kerala	**2031.60**	**804.00**	**207.80**	**3043.40**	**3.19**
Madhya Pradesh	3078.00	1120.20	22.00	4220.20	4.42
Maharashtra	9770.60	2027.90	7439.80	19238.30	20.14
Orissa	2304.50	1602.00	—	3906.50	4.09
Punjab	4528.90	1127.00	—	5655.90	5.92
Rajastan	3029.00	1472.00	9.70	4510.70	4.72
Tamil Nadu	5281.60	2179.00	1830.00	9290.80	9.73
Uttar Pradesh	4658.60	2944.00	—	7602.60	7.96
West Bengal	3754.80	1594.50	1201.50	6550.80	6.85
Total	57144.10	23179.50	15196.20	95520.00	100.00

Source: "Annual Report 2002-03", Ministry of Power, Government of India as reported in *Economic and Political Weekly*, Vol.39, No.4, p.310.

states look forward to the Central government to compensate for the backwardness arising from locational and infrastructural factors. However, in the case of Kerala, the trends in Central investment in the past few decades have belied such expectations (Table 4.11).

TABLE 4.11

Central Sector Investment in Kerala: 1970-2002

(Rs. Crores)

Years as on 31st March	Investment Gross Block		% of Kerala to India
	All India	Kerala	
1970	3795	116	3.06
1975	6242	202	3.24
1980	18161	423	2.33
1985	47323	831	1.76
1990	113430	1701	1.50
1995	227349	2906	1.28
1996	256200	3390	1.32
1997	284330	3992	1.40
1998	319829	4717	1.50
1999	353660	5962	1.69
2000	381365	6828	1.79
2001	411865	9893	2.40
2002	480518	13504	2.81

Source: "Reports of Public Enterprise Survey", Governemnt of India as reported in *Economic Review, 2003*, State Planning Board, January 2004, p. S.120.

Kerala's share in Central investment registered a consistent decrease from 3.06 per cent in 1970 to 1.28 per cent in 1995. From 1996 the share registered a slow but steady increase and reached a new peak of 2.81 per cent by 2002. Though the recent experience is an encouraging trend, the fact cannot be overlooked that the share of Kerala had registered an overall decrease during the period 1970-2002. In terms of employment offered by Central investment also, Kerala is way behind most other states (Table 4.12). In terms of employment provided by Central public sector enterprises Kerala occupied the lowest position among the ten major states.

Foreign Investment in Kerala

Kerala's inherent disadvantages from the point of view of attracting industrial investment, outlined earlier, equally apply to foreign investment (Table 4.13).

Kerala has been the third lowest among the states in India in attracting foreign investment during the post-liberalisation period (Table 4.13). Though the state has several favourable factors as an investment

TABLE 4.12

Central Sector Investment and Employment in Selected States as on 31-03-2002

Name of the State	*Investment in Gross Block (Rs. Crore)*	*Employment (in Lakh)*
Kerala	**13504**	**0.40**
Karnataka	18041	0.94
Andhra Pradesh	38172	1.11
West Bengal	28712	2.85
Gujarat	34418	0.63
Maharashtra	81278	2.43
Orissa	27131	0.75
Uttar Pradesh	33551	1.07
Assam	21192	0.60
Tamil Nadu	33058	1.10
All India	480518	18.84

Source: "Survey of Public Enterprises, 2001-02" as reported in *Economic Review, 2003*, State Planning Board, January, 2004, p. S.121.

TABLE 4.13

State-wise Flow of FDI Approvals during August 1991 to March 2003

State-wise Position	*No. of Approvals*	*Amount (Rs. Crore)*	*% to Total*
Northern Region			
New Delhi	2278	34087	11.9
Haryana	815	3622	1.3
Himachal Pradesh	97	1174	0.4
Punjab	185	1968	0.7
Western Region			
Gujarat	1107	18679	6.5
Maharashtra	4374	49587	17.4
Rajasthan	325	3005	1.1
Eastern Region			
Bihar	48	739	0.3
Orissa	137	8229	2.9
West Bengal	631	9014	3.2
North–Eastern Region	31	74	0.0
Central Region			
Madhya Pradesh	232	9271	3.2
Uttar Pradesh	760	4815	1.7
Southern Region			
Andhra Pradesh	1106	13218	4.6
Karnataka	2182	23689	8.3
Kerala	**288**	**1530**	**0.5**
Tamil Nadu	2346	23657	8.3
All Others	6611	79166	27.7
Total	23553	285525	100.0

Source: Ministry of Commerce and Industry, Government of India: "SIA Newsletter," April 2003 as reported in *Economic and Political Weekly*, October 25, 2003, p.4499.

destination, certain factors like investment climate and labour militancy nullify them to keep the state industrially backward. It appears that the challenge before the state is to take necessary corrective action on these fronts to emerge as an investment-friendly destination.

Structure of State Finances

In a federal set up the finances of an individual state have to be analysed against the background of the federal financial framework. The Indian Constitution has set forth the taxing powers and expenditure responsibilities of both Central and the State Governments. Some of the elastic sources of revenue like income tax and excise and custom duties are assigned to the Centre. Among tax and non-tax revenue sources assigned to the states, sales tax forms the major source. The Centre and the States are considered equal partners in the efforts at development of the country. However, the expenditure requirements of the states are disproportionately higher than their taxing powers. The imbalance inherent in the constitutional provisions relating to taxing powers and expenditure requirements has been sought to be rectified through the constitutional body called Finance Commission appointed every five years. An overview of the structure of Kerala's revenue and expenditure for the past two decades is presented in the following sections.

Composition of Kerala's Revenue

An analysis of the composition of revenues of Kerala and All States reveal that the proportion of own revenue in the total revenue of Kerala has been consistently higher than that of All States (Table 4.14). The state has thus been making earnest efforts to finance growing expenditures through mobilising own resources. The proportion of own resources has gone up from 68.18 per cent in 1980-81 to 74.43 per cent in 2003-04. The corresponding figures of all states are 60.65 per cent and 61.89 per cent respectively.

The proportion of tax revenue to total own revenue of Kerala has consistently increased during the period 1980-81 to 2003-04 (Table 4.15), from 77.08 per cent to 91.88. Conversely, the share of non-tax revenue in total own revenue of Kerala has registered a declining trend over the period. Though the share of tax revenue has increased over the years in the case of All States also, the rate of increase has been substantially lower than that of Kerala. It seems that excessive dependence on tax sources has significantly restricted the fiscal manoeuvrability of Kerala.

TABLE 4.14

Proportion of Own Revenue as a Percentage of Total Revenue of Kerala and All States

(Rs. in Lakh)

Year	*Kerala*					*All States*				
	*STR***	*SOTR***	*SONTR***	*SOR***	*SOR as % of STR*	*STR***	*SOTR***	*SONTR***	*SOR***	*SOR as % of STR*
1980-81	64038	33654	10005	43659	68.18	1629330	661618	326564	988182	60.65
1981-82	85048	37418	23233	60651	71.31	1845460	823432	323418	1146850	62.14
1982-83	81017	43835	11639	55474	68.47	2112554	948607	362526	1311133	62.06
1983-84	93424	48677	11826	60503	64.76	2401382	1075311	416023	1491334	62.1
1984-85	112499	62165	13342	75507	67.12	2742547	1225981	454960	1680941	61.29
1985-86	137117	73050	14173	87223	63.61	3342408	1455093	529063	1984156	59.36
1986-87	150253	81389	16386	97775	65.07	3822626	1671199	614549	2285748	59.8
1987-88	158609	92522	18854	111376	70.22	4400039	1932162	674394	2606556	59.24
1988-89	189706	106547	18136	124683	65.72	5042085	2240126	762365	3002491	59.55
1989-90	204764	123250	17444	140694	68.71	5653478	2599510	893996	3493206	61.79
1990-91	240293	134035	20881	154916	64.47	6646678	3034483	923719	3958202	59.55
1991-92	285212	167393	23472	190865	66.92	8053570	3575605	1270611	4846216	60.17
1992-93	331873	188697	27940	216637	65.28	9109113	3986828	1288388	5275216	57.91
1993-94	392205	234487	32322	266809	68.03	10556372	4642407	1556883	6199290	58.73
1994-95	466642	279910	39635	319545	68.48	12228371	5573453	2166006	7739459	63.29
1995-96	542356	338268	53549	391817	72.24	13680338	6386519	2289475	8675994	63.42
1996-97	614508	389850	51380	441230	71.8	15283638	7110152	2354258	9464410	61.93
1997-98	711820	450105	55210	505315	70.99	17030078	8122943	2443763	10566706	62.05
1998-99	719812	464956	55766	520722	72.34	17644774	8899525	2416781	11316306	64.13
1999-00	794176	519351	53072	572423	72.08	20720115	10258190	2987466	13245656	63.93
2000-01	873085	587026	65908	652934	74.78	23795293	11798100	3145450	14943550	62.8
2001-02	905639	592342	54338	646680	71.4	25567517	12809666	3228090	16037756	62.73
2002-03*	1145133	740363	73696	814059	71.09	29400869	14514114	3995638	18509752	62.96
2003-04#	1269961	868392	76787	945179	74.43	33171594	16392313	4138529	20530842	61.89

Note: *Denotes revised estimates; # Denotes Budget estimate
**STR - State's Total Revenue
**SOTR - State's Own Tax Revenue
**SONTR - State's Own Non-Tax Revenue
**SOR - State's Own Revenue

Source: *State Finances-A Study of Budgets* and *RBI Bulletin*, Reserve Bank of India, Various issues.

Kerala was top among the major states in India in respect of own tax-GSDP (Gross State Domestic Product) ratio in 1997-98 and 1998-99 (Table 4.16). However, in 2000-01, the latest year for which at least quick estimates of GSDP are available, the performance of four states, i.e. Gujarat, Haryana, Karnataka and Tamil Nadu is seen to have been ahead of Kerala. In considering own non-tax revenue-GSDP ratio, Kerala stands far behind the other states from the 1990s and the ratio has actually come down over the years. This finding points towards the need for raising the non-tax revenue-GSDP ratio of Kerala through additional resource mobilisation.

An enquiry into the buoyancy of own tax revenue and sales tax in the major states for two periods, 1980-1981 to 1992-93 and 1980-81 to 1999-00 shows that the own tax revenue of states has been, in general, more buoyant during the period 1980-81 to 1992-93 than during the entire period 1980-81 to 1999-00 (Table 4.17). Obviously, the buoyancy of own tax revenue of states in general has been decreasing during the post-liberalisation period. This has been particularly so in the case of sales tax. As already indicated, in terms of per capita own tax revenue, Kerala's position is one of the highest among the major states (Table 4.18).

The proportion of taxes on income came down from 2.66 per cent in 1980-81 to a mere 0.03 per cent in 2003-04 (Table 4.19). The percentage share of taxes on property and capital transactions registered an upward

TABLE 4.15

Percentage of Total Revenue of Kerala and All States

(Rs. in Lakhs)

Year	*Kerala*					*All States*				
	*SOTR***	*SONTR***	*SOR***	*SOTR as a % of SOR*	*SONTR as a % of SOR*	*SOTR***	*SONTR***	*SOR***	*SOTR as a % of SOR*	*SONTR as a % of SOR*
1980-81	33654	10005	43659	77.08	22.92	661618	326564	988182	66.95	33.05
1981-82	37418	23233	60651	61.69	38.31	823432	323418	1146850	71.8	28.2
1982-83	43835	11639	55474	79.02	20.98	948607	362526	1311133	72.35	27.65
1983-84	48677	11826	60503	80.45	19.55	1075311	416023	1491334	72.1	27.9
1984-85	62165	13342	75507	82.33	17.67	1225981	454960	1680941	72.93	27.07
1985-86	73050	14173	87223	83.75	16.25	1455093	529063	1984156	73.34	26.66
1986-87	81389	16386	97775	83.24	16.76	1671199	614549	2285748	73.11	26.89
1987-88	92522	18854	111376	83.07	16.93	1932162	674394	2606556	74.13	25.87
1988-89	106547	18136	124683	85.45	14.55	2240126	762365	3002491	74.61	25.39
1989-90	123250	17444	140694	87.6	12.4	2599510	893996	3493206	74.42	25.58
1990-91	134035	20881	154916	86.52	13.48	3034483	923719	3958202	76.66	23.34
1991-92	167393	23472	190865	87.7	12.3	3575605	1270611	4846216	73.78	26.22
1992-93	188697	27940	216637	87.1	12.9	3986828	1288388	5275216	75.58	24.42
1993-94	234487	32322	266809	87.89	12.11	4642407	1556883	6199290	74.89	25.11
1994-95	279910	39635	319545	87.6	12.4	5573453	2166006	7739459	72.01	27.99
1995-96	338268	53549	391817	86.33	13.67	6386519	2289475	8675994	73.61	26.39
1996-97	389850	51380	441230	88.36	11.64	7110152	2354258	9464410	75.13	24.87
1997-98	450105	55210	505315	89.07	10.93	8122943	2443763	10566706	76.87	23.13
1998-99	464956	55766	520722	89.29	10.71	8899525	2416781	11316306	78.64	21.36
1999-00	519351	53072	572423	90.73	9.27	10258190	2987466	13245656	77.45	22.55
2000-01	587026	65908	652934	89.91	10.09	11798100	3145450	14943550	78.95	21.05
2001-02	592342	54338	646680	91.6	8.4	12809666	3228090	16037756	79.87	20.13
2002-03*	740363	73696	814059	90.95	9.05	14514114	3995638	18509752	78.41	21.59
2003-04#	868392	76787	945179	91.88	8.12	16392313	4138529	20530842	79.84	20.16

Note: * - Denotes Revised Estimates; # - denotes Budget Estimate; **SOTR - State's Own Tax Revenue; **SONTR - State's Own Non-Tax Revenue; **SOR - State's Own Revenue

Source: *State Finances-A Study of Budgets* and *RBI Bulletin*, Reserve Bank of India, Various issues.

TABLE 4.16

State's Own Tax and Non-Tax Revenue GSDP Ratio of Kerala and Major Indian States

(in per cent)

States	*Own Tax/GSDP Ratio*				*Own Non-Tax/GSDP Ratio*			
	1997-98	*1998-99*	*1999-00*	*2000-01*	*1997-98*	*1998-99*	*1999-00*	*2000-01*
Andhra Pradesh	7.4	6.9	7.3	7.7	3.5	2.9	3.6	3.6
Assam	3.9	3.8	4.3	4.7	8.6	8.5	7.7	8.5
Bihar	7.1	6.9	8.6	6.3	6.6	5.6	9.1	4.1
Gujarat	7.3	7.3	7.7	8.1	3.3	3.3	3.8	4.6
Haryana	6.1	7.2	7.3	8.0	7.7	4.3	3.6	3.6
Karnataka	8.9	7.9	8.1	8.6	2.8	2.7	3.1	3.0
Kerala	**9.1**	**8.3**	**8.0**	**7.8**	**2.7**	**2.1**	**1.9**	**1.7**
Madhya Pradesh	7.6	7.4	7.6	7.8	5.6	4.8	5.5	4.5
Maharashtra	7.0	6.7	7.2	7.6	2.5	2.2	2.2	2.7
Orissa	4.5	4.4	4.7	6.0	2.5	4.0	6.7	5.8
Punjab	6.3	5.8	6.3	7.2	5.4	3.4	4.6	5.5
Rajasthan	5.6	5.4	5.7	6.9	4.7	3.7	3.8	5.6
Tamil Nadu	8.4	8.1	8.6	8.9	2.1	1.9	2.2	2.4
Uttar Pradesh	5.1	5.1	5.5	6.1	2.5	2.4	2.7	2.6
West Bengal	4.6	4.1	4.0	4.2	1.5	1.7	1.7	3.1
All States	5.8	5.6	5.8	6.2	3.5	3.0	3.4	3.7

Source: *Budget in Brief 2003-04*, Government of Kerala.

TABLE 4.17

Buoyancy of State Taxes of Major States

States	Own Tax Revenue		Sales Tax	
	1980-81 to 1992-93	1980-81 to 1999-00	1980-81 to 1992-93	1980-81 to 1999-00
Andhra Pradesh	1.03	0.93	1.08	1.07
Assam	1.30	1.22	1.35	1.23
Bihar	1.13	1.14	1.12	1.10
Gujarat	1.17	1.03	1.21	1.03
Haryana	1.08	0.98	1.08	1.07
Karnataka	1.14	1.07	1.22	1.13
Kerala	**1.17**	**1.08**	**1.23**	**1.14**
Madhya Pradesh	1.13	1.08	0.99	0.98
Maharashtra	1.03	0.98	1.00	0.95
Orissa	1.32	1.17	1.30	1.25
Punjab	0.96	0.92	0.98	0.93
Rajasthan	1.10	1.07	1.02	1.00
Tamil Nadu	1.05	1.03	1.06	1.09
Uttar Pradesh	1.17	1.10	1.14	1.09
West Bengal	1.19	0.98	1.17	1.02

Source: *Report on Currency and Finance 2001-02*, Reserve Bank of India, P.IV-II.

TABLE 4.18

Per Capita States' Own Tax Revenue of Major Indian States

(in Rupees)

States	1980-81	1990-91	1997-98	1998-99	1999-00	2000-01	2001-02*	2002-03**
Andhra Pradesh	109	417	970	1073	1201	1398	1539	1777
Assam	33	171	349	383	471	539	591	680
Bihar	40	134	251	276	369	294	295	339
Gujarat	113	591	1420	1617	1708	1875	1877	2045
Haryana	182	660	1245	1613	1788	2174	2360	2632
Karnataka	128	521	1275	1362	1499	1736	1918	2254
Kerala	**132**	**450**	**1431**	**1463**	**1618**	**1820**	**2071**	**2362**
Madhya Pradesh	74	276	600	660	735	707	845	938
Maharashtra	180	686	1554	1588	1906	2165	2403	2543
Orissa	56	161	407	421	478	609	708	753
Punjab	50	215	1335	1412	1687	2080	2043	2543
Rajasthan	209	656	707	757	855	990	1020	1244
Tamil Nadu	68	277	1441	1581	1776	1988	2089	2295
Uttar Pradesh	132	559	436	482	561	645	693	794
West Bengal	58	235	563	618	651	749	911	1028

Note: * Revised Estimate; ** Budget Estimate.

Source: *Budget in Brief 2004-05*, Government of Kerala, p.B-1.

TABLE 4.19

Percentage Share of Each Tax and Non-Tax Source in State's Own Revenue of Kerala

Year	Tax on Income	Tax on Property & Capital Transactions	Taxes on Commodities and Services	Of which Sales Tax	Interest Receipts	Dividends & Profits	General Services	Of which Lotteries	Social and Community Services	Economic Services	Of which Forest & Wild Life	Of which Industries
1980-81	2.66	6.67	67.75	46.71	2.05	0.14	3.07	0.86	3.77	13.88	10.47	0.52
1981-82	1.46	5.40	54.83	40.88	0.64	0.14	2.95	0.72	3.40	11.18	8.56	0.21
1982-83	1.96	6.56	70.50	49.61	1.84	0.16	2.69	1.10	3.92	12.37	8.95	0.65
1983-84	2.17	7.15	71.14	50.68	1.57	0.08	3.75	1.49	4.24	9.91	6.74	0.40
1984-85	2.48	6.65	73.21	49.69	4.06	0.08	3.21	0.00	3.22	7.46	4.49	0.31
1985-86	2.39	6.10	75.26	52.56	2.76	0.07	2.86	1.51	2.97	7.57	4.88	0.08
1986-87	1.66	6.38	75.20	52.85	3.63	0.09	2.86	1.07	2.77	7.41	4.93	0.34
1987-88	0.86	6.83	75.38	53.84	3.44	0.07	4.71	2.92	2.47	6.23	3.60	0.13
1988-89	1.11	8.89	75.45	55.37	2.09	0.06	4.64	3.14	2.39	5.36	2.71	0.12
1989-90	1.17	9.12	77.31	54.64	1.28	0.13	4.55	3.00	2.15	4.30	2.29	0.15
1990-91	1.55	8.84	76.13	57.93	1.38	0.17	5.41	4.32	2.01	4.50	2.41	0.10
1991-92	1.84	8.79	77.08	58.79	1.02	0.19	4.33	2.82	1.60	5.16	2.92	0.29
1992-93	0.58	9.65	76.88	60.27	1.07	0.18	4.05	2.64	1.58	6.06	3.63	0.65
1993-94	0.78	9.69	77.41	57.47	1.03	0.15	3.34	2.35	1.57	6.02	3.86	0.19
1994-95	0.54	10.19	76.87	58.36	1.18	0.14	3.39	2.26	1.44	6.26	4.28	0.19
1995-96	0.67	9.83	75.84	58.34	2.56	0.15	3.43	2.36	1.56	5.97	4.10	0.29
1996-97	0.27	8.88	79.02	62.83	1.26	0.09	3.58	2.42	1.07	5.64	3.67	0.42
1997-98	0.42	7.30	81.35	61.03	1.06	0.12	3.76	2.09	1.23	4.76	2.87	0.29
1998-99	0.52	6.72	82.05	64.65	1.36	0.14	3.57	2.16	1.27	4.37	2.32	0.13
1999-00	0.25	5.84	84.64	67.32	0.65	0.17	3.68	1.76	1.17	3.59	1.92	0.27
2000-01	0.06	6.21	83.64	66.54	0.56	0.19	3.88	2.05	1.18	4.29	2.16	0.32
2001-02	0.03	7.20	84.37	68.67	0.48	0.08	3.36	1.88	1.27	3.22	1.76	0.26
2002-03*	0.03	7.23	83.68	66.33	0.42	0.12	3.59	2.17	1.26	3.65	2.21	0.27
2003-04#	0.03	7.26	84.58	67.90	0.37	0.11	2.73	1.48	1.16	3.75	2.33	0.25

Note: *denotes Revised Estimates; # denotes Budget Estimate.

Source: *State Finances-A Study of Budgets* and *RBI Bulletin*, Reserve Bank of India, Various issues.

trend from 6.67 per cent in 1980-81 to 10.19 per cent in 1994-95. However, since 1995-96, the relative share of this revenue source has been exhibiting a downward trend and in 2003-04 its contribution was only 7.26 per cent. The taxes on commodities and services have increased from 67.75 per cent in 1980-81 to 84.64 per cent in 1999-00 and in 2003-04, it was 84.58 per cent. The share of sales tax, the largest single component, increased from 46.71 per cent in 1980-81 to 67.9 per cent in 2003-04. The major non-tax revenue sources are Interest Receipts, Dividends and Profits, General Services, Social and Community Services and Economic Services. Their combined share has come down from 22.92 per cent of total own revenue in 1980-81 to just 8.12 per cent in 2003-04.

The analysis of the rate of growth of tax and non-tax revenue sources (Table 4.20) shows that in the case of tax revenue, which contributes almost 90 per cent of total own revenue of the state, the rate of growth during the second period (1990-91 to 2003-04) was slightly lower than during the first period (1980-81 to 1989-90). The fall in growth rate has been very significant in the case of taxes on income and capital transactions. Sales tax, the foundation of the revenue structure of the state, has not experienced any significant change in both the periods. The overall rate of growth of non-tax revenue registered an improvement in the second period.

TABLE 4.20

Average Annual Growth Rates of Major Tax and Non-Tax Sources

(in per cent)

Revenue Source	*1980-81 to 1989-90*	*1990-91 to 2003-04*	*1980-81 to 2003-04*
Tax on Income	8.00	3.27	5.24
Tax on Property and Capital Transactions	17.44	13.37	15.07
Taxes on Commodities and Services	15.8	15.55	15.65
Of which Sales Tax	16.91	16.52	16.68
State's Own Tax Revenue	15.63	15.20	15.38
Interest Receipts	21.69	13.15	16.71
Dividends and Profits	14.67	20.07	17.82
General Services	104.79	11.48	50.36
Of which Lotteries	24.2	11.10	16.56
Social and Community Services	8.15	10.54	9.55
Economic Services	0.96	15.31	9.33
Of which Forest and Wild Life	-2.02	17.28	9.24
Of which Industries	49.07	42.85	45.44
State's Own Non-Tax Revenue	10.8	12.19	11.61

Note: The figures for 2002-03 and 2003-04 are revised estimates and budget estimates respectively.

Source: *State Finances-A Study of Budgets* and *RBI Bulletin*, Reserve Bank of India, Various issues.

Budgetary Trends

The analysis of the revenue structure of the state however provides only a partial picture of the finances of the state. Though not very remarkable, the revenue performance of the state compares favourably with that of the major Indian states. But the basic question is whether the resource mobilisation efforts of the state have been adequate to meet its expenditure requirements. From the mid-80s, Indian states in general have been facing fiscal strains of varying degrees. But in Kerala, budgetary deficits occurred much earlier than in other states and the magnitude of deficit was much larger (see George and Krishnakumar, 2003: 1). Expenditure, particularly revenue expenditure, has been growing at a faster rate than revenue receipts. The revenue expenditure as a percentage of total expenditure was 78.04 1n 1980-81 (Table 4.21). In 2003-04, it was 88.73 per cent. Revenue deficit as a percentage of revenue expenditure exhibits an increasing trend though there are year-to-year fluctuations. From just 4.01 per cent in 1980-81 it reached an all time high of 31.3 per cent in 1999-00 and the state managed to bring it down to 17.3 per cent in 2003-04.

Gross Fiscal Deficit, as a percentage of Gross State Domestic Product (GSDP) was 3.57 per cent in 1980-81 (Table 4.22). The difference between GFD-GSDP ratio and revenue deficit-GSDP ratio has considerably narrowed down over the years.

The GFD-GSDP ratio of Kerala is not very alarming when compared to that of states like Bihar, Gujarat and Orissa (Table 4.23). Kerala's GFD-GSDP ratio (5.62 per cent in 2000-01) is compared favourably with that of Bihar (10.56 per cent) and Orissa (9.14 per cent).

The financial situation of the state as indicated by the use of borrowed funds used for meeting revenue expenditure which has gone up from 52.8 per cent in1995-96 to 80.6 per cent in 2003-04 (Table 4.24). In 1995-96, 32.1 per cent of borrowed funds were used for capital purposes. It was only 17.9 per cent in 2003-04.

The factors contributing to the growth of revenue deficits and the resultant fiscal strains have been analysed by individual scholars and committees and commissions appointed by Government of Kerala from time to time (see for example, Bagchi and Rao, 1987; George, 1993). The root causes of Kerala's fiscal problems are attributed to her expenditure pattern. The predominance of social and community services over economic services is the major difference between the budgets of Kerala and of other states. The major

TABLE 4.21

Trends in Revenue Expenditure and Revenue Deficits of Kerala-1980-81 to 2003-04

Year	*Revenue Expenditure (Rs. lakh)*	*As % of Aggregate Expenditure*	*Revenue Surplus/Deficit (Rs. lakh)*	*As % of Revenue Expenditure*
1980-81	66760	78.04	2702#	4.0
1981-82	75450	69.5	9600#	12.7
1982-83	78339	78.63	2680	3.4
1983-84	99244	75.08	5820	5.9
1984-85	113866	72.44	1370	1.21
1985-86	144533	73.42	7420	5.1
1986-87	165477	76.55	15220	9.2
1987-88	178068	79.10	19460	10.9
1988-89	206100	81.76	16390	8.0
1989-90	229809	79.55	25050	10.9
1990-91	282495	83.67	42210	14.9
1991-92	321645	80.31	36430	11.3
1992-93	365614	83.80	33740	9.2
1993-94	429336	83.56	37130	8.6
1994-95	506630	85.02	39990	7.9
1995-96	582637	84.17	40280	6.9
1996-97	678811	85.47	64300	9.5
1997-98	824112	83.94	112290	13.6
1998-99	922808	86.97	203000	22.0
1999-00	1156597	89.66	362420	31.3
2000-01	1187791	90.34	314710	26.5
2001-02	1166203	88.80	260560	22.3
2002-03*	1335000	86.46	189870	14.2
2003-04**	1536465	88.73	266500	17.3

Note: * - Revised estimates; ** - Budget estimates; # - Revenue surplus

Source: Same as Table 4.1.

TABLE 4.22

Gross Fiscal Deficit (GFD) in Relation to Gross State Domestic Product (GSDP) of Kerala for Selected Years

Year	*GFD (Rs. Crore)*	*GFD as % of GSDP*	*Revenue Deficit as a % GSDP*
1980-81	179.00	3.57	0.54
1985-86	323.00	3.67	0.84
1990-91	799.00	4.85	2.56
1995-96	1302.70	3.36	1.04
1997-98	2413.90	4.88	2.27
1998-99	3012.20	5.36	3.61
1999-00	4536.60	7.26	5.79
2000-01	3877.80	5.56	4.51
2001-02 P	3269.40	4.11	3.28
2002-03 Q	2845.00*	3.13	2.09
2003-04	3306.90**	—	—
2004-05	5342.90#	—	—

Note: P and Q denote provisional and quick estimates respectively. *: Revised Estimates; **: Budget Estimates; #: Budget Estimates given in Budget in Brief 2004-05, Government of Kerala.

Source: (1) SDP figures for 1980-81 to1998-99 are taken from Domestic Products of States of India 1960-61 to 2000-01, Economic and Political Weekly Research Foundation, 2003. SDP figures for 1999-00 to 2002-03 are taken from *Economic Review, 2003*, State Planning Board, Government of Kerala, Thiruvananthapuram.
(2) *State Finances-A Study of Budgets* and *RBI Bulletin*, Reserve Bank of India, Various issues.

components of social and community services are education and health. By their very nature, these services have higher revenue content in the form of salary and pension payments. The salary component show a downward trend while that of pension and

TABLE 4.23

Gross Fiscal Deficit (GFD)-Gross State Domestic Product (GSDP) Ratio of Major States for Selected Years

States	*GFD in 1980-81 (Rs. Crores)*	*GFD as % of GSDP*	*GFD in 1990-91 (Rs. Crores)*	*GFD as % of GSDP*	*GFD in 1990-91 (Rs. Crores)*	*GFD as % of GSDP*	*GFD in 2000-01 (Rs. Crores)*	*GFD as % of GSDP*
Andhra Pradesh	222	2.55	967	2.73	2416.8	3.03	7305.9	5.31
Assam	28*	1.08	567	5.19	652.2	3.36	1540.0	5.13
Bihar	335	4.31	1595	5.71	1570.6	6.42	4884.3	10.56
Gujarat	246	3.04	1798	5.89	1745.6	2.43	7987.6	7.13
Haryana	112	3.07	385	2.62	986.0	3.31	2265.2	4.21
Karnataka	226	3.39	558	2.23	1456.8	2.59	4219.2	4.00
Kerala	**179**	**3.57**	**799**	**4.85**	**1302.7**	**3.36**	**3877.8**	**5.62**
Madhya Pradesh	337	3.70	1019	2.86	1633.4	3.41	2712.1	3.74
Maharashtra	464	2.70	1611	2.42	4150.8	2.63	8975.8	3.48
Orissa	135	3.48	616	5.41	1395.9	5.25	3325.3	9.14
Punjab	160	3.27	1242	6.75	1364.6	3.49	3903.8	5.70
Rajasthan	207	3.86	545	2.28	2574.3	5.44	4313.2	5.64
Tamil Nadu	211	2.36	1126	3.24	1255.9	1.60	5076.0	3.70
Uttar Pradesh	551	3.22	3068	5.02	4380.6	4.12	10179.5	5.63
West Bengal	290	2.60	1634	4.35	2696.3	3.65	10920.2	7.79

Note: SDP for 2000-01 are quick estimates.

Source: (1) *State Finances-A Study of Budgets* and *RBI Bulletin*, Reserve Bank of India, Various issues.
(2) For GSDP figures, *Domestic Products of States of India 1960-61 to 2000- 01*, Economic and Political Weekly Research.

TABLE 4.24

The Expenditure Pattern of Borrowed Funds to Cover Gross Fiscal Deficit

(in per cent)

Year	*Revenue Deficit/GFD*	*Capital Outlay/ GFD*	*Net Lending/ GFD*
1990-91	52.8	32.1	15.1
1995-96	30.9	43.3	25.8
1997-98	46.5	30.6	22.9
1998-99	67.4	21.6	11.0
1999-00	79.4	14.3	5.8
2000-01	81.2	14.9	4.0
2001-02	79.7	17.1	3.2
2002-03*	66.7	28.2	5.1
2003-04**	80.6	17.9	1.5

Note: * - Revised estimates; ** - Budget estimates.

Source: *State Finances-A Study of Budgets* and *RBI Bulletin*, Reserve Bank of India, Various issues.

interest payments shows an upward trend (Table 4.25). The expenditure on these three categories together accounted for 70.15 per cent of total revenue expenditure in 2003-04.

Trends in Public debt

A comparative analysis of Kerala and the other major states in terms of public debt outstanding as a percentage of Gross State Domestic Product shows that Kerala's position is not very alarming (Table 4.26). However, the high per capita debt position of Kerala is a cause of concern (Table 4.27).

Concluding Observations

The foregoing analysis shows that the fiscal situation of Kerala demands urgent reform and

TABLE 4.26

Debt Outstanding as Percentage of GSDP Ratio of Major States at the end of March

States	*1996*	*1997*	*1998*	*1999*	*2000*	*2001*
Andhra Pradesh	19.0	19.0	20.8	20.8	23.5	25.9
Assam	28.1	28.0	27.2	26.7	30.3	34.0
Bihar	67.7	56.0	59.9	59.7	69.9	73.1
Gujarat	15.5	15.0	16.6	17.8	21.6	26.6
Haryana	19.4	18.0	19.7	21.8	23.9	25.5
Karnataka	17.6	17.0	18.1	17.6	19.5	21.0
Kerala	**26.1**	**26.0**	**26.0**	**27.9**	**31.1**	**31.7**
Madhya Pradesh	25.7	25.0	26.7	28.0	30.4	36.2
Maharashtra	11.6	12.0	13.3	14.6	15.9	17.3
Orissa	35.3	42.0	39.2	42.2	50.5	60.5
Punjab	35.3	35.0	35.4	37.4	37.2	40.7
Rajastan	25.8	25.0	25.6	28.9	33.3	40.1
Tamil Nadu	16.0	16.0	15.7	16.4	18.7	20.9
Uttar Pradesh	28.2	27.0	29.2	31.5	35.2	36.7
West Bengal	20.8	22.0	22.5	24.8	28.9	33.7

Source: *Budget in Brief-2003-04*, Government of Kerala, p.B-26.

TABLE 4.25

Salary, Pension and Interest Payments as a Percentage of Total Revenue Expenditure of Kerala: 1990-91to 2002-03

Year	*Expenditure on Salary (Rs. Crore)*	*As % to Revenue Expenditure*	*Expenditure on Pension (Rs. Crore)*	*As % to Revenue expenditure*	*Expenditure on Interest Payments (Rs. Crore)*	*As % to Revenue Expenditure*	*Salary, Pension & Interest Payments Total (Rs. Crore)*	*Total as % to Revenue Expenditure*
1990-91	1682.65	59.56	293.76	10.40	340.64	12.06	2317.05	82.02
1991-92	1383.59	43.02	338.96	10.54	483.42	15.03	2205.97	68.58
1992-93	1419.46	38.82	371.87	10.17	542.51	14.84	2333.84	63.83
1993-94	1836.13	42.77	464.72	10.82	687.16	16.01	2988.01	69.60
1994-95	2194.25	43.31	565.45	11.16	819.67	16.17	3579.37	70.65
1995-96	2230.4	38.28	716.85	12.30	924.16	15.86	3871.41	66.45
1996-97	2616.66	38.55	753.48	11.10	1103.41	16.26	4473.55	65.90
1997-98	2803.26	34.02	913.02	11.08	1286.09	15.61	5002.37	60.70
1998-99	3254.68	35.27	1154.32	12.51	1446.26	15.67	5855.26	63.45
1999-00	4502.86	38.93	1808.29	15.63	1952.27	16.88	8263.42	71.45
2000-01	4491.61	37.81	1929.48	16.24	2257.60	19.01	8678.69	73.07
2001-02	4200.82	35.42	1837.93	15.50	2489.47	20.99	8528.22	71.91
2002-03	4678.99	31.71	2282.90	15.47	2946.77	19.97	9908.66	67.15
2003-04*	5147.46	33.50	2291.07	14.91	3340.74	21.74	10779.27	70.15

Note: * - Revised estimates.

Source: *Budget in Brief*, Government of Kerala, various issues.

TABLE 4.27

Per Capita Debt Outstanding of Major States at the End of March

(Amount in Rs.)

States	*1991*	*1997*	*1998*	*1999*	*2000*	*2001*	*2002(RE)*	*2003(BE)*
Andhra Pradesh	1062	2303	2722	3233	3882	4724	5711	6687
Assam	1072	2299	2457	2665	3294	3893	4508	4975
Bihar	1082	1909	2117	2392	2872	3384	4745	5387
Gujarat	1534	2754	3245	3941	4809	6173	7530	9228
Haryana	1741	3247	4013	4910	5875	6646	7376	8313
Karnataka	1043	2256	2574	3029	3623	4254	5100	6181
Kerala	**1491**	**3630**	**4090**	**4940**	**6285**	**7414**	**8342**	**9425**
Madhya Pradesh	1028	1871	2110	2489	2929	3296	5039	5647
Maharashtra	1320	2464	2931	3487	4229	4904	5538	6338
Orissa	1457	3050	3549	4265	5136	6140	6949	7957
Punjab	3482	6788	7551	9038	10112	11824	13710	15624
Rajasthan	1307	2798	3219	4058	5035	5721	6267	7241
Tamil Nadu	984	2352	2710	3216	3877	4644	5443	6593
Uttar Pradesh	1055	2135	2490	2964	3581	3902	4604	5246
West Bengal	1207	2386	2895	3704	4721	5980	7149	8490

Source: Budget in Brief-2003-04, Government of Kerala, p. B-27.

restructuring. The state has to examine its tax and non-tax sources afresh with a view to identifying their deficiencies and exploring avenues for reform and restructuring.

II. FINANCIAL SERVICES

Introduction

This section traces the evaluation of the system of financial services and seeks to set out policy directions for improvement of the financial services in Kerala for achieving rapid and equitable development. It also highlights` the achievements that the state has made.

The Financial System

A well-developed financial system is crucial to growth and development, both economic and social, of a region. A financial system comprises all the mechanisms, processes and institutional frameworks that facilitate the flow of funds from economic units with surpluses (the supply side) to economic units with deficits (the demand side). The efficient mobilisation of funds from economic units that have surplus funds, and the effective allocation of funds to the economic units that require funds, provides the *raison d'être* for a financial system and its services. On the supply side of the system, it is the household sector that predominates. The household sector generates the savings/surplus funds which the economic units on the demand side make use of for asset creation.

It is the business sector and the government sector that fall on the demand side of the system. It is these sectors that seek funds for investment. The financial system is constituted by intermediaries—in the organised as well as in the unorganised sectors—that facilitate the flow of funds from the supply side to the demand side. The intermediaries include banks, other financial institutions, insurance companies, the post office system, capital and money markets and moneylenders. The effectiveness and efficiency of these institutions determine the quality of the financial system.

The Approach and Scope

This section examines only the household sector and the business sector as clients of the financial system. Great diversity is observed in the needs of units within the household and the firm sectors, depending largely on geographic, economic, social and demographic characteristics of the society and the characteristics of its business sector. No financial system is capable of offering a complete range of services and products to meet all the diverse needs of its clientele. However, the success of the financial services sector would be measured by how best it is able to meet these varying needs efficiently. The section is limited to an analysis of the role of the two most important categories of financial intermediaries-banks and other financial institutions.

In the second part of this section the focus is on the effectiveness and efficiency of the financial services sector in mobilising funds from the supply side. In the third part the focus is on the effectiveness and efficiency of the financial services sector in deploying funds on the demand side. Finally, in the fourth part the constituents of the financial services sector other than banks and financial institutions that operate on both the supply and the demand sides of the system, namely Chit Funds, the capital markets and Insurance agencies, are discussed.

The Supply Side: Fund Mobilisation

The banking sector is the most important channel for mobilisation of funds. It is at once a vehicle both for mobilising funds and for allocating them. Since Independence, and particularly since 1969, the Government of India has been trying to use the banking system to effectively address the needs of all sections of the society, with special emphasis on the requirement sections of those disadvantaged by socio-economic, geographical and location factors. The effectiveness of the banking sector's performance in the state in terms of geographical, socioeconomic and functional coverage is discussed below. The banking sector in India may be broadly classified into the commercial sector and the cooperative sector. Recognising the fact that the scheduled commercial banking sector—in spite of its vast network and government-backed thrust—has limitations in meeting the requirements of a vast and diversified clientele, the Government has been encouraging the parallel development of the cooperative banking sector. As opposed to the scheduled commercial banks that operate on a national scale, cooperative banks have a more localised area of operation. With their extensive branch network and localised operational base, cooperative banks enlarge the reach of banking, both geographically and in a socioeconomic sense. Though the thrust of the cooperative banking sector has been more on the credit side than on the deposit mobilisation side, this sub-section analyses first the performance of the scheduled commercial banks and then of the cooperative banks on the deposit mobilisation front, in the state of Kerala.

Scheduled Commercial Banks

(a) Coverage at State Level

Though technological advancements have brought vast changes in the manner of provision of banking services, bringing in concepts of 'virtual' or 'anywhere-anytime' banking, physical presence is yet of crucial importance. Tables 4.28 and 4.29 show the state-wise distribution of commercial bank branches and population per bank office since 1969, the year of nationalisation of banks and for selected years since then till 2000-04. It is seen that Kerala had traditionally been a well-banked region in terms of the availability of bank branches. In 1969, Kerala accounted for 601 branches out of a total of 8,262 branches at the national level, accounting for 7.3 per cent of the total number of branches in the country. Similarly, in 1969 the average population per bank branch was only 34,000 in Kerala as compared to a national average of 65,000.

The pace of expansion of banking facilities across the country picked up momentum after the nationalisation of banks in all the states of India. By June 2004 the number of bank branches in Kerala

TABLE 4.28

The State-wise Distribution of Commercial Bank Branches: 1969 and 2000-04

	Number of Bank Branches as at the End of					
States	*Jun-69*	*Jun-00*	*Jun-01*	*Jun-02*	*Jun-03*	*Jun-04*
Andhra Pradesh	567	5112	5171	5207	5267	5293
Assam	74	1234	1237	1223	1220	1223
Bihar	273	5008	3561	3564	3564	3569
Gujarat	852	3642	3670	3657	3670	3667
Haryana	172	1494	1516	1551	1591	1624
Karnataka	756	4720	4761	4779	4804	4853
Kerala	**601**	**3255**	**3298**	**3334**	**3370**	**3427**
Madhya Pradesh	343	4497	3456	3458	3450	3461
Maharashtra	1118	6224	6294	6320	6317	6332
Orissa	100	2218	2220	2227	2227	2239
Punjab	346	2508	2534	2573	2615	2654
Rajasthan	364	3321	3323	3336	3342	3360
Tamil Nadu	1060	4767	4785	4784	4746	4769
Uttar Pradesh	747	8909	8155	8169	8212	8216
West Bengal	504	4394	4424	4430	4446	4475
Total	7877	61303	58405	58576	58841	59162
All India Total	8262	65621	66119	66355	66692	67097

Source: *Economic Review 2003*, State Planning Board, Government of Kerala and *Quarterly Statistics on Deposits and Credits of Scheduled Commercial Banks*, June 2004, Reserve Bank of India.

TABLE 4.29

The State-wise Population Per Bank Branch ('000s): 1969 and 2000-03

State	Jun-69	Jun-00	Jun-01	Jun-02	Jun-03
Andhra Pradesh	74	15	15	15	15
Assam	193	21	22	22	22
Bihar	207	20	21	21	21
Gujarat	34	13	13	14	14
Haryana	97	13	13	13	13
Karnataka	37	11	11	11	11
Kerala	**34**	**10**	**10**	**10**	**10**
Madhya Pradesh	106	18	18	18	19
Maharashtra	43	15	15	15	15
Orissa	211	16	S	16	17
Punjab	42	9	9	9	9
Rajasthan	68	16	17	17	17
Tamil Nadu	37	13	13	13	13
Uttar Prdesh	114	19	20	20	20
West Bengal	85	18	18	18	19
All India Total	65	15	15	16	16

Source: *Economic Review 2003* (State Planning Board, Government of Kerala, 2004) and *Quarterly Statistics on Deposits and Credits of Scheduled Commercial Banks*, June 2004, Reserve Bank of India.

became 3,427 while the total number of branches in India as a whole was 67,097, thus Kerala accounting for 5.1 per cent of the total number of bank branches in the country. Therefore while the number of bank branches in Kerala increased by around 5.7 times between 1969 and 2003, the corresponding growth at the all-India level was by 8.12 times. Similarly, by June 2004 the average population per bank branch in Kerala came down to only nearly 11,000 as compared to the national average of 16,000. Extensive banking expansion of the post-1969 period has thus reduced the disparities in bank facilities between Kerala and the rest of India. However, in terms of availability of banking facilities, Kerala has historically been and continues to be ahead of the rest of the stats in the country.The average population per bank branch has remained static at nearly 11,000 in Kerala over the past five years. At the national level too, the average population per bank branch has remained somewhat static at around 16,000.

(b) Distribution of Bank Branches

Table 4.30 shows the rural-urban distribution of bank branches in the different states. The proportions of branches in rural, semi-urban, urban and metropolitan population centres at the all-India level as of June 2004 were 47.7 per cent, 22.4 per cent, 16.58 per cent and 13.3 per cent respectively as against 10.1 per cent, 71.4 per cent, 18.5 per cent and 0 per cent respectively in Kerala. Amongst the states with very low population per branch, Kerala is the only state to have achieved this status in the absence of metropolitan population centres.

TABLE 4.30

Population Group-wise Distribution of Bank Branches, June 2004

State/Station	Rural	Semi-Urban	Urban	Metropolitan	Total No. of Branches	% of Total
Andhra Pradesh	2395	1258	1086	554	5293	7.9
Assam	793	261	169		1223	1.8
Bihar	2484	04	411		3569	5.4
Gujarat	1498	843	487	839	3667	5.5
Haryana	900	426	498		1624	2.4
Karnataka	2161	1058	826	808	4853	7.2
Kerala	**346**	**2446**	**635**		**3427**	**5.0**
Madhya Pradesh	1864	787	443	367	3461	5.2
Maharashtra	2231	1100	939	2062	6332	9.5
Orissa	1586	329	324		2239	3.3
Punjab	1130	726	577	221	2654	3.9
Rajasthan	1844	754	496	266	3360	5.0
Tamil Nadu	1719	1232	1021	797	4769	7.1
Uttar Pradesh	4847	1352	1957	560	8216	12.3
West Bengal	2271	566	628	1010	4475	6.7
Total	28069	13142	12892	7484	54309	88.2
All India Total	32027	15059	11059	8952	67097	100.0

Source: *Quarterly Statistics on Deposits and Credits of Scheduled Commercial Banks*, June 2004, RBI.

Table 4.31 gives the district-wise distribution of scheduled commercial bank branches within Kerala as of June 2004. Wide differences exist amongst the districts: the hilly districts of Wayanad and Idukki have only 74 and 99 branches respectively, as compared to 507 branches in Ernakulam district.

In order to examine the effectiveness and efficiency, the banking sector may be analysed first at the branch level and then in terms of the ratio between deposit growth on the one hand and population and economic activity on the other. Per capita branch deposits and deposits as a percentage of state domestic product, are also looked into.

TABLE 4.31

District-wise Distribution of Scheduled Commercial Bank Branches within the State of Kerala as of June 2004

District	*Number of Branches*
Alapuzha	215
Ernakulam	507
Idukki	99
Kannur	221
Kasargod	126
Kollam	191
Kottayam	275
Kozhikode	259
Malapuram	226
Palakkad	258
Pathanamthitta	241
Thiruvananthapuram	352
Thrissur	383
Wayanad	74

Source: Quarterly Statistics on Deposits and Credits of Scheduled Commercial Banks, June 2004, Reserve Bank of India.

(c) Deposit Mobilisation

Table 4.32 shows the amounts of deposits mobilised by the Scheduled Commercial Banks in Kerala during the period 1972-1995 and as of June 2004. The total amount of deposits mobilised by scheduled commercial banks in Kerala as of December 1972 was Rs. 247.33 crore accounting for 2.96 per cent of the all-India total of Rs. 8,359.65 crore. By June 2004, the amount of deposits mobilised by all scheduled banks from Kerala had grown by 265 times to Rs. 65,609 crore. At the all-India level, the corresponding increase was by 182 times, from Rs. 8,359.65 crore to Rs. 15,24,546 crore. By June 2004, Kerala accounted for 4.3 per cent of the total scheduled bank deposits in the country. The compound annual growth rate (CAGR) of deposits with scheduled commercial banks in Kerala has been approximately 19 per cent over the period 1972-2004 as against 17.7 per cent at the all-India level.

As of December 1972 there were 947 bank branches in Kerala and 14650 at the all-India level. The amount of deposits per branch in 1972 was Rs. 26 lakh in Kerala as against Rs. 57 lakh in all-India level. In June 2004, the deposits per branch in Kerala stood at Rs. 19.15 crore as against a national average of Rs. 22.72 crore. In terms of the amount of deposits per branch, the difference between Kerala and all-India has considerably narrowed.

TABLE 4.32

Deposit Mobilisation by Scheduled Commercial Banks in Kerala: 1972-1995 and 2004

Year	*Kerala (Rs. Crore)*	*All India (Rs. Crore)*
1972	247.33	8359.65
1973	284.13	9159.06
1974	339.17	10755.26
1975	406.65	12637.04
1976	485.73	15254.89
1977	670.98	18983.37
1978	890.00	23333.72
1979	1119.00	28683.59
1980	1287.86	33321.39
1981	1567.31	40412.76
1982	1816.04	45824.98
1983	2149.49	54447.50
1984	2632.74	64316.05
1985	3131.60	77767.48
1986	3693.52	92233.32
1987	4393.15	108343.38
1988	5002.87	127592.67
1989	5679.51	147031.29
1990	6554.82	171911.39
1991	7786.22	200568.36
1992	9607.69	237107.23
1993	12083.41	275850.47
1994	14770.17	323976.52
1995	17250.08	379174.14
2004	65609.00	1524546.00

Source: Banking Statistics 1972-1995, Reserve Bank of India and '*Quarterly Statistics on Deposits and Credits of Scheduled Commercial Banks*, June 2004, Reserve Bank of India.

The level of bank deposits in an economic system is determined primarily by the size of the population. A good measure, therefore, to assess the performance of the banking sector is the amount of bank deposits per capita. In 1981, the per capita deposits in Kerala was Rs. 614.63 (Rs. 1,567.31 crore deposits as on June 1981 and population 2.55 crore) as against the all-India average of Rs. 591.44 (Rs. 40,412.76 crore deposits as on June 1981 and population 68.33 crore) (See Table 4 of Banking Statistics 1972-1995, RBI and *Statistical Abstracts*, CSO). In 2001 the per capita deposits in Kerala was Rs. 13,892 (Rs. 44,178 crore deposits as on March 2001 and population 3.18 crore) as against the all-India average of Rs. 9,244 (Rs. 9,49,433 crore deposit as on March 2001 and population 102.7 crore) (See *Table 1.5 of Basic Statistical Returns of Commercial Banks in India*, March 2001, RBI and *Statistical Abstracts*, CSO).

Apart from population, the other driving force of bank deposits of an economic system is the level of its economic activity. The analysis is done by comparing the level of bank deposits to the State Domestic Product (SDP). For a state like Kerala, remittances from outside the state make the state domestic product much lower than the state's total income. Nevertheless, SDP gives a rough and ready measure. In 1981, bank deposits at the all-India level were 36.51 per cent of Net Domestic Product at Factor Cost at current prices (Rs. 1,10,685 crore in 1981, Source: CSO) and the bank deposits in Kerala formed 41 per cent of the State Domestic Product (Rs. 3,823 crore in 1981, source: CSO) at Factor Costs at Current Prices. By 2001 bank deposits at the all-India level formed 55.2 per cent of Net Domestic Product at Factor Cost at current prices (Rs. 17,19,868 crore in 2001, source CSO) and the bank deposits in Kerala were as high as 70 per cent of the State Domestic Product (Rs. 63,094 crores in 2001, Source: CSO) at Factor Costs at Current Prices.

Cooperative Banks—Coverage and Deposit Mobilisation

Structurally, cooperative banks in India may be classified into Urban Cooperative Banks (UCBs), State Cooperative Banks (SCBs), District Central Cooperative Banks (DCBs), Primary Agricultural Credit Societies (PACS), State Cooperative Agricultural and Rural Development Banks (SCARD) and Primary Cooperative Agricultural and Rural Development Banks (PCARDBs). The SCARDs and the PCARDBs were created essentially for providing long-term loans to the rural sector (both farm and non-farm); they have only a very limited role in deposit mobilisation. In the following discussion, the focus is therefore on the rest of the cooperative banking institutions, namely, UCBs, SCBs, DCBs and PACSs.

As of March 2003, there were 60 branches of UCBs in Kerala with deposits to the tune of Rs. 2,148 crore. As against the all-India figures of 1847 branches with deposits of Rs. 1,01,972 crore, the State accounted for 3.25 per cent of the branches and 2.11 per cent of the deposits. The deposit per branch in Kerala works out to Rs. 35.8 crore as against the all-India average of Rs. 55.21 crore. It should be noted here that the state of Maharashtra accounts for about 30 per cent of the total number of branches and 60 per cent of the total amount of deposits of UCBs in the country. However, Kerala's average deposit per branch (of Rs. 35.8 crore) compares favourably with the national average excluding Maharashtra, namely Rs. 33.19 crore.

In March 2003, there were 24 branches of SCBs in Kerala with a total deposit of Rs. 2,326.76 crore. The corresponding all-India figures were 931 branches and Rs. 39,111.78 crore as deposits. Kerala thus accounted for 2.58 per cent of the branches and 5.95 per cent of the deposits. The deposits per branch in Kerala work out to Rs. 96.95 crore as compared to the all-India average of Rs. 42.01 crore. Table 4.33 shows the state-wise deposits of SCBs as on 31st March 2003.

There were 495 branches of DCBs in Kerala with a total of Rs. 5,402.84 crore of deposits in March 2003. At the all-India level, the corresponding figures were 12957 branches and Rs. 72,394.43 crore of deposits, the

TABLE 4.33

State-wise Deposits of State Cooperative Banks, as on 31st March 2003

State	*Deposits (Rs. Crore)*	*State*	*Deposits (Rs. Crore)*
Andaman and Nicobar	152.29	Madhya Pradesh	1394.19
Andhra Pradesh	1359.63	Maharashtra	11238.23
Arunachal Pradesh	107.04	Manipur	24.12
Assam	502.71	Meghalaya	365.47
Bihar	730.34	Mizoram	104.75
Chandigarh	89.18	Nagaland	118.06
Chhattisgarh	730.20	Orissa	886.14
Delhi	554.30	Pondicherry	149.54
Goa	486.07	Punjab	1031.38
Gujarat	3050.14	Rajasthan	991.89
Haryana	949.74	Sikkim	11.22
Himachal Pradesh	1506.74	Tamil Nadu	2924.42
Jammu and Kashmir	256.31	Tripura	187.05
Karnataka	1727.91	Uttar Pradesh	3079.17
Kerala	**2326.76**	West Bengal	2076.79
		All India	39111.78

Source: Basic Data, State Cooperative Banks, National Federation of State Cooperative Banks.

TABLE 4.34

State-wise Deposits of District Central Cooperative Banks, as on 31st March 2003

State	*Deposits (Rs. Crore)*	*State*	*Deposits (Rs. Crore)*
Andhra Pradesh	2562.16	**Kerala**	**5402.84**
Assam	18.92	Madhya Pradesh	3288.05
Bihar	672.26	Maharashtra	21400.36
Chhattisgarh	1222.64	Orissa	1375.62
Gujarat	6729.30	Punjab	3686.43
Haryana	2013.98	Rajasthan	1856.90
Himachal Pradesh	1952.67	Tamil Nadu	7236.37
Jammu and Kashmir	672.96	Uttar Pradesh	4914.91
Karnataka	3334.92	West Bengal	2373.01
		All India	72394.43

Source: Basic Data, District Central Cooperative Banks, National Federation of State Cooperative Banks.

State accounting for 3.82 per cent of the branches and 7.46 per cent of the deposits. The deposits per branch in Kerala work out to Rs. 10.92 crore as compared to the all-India average of Rs. 5.59 crore. Table 4.34 shows the state-wise deposits of District Central Cooperative Banks as on 31st March 2003.

The phenomenal reach and influence of the cooperative sector in Kerala's financial services sector is observed also in the figures relating to the PACS (Table 4.35). In March 2003, there were 1961 PACS in Kerala with Rs. 7,160 crore of deposits as against an all-India total of 1,12,309 PACS with Rs. 19,120.23 crore of deposits. While accounting for only 1.75 per cent of the PACS in the country, the State had a share of 37.45 per cent of the total amount of deposits in PACS of the country. The deposits per PACS in Kerala were Rs. 3.65 crore as compared to the national average of only Rs. 0.17 crore. Out of the 1961 PACS in Kerala, 76.34 per cent (1,497) are classified as viable as compared to only 62.08 per cent at the all-India level.

Post Offices

In India, the Department of Posts plays a very important role in the mobilisation of savings. In March 2002, there were 5,073 post offices functioning under the Kerala Postal Circle which includes Lakshadweep and Mahe. The total number of post offices in India in March 2002 were 1,55,279. The Kerala circle accounted for 3.28 per cent of the total number of post offices in the country. There was one post office for every 6,276 persons in Kerala in March 2002 comparing favourably to the national average of one post office for every 6,630

TABLE 4.35

State-wise Number of PACS and Deposits of PACS, as on 31st March 2003

State	*Total Number of PACS*	*Deposits (Rs. Crore)*
Andhra Pradesh	4359	758.9
Assam	809	5.08
Bihar	7057	13.82
Gujarat	8176	111.22
Haryana	2418	192.35
Himachal Pradesh	2104	428.07
Jammu and Kashmir	425	0.50
Karnataka	4094	1082.13
Kerala	**1961**	**7160.00**
Madhya Pradesh	4568	361.63
Maharashtra	23340	1196.82
Orissa	3864	2157.66
Punjab	4002	422.71
Rajasthan	5941	91.87
Tamil Nadu	5381	3873.18
Uttar Pradesh	8929	68.20
West Bengal	19333	810.46
All India	112309	19120.23

Source: Basic Data, Primary Agricultural Credit Societies, National Federation of State Cooperative Banks.

persons. Of the 5,073 post offices in the State, 4,194 are located in rural areas and 879 in urban areas. Again, within the state there exist wide disparities amongst districts in the coverage of post offices. In March 2000, the Kerala Circle of Indian posts had a closing balance of Rs. 149.72 crore in the Post Office Savings Bank Accounts as compared to the all-India total of Rs. 7,978.3 crore.

Financial Services Sector in Kerala: Mobilisation of Resources

The financial services sector in Kerala has been very effective in carrying out the function of mobilisation of funds. Whether it be in terms of geographical reach, or efficiency of deposit mobilisation, the Kerala sector compares favourably with the rest of the country. Kerala has, in fact, been historically better placed on all these aspects. Kerala has managed to hold on to its leading position, and improve on its lead.

The Demand Side Asset Creation

This section of the report focuses on studying the performance of the financial services sector in Kerala in meeting the needs of its economic units.

TABLE 4.36

State-wise Deposits and Credits of Scheduled Commercial Banks Amount in Rupees lakh

State	*2004*		*2003*		*2002*		*2001*	
	Deposits	*Credit*	*Deposits*	*Credit*	*Deposits*	*Credit*	*Deposits*	*Credit*
SI	34648823	23745926	29460744	19524939	253619,93	16384658	21809325	14526813
AP	8475977	5585087	7302451	4553856	6378853	3950556	5444552	3512765
Karnataka	9365181	5913943	7532892	4692770	6295312	3879343	5474249	3336877
Kerala	**6812177**	**3097393**	**5952165**	**2546340**	**5166705**	**2236709**	**4417814**	**1910833**
TN	9740558	9064032	8448241	7663114	7328940	6257841	6306488	5711962
LD	9452	756	11073	510	7312	580	5509	575
PD	245478	84715	213923	68349	184871	59629	160714	53801
AI	151127339	88031203	127619570	75596882	112339332	65599308	94943329	53843379

Source: Table 1.5, (Deposits and Credit of Scheduled Commercial Banks according to State) *Basic Statistical Returns*, RBI Various years (SI - South India; AP- Andhra Pradesh; TN – Tamil Nadu; LD – Lakhsadweep; PD – Pondicherry; AI- All-India).

(a) Scheduled Commercial Banks

Table 4.36 shows the deposits and loans disbursed in Kerala by commercial banks over the period 2001-2004. It may be seen that though deposits have been growing, the growth rate in deposits decreased from 17.0 per cent to 14.4 per cent in 2003-04 over 2001-02. Meanwhile, the growth rate in credit disbursals increased from 17.4 per cent to around 21.6 per cent during the same period.

The general perception about the activities of commercial banks in Kerala is that they are focused more on deposit mobilisation than on credit expansion. Further, advances made by commercial banks in Kerala were lower than at the national level during the most part of the nineties. However, some improvement is observed in more recent years.

The credit-deposit (CD) ratio is an important measure of the efficiency of the banking sector and the health of the economy. Credit-deposit ratio is the proportion of financial assets created by banks on the basis of deposits received. Table 4.38 shows the credit-deposit ratio of the different states in 1990 and 2004. In several states, the ratios were already lower than 50 in the 1990s; the ratios have since then worsened for every state except states like Maharashtra and West Bengal and, marginally, Rajasthan. The all-India average itself has gone down in this period and so has the ratio for the state of Kerala. (The all-India ratios are lower than 100 per cent because a certain proportion of deposits is kept in the form of cash, and the banks make large investments in Government debt, shares, bonds and debentures).

The low CD ratio of banks in Kerala has remained a matter of concern for sometime now. When banks were nationalised in 1969, the CD ratio in Kerala was around 65.8 and was higher than in several other states. The CD ratio of Kerala showed a sharp decline of 19.1

TABLE 4.37

Average Growth Rates in Advances by Commercial Banks

Year/period	*Growth Rate in Advances (Kerala)*	*Growth Rate in Advances (All India)*
1985-1990	13.6	15.7
1991-1995	13.7	16.1
1996-2000	15.4	15.6
2001-2004	19.0	19.7

Source: State Economic Review, 2004.

TABLE 4.38

Credit-Deposit Ratios in States, 1990-2004 (percentage)

State	*March 1990*	*March 2004*	*State*	*March 1990*	*March 2004*
Haryana	75	59.6	Madhya Pradesh	68.1	50.1
Punjab	46.2	45.7	Uttar Pradesh	32.8	38.0
Rajasthan	61.5	62.8	Gujarat	63.2	54.8
Assam	78.4	35.7	Maharashtra	65.1	66.5
Bihar	39	26.9	Andhra Pradesh	82	70.9
Jharkhand	(Bihar)	26.9	Karnataka	84.6	69.0
Orissa	92.5	58.6	**Kerala**	**63.1**	**47.8**
West Bengal	44.6	53.8	Tamil Nadu	95.4	96.1
All India	60.7	58.2			

Source: Banking Statistics 1972-2002 and Basic Statistical Returns, RBI, Various Issues.

TABLE 4.39

Credit-Deposit Ratio in the Southern States, 1996-2004

(in percentage)

State	1996	1997	1998	1999	2000	2001	2002	2003	2004	Average
Andhra Pradesh	81.2	77.4	72.4	69.1	65.5	64.9	67.7	69.3	70.9	70.9
Karnataka	71.1	72.2	70.3	66.7	65.5	61.8	68.9	71.1	69	68.5
Kerala	**44.7**	**45.7**	**44.7**	**41.8**	**41.7**	**42.3**	**43.7**	**43.6**	**47.8**	**44.0**
Tamil Nadu	94.4	97.3	92.6	90.3	87.5	90.6	88.5	98.1	96.1	92.8
Pondicherry	50.2	53	48.3	41.4	38.7	35.8	39.2	39.6	42.6	43.2
South India	74.8	75.3	72	68.7	66.8	66.8	68.9	71.2	72.7	70.8
All India	59.8	56.8	55.3	54.8	56	56.7	58.4	59.2	58.2	57.2

Source: Banking Statistics 1972-2002 and Basic Statistical Returns, RBI, Various Issues.

percentage points by 2004. Though some degree of decline was witnessed for other southern states also (Table 4.39) (except Tamil Nadu), in those other states, the ratio stood higher than the national average. The latest figures available indicate that the CD ratio in Kerala has risen to more than 64 per cent in September 2005.

At the district level, the CD ratio was very low in Pathanamthitta and Thrissur districts; in fact it was way below the state's average. The reason for this was a high deposit base without proportionate credit off-take. On the other hand, the CD ratio was extremely high in the districts of Wayanad and Idukki. In most years, the CD ratio was above 130 per cent for Wayanad district. In the case of Wayanad, the high CD ratio is not due to high amount of lending but low deposit base. The CD ratio in 2004 is high and compared favourably with the national average in the districts of Ernakulam, Kozhikode, Kollam and Thiruvananthapuram.

Kerala typically attracts large amounts of non-resident deposits. The low CD ratio could either be due to this large quantum of deposits or could be due to low levels of economic activity that needs credit. A good idea of the extent to which the banking sector contributes to the economic activity in the state may be obtained by studying the ratio of credit disbursals to the State Domestic Product (Table 4.42). The credit off-take from the banking system as a proportion of state income compares reasonably well in the recent past with the national average.

In March 2004, the total (rural, semi-urban, urban) number of deposit accounts in banks in Kerala were 238.8 lakh (Table 4.43). Assuming Kerala's population on that date was 326.20 lakh (source: Statistical Pocket Book India 2003, CSO), the number of deposit accounts in Kerala works out to 73.21 per cent of its total population. At the all-India level with 4460.8 lakh deposit accounts for a total population of 10,682.14 lakh the number of deposit accounts were only 42.80 per cent of the total population.

In 2004, the average amount per deposit account in Kerala was Rs. 28,527, lower than the national average of Rs 33,058. In March 2004, the total number of credit accounts in Kerala were 40.69 lakh. The number of credit accounts in Kerala as proportion of total population were 12.47 per cent. In all-India there were 663.9 lakh credit accounts. At the all-India level, hence, the number of credit accounts as proportion of total population were only 6.22 per cent. However, in 2004 the average credit per account in Kerala was only Rs. 76,122; at the national level, the corresponding figure was Rs. 1,32,597.

Thus, both on the funds mobilisation side and on the funds utilisation side, the commercial banking sector in Kerala is well-developed. However, the average amount per credit account in Kerala is far below the national average. The demand for banking services on the credit side is a derived demand. Unless there is adequate underlying economic activity, there cannot be adequate demand for credit.

Tables 4.44 and 4.45 show the occupation-wise advances of scheduled commercial banks at the all-India level and in Kerala. Table 4.46 furnishes the same information in percentage terms. It is seen that Kerala fares better than all-India in the matter of agricultural and personal loans and retail loans. But in the case of industrial loans, Kerala's position is lower than one-fourth of that at the national level; in the case of trade, Kerala's figure comes to about one-half the national average in 2004.

TABLE 4.40

Deposit and Credit Disbursed in Kerala, 2000-2004

(in Rupees)

District	2004		2003		2002		2001		2000	
	Deposits	*Credit*	*Deposits*	*Credit*	*Deposits*	*Credit*	*Deposits*	*Credit*	*Deposits*	*Credit*
Alapuzha	479889	173068	426891	142518	373934	121117	323630	102455	292886	93874
Kannur	353776	141412	325471	116918	287079	107005	253870	92500	221331	79987
Ernakulam	1204114	759487	1020083	622842	881286	556133	752022	502181	660715	440444
Idukki	73942	66898	61108	54942	51560	48905	42766	35554	38745	33240
Kasaragod	123205	63642	109765	50587	94910	46899	79085	39768	70248	35176
Kollam	418910	199884	370749	166247	321033	148198	276671	138273	246652	127060
Kottayam	550651	219965	462337	183993	385643	156784	336118	130019	294707	111736
Kozhikode	350955	202130	307409	171094	267848	157923	225578	133470	202446	116230
Malappuram	335269	115857	293762	99833	255212	87175	208167	72811	183918	67264
Palakkad	309789	151584	273448	127705	241591	108874	196586	88000	176951	84760
Pathanamthitta	727250	128387	642677	105980	548888	85227	486182	65914	433308	57639
T'Puram	1011108	573906	881038	442347	778237	374660	666659	283554	577893	212156
Thrissur	839746	247026	749460	213601	655094	193124	548114	190476	482032	131836
Wayanad	33572	54147	27967	47734	24392	44685	22365	35859	22663	30086

Note: T'Puram – Thiruvananthapuram.

Source: Compiled from credit and deposit details extracted from *Basic Statistical Returns*, RBI, 2000-04.

TABLE 4.41

CD Ratio in Various Districts of Kerala, 2000-2004

(in Per Cent)

District	2004	2003	2002	2001	2000
Alapuzha	36.1	33.4	32.4	31.7	32.1
Kannur	40.0	35.9	37.3	36.4	36.1
Ernakulam	63.1	61.1	63.1	66.8	66.7
Idukki	90.5	89.9	94.9	83.1	85.8
Kasaragod	51.7	46.1	49.4	50.3	50.1
Kollam	47.7	44.8	46.2	50.0	51.5
Kottayam	39.9	39.8	40.7	38.7	37.9
Kozhikode	57.6	55.7	59.0	59.2	57.4
Malappuram	34.6	34.0	34.2	35.0	36.6
Palakkad	48.9	46.7	45.1	44.8	47.9
Pathanamthitta	17.7	16.5	15.5	13.6	13.3
Thiruvananthapuram	56.8	50.2	48.1	42.5	36.7
Thrissur	29.4	28.5	29.5	34.8	27.4
Wayanad	161.3	170.7	183.2	160.3	132.8

Source: Compiled from credit and deposit details extracted from *Basic Statistical Returns*, RBI, 2000-04.

These figures reflect the weakness of the credit absorption capacity of the economy due to its industrial slackness. In 2004, loans to the industrial sector contributed only 4.1 per cent of the total lending in Kerala whereas at the national, the corresponding rate was 20.2 per cent. The corresponding figures were 39 per cent for Tamil Nadu, 33.2 per cent in Karnataka and 29.7 per cent in Andhra Pradesh.

TABLE 4.42

Advances as Proportion of State Income

Year	Kerala	All India
1998	27.3	26.2
1999	26.6	25.4
2000	25.5	25.1
2001	27.5	26.9
2002	30.5	28.3
2003	33.4 (P)	34.1
2004	35.3 (Q)	NA

Source: *Economic Review 2004*, Government of Kerala.

TABLE 4.43

Analytical Decomposition of the CD Ratio, 2004

Parameter	2004		2003	
	Kerala	*All India*	*Kerala*	*All India*
Number of Deposit Accounts (Lakh)	238.8	4571.58	214.68	4460.8
Number of Credit Accounts (Lakh)	40.69	663.9	38.80	584.91
Deposit Accounts as % of Population	73.21%	42.80%	65.81%	41.76%
Total Deposits (Rupees Lakh)	6812177	151127339	5952165	127619570
Average Deposit Amount per Deposit A/C (Rupee)	28527	33058	27712	28609
Total Credit (Rupees Lakh)	3097393	88031203	2546340	75596882
Credit Accounts as % of Population	12.47%	6.22%	11.89%	5.48%
Average Credit Amount per Credit A/C (Rupee)	76122	132597	65602	129245

The number of industries registered in Kerala during 1991-2002 formed only 1.06 per cent of the total number of industries registered in India during the period; in terms of the amount of investment, they formed even lower, only one per cent of the all-India total. During this period, the shares of new industries registered in Tamil Nadu, Andhra Pradesh and Karnataka were 9.43 per cent, 6.95 per cent and 4.03 per cent respectively; in terms of the amounts invested, the corresponding figures were 6.4 per cent, 10.9 per cent and 5.6 per cent respectively. Kerala's low credit-deposit ratio seems to have arisen primarily from the apathy on the part of entrepreneurs. The marginal improvement in the CD ratio observed more recently is primarily due to rise in demand from the retail segment, more precisely from the housing and the personal loans segment. This is an indication of an important trend—of loans going for current consumption and to unproductive sectors.

TABLE 4.44

Classification of Outstanding Credit of Scheduled Commercial Banks according to Occupation of Borrowers, March 2004, All India

Occupation	*No. of Accounts*	*Credit Limit (Rs.)*	*Amount Outstanding (Rs.)*
Agriculture	20658570	5518416	4739393
Industry	2354885	790140	661438
Transport Operators	437372	216478	170412
Professional and Other Services	1353672	460091	362895
Personal Loans	25880914	11491256	7037110
Trade	4956003	1623563	1321739
Finance	58839	23534	17282
All Others	6199583	2327198	1959712
Total Bank Credit	61899838	22450676	16269981

Source: Basic Statistical Returns, RBI, 2004.

TABLE 4.45

Classification of Outstanding Credit of Scheduled Commercial Banks according to Occupation of Borrowers, March 2004, Kerala

Occupation	*No. of Accounts*	*Credit Limit (Rs.)*	*Amount Outstanding (Rs.)*
Agriculture	1578610	488172	436055
Industry	174414	963228	657427
Transport Operators	30954	47748	34545
Professional and Other Services	118857	229917	191268
Personal Loans	1320970	1313051	1100441
Trade	311870	578254	484452
Finance	3573	38830	37064
All Others	556141	398285	312403
Total Bank Credit	4095389	4057485	3253654

Source: Basic Statistical Returns, RBI, 2004.

(b) Cooperative Banks

Agricultural credit is disbursed through multiple channels in Kerala; with their vast network and wide outreach extending even to the remotest parts of the state, the cooperative credit institutions have remained an important institutional agency for agricultural and non-agricultural rural credit dispensation. As in the case of deposit mobilisation, the performance of the cooperative banking sector in Kerala on the credit dispensation front has been remarkable.

Table 4.48 presents a comparative picture of the cooperative banking sector in Kerala as of March 2004 *vis-à-vis* the cooperative banking sector at the all-India level. Kerala accounted for 3.61 per cent, 6.92 per cent and a huge 13.29 per cent of the total loans issued by SCBs, DCCBs and PACS respectively in India in 2004. Besides, the recovery performance of SCBs, DCCBs and PACS in 2003 in Kerala (represented by the 'percentage of over-dues to demand' figures) compared favourably with the all-India performance. The percentage of loans flowing to the non-agricultural sector in Kerala through the SCBs, DCCBs and PACS is far higher than the corresponding percentages at the national level (Table 4.48).

The truly spectacular performance of the cooperative banking sector in Kerala becomes obvious from the performance of the smallest units in the cooperative banking system, namely PACS. In the financial year 2004, Kerala with 144.65 lakh borrowers was the state with the highest number of borrowers in PACS. The

TABLE 4.46

Classification of Outstanding Credit of Scheduled Commercial Banks according to Occupation of Borrowers, March 2004

(in percentage)

Occupation	*Kerala*	*All India*
Agriculture	29.1	13.4
Industry	4.1	20.2
Transport Operators	1.0	1.1
Professional and Other Services	2.2	5.9
Personal Loans	43.3	33.8
Trade	8.1	14.9
Finance	0.1	1.1
All Others	12.0	9.6
Total Bank Credit	100.0	100.0

Source: Basic Statistical Returns, RBI, 2004.

TABLE 4.47

State-wise Outstanding Credit of Scheduled Commercial Banks according to Occupation, March 2004

(in percentage)

Occupation	*Andhra Pradesh*	*Karnataka*	*Kerala*	*Tamil Nadu*	*Average*
Agriculture	17.9	15.1	13.4	9.7	14.0
Industry	29.7	33.2	20.2	39.0	30.5
Transport Operators	1.7	1.1	1.1	0.8	1.2
Professional and Other Services	4.8	5.9	5.9	6.3	5.7
Personal Loans	26.1	27.1	33.8	23.8	27.7
1. Loans for Purchase of Consumer Durables	0.7	0.5	0.6	0.6	0.6
2. Loans for Housing	11.8	14.5	17.1	10.2	13.4
3. Rest of the Personal Loans	13.5	12.1	16.1	13.1	13.7
Trade	7.9	6.8	14.9	7.5	9.3
Finance	1.2	3.3	1.1	6.7	3.1
All Others	10.7	7.5	9.6	6.1	8.5
Total Bank Credit	100.0	100.0	100.0	100.0	100.0

Source: *Basic Statistical Returns*, RBI, 2004.

state with the next highest number of borrowers (Orissa) had only 62.39 lakh borrowers. The number of borrowers from the PACS in Kerala in 2004 formed 44.34 per cent of the total population of the state in 2003. Equally dramatic is the fact that it accounted for 28.22 per cent of the total number of borrowers from PACS (512.65 lakh) in the country.

Table 4.49 (a), 4.49 (b) and 4.49 (c) shows that the total amount of short-term loans issued in Kerala in 2004 through the PACS was Rs. 4,49,731 lakh; this was also the highest amount for any state. Similarly, in the case of medium term loans also, the state ranked first with an amount of Rs. 1,74,112.4 lakh dispersed through PACs. Only 18.97 per cent of PAC loans goes for agricultural purposes. At the national level, 62.72 per cent of the total loans issued are for the agricultural sector. The credit requirements of the agricultural sector are seen to be met by banks more than the cooperative sector.

TABLE 4.48

Comparative Picture of Cooperative Banking, March 2003: Kerala *versus* All India

Parameters	2003		2004	
	Kerala	*All India*	*Kerala*	*All India*
Total Loans: State Coop Banks (SCBs) (Rs. Lakh)	126032	3920286	125809	3486449
Of which Non-agri. Loans	115409 (91.57%)	2407197 (61.4%)	115266 (91.61%)	1877434 (53.84%)
Proportion of Over-dues to Demand: SCBs	9.47	17.74	6.29	16.82
Total Loans: District Central Coop Banks (Rs. Lakh)	277841	5919880	397826	5752901
Of which Non-agri. Loans (Rs. Lakh)	226505 (81.52%)	3519513 (59.45%)	287341 (72.23%)	2456510 (42.7)
Proportion of Over-dues to Demand: DCCBs	20.92	37.43	17.46	36.9
Total Loans: Primary Agri. Credit Societies (Rs. Lakh)	577246	3399586	588069.59	4423677
Proportion of Over-dues to Demand: PACS	24.35	38.23	25.17	36.84

Source: National Federation of State Cooperative Banks (NAFSCOB).

TABLE 4.49 (A)

Loans Issued by SCBs Purpose-wise During 2002-2004

(Rs. Lakh)

	2002-03				2003-04			
	Agriculture	*Non-Agri*	*Others*	*Total*	*Agriculture*	*Non-Agri*	*Others*	*Total*
Kerala	**10623**	**111437**	**3972**	**126032**	**10543**	**102387**	**12879**	**125809**
All India	1513089	2236320	170877	3920286	1609015	1789314	88120	3486449

TABLE 4.49 (B)

Loans Issued by DCCBs Purpose-wise During 2002-2004

(Rs. Lakh)

	2002-03				2003-04			
	Agriculture	*Non-Agri*	*Others*	*Total*	*Agriculture*	*Non-Agri*	*Others*	*Total*
Kerala	51336	182923	43582	277841	61999	298540	37287	397826
All India	2453072	2525884	993629	5972585	2472940	2416930	863031	5752901

TABLE 4.49 (C)

Loans Issued by PACs Purpose-wise During 2002-2004

(Rs. Lakh)

	2002-03			2003-04		
	Short Term	*Medium Term*	**Total (L & A)*	*Short Term*	*Medium Term*	**Total (L & A)*
Kerala	**395110.7**	**182135.8**	**577246.4**	**449731**	**174112.4**	**623843.4**
All India	2719992	679594.3	3399586	2932589	579334.6	3511924

Note: * Loans and advances
Source: NAFSCOB 2002-03, 2003-04.

All-India Financial Institutions and Kerala-based Institutions

All-India Financial Institutions

The all-India Financial Institutions (AIFIs) include development banks like IDBI, IFCI, ICICI (erstwhile), IDFC, SIDBI; specialised financing institutions like EXIM bank, NABARD and insurance companies like LIC, and general insurance companies and Tourism Financial Corporation of India. These institutions totalling 15 and 47 state level institutions together play a major role in providing industrial credit. These institutions disbursed a cumulative total of Rs. 6,57,221.4 crore as credit till March 2004. Over the past few years sanctions and disbursals have come down drastically because of a host of factors like subdued growth of the industrial sector and general drop in the GDP growth rates; however, sanctions and disbursals have picked up again due to a recovery of the national economy lately.

TABLE 4.50

Trends in Sanctions and Disbursals of AIFI

Year	*Sanctions (Rs. Lakh)*	*Growth (%)*	*Disbursals (Rs. Lakh)*	*Growth (%)*
1999-00	100437.5	25.9	70930	20
2000-01	116461.0	16	76439.8	7.8
2001-02	79001.4	-32.2	63822.2	-16.5
2002-03	39621.0	-49.8	33258.9	-47.9
2003-04	63609.2	60.5	40439.5	21.6

Source: Report on Development Banking, 2004, IDBI.

The amounts of assistance provided by AIFIs to various states during the period 1999-2004 are shown in Table 4.51. It may be noted that the top six states assisted by these AIFIs are Maharashtra, Gujarat, Delhi, Andhra Pradesh, Tamil Nadu, Karnataka; recently Haryana has also joined them. The sanctions and disbursals pattern shows that demand for loans from the industrial sector is the sole criterion for assistance and that loans are not decided based on other criteria like population or industrial backwardness.

Surprisingly, Tourism Finance Corporation of India (TFCI) which was set up to cater to the financial needs of tourism industry has not sanctioned or disbursed even a single loan to the state of Kerala in the past four years. Finance from this agency is going primarily to states like Maharashtra, Gujarat, Rajasthan, Delhi, Tamil Nadu and Andhra Pradesh. The reason for this might be lack of awareness of the Kerala tourism-related enterprises of the facilities being provided by TFCI.

Kerala State Financial Corporation (KFC)

State Financial Corporations (SFC) of various states are incorporated under the SFCs Act 1951, and were established with the objective of playing a major role in the development and industrialisation of states by extending financial assistance to entrepreneurs. SFCs were set up primarily to finance small and medium scale units. Their area of operation is in general restricted to the concerned States. SFCs also assist small-scale units for their modernization and technology up-gradation programmes by providing them soft loans and restructuring the sick small-scale units through rehabilitation schemes.

Currently, there are 18 SFCs (including TIIC which was set up as a company) in the country which have existed for more than 40 years. They provide financial assistance to industrial units by way of term loans, direct subscription to equity, guarantees, etc. Over the years, SFCs have expanded their activities and coverage of assistance. In tune with the other SFCs, Kerala State Financial Corporation (KFC) has been playing a major role in the field of industrial finance to service sector projects. KFC has achieved the status of Category A. The SFC was established during the financial year 1995-96, thus joining the elite list of the top six SFC in the country. By 2003-04, KFC had sanctioned industrial loans amounting to Rs.2600 crore to establish more than 40,000 industrial units, spread all

TABLE 4.51

State-wise Assistance Sanctioned and Disbursed by AIFIs: 1999-2004

(Rs. Crore)

S. No	State	Sanctions					Disbursements				
		1999-2000	2000-01	2001-02	2002-03	2003-04	1999-2000	2000-01	2001-02	2002-03	2003-04
1	Andhra Pradesh	8038.5	5011.8	5816.2	2187.3	3839.9	3935.5	3722.7	3394	1461.8	1732.7
2	Arunachal Pradesh	2.8	5.6	2.9	5.0	4.0	2.8	5.8	2.9	5.0	3.5
3	Assam	331.2	313.1	182.1	67.3	112.8	166.5	228.9	101.1	63.7	108.1
4	Bihar	440.8	175.0	65.3	38.3	17.8	431.4	178.1	76.1	38.4	16.2
5	Chhattisgarh	599.3	381.5	69.7	13.8	345.3	129.5	578.2	285.1	32.5	54.9
6	Delhi (National Capital Territory)	9079.4	10548.6	7941.0	4576.2	16154.4	6736.2	8032.9	6594.7	5276.7	7685.9
7	Goa	288.7	260.6	112.8	79.8	67.1	390.2	246.5	105.3	70.9	41.4
8	Gujarat	12178.0	13893.7	6880.3	2293.7	4611.3	8541.6	5079.6	3477.9	2117.4	2407.4
9	Haryana	1659.4	4765.4	990.5	628.8	6953.5	1430.1	1701.9	1696.9	471.1	362
10	Himachal Pradesh	712.0	572.0	460.5	291.0	1248.2	609	724.3	721.3	213.9	978.4
11	Jammu & Kashmir	340.5	406.6	759.3	94.6	247.4	109.2	274.6	429.1	119.7	122.7
12	Jharkhand	572.9	124.5	219.6	25.6	81.6	558.9	145.7	182	30.3	62.9
13	Karnataka	5374.2	6838.3	3770.4	2093.1	1566.3	4093.9	5246.4	4189.1	1978.4	1661.7
14	**Kerala**	**776.9**	**1209.7**	**1226.0**	**658.3**	**1043.4**	**878.4**	**1060.5**	**1007.8**	**570**	**724.9**
15	Madhya Pradesh	1712.9	2276.8	1157.9	398.1	637.7	1322.2	1258.1	743.2	306.3	439.6
16	Maharashtra	21409.7	31155.7	19887.7	10145.7	7438.7	16093.3	19781.3	15246.1	8359.2	9000
17	Manipur	5.3	21.5	1.7	4.5	2.8	4.7	22.4	51.7	3.2	3.9
18	Meghalaya	11.0	34.0	19.4	11.7	33.4	10.6	15.2	30.9	12.4	52.5
19	Mizoram	4.6	7.4	8.9	15.5	16.4	4.5	7.6	8.7	15.5	16.4
20	Nagaland	1.8	7.5	3.7	1.0	1.4	1.8	6.5	3.7	1.0	1.2
21	Orissa	2939.8	1558.6	819.6	306.0	493.1	1082.3	1055.6	716.7	310.5	367.2
22	Punjab	1973.7	2491.5	2536.1	780.5	536.4	1373.5	2098.6	1126.2	658.7	400.9
23	Rajasthan	1692.7	2730.1	872.2	1022.0	904.7	1442.1	1816.5	1115.8	434.5	772.4
24	Sikkim	3.8	1108.2	4.0	3.9	55.5	5.0	57	10.2	3.7	1.5
25	Tamil Nadu	7510.3	6777.4	4486.2	2530.6	3429.1	4456.3	5022.3	3226.8	1958.9	1942.7
26	Tripura	9.8	10.3	3.7	18.1	12.2	9.9	8.9	208.6	14.5	11.4
27	Uttaranchal	71.4	537.5	390.8	128.3	32.7	46.2	86.8	155.2	78.6	78.0
28	Uttar Pradesh	3317.7	3463.8	1593.6	903.9	797.9	2555.8	2593.2	1500.3	962.3	517.2
29	West Bengal	3790.3	4691.2	2437.4	1435.3	1232.7	3316.1	3840.2	2007.8	1177.4	1339
30	Union Territories	577.3	626.2	428.8	169.3	225.6	311.6	1020.3	496.5	93.5	100.3
31	Multi-State	10353.0	11385.8	10819.7	1088.7	1677.3	7246.5	7730.5	10712.1	1345.2	2083.1
	Total	95779.7	113389.9	73968.0	32015.9	53820.6	67295.6	73647.1	59623.8	28185.2	33090.0

Source: *Report on Development Banking*, IDBI, 2004.

TABLE 4.52

Assistance Provided by Tourism Finance Corporation of India

(Rs. Crore)

S. No.	State	Sanctions					Disbursements				
		1999-2000	2000-01	2001-02	2002-03	2003-04	1999 -2000	2000-01	2001-02	2002-03	2003-04
1	Andhra Pradesh	8.3	33.9	16.7	0.5	6.6	5.1	22.9	29.0	2.2	6.4
2	Delhi (National Capital Territory)	-	9.8	2.0	1.7	1.6	8.4	2.0	-	1.7	1.5
3	**Kerala**	**0.7**	-	-	-	-	**5.0**	-	-	-	-
4	Maharashtra	36.0	5.7	22.3	24.3	18.7	14.7	8.9	16.8	35.4	15.7
5	Rajasthan	6.0	7.5	8.1	6.0	0.5	7.1	2.3	-	3.1	0.5
6	Tamil Nadu	14.4	18.5	7.9	9.3	4.0	13.1	4.6	11.3	15.1	-
7	Andhra Pradesh	8.3	33.9	16.7	0.5	6.6	5.1	22.9	29.0	2.2	6.4

Source: *Report on Development Banking*, IDBI, 2004.

over the state. The kinds of assistance provided by KFC are term loans, project finance, working capital finance and asset finance. The maximum limit of assistance to individual private or public limited companies and cooperative societies is fixed at Rs. 5 crore and for others at Rs. 2 crore.

TABLE 4.53

Top Five SFCs in Terms of Annual Sanctions

(Rs. Crore)

SFCs	1999-00	2000-01	2001-02	2002-03	2003-04
APSFC	335.2	391.9	390.1	385.2	369.5
GSFC	364.8	282.0	93.9	3.9	0.2
KFC	162.1 (6)*	292.5 (3)	160.2 (4)	155.6 (5)	167.9 (5)
KSFC	336.7	461.4	289.5	331.7	289.8
RFC	198.8	178.2	157.3	192.4	215.8
TIIC	244.3	279.9	211.0	145.4	185.3
UPFC	65.6	107.2	152.7	196.5	71.6
Aggregate Sanctions of all SFCs	2237.8	2790.7	2078.6	1808.4	1545.4

Note: *Rank of KFC among all SFCs.

Source: Report on Development Banking in India 2000-01, IDBI

TABLE 4.54

KFC's Performance Over 2000-2004

(Rs. Crore)

Description Bottom of Form	2000-01	2001-02	2002-03	2003-04
Sanctions	292.5	160.2	155.6	167.9
All-India SFCs	2790.7	2078.6	1808.4	1545.4
Disbursements	226.9	175.9	112.3	121.0
All-India SFCs	2008.1	1770.9	1488.7	1291.4
Recovery	230.7	237.1	252.8	NA
Capital Adequacy Ratio (%)	13.90	10.16	11.05	NA
Recovery Ratio (%)	40.43	30.70	42	NA

Source: Report on Development Banking 2004, IDBI.

KFC has been figuring among the top five State Finance Corporations over the past few years because of its commendable performance in terms of sanctions and disbursals (Table 4.53). The performance has to be judged against the background of the small manufacturing base of the state. KFC ranks well on the other measures of capital adequacy ratio and recoveries as well (Table 4.54). Sanctions and disbursals in the past few years had come down; lately it has recovered

TABLE 4.55

District-wise Loans Sanctioned and Disbursed by KFC in 2003

(Rs. lakh)

District	Sanction		Disbursement	
	No.	Amount	No.	Amount
Idukki	30	892.77	28	790.33
Wayanad	47	357.26	37	316.24
Alappuzha	23	291.65	27	356.31
Malappuram	24	626.35	27	452.99
Kannur	21	365.60	22	353.76
Kasargode	32	285.39	33	277.70
Thiruvananthapuram	62	1887.23	49	1354.10
Thrissur	76	2370.06	61	1671.22
Pathanamthitta	19	574.02	20	314.24
Kollam	78	1257.22	87	975.17
Kottayam	21	700.85	20	393.30
Ernakulam	123	4034.17	117	2418.79
Palakkad	59	1156.39	38	888.49
Kozhikode	81	760.07	81	668.12
Total	696	15559.03	647	11230.76

Source: Department of Economics and Statistics, Govt of Kerala.

TABLE 4.56

Industry-wise Assistance Sanctioned (S) and Disbursed (D) by SFCs in Kerala and all-India

(Rs. Crore)

S. No.	Type of Industry	Kerala		All-India	
		S	D	S	D
1.	Food Products	8.4	9.7	162.2	140.9
2.	Textiles	2.1	3.6	86.4	68
3.	Paper & Paper Products	2.4	6.0	36.8	27.7
4.	Rubber & Rubber Products	6.2	6.7	40.8	38.6
5.	Chemicals & Chemical Products	3.5	3.0	57.7	48.6
6.	Fertilisers	—	—	5.5	3.4
7.	Cement	—	—	0.7	3.0
8.	Basic Metals	—	—	81.9	73.4
9.	Metal Products	17.0	7.7	66.4	31.2
10.	Machinery	1.7	1.0	37.5	27.7
11.	Electrical & Electronic Equipment	1.0	1.4	71.0	79.7
12.	Transport Equipment	—	—	17.6	10.7
13.	Infrastructure	4.6	3.8	23.6	12.9
14.	Services	88.9	63.5	314.1	269.3
15.	Other Industries	32.1	14.6	543.2	456.9
	Total	167.9	121.0	1545.4	1291.4

Source: Report on Development Banking in India 2003-04, Industrial Development Bank of India.

some lost ground (in the year 2004). A similar trend is observed in the aggregate disbursals of all-India SFCs also during the past four years, but the trend reversal witnessed by KFC is not reflected in the aggregate sanctions and disbursals at the all-India level.

Table 4.55 presents data on the assistance given by KFC to units located in various districts of Kerala and the Union Territory of Lakshadweep. The lion's share of the disbursals has gone to the district of Ernakulam while the district of Wayanad accounts for the lowest share. Ernakulam is well-known as the preferred location of most economic activity in the State of Kerala. As Table 4.56 shows, in tune with the trend of the all-India SFCs, KFC's disbursements also mainly flow to Food Products and Services with the Services sector getting the maximum assistance.

Kerala State Industrial Development Corporation

Among the 28 State Industrial Development Corporations set up by the state governments, Kerala set up in 1961 the Kerala State Industrial Development Corporation (KSIDC) to foster medium and large-scale industries in Kerala. KSIDC, a fully owned Government agency extends its services beyond financial support. KSIDC helps entrepreneurs identify investment ideas, translate them into business proposals and obtain for them the required government clearances and tie up infrastructure. This way KSIDC plays the role akin to a venture capitalist in conventional type of project financing. By October 2003, KSIDC promoted 448 units with a total investment of Rs 4235 crore. KSIDC almost achieved a steady increase in disbursals during the decade of the 1990s except for 1997-98. Disbursals by KSIDCs, however, declined alarmingly over the past four years consecutively.

Non-Banking Financial Institutions/ Companies (NBFI/Cs)

Any study of the activities and performance of Non-Banking Financial Institutions encounters definitional and data problems; the emergence of the multi-service companies accentuates the problem. RBI (Amendment) Act 1997 defines NBFC as an institution or agency whose principal business is to accept deposits under any scheme and to lend in any manner. Accordingly a large number of loan and investment companies established by corporate houses for the purpose of making investments in group companies became NBFI/Cs. The Act of 1997 made it mandatory for NBFCs to apply to the RBI for certificate of registration. NBFC/Is perform a variety of activities and have products that serve the needs of a variety of enterprises ranging from individuals to corporates. Based on the type of activities performed, the major categories (regulated by RBI) of NBFI/Cs are:

- Equipment Leasing Companies.
- Hire-Purchase Finance Companies.
- Loan Companies.
- Investment Companies.
- Residuary Non-Banking Companies, and
- Miscellaneous Non-Banking Companies.

Besides, there are other categories of NBFCs also *viz.*, Merchant Bankers and Housing Finance Companies. In India there are about 13,000 registered NBFCs rendering services in a variety of sectors such as transport and hire purchase. In Kerala, as many as 171 companies are operating among which 23 are public-deposit accepting NBFCs with a total asset size of Rs 221 crore (as on Dec 31st 2003). Hire purchase lending

TABLE 4.57

Assistance Sanctioned and Disbursed by all SIDCs and KSIDC

(Rs. Crore)

Year	*Sanctions*				*Disbursals*			
	All India SIDCs	*Growth Rate*	*KSIDC*	*Growth Rate*	*All India SIDCs*	*Growth Rate*	*KSIDC*	*Growth Rate*
1999-00	1601.4		115.3		1614.7		78.2	
2000-01	2047.4	21.78%	77	-49.74%	1631.2	1.01%	51.3	-52.44%
2001-02	1555.6	-31.61%	69.5	-10.79%	1679.5	2.88%	45.5	-12.75%
2002-03	926.0	-67.99%	57.1	-21.72%	1252.4	-34.10%	23.6	-92.80%
2003-04	895.3	-3.43%	44.1	-29.48%	818.0	-53.11%	27.0	12.59%

Source: Report on Development Banking in India 2003-04, IDBI.

has gone up to 62 per cent in 2003. The current trend is to advance loans against gold, which is considered less risky than hire purchase business. NBFCs had collected Rs. 72 crore of deposits by September 30, 2003.

TABLE 4.58

Sources of Funds of NBFCs in Kerala, 1999-00 to 2001-02

Funds	*1999-00*		*2000-01*		*2001-02*	
	Amount (Rs. Crore)	*Growth (%)*	*Amount (Rs. Crore)*	*Growth (%)*	*Amount (Rs. Crore)*	*Growth (%)*
1. Net Owned Fund	34.58 (30.45)	-	39.20 (29.46)	13.36	43.17 (26.23)	10.13
2. Public Deposits	32.56 (28.67)	-	35.80 (26.90)	9.95	50.47 (30.67)	40.98
3. Exempted Borrowings	46.43 (40.88)	-	58.07 (43.64)	25.07	70.92 (43.10)	22.13
4. Total	113.57 (100.00)	-	133.07 (100.00)	17.17	164.56 (100.00)	23.66

Note: Figures in brackets show percentage share.

Source: *Report of the Working Group on Study of NBFIs*, State Planning Board.

It is evident that the NBFCs are catering to the needs of hire purchase transactions and that they are sourcing their funds predominantly from borrowings (corporate borrowings, bonds, bank borrowing).

TABLE 4.59

Activity-wise Asset Pattern of NBFCs in Kerala, 1999-00 to 2001-02

Activity	*1999-00*		*2000-01*		*2001-02*	
	Amount (Rs. crore)	*Growth (%)*	*Amount (Rs. crore)*	*Growth (%)*	*Amount (Rs. crore)*	*Growth (%)*
1. Hire purchase	91.78 (64.74)	-	114.30 (69.77)	24.73	125.20 (62.71)	9.49
2. Loans and Advances	11.65 (8.22)	-	15.14 (9.24)	29.95	40.61 (20.34)	168.23
3. Investment	12.79 (9.02)	-	14.68 (8.97)	14.77	14.01 (7.02)	-4.56
4. Other Assets	25.54 (18.02)	-	19.68 (12.02	-22.94	19.85 (9.93)	0.86
Total	141.76 (100.00)	-	163.83 (100.00)	15.57	199.65 (100.00)	21.86

Note: Figures in brackets show percentage shares.

Source *Report of the Working Group on Study of NBFIs*, State Planning Board.

Other Constituents of Financial Services Sector

Chit Funds

A Chit Fund is basically an arrangement to promote savings for mutual benefit of its members. It is popular throughout South India. Chit means transaction and is variously known as chit or *kuri*. A Chit Fund enters into an agreement with a number of subscribers under which every member subscribes to the fund in a fixed number of monthly installments and every subscriber is entitled to a prize amount as agreed upon in the agreement when his/her turn comes. As long as the chit fund is organized precisely along the lines laid out above, the company can operate as a financial intermediary, regulated by the Registrar of Chit Funds in each state, rather than by the RBI Act. The stream of dividends reflect the competitive price of capital within the group. Chit Funds have been able to generate an interest rate that was a few percentage points higher than the conventional bank rate on deposits.

This process continues for as many months as there are participants, with an auction conducted each month. The dividend generated endogenously within the group, thus, acts as an interest payment. Participants who win the bid early are effectively borrowers, while those who wait until the end are effectively lenders: the participant who wins last receives his principal in full and all the dividends generated over the course of the group. In the current scenario, chit funds assume great importance because of the prevailing low interest regime in the economy; since returns in chits are attractive, many gullible investors are lured, by dubious chit fund companies, to become subscribers. To provide an alternative to private chit funds, and with a view to bringing social control over the chit fund business (for safeguarding the common man from possible unscrupulous operators in the field), the Government of Kerala established the Kerala State Financial Enterprises Limited (KSFE) in 1969. KSFE is a Miscellaneous Non-Banking Finance Company (MNBFC), which started with a paid up capital of Rs. 2 lakh, 10 branches and 40 employees. It has now grown into an institution doing business worth Rs. 3500 crore annually, employing over 3000 persons directly and thousands of persons indirectly, having a branch network of 230 branches and a net worth of Rs.10 crore. This company has been consistently maintaining a high credit-deposit ratio (CD ratio) of about 80. It is also notable that the company has been advancing funds entirely mobilised through its deposit schemes within Kerala. Table 4.60 gives a snapshot of the performance of KSFE during the period 1997-2003.

The number of Chit Funds run by cooperative societies is far higher than those run by KSFE and private chit funds, with a total capital Rs. 1240.5 crore.

TABLE 4.60

Registered Chits, 1999-2000

Name of the Institution	Number of Chits	Share of each to Total Percentage	Capital (Rs. Lakh)	Share of each to Total Percentage
1. KSFE	7446	37.5	95249	77
2. Cooperatives	8793	44.2	21101	17
3. Private Chits	3633	18.3	7701	6
Total	19872	100	124051	100

Source: *Report of the Working Group on NBFIs*, State Planning Board 2005.

Though KSFE is the leader in Kerala's chit fund business, the actual volume of chit business would be several times higher if the volume of business of chit funds in the unregistered sector and those with bases outside Kerala are included.

- The loans are mainly availed for meeting marriage expenses, construction of houses, medical expenses, etc particularly in the context of non-availability of adequate institutional credit for the purposes.
- The borrowers are predominantly the poor and the vulnerable sections of the society.

Population covered per money lending institution in the state is 5590 whereas on an average each branch covers 9431 persons (as per *Economic Review*, 2004). These pieces of evidence imply that there exists significant unmet demand for credit in Kerala. The purposes for which the loans are being availed again point out that the demand for retail loans is significant and that banks and other financial institutions would find enough demand if they tailor their products to meet the demands of individuals and small agencies. It might be difficult for banks to offer loans to meet

TABLE 4.61

Performance of KSFE, 1997-2003

(Rs. Lakh)

S. No.	Particulars	1997-98	1998-99	1999-00	2000-01	2001-02	2002-03	2003-04
1	Annual Chitty Turnover	629.17	804.48	989.73	1229.7	1454	1595.18	2257
2	Total Advance	391.1	534.2	5026.5	564	560	548.82	(includes advances)
3	Total Deposit	439.4	651.3	758	881	1207	1426.84	1432.25
	Total Business	1459.67	1989.98	2254.23	2674.7	3221	3570.84	3689.25

Source: KSFE website.

Moneylenders

Money lending in Kerala seems to be big business despite the state's well-developed banking infrastructure. No official data exist on this segment for the past; a recent survey done by the Working Group on NBFIs has, however, brought forth the following facts:

- There were 5696 moneylenders in the organised sector in Kerala in March 2004.
- Alappuzha alone accounts for around 17 per cent of them.
- A large proportion of loans given by moneylenders is charged interest rates ranging from 18 per cent to 20 per cent, against the collateral in gold.
- The money lenders source their funds predominantly from NRIs and local businesses.
- The flexibility and the minimum restrictions under which moneylenders give loans are a major attraction for borrowers.

TABLE 4.62

Moneylenders in Kerala, 2003-04

District	Moneylenders		Population Covered per Institution
	Number	%	
1. Thiruvananthapuram	570	10.01	5675
2. Kollam	675	11.85	3828
3. Pathanamthitta	785	13.78	1569
4. Alappuzha	976	17.13	2157
5. Ernakulam	225	3.95	13770
6. Kottayam	366	6.42	5336
7. Idukki	344	6.04	3281
8. Thrissur	488	8.57	6097
9. Palakkad	144	2.53	18174
10. Malappuram	162	2.84	22405
11. Kozhikode	601	10.56	4789
12. Wayanad	128	2.25	6145
13. Kannur	139	2.44	17355
14. Kasaragod	93	1.63	12939
State	5696	100.00	5590

Source: *Report of the Working Group on NBFIs*, State Planning Board, 2005.

TABLE 4.63

Credit to Small Borrowal Accounts of Scheduled Commercial Banks 2004

(Amount in lakh, No. of accounts in thousand)

State	*Total Credit*		*To Small Borrowers*		*Small Borrowers Proportion*		*Amt Lent Per Small Credit Account (Rs.)*
	No. of Accounts	*Amt Out Standing*	*No. of Accounts*	*Amt Out Standing*	*Number-wise*	*Amount-wise*	
South India	29808	23745926	28389	6267893	95.24%	26.40%	22079
Andhra Pradesh	7778	5585087	7444	1800368	95.71%	32.24%	24185
Karnataka	5967	5913943	5587	1508930	93.63%	25.51%	27008
Kerala	**4069**	**3097393**	**3826**	**1058663**	**94.03%**	**34.18%**	**27670**
Tamil Nadu	11891	9064032	11435	1871378	96.17%	20.65%	16365
All India	66390	88031203	61900	16269981	93.24%	18.48%	26284

Source: *Basic Banking Statistics 2004*, RBI.

cultural and family-related events like marriages especially to those sections which do not have consistent and productive means of repaying the loans, because banks are just custodians and are accountable to their depositors. At the same time, banks should seriously re-examine their credit approach to small businessmen who would repay loans from their economic pursuits. But a look at the following numbers in Table 4.63 shows that banks do fare better in servicing small borrowers in the state of Kerala, both in terms of the amount per credit account and the proportion of small credit accounts to all credit accounts. Kerala's average is higher than the average for the other southern states except Tamil Nadu. Nevertheless, banks have still greater opportunities to lend to small and retail borrowers.

Capital Markets

Stock markets promote economic growth and capital formation by creating liquidity for long term capital. For investors who may be reluctant to relinquish control over their savings for long periods, stock markets provide an opportunity for an exit route. But, the investment culture does not seem to have taken off as yet in Kerala. This can be gauged from the latest survey published with disaggregate level data, conducted by SEBI-NCAER in 2003. Kerala doesn't stand anywhere near the other southern states in the matter of investing in market-related instruments. Of all the market-related instruments, the preferred vehicle seems to be the mutual fund as the proportion of investors using mutual funds is higher for Kerala than the national figures. But when compared with its southern counterparts, market-traded instruments do not seem to have found much favour in Kerala.

The same inference can also be drawn by looking at the distribution of the number of beneficial accounts with the depositories. Data published for National Securities Depository Limited (NSDL) shows that Kerala has 76,793 beneficial accounts which come to 2.4 per cent of the total number of accounts in the country. The other southern states, Andhra Pradesh (6.08 per cent), Karnataka (6.10 per cent) and Tamil Nadu (7.10), fare better than Kerala.

TABLE 4.64

Proportion of Investor Households to All Households Owning Different Types of Instruments

(Per Cent)

State	*Total Investors*	*Only E**	*Only B**	*Only M**	*E & B*	*E & M*	*B & M*	*E, B & M*	*Total E*	*Total B*	*Total M*
Andhra Pradesh	24	4.7	14.7	3.8	1.7	1.0	0.8	1.2	8.5	18.4	6.7
Karnataka	8.1	0.4	5.6	6.2	0.5	0.1	1.3	0.2	1.2	7.7	7.8
Kerala	**4.9**	**1.3**	**0.7**	**6.5**	**0.2**	**0.8**	**1.1**	**0.7**	**3.1**	**2.7**	**9.1**
Tamil Nadu	7.7	2.4	1.8	16.7	0.4	0.8	1.9	0.5	3.9	4.5	19.9
South	13.2	2.6	7.0	8.6	0.9	0.7	1.3	0.7	4.9	9.8	11.2
All India	7.4	1.5	2.8	4.5	0.9	0.5	0.9	0.8	3.7	5.4	6.7

Note: Investors include households investing in equity or bonds or both.

*E – equity; B - bonds and M - mutual funds.

Source: *Handbook of Statistics*, SEBI.

TABLE 4.65

Distribution of Beneficial Accounts with NSDL (End of February 2003)

State	*Number of Accounts*	*% of Total*
Andhra Pradesh	194405	6.08
Karnataka	195159	6.1
Kerala	**76793**	**2.4**
Tamil Nadu	230407	7.2
All India	3197964	100

Source: Indian Securities Market Review 2003, National Stock Exchange.

At one point of time India had the largest number of organised and recognised stock exchanges in the world, all of them regulated by SEBI. The number of official stock exchanges were 23 at the end of Dec. 1997. But, the technology-driven National Stock Exchange (NSE) soon became the most popular exchange. Currently, apart from the Bombay Stock Exchange (BSE), NSE is the only major exchange. In Kerala, the Cochin Stock Exchange, established in the year 1978, was a premier regional exchange that played a major role in the securities market in southern part of the country. But, the Cochin Stock Exchange too, like the other 19 regional exchanges, is on the verge of collapse. The share of 19 regional stock exchanges (RSEs), which was as much as 45.6 per cent of the total all-India turnover of Rs. 2.39 lakh crore in 1995-96, declined progressively to 1 per cent of the total volume in 2001-02. At present, there takes place virtually no trading at any of the RSEs. Trading is thus confined to NSE and BSE only. The Cochin Stock Exchange did make valiant efforts to survive by introducing the facility of computerised trading, the Cochin Online Trading (COLT). There was some appreciable increase in the trade volume in the year 1997-98 but soon afterwards the volumes dwindled and in the past two years, the volume of trade virtually disappeared, as was the case with the other RSEs. To counter this mishap, CSE floated a subsidiary, the Cochin Stock Brokers Ltd (CSBL) and started trading in the National Stock Exchange and the Mumbai Stock Exchange. In fact, CSBL is the first subsidiary of a Stock Exchange to get membership in both NSE and BSE. At present CSBL offers trading in BSE and NSE with more than 150 registered brokers and each member is given separate terminal for online trading. CSE is also a founding member, along with 13 other RSEs, of the Interconnected Stock Exchange of India, which is another bid to revive the fortunes of the RSEs.

Insurance

While financial services, like deposit schemes and loan schemes, provided by banks and other financial institutions help an entity to transfer wealth across time, insurance services help an entity to cope with unanticipated need for financial support arising from adverse events that either impair earning capacity or increase expenditure.

The State of Kerala occupies a unique position in the demographic map of India. As Table 4.66 shows, the life expectancy in Kerala is far higher than the

TABLE 4.66

Expectation of Life at Different Ages

State	*At Birth Male*	*At Birth Female*	*Age 30 Male*	*Age 30 Female*	*Age 50 Male*	*Age 50 Female*	*Age 70+ Male*	*Age 70+ Female*
Andhra Pradesh	61.2	63.5	38.8	41.2	21.9	23.5	9.7	9.5
Assam	56.6	57.1	36.8	38.9	20.3	22.4	8.9	10.1
Bihar	60.4	58.4	40.6	40.8	23.8	24.3	12.0	12.3
Gujarat	60.9	62.9	38.8	42.2	21.8	24.3	9.2	9.7
Haryana	63.7	64.6	42.1	45.8	25.0	27.9	11.4	13.1
Himachal Pradesh	64.6	65.2	42.0	42.7	25.1	25.0	13.9	10.1
Karnataka	61.6	64.9	38.8	43.0	30.0	34.1	9.8	10.8
Kerala	**70.4**	**75.9**	**42.9**	**48.1**	**33.8**	**38.6**	**12.6**	**13.3**
Madhya Pradesh	55.6	55.2	38.0	39.0	29.3	30.2	9.5	9.5
Maharashtra	64.1	66.6	40.5	43.6	31.6	34.6	10.8	11.1
Orissa	57.1	57.0	38.8	38.8	30.1	30.2	10.6	9.9
Punjab	66.7	68.8	43.6	47.3	35.3	38.3	15.1	15.1
Rajasthan	59.1	60.1	38.9	41.8	29.9	33.0	8.9	9.6
Tamil Nadu	63.2	65.1	39.2	41.7	30.5	32.6	9.7	9.7
Uttar Pradesh	58.1	56.9	38.7	39.3	30.0	30.7	9.2	10.1
West Bengal	62.2	63.6	39.9	41.7	30.9	32.7	10.1	10.8

Source: Office of the Registrar General of India, Ministry of Home Affairs.

national average and in fact comparable to that in developed countries.

Given its demographic profile, the financial services sector in Kerala should be geared to meet its insurance needs. Table 4.67 shows the Life Insurance Penetration (defined as Life Insurance Premium as percentage of State Domestic Product) and Life Insurance Density (defined as Life Insurance Premium Per Capita) for various states and all-India for the period 1980-81 to 1999-2000.

It is obvious that insurance penetration and insurance density in Kerala are amongst the highest in India in the year 1999-2000. More importantly, Kerala's relative position has been improving over the years. The State Government has also been complementing the efforts of the Insurance sector through various welfare schemes (pension, welfare funds, insurance) targeted at groups like Agricultural Workers, Cashew Workers, Coir Workers, Construction Workers, Beedi Workers, Tree Climbers and Fishermen.

Deployment of Funds

The performance of banks and state sector financial institutions in Kerala as far as credit creation is concerned, has been satisfactory. As in the case of mobilisation of investable resources, the financial services sector in Kerala has been effective also in providing adequate credit services to meet the demand side.

With regard to access to credit two mutually contradictory facets are observed: the thriving of money lenders and the brilliant performance of the cooperative sector. Access to credit services of the formal sector seems to be restricted to certain sections of society. But the phenomenal performance of the cooperative sector in Kerala indicates that credit services are available to all classes of borrowers.

The low levels of credit per account and the strikingly different credit patterns in Kerala as compared to the levels attained by the rest of the country are nevertheless causes for concern. The low levels of credit creation and utilisation might adversely affect the state's long term growth prospects.

Conclusion

Kerala's financial services sector presents a complex image. Kerala is undoubtedly a state with a vibrant financial services sector. In terms of geographical and functional reach, Kerala seems to be far ahead of the rest of the country. The State continues to be ahead of

TABLE 4.67

Life Insurance Penetration & Density for Selected States and Years

States	*Life Insurance Penetration*			*Life Insurance Density*		
	1980-81	*1990-91*	*1999-00*	*1980-81*	*1990-91*	*1999-00*
Jammu & Kashmir	0.12	0.44	1.61	7.41	27.75	138.17
Himachal Pradesh	0.14	0.62	1.87	9.11	52.09	227.16
Rajasthan	0.20	0.61	1.97	9.53	45.91	192.72
Punjab	0.22	0.67	2.28	20.23	86.26	395.84
Delhi	0.56	1.32	3.50	83.58	264.83	917.59
Haryana	0.15	0.43	1.75	12.97	54.03	263.80
Uttar Pradesh	0.17	0.59	2.48	7.69	35.09	151.34
Madhya Pradesh	0.11	0.45	1.72	5.98	31.94	149.05
West Bengal	0.27	0.89	2.72	14.58	57.93	276.22
Bihar	0.12	0.53	2.51	4.35	24.88	115.05
Orissa	0.08	0.54	2.08	3.58	26.15	129.29
Maharashtra	0.37	0.85	2.09	28.99	95.48	356.04
Goa	0.31	1.21	2.73	34.69	211.35	872.04
Gujrat	0.30	0.99	2.28	21.94	99.58	344.83
Andhra Pradesh	0.24	0.84	2.42	12.04	63.26	257.14
Karnataka	0.31	0.91	2.24	16.93	67.33	281.27
Tamil Nadu	0.24	0.76	2.30	14.19	66.16	320.60
Kerala	**0.22**	**0.89**	**2.91**	**13.20**	**67.46**	**339.33**
All India	0.22	0.69	2.10	13.00	56.74	241.04

Source: *Annual Report & Yogakshema* (various issues), Life Insurance Corporation of India.

the rest of the nation in terms of indices like population per bank branch. In the matter of functional reach (providing services to clientele), Kerala's cooperative banking sector has been able to mobilize savings and provide credit services to the stratatum of society that normally would not be serviced by the traditional commercial banking sector. Kerala is also amongst the best states in India in terms of insurance penetration and density.

The extent of participation by Kerala's population in the savings mobilisation and credit dispensation services offered by the financial services sector also is far more than in the rest of the country. Besides, the participation does not seem to be limited to only certain strata: it is spread out far and wide and equitably too. In terms of deposit accounts as a percentage of population and the number of borrowers from PACS as a percentage of the population, Kerala's position is way ahead of the rest of the country.

The direction of the financial services sector in Kerala appears, in general, to have been towards overall socio-economic development. The financial services sector in Kerala has benefited from a number of characteristics unique to the state: 1) its unique demographic characteristics with widely diffused and densely populated habitations may have rendered provision of financial services easy; 2) its long history of social movements may have facilitated financial sector access to all sections of the society; 3) its high literacy levels may have enabled all strata of society with a complex of financial transactions, and 4) the large inflows of foreign funds in the form of emigrant's remittances may have resulted in large deposits and greater familiarity of the population with banking services.

In short, quite clearly, Kerala's achievements on the socio-economic development front cannot be attributed to the development of its financial services sector. On the contrary, the development of Kerala's financial services sector may be attributed to Kerala's prior achievements on the socio-economic front.

While the overall performance of Kerala's financial services sector seems to be impressive, there remain areas of concern. Having already achieved very high levels of penetration, the financial services sector in the state may not be able to do much more in terms of increasing its reach, in the mobilisation of savings and in the provision of credit services. Growth rates in deposits are flattening and they cannot be expected to provide the impetus for growth of the financial services sector indefinitely. And, finally, the greatest cause for concern may be the unique pattern of credit flow in Kerala. Unlike in the rest of the country, a large portion of the credit from the sector in Kerala seems to be flowing to non-agricultural and non-industrial uses. Moreover, the amount of credit per account is much lower than the national average. The demand for credit in Kerala is, by and large, consumption-driven rather than investment-driven.

In sum, the financial services sector in Kerala has to reorient the direction it has taken in terms of its relation with socio-economic development of the state. The financial services sector has now to begin on a path of providing the lead to the development of Kerala, more positively and directly.

III. FISCAL REFORMS IN KERALA: OPTIONS AND SOURCES

An attempt to propose major reforms in the tax and non-tax sources of revenue of Kerala is made below.

Suggestions for Tax Reform

Sales Tax

Like most Indian states, sales tax has been the single most important revenue source for the state of Kerala. The share of sales tax on total tax revenue of Kerala has increased from 46.71 per cent in 1980-81 to 66.47 per cent in 2002-03. Per capita consumer expenditure and the percentage share of the state in total sales tax collection for the major states of India for selected years for the period from 1972-73 to 1999-2000, are given in Table 4.68.

The manner in which sales tax is levied and collected has been a major factor that prevents the states from exploiting its full potential. It also causes serious distortions in the underlying economy. Value Added Tax (VAT) is universally accepted as the solution to complexities of sales tax administration. After considerable debates and discussions, Government of India decided to switch over to the VAT system from 1st April 2005. With the introduction of VAT, some of the teething problems of the state's sales tax structure like narrow base, multiplicity of rate categories, exemptions and concessions, and inter-state competition to attract investment are being sorted out to the satisfaction of all concerned.

Though some fears about fall in revenue in the initial years of VAT do exist, it is held in general that with the widening of the tax base, VAT would compensate for the possible revenue loss. Attempts

TABLE 4.68

Per Capita Consumer Expenditure and Percentage Share in Total Sales Tax Collection of Major States for Selected Years

States	C.E. as per 27th Round (1972-73)	Per cent Share in Total Sales Tax Collection in 1972-73	C.E as per 38th Round (1983)	Per cent Share in Total Sales Tax Collection in 1983	C.E as per 50th Round (1993-94)	Per cent Share in Total Sales Tax Collection in 1993-94	C.E as per 55th Round (1999-00)	Per cent Share in Total Sales Tax Collection in 1999-00
Andhra Pradesh	522.95	5.93	1512.08	8.25	3904.79	8.78	6572.96	10.6
Rank	12	7	9	5	9	4	10	3
Bihar	524.30	5.15	1208.56	4.89	2871.38	4.30	4961.57	3.92
Rank	11	8	14	10	14	10	14	11
Gujarat	649.11	9.16	1647.28	9.09	4323.46	10.47	8254.51	8.82
Rank	4	4	5	3	5	3	6	4
Haryana	852.11	2.64	1940.05	2.74	4950.73	2.90	9389.20	3.38
Rank	2	13	2	13	3	13	3	13
Kerala	**545.05**	**4.84**	**1837.65**	**5.03**	**5082.06**	**5.79**	**9843.55**	**6.62**
Rank	**8**	**10**	**3**	**9**	**2**	**8**	**1**	**7**
Karnataka	581.30	6.08	1569.65	6.54	3855.90	8.60	7780.71	8.04
Rank	6	6	8	7	10	5	7	5
Madhya Pradesh	537.37	5.52	1332.48	5.78	3506.23	4.59	5832.62	4.39
Rank	9	9	12	8	12	9	12	9
Maharashtra	631.77	19.11	1658.69	19.61	4527.81	17.91	8502.47	18.05
Rank	5	1	4	1	4	1	5	1
Orissa	453.37	2.23	1277.01	1.87	2971.72	1.94	4987.06	1.90
Rank	14	14	13	14	13	14	13	14
Punjab	917.29	4.83	2124.10	4.18	5547.64	3.63	9682.04	3.40
Rank	1	11	1	11	1	12	2	12
Rajasthan	657.93	3.88	1629.44	4.10	4207.31	4.00	7380.47	4.16
Rank	3	12	6	12	6	11	8	10
Tamil Nadu	518.77	11.95	1571.97	11.50	4173.48	12.13	8696.22	12.07
Rank	13	2	7	2	7	2	4	2
Uttar Pradesh	531.96	9.10	1338.97	9.03	3609.54	8.11	6242.92	8.76
Rank	10	5	11	4	11	6	11	5
West Bengal	557.48	9.56	1482.93	7.38	4045.00	6.85	6937.76	5.89
Rank	7	3	10	6	8	7	9	8

Source: *NSSO Publications*, relevant issues.

have been made to estimate the impact of VAT on the sales tax revenue of states on the basis of simple assumptions (Table 4.69). It shows that if 20 per cent value addition is assumed in retail trade, Kerala would have experienced a net revenue gain of Rs. 475 crores for the year 1997-98. The corresponding gains with 15 per cent and 10 per cent value addition are assumed to be Rs. 270 crores and Rs. 65 crores respectively.

To exploit the full potential of VAT, Kerala has to invest substantially in modernising tax administration. The major components of the reform proposal under the modernisation programme are discussed below.

ICT-Based Tax Administration

Information and Communication Technology (ICT) has offered tremendous possibilities for tax administration (Bagchi, 1993). Some of the Southern states like Tamil Nadu and Karnataka have made rapid strides in modernising tax administration through computerisation. A full-fledged e-governance concept of tax administration has been recommended for Karnataka (see government of Karnataka, 2001). Though Kerala has taken some concrete steps towards computerisation of Commercial Tax Department, not much progress has been achieved in this direction. Switching over to an ICT-based tax administration at the earliest is the first step towards reforming the revenue structure of Kerala.

As a consumer state, Kerala imports the lion's share of the consumer goods from other states and other countries. The geographical peculiarities of Kerala demand an integrated surveillance of the movement of goods into the state through different modes of

TABLE 4.69

Impact of Introduction of VAT

(Rs. Crores)

	Loss Due to			*Gains Due to Tax on Value Added*			*Net Impact (1997-98)*		
	Tax Credit	*Reduction in Value of Output*	*CST Withdrawal*	*20%*	*15%*	*10%*	*20%*	*15%*	*10%*
Andhra Pradesh	384.14	15.37	623.24	1628	1221	814	605	198	-209
Assam	47.13	1.89	0	277	208	139	228	159	89
Bihar	248.15	9.93	353.66	881	661	440	269	49	-171
Gujarat	851.91	34.08	677.93	954	716	477	-610	-848	-1087
Haryana	261.11	10.44	491.65	426	320	213	-65	-172	-279
Himachal Pradesh	30.81	1.23	21.85	99	74	50	77	53	28
Jammu and Kashmir	7.63	0.31	0	143	107	71	135	99	63
Karnataka	312.45	12.5	213.17	854	641	427	316	102	-111
Kerala	**174.55**	**6.98**	**163.13**	**820**	**615**	**410**	**475**	**270**	**65**
Madhya Pradesh	320.20	12.81	432.42	1128	846	564	362	80	-202
Maharashtra	1395.90	55.84	1278.28	2235	1676	1118	-495	-1054	-1612
Orissa	93.01	3.72	0	295	221	148	199	125	51
Punjab	228.71	9.15	276.31	588	441	294	311	164	17
Rajasthan	204.87	8.19	115.17	788	591	394	460	263	66
Tamil Nadu	611.81	24.47	1034.58	1543	1157	772	-128	-514	-899
Uttar Pradesh	532.94	21.32	237.06	2298	1724	1149	1507	932	358
West Bengal	274.27	10.97	332.09	1170	878	585	553	260	-32
Delhi	116.97	4.68	0	718	539	359	718	539	359

Notes: 1) The figures for CST collections are taken from RBI. For 1997-98, a few states have reported Zero collections .If this is a result of incorrect accounting, the loss from introduction of VAT in these states would be higher. 2) Delhi, Haryana, Himachal Pradesh and Punjab have modified versions of last point taxation, which eliminates input taxation in the existing regime. Therefore, these costs would not exist for these states. However, the gain to revenue is assumed to accrue since the present structure of taxes is recognised to result in tax leakage.

Source: Kavitha, Rao. R. (2004). "Impact of VAT on Central and State Finances", *Economic and Political Weekly*, June, 26, pp.2773-2777.

transport - sea, road and rail- to prevent tax evasion and tax avoidance. It has been pointed out that systems like Smart Card Technology have revolutionised tax administration in developed countries (Bagchi, 1993).

Human Resource Development

Introduction of VAT also presupposes a highly motivated and self- driven team of tax administrators. The entire staff should be imparted training in computer application, software package for tax administration and aspects like interpersonal relationship, customer service and public relations.

Lottery System of Preventing Tax Evasion in the Case of Gold and Jewellery

It is recognised that the use of gold ornaments and jewellery of all kinds in Kerala is one of the highest in the country. A large volume of gold ornaments is illegally brought into the state. However, the sales tax collections from gold and jewellery transactions are extremely low, a fact which baffles both tax administrators and the general public. The state has experimented with several systems to prevent tax evasion in gold and jewellery sales, but without much success. It has been suggested that the lottery system prevalent in some of the Latin American countries may be used to prevent tax evasion in high value items (Sebastian, 1995). It may also be noted that the Government of Andhra Pradesh has adopted in recent years a scheme on these lines known as "Mahabill Scheme".

Formation of Special Commodity Squads

The concentration of revenue receipts to the sales only of a few commodities is also a major constraint. The Task Force on Tax and Non-Tax Resources appointed by the State Planning Board had recommended the formation of Special Commodity Squads in 1997 (Government of Kerala, 1997). However this recommendation is yet to be implemented. Special

Commodity Squads would help tracking the trade pattern, the origins and the destinations of commodities and the *modus operandi* of evasion specific to each commodity. It seems that in the VAT regime this recommendation merits serious consideration.

Integrated System of Surveillance of Commodity Movements

The geographical peculiarities of the state and the presence of the centrally administered enclave inside the territorial jurisdiction of the state (Box 4.1) have necessitated an integrated system of surveillance of commodity movements. ICT offers tremendous potential for the state in this context.

BOX 4.1

Mahe: Kerala's Bane

Mahe, part of the Centrally administered Pondicherry is a small enclave within the geographical area of Kerala. Mahe is 9.7 square kilometres in area and had a population of 33,447 (1991 Census). Being a centrally administered area, Mahe does not have the botheration of mobilising resources for Plan purposes and therefore can afford to keep lower sales tax rates. But the lower sales tax rates in this enclave cause considerable diversion of trade from Kerala in which it is located. Mahe causes considerable revenue loss to Kerala through tax evasion. Mahe is approachable by road, rail or sea. Goods meant for Mahe are transported through the Manjeswaram and Valayar check-posts of Kerala. Since goods are taken to Mahe, they are not subjected to detailed scrutiny at the Kerala check-posts. It has been reported that trucks entering Kerala rarely reach Mahe as the goods are unloaded in various parts of Kerala. The annual loss of sales tax revenue to Kerala due to this practice is estimated at Rs. 400 crores (Report, Kerala Kaumudi Daily, December 6, 2003, p.1).

Performance Incentive to Staff

Tax administration in several countries has shown that by motivating officers through monetary and non-monetary incentives, it is possible to enhance efficiency and in turn improve revenue performance. There exists a performance incentive system in the Central Excise and Customs Department in India. Some of the Commissions and Committees appointed by the Government of Kerala have recommended the adoption of such practices in the state.

Incentives to Informants

Non-availability of reliable information on the various methods in use for suppression of facts relating to taxable sales turnover is a major handicap for tax administrators for taking effective steps for preventing tax evasion. This undue advantage could be overcome to a great extent if a system of rewarding informants of tax administrators is put in place. It may be noted that such systems do exist in Central Excise and Customs. Three Commissions/Committees appointed by the Government of Kerala also recommended the introduction of some form of incentives for informants.

Measures to Promote Voluntary Tax Compliance

a) Tax Payer Services

Taxpayer services are an essential component of the VAT system. The concept of voluntary tax compliance is practicable if only taxpayers are assisted with and offered several forms of services to help them comply. Taxpayer services create positive attitudes to tax payment. Simplification of the law and procedures for its implementation is the first step required for any system of taxpayer services to become successful.

b) Public Recognition for Compliance Performance

One of the widely used measures to promote voluntary tax compliance is public recognition of exemplary compliance performance. Taxpayers who have registered consistently high revenue growth over a period of time may be selected for public recognition. Though the Finance Minister of Kerala had announced such a scheme of public recognition in the budget speech in 2002, the recommendation has not been implemented so far (Government of Kerala, 2002).

Reforms in other Tax Sources

Stamps duty and Registration fee, Agricultural Income Tax, Motor Vehicle Tax and State excise together contribute almost 25 per cent of total state's own tax revenue. Though the scope for additional resource mobilisation from these sources is low compared to sales tax or VAT, the fiscal situation of the state demands that all these sources should be exploited fully.

Agricultural Income Tax

The contribution of Agricultural Income Tax has steadily fallen over the years. Government of Kerala widened the exemptions on Agricultural Income Tax in recent years as a measure to give relief to farmers who have experienced significant loss of income due to fall in the prices of agricultural products. However, recent trends suggest that the prices of crops like coconut and rubber are rising. Instead of across the board exemptions, a better policy option for the government would be to levy agricultural income tax selectively. Government may consider bringing farmers having holdings above a specified ceiling under the tax net.

Stamps and Registration

The Government of Kerala introduced major reforms in Stamps and Registration in 2003. The stamp duty was brought down to eight per cent in urban areas and five per cent in rural areas. However, due to certain problems in implementation the revenue from Stamp & Registration experienced a steep fall. As a result, the Government of Kerala reverted to the old system of stamp duty. The wide prevalence of under-valuation of property in the present system would be prevented only through major reforms in stamp duty and registration fees. Some of the reform proposals are discussed below.

Computerisation

The efficiency of Stamps and Registration Department can be considerably improved through computerisation and adoption of Management Information System. The proposal to institute a system of computerised generation of guidance values seems to be valid in the case of Kerala (see Government of Karnataka, 2001).

Motor Vehicle Tax

The system of a one-time motor vehicle tax exists in Kerala. A comparison of the rates of motor vehicle tax in Kerala with those in the neighbouring states reveals that the scope for additional resource mobilisation by raising the rates is rather limited. Some other measures to augment revenue have to be considered.

Increasing the Tax Rates on Motor Vehicles Entering the State for Short Periods

Vehicles from other states arrive Kerala in large numbers for short duration stay. Both pilgrimage tourism and pleasure tourism have picked up in recent years. There seems to exist a valid case for raising the rates of taxes on vehicles entering the state for short duration stay.

Raising the Penalty Rates for Violation of Motor Vehicle Act and Rules

Accidents involving motor vehicles have registered sharp increases in recent years primarily due to violation of traffic rules. In deciding the rates of penalties for violation of rules, a balance has to be struck between revenue considerations and crime deterrence.

State Excise

Since taxation on liquor is designed to achieve the twin objectives of discouraging consumption and mobilisation of resources, a balance has to be maintained between the two. The production of Indian Made Foreign Liquor (IMFL) inside the state meets only a small part of the demand in the state. Bulk of the IMFL consumed in Kerala is brought from other states. A comparative analysis of the rate structure of excise duty on alcoholic drinks in the southern states suggest that not much scope exists for mobilising additional resources through increasing rates. The wholesale and the retail distribution of IMFL is done by Beverages Corporation, a public sector enterprise. No large scale evasion of sales tax on Indian Made Foreign Liquor is therefore reported except perhaps in the case of the excise and sales taxes caused by the existence of the Mahe enclave. The Commercial Taxes Department has to strengthen surveillance on the border between Kerala and Mahe.

Non-Tax Revenue Sources

The non-tax sources together contribute nearly 10 per cent of the total state's own revenue receipts, a proportion considerably lower than the all-India average. As a result the state has to depend excessively on commodity taxes like sales tax. The expenditure pattern of the state has all along favoured social and community services. The major non-tax sources of the state are interest receipts, dividends and profits and cost recovery from social, economic and general services.

a. Interest Receipts, Dividends and Profits

The ratio of interest received by the Government of Kerala to its outstanding loans and advances varies between 1 per cent and 4 per cent (Table 4.70). The ratio of interest received by state government to its outstanding loans and advances came down from 3.1 per cent in 1991-92 to a mere 1 per cent in 2000-01. It may be noted that the average interest rate on state's market borrowings varied between 14 per cent and 11 per cent during the period1995-96 to 2000-01. There have been heavy arrears in the recovery of both principal and interest. The three statutory corporations, Kerala State Electricity Board, Kerala State Road Transport Corporation and Kerala Water Authority together account for the lion's share of the arrears (George and Krishnakumar, 2003). There is thus a strong case for taking steps to raise the revenue receipts from interest, dividends and profits.

TABLE 4.70

Trends in Interest Receipts and Dividends

Year	Interest as % of Outstanding Loans and Advances			Dividends Received as % of Outstanding Investments*				
	Interest Received (Rs. Crores)	*Loans & Advances @ Outstanding at the Beginning of the Year (Rs. Crores)*	*Col.2 as % of Col.3*	*Statutory Corporations*	*Government Companies*	*Other Joint Stock Companies*	*Cooperative Banks & Societies*	*Total*
1	2	3	4	5	6	7	8	9
1991-92	33.56	1083.99	3.10	0.00	0.70	11.28	0.09	0.57
1994-95	18.36	1641.29	1.14	0.00	0.65	11.18	0.17	0.53
1995-96	66.26	1641.29	4.04	0.00	0.74	10.68	0.31	0.60
1996-97	34.26	1975.96	1.73	0.00	0.40	6.86	0.22	0.35
1997-98	34.79	2255.09	1.54	0.00	0.55	8.66	0.33	0.47
1998-99	63.14	2801.05	2.25	0.00	0.60	8.32	0.29	0.48
1999-00	35.05	3129.46	1.12	0.00	0.81	8.73	0.28	0.61
2000-01	35.38	3391.04	1.04	0.00	0.89	9.31	0.16	0.63

Note: @ Interest received other than the interest on cash balances;

* Dividends received during the year and outstanding investments at the beginning of the year.

Source: (1) *Finance Accounts*, Comptroller and Auditor General of India, Government of Kerala.

(2) *State Finances, 2002-03*, Reserve Bank of India.

b. Cost Recoveries from Public Services

Another major factor behind the low proportion of non-tax revenue in the total revenue of the state is the extremely low recovery rates from public services in health, education and other social and community services. The aggregate cost-recovery ratio (excluding revenue and expenditure relating to State Lotteries, Forestry and Wild Life and Industries) in 2000-01 was only 4.4 per cent whereas the corresponding figures for all states was 5.7 per cent (Table 4.71). The cost recovery ratios for Kerala varied between 8 per cent for social services to 5.8 per cent for economic services. There is a strong case for raising the user fee on the services provided by the state in social and community services which accounted for about 40 per cent of the public services.

Other Avenues of Augmenting Non-Tax Sources of Revenue

A possible source of non-tax revenue is the judicious use of the assets and the capacity created by the state in terms of buildings, dams, irrigation canals and waterways.

Issues Relating to Expenditure Management and Debt Management

Resource mobilisation efforts should be supplemented with judicious management of expenditure because resources saved are equivalent to resources generated. The management of expenditure and debt assumes as much importance as mobilising resources.

Management of Expenditure

Revenue expenditure forms almost 90 per cent of the total government expenditure. Of this, expenditure on salaries, pensions and interest payments constitutes almost 73 per cent. Salaries alone account for almost 38 per cent of revenue expenditure. The proportion of capital expenditure in total expenditure has been continuously declining over the years due to the practice of using borrowed funds to finance revenue expenditure. The state is in need of a judicious policy of expenditure reduction and not across the board reductions. Some of the areas where there exists scope for better management of expenditure are highlighted below.

Redeployment of Staff

The Administrative Reforms Committee appointed by the Government of Kerala has identified 60,000 excess posts in government. The government may consider redeployment of the excess staff in departments experiencing staff deficiency due to retirement of personnel. Redeployment would reduce the need for fresh recruitment and increase in the wage bill.

TABLE 4.71

Head-wise Non-tax Revenue Receipts from Social and Community Services as Ratio of Revenue Expenditure: Kerala and All States

(Per Cent)

Heads	*1990-91*		*1995-96*		*2000-01*	
	Kerala	*All States*	*Kerala*	*All States*	*Kerala*	*All States*
A. Social Services	2.43	2.09	2.64	2.04	1.83	2.21
Education, Sports, Art and Culture	2.38	1.17	2.03	0.95	1.72	1.11
Medical, Public Health and Family Welfare	4.18	4.18	6.99	4.24	3.07	3.09
Water Supply and Sanitation	0.00	0.00	0.25	4.65	0.96	5.50
Housing	6.55	9.69	3.75	0.90	7.77	8.97
Urban Development	9.58	2.34	32.87	4.94	0.89	3.96
Social Security and Welfare	0.41	1.20	0.40	2.92	0.12	3.54
B. Economic Services	13.29	20.59	21.24	22.95	12.85	17.91
Economic Services excluding Forestry and Wild Life	6.33	10.04	6.04	8.94	5.78	8.97
Crop Husbandry	8.20	6.31	6.22	5.88	17.04	6.58
Animal Husbandry	10.00	3.90	8.71	3.73	5.82	4.00
Fisheries	9.04	11.67	3.16	10.76	0.51	16.55
Forestry and Wild Life	120.65	96.73	224.10	88.36	105.81	45.27
Cooperation	29.63	8.01	42.65	16.00	52.37	22.45
Major and Medium Irrigation	3.22	6.19	7.67	10.44	7.08	8.55
Power	0.00	18.33	0.00	9.13	0.00	6.22
Village and Small Industries	4.24	11.47	3.23	6.24	3.06	5.45
Industries	24.49	317.93	186.37	549.82	167.14	572.10
Tourism	12.05	20.59	14.44	20.33	3.86	8.87
C. General Services#	14.79	16.94	25.73	38.20	25.59	19.49
General Services excluding State Lotteries	3.47	14.56	9.42	25.33	13.41	11.90
Total of all Public Services (A+B+C)	7.79	11.30	10.91	15.53	8.29	9.94
Total excluding Forestry and Wild Life, Industries and State Lotteries	3.50	7.06	4.36	7.84	4.41	5.74

Note: # Here General Services include Organs of State, Administrative Services and Miscellaneous Services.

Source: George and Krishnakumar, 2003: 46.

Voluntary Retirement Scheme

With computerisation of major government departments, the excess staff in government service is likely to go up. Given the very few alternative employment opportunities outside the government sector in Kerala, the possibility of shedding the flab through a normal Voluntary Retirement Scheme (VRS) of the normal kind is rather bleak. The government may have to make the VRS scheme attractive to the employees. Since it will not be possible to honour the immediate financial commitments of conventional VRS schemes, government may have to devise schemes that will permit phasing out the payment obligations over a period of time.

Contributory Pension Funds

Pension payments accounted for 20.3 per cent of the total revenue expenditure of the state in 2001-02. This is a higher proportion than in most of the states (Table 4.72). Recently Reserve Bank of India formed a study group to examine the pension liabilities of state governments (Box 4.2). The study group recommended that the state governments should introduce contributory pension schemes for new employees in place of the existing non-contributory defined- benefit pension schemes. Considering the increasing life expectancy of Keralites, the commitments on account of pensions are likely to keep rising. It is in this context, that the Government of Kerala decided to implement the scheme for the employees recruited from 1st April 2005 onwards.

TABLE 4.72

State-wise Pension Payments as a Percentage of Revenue Receipts

States	*1989-90*	*1990-1995*	*1995-2000*	*2000-2001*	*2001-2002*
Andhra Pradesh	4.1	6.7	9.1	12.2	10.6
Assam	1.5	3.9	6.8	11.9	12.3
Bihar	2.4	4.3	9.5	14.5	17.4
Gujarat	3.3	4.9	7.8	9.1	9.4
Haryana	2.5	3.5	6.3	8.7	8.6
Karnataka	6.0	6.6	8.4	10.7	10.7
Kerala	**8.5**	**11.9**	**15.4**	**22.1**	**20.3**
Madhya Pradesh	2.3	4.3	7.7	7.7	9.0
Maharashtra	2.6	3.3	4.6	7.2	8.6
Orissa	2.3	4.1	8.0	12.1	14.2
Punjab	3.6	5.2	9.3	11.9	11.6
Rajasthan	3.8	4.5	8.5	13.6	13.9
Tamil Nadu	3.8	6.6	10.8	16.6	16.2
Uttar Pradesh	2.0	3.4	7.2	8.7	9.3
West Bengal	2.9	5.10	9.8	13.3	15.5
All States	3.2	4.8	7.8	10.7	11.0

Source: "Report of the Group to Study the Pension Liabilities of State Governments", *Reserve Bank of India Bulletin (supplement)*, February 2004, p.62.

BOX 4.2

Major Recommendations of the Group on Pension Liabilities of State Governments

Contributory Pension Schemes may be introduced for new employees of state governments in place of the existing non-contributory defined –benefit pension schemes.

In respect of states where pay, pension and interest burden has exceeded 90 per cent of state's total revenue receipts, the new contributory scheme may be made obligatory for even existing employees with less than 10 years of service.

Instead of fixing pensions on the basis of only last one month's pay, pensions may be determined on the basis of the average pay for a longer period.

The maximum permissible commutation amount should be brought down from 40 per cent of basic pension to 33.33 per cent.

There is need for setting up 'Dedicated Pension Fund' to meet at least partially the pension burden of the existing employees and pensioners.

The Pension Fund to be created under the proposed revised schemes should be kept completely outside the State's Consolidated Fund and Public Account.

Source: "Report of the Group to Study the Pension Liabilities of State Governments", *Reserve Bank of India Bulletin (Supplement)*, February, 2004.

Treasury Management System

A major problem that has affected the expenditure management of Government of Kerala is the growing laxity in following the procedures and formalities laid out in the Kerala Budget Manual. The Budget Manual requires that the heads of departments and controlling officers should report their commitments in time to the government in standardised formats so that sufficient provisions are made in the budget of the financial year concerned. Such systems and practices are being progressively abandoned, rendering thereby budget estimates unrealistic and cash management out of gear (Government of Kerala, 2001). It is therefore important to ensure that proper sanctions are obtained before expenditure commitments are made.

Zero-Based Budget

The present system of incremental budgeting emphasises financial targets as against physical targets. Consequently every year a certain percentage increase over the previous year's budgetary allocation is made irrespective of whether physical targets are achieved or not. The pitfalls of this system can be overcome only through introducing zero-based budgeting which makes it mandatory to take a fresh look each time at expenditures independent of past expenditure patterns. It may be noted that the Union Budget for 2000-01 proposed to subject all ongoing schemes to zero-based budgeting (Premchand and Chattopadhyay, 2002).

BOX 4.3

The Politics of Token Provision

A practice, which has led to gross inefficiency in the budget-making process in Kerala, is that of 'token provision'. All the competing claims for budgetary provision cannot be accommodated as there will not be resources enough. But compulsions of coalition politics and competitive populism force Finance Ministers to give accommodation to numerous schemes in the budget without sufficient budgetary provision for them, some times with small provision as Rs.1000 for each. The projects or the schemes concerned would actually require much larger provisions, say each a few hundred crores of rupees for implementation. Known as 'token provision', this practice is widely used to hoodwink the public. The fate of such projects/schemes depend upon the manoeuvring skill of the parties or groups concerned. Some succeed in procuring higher allocations through supplementary demands but the expenditures often take place during the last quarter of the financial year. In some cases the token provision may be allowed to lapse. The major pitfall of token provisions is that they open up umpteen avenues for manipulation and rent-seeking.

Practice of Inadequate Funding

A major factor of inefficiency of developmental projects in Kerala (and probably in other Indian States as well) is the practice of launching simultaneously large numbers of projects with resources thinly spread over them. Inadequate funding leads to inordinate delays and cost escalations. When a project is completed its total cost would be several times the initial estimate and the returns from the project are likely to be grossly insufficient to repay the debt incurred to finance it. Politicians and the public should be conscientised about the dangers of this practice.

Outsourcing and Leasing

Through outsourcing and leasing, revenue expenses could be curtailed substantially. This practice would also reduce the burden of acquiring and maintaining costly equipment and facilities. Expenditure may be reduced to a large extent if the following options are considered.

Instead of providing vehicles and home telephone to officials, government may reimburse the expenditures incurred on those items up to a ceiling.

Instead of purchasing computers, printers, scanners, fax machines and photocopiers in offices, government may outsource these services.

In government-run hospitals, private players may be provided the space to install and run diagnostic facilities at competitive rates.

Instead of spending money on construction of office buildings, government may lease in private buildings.

BOT and BOLT Schemes in Infrastructure Development

Another option for efficient management of public expenditure is the adoption of Build, Operate and Transfer (BOT) and Build- Operate-Lease and Transfer (BOLT) schemes especially in infrastructure projects. The Government of Kerala has already experimented with this option in some projects. The absence of a transparent regulatory mechanism is the major challenge facing the government in extending such schemes.

Public Debt Management

Kerala stands second among the major states in terms of per capita outstanding debts. In terms of Debt-GSDP ratio Kerala (52 per cent) stands ahead of most states in India, the all-India average being 32 per cent. Interest payments accounted for 19 per cent of revenue expenditure in 2000-01. Till recently the contingent liabilities of states were not taken into account while considering issues relating to the debt position of states. A major form of contingent liability is state government guarantees. State governments have been increasingly resorting to issuing guarantees on behalf of public sector enterprises undertaking infrastructure investment and other development activities. As a percentage to GSDP, guarantees of Government of Kerala stood at 12.68 per cent in 2000-01 which is on the higher side when compared with the situation in some of the states like Andhra Pradesh and Tamil Nadu (Table 4.73). Here the critical issue is not the absolute amount of guarantee but the financial position of the entities for which government has issued the guarantee and the capacity of the State government to honour the guarantee in the event of it being invoked.

Considering the importance of the issue, the Government of India formed a Technical Committee of State Finance Secretaries on State Government Guarantees. On the basis of the recommendations of the Committee, several states have taken initiative to fix a ceiling on guarantees. The Government of Kerala passed the *Kerala Ceiling on Government Guarantees Act, 2003* which envisages that the outstanding government guarantees as on the first day of April of any year shall not exceed Rs. 14000 crore. Recently, the Reserve Bank of India constituted a group consisting of Finance Secretaries of selected states to examine the fiscal risk of guarantees extended by state governments. The Group made several recommendations, which have an important bearing on the debt position of states (Box 4.4). All these suggest that states will have to devise strategies to bring down their debt to manageable levels. Substitution of high-cost borrowing with low-cost borrowing and formation of debt redemption fund are the two strategies suggested.

Substitution of High-Cost Borrowing with Low-Cost Borrowing

A major part of the state government loans are those taken from the Government of India and all-India Financial Institutions. Loans taken during the pre-liberalisation period generally carried higher rates of interest and more stringent repayment conditions than those of the post-liberalisation period. Interest rates have registered a steep fall in recent years. This fall offers avenues for state governments to clear away high-cost loans and avail low-cost loans instead. It has been pointed out that as on March 2004, the total bank deposits in the scheduled banks of Kerala were of the tune of Rs. 65,961 crore (*Economic Review*, 2004; 2005). The credit–deposit ratio was as low as 48.31 per cent.

TABLE 4.73

Comparative Analysis of State-wise Guarantees

States	*Guarantee in 1992 (Rs. Crores)*	*% to GSDP*	*Guarantee in 2001 (Rs. Crores)*	*% to GSDP*	*Per Capita Guarantee in 2001 (Rs.)*	*Growth Rate in Guarantee in 2001 Over 1992*	*Annual Compound Growth Rate in GSDP During 1993-2001*
Andhra Pradesh	3636	8.42	13138	9.55	1735.53	261.33	5.46
Assam	1008	8.27	1100	3.67	413.53	9.13	2.63
Bihar	1359	4.36	1157	2.5	139.57	-14.86	4.13
Gujarat	4514	13.52	17301	15.44	3419.17	283.27	6.16
Haryana	1264	7.17	8209	15.26	3890.52	549.45	5.73
Karnataka	3057	9.46	12989	12.32	2464.71	324.89	8.24
Kerala	**1744**	**8.51**	**8756**	**12.68**	**2753.46**	**402.6**	**5.28**
Madhya Pradesh	677	1.78	10482	14.44	1735.43	1448.3	4.29
Maharashtra	7351	9.7	44954	17.41	4644.01	511.54	5.92
Orissa	1090	7.44	3787	10.4	1031.88	247.43	3.27
Punjab	1303	5.85	6060	8.85	2493.82	365.08	5.07
Rajasthan	2727	10.26	11954	15.63	2115.75	338.36	6.8
Tamil Nadu	2895	7.06	12388	8.99	1994.85	327.91	6.23
Uttar Pradesh	4257	5.97	6391	3.53	384.77	50.13	4.25
West Bengal	2450	5.63	6982	4.98	870.57	184.98	7.21

Note: GSDP figures for 2000-01 are quick estimates.

Source: Worked out using the data from *RBI Bulletin* and *Domestic Product of States in India 1960-61 to 2000-01*, Economic and Political Weekly Research Foundation.

BOX 4.4

Major Recommendations of the Group on Fiscal Risk of State Government Guarantees

Those guarantees, which are in the nature of direct liabilities, should be clubbed with debt while assessing the debt profile of the states.

For such guarantees, repayment provision should be made in the budget.

Rest of the guarantees should be classified into high risk, medium risk and low risk categories and Finance Departments of states should assign devolvement probability to each risk category.

At least an amount equal to one percent of the outstanding guarantees may be transferred to the Guarantee Redemption Fund (GRF).

Debt service plus guarantee obligation of state government may be fixed as not exceeding 20% of revenue receipts.

Devolvement during the life of guarantee may be treated as normal debt and clubbed together with debt obligations. Together the liability could be measured as a ratio of State Domestic Product.

Source: Reserve Bank of India Bulletin, June 2003.

The Government of Kerala may explore the possibility of utilising these deposits to clear its high cost loans. The first step taken towards such policy options in financial management seems to be the creation of congenial atmosphere for private investment in the state.

Debt Redemption Fund

The mounting debt-servicing obligations of Kerala point towards the need for forming a Debt Redemption Fund (DRF). The following are some of the options to fom DRF.

A proportion of total revenue receipts transferred each year to the DRF.

A portion of tax and non-tax revenue sources earmarked exclusively for DRF.

Levy of a special cess exclusively for DRF.

The success of such schemes however is contingent upon the public conviction that in public expenditure there is both economy and efficiency. Government should publish the progress made each year in reducing its overall debt and interest payments burden.

An Outline of the Medium Term Fiscal Framework of Kerala

The *Kerala Fiscal Responsibility Act, 2003* passed by Government of Kerala envisages reduction of the revenue deficit to 'nil' and fiscal deficit to two per cent of GSDP by the end of March 2007. Evidence suggests that the state possesses the required fiscal capacity to achieve these goals; but to translate this into actual tax and non-tax revenue, fundamental changes in the institutional mechanism of administration and enforcement are called for. An attempt is made below to present a Medium Term Fiscal Framework in the light of the emerging fiscal scenario in the country.

Medium Term Fiscal Reforms Programme of Kerala

In view of the Kerala Fiscal Responsibility Act, 2003 and the need to reduce revenue deficit to nil, Government of Kerala is in the process of undertaking the following steps (Government of Kerala, 2003: 13).

- PSE reforms through VRS, reduction of budgetary support and restructuring;
- Phasing out of non-merit subsidies and better targeting of merit subsidies;
- Compression of administrative costs and effective economy and austerity measures. Enactment of legislation to promote transparency in government procurement;
- Modernisation of Government Programme to improve service delivery to the public;

Budgetary controls through on-line computerised treasury network.

Bringing forward of budget cycle to ensure passing of the full budget before March, from financial year 2005-06.

Ensuring of budget transparency through appending schedules on salaries, pensions and contingent liabilities;

Reduction of supplementary demands for grants to two in a fiscal year.

Forecasts of Receipts and Expenditure

A major challenge before outlining the fiscal framework of a state, or a country, is the making of realistic projections on revenue and expenditure. Projections are made based on past trends and assumptions. A major difficulty in projecting government receipts and expenditure is the unpredictability of political developments and their impact on policy. The successive Finance Commissions have adopted sophisticated econometric techniques to project the revenue and expenditure of states, and most often states have complained that they have suffered losses due to forecasts made by Finance Commissions. Severe data and methodological problems are constraints on the preparation of realistic estimates. Another major handicap is the difficulty in forecasting the implications of the reforms proposed in tax and non-tax resources and under various heads of expenditure.

On the expenditure side, much depends upon the way the state government conducts its affairs. If the state government has to adhere to the provisions of the Fiscal Responsibility Act, measures of reducing revenue expenditure are called for. It is almost impossible to accommodate the impact of policy changes in any model of forecasting. The best option would be to forecast receipts and expenditures on the basis of past trends. The projections made by the Government of Kerala as part of the Memorandum submitted to the Twelfth Finance Commission have also adopted such an approach. The forecasts of revenue receipts, revenue expenditure, capital receipts and capital disbursements are presented below.

Revenue Receipts

Modernisation of tax administration based on Information and Communication Technology (ICT) offers tremendous possibilities for Kerala. It is expected that with the introduction of VAT from April 2005, the tax buoyancy of the state will also go up. An emerging area of taxation particularly in the context of Kerala is the taxation of services. During the past few decades, the service sector registered tremendous growth in Kerala. But unless the centre enacts necessary legislations, the state will not be empowered to tap the tax potential generated by this growth. Several measures aimed at toning up the tax administration also hinge upon the political will of the government.

The Memorandum submitted by the Government of Kerala to the Twelfth Finance Commission has assumed an annual inflation rate of 5 per cent and a real growth rate of the economy at 6 per cent. On the basis of this assumption the State's Own Tax Revenue (SOTR) would grow at 13 per cent and the non-tax revenue at 11 per cent during the period 2005-06 to 2009-10. However, the growth rate for each individual tax and non-tax source is separately worked out based on the pattern of growth observed during the immediately preceding years and also the special circumstances of each source. The forecasts for the period 2004-05 to 2009-10 are presented in Table 4.74.

TABLE 4.74

Forecasts of Revenue Receipts of Kerala-2004-05 to 2009-2010

(Rs. in Lakhs)

Receipt Head	*Rate of Growth Assumed in %*	*Forecast*					
		2004-05	*2005-06*	*2006-07*	*2007-08*	*2008-09*	*2009-10*
Total Revenue (I+II)	—	1340785.14	1497614.85	1673556.43	1871026.56	2092762.93	2341863.85
I Tax Revenue (A+B)	—	1116309.4	1250127.45	1400599.66	1569868.67	1760362.57	1974834.48
A. State's Own Tax Revenue (1to 3)	—	905709.39	1022679.45	1154955.82	1304573.33	1473843.59	1665393.99
1. Taxes on Income (Agricultural Income Tax)	18	890.48	1050.77	1239.91	1463.09	1726.45	2037.21
2. Taxes on Property and Capital Transactions (i to iii)	5	72604.66	83057.19	95117.13	109048.89	125163.96	143829.92
i) Land Revenue	14	4233.74	4445.43	4667.70	4901.09	5146.14	5403.45
ii) Stamps and Registration Fee	25	63229.83	72082.00	82173.49	93677.77	106792.66	121743.63
iii) Urban Immovable Property Tax		5141.09	6529.76	8275.94	10470.03	3225.16	6682.84
3. Taxes on Commodities and Services (i to vi)	13	832214.26	938571.48	1058598.80	1194061.40	1346953.10	1519526.87
i) Sales Tax	10	682266.52	770961.16	871186.12	984440.31	1112417.55	1257031.83
ii) State Excise	14	80231.46	88254.60	97080.06	106788.07	117466.88	129213.57
iii) Taxes on Vehicles	5	66695.59	76032.97	86677.59	98812.45	112646.19	128416.66
iv) Taxes on Goods and Passengers	10	0.11	0.12	0.12	0.13	0.13	0.14
v) Taxes on Duties on Electricity	10	689.32	758.25	834.07	917.48	1009.23	1110.15
vi) Other Taxes and Duties		2331.26	2564.38	2820.82	3102.91	3413.20	3754.52
B. Share in Central Taxes		210600.00	227448.00	245643.84	265295.35	286518.97	309440.49
II. Non-Tax Revenue(C+D)		224475.75	247487.4	272956.77	301157.88	332400.36	367029.37
C. State's Own Non-Tax Revenue (1 to 5)	10	82803.75	91649.12	101534.31	112593.34	124979.06	138865.96
1. Interest Receipts	20	4339.25	4773.18	5250.50	5775.55	6353.10	6988.41
2. Dividends and Profits	—	1383.87	1660.64	1992.77	2391.33	2869.59	3443.51
3. General Services	—	32361.58	35998.87	40067.58	44622.25	49724.90	55446.09
4. Social Services	—	13619.25	15444.64	17533.83	19926.54	22668.60	25812.95
5. Economic Services		31099.80	33771.78	36689.63	39879.69	43362.87	47175.00
D. Grants from the Centre		141672.00	155838.28	171422.46	188564.54	207421.30	228163.41

Source: Worked out on the basis of Forecast of Revenue Receipts 2005-10 presented to Twelfth Finance Commission, Finance Department, Government of Kerala, November 2003.

Revenue Expenditure

Revenue expenditure forms almost 90 per cent of the total government expenditure. Of this, expenditure items like salaries, pensions and interest payments form almost 73 per cent of the total revenue expenditure. The salary and pension payments are likely to register substantial increase if the government chooses to go in for pay revision. Depending upon the inflationary price rise, dearness allowances will also have to be raised. All these would increase revenue expenditure unpredictably.

The forecast of revenue expenditure is based on pre-actual figures of Accountant General for the year 2002-2003. In a bold departure from the conventional approach of forecasting all expenditure at a flat rate, the Government of Kerala has disaggregated the expenditure under each head as salary and non-salary components. In order to accommodate the future commitments arising from increments in salary, an annual increase of 2.5 per cent is allowed to the salary component. Non-salary component of non-development services is assumed to grow at 7 per cent per annum whereas the correspondence rates for development services (social services) and economic services are 15 per cent and 11 per cent respectively. Of this 5 per cent is to take care of inflation. The forecasts for the period 2004-05 to 2009-10 are presented in Table 4.75.

Forecasts of Receipts and Disbursements on Capital Account

The major items of capital receipts are internal debt (i.e market loans and negotiated loans from institutional financiers like LIC and National

TABLE 4.75

Forecasts of Revenue Expenditure: 2004-05 to 2009-10

(Rs. In Lakhs)

Items	*2004-05*	*2005-06*	*2006-07*	*2007-08*	*2008-09*	*2009-10*
A. Social Services (1 to 12)	559272	648764	693252	727454	772263	820560
1.Education, Sports, Art and Culture	317443	332289	349306	366937	386406	407986
2. Medical and Public Health	74551.3	94730.2	97123.2	98089.9	101599	103994
3. Family Welfare	8493.48	9572.72	11289.4	12411.5	13647.5	15008
4. Water Supply and Sanitation	29149.7	51897.9	56729.2	56188.3	59988.5	64174.3
5. Housing	7591.09	13115.4	14734.6	16039.8	7481.18	19073.8
6. Urban Development	38241.3	42726.1	49690	54959.3	60811.7	67310.2
7. Welfare of SC, ST and BC	27938	31457.3	36523.3	40505.9	44962.2	49949.1
8. Labour & Labour Welfare	12381.6	13626.1	15313.5	16759.3	18378.1	20191.7
9. Social Security and Welfare	31278.1	45466.2	46708.8	47532.2	48436.8	49430.2
10. Nutrition	102.27	109.97	118.64	128.42	139.46	151.95
11. Relief on account of Natural calamities	9803.69	11274.3	12965.4	14910.2	17146.7	19718.7
12. Others	2297.8	2498.5	2750.46	2992.86	3265.29	3571.85
B. Economic Services (1 to 9)	378674	431619	494563	542357	593581	651148
1. Agriculture and Allied Activities	76984	84389.5	94231.4	102886	112579	123454
2. Rural Development	176877	197344	228968	253446	280661	310916
3. Special Area Programmes	1149.68	1295.77	1528.14	1680.02	1847.33	2031.5
4. Irrigation and Flood Control	15416.3	28477.5	33157.1	34470.1	34060	34255.2
5. Energy	4321.74	4870.35	5741.32	6312.37	6941.43	7633.96
6. Industry and Mineral	18526.6	20634.4	23854.5	26087.8	28545.9	31250.2
7. Transport and Communication	56965.4	62856.4	276.55	77142.3	4730.4	93116.7
8. Science, Technology and Environment	3362.26	3782.93	4431.67	4877.18	5368.35	5909.58
9. General Economic Services	25071.2	27968.2	32374.8	35455.1	38847.2	42581
C. General Services (1 to 6)	803017	906323	1010271	1103878	1194852	1304107
1. Organs of State	17169.5	29265.2	32171.3	30111.7	31241.8	31738.1
2. Fiscal Services	32004.1	37869.5	46258.2	48916.9	38677.2	40395.6
3. Interest Payments and Servicing of Debt	371083	409610	467721	532807	599634	670209
4. Administrative Services	93556.9	115660	22869.2	121876	123758	126183
5. Pensions	266321	288958	313520	340169	369083	400455
6. Miscellaneous General Services	22883.2	24959.8	27731.9	29998.1	32457.6	35126.6
D. Dearness Allowance	71613.3	111239	114563	138459	163478	189651
E. Dearness Relief	25673	42437.5	46751	59809.9	74751.1	91800
F. Fresh Expenditure	Nil	5480.38	36265.2	1729.7	21347.9	12314.9
Total Revenue Expenditure (A+B+C+D+E+F)	1838249	2145862	2395665	2603687	2820272	3069581

Source: Same as Table 4.68.

Cooperative Development Corporation, loans from the Centre, Centrally sponsored schemes, share of small savings collections, recoveries of loans and advances and Public Account.

The basis of the forecast in market loan is the actual receipt during the financial year 2003-04 and budget estimate for 2004-05. For forecasts for 2005-10, a 10 per cent increase over the net receipt in 2003-04 has been assumed. For the loans from LIC, GIC, RBI and other financial institutions, a 10 per cent growth rate over the actual receipt during 2003-04 is assumed. The Tenth Plan outlay has been fixed at Rs. 24000 crore. The Central assistance is estimated at Rs.7736 crore and 70 per cent of this is assumed as loan. On the basis of this approach, State Plan loans for each year during the 10th Plan period have been worked out. For Centrally sponsored schemes and share of small savings collections, the pre-actual figures for 2002-03 have been taken as the basis and the forecasts for the period 2004-05 to 2009-10 have been made assuming 10 per cent growth rate. Owing to the fluctuating pattern of the actual figures of recoveries of loans and advances, no growth rate is assumed over the budget estimates for 2003-04. In the case of savings deposit, the budget estimate for 2003-04 has been taken as the basis and the forecasts are made assuming 10 per cent annual growth rate. For State Provident Fund, the trends in net accretion during the past three years have been taken and the forecasts are based on 10 per cent annual growth rates. The forecasts of capital receipts for the period 2004-05 to 2009-10 are presented in Table 4.76.

The estimate of capital disbursements under State Plan and Centrally Sponsored Schemes have been made on the basis of total plan outlay approved for the 10th Five Year Plan (Table 4.77).

TABLE 4.76

Forecast of Capital Receipts: 2004-05 to 2009-10

(Rs. in Lakhs)

Items	*2004-05*	*2005-06*	*2006-07*	*2007-08*	*2008-09*	*2009-10*
Total Receipts (I to V)	498543	542382	590316	642738	700080	762820
I. Internal Debt	281062	309168	340085	374093	411502	452652
II. Loans and Advances from the Centre	116398	122217	128328	134745	141482	148556
III. Recovery of Loans and Advances	8060	8672	9345	10086	10901	11798
IV. Contingency Fund (Net)	—	—	—	—	—	—
V. Public Account	93023	102325	112557	123813	136194	149814
Small Savings, Provident Fund etc.(Net)	89258	98184	108002	118802	130682	143751
Reserve Funds (Net)	294	323	355	391	430	473
Deposits and Advances (Net)	2455	2700	2970	3268	3594	3954
Suspense and Remittances	1016	1118	1230	1353	1488	1637

Source: Same as Table 4.68.

TABLE 4.77

Forecast of Capital Disbursements: 2004-05 to 2009-10

(Rs. in Lakhs)

Items	*2004-05*	*2005-06*	*2006-07*	*2007-08*	*2008-09*	*2009-10*
Total Disbursements (I+II+III+IV)	183368	278004	317674	348982	383341	421176
I Total Capital Outlay (A+B)	65000	136800	162600	178900	196700	216400
A State Plan Schemes & Central and Centrally Sponsored Schemes	63126	134832	160534	176731	194422	214008
B Non-Plan (1 to 3)						
1. Social Services	30	31	33	34	36	38
2. Economic Services	1190	1250	1313	1378	1447	1520
3. General Services	654	686	720	757	794	834
II Discharge of Internal Debt (1 to 5)	21982	24180	26598	29258	32183	35402
1. Loans from LIC	8461	9307	10238	11262	12388	12627
2. Loans from National Agricultural Credit Fund/NABARD	6271	6898	7587	8346	9181	10099
3. Loans from National Cooperative Development Corporation	6050	6655	7321	8053	8858	9744
4. Loans from GIC	1189	1308	1439	1583	1741	1915
5. Others	11	12	13	15	16	18
III Repayment of Loans to Centre	78326	85852	94131	103238	113256	124276
IV Loans and Advances by State Government (A +B)	18060	31172	34345	37586	41201	45098
A State Plan Schemes and Central and Centrally Sponsored Schemes	10000	22500	25000	27500	30300	33300
B Non-Plan Loans (1 to 4)	8060	8672	9345	10086	10901	11798
1. Housing	141	155	171	188	207	227
2. Welfare of SC and ST	9	10	10	12	13	14
3. Short Term Loans for Agricultural Inputs	9	9	9	9	9	9
4. Others	7901	8498	9155	9878	10673	11548

Source: Same as Table 4.68.

Overall Medium Term Fiscal Scenario

The forecasts relating to the overall fiscal scenario for the period 2004-05 to 2009-10 are presented in Table 4.78. In the emerging fiscal scenario, fiscal deficit will not be wiped out completely. The forecasts show that revenue deficit and overall fiscal deficit will continue to persist though their rate of growth may register a moderate fall. As per forecasts, the ratio of revenue deficit to revenue expenditure shows a decreasing trend. This is also true of revenue deficit- fiscal deficit ratio. The overall fiscal scenario thus suggests that unless the state takes fundamental fiscal reforms, the fiscal situation is likely to aggravate in the medium term.

Concluding Observations

The overall medium term fiscal scenario of the state suggests that unless urgent corrective steps are taken it will be difficult to contain revenue deficits. Achieving the target envisaged in the Fiscal Responsibility Act passed by the Government of Kerala appears to be an uphill task. The past trends of carving out surpluses in the capital account to finance revenue deficit are likely to continue and this practice has grave consequences for the development of the state. The overall scenario points towards the need for bold innovations both in resource mobilisation and expenditure management on the part of the state government.

TABLE 4.78

Forecast of the Overall Medium Term Fiscal Scenario, 2004-05 to 2009-10

(Rs. in Lakhs)

Heads	*2004-05*	*2005-06*	*2006-07*	*2007-08*	*2008-09*	*2009-10*
I Revenue Receipts						
1 State's Own Revenue	988513	1114329	1256490	1417167	1598823	1804260
2 Transfer From the Centre	3522272	383286	417066	453859	493940	537603
Total: I (1+2)	1340785	1497615	1673556	1871026	2092763	2341863
II Revenue Expenditure	1838249	2145861	2395665	2603687	2820273	3069581
III Surplus(+) or Deficit(-) on Revenue Account (I-II)	-497464	-648246	-722109	-732662	-727510	-727718
IV Capital Receipts	398236	432351	469588	510242	554640	603143
V Capital Disbursements	83060	167972	196945	216486	237901	261498
VI Surplus(+) or Deficit(-) on Capital Account	315176	264379	272643	293756	316739	341645
VII Overall Budgetary Surplus (+) or Deficit (-) (III+VI)	-182288	-383868	-449466	-438905	-410771	-386074
VIII Fiscal Deficit						
A Receipt						
1 Revenue	1340785	1497615	1673556	1871026	2092763	2341863
2 Capital	8060	8672	9345	10086	10901	11798
Total-A (1+2)	1348845	1506287	1682901	1881112	2103664	2353661
B Expenditure						
1 Revenue	1838249	2145861	2395665	2603687	2820273	3069581
2 Capital						
i. Capital Outlay	165000	136800	162600	178900	196700	216400
ii. Loans & Advances	18060	31172	34345	37586	41201	45098
Total-B (1+2)	1921309	2313833	2592610	2820173	3058174	3331079
C Fiscal Deficit (A-B)	-572464	-807546	-909709	-939062	-954510	-977418
Revenue Deficit as % of Revenue Expenditure	27.06	30.21	30.14	28.14	25.80	23.71
Revenue Deficit as % of Fiscal Deficit	86.90	80.27	79.38	78.02	76.22	74.45

Source: Worked out on the basis of Forecast of Revenue Receipts 2005-10 presented to Twelfth Finance Commission, Finance Department, Government of Kerala, November 2003.

References

Aiyar, Ramalingam and K.N. Kurup (1992). in Amaresh Bagchi, J.L Bajaj and William A. Byrd (eds.), *State Finances in India*. New Delhi: National Institute of Public Finance and Policy.

Bagchi, Amaresh (1993). "Information Technology in Tax Administration: Recent Cross Country Experience", *Economic and Political Weekly*, Nos.32 & 34: 1640-44.

Bagchi, Amaresh and M.G. Rao (1987). *Review of Plan Financing in Kerala During the Sixth Plan*. New Delhi: National Institute of Public Finance and Policy.

Bagchi, Amaresh, J.L Bajaj and William A. Byrd (eds.) (1992). *State Finances in India*. New Delhi: National Institute of Public Finance and Policy.

Eleventh Finance Commission (EFC) (2000). *Report of the Eleventh Finance Commission for 2000-2005*. Ministry of Finance, Department of Economic Affairs, Government of India. July.

George K.K. (1988). *Centre-State Financial Relations and Inter-State Disparities*. New Delhi: Criterion Publishers.

———. (1990). "Kerala's Fiscal Crisis: A Diagnosis", *Economic and Political Weekly*, September 15, pp.2097-2105.

———. (1993). *Limits to Kerala Model of Development*. Thiruvananthapuram: Centre for Development Studies.

———. (1994). "Trends in State Finances", in Prakash (ed.), *Kerala Economy: Performance, Problems and Prospects*.

George, K.K. and K.K. Krishnakumar (2003). "Fiscal Management in Kerala: Constraints and Policy Options", *Working Paper* No. 9. Kochi: Centre for Socio-Economic and Environmental Studies.

Gopalakrishnan, P.K. (1986). *Kerala Finances: A Synoptic View*. Thiruvananthapuram: KPCC Publications.

Government of Karnataka (2001). *Final Report of the Tax Reforms Commission*. Bangalore.

Government of Kerala (1977). *Report of the Task Force on Tax and Non-Tax Sources of Revenue*. Thiruvananthapuram: State Planning Board.

———. (1993). *Report of the Resources Commission*. Thiruvananthapuram.

———. (1997). Task *Force Report on Tax and Non-Tax Sources of Revenue*, State Planning Board, Thiruvananthapuram.

———. (2001). *White Paper on State Finances*. Thiruvananthapuram.

———. (2002). *Economic Review 2001*. Thiruvananthapuram: State Planning Board.

———. (2003). *Budget Speech of the Finance Minister-2002-03*. Thiruvananthapuram: Finance Department.

———. (2004). *Economic Review 2003*. Thiruvananthapuram: State Planning Board.

———.(2006). *Economic Review 2005*. Thiruvananthapuram: State Planning Board.

Government of India (GoI) (2003). *Economic Survey 2002-2003*. Ministry of Finance, Economic Division.

Jacob, Jose (1997). "Fiscal Disequilibrium of Kerala: A Diagnosis", in P.R. Gopinathan Nair, K.N.S. Nair, Thampi Jose and K.V. Velayudhan (eds.), Dimensions of Economic Development: *Spatial and Sectoral Perspectives, C. Radhakrishnan Commemoration Volume.*

Kannan K.P. and K.S. Hari (2002). " Kerala's Gulf Connection: Emigration, Remittances and their Macroeconomic Impact-1972- 2000", *Working Paper* No.328. Thiruvananthapuram: Centre for Development Studies.

National Institute of Public Finance and Policy (1994). *Reform of Domestic Trade Taxes in India: Issues and Options*. New Delhi.

Premchand, A. and Saumen Chattopadhyay (2002). *Fiscal Adjustment and Expenditure Management, Discussion Paper No.3*. New Delhi: National Institute of Public Finance and Policy.

Rakhe, P.B. (2003). Esimation of Tax Leakage and its Impact on Fiscal Health in Kerala, *Working Paper* 347. Thiruvananthapuram: Centre for Development Studies.

Sebastian, Jose (1997). "Burden of Taxation and Benefits of Public Expenditure: A Comparison of Kerala with Major Indian States", in P.R. Gopinathan Nair, K.N.S. Nair, Thampi Jose and K.V. Velayudhan (eds.), Dimensions of Economic Development: *Spatial and Sectoral Perspectives, C. Radhakrishnan Commemoration Volume.*

———. (2002). "Implementation of VAT in India: The Tasks Ahead", *International VAT Monitor*, Vol.13(5): 352-60.

Srivastava, D.K., Chattopadhyay, Saumen and Pratap Ranjan Jena (1999). *State Fiscal Studies-Kerala*. New Delhi: National Institute of Public Finance and Policy.

Chapter 5

Agriculture

The agricultural scenario in Kerala is somewhat unique and distinct from that of many other states in India in terms of land utilisation and cropping pattern. The cropping pattern is predominantly of commercial crops hereby dependent on international markets. The size of operational holdings is extremely small. The contribution of agriculture to the state income has been steadily declining from 56 per cent in 1960-61 to 13 per cent in 2003-04. This Chapter provides a brief review of the performance of the agricultural sector in Kerala in three distinct phases: 1960-61 to 1975-76 corresponding to the early days of the state formation and increased emphasis on food crops; 1975-76 to 1995-96 corresponding to an expanding phase of non-food crops at the expense of food crops; and the period beginning with 1995-96 corresponding to the WTO era.

Topography, Climate and Soil

Kerala has three natural divisions: lowland, midland and highland, forming parallel belts across the length of the state. The lowland with stretches of sand and numerous backwaters on the western fringe of the state along the sea shore is ideally suited for the cultivation of coconut and rice. The midland region with hills and valleys presents an undulating tract of laterite soil cut across by numerous rivers is noted for a large variety of crops like rice, coconut, pepper, cashew, ginger, tapioca and rubber. The highland consists mainly of mountains covered by dense forests bordering the Western ghats, and has important export-oriented plantation crops like tea, cardamom, coffee, and pepper. The annual rainfall in the high land region ranges from 2540 to 5080 millimetres. The midland region also receives good rainfall ranging from 1400 to 3940 millimetres per annum. The annual rainfall in the coastal belt ranges from 890 mm in the south to 3560 mm in the north. Relative humidity is high in coastal areas.

Land Utilisation Pattern

The total geographical area of the state is 3885 thousand hectares, of which 1082 hectares are classified as forest land which includes all forested areas and land classified or administered as forests under any legal enactment dealing with forests, whether state-owned or private. Though the ground realities indicate that the forest area has dwindled on account of various factors such as encroachment, development projects etc., official statistics remain unchanged since land classified as forest retains the same status until fresh surveys and reclassification are implemented. In fact studies based on the Survey of India topographical sheets indicate that the area under forest declined from 44 per cent of the geographical area in 1905, to 27.7 per cent in 1965, and to 17.1 per cent in 1973.

The land use pattern in Kerala indicates a steady increase in land put to non-agricultural uses and an overall increase in total cropped area between 1960-61 to 2003-04. The total cropped area declined marginally since 1995-96. Increase in gross cropped area was due to increases in both net area sown and area sown more than once. While reductions in all other categories of land use had contributed to the increase in gross cropped area, the farmers' tendency of keeping land idle has declined sharply. Intensity of land use as reflected by the cropping density (total cropped area divided by net area sown) increased substantially during the period 1960-61 to 1975-76, but in the subsequent years, it remained stagnant. Changes in the cropping pattern in favour of perennial crops might have influenced this pattern (Table 5.1). Net area sown accounted for 49.5 per cent of total geographical area in 1960-61; the corresponding figures were 56.4 per cent in 1975-76, 58.3 per cent in 1995-96, and 56.5 per cent in 2003-04.

TABLE 5.1

Land Utilisation Pattern in Kerala

(1000 hectare)

	1960-61	1975-76	1995-96	2003-04
Total Geographical Area	3885	3885	3885	3885
Forest	1082	1082	1082	1082
Land put to Non-agricultural Use	205	259	313	388
Barren & Uncultivable Land	151	78	43	30
Permanent Pastures & Grazing Land	45	20	1	0.5
Land under Misc. Tree Crops	204	84	27	12
Cultivable Waste	144	113	74	71
Fallow Other Than Current	62	23	29	39
Current Fallow	67	37	51	71
Net Area Sown	1924	2189	2265	2194
Total Cropped Area	2349	2981	3067	2976
Area Sown More Than Once	425	792	802	783
Cropping Intensity	122.1	136.2	135.4	135.6

Note: All the tables and figures are compiled from various issues of the Annual Economic Reviews brought out by the Kerala State Planning Board and periodic issue of Statistics for Planning brought out by the Department of Economics and Statistics, Government of Kerala.

The net area sown increased by 14 per cent during 1960-61 to 1975-76, and by three per cent during 1975-76 to 1995-96; but it declined by three per cent during 1995-96 to 2003-04.

Land put to non-agricultural uses increased from 5.3 per cent in 1960-61 to 6.7 per cent in 1975-76, to 8.1 per cent in 1995-96 and to 10 per cent in 2003-04. The increase during all the three intervals was by more than 20 per cent. While all the other categories represented only very small percentages of change in the total geographical area, in each category taken independently; the decline during all the three intervals had been significant.

Size of Operational Holdings

The average size of operational holdings in Kerala is extremely small (George, 1986), only 0.74 hectare in 1966-67; by 1976-77, the size declined to 0.49 hectare and by 1990-91 to 0.33 hectare.

During 1990-91 about 93 per cent of the holdings were below one hectare with an average size of only 0.18 hectare. Another five per cent of the holdings belonged to the category of 1-2 hectares with an average size of 1.36 hectares. The number of holdings of more than four hectares was only less than one-half a per cent (Table 5.2).

TABLE 5.2

Distribution of Operational Holdings

Size of Holdings (ha)	*1966-67*		*1976-77*		*1990-91*	
	Number %	*Average Size (ha)*	*Number %*	*Average Size (ha)*	*Number %*	*Average Size (ha)*
Marginal (below 1)	81.8	0.28	87.1	0.24	92.6	0.18
Small (1 to 2)	10.1	1.43	8.4	1.37	5.2	1.36
Semi-medium (2 to 4)	5.6	2.79	3.4	2.70	1.8	2.60
Medium (4 to 10)	2.1	5.60	1.0	5.49	0.4	5.27
Large (above 10)	0.5	19.86	0.1	19.06	0.06	55.74
All	0.74		0.49		0.33	

Cropping Pattern

The cropping pattern in Kerala has undergone major changes over the past four decades. As indicated earlier, the total gross cropped area in the state increased from 2349 thousand hectares in 1960-61 to 3067 thousand hectares during 1995-96, and then declined to 2976 thousand hectares in 2003-04. During 1960-61 rice was the most extensive crop occupying 779 thousand hectares, and the next in importance was coconut which occupied 501 thousand hectares. Tapioca (242 thousand hectares), rubber (123 thousand hectares) and pepper (100 thousand hectares) were the other important crops. By 1975-76 all the important crops of Kerala had increased their area. Between 1975-76 to 1995-96 there was a rapid decline in the area under the food crops of rice and tapioca, and a substantial increase in the area under coconut, rubber and pepper. The declining trend of the area under rice continued during 1995-96 to 2003-04 with the result that the area under rice in 2003-04 was only about one-third of the area during 1975-76. While the area under coconut and tapioca had slightly declined during this period, the area under rubber and pepper continued their growth trend but at a diminishing rate (Table 5.3).

Changes in the share of area under major crops indicate that rice which had occupied the premier position during 1960-61 and 1975-76 slipped to the second position by 1995-96 and further down to the third position by 2003-04. Coconut had remained in the second position during 1960-61 and 1975-76 and rose to the first position during 1995-96 and 2003-04. Tapioca had occupied the third position during 1960-61 and 1975-76; but it moved down to the fifth position by 1995-96 and remained in the same position during 2003-04. Rubber occupied the fourth rank during 1960-1961 and 1975-76, moved upwards to the third rank during 1995-96 and rose to the second position by

TABLE 5.3

Area under Major Crops in Kerala

('000 hectares)

Crop	1960-61	1975-76	1995-96	2003-04
Rice	779	876	471	287
Coconut	501	693	914	906
Tapioca	242	327	114	111
Rubber	136	212	449	476
Pepper	100	108	192	207
Cashewnut	54	109	103	88
Arecanut	54	77	71	93
Plantains & Banana	44	52	73	107
Tea	38	38	37	37
Cardamom	29	54	44	32
Coffee	17	42	82	85
Ginger	12	12	13	9
Total Cropped Area	2319	2981	3067	2976

2003-04. During 1960-61 pepper which had been the fifth major crop, slipped down to the sixth position in 1975-76; it has since moved upwards to the fourth rank by 1995-96 and 2003-04. The changes in the cropping pattern indicate a clear shift away from subsistence-oriented crops (mainly rice and tapioca) from the mid-seventies in favour of more remunerative commercial crops such as rubber and coconut among tree crops and to some of the export-oriented other crops such as pepper and coffee. The relative positions of the different crops during the four periods are shown in Table 5.4.

Productivity

The yield levels of different crops have indicated mixed trends during the three periods considered here. The rice yield of 1371 kgs/ha in 1960-61 had increased to 1520 kg/ha in 1975-76, and further to 2023 kg/ha in 1995-96 before it declined to 1984 kg/ha in 2003-04. During 1960-61 to 1975-76 rubber had the maximum growth in yield (233 per cent) followed by ginger (164 per cent), tapioca (141 per cent), rice (11 per cent), tea (7 per cent) and plantains (2 per cent). Coconut, cashewnut, cardamom, pepper and coffee had experienced decline in yield levels ranging between—11.9 per cent for coffee and -32.4 per cent for cashewnut.

Between 1975-76 to 1995-96, rice, coconut, tapioca, rubber, pepper, tea, cardamom, coffee and ginger had experienced yield increases. The increase was the highest for cardamom (221 per cent), followed by 69.5 per cent for rubber, the lowest increase being for coconut (14 per cent). Cashewnut and plantains were the only two crops which had showed decrease in yield levels during this period. However, during 1995-96 to 2003-04, rice, pepper, cashewnut and tea experienced decline in yield levels ranging between -1.9 per cent for rice and -23.2 per cent for pepper. During this latter period cardamom recorded the highest increase in yield of about 70 per cent, followed by rubber (30 per cent). In fact rubber maintained steady increase in yield levels over all the three periods considered. Tapioca and ginger were the other two crops which experienced rising yield levels during all the three periods. Rice and

TABLE 5.4

Share of Major Crops in the Cropped Area and their Ranks

Crop	1960-1961		1975-1976		1995-1996		2003-2004	
	Share (%)	Rank	Share (%)	Rank	Share (%)	Rank	Share (%)	Rank
Rice	33.2	1	29.4	1	15.4	2	9.6	3
Coconut	21.3	2	23.3	2	29.8	1	30.4	1
Tapioca	10.3	3	11.0	3	3.7	5	3.7	5
Rubber	5.2	4	6.9	4	14.6	3	16.0	2
Pepper	4.3	5	3.6	6	6.3	4	7.0	4
Cashewnut	2.3	6	3.7	5	3.4	6	3.0	8
Arecanut	2.3	7	2.6	7	2.3	9	3.1	7
Plantains & Banana	1.9	8	1.8	8	2.4	8	3.6	6
Tea	1.6	9	1.3	11	1.2	11	1.2	11
Cardamom	1.2	10	1.8	8	1.4	10	1.4	10
Coffee	0.7	11	1.4	10	2.7	7	2.9	9
Ginger	0.5	12	0.4	12	0.4	12	0.3	12

tea had increasing yield levels during the first and the second periods, but falling yield levels during the third period. Though coconut, cardamom and coffee had recorded a decline in yield during the first period, they recorded rising yield levels during the second and the third periods. Cashewnut was the only crop which had falling yield levels during all the three periods (Table 5.5).

Production Trends of Major Crops

Between 1960-61 and 1975-76 most of the crops grown in Kerala had recorded increase in production levels. Between 1975-76 and 1995-96 three crops (rice, tapioca and cashewnut) experienced shortfalls in production. Tapioca experienced the highest rate of decline of about 54 per cent followed by cashewnut (31 per cent) and rice (28 per cent). During this period also rubber kept on increasing its production level by an astonishing 268 per cent; it was followed by lower rates of increase for pepper (179 per cent), cardamom (162 per cent), coffee(157 per cent), ginger (62 per cent) plantains and coconut (both 50 per cent) and tea (42 per cent).

During 1995-96 to 2003-04, five crops (rice, pepper, cashewnut, tea and ginger) experienced decline in production levels. The highest rate of decline was for

TABLE 5.5

Yield Levels of Major Crops in Kerala

(Kg/hectare)

Crop	*1960-61*	*1975-76*	*1995-96*	*2003-04*	*Percentage Change During*		
	A	*B*	*C*	*D*	*A to B*	*B to C*	*C to D*
Rice	1371	1520	2023	1984	10.9	33.1	-1.9
Coconut*	6430	4963	5638	6052	-22.8	13.6	7.3
Tapioca	6845	16491	22008	22484	140.9	33.9	2.2
Rubber**	187	623	1056	1377	233.2	69.5	30.4
Pepper	271	227	358	275	-16.2	57.7	-23.2
Cashewnut	1659	1122	801	737	-32.4	-28.6	-8.0
Plantains	7381	7556	6585	7446	2.4	-12.8	13.1
Tea	1073	1148	1762	1513	7.0	53.5	-14.1
Cardamom	45	38	122	208	-15.6	221.0	70.5
Coffee	442	345	546	754	-11.9	58.3	38.1
Ginger	938	2479	3594	3330	164.3	45.0	7.3

Note: * Coconut yield is reported in nuts/hectare.

** Rubber yield is based on planted area. When the tapped area is considered yield levels are higher.

TABLE 5.6

Production of Major Crops in Kerala

(thousand metric tonnes)

Crop	*1960-61*	*1975-76*	*1995-96*	*2003-04*	*Percentage Change During*		
	A	*B*	*C*	*D*	*A to B*	*B to C*	*C to D*
Rice	1050.7	1331.2	953.0	570.0	26.7	-28.4	-40.2
Coconut*	3220	3439	5155	5484	6.8	50.0	6.4
Tapioca	1656.5	5390.2	2500.1	2503.6	225.4	-53.6	0.1
Rubber	23.2	128.8	474.6	655.8	455.1	268.48	38.2
Pepper	27.0	24.6	68.6	55.9	-8.9	178.8	-18.6
Cashewnut	83.3	119.9	82.8	65.2	43.9	-30.9	-21.3
Plantains	322.7	395.0	592.4	775.4	22.4	50.0	30.9
Tea	40.0	45.8	64.8	55.9	14.5	41.5	-13.7
Coffee	7.0	17.5	45.0	63.8	150.0	157.1	41.7
Ginger	11.1	28.8	46.5	29.7	159.5	61.5	-26.1

Note: * Coconut production is reported in million nuts.

rice (40 per cent) followed by ginger (26 per cent), cashewnut (21 per cent), pepper (19 per cent) and tea (14 per cent). Cardamom had the highest rate of increase in production of about 62 per cent; the production levels of coffee (42 per cent), rubber (38 per cent), plantains (31 per cent) and coconut (6 per cent) also increased by lower rates. Tapioca had only a marginal production increase of 0.1 per cent. Thus coconut, rubber, plantains, cardamom and coffee maintained increased production levels during all the three periods considered. Rice production had reached a peak during 1975-76 after which there was continuous decline (Table 5.6).

Contribution of Area and Yield to Production

An analysis of the relative contributions of area and yield changes towards production changes indicate that during 1960-61 to 1975-76 both area and yield increase had contributed to the production increase of rice, tapioca, rubber, and plantains. Production increases of coconut, cashewnut, cardamom and coffee were associated with increase in area and decrease in yield. Yield increase was the sole contributing factor for production increase of tea and ginger since the area under these crops remained constant during this period.

During 1975-76 to 1995-96 eight commodities had recorded increased production and three commodities had decreased production. Among the commodities which showed increase in production levels were coffee, coconut, rubber, pepper and ginger which also experienced increase in both area and yield. The contribution from area increase of both plantains and cardamom more than compensated for the negative impact of falling yield levels. Increase in the production levels of tea was associated with positive contributions from yield increase but negative contributions from area decline. Among the three commodities which showed decrease in production levels, rice and tapioca witnessed negative contributions of area decrease which far exceeded the positive contribution of yield increase.

During 1995-96 to 2003-04, six commodities showed increase in production and five decreased production levels. Among the commodities with increased production were rubber, plantains and coffee which experienced increases in both area and yield. Coconut, tapioca and cardamom had achieved production increase on account of the larger positive contribution of yield over the negative contribution of area decline. Decreased production of pepper was on account of the dominant negative role of yield over the positive role played by area expansion. For rice and cashewnut both area and yield contributed to decline of their production levels.

Price Parity and Profitability

Between 1960-61 and 1975-76, farm costs of cultivation in Kerala had increased by 293 per cent, prices received by farmers increased by 256 per cent and prices paid by farmers increased by 249 per cent. Between 1975-76 and 1995-96 the increase in farm cultivation cost, prices received by farmers and prices paid by farmers increased by 620 per cent, 369 per cent and 462 per cent respectively. During 1995-96 to 2003-2004 also, the increase in farm cultivation cost was the maximum followed by increase in prices paid by the farmers. Thus between 1960-61 and 1975-76 though the farm cultivation cost increased at a more rapid rate than the prices received by farmers, the prices paid by farmers had increased at a lower rate. During both 1975-76 to 1995-96 and 1995-96 to 2003-04 the increase in farm cultivation cost was very high followed by prices paid by farmers and the lowest increase was for prices received by farmers (Table 5.7).

TABLE 5.7

Increase in Prices during 1960-61 to 2003-04

(per cent)

Period	*Farm Cultivation Cost*	*Prices Paid by Farmers*	*Prices Received by Farmers*
1960-61 to 1975-76	293	249	256
1975-76 to 1995-96	620	462	369
1995-96 to 2003-04	113	84	42
1960-61 to 2003-04	5931	3509	2265

During 1960-61 to 2003-04 the index of farm cultivation cost (1952-53=100) increased from 117 to 7056. During the same period the index of prices received by farmers increased from 108 to 2554 and the index of prices paid by farmers increased from 119 to 4295. The profitability index of farmers measured by the ratio between the prices received and the farm cultivation cost decreased from 92 in 1960-61 to 36 in 2003-04 indicating that the farmers were continuously and increasingly at a disadvantageous position in respect of profitability of agriculture. The traditional price parity measures obtained as the ratio of prices received by the farmers and the prices paid by the farmers indicate that the disadvantage for farmers had been small between 1960-61 and 1975-76, but that it grew to enormous proportions during the ensuing two periods (Table 5.8).

TABLE 5.8

Profitability Index and Price Parity Index

Period	*Index of Cultivation Cost (A)*	*Index of Prices Received (B)*	*Index of Prices Paid (C)*	*Profitability Index (B/A)×100*	*Price Parity Index (B/C)×100*
1960-61	117	108	119	92	92
1975-76	460	384	415	83	93
1995-96	3312	1802	2331	54	77
2003-04	7056	2554	4295	36	57

Share of Agriculture in State Income

The relative contribution of agriculture to the state income has been declining over the years since the other sectors were growing at rates much higher than those of the agricultural sector. In 1960-61, agriculture had accounted for 56.0 per cent of the state income. By 1975-76, its contribution declined by 23.8 per cent. Between 1975-76 and 1995-96 the share of agriculture declined further by 39.6 per cent. There was a drastic decline of 49.6 per cent in its share during the eight year period between 1995-96 and 2003-04. By 2003-04 agriculture's contribution to the state income was only 13 per cent (Table 5.9).

TABLE 5.9

Agriculture's Share in the State Income

Year	*Share (per cent)*
1960-61	56.00
1975-76	42.70
1995-96	25.78
2003-04	13.00

Irrigation

About 90 per cent of the precipitation of rain in Kerala occurs during the two monsoons spread over June to August and October to November. Half the annual rainfall is estimated to run off to the rivers in the state. It is estimated that about 16 lakh ha (net) or 25 lakh ha (gross) could be brought under irrigation through major and medium irrigation projects and nine lakh ha through minor irrigation projects.

Consistent with the national approach, Kerala has relied mainly on the surface water irrigation system operating on gravitational force for distribution. At the beginning of the Tenth Plan there were 18 completed irrigation projects and 7 projects were at different stages of implementation. The cumulative investment on irrigation was Rs. 3402 million of which 68 per cent was for major and medium irrigation projects. The gross area irrigated during 2003-04 was only about 4.27 lakh ha of which government canals accounted for about 14.4 per cent of the gross cropped area. Forty per cent of the gross irrigated area was under rice which accounted for 59 per cent of the area under rice cultivation; coconut accounted for about 37 per cent of the gross irrigated area and accounted for only 17 per cent of the area under coconut.

The experience of the irrigation projects in Kerala highlights the following aspects:

There have been long delays in the completion of irrigation projects. While the average time taken for completion of a project was 19 years, five projects had taken an average of 30 years. The average cumulative cost of infrastructure development per hectare of potential irrigated area was Rs.1.39 lakh.

Among the seven projects under implementation one was initiated 30 years ago, two 25 years ago, one 23 years ago, one 19 years ago, one 17 years ago and one 6 years ago. The revised cost estimates of these projects made in 1999 indicate that the cost escalation ranged between 40 per cent for the project started in 1998 and 3228 per cent for the project started in 1979, with an average of 1633 per cent for the 7 projects.

The irrigation projects in the state were technically oriented towards rice cultivation. In the context of rapid shift of land use from rice cultivation in the state to several other crops and the increasing dependence on sources of water other than canal irrigation for the crops substituted, there could have arisen a mismatch between the capital investment made on canal irrigation projects and the emerging cropping pattern in the state.

In view of the monsoon pattern in the state, irrigation requirements for crops are critical during the summer months. However, availability of canal water during the summer months is not assured and this pattern has introduced severe constraints on farmers.

Under-utilisation of the irrigation potential created by irrigation projects is attributed to non-implementation of appropriate land development and water management measures in the command areas. Field channels and field drains have not been completely laid down in some of the command areas.

An analysis of the working expenses for nine major irrigation projects in the state indicates that revenues from these projects accounted for only a small proportion of the costs incurred on them. The ratios between revenues and costs from 1998-99 to 2002-03 were 3.4 per cent, 3.2 per cent, 12.4 per cent, 2.6 per cent and 6.3 per cent in the successive years from 1998-99. This situation could be improved only with a realistic pricing policy for irrigation water.

Major Commodity Profiles

Coconut

India is the third largest country in terms of area and production of coconuts. Within India, Kerala has the highest concentration of coconut cultivation. Coconut is cultivated mainly by small farmers and it provides livelihood support for about 10 million persons. During 1955-56, the area under coconut cultivation in India was 647 thousand hectares and Kerala's share was about 70 per cent. Out of total production of 4226 million nuts, Kerala accounted for nearly 73 per cent. By 2003-04 the area under coconut cultivation in India went up to 1870 thousand hectares; but Kerala's share was reduced to 48.3 per cent; the all-India production was 11,986 million nuts, with Kerala's share at 47.6 per cent.

TABLE 5.10

Annual Growth Rates of Area, Production and Yield

(per cent)

Period	*Area*	*Production*	*Yield*
1961 to 1974	3.53	1.90	(-)1.23
1975 to 1995	1.50	2.49	0.90
1996 to 2003	0.09	1.11	1.02

The annual growth rate of area under coconuts had been 3.53 per cent during 1961 to 1974; the rate declined to 1.60 per cent during 1975 to 1995 and further down to 0.09 per cent during the globalisation period. Production growth rate had increased from 1.90 per cent during 1961 to 1974 and to 2.49 per cent during 1975 to 1995; but it declined to 1.11 per cent during the globalisation period. Growth rate of yield was negative during 1961 to 1974 and it has been continuously on the increase even since. During 1961 to 1974 the high growth rate in area was partially off set by the negative growth rate of yield. During 1975 to 1995, positive growth rates of both area and yield contributed to growth of production levels (Figures 5.1, 5.2 and 5.3). However, during the globalisation period, it was yield increases which mainly contributed to the growth of production (Table 5.10).

FIGURE 5.1

Area under Coconut

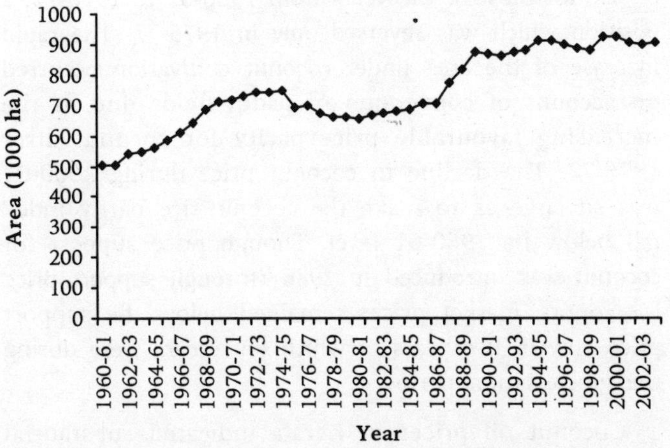

FIGURE 5.2

Production of Coconut

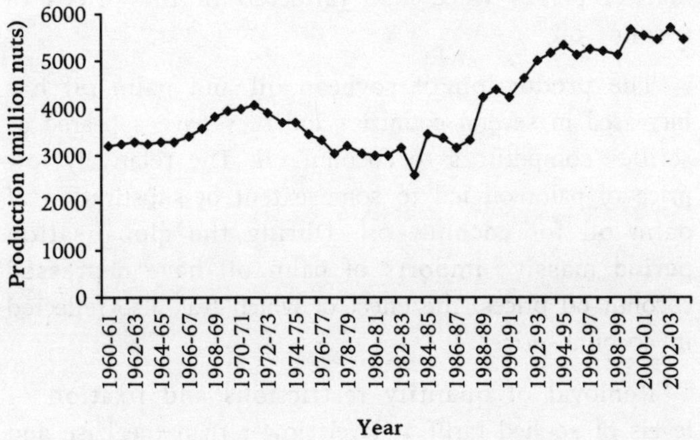

FIGURE 5.3

Yield of Coconut

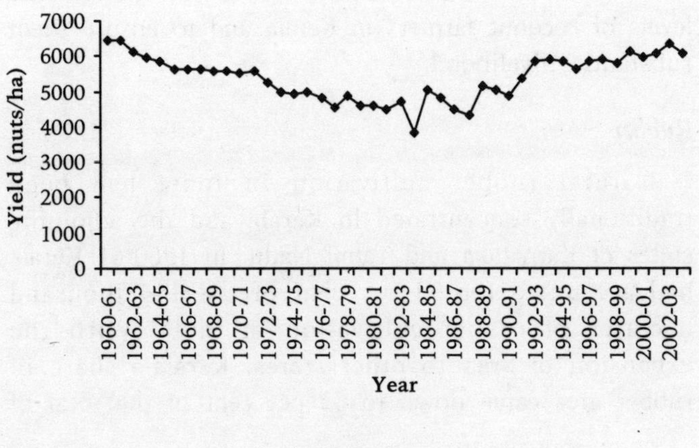

Prices: Farm level prices of coconut in Kerala indicate a general upward trend. Between 1960-61 and 2003-04 prices increased in 27 years, decreased in 15 years and remained stable for one year. During the globalisation period, price registered a sharp decline in 2000-01 following the crash in world edible oil prices. The relative prices of coconut and rice moved in favour of rice for most of the years from 1960-61 to 1976-77, a position which was reversed only in 1976-77. The rapid increase of the area under coconut cultivation occurred on account of conversion of paddy-fields due to the increasing favourable price parity for coconut after 1976-77. The decline in coconut price during 2000-01 was so large as to make the coconut-rice parity index fall below its 1960-61 level. Though price support for coconut was introduced in 1986 (through support price for copra), market prices remained below the support price only in five years of which four years were during the globalisation period.

Coconut oil prices in Kerala indicated substantial annual and seasonal fluctuations. A strong linkage existed between the quantity of oil imports and the domestic price level. Changes in the international market prices were also reflected in the prices of coconut oil.

The production of soybean oil and palm oil has increased in several countries and they have appeared as serious competitors to coconut oil. The relatively low price of palm oil led to some extent of substitution of palm oil for coconut oil. During the globalisation period massive imports of palm oil have depressed coconut oil prices, the effect of which was also reflected in coconut prices.

Removal of quantity restrictions and fixation of levels of applied tariff at levels lower than the base and bound levels forebode the strong possibility of repetition of the crisis created for coconut producers in Kerala during 2000-01. Several short-term and long-term measures are necessary to protect the income levels of coconut farmers in Kerala and to ensure them substantial livelihood.

Rubber

Natural rubber cultivation in India had been traditionally concentrated in Kerala and the adjoining states of Karnataka and Tamil Nadu. In 1960-61 Kerala had accounted for 94 per cent of the 144 thousand hectares of rubber cultivation in India. With the expansion of area to other states, Kerala's share of rubber area came down to 83 per cent of the total of 503 thousand hectares in the country. However, even during 2002-03 Kerala accounted for about 92 per cent of rubber production in India.

FIGURE 5.4

Tapped Area of Rubber

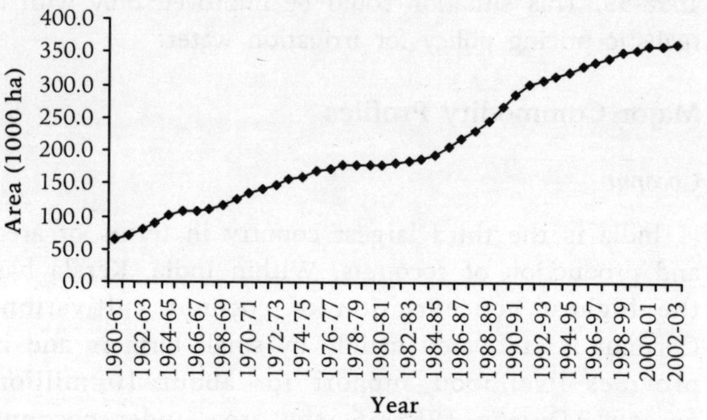

FIGURE 5.5

Production of Rubber

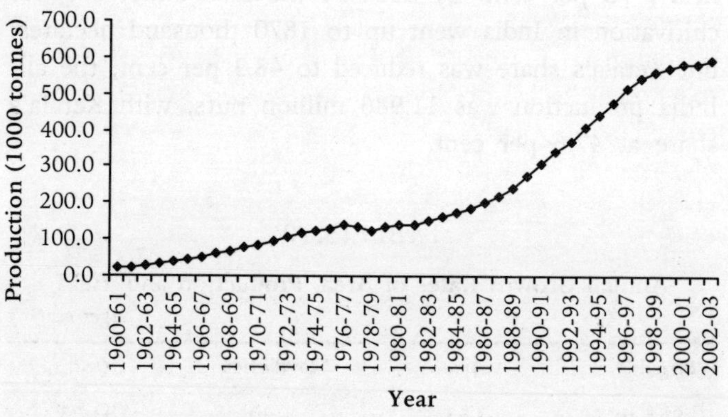

FIGURE 5.6

Yield of Rubber

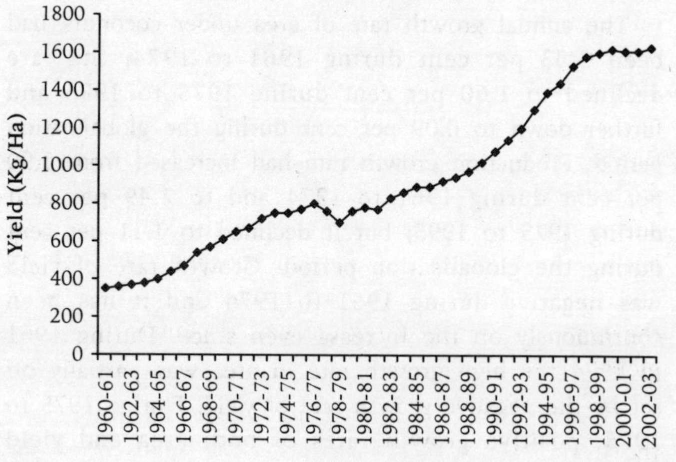

The growth rates of area under rubber cultivation in Kerala indicate a consistent downward trend during all the three periods of 1961 to 1974, 1975 to 1995 and 1996 to 2003. The growth rates of production and yield were falling too (Figure 5.4, 5.5 and 5.6). The growth rates of area, production and yield during the post-globalisation period were less than one-fourth of the growth rates during 1961 to 1974, though all these rates were positive (Table 5.11)

TABLE 5.11

Annual Growth Rates of Rubber Area, Production and Yield in Kerala

(per cent)

Period	*Area*	*Production*	*Yield*
1965 to 1974	6.62	13.73	6.70
1975 to 1995	3.71	6.80	2.99
1996 to 2003	1.47	2.93	1.45

Rubber price in Kerala used to be determined in isolation from international prices through government interventions in the forms of statutory prices, restrictions on imports and exports, and buffer stock operations. The government interventions were expected to control speculative tendencies in the market and to ensure remunerative prices to rubber cultivators. Most of these measures were either modified or straightway abolished with the introduction of the WTO regime.

Rubber prices in Kerala showed a consistent upward trend over the entire period but with some amount of annual fluctuations. Though market prices in Kerala were not directly linked to international prices, major fluctuations in international prices due to events such as changes in the demand for automobiles, the South-Asian currency crisis, changes in the world supply of natural rubber, exchange rate fluctuations, and changes in the stock level of natural rubber had their impacts on domestic prices. The rubber prices in Kerala remained well above world market prices during the 1970s and the 1980s; but the margin between the two narrowed down from the 1990s onwards, implying thereby that the integration of Kerala rubber market with the international market has gone ahead to a substantial extent. The annual variations in the price levels also indicate that the gap between the domestic and the international prices has been closed and that the range of annual variations has declined during the globalisation period.

The coefficient of variation for the Kerala market and the world market decreased during the 1990s from that during the previous decade. The variation was the lowest during the first five years of the present century. The variability in the world market price was more than in the Kerala market price. The gap between the two has narrowed however since 1995-96. While Kerala accounted for 90 per cent of the natural rubber production in India, bulk of its utilisation takes place in other states. This apparent paradox has given rise to conflicts of interests between rubber producers in Kerala and rubber product manufacturers outside Kerala, particularly on matters related to input tariff.

With the removal of quantitative restrictions, rubber may now be freely imported under OGL. The base customs duty on rubber imports was reduced to 20 per cent with effect from January 2004. Though about one-half the natural rubber consumption requirements used to be met from imports, with the expansion of domestic production, imports have declined. The tendency of imports was strong among manufacturers during the period when the domestic prices were substantially above international prices. However, during the recent months, imports have proved uneconomic since international prices have come to be higher than domestic prices. Further, exports exceeded imports in two years after 2000. Malaysia and Thailand were the major sources for import of rubber to India. Though the exports of rubber from India were low, efforts are being made to increase the volume of rubber exports; exports have picked up during the past two years. Increased awareness is at present evinced about the need for strengthening export efforts in order to put an end to the crisis situation which prevailed during 2002. AoA is not applicable to natural rubber since it is excluded from the list of agricultural commodities. It is considered advantageous to a large number of rubber cultivators in Kerala if rubber were reclassified as an agricultural commodity. Such classification would help protect domestic producers against dumping by major foreign producers of natural rubber.

Rice

Kerala has experienced a drastic decline in the area under rice, from 876 thousand hactares in 1975-76 to 287 thousand hectares in 2003-04. Consequently, the share of rice area in the total cropped area has declined from 29 per cent during 1975-76 to below 10 per cent during 2003-04. The declining trend has been quite steady during all the years. Since the yield increase during this period could not be compensated fully for the decrease in area, total production has also declined (Figures 5.7, 5.8 and 5.9). Considering the adverse impact of this decline on food security, employment opportunities and ecology, serious concerns have been voiced in the state; nevertheless the decline has taken place uninterrupted.

FIGURE 5.7

Area under Rice

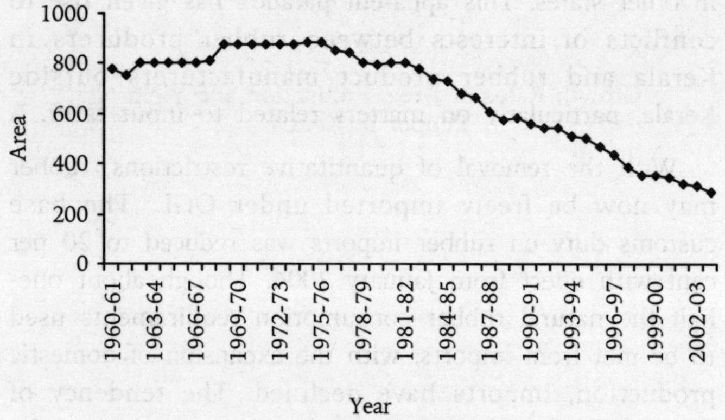

FIGURE 5.8

Production of Rice

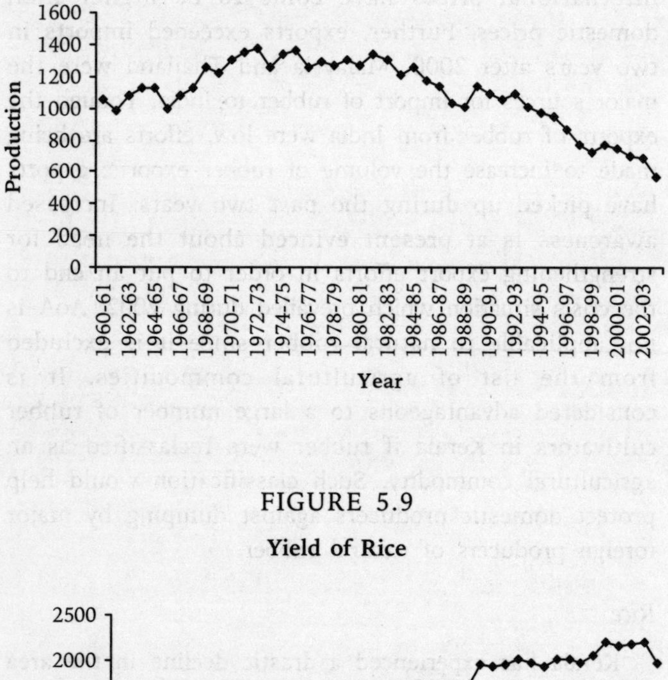

FIGURE 5.9

Yield of Rice

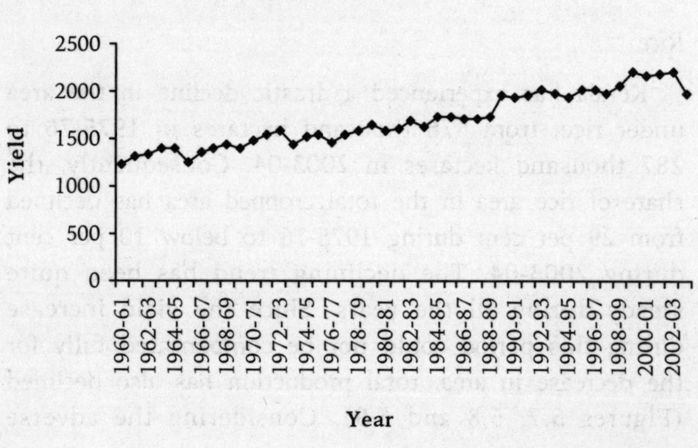

Annual growth rates of area, production and yield had positive values during the period 1960-61 to 1974-75. During 1975-76 to 1994-95 growth rates of both area and production were negative while the growth rate of yield was positive. However, from 1995-96 onwards there took place a rapid decline in the growth rates of area and production, with a substantially reduced growth rate of yield (Table 5.12).

TABLE 5.12

Annual Growth Rates of Rice Area, Production and Yield

(per cent)

Period	*Area*	*Production*	*Yield*
1961 to 1974	1.09	2.16	1.31
1975 to 1995	(-) 3.16	(-) 1.62	1.55
1996 to 2003	(-) 5.56	(-) 4.82	0.74

The nature of changes in area indicates that paddy land has been diverted either to other crops, mainly tree crops or to non-agricultural purposes such as sites for construction of buildings, brick-mining and infrastructural facilities such as roads, railways and canals (Kerala Statistical Institute,1984; and Gopinath and Sundaresan, 1994). The factors influencing the shift included large increase in cost of cultivation of rice without corresponding increase in its price, relative price changes in favour of competing crops, problems of managing labour, increased demand for housing and infrastructure, state policies relating to land tenure and tax structure (Jeemol Unni, 1983; Sivanandan, 1985; George 1982; Panikar, 1980; Kannan and Pushpangadan, 1988; Uma Devi, 1984). Though rice cultivators expect the state government to provide substantial price support, the measures adopted by government have not fulfilled this expectation. The land tenure system in vogue is another problem which has its adverse ramifications for effective land utilisation in the state, especially utilisation for rice cultivation.

Pepper

Pepper which is considered the king of spices is one of the most ancient crops of Kerala. It has played an important role in the Kerala economy since ancient times. Pepper trade was responsible for bringing at different stages in the history, Europeans, Persians and Arabs to the Malabar Coast (see Figures 5.10, 5.11 and 5.12)

FIGURE 5.10

Area under Pepper

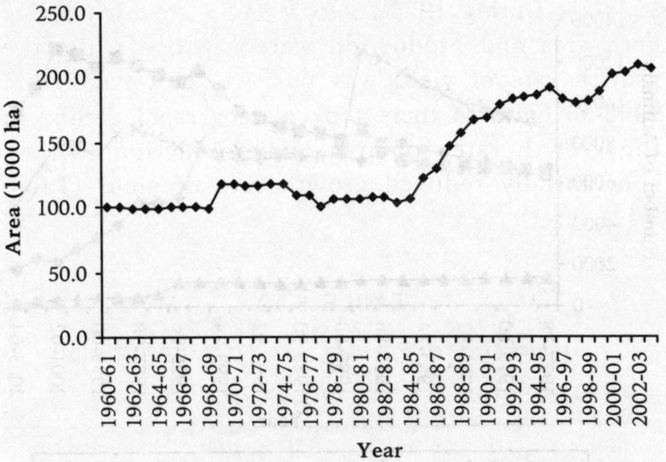

FIGURE 5.11

Production of Pepper

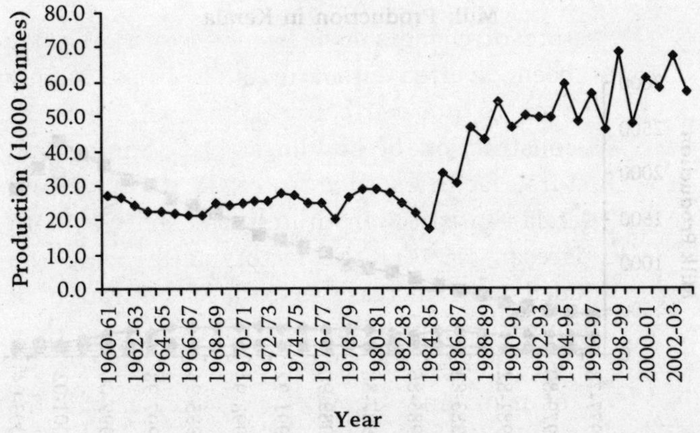

FIGURE 5.12

Yield of Pepper

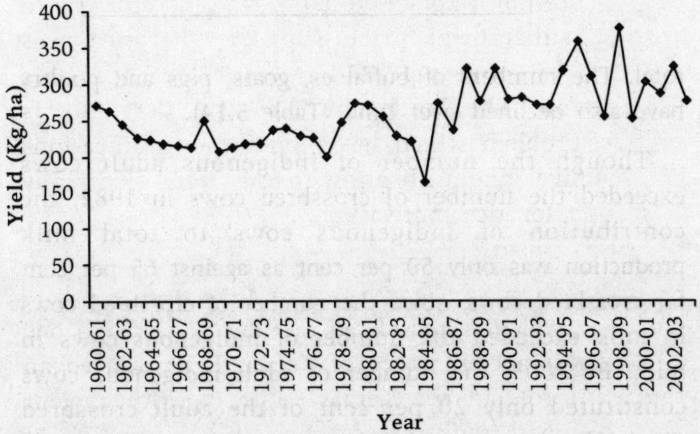

The growth rates of area, production and yield during the period 1975 to 1995 were higher than the corresponding rates for 1961 to 1974; but during 1996 to 2003 all these rates fell. While the growth rate of production was 4.90 per cent during 1975-1995, the corresponding rate for post-globalisation period (1996 to 2003) was a mere 0.21 per cent. Yield growth rate was negative during 1961-1974 and 1996-2003 (Table 5.13).

TABLE 5.13

Growth Rates of Area, Production and Yield of Pepper in Kerala

(per cent)

Period	*Area*	*Production*	*Yield*
1961 to 1974	1.62	0.40	(-) 1.18
1975 to 1995	3.37	4.90	1.42
1996 to 2003	1.76	0.21	(-) 3.31

The prices received by farmers underwent some degree of annual fluctuations. The average farm price of pepper in 1980-81which was Rs. 12.53/kg, declined to Rs. 12.04/kg during the next year. There was a gradual increase in the farm price during the ensuing six years to reach Rs. 52.62/kg in 1987-88. The next five years witnessed gradual decline to Rs. 26.16/kg in 1992-93. The increase which began from 1992-93 continued till 1996-97 when the price reached Rs. 87.80/kg. The year 1997-98 witnessed prices doubling; a course of moderate increase began and lasted until 1999-00 when the price reached its peak level.

Between 1960-61 and 2003-04, the quantity of pepper exports varied between 15.65 thousand tonnes in 1978-79 and 47.70 thousand tonnes in 1996-97. The average annual export for the 10 years prior to globalisation was 33.71 thousand tonnes and during the first 9 years of globalisation the annual average remained at 29.94 thousand tonnes. Export earnings between 1960-61 and 2003-04 varied between Rs. 5.89 crore in 1963-64 and Rs. 885.3 crore in 1999-00. Though export earnings were high during the second half of the 1990s, from 2000-01 onwards, there took place a rapid decline on account of the short-fall in the quantities exported. India could not take advantage of the emerging market opportunities on account of inadequate market development during the 1970s and the 1980s, and excessive dependence on bilateral government purchase agreements with the former Soviet Union. However, by 2002-03 about 56 per cent of India's pepper exports were to the American zone as against only 10 per cent during mid-1980s. The high production cost resulting from low yield levels in

Kerala, has contributed to the poor competitive position of the state in international markets in spite of the superior quality of its product. While there was an upward trend in the unit value of exports during the 1990s, a declining trend started in 2000-01 due to competition from the emerging pepper producing country of Vietnam.

There have been wide year-to-year fluctuations in the quantities and values of exports. The variability was in terms of quantity, but was quite high for export earnings. Over the years, variability has increased in quantities exported, unit value of exports and total export earnings; such variability has been particularly wide in the post-globalisation period.

With the liberalisation of imports in general under WTO provisions and of imports from Sri Lanka under the Indo-Sri Lanka Free Trade Agreement, imports of pepper to India have been expanding quite rapidly in recent years. The volume of imports increased from 4028 tonnes in 2000-01 to 15,750 tonnes in 2002-03. During this three year period, imports from Vietnam increased by more than 10 times while imports from Sri Lanka increased by 2.6 times. While the value of imports from Vietnam increased by 638 per cent and imports from Sri Lanka increased by 111 per cent, imports from Indonesia declined by 20 per cent. In 2002-03, the unit value of imports from Sri Lanka was 20 per cent higher than the unit value of imports from Vietnam.

Livestock

Kerala has witnessed a rapid progress in its livestock sector during the past three decades and a half, partly triggered by improvement in the genetic qualities of indigenous cattle through the cross- breeding technology popularised under the Indo-Swiss project (George and Nair, 1990). However, it appears that a declining phase of the livestock sector has already set in, which is manifested by reductions in the size of the cattle population and milk production (Figure 5.13 and 5.14).

According to livestock census data there was continuous decline in the number of both indigenous and crossbred male cattle in recent years. The numbers had increased until 1987 and rapidly declined subsequently. The number of female crossbred cattle recorded an increase until 1996 and declined thereafter. While crossbred cows accounted for about 50 per cent of the total number of cows in 1977, by 2003 crossbred cows accounted for as many as 82.5 per cent of the

FIGURE 5.13

Livestock Population in Kerala

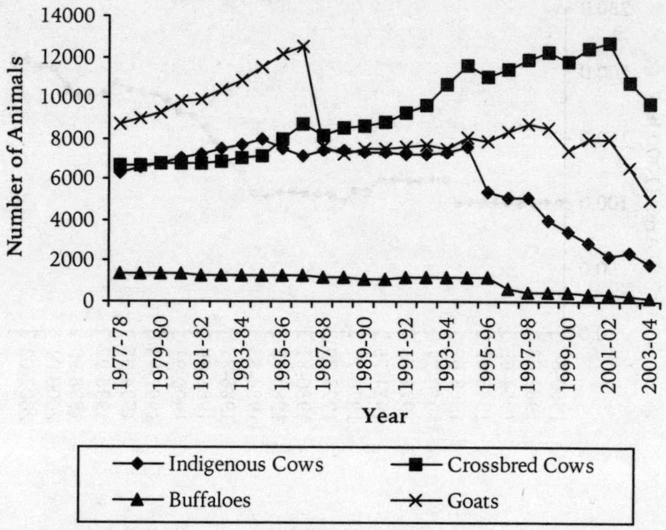

FIGURE 5.14

Milk Production in Kerala

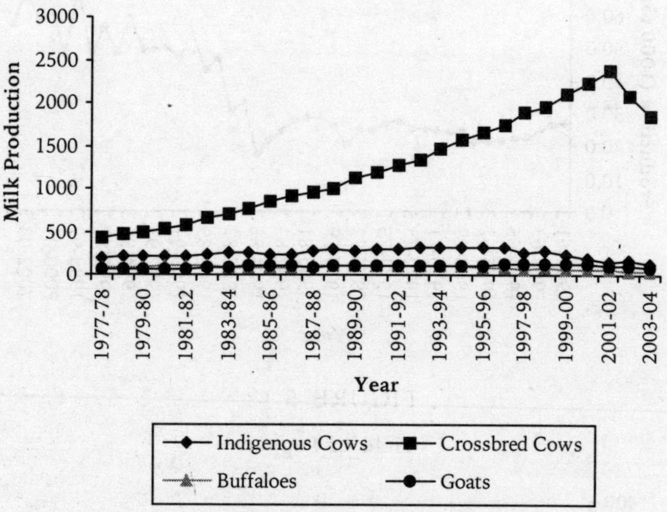

total. The numbers of buffaloes, goats, pigs and poultry have also declined over time (Table 5.14).

Though the number of indigenous adult cows exceeded the number of crossbred cows in 1982, the contribution of indigenous cows to total milk production was only 50 per cent as against 65 per cent for crossbred cows, since the number of crossbred cows in milk exceeded the number of indigenous cows in milk. By 2003, the number of adult indigenous cows constituted only 20 per cent of the adult crossbred cows. However, the gap between the proportions of indigenous and crossbred cows in milk has narrowed over the years (Table 5.15).

TABLE 5.14

Livestock Population in Kerala, 1977-2003

(in thousands)

	1977	*1982*	*1987*	*1996*	*2000*	*2003*
Indigenous Cattle						
Male	536	442	309	152	71	47
Female	1115	1202	1413	957	462	340
Total	1651	1644	1722	1109	533	387
Crossbred Cattle						
Male	217	217	199	232	144	135
Female	1138	1236	1503	2055	1813	1600
Total	1355	1453	1702	2287	1957	1735
Total Cattle						
Male	753	659	508	354	215	182
Female	2253	2438	2916	3012	2276	1940
Total	3006	3097	3424	3396	2491	2122
Buffaloes			329	165	111	65
Goats			1581	1861	1598	1213
Pigs			137	143	88	76
Poultry			17555	29525	16908	13189

TABLE 5.15

Population of Adult Cattle

(in thousands)

	Indigenous			*Crossbred*		
	In Milk	*Total*	*Per Cent*	*In Milk*	*Total*	*Per Cent*
1982	392.8	785.7	50.0	471.5	726.5	64.9
1987	451.8	812.0	55.6	563.2	889.3	63.3
1996	329.7	569.5	57.9	785.4	1226.4	64.0
2000	195.7	340.6	57.5	756.0	1182.0	64.0
2003	106.6	173.3	61.5	607.4	872.5	69.6

Milk Production in the state increased gradually from 778 thousand tonnes in 1977-78 to 2717 thousand tonnes in 2001-02; however the subsequent two years witnessed a drastic decline and milk production stood at 2110 thousand tonnes in 2003-04. In 1977-78 crossbred cows had accounted for 55 per cent of the total milk production and indigenous cows 25 per cent; the contributions from buffaloes and sheep were 11 per cent and 9 per cent respectively. By 2003-2004 the share of crossbred cows in total milk production increased to 88 per cent; the contributions from other sources declined in consequence: indigenous cows to six per cent, buffaloes to two per cent and sheep to four per cent. The increasing trend of milk production from 1977-78 was reversed for indigenous cows during 1995-96, for crossbred cows in 2001-02, and for buffaloes in 1993-94 and for goats in 1999-00.

The rapid increase in the population of crossbred cows in the state was facilitated by the measures adopted by the state government for providing the infrastructure for production and distribution of materials for artificial insemination. The declining trend in the livestock economy is attributed to a variety of factors including scarcity of feed and fodder, non-availability of family labour, uneconomic price level partly on account of the inflow of cheaper livestock products from the neighbouring states and the changing value system. In spite of the various measures initiated for increasing green fodder production, the supply of green fodder in 2005 is estimated to be less than 40 per cent of demand. The rapid decline in the area under rice cultivation has drastically reduced the availability of dry fodder (hay and straw). Farmers responded to these changes by first limiting the number of indigenous cows and of late even the number of high-yielding crossbreds.

In view of the declining trend in the livestock sector, there have arisen doubts about the viability of homestead-based livestock units maintained with technological support. Suggestions have come regarding the establishment of large commercial cattle farms for supply of milk and meat. However, it is livestock that provide the main source of livelihood for a large number of landless households, and small and marginal farmers in the state. Livestock are still considered a sure source of supplementary income by many poor households; in the absence of adequate support for maintaining livestock, these poor households may find even their very survival difficult. There is, therefore, an urgent need to balance commercial considerations and livelihood strategies. Organic farming has good potential in the state and the possibility of combining livestock-rearing with organic farming is worth exploring. There is also scope for realising user charges for certain services for improving the level of efficiency of the state veterinary institutions through selective involvement and privatisation (Ahuja Vinod *et al.*, 2000).

Fisheries

Kerala's abundant natural endowments for fisheries development include a long coastal belt of about 590 kilometres, inland water spread of about 4 lakh hectares consisting of 44 rivers, 30 major reservoirs,fresh water ponds and brackish inland backwaters. In 2003-04, there were 2.20 lakh active fishermen (1.79 in marine fisheries and 0.41 lakh in inland fisheries) in the state. The 222 fishing villages in the marine sector had a total population of 8.43 lakh and the population of the 113 fishing villages in the inland sector was 2.52 lakh.

During the 1980s, marine fish production in Kerala increased from 2.68 lakh tonnes in 1980-81 to 5.63 lakh tonnes in 1990-91. There were near- stagnant conditions of production during the 1990s with the annual average for the decade remaining at about 5.72 lakh tonnes. The average annual production during the first four years of the current century was 5.93 lakh tonnes. The substantial increase of motorised fishing crafts from 9914 in 1988-89 to 29395 in 2003-04 and a small increase in the number of non-motorised crafts from 24093 to 26106 during the same period have not contributed to any significant increase in fish production. However, the increase in the number of mechanised crafts has resulted in a reduction of the share of traditional crafts in total fish landings. An immediate outcome of this shift has been frequent confrontations between traditional fishermen and operators of mechanised boats and trawlers. The indiscriminate use of gears and nets in violation of the Marine Fisheries Regulation Act has also aggravated the problem.

Inland fish production increased from 0.26 lakh tonnes in 1980-81 to 0.36 lakh tonnes in 1990-91 and to 0.85 lakh tonnes in 2000-01. The average annual production of inland fish during the 1980's was 0.28 lakh tonnes and to 0.51 lakh tonnes during the 1990's and 0.79 lakh tonnes during the four years of the present century. There is scope for further utilisation of the potential of inland fisheries in the state (Figure 5.15)

FIGURE 5.15

Fish Production in Kerala

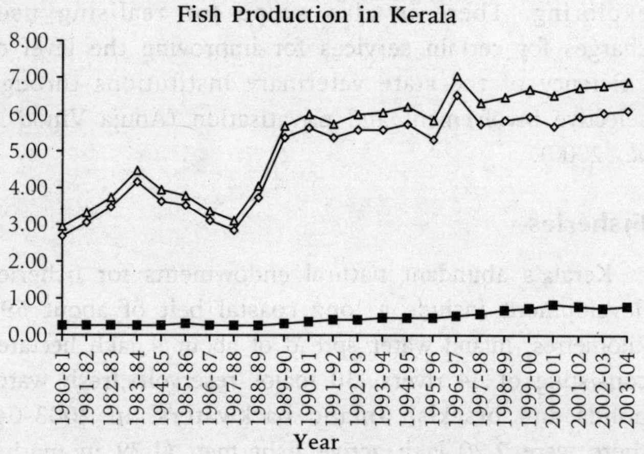

Exports of marine products from India had started on a modest level in the early 1950s with a turnover of Rs. 2.46 crore; they have grown up significantly during the past five decades to reach the level of Rs. 6092 crore in 2003-04. Kerala is the second largest marine products exporting state in India. During 1980-81 export of fish products from Kerala came to 29.1 thousand metric tonnes worth Rs. 95.3 crore. The upward trend in exports continued until 1996-97 at a peak level of 92.3 thousand metric tonnes. During the subsequent years there has been a steady decline in the quantity exported (with the exception of 1999-2000) and the level of 76.6 thousand tonnes was reached in 2003-04.

Kerala's share of exports of marine products from India has been continuously on the decline, from 38 per cent in 1980-81 to 19 per cent in 2003-04. The corresponding decline in the share of exports earnings was from 41 per cent in 1980-81 to 15 per cent in 2003-04 (Figure 5.16).

FIGURE 5.16

Kerala's Share

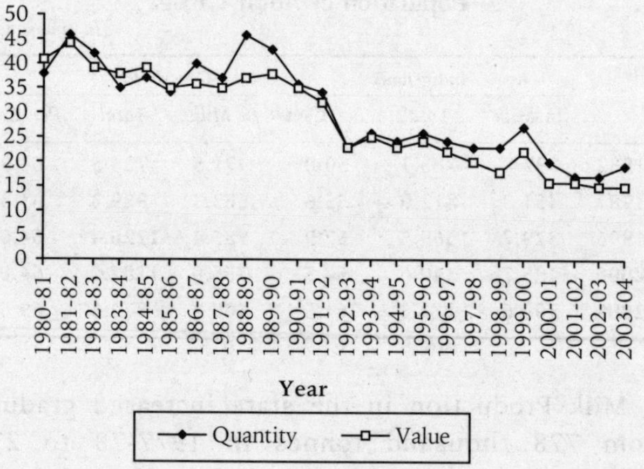

Frozen shrimp is the export item which accounts for about one-half the export earnings of marine products from the state. Acquaculture of shrimp has gained momentum as the share of acquaculture shrimp in the total shrimp exports increased from about 33 per cent in 1988-89 to 60 per cent in 2002-03, in quantity terms. In terms of value, the corresponding increase was from 49 per cent to 82 per cent. During 2003-04 Kerala accounted for only about 9.1 per cent of the area under shrimp culture in India and nearly 5.7 per cent of the total shrimp production. Kerala's annual productivity of 0.46 tonnes/ha was the lowest in India;

the highest productivity of 1.89 tonnes/ha being in Tamil Nadu; the national average was 0.73 tonnes/ha. The productivity of fresh water prawn (scampi) in Kerala was only 0.27 tonnes/ha against the highest productivity of 1.18 tonnes/ha in Andhra Pradesh and the national average of 0.86 tonnes/ha.

Traditional fishermen in Kerala belong to the most economically backward communities, their living standard depending mainly on the earnings from the fisheries sector. Stagnation in their production levels can only worsen their living standard. Effective measures to regulate the number of fishing crafts, and promotion of the use of proper gears and nets and other conservation measures are necessary to protect the interests of this impoverished community. While the marine fisheries sector is somewhat saturated, there is scope for expansion of inland fisheries, culture fisheries and ornamental fisheries. Increase in the productivity of acqaculture, promotion of inland fisheries and measures for maintaining quality standards are also important to regain their due share of the export market.

Perspective

The foregoing analysis has suggested that Kerala has reached the limits in terms of extension of cropped area and that there remains little further scope for agricultural development through extension. However, there is still scope for intensification of developmental efforts in agriculture since the productivity levels of most crops, probably with the exception of rubber, are well below their potential, even the realised levels in other states (Nair and Menon, 2004). Several constraints, structural, organisational and socioeconomic, could be identified in relation to individual crops; removal of suh constraints would be an essential pre-requisite for productivity enhancement. Both livestock and fisheries sectors are either stagnant or declining; effective steps to avoid further decline are required to safeguard the livelihood concerns of the very large numbers of poor households dependent on these activities. Structural changes in the livestock sector would necessitate changes in the livestock development strategy. The concept of one animal for each small farmer may have to give way to the emergence of small scale dairy entrepreneurs. Emphasis on value added products may be necessary in areas with sufficient organisational capability. In the fisheries sector, along with the stagnant marine fisheries sector, development of inland fisheries, cultural fisheries and ornamental fisheries is important.

The farming community in the state has been quick in shifting the cropping pattern in accordance with the changing economic opportunities. The rapid conversion of land under seasonal food crops such as rice and tapioca to perennial cash crops reflects the entrepreneurial skills of the local farmers. However, considerations of food security and ecological concerns would call for enforcement of some constraints on conversion of land. Organic farming is assuming importance and there is scope for integrating cattle-keeping with organic farming. Therefore the state policy should provide sufficient encouragement to farmers to adopt cropping patterns consistent with economic and social realities.

The dominance of crops dependent on world market conditions in the cropping patterns in the state, makes it highly vulnerable. Though it is too early to draw firm conclusions on the impact of globalisation on Kerala agriculture, on the basis of the experience during the post-globalisation period, it is inferred that the expectation of substantial benefits to the Kerala economy from expanded trade resulting from globalisation of agriculture, has not materialised. At the same time there have been disturbing tendencies in terms of increased imports of items such as pepper, palm oil and soybean oil which compete with local crops and products. Though there has been some integration of Kerala markets of the major agricultural commodities with the international markets, farmers in Kerala have not derived substantial gains of farm income. While the rising prices of coconut and rubber in the international markets during the past two years have contributed towards a recovery, pepper producers continue to live in distress. There is also a danger that the high volatility of international market conditions might impose further hardships on coconut and rubber producers during periods of downward trend in prices. Therefore it is important that adequate measures are initiated to take advantage of the opportunities open to Kerala on account of the changing international scenario and to provide appropriate safeguards to ensure the livelihood security of a large number of small farmers of Kerala engaged in the production of these commodities.

One of the most important concerns relating to expanded trade of commodities is the product profile offered. Traditional product profiles are fast changing and new products with high values are rapidly entering the market. In the absence of product diversification, the shift towards high value items would offer little scope for realising high income opportunities for domestic farmers. However, diversification to value-added products would require access to new technology, technical know how, quality control and effective entrepreneurial skills for market penetration. These requirements would be fulfilled only through active cooperation of all the concerned government agencies in close collaboration with the public and the private enterprises.

The main competitors, in respect of the major agricultural commodities exported from Kerala, in the international markets, include Vietnam, the Philippines, Indonesia, Malaysia and Sri Lanka. India's special relations with these countries make the formulation and implementation of suitable safeguards to farmers in Kerala, a highly sensitive issue. In order to honour national commitments through bilateral and multinational agreements, Kerala farmers are called upon to make huge sacrifices and forego compensating policies and programmes of income generation and measures in their support for product diversification and value addition.

Marketing support is crucial in areas of post-harvest technology and export promotion. In order to compete effectively in the international markets, products should conform to acceptable quality standards which can be maintained only through careful post-harvest operations using modern processing facilities. The changing profiles of supply and demand in the major exporting and importing countries and the response of individual countries to the changing marketing environment, should be made known and available to all those who are directly or indirectly involved in export marketing operations in major commodities. Timely availability of market intelligence is an important condition for successful operations in international markets.

One of the key elements affecting export competitiveness is the relatively high costs of production in Kerala caused mainly by low productivity. The perennial nature of the major crops introduces rigidities that make it difficult for adjustments in production conditions rendered necessary by changes in market conditions. Since crops such as coconut, rubber and pepper have long lives, measures involving activities like replanting with superior varieties and improved management (including irrigation where applicable), often tend to be adopted by farmers only under conditions of assured returns for investment. The experience of replanting incentives provided by the Rubber Board indicates that there is good scope for improving the productivity of pepper and coconut also through similar measures.

The sharp fall in prices of the major commodities during the early years of the present century has created a crisis in the state's agricultural sector. In addition to fall in international market prices, imports taking place under the liberalised trade regime also have been responsible for the crisis. Integration of domestic markets with international markets and high degrees of fluctuations in international prices are matters of grave concern for income stability of the farming community in Kerala. While the situation may improve with effective steps for product diversification and marketing support, there will be a long time lag involved for realising their results. Therefore suitable short-term measures are necessary to safeguard the interests of agriculture in Kerala. Two significant measures in this direction are those related to import duty adjustments and creation of a Price Stabilisation Fund. The applied tariff rates in vogue are well lower than the basic duty and the bound duty, and the applied rates should be suitably modified to regulate imports. Export subsidy offered for rubber was effective in its export promotion and extension of this provision to other commodities is worthwhile. A Price Stabilisation Fund with contributions from producers (during periods of high prices) and trade and government sources would be an effective device to compensate farmers during crisis periods. Further, crop insurance schemes would be able to protect farmers from loss of income due to shortfall in crop production levels.

There is need to evolve suitable measures to avoid misuse of the re-export provisions. Since there are existing notions regarding the quality of goods originating from particular locations, in the absence of proper certification of origin, inferior quality items from competing countries enter the Indian market and get re-exported under the guise of Indian goods. Such a practice is likely to spoil the image of high quality for the products from Kerala, especially for pepper. A stipulation regarding minimum value addition could be introduced as a control measure to check the flow of fake goods.

Reclassification of rubber as agricultural commodity would help rubber cultivators, especially in the context of a large number of small scale rubber producers involved in rubber production; such a measure would also be consistent with the treatment meted out to other plantation crops, such as tea and coffee. If it is difficult to pursue this option due to non-approval by the Government of India, some other suitable mechanism should be devised to compensate rubber producers for their loss of income during periods of abnormally low prices.

In view of the dynamic nature of the international markets, it is important to monitor changes systematically and evolve strategies consistent with the changing environment. For this purpose there should be a permanent mechanism at the state level with both administrative and advisory responsibilities.

Cooperatives

The Cooperative movement began in Kerala also in the early years of the 20th century. However, it has gained momentum only in the period since Independence. It was started basically as a credit movement but has diversified its activities to several areas of socioeconomic fronts in Kerala over the years. Today with more than 20,000 cooperatives, the cooperative movement in Kerala has spread its wings in almost all parts of the state and most spheres of life.

Cooperatives in Kerala are regulated by the provisions of the Kerala Cooperative Societies Act. During the early years of the movement, the societies were registered under separate Provisions and Acts. Madras and Travancore-Cochin had separate Cooperative Societies Acts during 1949-56. The need for a comprehensive act was felt after the formation of the Kerala state in 1956. Accordingly, the Kerala Cooperative Societies Act was passed in 1969. Even though many amendments have been made to the Act to retain the democratic nature of cooperatives, the Act continues to be in force and Cooperatives function as Government-sponsored institutions. Enormous powers are vested with the Registrar of Cooperative Societies. Amendments to the Kerala Cooperative Societies Act on the lines of Model Cooperative Societies Act as recommended by Chaudhary Brahma Prakash Committee have been for some time under the consideration of the Government.

Structure

The Cooperative credit structure in Kerala has two broad sectors *viz.*, the Agricultural Credit Sector and the non-Agricultural Credit Sector. The Agriculture Credit Sector comprises the Kerala State Cooperative Bank at the apex level, 14 District Cooperative Banks at the middle level and 1628 Primary Agriculture Credit Societies at the grassroots level. The Kerala State Cooperative Bank started functioning as the apex level institution from November 1, 1956, the very date of formation of the state of Kerala.

During the period 1956 to 2003, the share capital of the Kerala State Cooperative Bank increased from Rs. 9.85 lakh to Rs. 2268.82 lakh, reserves from Rs.0.91 lakh to Rs. 6994.20 lakh, deposits from Rs. 30.33 lakh to Rs. 232676.05 lakh, working capital from Rs. 42.9 lakh to Rs. 84886.63 lakh and loans and advances outstanding from Rs. 21.66 lakh to Rs. 123713.09 lakh. District Cooperative Banks also registered significant progress. The paid-up share capital of District Cooperative Banks increased from Rs. 78.15 lakh in 1960-61 to Rs. 9135.54 lakh in 2002-03; Reserves from Rs. 15.4 lakh to Rs. 4100.55 lakh, deposits and borrowings from Rs. 451.34 lakh to Rs. 617011.34 lakh, working capital from Rs. 544.90 lakh to Rs. 524496.69 lakh and loans and advances from Rs. 359.32 lakh to Rs. 369753.45 lakh during the same period.

The efficiency of the cooperative credit movement ultimately rests with the performance of the primary agricultural credit societies (PACS) functioning at the grassroots level. Now with its 1628 PACS covering all the panchayats of the state, the movement has built up an elaborate organisational network all over the state. The Primary Agricultural Credit Societies have emerged as significant democratic institutions at the grassroots level with a total membership of 2.26 crore. During the period from 1960-61 to 2002-03 the share capital of PACS increased by 290 times, deposit by 3117 times and loans and advances by 1323 times. Loans and advances issued by PACS in 1960-61 had been to the tune of Rs. 508.86 lakhs. However, the corresponding figure was Rs. 875051 lakh in 2002-03. Out of the total PACS, 52 per cent had made profits in 1960-61. But the proportion of profit-making societies declined to 46 per cent in 2002-03.

The long-term credit needs of the farmers are now met by Cooperative Agriculture and Rural Development Banks. The Kerala Central Land Mortgage Bank was established in 1956. The Bank raises its working funds through debentures, refinance from NABARD, deposits etc. The developmental activities supported by the Banks include loans for minor irrigation, farm mechanisation, land development, soil conservation, rural housing, etc. The total amount of loans issued by Kerala State Cooperative Agriculture and Rural Development Bank in 1960-61 was Rs. 19.86 lakh and by the Primary Agriculture and Rural Development Banks, Rs. 68.20 lakhs. The loans issued by Kerala State Cooperative Agriculture and Rural Development Bank have increased to Rs. 29331 lakh in 2002-03 registering a growth of 1477 times.

Non-credit societies such as marketing, consumer, housing, literary, transport, and weavers societies were also organised in Kerala as per provisions of the Cooperative Societies Act. Cooperative marketing in Kerala is a two-tier structure with Marketing Federation at the apex level and Primary Marketing Societies at the base level. The Federation which had been originally registered as Malabar Cooperative Wholesale Store and latter converted to Malabar District Cooperative Supply and Marketing Society, became the apex body of the Marketing Structure in 1960. The main functions of the Federation are distribution of fertilisers, procurement of copra, spices, cashew etc. In the cooperative marketing sector there are commodity marketing societies and their federations such as Kerala State Cooperative Rubber Marketing Federation, Kerafed, Coirfed and Milma.

The organisational set up under the consumer cooperative segment consists of the Kerala State Cooperative Consumer Federation at the state level with District Wholesale Stores and Primary Consumer Stores at lower levels. The Kerala State Cooperative Consumer Federation is the apex institution of consumer cooperatives. Its main objective is to procure and distribute consumer goods at reasonable prices through District Wholesale Stores, Department Stores named *Triveni* and primary stores. The total sales turnover of the Federation which had been Rs. 1474 lakh in 1980-81 increased to Rs. 30555 lakh in 2002-03.

The overall aim of consumer cooperatives is to supply goods and services for the welfare of the people. In order to achieve this objective, consumers have to be mobilised for strong participation in consumer cooperatives; and management of consumer business operations have to be strengthened with a view to profitability, viability of operations and integration of consumers with producers. Normally people organise consumer cooperatives to ensure steady supply of essential commodities and to ensure the quality of goods required at competitive prices and consumer protection to the extent possible.

Consumer Cooperatives are yet to take deep roots in Kerala. They are faced with several operational problems mainly in the field of procurement and supply, pricing and promotion of sales and general management. The commodity coverage of the stores is low reportedly due to non-availability of cash and credit facilities at required times, excessive expenses incurred in terms of administrative overheads, non-availability of a purchasing decision-making system and of methods of ascertaining consumer preferences, poor maintenance of stocks and accounts and lack of proper training of employees and of employee involvement. Factors like poor finance, poor service conditions, lack of commitment on the part of members and employees and of co-ordination among the cooperatives, competition from private traders and absence of dynamic policies have contributed to a situation of under-performance of consumer cooperatives.

Housing is an important activity supported by the cooperative sector. There are about twenty public agencies supporting housing schemes in the state. The major agencies are the Kerala State Housing Board, Rural Development Department, Kerala state Cooperative Housing Federation, Kerala State Cooperative Agricultural and Rural Development Bank and Nationalised banks. The Kerala State Cooperative Housing Federation at the apex level has 207 primary housing societies at its base. The Federation raises funds for lending by way of share capital from member societies and from Government and in the form of borrowings from institutions like LIC, HDFC, HUDCO and NHB. During 2003-04, the Federation received a total amount of Rs.100 lakh from the State Government. LIC and NHB gave out as loans an amount of Rs. 41.30 crore for the construction of 7562 house buildings. Since its inception in 1970 the Federation has advanced Rs. 766.85 crore for the construction of 144955 house buildings till the end of 2002-03.

Cooperatives have been organised with particular focus on the welfare of the weaker sections of society. There are 482 Scheduled Castes and 92 Scheduled Tribes Societies functioning under the apex body. The Kerala State Federation of Scheduled Caste and Scheduled Tribes Development Cooperative Limited undertakes the dispensation of credit, and the marketing of agricultural inputs. The Federation runs an *Ayurvedic* medicine manufacturing unit and a petrol pump. It also collects and markets minor forest produce from member societies. The federation provides employment to furniture-making member societies by distributing to them cane and seed. With the financial support of NCDS, the Federation has established a honey-processing unit.

The Cooperative movement has made a good beginning in the employment front also. Cooperative hospitals, cooperative dispensaries, cooperative transport societies, cooperative educational societies, autorickshaw/

taxi drivers cooperatives, labour contract societies, women cooperative societies, tailors' cooperative societies, washermen cooperative societies, and *chethuthozhilali* cooperative societies are some of the societies organised for the purpose of employment generation.

The Cooperative movement has been in existence in the state for nearly 100 years. The movement was introduced with high hopes and lofty expectations. It was expected to provide a lasting solution to the problems of our economy. All committees and commissions appointed for looking into the subject have reiterated their abiding faith in the efficacy of the movement as an enduring solution to the ills of our rural economy in general and of agricultural credit in particular.

The first cooperative law entitled "The Co-operative Credit Societies Act" heralded the beginning of formal cooperatives in the country. Under Article 246 of the Constitution of India, cooperation is recognised as a state subject. Various attempts in different forms have been made to make the Cooperative Societies member-driven, vibrant and autonomous institutions. But much remains to be done in this direction and the process of legal reforms must continue so that institutions could become fully democratic, independent and responsive business enterprises capable of facing the challenges of globalisation and fulfilling the aspirations of their members.

References

Ahluwalia, M.S. (1996). "New Economic Policy and Agriculture, Some Reflections", *Indian Journal of Agricultural Economics*, Vol. 51(3): 410-426, July-Sept.

Ahuja, V., P.S. George *et al.*, (2000). *Agricultural Services and the Poor: Case of Livestock Health and Breeding Services in India*. IIM-Ahmedabad, World Bank and Swiss Agency for Dev. Cooperation.

Bhalla, G.S. (1995). "Globalisation and Agricultural Policy in India", *Indian Journal of Agricultural Economics*, January-March, pp.7-26.

George, P.S. (1979). "The Coconut Economy of Kerala", in M.A. Oommen (ed.), *Kerala Economy Since Independence*. Oxford and IBH Publishing Company. pp.48-61.

———. (1986). "Emerging Trends in Size Distribution of Operational Holdings in Kerala", *Economic and Political Weekly*, Feb., pp.198-200.

George, P.S. and C. Mukherjee (1986). "A Disaggregate Analysis of Growth, Performance of Rice in Kerala", *Indian Journal of Agricultural Economics*, XLI(1): 1-16, Jan-March.

George, P.S. and K.N. Nair (1990). *Livestock Economy of Kerala*. Trivandrum: Centre for Development Studies.

George, P.S. *et al.* (1989). *Policy Options for Cattle Development in Kerala, India and Intercorporation*. Bern, Switzerland: Swiss Development Cooperation

George, P.S., K.N. Nair and K. Pushpangadan (1989). *Pepper Economy of Kerala*. Oxford & IBH Publications Co., Ltd.

Gopinath & Sundaresan (1994). *Cropping Pattern Changes and Employment Effects in Selected Districts of Kerala*. Trivandrum: Centre for Management Development

George T., V. Haridasan and B. Sreekumar (1988). "Role of Government and Structural Change in Rubber Plantations in India", *Economic and Political Weekly*, Vol. 23(48): M 158-166.

Government of Kerala (various years). *Statistics for Planning* (various issues). Department of Economics and Statistics.

———. (various years). *Economic Review* (various issues). State Planning Board.

———. (2004). *Report of the Integrated Sample Survey for Estimation of Production of Milk, Meat and Egg*. Directorate of Animal Husbandry.

Gulati, A. and A. Sharma (1997). "Freeing Trade in Agriculture: Implications for Resource Use Efficiency and Cropping Pattern Changes", *Economic and Political Weekly*, October 19, pp.2931-2942.

Harilal, K.N. and K.J. Joseph (1998). "India Sri Lanka Free Trade", *Economic and Political Weekly*, Vol.4(13): 750.

Jacob, Mathew (1978). "Trends and Fluctuations in Price of Coconut and Coconut Oil", Unpublished M.Phil Dissertation. New Delhi: JNU.

Jeromi, P.D. and A. Ramanathan (1993). "World Pepper Market and India: Analysis of Trend and Instability", *Indian Journal of Agricultural Economics*, 48(1): 89-97.

Jeemol, Unni (1983). "An Analysis of Changes in Cropping Pattern in Kerala with Particular Reference to the Substitution of Coconut for Rice", *M.Phil Dissertation*. New Delhi: JNU.

Joseph, T., and T. George (2002). *WTO and Natural Rubber Sector in India*. Kottayam: Economic Research Division, Rubber Research Institute of India.

Kannan, K.P. and K. Pushpangadan (1988). "Agricultural Stagnation in Kerala: An Analysis of Crops, Seasons and Regions", *Working Paper* 238. Trivandrum: Centre for Development Studies.

Kerala Statistical Institute (1984). *Conversion of Paddy Land in Kerala*. Thiruvananthapuram.

Mani, Sunil (1992). "Government Interventions in Commercial Crop Development, Indian Natural Rubber Industry", *Economic and Political Weekly*, June 27, pp.A83-92.

Nair, K.N., and S. Chattopadhyaya (2005). *Water Resources of Kerala: Issues and Case Studies*. Trivandrum: Centre for Development Studies.

Nair, K.N., and Vineeta Menon (2004). *Reforming Agriculture in a Globalising World: The Road Ahead for Kerala*. Trivandrum: Centre for Development Studies.

Narayana, D. *et al.*, (1994). *Coconut Development in Kerala*. Trivandrum: Centre for Development Studies .

Narayana, D. (2002). "Dairying in Malabar, A Venture of the Landowning Based on Women's Work", *Indian Journal of Agricultural Economics*, Vol. 57(4): 698-713.

Panikar, P.G.K. (1984). "Recent Trends in the Area and Production of Rice in Kerala", *Working Paper* 116. Trivandrum: Centre for Development Studies.

Rubber Board (2004). *Indian Rubber Statistics*, Volume 27. Kottayam.

Santhakumar, V. (2004). *Development of Livestock Sector in Kerala: Status and Constraints Against Future Growth*. Trivandrum: Centre for Development Studies.

Sivanandan, P.K. (1980). "Kerala's Agricultural Performance: Differential Trends and Determinants of Growth", *M.Phil Dissertation*. New Delhi: JNU.

Uma Devi, S. (1984). "Impact of Plantations on Kerala Economy with Special Reference to Rubber, Some Historical and Qualitative Aspects", *Ph.D Dissertation*. University of Kerala.

Varma, Poornima (2002). "Agriculture under Economic Liberalisation: A Case Study of Rubber and Coconut Prices in Kerala", Unpublished M.Phil Dissertation. New Delhi: JNU.

Veeraputhran, A. (1999). "Trends and Fluctuations in Indian Natural Rubber Prices, 1968-67 to 1997-98", Unpublished M.Phil Dissertation. New Delhi: JNU.

Viswanathan, P.K. (2002). "Irrigation and Water Development in Kerala: An Analysis of Missed Linkages", *Review of Development and Change*, Vol. 7(2): 279-312.

Chapter 6

Industrial Development

Introduction

The Kerala economy is at present in a state of industrial stagnation, with poor growth of industrial employment, low industrial contribution to per capita income and living standards, and paltry support to the revenues and the developmental resources of the state.

The Gulf boom, which provided employment to Keralites since the early 1970s has subsided. Not only has emigration slowed down; return migrants too find it difficult to find employment in Kerala. In addition, entrepreneurs are hesitant to invest in industrial establishments due to problems of labour militancy, unfavourable political attitudes and inadequate infrastructure facilities.

There is an increasing realisation in recent years that the industrialisation process should be stimulated in the state to solve the problems of slow growth and worsening unemployment.[1] The government's inability to support developmental activities actively due to fiscal constraints has led to a change in outlook towards private investment.

The government's realisation of the urgent need to rejuvenate Kerala's industrial economy manifested itself in recent efforts in the organisation of Global Investor Meet (GIM). Obviously, a lot more concerted effort is required to revive the industrial fortunes of Kerala.

Industrial Needs

The industrial need of the state is assessed with reference to the following:

Per Capita Industrial State Domestic Product (ISDP) of leading industrialised states of India, *viz.*, Andhra Pradesh, Gujarat, Karnataka, Maharashtra, Punjab and Tamil Nadu along with that of India as a whole; ISDP levels to be achieved by Kerala to eliminate unemployment backlogs in three-four years; and industrial production requirements of Kerala corresponding to the state's future projected power consumption needs.

Reaching Per Capita ISDP Levels of Leading Indian States

In Table 6.1, alternative ISDP targets for 2001-02 through 2010-11 are estimated for Kerala using per capita ISDPs of the six target states and population of Kerala projected for those years based on Kerala population data given in Census 2001. An explanation of the method used for making the estimates and a detailed analysis of the results of Table 6.1 are given in Appendix A-6.1.

Given the actual ISDP of Kerala in 2000-01, in order to catch up with Maharashtra by 2010-11, the ISDP of Kerala has to grow at a rate of 14 per cent per annum; to be on par with Tamil Nadu it has to grow at 12.8 per cent per annum, to achieve the same status as Punjab, it has to grow at a rate of 10.5 per cent annually, and to match the growth rate of Karnataka, to reach the national average of 6 per cent, ISDP of Kerala has to grow at a rate of 8.5 per cent annually to 2010-2011.

Removal of Unemployment Backlog

In Table 6.2, ISDP growth targets that help remove the unemployment backlog of Kerala are estimated till 2010-11. The unemployment rate has been taken as 8.6 per cent, which was the actual rate reported in the state in 1999-2000. The rate of unemployment is considered to have been continuing in the years

1. This point was echoed in earlier studies as well (e.g., in Subramanian, K.K. (1990). "Development Paradox in Kerala: Analysis of Industrial Stagnation", *Economic and Political Weekly*, September 15, pp.2053-8).

TABLE 6.1

Industrial SDP Projections for Kerala 2001-02 to 2010-11
(Based on Per Capita Industrial SDP of Leading States and Kerala Population in 2001)

Year	*Industrial SDP (ISDP) (Per Capita = Rs. 2,127) Kerala*		*Per Capita Industrial SDP = Rs. 4,585 Gujarat*		*Per Capita Industrial SDP = Rs. 4,929 Maharashtra*		*Per Capita Industrial SDP = Rs. 4,030 Tamil Nadu*	
	At Existing Growth Rate#	*At 6% Growth Rate*	*Required ISDP for Kerala@*	*Matching ISDP: At 6% Growth**	*Required ISDP for Kerala@*	*Matching ISDP: At 6% Growth**	*Required ISDP for Kerala@*	*Matching ISDP: At 6% Growth**
(1)	(2)	(3)	(4)	(5)	(6)	(7)	(8)	(9)
2000-01	6712	6712	6712	14467^	6712	15552^	6712	12715^
2001-02	6994	7115	7597	15165	7652	16300	7572	13457
2002-03	7288	7542	8600	15896	8723	17085	8542	14241
2003-04	7594	7995	9734	16663	9944	17907	9637	15072
2004-05	7913	8475	11018	17467	11336	18768	10872	15951
2005-06	8246	8984	12471	18309	12923	19671	12265	16881
2006-07	8593	9523	14116	19192	14732	20618	13837	17866
2007-08	8954	10094	15978	20118	16795	21610	15610	18908
2008-09	9330	10700	18086	21089	19146	22650	17610	20011
2009-10	9722	11342	20472	22106	21826	23740	19867	21178
2010-11	10131	12023	23172	23172	24882	24882	22413	22413
Growth Rate (%)$	4.2	6.0	13.2	4.8	14.0	4.8	12.8	5.8

Year	*Per Capita Industrial SDP = Rs. 3,523 Punjab*		*Per Capita Industrial SDP (ISDP) = Rs. 2,779 Karnataka*		*Per Capita Industrial SDP (ISDP) = Rs. 2,125 Andhra Pradesh*		*Per Capita Industrial SDP (ISDP) = Rs. 2,963 India*	
	Required ISDP for Kerala@	*Matching ISDP: At 6% Growth**	*Required ISDP for Kerala@*	*Matching ISDP: At 6% Growth**	*Required ISDP for Kerala@*	*Matching ISDP: At 6% Growth**	*Required ISDP for Kerala@*	*Matching ISDP: At 6% Growth**
(1)	(10)	(11)	(12)	(13)	(14)	(15)	(16)	(17)
2000-01	6712	11116^	6712	8768^	6712	6705^	6712	9349^
2001-02	7416	11678	7258	9231	7086	7079	7280	9809
2002-03	8195	12269	7848	9718	7480	7474	7896	10293
2003-04	9055	12889	8485	10231	7897	7891	8564	10800
2004-05	10005	13541	9175	10771	8337	8331	9288	11332
2005-06	11055	14226	9921	11339	8801	8796	10074	11890
2006-07	12215	14946	10727	11937	9291	9287	10927	12475
2007-08	13497	15702	11599	12567	9808	9805	11851	13090
2008-09	14913	16496	12542	13231	10355	10352	12854	13735
2009-10	16478	17330	13562	13929	10931	10930	13941	14411
2010-11	18207	18207	14664	14664	11540	11540	15121	15121
Growth Rate (%)$	10.5	5.1	8.1	5.3	5.6	5.6	8.5	4.9

Note: All estimates are based on Kerala's population in 2001 (3.1839 crore) extrapolated for subsequent years using annual population growth of 1991-2001 (0.9%). All per capita values relate to 2000-01. All values are in 1993-94 prices.

Existing growth rate is the trend growth rate during 1993-94-2000-01.

@ For 2000-01, the actual ISDP; for other years, (value of each preceding year) × (1 + CAGR implied between Required ISDP 2000-01 and Matching ISDP 2010-11).

* For 2000-01, (respective state's per capita ISDP) × (population of Kerala); for other years, (value of each preceding year) × (1 + assumed growth rate of 0.06) adjusted for population growth differentials between Kerala and the target state. While trying to achieve a comparable per capita ISDP, the burden of the assumed 6% growth rate of ISDP of respective states on Kerala is lower due to its favourable population growth differential over respective states.

$ CAGR (%) implied between ISDP 2000-01 and ISDP 2010-11.

^ Ideal ISDP for 2000-01 or ISDP Target for Kerala if ISDP matching the target state's has to be reached by Kerala in the first year (2000-01) itself.

Source: Population data are based on Census 2001; ISDP data are based on EPW Research Foundation: *Domestic Product of States of India 1960-61 to 2000-01*.

TABLE 6.2

Projection of Industrial SDP (ISDP) Growth for Removal of Unemployment Backlog

Year	*ISDP Target from 2001-02 $ #*	*Unemp. Backlog + Growth of Workforce*[1]	*Column (3) as % of Workforce*	*Unemp. Removal Target %*	*Extra ISDP (coefficient 0.000138)**	*Extra ISDP as % of Previous Year ISDP*	*Additional Normal Growth % (trend*[2]*)*	*Desirable Higher Growth (%)*	*Extra + Additional Normal ISDP Growth %*	*Extra + Desirable Higher ISDP Growth %*
(1)	(2)	(3)	(4)	(5)	(6)	(7)	(8)	(9)	(10)	(11)
2000-01	6712	8.74	8.6	0	0	0	4.2	6	4.2	6
2001-02	6994	8.85	8.6	0	0	0	4.2	6	4.2	6
2002-03	7288	8.96	8.6	0	0	0	4.2	6	4.2	6
2003-04	7594	9.17	8.6	0	0	0	4.2	6	4.2	6
2004-05	8202	10.44	9.45	2	144	1.9	4.2	6	6.1	7.9
				4	289	3.81	4.2	6	8.01	9.81
	(4% target of unemp. removal assumed)			6	433	5.7	4.2	6	9.9	11.7
				8	578	7.61	4.2	6	11.81	13.61
				9.45	682	8.98	4.2	6	13.18	14.98
2005-06	8835	7.34	6.34	4	289	3.52	4.2	6	7.72	9.52
2006-07	9517	4.09	3.33	3.33	240	2.72	4.2	5	6.92	7.72
2007-08	10265	1.5	1.14	1.14	82	0.86	4.2	7	5.06	7.86
2008-09	11063	1.57	1.1	1.1	79	0.77	4.2	7	4.97	7.77
2009-10	11916	1.71	1.09	1.09	79	0.71	4.2	7	4.91	7.71
2010-11	12828	1.87	1.07	1.07	77	0.65	4.2	7	4.85	7.65

Notes: Compounded growth rate of ISDP implied during 2001-02 to 2010-11 is about 6.69% per annum.

$ 2001-02 to 2003-04, growth rate at trend annual rate of 4.2% of 1993-94-2000-01; # 2004-05 onwards, growth rate at extra+additional normal or extra+desirable higher rates as accepted and indicated in bold figures in one of the last two columns (Analysis is useful from year 2004-05 only since other years have already passed) (Unemployment removal target)/(coefficient), where 'coefficient' is 2000-01 ratio of (employment/ISDP).

1. Number in lakhs.
2. Annual trend rate of growth of ISDP during 1993-94 - 2000-01.

Limitation: Underlying employment-ISDP ratio (0.000138) is an average and may be inappropriate since the incremental employment-ISDP ratio may be different from this average ratio.

Source: Population & labour force data are based on Census 2001; unemployment figure is taken from *Economic Review 2002*, Kerala; ISDP data are based on EPW Research Foundation: *Domestic Product of States of India 1960-61 to 2000-01*.

2000-01 to 2003-04. Our ISDP projection starts with the year 2004-05. The rate of growth of labour force assumed for making the estimate is the same as the annual growth rate of workforce of Kerala during 1991-2001 reported in Census 2001. This rate is assumed to continue during 2004-05–2010-11 as well, although it might imply a slight overestimation.

As per the projection method implied in Table 6.2, Kerala's ISDP needs to grow close to 7-8 per cent per annum during 2004-05–2006-07 to remove the unemployment backlog by 2006-07, while it should grow after 2006-07 annually at a minimum of 5 per cent to preempt creation of new unemployment backlog and preferably at 7-8 per cent to ensure matching of ISDP growth rates of leading Indian states.

Matching Future Power Consumption Needs

In Table 6.3, ISDP levels corresponding to the projected power consumption needs of Kerala during 2001-02–2010-11 are estimated based on the ISDP-Power Consumption Coefficient of Kerala for 2000-01. We have obtained alternative ISDP projections for 2001-2002–2010-11 with and without the power supply constraints impacting power consumption.

According to Table 6.3, the power consumption demand will grow in Kerala during 2001-02–2010-11 at a rate of 7.3 per cent per annum under power supply constraints and 10.5 per cent per annum under no power supply constraints. Given the actual ISDP of Kerala of Rs. 6,712 crore during 2000-01, the actual ISDP growth for Kerala during 2001-02–2010-11 that matches the power consumption projection for those years is 11.7 per cent and 22.1 per cent respectively under the two assumptions. The corresponding per capita ISDP growth requirement will be of 6.3 per cent and 9.5 per cent respectively per annum during 2001-

TABLE 6.3

Industrial SDP Projections for Kerala 2001-02 to 2010-11
(Based on Expected Power Demand$ of Kerala & Kerala Industrial SDP in 2000-01)

Year	*Kerala Actual Power Consumption in 2000-01: 10,117 MU**		*Kerala Industrial SDP in 2000-01: Rs. 6,712 Crore*		*Kerala Industrial SDP–Power Ratio 2000-01: 6.6344*	
	Power Demand: Constrained#	*Power Demand: Unconstrained#*	*ISDP: Constrained Estimate*	*ISDP: Unconstrained Estimate*	*PC ISDP[1]: Constrained Estimate*	*PC ISDP[1]: Unconstrained Estimate*
2000-01	15213	27422	10093	18193	3199	5766
2001-02	16316	30306	10825	20106	3400	6315
2002-03	17499	33493	11610	22221	3614	6917
2003-04	18768	37016	12451	24558	3841	7577
2004-05	20129	40909	13354	27141	4083	8299
2005-06	21589	45211	14323	29995	4341	9090
2006-07	23154	49966	15361	33149	4614	9956
2007-08	24833	55221	16475	36636	4904	10905
2008-09	26633	61029	17669	40489	5213	11945
2009-10	28565	67447	18951	44747	5541	13083
2010-11	30676	74551	20352	49460	5897	14331
Growth Rate (%)@	7.3	10.5	7.3(11.7)**	10.5(22.1)**	6.3	9.5

Notes: $ Power demand projections have been taken from *Plight of the Power Sector in India*, Kannan, K.P & N.V Pillai, CDS Trivandrum, May 2002, P. 147.

* Figure for 2000-01 was extrapolated from the actual data for the preceding years of 1990s.

\# Power demand projections in the source mentioned above are available under two categories, *viz.*, constrained and unconstrained.

@ Compounded annual growth rates implied between the estimates for 2000-01 & 2010-11.

** These figures are the growth rates per annum required till 2010-11 under the two conditions, given that the actual ISDP of Kerala during 2000-01 was Rs. 6,712 crores.

1 Actual per capita ISDP of Kerala in 2000-01 was Rs. 2,127.

2002–2010-11. Thus, the future power consumption needs projected for Kerala during 2000-01–2010-11 imply a huge ISDP growth requirement on Kerala economy.

Alternative Projections: A Summary

A comparison of the minimum and the maximum growth targets of Kerala under the three methods of estimation, as shown in Table 6.4, reveal that the ISDP of Kerala has to grow during 2001-02–2010-11 within a range of 6.69-11.7 per cent at the minimum and 14.0-22.1 per cent at the maximum. In comparison with such requirements, how has been Kerala's performance in the past? In the next section, we review Kerala's industrial performance and evaluate its current position in the industrial scenario of India.

TABLE 6.4

ISDP Growth Projections Compared Across Methods

	Method 1	*Method 2*	*Method 3*	*Overall*
Minimum	8.1$	6.69*	11.7#	6.69@1
Maximum	14.0	8.01	22.1#	8.01@

Notes: $ Excluding AP with lower per capita ISDP than Kerala.

* Compounded annual growth rate 2001-02 - 2010-11.

\# With respect to actual ISDP of Kerala in 2000-01.

@[1] Minimum of minimum (Minimin).

@ Minimum of maximum (Minimax).

The Current Status and the Gap

Industrial development of Kerala evinces several characteristics that testify its industrial weaknesses and gaps. Kerala's per capita income position in relation to that of a few leading Indian states is shown in Table 6.5(A). Indeed, Kerala had some edge over states like Tamil Nadu and Andhra Pradesh in the earlier years; but it lost this edge against Tamil Nadu after 1980-81, notwithstanding some gains in current price terms (Table 6.5(B)). This is despite Kerala's slightly better performance relative to national average during 1992-93-2000-01 in the annual growth rate of per capita income (Table 6.6(A) and 6.6(B)). Kerala's industrial problems are certain to have contributed to its low economic profile among the leading states.

A progressive economy is historically found to go through three stages of development: first, dominance

TABLE 6.5(A)

Per Capita SDP at Constant Price Over Different States

Year	*Andhra Pradesh*	*Gujarat*	*Karnataka*	*Kerala*	*Maharashtra*	*Punjab*	*Tamil Nadu*	*India*
1960-61		362	296	259	409	366	334	350
1970-71	585	829	641	594	783	1070	581	720
1980-81	1380	1940	1520	1508	2435	2674	1498	1741
1990-91	2060	2641	2039	1815	3483	3730	2237	2385
2000-01	9982	12975	11910	10627	15172	15390	12779	10306

Note: Base Year: 1960-61 at 1960-61 base
1970-71 at 1970-71 base
1980-81 & 1990-91 at 1981 base
2000-01 & 2003-04 at 1993-94 base

Source: Domestic Products of States of India, 1960-61 to 2000-01, EPW Research Foundation, 2003.

TABLE 6.5(B)

Per Capita SDP at Current Prices Over Different States

Year	*Andhra Pradesh*	*Gujarat*	*Karnataka*	*Kerala*	*Maharashtra*	*Punjab*	*Tamil Nadu*	*India*
1980-81	1467	2089	1644	1835	2492	2629	1666	1741
1990-91	4816	6343	4975	5110	7612	8177	5541	5365
2000-01	16708	18560	17806	19951	21871	24283	20361	16555
2002-03	18661	22047	18521	21853	26386	25855	21433	20989

Note: Base year: 1993-94.

Source: Economic Survey, different years.

TABLE 6.6(A)

Annual Growth Rates (%): Kerala & India

Indicator	*1980- 81–1990-91*		*1992-93–2000-01*	
	Kerala	*India*	*Kerala*	*India*
Domestic Product	3.2	5.8	6.3	6.3
Per Capita Income	1.8	3.4	4.9	4.4

Source: Jeromi, P.D. (2003). "Banking on Development", *Frontline*, Volume 20(18), August 30-September 12.

TABLE 6.6(B)

Annual Growth Rates (%): Kerala & India

Year	*Domestic Product*		*Per Capita Income*	
	Kerala	*India*	*Kerala*	*India*
2000-01	2.6	4.2	3.3	2.3
2002-03	7.3*	4.2*	6.3*	2.4*
2003-04	7.3@	9.0@	6.3@	7.1@

Note: * Provisional @ Quick Estimates.

Source: Based on *Economic Review 2004* (Kerala). *Economic Survey 2004-2005* (India)

of primary sector with low proportions of contribution from secondary and tertiary sectors; second, dominance of secondary sector with declining role of primary sector and rising contribution of tertiary sector; and third, dominance of tertiary sector with low share of primary sector but high significance of secondary sector. In Kerala, the primary sector share declined from over 55 per cent in 1960-61 to just below 25 per cent in 2000-2001. This is clear from Table 6.7(A) (For data on sectoral composition of GDP of India, see Table 6.7(B).

The tertiary sector contribution increased from about 29 per cent to over 55 per cent during this period. The

TABLE 6.7(A)

Percentage Sectoral Shares in Kerala SDP at Constant Prices

Period	*Industry*	*Agriculture*	*Services*	*Total*
1960-61	15.59	55.63	28.78	100
1970-71	20.42	45.57	34.01	100
1980-81	20.67	40.17	39.16	100
1990-91	26.61	32.65	40.74	100
2000-01	19.79	24.62	55.59	100
2003-04*	19.31	17.09	64.60	100

Note: * Quick Estimates

Source: Economic Review—Various issues, *Domestic Products of States of India, 1960-61 to 2000-01*, EPW Research Foundation, 2003.

TABLE 6.7(B)

GDP Growth Range: India (1993-94 prices)

Period	*India GDP Growth Range (%)*			
	Overall	*Primary*	*Secondary*	*Tertiary (3 sub-sectors)*
1950-52–1960-61	(-)1.2-7.6	(-)4.2-9.9	(-)1.0-10.5	1.4-8.5
1960-61–1970-71	(-)3.7-8.1	(-)10.2-14.3	1.8-10.6	1.8-7.1
1970-71–1980-81	(-)5.2-9.0	(-)12.2-12.9	(-)3.4-9.3	(-)0.4-9.0
1980-81–1990-91	3.1-10.5	(-)1.0-15.4	2.9-10.7	1.9-12.6
1990-91–2000-01	1.3-7.8	(-)1.5-8.8	(-)1.0-12.3	2.5-13.3
2000-01–2003-04	4.4-8.5	(-)5.6-9.3	3.7-7.0	3.5-11.8

Note: Base: 1993-94 Prices.

Source: Compiled from *Economic Survey 2004-05*.

TABLE 6.8

Annual Growth of Broad Economic Sectors

Sector	*1980-81–1990-91*	*1992-93–2000-01*	*2001-02–2003-04**
Primary	2.3%	2.3%	-0.25%
Secondary	3.3%	7.6%	3.4%
Tertiary	4.3%	8.3%	8.7%

Note: * Simple annual average, based on *Economic Review 2004*.

Source: As in Table 6.6 (A).

share of the secondary sector moved from about 16 per cent in 1960-61 to about 27 per cent in 1990-91, and then declined to below 20 per cent during the 2000s. This implies not only that the secondary sector never rose to its expected prominence, as has been the case with the national economy, but also that it declined. The fact that the secondary sector (including construction) grew at an annual average rate of 7.6 per cent during 1992-93–2000-01 as compared to 3.3 per cent during 1980-81–1990-91 did not help Kerala in reversing the decline in the share of the secondary sector in the SDP (see Table 6.8); in fact the growth rate came down after 2000-01 (to just 3.4 per cent during 2001-02–2003-04). Thus, Kerala has missed opportunities to create a strong industrial production base on which its services economy could have prospered.

SDP Growth

The SDP of Kerala has never grown impressively since the state formation; see Table 6.9. While during the 1960s the average compounded growth per annum was comparable to the national NDP growth, Kerala's annual compounded SDP growth since the 1970s always lagged behind the annual NDP growth of India. Further, the compounded annual industrial SDP growth

TABLE 6.9

Growth Rate (%) of SDP at Constant Prices@ in Kerala

	Period	*All India NDP*	*Kerala SDP*	*Kerala SDP Industry$*	*India NDP Industry**
1.	1960-61 to 1970-71 (1960-61 base)	3.38	3.99	7.21	6.05
2.	1970-71 to 1980-81 (1970-71 base)	3.57	1.87	4.71	3.78
3.	1980-81 to 1990-91 (1990-91 base)	3.80	3.13	2.91	6.71
4.	1993-94 to 2000-01 (1993-94 base)	7.87	5.31	4.23	5.45
5.	2001-02–2003-04#	6.07	5.81	3.40	5.55

Note: @ Only data in constant prices show the real growth in output; current price data is misleading when inflation rates are not stable.

$ Excluding construction

* Average for the period.

\# Based on provisional/quick/advance estimates for 2002-03 & 2003-04.

Sources: *Economic Review* (various issues), *Domestic Products of States of India, 1960-61 to 2000-01*, EPW Research Foundation, 2003.

(excluding construction) of Kerala was never very impressive after the 1960s, not even during the much-hyped 1990s.

Industrial Profile

During the 1960-61–1980-81 period, the average annual industrial (secondary sector) growth rate of Kerala exceeded Kerala's SDP growth rate; see Table 6.9. After 1980-81, the pace of industrial growth slowed down and became a drag on Kerala's SDP growth. Similarly, in per capita industrial SDP, Kerala had fared better than certain leading Indian states mentioned in Table 6.10, till the early 1980s. The situation changed

TABLE 6.10

Per Capita Industrial SDP at Constant Prices Over Different States

Year	*Andhra Pradesh*	*Gujarat*	*Karnataka*	*Kerala*	*Maharashtra*	*Punjab*	*Tamil Nadu*
1960-61		93	44	39	108	57	59
1970-71	80	100	64	61	153	83	85
1980-81	229	528	315	327	255	494	502
1990-91	460	914	485	430	1217	294	740
2000-01	2125	4585	2779	2127	4929	3523	4030
2002-03	11188	13218	11104	13101	15819	15501	12850

Note: 1960-61 & 1970-71 at 1960-61 base; 1980-81 & 1990-91 at 1970–71 base;

2000-01 at 1993-94 base; 2002-03 deflated with WPI (1993-94 base) for India.

Source: *Domestic Products of States of India, 1960-61 to 2000-01*, EPW Research Foundation, 2003.

since then, and Kerala's per capita industrial SDP continued to lag behind that of most others in 2000-01, although the state's position became better than that of at least Andhra Pradesh and Tamil Nadu by 2002-03.

Some of the major states of India differed from Kerala in their level of industrial progress as well as in changes in their industrial profile over time; see Table 6.11. In 1960-61, Maharashtra and Gujarat were the most industrialised among the seven states in terms of the share of the secondary sector in SDP. Punjab, Kerala and Karnataka had comparable percentage shares of the secondary sector in their SDP in that year; Tamil Nadu's secondary sector share in that year was just a couple of percentage points higher than that of the other three. Andhra Pradesh had the lowest share for its secondary sector. Gujarat and Maharashtra continued to have higher industrial profile in the subsequent years too, and the other states also considerably improved their industrial profile over the decades. However, Kerala ended by 2000-01 with the lowest secondary sector share among the given states, with very little net increase in the share over 1960-61. Clearly, Kerala turned out to be the industrial laggard among the leading Indian states.

TABLE 6.11

Share of Secondary Sector in the SDP at Constant Prices

(per cent)

Year	*Andhra Pradesh*	*Gujarat*	*Karnataka*	*Kerala*	*Maharashtra*	*Punjab*	*Tamil Nadu*
1960-61	10.65	25.73	15.16	15.59	26.42	15.62	17.59
1970-71	14.02	30.24	23.64	20.42	34.4	15.35	26.66
1980-81	17.64	28.12	21.41	20.67	35.45	18.49	33.97
1990-91	23.05	34.28	23.74	26.61	34.00	22.42	33.63
2000-01	22.96	38.15	23.47	19.79	32.73	22.46	31.75

Source: *Domestic Products of States of India, 1960-61 to 2000-01*, EPW Research Foundation, 2003.

The figures of annual compounded growth rate of the secondary sector of the same seven states given in Table 6.12 strengthen the findings of Table 6.11. During the 1960s Kerala had the highest annual growth rate of the secondary sector among the seven states. In contrast, the annual growth rate of the secondary sector of Kerala became the lowest among them in the subsequent decades (except for Maharashtra during the 1993-94–2000-01 period).

A summary profile of the factory sector of Kerala during 1962-2001 is given in Table 6.13. The number of factories is found to have grown about eight times while output grew by hundreds of times during the period. The average size of the factory also grew significantly in respect of output, value added and productive capital. During the same period, value added and productive capital grew at closely similar rates but not at rates commensurate with the growth in the value of inputs and (gross) output particularly after 1974, thus, resulting in a decline in the capital intensity of output on the one hand and an unsatisfactory value added-productive capital ratio on the other. At the same time, the slower growth rate of employment during 1962-2001 signifies a substantial rise in both employee productivity and the amount of productive capital per employee.

Table 6.14 throws some light on the changing profile of Kerala in the factory sector in India as well as the growth of various parameters of Kerala's factory sector. While in terms of number of factories and employment in the factory sector, Kerala experienced a relatively satisfactory position in India in 1999-2000 as against 1980-81, the proportion of both capital invested and net value added accounted for, by Kerala in the factory sector in India declined after 1980-81. Significantly, the annual growth rate of the number of factories, capital invested and employment in the factory sector showed substantial increases during 1990-91–1999-2000 as compared to the period 1980-81–1990-91, while the opposite (substantial decline in growth rate) happened in the case of net value added in the factory sector of Kerala during the same period.

TABLE 6.12

Growth Rates of Secondary Sector (Constant Prices)

Period	*Andhra Pradesh*	*Gujarat*	*Karnataka*	*Kerala*	*Maharashtra*	*Punjab*	*Tamil Nadu*
1960-61 to 1970-71	4.88	3.61	5.96	7.21	5.14	6.21	5.79
1970-71 to 1980-81	5.5	5.87	6.5	4.71	5.62	6.46	5.52
1980-81 to 1993-94	8.09	7.89	6.87	2.91	6.35	7.24	4.78
1993-94 to 2000-01	6.64	6.18	7.94	4.23	3.02	7.04	5.06

Source: *Domestic Products of States of India, 1960-61 to 2000-01*, EPW Research Foundation, 2003.

TABLE 6.13

Factory Sector Kerala: Profile

	1962	*1974*	*1981*	*1991*	*2001*
Number of factories (No.*)	2500	6036	9500	13255	18621
Output (Rs. Lakhs)	9015	52215	209141	608154	2671055
Inputs (Rs. Lakhs)	6602	38848	164691	469693	2252893
Employees (No.**)	180000	258960	310000	365000	434918
Value Added (Rs. Lakhs)	2413	15184	39063	122207	355381
Productive Capital (Rs. Lakhs)	5670	52728	128638	316842	934725

Note: * 1962, 1981 (fig. approx) ** 1962, 1981, 1991 (fig. approx)

Index of Growth Over Time

Number of Factories	1	2.41	3.8	5.3	7.45
Output	1	5.79	23.2	67.46	296.29
Inputs	1	5.88	24.95	71.14	341.24
Employees	1	1.44	1.72	2.03	2.42
Value Added	1	6.29	16.19	50.65	147.28
Productive Capital	1	9.3	22.69	55.88	164.85

Size Ratios (Per Factory)

Output	3.6	8.7	22	45.9	143.4
Inputs	2.6	6.4	17.3	35.4	121
Employees	72	42.9	32.6	27.5	23.4
Value Added	1	2.5	4.1	9.2	19.1
Productive Capital	2.3	8.7	13.5	23.9	50.2
Productivity Ratios					
Output-Input	1.37	1.34	1.27	1.29	1.19
Output-Employees	5008	20163	67465	166618	614151
Output-Productive Capital	1.59	0.99	1.63	1.92	2.86
Value Added-Output	0.27	0.29	0.19	0.2	0.13
Value Added-Productive Capital	0.43	0.29	0.3	0.39	0.38
Value Added-Employees	1341	5863	12601	33481	81712
Productive Capital-Employees	3150	20361	41496	86806	214920

Source: Compiled from the various annual publications of the Economic Review of State Planning Board, Government of Kerala, Thiruvananthapuram.

To understand the problems of Kerala on the growth of net value added in the factory sector in recent years, a comparison across selected states of the southern peninsula and with India would be useful; see Table 6.15. During the period 1980-81–1990-91, Kerala's annual growth rate of net value added in the factory sector was higher than in Karnataka and the all-India average. However, by 1990-91–1999-2000 the annual growth rate of net value added in the factory sector of Kerala became the lowest of all of them.

TABLE 6.14

Relative Profile: Growth of Factory Sector of Kerala

Parameters	*Share in India (%)*			*Growth Rate (% p.a.)*	
	1980-81	*1990-91*	*1999-2000*	*1980-81–1990-91*	*1990-91–1999-2000*
No. of Factories	3.2	3.2	3.7	1.2	3.6
Capital Invested	2.9	2.0	1.8	3.1	5.3
Employment	3.6	3.3	3.7	1.2	3.6
Net Value Added	3.3	2.4	2.3	7.6	3.5

Source: As in Table 6.6 (A).

TABLE 6.15

Annual Growth of Net Value Added in Factory Sector: A Comparison

State	*Growth (% p.a.)*	
	1980-81 to 1989-90	*1990-91 to 1999-2000*
Kerala	**7.6**	**3.5**
Tamil Nadu	8.0	5.3
Karnataka	7.0	7.4
Andhra Pradesh	8.1	9.2
All India	6.8	6.6

Source: As in Table 6.6 (A).

Table 6.16 provides some broad idea of the structure of the factory sector of Kerala during 1980-81–1997-98. Among the seven major industrial groups listed in the Table, food and the related industries and chemicals and the related industries increased their shares between 1980-81 and 1990-91 while all other segments within the factory sector declined in relative importance. Between 1990-91 and 1997-98, the traditional industries of wood, leather and paper as well as the modern engineering industries of machinery and transport gained prominence while chemicals and related industries lost their share. The recent performance of engineering industries is definitely an improvement over their past performance which had come up for adverse comments (see Subrahmanian, 1990 *op. cit.*). It was noted that "...Kerala had a lopsided industrial structure with its base consisting of a set of resource-based industries; ...capital goods related (e.g. engineering) industries do not have a 'fair' share. ...The analysis of recent ASI data for 1985-86... did not show any significant change in the industrial base of Kerala."

A comparison of the annual compound growth rates of different segments of the factory sector across selected leading industrial states of India during 1979-

TABLE 6.16

The Industry Categories & Net Value Added (Rs. lakhs) in Kerala (1997-98)

	Category	*1980-81*	*% to Total*	*1990-91*	*% to Total*	*1997-98*	*% to Total*
20-22	Food & Related	4906	12.56	24145	17.66	75545	23.24
23-26	Textile & Related	4535	11.61	11482	8.4	26327	8.1
27-29	Wood, Leather & Paper	2968	7.6	5389	3.94	18382	5.65
30-31	Chemical & Related	10760	27.55	54134	39.59	102900	31.65
32-34	Minerals, Metals & Metal Products	2950	7.55	8268	6.5	20443	6.29
35-37	Machinery & Transport	4320	11.06	11872	8.68	33584	10.33
38	Others	8624	22.1	21444	15.68	47905	14.74
	Total ASI	39063	100.0	136734	100.0	325086	100.0

Source: Computed from ASI data.

1980–1997-98 reveals that in terms of factory sector growth, Kerala's performance had not been very impressive during the 1980s; it was relatively high between 1990-91 and 1997-98. Similarly, in all the industrial segments except chemicals and related, Kerala's growth rates had been the lowest among the seven states referred to above earlier, during 1979-80–1990-91.

The technical ratios of certain segments of the factory sector of Kerala in comparison with selected states and India, during 1980-81–1997-98 are shown in Table 6.18. The technical ratios selected are personnel cost ratios defined as emoluments to net value added (Emol/NVA), capital intensity defined as fixed capital to value of output (FC/OP) and fuel cost ratio defined as fuel cost to value of output (Fuel/OP). Between 1980-1981 and 1997-98, personnel cost decreased in two states (Andhra Pradesh and Punjab) and all-India in textile and related products, in two states (Maharashtra and Andhra Pradesh) and all-India in chemicals and related products, in one state (Andhra Pradesh) and all-India in machinery and transport segments, and in two states (Maharashtra and Karnataka) and all-India in the 'others' category. Against this, Kerala showed no single

TABLE 6.17

Category-wise Compounded Growth Rate for Industrial States of India (1979-1998)

(Per cent)

Category	*Maharashtra*	*Kerala*	*Tamil Nadu*	*Andhra Pradesh*	*Karnataka*	*Punjab*	*India*
20-22 (i)	5.64	5.3	5.69	6.53	6.21	7.49	6.24
(ii)	7.11	8.03	7.34	5.8	6.54	5.61	6.68
23-26 (i)	3.74	-1.62	6.33	8.22	4.63	6.52	4.61
(ii)	11.69	8.85	9.53	8.95	9.65	5.63	7.44
27-29 (i)	5.13	4.85	6.16	7.29	7.72	10.83	5.99
(ii)	7.84	8.03	6.45	4.34	6.23	8.23	6.73
30-31 (i)	5.67	5.05	5.28	7.9	5.97	8.47	6.35
(ii)	5.48	6.52	7.28	8.54	9.14	5.35	13.34
32-34 (i)	5.99	6.49	6.24	8.78	5.65	6.33	6.21
(ii)	6.8	6.17	7.05	9.7	7.49	5.86	6.52
35-37 (i)	5.93	5.38	6.33	6.51	6.82	7.07	6.29
(ii)	7.92	5.19	6.51	5.84	8.12	6.03	7.43
38-99 (i)	7.66	4.34	7.88	7.6	6.01	7.78	7.27
(ii)	8.4	7.14	8.15	9.89	10.17	7.13	9.44
Total (i)	5.72	4.99	6.11	7.11	6.19	7.21	6.17
(ii)	7.29	6.89	7.47	8.08	8.1	5.93	7.41

Notes: 20-22 Food & related; 23-26 Textile & related; 27-29 Wood, Leather & Paper; 30-31 Chemicals & Related; 32-34 Minerals, Metals & Metal Products; 35-37 Machinery & Transport; 38-99 Others

(i) 1979-80 to 1990-91 (ii) 1990-91 to 1997-98

Source: *Annual Survey of Industries, 1973-74–1997-98*, EPW Research Foundation, 2002, Data Series at Current Prices.

trend in any of the industrial segments over the three time points noted in the Table except in the 'others' category in which the personnel cost increased. In the same manner, in terms of other technical ratios too, no discernible trend is found among the states (except for the increasing capital intensity of Maharashtra in most of the sectors listed) or in respect of Kerala either in any particular industry segment or in the listed industry categories in general.

Table 6.18(A) mentions the ranks of Kerala among the Indian states in respect of selected technical ratios of factory sector. While in both capital intensity and wage rate Kerala is not among the leading Indian states, Kerala indeed suffers from high labour cost (rank 1 in 1997-98 on share of emoluments in net value added) and poor employee productivity (rank 15 in 1997-98 on net value added per employee).

Traditional Industries

Traditional industries include coir, cashew-processing, handloom, handicrafts, rubber-processing, tea and coffee-processing, textiles and tiles. These industries are large sources of industrial employment as well as SDP in Kerala. Over the years, however, the traditional industries have declined in importance due to a variety of reasons such as technological stagnation, high costs of production, labour problems and competition. While it is a natural process for emerging industries to replace the dominance of old ones, there still exists a lot of scope for strengthening the

TABLE 6.18

Technical Ratios for High Growth Industries Over Different States

	23-26 (Textile & Related)			*30-31 (Chemical & Related)*			*35-37 (Machinery & Transport)*			*38-99 (Others)*		
States	*1980-81*	*1990-91*	*1997-98*	*1980-81*	*1990-91*	*1997-98*	*1980-81*	*1990-91*	*1997-98*	*1980-81*	*1990-91*	*1997-98*
Maharashtra												
Emol/NVA	0.57	0.5	0.68	0.36	0.27	0.2	0.47	0.48	0.41	0.43	0.36	0.27
FC/OP	0.2	0.23	0.48	0.11	0.13	0.15	0.11	0.23	0.32	1.69	1.28	0.69
Fuel/OP	0.07	0.12	0.08	0.04	0.03	0.03	0.02	0.01	0.02	0.17	0.11	0.02
Kerala												
Emol/NVA	0.5	0.44	0.44	0.29	0.19	0.32	0.45	0.5	0.46	0.44	0.65	0.75
FC/OP	0.27	0.25	0.4	0.18	0.35	0.27	0.81	0.39	0.26	2.31	2.41	2.43
Fuel/OP	0.04	0.04	0.06	0.03	0.04	0.04	0.02	0.02	0.02	0.01	0.02	0.03
Tamil Nadu												
Emol/NVA	0.53	0.42	0.47	0.44	0.31	0.4	0.52	0.4	0.48	0.51	0.58	0.6
FC/OP	0.22	0.26	0.3	0.17	0.3	0.38	0.21	0.21	0.28	1.16	1.68	1.24
Fuel/OP	0.05	0.07	0.07	0.05	0.07	0.07	0.01	0.01	0.03	0.14	0.33	0.34
Andhra Pradesh												
Emol/NVA	0.53	0.5	0.42	0.39	0.33	0.31	0.62	0.43	0.38	0.44	0.37	0.93
FC/OP	0.19	0.27	0.29	0.47	0.35	0.71	0.34	0.23	0.24	3.05	2.71	1.42
Fuel/OP	0.04	0.08	0.04	0.05	0.04	0.04	0.02	0.1	0.11	0.2	0.11	0.11
Karnataka												
Emol/NVA	0.55	1.59	0.32	0.25	0.27	0.31	0.57	0.46	0.53	0.65	0.53	0.31
FC/OP	0.18	0.2	0.31	0.49	0.31	0.65	0.23	0.34	0.26	1.52	0.99	1.06
Fuel/OP	0.05	0.05	0.04	0.05	0.08	0.06	0.02	0.02	0.02	0.03	0.02	0.02
Punjab												
Emol/NVA	0.42	0.35	0.31	0.5	0.33	0.4	0.41	0.41	0.33	0.39	0.97	1.02
FC/OP	0.24	0.34	0.57	1.59	0.65	0.41	0.26	0.41	0.47	4.26	3.88	2.25
Fuel/OP	0.02	0.03	0.06	0.15	0.13	0.14	0.03	0.03	0.03	0.13	0.33	0.31
All-India												
Emol/NVA	0.6	0.49	0.47	0.38	0.27	0.24	0.77	0.41	0.38	0.52	0.49	0.34
FC/OP	0.42	0.47	0.6	0.58	0.55	0.65	0.8	0.48	0.74	2.68	2.07	1.13
Fuel/OP	0.06	0.07	0.07	0.05	0.07	0.06	0.02	0.02	0.01	0.19	0.19	0.11

Note: OP- Output; FC- Fixed Capital.

Source: Computed based on the Annual Survey of Industries (ASI) published by the Ministry of Statistics and Program Implementation, Government of India, New Delhi.

TABLE 6.18(A)

Ranks of Kerala among the Indian States

	1980-81	*1990-91*	*1997-98*
FC/EMP	12	15	16
Wage/Wor	12	14	14
Emol/NVA	10	4	1
FC/NVA	12	11	11
NVA/EMP	9	14	15

Source: As in Table 6.18.

contribution of traditional industries in Kerala through new value addition and new uses and new markets. The status of traditional industries is examined below based on some selected aspects.

Table 6.18(B) presents a few items of information on traditional industries of Kerala for selected years, for which data are accessible. The industries covered include handloom, powerloom, coir, cashew-processing, Khadi & Village Industries (KVI), sericulture and a few others.

The traditional industries in Kerala have not been doing well in recent years. Sectors like coir, cashew, handloom and KVI are facing decline, stagnation or very slow growth. The performance of the cooperative sector has been particularly poor in a large number of cases. New efforts and approaches are being adopted for revitalising the traditional industrial sectors; but the results have remained imperceptibly low.

Problems

The traditional industries of Kerala are plagued by a variety of problems. Cheaper and better substitute products are rapidly displacing Kerala's traditional industrial products such as tiles and handloom textiles. Changes in tastes and preferences of Keralites taking place with increase in incomes and social status are major market-related factors affecting the prospects of several traditional industries in Kerala. Labour unrest has been for long a major problem affecting the operations and growth of many traditional industrial units in Kerala particularly in the coir and the cashew-processing and tiles manufacturing sectors. The small size of the producing units has led to low productivity and waste of resources thereby affecting their ability to adapt to changing market conditions and come up with new products and lower costs. The smallness of producing units and other factors also contributed to poor technological capabilities and consequent technological stagnation in most of these industries. Some of the remedial measures undertaken in recent years include development of new value added products, new uses for traditional products, infusion of technology and new investments and institutional support through promotional agencies.

Public Sector

In an economy with considerable handicaps to private investment and commercial activities, the public sector has to play the leading role in industrial

TABLE 6.18(B)

Traditional Industries of Kerala: Selected Statistics

Segment	*Number*		*Value of Production (Cr.)*		*Employment(No.)*		*Exports(Cr.)*	
	1995-96	*2003-04*	*1995-96*	*2003-04*	*1995-96*	*2003-04*	*1995-96*	*2003-04*
Handloom Units		48824		272		473		
SSI Units	180091#	275649		14550		1237422		
Industrial Cooperatives	1974	1238						
Power Loom Units		3800		7.35				
Coir Cooperatives	552	687	28.6	47.1	256940	154113	207@	357@
Cashew Industry								1211
KVI Board			138.3	184.7	209000	172007		
Sericulture Units		3216		4042$				
Tea & Coffee Processing								1383
Textiles								615
Marine Products								1205
Spices								660

Notes: * Lakh mandays; $ Silk production in kg; # 1997-98; @ Coir industry.

Source: As in Table 6.18.

development. As Table 6.19 reveals, Kerala's share in central sector investment in India had been declining after 1960-61, from nearly 3 per cent to just 1.43 per cent in 1989-90. This happened during a period when Kerala was in a state of industrial stagnation. As a welcome sign, recent years have shown (Table 6.19) some reversal of the trend.

Table 6.20 throws some light on the performance of Kerala's public sector enterprises (KPSEs) since 1981-82. The number of KPSEs increased from 77 in 1981-82 to 91 in 1991-92 and to 107 in 2003-04. The increase in the capital employed between 1981-82 and 2003-04 has been more than three-fold in companies and nearly seven-fold in statutory bodies. At the same time, employment in companies declined from 65,500 in 1981-82 to 60,129 in 2003-04 after increasing to 97548 in 1991-92. Employment in statutory bodies too behaved in a like manner. While the number of KPSEs making profits has remained nearly unchanged between 1981-82 and 2003-04, the number of loss-making companies went up from 37 in 1981-82 to over 50 in subsequent years. The behaviour of statutory bodies in this respect was worse. Given the losses of KPSEs, particularly in the statutory bodies over the years, the state PSEs of Kerala have continued to be significant destroyers of public wealth.

TABLE 6.19

Central Sector Investment in Kerala

Period	*Investment (Rs. Crore)*		
	India	*Kerala*	
		Amount	*%*
1969- 70	3885	116	2.99
1979- 80	21192	482	2.27
1989- 90	129713	1853	1.43
1999- 00	381365	6828	1.79
2002- 03	525303	14548	2.77

Source: Economic Review, Kerala, Various years.

TABLE 6.20

Performance of State Public Enterprises in Kerala

Item	*1981-82*	*1991-92*	*2003-04*
A. Govt. Companies			
(a) Number	77	91	107
(b) Employment	65500	97548	60129
(c) Capital Employed (Rs. Crore)	380.3	1387.0	1660.0
(d) No. of units on profits	34	32	32
(e) No. of units on loss	37	57	75
(f) Net profit/loss (-)	-5.0	-41.3	-38.0
(g) Loss per employee (Rs.)	763	4234	6320
(h) Loss per Re. of capital (paise)	1.3	3.0	2.3
B. Statutory Bodies			
(a) Number	7	8	6
(b) Employment	64455	69173	55568
(c) Capital Invested (Rs. Crore)	427.1	2638.7	3521
(d) No. of units on profits	3	1	2
(e) No. of units on loss	1	5	4
(f) Net profit/loss (-)		-96.1	-181.0
(g) Loss per employee (Rs.)		13893	32573
(h) Loss per Re. of capital (paise)		3.6	5.1

Source: Annual Reports on Performance of Public Enterprises in Kerala.

Industrial Exports

Products having primary sector origins such as cashewnut, spices, marine products, coffee and tea still dominate Kerala's industrial exports and account for about a two-fifth of the total value of exports. In 2003-2004, among the major categories, other major products with lesser degree of primary sector, *viz.*, coir and coir products (which also have primary connection, but whose processing drastically changes their primary character), textiles, garments and software accounted for just about a-tenth of the value of industrial exports. Other states in India have been able to benefit tremendously from several emerging industrial activities. States such as Andhra Pradesh, Karnataka and Tamil Nadu earn large amounts of exports of software revenues unlike Kerala. Similarly, under the WTO regime, especially after the dismantling of the quotas, the scope for exporting textiles and clothing has become unlimited; yet, despite a number of advantages in terms of infrastructure and human resources and despite the urgent need to ensure work and income to thousands of threatened traditional textile sector workers in the state, Kerala has not been able to show any commendable gains in the exports of textiles and garments. Kerala's textile sector has reportedly the potential to create employment for Rs. 25,000 workers on the whole; on the export front as well as the industrial production front, Kerala performance has been lukewarm and much lower than its potential.

Pattern of Investment

A rough idea about the changes in the pattern of capital investment in the manufacturing sectors of Kerala may be obtained from Table 6.20(A). The total investment in manufacturing grew between 1987-88 and 1996-97 by a substantial 183 per cent. While the cotton textiles sector received a much larger share of capital investment in 1996-97 than in 1987-88, traditional sectors like tea-processing, cashew-processing, coir products and rubber products also improved their shares to some extent. The decline in the share of plywood and chemicals is understandable given the environmental implications of those industries. In general, it is expected that the environmental factor might force Kerala to shift more and more of its manufacturing units to land, and environment-friendly industries, in which processing forms a predominant component.

TABLE 6.20(A)

Capital Invested in Major Manufacturing Sectors of Kerala (Selected Years)

Sector	*1987-88*		*1996-97*	
	Rs. Crores	*%*	*Rs. Crores*	*%*
Cotton Textiles	56.3	2.30	485.8	7.02
Tea Processing	28.6	1.17	118.6	1.71
Cashew Processing	33.4	1.37	132.3	1.91
Coir Products	11.1	0.45	83.5	1.21
Tile Products	21.9	0.90	63.7	0.92
Plywood	17.0	0.70	22.4	0.32
Soap & Glycerin	14.2	0.58	21.3	0.31
Tyres & Tubes	9.2	0.38	90.6	1.31
Chemicals	379.7	15.53	1028.1	14.85
Other Products	1874	76.65	4876.9	70.44
Total	2445	100	6923	100

Source: *Economic Review*, Kerala, Various years.

Plan Expenditures in Industry Sector

Ever since the First Five Year Plan period, plan expenditures on industry (and mining) have been on the increase. However, such increases have not been steady over the plan periods. Table 6.20(B) gives a fair idea about the trends in plan investment in the industrial sector in Kerala. Since the Fifth Five Year Plan period, plan expenditures on Industry and Mining ranged between 9 and 12 per cent of total plan expenditure. The Ninth Five Year Plan also made its allocation to Industry and Mining in approximately the same range, but closer to the upper limit.

Industrial Climate

Despite the liberalisation efforts of Kerala made in conformity with the liberalisation and globalisation trends at the national level since 1991, Kerala continues to be one of the least attractive investment destinations among the Indian states (Table 6.21). Kerala accounted for a mere 1.1 per cent of the total Industrial Entrepreneurs' Memoranda (IEM) and Letters of Intent (LoI) signed in India during August 1991-January 2002. Also, in the investment amount proposed, employment proposed and the FDI approved during this period, the share of Kerala was merely one per cent or even less. As Table 6.21 reveals, these figures compare very poorly with the shares of other southern Indian states such as Tamil Nadu. Recently Kerala has come out with a Global Investor Meet specifically to attract investors into the state. However, it seems that even such exercises did not give the needed impetus to the industrial investment activities in the state despite the euphoria and the initial positive signs the meet generated.

TABLE 6.20(B)

Plan Expenditures on Industry & Mining

Plan	*Expenditure (Rs.Crore)*	*% of Total Plan Expenditure*
First FYP	0.5	1.93
Second FYP	6.0	7.48
Third FYP	14.4	7.90
Annual Plan 1966-69	13.3	9.21
Fourth FYP	26.0	7.52
Fifth FYP	54.8	10.99
Annual Plan 1978-80	67.1	15.26
Sixth FYP	166.5	9.24
Seventh FYP	272.6	10.87
Annual Plan 1990-92	151.0	10.60
Eighth FYP	869.4	11.79
Ninth FYP	971.8	11.15

Source: Compiled from the annual reports of on Performance of Public Enterprises in India.

TABLE 6.21

Share in Industrial Investment Proposals- FDI (August 1991-January 2002)

State	*% Share*			
	IEM+ LOI	*Investment Proposed*	*Employment proposed*	*FDI Amount Approved*
Kerala	**1.1**	**1.0**	**1.0**	**0.6**
Tamil Nadu	9.5	6.4	8.5	8.4
Karnataka	4.0	5.1	4.0	7.8
Andhra Pradesh	6.9	10.9	6.5	4.6
India ('00s)	48138 units	1066534 crore	8629068 (no.)	2747149 crore

Source: *Economic Review*, Kerala, Various years.

Foreign Direct Investment (FDI)

The FDI policies in India have become increasingly liberal over the years since 1991. This was a result partly of the overall liberalisation policies and partly of the globalisation efforts induced by the liberalisation policies and by the WTO agreements. While the benefits of FDI have hardly come to Kerala, the few foreign investment commitments having Kerala as their destination pertain to the IT and the textile sectors. As the state carries out new initiatives in the league of Global Investor Meet, IT parks, Technology parks, Food parks, Special Economic Zones and Towns of Export Excellence, interests of foreign investors in the state are expected to grow.

As Table 6.22 suggests, while the number of factories increased in the public sector from 38 in 1961 to 538 in 2003 and in the private sector from 2436 to 17838 during the same period, factory sector employment rose from 5016 persons to 95580 persons in the public sector and from 166324 persons to 316169 persons in the private sector during 1961-2003. Thus, the total number of factories in Kerala showed an increase from 2474 in 1961 to 18376 in 2003 and total employment in the factory sector from 171340 persons in 1961 to 411749 persons in 2003.

TABLE 6.22

Working Factories (Reg. under FA) in Kerala-Number & Employment

Year	*Public Sector*		*Private Sector*		*Total Industry*	
	Number	*Employment*	*Number*	*Employment*	*Number*	*Employment*
1961	38	5016	2436	166324	2474	171340
1974	#	#	#	#	6036	258960
1992	495	127538	14113	248198	14608	375736
2001	553	96154	18068	338764	18621	434918
2003	538	95580	17838	316169	18376	411749

Note: #: Not Available.

Source: Economic Review, different years.

SSI Units

The progress of the SSI sector can be a good indicator of the spread of industries in a region that is constrained in industrial development by various factors. Table 6.23 presents the share of the unregistered manufacturing sector in net SDP in 1989-90 and 1998-99 for selected states in India.

Despite a decline in the ratio at the all-India level, the major industrial states are seen to have increased their shares of the unregistered manufacturing sector in net SDP; Kerala also followed this trend. It appears that under liberalisation of the 1990s, industrial activities have been spreading among small and tiny players indicating greater dispersal of the industrial benefits of liberalisation.

TABLE 6.23

Share of Unregistered Manufacturing in Net SDP: Selected States

(per cent)

State	*1989-90*	*1998-99*
Gujarat	6.0	9.2
Maharashtra	7.4	8.7
Andhra Pradesh	4.1	5.6
Karnataka	4.3	9.7
Kerala	**5.6**	**6.5**
Tamil Nadu	7.1	7.8
India	5.9	5.7

Source: Economic Review, Kerala, Various years.

Medium & Large Units

Kerala had 719 medium and large units in the public, private, cooperative and joint sectors as on March 31, 2004; 254 of them (35.2 per cent) in Ernakulam district alone and another 238 (33 per cent) in Thiruvananthapuram, Palakkad and Trichur districts together. The districts of Idukki, Pathanamthitta, Wayanad and Kasargod together hosted only 36 medium and large units. Also, Idukki and Wayanad were the only districts without any central or state public sector enterprises operating in them.

Support Systems

The industrialisation efforts of Kerala should have received substantial assistance from the elaborate support systems created for the purpose. There have been several agencies to assist the investors directly and indirectly and in financial and other terms. A brief evaluation of the assistance provided by various channels and agencies is given in this section.

SSI Cooperatives

Cooperative societies have been an important basis of industrialisation in Kerala. The number of SSI cooperatives in Kerala showed a steady decline since 1981. Between 1991 and 2004, large declines occurred in the number of industrial cooperatives in Trichur, Alappuzha, Kannur and Kollam districts, some of which used to be the traditional strongholds of industrial cooperatives. On the other hand, the number of industrial cooperatives registered impressive growth in Wayanad, Ernakulam and Kottayam districts during 1991-2004.

By the end of 2003-04, Kerala had 687 coir and 758 handloom societies. Of these, Kollam and Alappuzha claimed over one-half the number of coir societies and Thiruvananthapuram accounted for nearly one-half the handloom societies. Many of the societies are reportedly dormant and many others in serious problems threatening their very existence. There is need to ensure the survival and good health of the societies by modernising their technologies and changing their operational and marketing strategies.

KSIDC

KSIDC was set up to support the industrial development efforts of the state through lending assistance to identify investment projects in the state. In the past, KSIDC supported mainly small and medium enterprises. The involvement of KSIDC has increased over time, e.g., during in the second half of the 1990s as compared to the preceding half, in terms of the cost of projects at various stages of processing or execution as well of financial sanctions and disbursements (Table 6.24).

TABLE 6.24

Performance of KSIDC

Performance Indicators (Rs. Crores)	*1991-92 to 1995- 96*	*1996-97 to 2000- 01*	*2002-03 to 2003-04*
1. MoU signed (Private)			
(a) No.	212	206	42
(b) Total Cost	5242	9016	13585
2. Projects Cleared			
(a) No.	258	259	51
(b) Total cost	1593	3002	223
(c) Employment No.	24921	16314	3892
3. Projects Completed			
(a) No.	155	213	34
(b) Total cost	504	1592	168
(c) Employment No.	14042	16314	2048
4. Projects being Implemented*			
(a) No.	69	92	69
(b) Total Cost	323	1330	1527
(c) Employment No.*	5777	6541	6859
5. Financial Sanctions	284	464	96
(a) Disbursements	168	294	51
(b) Recovery	103	234	120
(c) Operating Profits	37	70	20

Note: * Annual Average over the years.

Source: Economic Review, different years.

Other Support Agencies

Other state-level agencies also participate in industrial promotion and support activities in Kerala. They include:

- Kerala Financial Corporation (KFC)
- Kerala Industrial Infrastructure Development Corporation (KINFRA)
- Kerala State Handloom Development Corporation (HANVEEV)
- Kerala Industrial and Technical Consultancy Organisation (KITCO)
- Kerala State Electronic Technology Parks (TECHNO PARK)
- Small Industries Development Corporation (SIDCO)
- Small Industries Service Institute (SISI)
- The existence of a large number of institutions in a few fairly related activities is bound to lead to duplication of services and confusion; it is difficult to demarcate the boundaries of different agencies in unambiguous terms. Further discussion about the industrial promotional agencies will be taken up presently.

Administrative Agencies

District Industries Centres (DICs) act essentially as the district-level extensions for government support at the project level especially for small enterprises. While DICs play a significant role, they need to be re-oriented from their current target-oriented approach to a success/stake-oriented approach. Further, there are various administrative arms of the government having functions related to industries such as providing various approvals, conducting inspections, and providing inputs such as electricity and water. Many of these functions are not properly manned (with trained and motivated personnel) or oriented (to play the role of a facilitator). Therefore, they fail to contribute effectively to realising the industrial goals of the state. All these agencies are in need of thorough revamping.

Recent Support Efforts

Several industrial support measures have been initiated or strengthened in recent years in tune with the renewed efforts of the state for rapid industrial progress. Such measures are meant for reforming the public sector, smoothing the operations of existing private enterprises and attracting new investments into vital and emerging industrial sectors of the state. Some of these recent efforts are examined below.

RIAB, ERC and KIRFB: Support to Public Sector

The state public sector enterprises have been suffering from several weaknesses. They were not therefore able to play a leadership role in the industrial development or rejuvenation in the state. Therefore, any efforts aimed at the state's re-industrialisation should have included policies for strengthening the public sector to become efficient. In recent years, the institutions of RIAB (Restructuring and Internal Audit Board), ERC (Enterprises Reforms Committee) and KIRFB (Kerala Industrial Revitalisation Fund Board) have been playing important roles towards strengthening the public sector enterprises. Till 2003-2004 ERC recommended case-based reform measures on 45 state level public enterprises (SLPEs). Voluntary Retirement Scheme was applied during 2003-04 in the case of 2348 employees of SLPEs, involving payments to the tune of Rs. 6403 lakh. KIRFB released by 2003-04, amounts of assistance of Rs.106.8 crore by way of long-term loans and Rs.164 crore in the form of short-term loans to SLPEs.

New Initiatives

Some of the new support initiatives undertaken in Kerala for industrial development—either under the auspices of the state or as part of the central schemes—are the Global Investor Meet (GIM), creation of Special Economic Zones (SEZ) and development of Towns of Export Excellence. The GIM indeed attracted large investor interest as the state had put in considerable effort in organising it; but the utility of the initiative in terms of actual investments induced by it is being questioned in several quarters. By gaining SEZ status, the relevant KINFRA Parks (e.g., electronics at Kochi and food-processing at Malappuram) have been able to provide to the operating units several tax benefits and concessions including those on customs duties and tariffs. The handloom industry in Kannur and seafood industry in Alappuzha are benefited from supportive investments and facilities due to the Towns of Export Excellence status accorded to Kannur in handloom textiles and to Alappuzha in seafood processing.

Cluster approach is another important development. It is a crucial element in the current efforts at developing particularly small enterprises facing constraints of infrastructural facilities. The Kerala Bureau of Industrial Promotion (K-BIP) is the state agency involved in cluster identification and related activities in Kerala. Under this approach, a cluster of units in a particular industry is identified and infrastructural facilities are provided to the units on a sharing and mutually supportive basis. Products having good potential for clustered development have already been identified in each of the 14 districts of Kerala. Development work on many product clusters is at different stages of progress. Another notable effort is promotional activities for the food-processing industry in Kerala. KINFRA has formed a separate Agency for Development of Food Processing Industry in Kerala (ADFIK).

Banking and Financial Support

Banks and financial institutions are expected to contribute significantly to the industrial development of a region as they constitute the major sources of financing industrial activities. The role of the commercial banks in Kerala has been, however, more in mobilising resources than in supporting investments in the state. While the share of Kerala in India in the matter of commercial bank deposits declined in June 2004 over March 2002, the share of credits improved a little during the period (Table 6.25). Similarly, while the credit-deposit ratio of commercial banks in Kerala had been 92 per cent of the all-India ratio in June 1969, it declined to as low as 68.5 per cent by March 2002, before again going up to 98.2 per cent by June 2004.

TABLE 6.25

Commercial Banking Profile of Kerala

Parameters	*% Share in India*		
	June 1969	*March 2002*	*June 2004*
No. of branches	7.3	5.0	5.1
Deposits	3.3	4.7	3.7
Credits	2.9	3.2	3.6
Per capita deposits*	83.0	151.9	119.8
Per capita credits*	73.5	104.1	117.5
Deposit per branch*	44.6	94.1	73.0
Credit per branch*	38.6	64.5	71.7
Credit-Deposit Ratio*	92.0	68.5	98.2

Note: * Kerala value as a % of All India value.

Source: Jeromi, P.D. *op.cit*; June 2004 based on *Economic Review 2004*.

Table 6.26 gives information about the extent of assistance provided by various all-India financial institutions to Kerala. Except for SIDBI and NABARD, the average share of Kerala in the total financial

TABLE 6.26
Financial Assistance Disbursed by Financial Institutions

Financial Institutions	*% Share of Kerala*		
	Since Inception to March 2001	*2000-01*	*2003-04***
IDBI	1.6	1.1	1.5
IFCI	0.8	0.9	0.8
ICICI	0.7	0.3	0.7
IIBI	1.4	2.8	
IDFC	1.7		
SIDBI	5.9	8.3	3.0
NABARD	11.7	10.8	4.5
Exim Bank	1.8	0.8	
Total*	1.5	1.3	

Note: * Per capita assistance of FIs received by Kerala is only 43% of Per capita assistance of FIs at all India level.

Source: Jeromi, P.D. *op. cit*; ** *Economic Review 2004*.

assistance disbursed by any of these institutions during their existence up to 2003-04, was less than two per cent. And, the average for all institutions including SIDBI and NABARD was also below that figure till 2000-01.

The Gap

It is thus fairly obvious that Kerala occupies a relatively low position among the states in India in industrial development and that the state encounters several barriers in this respect. The causes for the deficiencies or gaps are examined in the following sections by evaluating the constraints of the state in achieving industrialisation.

The causes of the industrial deficiencies or gaps of Kerala are basically the constraints on development operations in industry that the state faces. The analysis of the constraints is taken up after a short analysis of the past industrial policies of the state with a view to bringing out their salient features. The industrial promotion agencies set up under the industrial policies at various time points in the past are also examined.

Industrial Development Policy Under the Plans

Serious efforts at industrialisation of the state started only during the Second Five Year Plan period (1956-57-1960-61). A programme for the organisation of industrial cooperatives was introduced during this period. The industrial estates programme was also adopted during this period. By the end of the Third Plan (1961-62–1965-66), 18 industrial estates had been set up in the state. During the Third Plan, Kerala State Small Industries Corporation (KSSIC) was set up to assist industrialists for procuring raw materials and machinery. The Corporation was also entrusted with the management of industrial estates, sales emporia and production units run by the Industry Department. Later, KSSIC and Kerala Employment Promotion Corporation were merged to form Kerala State Small Industries Development and Employment Corporation Limited (SIDECO). During 1962-65, the Rural Industries Programme was implemented. Two projects, one at Alleppey and another at Kozhikode, were started under the programme. Under this programme, industrial units that cost up to Rs. one lakh were to be set up by the department and handed over to prospective entrepreneurs on hire purchase basis. The Fourth Plan (1969-70–1973-74) saw the emergence of functional and ancillary industrial estates. The functional estates started under this programme were at Changanassery for rubber and plastics, at Quilon for ceramics, at Karakulam for electronics, at Kalamassery as an ancillary industrial estate for HMT and at Veli as an industrial estate for ISRO-related works.

Industrial Promotion Programmes under FYPs

II FYP: Programme of industrial cooperatives; industrial estates programme.

III FYP: Setting up Kerala State Small Industries Corporation (KSSIC); Rural Industries Programme.

IV FYP: Setting up functional & ancillary industrial estates.

V FYP: Mini Industrial Estates Programme; District Industries Centre (DIC); Entrepreneurship Development Programme.

VI FYP: Attention to SSI sector; SSI infrastructure creation.

VII FYP: SSI development with private participation; Technological advancement efforts in SSI sector.

VIII FYP: Intensive Industrialisation Programme to promote SSI sector; State Investment Subsidy; Seed Capital Loan; Margin Money Assistance; Assistance to women entrepreneurs; KINFRA.

IX FYP: Energising KSIDC, KINFRA, TECHNOPARK, KFC & SIDCO; IT policy; Promoting Techno Parks.

X FYP: Cluster development approach, Establishment of technology incubation centres; Early warning system for sickness prevention; Modernisation & technology up-gradation; Industrial Development Zones with private participation.

Private industrialists and industrial cooperatives were provided with loans from commercial banks for development of industries. In addition, the Kerala

Financial Corporation and the Industries Department reached an agreement to provide loans to small industries at subsidised rates of interest. To ensure regional balance in industrial growth, in 1971 the Government of India also offered investment subsidy of 10 and 15 per cent in most backward districts of the country.

Under the Fifth Plan (1974-75-1978-79) the major change in policy was the thrust given to institutional financing of industries. The state's vital role lay in the creation of infrastructure, co-coordination of assistance to small industries sector and development of a climate of increased confidence among entrepreneurs. On the 1st of April 1975, the Mini-Industrial Estates Programme was launched for intensifying the industrialisation efforts in the state. In 1977, based on the Industrial Policy Resolution (1977) of the central government, the District Industries Centre (DIC) was started. DIC was envisaged as the hub of all financial and technical assistance and of the inputs and other services that entrepreneurs needed. Entrepreneurship Development Programme was also started for the weaker and marginalised communities of the society. Further, a number of incentives were also instituted.

During the Fifth and the Sixth (1980-81–1984-85) Plan periods, serious and concerted efforts were made to vitalise medium, large as well as small industries in the state with strong resource base. The success of this approach was reflected in the consistent growth in the number of registered factories and the vast employment generated during this period. Thus, between 1973 and 1980 the number of factories increased at an annual rate of 19.56 per cent and employment at the rate of 3.30 per cent; these growth rates were undoubtedly higher than the corresponding rates during the previous periods.

During the Sixth Plan period, the difficulties faced by the small-scale sector received utmost attention. Most of the infrastructure creation in the industrial sector was being made in tune with the specific needs of this sector. Yet, achievements remained far short of targets. According to the Task Force Report on Modern Small Scale Industries of the Ninth Five Year Plan (1997-98–2001-02), "The Sixth Plan target was to set up 17000 new units, against which the state could register only 13225 units. An amount of Rs. 25 crores was provided for small scale industries out of which only 11.59 per cent was utilised."

The Seventh Plan (1985-86–1989-90) envisaged development of the small-scale sector with the aid of private investment as the department concentrated its energies on infrastructure creation in industrial estates and development of plots and functional complexes in selected growth centres. It also aimed at reorganising the industrial promotional agencies in the areas of finance, raw material supply and infrastructure development. The Department also focused its attention on technological advancement in the sector. The achievements in this period included a total investment of Rs. 4310 crore, employment potential of 1.93 lakh persons and production of goods and services valued at Rs. 882.25 crore. By the end of 1989-90, there were 64675 registered small-scale units in the state with an investment of Rs. 854 crore, employing 3.82 lakh persons and producing goods and services worth Rs. 1745 crore.

During the Eighth Plan (1992-93–1996-97), several changes were brought about in industrial policy. The Industrial Policy (1991) paved the way for initiating structural changes in the sector. The government, while refraining from making direct investment in industrial ventures, stepped up its role of providing the necessary promotional services and infrastructural facilities required. Against an outlay of Rs. 500 crore set apart for large and medium industries, the actual expenditure was Rs. 500.2 crore. Without direct investment from the government, the public enterprises did very badly during the period in comparison to the private sector.

An Intensive Industrialisation Programme was launched in 1993 to promote small industries. The other schemes of this period included State Investment Subsidy, Seed Capital Loan, Margin Money Assistance and Assistance to Women Entrepreneurs.

Ninth Plan

The Ninth Plan priority areas included development of small-scale industries through provision of adequate infrastructure support, common facility centres, marketing facilities and investment subsidies. It was planned that the small-scale sector will receive substantial support from local bodies also. In the case of traditional industries, the focus was on modernisation, infrastructure support, training, marketing support, and provision of credit facilities etc, with a view to enhancing production, tapping the export potential and creating more employment.

Restructuring and consolidation of the public sector undertakings and making them more competitive was the primary concern of the plan in the large and the medium industries sector. The role of government as a facilitator rather than as a direct financier was emphasised. With a view to attracting more investment in the industrial sector, promotional agencies such as KSIDC, KINFRA, TECHNOPARK, KFC and SIDCO were energised. Efforts were also made to create an environment conducive to attract private capital investment in large amounts and to make Kerala an investor-friendly state.

Small industries in general performed well during the Ninth Plan. An amount of Rs.51.2 crore was spent under the investment subsidy programme. But the schemes like creation of industry-varsity linkage, rehabilitation of women from socially condemned professions, and installation of industry facilitation council, productivity council, tool room etc, which had been suggested, were dropped or merged with other schemes.

The government's IT policy announced in 1998 focussed mainly on the diffusion of information technology, enhancement of information technology base, creation of a robust state information infrastructure and human resource development for IT. The major schemes undertaken in the Ninth Plan period include establishment of 'FRIENDS' (Fast Reliable Instant Efficient Network for Disbursement of Services), PEARL (Package for Effective Administration of Registration) and ITES Habitat of the GCDA.

The Electronic Technology Parks – the Kerala Techno Park, which was the primary initiative of the state to promote the information technology ventures, now functions under the IT Department. The Techno Park campus in Thiruvananthapuram covers an area of 143.64 acres. An area of 56.08 acres was acquired to be developed into a support campus. The Park provides state-of-the-art facilities for the IT companies interested in setting up their houses in Kerala. At present 55 companies function in the campus with a total investment of Rs. 147.55 crore and employing 6800 persons.

Tenth Plan (2002-03–2006-07) Proposals

A package of financial incentives is recommended to provide marketing support to the small-scale sector. The salient features of the development policy are based on the cluster development concept, the establishment of technology incubation centres and the establishment of an early warning system for sickness prevention. In the coir sector, attracting private investment is taken as a crucial strategy. Modernisation and technology upgradation are given the highest emphasis, as they will reposition the industry with value addition in product line. In the handloom sector, activities that will remove the disparities between the spinning and the weaving sectors are envisaged. In the case of public sector undertakings, the plan proposes to proceed with the restructuring process in a time-bound manner and the disinvestment proceeds are proposed to be utilised in restructuring, including provisions for VRS and training the workforce retained for the new environment. The Kerala State Industrial Development Corporation is expected to transform itself into the Kerala State Industrial Investment Promotion Board. This transformation will entail a role change to promotion of private and public investments in industry and physical and social infrastructure in the state. It is also planned to set up a Technology Development Centre to cater to the private entrepreneurs of small, medium and large enterprises. In conjunction with the Industrial Policy 2001, Industrial Development Zones are being established with private sector participation. Strong linkages are to be developed between the DIC and the local Self Government Institutions for effective implementation of the programmes of the Department of Industries.

New Industrial Policies and Initiatives

The new industrial policies are aimed at giving further boost to the re-industrialisation efforts initiated in Kerala in the recent past. The new policies target improvements in industrial infrastructure, Kerala's labour image, development of traditional industries having good employment and export potential, accelerated development of emerging or sunrise industries such as electronics & IT, IT services and bio-technology and food-processing in addition to other high value-added activities. While the new policies are indeed attracting new investments, a large scale flow of investments into the state is yet to occur, probably because of the lingering problems of the past such as shortage of power and infrastructure bottlenecks as well as poor labour image and unfriendly political attitudes.

The new initiatives having great potential to contribute to the fast re-industrialisation of Kerala have been mentioned as promotion of Special Economic Zones, development of Towns of Export Excellence, setting up of a separate agency, ADFIK by KINFRA for development of food-processing industry and the cluster development approach. While the first two initiatives are likely to benefit specific localities coming under these schemes, the last two initiatives are likely to have their benefits throughout Kerala. The cluster approach is the most influential among the new initiatives as industries having potential for cluster-based development have been identified in every district in the state. Intensive efforts are also in progress to realise the cluster development benefits in many of the identified clusters.

Industrial Promotion Agencies

The various industrial promotion agencies and their functions are listed below:

1) Kerala State Industrial Development Corporation (KSIDC)

As already mentioned, KSIDC was set up as a fully government-owned company for the promotion, development and financing of medium and large industries in the state. It functions as an extended arm of the government in the implementation of industrial development programmes. It advises and assists the government in taking concrete steps to promote industrialisation of the state. The major activities of the Corporation include identifying viable projects, finding suitable investors, assisting entrepreneurs, assisting in getting clearance for projects, giving publicity to the facilities offered to investors, organising industrial promotion seminars and exhibitions, providing loan assistance and share capital assistance for implementing projects, creating infrastructure facilities, and monitoring growth and development of industries. KSIDC is envisaged to transform itself into the Kerala State Industrial Investment Promotion Board in due time.

2) Kerala Industrial Infrastructure Development Corporation (KINFRA)

KINFRA was established in 1993 with a view to providing infrastructure facilities required by industries for setting up units in Kerala. The Industrial Parks developed by KINFRA have facilities like developed land, dedicated power supply, continuous water supply and communication facilities in addition to supporting administrative facilities such as bank, post office, and round the clock security. Emerging industries such as electronics, IT, apparels, and food processing have been in the developmental priority list of KINFRA.

3) Kerala Industrial and Technical Consultancy Organisation (KITCO)

KITCO was set up with the objective of catering to the consultancy needs of small and medium entrepreneurs in the state, assisting them in the preparation of project reports, and asset valuation reports, special studies, turn key assignments, energy audits, engineering work and training programmes. The company has rendered engineering consultancy services and advice for infrastructure development projects of several state government undertakings. They also conduct skill development training for the SSI sector as well as entrepreneurship development training for industry in general.

4) Kerala State Industrial Enterprises Ltd. (KSIE)

KSIE acted as a holding company of the state government till 1999. In 1999, the subsidiary companies were de-linked from KSIE. The main functions of the KSIE are the management of the air cargo complexes at Thiruvananthapuram and Kozhikode, and operating their sales outlets at Thiruvanathapuram, Kochi and Kozhikode.

5) Kerala Small Industries Development Corporation (SIDCO)

SIDCO is a promotional agency established by the government of Kerala in 1975. It carries out activities through its five divisions: Raw Material Division, Marketing Division, Construction Division, Production Division and Industrial Estate Division. The Raw Materials Division is engaged in the distribution of raw materials to the SSI sector and the public sector undertakings. The number of SSI units benefited by this activity was 250 in the year 2001-02. The Marketing Division provides assistance to the SSI units in procuring orders from the government and the public sector undertakings and in marketing their products. Under the Production Division, 11 production units functioned in 2001-02. The government departments and the public sector undertakings purchase furniture and equipment produced by these units without undergoing the formalities of inviting tenders. In 2000-2001, 752 SSI units functioned in the industrial estates located in different parts of the state.

6) Small Industries Service Institute (SISI)

Small Industries Service Institute, established in 1956, is the field level arm of the Small Industries Development Organisation (SIDO) to take care of the needs of the small-scale sector in the state in the area of technological, economic and managerial consultancy services. It also extends common facility services to needy entrepreneurs.

7) Other Agencies

Several other important promotional agencies also operate in Kerala: KVIB, Serifed, Coir Board etc. KVIB industries provide substantial employment in Kerala; but the state accounts for only less than 2 per cent of KVIB production and about 2.5 per cent of KVIB employment in India. The task of Serifed is to promote sericulture and expand the production of silk in the state. Serifed has not been a big success. New approaches (e.g., a cluster development approach) are considered essential to promote sericulture and silk production. Despite the existence of specialised agencies for developing the coir industry, the industry has been facing a crisis in recent years. Developing new products and finding new uses for coir products have been the crucial considerations for revival efforts in this industry.

Suggestions for Effective Promotional Support

Apart from labour-related, political and energy-related factors, some other major reasons also work behind the poor performance of Kerala on the industrial front. They include multiplicity of agencies concerned with various aspects of industrial investment operations and the lack of a professional approach of these governmental agencies. The existing and potential investors complain about delays and administrative harassments (may be due to expectations of illegal gratification). Despite the recent efforts at reducing bureaucratic impediments and promoting single-window schemes, the approval process has remained lethargic and cumbersome. There is need to make much greater efforts on this front. There should be a true 'green channel' which will take care of all approvals and licences speedily and promptly without creating any feeling of hassle to investors. This channel should comprise experts from all areas relevant to industrial development including the government, the banking sector, specialised academic institutions and industry associations. Such a green channel agency, if given adequate authority to transact on behalf of investors with relevant agencies including KSEB, KWA and Pollution Control Board might even hold erring investors liable for their failures. The investment process as a whole would then become a pleasurable experience to investors.

There is also need to change the attitudinal orientation of the personnel of promotion agencies and other officials associated with industrial development. The industrial development official needs to be rather more than a manager, a regulatory authority or a control agent. Investors often find the bureaucratic approach unsuitable for meeting the requirements of the market. Further, the promotional agencies often rush to decisions and conclusions about what is the right promotional approach or initiative as they are often driven by targets or deadlines set for them. While targets and deadlines are useful, the quality of investment (in terms of viability, profitability and long-term potential for growth and success) should be the key consideration in dealing with investment promotion and approvals. There is need to develop market-related skills of officials of the promotional agencies especially at the sub-state levels so that they are able to guide investors on prospective investment avenues, appropriate scales of investment, suitable geographical entry points, correct timing of entry and productive market strategies.

Industrial Constraints

Industrial constraints of Kerala include unfavourable political factors and labour attitudes and dearth of land and natural resources and government's inability to give adequate support to industry[2]. Some of the major constraints are discussed in the following sections.

Economic Environment: Liberalisation, Globalisation & WTO System

The most important constraint is the environment, while it is also a major opportunity. Some important components of the external environment include the liberalisation of the Indian economy since 1991, the globalisation process and the emergence of the WTO system. The liberalisation process has led to an increase in domestic competition and a reduction in the government role. Globalisation has led to entry of multinationals in India's markets and an opening up of international markets to India's (and Kerala's) exports.

The emergence of the WTO system has forced India to open its markets to the entry of foreign goods and to reduce tariffs on imports. Kerala has started facing competitive pressures in the domestic market as well as abroad on several items of great importance for industrial development such as rubber, coconut, and tea. Several WTO provisions (such as reduction of tariffs, sanitary and phyto-sanitary measures, anti-dumping and countervailing measures) have been

2. Albin, A. (1990). "Manufacturing Sector in Kerala: A Comparative Study of its Growth and Structure". *Economic and Political Weekly*, Sept. 15, pp. 2059-70, had blamed regional factors for the unsatisfactory industrial performance of Kerala during the 1960s and the 1970s.

particularly stressful to producers in the state. At the same time, they also provided opportunities through liberal provisions for imports which have reduced prices of raw materials for industrial production.

Political Factors

There exists among the people of Kerala, a tendency to view the growth of private business enterprises as a manifestation of increasing exploitation. The fact that the growth of enterprises could support the progress of all stakeholders without jeopardising anybody's interest is lost sight of. What Kerala requires for its industrial development is a sober approach to enterprise and expression of disagreements.

Labour Attitude

Analysts have often viewed Kerala labour as militant[3] based on the number of industrial units closed or affected or production days lost due to labour problems in Kerala. The problem is partly an outcome of the excessive sensitiveness of the people of Kerala, thanks to high levels of mass education, and general awareness of the world affairs. Workers approach labour problems with a studied bias against both public and private ventures.

Industrial Disputes

Table 6.27 throws some light on the industrial disputes in the state between 1961 and 2003-04. The number of industrial disputes has continued to decline since 1961. However, the average number of man-days lost in the disputes during 2003-04 appear to have been higher than in 1980 though the number of disputes leading to work stoppage in 1980 had been close to double the number in 2003-04.

TABLE 6.27

Industrial Disputes in Kerala (Leading to Work Stoppage)

Year	*No. of Disputes*	*No. of Workers Affected*	*Man-days Lost*
1961	324	81318	442000
1974	225	285875	4794000
1980	103	73769	1431000
1992	41	7762	507000
2003-04	57	56745	1893078

Source: Economic Review, different years.

Different sectors witnessed losses of man-days in industrial disputes (Table 6.28). For instance, in 1961, the maximum number of man-days was lost in disputes in the tile and plantation industries. In 1974, it was in plantations and cashewnut; in 1980 and 1992 it was in plantations and the textiles sectors; and in 2001 it was in the textiles and the coir sectors, while plantation and tiles sectors also faced significant loss of man-days.

TABLE 6.28

Man-days Lost in Industrial Disputes in Kerala: Segment-wise ('000s)

Segment	*1961*	*1974*	*1980*	*1992*	*2001*
Plantaion	102	3180	284	172	248
Cashew	46	811	-	-	-
Textiles	30	141	176	130	561
Coir	17	29	-	-	400
Saw Mill	8	10	1	3	-
Tiles	154	252	7	20	208
Chemical & Pharma	-	-	-	-	-
Paper Mill	-	-	-	-	-
Rubber Factory	-	-	-	-	-
Others	85	371	963	183	197
Total	442	4794	1431	508	1614

Source: Economic Review, different years.

Development of Traditional Industries

While problems of the traditional industries continue to be serious, efforts to rejuvenate them with new strategies such as product development and finding new uses, have been in progress during the past few years. The problems related to technology, labour, productivity and product quality need also to be addressed rigorously. There exists growing interest in regions like European Union in natural products that are friendly to human health and environment. Our traditional industries such as coir, handloom and handicrafts are capable of meeting such needs. They have not so far succeeded in exploiting this opportunity adequately. The government has recently adopted a cluster approach under which facilities are set up near to the different industrial clusters identified. The cluster approach is beneficial to industries such as rubber, coir, plywood, plastics, tile, textiles and garments.

Mineral Resources

Production of several minerals substantially increased in Kerala during 1980-81–2003-04 (Table 6.29). But it has not led to growth of industrial activities. Proper exploitation of mineral resources through activities of value addition is yet to happen in Kerala.

3. Some studies in the past had tried to refute such views (see Subramanian, K.K and P Mohanan Pillai (1986). "Kerala's Industrial Backwardness: Exploration of Alternative Hypothesis", *Economic and Political Weekly*, April 5.; Subramanian, K.K. *op. cit.*).

TABLE 6.29

Mineral Production in Kerala

('000 tonnes)

Minerals	*Production*	
	1980-81	*2003-04*
Illmenite	126.3	164.6
Rutile	5.6	7.5
Zircon	1.5	10.9
Sillimanite	0.8	10.7
Luecoxene		0.5*
Glass & White Quartz Sand	69.5	1.2 (Qtz)*
China Clay	121.8	320.7
Lime Shell	112.1	78.7
Silica Sand		150.4
Bauxite		26.8
Graphite		0.1*
Limestone		192.8

Note: * 2001-02.

Source: Economic Review, different years.

Public Finance

Kerala's fiscal deficit and public liabilities have reached unmanageable proportions despite signs of some improvement in recent years, see Table 30. There exist several fiscal constraints on the government on promotion of industry in the state.

Land Resources

For large-scale industrialisation, several resources are essential among which availability of land is one of the foremost. Kerala has severe constraints in this regard. High population density and intensive efforts to enhance their social standard of living have left hardly any large tracts of unused lands in the state. Table 6.31 shows that except tracts of environmentally important lands whose exploitation could cause environmental problems and public outcry in the state, only agricultural lands remain, the further diversion of which to other uses would aggravate the precarious agricultural situation in the state. All the lands under non-agricultural uses are already occupied. Very little land in the form of waste and fallow lands remain. Obviously, Kerala cannot indulge in land-intensive industrialisation or go for large enterprises requiring large tracts of land. Therefore, a viable option for Kerala is to patronise small and medium enterprises or industries which do not require extensive use of land.

TABLE 6.30

Fiscal Position and Public Debts of Kerala

Year	*As % of State Domestic Product*	
	Gross Fiscal Deficit	*Total Liabilities*
1980-81	4.7	27.3
1990-91	6.6	38.7
2000-01	5.7	37.7
2003-04*	5.4	47.4

Source: Jeromi, P.D. *op. cit*; * *Economic Review* 2004.

TABLE 6.31

Land Use Pattern in Kerala

Category	*Area in '00 Hectares*				
	1960-61	*1970-71*	*1980-81*	*1990-91*	*2001-02*
A. Ecologically Important Lands					
1. Forest	10560	10550	10815	10815	10815
2. Permanent Pastures & Grazing Land	450	280	54	19	23.3
3. Land under Misc. Tree Crops	2040	1320	639	344	136.13
4. Current Fallow	670	240	436	442	792.7
B. Agricultural Land					
1. Net Area Sown	19240	21892	21796	22468	21906.9
C. Non-agricultural Use Land					
1. Land Put to Non-agri. Uses	2050	2750	2698	2974	3923.52
D. Waste & Fallow Lands					
1. Barren & Uncultivable Land	1510	800	858	583	297.28
2. Cultivable Wasteland	1440	1134	1290	946	637.71
3. Fallow other than Current Fallow	620	230	269	264	343.31

Source: *Economic Review* 1999, 2001.

Power Availability

Power is an essential input in industrial activities. Any effort at promoting industries should simultaneously ensure adequate and uninterrupted supply of power. However, Kerala has been notorious for its frequent spells of power shortages and failure. However, the state has a huge potential. Table 6.32 suggests that the supply capacity of power in 2000-01 was lower than one-half of the potential demand. Supply of power does not increase and becomes uninterrupted, efforts at industrialisation would not succeed.

TABLE 6.32

Power Constraints in the State

Period	*Per Capita Consumption kWh*	*Actual Consumption*	*Supply MU*	*Potential Demand MU*
1960-61	30	-	591	-
1970-71	72	-	2126	-
1980-81	109.4	2767	5242	3497
1990-91	185.1	5332	5490	10088
2000-01	311.67	10117	12484	27422
2003-04	386	8911	12569	-

Source: *Economic Review*, various years.
Kannan, K.P. & N.V. Pillai (2000). *Plight of Power Sector in India*. Thiruvananthapuram: CDS.

Marketing: Internal and External

Market success of any industry is dependent on compatibility of its product attributes with consumers' requirements, product quality, marketing efforts and the price factor. Efforts are on in Kerala industry to improve product quality and develop new features to meet consumer tastes and preferences. One relevant example is the coir industry, the R&D efforts of which are unusual to many traditional industries in India, and are made through the Centre for Development of Coir Technology and National Coir Research and Management Institute. The industrial marketing efforts in Kerala include the B2B meet in 2004 where international buyers and Kerala's small-scale suppliers met face to face to transact on the Kerala products on offer and to create international market links for the future. In the handloom sector, the state government has been extending substantial amounts of subsidy to make handloom products attractive to consumers and to help producers sell products at prices even lower than production costs. Another market support measure of the state is *SURABHI* in the handicraft sector. The Kerala Artisans' Development Corporation, Handicrafts Development Corporation, Kerala State Bamboo Corporation and Kerala Bamboo Fest 2004 make useful marketing efforts. Attempts are also on to incorporate the safety standards of foreign markets into Kerala's export products.

Technology

Kerala has been trying also to bring into the state and develop industries which employ emerging technologies. Such industries include Electronics, Information Technology, Bio-technology, Fashion-designing and Food-processing. Kerala has the potential to emerge as a major IT hub with Kochi's ascendance as an important link in India's international telecommunications and IT network. The total investment in optical fibre connectivity by various telecom and cable service providers amounted to Rs. 3,750 crore till March 2004. Despite these developments, the state still plays only a marginal role among the south Indian states, with Kerala's software exports in 2002-03 being US$36 million as against Karnataka's US$ 2,708 million, Tamil Nadu's US$ 1,385 million and Andhra Pradesh's US$ 804 million.

Human Resources

The spread of education including education at higher and technical levels and the existence of widespread educated unemployment in the state ensure ready availability of manpower for industrial development in the state. The quality of manpower and skill level provides a conducive environment for the expansion of high technology-intensive industries. There exist, of course, problems in the traditional industries such as skill obsolescence, low productivity and poor enterprise. Though Kerala has a multitude of technical and training institutions, many of them are in need of substantial modernisation and skill upgradation before they could be deployed to train human resources for the emerging industries.

Task Ahead

It is necessary to deal with these and several other relevant factors urgently and effectively if Kerala's hopes for a genuine and substantial industrial growth have to come true in the near future. For this purpose, the wholehearted support of political and social organisations including labour unions and workers is of paramount importance.

Industrialisation Strategies

A well planned industrialisation strategy for Kerala

should have the following components:

Land-friendly industries: Since Kerala is severely constrained on the issue of land, industries or units requiring vast tracts of land cannot be considered suitable for the state.

Ecology-friendly industries: Since Kerala has high population density, its fragile ecology is sensitive to developmental activities and its population intolerant to projects that may create adverse consequences for its natural environment; therefore, chemical, metal-processing or other pollutive units cannot be thought of as suitable for Kerala.

Industries uninfested by labour movements: Since Kerala's traditional industries are prone to labour-management problems, industries having limited possibility of labour-problems may be suitable.

Industries such as IT hardware and software, tourism products, health-care products, food products, and premium apparels, appear to be suitable for Kerala. Official studies are said to mention the following areas too as promising: rubber, mining, electronics, marine products, light engineering, biotechnology and pharmaceuticals. Of these, mining and pharmaceuticals (except Ayurvedic) are doubtful categories, mining due to its environmental ramifications and pharmaceuticals due to high competition. Further, industries that are basically exporters of raw (or semi-finished) natural resources (including minerals) may be undesirable in the long run; when the state develops capabilities of huge value addition on these resources, the state may no longer have these precious resources within the state.

Size of Industrial Units

Since Kerala has land and ecological constraints, and since labour problems are frequent particularly in large units, Kerala should promote with top priority small and medium units.

Power Supply

Power supply should be expanded adequately to ensure uninterrupted supply in adequate measure to industrial units.

Industrial Health

To ensure the health and the smooth functioning of industrial enterprises, the promotional agencies should be revamped for both functional and attitudinal changes, and the cumbersome bureaucratic system should be simplified.

Industrial Incentives

The best incentive all serious industrialists expect is an atmosphere in which they could operate without any hassles – bureaucratic, political or regulatory. The units that seek solace in monetary incentives and concessions even beyond a reasonable set up period, are the ones without adequate inherent strength and confidence. Such units do not deserve to be propped up. Therefore, industrial incentives need to be designed as support mechanisms to assist units set up firmly within reasonable time periods. Cluster development schemes and industrial parks have provisions for the sustenance of units. The Kerala Bureau of Industrial Promotion (K-BIP) prepared a detailed report on cluster development in Kerala in which it identified several possible industry clusters at the district level, deserving developmental support. Such initiatives should be strongly carried forward.

Policies, Programmes, Processes and Procedures

Several supportive policies, programmes, processes and procedures are required for rapid industrialisation of the state on desired lines. Existing special promotion efforts such as of KINFRA, K-BIP etc. need to continue. To the extent possible, the activities of the numerous institutions currently engaged in the promotion of industries and segments within industries need to be coordinated so that investors and entrepreneurs are not confused in seeking support. At present a single-window scheme is in existence, but practically only in name.

An industrialist venturing into Kerala witnesses *bandhs*, *hartals* and strikes off and on for silly reasons. The labour force of the state has to be rid of this scourge. Agitations cannot solve the major problem of unemployment, whereas industrialisation can.

Investment Requirements

As per available data, as in August 2004, Kerala had about 37.95 lakh job seekers. As on March 31, 2004, total investment in the KINFRA industrial parks was Rs.337.5 crore and the industrial parks generated employment for 9,930 persons. Based on the investment to employment ratio of the KINFRA parks, if KINFRA parks were to provide employment immediately to all the 37.95 lakh job seekers, then, the corresponding investment requirement would have been Rs.1,29,000 crore. Similarly, based on the investment to employment ratio of the small-scale units registered till March 31, 2004, in the state, the total investment requirement of Kerala industrial sector to generate enough activities to provide employment to all the 37.95 lakh job seekers would have been Rs. 12,365 crore. This is indeed an unmanageably wide range and the state would be better off if it can manage its industrial objective more with SSI sector units than with programmes and initiatives requiring heavy investments. At the same time, ventures like KINFRA parks would also be essential to meet the technology, value addition and export goals of Kerala's industrial sector. So, if five per cent of the additional jobs have to come from initiatives requiring KINFRA level of investments, with corresponding investment of Rs. 6,500 crore, the state would need about Rs. 19,000 crore.

Public and Private Sectors

Nearly, 75-85 per cent of the investment resources may have to come from the private sector. Obviously, the government may need to find out its own resources for the balance. The actual industrial investment need of the state over the years will, however, be dependent on (a) the time-frame the state to eliminate unemployment, (b) the rate at which the job seekers grow over time, (c) the proportion of job seekers getting absorbed in non-industry sectors and (d) the level of investments occurring in the small, medium and large sectors as well as in the traditional and new initiative segments.

Sunrise Industries

In various IT parks and facilities in the state, the total investment till March 2004 was of Rs. 252 crore and the employment created was 43,000 persons. Given the investment-employment ratio derived from these data, even for absorbing 5 per cent of the job seekers, the IT industry will require about Rs. 1115 crore of additional investment. Further, given the US$ 36 million exports achieved with the investment of Rs. 252 crore, and given the US$ 2708 million exports of Karnataka (2002-03), Kerala needs to make huge investments and efforts in the IT sector if in the near future Kerala's IT stature should become comparable to those of the other southern states. Large investments are also required in food-processing, biotechnology, etc.

Mobilisation of Resources

A large part of the investments required for industrialisation should come from the private sector with the government playing a strongly supportive role. By improving the political climate and the image of the state, a substantial part of the requirements could be attracted from outside the state and the country. Small entrepreneurs should continue to play a crucial role especially if the government makes the process of providing clearances, approvals and support facilities simple, short and pleasurable. Industrialisation of the state should receive the highest priority and the industrial sector should be rid from the shackles of disruptive agitations. Initiatives like KINFRA and SEZ should grow in importance, to attract new investors especially from outside Kerala, who may be sensitive to infrastructure deficiencies.

Public-Private Partnership

Partnership may be developed in the provision of infrastructure. There already exist many public-private partnership examples in India. The Cochin International Airport is one such instance. KINFRA is providing infrastructure while private investors are investing in the production and the service operations. In future, the government needs to give collaborative roles to private sector and to make use of the resources abundantly available with it. In such partnership ventures, the major role including management should vest with the private sector, with the government remaining a facilitator.

Accelerated Development of Industrial Infrastructure

There are several components to be attended with top priority. Power is the most important among them. Power should be available on demand. There should not be any disruption in supply. Quality of supply in terms of voltage stability and other parameters needs to be absolutely in conformity with industrial requirements. Given the population and the environmental factors, thermal or other polluting or ecologically sensitive sources of power do not seem to suitable for the state. Even large hydro projects may not be easy to implement without affecting the fragile ecosystem. In future growth in the power sector seems to lie in harnessing non-conventional and renewable sources as well as small and micro-hydro projects which will have only limited environmental ramifications. Even tiny captive power generation by industrial units from eco-friendly and prudential sources could be freely permitted.

Kerala is dependent predominantly on the Cochin port for exports. While there are other smaller ports, they serve limited purposes even with respect to local needs. There is need to develop alternative ports to ease the pressure on the Cochin port and to decentralise cross-border trade activities in the state. With the setting up of the Vallarpadam International Container

Transshipment Terminal, there needs to be further investment in railway transport and substantial growth in the railway carrying capacity. The telecommunications system has seen rapid improvements in the state during the past decade. At the existing rate of progress of this sector, Kerala is not expected to encounter any telecommunications constraints in its industrialisation process. The role of Cochin in the international telecommunication network of India has only increased Kerala's telecommunication prospects.

Although Kerala has a much better road network than many other regions of the country, there is a lot of scope to improvement. Traffic currently does not satisfy industrial requirements due to congestion routes and narrow stretches even on major highways. The proposed north-south highway might alleviate some of the difficulties. But other expansionary and maintenance measures will be essential too. The government has already declared its intention to involve the private sector in road and other infrastructure development activities.

Administrative infrastructure too needs upgradation to match the state's industrial challenges. The bureaucracy needs to be wellversed with management tools and approaches so that industrial facilitation and promotion are done on modern principles.

Initiatives & Participation of Local Governments

Local initiatives for promoting small-scale enterprises are underway in different districts and under several *panchayats*. Several *panchayats* have taken the lead in assessing, with the help of outside consultants, their industrial potential based on local resources. Some district *panchayats* have also been active in this matter. The *Kudumbashree* project is the manifestation of the changing nature of local efforts.

The local governments have in-depth knowledge of local resources, constraints and opportunities. Often, resources that could be used to fund industrial investments and used as materials for value addition, lie unused due to absence of local entrepreneurship and difficulties in finding markets for their products. Besides, when investments are done with borrowed resources, it is necessary to ensure the repayment potentials of borrowers. The local authorities would be able to find interested local entrepreneurs and ensure locally relevant investments which would fit into the local constraints and resources. Moreover, the local governments' role as providers of public utilities such as water and sewerage, is rapidly growing and the industries would become increasingly dependent on local governments for such utility services. Thus, the role of local governments in the industrialisation process is crucial.

Conclusions

After a prolonged period of industrial stagnation and accumulation of associated economic and social problems, Kerala has woken up to the urgent need to re-industrialise. However, since Kerala has lagged far behind the other major industrial states of India, in order to reach comparable levels of industrialisation within a period of not more than 10 years, Kerala's industrial growth should be about 10 per cent per annum. The feasibility of achieving such a high growth rate is doubtful at least in the next five years. Intensive efforts at industrialisation are being made at the government level; but the misadventures of the past still haunt the state. Other constraints such as those related to availability of land, fragility of the environment, and strategies and irregularities of the power supply situation set limit to the opportunities of Kerala for setting up of large enterprises. The industrialisation process in Kerala has therefore to be oriented towards small, environment-friendly and energy-efficient enterprises in areas such as IT hardware and software, health care, tourism, marine products, biotechnology and electronics.

All procedural formalities should be reduced into a single channel at which clearances and approvals are made; industrial investment should be made wholesome and pleasurable experience for prospective entrepreneurs.

APPENDIX 1

The alternative ISDP targets for Kerala for 2001-02 through 2010-11 presented in Table 6.1 are estimated using per capita ISDP of the six target states and India and the population of Kerala projected for those years based on Kerala population data given in Census 2001. The following method has been used for the estimation.

Step 1: Ideal ISDP for Kerala in 2000-01 = Per Capita ISDP of 2000-01 of target state x Population of Kerala in 2000-01.

Step 2: Target ISDP of Kerala for subsequent years if Kerala started at Ideal ISDP 2000-01 = ((Target state's actual ISDP 2000-01 × $(1+0.06)^t$ for t = 1 to 10 years from 2001-02 to 2010-11 (at assumed 6 per cent growth per annum))/Target state's population for corresponding subsequent year) x Kerala's population for corresponding subsequent year.

Step 3: ISDP growth rate Kerala actually requires for subsequent years to reach the 2010-11 target of Step 2 from the actual of 2000-01 = (((Kerala's ISDP target 2010-11/Actual ISDP of Kerala for $2000\text{-}01)^{0.1}) - 1)$

Step 4: Absolute target levels of ISDP of Kerala corresponding to Step 3, for subsequent years = $(1+\text{Target ISDP growth rate of Step 3})^t$ x Actual ISDP of 2000-01, where t = 1 to 10 for years 2001-02 to 2010-11.

Column (2) of Table 6.1 shows the levels of ISDP that Kerala would achieve in different years if ISDP continues to grow till 2010-11 at the trend rate of 4.2 per cent of 1991-92-2000-01. Column (3) presents estimates of ISDP growth at the rate of 6 per cent per year throughout 2001-02–2010-11.

Column (5) shows the ideal ISDP for Kerala if Kerala had reached the per Capita ISDP level of Gujarat in 2000-01 itself and if Kerala were to match Gujarat's per capita ISDP levels during 2001-02–2010-11 when Gujarat's ISDP grew at an assumed rate of 6 per cent per year. It is obvious that the burden of a 6 per cent growth of ISDP of Gujarat on Kerala (for matching Gujarat's ISDP in every year till 2010-11) will be only 4.8 per cent due to the favourable population growth differential of Kerala compared to Gujarat.

Column (4) of Table 6.1 suggests a Herculean task lying before Kerala: in 2000-01 Kerala achieved an actual ISDP of Rs. 6,712 crore instead of an ideal ISDP (compared to Gujarat) of Rs. 14,467 crore. So, in order to reach the 2010-11 ideal level of ISDP of Rs. 23,172 crore, Kerala has to travel all the way from Rs. 6,712 crores instead of from Rs. 14,467 crore. This implies that if Kerala has to achieve a per capita ISDP equivalent to that of Gujarat by 2010-11, the actual ISDP of Kerala has to grow from its 2000-01 level at a rate of 13.2 per cent per year throughout till 2010-11. Note that the actual trend growth rate of ISDP of Kerala till 2000-01 (4.2 per cent) does not come anywhere near this target.

Columns (6) to (11) and (15) to (20) may also be interpreted in a similar way. The findings are summarised below.

If Kerala were to be at the Maharashtra level of per capita ISDP in 2000-01, the Kerala ISDP should have been Rs. 15,552 crore in 2000-01 instead of the actual Rs. 6,712 crore. From this ideal ISDP, Kerala must have ensured just 4.8 per cent growth of ISDP per year till 2010-11 to match the Maharashtra per capita ISDP during this period with the Maharashtra ISDP growing at an assumed 6 per cent rate per annum. But, given the huge difference between the actual and the ideal ISDP of Kerala during 2000-01 (compared to Maharashtra), to reach the ideal ISDP level of 2010-11, the actual ISDP of Kerala is required to grow at a rate of a tremendous 14 per cent per annum till 2010-11.

To be at the per capita ISDP level of Tamil Nadu (TN) in 2000-01, Kerala's ISDP should have been Rs. 12,715 crores. Thereafter, to continue to have TN's level of per capita income every year till 2010-11 when TN's ISDP grows at 6 per cent per annum, Kerala's ISDP should have grown at 5.8 per cent. However, since actual ISDP of Kerala of 2000-01 remained much lower than the ideal level corresponding to that of Tamil Nadu, the actual ISDP of Kerala should grow at 12.8 per cent per year during 2001-02 – 2010-11 to reach TN's per capita ISDP level by 2010-11.

In the same way, to match a 6 per cent ISDP growth of Punjab, Kerala's ideal ISDP should grow at 5.1 per cent per year till 2010-11 from an ideal position of Rs. 11,116 crore in 2000-01. The actual ISDP of Kerala of 2000-01 should grow at a rate of 10.5 per cent annually till 2010-11 if Kerala were to achieve the per capita ISDP of Punjab by that year.

To match 6 per cent ISDP growth of Karnataka, the ideal ISDP of Kerala (at Rs. 8,768 crores in 2000-01) could have grown at 5.3 per cent between 2000-01 and 2010-11. But, to reach Karnataka's per capita ISDP level by 2010-11, Kerala's actual ISDP has to grow from its 2000-01 level by 8.1 per cent per year till 2010-11.

Since Andhra Pradesh's (AP's) per capita ISDP in 2000-01 was slightly lower than Kerala's, the ISDP of Kerala that matches the per capita ISDP of AP is also slightly lower than Kerala's. Given the favourable population growth differential of Kerala compared to AP, a target 6 per cent growth of ISDP of AP requires Kerala's 'ideal' ISDP to grow at 5.6 per cent if it were to match the per capita ISDP of AP till 2010-11. Further, the actual ISDP of Kerala of 2000-01 also has to grow only at 5.6 per cent per annum till 2010-11 if Kerala is happy to remain at the per capita ISDP level of AP in 2010-11.

Whereas, compared to the average per capita ISDP level of India in 2000-01, Kerala's ISDP should have been Rs. 9,349 crore. This ideal ISDP should have grown at 4.9 per cent per annum till 2010-11 to match the national per capita ISDP average till then when national ISDP supposedly grows annually at 6 per cent. In the same way, the actual ISDP of Kerala of 2000-01 should grow at 8.5 per cent per annum if Kerala's per capita ISDP were to reach the national average by 2010-2011.

In short, ignoring the case of AP, if Kerala has to reach respectable levels of per capita ISDP by 2010-11 by the national standard or the standards of leading industrial states of India, Kerala's ISDP has to grow from its 2000-01 level at a rate of 8.1 per cent at the minimum (to reach the Karnataka level) and 14 per cent at the maximum (to reach the Maharashtra level) annually till 2010-11.

Chapter 7

Infrastructure

In this chapter, the state of infrastructure is examined. In Section I, the discussion is with particular reference to road transport and the problems of that the road transport sector encounters as well as the schemes of transport improvement under way. Waterways, roadways, air transport and ocean transport are also touched upon. Section II deals with the power sector. The focus of the discussion is generation, distribution, consumption and pricing of electricity. The main problems of power sector are highlighted. The programme for the generation of alternative resources of energy is also mentioned in brief. Water supply resources of the state and water supply schemes at work receive attention in Section III. The organisational setup of water supply schemes and the financial performance of the Kerala Water Authority come under scrutiny. The discussion is concluded with an enumeration of the major strength and weakness of schemes operated by beneficiary groups and the identification of factors contributing to non-sustainability of existing water supply schemes. Telecommunications are discussed in Section IV. The origins and evolution are traced and the present state of the sector discussed in some detail. Most of the discussion is carried out on an inter-state comparative basis.

SECTION I: TRANSPORT

The backbone of industry in Kerala is its biomass and its human capital as well as information technology. The biomass includes agro-based, small-scale and traditional industries. Infrastructure and energy are catalysts of economic development, in particular of industrial development. A well developed infrastructure is a prerequisite for attracting investment and achieving development. The development of infrastructure requires coordination among various departments and agencies. Infrastructure projects typically involve high costs and long gestation periods. The inability to develop quality infrastructure is likely to stunt industrial as well as GDP growth. Kerala with its agriculture, and service-industry-based economy needs a high quality transportation network for achieving economic progress. Tourism, an important and growing economic sector in the state requires an extensive and efficient transportation network to attract visitors to its various exotic tourist destinations. Though Kerala stands fourth in the country in the matter of infrastructure penetration through transport, communication and energy related variables, the primary challenge that the state faces, is the upkeep, upgradation and expansion of the existing infrastructure to enable it to cater to the fast changing environment and socioeconomic development.

The Rate of Infrastructure Penetration

State	*Rate*
1. Maharashtra	2.8
2. Tamil Nadu	2.6
3. Punjab	2.5
4. Kerala	**2.5**
5. Karnataka	2.4

Source: Study of Confederation of Indian Industries, 2003.

Unlike the other parts of the country, urbanisation in Kerala is not limited to cities and towns. Barring a few *panchayats* in the hilly tracts and a few other isolated pockets, the entire state presents the picture of an urban-rural continuum. The Kerala society may be termed by and large urbanised. The urban spread demands heavy investment in infrastructure development. An urban spread may sometimes lead to the depletion of agricultural areas. Out-migration of people from rural areas may also raise transportation costs and energy consumption. However, the dispersed settlement systems that Kerala has, have certain positive aspects also. Kerala does not have separate processes of primate city development and metropolitan city development and the problems associated with such developments.

Transport within the state relies mainly on railways and, to a much greater degree, on roadways. The growing demand for door-to-door transport continues to boost road transport partly due to its inherent competitive advantage and partly to failure of other modes of transport. The state's transport sector has mixed ownership and management with public and private sectors participating in all development and operating services. The public sector is more into transport infrastructure while the private sector concentrates on road transport services and consultancy and construction works.

Kerala depends on all modes of transport—road, rail, air and water transport—for the movement of passengers and goods. The transport system consists of 1.46 lakh km of roads, 1,148 km of railways, 1,687 km of inland waterways and 111 statute miles of airways. There are 14 functional ports including the major port of Kochi. It is one of the most prominent ports on the western coast of India and is an ISO-rated port.

Roads

Kerala has a wide network of roads comprising 1,45,704 kms. The state has the highest road density in India with 374.9 km/100 sq.kms (the national average is 74.9 km/100 sq.km). Out of this, 1,12,551 kms (77.77 per cent) are owned by local governments (*panchayats*, municipalities and corporations); PWD, (Roads and Bridges) and PWD (NH) own 22,990 kms (15.78 per cent); the rest belongs to various departments and agencies (Forests, Kerala State Electricity Board (KSEB).

The major road network of Kerala (which comprises 1524 kms of National Highways (8 stretches) and 3785 km of State Highways) even though well-connected, faces severe constraints due to the urban sprawl and the haphazard ribbon development all along the routes. The existing traffic levels at most stretches are excessive and beyond the road capacity. The traffic on roads has been increasing at a rate of 10 to 11 per cent every year. Capacity augmentation of existing roads is beset with problems relating to limited right of way and land acquisition.

TABLE 7.1

Agency-wise Distribution of State Roads

Name of Department	*Length (Km)*	*Percentage*
Panchayats	98973	67.92
Municipalities	7696	5.82
PWD (Roads & Bridges)	21467	14.73
Corporation	5882	4.03
Forest	3926	2.69
Irrigation	2359	1.62
PWD (NH)	1523	1.04
Others (Railways, KSEB)	3874	2.65
Total	145704	100

Source: Government of Kerala (2005). *Economic Review, 2004*. State Planning Board, Thiruvananthapuram.

Of the 14 districts in the state, Ernakulum district has the largest share of PWD roads (with a length of 2182.217 km (10.17 per cent)) whereas Wayanad district has the lowest share with 515.897 kms (2.40 per cent). As on March 2004 there were 2024 bridges and 47,605 culverts on the PWD roads. Out of these, 182 bridges need reconstruction or renovation and 1,654 culverts are not in good condition.

The analysis of figures from 1980-81 onwards shows that the increase in the number of accidents was steady from 7064 in 1980-81 to 20,900 in 1990-91 and 34,387 in 2000-01. In 2003-04, the number stood at 40,312 (Table 7.2). However, the increase in the number of accidents has remained lower than the rate of increase of vehicle population in the state.

Public Transport

While most transport systems are made up of many modes—bicycle, bus, trains, car, autorickshaw, boat—bus forms the backbone of most urban transport systems. Road transport service also acts as the feeder service to rail, air and water traffic. In the case of Kerala, the major share of the passenger transport operations on roadways is vested with private operators. Kerala State Road Transport Corporation (KSRTC) holds only 13.54 per cent of the stage carriages in the state. The total number of stage carriages in the state were 31,889 in 2003-04; 11,453 lakh passengers travelled in the KSRTC buses during 2003-04. The average number of kms run by a bus in a day was 333 during 2003-04.

TABLE 7.2

Registered Road Accidents

Year	*No. of Accidents*
1980-81	7064
1985-86	10348
1990-91	20900
1992-93	27185
1993-94	32513
1994-95	36087
1995-96	37123
1996-97	34702
1997-98	33820
1998-99	33296
1999-00	34387
2000-01	37252
2001-02	38353
2002-03	38967
2003-04	40312

Source: Government of Kerala (2001). *Statistics for Planning*. Directorate of Economics and Statistics, Thiruvananthapuram; Government of Kerala. *Economic Review*. various years, State Planning Board, Thiruvananthapuram.

Out of 4199 buses of KSRTC, 545 buses (12.98 per cent) were aged 10 years or more in 2003-04.

Issues: Buses in the cities in Kerala as is the case in most Indian cities, are heavily overcrowded. Buses have to negotiate extremely congested, narrow streets, with no separate rights-of-way at all, fighting with an array of different types of vehicles—mini-vans, cars, taxicabs, motorised two-wheelers, auto rickshaws—and also pedestrians, cyclists, and street vendors. Severe congestion slows down most buses to a crawl during much of the day. Owing to insufficient number of vehicles and terrible service conditions, public transport has been losing its market share in many cities.

The deteriorating quality of public transport leads to a shift away from this mode towards individual motorised transport, a development that has worsened the problem of roadway congestion; it has reduced travel speed and endangered traffic safety arrangements. A possible solution to the crisis in the public transport sector is privatisation. Unfortunately, private operators are not adequately regulated and their services duly coordinated. Moreover, private buses are often poorly maintained and highly polluting, adding to problems of congestion and insecurity.

In the face of severe resource crisis, public authorities resort to cost-sharing devices such as privatisation and liberalisation of controls. A lasting solution to the problem can come only from enlargement and improvement of the public transport system.

Road Development Policy of the Government

Considering the great importance of the transportation network in the state and the key role of roadways, the Kerala government has evinced keen interest in development of transport of roadways. A *Road Development Policy* was prepared in 1999.

The Policy aims at "a sustainable road network providing connection to all cities, towns and villages, and allowing safe and efficient travel between them." The Government seeks to address the following key road sector issues:

(a) Alleviating Network Deficiencies and Improving Road Sector Financing:

It aims at rehabilitating existing high and medium density corridors in a phased and timely manner and upgrading the network to comply with modern highway design standards through provisions for the required funding.

(b) Enhancing Institutional Capacities

It seeks to improve the performance of the road sector through appropriate steps to modernise and improve the performance of the Public Works Department in order to keep pace with new developments and requirements.

(c) Reducing Accident Rates and Mitigating Adverse Environmental and Social Impacts

Kerala's high accident rates have prompted the government to address road safety problems; road safety audits for new road projects have been introduced and accident blackspot locations have been identified. The PWD has developed a draft comprehensive and integrated State Road Safety Action Plan with recommendations for road safety sub-sectors like coordination and management, accident data systems, safety publicity campaign, safety engineering, traffic legislation and enforcement, and safety research.

The plan also recommends the establishment of a PWD Road Safety Unit. For addressing environmental and social impact issues, the approach of the state government is to identify potential impacts early in the planning process and to programme accordingly so as to avoid or mitigate adverse effects of road development.

The policy is to prepare and implement Environmental Management Plans (EMP) whenever required and to develop codes for environmental practice related to road construction and maintenance.

The major stakeholders in the road sector of the state are Kerala Public Works Department (PWD) and Local Self Governing Bodies (LSG) including Corporations, Municipalities and *Panchayats*. The following organisations work under PWD:

- Kerala State Construction Corporation Ltd;
- Roads and Bridges Development Corporation of Kerala Ltd; and
- Kerala Road Fund Board

KSTP

- Commenced On: June 2002
- Completion Expected: Dec 2007
- Total Project Cost: Rs.1632 Crore
- World Bank–GoK Share: 80:20

The World Bank assisted Kerala State Transport Project (KSTP) implemented by PWD aims to improve traffic flow and road safety on Kerala State's primary road network, and to strengthen the institutional and financial capacity of Kerala's key transport sector agencies. The project consists of four main components: 1) The transport corridor improvement component will support upgrading of state highways (584 km), including related social and environmental mitigation measures, and rehabilitating inland water transport feeder canals (93 km). 2) The road maintenance component will provide periodic maintenance of state highways and major district roads (1143 km). 3) The road safety improvement component comprises consultant services for black spot identification, programming and designing of minor improvement works for State roads and minor mitigation measures and recommendations. Works identified through this service will be implemented through small contracts. 4) The institutional development and technical assistance component will provide services to implement the institutional strengthening action plan by appointing consultants in the areas of maintenance, management and data collection, and development of a road management system.

Institutional Strengthening Action Plan (ISAP): The action plan will implement the range of policy-based institutional strengthening measures to improve the capabilities of PWD and other concerned agencies in transport infrastructure development, maintenance and management.

GIS-based Road Information Management System (RIMS): A Road Information and Management System based on Geographical Information System (GIS) aimed at supporting the inventory management and developing long-term maintenance strategies for roads and bridges, is under preparation. Guidance to PWD in developing a vision and a plan for the road map for the state, adopting GIS in its day-to-day working, will also be provided.

Road Maintenance and Management System (RMMS): The Public Works Department of Kerala is establishing a Road Maintenance & Management System (RMMS) with the objective of controlling and monitoring construction and maintenance of bridges and roads. The RMMS aims at the promotion of overall decision-making and management capabilities with interfacing through the use of GIS technology for planning, reconnaissance and data acquisition as well as for management, design, budgeting, procurement, execution and maintenance of projects.

A Road-User Satisfaction Survey was initiated by PWD in the state to help improve road transport outcomes in Kerala. The study was intended to gain insights into people's perceptions of the existing road network and governing authority (PWD) and to obtain feedbacks.

Accident Management System (AMS): Geographical-knowledge-based Kerala Accident Management System is an accident data system that facilitates efficient recording and analysis of road accident data. Effective accident black-spot improvement works could be implemented only on the basis of a reliable and powerful accident database. This ensures collaboration among traffic police, road engineering departments, motor vehicles departments, insurance companies and non-government agencies involved in road safety. AMS was launched on 1st June 2004 by the Chief Minister of Kerala and was handed over to the Director General of Police.

A study was initiated in 2003 with the purpose of arriving at link-wise identification of the road network in Kerala to facilitate proper selection of road corridors for improvement. On the basis of the results of the study, a second State Road Project in Kerala PWD comprising State Road Improvement Project, Bypass Project, Hill Roads Improvement Project and Coastal

Road Improvement Project was prepared. Various strategic options were formulated, and links were short-listed based on socioeconomic and environmental impact assessment.

Recent Achievements in Road Transport

Some of the major achievements in the recent past in road transport are the following:

- Introduction of computer-aided issuance of Learners' Licence
- Improved service delivery system
- Hosting of website for the motor vehicle department
- Internet connectivity to various transport offices, and
- Intensification of awareness campaigns on road safety

Research and Development in Road Sector

Design, Research, Investigation and Quality Control Board (DRIQ Board), Kerala Highway Research Institute (KHRI) and National Transportation, Planning and Research Centre (NATPAC) are the major institutions in the state engaged in research and development of roadways.

Water Transport

Inland waterways in Kerala stretch to a length of 1687 kms (11.6 per cent of total inland waterways in the country). The major stretch in the state is the West Coast canal connecting Hosdurg in the north and Thiruvananthapuram (Poovar) in the south, having a length of 560 km. The 168 km stretch of West Coast Canal (Kollam-Kottapuram) along with the 14km stretch of Champakara canal and 23 km of Udyogamandal canal forms the National Waterway 3 (NW 3). The Central Government has initiated developmental activities for improvement and maintenance of fairway and provision of terminals, navigational aids, etc., through Inlands Waterways Authority of India. The cargo movement in this waterway during the year 2003-04 was 13,62,149 M.T.

Ninety-three km of the canal improvement is done with assistance of World Bank under Kerala State Transport Project (KSTP). On NW-3, capital dredging work in Kochi-Alappuzha sector has been completed and a depth of 2 metres has been provided in about 100 km length of the waterway between Kochi-Alappuzha and Udyogmandal and Champakara Canal. Canal dredging in the remaining part i.e. Alappuzha- Kollam and Kochi-Kottapuram, is in progress. A scheme for construction of terminals at 11 locations through CPWD is also in progress. A scheme for provision of night navigational aids on NW-3 has been approved and necessary action is being taken for its implementation.

The Government of India has accepted the extension of NW-3 from Kollam to Kovalam in the south and Kottappuram (Kodungalloor) to Kasargod in the north. These extensions along with the development of feeder canals will improve the inland water transport system in the state substantially.

The state's waterways sector has the potential to become a major source of employment, according to a study by the National Transportation Planning and Research Centre (NATPAC). Further, the study projects that 16.6 per cent of total goods traffic through road could be diverted to the water navigation system. According to this study, Kerala's inland waterways sector directly employs between 1.5 lakh and 2 lakh persons in the operation and maintenance of boats.

The State Water Transport Department operates passenger boats in Alappuzha, Kollam, Kottayam, Ernakulam, Kannur and Kasaragod. Even though revenue receipts increased by six per cent in the year 2003-04, revenue expenditure increased only by two per cent. The number of passengers who used water transport recorded an increase of 13.83 per cent during the year.

Railways

Kerala's major transport corridors, both rail and road, run the state's entire length. The total rail route length exceeds 1100 km for the strip of land of Kerala which extends for about 550 kms and has an average width of only 70 km. Railways in Kerala have grown substantially and stay well above the national figures in terms of route length. A major achievement in recent years has been the commissioning of the Konkan Railway in 1998.

The rail transportation system in Kerala is passenger-oriented. At present more than 120 passenger trains run daily on the rail network of the state; more than 1500 lakh passengers are carried annually by rail, the majority of whom are daily commuters for short distances (inter-city commuters).

The railway network in Kerala has been expanding over the years to accommodate the growth in passenger traffic. The performance of Thiruvananthapuram railway division is indicated in Table 7.3.

TABLE 7.3

Performance of Railway Division: Thiruvananthapuram

Route Length	625 km
Daily Number of Express Trains (in pairs)	57
Daily Number of Passenger Trains (in pairs)	58
Passenger Carried Daily	1.65 lakh
Annual Earnings from Passengers and Miscellaneous(Rs. Crore)	274.39
Goods (Tonnes)	126.93

Source: State Planning Board (1997). *Report of the Steering Committee on Transport and Communication*.

Fifty-six per cent of freight and 40 per cent of passenger traffic on Indian Railways are made by electric traction. The priority items to be taken up in the rail sector include the following:

- Early completion of all sanctioned doubling works.
- Rationalisation of long distance freight movements with linkages to container terminals at nodal points and efficient road connectivity.
- Electrification works and their extension up to Thiruvananthapuram.
- Introduction of a third line between Kayamkulam and Thiruvananthapuram and an additional line between Palakkad and Ernakulam.

Air Transport

Three airports are in service in Kerala—Thiruvananthapuram, Nedumbassery and Kozhikode. Of these, the Thiruvananthapuram and the Nedumbassery airports are "International Airports." The Kozhikode airport also has been declared an international airport in January 2006. Exports and imports are managed through air cargo complexes located at these airports. Nedumbassery airport became operational in 1999-2000. Though fluctuations are observed in the number of flights handled and passengers serviced in Nedumbassery and Kozhikode for the past five years, it is the Thiruvananthapuram airport that has shown a steady increase on both counts (Table 7.4).

The number of international flights handled at Thiruvananthapuram, which is ranked third in terms of revenue among the 120 airports in the country including five international airports managed by the

TABLE 7.4

Flights and Passengers from International Airports of Kerala

Year	*Thiruvananthapuram*		*Kochi*		*Kozhikode*	
	Flights	*Passengers*	*Flights*	*Passengers*	*Flights*	*Passengers*
1997-98	9610	1145154	-	-	6266	495753
1998-99	9066	1138185	-	-	6686	533011
1999-00	8448	1045654	5397	484475	6472	532704
2000-01	9079	996652	10301	751574	6211	481269
2001-02	9898	9598926	11478	832871	6871	512020
2002-03	10524	1012762	10301	751574	6211	481269
2003-04	15510	1357972	11478	832871	6871	512020

Source: Government of Kerala. *Economic Review* (Various years). State Planning Board, Thiruvananthapuram.

Airport Authority of India, has been higher (10,688 in 2003-04) than in the other two airports put together (7623 in 2003-04), even though the volume of investment made in the Thiruvananthapuram airport since 1991 has been lower than Rs.100 crore. Moreover, Thiruvananthapuram airport has the locational advantage of being used by international flights as a point for refuelling. This advantage is likely to enhance the revenue of the airport further in the years to come. But in order to realise its full potential, much larger investments are required for expansion of aircraft parking bays, extension of taxiways, etc., in addition to the already felt need for expanding the international terminal.

Shipping and Ports

In Kerala, only Kochi port falls in the category of major ports. Along its coastal line of 585 kms, Kerala has one major, three intermediate and 10 minor ports. Even though the hinterland of Kochi port spreads to parts of Tamil Nadu and Karnataka apart from the whole of Kerala State, a study shows that 97 per cent of the total volume of traffic from this port is accounted for by Kerala. The major share of (73.38 per cent) the cargo handled at Kochi port during the year 2003-04 relates to Petroleum and Allied Products. Table 7.5 gives a rough idea of the performance of the Kochi port.

Non-major ports are under the control of state government. The government agencies involved in port development activities in the state are Port Department, Harbour Engineering Department, Hydrographic Survey Wing and Kerala State Maritime Development Corporation. Among the non-major ports, only Beypore

TABLE 7.5

Performance of Kochi Port at a Glance

Parameters	*2002-03*	*2003-04*
Total Traffic in lakh tonnes		
(a) Import	108.99	111.19
(b) Export	21.25	24.53
Total	130.245	135.74
Container Traffic in TEUs	165687	169965
No. of Container Vessels Handled at the Port	483	381
Average Turn Round Time in Days	2.19	2.22
Average Pre-berthing Time in Hours	1.67	4.02
No. of Employees as on 31st March	4375 persons	4353
Net Surplus in Rs. Crores	19.40	21.34

Source: Government of Kerala (2005). *Economic Review 2004*. State Planning Board, Thiruvananthapuram.

port accounted for a major share of cargo handling. The number of steamers and sailing vessels that called at non-major ports was 361 with a net registered tonnage of 109701 in 2003-04. The activities of other ports are almost entirely limited to registration and licensing of harbour crafts, maintenance of local light houses, display of water warning signals for sea rescue operations and collection of revenue. During the year 2003-04, 2180 harbour crafts were registered.

The port at Kochi is administered directly by the Government of India. The three intermediate ports are located at Neendakara, Alappuzha and Beypore, while the 10 minor ports are at Vizhinjam, Thiruvananthapuram, Kollam, Kodungallur, Vadakara, Thalassery, Ponnani, Azheekkal, Kannur and Kasaragod.

TABLE 7.6

Number of Ships and the Total Tonnage Handled at Kochi Airport: 1995-96-2003-04

Year	*No. of Ships called at the Port*	*Net Registered Tonnage (in Lakhs)*
1995-96	921	73.49
1996-97	940	76.48
1997-98	1006	83.62
1999-00	1113	87.62
2000-01	1096	87.79
2001-02	1100	82.17
2000-02	1190	82.72
2002-03	1174	78.15
2003-04	1133	79.44

Source: Government of Kerala. *Economic Review* (various years). State Planning Board, Thiruvananthapuram.

The volume of business at the port at Kochi shows an upward trend of growth though inter-year fluctuations are observed. To improve its performance and to ward off competition from the nearby ports of Mangalore and Tuticorin, connectivity and accessibility of the port has to be improved. This could be done through expansion of the existing road and rail links to the port. The newly planned container facility transhipment at Vallarpadam Island would be a boost to the transport sector in general in the state. Since the island has not yet been connected to the mainland, immediate investments are required in the rail and the road sectors. Thus an overall development through investments in all these three sectors is envisaged.

TABLE 7.7

Performance of Non-Major Ports

Year	*Number*	*Net Registered Tonnage*
1995-96	418	150067
1996-97	407	100848
1997-98	333	112356
1999-00	375	106526
2000-01	390	118474
2001-02	370	86954
2002-03	360	65246
2003-04	361	109701

Source: Government of Kerala. *Economic Review* (various years). State Planning Board, Thiruvananthapuram.

The non-major ports handle only an insignificant tonnage of cargo. Over the years the picture has been one of a declining trend. Since trade in these regions is improving, these ports are bound to grow if basic facilities in them are improved. More private participation planned in the new 'Transhipment Hub' at Vizhinjam is likely to encourage trade.

The port-based Special Economic Zone agreed to in principle by the Government of India, establishment of LNG terminal at Putuvaiipin, and the ICTT at Vallarpadam are bound to increase the volume of rail/road traffic substantially and thereby to increase trade through these non-major ports.

Vision for Development—On the Road to the Future

Even though Kerala is comparatively better placed than most other states in India in terms of road length, the condition of many of its roads is poor. Therefore, the main emphasis under road development in Kerala has been on improvement and upgradation of existing roads rather than on construction of new roads. The investment needs in the road sector are of magnitudes far beyond the resources available with the state Government.

The road network in Kerala has the distinction of achieving connectivity to all villages in the state, connectivity has not been established in all its habitats, the establishment of which should be the future direction of efforts in road development in the state. The traffic density in National Highways and State Highways in the state has already surpassed the two-lane capacity; the traffic demand in most of the urban roads has reached the level of 30000-40000 PCUs thereby warranting the establishment of four and six lanes, especially in the high density corridors. Since widening of existing highways may pose problems, the development of alternative routes along new alignments free of utility hindrances is the solution to the inadequacy of the road sector in Kerala.

Apart from a road development policy, a comprehensive road transport policy is also urgently required in the state. Such a policy should take into full account the need for integration with other modes of transport and the resultant beneficial community outcomes in economic, environmental and social terms. It should also incorporate as its goal, the promotion of global technology standards in order to maximize opportunities. The possibilities of new forms of financing, road pricing, combined transportation, inter-modal platforms, corridors, etc. should also be looked into.

Efficient transport connectivity among urban centres within the state as well as with other states is essential for boosting economic development. The capital city has initiated development programmes by integrating them with the Capital Region Development Programme. The upcoming of Vizhinjam port and the Kochuveli railway terminal projects and the development of Technopark, will give a face lift to Thiruvananthapuram city. Likewise the Vallarpadam container terminal, LNG terminal, the KINFRA IT Park and the Smart City projects will further raise Kochi to the status of a megalopolis in a short time. These developments cannot become fruitful without establishing proper connectivity among urban centres and installation of an efficient transport system within cities. Apart from city development, considering the state's policy of economic development with emphasis on the state service industries including IT, tourism, education, health etc, transportation and the transport system of the region will have a very important role to play.

Despite its inherent advantages, inland water transport continues to be a neglected sub-sector of the transport system in Kerala. There is need to give greater attention to this mode of transport in plan allocations in the state.

The transport situation in Kerala can be improved by efficient planning and proper coordination among the multifarious agencies involved, and by augmentation of the public transport system. A meaningful urban transport policy needs to be formulated which should have the following objectives:

- Ensuring full use of available transport infrastructure through low-cost optimisation measures;
- Development of cost-effective road/rail/water-based forms of public systems and inter-modal integration;
- Reduction of emissions from motor vehicles;
- Land use – transport integration;
- Ensuring high levels of financial support for urban transport projects by both Central and State Governments and exploration of innovative sources of financing; and
- Development of suitable institutional mechanisms at national, state and local levels for planning, financing, construction and O&M of urban transportation systems.

Planning For Rail-Based Urban Transport: In cities with three million inhabitants or more, there exist several corridors of heavy peak hour and direction traffic. Provision of rail-based urban transport system on such corridors becomes inescapable, and institutional arrangements for introducing such systems in eligible cities are overdue. City-wise or region-specific projects for rail-based urban transport systems together with funds required for them need to be identified. Certain other measures required are the following:

Transport agencies of the state have not proved themselves to have adopted working with the public. The public feel alienated from transportation programmes (especially road projects). A holistic approach of project implementation, allowing the public to make a fair and impartial assessment of the programme and project trade-offs is urgently called for.

An effective system of citizen involvement requires a comprehensive approach mirroring all phases of transportation system planning, programme development, project planning and design, implementation and monitoring. Also, due attention needs to be extended on 'context based' environment and social issues in each project, through focused group discussions in order to secure the people's mandate for taking the projects forward and attaining their goals in full.

SECTION II: POWER

Introduction

Power generation in Kerala began in 1940 when the Government of Travancore began the 5 MW Pallivasal project. The development of Kerala's power sector is mainly the responsibility of the government-owned Kerala State Electricity Board (KSEB). KSEB is engaged in generation, transmission and distribution of power in the state.

Kerala's resource endowments in conventional power generation lie mainly in its vast hydel potential. Kerala's abundant hydro-potential derived from its 44 rivers, is estimated at 30,000 MU at 60 per cent load factor (Cyriac, 1988). But only a third of the state's resources has been utilised. Unfortunately, Kerala has hardly any known fossil fuel resources like coal or oil. Its energy source is, therefore, not diverse. Resource constraints and numerous socio-environmental concerns impede the growth and development of the power sector in the state.

Besides KSEB, the Agency for Non-Conventional Energy and Rural Technology (ANERT) and Energy Management Centre (EMC) facilitate the development of non-conventional energy and energy conservation measures in the state.

Kerala's Power Sector Development: An Overview

Till recently, power generation in Kerala has been rightly focused on tapping the hydro-power[1] potential of the state. There has been remarkable progress in the growth of the power system in Kerala since 1951 (See Table 7.8).

The power system of Kerala consists of 18 hydel stations, two captive power plants, three Independent Power Producers (IPPs), five major inter-state transmission lines, one 400 KV substation and two 220 KV substations with inter-connecting grid (GoK, 2005). The lion's share of the energy requirement of the state was being met till recently by the generation by 20 hydel power plants controlled and operated by KSEB. Though Kerala has a total hydel generation potential of about 4333 MW, only 1835 MW could be harnessed till now. While industrial development remained stagnant, there has been phenomenal growth in domestic consumption of power. As the state could not keep pace with increasing demand for energy by undertaking more hydel projects, it was forced to turn increasingly towards thermal energy either through import of power or through power generation within the state. On account of high transportation costs of coal and environmental problems, coal-based thermal power plants did not come up in a big way in the state. Kerala State Electricity Board established two diesel power plants: one at Brhmapuram near Kochi (106.6 MW) and another at Kozhikode (128 MW). NTPC established a naphtha-based thermal plant at Kayamkulam (360 MW). The Government of Kerala permitted establishment of diesel-based power generation stations at Cochin (157 MW) of BKPL and at Kasargod (20MW) of KPCL. The state has also been forced to purchase more power from central generating stations.

TABLE 7.8

Growth of Power Generation and Distribution in Kerala, 1951-2004

	1951	*2004*
Installed Capacity (MW)	37.5	2615.71
Annual Sales of Power (MU)	140	8910.84
Per Capita Consumption of Power (kWh)	13	386
EHT Lines (circuit KM)	910.7	9256.12
HT Lines (circuit KM)	1067	33280.22
LT Lines (circuit KM)	992	201637
Distribution Transformers	324	34758

Source: India: A Reference Annual, Government of India.

Installed Capacity

Generation of power by KSEB from its plants in 2003-04 stood at 4488.06 MU, out of which 87.17 per cent came from hydel sources (GoK, 2005).

Till the middle of the 1980s, Kerala had been a power surplus state. During 1974-85 the state had exported huge quantities of electricity to the neighbouring states due to low internal demand

1. Hydro power is a renewable, non-polluting and economical form of energy.

(presumably due to the industrial backwardness of the state), and sluggish household demand. This situation rapidly changed after 1985 since when the net import of power into the State began to increase steadily.

Kerala now experiences acute power shortage due to slow growth in installed capacity in relation to the internal peak demand. The possible reason for the poor growth in installed capacity is the near-total dependence on hydel sources. It has been observed that the state's power requirements could not be met fully from hydel projects alone (Parameswaran, 1990). Experts are of the opinion that at least 200 MW of non-hydel generating capacity has to be added every year if the state has to avoid energy crisis (Menon, 1990).

The total reliance on major hydro projects resulting in a virtual exclusion of other options has really contributed to the tardy growth of capacity. The state's enormous potential for mini-, and micro-hydel projects could have been positively tapped. Micro projects are environmentally sustainable and economically desirable. Small hydel projects have been mentioned as a solution to energy problems of remote and hilly areas where extension of grid system is non-economical.[2]

The hydro projects awaiting sanction from the Ministry of Environment and Forests are capable of contributing another 408 MW. Projects held up in inter-state disputes would add a generation capacity of 700 MW. The potential capacity of the exploitable schemes is of the order of 1181 MW.

Maximum Demand

Today, about 20 per cent of the demand for electricity in the state is for the lighting purpose. There are two forms of maximum demand viz., maximum internal demand and maximum system demand.[3] It was found that up to the Sixth Plan, the maximum system demand exceeded maximum internal demand. Thereafter the maximum internal demand tended to exceed the maximum system demand (Pavithran, 1999). In the context of Kerala, the system has been unable to meet the internal maximum demand from the mid-1980s onwards; therefore, load management techniques like load shedding and power cut are implemented to overcome persistent power shortages. The gap between system demand and internal demand is made up through power imports.

In the year 1980-81, the average generating capacity was 1011.50 MW, the maximum internal demand was 735.40 MW and the maximum system demand was 843.10 MW. By the year 2003-04 the average generating capacity went up to 2614.22 MW, the maximum internal demand to 2520.00 MW and the system demand to 2333.00 MW. KSEB now owns 20 hydel power stations, 2 thermal power stations and 1 wind farm. The naphtha-based thermal power plant situated at Kayamkulam is owned by NTPC. There are two privately owned hydel power stations, one at Maniar and the other at Kuthungal. The break up of the installed capacity of electricity in the state during the year 2003-04 was as shown below:

KSEB:	2044.23 MW
NTPC:	359.58 MW
Thermal(IPP):	178.90 MW
Hydel(Private):	33.00 MW
Total:	2615.71 MW

In addition, Kerala is entitled to its share from the central pool delivered through the lines of the Power Grid Corporation of India Ltd. The details are given in Table 7.9.

TABLE 7.9

Supply of Power from Central Pool

S No	*Name of Stations*	*Installed Capacity*	*Kerala's Share (MW)*
1	Ramagundam STPs	2100	245
2	NLC Stage I	630	63
3	NLC Stage II	840	90
4	MAPS	340	18
5	KAPP	440	38
6	Eastern Region	-	60
7	Western Region	-	15% of surplus power

Source: GoK, 2002.

Besides, Kerala is also entitled to get a share of 16 per cent from the unallocated portion of about 610 MW for all the stations put together. On an average the actual central share accounts for 415-450 MW and 10 to 11 MU. Except BSES, private generation is yet to come on a significant scale. Maniar and Kuthungal are hydel projects in the private sector having a total installed capacity of 33 MW. These projects cater to

2. Personal interview by the author with Prof. V.K. Damodaran.
3. The maximum internal demand refers to peak load of consumers and the maximum system demand is what the state can meet during the peak hours (6 pm to 10 pm).

EHT consumers and are therefore deemed captive plants.

A few hydel projects with a total installed capacity of 12.6 MW have been installed by KSEB with technical assistance from IN-SHP China. The micro-hydel projects commissioned under this arrangement in the year 2003-04 are listed in Table 7.10.

TABLE 7.10

Micro Hydro Projects with Assistance of IN-SHP China, Commissioned in 2003-04

Sl No	*Name of Projects*	*Capacity (MW)*
1	Chempukkadavu Stage I	2.7
2	Chempukkadavu Stage II	3.75
3	Urumi I	3.75
4	Urumi II	2.4
	Total	12.6

Source: GoK, 2002.

There has been unprecedented increase in the demand for power in the state of Kerala with rise in the standard of living, a flourishing construction sector and a thriving market for electrical and electronic goods. The 'Gulf boom', and the increasing NRI remittances from the Gulf, have triggered an unprecedented growth of the housing sector and encouraged an increasing demand for electricity appliances in Kerala since the mid-1970s. The number of electrified houses must have increased also a result of the several social security schemes of the government (IRTC, 1996). Although a serious power shortage situation had entailed restrictions on providing new connections since 1982-1983, energy consumption intensity in terms of the number of customers as well as of connected load, has been on the increase (Kannan and Pillai, 2002).

It was earlier mentioned that till the turn of the 1980s, Kerala had been a power surplus state, exporting power to neighbouring states. Since the drought of 1982-83, Kerala had been experiencing unprecedented power cuts and load shedding, constraining actual demand.

Sectoral Demands for Power in Kerala: Consumer Groups

The various types of demand for power in Kerala are classified into:

- Domestic, commercial and industrial low tension
- Industrial high tension and extra high tension
- Agricultural
- Public lighting
- Public works; and
- Licensees[4]

Consumer Demand & Connected Load

The demand for electricity for various categories depends upon their connected load. Connected load directly varies with the number of consumers and the installed electrical appliances. During the period 1970-1971 to 1995-96, the domestic sector registered the highest rate of increase in connected load, namely 10.34 per cent per annum. The household sector recorded quinquennial changes of more than 75 per cent during the first 15 years. The rate of increase in the connected load in the domestic sector declined thereafter due to KSEB's refusal to provide new connections to all applicants, for reasons of power shortage and rising backlog of applicants. The details of the total number of consumers and the connected load for selected years are given in Table 7.11.

TABLE 7.11

Consumers and Connected Load

Year	*No. of Consumers*	*Connected Load in KW*
1990-91	3449888	4642680
1995-96	4685880	5776094
2000-01	6446298	8551000
2001-02	6661724	8917060

Source: KSEB, Power System Statistics, 2001-02.

Commercial connected load has increased at an annual compound rate of growth of 7.8 per cent. It is observed that up to 1985-86, the rate of change in commercial connected load was higher than that of industrial (LT, EHT, HT) connected load. However, during 1985-90 the rate of change in commercial connected load fell behind that of household and industrial connected load. In the 1990s the commercial connected load showed higher rate of change than the connected loads for other sectors.

Connected load in the agricultural sector rose at a rapid rate till 1980-81; thereafter the rate tended to decline perceptibly. However, for the entire span of the

4. Licensees are a category of consumers who purchase electricity from KSEB and sells the same to various groups of consumers within a specified area.

past quarter of a century, the agricultural sector recorded a high rate of growth from 75.15 MW to 563.85 MW, next only to the domestic sector. The compound annual rate of growth of connected load in this sector was 7.8 per cent.

Sectoral Consumption of Power in Kerala

Kerala accounts for only 2.78 per cent of the total electricity consumed in the country (TERI, 1996-97). But the state has the highest share of household consumption (44.93 per cent), the reasons for which are electrification of all villages in the state, the high rate of urbanisation, high density of population, high literacy rate, impact of foreign remittances leading to a housing boom and high rate of use of electric gadgets. In the matter of energy consumption in the commercial sector too, Kerala ranks the highest (13.28). By contrast, in energy consumption in the agricultural sector, Kerala has the lowest position (3.91 per cent) as against the national average of 30 per cent. The industrial sector accounts for 33.47 per cent of the total energy consumption in the state which forms the highest figure in India (Table 7.12). This high figure may be attributed to the following factors.

Electricity is the major form of energy used by the industrial units in Kerala, while it is alternative energy sources like coal and oil that are significantly used in other parts of the country.

All the 34 EHT units operating in the state are said to be highly power-intensive.

TABLE 7.12

Power Consumption in Kerala

S No	Category	% of Consumers to Total	Consumption as % of Total
1	Domestic	78.79	44.93
2	Commercial LT&HT	14.22	13.28
3	Industrial LT	1.47	8.42
4	Industrial HT&EHT	0.02	25.05
5	Others	5.49	8.31
	Total	100.00	100.00

Source: GoK, 2005: 201, Table 7.10.

Energy Availability

The energy availability in the state for the year 2003-04 was 12279.92 million kWh (Table 7.13) of which 4488.06 million kWh was from generation of power on Hydel, Thermal and Wind Farm operations; 8014.46 million kWh was from purchases from the central pool and the private generating system. The total loss was to the extent of 174.5 million kWh and auxiliary consumption accounted for 48.1 million kWh.

TABLE 7.13

Energy Availability in the State During 2003-04

S No	Source	Power in Million kwh
1	Generation	
	A Hydel	3910.68
	B Thermal (BDPP+KDPP)	574.89
	C Wind Farm	2.49
	Total (1)	4488.06
2	Power purchases	
	A NTPC-Kayankulam	1034.00
	B NTPC-Ramagundam	2271.22
	C NLC-Neyveli Lignate Corporation	1348.11
	D MAPS- Madras Atomic Power Project	80.13
	E Eastern Region	467.52
	F Kaiga	373.60
	G BSES	992.21
	H KPCL-Kasargod	77.23
	I PTC Power	71.20
	J UI Units	682.15
	K GEL	12.03
	L Talcher Stage II	605.06
	Total (2)	8014.46
	Total (1+2)	125 02.52
	Less: Losses in MU	174.5
	Auxiliary consumption	48.1
	Total	222.6
	Net Availability in million Kwh	12279.92

Source: GoK, 2005: 203, Table 7.12.

Pattern of Power Consumption and Revenue Realisations

As on 31.3.2004, there were 7253866 consumers in Kerala which fetched a revenue of Rs. 275682.87 lakh to the exchequer. There were 4.74 lakh applications for power connection pending with KSEB (GoK, 2005: 205).

The household sector forms the largest consuming sector in Kerala, which continues to be heavily subsidised. Of the total number of consumers, 78.79 per cent belong to the household sector which consumes 44.93 per cent of the energy; the revenue realised from this sector is however only 25.52 per cent. Household consumers enjoy the lowest tariff next only to agriculture. HT and EHT consumers account 25.05

TABLE 7.14

Pattern of Power Consumption and Revenue Collected During 2003-04

Category	*No. of Consumers*	*Connected Load as on 31/3/04(MW)*	*Energy Sold (MU)*	*Consumption as % to Total*	*Revenue Collected (Rs lacs)*	*Revenue as % to Total*
Domestic						
(a) Paying group	5705904	5949.21	3995.52	44.84	70372.04	25.53
(b) Non paying	46212	15.06	8.36	0.06	57861.13	20.99
Commercial LT+HT+Non ind	1037815	1280.48	1312.75	14.73	2816.56	1.02
Public lighting	2325	83.61	165.68	1.86	1967.85	0.71
Irrigation & Dewatering	399044	721.78	211.03	2.37	30550.76	11.08
Industrial						
(a) LT	107754	1173.95	750.51	8.42	104564	37.93
(b) HT & EHT	1011	635.15	2232.5	25.05	1679.8	0.61
Railway Traction	4	24.5	46.12	0.52	5796.45	2.10
Bulk Supply to Licensee	9	26.41	188.37	2.11	73	0.03
Outside supply						
Total	7300078	9910.15	8910.84	100.00	275682.87	100

Source: Gok (2005).

per cent of the energy sold, but contribute 37.93 per cent of the revenue collected (Table 7.14).

Transmission and Distribution

Transmission

The transmission and distribution system in the state has not kept pace even with the slow and inadequate addition in generation capacity. Shortfalls in transmission and distribution have resulted in a very defective power system and a poor quality power supply.

TABLE 7.15

Power System Transmission Infrastructure Commissioned (2003-04 & 04-05)

Capacity	*Sub Stations (Nos.)*		*Transmission Lines (Nos.)*	
	2003/04	*2004/05 (upto31/8/04)*	*2003/04*	*2004/05 (upto31/8/04)*
1	*2*	*3*	*4*	*5*
220 KV	1	-	1	-
110 KV	6	2	7	2
66KV	3	-	3	-
33KV	7	3	8	3

Source: GoK, 2005, Table 7.12.

KSEB attaches prime importance to strengthening of infrastructure to match the installed capacity. Transmission infrastructure facility was substantially increased and strengthened during 2003-04. The details of the transmission infrastructure commissioned during 2003-04-2004-05 are given in Table 7.15.

The progress of the transmission works of the power system development in Kerala has been hardly satisfactory for the following main reasons:

Opposition from the public to alignment of transmission lines and acquisition of land for substations; in a few cases, non-availability of land to draw lines through forest areas.

Poor contract and project management and inadequate project monitoring.

Incomplete procurement or non-procurement of materials required for work.

Frequent deviations from plans due to ad hoc decisions to take up schemes of vested interests and consequent diversion of materials.

Distribution

It is officially declared that all the villages in the state are electrified. But, in reality, electricity is yet to reach about 40 per cent of the households in Kerala. (State Planning Board, 2002). KSEB is the sole distributor of power in Kerala except Thrissur Municipal corporation and Munnar where distribution is managed by licensees. In Thrissur the City

Corporation and in Munnar M/s Tata Tea Ltd are the licensees. The details of the distribution infrastructure of KSEB are given in Table 7.16. The details of achievements in the power distribution sector during 2003-04 and 2004-05 are given in Table 7.17. The performance of the distribution system is highlighted in Table 7.18.

TABLE 7.16

Distribution Infrastructure (2004-05)

No of consumers	7253866
11K V lines ckm	30296
LT lines ckm	189309
Distribution transformers	31579

Source: GoK, 2005.

TABLE 7.17

Distribution of Power in Kerala (2003-04 - 2004-05)

Particulars	*2003/04*	*2004/05 (Up to 31-8-04)*
No of Service Connections	391815	152132
11 K V Lines (ckms)	1269.10	249.22
LT Lines (ckms)	4429.23	2087.159
Distribution Transformers (Nos.)	1063	398
Street Lights (Nos.)	34383	20313

Source: GoK, 2005.

Inadequacies

There exist grave inadequacies in the generation, transformation and distribution sectors of the power system in Kerala. From the very beginning of the project implementation stage, inefficiencies have occurred in the form of time and cost overruns. Inordinate delays in project implementation and consequent cost escalation have become a regular feature in the electric power sector in Kerala. Normally the completion of a major hydro-power plant would take 8 to 10 years and of a mini hydel project, 2 to 3 years. But in Kerala, in both cases, much longer gestation periods are involved in the completion of projects; as a consequence, higher cost escalations have become a usual feature.[5]

Transmission and Distribution (T&D) losses are another matter of serious concern. The energy losses occur during the transmission of power from the generating station to the end users. Power losses are incurred due to technical factors such as power station auxiliary consumption, transformation and transmission consumption and sub-transmission consumption, and non-technical reasons like defective metering, out-moded billing, un-metered supplies, pilferage and theft.

Though Kerala had reportedly the minimum level of Transmission and Distribution losses of around 12 per cent during the 1970s, the proportion of losses started rising during the 1980s reaching the highest level of

TABLE 7.18

Physical Targets and Achievements in Distribution Sector During Ninth Five Year Plan

	1997-98		*1998-99*		*1999-2000*		*2000-01*		*2001-02*		*PA up to*
	PT	*PA*	*PT*	*PA*	*PT*	*PA*	*PT*	*PA*	*PT*	*PA*	*31-3-02*
Service connections including agriculture (Nos.)	2,00,000	287588	318015	392668	350000	390512	500000	410997	200000	330213	8743900
Agricultural connections	10000	14260	10000	21149	16000	20711	10000	16856	10000	13919	86895
Construction of 11KV lines (km)	3000	5827	1800	10069	1800	917.18	1100	1250.6	3800	881.09	9882.7
Construction of LT lines (km)	8000	5548	7000	5957	4000	6302.7	7550	6700.8	7000	4545.92	29055.23
Erection of transformers (Nos.)	2000	853	2000	1326	2000	1589	1750	1871	3300	1224	6854
Street light installation (Nos.)	17000	17076	17585	29233	18000	48859	28700	47522	58700	33141	175831

Note: PT-Physical Target

PA-Physical Achievements

Source: Government of Kerala, *Economic Review 2002*.

5. For example, the Kakkad power project was sanctioned in 1976 and originally scheduled to be commissioned in 1996. But work started only in 1979 and the estimated cost was revised to Rs.153.5 cr. against the original estimate of Rs.18.60 crore. The cases of the Kallada, Lower Periar, Pooyamkutty, Malampuzha, Mettupetty, Malankara, Chimony, Peppara. Azhutha diversion, Kuttiar diversion, Peringalkuth West Bank Extension, Vadakepuzha Diversion, Vazhikadave Diversion, Kuttiadi Tail Race and Kuttiady, Extension, have also been similar.

28.95 per cent in 1987-88. It moved downward to reach the level of 20.05 per cent in 1995-96 (Kannan & Pillai, 2002). But in more recent years it has again increased to 30 per cent (GoK, 2002; 2004). The poor status of T&D network such as insufficient distribution lines and inadequate transformers has been mentioned as the major reason for high T&D losses in Kerala (Pavithran, 1999). The technical reasons for the losses include energy dissipation in the conductors and equipments used for transmission and distribution of power (IRTC, 1996).

Transmission loss has been on the increase due to insufficient HT and LT lines. Though the length of circuit kilometres of HT lines increased from 1067 in 1951 to 33280 in 2004, it remains inadequate. Between 1951 and 2004 the circuit kms of LT lines increased to 201637 from 992. The distribution efficiency of a power system depends to a great extent on LT lines as they are mainly distribution lines. In Kerala, power is distributed through lengthy distribution lines, which lie in many cases in places far away from transformers. It is pointed that the ideal ratio between HT and LT is 1:1 which in Kerala has been a mere 1:6.3.[6] The installation of transformers at the load centre itself is another measure necessary to reduce T&D loss. The loss of energy due to poor T&D network affects the economic efficiency of the power system.

It is noted that 70 per cent of the total energy loss is due to technical reasons and 30 per cent due to non-technical reasons (IRTC, 1996:89). The transmission loss is different from distribution loss: the former happens through delivery of power at high voltage (220 KV and 66 KV) and the latter through delivery at low voltage (11KV, 200v) to the consumer end. There are voltage substations at various levels such as 220 KV, 110 KV and 66 KV. When the line length is beyond the stipulated circuit kilometres, voltage tends to drop at the tail end of the line. The energy loss could, therefore, be curbed through installing sufficient number of transformers.

The T&D loss in Kerala has been found to be 30 per cent (GoK, 2004). A major part of the commercial loss is due to the defective metering system as well as theft, pilferage and misuse. According to a study, approximately eight lakh meters in the state were defective. Replacement of these meters would cost of Rs 80 cr. Experiments made in sections have shown that replacement of faulty meters could bring down T&D loss to 20 per cent or even lower. Reduction in T&losses by 10 per cent could increase the revenue by about Rs 240 cr per annum (GoK, 2002). Hence, replacement of defective and sluggish meters as well as strengthening anti-theft activities, are to be given top priority.

In the performance of the power system, adequate supply of conductors of various voltage levels of transmission and distribution is essential. Because of the strained financial status of KSEB, this problem has hardly been addressed. The line loss in Kerala is heavy because hydro-projects are location-specific. The existing 10 hydro-projects are located in the eastern part of the state, while the consumers are concentrated in the coastal regions on the west. In order to transmit power at the stipulated ratings throughout Kerala, a large number of substations of various capacities are essential. But the rate of growth of substations and conductors has been lower than that of other variables like consumers, consumption and connected load. To evacuate high voltage power from the generating point to the various substations located in different parts of the state, 440/220 KV substations are required.[7] That transmission of power at very high voltage is more economical in the sense of minimising line losses is well-known; but Kerala woke up to this fact only in the year 1992 when the state commissioned its first 440KV substation. It has been proposed that at least three 440 KV substations are required in the State (KSEB, 1996). Unlike the other south Indian States, there exists no 440 KV feeder in Kerala to deliver power to various substations. All these factors contribute to poor level of T&D system in the state.

It is a matter of concern that the distribution loss is quite high in rural areas, amounting to more than 30 per cent on an average, approaching 40 per cent during peak hours (Suresh & Elachola, 2000). The main problem of the rural distribution system is its large number of low load consumers distributed over a large area. This is a consequence of the habitat patterns of the region in which the distance between homesteads is comparatively high. Another problem is that the length of LT lines far exceeds the length of HT lines. Still another factor is the lengthy single-phase lines that contribute to high distribution loss.

The distribution loss can be reduced by optimisation of the distribution system. The optimum distribution system is the economical combination of primary line

6. The ratio between HT and LT lines at the all-India level was 1:3 (IRTC, 1996: 9).

7. In developed countries power is transmitted through 750 KV lines in order to bring down power losses to the minimum extent possible.

(HT), distribution transformers and secondary line (LT), which depends on location, load density and diversity of the system, as well as capital cost. The lower the HT/LT line length ratio, the higher will be the voltage drop and the line loss. To reduce this loss and improve voltage, HT/LT line length ratio should be optimised. For this purpose, decentralisation is required under which the high capacity transformers (160 KVA, 250 KVA) will be replaced by transformers of low capacity (25 KVA, 30 KVA), resulting in optimal placement of transformers and reduction of distribution loss through optimisation of HT/LT line length ratio. KSEB has been adopting this strategy to reduce distribution loss and installing low capacity transformers (63 KVA) in rural areas.

In order to salvage the state from severe power crisis, KSEB suggests setting up of three 440 KV substations, 18 220KV substations, 50 110 KV substations and 120 33 KV substations. The financial outlay required for setting up of this number of substations would be around Rs. 20,000 crore. Details of additional transmission facilities required are given in Table 7.19. It is drawn that as part of loss reduction measures, 866936 faulty energy meters were replaced during 2003-04 and 236994 in 2004-05 (up to 30-11-04) (GoK, 2005).

TABLE 7.19

Additional Transmission Facilities Required

Voltage	*Substations*	*Lines (ckm)*	*Total Cost Rs. Million*
440 KV	3	600	3300
220 KV	18	900	5400
110 KV	50	3000	9500
33 KV	120	3000	1800
Total	191	7500	20000

Source: KSEB, 1996.

The wide gap between the cost of production and the selling price per unit of power causes heavy financial loss. It is stated that KSEB now spends more than Rs. four per unit of power produced from thermal projects. But it sells power at an average rate of Rs.2.34 per unit. The subsidised tariffs put heavy burden on KSEB. The price differentials in retail tariff are 795 ps per unit in extreme cases. While agriculture consumers are charged at the subsidised rate of 65ps/unit, high and commercial consumers are charged at 825ps/unit and non-domestic consumers in LT vi (c) category at 860 ps/unit. The average rate is 176 ps/unit, whereas average per unit cost is 359 ps and average tariff 309 ps/unit (GoK, 2005).

Inefficiencies of the state power sector are rooted in the high cost of electricity supply. For all SEBs in India, the unit cost of supply of electricity in 1974-75 had been 22.5 ps/unit, which increased to 41.9 ps/unit in 1980-81 (at an annual average compounded growth of 10.9 per cent) and further to 108.6 ps/unit in 1990-91 (at an annual rate of 10 per cent). The 1990s saw a sharp rise in the unit cost of supply from 116.8 ps/unit in 1991-92 to 227.89 ps/unit in 1997-98 (Kannan and Pillai, 2002:55).

If adequate and timely capacity additions were made, Kerala could have enjoyed the role of a net exporter, rather than of a state severely affected by power shortage. Kallada (15MW), Kakkat (50MW) and Lower Periar (180MW) were classic examples of project time overruns, which were to be commissioned during the 7th Five Year Plan, but could finally be put into operation only in the mid-1990s. The time overrun in the case of Idamalayar project and of Mattupetty was nine years. The consequent cost overruns were: Idamalayar 285 per cent, Kakkad 725 per cent, Kallada 53 per cent, Lower Periar 299 per cent, Peppara 74 per cent and Mattupetty 64 per cent (GoK, Economic Review, various issues).

Another factor of serious concern is the forced purchase provisions of Power Purchase Agreements which State Electricity Boards are sometimes compelled to enter into, in order to promote their own cheap generators. A clear case is the Power Purchase Agreement between NTPC and KSEB in respect of power from Kayamkulam thermal station.

The sub-transmission and distribution system in the state is inadequate to meet the rising demand for power within the state with the desired level of quality and reliability of power supply. The large expansion of the urban systems and of the rural electrification programmes have led to considerable expansion of the low tension distribution network. Resultantly, the distribution system in the state is characterised by high level of energy losses, low reliability of supply and frequent interruption. Therefore, there is urgent need to develop, expand and improve the power distribution system in the state.

The committee on Energy Development of the State Planning Board suggests the following measures to reduce losses in the distribution system with the minimum investment.

- Adoption of high voltage distribution system;
- Load-balancing;
- Installation of shunt capacitors based on technical studies;
- Use of Arial bunched cables;
- Installation of quality meters;
- Automatic meter reading system for high voltage consumers;
- Computerised meter reading system for high voltage consumers;
- Computerised metering and billing system;
- Adequate meter testing facility; and
- Regular testing of meters.

Financial Requirements

System losses (at 22 per cent) are reported to be relatively low compared with those of other Indian states; but in the absence of adequate and accurate metering, actual losses could be considerably higher. About 40 per cent of the meters are believed to be faulty. Residential and industrial consumptions are about 48.6 per cent and 32.8 per cent while agricultural consumption is about 4.7 per cent. The remainder consists of commercial uses and public lighting. KSEB is not burdened by a heavy power-consuming agriculture sector. However, with an average tariff of about Rs.1.87 and production cost in the range of Rs. 2.90-Rs. 3.26 per kWh, the cost recovery rate is less than 64 per cent. Since production costs are increasing as a result of increasing dependence on expensive thermal generation, the financial situation is likely to worsen unless tariffs are increased and KSEB's operations made more efficient (The government of Kerala had increased the tariff by an average of 25 per cent in August 2001).

KSEB is currently running on an operational deficit of $.418 million annually. At the same time, the investment requirements of the Kerala power sector are substantial; therefore, the sector must be turned around to make it financially self-sustaining and capable of self-financing at least a part of its investment costs. During the next 15 years capital investments needed for power generation would be about $ 5144 million and for transmission $ 544 million, while distribution would require about $ 8700 million.

Prospects: Power Sector Development Programme in the 10th Five Year Plan

For formulating any programme on power development, estimation of the power and energy requirements of the state is required. There are many authentic documents in this regard *viz.*, 16th Annual Power Survey of Central Electricity Authority, Load Forecast Reference Report prepared by KSEB in 1998-99 and Energy Infrastructure Services Project funded by CIDA and SNC-Lavelin International Inc. Canada. The 16th Annual Power Survey of CEA has assumed 10 per cent growth rate for power and energy. On this basis, the power demand of Kerala is expected to reach the level of 4728 MW by 2006-07, the final year of the 10th Five Year Plan.

The Energy Infrastructure Services Project and the Load Forecast Reference Report of the KSEB have projected two growth rates *viz.*, a constrained and an unconstrained. While the constrained growth projected a load demand of 3529 MW by 2006-07, the unconstrained load growth projected a demand of 4959 MW by that date. The power system in Kerala seems to have grown at an average rate of 7.5 per cent per annum; at this rate, the load demand would be 3575 MW. The given projections, however, do not include the demand likely to be grown in the IT sector, as envisaged in the recent IT policy announced by the Govt. of Kerala. The need of power of the IT sector development alone may come to about 200 MW. The total power requirement taking into account this additional demand would be around 3800 MW, based on a 7.5 per cent growth rate. It would, therefore, be appropriate to target a minimum power requirement of 3800 MW by 2006-07. The corresponding energy requirement is estimated at 20800 MU. But the desirable level of power development may be pegged at 4728 MW as envisaged by the 16th Annual Power Survey; industrial growth requirements of the state at rapid rates should be also taken care of.

After allowing for the availability of power from the existing and ongoing projects and the committed supply from central projects, the addition on a desirable scale during the Tenth Five Year Plan would not be less than 900 MW.

It is well known that the cost of petroleum-products-based power generation is escalating quite rapidly. Generation of electricity by using petroleum fuels is therefore hardly cost-effective and would be highly inflationary. The cost of such energy production depends mainly upon external factors like international price of fuel, import duties, and exchange fluctuations. It is therefore better to increase the proportion of hydel power in total power supply in order to minimize cost of power production.

The new projects envisaged to be undertaken and completed during the 10th Plan Period are Athirapally (163 MW), Kuttiadi Additional Extension (100 MW), Neriamangalam Extension (25 MW) and Pallivasal Extension (60 MW). The Committee on Energy Development, State Planning Board, in their Report on Energy Development for the Tenth Five Year Plan (June, 2002) strongly recommended to implement these projects and along with them a few projects envisaged to be completed under the private sector *viz.*, Bhoothathankettu (16 MW), Ullungal (7MW), Kakkayam (15 MW), and Barapole (9 MW).

The hydro generation programme envisaged for the Tenth Five Year Plan would, however, leave a gap of more than 500 MW in meeting the modest Tenth Plan capacity requirement. The gap is to be bridged through creation of thermal power generating capacity with private sector participation.

The financial outlay for the continuing projects of KSEB would be Rs 111.32 cr. And the proposed outlay for the new works would be Rs. 758 cr. (GoK, 2002).

Alternatives: Development of Renewable Sources of Energy:

Wind Mills

In Kerala there are 95 sanctioned Windmills, of which 75 Windmills have been installed. Eight area generators and hybrid systems were also installed. There are 198 identified SHP Projects of less than 25 MW capacity with a total capapcity of 466.85 MW.

Wind Energy Programme

Wind power has emerged as a promising source of renewable energy for power generation and is one of the most cost-effective options for grid connected power generation. Wind farms are becoming popular all over the world. Pasavaikumbe in Kasargod and Kallyanathandu in Idukki district are the two sites identified for study under the National Wind Energy Resource Assessment. The programme is to be implemented jointly by ANERT and Centre for Wind Energy Technology, Chennai (GoK, 2005).

Solar Photovoltaic Programmes (SPV)

Solar Photovoltaic technology helps direct conversion of sunlight into electricity. SPV systems are an option for meeting electrical energy needs of remote areas where grid electricity has not yet reached. There exist 302 unelectrified remote colonies in Kerala (GoK, 2005).

The projects under SPV include solar village electrification, line-interacting PV rooftop systems in government offices and hospitals, stand-alone power plants on rooftops of residential buildings and grid-interactive PV power plants in autonomous private institutions (GoK, 2005).

As part of the Remote Village Electrification Programme, a survey was carried out with the help of IREP offices. It is estimated that more than 1500 hamlets in Kerala still remain unelectrified or partially electrified (GoK, 2005).

Solar Thermal Energy Programme (STEP)

STEP envisages the promotion of the use of Solar heat energy to meet various thermal needs. The most popular solar thermal devices are solar water heating systems, solar cookers and solar dryers.

Bio-Energy Programme

The bio-energy programme includes bio-gas programme, bio mass gassification programme, alternate fuels, and waste-to-energy programme. ANERT is implementing the National Bio-gas Programme of MNES since 1999-2000 by installing community, institutional and night-soil-based bio-gas plants ranging from capacities of $15m^3$ to $35m^3$ for the production of bio-gas from bio-degradable wastes like animal waste and kitchen waste. National Biomass Resource Assessment Survey was conducted in all the districts of the state to assess the availability of biomass for conversion to energy.

Small Hydro Power (SHP) Programme

Hydro power is a renewable, non-polluting and environmentally benign source of energy. It is perhaps the oldest renewable energy technique known to mankind for mechanical energy conversion as well as for electricity generation. The first hydro-power plant in India was a small hydro-electricity station of 130 KW set up in 1897 at Sidrapong in Darjeeling.

With the advancement of technology and increasing demand for electricity, the thrust of electricity generation using small hydro projects was shifted to big hydro power stations. Today India has a total installed capacity of 108207 MW, which includes 76607 MW from thermal, 27010 MW from hydro and 2720 MW from nuclear sources. The hydro share declined from 44 per cent in 1970 to about 25 per cent in 2003. In order to arrest further decline, Government of India announced the Policy on Hydro Power Development in August 1998. Realising the fact that small hydro power projects are capable of providing a solution for the energy problem in remote and hilly areas where extension of grid system is uneconomical, promotion of small and mini hydel projects was one of the objectives of the Policy on Hydro Power Development (Saxena, 2003).

In India, hydro projects upto 25 MW of station capacity have been categorised as small. India has a broad potential of about 15000 MW of small hydro power projects. About 4233 potential sites of up to 25 MW of capacity, aggregating to a capacity of about 10,000 MW have been identified. State-wise details are given In Table 7.20.

Till 2002, 466 projects in 29 states aggregating to 1530.39 MW were set up and 196 projects in 22 states aggregating to 609 MW were under implementation (Table 7.21).

TABLE 7.20

State-wise Identified Small Hydel Sites up to 25 MW Capacity

S. No.	*Name of State*	*Identified Number of Sites*	*Total Capacity in MW*
1.	Haryana	22	30.05
2.	Himachal Pradesh	323	1624.78
3.	Jammu and Kashmir	201	1207.27
4.	Punjab	78	65.26
5.	Rajasthan	49	27.26
6.	Uttar Pradesh	211	267.061
7.	Uttaranchal	354	1478.235
8.	Goa	3	2.6
9.	Gujrat	290	156.83
10.	Madhya Pradesh	85	336.325
11.	Chhatisgarh	47	57.9
12.	Maharashtra	234	599.47
13	Andhra Pradesh	286	254.63
14.	Karnataka	230	652.61
15.	**Kerala**	**198**	**466.85**
16.	Tamil Nadu	147	338.92
17.	Bihar	92	194.02
18.	Jharkhand	89	170.05
19.	Orissa	161	156.76
20.	Sikkim	68	202.75
21.	West Bengal	145	182.62
22.	Arunachal Pradesh	492	1059.03
23.	Assam	46	118.00
24.	Manipur	96	105.63
25.	Meghalaya	98	181.50
26	Mizoram	88	190.32
27.	Nagaland	86	181.39
28.	Tripura	8	9.85
29.	A & N Island	6	6.40
	Total	4233	10324.37

Source: Saxena, 2003.

TABLE 7.21

State-wise SHP Projects (up to 25 MW) Setup & under Construction

S. No.	*State*	*Projects Set-up*		*Projects Ongoing*	
		Nos.	*Capacity (MW)*	*Nos.*	*Capacity (MW)*
1.	Haryana	4	4830		
2.	Himachal Pradesh	41	9324	13	6750
3.	Jammu and Kashmir	27	102.24	9	13.31
4.	Punjab	21	108.40	1	2.70
5.	Rajasthan	10	23.85		
6.	Uttar Pradesh	8	21.50	1	3.60
7.	Uttaranchal	70	64.60	31	33.02
8.	Goa	1	0.05		
9.	Gujrat	2	7.00		
10.	Madhya Pradesh	7	38.96	4	26.40
11.	Chhatisgarh	2	1.00		
12.	Maharashtra	27	207.08	4	15.75
13	Andhra Pradesh	49	155.61	12	26.50
14.	Karnataka	38	198.88	18	91.90
15.	**Kerala**	**10**	**72.02**	**10**	**73**
16.	Tamil Nadu	11	76.40	2	7.90
17.	Bihar	4	44.90	10	15.00
18.	Jharkhand	6	4.05	8	34.85
19.	Orissa	6	7.30	7	40.97
20.	Sikkim	12	35.60	5	15.20
21.	West Bengal	18	92.28	5	5.62
22.	Arunachal Pradesh	50	32.37	27	51.64
23.	Assam	3	2.11	8	51.00
24.	Manipur	8	5.45	3	2.75
25.	Meghalaya	3	30.71	9	3.28
26	Mizoram	16	14.78	3	15.50
27.	Nagaland	8	20.47	6	12.40
28.	Tripura	3	16.01		
29.	A & N Island	1	5.25		
	Total	466	1530.39	196	609.74

Source: Saxena, 2003.

While most investment in rural energy development has been in the modern energy system, electricity in adequate quantities has hardly reached the rural areas. In India, for example, although about 86 per cent of all villages have electricity supply, only 31 per cent of the households were able to afford the cost of connection to the grid, as well as to afford the internal connection and end use equipment costs such as wiring and purchase of light bulbs.

Even though India has a history of more than 100 years in the development and utilisation of small hydro power, it has tapped a total of only 22,000 MW of hydro power against an estimated potential of 90,000 MW and out of that the share of small hydro projects is hardly 500 MW.

Small hydro power involves only limited investment, short gestation periods and simple civil works; but it uses sturdy machines, which can be easily maintained at local levels with minimum operation and maintenance expenses. These small schemes can be an economical proposition from a long term point of view also, as they can sustain on their own by utilising water, which otherwise will go waste.

SHP is site-specific, which means that features of the project have to be decided on local site conditions. The size of the scheme is determined based on parameters including the head and the discharge available. In Kerala 61 SHPs are identified by KSEB with an installed capacity of 161 MW and an average annual generation of 436 MU. Of these, detailed project reports have been prepared for 30 projects.

Power Sector Reforms in Kerala

Objectives

- The objectives of the power sector reforms at the national level are the following:
- Promotion of development of the power sector by ensuring generation and supply at economic cost.
- Provision of reliable and high quality service to the consumer.
- Ensuring of the financial vulnerability of the SEBs (State Electricity Boards), thereby attracting private sector investments.

The power sector reforms that have swept over many other parts of India had made little impact on Kerala's power sector in the initial years.

In recent years, however, the government has decided to initiate a reforms process on the lines prescribed by the central government. In August 2001, the Government of Kerala signed a Memorandum of Understanding (MoU) with the central power ministry. The MoU requires the state government to divide KSEB and make it accountable for the functions of generation, transmission and distribution. Accordingly, KSEB was divided into three independent profit centres having separate administrative and accounts wings in April 2002. An independent State Electricity Regulatory Commission was also instituted as per the provisions of the enacted Central Electricity Act. But the power sector reforms still remain unfinished in Kerala.

The following reform measures were taken in Kerala during 2003-04:

Acceleration of the electrification programme to cover all the households by 2007 providing four lakh service connections per year;

T&D loss brought down to 26.07 per cent in July 2004.

Renovation and maintenance works in Pallivasal, Sengulam and Panniar projects completed.

Kerala State Electricity Regulatory Commission issued orders on Aggregate Revenue Requirement (ARR) for the year 2004-05 in April 2004. The Commission approved an ARR of Rs. 3492.46 cr. and total revenue receipts of Rs. 3196 cr. for the year 2004-05.

Privatisation

With the objective of bringing in additional resources for the capacity addition programme in the electricity sector, the government of India formulated a policy to encourage participation of private enterprises in the fields of electricity generation, supply and distribution. The policy has not only widened the scope of private investment in the electricity sector, but it has introduced modifications in the financial, administrative and legal environment, in favour of private enterprise participation.

Private sector units are entitled to set up thermal projects (coal, lignite or gas based) or hydel projects and wind/solar energy projects of any size. Private sector entrepreneurs may set up enterprises, either as licensees, or as generating companies.

In this liberalised environment, private enterprises may be encouraged to undertake power projects in Kerala to ensure uninterrupted supply of quality electricity to people at reasonable prices. Kerala State Electricity Board may be revamped by making it a public limited company for greater efficiency, profitability and accountability.

Policy Suggestions

In order to ensure reliable and dependable supply of quality power in Kerala, the state has to create an additional capacity of 3350 MW by 2010. For achieving this target, the state has to accomplish the following immediate tasks:

- Since large hydro projects affect ecological balance, it would be advisable to popularise micro, mini and small hydro power stations in Kerala;
- Micro power projects may be encouraged wherever possible with financial assistance of the local or the state government agencies;
- Independent Power Producers may be encouraged to install wheeling power projects and to act as power marketers to industrial units;
- Industrial units may be permitted to install captive power projects by stipulating to them specifications for environmental protection;
- In order to stabilise the financial position of KSEB, power tariff has to be restructured by taking into consideration short run and long run marginal cost principles;
- Demand forecasting mechanism should be revamped by developing a techno-economic model to identify energy demand of each consumer based on connected load, hours of consumption, use of electrical appliances, etc;
- Install electronic meters for all types of electrical connections;
- Use high quality conductors and underground cables of high voltage ratings for curbing T&D losses;
- Discourage diesel, gas and naphtha-based thermal stations for environmental reasons and in the larger interests of the nation for saving foreign exchange;
- Tap the enormous scope that exists for non-conventional sources of energy like sun, wind, waves and bio mass, to the maximum extent possible;
- In view of the financial crunch of the state government, make efforts to make use of the resources of IPPs and self–financing power producers who are able to raise funds and fuel inputs from international sources;
- In order to reduce T&D losses to 15.5 per cent (the norm stipulated by the World Bank), increase the number of sub-stations, transformers of various capacities and the length of HT lines;
- Revamp KSEB into a public limited company;
- Encourage private enterprises to undertake power projects in the state to ensure uninterrupted supply of quality electricity.

SECTION III: WATER SUPPLY

Introduction

This section presents a brief review of the developments in the water supply sector of Kerala and a discussion of the current status of this sector. Some projections for the future and suggestions for improvement are also presented.

Water Resources of Kerala

The state of Kerala is blessed with abundant rainfall, with two predominant rainy seasons – the southwest monsoon (June to August) and the northeast monsoon (September to December). The average annual rainfall is estimated to be about 3100 mm, of which about 60 to 65 per cent occurs during southwest monsoon, about 25 per cent occurs during northeast monsoon and the rest during the summer months. Annual rainfall shows, however, considerable spatial and temporal variation. Although the state receives about 2.8 times the national average rainfall, the population density in the state is also about 2.5 times the all-India average. Geographically, the state falls into three distinct zones: highlands (greater than 75m above MSL), midlands (between 7.5m and 75m above MSL) and low lands or coastal region (below 7.5m above MSL). The highlands slope on the western side of the Western Ghats and are characterised by relatively flat erosional plateau surfaces flanked by debris-mantled steep slopes. Most of the rivers in Kerala have their origin in this zone. The midlands lying between these mountains and the lowlands comprise undulating laterite-capped residual mounts and valleys. The lowlands or the coastal areas are mostly alluvial plains made up of river deltas, backwaters and the shores of the Arabian Sea. The average width of the state is around 50 km and consequently the average ground slope is very steep. According to a study, while the water (from rain): man ratio for India decreased four-fold, the corresponding decrease for Kerala was five-fold. The state has the lowest water-man ratio in the country—lower than that of even Rajasthan! The per capita water availability for India is about 15,600 lpcd, while for Kerala it is 12,500 lpcd and for Rajasthan 16,000 lpcd.

Kerala has 44 monsoon-fed rivers of length more than 15 km each. Most of these rivers are ephemeral since their only source of water is rainfall. Also, these rivers are short in length and their drainage areas are small compared to those of rivers like the Ganga, the Brahmaputra and the Godavari. In fact, Kerala does not have a single river that can be called a 'major river'. The annual discharge from all the rivers of Kerala is estimated to be 78,041 MCM (million cubic metres), which is about 30 per cent less than that of a single river like Godavari. Almost all these rivers suffer from the problem of saline water intrusion during summer months with seawater reaching up to about 26 kms upstream from the river mouths. Also, these rivers get polluted from industrial wastes, domestic wastes, pesticides and fertilisers. Estimates of surface and ground water resources of the state made by various agencies do not project a healthy scenario. The gross yield from rainfall for the entire state is reported to be around 115 cubic km/yr. The runoff from all rivers to sea is about 77.9 cubic km/yr and the annual replenishable groundwater resource is estimated at 7.5 cubic km. Taking into account interstate problems and other issues related to development, the total amount of utilisable water resources of the state is estimated at 50 cubic km/yr, with the surface and groundwater contributions being approximately 42.7 and 5 cubic km/yr respectively. Because of limited storage capacity and the dependence of river flows entirely on seasonal rainfall, only a very small portion of river flow is really utilised. However, CWRDM and some other agencies feel that these figures based on estimates of surface water resources in 1974 are not fully reliable. According to another estimate, the total surface water resource availability per annum, after accounting for losses due to evaporation, transpiration, and interception is about 54,410 MCM. Of this, about 10 per cent is stored in reservoirs and about 7900 MCM utilised for groundwater recharge. Hence, only about 41,000 MCM of water forms the surface runoff in rivers. This entire quantity of water cannot be utilised for several reasons. Some amount of fresh water is required for maintaining an environmental balance in the river systems, lakes and backwaters, and to maintain flow in the riverine systems to prevent salt water intrusion. According to official figures, at least 40 per cent flow is required to be maintained in rivers. Based on these estimates, the annual utilisable surface water resources come to about 24,600 MCM. There are two major fresh water lakes, about 19 reservoirs of irrigation and hydel projects and several ponds in the state. Also, there are about 995 ponds with a capacity of over 10,000 cubic metre each. Brackish water in lakes and canals is spread over an area of about 2400 sq. km.

The annual replenished groundwater resource is estimated at 7500 MCM. About 65 per cent of this quantity is available for utilisation without creating any adverse consequences. The utilisable groundwater resource is estimated at 6587 MCM. According to an estimate, the annual utilisable groundwater resource is 5135 MCM and the water collected in surface water reservoirs is 5500 MCM. Traditionally, most of the people in Kerala depend on open wells in their homesteads for meeting their domestic water requirements. There are about 4.5 million open wells in Kerala. The density of open wells is very high, perhaps the highest in the country or even in the world (150 to 200 wells/ sq.km). In coastal areas, the density rises to as high as 400 wells per sq. km. About 80 per cent of the population, especially in rural areas, depends on open wells for meeting their water requirements. Even in a city like Kozhikode, the figure is as high as 50 per cent.

It may, however, be recognised that the actual flow in the river systems, the storage in surface water reservoirs and the recharge into underground aquifers during a year depends on the quantum of rainfall received during that year. Although only about 15 per cent of total annual river flow takes place during the period from December to May, about 75 per cent of the annual water requirement is experienced during this period. This is the major problem that the state of Kerala faces with respect to utilisation of its water resources. Table 7.22 shows an estimate of availability of and demand for water in Kerala.

Although these figures show an overall water surplus of 8,506 MCM in a year, the state is facing acute water stress during summer months. A deficit of 7,142 MCM is experienced during the summer months.

Kerala has been experiencing severe drought conditions and drinking water shortages every summer over the past few years for several reasons. Topography exercises a major control over the water potential of the state. The highlands comprising the terraced segments of Western Ghats and the highly dissected hills on the

TABLE 7.22

Water Availability and Demand in Kerala (in MCM) in 2001

	Annual		*Summer*	
	Availability	*Demand*	*Availability*	*Demand*
Surface Water	24,600	-	3,690	-
Groundwater	5,135	-	5,135	-
Stored Surface Water	5,500	-	5,500	-
Domestic Demand	-	1,226	-	809
Birds and Animals	-	438	-	293
Industrial Demand	-	6,400	-	3,200
Conservation of Kari Land	-	5,000	-	3,500
Irrigation	-	13,665	-	13,665
Total	35,235	26,779	14,325	21,467
Surplus/Deficit	+8,506	-7,142		

Source: KRWSA (2004). *Jalasurakhsakku Mazhavellam.*

eastern regions are sources of all the rivers in Kerala. Since the gradient is steep and the degree of dissection high, the entire rain falling in the catchments drains down swiftly, the residence time being extremely small. This makes the construction of reservoirs essential for storage of water. But, unfortunately, the question of construction in most new sites identified for the purpose is bogged down in environmental controversies. Also, thick forest and vegetative cover that existed in earlier times in the highlands had acted as a means of protection and played a major role in the conservation of water. Large-scale encroachment, destruction of forests, reclamation of wetlands, ponds, paddy fields and changes in cropping pattern have aggravated the problem of water scarcity. Increase in impervious surfaces by activities such as paving of courtyards of buildings has increased the rate of runoff and reduced the retention time of water and consequently recharge. Besides, improvement in the general standard of living of the population has led to increase in water consumption and promoted wasteful usage of water. Uncontrolled pumping of groundwater in certain areas of the state has resulted in decline in the groundwater table. Unscientific and unregulated sand-mining activities in the river beds have led to large scale reduction in groundwater resources. The vagaries of monsoon are another reason for the water crisis in the state during the past few summers. A recent report states that Kerala has suffered seven years of deficient rainfall and another five years of below-normal rainfall since 1980. An analysis of rainfall during the period 1998 and 2003 indicates that all districts of Kerala except Thiruvananthapuram have been receiving grossly deficient rainfall since 2001. If the state receives normal rainfall from all three spells of rainfall – the two monsoons and the summer rains - every year, water scarcity may not become acute. The seasonal pattern of rainfall makes it necessary to conserve water during the rainy season to make it available for use during the dry season. The potential for groundwater recharge is also limited due to the topography of the state which facilitates rapid run-off and minimum retention. The soil cover is generally thin, with the basement rock exposed at several locations, minimising the prospects of infiltration and groundwater recharge. The thick laterites in the midlands, especially in North Kerala, are potential sites for storage by virtue of their high porosity. However, the hard crust at the surface limits infiltration and the poor permeability of this zone results in poor percolation. The little water that is stored is readily released by seepage and through springs due to the high degree of dissection. Nine out of fourteen districts of Kerala are coastal districts. It is estimated that the coastal alluvium comprising unconsolidated sediments have a potential of about 0.30 MCM/sq.km. However, this fresh water body is in close proximity to the sea and uncontrolled and unscientific pumping has already resulted in saltwater intrusion and associated problems, causing potable water scarcity. Not only wells but also watersupply schemes from surface water sources in the lower reaches of rivers in this zone are prone to the threat of salinity.

A large amount of freshwater flow into the backwater is required during summer months to flush off salinity ingress. During this period, fresh water requirement cannot be met by river flows. Often ponding in the upper reaches is required. The water that reaches the estuaries in the lower reaches becomes saline. Also, the quality of surface water is being adversely affected by contamination caused by industrial effluents, agricultural discharges and urban wastes. Drying up of sources adds to the problem.

The highland areas of Kerala have a different set of problems. Open wells are not in common use because dug wells are not economically viable, the groundwater table in these areas being in general, extremely deep (>15 m). Natural springs are in use to a great extent. However, this source does not meet the water supply requirements during summer months as springs get dried up. Wells constitute a major water source in the midland region.

Groundwater extraction through open walls takes place in Kerala at alarming rates especially in recent times. As a result, water table levels in several districts have drastically declined and saline water intrusion is experienced in the coastal belt. Indiscriminate sand-mining from river beds and conversion of paddy fields to non-agricultural uses have compounded this problem. According to the Central Ground Water Board (CGWB) and the State Groundwater Department (GWD), groundwater is being overexploited in 15 blocks of the state. In 33 other blocks, 70 per cent of the groundwater is being used up. It may be noted that groundwater recharge potential is limited due to geologic and topographical factors.

Water Policies of Kerala

The Government of India accords great importance to the supply of safe drinking water to the entire population for ensuring public health. In line with the National Water Policy document of 1987, the Government of Kerala announced a comprehensive State Water Policy in 1992, the first of its kind by any State in the country. The state government had set a target of extending safe water supply to its entire population by 2001 AD. The Water Policy (1992) stressed the need to harness and manage the water resources of the state to derive the maximum advantage, and maintain an ecologically healthy environment. It advocated a river basin/watershed-based planning for integrated development of land and water resources of various regions, pointed to an acute drinking water scarcity experienced for about half the year in various parts of the state and emphasised the need to conserve as much rainwater as possible. It also listed out short-term and long-term strategies for water management. Efforts to revise the State Water Policy are at their final stages.

Evolution of Water Supply Schemes in Kerala

During the pre-independence era, Trivandrum, Cochin and Alleppey were the only towns in the present-day Kerala that had protected water-supply. A protected piped water-supply system for Trivandrum (Wellington Water Works) was launched in 1933 by the erstwhile Travancore State. The scheme was designed to serve a population of 1.35 lakh (the prospective population of 1961 as envisaged in 1930) and an area of 11.22 square miles. The capital cost came to Rs. 57 lakh. The quality of water supplied was monitored continuously at supply points and quality standards were comparable with those of water supplied in the best schemes of the world. Protected water was supplied free of cost through street fountains and charges were levied on water supplied through metered house connections. The charge levied on water for domestic use was about a half of that for water supplied for non-domestic purposes. Production and purification costs as well as maintenance cost were continuously on the increase; but the pricing pattern and water-tax levied at the rate of three per cent of annual rental value of all buildings located within the limits of Trivandrum Corporation kept the system profitable. After independence, the Trivandrum Water-Supply Scheme was augmented a few times to meet the rising requirements caused by increase in population and expansion of the city. At present, against a demand of 217 MLD, actual supply is estimated at 203 MLD. The JBIC-assisted Kerala Water-Supply Project (KWSP) is expected to create an additional capacity of 42 MLD so as to tide over the shortage and equipping the system to meet future requirements for some period.

The Ernakulam Water-Supply Scheme was commissioned in 1934. It was a small scheme designed for supplying water to the Ernakulam town alone (for a population of 11.91 lakh) at an estimated cost of Rs.152 lakh with river Periyar as the source. Water demand for meeting domestic and industrial requirements has undergone manifold increase due to rapid development of Cochin following the setting up of a number of industries and establishments, the development of the Cochin Port, and the inclusion of nearby towns and villages in Greater Cochin. At present, as against a total demand of 400 MLD of water (domestic and others 326 MLD and Industrial, 74 MLD), the supply is only 205 MLD, resulting in a huge shortage. Even after completion of the HUDCO-assisted augmentation scheme and some other projects, Cochin still faces a shortage of about 120 MLD of water. The situation would improve only after proposals for retro-fitting existing water treatment plants and Kochi Metro Water Supply Project are implemented.

The Alleppey Water-Supply Scheme was commissioned in 1939. The Municipality met half the project cost with interest as well as the maintenance expenditure. The Kozhikode Water-Supply Scheme was commissioned in 1953 to meet water requirements of an anticipated population of 1.35 lakh living in the then municipal town. Augmentation schemes are being done to meet the increase in demand caused by increase in population and extension of city limits. These schemes are intended to serve an ultimate population of about six lakh. At present, as against a demand of 185 MLD of water, supply is only to the tune of 65 MLD. It is expected that the JBIC-assisted Kerala Water-Supply Project (KWSP) being implemented would create an additional capacity of about 151 MLD so as to provide a solution to the water scarcity problem in Kozhikode. Other schemes in Kerala taken up for implementation during the pre-independence period include the Kumarakam, the Shertallai and the Kuttanad Water-Supply Schemes.

After independence, though the Government of India formulated and implemented many programmes for installing piped public water-supply schemes, appreciable progress was not noticed in Kerala till 1964; significant efforts have been made to improve the situation only since then. After the formation of the State, public water-supply was managed by Kerala State Public Health Engineering Department till the formation of Kerala Water and Waste Water Authority; later it was rechristened as the Kerala Water Authority. In addition to direct financial assistance from the Government of India, state funds remained the dominant source for investment in the water-supply and sanitation sector over the years, with various financial institutions such as Life Insurance Corporation of India (LIC), and the Housing and Urban Development Corporation (HUDCO) also granting substantial loans for implementation of major schemes. As a result, during the period from 1970 to 1981, 33 urban water-supply schemes (UWSS) and 955 rural water-supply schemes (RWSS) were implemented in Kerala, aimed at benefiting 63 per cent urban and 29 per cent rural population. At the beginning of the International Drinking Water-Supply and Sanitation Decade, the situation in the state was not wide of the mark from the figures suggested by World Health Organization (WHO) for Third World countries, viz. 75 per cent urban and 31 per cent rural population coverage. Private investment in water-supply and sanitation sector has been minimal; the low degree of cost recovery being a major reason.

The Present Scenario

According to an estimate made in 2003, piped water reaches about 79 per cent of the urban population and 58.7 per cent of the rural population in Kerala. However, this is a norm-based estimate and the corresponding figures based on actual consumption of drinking water from public sources are much lower (Pushpangadan, 2003). The rest of the population depends on open wells, ponds, natural streams, etc. for meeting their water requirements. It is estimated that about 45 per cent of the rural population depends on privately owned wells. A survey on the status of water-supply in rural areas of the country conducted in 1993 showed that of the 991 *panchayats* (about 9776 habitations or wards) in Kerala, 2289 non-covered (NC) habitations and 7422 partially covered (PC) habitations existed. The corresponding figures at present are 994 NC habitations and 6889 PC habitations respectively. There are 53 Municipalities, one Township and five Corporations in addition to nearly 100 Classified Census Towns in Kerala. Nearly 20 municipalities have a supply level of less than 70 lpcd and as such require schemes for immediate augmentation. There exist 1858 rural water-supply schemes and 58 urban water-supply schemes in operation. The district-wise breakup of these is given in Table 7.23.

TABLE 7.23

District-wise Breakup of UWSS and RWSS in Operation as in 10/2003

Sl. No.	*District*	*No. of Urban Water Supply Schemes*	*Rural Water Supply Schemes*		*Total*
			Multi Panchayat	*Single Panchayat*	
1	Thiruvananthapuram	5	40	80	125
2	Kollam	3	31	57	91
3	Pathanamathitta	3	16	33	52
4	Alappuzha	5	1	72	78
5	Kottayam	5	50	99	154
6	Idukki	1	98	88	187
7	Ernakulam	11	53	81	145
8	Thrissur	6	141	103	250
9	Palakkad	3	130	48	181
10	Malappuram	5	105	46	156
11	Kozhikkode	2	108	77	187
12	Wyanad	0	29	29	58
13	Kannur	7	49	90	146
14	Kasargode	2	55	49	106
	Total	**58**	**906**	**952**	**1916**

Source: State Planning Board. *Report on the KWA 2002.*

Table 7.24 shows the service level of the existing water-supply systems. Apart from these schemes, there exist 1255 small schemes and extensions, which include schemes exclusively benefiting Scheduled Castes and Scheduled Tribes. In addition, there exist approximately 12000 public bore-wells fitted with hand pumps in Kerala, each serving an average of 50 to 100 persons. The local bodies have also constructed community dug-wells, ponds etc. Community wells in schools, *anganwadis* and other institutions also serve sections of the public. All these are in addition to domestic wells.

TABLE 7.24

Service Level of Existing Water Supply System in Kerala through House-taps and Stand-posts

Sl. No.	*Type of Use*	*No. of Connections*
1	Domestic	8,03,706
2	Non-Domestic	66,323
3	Industrial	1,208
4	Stand Posts	1,72,381
	Total	10,43,618

Source: Website of the KWA.

Formation of the Kerala Water Authority (KWA)

The Kerala Water Authority was constituted by the Government of Kerala on 1st April 1984 under Kerala Water-Supply and Waste Water Ordinance 1984 as a successor to the erstwhile Public Health Engineering Department of the Government of Kerala. At present, the KWA plays a leading role in all developments in the water-supply sector in the state. The major responsibilities of KWA are the following.

Design, construction, execution, promotion, operation, maintenance, and financing of schemes for supply of water and for collection and disposal of wastewater.

Rendering all necessary services to the government in relation to water-supply and collection and disposal of wastewater in the state of Kerala.

Establishment of necessary standards for water-supply and wastewater services.

Fixation and revision of rates for water-supply and sewerage maintenance with the approval of government.

Taking other measures necessary to ensure water-supply in times of emergency.

Table 7.25 presents the details of funds received from the Government of India and other agencies for public water-supply schemes since the formation of KWA.

TABLE 7.25

Funds Received from Government of India and Other Agencies for Public Water Supply Schemes (in Rs. Lakh) after Formation of KWA

Year	*LIC/HUDCO*	*External Agencies*	*Government of India*	*Total*
1983-1984	469.05	523.38	1571.30	2563.73
1984-1985	471.00	268.70	1471.30	2211.00
1985-1986	543.61	606.12	1085.00	2234.75
1986-1987	600.00	1533.24	1398.32	3591.56
1987-1988	660.00	1533.24	1938.32	3591.56
1989-1990	947.00	734.00	944.00	2625.00
1990-1991	1000.00	955.00	1290.00	3245.00
1991-1992	1347.00	2054.00	1634.00	5035.00
1992-1993	1000.00	1375.00	2710.00	5085.00
1993-1994	2404.00	226.00	-	2630.00
1994-1995	3600.00	372.00	-	3972.00
1995-1996	3088.00	498.00	2469.00	6055.00
1996-1997	2560.00	500.00	2414.00	5474.00
1997-1998	4055.00	6563.00	4071.00	14689.00
1998-1999	3953.00	7178.00	4942.00	16073.00
1999-2000	3621.00	1582.63	3668.00	8871.63
2000-2001	2777.00	2383.52	3846.00	9006.52
2001-2002	-	2100.00	5565.00	7665.00
2002-2003	5029.00	302.00	6204.00	11535.00

Source: Government of Kerala. *Economic Review and Report of the KWA 2003.*

Organisational Set up

The KWA functions under the overall control and supervision of its Board, consisting of Chairman, Managing Director, Secretaries to Government of Finance, Water Supply, Local Administration, and Rural Development, and two Members each representing local bodies, and two Members appointed by government, a Technical Member, and an Accounts Member. There are 8739 regular employees and around 2600 HR workers under 141 categories in the 483 offices of KWA.

The KWA is divided into three zones: namely, the Southern, the Central and the Northern. The Regional Chief Engineers look after project implementation, collection and distribution of water, and collection of revenue in their respective regions. There is also a group that takes care of issues related to maintenance of water quality standards. The functions of the regions are distributed among 10 circle offices, three to four circle offices under each region. The functions of circle offices are further distributed among Divisions, Subdivisions and Sections.

Evaluation of the KWA Set up

The present organisational structure of KWA is cumbersome with several layers of hierarchy, resulting in repetitive handling of office work and delay in decision-making and implementation. At present, the operation and maintenance of existing water-supply schemes and construction of new projects including distribution systems and treatment plants are done by the same technical personnel (including Engineers). The same office handles revenue collection also at many places. This undoubtedly leads to these functions getting mixed up without focus. Separating these tasks and assigning them to different groups of personnel will improve efficiency of implementation.

In view of advances made in various fields such as those in surveying, documentation, drafting, communication and computerisation, office staff in IPD and circles may be reduced. Also, with the adoption of new approaches such as decentralisation and community participation, especially in rural water-supply sector, manpower requirement in KWA has to be critically examined. There has been no system of maintaining performance reports in KWA ever since its inception.

There is an urgent need to equip water quality laboratories of KWA with modern testing instruments for enforcement of water quality. The regional water quality laboratories should be equipped with state of the art equipment for analysing contaminants of all kinds. Existing staff should be trained in the use of equipment and the conduct of microbiological tests.

There is no promotion committee in position either and promotions are done as in the Government of Kerala. The suggestion made in 1999 by the state government for improvement of the efficiency and to redressal of the grievances of employees of KWA has remained unattended.

KWA is required to seek directions from the government even for several minor issues, leave alone major ones. This type of management without accountability and operational independence is bound to cause delays in completion of water-supply schemes, resulting in cost escalation in all other spheres of activity.

Project and Materials Management in KWA

Projects completed remained with KWA after completion and the responsibility for their maintenance too rested with KWA. In the case of ongoing schemes, monitoring and implementation could not be properly done in many cases. Delay in finalisation of tenders, delay in execution resulting from material mismatch between supply and demand by contractors, and excess claims by contractors have adversely affected the pace of their progress. Overlap of projects has often resulted in too many projects being handled at a time causing further delay. As a result, some schemes had to be abandoned even after investments were made for procurement of material and part construction of network elements. Steep increase in maintenance expenditure due to increase in production cost and large number of schemes being maintained simultaneously have resulted in avoidable wastage of resources. The present system of material management is grossly inadequate and unscientific with no arrangement for monitoring non-moving items, excess stock availability at locations, and record keeping. Purchase procedure based on rough and ready estimates of material quantity results in project delays and piling up of huge quantity of unused materials at work for long periods. It is fairly difficult to rectify these weaknesses in a top-down system with several many layers of hierarchy.

Financial Performance of KWA

The Government of Kerala (GoK) allots its plan funds to KWA partly as loan and partly as capital and revenue grants every year. Revenue grants are meant for meeting non-plan requirements. Capital grants received directly from the government of India are utilised for implementation of centrally sponsored water-supply schemes. In addition, KWA avails of loans from LIC of India and HUDCO with guarantee from the GoK for implementation of water-supply and sewerage schemes. Repayment of loans and payment of interest on loans from the GoK have not yet been made. Table 7.26 and Table 7.27 summarise the financial position (as in March 2002) and the Plan and Non-plan expenditure (for 2002-2003) of KWA.

TABLE 7.26

Financial Position of the KWA as on 31st March 2002

Item	*Amount (Rs. Crores)*
A. Liabilities (as on 31-3-2002)	
1. Capital Employed	1705
2. Loans (GoK, LIC, HUDCO)	1331
3. Other Liabilities	89
Total Liabilities	3125
B. Assets (as on 31-3-2002)	
1. Fixed Assets	1850
2. Current Assets and Loans & Advances	413
3. Accumulated Losses	862
Total Assets	3125

Source: State Planning Board. *Report on the KWA 2002*.

As per annual accounts of KWA, up to 31-3-2002, accumulated excess of expenditure over income since its formation is Rs 862 crore (Table 7.26) after taking into account the non-plan grant of the GoK as income and the interest on loans and depreciation. Tables 7.28 and 7.29 present the data on income and non-plan expenditure in a typical year (2002-2003). KWA owes Rs. 510 crore to the State Government and about 293 crore to LIC/HUDCO. Non-plan expenditure of KWA on such items as establishment and other administrative expenses, power charges, operation and maintenance charges, interest and repayment of loans, has to be met from water charges collected and non-plan grant from the government. During the past few years, all expenses have been on the increase as shown in Table 7.30.

TABLE 7.27

Plan and Non-Plan Expenditure of Kerala Water Authority (Rs. Lakhs)

	1995-96	*1996-97*	*1997-98*	*1998-99*	*1999-00*	*2000-01*	*2001-02*	*2002-03*
Plan Expenditure								
Plan Schemes other than ARP, LIC/HUDCO	6713	7139	12138	12140	5381	5748	3965	5105.87
ARP Schemes	1498	2875	3916	3533	4228	4383	45233	4331.71
LIC/HUDCO	3236	2473	673	2930	6437	3346	4140	3706.07
Others (AUWSP-Central share and PMGY)	132	288	171	132	0	0	0	1416.21
Total Plan Expenditure	11579	12775	16898	18735	16046	13477	12338	14559.86
Non-plan Expenditure								
Salary & Establishments	5490	4742	5153	5950	9520	10069	10433	10259
Power	1940	2101	2900	3664	5451	5491	6600	4809*
Operation & Maintenance	1826	2191	2329	2439	3015	3068	3134	3131
Others	372	413	542	517	588	558	560	566
Interest on Loans (Excluding GoK)	2225	2217	2515	2859	3309	3422	3563	3521
Repayment of Loans (Excluding GoK)	884	948	1172	1267	1660	2177	2026	873
Total Non-Plan Expenditure	12737	12612	14611	16696	23543	24785	26316	23159
Grand Total	24316	25387	31509	35431	39589	38262	38654	37718.86

Note: *Power charges amounting to Rs. 86 crores are outstanding as on 31-03-2003.

Source: State Planning Board. *Report of the KWA 2002.*

TABLE 7.28

Income of KWA (2002-2003) (Rs. Crores)

Revenue from Water/ Sewerage Rates	*State Govt. Plan*	*State Govt. Non-Plan*	*GoI*	*LIC/HUDCO*	*Others*	*Total*
105.80	104.00	61.86	62.04	50.29	3.02	387.01

Note: Funds available for non-plan expenditure = 105.8* + 61.86 @ Rs. 167.66 crores (*This includes sewerage rates – one time sewerage connection charges).

Source: Government of Kerala. *Economic Review and Report of the KWA 2003.*

TABLE 7.29

Income and Expenditure (Non-Plan) for Year Ending on 31-3-2003

S. No.	*Item*	*Amount (Rs. Crores)*
1	Income	167.66
2	Expenditure (excluding depreciation and repayment of GoK loan)	231.59
	Excess of expenditure over income	64.43

Source: Government of Kerala. *Economic Review and Report of the KWA 2003.*

TABLE 7.30

Comparative Statement of Various Expenditures and Income

Year	*Establishment Expenditure (Rs. Crores)*	*Power Charges (Rs. Crores)*	*Other O & M Expenses (Rs. Crores)*	*Income from Water Charges (Rs. Crores)*
1996–97	51.55	21.01	21.92	50.84
1997–98	56.55	29.01	23.29	55.17
1998–99	64.66	36.64	24.39	68.89
1999–00	101.02	54.48	26.11	79.76
2000–01	111.38	60.48	30.59	90.63
2001–02	124.00	72.00	33.00	95.00
2002–03[2]	108.25	72.00	31.31	105.8
Average Annual increase	19%	27%	8.5%	14%

Source: Government of Kerala. *Economic Review and Report of the KWA 2003.*

High-tension consumers pay power tariff at the rate applicable to industrial consumers. The high burden to KWA from the pension component, repayment of loans and payment of interest, price preference offered by KWA to SSI units and government organisations, 22 per cent capital cost charged to revenue etc. upsets the balance in non-plan expenditures. As a result, KWA is forced to divert capital (plan) funds for meeting non-plan requirements. Diversion of funds from capital to revenue adversely affects implementation of capital works including centrally sponsored schemes. As targets for schemes supported by the Government of India could not be achieved due to such reasons, there has been considerable reduction in the allotments received in recent years and the trend is expected to continue until remedial measures are taken. The large amounts due to creditors like KSEB, HUDCO, and suppliers of materials result in further liability in the form of fines. If this situation continues, further delays and cost escalation will take KWA to a dead-end.

Water-Supply Schemes

Various schemes are being implemented by the Kerala Water Authority for extending the coverage of protected water-supply in the state. These include schemes funded from Plan Funds of the state, Accelerated Rural and Urban Water Supply Schemes sponsored by the Government of India, Technology Mission Schemes, Schemes approved under the XI Finance Commission, and Schemes with loan assistance from financial institutions like LIC, HUDCO and NABARD.

Accelerated Rural Water-Supply Programme (ARWSP)

Until the beginning of Third Five Year Plan, drinking water-supply in rural areas formed a major component of the Community Development Programme. In 1954, The Ministry of Health of the Government of India implemented the National Water-Supply and Sanitation Programme. ARWSP, a scheme sponsored by Government of India, was launched in 1972-73 in order to provide safe drinking water to areas identified as 'difficult' and 'problem villages' by an assessment survey conducted in 1972. Voluntary organisations were also encouraged to take up projects under this programme. In general, these projects were designed for a per capita demand of 40 lpcd. The Government of India provided funds to states for making provision of safe drinking water in rural habitations. The state governments were to provide matching funds from their own resources. To tackle water quality problems and to ensure source sustainability up to 20 per cent of funds could be utilised. Projects/schemes on sustainability of sources could also be taken up under this programme for rainwater harvesting, artificial recharge, revival of traditional systems, etc. Further, 15 per cent of funds released could be spent on operation and maintenance (O&M) of existing systems/sources of rural water-supply. A certain proportion of ARWSP funds was set aside for implementation of sector reforms projects for institutionalising community participation in Rural Water-Supply Programme. Under these projects, people's contribution amounting to at least 1.00 per cent of the capital cost and 100 per cent of O&M cost were also envisaged. Contribution towards capital cost could be in the form of cash, kind, or labour. At present, work on 121 schemes under ARWSP (89 schemes with central funds and 32 schemes with state funds) is in progress in the state.

Accelerated Urban Water-Supply Programme (AUWSP)

This programme was initiated in 1993-94 by the Government of India to provide safe and adequate water-supply facilities to the entire population of towns having a population of less than 20,000 according to the 1991 census. Fifty per cent of the funds are received from the central government and a matching contribution is made by the state government. Priority is given to towns with very low per capita supply of potable water, very distant or deep water sources, excess salinity, or fluoride, iron or arsenic content in water sources, high incidence of water-borne diseases, and drought-prone areas. At present, six schemes under AUWSP are under execution in the state.

Technology Mission Schemes

In 1986, during the Seventh Five Year Plan period, the rural water-supply component of the state sector Minimum Needs Programme (MNP) and the ongoing centrally sponsored ARWSP were brought together into the Technology Mission of Drinking Water and Related Water Management (also called National Drinking Water Mission—NDWM), with a view to increasing the coverage of problem villages under the Technology Mission strategy. It was one of the five Societal Missions launched by the Government of India. NDWM was renamed the Rajiv Gandhi National Drinking Water Mission (RGNDWM) in 1991. The Government of India, through Rajiv Gandhi National Drinking Water Mission (RGNDWM), supplements the efforts of the state governments by providing central assistance under the Accelerated Rural Water-Supply Programme (ARWSP). Further, in order to attain the goal of providing safe drinking water to all rural habitations in the country within five years in consonance with the National Agenda for Governance of the Government, a Department of Drinking Water-Supply was created under the Ministry of Rural Development in October 1999. Objectives of the mission are to cover residual not covered (NC), partially covered (PC) and quality-affected rural habitations, evolve appropriate technology mix wherever required, improve performance and cost effectiveness of ongoing programmes, create awareness on the use of safe drinking water, and take conservation measures for sustained supply of drinking water. These schemes are implemented in water quality affected areas (with alternative sources by providing treatment units for controlling excess iron, fluoride, salinity etc). According to a recent decision of the Government of India, the present allocation criteria of funds under ARWSP to states based on normative criteria would be replaced with a need-based approach. Accordingly, states having large number of habitations which are not covered and water quality affected and which are situated in drought prone, desert, and hard rock areas, would get more allocation than habitations well-endowed with water resources. In Kerala, two schemes had been sanctioned before 1-4-1998 with 50 per cent central share and 50 per cent state share; eight other schemes, one unit with equal sharing by the central and the state and seven schemes with 75 per cent central and 25 per cent state contribution, have also been sanctioned. Of a total 10 schemes sanctioned, one was commissioned in December 2002 and work on the remaining is in progress.

Finance Commission Award

The XIth Finance Commission Award for water-supply sector is Rs. 645 lakh. The empowered committee has approved proposals of KWA for projects costing Rs. 645 Lakh. An amount of Rs. 379.42 lakh was spent up to 30-09-03. The Govt. of Kerala has already sanctioned an amount of Rs. 534.58 lakh. Work on these schemes is in progress.

Water-Supply Schemes (WSS) to Rural Schools

KWA is implementing WSS to schools in rural areas. Fifty per cent of the expenditure is met from ARWSP funds and the remaining from the State Plan funds. Out of the 355 school projects taken up under this scheme, 86 were provided with water supply by 2002-03. The remaining work is in progress.

Swajaladhara

The Government of India launched a new, community-based, participatory, demand-driven Rural Water-Supply Scheme christened *Swajaladhara* in the financial year 2002-03 to cover all villages/habitations lacking drinking water facility. Block or *gram panchayats* or Beneficiary Groups following all fundamental reform principles are eligible to implement projects under the Scheme. These institutions or beneficiary groups shall plan, implement, operate, maintain and manage such projects. This central scheme, which is also applicable to educational institutions, provides for execution of projects with 90 per cent of funding from the Union Government and 10 per cent contribution from the public or from block or *gram panchayat* or a committee of parents or teachers, as the case may be. In the case of scheduled castes and scheduled tribes, the mandatory contribution from the public, parents or teachers has been reduced to 5 per cent, subject to the condition that they should form more than 50 per cent of the population in a village/habitation as per the 1991 Census. During the year 2002-03, 120 scheme proposals were sanctioned with an estimate amount of Rs. 887.88 lakh and for the year 2003-04, 82 scheme proposals were sanctioned with an estimate amount of Rs 504 lakh. As per directions from the Government of India, a District Implementing Agency—a District Water and Sanitation Mission (DWSM)—has been constituted in each district of Kerala with District Collector as Chairman and Executive Engineer, Kerala Water Authority, District Headquarters Division, as Member Secretary for implementing the schemes.

LIC-Aided Schemes

Rural and urban water-supply schemes have been under implementation with financial assistance in the form of loans from the Life Insurance Corporation of India (LIC) since 1967-68. An amount of Rs. 319.57crore has so far been received from LIC for financing the water-supply sector. 278 water-supply schemes have been completed with LIC assistance. As per the financing pattern of LIC, assistance provided is less than 50 per cent of the estimated cost of the scheme. Therefore, more than 50 per cent of cost of these schemes is borne by the State Government or KWA as matching assistance, for completion of these schemes. Now there are 80 rural water-supply schemes and 41 urban water-supply schemes under different stages of implementation with LIC assistance. They include 19 new rural and 8 new urban schemes sanctioned by LIC during March 2003.

HUDCO-Aided Schemes

Assistance in the form of loans from HUDCO has been received for 18 urban water-supply schemes. Out of them, 13 schemes have already been commissioned. The remaining schemes are at various stages of implementation. The total loan amount sanctioned for these schemes comes to Rs.157.27 crore while the amount of loan already received is about Rs. 119.71 crore.

NABARD's Loan Assistance for New Rural Water Supply Schemes

NABARD has already sanctioned eight new rural water-supply schemes costing about Rs. 4868.33 lakh. The total loan amount sanctioned is Rs. 3324.06 lakh and the amount to be contributed by the State Government is Rs. 1544.27 lakh. The date of completion of the projects is 31st March 2006.

Varsha (Rainwater Harvesting), and Jalavahinii

As mentioned previously, it is estimated that piped water has reached about 79 per cent of the urban and 58.7 per cent of the rural population in Kerala by 2003. The state government has set about the task of raising these levels to 100 per cent and 90 per cent respectively. It has formulated three drinking water schemes with this in mind, viz. *Varsha*, the rainwater harvesting (RWH) scheme, *Jalavahini*, which seeks to sustain and maintain conventional sources of water for meeting local needs and the ongoing *Jalanidhi*, the scheme involving *panchayat*-level ventures developed and maintained by local people themselves. The Government of Kerala intends to achieve the ambitious 'Water for All' target by 2007. The first model project under *Varsha* was launched in the state secretariat and a few other government buildings. The implementation of rainwater-harvesting schemes such as *Varsha* is done with active involvement of the local community. Each of the proposed units under *Varsha* is envisaged to serve five families. Ten per cent of the cost of the unit is to be borne by beneficiaries. Out of 623 units proposed, work of 170 units was completed during 2002-03.

Severe drought conditions in the state during the summer of 2004 brought out the need to have a holistic and continuous approach towards extraction, use, conservation, and management of water resources of the state. The necessity for chalking out an appropriate strategy for scaling up efforts for harvesting rainwater was re-emphasised. Several small and isolated initiatives in water management had been launched at different places within the state following the droughts in 1983 and 1987, mostly at individual, household and NGO levels. Most of them related to harvesting and using rainwater at the household and the micro-community level. Rainwater harvesting, irrespective of the technology used, essentially means harvesting and storing water in days of abundance, for use in lean days. Storing of rainwater may be done in two ways - storing in an artificial storage like a tank or storing in the soil as groundwater. The former is more specifically called rooftop water harvesting and is rather a temporary measure aimed to provide immediate relief from drinking water scarcity; the latter has the potential to provide sustainable relief from water scarcity, addressing the needs of all living beings in nature. Ideally, Kerala needs a combination of both the approaches with focus on site, and area-specific solutions i.e., rainwater harvesting and storage where there is acute seasonal scarcity of drinking water and recharge of groundwater in other areas.

The major objectives of the rainwater harvesting campaign are to sensitise stakeholders of the seriousness of the water scarcity looming over the state, to disseminate knowledge on existing good practices in rainwater harvesting, to demonstrate good practices in rainwater harvesting by adopting them in public buildings and institutions, to prepare ground for large scale adoption of RWH in the state of Kerala and to establish a Rain Centre at Thiruvananthapuram for promoting RWH and groundwater recharge measures. Although the idea is attractive in principle, it would be dangerous if implementation is not done scientifically and without utmost care. Harvested water may not be ideal for all uses and there is a physical limit to the amount of water that can be stored in tanks. In the Kerala context, limitations exist in the subsurface as well. Also, attempts are being made to create carbon copies of techniques adopted elsewhere without really looking into the ground realities at site.

Roof-top rainwater harvesting may be an ideal technique for meeting some of the water requirements in institutional, industrial, and office buildings, but may not be an ideal technique for residential use in the settings in Kerala. What Kerala needs to do is to look at the problem holistically and adopt an 'Integrated Water Resources Management' approach. Our actions such as unscientific, uncontrolled, and unscrupulous filling up of areas like paddy-fields, wetlands, marshes, and ponds, large-scale paving and creation of impervious surfaces, demolition of hillocks and mountains, uncontrolled pumping of groundwater, wasteful usage of water, and excessive sand-mining from river beds have all contributed to the water scarcity problem in the State.

Schemes under Japan Bank of International Cooperation (JBIC) Assistance

A package of five major water-supply schemes was approved by the Overseas Economic Cooperation Fund (OECF) of Japan for loan assistance. The funding agency is now known as JBIC. Loan agreement for the project was executed on 23rd February 1997 between OECF and the Government of India. According to the agreement, Government of India is the borrower and KWA is the implementing agency. The project, with an estimated cost of Rs.1787.45 crore (maximum loan amount Rs.1519.38 crore) aims at augmenting and rehabilitating water supply schemes of two urban areas *viz.*, Thiruvananthapuram and Kozhikode, and constructing new water-supply schemes in three rural regions viz., Meenad and adjoining villages in Kollam district, Cherthala and adjoining villages in Alappuzha district, and Pattuvam and adjoining villages in Kannur district. The design, estimates, tender preparation etc were done by consultants specially hired for this purpose. The project is scheduled for completion by the end of 2006 and, when completed, is expected to provide safe drinking water to a population of about 43 lakh. For a projected population of 9.39 lakh in 2021 within the Thiruvananthapuram city limits and six neighbouring *panchayats*, the ultimate water demand is expected to be 285 MLD as against the present supply capacity of 203 MLD. This project is expected to augment the present system in Thiruvananthapuram by 42 MLD. The project for Kozhikode covers an area comprising the city and 16 neighbouring *panchayats* and aims at using the water stored in the Peruvannaamoozhi reservoir for meeting the water-supply requirements. The scheme is expected to augment the present supply by 151 MLD in 2006 and by 188 MLD at its ultimate stage (2021).

Schemes Funded by External Agencies

A few other external agencies and countries also have provided assistance to strengthen the water-supply network in the state. As part of the Drinking Water-Supply and Sanitation Decade, several projects for supplying drinking water were launched with the support of bilateral and multilateral agencies during the 1980s. In 1985, the World Bank approved the Kerala Water-Supply and Sanitation Project aimed at strengthening the Kerala Water Authority, providing piped water-supply systems in selected rural areas, and introducing low-cost onsite sanitation pilot programmes in rural areas of the state. Under DANIDA assistance, three schemes were taken up during 1983-1998 covering three rural areas in Kerala. The Netherlands provided assistance to set up eight water-supply schemes in Kerala. The Dutch-assisted water-supply projects are coming up in Alappuzha and Idukki districts.

Decentralisation in Rural Water-Supply and Jalanidhi

Until a few years ago, KWA was the sole agency for execution of water-supply schemes, distribution of drinking water, and maintenance of water-supply schemes throughout the state. After the 73rd and the 74th Constitutional amendments, efforts to decentralise rural water-supply schemes were initiated. The centralised system of water-supply is ineffective in sparsely settled rural areas where provision of water through this system within reasonable distance or through house connection involves high networking costs. Identification of individual or group sources of drinking water is more attractive in such situations. In addition to KWA, several others have come into the water-supply sector over the past decade. Transformation from a centralised to a decentralised system, especially in the case of rural water-supply, is taking place in the state at a rapid pace.

The Government of Kerala launched a People's Planning Campaign as an instrument for decentralised planning in July 1996. In order to bring in people's involvement in planning and implementation of schemes for mitigating the inadequacy of coverage of drinking water-supply in several rural areas of the state, the government decided to permit local bodies (*Gram Panchayats*) to take up drinking water-supply schemes and issued orders in March 1998 stipulating procedures for implementation of certain types of water-supply schemes by local bodies. The Government of Kerala also issued guidelines on schemes that can be taken up by local bodies directly as well as those that can be taken up on behalf of local bodies by KWA. Local bodies were allowed to take up small water-supply schemes covering a single *panchayat* with technical assistance of KWA and other agencies. Subsequently, in November 1998, the Government of Kerala issued further guidelines for transferring existing small schemes within the boundary of a single *panchayat*, operated by Kerala Water Authority in rural areas, to local bodies. It was decided that KWA should hand over 1050 Rural Water-Supply Schemes that fall within the boundary of single *panchayats*, and having independent sources to local bodies. The Government agreed to provide necessary funds for carrying out maintenance of these schemes before their handing over. *Panchayats* were made responsible for operations, maintenance, quality control, augmentation, and improvement of the schemes thus undertaken and for meeting all the expenditures involved from their own resources by suitably modifying the tax/tariff structure. Work on handing over these projects is in progress. Table 7.31 gives the district-wise break-up of schemes to be transferred from KWA to various local self-government bodies.

Although various state governments and the Government of India have adequate investments in the water and sanitation sectors in the past, the resultant coverage in both was considered too low in terms of the investment levels due to a top-down approach to planning, non-involvement of users, highly inadequate levels of cost recovery, depletion of sources due to over-drawal, and frequent breakdowns due to poor operation and maintenance. Against this background, policy makers of all states met together for a Summit on Water Policy in 1999 and brought out the Cochin Declaration, which redefined the approach of the government towards provision of water security. The 1999 Cochin Declaration on Rural Water-Supply Policy Reforms make mention of (i) adopting "demand responsive approaches" through the use of participatory processes, (ii) changing the role of the government from that of a 'provider' to that of a 'facilitator', (iii) establishing financial viability and sustainability of rural water-supply services, and (iv) promoting integrated water resources management.

The Kerala Rural Water-Supply and Environmental Sanitation Project implemented under *Jalanidhi* scheme aims at improving water-supply and sanitation services for about 1.5 million persons, specifically targeting the poor and the disadvantaged communities in four districts of the state, viz. Kozhikode, Malappuram, Palakkad and Thrissur. *Jalanidhi*, the Rs. 380 crore World Bank-funded project, initiated in 1999 aims at establishing better water-supply systems, construction of sanitary latrines for below poverty line households, conversion of unsanitary latrines in *Gram Panchayats* to sanitary two-pit latrines, measures for efficient groundwater recharge, etc. The project is designed on the redefined premise of delivery of water and sanitation services. It is a demand-driven project, conceptualized, planned, and implemented by users themselves as against the conventional top-down approach. This will be owned, operated and maintained by users themselves on a total cost-recovery basis.

There are also other well-integrated components which make this project unique. The major objective of the organisation is to achieve sustained provision of adequate quantities of safe, drinking water to rural poor, the focus being on ensuring sustainability of source, sustainability of operations, adequacy of water,

TABLE 7.31

District-wise Break-up of Water Supply Schemes Transferred to Local Bodies

Sl. No.	*District*	*No. of Panchayats*	*No. of Villages*	*Total Number of Schemes*	*Population Benefited*	*Handed over (included in the list of 1050 schemes)*	*No. of Schemes Handed Over Outside the 1050 Scheme list*	*Total No. of Schemes Handed over*
1	Kasargod	26	37	54	78850	5		
2	Kannur	54	57	90	183565			
3	Wayanad	16	17	29	46575			
4	Kozhikkode	61	17	29	46575			
5	Malappuram	42	46	66	126835	20	6	
6	Palakkad	54	66	92	528401	44	34	
7	Thrissur	54	92	103	369091			
8	Ernakulam	41	49	82	300828	1		
9	Idukki	28	28	88	136825			
10	Kottayam	51	52	99	419280			
11	Alappuzha	48	52	72	543929			
12	Pathanamthitta	24	25	33	144561			
13	Kollam	32	39	57	403150			
14	Thiruvananthapuram	60	69	80	657953			
	Total	591	693	1050	4361455	98	46	144

Source: Government of Kerala. *Economic Review and Report of the KWA 2003.*

and quality of water. The project assists local and state level public agencies to shift the focus from direct service delivery to the supporting of community groups in planning, constructing, and operating of piped water-supply and environmental sanitation systems. It also assists the Government of Kerala and the Government of India in building their capacity to implement India's sectoral reform policies.

The core principle of the project is public ownership. While many of the government-sponsored water-supply schemes have turned into bad assets because of neglect by the general public, in the *Jalanidhi* scheme, the beneficiaries are participant stakeholders and therefore they ensure that the entire project is conceived and implemented economically and managed efficiently. Under this scheme, Beneficiary Groups (BGs) are responsible for planning, technology selection and construction of their RWSS facilities. They provide their part of the capital cost contribution, manage operation and maintenance of improved facilities, and levy and collect appropriate user charges.

Representative Beneficiary Committees (BCs) were to be set up by each of the participating BGs. Their composition, functions, method of selecting members, byelaws, legal framework, and the relationship with *Gram Panchayat* and KRWSA have been formulated. The project aims to make vigorous efforts to maximise women's representation in BCs. At least 50 per cent of the members of BCs are women, and 20 per cent of them from socially disadvantaged groups. At least one of the top management positions of BCs (President or Treasurer) is also held by a woman. NGOs and private sector consultants play an important role in these projects. While one group supports GPs, BGs and beneficiary committees (BCs) on a day-to-day basis in planning and implementing the project's activities and providing brief support to BGs during post-implementation to stabilise the operation of the scheme, another set draws up a range of programmes, or provides specialised assistance in such tasks as preparing groundwater recharge schemes, water-quality monitoring, or in developing strategies and materials for sanitation and hygiene promotion programmes.

The third category is the private sector consulting firms which provide assistance in computerised financial management systems, audits and accounts, design engineering of multi-*panchayat* water-supply schemes, organise independent construction, undertake quality monitoring, conduct management information systems (MIS) etc. *Gram panchayats* (GP) is the focal point for project activities in their respective domains. GPs are mainly responsible for seeking project assistance, preparing the implementation phase proposal during the planning phase, and for facilitating project implementation by BGs during the implementation phase. GPs also provide counterpart funding to BGs as a percentage of infrastructure building costs. During post-implementation phase, GPs monitor sustainability of the scheme's operations and ensure that BGs satisfactorily discharge their O&M management function including levying and collecting user charges from beneficiaries to fully recover the recurring O & M costs. In general, 75 per cent of project funding is taken up by *Jalanidhi*, and 10 per cent by *gram panchayats*; the remaining 15 per cent is obtained from beneficiaries of the scheme. Beneficiary groups meet 100 per cent of the recurring costs of operation and maintenance, thus, lightening the burden on the exchequer.

The project has been quite successful in the four districts (viz. Malappuram, Kozhikode, Thrissur and Palakkad), in which it is being implemented. Improvements achieved have resulted in better living conditions in 85 *gram panchayats*; 750 water-supply schemes out of 1750 are operational and the rest nearing completion. Also, 38,000 sanitary latrines and about 20,000 units of compost pits and soak pits have been constructed. About 26,000 unsanitary latrines have been converted into sanitary latrines as part of the project. Three villages—Pothukal in Malappuram district, Puthupady in Kozhikode district, and Ayroor in Palakkad district—have achieved 100 per cent sanitation in the process, an uncommon feat in the rural scenario in India. The Kerala Rural Water Supply and Sanitation Agency (KRWSA) has recently decided to extend the efforts to all over the state, implementing it in three *gram panchayats* each in the 10 remaining districts. Table 7.32 gives details of the district-wise coverage of the schemes under KRWSA (*Jalanidhi*) as on 30th September 2005.

In addition, 18 *gram panchayats* spread over nine districts of the state, (excluding Alappuzha district) are also being covered by this scheme. Overall, the *Jalanidhi* project covers 110 *gram panchayats* through 120 projects, of which 10 are tribal projects. In September 2005, there were 4193 active beneficiary groups and over 9 lakh people are being benefited. The project is estimated to cover about 27 per cent of the total households in *gram panchayats* facing shortage of

TABLE 7.32

District-wise Coverage of Schemes under Jalanidhi

Sl. No.	*District*	*Total No. of Grama Panchayats in the District*	*Grama Panchayats by Jalanidhi*	*Percentage Coverage*
1.	Palakkad	90	20	22
2.	Thrissur	92	16	17
3.	Malappuram	100	33	33
4.	Kozhikode	77	23	30
5.	**Total**	**359**	**92**	**26**

Source: Status Report of KRWSA, 2005.

potable water; 54 per cent of the total *Jalanidhi* membership is from families living below the poverty line (BPL) and 17 per cent from SC/ST households.

Community-Owned and Operated Water-Supply Systems

There are also a few cases of water-supply systems built, owned, and operated by Non-Governmental Organisations and Voluntary Agencies (e.g., Olavanna, Pazhakulam). All these schemes are self-supporting. The scheme in Olavanna *gram panchayat* in Kozhikode district has attracted considerable attention even at international levels. The *gram* panchayat commissioned the first piped water-supply scheme in 1987 in its Vettuvedankunnu Ward to serve 400 households, using funds from Government grants to the block *panchayat*. Since 1987, the *gram panchayat* and the block *panchayat* built 18 more such schemes. KWA too commissioned two schemes in 1990 and in 1998, serving 2400 households. Already in 1989 a retired schoolteacher had installed a small water-supply scheme serving five neighbouring families in Kambiliparamba with money collected from beneficiaries and with the support of the *panchayat*. The success of this scheme convinced the villagers that instead of agitating against KWA and the *panchayat*, they could themselves solve their drinking water problem by community action, and that too at low cost. Fifty-four households in the same ward thereupon got together the same year and with a contribution of Rs. 4500 from each household formed a registered cooperative society to meet their drinking water requirements. Table 7.33 presents some details pertaining to a few schemes.

From 1991 onwards several private societies have come up under which a large number of schemes have been commissioned. Today there are about 26 such schemes in the *panchayat*; 6 more societies are in the process of implementing their schemes. Although this type of actions is highly commendable, the government should step in to take necessary steps to ensure that pumping and other actions carried out by such societies do not lead to problems of groundwater depletion and that the quality of water supplied remains good.

Ongoing and New Water Supply Projects of KWA

There are a number of urban and rural water-supply schemes, which were sanctioned and are under various stages of implementation. These are being implemented with assistance received under various programmes or with soft loans. Some details pertaining to schemes targeted for completion before 31st March 2006 are presented in Table 7.34.

TABLE 7.33

Details Pertaining to Some of the Schemes in Water Supply

S. No.	*Name of Scheme*	*Implementing Agency*	*Source of Funding*	*Remarks*
1	Urban Water Supply Schemes (UWSS)	KWA	HUDCO/LIC	Approximate total no. of house connections 8 lakhs
2	Rural Water Supply Schemes (RWSS)	KWA	(LIC/World Bank/DANIDA) Rajiv Gandhi National Drinking Water Mission (RGNWDM)	
3	Swajaladhara	KWA	RGNWDM	With beneficiary participation
4	Varsha	KWA		With beneficiary participation
5	Jalanidhi	Kerala Rural Water Supply Agency (KRWSA)	World Bank	With beneficiary participation (20% FC)
6	Sector Reform	Grama and District Panchayats	RGNDWM	With beneficiary participation (15% FC)
7	Olavanna Model	NGOs	Self	With beneficiary participation (100%)

Source: Personal Communication.

TABLE 7.34

District-wise Breakup of Schemes Targeted for Completion Before 31st March 2006

Name of the District	*Number of Ongoing Water Supply Schemes*								
	Rural Water Supply Schemes (RWSS)					*Urban Water Supply Schemes (UWSS)*			
	Accelerated Rural WSP	*Technology Mission*	*PMGY*	*State Plan*	*LIC*	*Accelerated UrbanWSP*	*State Plan*	*LIC/HUDCO*	*Total*
Thiruvananthapuram	11			3	2		3	2	21
Kollam	4		1	1	3				9
Pathanamthitta	4			4				1	9
Alapuzha	4			6	7		1		18
Kottayam	8		1	5	3		1	2	20
Idukki	6			1	3				10
Ernakulam	4			2	10		2	1	19
Thrissur	12	2		2	4	3	3	4	30
Palakkad	8	2		1	6			4	21
Malappuram	11			2	8			3	24
Kozhikode	5	1		3	1			3	13
Wayanad	2			1					3
Kannur	4			4			2	7	17
Kasargode	2	3			5				10
Total	85	8	2	35	52	3	12	27	224

Source: State Planning Board. *Report on the KWA 2002.*

Demand for and Supply of Water

Public water-supply system, being an inevitable component of infrastructure required to attain developmental objectives, has to keep pace with growth in demand for water. Different approaches have been suggested in the literature for estimating public water demand. According to the 'requirement approach', water demand in an area is estimated based on per capita requirement of the population. Water-supply projects are so planned and designed that they have sufficient capacity to meet not only present demand but also demand for a reasonable number of years in the future, called the 'design period'.

The 'demand curve approach' takes into account economic factors that influence demand for water such as price of water and income of the consumers, besides several non-economic variables such as climate, season, life style, and losses in the distribution system. The 'requirement approach' for estimation of water demand has yielded satisfactory results at several locations in the past. KWA, the major agency in the water-supply sector in Kerala, follows this approach for estimating water demand.

The Manual on Water-Supply and Treatment published by the Government of India prescribes norms for calculating per capita requirement of water for urban and rural water-supply schemes, and these norms are followed by KWA. In the case of UWSS, the norms recommend 70 to 100 lpcd of water for communities with population below 10000, 100 to 125 lpcd of water for communities with population between 10,000 to 50,000 and 125 to 200 lpcd of water for communities with population above 50000. With regard to rural communities for whom house connections are not contemplated and supply is made through common taps, the rate of water use is calculated at not be less than 40 lpcd; where house connections are contemplated the rate shall at least be 70 lpcd. The Manual also suggests that requirement of each water-supply scheme shall be studied with reference to local factors governing various non-domestic needs before the optimum rate of supply is decided upon.

Figure 7.1 shows the present pattern of water consumption in the state. During the early stages of water development in the state in the independence era, people used to draw water from several traditional sources such as natural springs, streams, rivers, open wells, ponds and tanks. The quality of water was also good in those days. Conditions have changed vastly over the years. Water quality has deteriorated in many places due to human activities and neglect, and traditional sources like ponds and tanks have been extensively destroyed. At present, people increasingly turn towards piped water-supply even in rural areas. Table 7.35 shows details of the quantity of water supplied by KWA from 1999 to 2003.

Although the present level of production of water through piped water-supply schemes in the state is estimated to be approximately 1008 MLD, there is wastage due to leakage and losses including theft, which limits the present effective supply to approximately 800 MLD, as against a demand of approximately 2900 MLD. Thus, at present there is a huge demand-supply gap. Another disturbing feature is the huge quantum of losses occurring in transmission. For bridging the demand-supply gap, scientific assessment of requirements and estimation of capital investment are required.

FIGURE 7.1

Consumption of Drinking Water in the State in Percentage

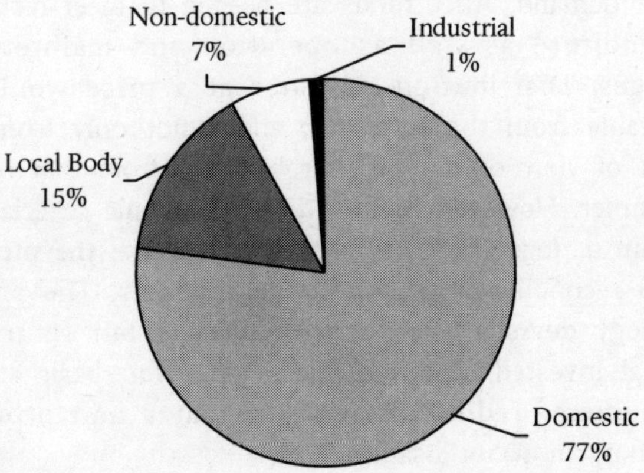

Source: GoK (2005).

Water demand of the state for 2001 was worked out as follows.

For 235.75 lakh rural population @ 70 lpcd	= 1650.25 MLD
For 82.67 lakh urban population @125 lpcd	= 1033.40 MLD
Non-domestic/ industrial demand	= 200.35 MLD
Total demand	= 2884.00 MLD

The sources of water are rivers, lakes, large reservoirs etc. Water is treated to standards conforming to drinking water requirements before it is distributed. Water supplied from open wells, bore wells, and tube wells by KWA is subjected to a minimum required level of purification whereas that supplied by other agencies are sometimes given no treatment at all. The treatment plants of KWA range in capacity from 1MLD to 100 MLD or even more. About 40 per cent of the total quantity of water produced goes unbilled or unaccounted for. This is mainly due to absence of a regular mechanism for measuring the actual quantity of water produced and used, poor billing mechanism, faulty metering system, and huge transmission losses.

The projected population of the state in 2051 is about 445 lakh where as the saturation population works out to be about 370 lakh. Assuming that the population stabilises at about 400 lakh with an urban population of about 25 per cent, water demand in 2051 is likely to be as shown below:

For 300.00 lakh rural population @ 70 lpcd	= 2100.00 MLD
For 100.00 lakh urban population @125 lpcd	= 1250.00 MLD
Non-domestic/ industrial demand	= 300.00 MLD
Total demand	= 3650.00 MLD

Meeting this water demand is going to be a herculean task and would need an integrated strategy combining traditional sources, systems, and wisdom with modern piped water supply systems.

Capacity Utilisation of Water-Supply Systems

Capacity utilisation may be defined as the ratio of actual to potential output. While actual output is clearly defined, there is no consensus on the method to measure potential output. While the engineering approach takes the maximum output that existing capacity can produce as the potential output, (i.e., a short term measure of potential output), the economic approach is based on the agency's average cost curves. Studies on capacity utilisation of water-supply systems have been rare. Table 7.36 shows capacity utilisation figures of a few water-supply schemes based on a study carried out by KWA in 1994. The major causes of underutilisation of capacity are reportedly fluctuations in power supply, power cuts, and shortage of operators.

TABLE 7.35

Details of Piped Water Supply by KWA

Year	*Water Available for Supply (MLD)*	*Actual Supply (MLD)*	*Leakage*
1999	1030 to 1050	770 to 800	25 to 30% of the production
2000	1030 to 1050	770 to 800	25 to 30% of the production
2001	1200 to 1300 (Capacity)	1000 to 1100	20 to 25% of the production
2002	1700 to 1800	1400 to 1500	17 to 22% of the production
2003	1720 to 1820 (Capacity)	756 to 856	Total Loss: 40%

Source: Government of Kerala. *Economic Review and Report of the KWA 2003.*

TABLE 7.36

Capacity Utilisation of Water-Supply Schemes

Name of the Scheme	*Potential Capacity (lakh lpd)*	*Actual Utilisation (lakh lpd)*	*Percentage Utilisation (%)*
Parassala WSS	7.9	5.9	74.68
Kumily WSS	40	34.5	86.25

Source: John, J. (1997). *Economics of Public Water Supply System.*

However, Pushpangadan (2003a) reported that the average capacity utilisation of rural water supply schemes in Kerala is as low as 49.5 per cent of design capacity. His study showed a marginal increase of about three per cent in RWSS in the southern districts of the State. The northern districts encounter serious voltage problems which reduce the number of their pumping hours. Capacity utilisation was found to be independent of the age of the scheme. It was the highest for bore-well-based schemes. There appears to be higher capacity utilisation for open well-based schemes in the north and for river-based schemes in the south.

The fact that only very few studies examined the problems of capacity utilisation of water supply schemes in the state, that wide divergences exist in the estimates of capacity utilisation of WSS reported, and that the reported values of capacity utilisation of RWSS are extremely low, leads to the conclusion that more comprehensive studies on this aspect are needed urgently. Also, measures to improve capacity utilisation rates have to be implemented.

Water-Pricing and Related Problems

Drinking water is neither a free gift of nature nor a purely private good. Residential water supply is a public utility and its output is an essential consumer good. However, it is not a pure public good either, as provision of this good based on pricing is possible and, to some extent, necessary. Production and distribution of drinking water is an economic activity as it involves costs. Total cost can be computed by pricing inputs. If costs are to be recovered from consumers, water distributed needs to be priced.

The pricing policy should be such that the norm of distributive justice or the welfare objective is adhered to. However, care has to be taken to ensure also fiscal and economic efficiency objectives. Water-supply is an economic activity that is highly capital intensive. It is not a 'once for all' type of investment as new projects or augmentation or modernisation schemes of existing projects have to be taken up along with growth in water demand. Also, funds are needed to meet recurring expenditure as well as operation and maintenance charges. Distribution of water at a price would be desirable from the economic angle, not only from the point of view of the supplier but also from that of the consumer. However, many a time, economic criteria may remain at loggerheads with welfare criteria; the problem is to reconcile these conflicting interests. The pricing strategy devised should bring back a fair return on capital invested, distribute costs on a fair basis among consumers, reduce wastage of water and promote economy in water usage.

In developed economies, recovery of costs is the major purpose of water pricing; questions of equity receive only secondary importance. The criterion for pricing is that "price should cover completely the capital investment and the recurring expenses". In Third World countries, even partial capital cost recovery may be difficult. In such countries, recovery of operation and maintenance cost may be the maximum that could be thought of. In spite of recommendations of several committees on the need for building up financial autonomy in operation of water-supply schemes, India, in general, Kerala in particular, does not follow any consistent policy on water pricing.

TABLE 7.37

Details of Water Tariff

Type of Demand	*Monthly Consumption(KL)*	*Rate from 1/10/91 to 31/5/93*	*Rate from 1/6/93 to 31/5/94*	*Rate from 1/6/94 to 31/3/99*	*Rate from 1/4/1999*
Domestic	0 – 10	Rs.1.00/KL subject to a minimum of Rs. 10/ month	Rs.1.50/KL subject to a minimum of Rs. 15/ month	Rs.1.70/KL subject to a minimum of Rs. 17/ month+ Rs.2.00 as MIC	Rs.2.00/KL subject to a minimum of Rs. 20 per month + Rs.2.00 as MIC
Domestic	10 – 30	Rs.10.00 + Rs.1.50/KL above 10 KL	Rs.15.00 + Rs.2.00/KL above 10 KL	Rs.17.00 + Rs.2.30/KL above 10 KL	Rs.20.00 + Rs.3.00 /KL above 10 KL
Domestic	30 – 50	Rs.40.00 + Rs.2.00/KL above 30 KL	Rs.55.00 + Rs.3.00/KL above 30 KL	Rs.63.00 + Rs.3.45/KL above 30 KL	Rs.80.00 + Rs.5.00/ KL above 30 KL
Domestic	Above 50	Rs.80.00 + Rs.3.00/KL above 50 KL	Rs.115.00 + Rs.4.00/KL above 50 KL	Rs.132.00 + Rs.4.60/KL above 50 KL	Rs.180.00 + Rs.7.35 /KL above 50 KL
Non-Domestic	0 – 50	Rs.3.00/KL subject to a minimum of Rs. 25/ month + Re. 1.00 as	Rs.4.00/KL subject to a minimum of Rs. 50/ month + Rs. 2.00 as service charge	Rs.4.60/KL subject to a minimum of Rs. 60/ month + Rs. 2.00 as MIC	Rs.7.35/KL subject to a service charge minimum of. Rs. 100/ month + Rs. 2.00 as MIC
Non-Domestic	Above 50	Rs.150.00 + Rs. 4.00/KL above 50 KL	Rs.200.00 + Rs. 6.00/KL above 50 KL	Rs.232.00 + Rs. 6.90/KL above 50 KL	Rs.370.00 + Rs.10.60/KL above 50 KL
Industrial	For the whole monthly consumption	Rs.5.00/KL subject to a minimum of Rs. 100/month	Rs.6.00/KL subject to a minimum of Rs. 100/ month	Rs.6.90/KL subject to a minimum of Rs. 115/ month	Rs.10.60/KL subject to a minimum of Rs. 200/ month + Rs. 2.00 as MIC
Panchayats	Rate per stand post per year		Rs. 1314.00		Rs. 2628.00
Municipalities and Corporation	Rate per stand post per year		Rs. 875.00		Rs. 1750.00

Source: Website of the KWA.

Studies have shown that several old water-supply systems have become inefficient because of obsolescence and poor maintenance and are in need of urgent repairs, augmentation or outright replacement. All over the country, including Kerala, funds generated by water charges fall short of recurring expenditure incurred.

At the time of formation of KWA, water tariff was low and it varied from place to place. There was a system of free allowance and local bodies used to collect water charges. Also, the billing system was highly irregular. To improve the situation, a Provisional Invoice Card System (PIC) was introduced in some places in 1988. A system for collection of water charges through banks was introduced later and KWA supplemented the PIC system with an adjustment bill system, based on actual measurements of water use every six months. With a view to unifying water tariff, the Government of Kerala issued orders in 1991, fixing a uniform tariff for the entire state. The minimum charge was fixed at Rs 10/ KL up to 10,000 lpm and the system of free allowance was withdrawn completely. The Financial Consultant (M/S Ferguson and Co.) recommended that if water rates were increased by 15 per cent every year from 1991, the KWA would become self-sufficient by 2001. Based on this recommendation, water tariff was revised in 1993. The minimum charge was raised to Rs 15.00/KL and the Government of Kerala agreed for an automatic upward revision by 15 per cent every year. But no annual increase was effected after 1994 when the minimum charge stood at Rs. 17.00/KL. The next revision was made in 1999. Some details of these water tariff revisions made since 1991 are presented in Table 7.37. The responsibility of collection of water charges from all consumers,

TABLE 7.38

Comparison of Domestic Water Charges

Quantity of Water (KL)	*Domestic Water Charges Levied by Various Water Supply Agencies (Rs.)*			
	KWA, Kerala	*BWSSB, Karnataka*	*CMWSSB, Tamil Nadu*	*HMWWSB, Andhra Pradesh*
15	35	90	75	90
25	65	200	375	150
50	180	600	1250	500

Source: Personal Communication.

including local bodies for street taps and stand posts, was vested with KWA after April 1991. In view of the steep increase in power charges and resultant increase in production costs, KWA requested for an increase in water tariff by 30 per cent in January 2000. However, a decision on this is yet to be taken.

In Kerala, the number of water-supply schemes in which water charges are levied and collected directly by KWA is small. In the case of most of the schemes, the responsibility rests with local bodies. *Panchayats* fix rates in cases of rural water-supply schemes operated by them whereas in cases of urban water-supply, this is done by the municipality or the corporation concerned. Water-supply through public taps and street fountains is not metered and no charge is levied. But water supplied to households and other consumers are metered and charged. Water charges levied in the state by KWA appear to be much lower than charges collected in neighbouring States (Table 7.38).

The High Level Committee on Social Infrastructure and Services constituted by the state Planning Board in 1982 recommended that it is possible to collect a substantial amount of money from consumers to meet operation and maintenance costs, as well as capital costs with interest thereon, over a reasonably long time period. However, this approach may be appropriate in developed economies, but infeasible in the Kerala context. There does exist great scope for mobilisation of funds through water-pricing. Unfortunately, no action has yet been taken to evolve and implement a good water-pricing policy. A comparison of costs *versus* average recovery is presented in Table 7.39. While the average cost is Rs. 8.54 per KL, the average recovery is only about Rs. 3.50 per KL.

An economic analysis carried out on the Neyyattinkara UWSS in Thiruvananthapuram district for a one-year period shows that only 26.9 per cent of the total current expenditure is collected by way of water charges and that the balance is borne by the state government through subsidies (Table 7.40). The situation is almost identical with other WSSs too.

TABLE 7.39

Comparison of Expenditure and Average Cost Recovery (2002-03)

	Rs./KL
Direct Variable Cost	
Operators Salary	1.58
Power Charges	2.83
Chemicals	0.39
Subtotal	4.80
Indirect Variable Cost	
Repairs and Maintenance	0.74
Administrative Overheads	1.27
Interest and Depreciation	1.73
Subtotal	3.74
Total Expenditure	8.54
Average Cost Recovery	3.50

Source: John, J. (1997). *Economics of Public Water Supply System.*

Table 7.41 provides information about the district-wise number of connections provided. At present, KWA is directly billing consumers and collecting water charges except in Thrissur, where the city corporation does this job. But, the corporation is required to pay the full cost of maintenance to KWA. Table 7.42 shows the income of KWA from water charges in 2002-03 while Table 7.43 presents details of payment dues from consumers as on 31st March 2003. Clearly, dues outweigh annual revenue. Consumer ledgers are found to remain un-updated. Also, there are reportedly a large number of unauthorised connections in many places. One of the major weaknesses of KWA is its inability to locate such connections and take appropriate legal action. Charge collection from local bodies for street taps and stand posts is not efficient either.

Although all connections have been, it is claimed, metered, about 50 per cent of the meters used are reportedly not working. According to Section 42 of Kerala Water-Supply and Sewerage Act, KWA has to provide meters. This provision makes it impossible to hold consumers responsible for replacement of faulty meters. A proposal to amend the Act is under consideration. Two monthly meter-reading and billing has been attempted in some places and the results are encouraging. KWA does not have sufficient staff for meter-reading, billing, and collection. Computerisation is getting delayed due to lack of trained and skilled manpower.

Studies on water use in some of the water-supply schemes have shown that, in general, consumers are averse to taking timely action to prevent wastage of water, particularly since the loss would not cost them much directly in terms of water use charges. Misuse of water treated exclusively for drinking purposes, for gardening and other cultivation purposes is widespread, especially during summer months when supply of water becomes scarce. Low water charges and neglect of misuse of water perpetuate this anomalous situation.

To Sum up: The prevailing pricing policy fails to meet the objectives of economy, efficiency, and welfare. In Kerala, water charges are uniform for all users irrespective of income status. Such a pricing policy is discriminatory against the lower income groups. Inadequate supply of water, low voltage and other power supply problems, non-availability of pumps and pump operators, etc also affect the poor adversely.

TABLE 7.40

Total Current Expenditure and Revenue (Neyyattinkara UWSS)

Item	*Amount (Rs.)*
Operation and Maintenance Cost (Monthly)	1,14,664.00
Monthly Interest on Capital	75,083.00
Recurring Cost (Monthly)	1,89,747.00
Monthly Depreciation	15,416.65
Current Expenditure (Monthly)	2,05,163.65
Monthly Revenue	55,194.05
Excess of Expenditure over Revenue	1,49,969.60

Source: John, J. (1997). *Economics of Public Water Supply System.*

Self-financing of Water-Supply Schemes and Policies of Water Pricing: Relevance to Kerala

According to the Manual on Water-Supply and Treatment, "Financial autonomy can be built into the operation of water-supply systems through revolving funds, reliance on bonds and debentures in the market, and loan assistance from various funding agencies. The

TABLE 7.41

District-wise Summary of Connections Provided

District	*Water Supply Connections*				*Street Taps*		
	Domestic	*Non-Domestic*	*Industrial*	*Total*	*Panchayat*	*Corporation or Municipality*	*Total*
Thiruvananthapuram	180137	20893	59	201089	10257	4198	14455
Kollam	60216	3691	95	64002	11373	3218	14591
Pathanamthitta	23510	2103	15	25628	8275	1433	9708
Alappuzha	57357	2285	42	59684	15088	4201	19289
Kottayam	44711	4025	27	48763	10074	2079	12153
Idukki	8882	858	4	9744	2784	496	3282
Ernakulam	202936	15395	755	219086	18792	14459	33251
Thrissur	71181	3112	35	74328	18441	3627	22068
Palakkad	46854	3928	92	50874	9797	2788	12585
Malappuram	30004	2126	13	32143	8437	2835	11272
Kozhikode	39822	2978	9	42809	5374	2549	7923
Wayanad	4683	909	1	5593	2647	186	2833
Kannur	20711	3251	46	24008	3766	1805	5571
Kasargode	12702	769	15	13486	3190	210	3400
Total	**803706**	**66323**	**1208**	**871237**	**128297**	**44084**	**172381**

Source: Government of Kerala. *Economic Review and Report of the KWA 2003.*

TABLE 7.42

Income of KWA from Water Charges during 2002-03

Consumer Category	*Income from Water Charges (Rs. Crores)*			
	Urban Schemes	*Rural Comprehensive Schemes*	*Rural Single Panchayat Schemes*	*Total*
Domestic, Non-domestic and Industrial Consumers	56.33	14.08	7.04	77.46
Street Taps	11.90	8.8	7.63	28.34
Total	**68.23**	**22.88**	**14.67**	**105.80**

Source: Same as Table 7.41.

TABLE 7.43

Dues from Various Categories of Consumers as on 31-03-2003

Sl No.	*Consumer Category*	*Amount (Rs. Crores)*
1	Domestic	47.82
2	Non-Domestic	79.62
3	Industrial	8.25
4	Panchayats	88.18
5	Municipalities	51.13
6	Corporations	45.30
	Total	**320.30**

Source: Same as Table 7.41.

use of these methods in isolation or combination has proven to be effective elsewhere in launching water-supply systems on the road to self-support, relieving the state and central governments of part of their burden of support and more importantly improving water-supply for the benefit of the consumers and for the development of the region concerned." It also emphasises that the revenue generated through sale of water should be adequate to meet annual recurring cost of operation and the maintenance of schemes and to leave a surplus for building up a reserve fund for investment in improvements and expansion. These recommendations have yet to be implemented in Kerala.

There are different methods adopted for pricing water. In the 'Flat Rate or Fixed Monthly Charge' method, a fixed charge per month is levied on the consumer, regardless of the quantum of water consumed. In the Kerala context, this method would promote inefficient and uneconomical usage of water and the method is highly discriminatory against poor consumers. The 'Constant Rate' method which charges a constant unit price from all consumers is in operation in Kerala at present. A minimum charge is fixed for consumption below a specified quantity of water. This system too does not ensure equity in water-supply. The third method is 'Block-Rate Pricing'. Two types of block-rates are employed—declining block-rates and increasing block-rates. The 'declining block-rate system' employs a minimum charge for an initial quantity followed by smaller unit prices in the higher discrete ranges of consumption. Average price decreases as consumption increases and vice versa. This pricing system is unsuitable for Kerala from the point of view of equity, as low-income groups who generally consume lower quantities of water will be charged higher average prices while high-income groups would pay lower average prices. In the 'increasing block rate' system, the unit price for water increases as a consumer uses more water. At a time when increasing water demands are stressing existing supplies, this policy will be advantageous from the point of view of both water conservation and equity in distribution. This system is ideally suited to the Kerala context, where per capita income level is lower than that in many other states of India and where wide disparities in income distribution exist. The pricing policy may be so evolved as to levy a lower charge on low-income groups and the subsidy involved may be partly or wholly recovered from high-income groups.

Performance of RWSS - Operated by Beneficiary Groups

Namboodiri and Thampi (2004) carried out a study on four different decentralised water supply schemes managed by Beneficiary Groups at Olavanna Panchayat in Kozhikode district. Detailed public opinion survey and field investigation were carried out to assess performance of these schemes in respect of the following aspects: customer satisfaction, sustainability of the system including that of source of water-supply, environmental sanitation, power consumption, level of public participation, and water tariff and its acceptability.

Table 7.44 presents a comparison of the four water supply schemes studied. A comparison of water charges in this Table with those in Table 7.37 for schemes operated by KWA shows that water charges in these systems are quite high, even in the absence of any water treatment. Besides, beneficiaries have to pay considerable amounts by way of connection charges. Economic viability of schemes operated by KWA could be considerably improved by evolving a proper pricing policy.

Singh *et al.* (1993) found, based on a study on rural water supply schemes in Kerala operated by KWA and local bodies, that these systems are caught in a 'low level equilibrium trap'. With very few connections and a low tariff, little revenue is generated beyond the subsidies provided by the government. The survey showed that respondents are deterred by high cost of connection. KWA may solve this problem by folding connection cost into water tariff, either partly or wholly. The study showed that the system could ratchet to a 'high level equilibrium' by making a few policy changes, encouraging more connections, and evolving a rational pricing policy.

Evaluation of Present System and Future Strategies

In general, the challenges that Kerala faces today in the water-supply sector are two-fold—reaching out to the uncovered sections of the population, and improving the quality and quantity of the existing schemes.

Issues

There are several factors contributing to non-sustainability of existing water-supply schemes such as the following:

Water-supply in cities, towns and rural areas of the state remains the primary responsibility of KWA or of local bodies. The financial status of KWA has become increasingly fragile over the past two decades. The organisation is finding it increasingly difficult to maintain even the existing level of water-supply services or to meet establishment expenditures from the revenue earned from water-supply charges and non-plan grants of the government. In the case of rural water-supply schemes managed by local bodies, the task of source development, maintenance of distribution system, and collection of water charges remain with them. Wherever transfer of created assets from the centralised system to the local bodies for operation and maintenance has taken place, the schemes perform badly for want of adequate assured plan assistance.

Even in the case of most of the Urban Water-Supply Schemes, the operating organisations do not have a proper vision in the formulation of strategies for operating and maintaining the existing schemes and their water-supply. Lack of reliable and accurate data makes it difficult to study the schemes and make suggestions for improvement.

TABLE 7.44

Comparison Among WS Schemes Operated by BGs in Olavanna *Panchayat*, Kozhikode District, Kerala State

Sl. No.	*Name of WSS*	*Source*	*No. of Beneficiaries*	*Present Share Value + connection Charge (Rs.)*	*Present Water Tariff (Rs.)*	*Pump Operator Charge Per Month (Rs.)*	*Meter Reader's Charge Per Month (Rs)*	*Remarks*
1	Kambili Parambil (Commissioned 1989)	Shallow Well	57	7000/-	10/-	Nil	No meters Installed	No regular disinfection; No women in the EC; No water metering system; No contribution from the government.
2	Nedumparamb Kunnu	do	135	13200/-	6KL(min) Rs. 35 10K L+3.33/KL 15KL+6.67/KL 17KL+10.0/KL Above 50.0/KL	1000/-	200/-	No regular disinfection; Perfect water metering system; No women in the EC; No contribution from the government.
3	Parayan Kadu Kunnu	do	130	7500/-	6KL Min Rs. 30/ Above Rs 20/KL	750/-	75/-	No regular disinfection; No women in the EC; No contribution from the government.
4	Kodal Nadakkavu	do	65	3000/-	6KL Min Rs. 30/ Above Rs 50/KL	400/-	100/-	No regular disinfection; No women in the EC; No contribution from the government.

Source: Namboodiri, T.V.N. and S.G. Thampi (2004).

A large section of the population of Kerala is 'water illiterate', resulting in a consumption pattern that causes considerable wastage of treated water.

In general, it may be said that the pricing mechanism has not been used to guide the decisions of consumers as to how much to consume, or how to balance supply with demand. The present water (connection) charges and water tariffs are heavily subsidised. The upward revisions of water charges and water tariff during the past half century have been minimal, not adequate even to compensate for the inflation rate. Being the guarantor of loans received by KWA from various financial institutions and agencies for implementation of water- supply systems, the State government comes to its rescue when questions of repayment of loans arise.

Organisations and local bodies which operate water-supply schemes do not take timely and appropriate action for maintenance. To assist local bodies operating these schemes, the Central Public Health Environmental Engineering Organisation (CPHEEO) of the Government of India has formulated a 'Manual on Water Supply and Treatment', which lays down guidelines as to how the systems should be maintained. However, in most cases these guidelines are seldom followed. Low water pressure at the supply point, poor water quality, and frequent pump failures are common in Kerala's water-supply schemes. Water- supply projects are capital intensive and their repayment periods are relatively long. Improper maintenance or lack of maintenance of these schemes has led to a progressive decline in the quality of services rendered, resulting in resistance from consumers of any proposal to effect an increase in water tariff and connection charges.

A considerable proportion of treated water is lost through leakages in the distribution system. Measures for reduction in loss due to leakages and theft are weak, inadequate and ineffective. Also, awareness about the use of conservation methods and equipment to ensure efficient use of water is generally lacking. It has been found that the major portion of leakages (about 82 per cent) occurs in the house-service connections through service-pipes and taps, and the remaining 18 per cent occurs due to leakage in pipelines.

Water supply is not metered in many areas; a significant proportion is supplied, particularly in low-income areas, through stand posts; leakages at public taps go unattended for days together; and breakage of distribution lines is also common. All these lead to huge wastage of water.

It is well known that illegal connections drawn from public water-supply lines abound and that a huge quantity of treated water is taken without payment, causing heavy revenue losses to the agency supplying water. Water meters are tampered intentionally at many locations by consumers themselves, leading to heavy loss of revenue.

KWA is responsible for investigation, planning, design, and implementation of water-supply projects. In the case of many RWSSs, operation and maintenance is the responsibility of local bodies, whereas in many others KWA itself carries out operation and maintenance. Administrative and supervision charges of most of the Water-Supply and Sewerage Boards, including KWA, are quite high. As administration and supervision charges are calculated and levied as a percentage of total project costs, officials of the implementing agency are in general unconcerned about project cost or time over-runs.

Often, treated water and untreated water are used indiscriminately. There exists substantial scope for segregated use of water and recycling of wastewater for further use such as gardening, industrial purposes, street cleaning, fire fighting and irrigation. Water used for purposes such as flushing, washing and gardening need not have to be of the same quality as of that used for drinking purposes and, hence, need not have to be treated to that level.

The responsibilities of local bodies include identification of water sources, generation of potable water from the sources, distribution of water, fixation of tariffs and charges, collection of revenue and operation and maintenance of schemes. Studies reveal substantial shortages of appropriately trained staff to deal with these tasks.

Poor cost recovery has been primarily attributed to irrational water charges, wastages and mismanagement. Although a National Policy towards 'Full Cost Recovery' in respect of water-supply and sanitation sector was adopted in March 1993, full or even realistic cost recovery still remains unachieved.

Water-supply schemes implemented hitherto are based on a supply-driven approach. However, projects implemented under *Jalanidhi* and other schemes involving public participation are based on a demand-driven supply philosophy. This latter type of projects is introduced only in areas in which interested groups of people show willingness to participate in the projects and to abide by conditions of cost-sharing. Source selection, technology selection, purchase, contracting, and implementation are done by the registered body, the beneficiary group, with technical help from support organisations. This inculcates a sense of ownership in the people. To ensure stakeholding of the project, 15 per cent of the capital costs is borne by the beneficiary community, 10 per cent by *gram panchayat* of the locality and 75 per cent by the govt. Beneficiary Groups themselves meet 100 per cent of recurring costs of operations and maintenance, thus lightening the burden on the state exchequer, and helping the government to utilise the money for other priority needs. An advantage of this scheme is that it helps develop a sense of public participation in terms of 'customer' rather than 'consumer'. Although the idea is appealing, actual implementation has shown that the goals have not been reached.

Gram panchayats have successfully shifted their role from being providers to facilitators. It was found that self-regulation is the key concept on which beneficiary societies functioned. In a few societies, consumers in a street were allotted timings for water collection in order to reduce peak demand. Sealing of additional taps to manage acute drought conditions in summer, and establishing special cells for repairing faulty water-meters are seen to have been followed. This type of RWSS is observed to have been effectively managed causing minimum wastage of water. Detection of leaks, if any, and rectification of these defects, are carried out within the shortest possible time. Consumer satisfaction is given top priority by Beneficiary Groups and the majority of customers expressed their overall satisfaction on the working of these schemes.

Energy audits are not being carried out in any of the schemes. Though people were aware about the sources of pollution, sanitary surveys were never carried out; nor were water quality tests conducted. Lack of database management pertaining to these schemes at the *panchayat* level was a serious constraint on planning.

Water-supply authorities should not penalise customers for inefficient management. A quick-response system to customer needs along with an efficient metering, billing and collection system would substantially enhance the 'willingness to pay' on the part of the public.

Suggestions

The following measures are suggested for making the water-supply sector financially viable and functionally efficient.

New schemes should be taken up only after detailed feasibility studies and careful planning. Proper and timely action should be taken for the operation and maintenance of all schemes in position. A detailed database of the system should be maintained and kept up-to-date.

Performance of existing schemes needs to be looked into and remedial action initiated on an urgent basis.

Immediate action should be initiated for detecting leaks and other forms of wastage and plugging them. Unauthorised connections should be identified and disconnected. Faulty watermeters should be replaced promptly. Measures should be taken for making beneficiaries responsible for proper maintenance of the metering system. Also, measures should be taken to clear outstanding water charge arrears.

Rural water-supply in Kerala is caught in a 'low level equilibrium trap'. By making a few critical policy changes such as folding the connection costs into monthly tariff, and encouraging new connections, inefficient systems could be made financially viable and the quality of their services improved.

Substantial investment has gone into the water-supply sector and huge infrastructure systems built over the past five decades. All of them have to be made functional and sustainable. Care should be taken to provide efficient service even if consumers have to be pay a little higher charges.

The present tariff policy has to undergo changes to minimise subsidies and to make the system financially viable. Measures for curtailing wasteful and unnecessary administrative overheads should be taken. At the same time, sufficient number of properly trained staff should be employed.

An action plan to make the public 'water literate' needs to be chalked to promote efficient and economical usage of water.

The feasibility of having a dual system for water-supply in which only water for drinking purposes is treated to a high degree, needs to be examined. Kerala needs a dual system with focus on site-and-area-specific solutions i.e., rainwater harvesting and storage wherever there is acute seasonal scarcity of drinking water and recharging of groundwater in other areas.

Rainwater harvesting is to be done scientifically. Roof-top rainwater harvesting may be an ideal technique for meeting water requirements at non-residential levels, but it may not be an ideal technique for residential use in Kerala. An 'Integrated Water Resources Management' approach has to be adopted. The unscientific, uncontrolled and unscrupulous practice of filling up of areas like paddy fields, wetlands, marshes and ponds, large scale paving and creation of impervious surfaces, demolition of hillocks and mountains, uncontrolled pumping of groundwater, wasteful usage of water, and indiscriminate sand-mining from river-beds followed in Kerala with impunity, in recent decades, have accelerated the water scarcity problem in the state. These issues should be boldly addressed and appropriate and stringent remedial actions taken. Advancing reasons for opposing construction of dams and then vouching for water tanks and pumps all over the state is, no doubt, preposterous.

The need for transformation from a target-based, supply-driven approach to a demand-based approach is urgent. Full cost recovery of operations and maintenance as well as replacement costs will be possible in such a system which would ensure financial viability and sustainability of the schemes.

Drinking water needs of people who cannot pay for the services, should become the responsibility of the government and the local bodies.

To conclude, the progress made by Kerala in the development of its water supply sector should not be evaluated purely in financial terms. Reforms in all allied activities are needed to protect the water-supply schemes in place from the plethora of threats looming large over them. The reform process should begin before it is too late.

SECTION IV: TELECOMMUNICATIONS

Introduction

This section focuses on the development of communications infrastructure in Kerala with respect to a set of parameters and analyses its strengths and weaknesses on a comparative basis with other states in India. A few emerging communication services that have an impact on infrastructure planning are identified and some potential areas for future development are discussed.

Brief History of Telecommunications in Kerala

Kerala had the first Telegraph offices at Thiruvananthapuram, Quilon and Alleppey in 1864. By 1947, almost all the District Head Quarters in Kerala State, Cochin State and the Malabar district of the erstwhile Madras Presidency had Post and Telegraph offices. Voice communication came to Kerala only in 1923, at Cochin with a 100-line Cross Bar exchange, followed by Calicut. But, Thiruvananthapuram had the first Telephone exchange, a 10-line Magneto Exchange only in 1930 and was managed by Travancore State Electricity Department. By 1947, the state had only about 2500 telephones. By 1950, New Auto Exchanges were installed at Quilon, Kottayam and Alleppey. In 1950-51, the Travancore Telephone System was integrated with the Indian Post and Telegraph Department.

In 1974, Kerala Telecommunications was detached from the Postal Department and a Kerala Telecommunications Circle was formed with Head Quarters at Thiruvananthapuram. Kerala Telecommunications Circle, which had been first formed as a combined Postal and Telecom Circle in 1961, provides services to a population of over 31 million in Kerala, the union territory of Lakshadweep Islands and parts of Pondicherry. The circle comprises 11 Major secondary switching areas and one minor secondary switching area at Lakshadweep.

Kerala Telecommunications has had an impressive record of growth and modernisation, especially during the past few years. Kerala is the first state in India to fully automate all telephone exchanges, the first to link all the exchanges through STD facility, the first to provide public telephone facilities in all *panchayat* headquarters, and the first to provide public telephones in every village. Kerala Telecommunications has a large network with modern digital switches linked through reliable and high-capacity optical fibre media.

As of 30 June 2005, the tele-density (number of telephones per 100 population) of Kerala was 19.5, a very high level compared to the national average of 9.37. Only Punjab and metropolitan cities have higher tele-density than Kerala. The Rural tele-density of Kerala is 9.74 whereas the corresponding national average is only 1.74. Urban tele-density of Kerala is as high as 47.61.

Owing to the ever-increasing demand for communications, Kerala has a relatively large waiting list of applicants for telephone connections. The per-line revenue in Kerala is one of the lowest in India. Telephone connections are available even in some remote areas without electrification.

Service Providers

The telecommunication service providers in Kerala are the following. The dates of authorisation to provide the service are shown in brackets.

Bharat Sanchar Nigam Ltd (BSNL), (29-2-2000 for Mobile Cellular Service)

Reliance Infocomm Ltd. (20-7-2001)

Tata Teleservices Limited

Bharti Cellular Limited (28-9-2001)

BPL Mobile Cellular Limited (19-12-1995)

IDEA Mobile Communications Limited (12-12-1995)

Among these service providers, the Reliance Infocomm Ltd., Tata Teleservices Limited, and the Bharti Cellular Limited are unified access service providers who are free to provide, within their areas of operation, services which cover collection, carriage, transmission and delivery of voice and/or non-voice messages over Licensee's network by deploying circuit and/or packet switched equipment. Also they provide wireline as well as wireless services in their service areas. Wireless services include Full Mobile, Limited Mobile and Fixed Wireless services. The licensees also provide various Value Added Services. BSNL is the key service provider in Kerala.

Telephone Connections

The total number of telephones and the tele-density values (number of telephones per 100 population) are given in Table 7.45. The number of fixed telephones including wired and fixed wireless local loop (WLL) exceeds the number of mobile telephones. The major service provider for fixed and mobile telephones is BSNL. As observed elsewhere in India, the number of cellular phone subscribers is growing in Kerala at a rapid rate as shown in Table 7.46. The contribution to tele-density in Kerala by cellular phone subscribers is relatively low compared to fixed (wired and wireless) telephones. However, in future, the relative contribution of the cellular phone subscribers to tele-density is expected to increase.

TABLE 7.45

Total Number of Telephones and Tele-density (As on 28.2.2005)

Circles	*Kerala*	*India*
Total Phones (Fixed + WLL FWT)	3658242	46334539
Fixed + WLL FWT Teledensity	11.1	4.29
Mobile GSM & WLL (M)	2525897	50805543
Mobile GSM & WLL (M) Teledensity	7.66	4.7
Total Telephones (Fixed+Mobile)	6184139	97140082
Overall Teledensity	18.76	8.98

Source: Lok Sabha Unstarred Question No. 4084, dated on 20.04.2005.

TABLE 7.46

Number of Mobile Phone Subscribers

City/Circle	*Kerala*	*All-India*
Dec-97	15197	794232
Dec-98	39712	1070603
Dec-99	80781	21997288
Dec-00	247617	3107449
Dec-01	348861	5478932
Dec-02	531464	10480430
Dec-03	1023096	24931697
Dec-04	1918180	37378807

Source: Cellular Operators Association of India.

Growth of Switching and Capacity and Demand in Kerala

There has been a dramatic growth in the network capacity of BSNL in Kerala during the past few decades. Between 1971 and 2003, the capacity grew by more than 600 per cent: from 49,000 in 1971 to 344,500 in 2003. The demand for connections has also been increasing at a very high rate (see Table 7.47).

TABLE 7.47

Comparison of Capacity and Demand

Year	*Equipped Capacity*	*Working Connections*	*Demand*
1996	812371	681234	1096555
1997	1062198	854009	1473964
1998	1305098	108419	1763198
1999	1704395	1355084	1933027
2000	2203954	1705139	2352304
2001	2584236	2161583	2935754
2002	2690584	2694156	3255627

Source: *Directory of Telecom Services 2002*, Kerala Telecommunications.

From 2003-04 onwards, the growth rate of telephones in Kerala increased quite rapidly. Of the 2055 thousand connections planned during 2005-06, 337,500 connections are targeted for rural areas and the rest for urban areas.

Allocation/Utilisation of Funds

The fund utilisation rate in Kerala is higher than in the other states of India. Among all the states of India taken together, only in Kerala did the utlisation of the funds far exceeded the allocation during the years 2002-03 to 2004-05.

Tele-density

The tele-density of Kerala in comparison with that in other states, is increasing at higher rates. However, it is increasing at lower rates in rural areas than in urban areas. The rates of rowth in Kerala began to leap particularly since 2000. BSNL has planned very high rates of expansion in rural communications in Kerala during 2005-06.

Kerala has one of the highest proportions of telephone connections in both rural and urban areas among all the states in India. While the national average of telephone connections was 29 per cent (as on 31.12.2004), Kerala's average was as high as 57 per cent.

Revenue

Table 7.48 shows the average revenue per direct exchange line in Kerala. Compared to other states, the revenue in Kerala is one of the lowest in India, probably due to the fact that a major portion of the telephones belong to rural areas where the tariff is lower than in urban areas. Also, the families of non-resident Keralites working in foreign countries use telephone instruments primarily to receive incoming ISD calls.

TABLE 7.48

Average Revenue per Direct Exchange Line (During 1997-98, 1998-99, 1999-2000)

Circle/ District	*Average Revenue per DEL per Annum on Actual Cash Basis*			*Average Revenue per DEL per Annum on Amount Billed for Basis*		
	1997-98	1998-99	1999-2000	1997-98	1998-99	1999-2000
Kerala	**7269**	**6897**	**6422**	**7283**	**6966**	**896.3**

Source: *Annual Report 1999-2000, 2000-01*. Ministry of Communications, Department of Telecommunications, Govt. of India.

Village Public Telephones, Public Call Offices

By 1994-95 itself, Kerala circle established public telephones in all villages, well ahead of many other circles. Kerala has the highest number of Public Call Offices (PCOs) after Andhra Pradesh and Maharashtra.

Waiting List for Telephone Connections

As shown in Tables 7.49, Kerala maintains a long waiting list for telephone connections. Most of the demand has come from rural areas.

TABLE 7.49

Waiting List for Telephone Connections in Kerala (As on 30.6.2002)

States/UTs	*Waiting List*
Kerala	**600635**
India	**2045886**

Source: Lok Sabha Unstarred Question No. 2607, dated 31.07.2002.

Emerging Communication Services and Their Impact on Infrastructure Planning

New communications services have an impact on infrastructure planning. Various services offered through the communications network include Internet, Integrated Digital services Network (ISDN), Intelligent Network services, Multi Protocol Label Switching Virtual Private Network (MPLS VPN), and I-Net, some of which are discussed below.

Internet Service

This is one of the faster growing services in Information Communication Technology. In future, this category of service is expected to become a major carrier of communication traffic. Compared to the growth rates of internet subscribers in India, the growth rate in Kerala has been relatively low. Nearly four per cent of the internet subscribers in India belonged to Kerala as on March 31, 2003.

BSNL and MTNL Broadband Connections

In the case of BSNL and MTNL, the proportions of registration are seen to have formed more than 10 per cent of the registration received for the country as a whole in 2005.

Postal Communication

The potential value of postal services as a basic communications provider and its relevance as part of the growing knowledge economy, is greater than it has been ever before. Statistics show that there exist more than 500 million internet users worldwide, 80 per cent of them in the developed world. Two out of every five persons in the developed world have access to Internet, compared to one in 50 in the developing world. The network of about 700 thousand postal outlets that exist worldwide provides a natural opportunity for helping people to have Internet access; some postal administrations are already facilitating such access by drawing customers to kiosks in their outlets, and partnering with other communication firms to offer convenient products and services.

As on 31.03.2001, the Kerala Circle had 5059 post offices, of which 876 were in urban areas and 4183 in rural areas. The population served on an average by a post office is 6294 persons and the area covered is 7.71 sq. km.

Opportunities and Challenges

Kerala has a significant advantage in international communication. Kochi is the landing point for two major under-sea cables, namely SEA-ME-WE 3 and SAFE, carrying international Internet and telephone traffic. There are only three points in India where high-bandwidth submarine cables achieve landfall: Bombay and Kochi westward, and Madras eastward. These two cables will enormously improve the bandwidth availability in the state; which will benefit the development of a range of bandwidth-intensive activities. A lot of data and voice traffic from southern India will be routed through Kochi. Not only is bandwidth abundant, it is also cheaper than at other locations. Nasscom has rated Kochi as one of the top two destinations in India for bandwidth-intensive IT-enabled services. VSNL's International Gateway Exchange with 15 Gbps capacity is located next to the Kochi Special Economic Zone. Recently, VSNL unveiled the SAT-3/WASC/SAFE submarine cable station in Kochi. With this facility, Kochi has become one of the 16 landing points across the world for submarine cable. The cable system has an ultimate capacity of 120 Gbps that enables it to convey a total of 5.8 million simultaneous telephone channels. VSNL operates a facility in the zone under co-location scheme, offering global connectivity support to zone units at low-entry costs. To make use of broadband connectivity, fibre optic network has been deployed by BSNL, VSNL, Bharti, and Reliance.

The major challenges include (i) providing telephone connectivity to the rural masses and (ii) equipping the backbone to handle the traffic from the emerging services.

The challenge of providing cost-effective connectivity to rural areas is being addressed by the service providers by deploying newer cost-effective technologies like WLL which can be deployed quickly. This is evident from the investment plan of BSNL for rural telephony.

The second challenge arises from the anticipated high growth of services like broadband internet and video communication. Since all telephone exchanges in Kerala are linked using OFC (e.g., 13137 Kms OFC by BSNL as of 31-03-2002), the traffic growth in the immediate future could be accommodated. In this case also, several initiatives have been taken in Kerala to meet future demand, such as the Rights of Way Policy explained below.

The Government of Kerala has declared a Rights of Way Policy, permitting private and public sector infrastructure providers (who propose to lay OFCs) to have the Rights of Way over public properties including National and State highways, village roads and other public properties for laying OFCs on a non-exclusive basis. Kerala Communications Private Limited (a Reliance Group Company) has already commenced laying of OFC from Walayar to Parassala. Bharti Telesonics Ltd. has also commenced its OFC cable-laying from Kasaragod. The Kerala IT Mission coordinates the establishing of Network among these companies.

Recommendations

Future development of infrastructure shall focus on broadband technologies, especially the emerging 3rd generation wireless communication technologies and high capacity optical fibre systems. Emphasis should be given to establish infrastructure in meeting the ever-growing demand for basic services in rural areas (as indicated by the large waiting lists) as well as in offering newer services through existing infrastructure to meet the demand in emerging application areas such as e-education, tele-medicine, e-governance and e-commerce. Also, the telecommunication infrastructure and services should be able to play a key role in balancing the developments in rural and urban areas through e-education, tele-medicine and e-governance.

References

Banerjee, Nirmala (1979). *Demand for Electricity*. Centre for Studies in Social Sciences and Calcutta: K.P. Bagchi and Co..

Basak, P. (1990). *Water Scarcity in Kerala*. Kozhikode: CWRDM. p.27.

———. (2004). *Water Resources and Watershed Management*, Lecture Notes of the AICTE-ISTE STTP on Water Conservation and Water Management. Kochi: Civil Engineering Division, CUSAT.

Bhattathiripad, T.N.N. (2004). *Water Conservation in Kerala*, Lecture Notes of the AICTE-ISTE STTP on Water Conservation and Water Management. Kochi: Civil Engineering Division, CUSAT.

CMIE (2001). *Energy*, April, Mumbai.

Cyriac, Mathew P. (1988). "Energy Pricing in a Developing State: A Case Study of Kerala". Unpublished Ph.D. Thesis. University of Kerala.

Department of Irrigation (1992). *State Water Policy*. Government of Kerala. p.15.

Dubash, N.K and S.C. Rajan, (2001). *The Politics of Power Sector Reforms in India*. World Resources Institute. April 2.

EIA (Energy Information Administration) (2003). *International Energy Outlook 2003*, US Dept. of Energy, Washington DC.

Energy Management Centre (2003). "Souvenir", *Asia-Africa Regional Seminar on Small Hydro Power*, Nov.11-15. Thiruvananthapuram.

Government of India (1996-97). "Public Electricity Supply, All India Statistics", *General Review*. New Delhi: CEA.

———.(2005). *India-A Reference Annual*

Government of Kerala (GoK) (1963-2002). *Economic Review*.

———.(1997). *Report of the Committee to Study the Development of Electricity*. (Chairman: E Balanandan). February.

———. (1997). *Report of the Steering Committee on Transport and Communication*. Thiruvananthapuram: State Planning Board.

———. (1998). *Report of the (K.P Rao) Expert Committee to Review the Tariff Structure of KSEB*, May.

———. (2002). *Economic Review 2002*. Thiruvananthapuram: State Planning Board.

———. (2004). *Economic Review 2003*. Thiruvananthapuram: State Planning Board.

———. (2005). *Economic Review 2004*. Thiruvananthapuram: State Planning Board.

Indira, T.R. (2004). "Water Supply to Cities: Issues and Constraints", Presentation at the *Kerala Science Congress 2004*.

Integrated Rural Technology Centre IRTC (1996). "Exercises for Integrated Resource Planning for Kerala End Use Analysis-An Empirical Study", *Technical Report-1, Electricity*.

Ishiguro, Masayasu and Takamas Akiyama (1995). "Energy Demand In Five major Asian Developing Countries: Structure and Prospects", *World Bank Discussion Paper*. Washington DC: World bank.

James, E.J (2003). "Water Management", in R. Sooryamoorthy and Antony Palackal (eds.), *Managing Water and Water Users*. New York: University Press of America Inc. pp.25-55.

Jayan, T. V (2004). *Hard Rain Down the Drain*. New Delhi: Centre for Science and Environment. pp.30-33.

———.(2004). "Water Woes in Wet Kerala", *Down to Earth*. New Delhi: Centre for Science and Environment. pp.26-29.

John, J (1997). *Economics of Public Water Supply System*. New Delhi: Rawat Publications. p.179.

Kannan, K.P and N.Vijayamohanan Pillai (2002). *Plight of the Power Sector in India: Inefficiency, Reform and Political Economy*. Thiruvanathapuram: Centre for Development Studies.

Kerala State Electricity Board (KSEB) (1996). *Annual Report 1995*. Thiruvananthapuram: Government of Kerala.

Krishnan, T.R (2004). *Water Resources of Kerala*, Lecture Notes of the AICTE-ISTE STTP on Water Conservation and Water Management. Kochi: Civil Engineering Division, CUSAT.

KRWSA (2004). *Jalasurakshakku Mazhavellam*. p.56.

Kumar, Arun, (2003). "Souvenir", *Asia-Africa Regional Seminar on Small Hydro Power*. Thiruvananthapuram: Energy Management Centre. Nov.11-15.

Lim, E.R. (2001). "Address", *World Bank Conference on Distribution Reforms*. Oct. 12-13.

Lonnorth, Mans, Steen Peter and Thomas Johansson (1980). *Energy in Transition: A Report on Energy Policy and Future Options*. California, Berkeley and Los Angeles: University of California Press.

Mathai, J. (2003), "Diverse Water Problems in Kerala: An Overview", in R. Sooryamoorthy and Antony Palackal (eds.), *Managing Water and Water Users*. New York: University Press of America Inc. pp.11-24.

Menon, R.V.G. (1990). "Electricity and Development", *Energy Debate*. Kozhikode: Kerala Sastra Sahithya Parishath.

Modi, P.N. (1998). *Water Supply Engineering*. Delhi: Standard Book House. p.776.

Morris, Sebastian (1996). "Political Economy of Electric Power in India", *Economic and Political Weekly*, Vol.31 (21&22), May 18 & 25.

Namboodiri, T.V.N and S.G Thampi (2004). "Necessity for Tuning Strategies for Efficient Management of Decentralised Water Supply Schemes Operated by Beneficiary Groups", Proc. of the *36th Annual Convention of the IWWA*. Ahmedabad.

Pachauri, R.K, (1975). *Dynamics of Electrical Energy Supply and Demand: An Economic Analysis*. New York: Praeger Publishers.

Parameswaran, M.P, (1990). "Kerala's Power Predicament: Issues and Solutions", *Economic and Political weekly*, September 15

Parikh, Jyoti K. (1981). *Modeling Energy Demand for Policy Analysis*. New Delhi: Planning Commission, Government of India.

Pavithran, K.V. (1999), "Power System of Kerala: A Techno-Economic Analysis", Unpublished Ph.D. Thesis. Pondicherry University

Pillai, P.P. (1981). *Dynamics of Electricity Supply and Demand in Kerala—A Macro Econometric Analysis*. New Delhi: Agricole Publishing Academy.

Planning Commission (2002-07). "'8.2 Power", *Tenth Five Year Plan*, Vol. 2, Ch 8. New Delhi: Government of India,

Prasad, M.N. (2003). *The Right Priorities for Railway Development in Kerala*. Chairman, Railway Board. March.

Prasad, M.N. (2003). *A Rational Approach to Transport Development in Kerala*, Chairman, Railway Board. January.

Pushpangadan, K. (2002). "Social Returns from Drinking Water, Sanitation, and Hygiene Education: A Case Study of Two Coastal Villages in Kerala", *Working Paper Series* No. 333. Thiruvananthapuram: Centre for Development Studies.

Pushpangadan, K. (2003). "Drinking Water and Well-Being in India: Data Envelopment Analysis", *Working Paper Series* No. 352. Thiruvananthapuram: Centre for Development Studies.

Pushpangadan, K., (2003a), "Rural Drinking Water: Capacity Utilisation and MeritGoods", in R. Sooryamoorthy and Antony Palackal (eds.), *Managing Water and Water Users*, University Press of America, Inc., New York, pp.103-119.

Rajagopal, V. *et al.* (eds.) (2004). *Watershed Based Approach for Sustainable Development, Kasaragod District Panchayat*, p.122.

Saxena, P. (2003), "Souvenir", *Asia-Africa Regional Seminar on Small Hydro Power*, Nov.11-15. Thiruvananthapuram: Energy Management Centre.

Singh, B. *et al.* (1993). "Rural Water Supply in Kerala, India: How to Emerge from a Low-Level Equilibrium Trap", *Water Resources Research*, pp.1931-1942.

State Institute of Languages, The (2000). *Keralam*. Thiruvananthapuram.

State Planning Board (Various years), *Report on the Kerala Water Authority*.

———. *Economic Review* (various issues), 1994-2004. Thiruvananthapuram

———. (1997). *Report of the Task Force Constituted by the State Planning Board-Kerala to Study and Make Recommendations on (A) Policy Issues relating to Power and (B) Power Sector Reforms*. Government of Kerala.

Suresh, P.R. and Shanavas Elachola (2000). "Distribution Loss of Electricity and Influence of Energy Flows: A Case Study of a Major Section in Kerala", *Discussion Paper* No. 23. Thiruvananthapuram: Kerala Research Programme on Local Level Development, Centre for Development Studies.

Tata Energy Research Institute (TERI) (1996-97). *Tata Energy Data Directory and Year Book (TEDDY)-1996-97*. New Delhi.

Tyner, W E, (1978). *Energy Resources and Economic Development in India.* Boston: Martinus Nighoff Social Sciences Division.

Vihari, Vijoy, (1979). *Energy Conservation.* New Delhi: National Productivity Council.

Western Ghats Cell (2004). *Jalam Jeevamrutham.* p.136.

————. (2004). *Watershed News Digest*. p.154.

World Bank and Public Private Infrastructure Advisory Facility (2000). *India:Country Frame Work Report for Private Participation in Infrastructure.* Washington DC. March.

World Bank (1979). *India: Economic Issues in the Power Sector*. A World Bank Country Study. November.

————.(1992). *World Development Report: Development and the Environment.* New York: Oxford University Press.

————. (2000a). *2000 World Development Indicators.* Washington DC: Development Data Centre.

————.(2000b). *World Development Report: Entering The 21st Century*. Oxford University Press.

Websites:

www.powermin.nic.in

www.kerala.gov.in

www.kseboard.com

www.teriin.org

Chapter 8

Education

In this chapter, both school education and education at the higher stages are discussed. In the first section, the progress of literacy in the state, and the status of education at the pre-primary, elementary, secondary and higher secondary stages are discussed. All the types of schools—government, private aided and private unaided—are also examined. In the second part, the growth patterns of the higher education institutions, the discernible questions relating to the quality of high education and the financial aspects of this sector are looked into in some detail.

SECTION I: SCHOOL EDUCATION

Introduction

'Universal Elementary Education' remains a dream in several states in the Indian Union. But Kerala has successfully tackled the first generation problems in education of illiteracy and low enrolment in schools. The net enrolment rate in elementary education is almost 100 per cent. School education has become equitable between the sexes and among social groups and regions in the state unlike in many other states in India. It is the first state to achieve total literacy in the country. Various agencies—social, political and missionary—during the pre-Independence and Independence periods have contributed to the spread of literacy and the development of school education (Tharakan, 1984). The state has accorded overriding importance to the development of school education.

Some policy measures implemented during the period since independence have been highly innovative and have expedited the process of expansion of school education. Compulsory and free school education, basic education, direct payment of salaries to private school teachers, reduction of regional and inter-community disparities in school education, promotion of female education, school-feeding programme, whole promotion policy and travel concessions to students are some of the significant policy interventions. The recent scheme of grading at the SSLC level may usher in a qualitative evaluation of academic performance of students. The schemes sponsored by the Union Government such as the District Primary Education Programme (DPEP) and the Sarva Shiksha Abhiyan (SSA) have also had remarkable impact on school education in the state.

This section aims to identify the issues confronting school education in the state. It traces the evolution of the education system in Kerala through spread of literacy, equitable distribution of school education among different social groups and across regions, improvement of the quality of school education and vocational education, encouragement of the private sector in school education and financing of school education.

Progress of Literacy

Kerala was recognised as a totally literate state on April 18, 1991. The effective literacy rate of Kerala, according to the 1991 Census, stood at 90 per cent (about 94 per cent for males and around 86 per cent for females). By 2001, Kerala attained the literacy rate of 91 per cent (94 per cent for males and 88 per cent for females). During 1961 to 2001, the overall literacy rate doubled.

The rate of growth of male literacy has been very high during the 1980s. The rate had grown by 18 percentage points during this period. Three districts, Palakad (65 per cent), Malapuram (66 per cent) and Wayanad (65 per cent) remained behind the state

TABLE 8.1

District-wise Literacy Rate

Sl No.	*District*	*1961*	*1971*	*1981*	*1991*	*2001*
1	*2*	*3*	*4*	*5*	*6*	*7*
1	Thiruvananthapuram	45.3	62.54	70.5	89.22	89.36
2	Kollam	50.49	64.67	74.11	90.47	91.47
3	Pathanamthitta	-	-	-	94.86	95.09
4	Alapuzha	56.9	70.44	78.52	93.87	93.66
5	Kottayam	61.52	72.88	81.66	95.72	95.9
6	Iddukki	44.33	56.42	67.44	86.94	88.58
7	Ernakulam	50.33	65.37	76.82	92.35	93.42
8	Thrissur	48.16	61.61	73.59	90.18	92.56
9	Palakad	33.69	46.69	58	81.27	84.31
10	Malapuram	34.29	47.9	60.5	87.94	88.61
11	Kozhikode	44.88	57.23	70.12	91.1	92.45
12	Wayanad	-	-	58.33	82.72	88.52
13	Kannur	41.29	54.84	65.74	91.48	92.8
14	Kasaragod	-	-	-	82.51	85.17
	Total	46.85	60.42	70.42	89.81	90.92

Source: Compiled from various Census Reports.

average (75 per cent) by about 10 percentage points in 1981. During 1991, all the three districts came close to the state average of 90 per cent. In 1991, the literacy rate was the lowest in Palakad (87 per cent). Malapuram (92 per cent) made significant progress. The overall literacy rate in the state 2001 remained almost the same as in 1991. It was lower than 90 per cent in Thiruvananthapuram (89 per cent), Idukki (89 per cent), Palakkad (84 per cent), Wayanad (86 per cent) and Kasargod (85 per cent).

The female literacy rate grew by more than 20 per cent points since 1981. Three districts Palakad (52 per cent), Malapuram (55 per cent) and Wayanad (52 per cent) had in 1981 rates lower than the state average (66 per cent) by about 10 to 14 percentage points. By 1991, all the three districts made significant improvement; however they still remained much behind the state average of 86 per cent. Even in 2001, the literacy rate was the lowest in Palakad (79 per cent). Malapuram (86 per cent) made significant progress.

The literacy rates of the scheduled castes and the scheduled tribes remain lower than that of the general population. The rates of scheduled castes lag behind the state average for them in Iddukki, Palakad, Wayanad and Kasargod districts. The literacy rate of the scheduled tribes is even lower; the rates are lower than the state average in Palakad, Thrissur, Malappuram, Kozhikode, Wayanad and Kannur districts.

TABLE 8.2

District-wise Literacy Rates for Males and Females during 1981-2001

Sl No.	*District*	*Males*			*Females*		
		1981	*1991*	*2001*	*1981*	*1991*	*2001*
1	*2*	*3*	*4*	*5*	*3*	*4*	*5*
1	Thiruvananthapuram	75.29	92.84	92.68	65.85	85.76	86.26
2	Kollam	78.1	94.09	94.63	70.21	87	88.6
3	Pathanamthitta	-	96.55	96.62	-	93.29	93.71
4	Alapuzha	82.12	96.79	96.42	75.1	91.12	91.14
5	Kottayam	83.96	97.46	97.41	79.35	94	94.45
6	Iddukki	72.15	90.82	92.11	62.55	82.96	85.04
7	Ernakulam	80.75	95.46	95.95	72.88	89.27	90.96
8	Thrissur	77.31	93.77	95.47	70.21	86.94	89.94
9	Palakad	64.81	87.24	89.73	51.55	75.72	79.31
10	Malapuram	65.93	92.08	91.46	55.34	84.09	85.96
11	Kozhikode	76.56	95.58	96.30	63.82	86.79	88.86
12	Wayanad	64.81	87.59	90.28	51.51	77.69	80.8
13	Kannur	72.2	95.54	96.38	59.48	87.65	89.57
14	Kasargod	-	88.97	90.84	-	76.29	79.5
	Total	75.26	93.62	94.2	65.73	86.17	87.86

Source: Compiled from various Census Reports.

TABLE 8.3

District-wise/sex-wise Literacy Rates for Scheduled Castes during 1981-1991

Sl No.	District	1981			1991		
		Male	Female	Total	Male	Female	Total
1	2	3	4	5	6	7	8
1	Thiruvananthapuram	64.41	53.84	59.01	86.84	77.72	82.13
2	Kollam	63.69	51.75	57.67	85.27	74.1	79.59
3	Pathanamthitta				90.08	83.01	86.47
4	Alapuzha	73.72	62.27	67.95	93.52	84.77	89.07
5	Kottayam	76.29	67.24	71.79	93.99	86.63	90.28
6	Iddukki	57.76	39.68	48.76	81.03	64.28	72.67
7	Ernakulam	68.89	57.34	63.1	87.29	77.55	82.37
8	Thrissur	63.52	53.02	58.16	84.19	73.8	78.82
9	Palakad	49.85	34.31	41.93	74.93	59.82	67.16
10	Malapuram	54.17	41.45	47.71	84.52	73.75	79.03
11	Kozhikode	69.27	55.36	62.26	91.02	80.54	85.71
12	Wayanad	55.67	39.96	48.09	81.75	68.55	75.27
13	Kannur	53.82	40.29	47.06	89.8	80.37	85.06
14	Kasaragod				70.47	56.73	63.61
	Total	62.33	49.73	55.96	85.22	74.31	79.66

Source: Compiled from various Census Reports.

TABLE 8.4

District-wise/sex-wise Literacy Rates for Scheduled Tribes during 1981-1991

Sl No.	District	1981			1991		
		Male	Female	Total	Male	Female	Total
1	2	3	4	5	6	7	8
1	Thiruvananthapuram	62.87	53.37	58.06	81.78	66.78	74
2	Kollam	53.84	46.99	50.3	68.53	56.24	62.42
3	Pathanamthitta	-	-	-	75.89	70.53	73.21
4	Alapuzha	58.67	48.75	53.71	79.74	69.17	74.48
5	Kottayam	75.51	71.78	73.63	89.98	87.44	88.69
6	Iddukki	47.23	39.33	43.35	68.16	57.28	62.78
7	Ernakulam	55.74	49.27	52.6	81.49	72.11	76.96
8	Thrissur	34.33	25.18	29.9	55.48	47.54	51.4
9	Palakad	16.02	7.97	12.04	40.11	29.49	34.87
10	Malapuram	19.94	12.9	16.33	50.12	37.99	43.93
11	Kozhikode	25.95	16.91	21.45	57.14	47.75	52.36
12	Wayanad	27.3	14.24	20.74	57.89	43.45	50.63
13	Kannur	43.04	23.02	33.18	65.26	51.92	58.61
14	Kasaragod	-	-	-	74.77	57.86	66.38
	Total	37.52	26.02	31.79	63.38	51.07	57.22

Source: Compiled from various Census Reports.

Pre-primary Education

The pre-primary stage of education does not find much significance in Kerala. The enrolment at the pre-primary stage as a proportion of enrolment in any category of schools is much lower than the national average. Many other states have higher percentage of enrolment at the pre-primary stage than in Kerala. For instance, the share of enrolment in the pre-primary classes to total enrolment in the independent primary schools was 1.12 per cent in Kerala, as compared to the national average of 2.7 per cent during 2002-03 (Metha, 2004). The share rose to 4.71 per cent in Kerala, as compared to the national average of 5.82 per cent, during 2003-04. Only in six states, have the corresponding figures remained lower than in Kerala. Development of pre-primary education at the government schools may contribute to increase in enrolment in those schools. Pre-primary education finds an important place in private unaided schools. Private unaided schools attract children right from the nursery stage. If government schools follow this practice, then the pre-primary children in them may choose to continue their education at the higher stages of the same schools.

Primary and Secondary Education

The Pattern of School Education

The dual system of school education followed in Travancore—Malayalam-medium stream and English-medium stream during the pre-Independence period at the upper primary and the secondary stages of school education—was abolished towards the end of the 1940s. The school system was streamlined by fixing Standards I to IV as the lower primary, Standards V to VII as the upper primary and Standards VIII to X as the secondary school stages. Following the recommendations of the Kothari Commission (1964-1966), most of the states adopted the 5+3+2+2 pattern in school education. Kerala is one of the few states which follow a pattern of school education different from the national pattern.

Infrastructure at Schools

Making schooling facilities available to larger student populations both in the rural and the urban areas is the first step towards universalising school education. Infrastructural facilities for schooling and other supporting facilities are more adequately and better distributed among regions and social groups in Kerala than in many other states in India (Gasper, 2003). But most of the school buildings and other supporting facilities, particularly in the government schools in the state are very old. Some of them require complete replacement; and others require renovation or major repairs.

Enrolment

In Kerala, the percentage share of enrolment in the government schools to total enrolment is low at all the stages—lower and upper primary, and secondary and higher secondary—of school. The percentage share of enrolment in the government schools to total enrolment is 13.7 per cent in upper primary schools,

TABLE 8.5

Growth of Students in Schools in Kerala

Year	*Students (in Lakhs)*				*Index of Growth*			
	LP Students	*UP Students*	*High Students*	*Total*	*LP Students*	*UP Students*	*High Students*	*Total*
1	*2*	*3*	*4*	*5*	*6*	*7*	*8*	*9*
1960-61	20.57	8.82	3.31	32.7	100	100	100	100
1970-71	28.08	12.67	7.25	48	136	144	219	147
1980-81	25.94	16.94	13.14	56.03	126	192	397	171
1985-86	25.25	17.77	13.43	57.16	126	202	406	175
1990-91	24.72	19.3	14.99	59.01	120	219	453	180
1991-92	24.21	19.33	15.53	59.07	118	219	469	181
1992-93	23.72	19.08	15.89	58.69	115	216	480	179
1993-94	14.78	15.78	27.33	57.89	72	179	826	177
1994-95	14.35	15.43	27.21	56.99	70	175	822	174
1995-96	13.99	15.15	26.95	56.09	68	172	814	172
1996-97	13.61	14.79	26.77	55.17	66	168	809	169
1997-98	13.19	14.47	26.54	54.2	64	164	802	166
1998-99	12.78	13.98	26.43	53.19	62	158	798	163
1999-00	12.26	13.69	26.39	52.34	60	155	797	161

Source: Directorate of Public Instruction, Kerala.

TABLE 8.6

Enrolment in School: Various Years

Year	Enrolment of Students			Index of Enrolment		
	All Communities	Scheduled Caste	Scheduled Tribe	All Communities	Scheduled Caste	Scheduled Tribe
1990-91	5901101	663418	65917	100	100	100
1995-96	5627753	619607	62431	95.37	93.4	94.71
1996-97	5534224	602653	61916	93.78	90.84	93.93
1997-98	5437091	587602	61657	92.14	88.57	93.54
1998-99	5335701	570843	60137	90.42	86.05	91.23
1999-00	5249047	557793	59836	88.95	84.08	90.77
2000-01	5219052	549060	58066	88.44	82.76	88.09
2001-02	5102038	539349	58859	88.46	81.3	89.29
2002-03	5001761	533488	59836	84.76	80.42	90.77
2003-04	4894005	524342	60339	82.93	79.04	91.54
2004-05	4842015	513820	64876	82.05	77.45	98.42

Source: Government of Kerala, *Economic Review* (various years), State Planning Board, Thiruvananthapuram.

TABLE 8.7

Index of Enrolment in Standard-1 of Various Years

Year	Enrolment of Students			Index of Enrolment		
	All Communities	Scheduled Caste	Scheduled Tribe	All Communities	Scheduled Caste	Scheduled Tribe
1990-91	601030	68822	9827	100	100	100
1995-96	519048	56380	7959	86.36	81.92	80.99
1996-97	507072	54630	8372	84.37	79.38	85.19
1997-98	475301	48794	7500	79.08	70.9	76.32
1998-99	464925	48205	6674	77.35	70.04	67.91
1999-00	443027	47133	6532	73.71	68.49	66.47
2000-01	450653	47522	5861	74.98	69.05	59.64
2001-02	451192	50397	7011	75.07	73.23	71.34
2002-03	456517	53165	8152	75.96	77.25	82.96
2003-04	441325	51778	7655	73.43	75.23	77.9
2004-05(P)	431981	47313	7727	71.87	68.75	78.63

Source: Government of Kerala, *Economic Review* (various years), State Planning Board, Thiruvananthapuram.

30.7 in upper primary integrated with secondary/higher secondary schools, 37.8 per cent in primary integrated with upper primary schools and 38 per cent in primary schools. It is the private aided schools which account for the major proportion of the enrolment.

Enrolment in absolute terms is declining in Kerala. During the period 1971 to 1999, the total enrolment in the first standard declined by 42 per cent. Enrolment declined more drastically in government schools than in private aided schools. During the same period, enrolment in the first standard declined to 49 per cent of the enrolment in 1971 in the government schools; Table 8.8. In the aided-private schools, the enrolment in Standard I declined to 60 per cent of the 1971 level; Table 8.9. Only in the unaided private schools, did the enrolment in the first standard increased from 1971 to 1999 by more than 630 per cent (Table 8.10)

The declining trend in the enrolment is noticeable in the first four standards at the state level (Table 8.11). Higher the standard, the lower is the decline. In all the four standards, the rate of decline in enrolment is higher than the state average in the government schools; it is lower than the state average in the private-aided schools. While an increase in enrolment is noted in the fifth standard at the state level for all schools and also in the private-aided schools, enrolment in the government schools in Standard V declined.

TABLE 8.8

Enrolment of Students in Government Schools in Kerala from 1971 to 1999

Standards	I		II		III		IV		V		VI		VII		VIII		IX		X		Total	
Year	Idx	No.s	Idx	No.s	Idx	No.s	Idx	No.s	Idx	No.s	Idx	No.s	Idx	No.s	Idx	No.s	Idx	No.s	Idx	No.s	Idx	No.s
1971	100	350656	100	319732	100	300003	100	283427	100	189792	100	142418	100	112391	100	108306	100	88796	100	54125	100	1948648
1973	84	294181	123	392735	103	309121	99	281742	103	194980	107	151913	108	121478	109	118403	103	91075	98	53107	149	2909738
1974	80	280199	100	320560	123	369587	105	296884	105	198665	115	164473	122	137558	92	99291	131	116674	134	72497	106	2056388
1975	79	278206	91	290242	101	302238	127	359184	115	218442	120	171575	136	153144	127	137531	96	85238	198	107032	108	2094832
1976	79	275456	84	268750	94	281166	104	294070	124	235596	140	199773	142	159447	135	146252	141	125600	150	81038	106	2067148
1977	80	280102	85	271629	88	263655	100	282888	130	247596	151	215654	153	172418	130	140554	142	126222	168	90794	107	2091512
1978	80	280815	89	285219	90	270656	95	268266	112	213260	136	193372	87	97863	148	160224	150	132779	194	104898	108	2108352
1979	76	267680	93	296339	95	284646	73	207929	143	270918	134	190471	162	182237	175	190009	168	149279	197	106443	110	2145951
1980	77	268363	90	287362	97	290362	97	276219	109	207490	132	188314	162	182062	177	191932	192	170554	209	113153	112	2175811
1981	76	267342	88	281494	94	280991	101	286762	114	216579	133	189751	163	182642	174	188333	198	176151	246	133381	113	2203426
1982	78	274709	87	278413	92	274879	88	249415	121	228882	142	201694	166	186318	183	197745	200	177583	254	137596	115	2237234
1983	76	264898	88	282509	90	269704	96	271893	120	227894	152	216240	176	198260	187	202333	205	181661	256	138477	116	2253867
1984	71	250000	85	272253	91	273054	94	266139	119	226323	152	216348	189	211979	193	208592	205	182345	262	141978	115	2249071
1985	73	255053	84	267837	89	267568	95	270398	118	224721	150	213938	182	204772	198	214294	208	184478	241	130659	115	2233718
1986	74	260874	87	277696	89	267529	95	268638	120	227210	149	211684	180	201889	194	210541	214	190390	50	27223	115	2243674
1987	72	253615	87	279531	90	269632	92	260523	122	231295	152	215875	179	200885	195	211021	213	189074	231	125241	115	2236692
1988	76	266257	88	281147	92	276461	95	269535	122	232015	155	220328	180	202742	194	209844	216	192088	233	126073	117	2276479
1989	71	248146	86	275421	92	275343	96	272741	122	230716	154	219276	193	216799	196	212025	215	191153	276	149357	118	2290977
1990	68	240043	80	256847	90	269077	95	270354	125	237588	154	219844	203	228077	109	118077	341	302530	282	152629	118	2295066
1991	69	241675	78	248853	85	253511	94	265248	125	237583	160	228333	198	222592	216	233577	235	208871	289	156329	118	2296572
1992	65	227117	79	251242	82	245374	89	251588	122	231029	160	227675	203	228315	222	240337	242	214871	306	165671	117	2283219
1993	64	222718	74	236927	81	244013	86	242837	117	221542	157	223856	204	229486	225	243953	244	216751	330	178828	116	2260894
1994	59	208257	72	231249	78	233723	86	243253	111	211505	150	213979	201	226289	229	248288	251	222805	504	272656	114	2212004
1995	58	202902	68	217162	76	227080	82	231957	112	212225	145	206606	193	217255	226	245121	254	225677	321	173590	111	2159575
1996	56	195579	66	210624	72	214658	79	225254	107	203728	145	206195	187	209774	219	237579	251	222783	325	175908	108	2102082
1997	54	188152	63	201935	69	206067	75	213064	103	195972	139	198197	186	208523	213	230178	245	217827	323	174835	104	2034750
1998	50	173878	61	195517	67	201055	73	206031	100	190070	135	192322	181	203602	211	228148	239	212077	316	171182	101	1973882
1999	49	170117	57	182062	65	194015	71	200518	97	184847	131	186955	177	198934	209	226309	239	212628	312	168984	99	1925368

Source: Directorate of Public Instruction, Thiruvananthapuram.

TABLE 8.9

Enrolment of Students in Aided Schools in Kerala from 1971 to 1999

Standards	I		II		III		IV		V		VI		VII		VIII		IX		X		Total	
Year	Idx	No.s	Idx	No.s	Idx	No.s	Idx	No.s	Idx	No.s	Idx	No.s	Idx	No.s	Idx	No.s	Idx	No.s	Idx	No.s	Idx	No.s
1971	100	446259	100	392704	100	366132	100	337902	100	320439	100	260553	100	224440	100	198761	100	168323	100	100732	100	2826225
1973	85	380014	128	501878	104	380459	103	349412	106	340198	112	291609	108	242621	106	210896	103	173175	101	101486	105	2971748
1974	81	362107	102	399190	119	434481	108	363539	108	347153	120	312832	123	276683	89	177109	127	213210	141	142183	107	3028487
1975	80	357211	93	365395	103	376190	126	424529	115	369541	124	321921	134	299643	114	226480	89	150443	197	198858	109	3090211
1976	79	353059	89	347692	93	339515	107	360324	127	405908	133	346722	136	305536	182	361541	120	201312	125	125798	108	3047405
1977	83	370420	88	347366	93	340151	97	326280	108	345689	139	362179	140	313829	138	274896	137	230301	149	149867	108	3060978
1978	85	379204	98	383170	97	355284	103	346414	115	369955	140	365541	164	368223	136	270751	138	232256	169	170118	115	3240916
1979	82	364847	97	379916	100	365316	103	346552	112	359091	151	393620	161	361684	150	299098	153	257047	182	183009	114	3220180
1980	82	367314	95	373726	101	369644	106	357809	116	370342	135	350932	157	352128	155	308561	166	280053	190	191022	118	3321531
1981	80	356921	95	373231	98	358311	107	362375	119	380489	137	358067	156	350970	151	300989	170	286931	210	211905	118	3339098
1982	81	363546	93	366416	99	362272	106	356940	120	385305	141	366797	160	359803	145	288729	163	275002	223	224660	119	3349470
1983	79	354307	93	366733	96	353149	105	356352	118	378351	143	372875	164	367907	146	290503	159	268241	215	216786	118	3325204
1984	77	344529	92	360620	97	355226	103	349050	118	378851	143	371628	168	376525	154	306831	162	272184	208	209230	118	3324719
1985	79	351110	94	368858	97	355844	104	352108	119	380198	143	371933	163	366477	163	324198	169	285221	205	206646	119	3362593
1986	80	355364	74	290806	100	367503	106	358385	182	582874	141	368146	158	355034	158	313502	172	289219	189	190636	190	5371469
1987	77	344902	99	390154	102	374816	105	355817	181	581593	143	371992	158	355191	156	309967	173	290934	187	188314	119	3363680
1988	78	345994	99	389748	103	378230	108	364997	120	383771	144	375130	159	356100	157	312284	172	289819	186	187286	120	3383359
1989	77	342720	92	363075	104	380044	110	372222	121	388627	141	367188	169	379599	155	308417	124	209105	225	226524	121	3427521
1990	75	335528	90	354848	97	356173	111	373983	126	402910	148	385228	172	385255	166	329762	173	290683	229	230390	122	3444760
1991	76	339294	89	348035	95	348021	105	355424	127	407512	152	396755	175	393812	168	333643	181	305326	227	228992	122	3456814
1992	73	327846	90	353177	93	341720	103	346930	123	393267	154	400750	181	406977	173	343222	186	312984	240	241521	123	3468394
1993	72	321984	87	341651	94	343554	100	338976	120	383753	150	390933	183	411690	177	351028	189	317629	243	244923	122	3446121
1994	69	309142	85	335008	92	336352	101	342378	117	374651	146	380460	183	409815	180	358045	192	322834	251	252485	121	3421170
1995	68	302742	82	322265	90	328188	98	332579	118	377674	143	373748	178	399187	180	357346	196	329809	252	253974	120	3377513
1996	67	299153	81	316278	87	316893	97	326388	115	369445	144	375531	175	392063	176	349019	196	330417	256	258274	118	3333461
1997	66	293700	80	313426	85	311711	93	315498	113	363039	141	368666	176	393972	174	345607	194	326047	259	261119	117	3292785
1998	62	275607	78	306956	84	307976	92	310115	110	353883	140	363862	173	389086	176	349763	192	323318	258	259796	115	3240362
1999	60	268705	73	287609	82	300021	90	304583	108	346449	135	352664	171	382814	175	347295	194	327372	256	257713	112	3175205

Source: Directorate of Public Instruction, Thiruvananthapuram.

TABLE 8.10

Enrolment of Students in Unaided Schools in Kerala from 1971 to 1999

Standards	I		II		III		IV		V		VI		VII		VIII		IX		X		Total	
Year	Idx	No.s	Idx	No.s	Idx	No.s	Idx	No.s	Idx	No.s	Idx	No.s	Idx	No.s	Idx	No.s	Idx	No.s	Idx	No.s	Idx	No.s
1971	100	3555	100	2985	100	2796	100	2394	100	2332	100	2037	100	1881	100	2628	100	2351	100	1690	100	24649
1973	144	5121	167	4971	154	4305	152	3641	183	4258	166	3383	154	2899	156	4090	146	3432	140	2360	156	38460
1974	150	5343	178	5304	168	4705	159	3806	182	4233	186	3796	189	3552	137	3608	170	3998	158	2674	166	41019
1975	142	5055	174	5187	170	4751	174	4163	175	4079	189	3855	176	3305	129	3394	119	2801	205	3472	165	40662
1976	142	5036	158	4704	167	4664	180	4310	170	3971	182	3708	176	3313	138	3626	166	3891	193	3264	164	40487
1977	196	6981	161	4819	162	4543	184	4412	161	3764	184	3743	195	3661	117	3063	141	3316	165	2787	167	41089
1981	203	7216	245	7314	238	6652	259	6194	260	6061	283	5755	323	6072	248	6507	229	5379	253	4279	245	60429
1982	214	7624	259	7727	262	7319	285	6828	285	6638	305	6217	296	5560	241	6343	236	5560	253	4278	26	6494
1983	200	7093	251	7505	267	7477	297	7122	315	7345	347	7064	333	6261	253	6646	256	6008	277	4681	273	67202
1984	231	8211	246	7340	263	7351	302	7239	361	8414	387	7887	395	7422	292	7662	282	6636	385	6503	303	74665
1985	324	11518	339	10114	321	8987	372	8914	390	9095	430	8758	431	8101	293	7712	276	6490	300	5076	344	84765
1986	405	14401	441	13168	397	11089	415	9943	455	10600	511	10410	491	9229	328	8614	336	7905	334	5649	410	101008
1987	453	16119	531	15846	501	14011	500	11965	473	11038	551	11225	564	10605	377	9912	375	8828	446	7536	475	117085
1988	501	17802	552	16486	575	16084	600	14353	54	1252	584	11892	610	11465	410	10776	419	9852	471	7956	523	128818
1989	500	17776	546	16290	572	15986	653	15624	551	12847	593	12083	622	11708	417	10955	453	10660	526	8894	541	133453
1990	534	18977	602	17980	614	17178	672	16080	621	14474	676	13776	662	12446	429	11279	471	11070	511	8630	580	142890
1991	564	20061	620	18493	636	17770	669	16018	642	14967	733	14941	708	13311	444	11670	466	10957	564	9527	599	147715
1992	589	20946	672	20071	652	18218	717	17169	678	15809	785	16000	758	14258	477	12545	493	11588	579	9788	630	155392
1993	611	21724	696	20772	691	19315	736	17614	715	16676	759	15470	751	14135	509	13388	526	12367	607	10260	656	161721
1994	652	23194	750	22381	745	20819	806	19298	774	18048	823	16770	814	15320	543	14276	556	13070	696	11757	710	174933
1995	651	23140	750	22382	770	21533	838	20052	802	18692	857	17460	869	16338	569	14956	581	13651	713	12053	731	180257
1996	684	24316	809	24155	822	22971	911	21815	851	19849	921	18764	926	17426	604	15867	628	14763	727	12284	776	191310
1997	709	25220	854	25496	849	23727	940	22514	957	22314	1020	20774	980	18433	702	18456	693	16298	794	13427	839	206689
1998	726	25816	855	25526	918	25656	1006	24074	1048	24451	1125	22923	1108	20846	769	20207	768	18044	906	15304	904	222847
1999	734	26104	856	25552	912	25488	1066	25511	1111	25901	1196	24353	1219	22937	854	22437	856	20125	989	16720	954	235128

Source: Directorate of Public Instruction, Thiruvananthapuram.

TABLE 8.11

Enrolment of Total Students in Kerala from 1971 to 1999

Standards	I		II		III		IV		V		VI		VII		VIII		IX		X		Total	
Year	Idx	No.s	Idx	No.s	Idx	No.s	Idx	No.s	Idx	No.s	Idx	No.s	Idx	No.s	Idx	No.s	Idx	No.s	Idx	No.s	Idx	No.s
1971	100	800470	100	715421	100	668931	100	623723	100	512563	100	414988	100	338712	100	308697	100	259470	100	156547	100	4799522
1973	85	679316	126	900584	104	693888	102	634795	105	539436	108	446905	108	366998	108	333389	103	267680	100	156953	105	5019944
1974	81	647649	101	725054	121	808773	106	664229	107	550051	116	481101	123	417793	91	280008	129	333882	139	217354	107	5125894
1975	80	640472	92	660824	102	683179	125	779876	116	592082	120	497351	135	456092	119	368005	92	238482	198	309362	109	5225705
1976	79	633551	87	621146	93	625345	106	658704	126	645475	133	550203	138	468298	133	411419	127	330803	134	210098	107	5155040
1977	82	657503	87	623814	91	608349	98	613580	116	597049	140	581576	145	489908	161	498513	139	359839	156	243448	108	5193579
1978	82	660018	93	667378	94	625940	99	615680	114	583215	135	558913	167	566086	140	430975	141	365035	176	275016	111	5349268
1979	79	632527	95	676255	97	649962	99	617470	111	567020	119	494091	161	543921	158	489107	234	606326	185	289452	112	5366131
1980	79	635677	92	661088	99	660006	102	634028	113	577832	130	539246	158	534190	162	500493	174	450607	194	304175	115	5497342
1981	79	631479	93	662039	97	645954	105	655331	118	603129	133	553573	159	538684	161	495738	181	468461	223	349565	117	5602953
1982	81	645879	91	652556	96	644470	103	643183	121	620825	136	564708	163	551681	160	492817	177	458145	234	366534	118	5650798
1983	78	626296	92	656747	94	630330	102	635367	120	613590	144	596179	169	572428	162	499482	176	455910	230	359944	118	5646273
1984	75	602800	89	640213	95	635213	102	635631	121	622428	148	613588	176	595863	193	595921	202	523135	295	461165	7	357711
1985	77	617681	90	646809	95	632399	101	631420	120	614014	143	594629	171	579350	177	546204	184	476189	219	342391	118	5681076
1986	79	630639	95	681670	97	646121	102	636966	121	620684	142	590240	167	566152	173	532657	188	487514	207	323508	119	5716151
1987	77	614636	96	685531	98	658459	101	628305	121	623925	144	599092	167	566681	172	530900	188	488836	205	321091	119	5717457
1988	79	630053	96	687381	100	670775	104	648885	136	697938	146	607350	168	570307	173	532904	190	491748	205	321315	121	5788656
1989	76	608642	92	655416	100	671373	106	660587	123	632190	146	607547	179	607106	172	531397	190	491918	246	384775	122	5851951
1990	74	594548	91	649675	93	622428	106	660417	128	654972	149	618848	185	625778	149	459118	233	604283	251	392649	123	5882716
1991	75	601030	86	615381	93	619302	102	636690	129	660062	154	640029	186	629715	188	578890	202	525154	252	394848	123	5901101
1992	72	575909	87	624490	90	605312	99	615687	125	640105	155	643425	192	649550	193	596104	208	539443	266	416980	123	5907005
1993	71	566426	84	599350	91	606882	96	599427	121	621971	152	630259	193	655294	226	698369	211	546747	277	434011	122	5868736
1994	68	540593	82	588638	88	590894	97	604929	118	604204	147	611209	192	651424	201	620609	215	558709	279	436898	121	5808107
1995	66	528784	79	561809	86	576801	94	584588	119	608591	144	597814	187	632780	200	617424	219	569137	281	439617	119	5717345
1996	65	519048	77	551057	83	554522	92	573457	116	593022	145	600490	183	619263	195	602465	219	567963	285	446466	117	5627753
1997	63	507072	76	540857	81	541505	88	551076	113	581325	142	587637	183	620928	193	594271	216	560172	287	449381	115	5534224
1998	59	475301	74	527999	80	534687	87	540220	111	568404	140	579107	181	613534	194	598118	213	553439	285	446282	113	5437091
1999	58	464925	69	495223	78	519524	85	530592	109	557197	136	563972	179	604685	193	596041	216	560124	283	443417	111	5335701

Source: Directorate of Public Instruction, Thiruvananthapuram.

In standards 7th to 10th, enrolment has been rising, but at a decreasing rate in government schools, in private-aided schools and at the state level for all schools taken together. In short, declining enrolment has been a problem in the LP and the UP schools/ sections of government schools. Students' demand for enrolment in high school classes in government schools has not fallen. If efforts are taken to restore the confidence of students in the LP and UP schools (for they are in large numbers), immediate collapse of the system of governmental provision of school education may be delayed, if not prevented altogether. It is of utmost urgency to restore the confidence of the students in the government provision of elementary education. However, the trend of falling in enrolment caused by falling fertility rates cannot be arrested by making admission to government schools attractive.

In the private-unaided schools, enrolment has been rising at all the stages of school. The enrolment in these schools in 1999 increased by 7 to 11 times the enrolment in 1971. The higher growth of enrolment in these schools may partially be explained by the fact that they have started from a low base in 1971. But it cannot be denied that they have lured a sizable portion of the student population from the aided and the government schools. So the explanation that falling fertility rate is the sole cause of falling enrolment in government schools is not correct (Retnakumar and Arokiasamy, 2003).

The total number of students in LP and UP classes is decreasing in all districts in Kerala. But the students' strength in LP classes has declined rapidly by 22 per cent in Kollam District, by 24 per cent in Pathanamthitta District and by 23 per cent in Idukki district during 1993 to 2000.

Teachers

Consequent upon falling enrolment in schools, the number of teachers in schools has also been declining both in government and private-aided schools. The problem is more severe in government schools than in private-aided schools. Further the decline has been high in the case of male teachers than female teachers in both government and private-aided schools; Table 8.12. Among the districts, the decline of the number of male teachers was very high in Alappuzha, Ernakulam and Kollam. The number of female teachers in government schools declined only in four districts—Kollam, Pathanamthitta, Alappuzha and Kottayam.

TABLE 8.12

The Percentage of Pass in SSLC Examination

Year	*Percentage of Students Passed SSLC*	
	Before Moderation	*After Moderation*
2000	48.89	56.18
2001	43.58	56.22
2002	49.91	60.62
2003	52.52	64.85
2004	56.69	70.06

Source: *Economic Review*, 2004.

The male teacher population decreased in all private-aided schools except in Malappuram and Wayanad districts. The decline has been high in Alappuzha (72 per cent), Ernakulam (63 per cent), Thrissur (68 per cent) and Kollam (66 per cent) during the period since 1965.

In the private-unaided schools, on the other hand, the number of teachers increased manifold in all districts. The increase was very high, by more than 11 to 12 times, in Idukki, Kottayam and Palakkad, by more than 15 times in Alappuzha, by more than 17 times in Kozhikode, by more than 19 times in Thrissur, by more than 21 times in Thiruvananthapuram and by more than 50 times in Malapuram. In all districts, the rate of growth of female teachers was much higher than that of male teachers during 1965 to 2005.

Size of Schools

There are no single-teacher schools in Kerala. Very few schools are small in size in the state. While enrolment is lower than 60 students in 30 per cent of the primary schools in the country, it is so only in 10 per cent of the primary schools in Kerala. The enrolment is lower than 100 students in 26 per cent of the primary schools in Kerala as against 52 per cent in the country (Metha, 2003). At the upper primary stage (UPS) also, the size of schools is much higher in Kerala than in the country as a whole.

Uneconomic Schools

Competition is rising high between private-unaided schools and the rest of the schools in the state. In the unaided sector, there are recognized and unrecognised schools. Many schools, mostly government schools, some of which had been large in size sometime ago, have found difficulty in getting even the minimum required number of students. Some such schools have turned out to be economically nonviable. The total number of uneconomic schools was 2622 in the year 2003 (GoK, 2004b). Of them 49 per cent were government schools and about 51 per cent private aided schools. About 81 per cent of the uneconomic schools were LPS schools, 16 per cent UPS schools and the remaining, high schools. Since the decline of enrolment has been very high in LPS schools, a larger number of them have turned out to be uneconomic.

Higher Secondary Education

Kerala has a separate department for administering Higher Secondary Education. The Plus Two courses were introduced in 1990-91. This stage of education had been known as the pre-degree stage and attached to the collegiate education system till the mid-1990s. During 2002-03, several new higher secondary schools were begun. In addition, 20 per cent seats were additionally allowed to all the existing schools with a view to providing admission to the maximum number of SSLC pass-outs possible. The annual intake of the students increased to 3.23 lakh and the number of schools to 1565 in 2004.

Private Participation

Private Secondary School (PSS Scheme), 1951

With the objective of improving the service conditions of private school teachers and the efficiency of private school management, a new scheme was introduced by the then Travancore-Cochin government in 1951. It provided for paying the salaries of teachers in private schools directly by the government at rates available for teachers in government schools. Under the scheme, the private school management was required to deposit 80 per cent of the total tuition fees collected by them into the treasury. The scheme was a step forward in promoting private participation in school education.

The Kerala Education Act, 1959

The Kerala Education Act introduced in 1959 extended more benefits to private school teachers. It granted the teachers in private schools with security of tenure. It paved the way for unifying different education codes of Malabar and the Travancore-Cochin regions. This Act also had a provision for checking the malpractices of the managements of private schools in the appointment of teachers and in granting admission to students for various courses of study. However, owing to stiff resistance from the managements of private schools, this clause was dropped. The bill was finally passed in 1960. The bill was not effective to check many of the wrong practices of the managements of private schools in school education.

Private-aided and Unaided Systems of Schools

Greater the proportion of schools managed by the government higher the financial liabilities for the government. But the government would thereby gain more control over the school education system. On the other hand, if private parties run larger number of schools in the system, the government will have lower financial burden, but the degree of its control over school education would come down. More than 86 per cent of the schools/sections are under direct government management at the all-India level. About 12 per cent of the schools in the country are in the private sector. Of this, the private-aided sector accounts for about 5 per cent and the private-unaided sector accounts for about 7 per cent (Metha, 2003).

In Kerala, only about 44 per cent of the schools/sections are under direct government management. About 56 per cent schools are in the private sector. Of this, the private-aided sector accounts for about 53 per cent and the private-unaided sector accounts for about 3 per cent only (Metha, 2003). The private-aided sector in Kerala is the largest in the country in terms of the proportion of schools and strength of students.

Student-Classroom Ratio

The student-classroom ratio in Kerala (32) is much lower than the national average of 48 at the primary level. At the primary with upper primary and secondary stages, not much difference is observed between Kerala and the rest of India, even though the ratio is definitely lower in Kerala.

Facilities in Schools

The facilities available in the schools in terms of drinking water and toilet facilities are much better in Kerala than the national average (Metha, 2003).

Drinking Water

At the national level, about 72 per cent of the primary schools have drinking water facility in the school. In Kerala, the corresponding figure is 86 per cent. Similarly, about 75 per cent of the UP schools have drinking water facility in the school in all-India as against 93 per cent in Kerala.

Toilet Facilities

In India, about 34 per cent and 22 per cent of the schools have common toilets and toilets for girls respectively. In Kerala, the corresponding figures are 74 per cent and 40 per cent respectively.

Electricity Connection

The percentage of schools having electricity connection in India is about 22 per cent. In Kerala, about 66 per cent of the schools have electricity connection. In fact, Kerala has the largest proportion of schools with electricity connection in the country.

Computer Education in Schools

Ever since 1994 efforts were on in Kerala to promote Information Technology Education in schools. An agency called 'IT@School' was started in 2001 to guide and strengthen computer education in schools. The aim was to enable the use of information technology for improving the quality of the teaching and learning environment in schools and to impart basic computer knowledge and computing skills to students in school. IT education was made compulsory at the secondary school stage. A nominal amount was collected monthly from students, except SC/ST students, to meet the teacher cost of IT education. Computer laboratories with a minimum of five computers functioned in more than 85 per cent of the High Schools during 2003-04. In establishing computer laboratories at schools, PTAs and the voluntary agency, the Kudumbasree, have extended substantial support.

Computers in Schools

About seven per cent of the primary schools in the country have computers installed for the benefit of school children. Kerala has the highest proportion of schools that have computers (about 23 per cent). The national average of primary with upper primary schools having computers is 10 per cent. Kerala (20 per cent) is in the third position (Metha, 2003).

The percentage of primary with upper primary and secondary/higher secondary schools having computers is high too (74 per cent as against the national average of 47 per cent).

Girls' Education

The Gender Parity Index (GPI)

The gender parity index (GPI) for India as a whole is 0.89 in primary classes and 0.79 in upper primary classes. Among the states, it is Uttaranchal that has the highest GPI (0.98). Kerala comes second. The GPI for Kerala in the primary classes is 0.97. Kerala has a very high GPI also in the case of UP enrolment (0.92) (Metha, 2003).

Share of Girls' Enrolment

At the all-India level, the shares of girls' enrolment at the primary and the upper primary levels of education are 47.2 per cent and 44.2 per cent respectively. In Kerala, the shares are much higher: 49.2 per cent at the lower primary and 48 per cent at the upper primary level.

Quality of Education

Teacher-pupil Ratio

The teacher-pupil ratio in schools in Kerala improved marginally from 1:28.5 in 2002-03 to 1:28.3 in 2003-04. The teacher-pupil ratio is 1:45 in lower primary schools, 1:33.4 in upper primary schools and 1:18 in high schools (GoK, 2004a).

Dropout in Schools

Dropout rates have been declining over the past several years. Total dropout rate of the students in general at the school stage is estimated as 1.46 per cent and that of SC students and ST students as 3.64 per cent and 4.66 per cent respectively for 2004-05. Overall, the dropout rate is negligible in Kerala. The problem is however, slightly higher in some districts. In Kasaragod, Ernakulam and Wayanad districts, the rates are around three per cent. The problem of dropout is more at the high school stage than at the LP and UP primary stages. For scheduled castes and scheduled tribes, the dropout rates are higher in Idukki, Wayanad, Eranakulam and Kasaragod.

Repetition Rate

At the national level, the repetition rate in Grade I is somewhat higher than in subsequent higher grades. It is true for both boys and girls. At all-India, the high repetition rate in Grade I is due to the larger number of over-aged and under-aged children enrolled. About 17 per cent of children in Grade I are below five years and above six years. The over-aged and under-aged children are about 18 per cent in elementary schools and about 16 per cent in higher secondary schools. The proportion of such children is the lowest in Kerala (4.5 per cent). The all-promotion policy has helped Kerala to reduce grade repetition rates.

Further, at the national level, the repetition rates in the terminal grades (such as Grade V and Grade VIII) are higher than in the rest of the grades. The majority of the grade repeaters across Grades I to VIII consists of failed students and long absentees. Failures and long absenteeism are more among boys than among girls. In the case of Kerala, failures are very few among boys (0.25 per cent) as well as girls (0.16 per cent) in the first grade. The number of failures increases gradually upto grade VII in the case of both boys (12.47 per cent) and girls (8.29 per cent). Long absenteeism is very rare among boys as well as girls in any class in Kerala.

Transition Rate

At the national level, about 64.5 per cent of children transit from the primary to the upper primary level of education. There is not much difference between the transition rates of boys (66 per cent) and girls (63 per cent). About 95 per cent of the children (boys or girls) transit from the primary to the upper primary level of Education in Kerala (Metha, 2003).

Examination Results

At the national level, there is not much difference between the educational achievement of boys (93.83 per cent) and girls (93.59 per cent). The percentage of students who pass out from class IV/V is about 94 per cent. The achievement tests conducted at class IV and V fails, however, to distinguish the quality of achievement of the students (Metha, 2004) Only about 44 per cent of the boys and girls passed Grade V with 60 per cent marks or more; 35 per cent boys and 37 per cent girls passed with 60 per cent or more marks from Grades VIII. In many states, the percentage of girls with 60 per cent or more marks was higher than that of boys. In Kerala, 41 per cent of the boys and 63 per cent of the girls passed Grade V with 60 per cent or more marks. The percentages of students who passed Grade VIII with 60 per cent or higher marks were 38 per cent among boys and 54 per cent among girls.

SSLC Examination Results

For a very long period, the proportion of pass in the SSLC examination remained much lower than 50 per cent. The SSLC examination results for the past five years show an upward trend in the percentage of students passed. The success percentage was 56 per cent during 2000. In 2004, it was 70 per cent. The rise in the pass percentages owes a great deal to the practice of moderation. The actual percentage of pass before moderation remains much lower; see Table 8.13. Around 2.68 lakhs SSLC students had failed in the examination before moderation. After moderation, it was only 1.45 lakh students who were declared as failed in SSLC in 2004. Thus, moderation in marks scored by SSLC students in the year 2004 helped rescue 1.23 lakhs of students from failure.

TABLE 8.13

District-wise Seat Strength in ITIs and ITCs

Sl No	*District*	*Seat Strength*		
		Total	*Govt. ITIs*	*ITCs*
1	2	3	4	5
1	Thiruvananthaouram	8228	3476	4752
2	Kollam	8064	1324	6740
3	Pathanamthitta	4127	209	3918
4	Alapuzha	6533	1109	5424
5	Kottayam	5007	1242	3765
6	Iddukki	1102	251	851
7	Ernakulam	8015	991	7024
8	Thrissur	5505	1328	4177
9	Palakkad	2644	1181	1463
10	Malapuram	1767	356	1411
11	Kozhikode	2185	527	1658
12	Wayanad	390	114	276
13	Kannur	2767	1162	1625
14	Kasargod	795	295	500
	Total	57149	13565	43584

Source: Government of Kerala (2004b).

Vocational Education

Basic Education

In accordance with the Educational policy of the government of India, the government of Kerala introduced the system of basic education at the elementary stage during the 1950s. The scheme was extended to the secondary stage later. As there were many problems in the implementation of the scheme, it was terminated during 1967-68.

Vocational Higher Secondary Education

Vocational Education was formally introduced in Kerala at the higher secondary level (+2 stage) in 1983-1984. There are 375 VHS Schools (247 govt. and 128 private-aided) handling 42 subjects during 2004-05. Subjects include agriculture (livestock management and fisheries), health and paramedical service, business and commerce, home science and humanities and service sectors in engineering and technology. Clothing and embroidery, cosmetology and management of beauty parlours, creche-pre-school management are courses meant exclusively for girls.

Some of the problems in the VHSE are the following: Most of these courses do no lead to jobs. There are 42 vocational subjects. Only 12 of them are recognised by Kerala Public Service Commission for appointments. Even apprenticeship is not available for many of the courses. Though some of the courses were intended to be terminal, a large number of students after completion of these courses are seen to seek admission in institutes of higher education, including professional education.

Several vocational high schools are staffed with temporary teachers for handling vocational subjects. Some teachers are on deputation from other government administrative departments. Appointment of permanent staff for vocational education may boost the morale of this sector; the falling demand for vocational courses may also get reversed. Giving opportunities to the teachers for pre-service and in-service training is sure to lead to the improvement of the quality of vocational education.

Resource allocation to this sector has remained poor. Paucity of finances is reflected in the quality of facilities available in VHSE institutions. The drop out rate remained high ranging between 11 to 15 per cent during the period 1994-95 to 2001-02. The quality of achievement of VHSE students has been very low. The percentage of VHSE students completing their education successfully in their first attempt was between 35 to 45 per cent (Kremer, 2000).

Vocational education has to be revamped. It requires more resource allocation, permanent teachers and periodical in-service training for teachers. The curriculum has to be updated. New courses may be introduced taking into account the developments in the fields of computer education and Information Technology. Between the vocational training imparted at the government institutions (ITIs) and at the private agencies (ITCs), it is observed that students' demand is high for private ITCs; Table 8.14. Almost in all trades, boys are better represented than girls; Tables 8.15 and 8.16. The achievement levels are very poor in both the ITIs and the ITCs. The failure rates are varied between 40 to 50 per cent in most of the courses.

Education for the Weaker Sections

Expansion of schooling opportunities may not by itself guarantee equitable access to primary education for

TABLE 8.14

Trade-wise in Take and Out Turn in Govt. ITIs as on 30.11.2004 (One-year course) (in Nos.)

S. No	*Name of Trade*	*Students Admitted in 2003*						*Students Passed*					
		Total		*SC*		*ST*		*Total*		*SC*		*ST*	
		Boys	*Girls*	*Boys*	*Girls*	*Boys*	*Girls*	*Boys*	*Girls*	*Boys*	*Girls*	*Boys*	*Girls*
1	Plumber	435	-	29	-	6	-	238	-	11	-	1	-
2	Mech. Diesel	243	-	33	-	7	-	191	-	26	-	4	-
3	Secretarial Practice		47	-	2	-	-	-	21	-	1	-	-
4	COPA	132	419	11	55	2	-	112	365	8	49	2	1
5	Steno (English)	56	292	2	60	-	1	29	140	1	20	-	-
6	Steno (Hindi)	5	78	-	13	-	4	4	51	-	2	-	-
7	Dress Making	1	90	-	7	-	-	1	76	-	7	-	-
8	Welder	735	-	48	-	3	-	561	-	24	-	1	-
9	Foundrymen	121	-	7	-	-	-	62	-	2	-	-	-
10	DTPO	-	69	-	5	-	-	-	68	-	5	-	-
11	FHT	2	-	-	-	-	-	-	-	-	-	-	-
12	Upholstery	33	-	3	-	1	-	21	-	1	-	-	-
13	SMW	255	12	16	3	-	-	146	9	10	1	-	-
14	Carpenter	343	-	14	-	1	-	175	-	8	-	-	-
15	PPO	55	3	5	-	-	-	47	3	4	-	-	-
16	Mech. Tractor	65	-	9	-	-	-	39	-	4	-	-	-
	Total	2481	1010	177	145	20	5	1626	753	99	85	8	1

Source: Government of Kerala (2004b).

TABLE 8.15

Trade-wise in Take and Out Turn in Govt. ITIs as on 2002-2004 (Two-year course) (in Nos.)

Sl No	Name of Trade	Students Admitted in 2002						Students Passed					
		Total		SC		ST		Total		SC		ST	
		Boys	Girls	Boys	Girls	Boys	Girls	Boys	Girls	Boys	Girls	Boys	Girls
1	MRTV	269	104	56	26	-	-	202	71	32	10	-	-
2	D/Civil	173	156	20	25	2	1	107	122	9	20	2	-
3	D/Mech.	58	10	2	3	-	-	32	6	1	1	-	-
4	MRAC	259	1	47	1	2	-	196	-	29	-	1	-
5	Surveyor	26	71	3	8	-	-	26	68	3	7	-	-
6	Fitter	551	-	58	-	5	-	449	-	39	-	3	-
7	Wireman	336	-	34	-	2	-	223	-	13	-	1	-
8	Electronic Mechanic	318	155	54	24	2	1	266	137	38	17	2	1
9	Electrician	405	1	38	-	5	-	360	1	30	-	4	-
10	MMV	441	-	55	-	10	-	401	-	48	-	6	-
11	Turner	275	1	30	-	1	-	248	1	23	-	1	-
12	Mechanist	253	1	25	1	-	-	227	1	19	1	-	-
13	Painter General	53	1	13	1	-	-	50	1	11	1	-	-
14	Instrument Mech.	77	-	6	-	2	-	77	-	6	-	2	-
15	Watch and Clock Maker	-	32	-	9	-	-	-	14	-	5	-	-
16	Mech./Agri. Mech.	11	1	2	1	-	-	9	-	2	-	-	-
	Total	3505	534	443	99	31	5	2873	422	303	62	22	1

Source: Same as Table 8.14.

TABLE 8.16

Expenditure on General Education (1956-57 to 2001-2002)

Year	Expenditure (Rs.in Crore)	Average Cost Per Pupil	
		Primary	Secondary
1956-57	6.35	11.06	21.50
1957-58	9.56	19.8	28.25
1958-59	12.4	23.47	36.25
1959-60	13.69	25.67	45.26
1960-61	16.23	28.6	52.62
1961-62	16.83	33.24	61.12
1962-63	17.11	36.25	73.14
1963-64	18.46	38.75	79.25
1964-65	19.88	41.25	85.36
1965-66	25.23	43.8	90.37
1966-67	29.33	54.17	103.81
1967-68	36.66	65.07	130.07
1968-69	42.21	73.23	139.71
1969-70	49.07	82.38	164.08
1970-71	52.53	85.91	176.23
1971-72	57.64	89.26	187.29
1972-73	59.71	94.51	194.15
1973-74	67.39	102.24	211.70
1974-75	86.17	117.52	217.90
1975-76	105.69	170.02	361.32
1976-77	116.73	186.16	356.40
1977-78	124.8	193.61	363.02
1978-79	134.14	206.21	356.43
1979-80	157.11	238.27	369.34
1980-81	179.66	265.24	454.25
1981-82	199.87	218.18	536.37
1982-83	223.96	326.13	589.41
1983-84	245.32	372.62	657.60
1984-85	279.44	414.43	737.31
1985-86	331.19	479.23	906.66
1986-87	386	563.03	1043.00
1987-88	409.34	596.67	1130.00
1988-89	463.55	638.32	1137.00
1989-90	506.92	732.43	1242.42

contd. ...

...contd. ...

Source: Same as Table 8.14.

all, particularly for the marginalised and the downtrodden sections. It has to be continuously monitored to ensure that the children belonging to these communities are able to make a fair choice of their school and attain education with reasonable quality to improve their quality of life. The DPEP and the Sarva Shiksha Abhiyan programmes are aimed at this goal.

In the country taken as a whole, the rate of enrolment of scheduled caste students has declined in recent years more rapidly than enrolment of children of other communities. The enrolment level of the Scheduled tribes during 2004-05 remains almost at the same level, as in 1990-91. This may imply that either this community has already reached 100 per cent enrolment and/or that the rate of growth of child population among them is declining. Both these reasons are untenable. The rate of decline in the enrolment of the scheduled tribe students in the first standard is high but slightly lower than the state average. The reasons for the decreasing rate of enrolment in the case of the weaker sections of the society have to be examined closely.

With the purpose of promoting the education of the Scheduled castes and tribes, various incentives are given by the government. The Tribal Welfare departments at the state level run schools specifically for the tribal people. The national average of schools run by the Tribal Welfare Department is 4.38 per cent. In Kerala, it is less than one per cent and the tribal population also comes to about one per cent of the state population (Metha, 2003). In view of the falling enrolment and the higher degree of dropout among the children belonging to these communities, the tribal welfare department takes deep interest in the issue.

Education for Disabled Children

Integrated Education of Disabled Children (IEDC) was started in 1974-75 with the objective of providing educational opportunities to all children with disabilities under the general school system, with 100 per cent Central Assistance. In 1998, IEDC was merged with DPEP. The total number of disabled children enrolled in the elementary schools was 54,874 during 2002-03, 32,037 boys and 22,837 girls (GoK, 2004a).

Science and Environmental Education

To improve the quality of science education and to promote scientific temper, a centrally sponsored scheme, 'Improvement of Science Education in Schools' became operational in 1987-88. Under the scheme 100 per cent assistance is provided to the States/Union Territories for provision of Science Kits to upper primary schools, upgradation of science laboratories and library facilities in senior/secondary schools and training of science teachers. The scheme also provides for assistance to voluntary organisations for undertaking innovative projects in the field of science education.

A centrally sponsored scheme to facilitate teaching on issues of environment in schools was initiated in 1988-89. The scheme envisages grants to States/UTs for various activities including review and development of curricula of various disciplines at the primary, upper primary and secondary levels with a view to infusing environmental concepts therein; review and development of textbooks on 'Environmental Studies' at the primary and upper primary levels; review of strategy for imparting environmental education at the upper primary level; development of teaching-learning materials; and organisation of suitable innovative work experience activities. To achieve these objectives, the scheme also envisages assistance to voluntary agencies.

Teacher Education and Training

Under the DPEP and now under SSA, teachers in the elementary classes get in-service training periodically. But the teachers in the secondary and higher secondary classes do not have much opportunity for in-service training. There is need for coordination of the activities of the SCERT and the DIETs in the state to extend training to these sections of the teachers also. Many new self-financing training colleges and colleges of Education have come up in recent years. The colleges of Education are affiliated to different universities in the state. Streamlining of the activities of these colleges will lead to a standardised educational and training programme suitable to the collective interests of the state.

Decentralisation of School Education

Though decentralisation is given more importance in Kerala, only a small percentage of schools come within the direct control of local bodies. Local Bodies run about 21 per cent of the total schools in the country. The corresponding percentage is only 2.56 per cent in Kerala (Metha, 2003).

Expenditure on School Education

The total plan and non-plan expenditure on education in Kerala has increased from Rs. 415 crore in 1985-86 to Rs. 2928 crore in 2002-03, by more than 600 per cent in nominal terms. Educational expenditure formed 4.12 per cent of the SDP of Kerala in 2002-03. During the period 1994-95 to 2001-02, the proportion of government's total educational expenditure devoted to Primary Education hovered around 50 per cent. The proportion has then declined and stood at 41.85 per cent in 2003-04. At the Secondary and the Higher Secondary stages, the proportions were 28.03 per cent and 8.23 per cent respectively in 2003-04. The growth of expenditure on school education for the periods 1956-57 to 1989-90, as well as the annual average cost per pupil in the primary and secondary sectors of school during the period, is shown in Table 8.17.

TABLE 8.17

Number of Institutions Offering Courses in Arts and Science

University	*1990*	*1995*	*2003*
Kerala	**44**	**44**	**59**
M.G	57	56	91
Calicut	71	70	99
Kannur	-	-	37
	172	170	286

Source: Directorate of College Education, First Year Intakes.

During the period 2002 to 2005, the state government's expenditure on school education inclusive of vocational higher secondary education (VHSE) has been 75 to 78 per cent of the state government's total expenditure on education. A large proportion (42 per cent) of this was spent on primary education. About 27 per cent was spent on secondary education. In terms of the government's spending on education, vocational higher secondary schools has received only a low priority. Only about 2 per cent is spent on VHSE. Kerala's per capita expenditure on primary and secondary education is one of the highest in the country.

Cost of Education

Compulsory and free education had been introduced in Kerala even before independence. Lower primary education had been free in the princely states of Travancore and Cochin. Fees had been abolished also in standards V to VII in the Travancore-Cochin state which came into existence in 1949 during the years prior to the establishment of the state of Kerala in 1956. The secondary stage of education was made free by the end of the 1960s. Tuition fees at the higher secondary education were abolished in the state in 1991. The entire institutional cost of education up to standard XII is borne at present by the state in the government and private aided schools. The constitutional mandate is to provide free education until the age of 14 years. But Kerala has achieved this goal and has even gone further ahead.

Though school education is free from the institutional point of view, it is not completely free for the consumers of education. The parents of school children incur costs of several types. Cost is incurred on purchase of reading and writing materials (other than those, if any, provided by the schools), clothing (other than those uniforms, if any provided by the schools), and on living costs of the children. The parents also have to incur daily travelling costs, costs of study tours, donations to PTA, special fees for learning moral science and computer literacy and costs of question papers and examination fees. Private tuition to students is another important item of costs to parents. The earnings foregone by children in school constitute the indirect private cost of school education. The private cost of education may differ from student to student depending upon the school and the levels of life of the households concerned. The private costs of school education were seem to have been in 2000, Rs. 2313, Rs. 2992 and Rs. 4676 in LP, UP and secondary section in government schools. The private costs of school education come to Rs. 3019, Rs.3357 and Rs. 4421 in LP, UP and HS in aided schools. In unaided schools, private costs were even much higher: Rs. 9100, Rs. 9281 and Rs. 10608 in LP, UP and HS unaided schools respectively (Nampoothiri, 2005).

Conclusion

As compared to other states, infrastructural facilities available for school education are much better in Kerala. There is extensive availability of schools in rural areas in the state. In fact, more than three-fourths of the schools are in rural areas. In terms of availability of facilities in schools, Kerala stands much ahead of most other states. The share of private management in school education is relatively higher in Kerala than in any other state in India. The proportion of participation of the private sector in school education is rising rapidly. But the type of privatisation in Kerala is such that it has little effect on reducing the financial burden of the state. Of late, the entry of the unaided sector has made a significant change to the situation. School discontinuation and repetition rates are very low in Kerala. However, the problems remain acute in the case of scheduled castes and tribes. In terms of educational achievements, girls do better than boys. However, the overall quality of educational achievement in school education in Kerala is not remarkable. Unlike in most other states of India, extremely small size schools are few in Kerala. Generally large size schools provide the appropriate environment for learning. But the terminal achievement of students in Kerala doesn't indicate that

Kerala has benefited any comparative advantage from having large sized schools. Better utilisation of resources at the school level has to be emphasised.

It is important to ensure that the available resources are made efficient use of. For instance, while DPEP was in operation, many schools in Kerala failed to use the teacher grants fully and the unutilised funds were returned to the directorate. This means that the actual beneficiaries, the students, were unknowingly denied of improved teaching-learning processes at school. But during the SSA period, no cases of teacher grants being returned to the directorate have arisen. What is more important is that these grants should be used well by the school for the benefit of students. There should be some mechanism to ensure that the flow of resources to schools creates a new environment at the schools, better maintenance of school buildings and better facilities at school. Students should benefit from all the facilities at school inclusive of computer, TV, public address system, teaching-learning materials, library facilities, facilities for recreation and physical education and the facilities for hygiene and public convenience.

Development of pre-primary education in the government schools may help reducing the number of schools getting closed down every year. This may also be helpful in utilising the services of surplus teachers. Falling rate of enrolment in the government and the government-aided schools cannot completely be attributed to fertility decline. The mushrooming of English medium schools is partly responsible for the declining students' strength in the Malayalam-medium schools. Stock-taking of unrecognised private schools in the state will throw more light on the issue of decreasing enrolment. Improvements of levels of students' achievement at the different levels of school education and vocational education have to be given priority. Achievements at the SSLC or the HSE levels mark the target of learning at school which begins from the pre-primary classes. Hence ensuring the quality of achievement right from the earliest level of school is of primary importance. Parents, teachers, students and the educational administers should move collectively towards this end. It is in the qualitative aspects of schooling that Kerala already lags behind.

SECTION II: HIGHER EDUCATION

Introduction

This section on the state of higher education in Kerala has the following objectives:

- To document the progress achieved during recent years.
- To highlight the constraints—financial, organisational and other—that hamper further desirable developments in institutions of higher learning, particularly the ones which are currently below par compared with the best in the state.
- To make a comparison of the momentum achieved in the field of tertiary education in Kerala with that visible in other leading states of the Union.
- To evaluate the capabilities of the higher education system in the state to respond to the new demands and challenges posed by globalisation.
- To evaluate the ability of the system to create links with the world of industry and employment, and to function as a vehicle for individual development as well as for the sustainable development of the state as a whole.
- To design and maintain a website for easy reference and for updating of information and data on individual institutions in higher education.

Institutions of Higher Learning: Growth Patterns

The conventional definition of an institution of higher learning encompasses all institutions offering education beyond the higher secondary school level including colleges of humanities and arts; institutions offering degrees in engineering, medicine and paramedical courses, and colleges of Ayurveda and Homoepathy.

Kerala has at present seven universities: University of Kerala, University of Calicut, Mahatma Gandhi University, Sree Sankaracharya University of Sanskrit, Cochin University of Science and Technology, Kannur University, and Kerala Agricultural University. There are also two deemed Universities.

There are 290 arts and science colleges affiliated to four of those Universities namely, Kerala, Calicut, Mahatma Gandhi and Kannur. Out of these, 38 are government colleges, 148 private aided colleges and 104 unaided colleges. There were nearly 1.7 lakh students in the Arts and Science colleges during 2003. Of the total students, girls constitute 65.6 per cent. Nearly 91 per cent of the students are in various undergraduate courses and the rest in postgraduate Courses.

Out of the total number of students (1.53 lakh) for under-graduate courses, 0.64 lakh (41.8 per cent) were undergoing B.A. courses, 0.66 lakh (42.5 per cent) B.Sc. courses and 0.24 lakh (15.7 per cent) the B.Com. course. Girls accounted for nearly 66 per cent of the enrolment for B.A. course, 68 per cent for B.Sc. courses and 53 per cent for the B.Com. course. In all, girls constituted 65 per cent of the total enrolment at the undergraduate stage. There are 16 subjects in B.A. courses and 15 subjects in B.Sc. courses. In B.A. degree courses, 30.4 per cent students are in economics and 15.4 per cent in history. Similarly, in B.Sc. courses 25 per cent students are in Mathematics and 19 per cent are in Physics.

During 2004 there were 16618 students for post-graduate courses; out of them 12365 (74 per cent) were girls; 7164 students (43 per cent) were for M.A. courses, 6953 (41.8 per cent) for M.Sc. courses and 2501 (15.1 per cent) for the M.Com. course. There are 16 subjects for M.A. courses and 10 subjects for M.Sc. courses. Out of the total number of students in M.A. courses, 25.4 per cent were in economics and 18.2 per cent in english. Out of the total number of students in M.Sc. courses, 21 per cent were in Mathematics and 17 per cent in Physics. In addition to this, there was a total of 19346 seats sanctioned under the engineering colleges in the state in the academic year 2004-05.

The number of institutions catering to the demand for higher education and the number of students enrolled in them have been steadily increasing, as may be seen from Tables 8.18 to 8.23.

As may be observed from Table 8.18, the number of colleges offering degree programmes in Arts, Humanities and Sciences decreased from 172 in 1990 to

TABLE 8.18

Enrolment in Arts and Science, Graduate Level

University	*1990*	*1995*	*2002*
Kerala	**14682**	**16062**	**15712**
M.G	13241	17347	17172
Calicut	13705	17948	13539
Kannur	-	-	4730
	41628	51357	51153 (2003: 50895)

Source: Directorate of College Education.

TABLE 8.19

Enrolment in Arts and Science, Post Graduate Level

University	*1990*	*1995*	*2002*
Kerala	**1498**	**1712**	**1948**
M.G.	2159	1793	1863
Calicut	1537	2462	1987
Kannur	-	-	418
	5194	5967	6216 (2003: 8398)

Source: Directorate of College Education, First Year Intakes.

TABLE 8.20

Number of Institutions and Seats in MBBS Degree Programmes

Year	*Government*		*Private Self-Financing*		*Total Number of Seats*
	Institution	*Seats*	*Institution*	*Seats*	
1989-1990	5	700	-	-	700
1999-2000	6	800	-	-	800
2002-2003	7	900	-	-	900
2003-2004	7	900	3	300	1200
2004-2005	7	900	6	600	1500

Source: Commissioner of Entrance Examination.

TABLE 8.21

Enrolment in Engineering Colleges

Year	*Government*				*Private Institutions*		*Total Institutions*	
	Government Institutions		*Government–Self-financing Institutions*					
	Number	*Seats*	*Number*	*Seats*	*Number*	*Seats*	*Number*	*Seats*
1989-1990	7	2656	-	-	-	-	7	2656
1995-1996	7	2741	6	1620	-	-	13	4361
1999-2000	12	4203	17	4220	-	-	29	8423
2002-2003	14	3993	17	3520	34	7970	65	15483
2003-2004	14	4013	18	3205	44	9860	76	17079
2004-2005*	14	4013	17	3670	47	10760	78	18443

Note: *-Projected number of seats

Source: Commissioner of Entrance Examination.

TABLE 8.22

Number of Institutions and Seats: Paramedical Courses

Year	Govt. Institutions		Private Institutions		Total	
	Number	Seats	Number	Seats	Institutions	Seats
1995-1996	9	280	-	-	9	280
1999-2000	11	492	-	-	11	492
2002-2003	13	532	-	-	13	532
2003-2004	13	610	7	360	20	970
2004-2005	13	610	11	580	24	1190

Source: Commissioner of Entrance Examination, Directorate of Medical Education.

TABLE 8.23

Number of New Courses Started and their Annual Intake in Universities in Kerala during 2002-03 and 2003-04

University	New Courses		Annual Intake	
	2002-03	2003-04	2002-03	2003-04
Kerala	**40**	**4**	**2600**	**100**
Calicut	24	9	710	314
Kannur	7	21	195	845
Mahatma Gandhi	60	30	7090	2084
Total	131	64	10595	3343

Source: *Economic Review 2003.*

170 in 1995, but increased rapidly to 286 by year 2003. Enrolment in arts and science courses increased from 41628 to 51357 (during 1990-1995) and decreased to 50895 in 2003. The decrease of students in srts and science course in recent years is mainly due to the increase of seats in professional and technical courses (medical, engineering), as shown in Table 8.21 to 8.23. A much larger increase is evident in the number of institutions and seats in technical colleges, especially in engineering colleges.

The number of institutions increased from 7 to 78, and seats from 2656 to 18443 during 1990-2004. This trend can also be observed in medical and allied sectors also, but to a lesser extent. There is also one self-financing Siddha College, with an annual intake of 50 students functioning in the state.

The trend over the years points to a shift in emphasis—and in student interestvfrom arts and sciences as subjects of study to technical, job-oriented courses. While enrolment in technical courses has risen by 594 per cent between 1990 and 2002, the corresponding increase in liberal arts and sciences courses has been only by 20 per cent. A number of new courses have been introduced in technical subjects. The number of new courses started in 2002-03 were 131; and 64 new courses were started in 2003-04 in modern disciplines such as bio-chemistry, micro-biology, bio-technology, computer science and polymer chemistry. The intake capacity for the new courses started in 2002-03 was 10595, and 3343 seats are available for the new courses started in 2003-04. Table 8.24 gives the university-wise break-down of the new courses started during 2002-03.

TABLE 8.24

Enrolment Trends in Arts and Science Graduate Level

Year	Total Enrolment (Arts, Sciences and Humanities)	Female Enrolment (in percentage)
1990	41628	54.03
1995	51357	55.28
2003	50895	61.05

Source: Directorate of Collegiate Education.

Profile of Student Enrolment and Faculty Resources

Gender-wise enrolment pattern in under-graduate and post-graduate programmes is shown in Tables 8.25 and 8.26. While enrolment at the under-graduate level in technical courses increased by 322.9 per cent between 1995 and 2003, the corresponding increase in Arts, Humanities and Sciences streams was only 0.99 per cent. For the system as a whole, the proportion of female enrolment increased in Arts and Humanities from 54.03 per cent to 61.05 per cent during 1990-2003.

Female enrolment increased in general, particularly in technical and professional courses, a healthy sign for a state, which has been always in the forefront of

TABLE 8.25

Details of Enrolment of Students in Arts & Science Colleges for Graduate and PG Courses

Graduate/PG Course	Boys	Girls	Total
B.A.	22914	38239	61153
B.Sc.	22733	38206	60939
B.Com.	10856	11251	22107
M.A.	2306	4358	6664
M.Sc.	1597	4315	5912
M.Com.	968	1224	2192
Total	61374	97593	158967

Source: *Economic Review 2003.*

TABLE 8.26

Proportion of Female Enrolment in Postgraduate Courses

Year	*Proportion of Female Postgraduate Students*
1990	58.9
1995	62.8
2003	70

Source: Directorate of Collegiate Education.

female empowerment. A corresponding pattern is observed in the case of teachers also, with female teachers far outnumbering male teachers in arts and science subjects. Around 52.52 per cent of the teaching staff in arts and science Colleges is females. But, in technical institutions, the ratio is in favour of males; 75.73 per cent of the teachers in Polytechnics are men.

In postgraduate education, female enrolment has been all the more evident. In 2003, it was 70 per cent at this level in undergraduate education as against 60 per cent in Arts and Science courses in general. Table 8.26 gives details of female and male enrolment for the different undergraduate courses.

Faculty and Non-Faculty Resources

Table 8.27 shows the number of faculty members and the faculty-student ratio in some of the leading institutes of higher education in the state. The student-faculty ratios for the Arts and Sciences undergraduate colleges in the state came to about 14 for institutions in the government sector, and 13.2 for private, aided colleges.

TABLE 8.27

Student-Faculty Ratio, 2004

Name of Institution	*Faculty Strength*	*Student–Faculty Ratio*
NIT	169	10
TKM	227	10
College of Engineering (TVM)	235	13
AITEC	28	12

Source: Study Conducted by IIM-Kozhikode.

While there do not exists wide differences in student-faculty ratios among various institutions, the existing differences are likely to have a marked impact on the quality of education imparted. Table 8.28 provides information on the qualification levels of the faculty of selected colleges.

TABLE 8.28

Faculty and Qualifications, 2003

Name of College	*Faculty with Doctoral Degrees (2003)*		*Faculty with Postgraduate Degrees (2003)*	
	Strength	*Percentage*	*Strength*	*Percentage*
NIT	87	51.47	58	34.31
College of Engineering (Tvm)	30	12.76	159	67.65
AITEC	1	3.5	14	50

Source: Study Conducted by IIM Kozhikode.

It is not a straightforward task always to judge the quantity and quality of non-faculty resources. Land area and buildings, for instance, need not be reliable indicators of quality. The availability of necessary equipment such as computers and laboratory facilities is a better indicator. Library resources (as measured by the number of books and journals), digital equipment and inter-library connectivity also have positive impact on the quality of education. Some information on their infrastructure and staff strength in a few selected technical institutions in the state is given in Table 8.29. Table 8.30 gives information about a larger number of such institutions about faculty and non-faculty resources.

TABLE 8.29

Non-Faculty Staff Resources, 2004

Institution	*Non-Faculty Staff Total*	*Faculty/Non Faculty Ratio*	*Number of Laboratories*
College of Engg, Tvm.	258	0.91	36
T.K.M College of Engg.	152	1.5	29
AITEC	22	1.25	10

Source: Study Conducted by IIM-Kozhikode.

Unfortunately, the expansion in staff resources in universities and colleges seems to have been influenced by several criteria, some of which have no bearing on the quality of education. The burgeoning share of salaries in total expenditure could be an indication of such an undesirable development. There is a need to adhere to UGC and AICTE norms in fixing the faculty and staff strength of institutions in the state.

The Quality of Higher Education: Discernible Trends

In this section, some of the major constraints faced by state–level institutions of higher education (i.e., not

TABLE 8.30

Comparison of Faculty & Non-Faculty Resources in Various Institutions in Kerala

Parameters	*AITEC*	*TKM College of Engg.*	*Trivandrum Engg. College*	*NIT Calicut*
ESTD	2002	1958	1939	1961
University	Kerala University	Kerala University	Kerala University	Autonomous
Type of Institution	Self Financing	Govt. Aided	State Govt.	Central+State Govt.
Branches in Engg. Graduate	3	8/3#	8/5#	7
Student Intake/Year (Graduate)	180	480/125#	593/170#	372
Post Graduate If any	NA	1/3#	3/17#	15
Student Intake/Year (PG)		30/43#	70/190	227
Average Placements	NA	66.5	210	229
Library[2]	7685/52/37/15	48000/75/50/25	84,000/15000^^	91580/83/20/1
Teaching Staff	1/14/13		30/159/46	87/58/24
Internet/Intranet Facility	Limited Internet Facility/Office Administration has intranet	Limited Internet Facility/NO	Limited Internet Facility/NO	Limited Internet Facility/NO

Note: #: Post graduate branches and student intake.

2: Books/National Journals/International Journals/Others.

^ ^ should go in the Trivandrum Engineering college.

Source: Study conducted by IIM-Kozhikode.

funded by the central government) are highlighted, by making comparisons with nationally funded institutions such as NIT and IIM Kozhikode. Comparison of resource availability is also made against selected institutions in other states—at similar overall development levels—such as in Tamil Nadu and West Bengal.

Impacts of Financial Constraints on Quality

The degree of dependence of universities on state government grants has been increasing over time. The income-expenditure gap has also been widening, the cause for which may be traced to falling internal receipts. State government grants accounted for 22.7 per cent of the total income of institutions of higher education in 1980-81; the proportion became more than 70 per cent by the 1990s; own resources declined from 67 per cent to 28 per cent during the same period. This trend has continued unabated even since then. Internal receipts which had constituted 70 per cent of total receipts in 1981, declined steeply to 21 per cent by 2001-02; but they rose to 28.9 per cent in 2002-03, following an upward revision of the fee structure.

Tuition fees collected cover hardly 10 per cent of the salary requirements of these institutions, while the corresponding figure in industrialized countries is in the range of 35 per cent to 45 per cent. An increase in tuition fees was recommended earlier for *new* courses; a general increase in the tuition fees structure seems essential. Owing to severe paucity of resources, spending on salaries is virtually the only item of expenditure that institutions could possibly undertake. Salaries account for as high as 90 per cent of the income in a few cases. For the three major universities, salaries account for close to 60 per cent of total expenditure, while the spending on library and laboratories together account for only less than 3 per cent.

Incredibly large amounts are spent by students on private tuition. The total amount spent by the student community works out to more than the entire state expenditure on higher education. In contrast, students spend only about four per cent of their total expenditure on university tuition fees. Such a situation also points to the need for increasing tuition fees which would make it possible to give the students high quality faculty inputs thus reducing their propensity to look for private tutors.

Examination fees also should be raised, considering the fact that now the fee covers only about 25 per cent of the cost of conducting examinations. The details of receipts and expenditure, university-wise, are provided in Tables 8.31 and 8.32.

TABLE 8.31

Proportion of Internal and UBC Sources of Funds of Universities, 2002-03

University	*Internal*	*UGC & Other*
Kerala	**26.2**	-
Calicut	38.5	2.82
M.G	25.95	2.69
Kannur	25.83	-
Sree Sankara	6.26	7.48
All universities	28.28	2.0

Source: Economic Review 2003, Government of Kerala.

TABLE 8.32

University-wise Expenditures as Percentages of Total, 2002-03

University	*Expenditure on Staff*	*Conducting Exam*	*Others*
Kerala	**41.77**	**22.69**	**35.54**
Calicut	51.16	9.97	38.86
M.G	76.67	8.89	14.43
Kannur	34.69	6.30	59.00
S. Sankaracharya	50.40	0.58	49.04
All	51.87	13.05	35.09

Source: Economic Review 2003, Government of Kerala.

Table 8.33, referring to faculty and non-faculty resources of a few premier institutes indicate a state of acute shortage of funds. These data may be compared with those furnished in Tables 10 and 11 about state level institutions.

It is observed that leading institutions have more faculty members with advanced qualifications, and also have better infrastructure in terms of computer and library facilities. This information on vital resource accessibility of students points to the need for upgrading in state-level colleges and universities in Kerala. Past trends indicate that improvements in quality have not kept pace with the multiplication of the number of institutions. The situation prevailing in national institutes should serve as a benchmark to be reached and eventually, surpassed. The existing resource gaps are the main impediments for achieving this goal.

An Expert Committee (Report of The Expert Committee on Financial Aid and Surplus Manpower in The school Education and The Higher education Sector in Kerala, March 2000) made several recommendations for easing the financial and budgetary constraints in universities in the state. The main recommendations were the following:

- Reduction in dependence on state grants
- Generation of additional revenue by engagement of faculty and students in society.
- Increase in examination and tuition fees.
- Additional income generation from endowments.
- These suggestions have to be acted upon if the current declining trend of internal revenue has to be arrested and the trend has to be reversed.

An increase in state support to higher education is also vital, since the current expansion in the number of self-financing colleges is not meeting societal or industry needs in the State. Unfortunately, government support to education (including higher education) as a proportion of total government expenditure has been showing of late, a downward trend.

A Comparison with Quality of Education in Private Colleges

Faculty appointments in private Arts and Sciences colleges do not seem to have been made in a flawless manner and instances of payment of donations to secure appointments have been fairly common. Such an environment is bound to have affected the quality of education. One way to check this malady is to improve the qualifications levels of teachers in private colleges.

TABLE 8.33

Faculty and Non-Faculty Resources in Premier Institutions

Institution	*Student-Faculty Ratio*	*Faculty with Ph.D.*	*Computers per Student*	*Books & Journals*
IIMK	8.5	21 (100%)	1	15375+360
NIT	10	87	0.3	91580+234
PSG College, T. Nadu	12	69	-	1,04,512+ 416
CIT, T. Nadu	15	23	0.1	40,000
Bengal Engg. College	9.45	-	0.1	2,00,000

Source: Same as Table 8.30.

Table 8.34 gives information on teacher's qualification levels and few other quality aspects in a few private colleges and selected university departments. Data on professional colleges such as engineering and medical colleges are also included.

The data do reveal serious shortages of quality resources in private arts and sciences colleges. The proportion of faculty members with doctorate degrees, the proportion engaging in research, and the annual funding for research, are all much higher in university departments. Only with regard to library resources, books and journals, do the private colleges come to a level with university departments.

Private professional engineering and medical colleges are not much better either. The number of doctorate or PG holders is higher in university departments in percentage terms than in private Arts and Sciences colleges, and a fair number of them are also engaged in research. But the amount of research funding is much lower than in university departments. The only function in which private professional colleges outperform the government sector colleges may be in terms of placement, presumably because of the emphasis given to that activity in order to attract enrolment. The most recent data indicate that Rajagiri engineering College places around 80 per cent of its students with campus recruiters, while the corresponding proportion is only 13 per cent at the Government Engineering College, Kannur.

The overall picture that emerges is that of an unbalanced growth in the private educational sector, with inadequate resources being earmarked to key activities on which the long-run performance of the colleges would depend. Even benchmarking these institutions with university departments will ensure higher quality levels for the higher educational system in the state as a whole.

State Higher Education Policies: Changing Budgetary Emphasis

Kerala has been a state known for a strong commitment to full literacy and primary education for all, but is less prominent in the area of higher education among the states of India. Table 8.35 shows the allocation for higher education in a relative perspective.

TABLE 8.35

Proportion of Expenditure on Higher Education in Kerala on a Comparative Basis (%)

Year	*Total Expenditure on Education*	*Expenditure on Higher Education*	*Expenditure on Technical Education*	*Interest Payments*	*Pension Payments*
1993-94	26.70	N.A	N.A	16.00	10.80
1999-2000	22.60	N.A	N.A	16.90	15.60
2000-01	22.06	3.30	1.02	19.00	16.24
2001-02	21.18	4.25	1.10	21.40	15.80
2002-03	17.30	2.60	0.99	-	-

Source: Various issues of *Economic Review* and *Sambathika Avalokanam*, Government of Kerala.

The proportion of expenditure on education in total revenue expenditure of the state fell from around 27 per cent in 1993-94 to about 17 per cent in 2002-03. Spending on higher and technical education constitutes only a small part of the total government expenditure.

TABLE 8.34

Quality Indicators: Comparison of Private Colleges and Universities

College/ Department	*Permanent Faculty (Number)*	*Ph.D Holders (Number)*	*Number of Teachers Engaged in Research*	*Number of Books/Journals in Library*	*Annual Funding for Research*
St. Alberts College, Ernakulam	84	32	5	41,000/37	Rs. 1 lakh
St. Teresa's College, Kochi	87	32	6	72,825/60	Not available
Payannur College, Payannur	65	15	15	37,767	Rs. 3.45 lakh
Dept of Physics, Cochin University	11	10	10		Rs. 100 lakh
Applied Chemistry, Cochin University	9	8	9	3600/9	Rs. 40 lakh
Polymer Science and Rubber Technology, Cochin University	7	6	7	2300/15	Rs. 40 lakh
Calicut Medical College	380	202 (post-MBBS)	-	-	-
Academy of Medical Sciences, Pariyaram (private)	142	139 (post-MBBS)	42	-	Rs. 8 lakh
Rajagiri College of Engineering (private)	82		8		Rs. 3 lakh

Source: Interviews and questionnaires given to College authorities.

But, the share of spending on higher education within total expenditure on education has shown a marginal increase from 13.44 per cent in 1990 to 14.98 per cent in 2002-03. Out of the total spending on education in 2002-03, primary education accounted for 40.8 per cent, secondary education 24.7 per cent, technical education 5.6 per cent and university and higher education 14.97 per cent.

The decline in expenditure on education as a proportion of revenue expenditure of the government may be contrasted with the increasing shares of interest and pension payments from 16.0 per cent and 10.8 per cent in 1993-94 to 21.4 per cent and 15.8 per cent respectively in 2001-02 (Table 8.36).

TABLE 8.36

Break-up of Expenditure on Education (Percentages)

Sector	*1989-90*	*1992-93*	*2000-01*	*2001-02*	*2002-03*
Primary + Secondary	82.6	81.7	79.6	79.7	77.5
Higher Education	13.44	14.7	14.9	15.1	14.97
Technical	4.0	3.08	4.62	4.73	5.6
Higher + Technical	17.44	17.8	19.5	19.9	20.6

Source: Various issues of *Economic Review* and *Sambathika Avalokanam*, Government of Kerala.

Capital Expenditure

In terms of capital expenditure, education (including higher education) receives much lower government funds, hardly about 3.4 per cent, including allotments for sports and culture. Within capital spending itself, the main item is 'construction'. The allocations for construction have been significant, and are obviously related to the provision of infrastructural facilities for new courses. In contrast, other items such as libraries, laboratories, faculty development and research have remained practically unfunded. During the 8th and the 9th plans, spending on construction stood at around 15 and 16 times higher than that on faculty development and research, and libraries. The direct expenditure on new courses also exceeds expenditure on faculty development and research. Thus, it looks as though development of new professionally oriented courses was done primarily at the cost of investment in other important requirements.

Expansion in Higher Education: Quality and Mode of Selection

The past few years have seen an unprecedented expansion in higher education in the state. The number of self-financing colleges went up from 33 in 1996 to 186 in 2003. However, it is doubtful if this increase was associated with a commensurate improvement in quality and direction of the process. The increase in colleges and courses has not taken place in response to the rising demand from the industrial sector in Kerala. The job prospect for the additional degree holders is bleak within the state.

While it is a positive fact that excessive outflow of capitation fees (donations) from the state has been arrested by the expansion of higher level educational institutions, the absence of any vital link between the growth of higher education and the growth of demand for high quality manpower from within the industrial sector in the state renders the whole exercise hardly remunerative. The concern becomes all the more disturbing since the newly started colleges offer professional, job-oriented courses. If the expansion were made in consultation with the State Planning Board, some pre-condition for compulsory education – industry linkages could have been planned and insisted upon.

Trauma of Entrance Examinations and the Link to School Education

It has already been shown that students pay more by way of private tuition fees than as regular tuition fees to colleges or university departments. It is also observed that students at the Plus 2 level and even at lower levels spend considerable amounts of money and time on coaching for the entrance examination. Further, it is possible that students are little concerned about regular attendance in classes or even obtaining high marks in class examinations. Thus, the mode of selection to institutions of higher learning appears to have a negative effect on education at the high school level. A lack of interest in the school curriculum seems to be a direct effect of the system of selection being followed for entry into universities and professional colleges.

A feasible solution to this problem would be to give weight to marks obtained by intending scholars in their school examinations; it may be desirable to allocate more weight to SSLC level marks, which are usually a good indicator of overall student capability and performance.

There are also doubts raised about the direction of expansion of higher education. The Report of The Steering Committee on Education (September 1998), set up by the State Planning Board, recommended that considering the number of unemployed graduates, the number of seats in courses like history, sociology, economics and political science may be reduced, even as the number of job-oriented courses were increasing. But, this suugestion raises questions about the ultimate purpose of higher education, which is usually taken to be the creation of a good, informed and responsible citizen. Given such an objective, the slashing of courses in arts and humanities should be considered ill-advised. Besides, the new professional courses have themselves contributed to the numbers of the educated unemployed, given the lack of industry demand in the state.

References

Mathew, E.T. (1999). "Growth of Literacy in Kerala: State Intervention, Missionary Initiatives and Social Movements", *Economic and Political Weekly*, Sept. 25.

Gasper, Chinnappan (2000). "Financing Education in Kerala", Paper presented in the National Conference on *Education in Kerala's Development: Towards a New Agenda*, Trivandrum, December 26-28. New Delhi : Institute of Social Studies and Kochi: CSES. Sponsored by UNICEF.

———. (2003). "Vocational Education in the Context of Globalization and Technological Change in Kerala, India", Paper presented in The Journal of Vocational Education and Training's Fifth International Conference on *Researching Policy and Practice in Vocational Education and Training*. London: University of Greenwich. 16-18 July.

George, K.K., George Zachariah, N. Ajith Kumar (2002). *Grants-in-Aid Policies and Practices Towards Secondary Education in Kerala*. Kochi: Centre for Socio-economic and Environmental Studies.

Government of Kerala (2000). *Report of the Expert Committee on Financial and Surpuls Manpower in the School Education and Higher Education Sector in Kerala*. Thiruvananthapuram: Planning Board.

———. (2003a). *A Study on Vocational Higher Secondary Education in Kerala*. Thiruvananthapuram: Planning Board.

———. (2003b). *Economic Review*. Thiruvananthapuram: Planning Board.

———. (2004a). *Education for the New Age: Kerala State School Education Commission 2003-2004*. Thiruvananthapuram: Planning Board.

———. (2004b). *Economic Review*. Thiruvananthapuram: Planning Board.

Kremer, Oliver (2000). *Vocational Higher Secondary Education (VHSE) in Kerala, India*. Bonn: Witterschlick.

Metha, Arun C. (2003). *Elementary Education in India-Analytical Report 2002*. New Delhi: NIEPA.

———. (2004). *Elementary Education in India-Analytical Report 2003*. New Delhi: NIEPA.

Nair, Gopinathan P.R. (1981). *Primary Education, PopulationGrowth and Socio-economic Change in Kerala*. New Delhi: Allied Publishers.

———. (1989). "Universalization of of Primary Education in Kerala", P.R. Panchamukhi (ed.) *Studies in Educational Reforms in India*, Vol.II. New Delhi: Himalaya Publishing Co.

Nampoothhiri, N. (2005). "Costs of Schooling in Kerala: A Study of Private and Instituional Costs under Different Types of Management", *Disscussion Paper* No. 77. Thiruvananthapuram: KRPLLD, Centre For Development Studies.

PEDSK (2005). *Sarva Shiksha Abhiyan (SSA)-Annual Report 2004-05*. Thiruvananthapuram.

Retnakumar, J. and P Arokiasamy (2003). "Fertility Decline and Falling School Enrolment", *EPW Commentary*. November 15.

Retnakumar, J. (2003)."Declining Fertility and Excess School Infrastructure: A Study of Pathanamthitta District, Kerala". Unpublished M.Phil Dissertation. Mumbai: International Institute for Population Sciences.

Salim, A. Abdul (2002). *Educational Development In India: The Kerala Experience Since 1800*. Anmol Publilcations Pvt. Ltd.: New Delhi.

Tharakan, Michael (1984). "Economic Factors in Educational Development: A Case of Nineteenth Centuary Travancore", *Economic and Political Weekly*. November 9 & 17.

Verghese, N.V & K.S. Sajeev (1997). *Educational Process and Progress: A Study of Primary Schools in Kasaragode District, Kerala*. New Delhi: NIEPA.

Chapter 9

Science and Technology

Introduction

Kerala has the highest population of Science and Technology (S&T) manpower in the country. Even prior to the formation of the Kerala State in 1956, the rulers of the princely States of Travancore and Cochin had provided adequate support measures to nurture science and technology activities in their states. The Travancore University set up by the Maharajah of Travancore in 1937 played a catalytic role in promoting Science and Technology education and research in the State. After the formation of Kerala in 1956, successive governments have continued to stress on S&T education by setting up institutions focusing on various aspects of S&T, to keep the state abreast of developments around the globe. This chapter takes a look at the progress made by the state in the promotion of science and technology activities.

S&T activities in Kerala take place both in the formal and the informal sectors. The State-run Scientific Research Institutions in Kerala are well developed and they work on a sustainable basis. The six universities including a University dedicated exclusively for S&T and an Agricultural University that function within the state are expected to help develop high quality manpower. The Government of India has also set up several research institutions in the State. Kerala has so far pioneered several achievements in diverse fields of S&T. Being a state with abundant natural resources, there is scope for application of the findings of scientific research on the ground.

S&T activities may be divided broadly into three categories:

- Basic and applied research to develop effective solutions to the socioeconomic problems of the state;
- Production of highly capable S&T manpower to facilitate rapid growth of the economy;
- Development of systems for storing and disseminating the wealth of knowledge developed through S&T activities.

Research Institutions set up by the Govt. of Kerala under its S&T policy have focused on objectives (a) and (c) while Universities intend to develop S&T manpower required for managing these institutions. The function of the government is to encourage such development activities and to implement the results of R&D at the grassroots of society.

The social infrastructure of the state is well-developed and the State is ahead of the Indian states in Human Development Index (HDI). HDI of Kerala is almost 20 per cent above that of Punjab, which has the second highest in India. However, this spectacular performance in Human Development could not be translated into economic gains and the state is ranked among the lowest in India in terms of per captia state Domestic Product (SDP). The high population density of 819 persons per square kilometers in 2001 and the high level of social awareness of its people have discouraged the growth of large industries in the state. Hence, the human resources of the state have migrated to greener pastures in developed nations in Europe, the Middle East and South East Asia seeking high income-earning opportunities. In consequence, large amounts of foreign remittances flow into the state making it one among the top Indian states in terms of per capita consumption, despite low levels of SDP.

The successive governments in Kerala have been fully aware of the crucial role that S&T plays in the economic positioning of the state (Figure 9.1). Research and Development activities conducted in the state have resulted not only in developing quality manpower but also in modernising the social and physical infrastructure of the State.

The S&T System in Kerala is highly structured. The major S&T Institutions in Kerala are mentioned in Figure 9.2. Figure 9.3 gives the organisational structure of S&T institutions under the Govt. of Kerala. The Department of Science and Technology is placed directly under the stewardship of the Chief Minister and all scientific institutions functioning under this Department are under the common umbrella of the Kerala State Council of Science and Technology and Environment (KSCSTE). The main areas of the activity of the science and technology institutions in the state comprise the following:

- Water Management.
- Earth Science Studies.
- Non-Conventional Energy.
- Forest Research.
- Bio-technology.
- Transportation Research.
- Agricultural Research, and
- Mathematical Studies

Brief details of these establishments are given in Table 9.1. An analysis of the activities of these institutions is given in the next section

TABLE 9.1

Research Institutions Sponsored by Government of Kerala under KSCSTE

S. No.	*Institute*	*Year of Establishment*	*Research Area*
1	Kerala Forest Research Institute (KFRI)	1975	Forestry Sciences
2	National Transportation Planning Research Centre (NATPAC)	1976	Transportation Planning
3	Centre for Water Research, Development and Management (CWRDM)	1978	Water Management
4	Centre for Earth Science Studies (CESS)	1978	Earth Science Studies
5	Tropical Botanical Gardens Research Institute (TBGRI)	1979	Plant Research
6	Agency for Non-Conventional Energy and Rural Technology (ANERT)	1986	Non-Conventional Energy
7	Rajiv Gandhi Centre for Bio-technology (RGCB)	1994	Bio-Technology
8	Kerala School of Mathematics	2004	Mathematical Sciences (under assistance from Department of Atomic Energy Govt. of India)

Source: Documents compiled from various reports of Kerala State Council of Science and Technology and Environment (KSCSTE).

FIGURE 9.1

Major Milestones in the History of S&T Development in Kerala

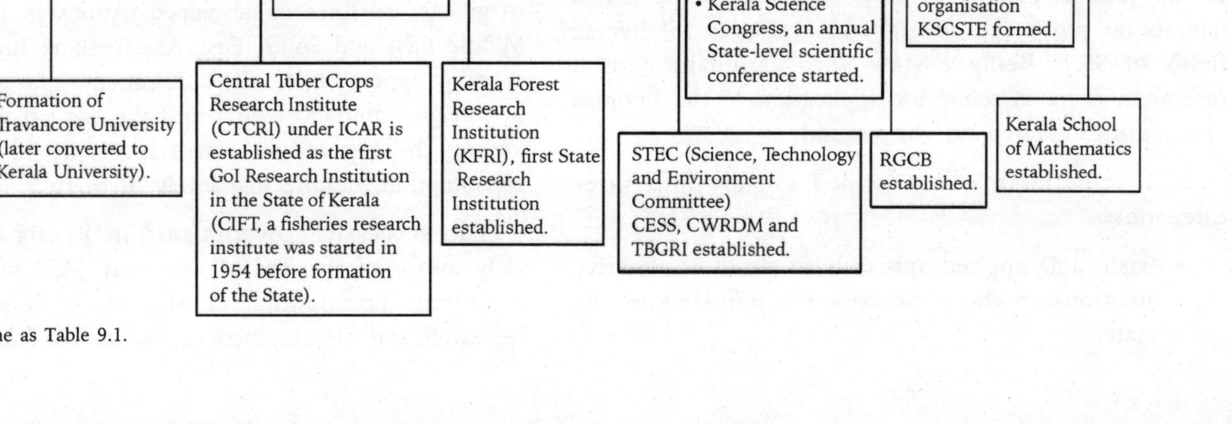

Source: Same as Table 9.1.

FIGURE 9.2

S&T Institutions in Kerala

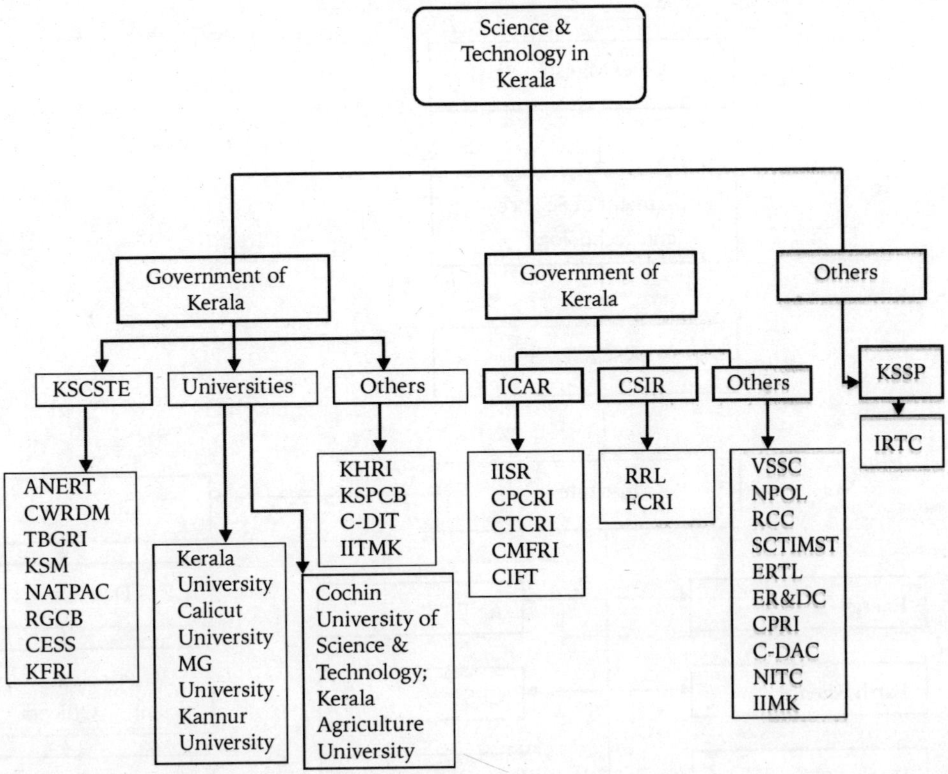

Notations Used:
KSCSTE: Kerala State Council of Science, Technology & Environment
ICAR: Indian Council of Agriculture Research
CSIR: Council of Scientific and Industrial Research
KSSP: Kerala Sastra Sahitya Parishad
IRTC: Integrated Rural Technology
ANERT: Agency for Non-conventional Energy and Rural Technology
CWRDM: Central Water Resources Development & Management
TBGRI: Tropical Botanical Garden and Research Institute
KSM: Kerala School of Mathematics;
NATPAC: National Transportation Planning Research Centre
RGCB: Rajiv Gandhi Centre for Bio Technology
CESS: Centre for Earth Science Studies
KFRI: Kerala Forest Research Institute
KHRI: Kerala Highway Research Institute
C-DIT: Centre for Digital Imaging Technology
IIITMK: Indian Institute of Information Technology and Management Kerala
IISR: Indian Institute of Spices Research
CPCRI: Central Plantation Crops Research Institute
CTCRI: Central Tuber Crops Research Institute
CMFRI: Central Marine Fish Research Institute
CIFT: Central Institute of Fisheries Technology
RRL: Regional Research Laboratory
FCRI: Fluid Control Research Institute
VSSC: Vikram Sarabhai Space Centre
RCC: Regional Canacer Centre
ERTL: Electonics Research & Testing Laboratory
SCTIMST: Sree Chitra Thirunal Institute of Medical Science and Technology;
ER&DC: Electronics Research & Design Centre
CPRI: Central Power Research Institute
C-DAC: Centre for Advanced Computing
NITC: National Institute of Technology
IIMK: Indian Institute of Management Kozhikode
IIITMK: Indian Institute of Information Technology Kerala

Source: Same as Table 9.1.

FIGURE 9.3

Organisational Structure of S&T Institutions under Kerala Government

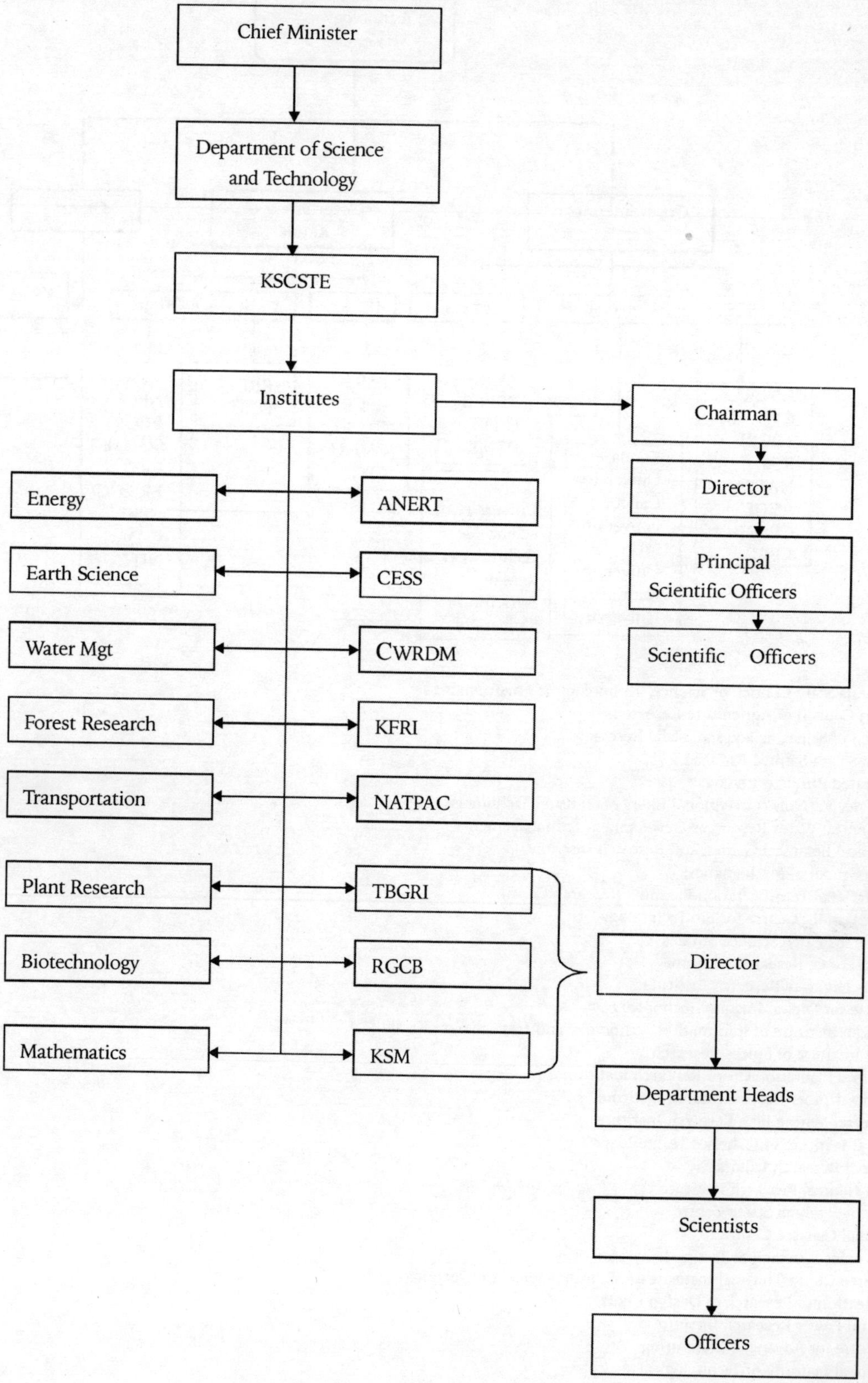

Source: Same as Table 9.1.

Science and Technology Institutions

A large number of S&T Institutions function in Kerala under the State and the Central Governments, Universities and several quasi-governmental and non-governmental organisations. In this section, performance of some of the major Institutions is analysed.

Institutions under Kerala State Council of Science, Technology and Environment (KSCSTE)

Institutions focusing on different areas of Science and Technology were established by the Government of Kerala under the broad guidelines of its S&T policy (1977) during the past two decades. These Institutions focus on areas relevant for the State's overall development such as Water Resources (CWRDM), Forest (KFRI), Environment (CESS), Energy (ANERT), Agriculture & Bio Technology (TBGRI, RGCB) and Transportation (NATPAC). The major activities of these Institutions are reviewed in the following sections in order to assess their contributions.

Agency for Non-conventional Energy and Rural Technology (ANERT)

The agency for Non-conventional Energy and Rural Technology (ANERT), a nodal agency for implementation of integrated rural energy programme in Kerala, was established in 1986 by the Govt. of Kerala as an autonomous body, with its headquarters at Thiruvananthapuram. The objective of the agency is to gather and disseminate useful knowledge in various fields of non-conventional energy, energy conservation and rural technology, and the conduct of studies, demonstration, implementation and support of projects in these fields, with a view to encountering problems arising out of rapid depletion of conventional energy sources. ANERT is active in updating technologies used in rural areas as well as in introducing appropriate new technologies for the purpose of reducing drudgery, increasing productivity and improving the quality of life of rural households and workplaces. Some of the major projects being carried out by ANERT are given in Table 9.2.

Centre for Earth Sciences Studies (CESS)

Kerala's terrain consists of highlands, midlands, low lying lands (below sea level), long coastline, thick forest areas and marshy lands. This terrain has posed several developmental challenges to the State. Landslides, soil erosion, sea erosion and floods are some of them. To focus research on four related areas (namely, Earth Systems Studies, Natural Resources Management, Natural Hazards Management, and Earth Science Applications), the Centre of Earth Science Studies (CESS) was established in 1978. The major activities of CESS include Research and Development in the areas of :

- Earth Processes.
- Carrying-Capacity-Based Studies.
- Micro-level Watershed Planning.
- Air/Water/Land/Noise Pollution Studies.
- Natural and Other Hazards Management.
- GIS/GPS, and
- Training.

Figure 9.4 gives the composition of research activities of CESS.

Centre for Water Resources Development and Management (CWRDM)

Kerala is one of the geographical areas of India that receives heavy rainfall. The state receives precipitation during both the monsoons, namely Southwest Monsoon during May-August and Northeast Monsoon during October–December. These two major monsoons, which extend up to around 120-140 days during a year

TABLE 9.2

Major Projects Undertaken by ANERT

Area	Projects Carried Out by ANERT	Significant Achievement
Energy	Solar Photovoltaic Programme, Wind Energy Programme, Bio-Energy Programme, Integrated Rural Energy Programme (IREP)	Responsible for wide spread acceptance of solar lanterns among households in Kerala. Numerous bio-gas plants and windmills have been established throughout the State
Rural Technology	National Programme on Improved Chula Rural Technology Development Micro Hydel Power Plants	Developed expertise in producing energy-efficient 'smokeless' *chulahs*, which received widespread acceptance in rural households

Source: Documents compiled from various reports of Agency for Non-Conventional Energy and Rural Technology (ANERT).

together give 1250 mm to 5000 mm of rainfall, resulting in an average yield of 70.3 bn cubic mts. of rainwater.

FIGURE 9.4

Research Activities of CESS as per the Classification Framework

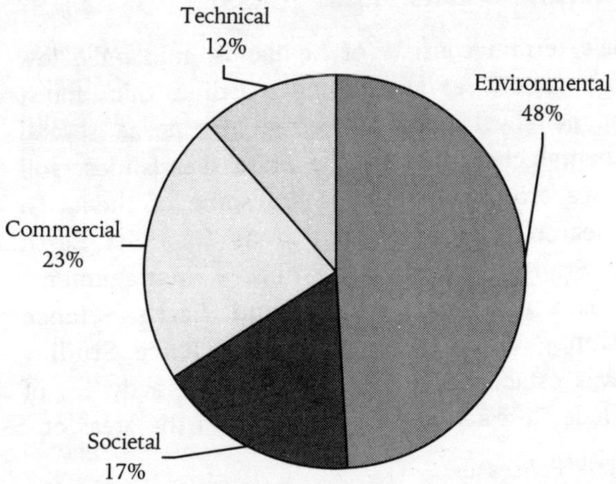

Source: Based on data collected from Centre for Earth Science Studies, Thiruvananthapuram.

The hilly terrain of the state is the source of a large number of rivers that flow in Kerala and the neighboring states. Water is one of the major resources available with the state. The S&T policy makers of the state identified the need for scientifically developing and managing this resource, which is fast depleting all the world around. The Centre for Water Resources Development and Management (CWRDM) was established in 1978 with this objective. While the Centre's focus is on conducting research on developing the state's water resources, it also provides extensive consultancy to other parts of India in developing water resources. CWRDM also has a major extension service activity to disseminate its research information.

During the past 25 years, the Centre has substantially contributed to scientific hydrologic studies and water management in the region. The Centre has tackled problems pertaining to forest and urban hydrology, estuarine management, groundwater development, water quality management, water-related environmental issues, wetland management, watershed development, agriculture water management, irrigation and drainage issues, etc. Several tools like mathematical modelling, systems approach, isotope hydrology and remote sensing techniques are made use of in these studies. More than 2000 scientific papers and 500 research reports were brought out based on these studies. The hydrologic data generated by CWRDM are expected to be of immense use to the water managers of Kerala. CWRDM has played a key role in supporting the Kerala Government in sorting out several water management issues. One of the significant achievements of CWRDM is the formulation of the State Water Policy which provides a broad framework for streamlining the water resources development projects of Kerala. The composition of research activities in CWRDM as per the classification framework is given in Figure 9.5.

FIGURE 9.5

Composition of Research Activities Carried Out by CWRDM

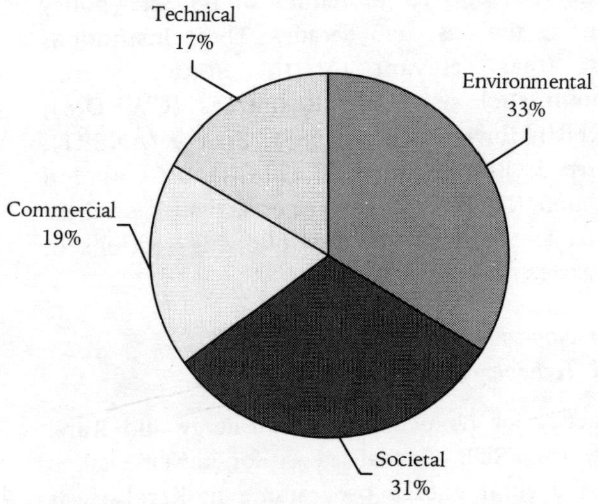

Source: Based on data collected from Centre for Water Resources Development and Management.

Kerala Forest Research Institute (KFRI)

KFRI was established as an autonomous research institution to focus on forestry and bio-diversity of Kerala, which are of vital importance for the development of the state. Located in Peechi, Trichur district, close to the Kerala Agricultural University, the institution serves numerous economic, social and environmental purposes set by the Government. KFRI has a major role in protecting the forest areas of Kerala. It has published 225 Research Reports, 1005 Scientific Papers, 18 Information Bulletins, 8 Handbooks, 30 Books, 1 CD, 2 Videos, and 2 pieces of Software, useful in forest resources planning and management.

National Transportation Planning and Research Centre (NATPAC)

NATPAC is an autonomous research institute under the Government of Kerala. It was established in 1976 as a Division of Kerala State Electronics Development Corporation (KELTRON), a public sector enterprise under the Government of Kerala. In 1982, it was reconstituted as an R&D institution under the Department of Science, Technology and Environment. In February 2003, NATPAC was merged with the new Council and, accordingly, it is functioning as an R&D unit under KSCSTE, which is fully funded and supported by the government. The Centre is undertaking research and consultancy works in the fields of traffic engineering and transportation planning, highway engineering, public transport system, inland water transport, tourism planning, rural roads, environmental impact assessment and transport energy. The typical portfolio of research activities at NATPAC as per the classification framework is given in Figure 9.6.

FIGURE 9.6

Research Activities of NATPAC as per the Classification Framework

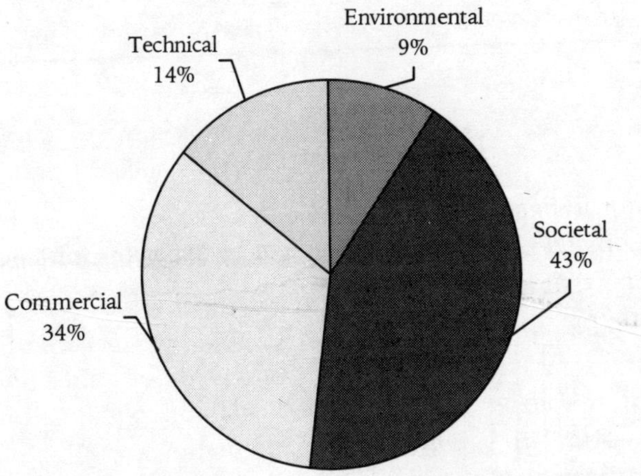

Source: Based on data collected from National Transportation Planning and Research Centre.

Rajiv Gandhi Centre for Biotechnology (RGCB)

The S&T Policy of Kerala focuses on developing expertise on frontier areas of scientific knowledge. Kerala is one of the few regions in the world to have its own separate policy for developing biotechnology, a typical sunrise technology. RGCB in Thiruvananthapuram was established in 1990 as Centre for Development of Education, Science and Technology and later converted to a focused R&D Centre in 1994. The Centre has a mandate for research and manpower development in biotechnology, healthcare, animal science, agriculture, environment and basic sciences. The Centre is focusing its research on cutting edge areas of bio-technology like molecular biology, environmental biotechnology, plant molecular biology, transgenic plants and animals, genetic control of diseases, molecular human genetics, neurobiology, cancer biology, molecular endocrinology and other areas of genetic engineering. The composition of research activities in RGCB as per the classification framework is given in Figure 9.7.

FIGURE 9.7

Research Activities of RGCB as per the Classification Framework

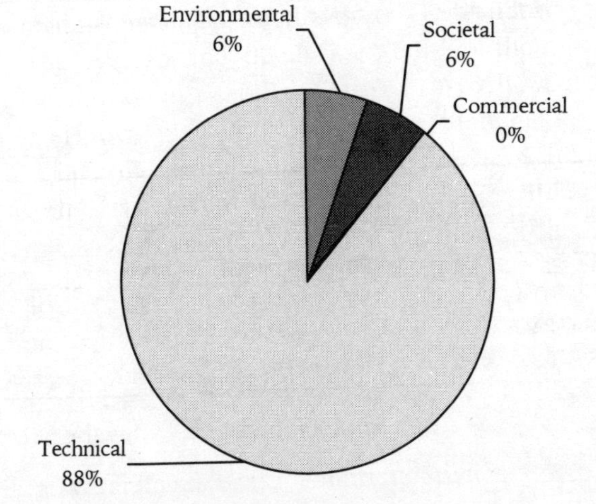

Source: Based on data collected from Rajiv Gandhi Centre for Biotechnology.

Tropical Botanic Garden & Research Institute (TBGRI)

TBGRI was established in 1979 as an autonomous Institute under the Government of Kerala. The Institute was established with the purpose of doing extensive and focused research on the rich flora and fauna of the state. Currently, it is functioning as the National Gene Bank for Medicinal and Aromatic Plants in Peninsular India. The Centre is also credited with the status of a National Centre of Excellence for *ex situ* Conservation and Sustainable Utilisation of Plant Resources of Tropical India. TBGRI, through its excellent performance, has earned the status of a National Coordination Centre for Biosphere Inventorying and Monitoring. The Centre has also obtained several patents for its works and is providing key support in preserving the IPR of tropical bio-genetics of India, which is a major area of research in the context of WTO agreements.

Analysis of Research Done by Various Institutions under KSCSTE

The Institutions under KSCSTE were set up by the Government of Kerala for conducting state-of-the-art research in their functional domains relevant to the development of the State. Most of the institutions have formulated their mission statement in conformity with

TABLE 9.3
Type of Projects Carried out by Select Institutions

Institution	*Kerala Specific Projects*		*Applied Projects for Other Domains*		*Projects Focussing on Basic Research*		*Total Number of Projects*
	No.	*%*	*No.*	*%*	*No.*	*%*	
CESS	157	96.32%	3	1.84%	3	1.84%	163
CWRDM	160	62.75%	17	6.67%	78	30.59%	255
NATPAC	37	56.06%	21	31.82%	8	12.12%	66
RGCB	2	11.11%	0	0.00%	16	88.89%	18

Source: Compiled from various reports of the above institutions.

TABLE 9.4
Composition of Projects Carried out by Major Institutions

Institute	*Environmental*		*Societal*		*Commercial*		*Technical*		*Total*
	No.	*%*	*No.*	*%*	*No.*	*%*	*No*	*%*	
CESS	80	49.08%	28	17.18%	37	22.70%	18	11.04%	163
CWRDM	86	33.73%	78	30.59%	48	18.82%	43	16.86%	255
NATPAC	6	9.09%	27	40.91%	22	33.33%	11	16.67%	66
RGCB	1	5.00%	1	5.00%	0	0.00%	18	90.00%	20

Source: Same as Table 9.3.

this objective laid down by government in the S&T Policy of the state. An analysis was conducted on the projects carried out by four of these seven institutions since their inception for which data are available; see Table 9.3.

While the main focus of most of the institutions has been on Kerala-based projects, except in the case of RGCB, which is focusing mainly on basic research, the projects have been in general applied in nature. For reasons of scarcity of funds (explained in the next section), many of these research institutions had to diversify their activities into commercial areas like consulting and training. The composition of projects according to their social and commercial relevance is given in Table 9.4 and Figure 9.8.

FIGURE 9.8
Type of Projects Carried out by Major Institutions

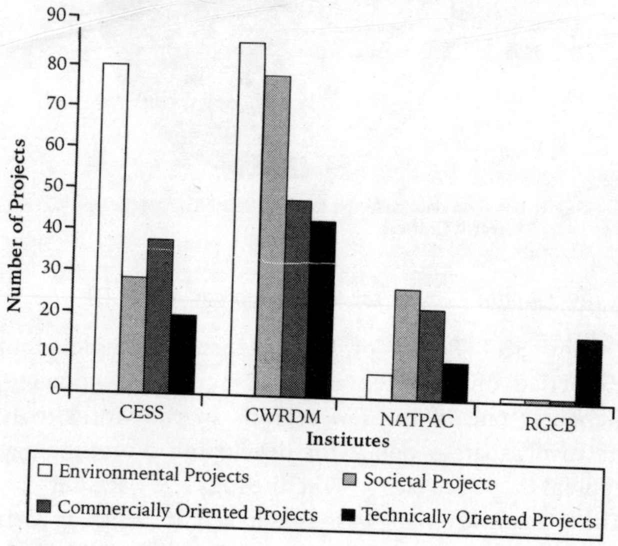

Source: Same as Table 9.3.

From Figure 9.8 it may be seen that older Institutions like CESS and CWRDM have gained enough expertise to initiate commercially viable projects as well as to provide consultancy services for generating revenue. RGCB, which is working on the cutting edge of biotechnology, is focusing more on technical projects as the majority of its projects fall under the basic research category.

Other Major Institutions in Kerala

In addition to the Institutions under KSCSTE, which are fully funded by Govt. of Kerala, there are many other institutions sponsored by both governmental and non-governmental bodies. Some of the major Institutions under this category are mentioned below.

Kerala Highway Research Institute (KHRI)

KHRI was established in 1974 for meeting the laboratory and R&D needs of the Kerala Public Works

Department. KHRI is basically a testing institute for materials related to road facilities and has done a large number of material-testing projects for clients in public and private sectors. Apart from this, it has also carried out a few technological training programmes, and other knowledge-dissemination activities.

Centre for Digital Imaging Technology (C-DIT)

C-DIT was established in 1989 for meeting the increasing needs of exploring the horizons of digital imaging technology in Kerala state. It was started as a software development institute; later it became well known for application of digital imaging technology and holography technology.

C-DIT has so far undertaken 10 major basic research projects and conducted many industry and academic training programmes. C-DIT is also active in knowledge dissemination through seminars, conferences, exhibitions, etc.

C-DIT is the only one of its kind in India with its production and R&D facilities under a single roof. C-DIT is also known for cost-effectiveness of its services. C-DIT plays a major role in the IT projects of the state especially in the e-governance area.

Vikram Sarabhai Space Centre (VSSC)

VSSC, a premier research centre under Indian Space Research Organisation (ISRO), is world-renowned in space sciences. Located in Thumba, near Thiruvananthapuram, VSSC was instrumental in making India one of the five nations in the world to design and develop own satellite launch vehicles. From a humble beginning of sending rockets for meteorological purposes, the unit has grown substantially to gain expertise in developing Polar Satellite Launch Vehicles (PSLV which placed the indigenous 1000 KG class Indian Remote Sensing satellite IRS-P2 in orbit on October 15, 1994) and Geo-Synchronous Satellite Launch Vehicles (GSLV). VSSC has stimulated the growth of S&T activities in Kerala.

Naval Physical Oceanographic Laboratory (NPOL)

The origin of naval system technology in India may be traced to the establishment of the Indian Naval Physical Laboratory (INPL) by the Indian Navy in 1952 at Cochin in Kerala. INPL work began as a field laboratory mostly for fleet support activities. Later it was merged with DRDO in 1958 and started working on underwater systems. INPL has been rechristened as Naval Physical Oceanographic Laboratory (NPOL).

Regional Research Laboratory (RRL)

Regional Research Laboratory, Thiruvananthapuram, functioning under the Council for Scientific and Industrial Research (CSIR) was established in 1978. It is the leading laboratory of CSIR devoted to multidisciplinary R&D work for optimum utilisation of regional/national resources. The laboratory focuses its activities on agro-processing and material sciences and has carried out more than 50 projects on Kerala. It holds over 150 patents and has published over 5000 monographs, books and other knowledge dissemination material. Some of the technologies developed by RRL, like ageing treatment of coconut leaves for improving the life of thatched roofs, etc. have been commercially exploited and have yielded substantial economic dividends.

Fluid Control Research Institute (FCRI)

Fluid Control Research Institute (FCRI), another CSIR Institution in Kerala, set up with techno-economic inputs from UNDP, provides measurement standards in Fluid flow and related areas for efficient operation of national and international trade. Standard artifact for measurement of fluid flow is related to basic parameters of length, mass, time and temperature. Flow measurement in all industries is a key constituent of quality, safety and efficiency and it plays a critical role in custody transfer and fiscal metering of fluids. It is therefore necessary to have authentic flow reference systems. In addition to research in basic and applied areas related to fluid control, oil hydraulics etc., FCRI also conducts training programmes for industry, academia and NGOs.

Central Power Research Institute (CPRI)

The Ministry of Power, Government of India established this Institute in 1993 to focus on power-related problems of Kerala. The power needs of the state are met mainly by Hydro-electricity projects situated in the hilly ranges of the state. Construction of long lines of high voltage carriers and complex distribution network are necessary for such projects. The transmission and distribution losses in this power-scarce state are extremely high due to the complexity of network (T&D losses in Kerala are around 33 per cent during 2002-2003, much higher than the national average of 23 per cent). CPRI is expected to focus its research on finding viable solutions to this sort of problems. The unit has completed more than two dozens of specialised projects sponsored by national and international agencies. It holds a patent for technological innovation.

Among the eight power research institutes in India, CPRI, Thiruvananthapuram is the oldest and is currently the leading energy consultant in the country. It is well known for its path-breaking development of novel tools for thermal power stations and for energy conservation.

Central Plantation Crops Research Institute (CPCRI)

CPCRI was established in 1970 by the Indian Council of Agricultural Research at Kasaragod. Focusing mainly on Coconut, the major homestead crop of Kerala, CPCRI has developed several harvesting and post-harvesting technologies for development of Coconut farming as well as for diversifying its use. CPCRI conducts training programmes and publishes its research findings. The institute has a sub-centre in Kayamkulam in southern Kerala.

The Central Marine Fisheries Research Institute (CMFRI)

The Central Marine Fisheries Research Institute established by the Government of India under the Ministry of Agriculture in 1947 became a member of the Indian Council of Agricultural Research (ICAR) in 1967. CMFRI has contributed significantly to the development of marine resources of the state, which has a lengthy coastline. With the fast changing marine fisheries scenario and the emergence of Mari-culture as a viable proposition for enhancing production, the Institute has over the years, fine-tuned its mandate in consonance with the needs of the times. CMFRI is the first among the seven marine research institutions in India. The pioneering efforts of CMFRI have resulted in several patents and publications useful for sustainable development of marine resources of Kerala.

Central Institute of Fisheries Technology (CIFT)

CIFT is another marine research institute in Kerala, situated in Wellington Island, Cochin and established in 1954 under ICAR. CIFT conducts several projects relevant to the specific needs of Kerala and training programmes for the personnel involved in development and management of fishery resources.

Central Tuber Crops Research Institute (CTCRI)

CTCRI, the lone tuber crops research Institute in the World, began functioning as a research institute under ICAR in July 1963 with its headquarters at Sreekariyam, near Thiruvananthapuram. It has a regional centre, which is functioning in Bhubaneswar. The All-India Coordinated Research Project on Tuber crops operates from this institute and has 15 centres spread throughout the tuber-crop-growing areas of India. The Institute is also one of the centres of the All India Coordinated Research Project on Harvest and Post-harvest Technologies. In 2002-03, CTCRI had 86 ongoing projects and 17 consultancy projects. It has also conducted four technological training programmes, one general training programme, three awareness programmes, nine conferences, and 10 extension activities. It is maintaining its own museum. CTCRI has acquired four registered patents. It had 85 publications by 2002-03. Most of the projects of CTCRI are funded by ICAR. However, a few projects receive funding from other national and international agencies also.

Centre for Development of Advanced Computing (C-DAC)

Centre for Development of Advanced Computing, (formerly ER & DCI), Thiruvananthapuram, is a national Centre of Excellence, pioneering in application-oriented research, design and development in the areas of Electronics and Information Technology.

The Centre has contributed significantly to the growth of industry in general and the electronics sector in particular through indigenous development of commercially viable systems and products, foreign technology absorption, adaptation and upgradation, consultancy and training, and turnkey implementation of contract projects. The Centre has several firsts to its credits and is a recipient of prestigious national level awards for excellence in application-oriented R & D.

Sree Chitra Tirunal Institute for Medical Sciences and Technology (SCTIMST)

SCTIMST is an Institute of national importance. It is an autonomous Institute under the administrative control of the Department of Science and Technology, Government of India.

The Institute signifies the convergence of medical sciences and technology and its mission is to enable indigenous growth of biomedical technology, besides demonstrating high standards of patient care in medical specialities, and evolving postgraduate training programmes in advanced medical specialities, biomedical engineering and technology, as well as public health. It has a hospital with 236 beds for tertiary care of cardiovascular and neurological diseases, a biomedical technology wing with facilities for developing medical devices from the conceptual to the commercialisation stage, and a centre of excellence for training and research in public health.

The Institute has the status of a University and offers post-doctoral, doctoral and postgraduate courses in medical specialties, public health, nursing, basic sciences and healthcare technology. It is a member of the Association of Indian Universities and the Association of Commonwealth Universities.

The bio-medical technology wing of SCTIMST has done pioneering work in the establishment of a Medical Device Industry by successfully developing and transferring technology for diverse medical products such as the disposable blood bag system, medical heart valve prosthesis, blood oxygenates, ophthalmic sponge, concentric needle electrode, and hydroxyapatite-based bioceramic porous granules. Many more products are in the pipeline and they are developed with industrial collaboration. The Institute also holds a number of international patents for devices and processes.

Integrated Rural Technology Centre, Mundoor (IRTC)

Integrated Rural Technology Centre, Mundoor, is the R&D agency of Kerala Shastra Sahitya Parishat, an independent voluntary organisation established for the promotion of S&T in Kerala. IRTC started operations in 1987 and is playing a key role in the revival of several rural technologies in Kerala, modernising them and making them available to modern society. IRTC has been conducting research activities and producing fruitful results in several fronts.

IRTC has so far done 66 Kerala-specific research projects and 3 basic research projects. Most of these projects were funded by national agencies. A few projects were carried out with own funding. Apart from these research activities, IRTC conducts academic training programmes and general awareness programmes. IRTC is also involved in counselling for various government organisations in Kerala and has conducted detailed resource mapping exercises for facilitating decentralised planning, an exercise which is proving to be of vital importance in the development of the state.

Analysis of S&T Sector in Kerala

The overview of research institutions has shown that Kerala is well endowed with S&T establishments that encompass a variety of scientific and technological

TABLE 9.5

S&T Institutions in Kerala

Main Sector	*Sub-sector*	*State Govt. Institutions*	*Central Govt. Institutions*	*Other Institutions*
Agriculture	Plantation Crops		CPCRI	Coconut Board; Central Coir Research Institute (Coir Board)
	Tuber Crops		CTCRI	
	Fisheries		CMFRI, CIFT	
	General	KAU		
	Cash Crops (Spices)		IISR	Rubber Board; UPASI (Tea); Spices Board
Botany	Tropical Flora	TBGRI		
	Forests	KFRI		
Bio-Medical		RGCBT		
Bio-Tech		CU	SCTIMST	
Earth Sciences		CESS		
Electronics		C-DIT, STIC	CDAC, ERTL	
Fluid Control Research, Process Automation			FCRI, RRL, DOEACC (former CEDTI)	
Mathematical Sciences		KSM		
Medical Sciences			SCTIMST, RRL, RCC	Amritha Institute of Medical Sciences Cochin
Marine Research		Cochin University of Science and Technology (CUSAT)	CMFRI, CIFT	
Oceanographic Research		CUSAT	NPOL	
Power/Energy/ Rural Development	Non-conventional Energy	ANERT		
	Power Transmission			CPRI
Transportation & Roads		NATPAC, KHRI		
Space Research			VSSC	
Water Resources		CWRDM		
Development of Local Technology		ANERT	RRL	IRTC

Source: Based on the study of the institutions for the State Development Report.

areas (see Table 9.5). It does not however include the academic departments of universities which also carry out research in several fields of S&T.

The issues related to Kerala government's S&T spending over the past two decades are discussed below. The Government of Kerala began to include science, technology and environment under its Five Year Plans only from the 5th Five Year Plan period onwards. The outlays and expenditures under the Five-Year Plans are given in Table 9.6.

TABLE 9.6

Plan Outlay and Actual Spending on S&T

Five Year Plan	*Outlay (Rs. Lakhs)*	*Expenditure (Rs. Lakhs)*	*% of Total Outlay*	*% of Total Expenditure*
V (1974-1978)	798	592	1.40%	1.22%
VI (1980-1985)	1746	1658	1.14%	0.93%
VII (1986-1990)	2560	2721	1.12%	1.08%
VIII (1992-1997)	2923	4308	0.54%	0.58%
IX (1997-2001)	7500	NA	0.74%	NA
X (2002-2007)	12000	NA	0.50%	NA

Source: Compiled various annual reports of the State Planning Board, Government of Kerala, Thiruvananthapuram.

The figures shown in the Table are in current prices and not in constant prices. From Table 9.6 and Figure 9.9, it may be seen that while the budget outlays as well as expenditures on S&T have been increasing, the relative share of this vital sector (which remained roughly at around one per cent till 1987) has been decreasing.

Distribution of Plan Outlay

The proposed spending for various S&T activities during the 10th Plan period is given in Table 9.7 and Figure 9.9 In addition to units under KSCSTE, the state provides fiscal support to various other governmental and voluntary institutions as well as for specific programmes (Figures 9.12a and 9.12b). A substantial amount (Rs. 900 lakh) is earmarked for environmental protection through plan assistance to Kerala State Pollution Control Board.

The emergence of Biotechnology as a major area has prompted the government to allocate more resources to RGCB.

Figure 9.16 shows the total funds allotted to the top five institutions (the amounts indicated are at current prices and are not based on a base year prices). From the graph it is seen that, on an average, five

FIGURE 9.9

Outlay and Expenditure on S&T

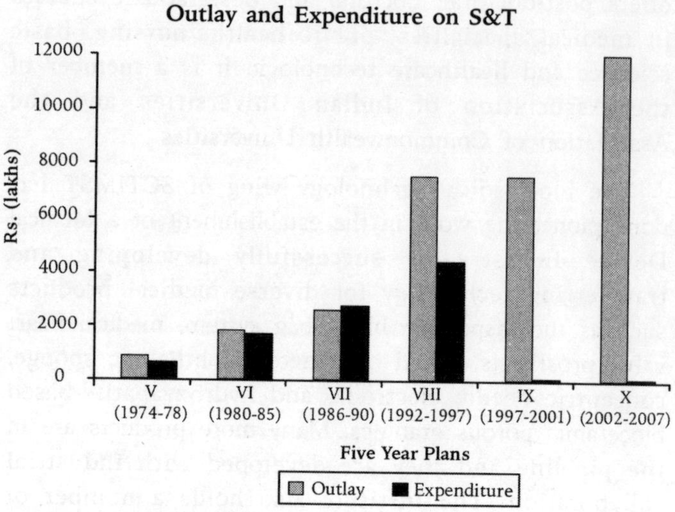

Source: Same as Table 9.6.

FIGURE 9.10

S&T Spending as Percentage of Total Outlay

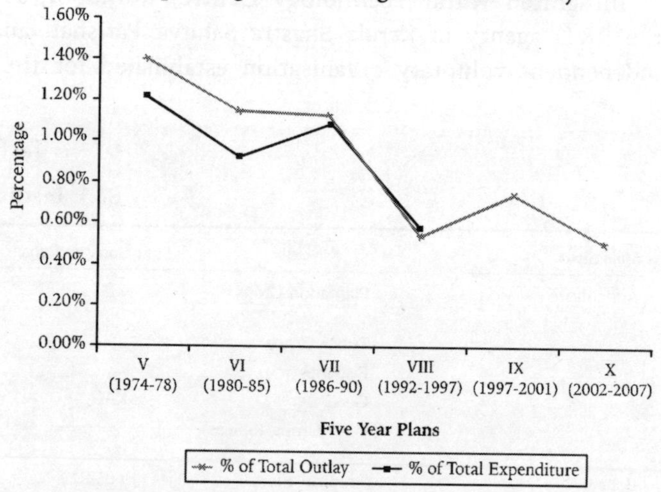

Source: Same as Table 9.6.

FIGURE 9.11

Tenth Plan Outlay for Various S&T Institutions

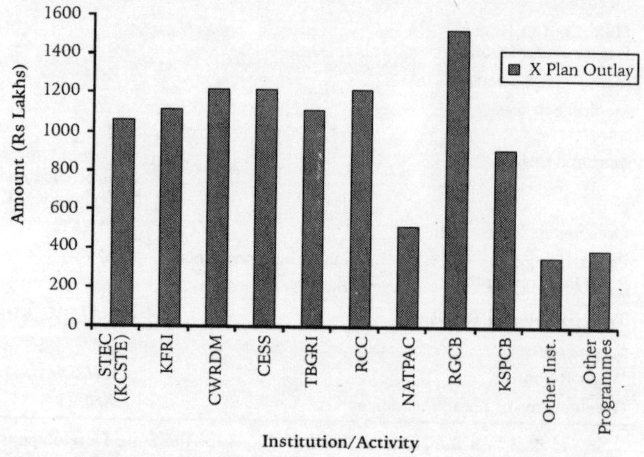

Source: Same as Table 9.5.

TABLE 9.7

Distribution of Plan Outlay across Institutions

(Rs. in Lakh)

Unit	*X Plan Outlay*
STEC (KSCSTE)	1050
KFRI	1100
CWRDM	1200
CESS	1200
TBGRI	1100
RCC	1200
NATPAC	500
RGCB	1510
KSPCB	900
Other Institutions	345
Other Programmes	375
Others	1520
Total	12000

Source: Same as Table 9.5.

FIGURE 9.12a

State Government Support during Tenth Plan for Various Schemes for S&T Sector

Support to S&T Programmes
(Value in Rs. Lakhs & Corresponding Percentage)

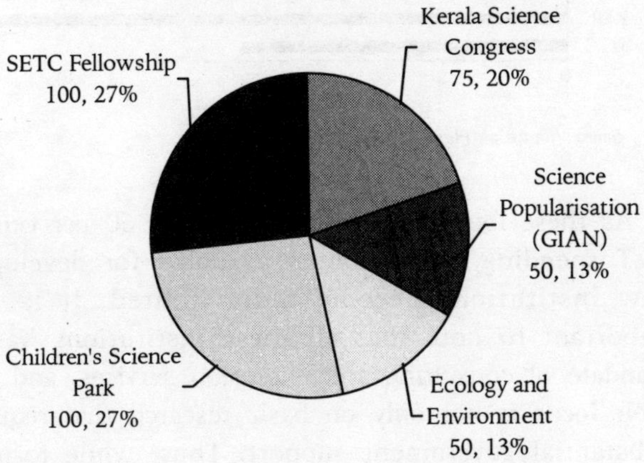

Note: Figures in Rs. lakh and corresponding percentages.

Source: Planning Board documents, Government of Kerala.

institutions have accounted for more than 70% of the S&T spending during the past 5 years.

Based on the spending pattern, the list of the top 10 Institutions that get support from government is given in Figure 9.15. RGCB, as explained earlier, accounts for the highest share of spending. This is basically due to the capital expenditure involved in setting up a reputed institution in the area of Biotechnology.

FIGURE 9.12b

State Government Support during Tenth Plan for Various S&T Institutions

State Support to Other S&T Institutions

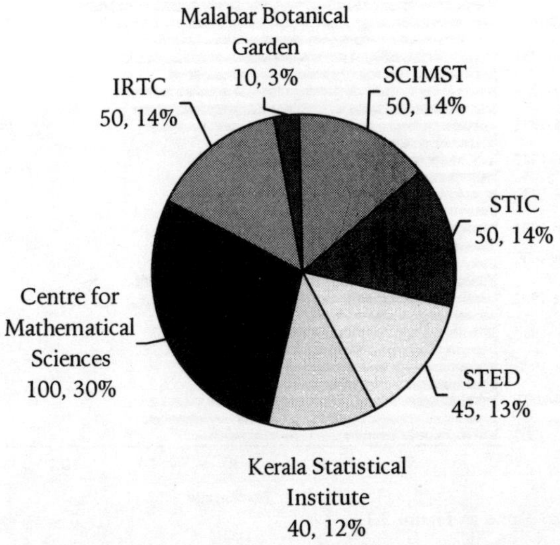

Note: Figures in Rs. Lakh and corresponding percentages of overall spending.

Source: Same as Figure 9.12a.

FIGURE 9.13

Distribution of Plan Outlay Over the Period 1975-2003

Percentage of Institutes Getting 50 per cent Allocation

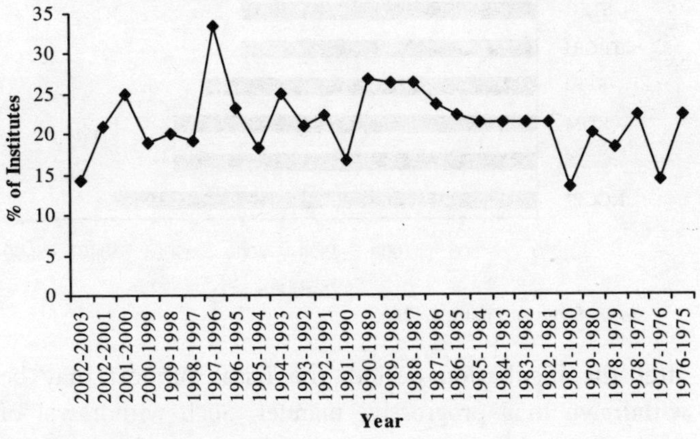

Source: Same as Figure 9.12a.

Economic Viability of Institutions

The S&T Institutions directly under KSCSTE as well as those supported by the Government need some amounts by way of initial assistance from government, to support their basic research activities. Every Institution would normally face an 'incubation' period during which it would need external support. However,

FIGURE 9.14

Distribution of Plan Outlay across S&T Institutions

Percentage of S&T Spending on Top Five Institutions

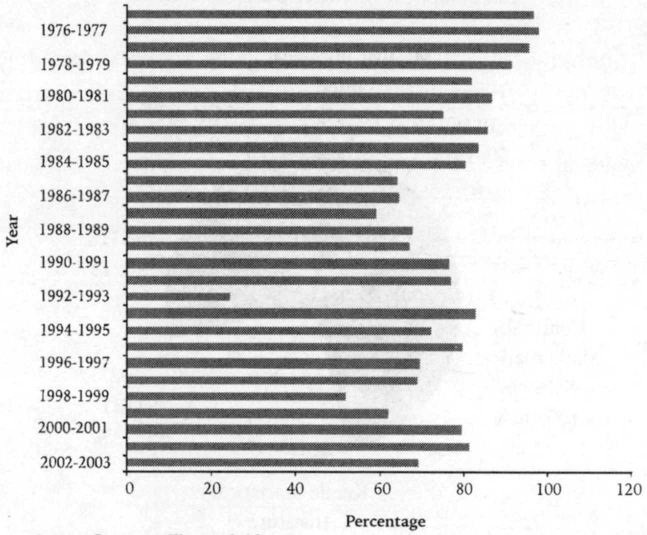

Source: Same as Figure 9.12a.

FIGURE 9.15

Top 10 Institutions based on Spending on S&T

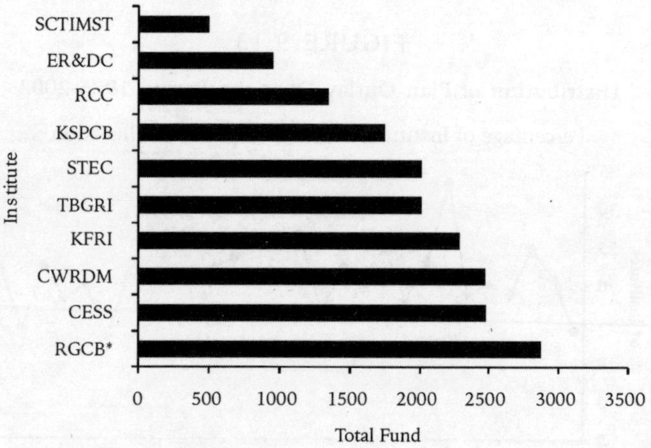

Source: Same as Figure 9.12a.

after the incubation period, the fiscal support may be withdrawn in a progressive manner. Such withdrawal of support would provide the resources which could be devoted to help institutions which focus their attention on other areas of applied research relevant to Kerala. While sustained government funding of S&T institutions may not be desirable, the role of government funding at the incubation stage of S&T institutions is indisputable.

The pattern of spending by the government on S&T Institutions in Kerala during the past 25 years is shown in Figure 9.14. It is observed that four out of the seven institutions, namely, KFRI, CWRDM, CESS and TBGRI, have been depending on substantial government support for more than 15 years implying thereby that these institutions have been cornering most of the government's funds spent on S&T. This fact raises serious questions on their scope for self-sustenance. On the other hand, if these institutions have not already thought seriously about self-sustenance, it is high time that they thought about it.

FIGURE 9.16

Number of Years in which an Institute is among Top 5 in Receiving Government Support

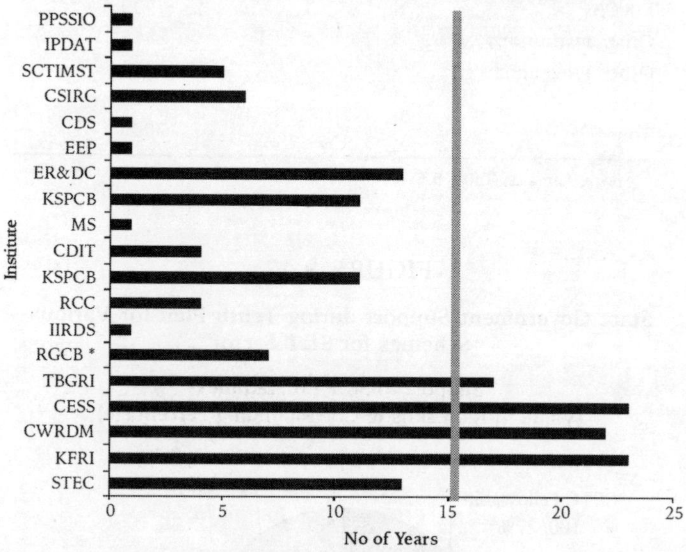

Source: Same as Figure 9.12a.

As these four Institutions claim over 60 per cent of S&T spending, the amounts available for developing new institutions become quite limited. It is also important to note that all these institutions have a mandate of consulting and extension services, and that their focus is not only on basic research that requires substantial government support. Thus, while forming policies for improving S&T activities in the state, it is necessary to make concerted efforts to render the S&T institutions financially self-reliant.

S&T Development in Kerala: A Road Map

S&T spending of Kerala is around 1 per cent of the total capital outlay of the government. Even the central government has achieved this level of spending in S&T only by 2003. According to the S&T policy, the annual spending on research and development by the central government should reach a figure of about 2 per cent of the total spending by the end of the Tenth plan period. It is estimated that at present, less than 20 per cent of the S&T expenditure in India is being met by the private sector. While, due to data unavailability, it is difficult to calculate the corresponding figure for Kerala, it may be safely assumed that it may not be much higher given the limited contribution of large scale private enterprises to the economy of Kerala. Therefore, there is substantial scope in Kerala for increasing expenditure on S&T activities both through governmental allocation as well as through private sector participation.

While Kerala has a large number of research institutions funded by the state government, it has not gained an image as a hub of research or technology development even within India. Most of the institutions are still dependent heavily on governmental funding making it difficult for the state to develop new areas of research. While most of the research organisations are satisfactorily carrying out their mandate, the number of innovations and patents generated by the institutions are quite limited indicating the need for refocusing their activities. The formation of KSCSTE in 2002, by the government of Kerala has been basically to tackle this issue. Only a few institutions are observed to have been involved in consulting and training activities. Research dissemination activities need to be strengthened to make Research institutions of international standards. S&T activities in Kerala should translate into generation of a large pool of talented manpower which is capable of taking up developmental challenges and thereby strengthening the economy.

Very few institutions have high-quality skill development programmes required to create high-calibre human resources. Thus, to develop Kerala as the Technology/R&D hub of India, a two-pronged strategy has to be adopted: a) increasing the spending on S&T activities to levels at par with those of countries with comparable HDI (about 2 per cent of total outlay); b) strengthening the institutions by focusing on applied research and training activities with a view to generating high quality manpower and reducing budgetary support from the government progressively, so that the scarce resources at the disposal of the government could be devoted to innovation and development.

Areas of Future Development

S&T activities of Kerala are focusing, in general, on issues concerning agriculture, forest resources, water, biotechnology, energy, rural technology, environment and transport. rgcb focusing on biotechnology and iiitm and c-dit focusing on information technology are examples of the proactive measures undertaken by the state. Innovations like nano-technology and Communications Technology will have to be fostered in the near future. Interdisciplinary research across institutions to ensure holistic growth will also have to be encouraged. Another area for development is basic research. While the proposed Kerala School of Mathematics is expected to carry out fundamental research in mathematics and related sciences, very little contribution is made by Kerala-based R&D Institutions so far on areas of fundamental research. As Universities have not succeeded in areas of fundamental research, may be, for reasons ranging from financial to political, it is important that government focuses on measures to attract quality manpower for the purpose by providing adequate infrastructure and support.

Knowledge Management Systems

Another area which calls for support and encouragement is the documentation of research. It has been observed that very few research institutions in Kerala have adequate systems of recording the knowledge generated through their research. Several institutes do not have even a compendium of research studies completed. Such a sorry state of affairs led to situations in which the critical learning accumulated through research is totally lost. As a consequence, the possibilities of technology transfer are lost too, to the present era of intellectual property rights and patent protection for which the loss of critical knowledge could prove to be highly costly. Besides, lack of documentation and records would hamper extensions of research studies already done. A statewide knowledge management system linking all the S&T institutions in the state would make a good beginning in arresting the ruinous trend. The knowledge management system would be able to ensure dissemination of learning and development of a knowledge library for future researchers to use. The lack of a knowledge base is in fact hampering multi-disciplinary research and sharing of knowledge across institutes. Even the different departments within the same institution have found it difficult to share knowledge. The knowledge management system will lead to greater interdisciplinary research thereby generating fertile ideas and opportunities for promotion of research and development.

Chapter 10

Healthcare

The state of Kerala is well known the world over for its remarkable achievements in the field of fertility and mortality transitions. The achievement is often attributed to the open society characteristic of the state, where "successive elections resulted in electors demanding educational and health services and in competing political parties offering to provide such services" (Caldwell, 1986). This chapter presents the health achievements of the state of Kerala, the main policy ingredients guiding the evolution of the public healthcare sector, the private sector, and the public-private mix, the utilisation of healthcare services and the healthcare costs incurred by households and their economic consequences.

Evolution of Health Status

Decline in Mortality

Kerala had one of the lowest mortality rates among the Indian states even as early as by 1951-60[1] and occupied a position among the top four or five states in the country. In terms of crude death rate (CDR), Kerala (16.1) compared well with Punjab (18.9), Rajasthan (19.4) and Maharastra (19.8). In terms of infant mortality rate (IMR), the state (IMR-120) was no different from the above three states and Andhra Pradesh, Gujarat, Karnataka, Tamil Nadu and West Bengal where IMR lay between 110 and 120. By 1971, when Sample Registration System (SRS) estimates became available, in terms of CDR, Kerala (9.0) stood ahead of all other states with Punjab (10.4), Haryana (9.9), Karnataka (12.1) and Maharastra (12.3) closely following (Table 10.1). In terms of IMR, Kerala (58) had already gone even further ahead leaving behind Haryana (72), Karnataka (95) and Punjab (102), the states which followed in that order, far behind.

The next three decades saw this picture changing further with Kerala making considerable strides in reducing mortality. The CDR dropped to 6.4 in Kerala by 2002, the next closest states being West Bengal (6.6), Maharastra (7.3), Punjab (7.1), Karnataka (7.2) and Gujarat (7.6). The IMR showed a sharp drop to 10 in Kerala with Tamil Nadu (44) and Maharastra (45), almost 35 points higher, as its immediate followers. Punjab (51) and West Bengal (49) were not far behind (Table 10.2).

How has Kerala achieved such remarkable reduction in mortality? For answering the question, an analysis of the age-specific death rates by broad age groups is necessary to identify the specific age groups that have gained in health status and the proximate causes of such gains.

The mortality reduction trends of the population in the ages from 10 to 54 years do not show any discernible pattern across the states of India over the period 1971 to 1996. The age-specific death rates of above 55 years age groups of the population show that Kerala has not been different from half a dozen other Indian states. For the 55-59 years group, the death rate had dropped from below 20 per 1000 population in 1971 to below 15 in 1996 for Kerala, Maharastra, Punjab and Haryana (Table 10.2). For Tamil Nadu and Rajasthan, the drop was from above 20 to below 15. The death rate of 60-64 years group remained at below 25 throughout the period in Haryana, Punjab and Kerala; in Gujarat and Rajasthan, it dropped, however, from 25-40 range to below 25. For the 65-69 years group, in Punjab and Haryana the death rate remained below 40 throughout the period while in Gujarat, Kerala Maharastra and Uttar Pradesh, it dropped from the 40-50 range to

1. For this early period only estimates based on Population Census data are available. Such estimates are not considered very reliable.

TABLE 10.1

Crude Death Rates and Death Rates of the Young in the Indian States, 1971-2002

State	Crude Death Rate		Infant Mortality Rate		Death Rate 0-4 Years		Death Rate 5-9 Years	
	1971	2002	1971	2002	1971	1996	1971	1996
All-India	14.9	8.1	129	63	51.9	23.9	4.7	2.3
Andhra Pradesh	14.6	8.0	106	62	44.9	17.8	4.7	1.6
Assam	17.8	9.2	139	70	45.7	24.0	7.2	3.5
Bihar	13.9*	7.9	118*	61	42.5*	27.9	5.3*	3.9
Gujarat	16.4	7.6	144	60	64.9	23.3	4.1	1.3
Haryana	9.9	7.0	72	62	32.5	23.4	3.0*	1.9
Karnataka	12.1	7.2	95	55	37.5	16.6	4.3	0.9*
Kerala	**9.0**	**6.4**	**58**	**10**	**24.5**	**3.8**	**2.3***	**0.9***
Madhya Pradesh	15.6	9.7	135	85	49.8	33.5	5.0	3.0
Maharastra	12.3	7.3	105	45	44.6	13.1	3.2	1.0
Orissa	15.4	9.8	127	87	54.2	30.6	5.4	2.9
Punjab	10.4	7.1	102	51	38.9	15.2	1.6*	1.2
Rajasthan	16.8	7.7	123	78	55.9	31.4	5.3	2.0
Tamil Nadu	14.4	7.7	113	44	40.7	12.6	4.6	0.6*
Uttar Pradesh	20.1	9.7	167	80	83.7	31.4	5.4	3.0
West Bengal	11.0*	6.6	91*	49	33.5*	18.1	2.6*	1.6

Note: * The figures are for the year 1981.

Source: Registrar General of India (1999). *Compendium of India's Fertility and Mortality Indicators 1971-97*. New Delhi; *Sample Registration Bulletin*.

below 40. And in Andhra Pradesh, Karnataka and Rajasthan, it dropped from above 50 to below 40. For the above 70 years, the death rate dropped from below 100 in 1971 to below 80 in 1996 for Punjab and Rajasthan, and from above 100 to below 80 for Gujarat and Haryana. Kerala does not at all appear in this group of states but remained along with Karnataka, Maharastra and Uttar Pradesh with death rates lying between 80-90 in 1996. Thus, at ages above 54 years, the mortality record of Kerala does not look different from those of most other Indian states.

At the lower age groups also, Kerala does not look widely different from other states in India with regard to the reduction in mortality rate among the population in the age group of five to nine years. According to Table 10.1, Kerala stood in 1971 along with Haryana with a death rate of two-three and Punjab with a death rate below two. By 1996, Karnataka and Tamil Nadu joined Kerala with a death rate below one. For the 0-4 years age group, Kerala had achieved a death rate of less than 30 by 1971. Haryana, Karnataka and Punjab had been in the 30-40 death rate range. Madhya Pradesh, Assam, Andhra Pradesh, Maharastra and Tamil Nadu had been in the 40-50 rate range. By 1996, the death rate for this age group dropped to less than 5 in Kerala, and between 10-20 in Andhra Pradesh, Maharastra, Tamil Nadu, Karnataka and Punjab. Thus Kerala stood out among the states in the matter of reducing mortality of the very young population.

Within the 0-4 years age group, by confining the discussion to the 0-1 year age segment, and taking the two components of infant mortality rate, namely neonatal mortality rate (NNMR- deaths of less than 29 days after birth) and post-neonatal mortality rate (PNMR-deaths during the period of 29 days to less than one year), some unique features of Kerala may be brought out. States with a higher level of NNMR in 1975 reported higher percentage reductions and the states with lower level of NNMR in 1975 reported smaller reduction in mortality (Table 10.3). The exceptions to this general trend are Kerala showing one of the largest reductions (78 per cent) despite having had a fairly low level of NNMR by 1975 (34) and Madhya Pradesh and Orissa showing low rates of reductions (less than 25 per cent) at high initial levels of NNMR (over 80). Punjab and Maharastra tended towards the level of Kerala while Rajasthan tended towards the levels reached by Madhya Pradesh and Orissa. Overall, a strong tendency among the states to gravitate towards a certain average level of NNMR—the

TABLE 10.2

Death Rates of the Elderly in the Indian States, 1971-1997

State	*Death Rate 55-59 Years*		*Death Rate 60-64 Years*		*Death Rate 65-69 Years*		*Death Rate Above 70 Years*	
	1971	*1996*	*1971*	*1996*	*1971*	*1996*	*1971*	*1996*
All-India	21.2	15.7	34.9	26.7	48.4	36.9	109.3	86.4
Andhra Pradesh	25.2	17.7	40.6	28.7	52.7	33.5	122.0	82.5
Assam	29.5	21.5	45.1	36.7	77.1	51.8	131.4	101.1
Bihar	21.2*	17.7	40.7*	29.0	49.2*	44.5	100.0*	85.9
Gujarat	21.8	16.6	36.1	24.2	41.0	29.9	126.9	76.2
Haryana	13.0	11.3	21.0	19.2	24.4	25.7	103.7	70.1
Karnataka	22.1	16.4	31.9	26.1	55.3	36.7	100.1	81.4
Kerala	**16.3**	**11.0**	**23.6**	**20.6**	**43.5**	**28.0**	**103.8**	**81.1**
Madhya Pradesh	17.5	18.3	31.2	27.9	40.1	38.7	100.1	102.3
Maharastra	18.3	13.4	30.8	25.8	43.2	35.7	94.0	88.5
Orissa	25.5	17.0	46.2	32.2	69.3	41.7	140.6	91.2
Punjab	11.0	11.5	23.0	17.6	22.7	25.3	85.0	73.0
Rajasthan	20.8	12.2	32.9	23.5	52.4	36.1	93.0	83.3
Tamil Nadu	25.6	14.7	46.2	26.6	51.8	43.0	115.8	97.9
Uttar Pradesh	18.7	16.1	36.7	26.5	48.1	36.1	94.1	82.5
West Bengal	15.8*	16.5	38.5*	29.4	53.9*	40.0	115.4*	94.8

Note: * The figures are for the year 1981.

Source: Registrar General of India (1999). *Compendium of India's Fertility and Mortality Indicators 1971-97*. New Delhi.

TABLE 10.3

Reduction in Infant Mortality in the Indian States, 1975-97

NNMR in 1975	*Per cent Reduction in NNMR 1975-97*				*PNMR in 1975*	*Per cent Reduction in PNMR 1975-97*		
	>50	*40-50*	*30-40*	*20-30*		*>60*	*40-60*	*<40*
>80	Guj. UP	AP Assam	Raj.	MP Ori	>60	TN UP	MP Ori Raj.	
70-80		Bi			40-60	AP Guj.	Assam Punj. Har	Bi
60-70		Maha WB	Har		30-40		Maha	
50-60		Punj.	Kar	TN	<30	KER		Kar WB
<35	KER							

Notes: Abbreviations have their full forms in Table 10.1. For WB and Bihar, the series begin in 1981.

Source: Registrar General of India (1999). *Compendium of India's Fertility and Mortality Indicators 1971-97*. New Delhi.

range of roughly 40 to 50—is evident. Kerala alone has succeeded in breaking away from this tendency.

The inverse relationship observed between the initial level and the extent of reduction in the case of NNMR is not to be found in the case of PNMR. Some states with high levels of PNMR in 1975 have reported high rate of reduction in mortality (Tamil Nadu and Uttar Pradesh) whereas other states with similar levels of PNMR in 1975 have reported lower rates of reduction (Orissa, Madhya Pradesh and Rajasthan). The states with slightly lower level of PNMR in 1975 also reported similar pattern. On the whole, except for Kerala and Karnataka, all the states reported more than 50 per cent reduction in PNMR during 1975-97 irrespective of the levels reached in 1975. The result has been that in 1997 almost all the states, except Kerala, reported PNMR in the range 15-35. Already by 1975, Kerala had the lowest PNMR at 22, which fell by close to 80 per cent during 1975-97, the highest rate of reduction for any state in India. Thus, the remarkable achievement of Kerala in mortality reduction is almost entirely confined to the 0-1 year segment. The high survival rate of newborn children is the unique achievement of Kerala; the other major Indian states even in 1997 stood far away from the level reached by Kerala already by as early as 1975.

Factors of Mortality Decline in Kerala

As already indicated, the IMR in Kerala had been significantly lower than the all-India average by 1971 and the declining trend continued beyond that period. The long-term decline of IMR in Kerala falls in three phases: 1956 to 1966; 1967 to 1976; and beyond 1976. The decline in the first phase was of the order of 50 per 1000 live births. In the second phase it was just about 10 points, and in the third phase between 1976 and 1997, 44 points. Between 1976 and 1997, neonatal mortality declined from 33.9 to 7.5 and post neo-natal mortality from 22.1 to 4.7. And by 1997 infant mortality rate in Kerala was a mere 12 per 1000 live births. According to T.N. Krishnan, "the first phase of decline in Kerala's infant mortality can be attributed largely to the expansion in vaccination programmes against smallpox and other infectious diseases and possibly an expansion of health facilities in the northern region." The mortality decline beyond 1976 is attributed to two sets of factors: the epidemiological data seem to indicate that already by 1980, there had happened a decline in the proportion of children treated for diphtheria, whooping cough, measles and enteric fever in southern Kerala. The immunisation programmes launched by Kerala in the late 1970s seem to have played a role in this. It may be noted that in Kerala, maternal and child health programmes had been initiated a decade earlier than the launching of the WHO-sponsored Universal Immunization Programme in 1985, at the all-India level. TT immunisation (against tetanus) for pregnant women (1975-76), polio and typhoid vaccination (1980-81), BCG vaccination (1981-1982) and measles vaccination (1985-86) had already been launched in Kerala. The expansion of immunisation into the whole of Kerala during the 1980s must have played an important role in bringing down infant mortality.

Immunisation explains the decline in infant deaths caused by exogenous factors. The neonatal infant deaths declined substantially by about one-third in Kerala during this period. The causes of death peculiar to infancy, such as malposition, birth injury, cord infection and malnutrition, have obviously been controlled in Kerala. One of the factors accounting for this achievement could have been the availability of medical attention during pregnancy and childbirth. Some evidence to this effect is available in terms of institutional deliveries and medical attention during childbirth. In Kerala in 1973, 26 per cent of rural childbirths took place in medical institution. The proportion of births delivered in medical institutions in Kerala increased to 47 per cent by 1980, 88 per cent by 1992-93, and to 93 per cent by 1998-99.

It may be seen from Figure 10.1 that higher the proportion of institutional deliveries, lower is the NNMR. The lower proportion of institutional deliveries does not necessarily lead to higher NNMR as the states falling at the left hand corner of the chart suggest. Probably, there are other processes at work, which also bring down NNMR. But higher institutional deliveries necessarily bring down NNMR. Kerala and Goa with close to 90 per cent institutional deliveries in the 1990s report NNMR of lower than 20. Thus, the importance of immunisation and medical attention during pregnancy and childbirth in explaining the infant mortality reduction in Kerala beyond 1976, cannot be underestimated.

FIGURE 10.1

Relation between Medical Attention during Childbirth and NNMR Indian States, 1992-93 and 1998-99

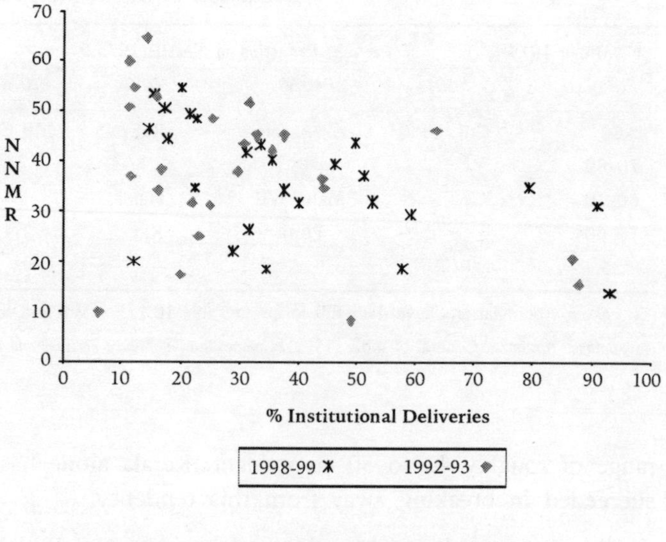

Source: National Family Health Survey, India 1992-93 and 1998-99.

Changing Disease Composition

As already indicated the load of communicable diseases has come down in Kerala; the load of lifestyle diseases and neoplasm has however been increasing. While a long-term analysis of the trend is not attempted owing to lack of evidence, the analysis of the trend during 1989-98 points to the transition that has

TABLE 10.4

Distribution of Medically Certified Deaths by Sex and Major Cause, Kerala, 1989-98

Major Cause Groups (ICD-9)	*Distribution (%) of Medically Certified Deaths by Sex and Major Cause during the Year*					
	1989		*1994*		*1998*	
	Male	*Female*	*Male*	*Female*	*Male*	*Female*
I. Infectious and parasitic diseases	14.8	16.2	11.7	13.5	8.2	7.1
II. Neoplasms	9.1	8.0	9.5	9.5	13.0	10.9
III. Endocrine nutritional and other diseases	2.5	2.1	4.1	4.1	4.6	5.0
IV. Dis. of blood and blood forming organs	0.8	1.2	1.1	1.1	0	0
V. Mental disorders	0	0	0	0	0.2	0.1
VI. Dis. of the nervous system	.4	4.0	1.9	2.1	2.8	3.0
VII. Dis. of the circulatory system	36.3	32.7	37.7	32.4	30.9	31.7
VIII. Dis. of respiratory system	7.3	7.9	7.5	6.5	7.2	5.9
IX. Dis. of digestive system	5.1	2.4	6.1	3.4	8.5	5.2
X. Dis. of the genito urinary system	1.9	1.8	1.5	1.1	2.8	3.3
XI. Complications of pregnancy		1.2		4.0		0.6
XII. Dis. of the skin etc	0	0	0	0	0.3	0.7
XIII. Dis. of the musculoskeletal system etc	0	0	0	0	0.2	0.7
XIV. Congenital anomalies	0.8	1.3	0.8	0.8	2.3	3.9
XV. Conditions originating in perinatal period	8.8	11.9	8.9	13.2	3.7	8.4
XVI. Ill defined conditions	1.8	1.2	0	0	1.4	1.1
XVII. Injury and poisoning	8.3	6.9	9.3	8.3	13.9	12.6

Source: Central Bureau of Health Intelligence. *Health Information of India* (various years). Ministry of Health and Family Welfare, New Delhi.

taken place in Kerala (Table 10.4). It is evident that the proportion of deaths owing to infectious and parasitic diseases has come down sharply and that the trend has been continuing also since then; in fact their share in the total had come down to less than 10 per cent by 1998. A similar trend is observable with regard to perinatal causes as well (group xv). The major causes of death are diseases of the circulatory, respiratory and digestive systems (Groups vii, viii and ix), that account for over 40 per cent of all deaths; Kerala has thus moved into a phase of predominance of non-communicable diseases. Two striking aspects of this transition are the increasing share of neoplasms and of deaths due to injury and poisoning. While neoplasms had accounted for about 8 per cent of the deaths by 1989, the next 10 years saw its share increasing to 13 per cent for males and 11 per cent for females. Injury and poisoning accounted for about 8 per cent of the deaths in 1989 and close to 14 per cent by 1998.

While at the all-India level, infections and parasitic diseases accounted for about 17 per cent of all deaths and in Madhya Pradesh for over 30 per cent of the deaths, in Kerala and Tamil Nadu they accounted for less than 9 per cent (Table 10.5). Similar is the case with perinatal conditions. At the other end, diseases of the circulatory and respiratory system accounted for close to 40 per cent of the total deaths in Kerala compared to about 30 per cent at the all-India level and around 25 per cent in Madhya Pradesh and Orissa. Most significant is the difference with regard to neoplasms; while no other state reported a share higher than 5 per cent, in Kerala they accounted for around 13 per cent. Thus, there has been a shift away from communicable diseases to life style diseases in Kerala.

Low Mortality and High Morbidity

Kerala is well known the world over for achieving high levels of life expectancy and low levels of mortality, in particular infant mortality, at fairly low levels of income. There are few regions in the world with comparable achievements. However, along with such achievements, Kerala reports one of the highest levels of morbidity (perceived ill-health). The morbidity rate for Kerala is twice the all-India average in the rural areas and over 50 per cent higher in the urban areas (Table 10.6). Further, the rural morbidity rate is more than 40 per cent higher than the urban morbidity rate; such a huge differential is not found in any of the other major Indian states.

TABLE 10.5

Proportion in Total Deaths by Some Major Cause of Death by States, 1998

State	*Infectious and Parasitic Diseases*		*Neoplasms*		*Diseases of the Circulatory System*		*Diseases of the Respiratory System Perinatal Period*		*Certain Conditions Originating in the*		*Injury and Poisoning*	
	Male	*Female*	*Male*	*Female*	*Male*	*Female*	*Male*	*Female*	*Male*	*Female*	*Male*	*Female*
All-India	17.2	15.2	3.0	3.4	25.7	24.3	7.5	7.1	7.7	8.2	11.8	12.8
Andhra Pradesh	9.8	9.2	2.8	3.1	33.0	28.7	13.0	9.3	8.3	9.4	10.5	16.4
Gujarat	15.7	14.8	1.6	1.2	21.5	18.5	5.0	2.5	8.4	9.5	16.4	22.9
Haryana	15.2	12.5	2.4	2.2	28.0	26.5	7.1	6.3	7.3	5.8	20.4	21.4
Karnataka	16.5	13.7	4.4	4.6	22.6	21.3	7.1	5.3	9.0	9.9	14.1	17.4
Kerala	**8.2**	**7.1**	**13.0**	**10.9**	**30.9**	**31.7**	**7.2**	**5.9**	**3.7**	**8.4**	**13.9**	**12.6**
Madhya Pradesh	34.2	30.5	1.7	1.6	24.0	19.6	8.3	7.4	8.4	6.1	9.5	13.7
Maharastra	17.8	13.9	2.8	3.9	26.4	26.7	8.6	8.8	7.3	8.5	9.3	9.8
Orissa	20.9	19.5	2.1	1.9	17.5	17.4	8.2	6.9	11.9	9.2	10.4	9.1
Punjab	10.2	9.0	3.3	3.8	44.1	56.4	4.4	4.0	3.5	1.5	14.1	8.8
Rajasthan	17.2	16.6	2.1	1.8	12.7	12.7	7.7	7.9	11.7	9.9	19.2	17.2
Tamil Nadu	8.9	8.3	3.7	4.5	38.0	31.9	4.9	4.9	6.4	7.7	13.6	16.9

Source: Central Bureau of Health Intelligence. *Health Information of India 2004*. Ministry of Health and Family Welfare, New Delhi.

The morbidity pattern by age and residence suggests that, in Kerala rural morbidity - both acute and chronic—is higher than urban morbidity for all age groups (Table 10.7). Acute morbidity is significantly higher in Kerala among the young (0-14 years) and the productive age groups (15-59 years); but among the elderly (60+ years), acute morbidity is lower than the all-India average. Unlike acute morbidity, chronic morbidity increases with age and is higher in both rural and urban Kerala than in other states. However, urban morbidity by age groups in Kerala is comparable to that in Punjab; but as regards rural morbidity the figures for Kerala are higher (Table 10.8).

TABLE 10.6

Number (per 1000) of Persons Reporting ailment (PAP) and Number Reporting Commencement of any Ailment (PPC) During Last 15 Days, 1995-96

State	*Rural*		*Urban*	
	PAP	*PPC*	*PAP*	*PPC*
Andhra Pradesh	64	35	61	31
Assam	80	52	86	57
Bihar	36	18	41	22
Gujarat	46	27	36	21
Haryana	61	34	63	24
Karnataka	45	24	40	22
Kerala	**118**	**60**	**88**	**43**
Madhya Pradesh	41	26	38	22
Maharastra	52	29	48	26
Orissa	62	43	62	47
Punjab	76	33	85	37
Rajasthan	28	15	33	19
Tamil Nadu	52	31	58	37
Uttar Pradesh	61	33	72	41
West Bengal	65	38	65	42
India	55	31	54	30

Source: National Sample Survey Organisation. "Morbidity and Treatment of Ailments", *NSS 52nd Round*, July 1995-June 1996, Report No. 441(52/25.0/1).

Healthcare in Kerala

The Public Healthcare Sector

The state has been devoting the bulk of public funds on infrastructure and social services, and in particular on health. The investment on health is guided by three policy coordinates: a public (allopathic) medical institution[2] in every *panchayat* (a development administration unit equal to or larger than a revenue village), medical education under the government to ensure adequate supply of medical personnel and encouragement to traditional medical systems.

At the time of reorganisation of the state in 1956, the Travancore-Cochin part had been far advanced in terms of the number of government medical

2. The healthcare sector in Kerala consists of three distinct systems of medicine, namely allopathy, ayurveda and homoeopathy. Tables 10.9 and 10.10 provide information on the allopathic system only, where as Table 10.14 provides information on all the three systems.

TABLE 10.7

Number of Persons Reporting Ailment During the Last 15 Days per 1000 Persons by Age Type of Ailment, Acute, 1995-96

State	Rural by Age in Years					Urban by Age in Years				
	0-14	*15-39*	*40-59*	*60+*	*All*	*0-14*	*15-39*	*40-59*	*60+*	*All*
Andhra Pradesh	51	33	38	98	43	53	32	37	69	41
Assam	95	40	79	148	72	90	51	63	226	74
Bihar	26	21	27	61	26	34	27	31	54	32
Gujarat	37	25	38	93	35	36	16	26	46	26
Haryana	53	33	54	87	47	38	43	51	106	46
Karnataka	25	24	43	77	31	32	23	26	59	28
Kerala	**114**	**57**	**80**	**88**	**80**	**85**	**51**	**51**	**66**	**61**
Madhya Pradesh	35	30	40	69	36	33	24	29	74	30
Maharastra	33	27	45	92	37	46	29	30	50	35
Orissa	52	50	62	102	56	72	41	39	72	52
Punjab	59	51	56	73	56	71	57	45	83	60
Rajasthan	22	17	15	84	22	29	15	28	48	24
Tamil Nadu	42	29	43	92	39	61	31	43	74	44
Uttar Pradesh	52	36	52	100	49	65	45	60	88	57
West Bengal	54	31	48	126	47	61	36	51	81	49
India	45	32	45	93	42	49	32	39	69	41

Source: Same as Table 10.6.

TABLE 10.8

Number of Persons Reporting Ailment During the Last 15 Days per 1000 Persons by Age Type of Ailment: Chronic, 1995-96

State	Rural by Age in Years					Urban by Age in Years				
	0-14	*15-39*	*40-59*	*60+*	*All*	*0-14*	*15-39*	*40-59*	*60+*	*All*
Andhra Pradesh	4	12	30	205	22	3	11	38	154	20
Assam	1	3	15	112	9	3	7	27	82	13
Bihar	2	7	17	77	10	2	5	20	88	10
Gujarat	3	8	20	54	11	2	5	21	77	10
Haryana	3	10	36	50	14	3	13	34	84	17
Karnataka	2	6	17	124	14	1	4	23	121	12
Kerala	**10**	**16**	**65**	**161**	**38**	**7**	**14**	**37**	**129**	**27**
Madhya Pradesh	1	4	10	32	5	2	5	18	39	7
Maharastra	4	5	25	90	15	2	7	23	87	13
Orissa	3	3	19	15	6	3	8	21	33	10
Punjab	5	11	39	102	20	6	17	52	137	25
Rajasthan	1	5	12	33	6	2	5	22	58	9
Tamil Nadu	3	9	21	60	13	3	7	26	87	14
Uttar Pradesh	3	11	26	44	12	2	11	30	101	15
West Bengal	6	14	44	94	19	4	8	34	71	16
India	3	9	24	80	13	3	8	27	89	14

Source: Same as Table 10.6.

TABLE 10.9

Distribution of Government Medical Institutions (Allopathy) by Districts, Kerala

District	*1960*	*1965*	*1970*	*1975*	*1980*	*1985*	*1990*	*2002*
Thiruvananthapuram	53	57	53	80	91	97	121	118
Kollam	35	50	53	90	92	97	121	91
Alappuzha*	38	48	54	78	81	84	100	94
Kottayam	27	39	42	59	61	64	95	90
Idukki	14	19	16	41	46	50	59	64
Ernakulam	42	57	62	81	87	100	116	120
Thrissur	38	62	62	86	87	105	113	123
Palakkad	30	45	55	76	90	97	113	115
Malappuram	19	31	44	71	74	90	114	125
Kozhikode	14	23	31	60	59	67	87	96
Wayanad	11	10	15	23	24	30	42	40
Kannur	20	26	33	72	72	84	97	106
Kasaragod	7	16	21	44	49	51	61	60
Kerala	**348**	**483**	**541**	**861**	**913**	**1016**	**1239**	**1310***

Note: *- including Pathanamthitta till 1990, for the year 2002, Alappuzha figure does not include Pathanamthitta.

Source: Government of Kerala, *Administration Reports of the Health Department*, Various Years.

Government of Kerala, *Economic Review*, various years.

institutions in comparison with Malabar, which had been part of the erstwhile Madras presidency. In 1960, while the districts south of Palakkad constituting the erstwhile Travancore-Cochin region, had one medical institution (allopathic) each for less than 45,000 population, the corresponding rate had been one medical institution for over 65,000 population in the northern districts, comprising erstwhile Malabar district of Madras Presidency, the Kerala average having been one institution per 50,000 population.

The period 1960-1975 witnessed two developments. The density of medical institutions increased rapidly to reach the level of one institution per 25,000 population by 1975. Secondly, inter-district variations were greatly reduced with almost all the *panchayats* in the state having at least one institution (Table 10.9). The period beyond 1980 witnessed further equalisation and expansion. Following the recommendations of the Pai Committee (The High Power Committee)[3] in 1979, popular demand arose for the provision of equal facilities in all *taluk* hospitals and a medical institution for every 20,000 population. Note the government reply on these issues in 1981 following the vociferous demand by the members of the subcommittee on social services. The government reply ran as follows:

"The High Power Committee in their report had suggested to improve the services of all *taluk* hospitals and to bring them on an equal footing. The Committee had also recommended that the *taluk* level hospitals should be provided with basic specialties like medicine, surgery, gynaecology and pediatrics and subspecialties like ENT, dental, eye, orthopedic and STD. When these recommendations were implemented, the present state of affairs would be completely changed and more or less equal facilities and status would be available in all of them. Steps had been taken to implement the recommendations of the High Power Committee" (Government of Kerala, 1981: 4).

Regarding the second issue, the Government said:

"It was stated on behalf of the government that Pai Committee had recommended that, in stages, a second dispensary may be started in each *panchayat* having a population of 20,000 or more. The report, the committee was informed, was being considered by the government" (Government of Kerala, 1981: 13).

The policy was gradually implemented and by 1990 most of the districts had one medical institution for about 20,000 population.

The expansion of facilities under the Indian system of medicine (Ayurveda) has also made progress more or

3. The High Power Committee was constituted by the Government of Kerala in 1977 to review the working of the hospital sytem under the Health Services Department and suggest measures for the rational development of health services in the state.

TABLE 10.10

Distribution of Government Hospital Beds (Allopathy) by Districts, Kerala

District	*1960*	*1965*	*1970*	*1975*	*1980*	*1985*	*1990*	*2002*
Thiruvananthapuram	3131	3918	4065	4910	5094	5684	6384	7483
Kollam	810	1182	1310	1755	2012	2188	2539	2476
Alappuzha*	1607	2027	2343	3164	3336	3690	4220	4887
Kottayam	775	1292	1720	2300	2603	2816	3098	4398
Idukki	71	116	118	261	351	446	795	872
Ernakulam	1633	2064	2174	2456	2748	3159	3768	5328
Thrissur	1947	2825	2839	3097	3462	3666	4322	4442
Palakkad	605	917	1017	1277	1537	1775	2230	2450
Malappuram	245	411	720	819	1036	1242	1830	2379
Kozhikode	1215	1905	2673	3314	3502	3798	4284	5757
Wayanad	90	127	163	227	336	446	749	811
Kannur	749	1076	1203	1692	1825	2288	2374	2815
Kasaragod	98	149	167	364	552	581	660	755
Kerala	**12976**	**18009**	**20512**	**25636**	**28394**	**31779**	**37253**	**46800**

Note: *- Including Pathamthitta. Also, Alappuzha figure does not include Pathamthitta for 2002 but the total includes Pathanamthitta.

Source: Same as of Table 10.9.

TABLE 10.11

Distribution of Medical Institutions (Ayurveda) by Districts

District	*1960*	*1970*	*1975*	*1980*	*1985*	*1991*	*2002*
Thiruvananthapuram	18	43	46	51	58	61	78
Kollam	24	35	42	45	40	46	60
Alappuzha*	28	39	50	49	41	46	65
Kottayam	16	19	23	29	31	35	50
Idukki			18	19	22	28	34
Ernakulam	30	42	34	43	50	58	74
Thrissur	51	57	61	63	71	78	94
Palakkad	22	34	44	45	46	54	79
Malappuram		24	45	48	54	61	76
Kozhikode	16	29	44	41	35	41	59
Kannur	15	39	75	66	38	46	68
Kerala	**220**	**361**	**482**	**499**	**551**	**554**	**845**

Note: *- includes Pathanamthitta till 1980, and the Kerala total includes Pathanamthitta.

Source: Same as of Table 10.9.

less on similar lines. The distribution of facilities across the districts had been, at the beginning, skewed in favour of the southern districts. By the mid-1970s equality was achieved; the northern districts became comparable with the southern districts and the distribution corresponded with that of allopathic institutions. Whereas in the case of allopathic institutions, a further expansion took place between 1980 and 1990 to achieve the Pai Committee norm, the expansion of Ayurvedic institutions followed the earlier norm (Table 10.9 and 10.11).

It is evident from the deliberations of the Committee that public accountability conforms to the three features discussed by Paul (Paul, 1992). Government accountability to the public rested with the political leadership at the macro level. Public accountability has been on inputs and not on outputs; and accountability is enforced in a top-down fashion. It is hardly ever the case that quality of care is discussed in any detail.

Kerala started its first medical college in 1951 with about 100 seats. The number of medical colleges increased to five by the mid-1980s with about 750 seats for the bachelors training and about 200 seats for postgraduate specialty training in about 18 specialties. The number of teachers increased from around 200 in 1960 to over 1000 in 1990. The standards of medical education in India are set by the Medical Council of India, which has been enforcing these standards. This would mean maintaining certain norms regarding the student-teacher ratio, infrastructure facilities and hospital beds over which expenditure had to be incurred.

In a situation of developing fiscal crisis, the health sector has escaped any sharp cut in expenditure. Government expenditure on health as a percentage of total government expenditure has shown only a very mild decline since the late 1980s. But the per capita government expenditure on healthcare has not fallen as the total expenditure has been rising in Kerala. In the face of an expenditure squeeze and growth in medical education, and facilities under the two systems of medicine, the share of the allopathic sector in the total expenditure has fallen.

The three policy coordinates have come with three distinct types of expenditures. Expansion of medical education has come with a proportionate increase in expenditure on account of expanding facilities and teaching staff in accordance with the standards set by the Medical Council of India. Any failure on this count would have run the risk of losing recognition for the degrees awarded. The result is a steady increase in the share of expenditure on medical education in the total expenditure on curative services from 10.21 per cent in 1977-1979 to 17.05 per cent in 1990-1992 (Table 10.12).

TABLE 10.12

Distribution (%) of Expenditure on Curative Services

	1977-79	*1980-89*	*1990-92*
Allopathic Medical Services	70.16	67.06	58.32
Other Systems of Medicine	7.96	9.24	12.32
Medical Education	10.21	12.89	17.05
Employees State Insurance	10.11	8.99	10.08
Direction & Administration	1.56	1.82	2.45
Total	100.00	100.00	100.00

Source: Ramankutty and Panikar, 1995.

The steady expansion of services under the Indian system of medicine led to its share in total expenditure going up steadily from less than 8 per cent in 1977-1979 to about 13 per cent in 1990-1992. The share of allopathic services fell from over 70 per cent of the total in 1977-1979 to about 58 per cent in 1990-92. As the number of allopathic medical institutions increased during this period by over 40 per cent, the expenditure largely went into disbursement of pay and allowances. The share of pay and allowances which had been only 37 per cent in 1960 increased to 55 per cent by 1975 and further to 63 per cent by 1990. Such an increase has left little resources for medicines (the share of which fell from 39 per cent in 1960 to 25 per cent in 1990), or maintenance and upgradation of facilities (Sadanandan, 1993).

The three policy coordinates have led to a situation in which locational access to institutions and doctors has been provided but the supply of medicines and facilities has steadily come down. Quality of care has obviously been on the decline. A clear indication of such a decline is the trend in the total number of patients being treated in government facilities (allopathic) under the Directorate of Health Services (DHS). The total number of outpatients treated in the facilities of the DHS had increased from about 11 million in 1957-58 to about 31 million in 1977-78; from then on the number declined and stood below 27 million in the early 1990s. There has been some reversal of this trend in more recent years, the number of outpatients treated in public facilities having increased to 40 million by 2004. The total number of inpatients treated in the facilities of the DHS also showed a similar trend. The number had increased from about half a million in 1957-58 to over 1.5 million in 1980-81; from then on the number declined reaching a level of below 1.4 million in 1991-92 and increased to 1.84 million in 2002. The decline in the number being treated during a period when the population has been growing and ageing is a clear sign of disenchantment of the people with the public healthcare sector.

The disenchantment with the public healthcare sector has led to the phenomenal expansion of private medical institutions. Kerala had 1016 medical institutions (allopathic) and about 32,000 beds under the government in 1986; the corresponding figures were 1278 institutions and 43619 beds by 2004. The private sector had 3565 institutions with 49,000 beds in 1986; the number increased to 4288 institutions and 68,000 beds by 1995 (Government of Kerala, 1986; 1996), the latest year for which details of private sector health institutions are available. More than the numbers, it is the specialities and other facilities the private institutions offer that give an indication of the nature of demand that was going unmet by the government institutions. In 1995, nearly 45 per cent of the institutions had inpatient facility, 25 per cent had operation facilities, 40 per cent of the doctors had postgraduate degrees, and 30 per cent had at least one of the higher specialities. Already in 1986-87, of the total number of patients hospitalised, only 43.38 per cent in rural areas and 55.65 per cent in urban areas were hospitalised in government hospitals. The proportions must have come down further by now. More importantly, in the rural areas, the proportion did not show much of a variation across decile groups; in the urban areas a relatively higher proportion of the poor approached government hospitals, than the rich (Sarvekshana, 1991).

In sum, there has been a squeeze on recurrent non-wage expenditure of the curative services (under allopathy). Two factors have led to such a development: Firstly, medical education is not amenable to cuts in expenditure as recognition of the medical degree is regulated by a national level organisation. Secondly, public accountability of the healthcare sector has largely been in the hands of the political leadership at the macro level and has been only in terms of inputs, such as number of health posts and number of specialities, and not in terms of processes or outcomes. Thus, the emerging situation is one in which there is an adequate supply of medical personnel and universal access to healthcare but the quality of service has gone on deteriorating.

The high differentiability of the product, its infrequent use (in contrast with water supply, electricity or telecommunication) and the easy availability of private healthcare services have considerably weakened the 'voice' response of the public. The 'exit' response has been further speeded up by the growing private practice by physicians employed in government service (Jayachandran, 1996), a factor which would have brought down the cost differential between the 'voice' and the 'exit' options even further.

The Private Healthcare Sector

Historically, there were three aspects to the introduction of allopathic medicine in Kerala, especially in the Travancore and Cochin part: compulsion in public health programmes, support to private medical practitioners and encouragement to people from all classes of society to take up the profession. Although systematic information has been available on the private healthcare sector (allopathy) supported by the government under the head of grants-in-aid institutions, information is lacking on the private sector as a whole.

A glimpse of the size of the private sector is provided in the candid admission by the government in the Second Five Year Plan document (1958). The Second Plan set the general aim of health programmes as the expansion of health services to bring them within the reach of all the people. Having set the aim thus, it admitted that, "The emphasis is not so much on multiplying the number of institutions as on consolidation since the field will be *served by private practitioners* as also by other systems of medicine" (emphasis added) (Government of Kerala, 1958: 47). Obviously, the field was already being served by a large number of private practitioners and their number was growing in the face of which planned investment by the public sector in such endeavours was thought of as mere duplication.

A comparative picture of the size and share of the private sector in the total is available for the year 1979. At the all-India level, in the early 1980s, out of about 29,000 hospitals and dispensaries, 33 per cent were in the private sector; in terms of hospital beds, of the 536,000 beds, about 27 per cent were in the private sector (Table 10.13). There was considerable variation in the number and the share of the private sector in terms of facilities and beds across the states of India. Almost 50 per cent of the facilities were located in the four states of Maharashtra, Gujarat, Karnataka and Kerala. In terms of the number of beds, these four states accounted for almost 40 per cent of the total. The share of the private sector in the total number of facilities was the highest at 78 per cent in Gujarat followed by Maharashtra (69 per cent) and Kerala (47 per cent); West Bengal and Andhra Pradesh (about 22 per cent) followed Kerala, but at a great distance. In the rest of the states, only less than 10 per cent of the facilities were in the private sector. In terms of hospital beds, Gujarat topped with the share of the private sector at 51 per cent; Kerala came second at 41 per cent, and Maharashtra with 37 per cent. In the rest of the states, the share of the private sector was below 30 per cent. Thus, the overall share of the private sector in India in the early 1980s was not insignificant. Kerala, which had a large healthcare sector compared to the other states of India, also had one of the largest private healthcare sectors in India.

One of the distinct characteristics of the private sector and the overall healthcare sector in Kerala is its rural orientation. As is evident from Table 10.13, while

TABLE 10.13

Distribution of Hospitals and Beds in the Indian States (1984)

States	*Hospitals and Dispensaries*			*Beds*			*Share of Pvt. in Total (%)*		*Share of Rural in Total (%)*	
	Govt.	*Pvt.*	*Total*	*Govt.*	*Pvt.*	*Total*	*Hospitals*	*Beds*	*Hospitals*	*Beds*
Andhra Pradesh	1080	303	1383	24904	11103	36007	21.91	30.84	26.67	0.33
Assam	517	30	547	7691	2086	9777	5.48	21.34	34.23	2.88
Bihar (1981)	1011	217	1228	19053	8447	27500	17.67	30.72	8.41	2.61
Gujarat	637	2207	2844	19484	20600	40084	77.60	51.39	8.32	9.09
Haryana	306	23	329	4548	2566	8114	6.99	31.62	9.20	5.69
Himachal Pradesh	290	10	300	3863	447	4310	3.33	10.37	40.00	4.21
Jammu & Kashmir (1980)*	30	5	683	3667	276	4128	0.73	6.69	5.71	1.52
Karnataka	1727	54	1781	26931	6588	33519	3.03	19.65	20.17	9.12
Kerala (1979)	804	704	1508	26338	18439	44777	46.68	41.18	78.50	0.22
Madhya Pradesh*	921	—	—	17213	—	—	—	—	—	—
Maharashtra	310	220	7530	53249	31343	84592	69.32	37.05	12.48	8.37
Orissa (1983)	549	56	605	10111	1471	11582	9.26	12.70	47.23	0.09
Punjab	958	47	2005	18145	2925	21070	2.34	13.88	43.36	2.12
Rajasthan	493	94	1587	17853	2059	19912	5.92	10.34	10.00	5.92
Tamil Nadu (1982)	963	79	1042	32606	8652	41258	7.58	20.97	25.80	9.10
Uttar Pradesh	205	223	2428	39882	11875	51757	9.18	22.94	10.35	5.40
West Bengal	637	186	823	43800	6372	50172	22.60	12.70	36.14	18.33
Total _	18619	694	28961**	393217	142988	536370**	33.47	26.65	26.38	13.63

Note: Govt. includes local bodies.
Private includes voluntary organisations.
* Data incomplete
** Some facilities and beds not classified are included in the total.

Source: Government of India, *Health Statistics of India 1984*, Central Bureau of Health Intelligence, Ministry of Health and Family Welfare, New Delhi.

Gujarat and Maharastra with fairly high shares of private health facilities in the total had one of the lowest rural shares, Kerala had almost 80 per cent of all the hospitals and over 50 per cent of the beds in the rural areas. Given the share of the private sector in the total, an overall 80 per cent of the hospitals in the rural areas could only be consistent with at least 60 per cent of the private facilities in the rural areas. Obviously, in Kerala, private healthcare facilities are located predominantly in the rural areas.

The private healthcare sector in Kerala showed a phenomenal growth in the 1980s and the 1990s. For 1986 and 1995, authentic information on the private sector is provided by the surveys conducted by the Bureau of Economics and Statistics of the Government of Kerala. By 1986, the share of the private sector had increased to 78 per cent of the institutions and 58 per cent of the hospital beds. By 1995, while the share of the private in the total number of institutions had remained almost unchanged at 77 per cent, the share in the total number of beds rose to 62 per cent. Thus, the private sector continued its vigorous growth in the 1980s and the 1990s overtaking the government sector in terms of the number of institutions and beds.

The vigorous growth of the private healthcare sector has meant that by the mid-1990s, Kerala had one medical institution per 2.60 square kilometre area (Table 10.14). The high density of private healthcare institutions provided high physical access to healthcare. As already indicated, the private healthcare facilities are not confined to a few districts or urban pockets in Kerala. They are spread all over the state.

The available information on the number of facilities and beds does not permit a review of developments for the period preceding 1979. But the information on the number of medical practitioners registered with the Medical Council together with the numbers working in the public sector may be used to develop an approximate picture of the size of the private healthcare sector. Both the surveys of 1986 and 1995 of private

TABLE 10.14

The Density of Health Care Facilities (All Systems) in Kerala, 1995

District	*GMI*	*PMI*	*TMI*	*G Bed*	*P Bed*	*T Bed*	*Area/ GMI*	*Area/PMI*	*Area/TMI*
Thiruvananthapuram	7	32	39	250	177	427	9.92	2.36	1.9
Kollam	7	42	49	97	312	409	15.1	2.47	2.13
Pathanamthitta	11	53	64	96	378	475	19.57	4.21	3.46
Alappuzha	8	52	60	208	192	400	8.78	1.35	1.17
Kottayam	9	78	87	202	432	633	13.68	1.54	1.38
Idukki	11	51	62	93	371	464	41.14	9.04	7.41
Ernakulam	8	50	58	150	412	562	10.89	1.7	1.47
Thrissur	9	34	43	159	325	484	13.01	3.21	2.58
Palakkad	8	32	40	94	94	187	22.74	5.89	4.68
Malappuram	7	32	39	77	128	205	15.99	3.63	2.96
Kozhikode	7	51	58	177	155	331	13.47	1.76	1.56
Wayanad	11	35	46	139	269	408	28.8	9.15	6.94
Kannur	8	41	49	104	182	286	16.66	3.19	2.64
Kasargod	11	39	50	79	122	201	17.32	4.71	3.7
Kerala	**8**	**43**	**51**	**143**	**244**	**387**	**16.34**	**3.08**	**2.59**

Note: GMI: Government Medical Institution per 100,000 population.
PMI: Private " " " "
TMI: Total " " " "
G Bed: Government Number of Beds per 100,000 population
P Bed: Private " " " "
T Bed: Total " " " "
Area: In Square Kilometres.

Source: Government of Kerala, 1986.

institutions provide data on the number of doctors in the private institutions (6345 in 1986 and 10388 in 1995). Information on the number of doctors working in the government institutions, including the medical colleges, is available from government publications: over 4500 in 1986 and close to 5000 in 1995. The total number of medical practitioners registered with the Medical Council is also available: 15,470 in 1986 and 23,813 in 1995. The number of doctors in private institutions bears a ratio of approximately 0.55 to the number registered with the Council less the number working in the public institutions in 1986 and 1995. If we use this ratio[4] to extrapolate backwards, it may be inferred that by 1970 the private healthcare sector had been almost as large as the public sector. In 1960, for every six doctors working under the government, there were four working in the private sector. The early 1960s being a period of rapid expansion of the healthcare sector under the government, the relative share of the private sector declined to some small extent. Growth picked up in the 1970s and accelerated in the 1980s and the 1990s (Table 10.15).

TABLE 10.15

Estimated Size of the Private Health Care Sector in Kerala (Allopathy)

Year	*Number of Medical Practitioners*	*Doctors in Govt. Service*	*Doctors in Private Sector*
1995	23813	5000	10388 (0.55)
1986	15470	4500	6345 (0.58)
1971	5516	2000	1934
1965	2807	1500	720
1960	1842	860	550

Notes: The figures in parentheses are the ratio of number of doctors in the private sector to the number of medical practitioners less those in government service. The figures for 1971, 1965, and 1960 in column 3 are obtained by applying the ratio of 0.55 on the figures of columns 1 and 2.

Sources: For Column 1, and for 1971, 1986, and 1995 in Column 2, Government of Kerala. *Economic Review* (various issues).

Government of Kerala. *Statistics for Planning* (various issues).

For 1960 and 1965 in Column 2, Sadanandan, Table III. 10.

For 1986 and 1995 in Column 3,

Government of Kerala. *Report on the Survey of Private Medical Institutions in Kerala*, 1986 and 1995 respectively.

4. The number of doctors in the private sector for 1988 and 1995 could be underestimates. Hence, the ratio of 0.55 allows for 'leakage' from the system on account of out-migration, non-practice, etc.

The share of the private healthcare sector reckoned in terms of the number of institutions, the number of beds, or the number of doctors, has been very large for a long time. In this respect it is comparable to the school system in Kerala: By the late 1950s, the school system consisted of 9500 primary and secondary schools, more than 60 per cent of which were run by private management (Jeffrey, 1992: 155). The bulk of the healthcare and the educational institutions in Kerala have come up in the private sector. The number of private healthcare institutions exceeded their public sector counterparts by the early 1980s.

The Public-Private and the System Mix in Kerala

The healthcare environment in Kerala has become a vast and complex infrastructure over the past four decades. It has a public-private mix with the private growing both in the urban and the rural areas. The health infrastructure is also characterised by various systems. This section seeks to present a picture of the health infrastructure in terms of its public-private and system mix across the districts of the state in the mid-1990s.

The health infrastructure under the state government has more than 6000 institutions, including subcentres. At the apex of the system are the medical colleges, geographically dispersed over the length of the state. All the 14 districts of the state have a general/district hospital each and numerous *taluka* hospitals. The most numerous are the PHCs and their subcentres. There are also institutions attending to infectious diseases, such as TB and Leprosy, and for both women and children. There are hospitals with beds attached to most of these institutions, totalling over 30,000. In addition, the medical college hospitals have close to 8000 beds in all.

More than 90 per cent of the government medical institutions are located in rural areas (Table 10.16). About 40 per cent of the hospital beds are also located in rural areas. Rural concentration is very high (over 65 per cent) in Idukki, Wayanad and Malappuram, and very low (less than 30 per cent) in Kannur, Kozhikode and Thiruvananthapuram.

The government has also supported the traditional systems of medicine, Ayurveda and Homeopathy, by establishing medical colleges and by setting up dispensaries and hospitals in these systems. There are altogether 690 Ayurvedic institutions and 415 Homeopathy institutions in the state. The total number of beds are limited compared to Allopathy but are fairly well-distributed over the districts of the state.

The private sector has grown phenomenally in Kerala and has facilities under all the three systems of medicine. Out of a total of 12618 private medical institutions, 4288 are Allopathic, 4922 Ayurvedic and 3118 Homoeopathic. But across the districts there exists considerable variation in the relative position of the different systems. While the districts south of Ernakulam have almost equal number of institutions of the three systems, the northern districts have relatively more of Ayurvedic and Homoeopathic facilities. In the south, Thiruvananthapuram is an exception.

In contrast to the number of institutions, the number of hospital beds is confined mainly to the Allopathic hospitals. Out of 70924 hospital beds in the private sector, 67517 are under the Allopathy system. Nearly 50 per cent of the hospital beds in the private sector are located in the four districts of Ernakulam, Thrissur, Kollam and Kottayam. Only less than 25 per cent of the total number of beds are located in the six northern districts taken together.

Taking public and private facilities under all the three systems of medicine for all the districts in Kerala as a whole, it may be seen that there is one medical institution per 2000 population and one hospital bed

TABLE 10.16

Distribution of Government Institutions and Beds (Allopathy) by Districts and Location, 1997

District	*Medical Institutions*			*Hospital Beds*		
	R	*U*	*T*	*R*	*U*	*T*
Thiruvananthapuram	92	23	115	1559	5657	7216
Kollam	83	5	88	1151	919	2070
Pathanamthitta	59	4	63	467	474	941
Alappuzha	81	9	90	1706	2300	4006
Kottayam	77	7	84	1228	2126	3354
Idukki	62	2	64	566	274	840
Ernakulam	95	21	116	1397	2641	4038
Thrissur	112	10	122	1990	2129	4119
Palakkad	105	7	112	1311	877	2188
Malappuram	114	9	183	990	1171	2161
Kozhikode	83	12	95	487	3908	4395
Wayanad	37	2	39	768	43	811
Kannur	94	9	103	573	1542	2115
Kasargod	56	4	60	288	401	689
Kerala	**1150**	**124**	**1274**	**14481**	**24482**	**38943**

Source: GoK, *Economic Review, 1998*. State Planning Board, Thiruvananthapuram.

per 250 population (Table 10.14). On an average a person could access a medical institution within a distance of one kilometre.

The variation in the density of medical institutions across the districts of Kerala is considerable. The density of government medical institutions (per lakh population) is higher in Pathanamthitta, Idukki, Wayanad and Kasargod, largely because the density of population in these districts is lower, as is evident from the area covered per government medical institution. The density of private medical institutions is lower than the state average in Wayanad, Malappuram, Palakkad, Thrissur and Thiruvananthapuram. It is significantly higher in Kozhikode and the geographical belt from Pathanamthitta in the south to Ernakulam in the central region. The distribution of the total (public and private) medical institutions across the districts shows that Kozhikode and the geographical belt from Pathanamthitta to Ernakulam have a density of over 58 institutions per one lakh population. The districts of Thiruvananthapuram, Thrissur, Palakkad, and Malappuram belt stand at the lower end with around 40 institutions per one lakh population. The other districts are close to the state average.

The distribution of hospital beds follows a pattern slightly different from that of medical institutions. The districts south of Thrissur report more than 400 beds per lakh of population while the northern districts report less than 300 beds per lakh of population, with the exception of Wayanad which reported 408 beds per lakh of population. The inequality in the distribution of beds in government institutions across the districts would explain only part of the overall inequality in distribution. In general, the southern districts have a density of institutions and beds higher than that of the northern districts.

The geographical area to be covered per government institution in the southern districts is well below 15 square kilometres, with the exception of Idukki and Pathanamthitta. In the northern districts, only Kozhikode reports an area per government institution below 15 square kilometres. Similar is the picture with regard to the geographical area covered per private institution. All the districts south of Thrissur, except Pathanamthitta and Idukki, report a figure below 3.2 square kilometres. In the north, only Kozhikode has a lower figure. Putting the two together, it may be seen that in the south, five out of the eight districts have a medical institution at an average distance of less than 0.8 kilometres. In the north, only Kozhikode falls in this category.

On the whole, Kerala reports a fairly high density of medical institutions and hospital beds. High density has existed, however, along with considerable inter-district variation, with the southern districts reporting densities higher than that of the northern districts. Among the districts, while Alappuzha reports the highest level of physical access to both government and private institutions, Kasaragod reports fairly poor access in terms of both.

A long tradition of education, especially of female education, and female autonomy and enlightened political process have facilitated higher levels of utilisation of healthcare facilities in Kerala than in many other parts of India. The higher utilisation levels of healthcare facilities, however, have not been exclusively those provided by the public sector, more so since the mid-1960s when people began exiting from public health services and seeking healthcare from a rapidly growing private sector. The exit process has reduced the role of the public sector in every aspect of healthcare. The private sector fills the increasing demand for healthcare in the state.

Access to, and Utilisation and Cost of Healthcare

Utilisation of Healthcare Services

A fairly high proportion of all ailments, in both rural and urban Kerala, receive medical treatment. There is hardly any variation across the fractile groups in the proportion of diseases receiving treatment, except in the rural areas in which among the lower 60 per cent of the population, the proportion receiving treatment is slightly lower (Tables 10.17 and 10.18). This would imply that irrespective of the level of household income, individuals do seek treatment.

The number of persons hospitalised (per 1000 persons) in Kerala is also one of the highest among the Indian states. In rural areas, the rate of hospitalisation is more than five times the Indian average. The next closest state is Haryana reporting a rate of hospitalisation which comes to one-third the Kerala average. In urban Kerala, the rate of hospitalisation is more than three times the all-India average; the closest to Kerala is Maharashtra which reports 40 points lower. In both the rural and the urban areas of Kerala, hospitalisation rates do not vary with income levels unlike in the other states of India (Tables 10.19 and 10.20). Thus, with regard to both outpatient and inpatient treatment, the variation across income classes is very small.

TABLE 10.17

Number of Persons Reporting Medical Treatment of Ailment During the Last 15 Days per 1000 Ailing Persons by Fractile Group of Mpce-rural; July 1995-June 1996

State	Mpce Fractile Group							
	0-10	10-20	20-40	40-60	60-80	80-90	90-100	All
Andhra Pradesh	709	746	702	727	757	794	793	745
Assam	426	469	573	509	553	644	861	560
Bihar	718	731	783	818	759	820	850	781
Gujarat	899	688	883	906	929	873	981	921
Haryana	—	1000	1000	935	976	952	979	970
Karnataka	799	624	816	705	783	854	851	775
Kerala	**900**	**734**	**824**	**845**	**897**	**880**	**906**	**883**
Madhya Pradesh	770	775	807	836	831	922	928	837
Maharastra	861	912	891	780	872	911	971	886
Orissa	488	674	611	716	704	899	898	677
Punjab	1000	1000	949	972	995	993	992	990
Rajasthan	994	514	942	876	935	901	922	898
Tamil Nadu	590	722	797	825	804	707	797	776
Uttar Pradesh	878	941	908	912	895	904	905	906
West Bengal	690	770	744	773	801	911	907	801
India	741	773	803	812	830	860	905	827

Source: National Sample Survey Organisation, "Morbidity and Treatment of Ailments", *NSS 52nd Round*, July 1995-June 1996, Report No. 441(52/25.0/1).

TABLE 10.18

Number of Persons Reporting Medical Treatment of Ailment during the Last 15 Days per 1000 Ailing Persons by Fractile Group of Mpce-urban, July 1995-June 1996

State	Mpce Fractile Group							
	0-10	10-20	20-40	40-60	60-80	80-90	90-100	All
Andhra Pradesh	786	746	817	843	899	914	920	850
Assam	907	409	519	616	677	860	847	636
Bihar	698	786	918	892	901	915	745	845
Gujarat	906	961	979	940	977	983	939	984
Haryana	1000	1000	1000	1000	996	971	939	984
Karnataka	734	901	866	940	984	931	996	914
Kerala	**696**	**857**	**928**	**906**	**929**	**974**	**803**	**892**
Madhya Pradesh	794	969	926	944	958	915	976	933
Maharastra	950	982	880	879	931	964	932	923
Orissa	525	842	906	847	995	980	898	866
Punjab	1000	820	964	970	960	997	961	965
Rajasthan	1000	793	872	934	862	967	970	896
Tamil Nadu	831	792	923	954	926	932	964	920
Uttar Pradesh	823	974	938	929	929	988	985	935
West Bengal	883	867	884	916	854	960	940	899
India	813	870	902	912	923	954	914	907

Source: Same as Table 10.17.

TABLE 10.19

Number of Persons Hospitalised During the Last 365 Days per 1000 Persons by Fractile Group of Mpce-rural, July 1995-June 1996

State	Mpce Fractile Group							
	0-10	*10-20*	*20-40*	*40-60*	*60-80*	*80-90*	*90-100*	*All*
Andhra Pradesh	3	5	6	9	17	27	64	14
Assam	13	5	5	8	8	10	29	9
Bihar	2	3	5	4	9	12	23	5
Gujarat	4	5	6	10	15	14	25	14
Haryana	—	7	9	22	16	29	40	25
Karnataka	3	4	10	9	14	26	56	14
Kerala	**9**	**70**	**62**	**52**	**66**	**77**	**83**	**70**
Madhya Pradesh	2	2	4	5	9	15	25	7
Maharastra	10	9	11	14	19	34	40	19
Orissa	3	6	12	11	18	33	58	13
Punjab	—	—	3	4	12	10	19	14
Rajasthan	1	2	5	4	6	13	18	8
Tamil Nadu	5	13	10	15	20	24	52	18
Uttar Pradesh	3	6	6	8	11	10	23	8
West Bengal	4	8	9	10	14	15	27	11
India	4	6	8	10	15	21	37	13

Source: Same as for Table 10.17.

TABLE 10.20

Number of Persons Hospitalised During the Last 365 Days per 1000 Persons by Fractile Group of Mpce-urban, July 1995-June 1996

State	Mpce Fractile Group							
	0-10	*10-20*	*20-40*	*40-60*	*60-80*	*80-90*	*90-100*	*All*
Andhra Pradesh	12	13	12	19	19	24	31	17
Assam	7	10	14	19	13	26	33	16
Bihar	4	10	10	11	20	28	27	12
Gujarat	17	9	19	19	20	23	39	21
Haryana	6	20	12	25	24	20	78	25
Karnataka	10	8	18	14	24	21	36	18
Kerala	**73**	**58**	**69**	**58**	**56**	**80**	**78**	**65**
Madhya Pradesh	9	6	14	14	19	23	51	15
Maharastra	17	20	22	24	22	33	39	26
Orissa	10	16	16	16	11	20	40	16
Punjab	7	6	13	14	15	23	29	17
Rajasthan	6	5	10	11	19	21	36	14
Tamil Nadu	20	16	18	23	25	30	44	23
Uttar Pradesh	4	7	9	17	17	26	37	14
West Bengal	16	20	17	20	23	25	39	22
India	12	13	16	19	21	27	38	20

Source: Same as Table 10.17.

TABLE 10.21

Per 1000 Distribution of Treatments (not Treated as Inpatient) During Last 15 Days by Institution Medical Service: Medicine Rural, July 1995-June 1996

State	*Government*			*Other*		
	Free	*Partly Free*	*Paying*	*Free*	*Partly Free*	*Paying*
Andhra Pradesh	173	11	49	28	3	735
Assam	41	121	288	85	26	438
Bihar	4	1	46	11	2	936
Gujarat	77	32	75	18	12	787
Haryana	29	29	76	8	2	856
Karnataka	123	45	148	4	10	669
Kerala	77	58	163	16	8	676
Madhya Pradesh	26	26	206	7	1	734
Maharastra	63	12	44	23	2	856
Orissa	43	57	278	37	25	560
Punjab	6	11	53	0	3	927
Rajasthan	1	6	400	0	0	593
Tamil Nadu	250	23	28	28	17	654
Uttar Pradesh	6	2	34	12	2	945
West Bengal	29	48	52	8	7	856
India	60	26	96	17	6	796

Source: Same as Table 10.17.

About one-third the total number of persons seeking treatment get treated in government facilities and less than 10 per cent get free treatment. There is not much difference between the rural and the urban areas in this regard. One of the striking aspects with regard to the proportion paying for treatment in the government facilities is that it is one of the highest among the Indian states (Tables 10.21 and 10.22).

The proportion of persons seeking inpatient treatment at government facilities is about 40 per cent of the total in both the rural and the urban areas of Kerala. Of those seeking treatment in government facilities, almost 90 per cent in the rural areas and 80 per cent in the urban areas receive free treatment (Tables 10.23 and 10.24). The proportion of the poor (population below the poverty line) in 1993-94 in Kerala is estimated to have been around 30 per cent in the rural areas and about 20 per cent in the urban areas. It may then be presumed that it is mostly the poor who avail themselves of the free treatment given in the government facilities.

Healthcare Expenditure in Kerala

Kerala's healthcare system used to be characterised by the expression 'good health at low cost'. This euphoria no longer exists. Today Kerala reports one of the highest figures of per capita healthcare expenditure in the country. Whether institutional, non-institutional or out-patient care, Kerala reports the highest per capita spending (Table 10.25) in both the rural and the urban areas.

The information on household healthcare expenditure based on the national health accounts extrapolated to the year 2004-05 by the National Commission on Macroeconomics and Health

is in conformity with the findings of NSS 55th Round. Among the major states, Kerala reported per capita annual household expenditure of Rs. 2548, which is two-and-a-half times the national average. Most of the household expenditure on healthcare is of the nature of out- of- pocket expenditure as insurance coverage of any form is non-existent or insignificant.

Impoverishment Due to Lack of Financial Protection

The exorbitantly high healthcare expenditure incurred in the absence of insurane cover of any sort could lead to impoversihment. The analysis carried out by Thomas George (2005) draws the following conclusions. The percentage-point increase in incidence of poverty (poverty head count) due to out-of-pocket expenditure in rural Kerala is 3.82 per cent whereas

TABLE 10.22

Per 1000 Distribution of Treatments (not Treated as Inpatient) During Last 15 Days by Institution Medical Service: Medicine Urban, July 1995-June 1996

State	*Government*			*Other*		
	Free	*Partly Free*	*Paying*	*Free*	*Partly Free*	*Paying*
Andhra Pradesh	61	26	28	24	3	857
Assam	46	151	152	14	11	626
Bihar	74	15	102	30	27	752
Gujarat	90	16	76	12	9	797
Haryana	17	10	74	..	5	895
Karnataka	60	23	104	22	4	788
Kerala	**74**	**50**	**181**	**13**	**4**	**677**
Madhya Pradesh	61	16	123	17	6	778
Maharastra	72	8	36	16	4	863
Orissa	31	13	280	19	..	657
Punjab	15	3	54	8	20	899
Rajasthan	76	24	309	22	..	569
Tamil Nadu	205	16	22	46	6	705
Uttar Pradesh	24	10	69	16	5	875
West Bengal	67	26	45	15	9	938
India	73	20	81	20	7	799

Source: Same as Table 10.17.

that due to pre- healthcare expenditure was 9.37 per cent. When the expenditure was decomposed between inpatient care and outpatient care expenditures, it was seen that the latter accounted for 2.34 per cent of the 3.82 per cent increase in poverty. In urban Kerala the increase in the incidence of poverty owing to healthcare expenditure is 4.48 per cent. Here too, the major source of impoverishment was the cost of outpatient care (2.72 per cent out of 4.48 per cent). Viewed from another angle, it is seen that in rural Kerala the proportion of those who had fallen below the poverty line due to expenditure on healthcare constitutes about 29 per cent of those who are below the poverty line in the post healthcare payment scenario. The remaining 71 per cent were already below the poverty line. In urban Kerala, 18 per cent fell below the poverty line owing to catastrophic healthcare spending.

Summing Up

In the foregoing discussion, an attempt has been made to trace the evolution of the health status of Kerala since the end of the 1960s. It was pointed out that in terms of bringing down mortality rates and in particular, infant mortality rates, Kerala stands ahead of all the Indian states. The difference between Kerala and the other states in respect of mortality rates lies mainly in the mortality rates of children in the 0-4 age group. Within this age group, it is in infant mortality in general and neo-natality in particular that Kerala has registered substantial gains. The decline in infant mortality during the past three decades has been mainly due to the decline in infectious diseases such as diphtheria, whooping cough, measles and enteric fever, the widespread acceptance of the immunisation programme and the practice of having childbirth in medical institutions.

In recent decades, while the incidence of communicable diseases has decreased, that of life style diseases and neoplasm has been increasing. The morbidity level of Kerala has become twice that of All-India in the rural areas and 50 per cent higher in the urban areas. Chronic morbidity is higher among the elderly population.

In Kerala, healthcare facilities in the three systems of medicine, namely Allopathy, Ayurveda and the Homeopathy are widespread across all the districts. Total government expenditure and per capita expenditure on healthcare have not declined; however, a part of the expenditure on medicines has given way to establishment expenditure in the Allopathic sector. The quality of medical care has also been on the decline in

TABLE 10.23

Per 1000 Distribution of Hospitalised Cases During Last 365 Days by Institution Medical Service: Medicine Rural, July 1995-June 1996

State	Government			Other		
	Free	Partly Free	Paying	Free	Paying General	Paying Special
Andhra Pradesh	204	17	—	15	622	126
Assam	607	85	0	158	75	14
Bihar	181	56	4	19	615	99
Gujarat	224	80	11	37	552	76
Haryana	279	23	2	17	622	50
Karnataka	364	76	11	14	424	95
Kerala	**351**	**27**	**17**	**24**	**408**	**158**
Madhya Pradesh	373	22	10	19	272	63
Maharastra	273	34	1	14	542	124
Orissa	827	15	0	4	53	29
Punjab	235	135	7	33	529	17
Rajasthan	614	13	6	44	270	30
Tamil Nadu	397	6	1	32	479	68
Uttar Pradesh	340	99	21	58	368	92
West Bengal	771	21	8	25	122	28
India	388	41	8	28	411	91

Source: Same as Table 10.17.

TABLE 10.24

Per 1000 Distribution of Hospitalised Cases During Last 365 Days by Institution Medical Service: Medicine Urban, July 1995-June 1996

State	Government			Other		
	Free	Partly Free	Paying	Free	Paying General	Paying Special
Andhra Pradesh	321	22	10	47	427	149
Assam	557	72	2	23	241	66
Bihar	248	60	11	141	390	73
Gujarat	241	110	12	13	473	135
Haryana	136	112	122	31	514	78
Karnataka	235	33	24	18	430	243
Kerala	**307**	**48**	**18**	**10**	**363**	**226**
Madhya Pradesh	469	66	12	22	327	80
Maharastra	251	50	5	35	435	188
Orissa	733	39	7	19	115	49
Punjab	159	102	5	28	608	61
Rajasthan	656	36	29	49	166	50
Tamil Nadu	312	25	5	77	375	164
Uttar Pradesh	287	74	30	39	418	135
West Bengal	626	68	19	19	189	67
India	347	55	16	35	372	147

Source: Same as Table 10.17.

TABLE 10.25

Monthly Per Capita Medical Expenditure in India by States, 1999-2000 (Rs.)

State	Rural		Urban	
	Inpatient care	*Non-inpatient care*	*Inpatient care*	*Non-inpatient care*
Andhra Pradesh	7.63	22.08	6.43	25.36
Assam	2.99	7.23	10.54	34.70
Bihar	2.00	14.57	2.46	17.84
Gujarat	10.35	17.62	12.29	28.19
Haryana	12.96	35.85	23.27	40.05
Karnataka	6.68	17.62	16.36	27.10
Kerala	**21.56**	**39.27**	**27.37**	**41.08**
Madhya Pradesh	5.33	18.79	8.86	29.70
Maharastra	11.04	26.54	19.72	35.27
Orissa	3.77	18.07	6.84	23.99
Punjab	15.5	40.38	13.88	40.11
Rajasthan	5.57	21.56	8.00	29.05
Tamil Nadu	7.80	22.18	13.90	29.36
Uttar Pradesh	5.73	32.96	7.20	35.31
West Bengal	3.72	16.63	10.26	32.12
India	6.66	22.92	12.33	30.95

Source: NSSO (2001). *Consumption of Some Important Commodities in India, 1999-2000*. (55th round), NSSO Report 461.

Allopathic institutions in the public sector. Since the beginning of the 1990s, there has taken place a steady decline in the number of patients in government medical care institutions under the Allopathic system, particularly in the number of out-patients; in the case of inpatients also there has been a decline, but of a lower order.

The decline in the popularity of public sector medical care institutions has been more than compensated by the steep increase in private medical care facilities. Even in the government institutions, physicians do private practice, thus bringing down further the glamour of the public sector.

Nearly 80 per cent of all the private hospitals and more than 50 per cent of the private hospital beds, are in rural areas. The private health sector in Kerala registered high rates of growth during the 1980s and the 1990s. Private healthcare institutions are spread all over the state and their number exceeds that of public healthcare institutions. Out of the total number of 12618 private medical institutions, about one-third are Allopathic, nearly two-fifths are Ayurvedic and around one-fourth are Homoeopathic. Ayurvedic and Homeopathic institutions under the private sector come to 690 and 415 respectively.

Of the total number of 70921 hospital beds in the state, more than 95 per cent are in Allopathic hospitals. As a result of developments under all the three types of institutions, Kerala has at present one medical institution per 200 persons and one hospital bed per 250 persons. A medical institution exists on the average, for a Keralite within a distance of one kilometre from his residence. Considerable inter-district variations however exist with regard to these facilities.

Medical expenditure per person is one of the highest in Kerala among all the states of India. Exorbitant levels of healthcare expenditure tend to push down nearly four per cent of the people both in the urban and the rural areas to levels below the poverty line.

References

Caldwell, J.C. (1986). "Routes to Low Mortality in Poor Countries", *Population and Development Review*, Vol. 12(2): 171-220, June.

Government of India (1991). "NSS Consumption Survey, 44th Round", *Sarvekshana*, Vol.XIV(3). New Delhi.

Government of Kerala (1979). *Report of the High Power Committee on Health Services*. Trivandrum.

———. (1958). *Second Five Year Plan: Kerala*. Trivandrum: Government Press.

———. (1981). *Subject Committee VI Social Services, Report*. Trivandrum: Secretariat of the Kerala Legislature.

———. (1986). *Report of the Survey of Private Medical Institutions in Kerala*. Trivandrum: Department of Economics and Statistics.

———. (1996). *Report on the Survey of Private Medical Institutions in Kerala*. Thiruvananthapuram: Department of Economics and Statistics.

Jayachandran, T.N. (1996). *Report of the Commission on Private Practice by Doctors in Government Service*. Thiruvananthapuram: Government of Kerala.

Jeffrey, Robin (1992). *Politics, Women and Well-being: How Kerala Became 'a Model'*. London: The Macmillan Press.

Krishnan, T.N. (1985). "Health Statistics in Kerala State, India:, in S.B Halstead, J.A Walsh and K.S. Warren (eds.), *Good Health at Low Cost*. New York: The Rockefeller Foundation.

Paul, S. (1992). "Accountability in Public Services: Its Voice and Control", *World Development*, Vol. 20(7): 1047-60.

Ramankutty, V. and P.G.K. Panikar (1995). *Impact of Fiscal Crisis on the Public Sector Healthcare System in Kerala*. Trivandrum: Achuta Menon Centre for Health Science Studies.

Sadanandan, Rajeev (1993). "The Role of Government in the Development of the Healthcare System in Kerala", M Phil dissertation (submitted). New Delhi: Jawaharlal Nehru University and Trivandrum: Centre for Development Studies.

Thomas George, Ashish (2005). "Catastrophic Healthcare Expenditure and Impoverishment in Kerala: An Analysis based on NSSO 55th Round, 1999-2000", M. Phil thesis (submitted). New Delhi: Jawahar Lal Nehru University

Chapter 11

Food Security and Public Distribution

To gain the goodwill of the people, Sancho, two things, among others, thou must not fail to observe. One is to be courteous to all... the other is to take special care that the people be exposed to no scarcity of food; For the poor, hunger is, of all afflictions, the most unsupportable.

— (Cervantes: Don Quixote)

Freedom from hunger and malnutrition constitutes the defining objective of food security. It implies access to all individuals at all times to enough food (Sen 1981; Dreze and Sen, 1989; Ravallion, 1987, 1997; Stringer, 2001). Access to food is determined by distribution of, and access to, resources, market, prices, social networks, and food transfer programmes (Stringer, 2001).

Kerala has long remained deficient in the production of food. The two major constituent regions of present-day Kerala, Travancore and Malabar had become net importers of food as early as 1848 (Kabir, 2002). Ever since then, food imports to the region have kept on steadily increasing. It is through imports that Kerala managed to overcome severe shortages of food grains; the state never witnessed severe famines of magnitudes comparable to those which afflicted many other parts of India. The state has earned acclaim for having introduced informal rationing of food at a date earlier than in any other state of India and achieved universal coverage under a comprehensive system of public distribution network.

Nevertheless, the performance of Kerala judged in terms of nutritional security and measured by targeted consumption levels, has been poor. An earlier study, which used the NSSO's consumption estimates for the early 1960s, had found that Kerala stood the lowest among the Indian states in terms of calorie intake (Dandekar and Rath, 1971). The norm used by this study was subjected to scrutiny by a subsequent study made by CDS, which noted the omission from the estimates of many items present in the Kerala food basket (CDS/UN, 1975). Based on a food balance sheet, this latter study argued that the average calorie intake in Kerala was much higher than what had been reported in the earlier study and that it did 'not seem to be lower than the national average'.

Though the state has made considerable strides in reducing poverty in recent years, the process has not been accompanied by commensurate improvement in the average calorie intake. According to the estimates made by the Planning Commission, based on the 55th Round of the NSS (1999-2000), rural Kerala had a head count poverty ratio of 9.4. Urban Kerala had a higher incidence of poverty, 20.3. In terms of relative ranking rural Kerala held the fourth position among the Indian states, the lowest poverty ratio being recorded by Punjab, followed by Himachal Pradesh and Haryana. The urban areas of Kerala held a still lower, namely the eighth position. However, considerable debate has followed regarding the estimates for 1999-2000. A re-estimation of the poverty figures by Deaton, using NSS data, has shown that the poverty ratio for rural Kerala had been 12.6, which is higher than, and for urban Kerala, 18.7, which is lower than the official estimates. In terms of relative ranking, Deaton places rural Kerala as the second, only after Punjab. For urban Kerala, Deaton's ranking places it as the eighth (Deaton, 2003). However, the relative position in terms of per capita calorie intake shows that rural Kerala had, in 1999-2000, the third lowest position among the Indian states, the lowest being Tamil Nadu; but Kerala stood the lowest in terms of urban per capita calorie intake.

It has been shown that there have taken place considerable changes in the composition of the food basket across all Indian states in recent years in the form of movement away from traditional articles of food consumption, particularly cereals, to costlier foods with lower calorie content (Suryanarayana, 2000; Meenakshi, 2000). For instance, expenditure on cereals in total household food expenditure, at the all-India level, fell from 40.8 per cent in 1977-78 to 31.8 per cent in 1999-2000 in urban areas and from 50 per cent to 44.1 per cent in rural areas (Bansil, 2003). While this shift in the consumption pattern has been seen as a positive trend, considerable differences are evinced in the explanation of the phenomenon.[1] Since each explanation is based on a particular set of assumptions each leads to a separate set of policy implications. But what becomes a matter of concern is the fact that the shift to higher priced food with lower calorie values than of cereals, raises the unit cost of calorie and slows down the growth of calorie intake, even with increases in food expenditure. What is of more serious concern is the observation that such shifts in food habit are taking place even among the poor (Meenakshi, 2000).

Some of the food security concerns in Kerala are examined in the following sections in the light of these trends. They specifically examine the recent trends in the production and consumption of cereals and cereal substitutes, which constitute the staple food items in the state. Secondly, they discuss the trends in the calorie intake across income classes over the past three decades. Thirdly, the trends in the sources of calorie intake and the changes in the commodity composition of the food basket, along with their implications for food expenditure are enquired into. Fourthly, an analysis is made of the changes in income and prices in the state since 1972 in an attempt to examine changes in the patterns of consumption. Fifthly, some aspects of state intervention in the food market are discussed. In this section, their significance in safeguarding the food security in the state is also examined. Some major implications of the findings for future food security in the state are discussed in the final section.

Trends in Food Production and Food Availability

Foodgrains are not the only item that enters into the food basket of the Keralite. The data mobilised by an expert committee on the basis of a survey on household consumption in selected localities in Kerala, indicate that, during the 1990s, in several items, out of the 15 for which actual consumption data were collected, consumption exceeded production (Table 11.1). Kerala's food deficiency pertains mainly to inadequacy in food production.

TABLE 11.1

Major Food Items in Kerala: Consumption and Production, 1991 and 1996

Item		*1991*		*1996*	
	Consumption/ week/person (in gms.)	*Consumption ('000 tonnes)*	*Production ('000 tonnes)*	*Consumption ('000 tonnes)*	*Production ('000 tonnes)*
Rice	2249	3403	1087	3637	953
Other Cereals	228	345	4	369	6
Tapioca	245	371	3803	396	2602
Pulses	108	163	16	175	15
Vegetables	499	755	143	807	154
Milk	521	788	1690	843	2246
Sugar	192	291	0	311	0
Tea	20	30	61	32	65
Coffee	8	12	21	13	22
Gur	19	29	52	31	51
Fish	308	466	607	498	851
Meat	60	91	117	97	138
Eggs	0.56*	847**	1550**	905**	1991**
Cooking Oil	59	89	***	95	***
Coconut	0.93*	1407**	4232**	1504**	5906**

Note: *in numbers, ** in million numbers, *** data not available. Coconut oil is the major vegetable oil used in the state and it may be safely assumed that consumption is more than production as the state is a net exporter of coconut oil.

Source: Kannan, 2000.

In Kerala, as in many other parts of southern and eastern India, rice is the staple food item. Rice constitutes nearly 92 per cent of the total cereal consumption in Kerala. A large number of roots and tubers also enter into the food basket in Kerala, supplementing energy intake, and sometimes even substituting for rice. Of particular significance among the items is tapioca (cassava), which till recently formed an important food item among the lower income groups. According to a food balance sheet prepared by the Centre for Development Studies (CDS) in 1975, tapioca accounted for 27 per cent of the calorie intake in the state. In this section we examine the trends in the production of cereals and their principal cereal substitute, tapioca.

In general, the area under food production has remained low in Kerala, thanks to the cropping pattern determined largely by its climatic and topographic conditions. In 1961, the area under food production accounted for more than 41 per cent of the total area cultivated in the state. The area under tapioca came to

1. For a brief summary of these explanations, see, Qadeer and Priyadarshi, 2005.

another 11.25 per cent. The rest of the area was cultivated under several cash crops, such as rubber, tea, coffee, pepper, coconut, arecanut, cashew and cardamom (Table 11.2). The area under food crops registered a marginal increase during the 1960s, apparently in response to the phenomenal rise in food prices in the late 1960s following imposition of inter-zonal and interstate restrictions on the movement of food grains. Thereafter, the area under food crops registered continuous decline as a result of the large-scale conversion of paddy fields into garden lands and for residential purposes and of lands used for tapioca cultivation for cultivation of cash crops. The area accounted by cultivation of rice and tapioca in 2001 fell to about 15 per cent of the cultivated area (Table 11.2).

In consequence, there has taken place a decline in the production of food in the state, the increase in productivity not fully compensating for the loss in area (Table 11.3).

The fall in production was taking place during a period when population in the state had been increasing rapidly. In 1961, the per capita production of rice was estimated at 165.23 grams per day. The production of tapioca was slightly higher (265.42 grams). Between 1961 and 1971, the production of rice and tapioca had gone up at annual rates of 2.65 per cent and 11.86 per cent respectively, as against an annual population increase of 2.36 per cent. As a result, the per capita production of rice in 1971 rose to 170.05 grams and that of tapioca to 644.52 grams. However, the rate of growth of production fell short of

TABLE 11.2
Area Under Major Crops in Kerala, 1961-2001

(in '000 hectares)

(1)	*1961* (2)	*1971* (3)	*1981* (4)	*1991* (5)	*2000-'01* (6)	*Col. (6) as % of Col. (2)*
Rice	762.42 (32.66)	874.95 (29.83)	804.31 (28.88)	550.39 (18.22)	347.46 (11.50)	45.57
Other Cereals and Millets	(0.56) 13.07	N.A	N.A	7.99 (0.26)	3.40 (0.11)	26.00
Pulses	43.63 (1.87)	N.A	33.69 (1.21)	23.15 (0.77)	10.81 (0.36)	24.78
Tapioca	238.28 (10.21)	298.40 (10.17)	243.87 (8.76)	144.18 (4.77)	111.18 (3.68)	46.66
Banana and Plantains	43.36 (1.86)	48.35 (1.65)	49.44 (1.78)	65.35 (2.16)	92.89 (3.07)	214.24
Coconut	500.57 (21.44)	724.70 (24.71)	659.55 (23.68)	866.54 (28.69)	936.30 (30.98)	187.05
Pepper	99.36 (4.26)	N.A (3.84)	106.92 (5.74)	173.32 (6.60)	199.37	200.65
Cardamom	28.52 (1.22)	47.50 (1.62)	56.38 (2.02)	55.28 (1.83)	41.29 (1.37)	144.78
Cashew	54.43 (2.33)	101.70 (3.47)	142.28 (5.11)	113.84 (3.77)	86.23 (2.85)	158.42
Tea	37.36 (1.60)	37.35 (1.27)	36.14 (1.30)	34.66 (1.15)	36.85 (1.22)	98.64
Coffee	17.72 (0.76)	31.60 (1.08)	57.95 (2.08)	79.54 (2.63)	84.74 (2.80)	478.19
Rubber	127.41 (5.46)	183.95 (6.27)	233.93 (8.40)	404.88 (13.40)	474.36 (15.70)	372.32
Others	368.56 (15.79)	584.5 (19.93)	360.66 (12.95)	501.42 (16.60)	597.14 (19.76)	162.02
Gross Cropped Area	2334.68 (100)	2933.00 (100)	2785.13 (100)	3020.55 (100)	3022.00 (100.00)	129.44

Note: (1) The figures for 1961 through 1991 are the averages of the two consecutive years. For instance, the figure for 1961 is the average for 1960-61 and 1961-62. For 2001, the figures relate to 2000-2001. (2) Figures in parentheses show the percentage share in the gross cropped area.

Source: Kerala State Planning Board (2004). *Economic Review* (Various issues).

TABLE 11.3

Production of Rice, Other Cereals and Millets and Tapioca in Kerala, 1961–2001

(in '000 tonnes)

	1961	*1971*	*1981*	*1991*	*2001*
Rice	1019.44 (165.23)	1325.00 (170.05)	1305.92 (140.56)	1073.46 (101.07)	751.33 (64.65)
Other Cereals and Millets	17.08 (2.77)	N.A	22.45 (2.41)	16.36 (1.54)	8.37 (0.72)
Tapioca	1637.61 (265.42)	5023.00 (644.65)	4075.43 (438.66)	2730.43 (257.07)	2512.15 (216.15)

Note: (1) The figure for each year, except for 2001, is the average of the two consecutive accounting years. The figure for 2001 relates to the accounting year 2001-02. (2) Figures in parentheses show the per day availability per person from domestic production in grams

Source: Kerala State Planning Board. *Economic Review (various years).*

the population growth in all the subsequent decades, though the rate of population growth itself was registering continuous decline. By 2001 the per capita production of rice fell to as low as just one-third, and that of tapioca to one-fourth, of their levels in 1971.

A better picture of the fall in per capita availability of cereals from internal production can be obtained by converting the tapioca produced in the state to its rice equivalent. It has been estimated that one kilogram of tapioca gives an energy equivalent of 0.46 kilogram of rice (CDS/UN, 1975). The per capita availability of starch-based food per day obtained from domestic production came down from 288.78 grams in 1961 to 163.43 grams in 2001.

The decline in rice production would have led to a fall in the level of food intake in the state, were it not compensated by imports. The fall in the production of rice was compensated to a small extent by the production of tapioca. In 1961, the rice equivalent of tapioca produced stood below total rice production. But, in subsequent decades, the rice equivalent of tapioca produced in the state tended to exceed rice production. In 2001, rice produced in the state came to 7.51 million tonnes, while the rice equivalent of tapioca produced was 11.43 million tonnes. However, all the tapioca produced in the state is not consumed within the state; a part of the production goes as animal feed and another part to production of industrial starches and glucose. According to an earlier study, which used the consumption data for 1981, only 70 per cent of the tapioca produced in the state went into direct human consumption (George, 1979). If we assume that these proportions still hold, the actual availability of tapioca in 2001 would have been 151.31 grams per person per day, which is equivalent to 69.60 grams of rice. By adding this quantity to the per capita domestic production of rice and other cereals, the total production of cereal equivalent could have been a mere 134.97 grams, which forms only about 36.48 per cent of the consumption norm of 370 grams a day prescribed by the ICMR. In the next section, the trends in the consumption of cereals and cereal substitutes in Kerala are indicated.

Trends in the Consumption of Cereals and Cereal Substitutes

The contribution of tapioca has been significant in providing food security to the state, particularly during a period of declining cereal production. According to the First Quinquennial Consumer Expenditure Survey of the NSS (1972-73), cereal intake in Kerala was the lowest among the Indian states. On the contrary, the state stood the highest in terms of the consumption of cereal substitutes. The subsequent surveys of the NSS showed little change in the relative position of the state. The latest NSS round on consumer expenditure (1999-2000) indicates that the daily per capita cereal intake in rural Kerala was only 9.89 kilograms per person per month (329.67 grams per day) and was the lowest among the Indian states. In the case of consumption of cereal substitutes, the state, with an intake of 0.96 kilograms per person per month, stood the highest. In the urban areas also, Kerala held the highest rank in terms of the consumption of cereal substitutes; however, in terms of cereal consumption, the urban areas of the state remained the third lowest, after Gujarat and Punjab.

Consumption data from the six rounds of the quinquennial consumer expenditure surveys of the NSS, from 1972-73 through 1999-2000, give an idea of the trends in the consumption of cereals and cereal substitutes in the state. Tables 11.4 and 11.5 give separate estimates for rural and urban areas and for three broad consumer expenditure classes *viz.* the poorest 30 per cent, the middle 40 per cent and the top 30 per cent.

Table 11.4 shows improvement in the cereal intake in rural Kerala over the entire period despite steady fall in the state's cereal production. Cereal consumption in the state in 1972-73 was as low as 7.97 kilograms per person per month or 265.67 grams per person per day, as against the ICMR norm of minimum requirement of 370 grams (11.1 kg per month). The cereal intake per person went up to 10.36 kilograms per month (or 345.33 grams per day) in 1987-88. Thereafter, the per person intake of cereals registered continuous decline, down to 337 grams per day in 1993-94 and 329.67 grams per day in 1999-00.

In the case of rice, the staple item of food in the state, the trends in consumption have been similar to those of cereals as a whole. However, the decline in consumption shown by the NSS Surveys in 1993-94 and 1999-2000 was sharper for rice than for cereals as a whole, thanks to the increase in the consumption of wheat. In fact, the per capita consumption of wheat, the cereal that takes the second position in consumption after rice in the state, has registered continuous increase (with the exception of 1977-78 when there was a decline) since 1972-73. Though wheat constitutes only a small proportion of the total cereal consumption in the state, its relative importance in the consumption basket has steadily been going up. Wheat had constituted only seven per cent of the total cereal consumption in the state in 1972-73. By 1999-2000, the corresponding figure went up to 10 per cent. The increase in the consumption of wheat is partly explained by its availability through the public distribution system and partly by the changing morbidity pattern in the state. The increase in the incidence of diabetes mellitus in the state has made large numbers of the population shift to wheat, which takes more time for the release of sugar into the blood system than rice does.

The fall in cereal consumption since 1987-88 might probably be explained by the overall increase in income in the state since the mid-eighties, consequent on

TABLE 11.4

Consumption of Cereals and Cereal Substitutes in Rural Kerala, 1972/73 to 1999/2000 (selected years)

(kg./person/month)

Class	*1972-73*	*1977-78*	*1983*	*1987-88*	*1993-94*	*1999-2000*	*Rate of Growth (72/73–99-2000)*
a. All Cereals							
Bottom 30%	5.11	6.09	7.63	8.26	8.55	8.43	1.87
Middle 40%	7.57	8.91	9.80	10.28	10.21	10.1	1.07
Top 30%	11.37	15.96	12.66	12.56	11.53	11.07	-0.10
All	7.97	10.18	10.01	10.36	10.11	9.89	0.80
b. Rice							
Bottom 30%	4.64	6.04	7.32	8.00	7.91	7.97	2.02
Middle 40%	6.98	8.78	9.22	9.78	9.46	9.16	1.01
Top 30%	10.69	15.32	11.72	11.43	10.45	9.58	-0.40
All	7.39	9.92	9.4	9.74	9.29	8.93	0.70
c. Wheat							
Bottom 30%	0.42	0.05	0.31	0.28	0.51	0.44	0.25
Middle 40%	0.53	0.12	0.58	0.50	0.72	0.93	2.09
Top 30%	0.71	0.65	0.95	1.15	1.26	1.48	2.77
All	0.55	0.26	0.61	0.63	0.82	0.95	2.04
d. Cereal Substitutes							
Bottom 30%	5.26	4.63	1.57	1.63	1.26	0.55	-8.02
Middle 40%	6.69	5.90	2.37	2.21	1.73	1.48	-5.43
Top 30%	6.42	6.00	2.64	2.13	1.83	0.68	-7.98
All	6.18	5.55	2.21	2.01	1.62	0.96	-6.66

Source: NSSO Reports/*Sarvekshana*.

steadily rising remittances from abroad (Kannan and Hari, 2002) and substitution of cereals by other food items. It may be noted that the consumption of cereals among the top 30 per cent of the population began declining from 1977-78 and the per capita consumption of cereals in 1999-2000 formed barely three–fourths of what it had been in 1977-78. On the contrary, cereal consumption by the bottom 30 per cent increased steadily till 1993-94 and showed some decline only in 1999-2000.

It is seen from Table 11.4 that the per capita monthly consumption of cereal substitutes declined from 6.18 kg. in 1972-73 to 0.96 kg. in 1999-2000, the rate of decline working out to 6.66 per cent per annum. The decline was continuous, spread across all income groups, though it had been the sharpest among the bottom 30 per cent of the population, at an annual rate of 8.02 per cent, from 5.26 kg. in 1972-73 to 0.55 kg. in 1999-2000.

The fall in the consumption of cereal substitutes might, by all means, be accounted for by the fall in the consumption of tapioca, the principal cereal substitute in the state. Tapioca is an inferior item of consumption (Pushpangadan, 1988); the fall in its consumption is therefore partly accounted for by increase in income. The fall in the production of tapioca has led to sharp increases in its relative price and forced even the poorest sections to reduce its consumption and to switch on to cereals. According to a study made by the Centre for Development Studies, the calorie value derived per rupee spent on tapioca during the 1960s and the early seventies had been more than two times the calorie value derived per rupee spent on rice. In recent years, the calorie value derived per rupee spent on tapioca has gone down to lower than that of rice.

Assuming that the cereal substitute used in the state consists only of tapioca[2] and converting the quantity of tapioca consumed into its rice equivalent, it is found that the per capita monthly consumption of cereal substitutes in rural Kerala must have declined from 2.84 kg. in 1972-73 to 0.44 kg. in 1999-2000. Inclusive of these figures, the overall consumption of cereals and cereal equivalent in the state might have come down from 10.81 kg. per person per month to 10.33 kg. in 1999-2000. Nevertheless, the decline in consumption was accounted for entirely by the richest 30 per cent—from 14.32 kg. in 1972-73 to 11.38 kg. in 1999-2000. In the case of the middle 40 per cent, the per capita monthly consumption increased from 10.65 kg. to 10.78 kg. and for the poorest, it registered an increase of 30 per cent, from 7.53 kg. to 8.68 kg.For the latter two groups, the increase was more than compensated by the decline in the consumption of cereal substitutes. To the poorest 30 per cent, however, the overall consumption of cereals and cereal substitutes registered steady increase till 1993-94, but it declined thereafter since the fall in the consumption of cereal substitutes was accentuated by the decline in cereal consumption reported in 1999-2000.

The trends in the consumption of cereals and cereal substitutes in urban areas in the state have more or less been similar to those in rural areas with the exception that it came down slightly earlier. The per capita monthly cereal intake in 1972-73 had been 8.17 kg. This works out to 272.33 grams per person per day. The consumption rose to 337.77 grams in 1983 and the increase was spread over all the expenditure classes. The intake of cereals registered steady decline thereafter, coming down to 308.83 grams in 1999-2000. However, in the case of the poorest 30 per cent, consumption increased till 1993-94 and declined thereafter, due mainly to the fall in the consumption of rice.

The increase in the average consumption of cereals between 1972-73 and 1999-2000 was offset by the decline in the consumption of cereal substitutes. The per capita monthly intake of cereal substitutes had been 3.24 kg. in 1972-73. It declined to 0.45 kg. in 1999-2000. In terms of rice equivalent, the decline had been from 1.49 kg. to 0.27 kg. Adding these figures to the quantity of cereals consumed, we find that the per capita overall consumption of cereals and cereal substitutes per diem was 322.01 grams in 1972-73 and 315.23 grams in 1999-2000.

The decline in the consumption of cereal substitutes had been the highest for the poorest 30 per cent, followed by the middle 40 per cent and the top 30 per cent. In fact, the bottom 30 per cent had higher consumption of cereal substitutes than the top 30 per cent in 1972-73. By 1999-2000, the consumption of cereal substitutes by the bottom 30 per cent had become the lowest of all the three categories. Nevertheless, for this group, the fall in the consumption of cereal substitutes during 1972-73 to 1993-94 was compensated by the increased

2. This is an extreme assumption since the cereal substitutes consumed in the state consist also of many other stems and tubers. According to a survey conducted by the Kerala Statistical Institute in 1991 in six selected areas of the state, the per capita consumption of tapioca was only 35 grams per day while, according to the 1993-94 NSS Survey, cereal substitutes consumed in the state was 54 grams per person per day. However, in terms of calorie content the other tubers stand approximately equivalent to tapioca.

consumption of cereals. As a result, the overall consumption registered an increase till 1993-94. Since then, the overall consumption has declined, thanks to fall in the consumption of cereals.

The consumer expenditure surveys from 1972-73 through 1999-2000 indicate that the cereal intake in urban and rural Kerala remained consistently below the ICMR norm for the bottom 30 per cent and the middle 40 per cent. Only the top 30 per cent in the rural areas, registered consumption above the norm. For the top 30 per cent in the urban areas consumption remained above the norm till 1987-88, but the subsequent two NSS rounds showed that consumption had fallen below the norm. The picture does not change even when cereals and cereal substitutes are taken together.

All the income groups in the rural areas and the top two groups in the urban areas had shown positive growth rates in consumption between 1972 and 1977. In all the subsequent periods, the growth rate recorded by the rural and the urban top 30 per cent and the rural middle 40 per cent (with the exception of 1983-1987) remained negative. For the poorest in urban areas, growth had been positive only during 1977-1983 and 1987-1993. In the rural areas, the per capita consumption among the lowest 30 per cent went up, though at a decreasing rate, till 1993-94, and then declined absolutely. It may be noted that the fall in consumption between 1993-94 and 1999-2000 was spread across all the income groups. For the poorest 30 per cent, per capita consumption of starchy foods had consistently remained below the minimum, in both rural and urban areas.

Trends in Calorie Intake

According to the NSSO, the per diem calorie intake in Kerala was only 1620, the lowest among all the states in India in 1961-62. NSS data have shown some improvement in the relative position of the state since then. The latest NSS round on consumer expenditure (1999-2000) indicates that the daily per capita calorie intake in Kerala was only 1982 for rural areas (the third lowest among the Indian states after Tamil Nadu (1826) and Assam (1915)). And the figure for urban Kerala (1995 calories) was the lowest among the Indian states.

TABLE 11.5

Consumption of Cereals and Cereal Substitutes in Urban Kerala, 1972/73–1999/2000

(kg./person/month)

Class	*1972-73*	*1977-78*	*1983*	*1987-88*	*1993-94*	*1999-2000*	*Rate of Growth (72/73–99-2000)*
a. All Cereals							
Bottom 30 %	5.55	5.66	7.78	7.53	8.25	8.06	1.39
Middle 40 %	8.16	9	10.4	9.66	9.76	9.7	0.64
Top 30 %	10.81	12.05	12.09	11.58	10.26	9.84	-0.35
All	8.17	8.91	10.12	9.6	9.46	9.25	0.46
b. Rice							
Bottom 30 %	4.88	5.55	7.2	7.21	7.61	7.24	1.47
Middle 40 %	7.33	8.59	9.48	8.96	8.87	8.48	0.54
Top 30 %	9.38	11.22	10.53	9.62	8.72	8.12	-0.53
All	7.21	8.47	9.11	8.63	8.45	8	0.39
c. Wheat							
Bottom 30 %	0.64	0.02	0.76	0.32	0.64	0.81	0.88
Middle 40 %	0.81	0.06	1.2	0.66	0.88	1.23	1.56
Top 30 %	1.41	1.33	1.01	2.02	1.52	1.69	0.67
All	0.94	0.43	1.01	0.97	1	1.24	1.03
d. Cereal Substitutes							
Bottom 30 %	3.61	2.65	0.49	0.66	0.68	0.39	-7.91
Middle 40 %	3.78	2.93	0.98	0.64	0.73	0.5	-7.22
Top 30 %	2.15	2.08	0.77	0.49	0.61	0.45	-5.62
All	3.24	2.59	0.77	0.6	0.68	0.45	-7.05

Source: NSSO Reports/*Sarvekshana*.

An earlier study by the CDS had noted that the 1960-61 NSSO survey had underestimated the consumption of many items that appear in the food basket in Kerala and that the actual level of food intake in the state had been higher than that reported based on the NSS. Survey. Based on a food balance sheet prepared by the Centre for the 1960s, it was estimated that the per capita intake of calories in the state was not lower than 2339 per day.

Even while granting the possibility for underreporting of certain items in the consumption basket, the NSSO surveys throw light on the long-term trends in the magnitude of food intake in the state. The consumption estimates prepared based on the data of the 27th (1972-73), 38th (1983), 50th (1993-94) and 55th (1999-00) rounds of the NSS are given in Table 11.6. The annual growth rates in per capita consumption (cereals plus cereal equivalent of cereal substitutes) for the periods 1972-1983, 1983-1993 and 1993-2000 are also given.

Despite decline in the intake of starchy foods, perceptible improvement is observed in the levels of calorie intake in both rural and urban Kerala from 1972-73 through 1999-2000. The calorie intake per person in rural Kerala which was as low as 1559 per day in 1972-73, rose to 1846 in 1983-84, 1965 in 1993-94 and 1982 in 1999-2000 at an average annual growth rate of 0.89 per cent over this 27 year period. The urban areas had a slightly lower growth rate of 0.54 per cent per annum.

Though there has taken place significant reduction in inequality in calorie intake between 1972-73 and 1999-2000, there still exist wide differences between the poorest and the richest. In rural areas, for example, the bottom 30 per cent (the poorest) of the population accounted for only 18.68 per cent of the total calorie intake in 1972-73, while the top 30 per cent accounted for 44.10 per cent, and the per capita calorie intake of the top 30 per cent in 1972-73 had been 2.36 times the intake of the poorest 30 per cent. The share of the bottom 30 per cent went up to 20.66 in 1983-84, 21.79 in 1993-94 and 21.83 in 1999-2000. Correspondingly, the share of the top 30 per cent declined to 40.47 per cent, 38.51 per cent and 38.43 per cent in 1983-84, 1993-94 and 1999-2000 respectively with the result that the per capita calorie intake of the top 30 per cent which had been higher than that of the poorest thirty per cent by 1.95 times in 1983, declined to 1.76 times in 1993-94 and 1999-2000. This meant that the differences between the share of the bottom 30 per cent

TABLE 11.6

Calorie Intake in Kerala, 1972-73 to 1999-2000

	A. Per Capita Calorie Intake Per Diem (K. Calories)							
	Rural				*Urban*			
M.P.C.E. Class	*1972-73*	*1983*	*1993-94*	*1999-2000*	*1972-73*	*1983*	*1993-94*	*1999-2000*
Bottom 30%	970.69 (18.68)	1271.55 (20.66)	1427.20 (21.79)	1442.48 (21.83)	1008.05 (17.55)	1301.07 (19.63)	1473.58 (22.49)	1486.98 (22.36)
Middle 40%	1450.57 (44.10)	1793.77 (40.47)	1950.20 (38.51)	1968.85 (38.43)	1605.65 (45.17)	1915.83 (41.82)	1926.82 (38.31)	1980.48 (37.93)
Top 30%	2291.88 (44.10)	2490.09 (40.47)	2522.53 (38.51)	2539.05 (38.43)	2594.42 (45.17)	2771.16 (41.82)	2510.66 (38.31)	2522.38 (37.93)
All Classes	1559 (100.00)	1846 (100.00)	1965 (100.00)	1982 (100.00)	1723 (100.00)	1988 (100.00)	1966 (100.00)	1995 (100.00)
	B. Annual Growth Rates of Per Capita Calorie Intake Per Diem (per cent)							
	Rural				*Urban*			
	1972-1983	*1983-1993*	*1993-1999*	*1972-1999*	*1972-1983*	*1983-1993*	*1993-1999*	*1972-1999*
Bottom 30%	2.48 (0.95)	1.16 (0.89)	0.18 (-0.83)	1.48 (0.53)	2.35 (0.96)	1.25 (0.68)	0.15 (-0.64)	1.45 (0.50)
Middle 40%	1.95 (0.21)	0.84 (0.11)	0.16 (-0.34)	1.14 (0.05)	1.62 (0.84)	0.06 (-0.72)	0.46 (-0.28)	0.78 (0.01)
Top 30%	0.76 (-0.29)	0.13 (-1.14)	0.11 (-1.38)	0.38 (-0.85)	0.60 (0.49)	-0.98 (-1.65)	0.08 (-0.80)	-0.10 (-0.59)
All Classes	1.55 (0.18)	0.63 (-0.16)	0.14 (-0.82)	0.89 (-0.17)	1.31 (0.74)	-0.11 (-0.69)	0.24 (-0.55)	0.54 (-0.08)

Note: Figures in parentheses in the upper panel show relative shares and in the lower panel show the rate of growth of per capita combined consumption of cereals and cereal equivalent of cereal substitutes.

Source: NSSO Reports/*Sarvekshana*.

TABLE 11.7

Sources of Calorie Intake in Rural and Urban Kerala, 1972-73 to 1999-2000

(Percentages)

% of Calorie derived from/M.P.C.E. Class	*Rural*					*Urban*				
	1972-73	*1983*	*1993-94*	*1999-2000*	*Rate of Growth 1972-99*	*1972-73*	*1983*	*1993-94*	*1999-2000*	*Rate of Growth 1972-99*
Cereals										
Bottom 30%	60.71	68.96	68.24	62.99	0.14	63.50	70.19	64.78	62.62	-0.05
Middle 40%	60.19	63.3	60.34	59.24	-0.06	58.61	63.03	48.59	56.42	-0.14
Top 30%	57.22	49.84	48.61	49.42	-0.54	48.06	33.81	41.7	39.55	-0.72
All	58.96	60.96	59.19	57.42	-0.10	54.69	56.41	55.3	53.22	-0.10
Cereal Substitutes										
Bottom 30%	28.36	7.14	4.85	2.39	-8.75	18.74	2.19	2.76	1.84	-8.24
Middle 40%	24.14	7.66	5.2	3.76	-6.65	12.32	2.97	2.07	1.76	-6.95
Top 30%	14.66	5.45	4.02	3.82	-4.86	4.34	1.25	0.93	1.04	-5.15
All	20.75	6.84	4.74	3.37	-6.51	9.84	2.22	1.98	1.57	-6.57
Others										
Bottom 30%	10.93	23.90	26.91	34.62	4.36	17.76	27.62	32.46	35.54	2.60
Middle 40%	15.68	29.04	34.46	37.00	3.23	29.07	34.00	49.34	41.82	1.36
Top 30%	28.12	44.71	47.37	46.76	1.90	47.61	64.94	57.37	59.41	0.82
All	20.29	32.20	36.07	39.21	2.47	35.47	41.37	42.72	45.21	0.90

Source: NSSO Reports/*Sarvekshana*.

and the top 30 per cent came down sharply between 1972-73 and 1993-94 and remained almost stable since then. And the per capita calorie intake of the poorest 30 per cent in 1993-94 and 1999-2000 had been only 57 per cent of that of the richest 30 per cent.

Urban Kerala had a similar trend, though the reduction in the degree of inequality was sharper. The difference between the per capita consumption of the richest and the poorest in urban areas came down by 2.57 times in 1972-73 to 2.12 times in 1983 and the succeeding years. Only the richest 30 per cent of the population, in both rural and urban Kerala, had intake levels above the required minimum, according to the intake levels in all the NSS Rounds.[3] Starchy foods constitute the principal source of energy among the poorer classes; in the rural parts of the state, cereals and cereal substitutes contributed 65 per cent and 62 per cent of the calorie intake of the poorest 30 per cent and the middle 40 per cent respectively in 1999-2000.

Sources of Calorie Intake

There has taken place among the Keralites a steady movement away from cereals and cereal substitutes to other food items which have lower calorie value. Table 11.7 shows the relative contribution of cereals, cereal substitutes and other foods to the total calorie intake in Kerala from 1972-73 to 1999-2000. In 1972-73, nearly 21 per cent of the average per capita calorie intake was contributed by cereal substitutes and 58.96 per cent by cereals. The relative contribution of cereal substitutes came down by nearly 14 percentage points in 1983, while that of cereals went up marginally by 2 percentage points.

The decline in the percentage contribution of cereal substitutes in rural areas continued during each subsequent NSS. Round, though at a diminishing rate. Interestingly, the decline in the relative contribution of cereal substitutes was not accompanied by commensurate increase in the contribution from cereals. In 1999-2000,

3. It is possible that many locally collected food items (like different kinds of yams, jack fruit, bananas, jack fruit nuts, coconuts and locally collected vegetables) which find a place in the ordinary Kerala kitchen, were underestimated in the NSS. Consumer Expenditure Surveys. It is also possible, moreover, that the food consumed from the mushrooming number of tea shops which cater to the poorer sections of the population was not fully captured either, in the NSS consumption expenditure surveys. Nevertheless, food consumption surveys conducted by other agencies also indicate nutrition deficiency among all groups of the population in the state. For example, the National Nutrition Monitoring Bureau (NNMB) has been collecting data on diet and nutritional status of representative population groups on a continuous basis. One of the important conclusions that emerge from these surveys is that there has been steady improvement in the intake of energy and protein in the state, even though the consumption of energy and protein remains significantly lower than the recommended daily allowance.

TABLE 11.8

Per Capita Monthly Food Expenditure in Kerala, 1972-73/1999-2000

M.P.C.E. Class	Monthly Food Expenditure (in Rupees) at Constant Prices (1972-73=100) Rural					Urban				
	1972-73	*1983*	*1993-94*	*1999-2000*	*Growth Rate 72-73/99-2000*	*1972-73*	*1983*	*1993-94*	*1999-2000*	*Growth Rate 72-73/99-2000*
Bottom 30%	15.68	22.37	23.05	26.45	1.96	17.70	21.86	25.26	25.82	1.41
Middle 40%	26.13	35.35	36.48	40.59	1.64	31.38	37.57	38.67	40.74	0.97
Top 30%	48.51	61.98	55.83	62.95	0.97	66.43	72.30	62.73	65.47	-0.05
All Classes	29.71	39.44	38.25	43.06	1.38	37.79	43.28	41.87	43.68	0.54

Source: NSSO Reports/*Sarvekshana*.

TABLE 11.9

Calorie-Rupee Ratio in Kerala, 1972/73–1999/2000

M.P.C.E. Class	Calories per Rupee Spent on Food Rural					Urban				
	1972-73	*1983*	*1993-94*	*1999-2000*	*Growth Rate 72-73/99-2000*	*1972-73*	*1983*	*1993-94*	*1999-00*	*Growth Rate 72-73/99-2000*
Bottom 30%	61.92	56.83	61.93	54.53	-0.47	56.95	59.52	58.34	57.59	0.04
Middle 40%	55.51	50.74	53.46	48.50	-0.50	51.17	51.00	49.82	48.62	-0.19
Top 30%	47.24	40.18	45.18	40.34	-0.58	39.05	38.33	40.02	38.53	-0.05
All Classes	52.47	46.80	51.37	46.03	-0.48	45.59	45.94	46.96	45.67	0.01

Source: NSSO Reports/*Sarvekshana*.

cereals supplied 57 per cent of the total calorie intake. Correspondingly, the relative contribution of items other than cereals and cereal substitutes, went up from 20.29 per cent in 1972-73 to 32.20 per cent in 1983 and to 39.21 per cent in 1999-2000.

The trends were similar in the urban areas. But, urban Kerala had lower rates of growth in the relative share of 'other' food articles in total calorie intake than rural areas had. The propensity for food diversification was greater in the rural areas than in the urban areas.

The increase in the relative contribution of non-starchy food items in rural and urban Kerala had been shared by all income classes. The increase had been the highest in the lowest income group. By 1999-2000, the pattern of food intake of the rural poor became almost the same as that of their urban counterpart.

The foregoing discussion shows that the pace of the shift away from cereals and their substitutes into other foods was higher in the rural than in the urban' areas and that in the poorer income groups than in the richer groups. Cereals and cereal substitutes still constitute the cheapest source of energy[4] and the movement away from these sources would suggest an increase in the share of food expenditure, unless accompanied by increase in income, and unit calorie cost.

Trends in Food Expenditure

Table 11.8 gives the per capita monthly food expenditure of the three expenditure classes at constant prices.

Food expenditure went up between 1972-73, in all income classes almost consistently, except the top 30 per cent in the urban areas. The implications of these trends in food expenditure for the cost of energy have been adverse to all income classes (Table 11.9). The decline in the calorie-rupee ratio was the lowest in the poorest 30 per cent. However, in the urban areas a marginal increase is noticed in the calorie-rupee ratio between 1972-73 and 1999-2000. The shift to food items other than cereals and cereal substitutes of the

4. Calculations made from the 55th Round (1999-2000) NSS estimates for Kerala show that one rupee spent on cereals gave 2.2 times the calorie obtained from one rupee spent on food other than cereals and cereal substitutes.

TABLE 11.10

Trends in Relative Prices

Year	*Price Index of*						*Relative Price Index of*			
	Cereals		*Cereal Substitutes*		C.P.I.A.L. (Food)	C.P.I.I.W. (Food)	*Cereals*		*Cereal Substitutes*	
	Rural	*Urban*	*Rural*	*Urban*			*Rural*	*Urban*	*Rural*	*Urban*
	2	3	4	5	6	7	2:6	3:7	4:6	5:7
1972-73	100	100	100	100	100	100	1	1	1	1
1983	206	201	285	294	227	242	0.91	0.83	1.26	1.21
1993-94	401	391	695	703	617	636	0.65	0.61	1.13	1.11
1999-2000	662	660	1338	1269	955	1047	0.69	0.63	1.40	1.21

Source: 2-5: NSSO Reports; 6-7, Labour Bureau, Shimla.

urban bottom 30 per cent had been lower than of their rural counterparts.

The decline in the calorie-rupee ratio of the relatively poor sections calls for attention since the per capita calorie intake of these income groups is lower than the required minimum. Any increase in food prices is likely to erode the fragile calorie intake of these groups further unless accompanied by a proportionate increase in income. Of particular importance would be the price of cereals, which continues to be the major source of calorie intake for these groups.

Price, Income and Taste

Systematic shifts in consumption, away from cereals which are not explained by movements in relative price and income, have been observed at the all-India and the state levels (Radhakrishna and Ravi, 1992; Meenakshi, 2000). These shifts appear to have been 'not merely a reflection of increased prosperity', but 'of changing food preferences'.

Table 11.10 gives the trends in the relative prices of cereals and cereal substitutes, for rural and urban Kerala separately, for the periods corresponding to the 27th, 38th, 50th and 55th rounds of the NSS.. Unit prices of cereals and cereal substitutes have been obtained from the corresponding NSS Reports by dividing respective values by quantities for the rural and urban areas separately. For constructing the relative price indices for the rural areas we have used the Consumer Price Index for Agricultural Labourers (Food) for Kerala and, for the urban areas, the average of the Consumer Price Index for Industrial Workers (Food) for the four centres in Kerala. All the indices are expressed at constant (1972-73=100) prices. The relative price of cereal substitutes increased in all the years, except in 1993-94. The relative price of cereals declined continuously during the period till 1993-94, and registered a marginal increase since then. This should imply that the shift in the pattern of consumption away from cereals to costlier food articles was induced by improvement in income and/or changes in preferences and tastes.

The trends in total expenditure of the three income groups and in their budgetary shares across the three broad groups of food-cereals, cereal substitutes and 'other' food, for rural and urban areas separately have been analysed. The results are summarised in Table 11.11. All the calculations are based on constant (1972-1973=100) prices.[5]

Panel A of the Table presents the real expenditure of the three income groups, for the rural and the urban areas separately, along with the annual growth rates. It shows that urban areas had positive income growth during all the sub-periods. For the rural areas also, the income growth had been positive except during 1983/1993-94. Even during this period, the negative growth was due to the decline in the income of the top income group. The rural areas recorded higher growth than the urban areas during the period, except between 1983 and 1993-94. In both the areas, the poorest had the highest growth rate of income, followed by the middle and the top expenditure classes in that order. In consequence, the differences in total expenditure as between rural and urban areas and among the income classes declined.

5. The CPIAL (General) and the CPIIW (General) for Kerala form the bases for the conversion of total expenditure into real terms. The expenditure on cereals and cereal substitutes were converted into constant prices using Laspryel's index constructed with unit prices of cereals and cereal substitutes derived for each expenditure class with quantity weights from the NSS 27th Round (1972-73) data.

TABLE 11.11

Total Expenditure and the Shares of Food, Cereals, Cereal Substitutes and Food Other than Cereals and Cereal Substitutes in Total Expenditure, Rural and Urban Kerala, 1972/73-1999/2000

	Total Expenditure (in Rupees)									
	Rural					*Urban*				
M.P.C.E. Class	*1972-73*	*1983*	*1993-94*	*1999-2000*	*Growth Rate 1972-73/ 1999-2000*	*1972-73*	*1983*	*1993-94*	*1999-2000*	*Growth Rate 1972-73/ 1999-2000*
A: Total Expenditure (in Rs.)										
Bottom 30%	20.69	30.35	32.32	42.37	2.69	23.17	28.83	37.49	41.44	2.18
	(3.55)	(0.63)	(4.62)			(2.01)	(2.42)	(0.91)		
Middle 40%	35.11	50.41	53.99	67.77	2.47	42.99	51.71	62.87	74.48	2.06
	(3.34)	(0.69)	(3.86)			(1.69)	(1.79)	(1.55)		
Top 30%	73.14	113.79	106.27	132.87	2.24	113.75	130.96	144.18	158.75	1.24
	(4.10)	(-.69)	(3.79)			(1.29)	(0.88)	(0.88)		
All Classes	42.19	63.41	63.17	79.68	2.38	58.27	68.62	79.65	89.85	1.62
	(3.77)	(-0.04)	(3.94)			(1.50)	(1.36)	(1.10)		
B: Share of Food (Percentages)										
Bottom 30%	75.78	73.73	71.30	62.43	-0.72	76.39	75.82	67.38	62.31	-0.75
Middle 40%	74.44	70.12	67.57	59.90	-0.80	72.99	72.65	61.51	54.70	-1.06
Top 30%	66.33	54.47	52.54	47.38	-1.24	58.40	55.21	43.51	41.24	-1.28
All Classes	70.42	62.21	60.55	54.04	-0.98	64.85	63.07	52.56	48.62	-1.06
C: Share of Cereals (Percentages)										
Bottom 30%	36.54	40.23	42.69	31.45	-0.55	36.30	42.23	40.20	30.72	-0.62
Middle 40%	35.32	33.28	32.73	25.44	-1.21	32.44	33.48	17.98	22.48	-1.35
Top 30%	28.54	20.50	20.04	15.46	-2.25	17.75	16.79	14.69	11.87	-1.48
All Classes	31.97	27.40	27.85	21.40	-1.48	24.30	25.03	23.20	18.00	-1.11
D: Share of Cereal Substitutes										
Bottom 30%	8.81	1.94	1.37	0.46	-10.37	5.78	0.62	0.79	0.34	-9.92
Middle 40%	7.03	1.76	1.19	0.60	-8.72	3.43	0.66	0.50	0.27	-8.98
Top 30%	3.49	0.88	0.67	0.35	-8.21	0.79	0.20	0.19	0.11	-6.95
All Classes	5.45	1.31	0.96	0.45	-8.83	2.16	0.39	0.38	0.20	-8.49
E: Share of Other Food										
Bottom 30%	30.44	31.56	27.25	30.52	0.01	34.32	32.97	26.38	31.25	-0.35
Middle 40%	32.09	35.08	33.65	33.86	0.20	37.12	38.51	43.03	31.94	-0.56
Top 30%	34.29	33.09	31.82	31.57	-0.31	39.86	38.22	28.63	29.26	-1.14
All Classes	32.99	33.50	31.74	32.18	-0.09	38.39	37.65	28.98	30.43	-0.86

Note: Figures in parentheses indicate the annual growth rates from the immediately preceding period. The real expenditures for rural and urban areas are based on the N.S.S. current price data deflated respectively by the C.P.I.A.L. (General) and C.P.I.I.W. (General) for Kerala.

Source: NSSO Reports/*Sarvekshana*.

As a sequel to the increase in income[6], the share of food in the total budget declined across all income groups. But inequality in the budget shares devoted to food across income groups widened caused mostly by changes in the share of cereals. The decline in the share of income devoted to cereals was the highest in the top 30 per cent. In 1972-73, this group was seen to be devoting 28.54 per cent of its total expenditure on cereals, as against 36.54 per cent by the poorest 30 per cent. By 1999-2000, the share of cereals in the budget of the poorest was 31.45 per cent, which was more than two times that of the richest.

Interestingly, while there was considerable inequality among income groups in the budget shares of cereals, the inequality in the share of 'other' foods was small. In 1972-73, the shares of expenditure devoted to 'other' foods by the three classes stood close to one another. The share of expenditure devoted by the rural poorest to 'other' foods came close to that of the richest in 1999-2000; in the urban areas the corresponding share exceeded that of the richest.

6. Engel's formulation of the relationship between income and food expenditure clearly states that the proportion of income spent on food declines as income increases and the share of income spent on food by the richer classes would be lower than that of the poorer ones.

TABLE 11.12

Per Capita Per Diem Consumption of Some Important Commodities in Kerala, 1987-88 to 1999-2000

Item Consumed and Unit of Consumption	*Per Capita Consumption per day*							
	Rural				*Urban*			
	1987-88	*1993-94*	*1999-2000*	*Growth Rate per annum 87-88/99-2000*	*1987-88*	*1993-94*	*1999-2000*	*Growth Rate per annum 87-88/99-2000*
Milk (ml.)	72.00	78.30 (1.41)	110 (5.83)	3.59	102.33	109.00 (1.06)	129.33 (2.89)	1.97
Oils (gm)	8.67	8.67 (0.00)	14.00 (8.31)	4.08	0.01	10.00 (216.23)	15.33 (7.38)	81.92
Meat (gm.)	6.33	8.00 (3.98)	8.67 (1.35)	2.65	6.67	8.00 (3.08)	11.00 (5.45)	4.26
Eggs (no.)	0.06	0.20 (22.22)	0.25 (3.79)	13.00	0.10	0.24 (15.71)	0.31 (4.36)	10.10
Fish (gm.)	35.33	45.00 (4.11)	58.33 (4.42)	4.27	53.00	54.00 (0.31)	62.67 (2.51)	1.41
Fruits (gm.)	N.A	43.41	75.33 (9.62)	N.A	N.A	69.00	87.75 (4.09)	N.A
Sugar (gm.)	26.33	27.67 (0.83)	28.33 (0.39)	0.61	29.67	30.33 (0.37)	29.33 (-0.56)	-0.10
Vegetables (gm.)	N.A	35.67	145.33 (26.38)	N.A	N.A	51.67	136.00 (17.50)	N.A
Pulses (gm.)	11.67	14.33 (3.48)	18.33 (4.19)	3.84	16.67	16.00 (-0.68)	23.00 (6.24)	2.72
Cereals (gm.)	345.33	337.00 (-0.41)	329.66 (-0.37)	-0.39	320.00	316.67 (-0.17)	308.33 (-0.44)	-2.78
Cereal Substitutes (gm.)	67.00	54.00 (-3.53)	32.00 (-8.35)	-5.97	20.00	22.67 (2.11)	15.00 (-6.65)	-2.37

Note: Figures in parentheses show the annual rate of growth from the preceding period.

Source: NSSO Reports.

In 1972-73, the bottom 30 per cent and the middle 40 per cent in the rural areas utilised lower proportions of their total budget on other foods than on cereals. The changes in the budget allocation of the poorest and the middle income groups indicate that it was not income alone that was responsible for the shifts in the pattern of consumption; rather they were due to changes in tastes and preferences. As Shaw has noted, 'poor people for reasons associated with status, mimic the taste patterns exhibited by the richer income groups, even if it meant less than adequate nutrition' (Meenakshi, 2000). However, it may be noted that changes in tastes are not independent of changes in income, which also had gone up, among all groups, and at higher rates for the poorest sections.

Shift to 'Other' Foods: A Further Exploration

The tendency to switch on to preferred foods has occurred even among the poorest income group and this tendency has been induced by changes in income and in tastes, Kerala being not an exception in this matter to the rest of India (Bansil, 2003; Viswanathan and Meenakshi, 2000-2001; Meenakshi, 2000). However, the 'other' food category to which the shifts were made does not specify the commodities involved. Detailed analysis of individual food items or groups of food items is necessary for identifying them. Adequate data on prices of individual commodities or of groups of food items for periods corresponding to the NSS Rounds[7] are however not readily available.

The data on the per capita quantity of consumption of the important food articles provided by the NSS give some idea of the directions in the consumption pattern. But such data are not available for the different MPCE classes, or for the period prior to 1987. Even the 1987 data do not include all the items on which information is provided in 1993-94 and 1999-2000. Table 11.12 gives some idea about the broad directions of the changes in demand.

7. A solution would lie in the analysis of the long-term trends in the shares of different food items in the total food expenditure. Such an analysis is rendered difficult for want of data on prices of food groups for the period after 1987-88. The series worked out by Minhas covers only the period 1972-73 to 1983 and that by Tendulkar and Jain only up to 1987-88.

The shift in consumption away from cereals and cereal substitutes between 1987-88 and 1999-2000 was characteristically towards a wide spectrum of food items such as milk, meat, eggs, fish, fruits, vegetables and fatty oils. The pattern of shift was more or less similar in both rural and urban areas and across income groups.

The income gain from purchase of rice in the rural areas from the public distribution system in 1972-73 had been to the tune of Rs. 32.85 per capita per annum for the poorest; the corresponding figures for the middle and the richest groups were Rs. 31.82 and Rs. 7.70 respectively.[8] These work out to 1.59, 0.90 and 0.10 per cent of the total expenditure of the respective income groups. The P.D.S. also covered articles other than rice such as wheat, sugar and kerosene. If all these items are considered, the gain would be much higher. This income gain might have had a significant effect on the consumption pattern of all groups, particularly of the poorest.

The Public Distribution System

Public Distribution of food takes place in Kerala at three levels: school children, expecting mothers and pre-school children and the general population. The first two are targeted programmes with small coverage. While the distribution to these two groups has improved in terms of coverage in recent years, the distribution of food to the general population through fair price shops has declined in scope and operation. Besides, supply of food articles is done through the Kerala State Civil Supplies Corporation also.

Other public programmes and schemes for food distribution are also in operation in the state. For instance, under the *Annapoorna* scheme,[9] rice at the rate of 10 kg. per month is distributed free to nearly 49 thousand destitute above the age of 65 years who do not receive the National Old Age Pension; under the *Anthyodaya Anna Yojana* Scheme, 2,74,109 'most disadvantaged' families, including all tribal families, are entitled to receive 35 kg. of rice per family per month at a price of Rs. 3 per kg.[10] But, in terms of the total quantity involved, these programmes are not of significance.

The School-Feeding Programme

The school-feeding programme is, by and large, the most comprehensive food support programme in Kerala to children in the age group 5-12 years. This programme had not been in effect in the state as a whole until 1961; parts of Kerala had adopted however a scheme of free mid-day meal to support needy children in the lower primary classes even during the colonial period.[11] The system was given coverage throughout Kerala in 1961. From 1961 to the middle of the 1970s, the scheme was supported under the commodity assistance programme from CARE (Cooperative for American Relief Everywhere), a consortium of US voluntary agencies.

Under the school-feeding programme, eligible children in all government and aided schools, whose parents give, in the beginning of the school year, a statement that their wards would like to be included in the scheme, are entitled to a cooked mid-day meal at school. Until the mid-eighties, only children in the lower primary classes were eligible. These children belonged roughly to the age group five to nine years. In the mid-eighties, the operation of the scheme was extended to cover children in standards V to VII also, roughly corresponding to the age group 9-12 years. In most of the years the scheme covered more than 70 per cent of the total number of children enrolled, of the relevant stage of schooling and age groups (see, Table 11.13).

At present, the school-feeding programme gives 60 grams of rice and 30 grams of pulses per day to each child under the programme; the scheme operates on all school working days (190 days in a year).[12] In addition to this regular supply, each child who is enrolled under the noon- meal scheme, is provided (from the closing years of the past millennium) with a free supply of five kilograms of rice during each of the four festival seasons in the state; Onam, Christmas, Id and Bakrid.[13]

8. For working out these figures, we, first multiplied the NSS 27th round figures on the quantity consumed per capita per annum (from the NSS) by the open market prices and then subtracted it from the expenditure on rice reported by NSSO. This seems to be a rational exercise because the NSSO's figures on expenditure also include the value of consumption out of home grown stock, arrived at on the basis of information on retail prices collected separately.

9. This was introduced as a central scheme with effect from 14-2-2001.

10. This was introduced as a central scheme on 25-2-2001. The target of beneficiaries fixed by the central government was 2,38,200, while the state government has enhanced the number to 2,74,109. See, Government of Kerala, *Economic Review*, 2003.

11. In the early 1940s, the then princely state of Travancore, on the basis of the recommendations of the Travancore Education Reforms Committee, which found widespread prevalence of 'class room hunger', introduced a system of providing free noon meal to poor children in lower primary schools. Cochin adopted a similar programme in the mid 1940s.

12. In addition, the state government has introduced the supply of one egg per week to each beneficiary from the current year (*viz.* 2005-06)

13. The system did not operate during the Id season of 2005, apparently due to the unwillingness of the State Civil Supplies Corporation, which supplies food materials to the schools, to make the supplies; on account of the heavy arrears due to the Corporation for supplies made during earlier years.

TABLE 11.13

Coverage of the School Feeding Programme in Kerala, 1961-62/2002-03

Year	*Number of Eligible Pupils ('000s)*	*Number of Pupils Covered under the Scheme ('000s)*	*Percentage of Pupils Covered*
1962-63	2184	1567	71.75
1970-71	2868	2084	72.66
1979-80	2576	1812	70.34
1984-85	2501	1481	59.21
1987-88*	4376	3200	73.12
1992-93	4354	2342	53.78
1996-97	4011	2375	59.21
1998-99	3736	2358	63.12
1999-00	3637	2484	68.28
2000-01	3613	2825	78.20
2001-02	3494	2702	77.34
2002-03	3414	2604	76.27

Note: * The scheme was extended to students up to class VIII.

Source: UN/CDS, 1975: 42; Kannan, 2000: 16, Government of Kerala, *Economic Review, 2003* and Government of Kerala, Educational Statistics Since Independence, 2004.

If we assume that all the children were supplied with free noon-meal every day at the prescribed rate and that all children who enrolled under the scheme availed of the 'five kilogram festival gift', the total quantity of rice supplied in the state under the school-feeding programme in 2002-03 would have been around 81.76 thousand tonnes[14] and that of pulses around 14.84 thousand tonnes. But the actual supply fell far short of these quantities and stood at 46.48 thousand tonnes of rice and 9.51 thousand tonnes of pulses.

As already noted, the school-feeding programme operates only in the government and the aided schools. Children enrolled in these schools come mainly from poor and low middle class families. The school-feeding programme constitutes therefore a form of food support to the relatively poor sections of the society. As was noted by the earlier CDS study, 'the programme is so designed as to secure redistribution in favour of the lower income groups only through the lower ages' (CDS/UN, 1975).

Supplementary Nutrition for Pre-School Children and Nursing Mothers

While the school-feeding programme addresses the problem of malnutrition among children in the age group 5-12 years, other programmes address other vulnerable groups. Of them, the supplementary nutrition programmes for pre-school children upto five years of age and for nursing mothers are the most significant in terms of coverage and the quantity of food supplementation involved. These programmes assumed significance only from the 1970s (CDS/UN, 1975). By the late 1970s, the programme covered more than a million pre-school children—close to 40 per cent of children upto five years of age.[15] By March 2003, the programme covered 8.74 lakh children and 1.42 lakh mothers.

The free supply of food to pre-school children and nursing mothers takes place through the *anganwadis* and *balavadis* set up with the help of local women's organisations spread over the whole state.[16] The *anganvadi* workers, who work on a nominal honorarium, identify all eligible persons of poor income groups. Each child enrolled in the scheme is entitled to food equivalent to 300 calories and 8.15 grams of protein per day. For nursing mothers the provision is 500 calories and 15 grams of protein per person per diem. These rates are roughly equivalent to one-fourth of the requirements of the beneficiaries; these supplies are expected to be provided 300 days a year. No reliable estimates of the food actually supplied are, however, available. If all the beneficiaries had access to food at the rates specified, 10.16 lakh beneficiaries (of which 8.74 lakhs were children)

14. If we exclude the five kilogram gift, the total supply of rice supplied, would be around 29.68 thousand tonnes, a figure which is only higher by 6.47 thousand tones than the actual figures in 1972-73 (CDS/UN, 1975, Table 18: 42).

15. The number of beneficiaries of nutritional programmes for children and women

Year	Number of Beneficiaries (in '000s)
1977-78	457
1980-81	1903
1991-92	1201
1995-96	1083
2002-03	1016

Source: Kannan, 2002; Government of Kerala. *Economic Review 2003*.

16. In March 2003, there were 25393 *anganwadi* centres spread across the state.

would have received a food equivalent of 28.89 thousand tonnes of cereals and 12.61 thousand tonnes of pulses a year, which work out to 0.71 per cent and 5.37 per cent respectively of the total quantity of cereals and pulses consumed in the state. If we add these figures to the free supply of food through the school-feeding programme, the total quantity of free supply through the two schemes would constitute around 2.71 per cent and 12 per cent respectively of the total quantity of cereals and pulses consumed in the state.[17]

Food Distribution through the Civil Supplies Corporation

Sale of foodgrains through the Civil Supplies Corporation is intended for improving the availability of foodgrains in the state.[18] The Corporation operates as a mechanism to control prices in the open market through the supply of foodgrains at prices lower than those in the open market. In fact, the Corporation deals not only in foodgrains, but also in other articles of consumption, like provisions (including chilies, onions, spices and condiments and various types of pulses) stationery like soaps, tea, coffee, toothpastes and cosmetics, edible oils, cooking gas, medicines and even petrol.[19]

The Corporation expanded its sale network from 1980, when it embarked on sale of articles through *maveli* stores. By 1992, the Corporation had 500 *maveli* stores; by 2002, the number increased to 950.[20] In addition, the Corporation also operates Festival markets during major festival seasons in the state.

The prices that the Corporation charges for food articles are below costs. For rice, under a government stipulation in 1993, the Corporation fixes prices subject to the condition that they are 10 per cent below open market prices.[21] Part of this operations is managed by cross subsidisation, through profits from supermarkets, petrol bunks, L.P.G. outlets and *maveli* medical stores.[22]

The Corporation's supply of rice in the state has ranged from 2 per cent to 6 per cent of the total food grain availability in the state (Mooij, 1999: 168). This includes not only sale through *maveli* stores, but also grain supplied to the school-feeding programme and also to jail inmates.

Food Distribution through Fair Price Shops

Sale of Foodgrains through fair price shops in Kerala is probably the most comprehensive scheme under food distribution. Unlike in any other state in India, its coverage has been universal. Ever since the introduction of universal statutory rationing in the state in 1965, the system has registered significant expansion (Table 11.14).

Distribution of food takes place through a wide network of fair price shops spread throughout the state.[23] Fair price shops distribute rice, wheat, sugar and kerosene. At times of scarcity and distress, they distribute tapioca and cloth too. These commodities are sold at controlled prices, much lower than market prices. Till changes were introduced in 1997, the prices charged by fair price shops had been uniform for all income groups. Studies made earlier (UN/CDS, 1975; George, 1979; Koshy, 1989; Suryanarayana, 1996) showed that nearly two-thirds of the purchase of rice of the poor in Kerala came from the fair price system. For the whole population, the proportion was around one-half.

17. Taking this quantity along with the 5.4 thousand tonnes of cereals, which the 44980 destitutes above 65 years of age are entitled to receive under the *Annapoorna* Scheme, around 2.1 per cent of the cereals consumed in the state would be free government supplies.

18. E.Chandrasekharan Nair, Minister for Civil Supplies in the Left Front Government in 1980, gave the following narrative, which quintessentially summarises the objectives of the Corporation: 'Kerala is a very food deficient state. Since the food security in 1964, we receive food grains from the Centre through P.D.S. The problem, however, is that this F.C.I rice is of very bad quality. We are here at the receiving end; we have to accept it. Open market prices are uncontrolled. The prices are set by important traders in Bombay and elsewhere...Kerala traders are relatively small compared to the large companies outside the state. We felt that we should organise a countervailing power against the traders. In 1980, when we came to power, prices were rising and the opposition claimed that we cooperated with the traders and that we tolerated hoarding. My idea was that one cannot solve economic problems with coercive power. We had to find an economic solution. I thought, if we had a market share of 10–15 per cent, that would be sufficient to control private trade. In principle, P.D.S. could have taken up this function, but the quality of food supplies is not good. P.D.S. has a downward effect on the price of low-quality rice. But so far nothing has happened to the piece of good quality rice. The Kerala State Civil Supplies Corporation could fill that gap. A second motive was the general price rise experienced during festival season...In 1980 the Corporation started to organise temporary shops and vegetable fairs, where people can purchase all the special requirements for the festival.' (Quoted in Mooij, 1999: 166)

19. The Memorandum setting out the objectives of the Corporation mention procurement, distribution, trade, storage and transport etc of food grains and other essential commodities as its main tasks.

20. In addition, the Corporation had, in 2003, 10 supermarkets, 35 medical stores, 10 petrol bunks, 4 L.P.G. outlets and one Kerosene Depot (GoK, *Economic Review*, 2002-2003).

21. The Corporation's procurement is direct and it helps keeping prices low. Internal procurement by the Corporation is negligible since most of the items sold come from other states. In 2005, the Corporation embarked on the procurement of surplus rice from the growers in the state through the Paddy Producers' Cooperative Societies.

22. However, the accumulated loss of the Corporation exceeds Rs. 350 crore; since the inception of the Corporation in 1974, the Government of Kerala has provided the Corporation Rs. 240 crore as grants.

23. The first economic census of India, carried out in 1977, showed that 99 per cent of villages in Kerala were covered by fair price shops within two kilometre distance; Maharashtra came second with 67 per cent. The all-India average was a mere 35 per cent (Kannan, 2000).

TABLE 11.14

Food Distribution through Fair Price Shops, Kerala, 1975-2002

Year	Household Ration Cards (lakhs)	Ration Permits to Institutions (nos.)	Population Covered by Ration Card (in million)	Quantity Distributed		
				Rice ('000 MTs)	Wheat ('000 MTs)	Sugar ('000 MTs)
1975	36.16	7634	N.A	531	490	97
1985	43.73	7922	N.A	1412	110	142
1993	54.75	N.A	28.23	1647	228	N.A
1994	55.70	N.A	28.39	1152	291	N.A
1995	56.54	13173	28.41	1130	423	150
1996	57.75	N.A	29.82	1404	492	N.A
1997	59.52	15015	30.23	1608	353	154
1998	61.09	17448	30.46	1639	458	N,A
1999	61.62	17663	30.47	1358	271	15.4
2000	62,62	17528	30.44	656	64	15.2
2001	63.44	17127	30.44	461	78	7.2
2002	63.83	16769	30.84	423	140	4.5

Source: Government of Kerala. *Economic Review*, various issues; Statistics for Planning, 1983; Statistics for Planning, 2003.

TABLE 11.15

P.D.S. Issue Prices and Open Market Prices for Rice In Kerala

Year	Off-take of Rice ('000 MTs)		P.D.S. Price		Open Market Price	Relative Price of Rice Supplied Through the P.D.S.	
	APL (1)	BPL (2)	For APL (3)	For BPL (4)	(5)	APL (3)/(5)	BPL (4)/(5)
1997	N.A	N.A	7.50	3.90	11.27	0.67	0.35
1998	1439	184 (92.23)	7.50 (100.00)	3.90	12.58	0.60	0.31
1999	1081	172 (71.92)	9.60 (93.47)	4.50	13.90	0.69	0.33
2000	115	370 (7.7)	12.40 (100.00)	6.40	13.34	0.93	0.48
2001	22	368 (1.56)	8.90 (100.00)	6.20	12.20	0.73	0.51
2002	N.A	N.A	8.90	6.20	12.90	0.69	0.48
2003	N.A	N.A	8.90	6.20	13.74	0.65	0.45

Note: Figures in column 1 and 2 relate to financial years. Figures in parentheses show off take as a percentage of allotment.

Source: Col.1 and 2: Pillai (2004); Col.3 to 5: GoK. *Economic Review 2003*; Statistics for Planning, 2002.

Nevertheless, the system of equal prices charged by fair price shops was discontinued in 1997, in pursuance of the changes in policy of the Union government. The Targeted Public Distribution System (T.P.D.S.) introduced by the Government of India with effect from 1st June 1997, limited food subsidy to households below the poverty line. The states were allowed to access from the central pool only to that part of the grain required for distribution among households below the poverty line (based on the Planning Commission's estimates on poverty) at subsidised prices. Additional supplies could be obtained at the 'issue price' fixed by the Union government. For Kerala, 25 per cent was taken as the proportion of population below the poverty line, based on the findings of the 50th round of the NSS. However, the Government of Kerala, on the basis of a survey conducted for IRDP, extended the subsidy to another 17 per cent, bearing the additional financial burden all by itself. Thus, at present 42 per cent of the population of Kerala are able to access the fair price system at prices below the market price. The remaining households are allowed access to food from the fair price shops at prices that covered the cost of acquiring it from the Food Corporation of India plus transportation and handling charges.

The Impact of Targeting

The off-take from the fair price system, therefore, is significantly influenced by differences in the open market prices and prices charged under the P.D.S. It also depends on the quality of food supplied through fair price shops *vis-à-vis* of that available in the open market.

The prices of food sold under the fair price system are fixed by the Union government and the main consideration in fixing these prices is the prices at which the items are procured from cultivators. The 'issue price' underwent revision four times between 1997 and 2002. As a result, the price of rice distributed through the fair price system showed considerable increase between 1997 and 2000 and declined thereafter. But, the issue price of rice in the fair price system (as shown by the price charged from the A.P.L. population) remained lower than open market prices, except in 2000 (Table 11.15). The difference in the prices between the open market and the fair price system is accounted for by several factors, the most important being the traders' margin and the quality of rice sold.

Table 11.15 shows considerable increase in the degree of dependence of the B.P.L. population on the P.D.S. for their rice requirement since the introduction of targeting. On the contrary, the off-take of rice by the A.P.L. population registered continuous decline. In 2001, it was as low as 1.56 per cent of the allotted quantity and only 1.53 per cent of the off-take in 1998. The decline in the off-take does not seem to have been the result of a rise in the P.D.S. price. P.D.S. rice continues to be relatively cheap. Moreover, the relative price of rice sold through P.D.S. in the post -targeting period has not been very much higher than during the 1960s, 1970s and 1980s.[24] However, studies conducted prior to the introduction of targeting noticed the relationship between P.D.S. purchases and the quality of the grain supplied,[25] poor quality of grain being cited as a reason for some households not lifting the ration to which they were entitled (Nair, 2000). It might appear that prosperity-induced changes in tastes have been taking place not only between cereals and other food items but also between better quality cereals and poorer quality cereals.

But there are strong reasons to believe that the policy of increasing the issue prices has proved to be inflationary and had a strong push effect on the open market prices.[26] The impact of these changes in the open market prices, in all probability, would be more on the households which fall on the border-line of poverty and remain outside the protection of subsidy.

Dependence on the Open Market

The supply of foodgrains to Kerala from outside sources consists of two parts: the quantity of grain lifted from the central pool on government accounts (and distributed through the public distribution system) and, the supply of grain through private trade channels. However, no reliable information is available on the latter though it is possible to make some rough and ready estimates. Using NSS data on per capita cereal consumption, it is possible to arrive at the total quantity of cereals consumed in the state. This quantity may be taken as the total availability. To calculate the

24. P.D.S. Price and Open Market Price of Rice in Kerala, 1965-2000 (Rs./ Kg.)

Year	P.D.S. Price	Open Market Price	Relative Price of P.D.S. to Open Market Prices
1965	0.70	1.13	0.62
1970	1.06	1.61	0.66
1980	1.77	2.58	0.69
1985	2.49	4.13	0.60
1990	3.31	5.25	0.63
1995	6.00	9.67	0.62
2002	8.90	12.85	0.69

Source: UN/CDS (1975); GoK. *Statistics for Planning, 1993 and 2002*, GoK, Department of Civil Supplies, *Statistical Hand Book of Rationing*.

25. Pulapre Balakrishanan and Bharat Ramaswami had put foreword a theoretical argument to suggest that consumer perception of the differences in the quality of cereals supplied by the two agencies, the P.D.S. and the open market, induces demand-switching between the two agencies (Balakrishnan and Ramaswami, 2000).

26. This can happen in two ways. As Balakrishnan and Ramaswami have argued, when issue prices rise and get closer to market prices, demand switch-over take place in favour of the open market; the demand pressure tends to push up market price. Another line of reasoning, which seems to have been more valid, is that when market prices of food grains rise, other prices, including those of agricultural inputs, follow suit, bringing in pressure from farm lobbies to raise the procurement prices, which, in turn, is taken by the government for raising issue prices. (See, Balakrishanan and Ramaswami (2000) and Krishnaji and Krishnan (2000).

supply of grain through private trade channels, we subtract from the total grain consumed in the state, the supply of grain from internal production, after making an allowance of 10 per cent for seed, and the quantity of grain lifted by the state government from the central pool. The results are summarised in Table 11.16.

Nearly 38 per cent of the rice and a slightly higher percentage of cereals consumed in the state in 1972-73 came from the public distribution system. Internal production contributed a slightly higher proportion; the contribution from imports through private trade channels was almost negligible. The availability of grain from internal production showed almost continuous decline in the subsequent years. But the decline in the contribution of internal sources was not matched by a proportionate increase in government supplies, the gap being filled by private imports of grain into the state.

The contribution of P.D.S. supplies to total grain availability in the state declined in 1993. The shift in the consumption pattern of the middle-income classes away from cereals referred to earlier, had begun in the mid-eighties; the shift also was from low quality cereals to high quality cereals. However, the decline was not conspicuous till 1999, till about the introduction of the T.P.D.S. Decline in the contribution of internal production meant increase in the relative contribution of private trade. By 1999, nearly 52 per cent of the grain market in Kerala was in the hands of private traders.

The decline of the fair price system and the corresponding rise in private trading in the grain market are causes for serious apprehension about the future of food security in the state. Not only has it left the market for grain to the manipulations of the private traders but also given clout to traders. The state has become, as a result, vulnerable to unexpected and transitory episodes of food insecurity.

Summary and Implications

Life expectancy and infant mortality rate in Kerala stand close to those of countries at much higher levels of income and certainly higher levels of nutrition. Kerala's deficiency in food production is related mainly to cereals, the cheapest and the richest source of energy. Unlike in/other parts of India, particularly the North, the principal energy sources in Kerala consist besides cereals, also of several tubers, of which the most important, in terms of quantity consumed, is tapioca. Till recently, tapioca constituted an important part of the Malayali dish, particularly among the poor. Therefore, the question of food intake was analysed with consumption of cereals and tapioca taken together. Though per capita consumption of cereals in the state increased over the period 1972-73 to 1999-2000, the overall calorie consumption did not register a corresponding increase, due to a steady fall in the consumption of cereal substitutes.

Nevertheless, despite fall in the intake of starch-based foods, the average calorie intake in the state registered improvement during the period studied (1972-73 to 1999-2000). But, only the richest 30 per cent of the population were found to have calorie intake above the required minimum. The calorie intake of 70 per cent of the population (comprising middle 40 per cent and the bottom 30 per cent) was found to be lower than the minimum requirement. The improvement in calorie intake is seen to have spread across all the income groups. In fact, the bottom 30 per cent registered the highest growth rate in both the rural and the urban areas. Consequently, inequality in calorie intake across income groups has declined over time. The rate of growth of calorie intake has been, however, declining for all the income groups.

Considerable shifts in the consumption pattern have taken place during 1972-73 to 1999-2000; there has

27. Information on the production of some commodities in Kerala during 1985-86 to 1999-2000 are shown in the table below:

Items	Production			Annual Growth Rates		
	1985-1986	1993-1994	1999-2000	1985-1993	1993-1999	1985-1999
Pulses (TT)	20.48	15.32	10.99	-3.56	-5.39	-4.35
Milk (M.T)	1.28	2.01	2.53	5.71	3.95	4.95
Eggs (M.N.)	1360	1844	2044	3.88	1.73	2.95
Meat (TT)	89.11	129.22	155.08	4.76	3.09	4.04
Fish (L.MT)	3.80	6.05	6.68	6.00	1.67	4.12
Fruits (TT)	551.10	907.49	1037.86	6.43	2.26	4.63

Note: (1) TT stands for thousand tonnes, MT for Million tonnes, M.N. for million numbers and LMT for Lakh million tonnes.

(2) Figures for fruits include only banana, plantains and mangoes.

Source: Statistics for Planning, 2001; *Economic Review 2003*.

been a movement away from cereals and cereal substitutes to 'other' foods which are costlier but are of lower calorie value. Such diversification was seen to have taken place among all income groups. These changes in Kerala are observed to be similar to those at the all-India level. The shifts were partly prosperity-induced. It has recently been shown that remittances made by emigrants began increasing steadily from the mid-seventies onwards and that the growth of this source accelerated from the mid-eighties.

The shift in the consumption pattern has been in favour of high-value products such as milk, meat, egg, fish, vegetables and fruits. The production of most of these items within the state is adequate to meet the current demand. However, the growth rates for some of these items between 1985/86-1993 and 1993/94 and 1999/2000 have been declining.[27]

However, the absolute demand for cereals is hardly likely to decline. The consumption of cereals by the highest income group has more or less been stabilised. But the consumption levels of the poorer groups fall short of requirements. Nevertheless, the possibility for raising cereal production within the state appears to be bleak. But, dependence on outside supplies for cereals makes food security in the state vulnerable to fluctuations in production elsewhere. Any fall in the production of cereals elsewhere in the country is likely to set in inflationary pressures on grain in Kerala. The policy at the distribution level should be able to manage the price system and it is in this context that the role of an effectively managed public distribution system arises.

The public distribution system has been facing crisis conditions in recent years. The off-take of grain by the A.P.L. population from PDS has become marginal. The decline has not been a result of changes in issue prices but deterioration in the quality of grain sold. It would seem that changes in the prosperity-induced shifts in the consumption pattern are not restricted to a movement from cereals to non-cereals, but also from poor quality cereals to high quality cereals. But, the withdrawal of the A.P.L population from the fair price system has raised the degree of their market dependence. After the introduction of targeting, the proportion of the quantity of food grains imported by private traders into the state has gone up from 28 per cent to 52 per cent. Left to the manipulations of the private traders, the food security in Kerala would be exposed to greater vicissitudes and vulnerability. The mounting losses of the Civil Supplies Corporation raise serious questions regarding its viability. It may be possible to overcome this crisis situation by cross-subsidisation, whereby the Corporation would expand its operations in proven profit-making activities and financing its operations in the food front, particularly that of grains, from such profits.

References

Balakrishnan, Pulapre and Bharat Ramaswami (2000). "Food Consumption Trends in India: A Regional Analysis", in N. Krishanaji and T.N. Krishnan (eds.), *Public Support for Food Security, The Public Distribution System in India.* New Delhi: Sage Publications.

Bansil, P.C. (2003). "Demand for Foodgrains by 2020 A.D", in Mahendra Dev. S, K.P. Kannan and Nira Ramachandran (eds.), *Towards a Food Secure India, Issues and Policies.* New Delhi: Institute for Human Development and Hyderabad: Centre for Economic and Social Studies.

Centre for Development Studies (1975). *Poverty, Unemployment and Development Policy, A Case Study of Selected Issues with reference to Kerala.* New York: United Nations.

Dandekar N.M. and N. Rath (1971). *Poverty in India.* Bombay: Indian School of Political Economy.

Deaton, Angus (2003). "Adjusted Indian Poverty Estimates for 1999-2000", *Economic and Political Weekly,* Vol. 37(4): 322-26.

Dreze, Jean and Amartya Sen (1989). *Hunger and Public Action.* Oxford: Oxford University Press.

George, P.S. (1979). Public Distribution of Foodgrains in Kerala—Income Distribution Implications and Effectiveness, *Research Report* 7. Washington: International Food Policy Research Institute.

Government of Kerala (Various years). *Economic Review.* Thiruvananthapuram: State Planning Board.

———. (2003). *Statistics for Planning: 2001.* Thiruvananthapuram: State Planning Board.

Indian Council of Medical Research (1998). *Nutritional Requirements and Recommended Dietary Allowances for Indian.* A Report of the Expert Group of the Indian Medical Research. New Delhi.

Kabir, M. (2002). "Growth of Service Sector in Kerala, A Comparative Study of Travancore and Malabar, 1901-1951", Ph.D Thesis (unpublished). Thiruvananthapuram: Centre for Development Studies.

Kannan, K.P. (2000). "Food Security in a Regional Perspective, A View from Food Deficit Kerala", *Working Paper* No. 304. Thiruvananthapuram: Centre for Development Studies.

Kannan, K.P. and K.S. Hari (2002). "Kerala's Gulf Connection, Emigration, Remittances and Their Macroeconomic Impact, 1972-2000", *Working Paper* No. 328. Thiruvananthapuram: Centre for Development Studies.

Koshy, Abraham *et al.* (1989). *Report of the Study on Evaluation of the Public Distribution System in Kerala.* Thiruvananthapuram: Centre for Development Studies.

Krishnaji, N. and T.N. Krishnan (2000). "Introduction", in N. Krishanaji and T.N. Krishnan *op. cit.* New Delhi: Sage Publications.

Meenakshi, J.V. (2000). "Food Consumption Trends in India: A Regional Analysis", in N. Krishanaji and T.N. Krishnan *op. cit.* New Delhi: Sage Publications.

Mooij, Jose (1999). *Food Policy and the Indian State: The Public Distribution System in South India.* New Delhi: Oxford University Press.

Nair, K.N. (2000). "Food Security and the Public Distribution System in Kerala" in N. Krishanaji and T.N. Krishnan *op. cit.* New Delhi: Sage Publications.

Pushpangadan, K. (1988). "Agricultural Stagnation in Kerala: An Econometric Study of Tapioca", *Working Paper* No. 226. Thiruvananthapuram: Centre for Development Studies.

Qadeer, Imrana and Anju P. Priyadarshi (2005). "Nutrition Policy, Shifts and Logical Fallacies" *Economic and Political Weekly,* Vol. XL(5), January 29.

Radhakrishna, R. and C. Ravi (1992). Effects of Growth, Relative Prices and Preferences on Food and Nutrition, *Indian Economic Review,* Vol. 27, Special Number 303-23.

Radhakrishna R. and K.V. Reddy (2004). *Agricultural Growth, Employment and Food Security: An Overview.* Mumbai: Indira Gandhi Institute for Development Research.

Ravallion, M. (1987). *Markets and Famines.* Oxford: Oxford University Press.

———. (1997). "Famines and Economics", *Journal of Economic Literature,* Vol.35: 1205-42, September.

Sen, Amartya (1981). *Poverty and Famines: An Essay on Entitlement and Deprivation.* Oxford: Clarendon Press

Stringer, Randy (2001). "Food Security in Developing Countries", in B.N.Ghosh (ed.), *Contemporary Issues in Development Economics.* London: Routledge.

Suryanarayana M.H. (2000). "Food Consumption Trends in India: A Regional Analysis", in N. Krishanaji and T.N. Krishnan *op. cit.* New Delhi: Sage Publications.

———.(1996). "Food Security and PDS in Kerala: Form and Scope for Reform", Paper presented at the International Conference on *Kerala's Development Experience: National and Global Dimensions,* December 9-11. New Delhi.

Viswanathan, Brinda and J.V. Meenaksi (2000-2001). "Developing Country Nutrition Does Improve with Income: A Look at Calorie and Protein Intakes, 1983 to 1993-94", *Sarvekshana,* 85th Issue, Vol. XXIV(2&3), October-March.

Chapter 12

Ageing and Social Security

Introduction

The process of ageing starts at the point of birth itself although the aged are persons who live through the life course and are chronologically old in the number of years lived. While this process is temporally compared along with the evolving process of demographic transition, it is often found that the number of the 'old' or the 'aged' keep steadily increasing. Apart from this numeric feature, old individuals represent distinctions in socioeconomic and physical make-ups from other individuals. This phenomenon occurring as a consequence of the differential paces of demographic transition across Indian states identifies the southern states to be ahead in the race. After the next 30 to 50 years, South India will undergo a distinct transformation in the age structure of its population with the proportion of its elderly population quite high.

Although the increasing proportion of elderly persons in total populations is a global phenomenon, the pace and patterns of ageing are relatively distinct in south India given the rapid pace, especially in the state of Kerala in contrast to the evolutionary trends in the northern states (Irudaya Rajan, 2005). The precipitous increase in the numbers of elderly persons and in their proportions in relation to those of the working age population have serious economic and social implications for Kerala, a state in which families have customarily supported their elderly. However, of late, the care-givers in families are on the decline due to reduction in family size, national and international migration and rising work participation rates of women opting for gainful employment outside home. The increasing presence of elderly persons in Kerala is making people of all ages increasingly aware that the present situation constitutes a diverse and multigenerational society. It is no longer possible to ignore the phenomenon of ageing, regardless of whether one views it positively or negatively. If current trends in ageing continue as predicted, the proportions of the young and the old will undergo a historic crossover around 2021 in Kerala.

As Kerala stands ahead by 25 years of the rest of the country in its achievement in reaching the final stage of demographic transition (low fertility and mortality), the ageing scenario of Kerala calls for special research unlike that in any other state in India (Zachariah and Irudaya Rajan, 1997; Irudaya Rajan and Zachariah, 1998). For instance, on an average, a woman in Kerala ends up producing just 1.6 children–lower than the replacement level of fertility. A male child born today in Kerala is expected to live more than 71 years of age and the female child for 76 years, five more years than her male counterpart. The infant mortality rate in Kerala is reported to be extremely low at 11 per 1000 live births. The number of children in Kerala's population is fast declining.

Even when families can support their older generation, they have difficulty in doing so because persons above 60 years of age today live much longer than their counterparts of earlier generations and may require care and medical treatment for many years as they endure into very old age. The recently released 2001 Census data which show that Kerala has more than 10 per cent of its population consisting of the elderly, focus on the needs to set in for enduring the welfare of this segment given the socioeconomic and health-related vulnerability of old age. Many elderly persons in Kerala who had worked in the formal sector and are recipients of pension or other income-security benefits would be able to economically support themselves in varying degrees during their post-

TABLE 12.1

Elderly in India, 2001 Census

Rank	*States*	*60+*		*70+*		*80+*	
		Population	*Percentage*	*Population*	*Percentage*	*Population*	*Percentage*
	India	76826245	7.5	29376651	2.9	8060098	0.8
01	**Kerala**	**3338428**	**10.5**	**1402678**	**4.4**	**389332**	**1.2**
02	Punjab	2200153	9.0	939859	3.9	299106	1.2
03	Himachal Pradesh	548890	9.0	245121	4.0	81152	1.3
04	Tamil Nadu	5545499	8.9	2097100	3.4	557029	0.9
05	Maharashtra	8464895	8.7	3094957	3.2	780039	0.8
06	Goa	112858	8.4	41928	3.1	10969	0.8
07	Pondicherry	81082	8.3	31939	3.3	8223	0.8
08	Orissa	3044221	8.3	1168791	3.2	293770	0.8
09	Uttaranchal	655726	7.7	258515	3.0	70331	0.8
10	Karnataka	4065985	7.7	1611495	3.0	457643	0.9
11	Andhra Pradesh	5798171	7.6	2082435	2.7	505185	0.7
12	Haryana	1590118	7.5	656182	3.1	184587	0.9
13	Tripura	232896	7.3	106606	3.3	35296	1.1
14	Chhattisgarh	1506393	7.2	534077	2.6	135486	0.7
15	West Bengal	5708014	7.1	2275599	2.8	670812	0.8
16	Madhya Pradesh	4292242	7.1	1609752	2.7	436919	0.7
17	Uttar Pradesh	11701369	7.0	4470314	2.7	1273057	0.8
18	Gujarat	3502295	6.9	1310502	2.6	374579	0.7
19	Rajasthan	3829791	6.8	1473636	2.6	394208	0.7
20	Manipur	145775	6.7	61569	2.8	17211	0.8
21	Jammu & Kashmir	678384	6.7	274603	2.7	82415	0.8
22	Bihar	5513117	6.6	2046843	2.5	566871	0.7
23	Lakshadweep	3732	6.2	1288	2.1	381	0.6
24	Jharkhand	1580601	5.9	553844	2.1	148144	0.5
25	Assam	1562062	5.9	601856	2.3	169824	0.6
26	Mizoram	49066	5.5	20108	2.3	5313	0.6
27	Sikkim	29144	5.4	11018	2.0	2716	0.5
28	Delhi	720743	5.2	269146	1.9	70929	0.5
29	Daman & Diu	8045	5.1	2930	1.9	811	0.5
30	Chandigarh	44977	5.0	18170	2.0	5216	0.6
31	Andaman & Nicobar Islands	17478	4.9	6222	1.7	1676	0.5
32	Meghalaya	105870	4.6	39790	1.7	11258	0.5
33	Arunachal Pradesh	49967	4.6	18063	1.6	5655	0.5
34	Nagaland	90540	4.5	37709	1.9	13644	0.7
35	Dadra & Nagar Haveli	8818	4.0	2618	1.2	611	0.3

Note: Estimates based on the 2001 Census.

Source: Irudaya Rajan and Aliyar, 2004.

retirement years. However, a majority of them who are not covered by any such schemes and who had earned their livelihood by work in the informal sector, continue to remain in the work force till about the age of 80 years. Shockingly, the majority of them are women. They have not been able, for one reason or another, to accumulate sufficient savings to ensure their well-being in old age. This situation makes a case for extension of social safety nets to cover all elderly persons.

TABLE 12.2

Sex Ratio Among Elderly, 2001 Census

States	*Sex Ratio (females per 1000 males)*		
	60+	*70+*	*80+*
India	1028	991	1051
Andaman and Nicobar Islands	766	827	932
Sikkim	772	734	752
Nagaland	780	786	765
Jammu and Kashmir	846	820	837
Bihar	882	827	811
Uttar Pradesh	886	821	830
Arunachal Pradesh	889	892	900
Chandigarh	891	887	953
Assam	949	876	923
Meghalaya	957	991	1050
Delhi	963	925	996
Punjab	971	865	922
Mizorzm	977	1019	1184
Lakshadweep	979	1024	1177
Manipur	986	988	1033
Haryana	991	863	884
Uttaranchal	1002	952	984
Jharkhand	1005	945	891
Tamil Nadu	1013	977	1040
Himachal Pradesh	1021	997	1027
Orissa	1022	958	892
West Bengal	1047	1032	1093
Tripura	1064	1105	1230
Rajasthan	1084	1108	1261
Madhya Pradesh	1084	1112	1240
Andhra Pradesh	1099	1051	1215
Karnataka	1111	1137	1258
Gujarat	1148	1239	1410
Maharashtra	1150	1063	1218
Chhattisgarh	1181	1182	1175
Pondicherry	1222	1239	1249
Daman & Diu	1239	1370	1886
Kerala	**1247**	**1319**	**1472**
Goa	1260	1424	1553
Dadra & Nagarhaveli	1270	1381	1406

Note: Estimates based on the 2001 Census.

Source: Same as Table 12.1

Population Ageing: Inter-state Analysis

As of 2001, India accommodates 77 million elderly persons, second only to China, representing 7.5 per cent of the total population. Among them, 29 million are above 70 years and 8 million above 80 years of age (Irudaya Rajan, 2006). Among the states, Uttar Pradesh led with 11 million elderly, followed by Maharashtra (8.5 Million), West Bengal (5.7 million) and Tamil Nadu (5.5 Million). The smallest number of the elderly is found in the union territory of Lakshadweep. The low fertility state of Kerala ranks number one with the highest proportion of the elderly in the country (10.5 per cent in 2001). Punjab and Himachal Pradesh occupy the second largest position in terms of percentage of the elderly, followed by states of Tamil Nadu (8.9 per cent) and Maharashtra (8.7 per cent). Dadra-Nagar Haveli registered the lowest proportion (4 per cent) of the elderly. The highest percentage of the population 80 years of age and above is seen in Himachal Pradesh (1.3 per cent), followed by Kerala (1.2 per cent); see Table 12.1.

India is one of the few countries in the world in which males outnumber females. Among the elderly, there are more widows than widowers. According to the 2001 Census, the sex ratio among the Indian elderly of 60 years and above is 1028 females for 1000 males. However, the trend is in favour of males among persons above 70 years; it is reversed in favour of females among the persons of 80 years of age and above. Among the states, Kerala has recorded one of the highest sex ratio—1247 females per 1000 males among the elderly. The ratio improves further to 1319 among the population above 70 years, and to 1472 among persons of 80 years and above (Table 12.2). Table 12.3 shows various indices of population ageing in India. Kerala has registered the highest median age (27.9 years) in India indicating a final phase of demographic transition, followed by Goa (27.6 years), Tamil Nadu (27 years) and Pondicherry (26.5 years).

The highest Index of ageing in the country is also reported for Kerala (40.2) followed by Goa (33.9), Tamil Nadu (33.0) and Pondicherry (30.8). This is also true of alternative indicators of ageing like median ageing and the aged dependency ratio. As Kerala is ahead by 25 years from the rest of the country and is in the final stages of demographic transition, the ageing scenario of Kerala is much more important than of any other state in India.

Ageing in Kerala

In the above context, it is quite interesting to note that the major features of the Kerala statistics are entirely different from those of the country as a whole. According to the first Census taken after the reorganisation of states in 1956, (in the 1961 Census),

TABLE 12.3

Indices of Ageing, 2001 Census

State	*Median Age*	*Index of Ageing*	*Age Dependency Ratio*
Jammu and Kashmir	21.6	18.7	11.6
Himachal Pradesh	24.5	29.1	15.1
Punjab	24.2	28.8	15.2
Chandigarh	24.6	17.2	7.6
Uttaranchal	21.5	21.2	13.8
Haryana	21.8	20.9	13.3
Delhi	23.5	16.0	8.4
Rajasthan	20.1	16.9	12.8
Uttar Pradesh	19.6	17.2	13.6
Bihar	19.5	15.8	13.0
Sikkim	21.6	15.4	9.0
Arunachal Pradesh	19.8	11.3	8.3
Nagaland	20.0	12.4	7.7
Manipur	23.1	20.6	11.1
Mizoram	21.7	15.6	9.3
Tripura	23.3	21.6	12.3
Meghalaya	18.1	10.8	8.6
Assam	21.6	15.7	10.3
West Bengal	24.1	21.4	11.9
Jharkhand	20.6	14.7	10.8
Orissa	24.1	24.9	14.1
Chattisgarh	22.3	19.6	13.0
Madhya Pradesh	21.1	18.4	13.1
Gujarat	23.6	21.0	11.5
Daman and Diu	23.7	18.6	7.5
Dadra and Nagar Haveli	22.3	11.3	6.6
Maharashtra	24.4	27.2	14.8
Andhra Pradesh	24.4	23.7	12.6
Karnataka	24.3	24.1	12.7
Goa	27.6	33.9	12.5
Lakshadweep	23.0	18.0	10.3
Kerala	**27.9**	**40.2**	**16.5**
Tamil Nadu	27.0	33.0	13.9
Pondichery	26.5	30.8	12.6
Andaman and Nicobar Islands	24.5	16.7	7.5
All India	22.7	21.1	13.1

Note: Estimates based on the 2001 Census.

Source: Same as Table 12.1

the number of elderly persons in Kerala of 60 years of age and above was only 10 lakh; the number increased to 26 lakh in 1991 (a 160 per cent increase). According to the latest 2001 Census, Kerala had 33 lakh elderly persons. Their number is expected to increase to 57 lakhs in 2021 and to 120 lakhs in 2061 and the proportion is likely to reach 40 per cent in 2061. Though the Kerala population is growing at less than one per cent, the growth of the elderly during 1991-2001 has been much higher and the trend is likely to continue for the next few decades; see Table 12.4.

Similarly, the old-old population (above 70 years of age) was just 10 lakhs in 1991. Our projections indicated that the old-old would reach 25 lakhs in 2021 and 72 lakhs in 2061. During 1961-1991, the growth rate among the old-old hovered around 3 per cent; it is expected to register a growth rate of around 4 per cent in the coming decades. The oldest-old (aged 80 years and above) in Kerala was a mere 2.9 lakhs in 1991; their number is expected to increase to 8 lakhs in 2021 and further to 27 lakhs by 2061.The growth rates among the oldest-old have been higher than of the young-old and the old-old in Kerala over the past 40 years; the growth rate is expected to slow down in the coming decades. The age pyramids for Kerala are presented (2001 and 2061) in Figure 12.1 to indicate the speed of ageing in Kerala. Though the number of the elderly in Kerala is much lower than those of a few populous states in India, Kerala leads with the highest proportion of the elderly among all the Indian states and union territories. Further, the number of women among the elderly far exceeds the number of men. Kerala also leads with the highest female expectation of life at birth and the gender gap was around six years around 2000. At the age of 60 years, a Malayali woman was expected to live 21 years against her male counterpart 19 years; see Figures 12.2 and 12.3.

FIGURE 12.1

Age Pyraminds for Kerala, 2001 and 2061
All Age Groups

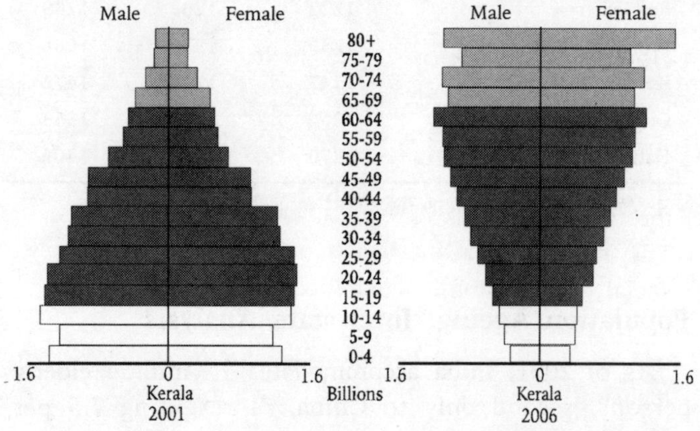

TABLE 12.4

Demographic Profile of Elderly, 1961-2061

Year	*Number of Aged (Millions)*			*Percentage Total*			*Growth Rate (Per cent)*		
	60+	*70+*	*80+*	*60+*	*70+*	*80+*	*60+*	*70+*	*80+*
1961	0.99	0.36	0.09	5.1	1.9	0.4	-	-	-
1971	1.33	0.50	0.13	6.2	2.3	0.6	3.47	3.66	4.71
1981	1.91	0.71	0.19	7.5	2.8	0.7	4.38	4.35	4.88
1991	2.57	1.00	0.29	8.9	3.4	1.0	3.48	4.06	5.59
2001	3.33	1.40	0.39	10.5	4.4	1.2	2.94	3.99	3.45
2011	4.20	1.94	0.54	12.2	5.6	1.6	2.61	3.86	3.85
2021	5.75	2.46	0.76	16.0	6.8	2.1	3.69	2.68	4.07
2031	7.78	3.52	1.01	21.3	9.7	2.7	3.53	4.31	3.29
2041	9.88	4.86	1.48	27.8	13.7	4.2	2.70	3.81	4.65
2051	11.48	6.22	2.11	34.4	18.6	6.3	1.62	2.80	4.26
2061	11.95	7.18	2.76	39.6	23.8	9.1	0.41	1.54	3.08

Note: Compiled by the authors for the periods 1961-2001 using the Indian Censuses. The figures for the years from 2001 to 2061 are extracted from the population projections done by the authors (more details, Irudaya Rajan and Sabu Aliyar, 2004).

FIGURE 12.2

Sex Ratio among Elderly in Kerala, 2001 and 2061

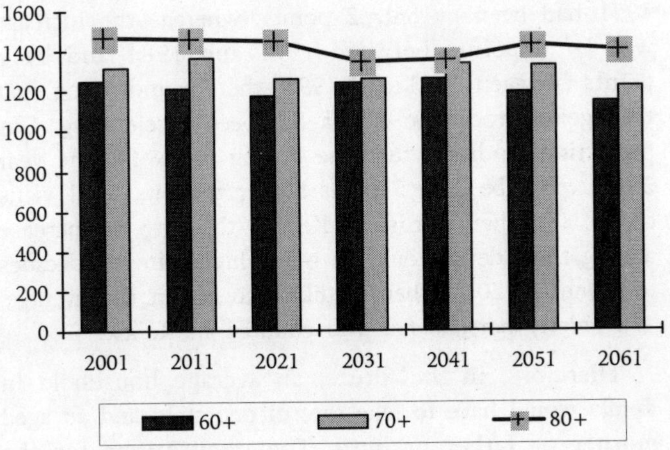

FIGURE 12.3

Expected Crossover between and the Aged in Kerala

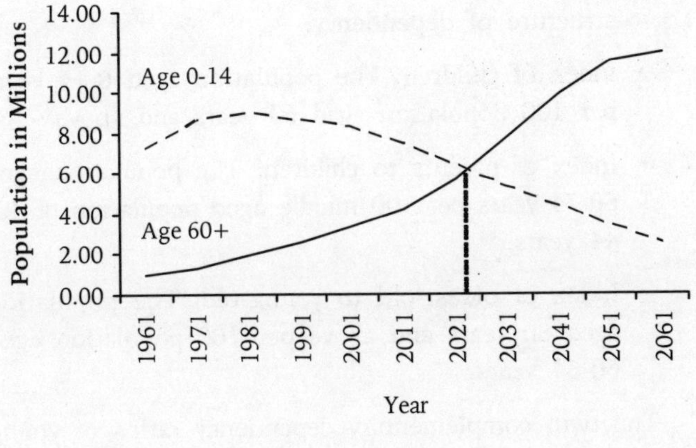

Dependency Ratios

Gerontologists are more concerned with the personal support systems and 'social convoys' of the elderly since the support systems have important implications for their social, psychological and economic well-being. The need for national measures of protection of the social and economic dependency of older persons has partly been highlighted by demographers through the use of various measures of 'age dependency'. These measures relate the numbers in various age categories to one another. Some of them serve as measures of dependency of the elderly on their families, particularly on their children, while others serve as measures of dependency on the society as a whole. The former tend largely to be surrogates for measures of social and psychological support of the elderly whereas the latter tends largely to be surrogates of economic support.

The ratio of persons aged 60-74 years to persons aged 40-44 years is a type of familial dependency ratio relating the elderly to their middle-aged children. The ratio of persons aged 80 years and above to persons 60-64 years is a type of familial dependency ratio relating the extremely aged persons to their young-old off-springs. The ratio of persons aged 60 or above to persons aged 15-59 is the most commonly used type of societal dependency ratio. The prospective shifts in the age structure of the population suggest that the extent of the problems of familial support for the aged will deteriorate in the future reflecting mainly the impact of the past trends in fertility rates, and that, in general, they will tend to become greater than at present and probably would become severe around 2025.

The following familial and societal dependency ratios are presented for Kerala for the periods 1961 to 2061.

- Young Dependency Ratio: The number of persons aged 0-14 years per 100 persons of intermediate age (working age 15-59 years).
- Aged Dependency Ratio: The number of persons aged 60 years and above per 100 persons of working age (15-59 years).
- Total Dependency Ratio: The number of persons in the non-working age group (0-14 years and 60+ years) per 100 persons of working age (15-59 years).
- Index of Ageing: The proportion of the population aged 60 years and above to the population aged 0-14 years. It is intended to measure the structure of dependency.
- Index of children: The population aged 0-14 years per 100 population aged 60 years and above.
- Index of parents to children: The population aged 60-74 years per 100 middle aged population of 40-44 years.
- Index of oldest-old to young-old: The population aged 80 years and above per 100 population aged 60-64 years.

The twin complementary dependency ratios of young dependency and old age dependency seem to have been moving together with the former registering a consistent decline and the latter a modest increase, in the state of Kerala during 1961-1991.The trends in the young dependency ratio registered a decline from 82.7 in 1961 to 49.9 in 1991 while the old age dependency ratio improved from 11.3 to 14.4 during the same period. At the present juncture, households in Kerala have gained in terms of the reduced burden of dependents, and caring for fewer children, without at the same time having to take too much strain to take care of their elderly. At the moment, 100 persons in the working age group take care on the average 17 old persons.

The decline in fertility reduced the overall dependency burden from 94.0 in 1961 to 64.3 in 1991.Though the aged dependency ratios are on the increase, the overall dependency ratio has shown a decline of 30 points during 1961-1991; see Table 12.5.

The projected age dependency ratios for the period 2001-2061 are also shown in the Table. During this period, the young dependency ratios are expected to decline from 41 in 2001 to 16 in 2061. On the other hand, the aged dependency ratio is expected to increase from 17 in 2001 to 76 in 2061. The implication of these ratios for the future is that instead of six working age persons now, there would be only two working persons in 2061 on the average, who will have to share the responsibility of taking care of at least one aged person. Moreover, the probability of this aged person being a woman, who is a widow, unskilled, little educated and non-working, non-recipient of any social security benefit and unhealthy without health insurance, is also high.

The index of ageing was nearly 14 in 1961; it increased to 15 in 1971 and to 29 in 1991.We also see from Table 12.5 that the increase between 1961 and 1971 had been by only 2 points, whereas the increase was by 6 points between 1971 and 1981 and by 7 points between 1981 and 1991, thereby indicating that the ageing process in Kerala has been accelerating. Our projections indicate that the ageing index for the year 2041 would be 228, 5 times higher than its 2001 value of 40. In other words, in Kerala, the rate of increase among the elderly would be much higher in the decades to come. In 2061, there is likely to be on the average, 476 elderly persons per 100 children in Kerala.

Therefore, in the future, an average household in Kerala would have to take care of one child and an aged mother or father or both. The implications for the burden of the family would be quite substantial as the cost of care of an older person is different from that of a child. For the society, this shift in the dependency structure would call for a substantial change in the pattern of public sector expenditure. Furthermore, while the care of the child is the direct responsibility of the parents, the care of old persons is only a social obligation which does not carry with it any legal sanction.

Migration Surveys, 1999 and 2004

The Centre for Development Studies has completed two migration surveys in Kerala covering 10,000

TABLE 12.5

Dependency Ratios, Ageing Index and Familial Dependency Ratios for Kerala, 1961-2061

Year	Dependency Ratio			Index of Ageing	Familial Dependency Ratio		
	Young	Old	Total		0-14/60+	60-74/40-44	80+/60-64
1961	82.7	11.3	94.0	13.7	731	105	23
1971	75.2	11.6	86.9	15.5	647	107	26
1981	61.5	13.2	74.7	21.6	466	134	27
1991	49.9	14.4	64.3	28.9	370	136	33
2001	41.1	16.5	57.6	40.1	250	130	38
2011	32.8	18.4	51.2	56.1	178	123	42
2021	26.6	24.0	50.6	90.4	111	148	44
2031	22.8	33.3	56.1	146.2	68	194	45
2041	20.3	46.3	66.6	228.2	44	255	55
2051	18.1	61.9	80.0	342.7	29	332	78
2061	16.0	76.1	92.0	476.1	21	377	109

Note: All ratios refer to 100.

Source: Same as Table 12.4

households throughout Kerala in 1999 and 2004 (Zachariah, Mathew and Irudaya Rajan, 2003; Zachariah and Irudaya Rajan, 2004). The raw data of these surveys have been re-tabulated for the present purpose of assessing issues pertaining to the elderly.

In 1999, around 58 per cent of households in Kerala did not have any elderly person; the corresponding proportion was 52 per cent in 2004 indicating a decline of six percentage points. This piece of evidence suggests a changing household atmosphere in which the elderly do not stay with the rest of the members of the family. In one of the recent discussions with a group of elderly persons living in an institutional set up, an elderly couple (they live alone as old couples) remarked thus: "We are interested to stay with our children and grandchildren but they are not interested in us; thus we are staying alone here managing our day-to-day affairs" (Irudaya Rajan, 2006). As almost half the households in Kerala have no elderly persons to live with, they do not realise the advantages and the disadvantages of elderly persons living with them. Another 33 per cent of the households in Kerala accommodate one elderly person, either a widow or a widower from either the husband's or the wife's side. In other words, almost all the elderly living in such households are just widows or widowers. The practice of two elderly persons living in the same household has gone up slightly from 11 per cent to 14 per cent, indicating the fact of the increase in life expectancy among the elderly, both males and females. Almost one in six couples in Kerala lives beyond 60 years of age as couples without loss of their partners. Households with more than three elderly persons formed less than one per cent in 2004; see Table 12.6.

TABLE 12.6

Distribution of Households by the Number of Elderly, 1999 and 2004

No of Elderly	2004	1999
Nil	51.46	58.00
One	33.47	31.00
Two	14.19	10.50
Three	0.76	0.50
Four	0.12	0.00

Note: Special Tabulations from the *Kerala Migration Survey* and *South Asian Migration Survey*.

To understand the district profile, the proportions of the elderly in all the districts of Kerala for the years 1999 and 2004 have been calculated from the migration surveys; see Table 12.7. Between 1999 and 2004, the proportion of the elderly to the total population in Kerala increased from 11 per cent to 14 per cent. Among the districts of Kerala in 2004, the highest proportion of the elderly is found in Pathanamthitta followed by Alappuzha, Kottayam, Ernakulam and Thiruvananthapuram in that order. All these districts had figures above the state average. The lowest percentage is found in Wayanad. However, 12 out of 14 districts in Kerala have already crossed the 10 per cent mark with Pathanamthitta district showing the

TABLE 12.7

District-wise Proportions of Elderly Population in Kerala: 1999 and 2004

Districts	*1999*			*2004*		
	Male	*Female*	*Total*	*Male*	*Female*	*Total*
Thiruvananthapuram	10.60	11.10	10.90	13.62	13.92	13.77
Kollam	10.70	12.00	11.40	13.21	12.27	12.73
Pathanamthitta	17.50	13.60	15.50	20.48	21.21	20.86
Alappuzha	13.90	13.10	13.40	14.29	15.60	14.97
Kottayam	12.80	12.60	12.70	17.30	19.34	18.32
Idukki	8.90	6.10	7.60	11.43	9.47	10.47
Ernakulum	12.00	13.30	12.70	15.01	16.31	15.67
Thrissur	10.50	12.00	11.30	12.25	13.89	13.11
Palakkad	11.70	11.30	11.50	12.57	14.27	13.47
Malappuram	7.90	7.70	7.70	9.64	9.58	9.61
Kozhikode	10.00	11.00	10.50	13.15	13.07	13.11
Wayanad	7.40	7.60	7.50	8.57	10.14	9.38
Kannur	8.70	10.20	9.40	12.06	13.60	12.87
Kasargode	8.00	8.60	8.30	10.51	10.53	10.52
Kerala	**10.70**	**11.00**	**10.90**	**13.17**	**13.85**	**13.52**

Note: Special Tabulations from the *Kerala Migration Survey* and *South Asian Migration Survey*.

maximum of 21per cent—double that of Malappuram district. Districts, which were the forerunners in the fertility and mortality transition, have reported higher proportions of the elderly (Guilmoto and Irudaya Rajan, 2001; 2002; 2005). In 2004, almost all the districts of Kerala have reported higher proportions of the female elderly in the population than of males, except in the three districts of Kollam, Idukki and Malappuram. Any social policy measures to augment the welfare of the elderly should take note of this phenomenon.

TABLE 12.8

Age Structure of Elderly in Kerala, 2004

Age	*Male*	*Female*	*Total*	*Sex Ratio m/f*1000*
60-64	30.44	31.02	30.75	869
65-69	25.24	25.86	25.57	865
70-74	19.45	17.67	18.50	975
75-79	12.60	12.13	12.35	921
80-84	7.86	7.29	7.56	956
85+	4.17	5.61	4.94	647

Note: Special Tabulations from the *South Asian Migration Survey*.

Among the elderly in Kerala, close to 56 per cent belong to the young-old age group (60-69 years), another 31 per cent are old-old (70-79 years) and only 13 per cent are oldest old (80 years and above); see Table 12.8. Among the elderly in general, there are more females than males (Gulati and Irudaya Rajan, 1999). In the age group 85 years and above, there are only 647 males per 1000 females. Most of the women lose their husbands in old age due to sex differentials in mortality and age differentials at marriage. All these dimensions of widowhood among the aged should be considered seriously when formulating economic and social security measures.

The majority of the men (86 per cent) were married; but among women, the majority (56 per cent) came under the widow category. Similarly, close to 5 per cent of women were reported either as single or as divorced or separated as against 2.5 per cent among men; see Table 12.9. Women require more social and economic

TABLE 12.9

Marital Status of Elderly in Kerala 2004

Marital Status	*2004*		
	Male	*Female*	*Total*
Single	2.0	3.1	2.6
Married	85.9	39.4	61.2
Widowed	11.5	55.9	35.1
Divorced/Separated	0.4	1.4	1.0

Note: Special Tabulations from *South Asian Migration Survey*.

attention in later life, as most of them have no property or assets in their names. In an earlier study, it was reported that around 60 per cent of the elderly females and 30 per cent of the elderly males in India had no valuable assets in their names. Among the major states in India, Kerala ranks first with 76 per cent of its elderly women reporting no financial assets in their names (Irudaya Rajan, 2006)

The status of current co-residence arrangements among the elderly in Kerala by sex, as of 2004 has been analysed. In both all-India and Kerala, 2.5 per cent of the elderly live alone in their respective households (Irudaya Rajan and Sanjay Kumar, 2003). Among them, 4 per cent are females and, most likely, all of them are widows; another eight per cent of the elderly live with spouse. Among the elderly, three-fourths of the males live with spouses, children and grandchildren compared to only 50 per cent of females. On the other hand, almost 40 per cent of females live in Kerala without spouses but live with children and grandchildren as against just 11 per cent among males. The practice of the elderly living with strangers or non-relatives in a household is not common in Kerala. The number of old-age homes in Kerala is 134, one-fifth of the total number of old age homes in India. Currently, at least five old age homes are coming up in Kerala every year. The number of inmates reported in the survey was 5076 persons, of which 60 per cent were women (Irudaya Rajan, 2002)

TABLE 12.10

Living Arrangements among Elderly in Kerala, 2004

Living Arrangement	*Male*	*Female*	*Total*
Living Alone	0.95	3.94	2.54
With Spouse Alone	10.56	5.07	7.65
With spouse, children and grand children	76.11	50.51	62.54
Without spouse but with children, grand children	11.42	38.47	25.76
Without spouse, but with relatives other than children and grand children	0.79	1.87	1.36
With non relatives	0.17	0.15	0.16
Total	100	100	100

Note: Special Tabulations from the *Kerala Migration Surveys*.

Social Security

Social security comprises welfare measures intended for the benefit of the public in general and the poor or the needy in particular. It necessarily serves as a mechanism to ensure basic entitlements for persons who are not able to meet their basic needs due to unemployment, illness, or old age. Social security affords, in short, protection against adversity. Social security measures are intended also to raise basic human capabilities such as health and education. Social security arrangements are collective remedies against adversity and deficiency (Swan, 1998). The present discussion on social security is mostly concerned with adversity among the elderly. It has already been noted that Kerala has made remarkable progress in its demographic transition. The state has achieved below-replacement level of fertility two decades ahead of the all-India target year of 2011. TFR (Total Fertility Rate) which denotes the average number of children that would be born to a woman during her life time, if she passes through her child-bearing years in conformation with the current age- specific fertility rates, declined from a high level of 5.6 in 1951-1961 to about 1.7 in 1993, a level which is much lower than replacement level of 2.05. The population growth rate declined to about 1 per cent per annum by 1995 from 2.3 per cent during 1961-1971. Among all the states in India, longevity is the highest in Kerala, for both men and women (Zacharaih and Irudaya Rajan 1997; Irudaya Rajan and Zachariah, 1998). While Kerala has the unique distinction of being the first state in India to complete the demographic transition, it is noted that one of the immediate consequences of the successful completion of the demographic transition has been population ageing. In the following sections, a brief discussion of the social security programmes for the elderly in Kerala is attempted.

Successive governments in Kerala have introduced social security and welfare assistance schemes during the past few decades. At present, there exist more than 35 such schemes in the state. Kerala spends close to 3 per cent of its state budget for social security programmes while the neighbouring states of Tamil Nadu and Karnataka spend only about 2.3 and 2.5 per cent respectively of their state budgets. During the financial year 2004-05, the allocation in the Kerala state budget for social security programmes was Rs. 21185 crore. The outlay for the development and welfare of the aged in Kerala in the budgets of local self- government institutions amounted to Rs. 18 crore during 2004-05. This expenditure was incurred on activities taken up by them such as provision of day-care centres as well as organisation of medical camps for the aged. Brief details about each scheme such as eligibility criteria, year of introduction, and annual expenditure incurred have come out in earlier publications (Irudaya Rajan, Mishra and Sarma, 1999; Irudaya Rajan, 1999; 2002a; 2002b. The schemes are classified into four categories as shown below:

- Schemes which are fully financed by the State and Central Governments:
  - o National Old-Age Pension
- Schemes which are fully financed by the State:
  - o Kerala Destitute and Widow Pension Scheme
  - o Kerala Agricultural Workers Pension Scheme
- Special Pension Scheme for the physically handicapped and mentally retarded:
  - o Old-age Pension to craftsmen
  - o Pension to Sportsmen in Indigent Circumstances
  - o Pension to Journalists in Indigent Circumstances
  - o Pension to Cine Artists in Indigent Circumstances
  - o Pension to Freedom Fighters
  - o Pension to Second World War Veterans
- Major schemes which are financed with partial state support:
  - o Kerala Coir Workers Welfare Fund
  - o Kerala Construction Workers Welfare Fund
  - o Kerala Fishermen Welfare Fund
- Schemes which are financed outside the budget and operated by respective Boards:
  - o Kerala Head Load Workers Welfare Fund
  - o Kerala Abkari Workers Welfare Fund Scheme
  - o Kerala Toddy Workers Welfare Fund
  - o Kerala Agricultural Workers Welfare Fund

Among the programmes, the highest number of beneficiaries is reported for the agricultural worker pension scheme (5.3 lakh), followed by widow/destitute pension scheme (2.1 lakh), pension for persons with disabilities scheme (1.5 lakh) and national old age pensions scheme (1.4 lakh) (see Table 12.11). Also, the share of the agricultural worker pensions came to about 21 per cent of the total amount earmarked for pension schemes during 2004-05 (Table 12.12). In total, close to 12 lakh elderly persons are receiving financial assistance from the Kerala government. Do they get the money regularly? Is it enough for sustaining their livelihood? In-depth field level research is required to ascertain the facts. In the discussion which follows, the agricultural worker pension scheme is dealt with in some detail.

TABLE 12.11

Social Assistance and Security Programme Beneficiaries in Kerala, 2003

Schemes	*Beneficiaries*
National Old Age Pension	134600
Agricultural Workers	527647
Widow/Destitute Pension Scheme	208445
Special Pension for Persons with Disabilities	148553
Building and Construction Workers	37969
Second World War Veterans	5690
Handloom Workers	7407
Tailoring Workers	5450
Pension to Journalists	398
Pension to Toddy Workers	14929
Coir Workers	67000
Fishermen	28190
Ration Dealers	252
Abkari Workers	97
Cine Artists	146
Khadi Workers	17
Freedom Fighters	8888
Kerala	**1195678**

Source: Compiled from the latest *Economic Review* published from the State Planning Board, Government of Kerala, Thiruvananthapuram.

TABLE 12.12

Financial Assistance from State Budget on Social Security Schemes, 2004-05

Name of the Scheme	*Percentage Allocation*
Destitute Pension	14.0
Agricultural Worker's Pension	21.1
Welfare Fund for Journalists	0.0
Relief to TB Patients	0.0
Welfare Measure for Coir Workers	1.4
Pension Scheme for Physically Handicapped	9.9
Freedom Fighter's Pension	18.4
Financial Assistance for Leprosy/Cancer Patients	0.0
Marriage Assistance to the Daughter of Widows	0.8
Assistance to the Orphanage Home for Aged and infirm and Beggar Homes	1.1
Journalist Pension	0.0
Welfare Scheme for Eminent Journalists	0.0
Kerala Non-journalist Pension Scheme	0.0
Self Employment Assistance	33.0
Total	100.0

Source: Economic Review 2004.

TABLE 12.13

Major Pension Scheme Beneficiaries in Kerala by Districts, 2003

Districts	*Agricultural Workers*	*Widow/Destitute Pension*	*National Old Age Pension*
Thiruvananthapuram	91024	26484	9292
Kollam	33077	28133	15971
Pathanamthitta	17933	6636	3641
Alappuzha	68500	13969	7569
Kottayam	33560	10770	8890
Idukki	7979	2792	3930
Ernakulum	33870	16426	13994
Thrissur	50650	19143	11708
Palakkad	57154	19593	18748
Malappuram	52846	29345	15175
Kozhikode	62085	27290	9454
Wayanad	11843	4475	1448
Kannur	42908	15195	9171
Kasargode	15635	10131	5609
Kerala	**527647**	**208445**	**134600**

Source: Economic Review 2004.

The district level profiles of beneficiaries for the three major pension schemes are presented in Table 12.13. The highest number of agricultural pension beneficiaries is reported for Thiruvananthapuram, followed by Alappuzha and Kozhikode. On the other hand, Malappuram leads with the highest number of widow/destitute pension beneficiaries, followed by Kollam and Kozhikode. In terms of the national old age pension schemes, Palakkad tops the list, followed by Kollam and Malappuram. This regional distribution of beneficiaries is likely to have a bearing with the number of the elderly in these regions, a matter which needs further confirmatory analysis.

Agricultural Workers Pension Scheme

One of the major social assistance schemes implemented in Kerala is the Kerala Agricultural Workers Pension Scheme, which came into existence in 1980 (see Gulati, 1990; Irudaya Rajan, 1999). The monthly pension amount was originally fixed at Rs. 45; it was raised to Rs. 60 in 1987, to Rs. 70 in 1991 and again to Rs. 100 in 1996. According to the provisions of the scheme, the beneficiaries should be agricultural workers above the age of 60 years and whose annual incomes do not exceed Rs. 11000 (State Planning Board, 2004). An agricultural worker is defined as a worker, not covered by the plantation labour Act, depending principally on agricultural wages for livelihood and residing within the state for a continuous period of at least 10 years, immediately preceding the date of application. Agricultural workers with physical infirmity are also eligible for pension. The State Labour Commissioner is the administrator of the scheme. The amount is payable once in three months, in January, April, July and October by money order.

TABLE 12.14

Expenditure and the Number of Beneficiaries, 1980-81 to 1999-2000

Year	*Beneficiaries*	*Expenditure (in lakh)*
1980-81	293778	1092.3
1981-82	172376	744.2
1982-83	139817	446.0
1983-84	217659	1188.0
1984-85	250116	1132.0
1985-86	277821	1801.0
1986-87	261584	1615.0
1987-88	286733	1469.5
1988-89	299758	1925.7
1989-90	308346	2197.1
1990-91	316509	3062.3
1991-92	344301	2515.8
1992-93	340776	2690.3
1993-94	345650	3551.0
1994-95	344946	2000.0
1995-96	312944	3457.3
1996-97	312944	3457.3
1997-98	300784	4301.0
1998-99	304638	3720.0
1999-2000	436452	NA

Source: Various (annual) issues of *Economic Review*, State Planning Board, Government of Kerala, Thiruvananthapuram.

In 1999, 3.1 lakh persons benefited from the scheme of which, 58 per cent were women. Kerala had 19.47 lakh agricultural labourers and the scheme covered 16 per cent of them. The expenditure on this pension scheme increased sharply from Rs. 1615 lakh in 1986-87 to Rs. 2690 lakh in 1991 and to Rs. 3720 lakh in 1999. The increase was due to extension in the coverage of workers and the upward revisions of the rates effected in 1988 and 1991.

The State of Civil Service Pension in Kerala

The elderly in the state eligible for pension benefit also include persons who benefit from civil service pensions. In fact in the context of the low retirement age of 55 years in the state along with increasing longevity, it seems that the civil service pensioners in Kerala are receiving pensions for about the same duration of their years in civil services. The number of such pensioners in the state has multiplied 2.5 times during the past three decades (Table 12.15).

TABLE 12.15

Number of Service Pensioners in Kerala

Year	*Number of Pensioners*
1970-71	112365
1980-81	146985
1990-91	209546
1991-92	215325
1992-93	216580
1993-94	232465
1994-95	238450
1995-96	239500
1996-97	242654
1997-98	245200
1998-99	246950
1999-2000	248920
2000-01	252768
2001-02	253125
2002-03	259040
2003-04	263895

Source: Prasad, 2005.

Concluding Observations

Can Kerala afford to provide social security or other financial security for all the elderly whose number is growing rapidly? According to the 2001 Census, the number of the elderly in Kerala was 33 lakh. Kerala has approximately 4 lakh pensioners (retired from the Kerala government services plus retired from state governments outside Kerala and returned to Kerala after retirement plus retired from the military, railways, and the post and telegraph departments. In other words, close to 15 per cent of the elderly in Kerala constitutes the creamy layer of the senior citizens. They are not looking for any assistance from the Kerala government.

The work participation rates among the elderly estimated on the basis of the NSS 1999-2000 round was around 50 per cent of the total number of the elderly in Kerala. In Kerala, even at the age of 80, 10 per cent of the elderly continue to work. As long as they work, theoretically speaking, they do not look for free monetary assistance from the Government (Irudaya Rajan, 2006).

The other important observation that can be made in this context relates to the restructuring of the financial allocation to accommodate this urgent need for financial assistance to this group. The absolute number of children has come down in Kerala resulting in closure of uneconomic schools by the Kerala government. The savings accruing from this account could perhaps be of help to government to divert some amount of resources from primary education to social security.

Similarly, the fertility levels in Kerala are extremely low and according to predications, they would be hovering around 1.5 children per woman for several decades to come. Recent studies have indicated that more than 70 per cent of women in Kerala are protected by various family planning methods and that 80 per cent among them are sterilised. These facts point to the need for lowering the emphasis on the family planning programme in Kerala. The government could also divert some money from family planning to social security.

Around 12 lakh persons from among the elderly are beneficiaries of social security and assistance schemes in Kerala. They account for 40 per cent of the elderly population. There remains an urgent need for a systematic study to explore the characteristics and composition of the beneficiaries of these schemes and comment on the bona fides of the recipients of these entitlements.

If the government is able to implement all the schemes effectively and provide assistance to the really needy among the elderly, Kerala would be in a position to continue to run the social assistance schemes without much financial constraints. The budget for social welfare and security could be enhanced through diverting resources from the departments of family planning and primary education. We hope that the government through *panchayat* level institutions would be able not only to identify the genuinely needy but also to raise the financial assistance from the current level of Rs. 110 to Rs. 300 per month (Incidentally, it may be noted that West Bengal pays Rs. 300 as old age pension). A bold step in the right direction is urgently needed.

References

Guilmoto Christophe, Z. and S. Irudaya Rajan (2001). "Spatial Patterns of Fertility Transition in Indian Districts", *Population and Development Review*, Vol. 27(4): 713-38.

———. (2002). "District Level Estimates of Fertility from India's 2001 Census", *Economic and Political Weekly*,Vol. 37(7): 665-72, Feb. 16-12.

———. (2005). *Fertility Transition in South India*. New Delhi: Sage Publications.

Gulati, Leela (1990). "Agricultural Worker's Pension in Kerala: An Experiment in Social Assistance", *Economic and Political Weekly*, Vol. 256): 339-44.

Gulati, Leela and S Irudaya Rajan (1999). "The Added Years: Elderly in India and Kerala", *Economic and Political Weekly*, Vol. 34(44): WS-46-51.

Irudaya Rajan, S. (1989). "Ageing in Kerala: One More Population Problem?", *Asia-Pacific Population Journal*, Vol. 4(2): 19-48, June.

———. (1999). "Aging and Social Security", in B.A. Praksah (ed.), *Kerala's Economic Development: Issues and Problems*. Chapter 3: 49-71. New Delhi: Sage Publications.

———. (2001). "Social Assistance for Poor Elderly: How Effective?", *Economic and Political Weekly*, Vol. 36(8): 613-617, February 24.

———. (2002a). "Home Away from Home: A Survey of Old-age Homes and Inmates from Kerala, India", *Journal of Housing for the Elderly*, Volume 16(1&2): 125-50.

———. (2002b). "Social Security for the Unorganized Sector in South Asia", *International Social Security Review*, Volume 55(4): 143-156.

———. (2004). "Chronic Poverty among Indian Elderly", *Chronic Poverty Research Centre and Indian Institute of Public Administration Working Paper* 17. New Delhi: Indian Institute of Public Administration.

———. (2005). "Chronic Poverty among the Indian Elderly", in Aasha Kapur Mehta and Andrew Shepherd (eds.), *Chronic Poverty and Development Policy in India*. Chapter 5: 168-97. New Delhi: Sage Publications.

———. (2006)." Social Safety Nets for the Vulnerable Poor and Elderly in India", in Nisha Srivastava and Pravesh Sharma (eds.), '*Protecting the Vulnerable Poor in India: The Role of Social Safety Nets*. Chapter 11: 233-60. New Delhi: World Food Programme.

Irudaya Rajan, S. and K.C. Zachariah (1998). "Long Term Implications of Low Fertility in Kerala", *Asia-Pacific Population Journal*, Vol. 13(4): 41-66.

Irudaya Rajan, S. and Sabu Aliyar (2004). "Demographic Change in Kerala in the 1990s and Beyond", in B.A. Prakash (ed.) *Kerala's Economic Development: Performance and Problems in the Post-Liberalization Period*, Sage Publications, New Delhi.

———. (2004). "Gender, Ageing and Social Security", *SAMYUKTA, Journal of Women's Studies*, Vol. 4(2), July.

———. (2005). "Fertility Change in Kerala", in Christophe Z. Guilmoto and S. Irudaya Rajan (eds.) *Fertility Transition in South India*. New Delhi: Sage Publications.

Irudaya Rajan S. and Sanjay Kumar (2003). "Living Arrangements among the Indian Elderly: New Evidence from the National Family Health Survey", *Economic and Political Weekly*, Vol. 38(1): 75-80, January 4.

Irudaya Rajan, S., U.S. Mishra and P.S. Sarma (1995). "An Agenda for National Policies on Ageing in India", *Research and Development Journal*, Vol.1(2): 38-53. Journal of Helpage India.

———. 1999. *India's Elderly: Burden or Challenge?*. New Delhi/Thousand Oaks/ London: Sage Publications.

Jhabvala, Renana and R.K.A. Subrahmanya (eds.) (2000). *The Unorganized Sector: Work Security and Social Protection*. New Delhi: Sage Publications.

Liebig Phoebe, S. and S. Irudaya Rajan (eds.) (2003). *An Ageing India: Perspectives, Prospects, and Policies*. New York: The Haworth Press Inc.

Palacious, Robert J. and S. Irudaya Rajan (2004). "Safety Nets for the Elderly in Poor Countries: The Case of Nepal", *World Bank Pension Primer Working Paper* No. 44.

Prasad, Syam (2005). "A 'Crisis in Making': The Pension System in India with Special Reference to Kerala", Unpublished M.Phil. Dissertation, Centre for Development Studies, Trivandrum.

State Planning Board (1996). *Social Security Initia-tives in Kerala*, Report of the Expert Committee. Trivandrum: Government of Kerala.

Swan, Abram De (1998). *In Care of the Stat*, Polity Press, Cambridge.

Zachariah, K.C., and S. Irudaya Rajan (eds.) (1997). *Kerala's Demographic Transition: Determinants and Consequences*. New Delhi/Thousand Oaks/ London: Sage Publications.

———. (2004). *Gulf Revisited. Economic Consequences of Emigration from Kerala– Emigration and Unemployment*. Thiruvananthapuram: Centre for Development Studies.

Zachariah, K.C., E.T. Mathew and S. Irudaya Rajan (2003). *Dynamics of Migration in Kerala: Determinants, Differentials and Consequences*. Orient Longman Private Limited.

State Planning Board (2004). *Economic Review 2003*. Thiruvananthapuram: Government of Kerala.

Chapter 13

Outlier Communities

A) *ADIVASI* COMMUNITIES

Demographic Features

Kerala is one of the states with the lowest *adivasi* population consisting of 1.14 per cent of its general population. It accounts for only 0.43 per cent of the total ST population in the country. The percentage of *adivasi* population in the state has remained at around one per cent during the past four decades; this is as against a small increase in the proportion of ST in the country (Table 13.1). There is a concentration of *adivasi* in the district of Wayanad accounting for 37 per cent of the total *adivasi* population in the state and constituting around 17 per cent of the district population; Idukki comes next with 14 per cent and Palakkad comes third with nearly 11 per cent of the total Scheduled Tribe population in the state.

TABLE 13.1A

Demographic Profile of the *Adivasis* in Kerala and India, 1961-2001

S.No.	*Indicators*		*Kerala*			*All-India*		
			SC	*ST*	*Gen*	*SC*	*ST*	*Gen*
1	% of Population	1961	8.5	1.3	90.2	14.7	6.9	78.4
		1971	8.3	1.3	90.4	14.6	6.9	78.5
		1981	10.0	1.0	89.0	15.8	7.8	76.4
		1991	9.9	1.1	89.0	16.5	8.1	75.4
		2001	9.8	1.1	89.1	16.2	8.2	75.6
2	Rural	1961	9.15	1.42	89.43	15.95	8.1	75.95
		1971	9.5	1.57	88.90	16.10	8.37	75.53
		1981	11.0	1.24	87.9	17.34	9.54	73.12
		1991	10.98	1.45	87.57	18.04	10.08	71.88
		2001	10.83	1.48	87.68	17.49	10.92	71.59
3	Urban	1961	4.77	0.36	94.87	8.7	0.98	90.32
		1971	5.0	0.31	94.7	8.75	1.19	90.05
		1981	6.5	0.10	93.41	10.63	2.03	87.34
		1991	6.96	0.15	92.89	12	2.32	85.68
		2001	6.90	0.17	92.93	11.14	2.71	86.15
4	Sex Ratio	1961	1014	1006	1022	957	987	941
		1971	1009	975	1016	935	982	930
		1981	1022	922	1032	932	983	934
		1991	1029	996	1037	922	972	928
		2001	1048	1021	1058	941	977	938

Sources: Census of India, various years.

TABLE 13.1B

Regional Pattern of Growth and Distribution of Kerala's Tribal Population 1991-2001

District	*Total*	*SC Total*	*SC %*	*ST Total*	*ST %*
Kasaragod	1204078	90218	2.89	30338	8.33
Kannur	2408956	98991	3.17	19969	5.48
Wayanad	780619	33364	1.07	136062	37.36
Kozhikode	2879131	200983	6.43	5940	1.63
Malappuram	3625471	285442	9.14	12267	3.37
Palakkad	2617482	432578	13.85	39665	10.89
Thrissur	2974232	354226	11.34	4826	1.33
Ernakulam	3105798	263518	8.44	10046	2.76
Idukki	1129221	159362	5.10	50973	14.00
Kottayam	1953646	150282	4.81	18340	5.04
Alappuzha	2109160	199231	6.38	3131	0.86
Pathanamthitta	1234016	162002	5.19	6549	1.80
Kollam	2585208	322887	10.34	5190	1.43
Thiruvananthapuram	3234356	370857	11.87	20893	5.74
Kerala	**31841374**	**3123941**	**9.81**	**364189**	**1.14**

Source: Census 2001.

The 3.18 lakh population of *adivasis* in the state belongs to clans/communities as notified in the list of Scheduled Tribes in Kerala. They are broadly classified into four categories, *viz.* hunters & gatherers, agricultural labourers, shifting cultivators and settled cultivators. Among the *adivasi* population, Paniyans, dispersed largely in Wayanad, Kozhikode and Malappuram districts, form the single largest community with 21.1 per cent of the total *adivasi* population in the state. They were bonded labourers by tradition; with the abolition of bonded labour in the state, they are now regarded as agricultural labourers. Nearly five per cent of the total *adivasi* population in the state is still constituted by 'primitive' tribes (see GoK, 2002; also see Mathur 1977; Menon, 1986)[1] living in 398 settlements, largely in Kasargod, Wayanad, Malappuram and Palakkad districts. The recent amendment of the ST list includes a few Other Eligible Communities who avail of the concessions normally allowed to the ST population.

The *adivasi* population in Kerala is the only social section in the state with a low sex ratio. Unlike the rest of India, they are not only geographically concentrated, but are overwhelmingly rural. Access to land resources and autonomous control over territory—forests, forest fringes, wildlife sanctuaries, mines, water, local level institutions etc.—are more of a concern among *adivasis* than among other minorities in the state.

Literacy: Efforts to be Strengthened

Kerala ranks first among the Indian states in respect of both male and female literacy among STs in India as well as the general population; ST literacy rate of 57.22 per cent is far lower than the state's general literacy rate of 89.81 per cent in 1991. Further, with respect to certain *adivasi* communities such as Muthuvar and Adiyan, literacy is as low as 24.25 per cent and 36 per cent respectively.

The differences in literacy level as between the general population and the STs in Kerala have been declining over time (Table 13.2). Literacy efforts for STs in Kerala have been lagging behind those of many other states, which are otherwise more backward than Kerala with respect to many social indicators.

In respect of two prominent sets of human development indicators, namely, quality of housing and access to basic education, Kerala is ahead of the rest of the states not only for the general population but for ST and SC population also. Yet the *adivasis* of Kerala appear to be struggling, with meagre access to basic resources, particularly land, as is evident from the numerous ongoing land struggles.

Adivasi Settlements as Pockets of Poverty?

Kerala has reportedly registered remarkable success in poverty reduction among all its social sections, including its *adivasi* population. The level of poverty among *adivasis* declined from 37 per cent to 24 per cent from 1993-94 to 1999-00, while the corresponding for all-India has been from 52 per cent to 46 per cent only (Table 13.3). The incidence of poverty among the *adivasis* of Kerala is only half that of all-India. The decline in the incidence of poverty registered in the state could be broadly attributed to the agrarian reforms and the large number of anti-poverty measures undertaken by governments on the one hand and the growth of the economy as a whole, on the other. However, rural poverty among *adivasis* in Kerala persists and comes to more than two-and-a-half times that of the rural population of Kerala in general. It is also observed that there exists over-representation of *adivasis* in the BPL population in the state; while the *adivasis*

* In this section, the terms 'indigenous population' and 'adivasis' are used interchangeably. 'Tribe' and ST are terms avoided other than in reference to state procedures.

1. The *Kurumba, Koraga, Kadar, Kattunayakan* and *Cholanaicken* clans are not included in the Scheduled Tribes list of Kerala; their population is estimated at around 16,000 in 1991.

TABLE 13.2

Literacy Rate and Disparity among Social Groups, Kerala and India

Indicators	*Kerala*				*All India*			
	1961	*1971*	*1981*	*1991*	*1961*	*1971*	*1981*	*1991*
SC: Person	24.4	40.2	56.0	69.4	10.3	14.7	21.4	30.1
Male	31.6	47.0	62.3	73.9	17.0	22.4	31.1	40.2
Female	17.4	33.4	49.7	65.0	3.3	6.4	10.9	19
ST: Person	17.3	25.7	31.8	48.6	8.5	11.3	16.4	23.6
Male	21.7	30.0	37.5	53.7	13.8	17.6	24.5	32.5
Female	11.9	19.4	26.0	43.5	3.2	4.9	8.0	14.5
Gen: Person	46.4	60.4	70.4	78.0	24.0	29.5	36.2	34.4
Male	55.0	66.6	75.3	80.81	34.4	39.5	46.9	52.8
Female	38.9	54.3	65.7	75.2	13.0	18.7	24.8	32.1
Disparity between All& ST								
Person	36.9	42.5	45.1	62.4	35.4	38.3	45.1	55.1
Male	41.1	48	49.9	66.5	40.1	44.5	52.3	61.5
Female	30.6	35.7	39.6	57.9	24.6	26.2	32.4	45.2

Note: The disparity index measures the performance of SC and ST relative to the general population. If literacy in one social section is low relative to the other, the index will have a low value of less than 100. As literacy rates among SCs rise relative to that in the general population, the value of the index rises, reaching 100 when literacy levels of the two groups are equal.

Source: Chakrabarty, G. and P.K Ghosh (2002). *Human Development Profile of Scheduled Castes and Tribes in Rural Indi: A Bench Mark Survey*. New Delhi: NCAER.

TABLE 13.3

Poverty among Different Social Groups of Rural Population, 1983-1999-2000 Percentage of Population Below Poverty Line (Rural) in 38th, 50th and 55th NSSO Rounds

States/India	*38th Round (1983)*			*50th Round (1993-94)*			*55th Round (1999-2000)*				
	ST	*SC*	*All*	*ST*	*SC*	*All*	*ST*	*SC*	*OBC*	*Oth.*	*All*
Andhra Pradesh	35.0	37.2	26.6	25.6	26.0	15.8	23.8	16.5	10.4	4.1	11.1
Assam	47.2	43.1	42.6	42.2	45.3	45.0	38.7	44.0	39.4	40.0	40.2
Bihar	74.9	80.8	64.4	70.0	70.9	58.3	59.7	59.8	42.9	26.5	44.2
Gujarat	57.8	39.2	29.8	31.1	32.2	22.2	29.1	17.8	11.7	4.8	13.2
Haryana	-	36.1	20.6	41.5	46.5	27.7	0.0	19.0	11.9	1.2	8.3
Karnataka	57.7	52.7	36.3	37.5	46.6	29.9	25.5	26.2	16.1	11.8	17.4
Kerala	-	**62.3**	**39.1**	**37.3**	**36.3**	**25.5**	**24.2**	**14.6**	**10.8**	5.4	9.4
Madhya Pradesh	66.4	58.4	48.9	56.9	46.0	40.8	56.3	41.3	32.5	12.2	37.1
Maharashtra	62.2	59.3	45.2	50.8	51.7	38.0	43.6	33.3	22.2	13.6	23.8
Orissa	86.0	76.0	67.5	71.5	49.1	50.0	73.9	51.8	39.5	23.4	48.1
Punjab	-	25.8	13.2	26.9	21.8	11.6	18.0	12.4	7.4	0.7	6.4
Rajasthan	61.4	40.4	33.5	46.2	38.3	26.4	25.3	19.6	10.2	6.3	13.6
Tamil Nadu	-	67.5	54.0	44.4	44.1	32.4	43.2	32.6	15.0	11.7	20.5
Uttar Pradesh	-	57.3	46.5	37.0	59.3	42.3	34.1	43.7	33.1	17.7	31.2
West Bengal	76.0	72.0	63.1	62.0	45.3	40.8	50.0	35.1	20.4	29.7	31.8
India	63.8	58.1	45.6	52.2	48.1	37.1	45.8	36.2	27.1	15.2	27.1

Source: (i) *Sarvekshana*, Vol.12 (3).
(ii) *Sarvekshana*, Vol.21 (1).
(iii) Differences in levels of consumption among socioeconomic groups 1999-2000, NSS 55th Round, NSSO, Government of India.

constitute only around one per cent of the state's population, nearly one-fourth of them still live below the official poverty line; the actual incidence of poverty among them could be even higher. This high incidence of poverty among *adivasis* points to the various dimensions of social inequalities prevalent in the state such as lack of access to land resources, lack of employment and the state's failure to provide adequate social security safeguards. Reports of starvation deaths and deaths due to poor access to medical facilities and poor levels of living have been numerous. They still suffer from tuberculosis, leprosy, scabies and several water-borne diseases. Studies carried out by the state department of health services and the AIIMS, New Delhi show that nearly 15 per cent of *adivasi* families in Wayanad and Palakkad suffer from sickle-cell anaemia.[2] It is not clear to what extent the various *adivasi* health projects including the one launched by UNICEF, have improved the situation. The state should get better equipped before setting up multi-specialty hospitals in *adivasi* regions; priority should be given to the strengthening of quality of the existing health infrastructure and the assurance of committed services from the health service personnel.

Labouring Hard but in Non-Accumulative Domains?

Deprived of their community resources, fragmented in identity owing to European penetration which had begun from the mid-19th century and large scale encroachments by native peasants from the plains from the early 20th century onwards, the *adivasis* in Kerala had been turned to bonded labour. They were perhaps the only community which was forced to suffer bondage for decades together, long after legal abolition of slavery in the mid-19th century; decades of state-led development initiatives in the post-1950s could not abolish bonded labour from among them, at least, not until the early 1970s. Rare instances of bondage are still seen to prevail in certain pockets of absolute deprivation. There is over-representation of *adivasi* population in the agricultural labour force of Kerala: 55 per cent as against 26 per cent for the general population. While the proportion of agricultural labourers among them increased in the 1960s in both Kerala and in the country as a whole, the proportions in all-India remained unchanged in the successive decades since then. But in Kerala, though there was a decline in the total number of agricultural labourers in the state since the early 1970s, the proportions among *adivasis* became progressively higher in the 1970s and the 1980s. An increase in the agricultural labour force is reflected in the decline in the proportion of cultivators among *adivasis* over the years since the 1960s. If a quarter of *adivasi* households had been cultivators in 1961, in 1991 the corresponding proportion was only 17 per cent. Among the general population, the proportion of cultivators is 12 per cent.

The fact that the percentage of cultivators among *adivasis* is much lower in Kerala than in all-India reveals the high degree of landlessness among them. Relatively low levels of economic and social attainment force both men and women among *adivasis* to high work participation rate (WPR) namely 46.04 per cent as against the state average of only 31.43 per cent. The average Women Work Participation (WWPR) in the state is found to be 15.85 per cent but the corresponding rate for the *adivasis* women is more than double, 36.90 per cent.

The high WPR in association with a higher incidence of poverty and lower levels of education is an indicator of deprivation. Both men and women among the *adivasis* do engage in low-skilled, low-paid economic activities as part of their survival strategy. The dual wage system in the *adivasi* regions, that was quite prevalent in the 1960s (see GoK, 1979; Kunhaman, 1982:51-55) has not been weaned out even now, with *adivasis* being paid lower wages than agricultural labourers belonging to other communities in the same areas. Women among *adivasis* suffer gender discrimination. Higher WPR particularly of women of weaker social groups obviously reflect certain aspects of gender equality, womens' empowerment and a consequent reduction in family violence and patriarchal conflicts; these aspects need to be examined more intensively. At the policy level, the necessity of strengthening the *adivasi* asset base and earning opportunities is obvious.

Land Alienation

Increasing land alienation of *adivasis* was noted by the *Evaluation Committee on the Welfare of the Scheduled Castes, Scheduled Tribes and the Backward Communities* as early as in the 1960s. The Committee noted that the extent of the land of the tribes is steadily on the decrease due to alienation, lease or mortgage and above all to unauthorised occupations of tribal lands by the non-tribal people (GoK, 1962: 53). The *Report on Socioeconomic Survey of Tribals in Kerala, 1976-1978* conducted by the Government of Kerala, found that the lands alienated during the period 1966-1976 worked out to 9859 acres (GoK, 1979). The pattern of land transfer, with 86 per cent of the cases and 92 per cent of the area being transferred to non-tribals, points to the

2. Some of these items of information have been collected from the Scheduled Tribes Development Department, Government of Kerala, Thiruvananthapuram.

TABLE 13.4

Extent of Land Alienated to Non-tribals during the Period 1962-1982

	Land Alienated (Area in Acres)										
	During Last 10 Years (1972-82)				*10 - 30 Years (1962-1982)*				*Total*		
I.T.D.P.	*No. of Households*	*% of Huseholds*	*Area*	*Land Lost per Household*	*No. of Households*	*% of Household*	*Area*	*Land Lost per Household*	*No. of Households*	*Area*	*Land Lost per Household*
(1)	(2)	(3)	(4)	(5)	(6)	(7)	(8)	(9)	(10)	(12)	(13)
Punalur	242	84.91	306.99	1.27	43	15.09	83.16	1.94	285	390.15	1.39
Idukki	311	91.74	594.60	1.91	28	8.26	67.80	2.42	339	662.40	1.95
Attappady	376	56.63	1443.86	3.84	288	43.37	1420.17	4.93	664	2864.04	4.31
Nilambur	62	61.39	117.08	1.88	39	38.61	119.87	3.07	101	236.95	2.35
Mananthavady	68	87.18	47.05	0.69	10	12.82	19.27	1.92	78	66.31	0.49
Total	1059		2509.58	2.37	408		1710.27	4.19	1467	4219.85	2.88

Source: Calculated from Table IX in GoK (1984). *A Bench Mark Survey of Integrated Tribal Development Project in Kerala, 1982*. Thiruvananthapuram: Government Press, p. 182.

enormity of sequestering *adivasis*. The extent of lands alienated by lease accounts for 29 per cent of the cases, the corresponding ratio for the land sold and mortgaged being 45 per cent and 16 per cent respectively. The survey conducted by the Government of Kerala in Integrated Tribal Development Project (ITDP) area of Attappady in 1982 revealed that nearly 39 per cent of the lands in the area originally owned by *adivasis* were alienated to non-*adivasis* already by the year 1977. The process of land alienation ran parallel to the process of deforestation in various parts of Kerala (see Viswanathan 1978; Sivanandan, Narayana and Nair, 1985).

Alienation of tribal lands in Kerala was hectic during the period 1972-1982 (Table 13.4). Nearly 92 per cent of the alienation occurred in Idukki in the early seventies. The percentage of land lost prior to 1977 to certain communities such as Irulas and Mudugas in Attappady had been as high as 67 per cent (GoK, 1982). In other words, the most blatant encroachments occurred after 1970, the year of passing of the Land Reform Act. The Patent Act of 1975 provided legal invalidation provision for any transfer of *adivasi* lands to non-*adivasis*. The loss of land for the tribals continued unabated in the whole of Kerala, the average size of cultivated land per scheduled tribe households declining from 0.8 hectares in 1987-88 to 0.2 hectares in 1992-1994.

The leaden-footed approach of government to the tribal land question would be clear from Table 13.5; hardly 9 per cent of the disputed cases have been settled so far. Out of the 19059 acres of area under dispute, only 1088 acres were restored. At the same time, the state has gone ahead with the policy of regularisation of unauthorised occupation of forest and tribal lands by settler farmers, by passing special rules.

Adivasi Land Question: Derailing the Law and the Constitution

The Kerala Agrarian Relations Bill (KARB) passed by the first Communist ministry in July 1959 was silent on the question of *adivasi* land rights; but it exempted plantations and private forests from the ceiling provisions (Raj & Tharakan, 1983). The possibility of release of any surplus land in the High Ranges, which would have brought partial relief to the land-hungry *adivasis* and the plantation workers, was thus forestalled. But, when the Act began to be amended by successive governments, the plight of *adivasis* became increasingly worse. Plantation empires continued to remain exempt from ceiling provisions. All contiguous and interspersed agricultural land within the boundaries of plantations was also exempted from ceiling provisions. The act also allowed the owners of such plantations and agricultural lands to evict households from the small allotments of land they had received for construction of hutments within the enlarged plantation boundary areas. Kerala Reforms (Amendment) Act of 1969 conferred tenant status to settler farmers who had acquired tribal lands (Ravi Raman, 2002; 2004). In brief, land reforms in Kerala not only failed to yield any benefits to the tribals but also marginalised them further.

The Dhebar Commission of 1960 had suggested that all lands that had been seized since January 26, 1950,

TABLE 13.5

Alienated Land (Acres) Under Disputes as on 30.6.1996

Revenue Divisional Offices (RDO)	*Disrict*	*No. of Applicants*	*Extent of Land under Dispute*	*Number of Cases Disputed/ Settled*	*Land Restored*	*Remaining Number of Cases*	*Remaining Land under Dispute*	*P/Capita Area under Dispute*
Manandavadi	Wayanad	2253	3792.60	17	8.69	2236	3783.91	1.69
Idukki	Idukki	1495	2000	0	0	1495	2000	1.34
Ottapalam	Palakkad	2522	10000	126	393.36	2396	9606.64	4.01
Palakkad	Palakkad	101	166	2	0	99	166	1.68
Kottayam	Kottayam	482	402.58	0	0	482	402.58	0.84
Thiruvalla	Kottayam	334	933.50	17	90	317	843.50	2.66
Thiruvananthapuram	Thiruvananthapuram	437	589.74	132	96.16	305	493.58	1.62
Kasaragode	Kasaragod	131	323.97	6	28.91	125	295.06	2.36
Perunthalmanna	Malappuram	120	178	95	135.39	25	43.30	1.73
Kannur	Kannur	115	483.54	72	126.99	43	92.15	2.14
Kollam	Kollam	218	248.45	154	147	64	101.45	1.59
Others		254	204.12	130	61.70	124	142.95	1.15
	Total	8462	19059.34	751	1088.03	7711	17971.12	2.33

Source: Various Revenue Divisional Offices, Kerala.

the day on which India became a Republic, be restored; but this was of no avail. The Kerala Scheduled Tribes Act (Restriction on Transfer of Lands and Restoration of Alienated Lands) of 1975 had a provision to restore all lands alienated on or after 1st January 1960; but the provision remained dormant for another 10 years. The rules and regulations governing the Act were finalised only in 1986. It then was decided that all transactions of tribal lands to non-tribals made between 1960 and 1982 would be invalidated and that the lands would be restored to the concerned tribals. The latter in turn were required to pay compensation and the amounts required would be provided to the tribals by the government in the form of loans. In order not to re-enact the process of alienation, it was also decided that any transfer effected by an *adivasi* to a *non-adivasi*, without the previous consent in writing of a competent authority, shall be considered invalid.

But the implementation of the legislation was jeopardised at the very outset by the settler farmers whose representatives themselves had supported the bill on the floor of the legislature. They even resorted to physical violence in their bid to stall official proceedings. The Government, both of the Leftist and the Rightist persuasions responded with silence and withheld implementation in spite of repeated warnings by the Judiciary. A quarter of a century has elapsed since the bill was passed but the Government has remained impotent, an instance of "a grave and great constitutional issue of the executive flouting the expressed will of the legislature" as observed by Justice K. Sukumaran of the Kerala High Court. In the face of repeated warnings from the judiciary, the government has been compelled to act; this it did by making amendments that simply reversed the whole proceedings—the settler encroachers came to be protected instead of the actual sufferers (Ravi Raman, 2002; Bijoy and Ravi Raman, 2003).

Successive governments that took up the reins of the state after 1975 twisted the issue of tribal land rights beyond recognition. After assuming power in 1996, the Left-led government, for instance, attempted to push through certain amendments on two occasions, in September 1996 and March 1999 (see GoK, 1996 and 1999). While the first amendment amounted itself to a breach of promise, the second all but rewrote the parent bill to the extent of extinguishing all tribal land rights. For instance, the 1996 amendment exempted the lands encroached upon during the period 1960-86 and which did not exceed a hectare each from the restoration drive. However, the majority of the lands alienated were of less than a hectare in area each and the greatest number of encroachments had occurred before the year 1986. Those lands and the lands usurped later by the settlers on payment of the stipulated compensation, also could be retained by them. In essence every single instance of encroachment got legitimised in the process. It was the tribals now who were expected to relocate themselves. The 1999 amendment confounded the tribal land question further. The amended bill exempted transactions involving less than two hectares of land and condoned encroachments of up to five acres of land. This amendment has invited resistance from the *adivasis* and their supporting agencies.[3] The rank injustice inherent in the act did not escape the notice of the President of India who refused to give his assent, thus forcing the state to go in for a further amendment.

The 1996 amendment which itself had raised a furore legalised encroachments only up to a hectare each. The extent of land to be given in compensation to the *adivasis* was reduced to one-half, that is from more than two acres to one acre. Furthermore, from the new bill, the Kerala Restriction on Transfer and Restoration of lands to Scheduled Tribes 1999—the word 'alienated' (denoting the lands captured by the settlers) was quietly dropped. Again, the term land indicated in the bill is taken to mean only 'agricultural land' a shift in scope which takes the legislation from the purview of the Central Government, with the State enjoying full freedom in the making of laws pertaining to it (Ravi Raman, 2002; 2004). The protection offered to the tribal population by the 9th schedule of the Constitution has thus been done away with a frank violation of the Civil Rights Act and the Scheduled Castes and Scheduled Tribes Prevention of Atrocities Act, 1989—a fact that the government is only too well aware of. The state also sidestepped the rule that the Commissioner for the Scheduled Castes and Scheduled Tribes should be consulted on all matters concerning the latter.

However, the implementation of even this legislation was jeopardised by the settler-encroachers who took to physical violence in their bid to foil official proceedings. Even the High Court had to question their onslaught.[4] Yet, the state made no move against settler interests. Whenever, the *adivasis* tried to assert their land rights, they were peremptorily crushed as had been done in Cheengeri in 1995, and in Panavally in 1997, the latest in this series of state violence being at Muthanga.[5]

Land Reforms and the Redistribution of Surplus Land

Knowing fully well the significance of land ownership in the amelioration of poverty and the empowering of weaker sections, both the Government of India and the state governments have made various efforts to protect and promote the land rights of the SC and the ST population. Yet, the outcome has been far from satisfactory, a state of affairs that has led to the recent struggles for land rights by the *adivasi* organisations.[6]

Aspects of access to land—cultivated land—for the 1990s as given by NSSO give additional insights on the land question in Kerala. In 1999-00, nearly 37 per cent of the *adivasi* households were found to be landless (Table 13.6). The proportion of households which possess more than one hectare of land has declined even further since then. This implies that cultivable land and economically viable farms of the tribals are being increasingly lost/alienated, making their life increasing vulnerable. At the all-India level, the proportion of land owned by the *adivasi* population remained a little higher than their share in population; but in Kerala their share in land is a little lower than their share in population.[7]

The extent of surplus land declared in Kerala following land reforms was low, only 1.35 lakh acres. Out of this, 47 per cent was distributed among vulnerable sections as on March 1996. The distribution benefited nearly 43 per cent of the SC and 5 per cent of the ST population in the state. The average area of land made available to the SC households was only 41 cents; and for STs, it was 71 cents. As per the national guidelines, 50 per cent of the surplus land declared surplus is to be distributed among SCs and STs. While the all-India situation meets this stipulation, Kerala lags behind with only 47 per cent of the area declared as surplus having been made available to scheduled castes and tribes.

In many cases, the government has adopted a very lackadaisical approach to the question of surplus land and its redistribution. As early as in 1971, the Government of Kerala passed an order for acquisition of half the Kannan Devan lands—owned by Tata Tea. But to date, this land has not been redistributed, neither to

3. In Kannur, the Collectorate was stormed by a group of tribal activists; in certain pockets, the tribals blocked the entry of the non-tribals who tried to do so without prior permission. The amended Bill was cremated in various tribal belts. The Palakkad District Collector was taken hostage on October 4, 1996 for nine hours by four captors who brandished toy guns and country bombs and who belonged to the Ayyankali Pada, a Maoist group, named after the radical Dalit leader Ayyankali.

4. Cited in Bijoy *op. cit.* p.1330.

5. In October 1997, the LDF, for instance, declared that more than 72000 adivasis would be vested with property rights but the declaration had no effect.

6. For detailed accounts, see Ravi Raman, 2002; Bijoy and Ravi Raman, 2003; Ravi Raman, 2004.

7. See Report on Landholdings (1); 37th Round, NSS Report No. 330, "Report on Some Aspects of Ownership Holdings (1)", 48th Round, NSS Report No. 399; for details, Ravi Raman, *op. cit.*

landless plantation workers nor to the *adivasis* (Ravi Raman, 1998). The area of land owned by two major corporate capital entities now in Kerala (Tata Tea and Harrisons Malayalam) is more than 50000 hectares, twice the land area redistributed under the ceilings legislation. Had the state at least confiscated the surplus land of these companies, nearly 1.3 lakh acres could have been mobilised i.e. almost an equivalent of the area already declared surplus. Unfortunately, the tribals themselves have failed to adopt a focused approach in their struggle for lands.

The state's present claim to be in possession of adequate confiscated lands—obviously forest areas and forest lands—to resettle the tribals is indeed surprising. It is likely that the state would make available lands already confiscated from monopoly planters and others—which would be five times more than the area under dispute - to resettle settler-farmers and not the tribals. In certain cases the settlers themselves have agreed to leave the disputed lands provided they are given adequate compensation, a suggestion to which the state seems always to turn a blind eye. As recent a case as that of the takeover of the Aralam Farm is a case in point. The state government had taken over the Central State Farm, Aralam from the Government of India comprising 3060 hectares in early 2004. It was also decided that 50 per cent of the farm area would be allotted to the landless *adivasis*, both in Kannur where the farm is situated and also in Wyanand, and that the remaining area would be retained as farm. Despite the fact that the funds required to take over the farm were met from the Tribal Sub Plan—worth more than Rs. 42 crore—there seems to have been no progress in the implementation of the scheme. More importantly, the state and the Tribal Rehabilitation and Development Mission (TRDM) appear to plan an outright distribution of land to *adivasis* without looking for more viable and imaginative alternatives such as bringing such area(s) under "scheduled areas."

It had become evident that the Act of 1975, even in its original form, did not address the issue of landlessness of the vast majority of *adivasi* families, and that a series of steps taken to scuttle its implementation have narrowed the scope for its implementation even further. The Act applied to only those cases in which *adivasis* were able to furnish records in proof of their past ownership; this stipulation obviously worked totally against the interests of *adivasis* who were quite ignorant of the complex laws and procedures involved and while settler-encroachers and officials easily manipulated records to their own advantage. Of the 45,000 landless tribal families in the state, only 8879 have applied for the restoration of their lands; of these only 4524 applications have escaped rejection, and they now contest for a meagre 7640 acres of land.

TABLE 13.6

Size Class of Land Cultivated (in Acres) by Caste and Sector: Kerala, NSSO (1999-2000) 55th Round

Acres	*Rural*	*Urban*	*Total*
Less than 0.05	11362 (2.95)	3525 (4.96)	14887 (3.26)
0.05 to 0.10	17155 (4.45)	9122 (12.83)	26277 (5.76)
0.10 to 0.50	97467 (25.31)	17134 (24.11)	114601 (25.12)
0.50 to 1.25	51178 (13.29)	3538 (4.98)	54716 (12.00)
1.25 to 2.47	50418 (13.09)	1513 (2.13)	51931 (11.38)
2.47 to 3.50	4624 (1.20)	—	4624 (1.01)
3.50 to 4.94	15944 (4.14)	—	15944 (3.50)
9.88 to 24.72	4624 (1.20)	—	4624 (1.01)
Landless	132307 (34.36)	36244 (50.99)	168551 (36.95)
Total	385079 (100.00)	71076 (100.00)	456155 (100.00)

Note: The percentages are given in brackets.

Source: Computed from NSSO (1999-2000) 55th Round, Employment and Unemployment Survey Unit Level Record Data. GoI, New Delhi.

Land Struggles and the Question of Autonomy: The New Turn

By the year 2000, many of the *adivasi* groups came to realise that their legal battle over the 1975 Act gave scant consideration to the fundamental question of rehabilitation of the 45,000 landless families on the one hand and totally disregarded the larger question of bringing the entire *adivasi* community under the protection of Schedule V on the other. They also realised the limitations in their approach which treat settlers as a single category (the latter also included small farmers), as well as the communal tension such treatment entailed.[8] The newly constituted Adivasi-Dalit Samara Samithi (which later initiated the formation of the AGMS), led by Janu and Geethanandan, thus negotiated a fresh pact—after a 48 day struggle—with the state government in October 2001. The major

8. Interview with M. Geethanandan dated October 17, 2001, Thiruvananthapuram.

components of the commitment undertaken by the government were the following (Bijoy and Ravi Raman, 2003):

Five acres of land would be given to all *Adivasi* families having less than one acre of land. To begin with, 42,000 acres of land of between 1-5 acres would be distributed while the rest would be distributed as and when lands were located and made available. This work would begin from Jan. 1 to Dec. 31, 2002 giving five acres wherever it was possible to do so and lesser extents of land in cases in which it was not possible and in which suitable lands were found.

A master plan would be prepared before December 2001 and included in the 10th Five year plan beginning from 2002 in which focus would be to provide support to the beneficiaries for a maximum of five years, until they reached a state of self-sufficiency.

A cabinet decision would be taken to include *Adivasi* areas in the V Schedule and a proposal would be sent to the Centre for notification by the President. Meanwhile suitable legislation at the state would be made to protect lands being allotted under this agreement.

Judgment by the Supreme Court on pending cases wherein the government had challenged the High Court judgment striking down the repeal of the Kerala Scheduled Tribes (Restoration of Alienated Lands and Restriction on Transfer) Act 1975 and declared contempt of court for not having implemented the High Court judgment of 1993 to implement the 1975 Act, would be abided by the Kerala Government.

A Tribal Mission would be constituted to carry out all the above components of this agreement headed by a senior IAS officer.

The term 'Scheduled Areas' has been defined in the Indian Constitution as "such areas as the President may by order declare to be Scheduled Areas." The specification of Scheduled Areas in relation to a particular State/Union Territory is made by a notified Order of the President, after consultation with the state governments concerned. The same procedure was to apply while altering, increasing or rescinding any order(s) relating to "Scheduled Areas." The criteria followed for declaring an area as "Scheduled Area" are: preponderance of tribal population; compactness and reasonable size of the area; underdeveloped nature of the area; and marked disparity in the economic standard of the people. These criteria are not spelt out in the Constitution of India but have become well established. At the time of devising and adopting the strategy of the Tribal Sub Plan (TSP) for socioeconomic development of Scheduled Tribes during Fifth Five Year Plan (1974-1979), certain areas besides Scheduled Areas, were also found to have a preponderance of *adivasi* population.

However, the state bureaucracy and its political leadership in collusion with other sectarian interests kept the 2001 agreement with the *adivasis* in a limbo: the forest department would not part with its forest lands even if they were degraded areas; the state farms would not hand over farm lands that lay fallow; the environmentalists made a great show of shielding the forest against its own children; and all the while the surplus land that lay sequestered under big capital remained untouched. It would be worthwhile to examine these isues, particularly in the light of the AGMS's claim that they had given the government a year's time to fulfill the agreement and that the latter had let them down miserably. The key operative part of the 'agreement' included distribution of land, the master plan and the inclusion of *adivasi* areas under the Vth Schedule.

Prior to 1st January 2002, the Tribal Mission set up by the state government had officially identified the number of landless tribal families to be 22,491 while the number of families having less than 5 acres of land were 30,981. In other words, a total of 53,472 families were found eligible to receive land up to 5 acres each. The government had also identified 59,452 acres[9] (the ADSS had identified upto 12 lakh acres of land that lay with the government itself) as on 1st January 2002. The report sent to the National Human Rights Commission by the Chief Secretary on behalf of the Kerala government states that as on April 2002, 568 families had been provided 1308 acres of land since 1st January 2002 when the state commenced the first land distribution at Marayur in Idukki district.[10] It means that only 1.06 per cent of the families were provided land which came to 2.2 per cent of the identified land within the first 4 months of the stipulated 12 month period. Since then, till date, there has not been any substantial or significant change in these figures except that the land actually allotted has been reported in the

9. The figures of beneficiaries and lands identified are elaborated in Adivasi Punaradhivasa Vikasana Paripadikkulla Prathyeka Suparsakal (Special Recommendations for the Rehabilitation and Development of Adivasis) Submitted by the Tribal Master Plan Committee with Sri. T. Madhavamenon IAS (Rtd.) as Chairman to the State Planning Board (Draft for Discussion), January 1, 2002, p.18.

10. "Report of Government of Kerala on the Petition dated 18.9.02 submitted by the All India Coordinating Forum of Adivasis/Indigenous Peoples before Honourable Justice Verma, National Human Rights Commission", pp.5-6.

media as 1770 to 848 families. At this rate it would take the government another 33 years to complete the task (Bijoy and Ravi Raman, 2003). Also the rate of allotment has gone down drastically as only around 462 acres have been distributed since April 2002 to January 2003 as compared to over 1300 acres in the first 4 months. Does this not mean that it would take another half century or more for the land distribution to be completed, if indeed it does take place at all? When it is acknowledged that the vast majority of the *adivasis* are facing poverty, exploitation, hunger, malnutrition and starvation (though the Kerala government refuses to officially acknowledge the starvation deaths), should it not also lend a sense of urgency to the implementation of the agreement?

In May 2002, the head of the Tribal Mission was virtually 'dismissed' and was replaced by a civil servant of the Indian Forest Service. The lands identified for distribution plummeted from 59,452 acres to a mere 2300 acres by June 2002 and further to 1223 acres when the issue came to the cabinet sub-committee.[11] That this country does not provide incontrovertible, firm and clear title to lands and that they are presumptive in nature is well known and accepted.[12] This caveat applies to government-owned lands too; executive and/or departmental orders are sufficient for official purposes as far as government lands are concerned, this having been the official routine with respect to both the state as well as the centre. The government's attempts at citing legal hurdles as an excuse to stall proceedings have thus fallen flat. The fact that the *adivasis* had prior claims to most of these lands before they were declared state property is a historical point that the government conveniently glosses over. Another major hurdle is said to be the fact that a large portion of lands identified earlier is disputed land with the forest department and the revenue department fighting it over. It is also mentioned that the Forest Conservation Act 1980 stands in the way of denotifying and transferring these lands to the *adivasis*. This is totally misleading misrepresentation of legal facts and the rights of *adivasis* on forests.

The Muthanga occupation was a symbolic gesture to signal the discontent rampant among *adivasis* and to assert their right to ownership and autonomy. Other *adivasi* organisations too, have initiated similar attempts during the same period, as in the case of the state-owned Orange Farm at Nelliampathi (Ravi Raman, 2004). It would be difficult to negate their long history of neglect and deprivation on the one hand and their deprivation of the outcomes of the developmental projects implemented, on the other (see Kunhaman, 1989; Velluva, 2004). In the new context of neo-liberal agenda of globalisation, the indigenous people face with corporate capital gaining importance, and, on occasion, and are being aided by even the legal institutions.[13]

Decentralisation and the SC/ST Population

As part of the democratic decentralisation process that was launched during the Ninth Five Year Plan (1997-2002) period, the funds for the Special Component Plan (SCP) and the Tribal Sub-plan (TSP) were devolved on the Local Self-Government institutions. This was to assure greater participatory development of the SC and ST population in the state. In the Ninth Five Year Plan, the plan funds for SCP and TSP were earmarked in proportion to the SC and ST population, and the earlier practice of notional flow of funds was discontinued. Further, re-appropriation of funds from SCP and TSP was forbidden. Owing to complaints about non-utilisation, mis-utilisation and biases in the utilisation of TSP funds, some *adivasi* organisations themselves demanded the resumption of TSP funds to the state from local bodies. In 2001-02, the state resumed TSP funds and entrusted the ST Development Department to transact the funds. In 2002-03 too, no TSP grant-in-aid was given to *panchayats*. But in 2003-04, one-half of total funds began to be channelled once again to *panchayats*. Neither the state nor the *panchayats*, not even *adivasi* organisations, are clear about the channel through which the funds could be most productively used. Special training was imparted to representatives of the SC/STs for the preparation and implementation of projects. In contrast to the *Grama Sabhas* of the SC, *Oorukuttams* were convened for STs in their settlements themselves for identification of projects and selection of beneficiaries. The staff of the SC department was redeployed to block *panchayats* and muncipalities for implementing the SCP.

The series of developmental programmes for advancement of education of SC/STs which the

11. Krishnadas, N.V. (2003). "Kanakkeduppum Kadukayari, Kanakkukoottalukal Paali", Malayala Manorama, 21 February, p.8.

12. The anarchic nature of land-related laws in the country is elaborated in Wadhwa, D.C. (2003). "Guaranteeing Title to Land", *Economic and Political Weekly*, 23 November.

13. One such issue is with respect to the struggle for water rights in Plachimada wherein the adivasis and the Dalits, with the help of several social organisations fight not only with the global Coca Cola but also with the state judiciary, see, Ravi Raman 2004; 2005.

government has been implementing may be broadly divided into three: (i) educational development programmes, (ii) employment oriented programmes and (iii) social development and welfare programmes. These programmes include opening up of nursery schools, granting of pre-matric and post-matric concessions, promotion of adult education, supply of clothes, provision of special incentives to talented students, conducting pre-and post-matric hostels, model residential schools and sports hostels, pre-examination training centres, Institute for Civil Services Examination Training, and ITCs and production-cum-training centres, granting of financial assistance to failed students and giving of educational concessions. In addition to financial assistance for education and social advancement, a large number of economic programmes are also being implemented in the state such as interest-free loans for industrial units, cottage units, etc. The social upliftment and welfare programmes include social security programmes such as enforcement of PCR Act, implementation of Prevention of Atrocities Act, interest-free housing loans, etc. A Calamity Relief Fund has been created from which assistance is provided for prolonged treatment and also as support to families in difficulties due to natural calamities. Anti-poverty measures that have been strengthened in the state are oriented towards generation of employment, income, and productive assets; these include the Swarnajayanthi Grama Swarozgar Yojana (SGSY), Indira Awas Yojana (IAY), Sampoorna Gramin Rozgar Yojana (SGRY), Kudumbashree, Ashraya, Food Support Programme during lean seasons, Attappady Environmental Conservation and Wasteland Development Project (AHADS), and Tribal Rehabilitation and Development Mission (TRDM).[14] The Kerala State Development Corporation for Scheduled Castes and Scheduled Tribes (begun in the state since 1972) implements many of these schemes.

Failure of Welfare Measures

In spite of various welfare measures and constitutional protection, the *adivasi* population in the state remains marginalised. They are subjected to many forms of deprivation and oppression. Therefore, more rigorous measures are required for them to realise equality with the rest of the population. Any attempt to launch further development programmes among *adivasis* should take into account the outcomes of the large number of projects already implemented in the state, particularly those that are launched during and after the Fifth Plan period. Most of such projects have either deviated from their original objectives or have simply met with catastrophic results. The Sugandhagiri Cardamom Project, for instance, was started under the Western Ghats Development Programme in 1976-77. The scheme was originally envisaged to rehabilitate 750 *adivasi* bonded labourers in Wayanad in 1500 hectares of vested forest land; a joint farming co-operative society was formed in 1978. All these bonded labourers were provided with permanent houses and employed as wage laboureres. The Society which received Rs. 1223 lakh by 1998-99, began cultivation of cardamom, coffee, pepper and mulberry. But gross mismanagement of the farm, absence of adequate multi-cropping and crop diversification, and inadequate capital investment made the project unsustainable; it was finally closed and the TRDM distributed the land to the families of all the eligible members. The performance of other projects such as the Pookot Dairy Project, the Attappady Farming co-operative Society and the Tribal Collective Farm, Vattachira, which were started by settling the bonded and landless *adivasi* families, has also been indifferent. The Priyadarshini Tea Estate at Pancharakolly which began in 1984 by rehabilitating 118 freed bonded labourers too faces severe crisis due to poor management and unsuitability of the crop they were entrusted with, namely tea. Tea happens to be one of the most crisis-ridden crops in Kerala particularly due to neo-liberal trade relations (Ravi Raman, 2004).

The draft Scheduled Tribes (Recognition of Forest Rights) Bill 2005 by the Government of India appears to be a sincere attempt to provide tribals access to forest resources on the one hand and protect their cultural and social identities, on the other. The Bill has advanced commendable propositions on critical questions of tribal livelihood such as restoration of land and protection of "traditional knowledge" and "community forest resources." The Bill also seeks to strengthen the *gram sabha* to stall any activity adversely affecting wildlife, forests and biodiversity. It contains a large number of valuable suggestions which would, if implemented properly, positively help the *adivasi* population. However, the Bill has left unaddressed a few vital issues pertaining to the jurisdiction of

14. The SGSY is intended to assist the beneficiaries above the poverty line by providing them with income generating assets through bank credit and government subsidy; the IAY is intended to help construction of dwelling units by members of SC/ST, erstwhile bonded labourers and non SC/ST rural poor below poverty line by providing them with grant-in-aid (currently at Rs. 27,500 per house). While the SGRY is intended to provide additional wage employment, food security, and creation of durable community, social and economic infrastructure in rural areas, the Ashraya is largely oriented towards rehabilitation of destitutes.

authorities to be vested with a *gram sabha,* protection to *adivasis* against maltreatment by forest officials and the state, and a "prior informed consent" clause for undertaking developmental projects.

Conclusions

A few suggestions are made in this concluding section for enrichment of the Bill, largely in the context of the upliftment of the tribals in Kerala with their own specific but varying degrees of deprivation and underdevelopment.

1. The Kerala government would do well to take note of the progress made in the restoration of alienated lands to the tribals as had been recommended by the Dhebar Commission and also as implicit in the parent Act of 1975. There is an urgent need to provide land for the landless *adivasi* families by identifying cultivable lands. The untoward consequences of spread of cash crops, settler encroachments, displacement due to 'developmental' projects and land reforms implemented in the state, need to be countered either through the restoration of alienated lands to the original owners or through assignment of fresh lands. It is quite unfortunate that the state has failed to initiate a policy of social dialogue in the case of the *adivasi* land question and livelihood. New organisational forms with the participation of *adivasis* should be worked out in different regions such as Muthanga, the Aralam Farm and the Orange Farm.

2. The question of bringing *adivasi* areas under Schedule V in states, which have not yet done so, needs attention. Specifically, Article 244 Clause (1) V Schedule makes it mandatory for the state to ensure (Para 5 (2) of Schedule V) total prohibition of transfer of immovable property to any person other than a tribal in lands held in the past by tribals. The provisions under Schedule V of this clause are not only applicable to the administration and control of areas notified by the President of India as 'Scheduled Areas' but also to those notified as 'Scheduled Tribes in any state'. This is to be achieved through suitable legislation as well as by the declaration of tribal majority areas as 'Scheduled Areas' with provisions for certain degree of self-governance on the strength of Panchayat Raj (Extension to the Scheduled Areas) Act 1996.

   Kerala is a state in which *adivasi* habitats or groups of habitats have not yet been declared as areas under Schedule V, despite the Bhuria Committee recommendation for the same; the fact is that the state government itself had agreed to initiate the process of scheduling the *adivasi* areas 1,064 sq. miles (3750 sq. kms) with a total population 71,76,129 including 1,12,000 *adivasis* (63.5%) earlier in the context of the Dhebar Commission Report in 1960 and also as part of settling the *adivasi* struggle as recently as in 2001. The state needs to win the confidence of the *adivasis* by keeping its promises. The Government of India, as part of its new drive towards the upliftment of the *adivasis* through the Forest Bill bears the onus to look into the matter and provide proper guidelines to states like Kerala. This would also make the ongoing process of decentralisation more meaningful for the weakest of social sections.

3. There is evidence of declining opportunities for employment for the *adivasis* in the agricultural sector—both plantations and non-plantations of Kerala. Issues such as social security measures—both 'protectional' and 'promotional'—health insurance, old age pension etc. need to be addressed seriously by bringing more and more social institutions such as educational institutions and medical centres closer to the *adivasi* settlements; it should be possible to make them an integral part of *adivasi* upliftment.

4. The state should ensure that the existing social policy with respect to tribals is enriched and that a critical minimum percentage of public expenditure is earmarked for the developmental activities in *adivasi* areas. The performance of local level institutions and their developmental programmes should be subjected to continuous scrutiny based on participation and outcome criteria of development.

5. The developmental projects in the *adivasi* belts should ensure permanent livelihood sources for *adivasis* through provision of employment, sustainable agricultural and non-agricultural activities and traditional industries. In the present context of the withdrawal of the state from developmental activities, special provision should be made for the protection of tribal communities which were rehabilitated in state farms and enterprises.

6. An analysis should be undertaken to explore the possibility of strengthening the traditional knowledge systems of *adivasis*. While chalking out strategies related to intellectual property rights, the success stories/models of sharing the benefits of intellectual property between the scientists involved and the tribals who inherit the traditional knowledge should be considered. The agreement between the *Kannikkars* of Kerala and the public sector TBGRI could act as a guide for the formulation of patents connected with intellectual property rights.
7. The Ministry of Environment and Forest had issued a number of orders (No.13-1/90-FP (1), No.13-1/90-FP (2), No.13-1/90-FP (3) and No.13-1/90-FP (5) dated 18.09.1990) regarding encroachment on forest lands, review of disputed claims over forest lands arising out of forest settlement, disputes regarding pattas/leases/grants involving forest land, conversion of forest villages into revenue villages and settlement of other old habitations. The Commissioner for Scheduled Castes and Scheduled Tribes issued a monograph describing how acts of omission and commission over the years have resulted in violation of rights of scheduled tribes. These orders attempt to rectify these violations. The Supreme Court (Pradip Prabhu Vs. State of Maharashtra and others) had, in March 1995, directed the states of Maharashtra and Madhya Pradesh to decide on the people's claims in the light of these orders. The Inspector General of Forests, Ministry of Environment and Forests further clarified and reiterated on 30th October 2002 that the guidelines issued earlier (in September 1990) relating to regularisation of encroachments of forestlands should be followed.
8. Human rights violations of the *adivasis* and the other Dalit groups in the country, are a blot on the face of the democracy. Compulsory family planning measures almost tantamount to ethnic cleansing, spread of alien diseases among *adivasis* and irresponsible tourism in the high ranges; its far-reaching consequences, such as the increasing incidence of unwed mothers among *adivasi* women, are social evils which the Bill should address in depth.
9. The GoI should form a high level Committee—with representatives from tribals, the Ministry of Tribal Affairs, National Commission on SC/ST, representatives from the state-level Tribal Missions, public figures and academicians—to supervise the implementation of legislations passed by the state and the centre. The committee should also look into whether the state/centre violate Articles 3, 13 and 14 of the ILO Convention 107 (ratified by India) and the UN declaration of human rights that relate to protection of property rights, respect of customary procedures of transmission of traditional ownership of lands, prevention of non-tribes from securing ownership or use of lands belonging to tribals, and provision of additional land when they do not have adequate land necessary for procuring the essentials of normal existence. The committee should also ensure adequate protection of human rights. The state should explicitly take a position with respect to Section 2 of the ILO Convention 169 on Indigenous and Tribal Populations which India is yet to ratify, and which clearly acknowledges the concept of territoriality of the indigenous people and the relationship they have with their identity and their right to ownership and possession over lands traditionally occupied. Unless the society at large is re-oriented towards re-distributive justice, the marginalised sections are unlikely to empower themselves for a struggle for identity.

B) MARINE FISHING COMMUNITIES

Introduction

The poverty of fishing communities is proverbial. Fishery seems to rhyme with poverty. This is not only true in Kerala or India. This is an issue that has engaged the minds of many researchers and policy makers world over. In several developed countries, where fisheries have contributed to societal well-being and economic growth—such as Norway, Canada and Iceland—the question of the poverty of fishermen was a matter of concern at the early stages of economic development.

However, in these developed countries, the post-second World War period witnessed a major change in the socioeconomic conditions of fishing communities. A combination of state and community initiatives—across the institutional, organisational and technological spectrum—was an important factor in giving a major boost to incomes and living conditions.

A defining feature of these development initiatives pertained to the rules restricting access to the sea, to the organisational arrangements for selling fish and obtaining credit and to the implementation of significant technological changes in fishing activities and fish processing.

The process of creating socioeconomic change in fishing communities in Kerala was also initiated along similar lines. However, the tempo of the process could only be maintained for two decades between 1956 and 1975. In the marine sector alone the value of output increased from Rs. 20 million in 1956 to Rs. 740 million in 1975 (Kurien, 1978). Thereafter, a radical shift in both the priorities of the state and of the dominating economic interests in the sector created conditions for fisheries development without fisherfolk development (Kurien, 1985).

A decade ago, an analysis was made of the process whereby the fisherfolk in Kerala state (particularly the marine communities) were left out from the mainstream of the much acclaimed benefits of Kerala's 'high quality of life' development experience (Kurien, 1995). In that analysis, it was pointed out that in terms of income, land holdings, housing quality, health conditions and literacy levels the fishing communities were clearly 'outliers'. They stood far behind the all-Kerala averages. Why were fisherfolk being left out of the development process and confined to poverty despite the richness of the natural resource that they harvested? An attempt was also made in that analysis to provide some of the salient reasons accounting for this anomaly.

Important among the reasons cited were: (1) the open access mode of resource use and the communities' lack of awareness of undergoing exploitation by merchants, (2) the particular pattern of export-oriented, capital-intensive fisheries development fostered by the state resulting in technological dualism, (3) the low educational attainments and the lack of associative physical and social conditions conducive to provide the incentive to acquire education, (4) the role of organised religion in denying the fishing folk a class identity, and (5) the lack of any sociopolitical movements in the communities.

That analysis however, concluded on an optimistic note. It conjectured that the independent socio-ecological movement of the fishing communities, which arose in the 1980s as a reaction to many of the above-mentioned reasons, compelled the state towards greater public action. The movement was also leading to capability-building by the community itself in an effort to enhance its entitlements for a better quality of life.

In this section, an attempt is made to assess the results of the actions taken by the state and the community. Macro-evidence to show that socioeconomic change and poverty alleviation is possible and that it has really occurred in fishing communities in the early 1980s following appropriate technological change, state support and community initiative, is given in the first instance. Secondly, using the available data for the state as a whole, it is shown that the fishing communities (marine and inland) have made some progress in 'catching up' with the rest of Kerala's population. The gaps that remain within communities across space and religious groupings are also highlighted. Finally, the measures that should be taken to sustain these improvements and allow the fishworkers of Kerala to follow the path of their counterparts in Norway, Iceland and Canada, are discussed.

Is Change Possible?

The study by UNRISD made in collaboration with the Kerala Statistical Institute between 1979 and 1984 provides hope that poverty in fishing communities can be alleviated by a combination of private and public interventions (UNRISD, 1980; 1983; 1985). The study examined poverty from a holistic perspective which took into account besides income and calorie intake variables such as health, nutrition, education, conditions of work, consumption and savings, housing, clothing, recreation, social security and human freedoms (UNRISD, 1983).

Of the 12 locations selected in Kerala—three each from the state's three eco-types— the lowlands, the midlands and the highlands—the fishing village (called TKA, in Alleppey district) was at the outset the poorest adjudged on the basis of selected variables. The poverty score which the study developed showed that the fishing village had the lowest score in 1979. At the end of the five year period of continuous monitoring, the study team found that the fishing village made significant reduction of poverty levels. Income and food consumptions improved at a much higher rate than in the other selected villages. The improvement was due to a variety of factors—large scale motorisation of fishing craft during the period, widespread employment assistance under the Government's National Rural Employment Programme and continued migration to the Gulf States (UNRISD, 1985). In TKA, the low-income households made greater improvement in income than the rest, and they benefited from the dramatic change in drinking water supply (Ibid.: 27). The housing sector benefited from government assistance as well as schemes of private organisations (including churches) and private initiative. The Fisheries Corporation's loans were generous, varying between Rs. 2000 and Rs. 5,000 of which about half is subsidy (Ibid.: 59). The proportions of households obtaining their drinking water from definitely unsafe sources such as open streams or pools declined. Through a government scheme the piped water system was extended to cover virtually the entire area, so that only a small proportion of households need now have recourse to unprotected sources (Ibid.: 59).

The low-income group, mainly fisherfolk which had accounted for about 7.1 per cent of the population, advanced more quickly than the rest. The average incomes rose by 93 per cent in monetary terms. Supply of electricity went entirely to the advantage of the low-income households, who also benefited from the marginal changes in land distribution (Ibid.: 99).

The systematic analysis of the changes showed significant improvements in the well-being of the population in the fishing village. Change is, therefore undoubtedly possible. Have such changes in fishing communities of Kerala happened throughout Kerala? The secondary data from the Census of India, the Department of Economics and Statistics and the census surveys conducted by the Department of Fisheries of the Government of Kerala throw light on this question.

The Aggregate Picture

Income levels and the quality of life for fishing communities show significant improvements—both at the state and at the district levels, thanks to the collective actions from below and the positive response from the state from above towards these actions.

(a) Changes in Income Levels

The economic fortunes of fishing communities are integrally linked to the quantum and the composition of their catch. Prices at the fishing landing centres are very sensitive to the quantum landed. The lack of any organised sales procedures and the control which merchants and middle-men exercise over credit and output markets make matters worse. As a result, increases in physical productivity consequent upon technological changes do not always translate into higher economic returns. Moreover, the open access nature of the sea and inland waters creates a race for fish. This phenomenon is particularly evident in the marine sector where capital intensifications of fishing operations after 1990 have not yielded sustained enhancement of harvests. The increases in the shore prices from burgeoning demand for fish in Kerala have been far in excess of its supply. (Table 13.7).

TABLE 13.7

Value of Output in the Fisheries Sector

Year	*Marine Capture (mt)*	*Inland Capture (mt)*	*Combined Average Price/ Tonne (Rs.)*	*Combined Value of Output (Rs. Million)*
1970/71	379865	12845	751	295
1980/81	268083	25526	4177	931
1985/86	350826	28578	7064	1454
1990/91	677554	36342	10926	5120
1995/96	532550	49586	31997	10826
1999/00	593720	74130	29470	19682

Source: GoK (2001a). *http://www.ecostatkerala.org/html/statplanning.html*

Both per capita state domestic product and per fisherman fishery sector product have increased substantially over the years. (Table 13.8) However, the members of the fishing communities, on average, have always remained worse off than the average person in the state. During the period when overall economic growth was slow (1970-1985), the difference between the per capita income of the state and the fishery sector product per fisherperson increased from 29 to 47 per cent. The narrowing of the gap observed in 1975 was due to the phenomenal increase in that year in marine fish production. During the period 1970-1985, the difference was getting sharper, and the fish catch in the marine sector dropped below its 1970 level.

It is significant that this period also witnessed intensification of the socio-ecological and political movement in the fishing communities across the state. This movement played an important role in focussing attention on the plight of the community and resulted in a change in state budget priorities. Greater emphasis was given to promotional social security and livelihood-oriented schemes. There was also a conscious attempt to support and promote technological change.

However, during the period after 1985, divergent trends were observed. During the 1990s, when the state economy was doing reasonably well, there was initially a narrowing of the gap between the per capita income of the state and the per fisherman income of the fishery

TABLE 13.8

State Domestic Product and Per Fisherman Fishery Sector Product and their Per Capita Distribution in Kerala

	1970	*1975*	*1980*	*1985*	*1990*	*1995*	*2000*
Net SDP (Rs. Mill)	12,546	21568	38,227	56,372	121,735	220,243	587,048
Population (million)	21.08	23.14	25.31	27.15	28.98	30.58	32.14
Fishery Sector Product (FSP) (Rs. Mill)	257	570	774	932	3,719	6,286	11,437
Fisher Population (lakhs)	6.12	6.92	7.79	8.47	9.36	9.92	10.50
Percapita SDP (Rs.)	595	932	1,510	2,076	4,200	7,200	18,262
FSP/fisherperson (Rs.)	420	823	993	1,100	3,970	6,334	10,885
Percentage Difference	29	12	34	47	6	12	40

Source: Kurien, 2000; GoK, 1988; GoK, 2001a.

sector. From the mid-1990s, the gap however widened and stood at 40 per cent by 2000 (Table 13.8).

The marine fish production peaked to an all-time high in 1990 to more than 670 thousand tonnes; thereafter it dropped to an average of around 555 thousand tonnes during the 1990s. The widening of the gap between per capita SDP and per fisherman FSP was due to rising fixed capital costs consequent on the rapid diffusion of mechanical propulsion (the outboard motors), increase in improved fishing gear, and development of new boat models to suit these changes. The shift from total dependence on renewable energy (wind and human) to total dependence on non-renewable sources (kerosene and petrol) has substantially raised the recurring costs of fishing. Consequently, despite rising shore prices of fish and hence higher values of output, value added in the sector has not risen proportionately as evident from the declining ratio of the fishery sector product to the value of fishing output. This reveals the poor transformation efficiencies in this state (See Table 13.9)

TABLE 13.9

Value of Output (VO) and Fisheries Sector Product (FSP) of Kerala

Year	*VO (Rs. Mill)*	*FSP (Rs. Mill)*	*FSP/VO (%)*
1970/71	295	257	87
1980/81	931	774	83
1985/86	1454	932	64
1990/91	5120	3719	72*
1995/96	10826	6286	58
1999/2000	19682	11437	58

Note: * This improvement was due to phenomenal increase in fish production that year. The triennial average value is 61.

Source: Same as for Table 13.1 for VO; GoK, 2001b for FSP.

The transformation efficiencies are more pronounced in the marine sector in which the open access nature of the coastal waters necessitates huge fixed and recurring costs. Costs increased also by the feverish race for fish. The economic outcomes and their distribution across fish worker households are important factors determining assets, wealth, poverty levels and livelihood patterns in the fishing sector.

(b) Changes in Quality of Life

As with value of output and value added, there have also happened noticeable improvements in the quality of life in the fishing communities.

(i) Improvements in Literacy

Data on the literacy levels of the fishing communities as a whole are not available for periods long enough to analyse trends within communities. However, Censuses provide data on 'workers' of these communities—persons gainfully employed in fishery and related activities. Since data are restricted to persons of the working ages, the rates of literacy for workers are likely to be higher than those for the population as a whole. We assume however that the difference is not large, particularly in recent periods.

The data suggest that there have taken place marked improvement in the levels of literacy of fish workers during 1971-1991, from 55 per cent to 81 per cent. The gap between the literacy level of workers in general and that of fish workers which had been 23 percentage points in 1971, declined to 18 percentage points in 1981 and 13 percentage points in 1991 (Table 13.10).

A spatial analysis of the literacy attainments highlights some significant differences. The major

TABLE 13.10

Literacy Rates of Population, All Workers and Fishworkers in Kerala

Year	1961	1971	1981	1991
Population	32	60	70	78
All workers#	60	78	85	94
Males	70	83	89	95
Females	34	58	71	85
Fishworkers (Total)	(50)*	55	67	81
Males	(57)*	56	67	82
Females	(19)*	36	44	67

Note: # excluding cultivators and agriculture labourers.

* Not for fishworkers alone but for all workers in mining, quarrying, livestock, forestry, fishing, hunting and plantations.

Source: Census of India, several volumes.

common feature between the three selected districts of Thiruvananthapuram, Thrissur and Malappuram is that the majority of the fishworkers and the fishery are marine based. The major differences among them lie in religious composition—Thiruvananthapuram being the district with the highest Christian fishworker population, Trichur with the highest Hindu fishworker population and Malappuram with the highest Muslim fishworker population. An important technological difference among them which has a possible bearing on the literacy rates is of the nature of the fishing craft used. In Thiruvananthapuram, the use of the *kattumaram* necessitates induction of fishermen into the occupation at a very early age to acquire the skills of operation of this craft. As a result, workers are deprived of the opportunity of schooling and acquisition of literacy. In the other two districts of Thrissur and Malappuram, the nature of the fishery and the type of craft in use make such compulsions less stringent. In fact, in these latter districts many marine fishermen do not necessarily know how to swim—a condition unthinkable to exist among fisherman in Thiruvananthapuram.

In Thrissur where Hindu fishermen are the dominant group and the canoe is the main fishing craft, literacy levels of fishworkers are very close to the average for fishworker population of Kerala as a whole across the whole period 1971 to 1991. However, in Thiruvananthapuram and Malappuram, the literacy levels (of the Christian and the Muslim fish workers) are significantly lower than the average. The literacy

TABLE 13.11

Literacy Rates Among Fishing Communities in Kerala

District	Trivandrum			Trichur			Malappuram		
Year	1971	1981	1991	1971	1981	1991	1971	1981	1991
Total	32	38	60	52	69	81	27	38	71
Male	33	38	60	52	69	82	27	38	71
Female	30	27	49	43	56	63	13	17	62

Source: Same as Table 13.10.

levels of women fish workers in these districts leave much to be desired. However, the increase in the literacy rates between 1981 and 1991 in Malappuram for both men and women fishworkers has been more significant than in Thiruvananthapuram. Despite the greater state support for education, the continued use of the *Kattumaram* in Thiruvananthapuram may be a significant factor for the slower rise in literacy rates of fishermen in this district. In Malappuram, large scale migration of fishermen to the Gulf countries may be an important reason for higher literacy achievements between 1981-1991 among both men and women fishworkers.

(ii) Ownership of Land

Between 1980 and 1990 the share of households among the fisherfolk with no land has more than halved, from 16 to 7 per cent. The landholdings are however very small and primarily cater to the need for housing alone. Even in 1990, as many as two-thirds of the households owning land possessed less than 10 cents each (Table 13.12)

TABLE 13.12

Size Distribution of Landholdings of Fishing Households: 1980 and 1990 (%)

	Landless	Landed	0-5 cents	6-10 cents	11-50 cents	50+ cents
1980	16	84	32	28	21	3
1990	7	93	30	37	22	4

Source: Govt. of Kerala, 1982; 1990.

The district-wise variations in land ownership also reveal that between 1980 and 1990, only small changes in land ownership took place; the size of a holding of one-half the total number of households was below five cents. If land is a major asset and its primary use is for housing, the quality and the size of housing are much poorer in Thiruvanathapuram district than in Thrissur and Malappuram where the size of holdings is larger (Table 13.13).

TABLE 13.13

Size Distribution of Land Holdings of Fishing Households by Districts: 1980 and 1990 (%)

Dist	*Year*	*Landless*	*Landed*	*0-5 cents*	*6-10 cents*	*11-50 cents*	*50+ cents*
Tvm.	1980	24	76	53	12	10	1
	1990	17	83	51	22	9	1
Tri.	1980	3	97	13	35	39	7
	1990	3	97	9	39	38	9
Mal.	1980	10	90	35	27	22	3
	1990	2	98	26	38	28	4

Source: Govt of Kerala, 1982; 1990.

An earlier study (Thomas, 1989) highlighted the important role played by associative physical conditions (housing, amenities like electricity, overall habitat etc.) in achieving and maintaining educational attainments in the fishing communities. Where these conditions were poor, the children's motivation to study was low and the rate of dropout was high.

(iii) Housing Conditions

The fishing settlements have population densities four to six times as high as the Kerala average. The population density in the state as a whole in 2001 was 819 persons per square kilometre. In 1980 the population density of the coastal fishing village tract (taking a quarter kilometre width across the coastline to represent this area of habitation) had been 4070; in 1990 the corresponding figure increased to 4392. The primary reason for high density is the desire of the fishermen to stay close to the sea. Fishermen had wanted since early times to be able to observe from day to day the nuances of the sea in order to decide the timing and the nature of fishing activities to be undertaken. However, over time this proclivity meant that all land, which was not away from the high tide line, was occupied (legally and not so legally) by better-off groups from non-fishing communities. Fish workers had to squeeze in on inconvenient places and undergo all the highly negative reciprocal externalities. The implications of this for the health status and the overall community well-being are obvious. The greater incidence of intra-community conflicts in fishing villages is mainly due to such over-crowding and its adverse impacts.

The relationship between size and location of landholdings and the quality of housing is obvious. In 1980, the fishing villages had twice as many thatched huts (48 per cent compared to 24 per cent) and nine times as many mud and semi-thatched huts (36 per cent as compared to 4 per cent) as the state as a whole had (Kurien, 1995). People who do not have ownership rights of the lands they occupied and where the lands are situated close to the high tide line of the sea, seldom venture to go in for good housing.

The available data for 1980 and 1990 however indicate a certain degree of improvement in the housing conditions and other basic facilities of the fisherfolk. Nearly 95 per cent of the fishing households have become owners of their houses. The numbers, which live in huts, declined to one-half of their earlier level—from 48 to 27 per cent. The number of persons living in semi and *pucca* structures increased nearly three-fold—from 16 per cent to 46 per cent. The number of households with electricity connection has more than doubled from 10 to 26 per cent; those with latrines increased from 5 to 15 per cent and, most importantly, more than one-half of the total had easy access to water in 1990 compared to only a third in 1980.

Between 1964 and 1980 the annual average amount of state support for housing, sanitation and health had been Rs. 1.28 million. The corresponding amounts were Rs. 6.66 million in 1981-85 and Rs.12.45 million in 1986-1998 (Kurien and Paul, 2000). It is unlikely,

TABLE 13.14

Housing Tenure, Type and Facilities in the Fishing Villages of Kerala

Year	*Tenure*			*Type*			*Facilities*		
	Own	*Rent*	*Other*	*Hut*	*Katcha*	*Pucca**	*Electrified*	*Latrine*	*Water Easy Available*
1980	80	5	15	48	36	16	10	5	33
1990	95	2	3	27	27	46	26	15	58

Note: * includes semi-*pucca*.

Source: Govt. of Kerala, 1982; 1990.

however, that government support alone was the major contributor to the increase in the number and the quality of housing.

Secondary survey data indicate that of the total amount of loans taken by the marine fisherfolk households, only 15 per cent came from direct government sources. In the case of the inland fisherfolk households, the corresponding share was 22 per cent. As much as 25 per cent of the loans taken by marine fishermen and 35 per cent of the loans taken by inland fishermen in 1985 were spent on house construction. In both the cases, this was the single most important item of expenditure on which loans were utilised (Government of Kerala, 1990). Fisherfolk households are thus found to be making attempts to improve their housing conditions.

Among the selected districts, Thiruvananthapuram presented a relatively poor performance. While the number of huts and *kutcha* structures did come down, the figures were still far above the Kerala average. The number of semi-*pucca* and *pucca* houses was also below the Kerala average. While there was slight improvement in the availability of electricity and latrine facilities, the easy availability of water did not improve much with half the number of households remaining without easy access to clean water. Clearly housing conditions of the fishing communities in Thiruvananthapuram left much to be desired. In short, the housing conditions of fisherfolk in Thiruvananthapuram district remained poor.

In the districts of Thrissur and Malappuram the quality of housing and the accessibility to facilities for fisherfolk greatly improved over time. Estimates of the total number of houses and percentage of houses built between 1985 and 1996 in the three districts of Thiruvananthapuram, Thrissur and Malappuram were reported for the year 1997. The percentage increase during the period 1985-1996 in respect of built houses was 11 per cent in Thiruvananthapuram, 21 per cent in Thrissur and 19 per cent in Malappuram (Government of Kerala, 1997).

TABLE 13.15

Population Density in Coastal Districts and Marine Fishing Villages

State/District	*Overall Population Density (1991)**	*Population Density in Marine Fishing Villages (1990)#*
Kerala State	749	4392
Trivandrum District	1344	5856
Trichur District	903	3712
Malappuram District	872	4355

Note: # - Calculated from Fisherfolk Census Data assuming the village habitation area to be the length of the district coastline and a width of 250 mts.

Source: * GoK, 2001b.

Despite changes, the overall location of marine fishing households close to the sea and the high tide line, makes their houses vulnerable to high tides during monsoons. Numerous reports of fishermens' houses getting destroyed by the fury of the tides and sea erosion are an annual feature. Earlier, destruction used to be confined to huts. Now, even *pucca* houses do not escape nature's fury.

(iv) Health Conditions

Poor health conditions have always dogged fishing communities. Undoubtedly, there is likely to have taken place some improvement in the conditions of health of the fishing communities over time—particularly of the marine fishers—with improvement in their income and literacy levels, and housing conditions and amenities

TABLE 13.16

Housing Conditions of Fisherfolk: Tenure, Type and Facilities 1980 and 1999 (%)

Dist.		*Tenure*			*Type*			*Facilities*		
	Year	*Own*	*Rent*	*Other*	*Hut*	*Katcha*	*Semi-pucca & pucca*	*Electrified*	*Latrine*	*Water Easy Available*
Tvm.	1980	66	3	31	45	43	12	15	7	51
	1990	87	4	9	31	40	29	23	20	48
Tri.	1980	96	1	3	53	33	14	4	4	18
	1990	97	1	2	30	20	49	19	17	53
Mal.	1980	87	5	8	64	28	8	6	2	28
	1990	98	1	1	40	28	31	21	20	46

Source: Govt. of Kerala, 1982; 1990.

such as water supply and sanitation. However, some studies made in recent years point to the fact that households with higher income levels do not necessarily have low morbidity levels (Charles, 1997). The main reason for such a state of affairs is the high reciprocal negative externalities prevalent as a result of excessive crowding. Isolated, individual efforts to improve health are rendered, by and large, futile particularly in the absence of overall participation of community initiative and commitment.

News papers have reported in 2003 and 2004 of the return of cholera, malaria, dengue fever, and TB to the coastal tract of Kerala. These reports have focussed on the higher incidence in coastal areas of Thiruvananthapuram district. Micro level studies (FRC/PCO, 2000) in the coastal urban fishing areas of Thiruvananthapuram district have highlighted morbidity patterns—of high levels of asthma, diarrhoea and fever—related to their poor environmental conditions. Owing to the lack of drainage, high water table and porous nature of beach soils, wells in the coastal areas easily get polluted with seepage from septic tanks. The problem is aggravated by the non-availability of land to build individual toilets, particularly if the technology of the pit latrine is to be adhered to.

Several NGOs have successfully taken the initiative to find answers to the sanitation problems; their efforts have been particularly focused on the needs of women who are the worst sufferers. The lack of toilet facilities is known to be the cause for women eating less during day time (Charles, 1997), a curse which accounts for the high incidence of reproductive tract disorders among women. The impact of this malaise on nutrition and health conditions is obvious. Initiatives to run 'pay and use' toilets managed by village- level women's organisations have proved socially successful and financially viable in some over-crowded fishing villages. The need for privacy was the most compelling factor for the crying demand for sanitation facilities (Kurian, n.d.).

Clean drinking water and hygiene education are the two other requirements to ensure good health conditions and thus to contribute to poverty alleviation in coastal areas. A study conducted in Thiruvananthapuram district in two of the most crowded fishing villages supports strongly the view that provision of clean potable water, environmental sanitation and hygiene education in poor regions brings out the gender aspect of poverty arising from the lack of these provisions. It further pointed out that improvement in health due to elimination of water-borne and sanitation-related illnesses reduced annual public expenditure per household by Rs. 682 and resulted in an annual saving per household on medicines and other related expenses to the tune of Rs. 510 (Pushpangadan, 2002). Given the low levels of income in fishing communities, this order of reduction in health related costs is highly significant.

Poor health is also related to poor food intake. Marine fishing families depend almost entirely on the market for their food items. Unlike for agriculture communities, there is no possibility of raising a kitchen garden for fishing households which may even possess land. Nothing except coconut palms grows in the sandy soil. Moreover it is much against their temperament to grow crops. Their diet is also largely unbalanced and deficient. It is generally devoid of vegetables and consists mainly of large quantities of rice or tapioca and fish.

According to a rapid appraisal of healthcare facilities in the fishing villages, 19 per cent had neither provision for government nor private health facilities in 1997. A mere 17 per cent had some private health facilities. Only in 44 per cent of the villages did government or private health institutions take some form of public health activity.

What's to be done?

Despite positive changes in average incomes and the quality of life in general of the fisherfolk in Kerala during the past four decades, particularly after 1980 during when public action was relatively strong and sustained, efficiencies of transforming rising output value into value added were declining (See Table 13.9). Investment and recurring costs of fishing were disproportionately on the increase. The traditional approach to solve this lacuna would be reduction of costs. In the fishery sector today, particular in marine fisheries in which the problem of rising costs to individuals and the sector as a whole remains excessively burdensome, the root cause of the problem has to be sought. It is the 'race for fish' arising from the open access nature of the coastal waters that constitutes the source of the problem, which must be tackled first if the larger issue of improving incomes were to be addressed at all.

Much needs to be done to enhance the quality of life. A radical approach is needed to address questions of land for housing, water, sanitation and literacy. Some of these questions are discussed below.

How to Improve Incomes

(i) Setting Limits to Access to the Resource

Setting limits to access to the coastal waters is not a decision that a fisherman can take for himself—or to impose on others. This is essentially a matter that must be decided upon by the state, with or without the collaboration of persons involved in fishing.

The challenge before the Government of Kerala today is to recognise this fact, accept it as a matter of priority and implement the decisions expeditiously. Needless to say, in Kerala, such actions cannot be taken unilaterally. They must necessarily be negotiated decisions taken with the full participation of all the stakeholders.

Setting limits to access has two important dimensions. Firstly, the question of who should be allowed to fish in coastal waters. Secondly, once this question is decided, what would be the technical specifications and investment limits to be imposed on persons who are granted access. In Kerala, attempts have been made to implement decision on the second question and turned a blind eye to the first question because of the political sensitivity attached to it. It is now abundantly clear, both from macro data and real hardships faced by fishermen, that postponement of decision on the limits of access will be at the collective peril of all concerned. It will have a long-term adverse impact on both the fishing communities and on the state in general.

The UDF Government of Kerala made in its Fisheries Development and Management Policy of 1994 specific recommendations for aquarian reform in the state which would ensure that the right to fish is restricted only to persons who actually fish—in other words a ban on absentee ownership of fishing equipment was envisaged. This policy suggestion was followed up by the LDF Government of 1997 and 2001 with two major initiatives: (i) Preparation of a Task Force Report on Livelihood-Secure Fishing Communities (TFR) and (ii) formulation of and Aquarian Reforms Committee (ARC).

The TFR reiterated commitment to the 1994 Policy, particularly to the aquarian reforms. It spelt out how, through a decentralised area approach, organisational arrangements for this purpose could be put in place. The ideas of *Matsyabhavans* (Fish Houses) and *Janakeeya Samitis* (People's Forums) in each coastal and inland *panchayat* were suggested. While the concept of *Matsyabhavans* was implemented (single-window set-up for all fishery-related welfare, development and management activities), the participative element of *Janakeeya Samitis* was overlooked.

Several meetings of the ARC were conducted and public hearings held across the state to inform people of the fishing sector and to get their reactions to the idea of aquarian reforms. A drafting committee was then requested to make a draft report. The consolidation of the report lay undone with the chairperson of the committee. When elections in May 2001 resulted in the defeat of the LDF, interest in ARC waned and the idea was kept in cold storage.

The UDF coalition government, which came to power in 2001, posted a Draft Fishery Policy (2004) on the official government website. This draft policy (poorly drafted and faulty with regard to terminology and references etc) makes no mention of the 1994 GoK-approved fishery policy (initiated by the UDF itself) nor of any later documents. It is a stand-alone piece with no reference to the past. It contains no mention of aquarian reforms or any measure to set limits to access to the resource. However, it has discussion on technical specifications with regard to the access – specifying horsepower type of nets and numbers of boats.

(ii) Lowering Costs of Fishing

Costs of fishing have been steadily on the rise after 1991, mainly due to the widespread use of outboard engines in fishing boats. Data available for the period between 1991 and 1998 (Kurien, 2000a) from two censuses of fishing crafts, gears and motors reveal that the total engine horsepower in Kerala's motorised fishing units rose from 1.30 lakh HP to 2.54 lakh HP. The average power of an outboard engine is thus seem to have increased from 11 HP to 16 HP. The increase in costs has not resulted in a commensurate increase in the production of marine fish. In fact, production has dropped significantly from the peak level of 1991. During the 1990s, average fish production stagnated at around 550,000 tonnes. The levels after 2000 are not very significantly higher. The total marine fish landings in Kerala during 2003-04 were 608.5 thousand tonnes. In this context, it is essential to formulate and implement measures to ensure lower costs.

There must be a ceiling on the outboard motor HP used by a fishing unit. Subsidies should be provided to convert fishing units for use of diesel-run inboard engines. But in this case too a ceiling on the HP should be prescribed. Reversion to the use of sails should be encouraged. Provisions for getting sails of good, durable materials need to be considered. The usage of information enhancing devices such as GPS and cell phones that aid efficient fishing in areas of the sea not hitherto explored, without exorbitant recurring costs, should be encouraged too.

Measures to Improve Quality of Life

(i) Priority Access to Land

The current approach of seeking modification in the CRZ rules regarding house construction for fisherfolk appears to be unwise. The solution sought for is at best valid only for the short-term. It only adds to the density on the riparian tracts and creates 'slum-like' conditions. It also forecloses the possibility of developing a buffer zone (which is the intention of CRZ) along coastal and other riparian areas. It is the lack of such buffers that compels marine fishing communities to build houses close to the high tide line. They thus continue to expose themselves to the risk of the sea eroding their land and 'eating away' their houses (Kurien and Nandakumar, 2000).

The viable long-term solution for housing in fishing villages is the planning for fishery settlements on land *outside the bounds* of CRZ. If necessary, private and government lands that lie outside the bounds of the CRZ, but close to the sea/inland waters, should be acquired by government and allotted for creation of planned housing estates for active fishermen (See Govt. of Kerala 1997 for suggestions on the planning and layout of such schemes). Steps need to be taken to identify such lands near major fishing centres. The required information on the availability of suitable lands is readily available in the coastal *panchayat* resource maps with the Land Use Board. In planning, priority should be given to coastal districts in which population density is high and rising. The fishing villages in Thiruvananthapuram district fall in this category.

Proposals for land acquisition are often disregarded because of the high financial costs involved and the high transaction costs arising out of litigation, etc. An analysis of the social cost of annual disaster relief (for housing, free rations, etc.) during the monsoon months should help place these costs in proper perspective.

(ii) Drinking Water, Sanitation and Hygiene Education

The most important contributors to improved quality of life, other than housing, are clean drinking water, satisfactory sanitary conditions and proper upkeep of personal hygiene. It is of great importance to ensure that all these factors are given in an integrated package and are best undertaken together.

Given the high water table and porous soils in the coastal tracts, there is need to examine alternatives for provision of potable water and high level of sanitation. Rainwater-harvesting and desalination plants are two possible solutions. The costs and organisational implications of these two alternatives are different. The option of dry composting (see Govt. of Kerala, 1997 for details of this option) for toilets has been tested in some of the overcrowded fishing villages in Thiruvanathapuram district with reasonable success. As has been shown by recent studies (Pusphangadan, 2002), the social benefits of undertaking investment in dry composting is very high. The toilets already provided have a strong pro-female disposition that is a welcome feature.

(iii) Literacy and Empowerment

The need for sustained efforts to ensure universal literacy is obvious. Once the associative physical conditions, housing and health, are improved, the literacy objective would become achievable and sustainable. The focus of the efforts needs to be on the girl-child and the woman.

Human resources for producing educated and responsible persons in the fishing communities should be found from within the fishing communities themselves. Training of girls who have gone through a minimum of 10 years of schooling as primary village workers would provide a major pool of human capital for the purpose. Girls trained in this manner may be given priority consideration in the setting up of child-care centres, local small-scale employment programmes and saving and credit unions. The financial and organisational resources available with the state government, the central social welfare boards and other poverty alleviation programmes should also be tapped for the purpose of development of human resources.

The eight Regional Fisheries Technical High Schools functioning in the state have a total intake of only less than 200 students. However the pass percentage at the SSLC examination during the 1980s in these schools was between 85 and 97 per cent. This is adequate proof to the fact that right environment provides good results. However, since these institutions do not have the elementary sections attached to them, they tend to keep away children from among poor fisherfolk families.

In general, only those who manage to secure a pass from the secondary level, would be able to make it into these schools. Such children tend to be children from the well-to-do sections in the community. The educational attainment of the poor continues to be low. The fisheries high schools should therefore be given their primary and middle school sections also. It would be an important means of ensuring that all children from the fishing communities are properly educated and that they continue to have close association with and adequate orientation towards the occupation of fishing. It is necessary to produce fishworkers who have the advantage of the traditional knowledge systems and who are conversant with the latest technological and institutional developments in the trade, choices and appropriate blending of systems.

Training of fishworkers in technical matters such as sea safety measures and use of communication and location-seeking equipment (cell phones and GPS) is of great importance. Such training courses should be organised by the Department of Fisheries of the state in collaboration with fishing technology institutions of the Central Government located in Kerala. This will make fishworkers better equipped and qualified to take on fishing jobs in the Gulf countries. Currently many fishermen go to the Gulf countries and get jobs in the fishing sector based on their traditional skills. Providing them with new technical skills will greatly increase their job opportunities abroad. There should be an active programme of encouraging qualified fishermen to take up jobs outside the country.

Conclusion

The changes that have taken place in the fish economy of Kerala, particularly in the post-1980 period, have contributed positively to improvement in their incomes and quality of life. During the pre-1980s, both incomes and quality of life had been far lower than the all-Kerala standards. However, during the 1980s, there was significant improvement in both. During the 1990s, while gross national incomes showed steady improvement, the indications are that their real earnings were not improving to any remarkable extent. Questions about the sustainability of the initial gains in the quality of life also remain unaddressed.

Fishing communities can and are slowly catching up with the rest of the population of Kerala. The current (2004) scenario indicates, however, that if their real incomes are to improve on a sustained basis and their quality of life is to be raised to fairly high levels, more radical institutional and organisational changes need to be made both in their fishing sector activities and in the physical and social ambience. For this purpose, greater political will and collective action are required.

References

Amnesty International. (2001). *Rascism and the Administration of Justice*. New York: Amnesty International.

Bijoy, C.R. (1999). "Adivasis Betrayed: Adivasi Land Rights in Kerala." *Economic and Political Weekly*, May 29 , pp.1329–1335.

Bijoy, C.R. and K. Ravi Raman (2003). "Muthanga: The Real Story—*Adivasi* Movement to Recover Land", *Economic and Political Weekly*, No. 31–33: 975–982, May 17.

Chakravarthi, G and P Karjan Ghosh (2002). *Human Development Profile of Scheduled Castes and Tribes in Rural India: A Benchmark Survey*. New Delhi: NCAER.

Census of India (1961). "Kerala", Vol VII, Part II B (i). Trivandrum

———(1971). "Series 9: Kerala", Part II B (ii). Trivandrum

———(1981). "Series 10: Kerala" Part III A & B (iii). Trivandrum

———(1991).."Series 12: Kerala", Part III-B, Vol 3. Trivandrum

Charles L, (1997). "Health Status and Health Care System Among the Fisherfolk: A Micro-Level Analysis", M.Phil Thesis. Trivandrum: CDS.

Dreze, Jean, and Amartya Sen. (1995). *India: Economic Development and Social Opportunity*. Delhi: Oxford University Press.

Franke, Richard W. and Barbara H. Chasin. (2000). "Is the Kerala Model Sustainable? Lessons from the Past, Prospects for the Future", in Govindan Parayil *(ed.), Kerala: The Development Experience*. London: Zed Books. pp.16–39.

FRC/PCO (2000). *Status of Education, Employment and Health in the Coastal Area of Thiruvananthapuram Corporation*. Trivandrum

GoI (1998). "Rural Labour Enquiry", *Report on General Ccharacteristics of Rural Labour Households (50th Round of NSS), 1993-94*. Shimla: Labour Bureau, Ministry of Labour.

Government of Kerala (GoK) (1962). *The Evaluation Committee on the Welfare of the Scheduled Castes, Scheduled Tribes and other Backward Communities*. Thiruvananthapuram: Government Press.

———(1979). *Report on Socio-economic Survey of Tribals in Kerala*. Thiruvananthapuram: Bureau of Economics and Statistics.

———(1982). *Survey Report of Tribal Land and Collection of Data of the Tribals at ITDP, Attappady*, Government Press Eranakulam, 1982.

———(1982). *Census of Fisher Folk in Kerala*, Directorate of Fisheries, Trivandrum

———(1986). *The Kerala Scheduled Tribes (Restriction Transfer and Restoration of Alienated Lands) Act 1975* and *Kerala Gazette Extraordinary* No. 89 dt. 24 January.

———(1988). *Statistics for Planning*. Thiruvananthapuram: Bureau of Economic and Statistics.

———(1996). *The Kerala Scheduled Tribes (Restriction on Transfer and Restoration of Alienated Lands) Amendment Bill, 1996*. Thiruvananthapuram: Government Press.

———(1997). *Report of the Task Force on Livelihood Secure Fishing Communities*, State Planning Board, Thiruvananthapuram.

——— (1990) *Techno Socio Economic Survey of Fisher Folk in Kerala*, Department of Fisheries, Thiruvananthapuram.

——— (1999). *The Kerala Restriction on Transfer by and Restoration of Lands to Scheduled Tribes Bill, 1999*, Government Press, Thiruvananthapuram

———(2001a). *Statistics for Planning*. Thiruvananthapuram: Bureau of Economic and Statistics.

——— (2001b). *Economic Review 2001*, State Planning Board, Thiruvananthapuram.

———(2002). *Report of the Socio Economic Survey of Primitive Tribes 1996-97*. Thiruvananthapuram: Directorate of ST Development.

Kannan, K.P. (2000). "Poverty Alleviation as Advancing Basic Capabilities: Kerala's Achievements Compared" in Govindan Parayil (ed.), *Kerala: The Development Experience*. Zed Books. pp.40-65

Krishnadas, N.V. (2003). *"Kanakkeduppum Kadukayari, Kanakkukoottalukal Paali"*, *Malayala Manorama*, 21 February

Kunhaman, M. (1982). "Bonded Labour in Kerala Among the Hill Tribes of Wynad", *State Society*, Vol. 3(2): 51-55.

——— (1986). "Tribesmen being cheated out of their lands", *Indian Express*.

——— (1989). *Development of Tribal Economy*. New Delhi : Classical Publishing Company

Kurian, C.O. (n.d.) "Community Latrines as a Viable Option". Trivandrum : SEUF. *(Mimeo)*

Kurien, J. and D. Nandakumar (2000). "Littoral Regulation Zone: A New Concept for an Integrated Approach to Resource Planning in Kerala State", in Eapen M *et al.* (eds.), *Development Perspective: First Step in Formulation of a District Plan*. Trivandrum: State Planning Board.

Kurien. J. and A, Paul (2000). *Nets for Social Safety: An Analysis of the Growth and Changing Composition of Social Security Programmes in the Fisheries Sector of Kerala State, India*. Chennai: ICSF Publications.

Kurien, J. (1978). "Towards an Understanding of the Fish Economy of Kerala State", *CDS Working Paper* 68. Trivandrum

———(1985) *Technical Assistance Projects and Socio-Economic Change: The Norwegian Intervention in Kerala's Fisheries*.

———(1995) "The Kerala Model: Its Central Tendency and the 'Outlier'", *Social Scientist*, Vol.23 (1-3). New Delhi

———(2000) "The Kerala Model: Its Central Tendency and the 'Outlier'", in Parayil G (ed.), *Kerala: The Development Experience*. London: Zed Books

———(2000a) "Capacity, Costs and Output Changes in the Small-Scale Fisheries Sector of Kerala State", SIFFS. *(Mimeo)*

Lieten, G. K. (2002). "The Human Development Puzzle in Kerala." *Journal of Contemporary Asia*, Vol.32(1): 47–68.

Mathur, P.R.G. (1977). *Tribal Situations in Kerala*. Trivandrum: Kerala Historical Society.

Menon, Madhava, T. (1996). *The Encyclopedia of Dravidian Tribes*, Vol. 1. Thiruvananthapuram: International School of Dravidian Linguistics.

Omvedt, Gail (1998). "Disturbing Aspects of Kerala Society", *Bulletin of Concerned Asian Scholars*, Vol.30(3), July–September.

Pushpangadan, K. (2002). "Social Returns from Drinking Water, Sanitation and Hygiene Education: A Case Study of Two Coastal Villages in Kerala", *Working Paper* 333. Trivandrum: CDS.

Raj, K.N. and Michael Tharakan (1983). "Agrarian Reforms in Kerala and Its Impact on the Rural Economy: A Preliminary Assessment", in Ghose Ajithkumar (ed.), *Agrarian Reforms in Contemporary Developing Countries*. London: Croomhelm pp.31–90.

Ram Mohan (1991)."Understanding Keralam: The Tragedy of Radical Scholarship", *Monthly Review*, January.

Ramachandran, V.K. (1997). "On Kerala's Development Achievements", in Jean Dreze and Amartya Sen (eds.), *Indian Development: Selected Regional Perspectives*. Delhi: Oxford University Press. pp.205–356.

Ratcliffe, John (1978). "Social Justice and Demographic Transition: Lessons from India's Kerala State", *International Journal of Health Services*, Vol. 8(1): 123–144.

Ravi Raman, K. (1998). "Intervention in the Western Ghats: An Inquiry into the Historical Processes of Loss of Biodiversity and Community Sources of Livelihood." in P. Pushpangadan et al (eds.), *Conservation and Economic Evaluation of Biodiversity*. New Delhi: Oxford—IBH Publishing Co. pp.525–544.

———(2002). "Breaking New Ground: Adivasi Land Struggle in Kerala", *Economic and Political Weekly*, March 9 , pp.916–918.

——— (2004). *Global Capital and Peripheral Labour: Political Economy of Tea*.

——— (2004)."Muthanga: A Spark of Hope", *Social Analysis: The International Journal of Social and Cultural Practice*, Vol 48(1).

——— (2004). "Commodity Chain-*Trap?* Livelihood Struggles in the Tea Plantations of Kerala", Paper read at the International Seminar on *Commodity Chain* at the School of Management, CUSAT, September 2003 and at the International Labour History Conference, V.V. Giri National Labour Institute, New Delhi, 6-11 March

——— (2005). "The Myth of Decentralisation: Situating Perumatty Panchayat, Coca-Cola and the New Social Movement", Paper presented at the *International Seminar on Decentralised Planning in Kerala*, Thiruvananthapuram.

——— (2005). "Corporate Violence, Legal Nuances and Political Ecology: Cola War in Plachimada", *Economic and Political Weekly*, June 18, pp.2481-86

Sivanandan, D. Narayana and K. Narayanan Nair, (1985). "Land Hunger and Deforestation: A Case Study of the Cardamom Hills in Kerala", *Working Paper* No. 212. Thiruvananthapuram: Centre for Development Studies.

Tharakan, Michael (1978). "Dimensions and Characteristics of the Migration of Farmers from Travancore to Malabar, 1930–1950." *Journal of Kerala Studies*, Vol. 5 (June): 287–305.

Thomas, J. (1989) "Socio-Economic Factors Influencing Educational Standards in a Marginalised Community: A Case Study on the Marine Fisherfolk of Kerala", M.Phil Thesis. Trivandrum: CDS.

Uma Devi, S. (1997). "Plantations in Southern India, c.1850-1950", Doctoral thesis (submitted). Thiruvananthapuram: Centre for Development Studies.

UNRISD (1980). "Socioeconomic Observation Areas in Kerala", Vol. 1, *Development Monitoring Service at the Local Level*. Geneva.

———(1983). "Level of Living and Poverty in Kerala", Vol. 2, *Development Monitoring Service at the Local Level*. Geneva.

———(1985). "Monitoring Change in Kerala: The First Five Years", Vol. 3, *A Development Monitoring Service at the Local Level*. Geneva.

Velluva, Sanathanan (2004). "Developmental Effects on Livelihood Strategies of Tribespeople in Attappady, Kerla," *Discussion Paper*. Thiruvananathapuram: KRPLLD, CDS.

Viswanathan, T.P. (1978). Brief History of Cardamom Hill Reserve (*mimeo*).

Wadhwa, D.C. (2003). "Guaranteeing Title to Land", *Economic and Political Weekly*, 23 November.

Chapter 14

Migration and Development

Introduction

This chapter deals with the consequences of migration on the Kerala economy. The principal means by which emigration impacts on socioeconomic situation in Kerala is remittances, which the emigrants send/bring back home. Several other factors also contribute to the totality of economic consequences of emigration. In this chapter, the main focus is remittances and the factors determining them. The main factor determining remittances to the state is the size and composition of the emigrants and return emigrants (together they are referred to as non-resident Keralites or NRKs).

The objective is to provide the overall impact on migration on development issues such as investment on education and health, macro economic assessment of remittances, consumption behaviour of migrants *versus* non-migrants, housing quality and the impact of emigrants on income distribution, employment and education.The data sources for this paper come from the two surveys conducted on Kerala migration, one in 1999 and the more recent one in 2004 (Zachariah, Mathew and Irudaya Rajan, 2003; Zachariah and Irudaya Rajan, 2004).

Design of SMS

The South Asia Migration Study (SMS) of 2004 was designed after the Kerala Migration Study (KMS) of 1999. The basic data used in both the studies were of the same order: primary data collected from 10,000 households from 225 localities (200 localities in KMS) selected at random from the 14 districts of the state. The questionnaire used in the two studies and the data-collecting agency were the same. The methodology of analysis followed in both the studies was quite similar, but the objectives were slightly different. In the KMS, the main concern had been the assessment of the migration situation in 1998-99. In SMS, the concern was not only assessment of the situation in 2003-04, but also a review of changes (dynamics) during 1999-2004. The two studies are therefore quite comparable.

TABLE 14.1

Sample Size by Districts, 2004

Districts	*Number of Households as per 2001 Census*	*No. of Sample Localities*	*No. of Sample Households*
Thiruvananthapuram	759,382	25	1,110
Kollam	593,314	20	891
Pathanamthitta	297,134	11	490
Alappuzha	483,960	16	710
Kottayam	434,520	15	671
Idukki	265,344	9	400
Ernakulam	693,161	23	1020
Thrissur	639,871	21	930
Palakkad	530,216	18	800
Malappuram	612,413	20	900
Kozhikode	567,658	19	850
Wyanand	166,763	5	220
Kannur	457,368	16	710
Kasargod	225,252	7	310
Kerala	**6,726,356**	**225**	**10,012**

Source: Zachariah and Irudaya Rajan (2004a).

Although the coverage is limited in the SMS compared with that of the KMS, the analysis of the selected problems of inquiry is much more comprehensive for two reasons mentioned below:

First, SMS is quite comparable with KMS taken five years earlier. Therefore, it has been possible to compare every aspect of emigration and the socioeconomic situation in 2004 obtained from SMS with that in 1999.

Secondly, in SMS about 5000 (half the total) sample households were the same as those included in KMS. This has given a unique opportunity for an analysis of the dynamics (change) of migration and socioeconomic characteristics in Kerala during 1999-2004 using the same set of households. In this way, the effect of sampling error on the comparisons could be almost entirely eliminated.

DIMENSIONS OF EMIGRATION

Demographic Dimensions

Contrary to expectations, emigration from Kerala continued unabated during 1999-2004. The number of emigrants in 2004 were 18.4 lakh persons, roughly 27 emigrants per 100 households. The comparable figure in 1999 (KMS) was 13.6 lakh persons, roughly 21 emigrants per 100 households. There has taken place a relatively large increase of about 35 per cent, in the number of emigrants from Kerala during the past five years.

The number of return emigrants was 8.9 lakh persons in 2004 as against 7.4 lakh persons in 1999. They represented 13.0 persons per 100 households in 2004 and 11.6 persons per 100 household in 1999. The return emigration showed a slower rate of growth, about 21 per cent in the 5 year period. The number of non-resident Keralites (NRKs), defined as the sum of emigrants and return emigrants, was 27.3 lakh in 2004 and 21.0 lakh in 1999 indicating an increase of 30 per cent during 1999-2004. There were about 40 NRKs per 100 households in 2004 but only 33 in 1999. The number of NRKs per 100 households increased by 7 persons during the period.

Although there were 40 NRKs per 100 households in 2004, only about 26 per cent of the households were direct beneficiaries of emigration. The proportion of households with at least one emigrant or one return emigrant (NRK > 0) was 24 per cent in 1999 as against 26 per cent in 2004. There was thus a slight increase in the spread of emigration among the households in Kerala. At the same time, the total number of households without an NRK actually

TABLE 14.2

Migration Trends in Kerala 1982-2003

Year	*Emigrants*	*Return Emigrants*	*Non-Resident Keralites*
1982	230740	39408	270148
1983	274804	51853	326657
1984	273342	67754	341096
1985	313980	85039	399019
1986	329083	99557	428640
1987	364909	120298	485207
1988	405513	151410	556923
1989	449611	163855	613466
1990	510214	197732	707946
1991	566668	219856	786524
1992	637103	253733	890836
1993	754544	287610	1042154
1994	819025	331166	1150191
1995	957388	379562	1336950
1996	1062376	433489	1495865
1997	1178589	486033	1664622
1998	1318489	553096	1871585
1999	1412649	620851	2033500
2000	1501917	684457	2186374
2001	1600465	739766	2340231
2002	1717695	794385	2512080
2003	1844023	893942	2737965

Source: Same as Table 14.1.

TABLE 14.3

Emigrants (EMI), Emigrants per 100 Households and Percentage Distribution by Districts, 2004

Districts	*Emigrants*		*EMI Per 100 HHs*		*Percentage to Total*	
	2004	*1999*	*2004*	*1999*	*2004*	*1999*
Thiruvananthapuram	168046	130705	21.5	19.9	9.1	9.6
Kollam	148457	102977	24.4	18.4	8.1	7.6
Pathanamthitta	133720	97505	44.3	33.1	7.3	7.2
Alappuzha	75036	62870	15.2	13.2	4.1	4.6
Kottayam	106569	35494	24.0	9.1	5.8	2.6
Idukki	7880	7390	2.9	2.9	0.4	0.5
Ernakulam	121237	103750	16.9	17.0	6.6	7.6
Thrissur	178867	161102	27.2	25.6	9.7	11.8
Palakkad	177876	116026	32.6	21.8	9.7	8.5
Malappuram	271787	296710	45.0	49.2	14.8	21.8
Kozhikode	167436	116026	28.6	22.0	9.1	8.5
Wyanand	7704	4552	4.4	2.9	0.4	0.3
Kannur	202414	88065	43.2	19.0	11.0	6.5
Kasargod	71449	38747	30.6	19.1	3.9	2.8
Kerala	**1838478**	**1361955**	**26.7**	**21.4**	**100.0**	**100.0**

Source: Same as Table 14.1.

TABLE 14.4

Return Emigrants (REM), Return Emigrants per 100 Households and Percentage Distribution by Districts, 2004

Districts	Return Emigrants		REM Per 100 HHs		Percentage to Total	
	2004	1999	2004	1999	2004	1999
Thiruvananthapuram	103059	118878	13.2	18.1	11.5	16.1
Kollam	69314	74106	11.4	13.2	7.8	10.0
Pathanamthitta	83502	54537	27.7	18.5	9.3	7.4
Alappuzha	43109	34572	8.7	7.2	4.8	4.7
Kottayam	28368	18164	6.4	4.6	3.2	2.5
Idukki	3766	5017	1.4	2.0	0.4	0.7
Ernakulam	74435	45028	10.4	7.4	8.3	6.1
Thrissur	86029	116788	13.1	18.6	9.6	15.8
Palakkad	55008	39238	10.1	7.4	6.2	5.3
Malappuram	141537	123750	23.5	20.5	15.8	16.7
Kozhikode	109101	60910	18.6	11.5	12.2	8.2
Wyanand	3852	3327	2.2	2.1	0.4	0.5
Kannur	45394	28263	9.7	6.1	5.1	3.8
Kasargod	47468	16667	20.3	8.2	5.3	2.3
Kerala	**893942**	**739245**	**13.0**	**11.6**	**100**	**100**

Source: Same as Table 14.1.

increased by about 2.7 lakh during the 5 year period, from 48.39 lakh in 1999 and 51.08 lakh in 2004.

This analysis provides a good reminder of the fact that direct beneficiaries of emigration are a relatively small minority in Kerala; that the vast majority of the households in the state are exposed to the ill effects of emigration such as price increase without having been in receipt of any direct benefits at all. Contrary to the common belief, Kerala is not flooded with NRKs and NRK households, even today.

Although emigration has not decreased, the rate of its increase has declined significantly in recent years, from 74.7 per cent during 1993-98 to 39.9 per cent during 1998-2003. The same pattern holds for return emigrants and non-resident Keralites also, but the rates of growth have been higher. The decline in the rate of increase is higher for emigrants than for return emigrants.

Though not unexpected, between 1999 and 2004, women, especially married women, have increased their presence significantly among the emigrants, On the contrary, married men lost out to unmarried men. The new emigrants included a relatively larger share of unmarried men and married women

The increase in the number of 'Gulf wives' (married women whose husbands are away in the Gulf), has not kept up with the increase in the number of emigrants. The number of 'Gulf wives' has remained almost unchanged at about one million between 1999 and 2004. The increase in the proportion of married women among the emigrants could have compensated for the increase in the total number of emigrants.

TABLE 14.5

Distribution of Non-Resident Keralites (NRK) by Districts, 2004

Districts	Non-Resident Keralites (NRK)			NRK per 100 HHs		Percentage to Total	
	2004	1999	Percentage Increase	2004	1999	2004	1999
Thiruvananthapuram	271105	249583	8.6	34.6	38.0	9.9	11.9
Kollam	217771	177083	23.0	35.8	31.6	8.0	8.4
Pathanamthitta	217222	152042	42.9	72.0	51.6	7.9	7.2
Alappuzha	118145	97442	21.2	24.0	20.4	4.3	4.6
Kottayam	134937	53658	151.5	30.4	13.7	4.9	2.6
Idukki	11646	12407	-6.1	4.3	4.9	0.4	0.6
Ernakulam	195672	148778	31.5	27.4	24.4	7.2	7.1
Thrissur	264896	277890	-4.7	40.3	44.2	9.7	13.2
Palakkad	232884	155300	50.0	42.6	29.2	8.5	7.4
Malappuram	413324	420460	-1.7	68.5	69.7	15.1	20.0
Kozhikode	276537	176936	56.3	47.3	33.5	10.1	8.4
Wyanand	11556	7879	46.7	6.6	5.0	0.4	0.4
Kannur	247808	116328	113.0	52.9	25.1	9.1	5.5
Kasargod	118917	55414	114.6	50.9	27.3	4.4	2.6
Kerala	**2732420**	**2101200**	**30.0**	**39.7**	**33.0**	**100**	**100**

Source: Same as Table 14.1.

Geographic Dimensions

During the past five years, Kerala emigrants have spread their wings over a much wider spectrum of countries in the world—North America, Europe and South East Asia. Within the Gulf region itself there were some significant realignments, some countries gaining ground at the expense of others. Within Kerala there were signs of realignment as far as the districts of origin are concerned, some districts gaining ground, at the expense of some traditionally important districts of emigration.

In 1999, about 95 per cent of Kerala emigrants went to the Gulf countries; and the other 5 per cent went mainly to the USA and Africa. By 2004, the share of the Kerala emigrants in the Gulf declined to about 90 per cent and that in countries other than the Gulf increased to 10 per cent. The principal destinations of Kerala emigrants outside the Gulf were the United States of America, England, Singapore and Maldives Islands. Within the Gulf region, the principal destinations were the United Arab Emirates and Saudi Arabia, which together accounted for more than two-thirds of all emigrants in the Gulf. In 2004 the share of the UAE increased to 36.5 per cent, up from 31.0 per cent in 1999. On the contrary, the share of Saudi Arabia declined to 26.7 per cent from 37.5 per cent in 1999.

TABLE 14.6

Country of Residence of Kerala Emigrants, 2004

Country	*2004*	*1999*
United Arab Emirates	670150	421758
Saudi Arabia	489988	510652
Oman	152865	132443
Kuwait	113967	68130
Baharin	108507	74619
Qatar	98953	70001
United States of America	98271	29848
Other Countries	105777	54504
Kerala	**1838478**	**1361955**

Source: Same as Table 14.1.

Along with the change in destinations, there were also changes in the relative importance of districts as the places of origin of Kerala emigrants. Although Malappuram district continued to send out the largest number of emigrants, it lost some ground to other northern districts. Between 1999 and 2004 there was a slight northward shift in the centre of location of emigrants from Kerala.

Remittances

Remittances are the principal means by which emigration impacts upon the economy. There are of course other ways such as on-the-job development of technical and management skills, change in life style and work culture and exposure to better and more modern tools and equipment. However, in this study the focus is on the consequences brought out through remittances and on their disposition.

We have made a distinction between total remittances and household remittances. Secondary data from official statistics of the Reserve Bank of India (RBI) and other sources are used to arrive estimates of the total remittances. On the other hand, household data collected for this study were used to estimate household remittances, that is, remittances received by households in Kerala directly from emigrants abroad.

Total Remittances

Our best estimate of the total remittances for 2004 was Rs. 18,465 crore. This bears comparison with the estimate of Rs. 13,652 crore for 1999. Thus, the total remittances that Kerala receives annually have increased by 35 per cent during 1999-2004.

The infusion of Rs. 18,465 crore a year to Kerala via remittances should have had considerable impact on the Kerala economy. Rs. 18,465 crore per year distributed among the 32.5 million persons of Kerala would give each person in Kerala, young and old, men and women about Rs. 5,680 per year or Rs. 473 per month sufficient to buy at least one kg. of rice per day per person. This calculation clearly indicates how important remittances are for the Kerala economy.

The net state domestic product (NSDP) for Kerala was Rs. 83,782 crore for 2002-2003. The remittances (Rs. 18,465 crore) come to about 22 per cent of the NSDP of Kerala. The past five years experienced a general decrease in the ratio of remittances to NSDP, from about 25 per cent in 1999 to 22 per cent in 2003.

The per capita domestic income for Kerala was about Rs. 25,764 in 2003. This estimate does not include remittances. The modified state domestic income, including remittances, would be Rs. 102,248 crore and the modified per capita income, including remittances, would be Rs. 31,442. The effect of remittances on

TABLE 14.7

Remittances to Kerala, 1981-2003

Year	*Kerala (Rupees in crores)*
1981	337
1982	432
1983	568
1984	780
1985	523
1986	861
1987	891
1988	824
1989	1156
1990	873
1991	2428
1992	3025
1993	3882
1994	6084
1995	7069
1996	9521
1997	10761
1998	10817
1999	13652
2000	14438
2001	15732
2002	17362
2003	18465

Source: Same as Table 14.1.

FIGURE 14.1

Trends in Remittances Kerala, 1981-2003

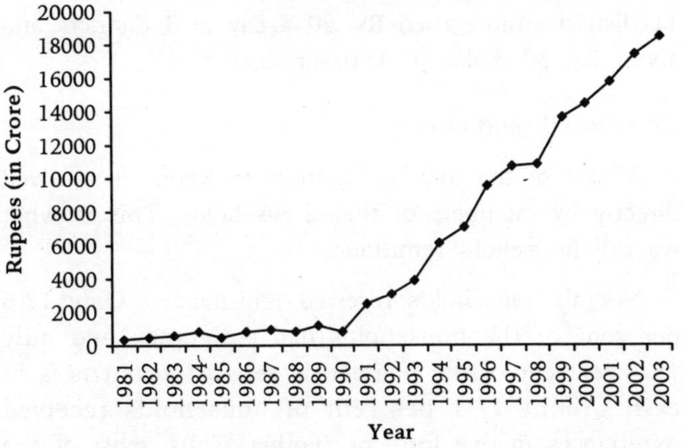

Source: Same as Table 14.1.

Kerala's per capita annual income in 2003 was an increase of Rs. 5678.

The importance of remittances in the Kerala economy becomes more evident from a few other comparisons too. The remittances were 1.74 times the revenue receipts of the state, 1.8 times the annual expenditure of the Kerala Government and 7 times the amount the state received from the Central Government. Remittances were sufficient to wipe out 60 per cent the state's debt in 2003.

Export of cashew kernels and marine products are two important earners of foreign exchange in Kerala. The total amount received by way of remittances in 2003 was 15 times the export earnings from cashew and 18 times that from marine products.

At the district level, remittances were the highest in Thrissur district with Rs. 3,234 crore. Malappuram district came next with Rs. 2892 crore. As expected, Idukki and Wayanad received the lowest amounts.

Remittances constituted 22 per cent of the states' NSDP. However, considerable variations were observed among districts. In Malappuram district, remittances formed about 46 per cent of the district domestic income. It was a meagre one per cent in Idukki district. Thrissur (38.2 per cent), Pathanamthitta (28.6 per cent) and Kollam (26.9 per cent) received relatively high proportions of their domestic incomes from remittances.

FIGURE 14.2

SDP Per Capita and Remittances Per Capita

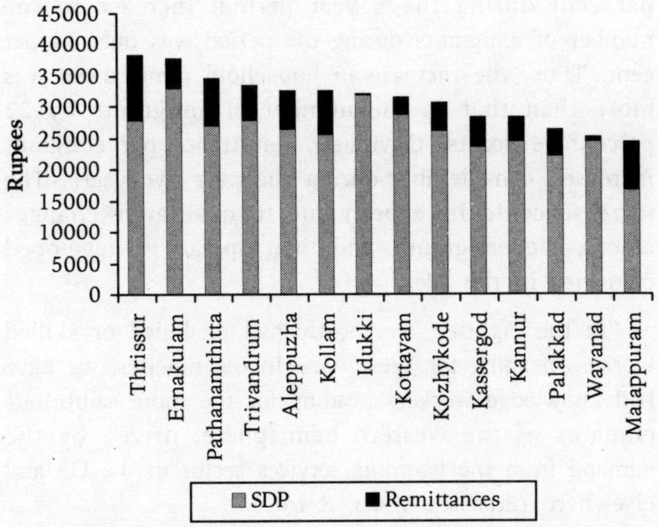

Source: Same as Table 14.1.

The impact of remittances on district level per capita income was the highest in Thrissur where remittances raised per capita income to Rs. 38,525 or by Rs. 10,654. Six districts where the impact was higher than the state average were Thrissur, Malappuram,

Pathanamthitta, Kollam, Alappuzha and Thiruvananthapuram. Remittances contributed more than Rs. 10 a day on the average income of persons in 11 districts, more than Rs. 20 a day in 3 districts and about Rs. 30 a day in Thrissur district.

Household Remittances

A part of the total remittances to Kerala is received directly by members of their households. This is what we call household remittances.

Not all households received remittances. Only 17.6 per cent of the households had emigrants, and only 16.7 per cent of the households received remittances in cash. About 17.1 per cent of households received remittances in one form or another. Thus, most of the households, which had emigrants from them, received remittances. At the same time, it is important to underline the point that 83 per cent of the Kerala households were not direct beneficiaries of workers remittances from abroad.

An estimate of the total household remittances (cash, commodities, and funds received mainly for consumption but also for buying land, houses, scooter etc.) received by Kerala households for various purposes were Rs. 7,965 crore. Of this total, cash remittances were Rs. 5,509 crore. The corresponding figure for 1999 had been Rs. 3,530 crore indicating an increase of 56 per cent during the 5 year period. Increase in the number of emigrants during the period was only 34 per cent. Thus, the increase in household remittances was more than that in the number of emigrants by 22 percentage points. Obviously, remittance per emigrant increased considerably during the past five years. The increase could have been due to qualitative changes among the emigrants, and their spread to developed countries in the West.

"In the eighties, we mostly had unskilled or skilled workers heading for West Asia. In the nineties, we have had knowledge workers heading for the more salubrious climates of the western hemisphere, driven by the demand from the booming services sector in the US and elsewhere *(Economic Times, 8/4/04)*."

The total cash value of goods (clothes, electrical and electronic goods and gold, etc.) received from emigrants was Rs. 562 crore in 2004 and Rs. 541 crore in 1999 indicating an increase of a mere four per cent. In 1999, remittances in kind came to 15 per cent of cash remittances. The corresponding proportion in 2004 was 10 per cent. Thus, the practice of bringing household goods, gold, clothes etc for the use of members of their households has not kept up in proportion with increase in the number of emigrants. Increase in the local availability of goods, which used to be imported, could have been the reason behind this slowdown.

In addition to cash and commodities, households received Rs. 1,575 crore by way of funds for investment in land and buildings. Of this amount, 87 per cent (Rs. 1367 crore) was used for the purchase of land and the balance Rs. 208 crore for construction/purchase of residential buildings.

An amount of Rs. 319 crore was received by households for the purpose of buying vehicles – cars and motor cycles -, for starting small scale industries and for paying dowry etc. Much of this amount (90 per cent) was spent on dowry payments and meeting miscellaneous expenses. Only less than half of one per cent of this Rs. 319 crore was spent on starting small-scale industries. About 10 per cent (Rs. 32 crore) was spent for buying vehicles.

Much of the cash value of commodities bought by emigrants (about Rs. 562 crore) was the value of clothing brought by the emigrants on their home visits. The next item in importance was gold ornaments. Another equally important item brought in by emigrants was electrical and electronic goods.

Household remittances were meant mainly for subsistence of the emigrant's relatives back home. About 50 per cent of the cash remittances was indeed used for subsistence. About half of that amount (25 per cent or 1,400 crore) was used for educational purposes.

Geographical Aspect of Remittances

Out of the total household remittances of Rs. 7,965 crore to Kerala in 2004, Rs. 1,368 crore (or 17.1 per cent) was received by households in Thrissur district. This is the largest proportion for any single district, among the 14 districts of the state. Households in Malappuram district received 1,257 crore (15.8 per cent of the total). The other districts which received substantial shares of the remittances were Kollam (10.6 per cent,) and Thiruvananthapuram (10.2 per cent).

In 1999, the district which received the largest amount by way of household remittances had been Malappuram, which received Rs. 766 crore or 18.8 per cent of the total. The share of Malappuram district decreased to 15.6 per cent in 2004. On the other hand, Thrissur's share increased from 14.0 per cent in 1999 to 17.1 per cent in 2004. The other districts, which experienced significant increases in their shares, are

Kollam and Thiruvananthapuram. On the other hand, some districts experienced decline in their shares: from 11.9 per cent to 7.7 per cent in Ernakulam, from 6.6 per cent to 5.0 per cent in Pathanamthitta and from 8.7 per cent to 6.6 per cent in Palakkad.

All the 14 districts experienced increases in the amounts received by households by way of remittances. The largest increase was in Thrissur district (Rs. 826 crore). The other districts of importance in this respect were Malappuram (Rs. 481 crore), Kollam (Rs. 467 crore) and Thiruvananthapuram (Rs. 456 crore).

Remittances per emigrant were the highest in Thrissur district, Rs. 51,750. Idukki district came close with Rs. 50,000. Ernakulam and Kollam are next in importance with about Rs. 40,000. Per emigrant remittances were the lowest in Kannur, only Rs. 15,000.

It was mentioned earlier that remittances in any form were received only by 17 per cent of the households in Kerala. The distribution of emigrants per households differed widely among the districts. At one extreme was Idukki district where only 1.5 per cent of the households received remittances in any form. On the other hand, in Malappuram district as much as a-third of all the households were direct beneficiaries of remittances from abroad. Pathanamthitta and Kasaragod were the other two districts, which had relatively large proportions of households receiving remittances.

Remittances by Religion

The total amount of remittance of Rs. 7,977 crore consisted of Rs. 2,365 crore received by Hindu households, Rs. 2,021 crore received by Christian households and Rs. 3,590 crore received by Muslim households. The average remittances per emigrant were Rs. 43,220. There was not much variation in this respect across religious communities. On the other hand, average remittances per household varied considerably by religion. Muslim households had an average remittance of Rs. 24,000 (Muslim households had larger number of emigrants per household) while Hindu households had an average of only Rs. 6,134 per household.

Remittances by Community

We have seen that the amount of remittance per household was the highest among Muslims. But Mar Thomite Christian households received even larger amounts. An average Mar Thomite Christian household received Rs. 26,098 as remittances in 2003-04, an

FIGURE 14.3

Per cent of Households Directly Benefited From Remittances

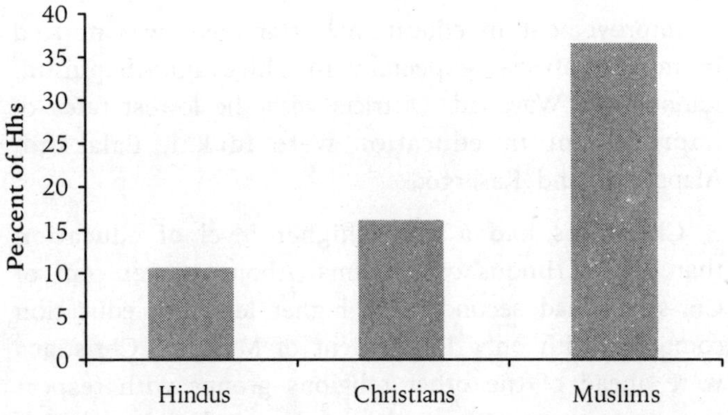

Source: Same as Table 14.1.

amount higher than the average for Muslims, Rs. 24,350.

In the order of remittances per household, the Mar Thomite community stood first followed by Muslims, Jacobite/Orthodox Christians, Latin Catholics, Roman Catholics, Nairs, and followers of the Church of South India in that order. The SC/ST group came last with only Rs. 725 per household.

Human Resources

Education, Employment and Unemployment

Other than the size of emigration, emigrants' human resources, education and employment pattern in particular, have a major role in determining the volume of remittances, the levels and patterns of consumption and disposition of remittances including all the economic consequences of emigration. Emigration also has a very important role in the human resource development of the population at the places of origin. Thus, human resources are simultaneously determinants as well as consequences of emigration.

Education

An important attribute of human resources is educational attainment. In this matter Kerala leads all other states of India. Yet, earlier, Kerala emigrants to the Gulf had not been well-educated, especially in comparison with their counterparts from other countries of origin. To what extent, has this situation changed in recent years?

During 1999-2004, the educational level of the population improved considerably in Kerala. The proportion of the population with secondary level of education or a graduate degree increased from 23.6 per cent to 27.1 per cent. Correspondingly, the proportion with primary level of education or below decreased.

Improvement in educational attainment was noticed in most districts, especially in Thiruvananthapuram, Kannur and Wayanad. Districts with the lowest rates of improvement in education were Idukki, Palakkad, Alappuzha and Kasargod.

Christians had a much higher level of education than either Hindus or Muslims. About 36 per cent of Christians had secondary or higher levels of education compared with only 15 per cent of Muslims. Christians were ahead of the other religious groups with respect also to improvement in the levels of education during 1999-2004.

Among Hindus, the Brahmin community was the most highly educated (51 per cent with high levels of education). Among Christians, the Mar Thomite Syrians were the most highly educated (47.5 per cent with high levels of education). Muslims were at the bottom and at par with the Scheduled Castes; only 15 per cent of them belonged to the high education group.

Emigrants were no doubt better educated than the general population. While 50 per cent of the emigrants, 36 per cent of the return emigrants and 45 per cent of the Non-Resident Keralites above the age of 15 years had secondary or higher levels of education, the corresponding proportion in the general population was only 32 per cent.

During 1999-2004, the educational level of the emigrants showed remarkable improvement. A notable feature of this improvement was the increase in the proportion of degree holders among emigrants, from 10.5 per cent in 1999 to 19.4 per cent in 2004.

Such increases were observed, not only in terms of proportions, but also in terms of absolute numbers. During 1999-2004, while the number of emigrants increased by 35 per cent, the number of degree holders among them increased by 144 per cent, from 1.36 lakh in 1999 to 3.33 lakh in 2004. Similar increases were noticed also among emigrants with the secondary levels of education, but their increase in numbers was not very much different from that of the total number of emigrants. Improvement in the educational level of the emigrants could have been therefore an important factor in the increase in the volume of remittances during 1999-2004.

FIGURE 14.4

Proportion with Secondary Level or Higher Level of Education

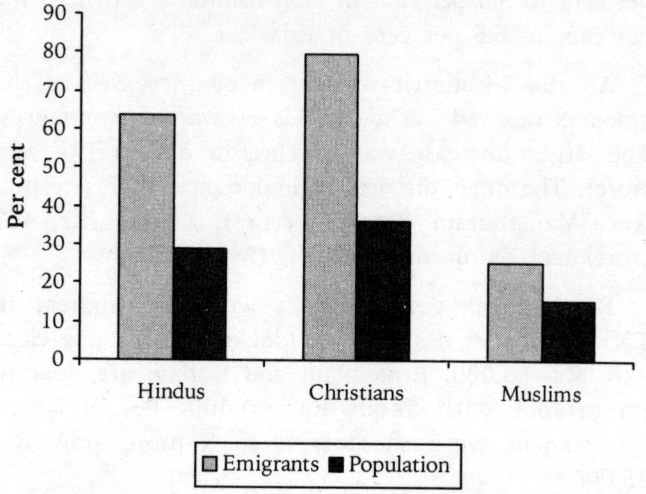

Source: Same as Table 14.1.

Expenditure on Education

Expenditure on children's education is a major item in the household budget. In recent years, the expenditure on education has been steadily on the rise.

A few households did not have, however, school-(college-) going children. The average expenditure on education for all households, including those without school children, was Rs. 3,739 while the average for households with children was Rs. 6,600. Christian households spent Rs. 10,315 per household, more than twice the average for Muslim households, which spent only Rs. 4,834.

Within the Hindu and the Christian religious groups there were very large variations in educational expenditure among communities. The Mar Thomite Christians spent the highest amount, Rs. 16,000 per household with children. The Orthodox/Jacobite Christians came next with Rs. 14,642 per household. They were followed by Roman Catholics, Nairs, etc. in that order.

Emigration has an impact on the amount that the households spent on education. The average expenditure per NRK household was Rs. 7731 and that per Non-NRK household was Rs. 6143. Such differentials existed in all religious groups, but they were the largest among Christians. NRK Christian families spent on an average Rs. 5754 more for education of their children than Non-NRK Christian families. The differential was the lowest among Muslims.

FIGURE 14.5

Expenditure on Education Per Household, by Migration Status and Religion

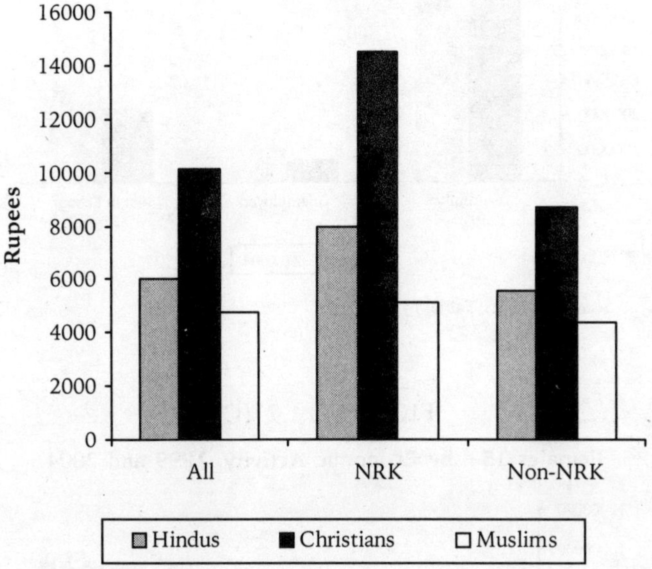

Source: Same as Table 14.1.

Expenditure for Health Services

Expenditure on family healthcare is an equally important item in the budget of Kerala households. In recent years, this item in the household budget has been on the rise. The average expenditure on healthcare per household was Rs. 4,953. As expected, the expenditure on healthcare also was higher among the NRK families than among the Non-NRK families. It was higher among Christians than among Hindus or Muslims. The difference was really large among NRK households. The Christian NRK households spent almost double the amount which the corresponding Hindu households spent. Hindus spent less on healthcare than Muslims did, both by the migrant and the non-migrant households.

As in the case of education, Mar Thomite Christian NRKs spent the maximum amount on healthcare, about Rs. 14,400 per household. The Orthodox/Jacobite Christian community came a close second. The effect of emigration, as measured by the difference between the NRK and the Non-NRK households was the largest among the Orthodox Christians. They were followed by the SCs/STs communities among whom emigration status made a big difference in the matter of

FIGURE 14.6

Expenditure per Household on Health, by Religion and Migration Status

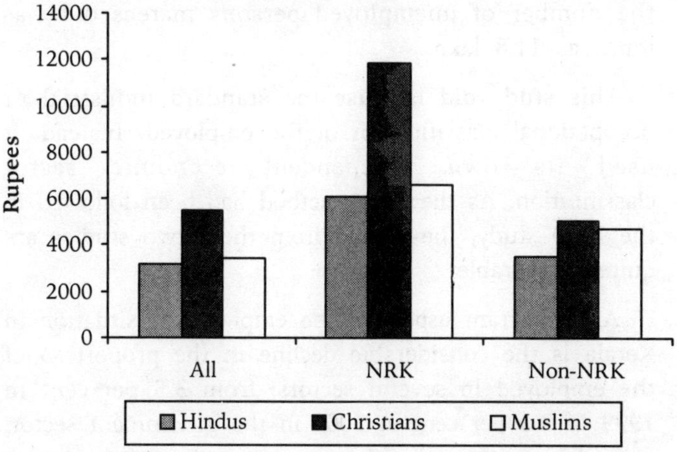

Source: Same as Table 14.1.

expenditure on healthcare. The migration effect was the lowest among the Latin Catholic, the Muslim and the Ezhava communities.

Economic Activity

The relation between emigration and economic activity is very close. Directly or indirectly, emigration from Kerala affects economic activity, and the levels of employment and unemployment in the state. In turn, the level of economic activity in the state does have some impact on the magnitude of emigration and its trends and characteristics.

According to SMS, there were about 25 million persons of employable age (taken as 15+ years in this study) in Kerala in 2004. Of them 12 million were in the labour force. Out of the 12 million, 10 million were gainfully employed and 2 million remained unemployed. Nearly 67 per cent (72 per cent in 1999) of the males and 15 per cent of the females (17 per cent in 1999) were gainfully employed; 24 per cent of males (22 per cent in 1999) and 75 per cent (78 per cent in 1999) of females were not in the labour force. About 8.5 per cent (5.8 per cent in 1999) of persons of 15+ years and 10 per cent of females of 15+ years (5.1 per cent in 1999) remained unemployed and were seeking jobs.

Between 1999 and 2004, the proportion of persons gainfully employed registered a decline, the proportion outside the labour force showed some increase and the proportion unemployed and seeking employment increased substantially.

During 1999-2004 while the number of employed males increased by 4.8 lakh, the number of employed females decreased by 43 thousand. At the same time, the number of unemployed persons increased by as much as 11.8 lakh.

This study did not use the standard industrial or occupational classification of the employed. Instead, it used its own independent economic sector classification. As the same method had been followed in the 1999 study, the results from these two studies are quite comparable.

An important aspect of the employment situation in Kerala is the considerable decline in the proportion of the employed in several sectors: from 3.5 per cent in 1999 to 3.2 per cent in 2004 in the government sector; from 4.1 per cent to 2.5 per cent in the private sector and from 13.1 per cent to 8.8 per cent in the self-employment sector. One major exception is employment in the casual labour sector, which registered an increase from 20.5 per cent to 22.7 per cent. Casual labour was the largest group among the employed. Next in the line was the self-employed. The net change among all the sectors combined was a decline from 43.4 per cent to 39.7 per cent.

In terms of numbers, the largest increase was found among non-agricultural labourers and the largest decrease among persons employed in the private sector. Employment in the semi-government sector experienced a robust increase of almost 70 per cent.

Kerala experienced a large increase in the number of pensioners during 1999-2004, by a whopping 433 per cent.

FIGURE 14.7 (A)

Population 15+ by Economic Activity, 1999 and 2004

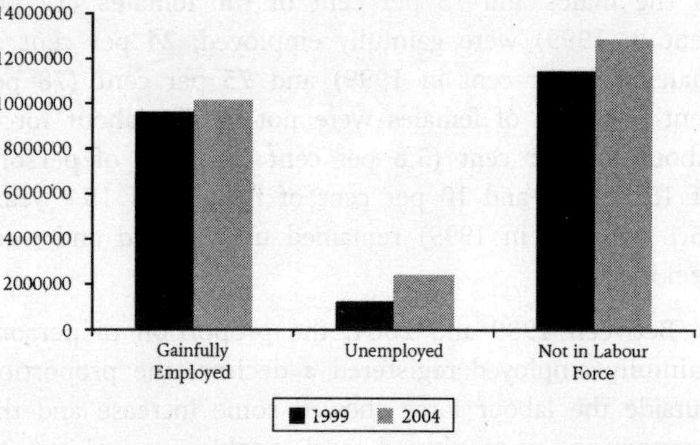

Source: Same as Table 14.1.

FIGURE 14.7 (B)

Males 15+ by Economic Activity, 1999 and 2004

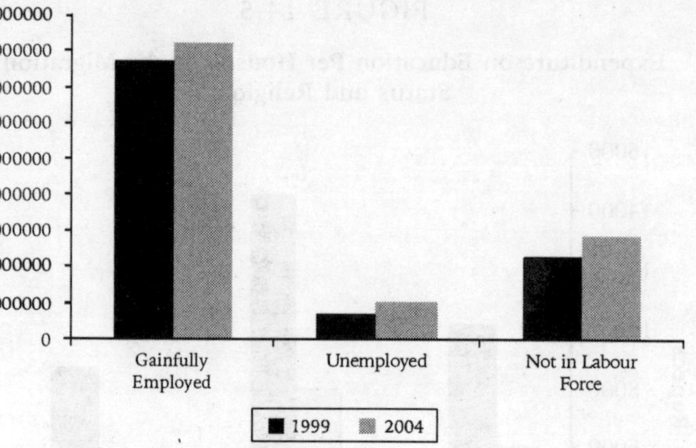

Source: Same as Table 14.1.

FIGURE 14.7 (C)

Females 15+ by Economic Activity, 1999 and 2004

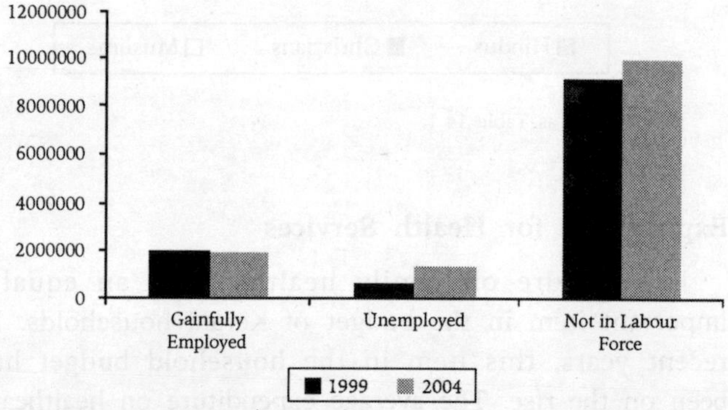

Source: Same as Table 14.1.

Unemployment

Of particular concern in this study is unemployment, which seems to have almost doubled during the past five years. The number of the unemployed persons had been 1.214 million in 1999 (619 thousand males and 594 thousand females) but was 2.389 million in 2004 (1.033 million males and 1.356 million females). The figures for 2004 represented an increase of 67 per cent among males, 128 per cent among females and 97 per cent among males and females taken together. The unemployment rate (unemployed per 100 persons in the labour force) was 11.2 per cent in 1999 and 19.2 per cent in 2004.

Thus the most dynamic element in the employment sector in Kerala during 1999-2004 was an extraordinary increase of the number of unemployed persons, stagnancy in the total number of employed persons and decline in the number of employed women.

Another interesting feature of the unemployment situation in Kerala in 2004 is its wide spatial variations. The unemployment rate was as high as 34.3 per cent in Thiruvananthapuram district and 27.8 per cent in Kasargod district but only 9.6 per cent in Idukki district and 10.4 per cent in Thrissur district. The number of the unemployed increased by 413 per cent in Thiruvananthapuram and 361 per cent in Kasargod, but decreased by 22 per cent in Palakkad and by 10 per cent in Thrissur. Such wide variations within this small state deserve careful analysis. The educational factor alone does not seem to account for such wide inter-district differences.

Unemployment was the highest among Christians and the lowest among Hindus. Among the different communities within each religious group, it was the highest among the Mar Thomite Christians and the Nairs. A close association is observed between unemployment rate and educational attainment. It was in the religious group and the community with a high proportion of persons with secondary or higher levels of education that unemployment rate was also the highest. A relatively high positive association existed between unemployment and higher education levels.

FIGURE 14.8A

Unemployment Rate By Education and Age

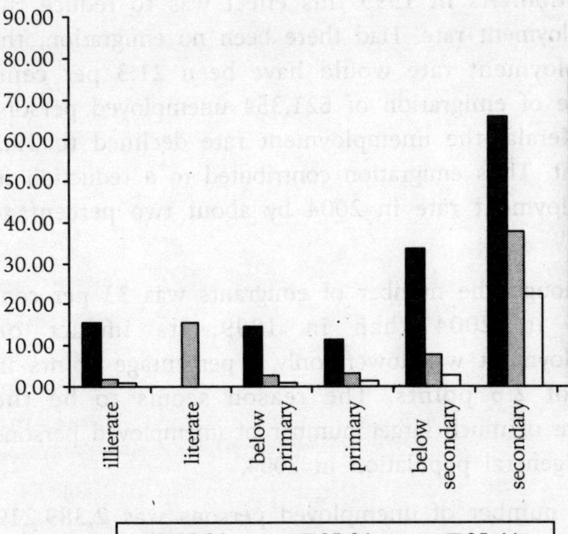

Source: Same as Table 14.1.

FIGURE 14.8B

Unemployment Rate by Age and Education

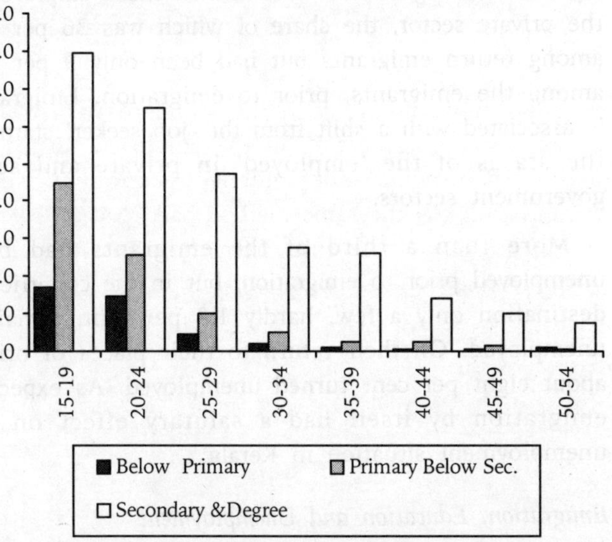

Source: Same as Table 14.1.

FIGURE 14.9

Per cent with High Education and Per cent Unemployed by Community

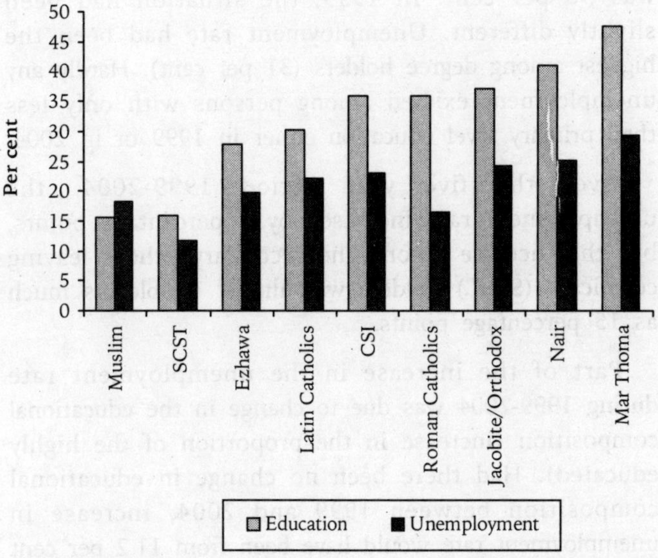

Source: Same as Table 14.1.

Emigration, Employment and Unemployment

Prior to emigration, about one-third of the emigrants had been employed as casual labourers. Among the rest, 9 per cent had been working in the private sector and 7 per cent had been self-employed. Among the return emigrants, the proportion of labourers increased a little to 36 per cent. But the most significant change was in the case of those employed in the private sector, the share of which was 36 per cent among return emigrants but had been only 9 per cent among the emigrants, prior to emigration. Emigration is associated with a shift from the 'job seeker' status to the status of the 'employed' in private and semi-government sectors.

More than a third of the emigrants had been unemployed prior to emigration; but in the countries of destination only a few, hardly 1.8 per cent, remained unemployed. On their return to their places of origin, about eight per cent turned unemployed. As expected, emigration by itself had a salutary effect on the unemployment situation in Kerala.

Emigration, Education and Unemployment

Education is an important factor in determining the level of unemployment in Kerala, as most of the unemployed were educated. In 2004, the highest unemployment rate of about 40 per cent was among persons who had the secondary level of education. The rate among the degree holders was not much lower; it was 36 per cent. In 1999, the situation had been slightly different. Unemployment rate had been the highest among degree holders (31 per cent). Hardly any unemployment existed among persons with only less than primary level education either in 1999 or in 2004.

Over the five year period 1999-2004, the unemployment rate increased by 8 percentage points, but the increase among the secondary school leaving certificate (SSLC) holders was almost double, as much as 15 percentage points.

Part of the increase in the unemployment rate during 1999-2004 was due to change in the educational composition (increase in the proportion of the highly educated). Had there been no change in educational composition between 1999 and 2004, increase in unemployment rate would have been from 11.2 per cent to 16.6 per cent only or just by 5.4 percentage points, instead of the observed 8.1 percentage points. Thus 33 per cent of the increase in the unemployment rate during 1999-2004 was due to change in the educational composition.

In terms of the number of the unemployed, the largest was among persons with secondary education, 11.9 lakh. The corresponding number in 1999 had been only 5.45 lakh. The increase was thus 6.5 lakh or 119 per cent. Unemployment among persons with primary level education showed a decline, by about 20 per cent. The overall increase was 97 per cent.

Factors Associated with the Increase in Unemployment

The relationship between migration and unemployment at the place of origin is rather complicated. There are both direct and indirect effects (spin-off effects). The direct effect is easy to estimate, but it is more difficult to measure the spin-off effects. As mentioned earlier, the unemployment rate, according to the KMS had been 11.2 per cent in 1999. The corresponding rate according to SMS was 19.2 per cent in 2004. The method used to estimate unemployment rate was the same in both the studies. Therefore, the observed increase is real. What are the factors underlying this increase?

In the KMS, it had been argued that emigration contributed to a decline in the unemployment rate in Kerala. Had there been no emigration, the unemployment rate in Kerala would have been 14 per cent instead of 11 per cent as recorded by KMS. Thus emigration had contributed to a reduction of the unemployment rate. This is the direct effect, or effect contributed by the departure of a large number of the unemployed from Kerala. In 1999, the indirect effect also would probably have been positive, favouring a reduction in the unemployment rate.

In 2004 also, there was this direct positive effect of emigration. As in 1999 this effect was to reduce the unemployment rate. Had there been no emigration, the unemployment rate would have been 21.3 per cent. Because of emigration of 621,354 unemployed persons from Kerala, the unemployment rate declined to 19.2 per cent. Thus emigration contributed to a reduction in unemployment rate in 2004 by about two percentage points.[1]

Although the number of emigrants was 33 per cent higher in 2004 than in 1999, its impact on unemployment was lower, only 2 percentage points in place of 2.6 points. The reason seems to be the presence of much larger number of unemployed persons in the general population in 2004.

The number of unemployed persons was 2,389,219 in 2004 as against 1,213,623 in 1999. The 2004 figure is higher by 97 per cent. The number of unemployed

1. The reported reduction of three percentage points in 1999 had been arrived by taking into consideration not only emigration but also out-migration to other states in India. If internal migration were excluded, the decline would have been only 2.6 percentage points.

persons among emigrants (before emigration) was 621,354 in 2004 and 360,917 in 1999. The 2004 figure is higher by 72 per cent. The impact of emigration of the unemployed is thus lower than the increase in the number of the unemployed.

Indirect Effects

The direct effect of emigration on unemployment would be relatively small compared with the indirect effects or spin-off effects. The net direct effect could at most be an increase of one percentage point as the gross effect in 1999 had been three percentage points and that in 2004 was two percentage points. We have to search for other factors for explaining the increase in unemployment (see later, in the section on Economic Consequences of Emigration)

Emigration and Acquisition of Consumer Durables

One of the inevitable consequences of emigration is the substantial increase in the disposable funds at the household level. This increase has had considerable impact on the consumption pattern of Kerala households. After repaying loans raised for meeting the cost of emigration, remittances are used to acquire a variety of consumer goods as well as land and houses, vehicles and household accessories. We have indicated earlier, how the remittances are used for housing, purchase of land, paying back debts, education of dependents and meeting the dowry payments of children and other relatives. Here we discuss the effect of remittances' on acquisition of housing amenities, household gadgets and consumer durables.

Housing and Household Amenities

Electrification

One important housing amenity is electrification. In Kerala, most houses are electrified, and therefore, the impact of emigration on electrification of houses could not have been very significant. According to this study in 2004, 85 per cent of its households were electrified, up from 74 per cent in 1999. About seven lakh houses were newly electrified during 1999-2004.

Although the overall percentage increase is very high, there existed differences across districts and religious groups. The proportion of houses electrified was nearly 90 per cent in Kottayam but only 66.4 per cent in Wayanad. Other districts with low rates (less than 85 per cent) of electrification are Idukki, Malappuram and Palakkad.

Emigration could have had a significant impact on the electrification of houses. Among households with an emigrant or return emigrant or an NRK, the proportion of houses electrified was as high as 96.9 per cent while the corresponding proportion among non-NRK households was only 81.9 per cent, a difference of 15 percentage points. The corresponding difference in 1999 had been higher, 19.7 percentage points. Thus, the differential between emigrants and non-emigrants in the matter of electrification of houses has become lower in more recent years. The reason is of course the fact that Kerala has reached a near-saturation level in the matter.

A significant point to note in this matter is that the increase in the proportion of electrified households among NRKs was 8.5 percentage points, while that among non-emigrants was 13.2 percentage points. Thus, the increase was much larger among the non-migrant households. The reason is that the initial level was much lower among the non-migrants and that there was scope for a higher rate of increase for them. On the other hand, among the migrant households, the level had been already very high and the scope for further increase was limited.

Emigration or no emigration, Kerala houses were getting electrified according to the facilities available with the KSEB. Emigration has not been a significant factor in this matter in recent years.

Cooking Fuel

The principal fuel used for cooking in Kerala households is wood. Nearly two-thirds of the households use wood alone or wood in combination with other fuels. Next in importance is LPG. About 31 per cent of the household use LPG alone or in combination with other fuels. Only about four per cent use kerosene oil.

In 2004, among the NRK households about 42 per cent used LPG compared with only 26.5 per cent among the non-NRK households. During the five year period 1999-2004, the proportion of households using LPG increased by 11.6 percentage points.

In 1999, the proportion of households using LPG had been 29.2 per cent among NRKs and 15.6 per cent among non-NRKs. The difference between NRK and non-NRK households in 1999 had been the same as was the case in 2004. Like in the case of electrification of houses, emigration has not been a significant factor in the use of LPG for cooking either. The differences between the proportion of households of migrants and of non-migrants with respect to the rates of increase in the use of LPG were not significant.

Housing

A major sector in which emigration seems to have had a very significant effect is housing. About 22 per cent of the houses in the sample were categorised as, 'luxurious' or 'very good' in 2004. The corresponding percentage in 1999 had been 14.5 per cent. Thus, during the 5 year period the housing quality improved considerably. However, there were large differences in the quality of houses occupied by the three religious groups. The proportion of luxurious or very good houses was 18.3 per cent among Hindus, 25.8 per cent among Christians and as much as 28.7 per cent among Muslims. This is one area in which Muslims stand much ahead of the other religious groups.

FIGURE 14.10

Per cent of Houses that are Luxurious or Very Good by Community

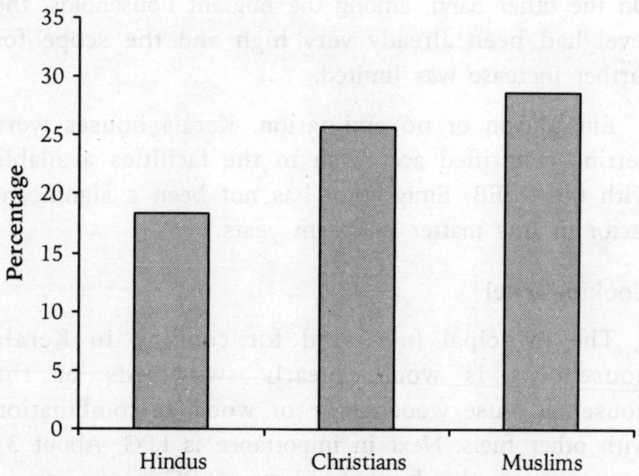

Source: Same as Table 14.1.

Emigration has had considerable impact on the quality of housing. Perhaps housing has been the very first requirement to receive emigrants' attention. About 58.3 per cent of the houses of the NRKs in 2004 were either luxurious' or 'very good'. Among the non-NRKs the corresponding proportion was only 17.1 per cent. The difference is as high as 41.2 percentage points. The corresponding difference had been only 13.1 percentage points in 1999. Thus, the effect of emigration on housing has become much stronger in recent years.

Comparison between the situation in 2004 and 1999 is highly revealing. In 1999 only 2.4 per cent of the NRK houses had been luxurious, but by 2004 as much as 17.2 per cent of them became luxurious. Similarly only 22 per cent of the NRK houses had been 'very good' in 1999. But by 2004 as much as 41 per cent of the houses of NRKs became 'very good.'

Even among the non-migrant households, some improvements have been observed in the quality of houses. Among them, 11.3 per cent of the houses had been 'luxurious' or 'very good' in 1999. The corresponding percentage was 17.1 in 2004. But unlike in the case of electrification and the use of LPG, the improvement in the quality of houses during 1999-2004 is seen to have been much stronger among emigrant households than among non-emigrant households. Emigration has had indeed an independent positive effect on housing quality. This positive effect of emigration on housing quality is independent of the district of origin of the emigrants or their religious affiliation. It is pervasive.

Acquisition of Consumer Durables

Remittances from emigrants, and money brought back by them on return increase the amount of disposable income of the NRK households. These households are, therefore, in a position to acquire consumer durables much more than their non-NRK counterparts are.

In 2004, 60 per cent of the Kerala households possessed television sets, 45 per cent had telephone connection and 30 per cent had refrigerators. All the corresponding proportions had been much smaller in 1999. Between 1999 and 2004, the proportion of Kerala households with television sets increased from 38 per cent to 60 per cent. The corresponding change in the case of telephones was from 15 per cent to 45 per cent, and in the case of refrigerators from 19 per cent to 30 per cent.

In terms of actual numbers the increases between 1999 and 2004 were 2,048 thousand telephone connections, 1,720 thousand television sets, 852 thousand refrigerators, 548 thousand VCRs, 509 thousand scooters/motor cycles and 330 thousand motor cars.

The effect of emigration on the possession of consumer durables could be understood better by comparing the increases during 1999-2004 as between emigrant households and non-emigrant households. The increase in the percentage of households with telephones among emigrants was by 40.9 points but only by 24.1 points among non-migrant households. In the case of television sets, the increases were 31.4 percentage points among emigrant households, but only by 21.1 percentage points among non-emigrants households. In all other items of consumer durables also, the increases were markedly higher among the emigrant households. Emigration indeed contributed significantly to the acquisition of consumer durables.

On the whole, the vast majority of Christian households owned most of these consumer durables more than the households of the other two communities. Seventy per cent of the Christian households had television sets compared with only 60 per cent of Hindu households and 51 per cent Muslim households. Hindus had the lowest proportion in the case of ownership of cars, scooters, telephones, cell phones, VCRs and refrigerators. Muslims came last with respect to the possession of television sets and cars. But they lead others with respect to the ownership of taxi cabs.

As shown earlier, emigration has had significant effect on the acquisition of consumer durables. The effect is significant among all the three communities; but it is the highest among Christians with respect to possession of telephones and refrigerators. In the case of television sets, the largest impact of emigration has been on the Muslim community. The difference between migrant and non-migrant households in the matter of possession of television sets is as much as 35 percentage points.

Economic Consequences of Emigration

Emigration and Unemployment

The 1999 KMS report concluded with a strong sense of euphoria about the impact of emigration on Kerala society. It said:

> Kerala has entered the new millennium with some cheer in many of its homes, thanks to migration and the economic returns that it brings (Zachariah, Mathew and Irudaya Rajan, 2000).

Emigration had brought into Kerala about Rs. 12 to 13 thousand crore by way of remittances in 1999, raising the State Domestic Product by 25 per cent, and per capita income by Rs. 4,351; directly reducing the unemployment rate by three percentage points (in consequence of the emigration of the unemployed); indirectly reducing unemployment through a number of spin-off effects, especially in the construction industry and the travel related service sectors; improving the educational level of the youth; restructuring the labour force by shifting a good many of its members from the category of general labour to self-employment; improving the housing condition in the state; and modernising housing facilities and enabling households to acquire many of the modern household amenities, and gadgets of luxury. As most of the emigrants of the late eighties and the early nineties came from relatively poor families, emigration and emigrants' remittances reduced the gap between the rich and the poor, thus leading to a more egalitarian society in Kerala.

Emigration of married men who left behind the responsibility of the management of the households to women in the family, has over the years, transformed about one million 'Gulf Wives' from the status of modest housewives to that of efficient managers of household affairs, capable of dealing with the outside world, maintaining family accounts, transacting business in banks, planning and pursuing the education of children and taking care of the health and well-being of the entire family.

The negative consequences of emigration had not altogether escaped the attention of the 1999 KMS report. But they did not receive much emphasis. The social and psychological problems of the 'Gulf Wives' and the loneliness of the 'Gulf Parents' which received some attention were considered to be minor spots in an otherwise brilliant picture of all-round benefits from emigration. The general surmise was, on the whole, one of euphoria.

Such euphoria was perhaps appropriate and warranted at that time, as large-scale emigration was at its early stage in Kerala. Possessing passports, buying air tickets from travel agents, travelling by plane to distant countries, etc. were new experiences for the ordinary labouring class of Kerala. Emigration brought in benefits beyond the wildest imagination of the emigrants themselves, not to speak of their families and neighbours.

The situation in 2004 was somewhat different. Kerala emigration had by then reached a more mature stage. It was no longer looked at with awe by most Keralites. Many of them had first hand experience, howbeit, at least for short periods. Emigration became one of the activities considered normal for the youth of the state, both men and women. The non-formal educational system in Kerala became especially geared to helping its youth to emigrate.

Did emigration deserve the same degree of euphoria in 2004 as it had in 1999? Our analysis showed that even today most consequences of emigration are highly beneficial to the Kerala society. At the same time, some of the secondary effects of emigration, the so-called spin-off effects, had begun to create problems. This report, while describing the beneficial consequences of emigration has taken particular care to point out some of these emerging adverse effects of emigration. In fact, this section deals more with the negative aspects of emigration than with its positive aspects, which had been well articulated, in the 1999 KMS.

First, a quick recapitulation of the positive aspects. During 1999-2004 emigration from Kerala continued to grow albeit at a slower rate. Return emigration was rapid but was at a rate slower than earlier expected. About 26 per cent of the Kerala households had an NRK in 2004 compared with 24 per cent in 1999.

Remittances by emigrants kept pace with the trend in emigration. The total number of emigrants were 18.4 lakh in 2004, up from 13.6 lakh in 1999. Remittances were Rs.18.5 thousand crore in 2004 as against Rs.13.6 thousand crore in 1999.

While the total amount of remittances kept pace with emigration, cash remittances received by households out paced emigration; they increased by 56 per cent. Two factors could be associated with the increase: First, emigrants in 2004 had educational levels, employment profiles and salary levels much more favourable than in 1999 for making remittances; second, many more of the emigrants of 2004 went to developed countries in America, Europe and South Asia where the salary levels are much higher than elsewhere.

With the increase in remittances and the consequent increase in disposable income at the household level, consumerist tendencies soared by alarming proportions in Kerala. People back home had no qualms to spend money earned by their relatives abroad on festivals and celebrations, on ornaments and jewellery, on costly apparel and on various other items of conspicuous consumption. Had they been spending money they themselves earned, they would not have indulged in such a spending spree. This is an important factor in the unfettered spending habits of many Kerala households.

Rabid spending was reflected most in housing, and acquisition of modern household gadgets and fancy household durables. The quality of housing is one area in which emigration had its greatest impact. Muslims had the highest emigration rate; they also had the highest proportion of 'luxurious or very good' houses back home.

Emigration had a very positive impact on human resource development also. Emigrants were better educated and their families spent much more on education of their children than non-emigrant families did.

Yet unemployment rate in 2004 was almost twice than that of five years earlier. Here in lies a paradox. Did emigration play any role in the increase in the unemployment rate? This is the '64 million-dollar question.' Before coming to the question of the effect of emigration on unemployment, we take up a discussion of a few other dimensions.

Income Redistribution

It was mentioned earlier that the direct beneficiaries of emigration were only 26 per cent of the total number of households in the state, the ones with NRKs. The balance 74 per cent received no direct benefit from emigration; if at all, they did only indirectly. If 26 per cent households received direct benefits and 74 per cent did not, what has been the impact of remittances on income or wealth distribution in the state? The answer would depend on who this 26 per cent were. If they were of the bottom stratum of the income ladder, as had been the case in the early nineties, probably emigration would have contributed to reducing inequalities in income distribution of the Kerala economy. On the other hand, if the 26 per cent were from the top stratum of the society, emigration would have contributed to greater concentration of income. We don't have any information on the income level of the Kerala emigrants. The best approximations that could be gathered from our survey were the educational level of the emigrants, the type of houses they lived in, the type of fuels they use for cooking, etc.

One evidence is provided by the relative amounts of remittances received by households of the well-educated (secondary level or degree) versus of the less-educated (below secondary level). In 1999, households with well-educated emigrants had received 54.8 per cent of the total 'household cash remittances.' By 2004, the share of the well-educated emigrant households increased to 64.2 per cent. Thus, more of the remittances received by the Kerala households in recent years went to households with well-educated emigrants (assumed to be from wealthy households). Similarly, in 1999, households with 'luxurious' or 'very good' houses had received only 39.5 per cent of the remittances. By 2004, the corresponding proportion was 56.4 per cent, an increase of 17 percentage points in five years. Another statistics supporting this conclusion is the increase in the share of remittances, received by households with LPG connection (presumably the richer households). In 1999, LPG-households had received 42.1 per cent of the total remittances. By 2004 more than 60 per cent of the remittances went to households which used LPG, an increase of 18 percentage points.

All these indirect pieces of evidence point to the conclusion that in more recent years, emigration and remittances were not helping to reduce inequalities in the society of Kerala.

The New Rich Versus the Old Rich Controversy

An adverse impact of Gulf emigration, which has received considerable public attention in recent days, is the emergence of social and political problems arising from the class of the 'New Rich' (*puthan panakkar*). Gulf money has played a major role in restructuring the Kerala society, at a rate never before experienced in the state. From the bottom five per cent of the income ladder, some of the Gulf NRKs have gone up all the way to the top five per cent, transcending family background, caste or creed. In fact, most of the transformation took place among the minority communities. Such overstepping of the traditional hierarchy is not liked by the 'Old Rich'" and has resulted in some resentment and social tension.

Sometime ago, the Chief Minister of Kerala, Sri A.K. Antony was 'accused' of being 'anti-minority' when he is alleged to have observed that minority communities in Kerala were cornering 'undue benefits' using their political and economic clout gained through Gulf remittances and influential Gulf emigrants.

Emigration brings money; and money brings power and the appetite for power, resulting in conflicts between the new rich and the old rich, between the traditional centres of power and the aspiring centres of power. This is one of the inevitable consequences of emigration taking place not only in state politics but also in local level politics, religious organisations, etc. It is instructive at this juncture, to recall what we have learned in this study about the community factor in Gulf migration. According to SMS, more than half the population of Kerala is Hindu, about 56 per cent. However among the emigrants from Kerala, only 31 per cent were Hindus. Muslims constituted less than 25 per cent of the total population, but as much as 44 per cent of the emigrants were Muslims. About 20 per cent of the population was Christian, but as much as 25 per cent of the emigrants belonged to this community.

Within the Hindu and the Christian religious groups themselves, there existed vast differences with respect to emigration and remittances. For example, among Hindus, the emigration rate (emigrants per 100 households) varied from 36.1 among Brahmins to 3.1 among the Scheduled Castes/Tribes. Among Christians, the Mar Thomite Syrians had an emigration rate of 70 while among the Latin Catholics and the followers of the Church of South India, the emigration rate was only 22.

What we have described above about emigration is also true of remittances. Hindu households received only 30 per cent of the total remittances. On the other hand, Muslim households received 45 per cent and Christian households received 25 per cent. Within the Hindu group, remittances per household varied from Rs. 725 among the Scheduled Castes/Tribes to Rs. 9,225 among Nairs. Within the Christian group, remittances per household varied from Rs. 9,198 among households belonging to the followers of Church of South India to Rs. 26,098 among the Mar Thomite Syrians.

Thus, according to SMS, remittances from emigrants were certainly benefiting the minority communities much more than the majority communities.

The accusation of exerting undue pressure by the minorities should be viewed in the light of their current status in society and their inherent aspiration to better their socioeconomic status. Muslims are the most backward community in Kerala with respect to human resources. While 29 per cent of the Hindus and 36 per cent of the Christians are educated up to the secondary or higher levels, only 15 per cent of the Muslims received secondary or higher levels of education.

In the 1999 KMS we observed:

"Nearly 51 per cent of the emigrants were from Muslim households; and Muslim households have received nearly 50 per cent of the remittances from abroad. At the same time, Muslims have the highest illiteracy rate, and the lowest proportion of persons with a secondary school certificate."

"Of all the districts in Kerala, Malappuram sent out the largest number of emigrants (270,000) and received the largest amount (Rs. 6,295 million) by way of remittances from abroad. Malappuram has the highest birth rate, the highest rate of population growth, the highest average family size, the highest proportion of illiterates, and the lowest proportion of persons with a secondary school certificate or a degree."

"These facts establish a very strong case for development of public policies, which would enhance this educationally backward population to use part of the remittances it receives for improvement of its educational level."

There had been a time (more than 100 years ago), when personal achievements in terms of education or wealth were not as important as the situation into which a person was born or the community he/she belonged to. It was not acquired factors such as education or remittances from abroad or contacts with prominent emigrants, but ascribed characteristics such as religion, caste or family background, over which a person has no control, that mattered most for achieving positions of influence. But now money power has become more important. Is there much of a difference? Is there anything basically wrong if a backward community asserts itself with its newly acquired money power and connections for its betterment in social and political terms?

Consumerism Gone Amok

Kerala has emerged as the hottest place to sell new products from all over India and even from abroad. There is hardly a day when one is not woken up from one's *seista* by a smart-looking sales person to sell/demonstrate a 'new product.' Some of the Keralites, especially housewives, fall easy prey to these smart guys. In the course of a few years, Kerala households have ended up possessing all the necessary and even unnecessary wares, much of which are not the products of the state. Not only are the goods made in other states, they are transported to Kerala in trucks belonging to non-Keralites and driven by non-Keralite drivers.

Higher levels of consumption did not result in larger economic activity in Kerala other than in sales and services. The point we want to stress here is that, the potential multiplier effect of the disposition of remittances (on production and employment) is leaking out to the rest of the world. Workers outside the state benefit much more than workers in Kerala.

Consumerism is said to be leading many a Keralite to financial ruin and even to suicide. When the buying spree is financed by borrowed money, disaster is not far off.

Stagnancy in Employment and Buoyancy in Unemployment

The employment sector in Kerala has experienced some unwelcome tendencies during 1999-2004. Employment stagnated while unemployment galloped. Both the tendencies are the two sides of the same coin and are best discussed together under unemployment.

Unemployment

While the direct effect of emigration of a large number of unemployed persons from Kerala has been the reduction of unemployment rate in the state, the overall effect of emigration on unemployment need not necessarily have been on the same direction. In fact, a point of view, which this study puts forth is that emigration is a causative factor for the high unemployment rate prevailing in the state.

The spin-off effects of emigration through remittances from emigrants and the cash brought by return emigrants should be expected to have increased the employment opportunities in the state and contributed to reduction of the state's unemployment rate. Investments made by return emigrants should have been an important factor for creation of employment opportunities in the state. From these points of view, the effect of emigration should have been to decrease the unemployment rate, not at all to increase it. To understand the increase in the unemployment rate simultaneously with the increase in emigration rate, we have to take a deeper look and search for other factors. Two such factors are discussed below - education and replacement migration.

Impact of Education on Unemployment

The unemployment problem in Kerala is essentially the problem of the educated unemployed. Nearly a third of the persons with secondary or higher levels of education remain unemployed. If the proportion of secondary level educated persons increases, the unemployment rate would increase. We have shown that nearly a third of the increase in the unemployment rate during 1999-2004 was due to structural changes, that is, increases in the proportion of persons with higher levels of education. Otherwise, the increase would have been only two-thirds (or 5.3 percentage points) out of a total increase of 8 percentage points.

A four-way analysis of variance using unemployment rate as the dependent variable and sex, district, religion and education as independent variables indicated that education and sex have statistically significant association with unemployment rate at less than 1 in 1000 per cent level of significance. Religion has also significant association but only at five per cent level.

Neither sex nor religion has any operational significance as they are both fixed variables. Hence the only variable of any significance is education.

Admitting that increase in the number of educated youths is a factor in the higher unemployment rate in Kerala in recent years, how does emigration come in the picture? We hypothesise that emigration has a role in increasing the population with higher level of education through what we call the demand factor and the income factor (see Flow Chart).

Demand Factor

A common aspiration among the youth in Kerala is emigration to the Gulf, earning of a lot of cash, getting married and living happily ever thereafter. In recent years many Governments in the Gulf region have made the secondary level of education mandatory to be eligible for becoming an immigrant to their countries. For instance, the United Arab Emirates made it mandatory that immigrants to that area should have a minimum of secondary level education. This requirement, which was laid down relatively recently, has increased considerably the demand for education at the secondary level in Kerala.

In 2003, 8.78 lakh students appeared for SSLC or higher secondary examinations. Five years ago, the corresponding number had been 5.71 lakh. The increase during 1999-2004 was 3.17 lakh. Such increases took place in the background of a decrease in the total number of youth in the age group of 15-19 years. Demographic transition was favouring a decrease in the numbers appearing for SSLC and higher secondary examinations. In fact, however, the numbers increased.

Most of the youth who passed the SSLC or higher secondary examinations, however, did not get a chance to emigrate and, therefore, have either remained unemployed in Kerala or gone for higher education. Much of the recent increase in the number of the educated unemployed could be attributed to the large increase in the number of the educated youth.

Income Factor

Education is costly. The costs of building new schools and colleges are high. Private costs of education at all levels are increasing by the day. Without external sources of funds, a large majority of the new schools would not have been built and many of the Kerala youth would not have gone for higher education. Without external funds, many children would not have gone for studies in self -financing schools and colleges. The required funds came by way of emigrants' remittances. In that way, emigration fuelled the demand for higher education and supplied the means to achieve it. The increase in the number of schools and colleges (built with emigrants' remittances), indirectly contributed to Kerala's unemployment problem. The increase in the number of youth going for higher education (paid for by emigrant's remittances) contributed indirectly to swell the ranks of the unemployed in the state.

In this study we estimated that the average cost of education of a family was about Rs 6,540 per year. Our analysis also showed that 24 per cent of cash remittances was used for educational expenses. This works out to be about Rs. 1,400 crore annually if we consider only the household remittances of Rs. 7,965 crore (or Rs. 4,434 crore if we consider the total remittances of Rs. 18,475 crore). Thus, emigration through remittances played an important role in increasing the proportion of the Kerala population with high levels of formal education, which in turn played an important role in increasing the level of unemployment in the state in recent yea.

The income factor also favoured growth in the unemployment rate but in another way. If a person gets cash from his/her relatives abroad, he/she would be able to remain unemployed for a longer period. Why should the unemployed youths work when they can live comfortably from money received from abroad?[2]

Replacement Migration

In the early phase of Gulf emigration from Kerala, the emigrants had been mostly non-agricultural labourers with low levels of education. They also included some skilled workers like carpenters, masons, and electricians. The emigration of the unemployed

2. A cross-classification of the 10000 sample households by the number of unemployed in the household and the number of emigrants in the household indicated that among households **without an emigrant**, the proportion of households with an unemployed was 26.9 percent. On the other hand, among households **with one emigrant**, the corresponding proportion was as much as 29.2 per cent. Thus, the existence of an emigrant in a household tends to increase the incidence of unemployment in that household.

FLOW CHART

Emigration and Unemployment in Kerala

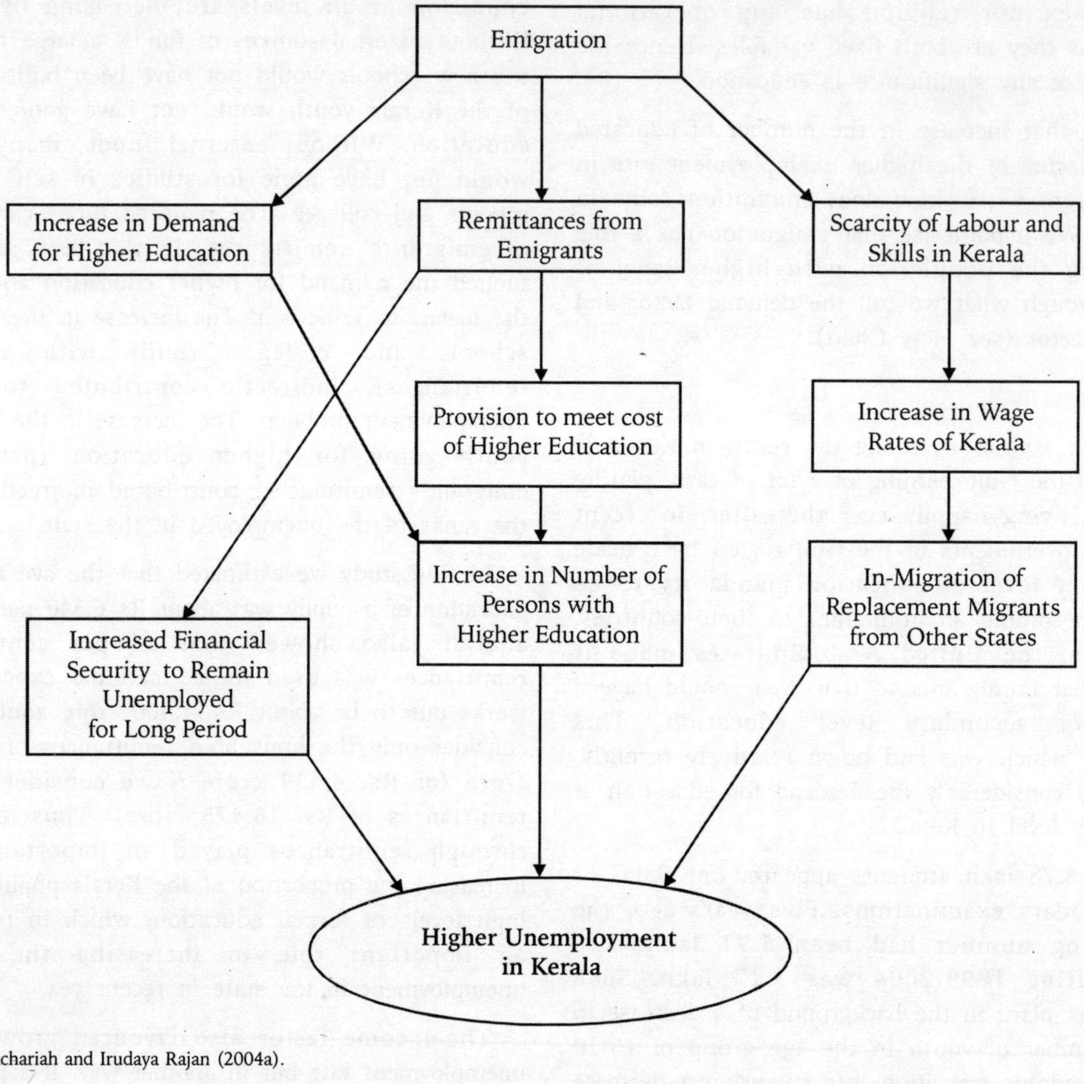

Source: Zachariah and Irudaya Rajan (2004a).

unskilled workers had helped reduction of unemployment. The money they sent home accelerated the construction industry and thus helped further reduction of unemployment.

Initially, emigration of skilled labour had not created any major bottleneck back home, but their continued emigration resulted in significant scarcity of skilled workers in the state. It is often said that it is easy to find a plastic surgeon in Kerala than a good carpenter. The scarcity was followed inevitably by increases in wage rates.

At present Kerala has the highest wage rates among the states in India. The increasing wage rates in agriculture along with stagnant or declining prices of agricultural products in Kerala have resulted in decreasing employment opportunities in agriculture. Costs incurred on high wages could not be recovered from the sale proceeds of agricultural products because of their falling prices. It was cheaper to buy imported rice from Andhra Predesh or imported bananas from Tamil Nadu than to produce them locally. The result is shrinkage in the agricultural activities and the employment opportunities in agriculture.

The differentials in wage rates between Kerala and the neighbouring states received the attention of workers in other states. And they began to infiltrate into Kerala and to take up work, which had used to be done by Kerala workers, especially in the construction sector. What started as a trickle soon assumed the dimensions of a torrent in the course of a few years. Thus started the era of replacement migration to Kerala.

After a lapse of about 60 years, Kerala is again becoming a net in-migrating state. As soon as a contractor takes up a construction or road work, he appoints an agent to recruit workers not only from neighbouring states but also from states as far away as Uttar Pradesh, Bihar and West Bengal. In many construction sites in Kerala the language used is not Malayalam but Hindi, Bengali or Tamil. Emigration of workers from Kerala, demographic contraction of the supply of young workers brought about by rapid demographic transition in the state, higher wage rates of Kerala workers, ability of Kerala workers to sustain themselves with remittances from relatives even without work for long periods, reluctance on the part of Kerala workers to do hard physical work—all these have engendered the era of replacement migration in Kerala. For the in-migrant workers, Kerala is, for all practical purpose, their promised land, the 'Gulf.' The way Kerala workers have penetrated into every economic sector in the Gulf region, the replacement workers from other states have started penetrating into most economic sectors in Kerala. Are they to blame for this intrusion? Nor is it an unwelcome development in our federal economy.

It is true that remittances from the Gulf kept up economic activity in the construction and the service sectors in Kerala. Normally the additional jobs thus created should have gone to the Kerala workers. But, given the large differences existing between the current wage rates in Kerala and in the rest of the states in India, and the unwillingness of Kerala workers to do certain types of hard physical work, workers from other states have grabbed the unfilled employment opportunities in Kerala. Thus, replacement migrants have taken the places which Kerala workers could have filled.

The so-called spin-off effects benefited outside workers more than Kerala workers. Thus, emigration, which initially had helped reduce unemployment in Kerala, has in fact, become a significant factor for the higher unemployment situation in the state at present.

References

Irudaya Rajan, S. (2004). "From Kerala to the Gulf: Impacts of Labour Migration", *Asia Pacific Migration Journal*, Vol. 13(4): 497-510.

———. (2006). "Economic Impact of Remittances in India", in Brij Lal and Rajesh Rai (eds.), *The Encyclopedia of Indian Overseas*. Singapore: National University.

Irudaya Rajan, S. and P.R. Gopinathan Nair (2006). "Indians in Gulf States", in Brij Lal and Rajesh Rai (eds.), *The Encyclopedia of Indian Overseas*. Singapore: National University.

Zachariah, K.C. and S. Irudaya Rajan (2001a.) "Gender Dimensions of Migration in Kerala: Macro and Micro Evidence". *Asia Pacific Population Journal*, Vol.16 (3): 47-70.

———. (2001b). "Migration Mosaic in Kerala. Trends and Determinants", *Demography_India*, Vol. 30 (1): 137-165.

———. (2004). *Emigration and Unemployment in Kerala*. Thiruvananthapuram : Centre for Development Studies and New Delhi : South Asian Network of Economic Institutes, (mimeographed).

———. (2004a) "Gulf Revisited Economic Consequences of Emigration from Kerala, Emigration and Unemployment", *Working Paper* No. 363, Centre for Development Studies, Thiruvananthapuram,. *www.cds.edu.*

———. (2004b) "Unemployment in Kerala at the turn of the Century Insight from CDS Gulf Migration Studies", *Working Paper* No. 374. Thiruvananthapuram: Centre for Development Studies. *www.cds.edu.*

———. (2004c). "Emigration Moving in to a Higher Orbit", *Passline*, Vol. 8(7 & 8), August 15-31.

Zachariah, K.C., B.A. Prakash and S. Irudaya Rajan (2003). "The Impact of Immigration Policy on Indian Contract Migrants: The Case of the United Arab Emirates", *International Migration*, Volume 41(4): 161-172.

———. (2004). Indian Workers in UAE: Employment, Wages and Working Conditions. *Economic and Political Weekly*, Volume 39(22): 2227-2234, May 29.

Zachariah, K.C., E.T. Mathew and S. Irudaya Rajan (1999). "Migration in Kerala State, India: Dimensions, Determinants and Consequences", *Working Paper I*. Thiruvananthapuram: Centre for Development Studies (CDS), Kerala and Indo-duch Programme on Alternatives in Development (IDPAD).

———. (2000). "Migration in Kerala State, India: Dimensions, Determinants and Consequences", *Working Paper II*. Thiruvananthapuram: Centre for Development Studies (CDS), Kerala and Indo-duch Programme on Alternatives in Development (IDPAD).

———. (2001a) "Impact of Migration on Kerala's Economy and Society" *International Migration*, Vol. 39(1): 63-88 (first published as a *CDS Working Paper* No. 297, *www.cds.edu*)

———. (2001b) "Social, Economic and Demographic Consequences of Migration on Kerala". *International Migration*, Vol. 39(2): 43-71 (first published as a *CDS Working Paper* No. 303. *www.cds.edu)*

———. (2003) *Dynamics of Migration in Kerala: Dimensions, Determinants and Consequences*". Hyderabad: Orient Longman Pvt. Limited.

Zachariah, K.C., K.P. Kannan and S. Irudaya Rajan (2002). *"Kerala's Gulf Connection: CDS Studies on International Labour Migration from Kerala State in India"*. Monograph Series. 2002. Thiruvananthapuram: Centre for Development Studies.

Zachariah, K.C., P.R. Gopinathan Nair and S. Irudaya Rajan (2001). "Return Emigrants in Kerala: Rehabilitation Problems and Development Potential", *Working Paper* No.319. Thiruvananthapuram: Centre for Development Studies.*www.cds.edu.*

———. (2006). *Return Emigrants in Kerala: Welfare, Rehabilitation and Development*. New Delhi: Manohar Manohar Publishers & Distributors.

Chapter 15

Gender and Development

The much lower gender gap in terms of basic capabilities in Kerala than in other parts of India has been widely acclaimed as indicative of the 'high status' for women in the state. Recently, however, this conventional wisdom regarding development has come in for questioning. New questions are being raised about the conventional indicators of well-being—education, health and employment—particularly about the ways in which they serve larger patriarchal interests. For instance, it is now being recognised that educational and health capabilities of women in Kerala have been harnessed within a familial ideological structure that has served to reinforce gender divisions rather than to expand freedoms for men and women. This awareness is linked to efforts to go beyond conventional indicators of well-being to hitherto less examined sites such as mental health, crime against women, political participation or property rights. These efforts have lately shown reverse trends such as rising crimes against women, growing practice of dowry and declining women's property rights.

Kerala is considered relatively free from the conventional restrictions against women's education, employment, or property ownership. This achievement is associated with the early 20th century social reforms, which widened access to education across genders and matrilineal forms of family and sanctioned women's rights to inherit property. However, the contention that social and legal reforms were instrumental to sanctioning of a new form of marriage, grounded in modern patriarchal relations, has received little attention. An important part of this process towards patriarchal relations was the abolition of matriliny and the strengthening of patriarchy among all social groups (Kodoth and Eapen, 2005). Today patriarchy is reflected in a general form of social commitment to women's domesticity in the state, implicit in their poor visibility in the public sphere. The questions that come to mind in this context are: what have women in Kerala done with their impressive gains in education, health and demographic advantage? Where have these 'achievements' been directed? A decomposition of the GDI is very revealing: high scores on education and health in 15 states of India (ranking Kerala first) mask women's poor employment profile.[1] Kerala ranked only 10 or 15 according to different measures of income shares based on gender work participation rates and wage rates (Prabhu Seeta *et al.*, 1996). High rates of literacy and impressive levels of female education did not translate into rapid growth of paid employment for women nor into upward occupational mobility. On the other hand, the state was witnessing downtrends in women's property rights, high levels of gender-based violence, particularly domestic violence, and rapid growth and spread of dowry and dowry related crimes even while levels of education continued to rise.

This chapter examines the contemporary trends in education and employment, demographic and health status, violence against women, property rights, and political participation in Kerala as important aspects of women's status. Some analytical focus has been brought to bear upon women of the marginalised groups, particularly Scheduled castes and Scheduled tribes but also women of low status occupational groups. As migration and ageing are two population related processes of importance in Kerala, we have also attempted a gendered assessment of these processes.

Women's Autonomy

The GDI estimated at the regional level by several scholars places Kerala at the top. In respect of GEM

1. Work participation, particularly access to earned incomes, is an important aspect of empowerment though by itself it does not ensure control over earnings or ability to take 'self-interested' decisions.

too, which attempts to measure empowerment or autonomy in terms of the extent to which women are able to use their basic capabilities to acquire decision-making powers, both economically and politically, Kerala is at or near the top (Mehta, 1996). Yet it is significant that on more direct measures of autonomy, including household decision-making, mobility and access to/control over money, Kerala trailed Gujarat, which had much lower levels of literacy (Visaria, 1996; Irudaya Rajan *et al.*, 1996). Indeed, the second National Family Health Survey, 1998-99, which incorporated measures of autonomy for ever-married women for the first time, for 25 states, also revealed that Kerala trailed behind Gujarat, Tamil Nadu, Goa and the North-eastern states (Table 15.1). Findings of this nature have called into question the much glorified, one-to-one relation between literacy and women's autonomy. Therefore, women's educational attainment and access to other resources need to be located within the extant patriarchal social structures, specifically the family.

Contemporary Trends in Education and Employment

To what extent has education broken down patriarchal structures in Kerala? This question has rarely been pursued beyond examining gender parity in outcome indicators of literacy and education. The attempt in this section is precisely to go beyond happy conclusions emerging from interpretation of near-gender-parity in literacy or girls' advantage in school enrolment in arts and science courses in college.

TABLE 15.1

Women's Autonomy by State

Ever-married Women Involved in Household Decision-making, with Freedom of Movement, and Access to Money by States, 1998-99 (in percentage)

	State	*Not Involved in any Decision-making*	*Involved in Decision-making on*				*Do not need Permission to*		*Percentage with Access to Money*
			What to Cook	*Own Healthcare*	*Purchasing Jewellery etc.*	*Staying with her Parents/ Siblings*	*Go to Market*	*Visit Friends/ Relatives*	
	India	9.4	85.1	51.6	52.6	48.1	31.6	24.4	59.6
North	Delhi	5.3	83.0	68.7	58.5	46.5	51.7	33.9	82.3
	Haryana	3.4	93.5	67.2	77.8	64.5	36.7	20.8	70.8
	Himachal Pradesh	0.8	95.1	80.8	93.4	91.4	32.5	31.1	80.1
	Jammu & Kashmir	12.4	80.0	55.5	58.2	48.9	12.0	7.8	58.1
	Punjab	1.0	96.7	78.5	75.3	67.6	50.1	28.0	78.3
	Rajasthan	13.3	82.3	40.6	42.7	39.3	19.0	17.0	40.5
Central	Madhya Pradesh	12.5	81.7	36.6	44.3	38.1	21.0	19.5	49.3
	Uttar Pradesh	16.4	77.8	44.8	41.4	36.1	17.4	12.4	52.3
East	Bihar	13.5	82.4	47.6	42.9	44.0	21.7	20.5	66.7
	Orissa	10.6	86.3	38.6	54.8	48.3	18.2	15.4	46.3
	West Bengal	8.0	87.4	45.1	48.4	46.7	17.8	14.1	51.4
Northeast	Arunachal Pradesh	1.4	93.6	70.0	76.5	74.8	46.8	53.7	78.6
	Assam	4.6	88.4	65.1	54.3	45.4	13.2	13.9	35.0
	Manipur	3.3	87.4	43.3	66.3	63.2	28.6	28.3	76.8
	Meghalaya	2.6	91.7	78.9	70.6	78.4	46.5	48.5	81.5
	Mizoram	5.8	88.2	73.2	77.8	77.0	64.2	59.5	55.0
	Nagaland	0.4	97.4	69.4	77.3	80.0	17.3	20.1	27.9
	Sikkim	2.7	92.1	60.2	57.9	56.7	38.2	41.6	78.9
West	Goa	3.6	89.9	61.6	62.5	72.4	66.7	58.7	82.4
	Gujarat	4.1	90.4	71.4	73.6	65.1	55.1	50.6	73.6
	Maharashtra	7.2	87.5	49.9	50.3	44.4	48.5	32.1	64.2
South	Andhra Pradesh	7.4	86.2	56.1	61.4	47.7	20.1	14.6	57.7
	Karnataka	8.1	88.4	49.3	47.3	44.5	43.0	34.3	67.0
	Kerala	**7.2**	**80.9**	**72.6**	**63.4**	**59.7**	**47.7**	**37.9**	**66.2**
	Tamil Nadu	2.4	92.1	61.1	67.4	62.4	78.5	55.9	79.0

Source: *NFHS, India* 1998-99.

Pattern of Education by Gender

The high levels of female literacy in Kerala have been well-documented. However, what gets obscured is (a) the lower (than all-India) proportion of 'graduate and above' category, among both men and women in Kerala and (b) the gender differentiated pattern of higher education as it has evolved over time. Although gender disparity is extremely low in the 10th standard, (even reversed to some extent at the pre-University and non-technical diploma levels) and currently women far exceed men in graduate and post-graduate education in the arts and science courses,[2] they lag far behind men in professional/technical education except in nursing in which there are few men, and in teaching in which the ratio is in favour of women (Table 15.2). Women formed less than one-third of the students enroled in engineering colleges (in 1997). Similarly in the lower technical educational institutions which are job-oriented, the intake of girls is below 10 per cent in technical schools, between 13 and 23 per cent in Industrial Training Institutes (ITIs) and Industrial Training Centres (ITCs) (two year course) and between 30 and 40 per cent in polytechnics during the 1990s. In striking contrast, in the ITIs and ITCs (one year course) data on trade-wise intake for the year 2000-01 reveal a preponderance of women in stenography, dress-making, cutting and tailoring, secretarial practice and data preparation (Table 15.3). Clearly women have limited entry into 'masculine' specialisations but dominate in

TABLE 15.2

Percentage Distribution of Girl Students in Kerala at Various Stages 1999-2004

Year	*LP*	*UP*	*HS*	*+2*	*Degree*	*Post-graduate*
1999	49.0	48.5	50.4	55.6	63.4	75.0
2000	49.1	48.2	50.2	57.0	64.1	73.3
2001	-	-	-	-	-	-
2002	49.3	48.1	49.5	57.4	61.4	66.7
2003	49.4	48.2	49.4	-	61.1	66.7
2004	49.7	48.3	49.2	55.6	64.7	75.0

Source: Economic Review 2004.

TABLE 15.3

Trade-wise Seats Strength in Government ITIs and Private ITCs 2000-2001 (One Year Course)

Sl. No.	*Name of Trades*	*Industrial Training Institutes*			*Industrial Training Centres*		
		Total Intake	*Girls*	*% of Girls to Total*	*Total Intake*	*Girls*	*% of Girls to Total*
1.	Forger & Heat Treater	352	-	-	16	-	-
2.	Carpenter	364	-	-	32	-	-
3.	Mechanic Diesel	192	-	-	1072	-	-
4.	Plumber	366	-	-	1616	-	-
5.	Sheet Metal Works	272	-	-	32	-	-
6.	Welder	708	-	-	336	-	-
7.	Steno (Eng)	448	191	42.63	1664	1608	96163
8.	COPA	440	110	25.00	3220	3002	93.23
9.	Steno (Hindi)	96	96	100.00	32	20	62.50
10.	Secretariat practice	48	42	87.50	272	190	69.85
11.	Dress making	96	96	100.00	64	24	37.50
12.	D.T.P.O.	100	50	50.00	80	5	6.25
13.	Plastic processing operator trade	64	-	-	-	-	-
14.	Mechanic Tractor	80	-	-	-	-	-
15.	Upholstry	32	-	-	16	-	-
16.	Foundryman	192	-	-	32	-	-
17.	Photography	-	-	-	16	-	-
18.	Preservation of fruits &Vegetables	-	-	-	16	-	0
19.	Hair & skin care	16	16	100	48	10	20.83
20.	Cutting and Tailoring	-	-	-	256	211	82.42
	Total	**3888**	**601**	**15.46**	**8820**	**5070**	**57.48**

Source: Government of Kerala. *Women in Kerala 2001.*

2. About two-thirds of the students enrolled in graduate courses and almost three-fourths enrolled in post-graduate courses are girls (*Economic Review 2004*).

professions identified as 'feminine'. This orientation of women's education, in particular the overwhelming crowding of women in general arts and science courses at the graduate and post graduate levels, is found largely a reflection of the hope of white collar employment.

Level and Pattern of Employment

Women in Kerala have scored poorly in terms of participation in paid employment, both in relation to women at the all-India level and in relation to men at the state level. Women's work participation rates (WPRs) in terms of usual principal and subsidiary status in Kerala used to be among the lowest in India. Currently while over a quarter of the female population is recorded as economically active at the all-India level, the corresponding proportion is about 23 per cent in the state. The difference is primarily due to lower rural female WPRs in Kerala; the urban situation in the state seems relatively favourable. About one-fifth of women in urban Kerala are employed compared to less than 14 per cent at the all-India level. And, unlike at the all-India level, which has witnessed a decline in female WPRs in both rural and urban areas in the 1990s (Sundaram, 2001), there has been greater stability in Kerala (Table 15.4). However, it needs to be noted that decomposition of usual employment by activity status shows the number of days of work to be much higher for women in rural and urban India and to have increased during 1993-94 and 1999-00. In Kerala the number of working days declined in rural areas and showed no change in urban areas. In urban areas there was an increase in the number of days reported by women as 'not seeking/not available for work', i.e., were not in the labour force (Table 15.5). This suggests a revealed preference of urban women for withdrawal from paid work as also a higher incidence of short-duration employment for women in Kerala.

TABLE 15.4

Work Force Participation Rates (Usual Principal and Subsidiary Status)

	Kerala			*All-India*		
	1987-88	*1993-94*	*1999-00*	*1987-88*	*1993-94*	*1999-00*
RM	50.6	53.7	55.3	53.9	55.3	53.1
RF	28.6	23.8	23.8	32.6	32.8	29.9
UM	53.0	55.9	55.8	50.6	52.1	51.8
UF	19.8	20.3	20.3	15.2	15.5	13.9
Total M	51.2	54.3	55.4	53.1	54.4	52.7
F	26.5	22.9	22.9	28.1	28.3	25.4
P	38.6	38.3	38.7	41.1	41.8	39.5

Note: RM (Rural Male), RFL (Rural Female), UM (Urban Male), UF (Urban Female).

Sources: 1) 1987-88: *Sarvekshana*, September 1990; 2) 1993-94: *Sarvekshana*, July-September 1996 and 3) 1999-00: *Sarvekshana*.

Women in Kerala enjoy higher wage rates for casual employment in both rural and urban areas than in other parts of the country; their annual earnings may also be higher. Bolstered by increasing male WPRs, as we see later, and higher household earnings, it is entirely likely that women are withdrawing into full-time domesticity for significant parts of the year. This could reflect an 'informed' choice, an option reflecting greater leisure or time to attend to household/family concerns. Such a choice entails considerable risk of vulnerability by reducing women's direct access to earned incomes and increasing the extent of their dependence on husbands or others.

TABLE 15.5

Activity -Status Distribution of Person-days per Year of Usually Employed (Principal plus Subsidiary Status) Workers

Activity Status	*Rural Females*			*Urban Females*		
	1987-88	*1993-94*	*1999-00*	*1987-88*	*1993-94*	*1999-00*
Kerala						
Employed	193	216	211	213	248	248
Unemployed	20	16	26	31	19	14
Not in Labour Force	152	133	128	122	99	103
India						
Employed	233	242	247	261	280	289
Unemployed	9	15	14	14	8	8
Not in Labour Force	123	112	104	90	77	68

Source: Estimated from data for the Three Rounds.

TABLE 15.6

Education-specific WPR for Persons of Age 15 Years and Above

Year	*Education*	*Kerala*				*All India*			
		RM	*RF*	*UM*	*UF*	*RM*	*RF*	*UM*	*UF*
1987-88	Not Literate	76.9	45.9	71.9	30.3	91.1	91.1	52.6	29.2
	Literate, upto								
	Primary	85.1	46.2	82.4	24.1	89.0	80.0	39.1	17.5
	Middle	72.3	31.7	73.2	22.4	73.9	73.9	28.6	11.3
	Secondary	57.2	28.3	58.5	25.3	72.9	72.9	26.2	15.1
	Graduate & Above	75.3	45.3	83.7	51.8	82.7	82.7	30.7	31.5
1993-94	Not Literate	77.9	37.2	74.2	28.6	91.8	54.0	87.0	
	Literate, upto								
	Primary	89.1	39.6	84.1	31.3	90.9	41.6	85.0	
	Middle	78.9	24.9	77.2	22.0	77.0	29.0	72.3	
	Secondary	63.6	27.4	66.6	20.4	72.8	25.8	67.7	
	Higher Secondary	44.2	17.7	52.9	27.5	68.6	23.4	60.7	
	Graduate & Above	73.1	38.2	82.2	40.2	83.4	36.6	81.8	
1999-2000	Not literate	72.0	35.9	54.6	20.1	89.5	51.3	83.9	27.1
	Literate, upto								
	Primary	83.2	37.0	81.5	31.2	88.0	40.3	83.0	17.7
	Middle	78.9	29.2	80.5	33.3	76.8	29.0	17.7	12.9
	Secondary	68.7	24.4	68.2	27.3	73.7	25.7	66.8	12.4
	Higher Secondary	56.7	19.6	48.8	21.6	71.3	70.6	60.8	12.4
	Graduate & Above	81.5	32.1	86.9	36.8	83.6	31.0	80.6	27.3

Source: Same as Table 15.5.

Male WPR in Kerala is more than twice that of females—55 per cent for females *vis-à-vis* 23 per cent for females; while the former rate increased since 1987-88, female WPR remained constant during the 1990s (see Table 15.4). The worker sex ratio (female workers per 1000 male workers) which had declined from almost 536 in 1987-88 to 439 in 1993-94, further declined to 436 in 1999-00. The decline is reflected also in the proportion of women in the total work force, from 35 per cent to 30.5 per cent in the early nineties and to 30.3 per cent in 1999-00.[3]

Even among the highly educated women in Kerala, (that is, women with graduation and above) the latest data reveal that worker participation rates were 37 per cent (urban) and 32 per cent (rural) compared with 87 per cent and 82 per cent respectively for men. Further, gender disparity in the levels of educated employment (ratio of male graduate WPR to female graduate WPR) widened marginally from 2.0 to 2.4 during the 1990s (Table 15.6). Table 15.6 also shows the very low levels of female participation among the secondary and higher secondary education categories, apparently with no other skill acquisition and hence very little potential for a 'status' job. Not surprisingly this segment records the highest incidence of educated unemployment among women.

Levels of Unemployment

Unemployment, crucially educated unemployment, is clearly a serious problem in Kerala. Attempts to explain low female work participation rates in terms of high overall unemployment rates in Kerala are inadequate in a situation in which the female unemployment rate far exceeds that of men; this is particularly so in the case of the educated. Educated unemployment of women is as high as 34 per cent in urban areas (in 1999-2000) compared to about 7 per cent for men. And while educated unemployment declined for men in the 1990s, it increased for women, particularly in rural areas (Table 15.7). Women's job preferences have also played a role in constraining their opportunities for work.

3. These percentages have been estimated on the basis of absolute numbers in the work force and its composition derived from WPRs and population data.

TABLE 15.7

Unemployment Rates for the Educated (15 years & above)

(per cent)

	Kerala		All-India	
	1993-94	*1999-00*	*1993-94*	*1999-00*
UPSS Rural Male	15.6	11.2	6.5	5.6
Rural Female	32.3	36.7	15.0	14.6
Urban Male	11.2	7.4	6.0	6.2
Urban Female	34.9	34.2	18.2	14.3
UPS Rural Male	18.5	15.0	8.8	6.8
Rural Female	49.6	49.1	24.9	20.4
Urban Male	12.6	9.9	6.9	6.6
Urban Female	40.6	41.9	20.6	16.3

Source: Same as Table 15.5.

Given high levels of educated unemployment it is entirely likely that women are unable to procure jobs commensurate with their educational skills and preferences and are constrained to remain unemployed. It has been argued (Nagaraj, 1999) that high unemployment rates for women (and men) in states such as Kerala *vis-a-vis* relatively backward states such as Uttar Pradesh, Madhya Pradesh and Rajasthan, are largely due to constraints in 'skill utilisation': work seekers may not be willing to accept employment at the wages being offered. It has also been suggested that women in Kerala continue to remain in the educational stream in the absence of 'desired' employment opportunities. However, men, both highly educated and less educated, are far more successful in finding employment, as is evident from nature of their employment, increasingly away from agriculture and with considerable options like migration. Nearly three-fourths of the unemployed women, according to a recent study of women's education, employment and job preferences, reported that they remained unemployed because they had not been able to find jobs of their preferences (Lakshmi Devi, 2002). Of the factors constituting preference, social status and proximity to home were the most important.

Industrial and Occupational Structure

The historical specificity of the region has thrown up a differentiated industrial structure for women compared to all-India (Table 15.8), with a much larger

TABLE 15.8

Industrial Distribution of Usual (P+S) Status Workers: Kerala

		Male				Female			
		1993-94		1999-00		1993-94		1999-00	
		% Share	No. of Workers ('000)	% Share	No. of Workers ('000)	% Share	No. of Workers ('000)	% Share	No. of Workers ('000)
Agriculture	R	53.2	3068	42.8	2676	63.0	1679	59.8	1698
	U	22.3	478	7.4	164	33.3	270	14.6	124
Mining & Quarrying	R	2.0	115	2.1	13	0.4	11	0.8	23
	U	0.5	11	0.4	19	0.4	3	0.2	2
Manufacturing	R	9.7	559	9.4	588	19.2	512	19.3	549
	U	16.3	349	17.4	386	25.1	203	27.2	232
Electricity, Gas, Water	R	0.4	23	0.3	19	0.1	3	0	0
	U	0.6	13	0.6	13	0.6	5	0.2	2
Construction	R	7.5	433	12.6	788	2.1	56	2.7	77
	U	10.0	214	14.1	313	3.0	24	2.1	18
Trade & Hotel	R	11.6	669	15.8	988	3.6	96	3.7	105
	U	20.6	442	32.7	726	6.5	53	25.1	214
Transport	R	5.8	334	9.0	563	0.4	11	0.2	6
	U	10.4	223	11.5	255	1.0	8	1.8	15
Services									
i. Financial	R	10.0	577	8.1	506	11.1	296	13.6	386
	U	19.4	416	15.8	351	30.0	243	28.8	245
ii. Pub. Adm.	R	1.4	81	2.1	131	0.5	13	1.1	31
	U	3.5	75	4.6	102	1.6	13	3.7	32
iii. Special & pers. Services	R	8.6	496	6.0	375	10.6	282	12.5	355
	U	5.9	341	11.2	249	28.4	230	25.1	214

Source: Same as Table 15.5.

proportion of women in non-agricultural employment (40 per cent, the highest among the states of India). Agriculture still accounts for about 60 per cent of female employment in rural areas though absolute numbers of the employed have been declining in Kerala, partly due to a changing cropping pattern and partly, as micro studies have shown (some of which are cited later), the unwillingness of young, literate work seekers to work in low status occupations. Non-agricultural segments which absorb a high proportion of women are manufacturing, trade, restaurants, public administration and social and personal services; in all these three sub-sectors, women' employment has grown in the 1990s. However, direct estimates of employment in the informal sector[4] in 1999-00 show that the industry divisions in which the proportion of the informal sector is high, such as manufacturing, construction and trade, absorb higher proportions of women workers; over three-fourths of the female workers in manufacturing are in the informal sector compared to less than 70 per cent for males and 81 per cent are in construction *vis-à-vis* 70 per cent for males. Among public, social and personal services, the proportion is the highest in the formal sector.

However, within an overall context of low work participation rates, higher levels of literacy have certainly enabled women to procure a higher share of organised sector employment in Kerala than in other states in India. The worker sex ratio (female employees per 1000 male employees) in the organised sector was 542 for Kerala (highest among the 15 major states) *vis-à-vis* 188 for all-India. However, worker sex ratio was very high (848) in the private organised sector compared to 344 in the public sector (Srivastatva, 1999). The figures over time reveal that bulk of the growth in the proportion of women in organised sector employment in Kerala like in the rest of India has taken place in the private sector. The proportion of public sector employment declined from almost 33 per cent in the early 1990s to about 30 per cent in 2000 (GoK, 2001). Private sector employment is in general, less secure and does not always carry non-wage benefits.

The occupational structure suggests that the majority of women in the formal sector are located at the lower rungs of the employment hierarchy, rendered easy by the generalised orientation of women's education thus facilitating occupational segregation; see Table 15.9). In urban Kerala, the share of women in professional categories is 21 per cent, higher than that for all-India, nearly 13 per cent. Most of the women at work are engaged in teaching in schools (Eapen and Kodoth, 2003). In the medical profession a larger number appears to be employed as nurses or other paramedical personnel. Other occupations comprise ministerial jobs such as clerk, stenographer, typist, steno/typist, computing machine operator, with few chances of career advancement, corresponding closely to the training they have opted. Among workers in the service occupations, a very high proportion of women in urban areas are employed as housekeeper, maid, cook, launderer, beautician, etc; very few are in managerial and administrative occupations in which it is men who score. In fact the proportion of women workers in these decision-making positions in urban Kerala is lower than for all-India. The large proportion of women work as agricultural labourers and plantation workers in rural areas and as production process workers in urban areas.

Some information on occupational mobility by gender in the 1990s at the state level is thrown up by the NSSO report for the year 1999-2000. Estimates for the number of usual principal status employed persons per 1000 workers who changed their establishment of work, status/ industry of work and occupation of work during the last two years of the decade appear to be extremely unfavourable to women: not a single woman worker per 1000 employed women in urban areas changed her status during this period; in terms of occupation the proportions were barely one-fifth of those for men in both rural and urban areas. However, the proportions of men and women changing establishments were not much different (NSSO 1996, 2001). Women are more mobile among establishments while they hardly achieve any upward mobility. Changes in women's employment by status—self-employed, regular and casual—particularly in urban areas, formed about 26 to 32 per cent between 1993-94 and 1999-2000, are surprising (Table 15.10). With such large proportions of women in the manufacturing, construction and trading activities in the informal sector, and in a context in which the formal sector is becoming 'informalised' (Unni, 2001) there is reason to revisit this whole notion of 'regular' employment as defined by the NSSO (Eapen, 2001).

Besides these macro data highlight, findings of micro studies covering several decades provide insights into the nature of the gender-differentiated occupational mobility pattern. Greater diversification of household incomes and significant out-migration of males are

4. These data are brought out for the first time by the NSSO in the 55th Round on Employment and Unemployment in India.

TABLE 15.9

Percentage Distribution of Usually Working by Occupation Group

1987-88	*Kerala*				*India*			
	Rural		*Urban*		*Rural*		*Urban*	
	Male	*Female*	*Male*	*Female*	*Male*	*Female*	*Male*	*Female*
0 and 1 prof, tech rel wkrs	2.2	6.5	7.1	21.2	2.1	1.1	6.9	12.9
08 nursing, other med/hlth technician	0.1	0.5	0.3	3.9	0.1	0.2	0.4	2
15 teachers	1.9	5.3	1.7	14.2	1.3	0.8	2.1	9.4
div 2 adm, exec, manag wkrs	1.7	1	4	1.3	0.8	0.4	5.5	2.6
div 3 clerical and related wkrs	3.3	2.4	10.6	18.8	1.8	0.2		
30-35 cler & oth supervisors, vill off			9.1	13.3			10	5.6
36-39 steno/typists, computing mach oper			1.5	5			1.2	0.4
div 4 sales workers	15.5	3	17.4	6.3	4.7	2.2	18.6	8.9
40 merchants, shopkeepers, wsale/ret	7.2	2	10.5	4.3	3.5	1.5	11.9	5.9
43	2.3	1			1	0.6		
42-44			6.1	1.8			5.7	2.5
div 5 service workers	4.2	7.7	6.6	14.1	4.2	7.7	8.2	17.7
51-56 hkeeper, maid, lunderer beautician	0.3	0.6	3.3	12.9	0.3	0.6	4.4	15.8
div 6 farmer, fishermen, hunter	50.8	50.7	14.9	20.6			8.5	21.2
610 and 611 cultiv (owner/tenant)	10	6.5			41	36.2		
63 agric labourer	17.1	25.5			26.9	35		
64 plantation labour	8.8	5.9			0.8	1		
619, 65	0.3	0.3			0.8	0.7		
62, 66, 67, 68	14.6	12.5			3.9	5.3		
div 7-9 prod/rel wkr, transp equip oper	24.2	23.3	38.8	22.1	14.3	9.3	28.3	30.5
72 metal processors			0.4	0			0.8	0.1
75 spinner, knitter, weaver, dyer	0.9	6.8	2.1	3.8	1.3	1.7	3.9	5.5
79 tailor, dressmaker, sewer, uphosterer			2.8	5.7			2.6	3.8
73, 74, 76, 78			2.4	3.6			1.2	6
80, 81 shoe/leath gdmaker, carpenter & 82-89			13	1.6			12.1	2.2
95 bricklayer/oth constrn wkr			3.9	2.1			3	3
98 engine/rel equipment oper, oiler			5.4	0			5.6	0.1

Source: National Sample Survey Organisation (1992). *Results of the Fourth Quinquennial Survey on Employment and Unemployment*. NSS 43rd round. July 1987-June 1988. Kerala Special Issue. Department of Statistics, Ministry of Planning, Government of India.

observed to have been associated with high levels of male occupational mobility but confinement of women to low-paying conventional occupations or to 'household duties'.

Chasin (1990) points out that between 1971 and 1986-87 in a central Kerala village, which was predominantly rice-cultivating and little affected by Gulf remittances, women registered much lower occupational mobility than men. In 1986-87, the largest proportion of women was engaged in household duties (36 per cent, though this signified a decline from 54 per cent in 1971), and the proportion of unemployed women came to 32 per cent as against 19 per cent for men. Despite unemployment, Chasin noticed that the demand for female agricultural labour went unmet "as women seem to prefer unemployment to labouring in the paddy fields." Nevertheless, agricultural labour continued to be the major type of female, but not of male, employment. Franke and Chasin (1996) analysed the main occupations of household members in 1986-87, in the same village, but with a higher sample size – 676 persons as against 548 persons in Chasin (1990). Their findings support the diverging trends of male and female employment; women were almost on par with men as students; but petty trade, skilled labour, white collar jobs and service sector and professional employment were dominated by men at an average ratio of 10: 1 (Franke and Chasin, 1996).

Male out-migration has had a powerful influence on the resource position and work patterns of women

(Sivanandan, 2003, Zachariah *et al.*, 2003, Kurien, 2002, Osella and Osella, 2000). Sivanandan found in 1999 in a south Travancore village which had been studied in the census of 1961, that women significantly involved in coir manufacturing. Over time, access to other incomes, particularly through remittances from the Gulf, has had a strong impact on women's work patterns. While the overall female work participation had plummeted from 43 per cent in 1961 to 27 per cent in 1999, women in 'household duties' had risen from 16 per cent of women non-workers in 1961 to 32 per cent in 1999. A second feature is that women in upwardly mobile or affluent households withdrew from poorly paid manual work and informal sectors but took to employment considered 'respectable', particularly regular jobs in government.

A much higher proportion of women in Kerala (than at the all-India level) whose main occupation was of housewife, did also subsidiary work at home such as kitchen-gardening, poultry and cattle farming, activities accepted within the domain of extended-SNA activities[5] (Table 15.10). Such work being home-bound, is rid of the negative associations of paid manual work. As many as 639 per 1000 women were engaged in domestic duties in rural Kerala and in poultry farming compared to less than 550 in rural India; in urban Kerala 458 women were engaged in maintenance of kitchen garden etc. compared to only 80 women in urban India; the corresponding figures were 331 women and 164 women in rural Kerala and in rural India respectively. Similarly, 142 per 1000 women in Kerala (compared to 48 per 1000 in India) participated in free tutoring of own/others' children. These pieces of evidence suggest that, 1) in literate Kerala too, women are largely involved in unpaid work in household premises and 2) women are directing their educational skills towards largely invisible, home-bound and unpaid services. Women's educational qualifications were being, by and large, used in the interests of family.

However, women from poor households with a disproportionately high representation of SCs and STs and of low status occupational groups, do not partake of the mainstream development gains. Perhaps the most telling indication lies in the fact that low economic status brings pressure on women to seek work for pay, even if it is in poorly paid and low status manual occupations. This fact is reflected in the much higher WPRs among the SC/ST categories of women. Table 15.11 shows that male and female work participation rates are distinctly higher among the SC and ST populations than among OBCs and the general population.

TABLE 15.10

Number of Women of Age 15 Years and Above Usually Engaged in Household Duties (principal status) and also Participating in Specified Activities per 1000 Women (age 15 years and above) Usually Engaged in Household Duties

Sl. No.	*Specified Additional Activities*	*Kerala 1999-2000*		*All India 1999-2000*	
		Rural	*Urban*	*Rural*	*Urban*
1.	Maint. of kitchen garden etc.	331	458	164	80
2.	Work in hh. Poultry etc.	639	377	543	219
3.	Free collection of fish etc.	38	24	179	46
4.	Free collection of firewood etc.	250	140	534	164
5.	Any of items 1, 2 4 or 5	789	685	817	355
6.	Husking of paddy (own produce)	4	22	111	9
7.	Grinding foodgrain (own produce)	30	44	86	14
8.	Preparation of gur (own produce)	4	0	8	0
9	Preservation of meat (own produce)	5	0	6	1
10.	Making basket etc. (own produce)	10	0	41	15
11.	Any of items 1, 2, 4, 5 & 8 to 12)	796	786	834	369
12.	Husking of paddy (acquired)	51	80	61	93
13.	Grinding foodgrains (acquired)	397	447	89	149
14.	Preparation of gur (acquired)	46	82	36	81
15.	Preservation of meat etc. (acquired)	140	152	42	92
16.	Making basket etc. (acquired)	33	87	38	84
17.	Preparing cow dung cakes	0	0	119	206
18.	Sewing, tailoring etc.	96	158	273	314
19.	Free tutoring of own/others' children	142	258	48	124
20.	Bringing water from outside hh. Premises	242	145	585	343
21.	Bringing water from outside village	9	0	18	0

Source: Same as Table 15.9.

TABLE 15.11

Rural Work Participation (UPSS) by Social Category

Year	*Scheduled Tribe*		*Scheduled Caste*		*OBC*		*Others*	
	M	*F*	*M*	*F*	*M*	*F*	*M*	*F*
1987-88	58.2	37.6	50.2	39.5			50.5	26.9
1999-00	72.1	40.8	58.0	32.7	52.8	22.6	57.2	22.1

Source: 1. *Sarvekshana*, Vol 15, No. 2, 1987-88. 2. Employment and Unemployment Situation among Social groups in India, 1999-00; NSS 55th Round, Report No. 469, September 2001.

5. Extended SNA (system of national accounts) activities are activities falling outside the SNA production boundary but within the general production boundary, a major part of which consists of unpaid services.

TABLE 15.12

Poverty among Scheduled Castes and Scheduled Tribes in the Indian States

State (Population 1991) (in million)	*% SC in Total Population*	*% ST in Total Population*	*% Agricultural Labourers in the Population-1991*			*% Population Below the Poverty Line (Rural)-1993/94*		
			Total	*SC*	*ST*	*Total*	*SC*	*ST*
Kerala 29.10	**9.9**	**1.1**	**25.5**	**53.8**	**55.5**	**25.76**	**36.43**	**37.34**
India 846.3	16.5	8.1	26.1	49.1	32.7	37.27	48.11	51.94

Source: *Tribes in India* (A Data Sheet). Planning Commission, Government of India, 2000. *Scheduled Castes in India* (A Data Sheet). Planning Commission, Government of India, 2000 cited in Narayana, 2002.

TABLE 15.13

Literacy among Population Groups by Sex in Kerala and India, 1991

State	*% Literate-All Population*			*% Literate-Scheduled Caste*			*% Literate-Scheduled Tribe*		
	Male	*Female*	*Persons*	*Male*	*Female*	*Persons*	*Male*	*Female*	*Persons*
Kerala	**93.62**	**86.13**	**89.81**	**85.22**	**74.31**	**79.66**	**63.38**	**51.07**	**57.22**
India	64.13	39.29	52.21	49.91	23.76	37.41	40.65	18.10	29.60

Source: GoI (2002). *National Human Development Report 2001*. Planning Commission, March.

Further, these groups have a distinctly higher representation among agricultural labourers and among households below the poverty line (Table 15.12).[6] This is a reflection of the distressed socioeconomic position of SC and particularly ST groups in the state. In a state in which STs constitute only one per cent of the population, their literacy level remains distinctly lower than that for the general population; differences in the level of female literacy are even starker (Table 15.13). Some aspects of patriarchy breakdown in families of poor women are noticed caused by their need for greater mobility and earning power and by their responsibility for provisioning the household. However poor working women have to contend with the larger structures of patriarchy demonstrated in discriminatory wage patterns and occupational segregation. Besides, in poor households, women seem to have much less access, than men or women from more affluent households, to resources such as literacy and education.

Gender and Migration

While migration to destinations both outside and within the country, is a significant employment option for men, it is certainly a factor in the intensity of female unemployment in the state. A Gulf migration study undertaken in 1998 found that only 10 per cent of the 3,752,000 migrants from the state were women. Significantly, nearly half (46 per cent) the number of the economically active female emigrants had been job seekers prior to emigration. The corresponding proportion among males was only 27 per cent. The differentials had persisted at the destination too but at much lower levels—5.6 per cent among females and 0.5 per cent among males. "Female migrants are better qualified than male migrants, but lower proportions of them get gainfully employed. Migration causes separation of wives from husbands. Few husbands are left behind by migrating wives but most wives are left behind by migrating husbands." While emigration was essentially a male affair, there were more women among out-migrants than among emigrants. More than half the number of emigrants was Muslim but only one-fourth of the total number of female emigrants was from this religious goup. The Christian community contributed nearly half the number of female emigrants and around 75 per cent of all female out-migrants (Zachariah and Irudaya Rajan, 2004).

Demographic and Health Status of Women

The role of women's literacy in achieving health transition in Kerala has been well documented. Health achievements are reflected in life expectancy and infant and maternal mortality figures (Table 15.18). Life expectancy of women in Kerala is clearly higher than

6. According to the 1991 Census, nearly 32 per cent of SC women and 37 per cent of ST women were recorded as working *vis-à-vis* 15 per cent of total female population in the state.

TABLE 15.14

Percentage of Females Migrants with Marital Status, in Kerala

Marital Status	*Female Migrants*	*Unemployed Female Migrants*
Married	60.0	50.5
Unmarried	35.3	44.9
Widow	2.3	2.3
Divorced	1.7	1.8
Separated	0.8	0.5
Total	100	100

Source: *Economic Review 2004*.

TABLE 15.15

Percentage of Females among Emigrants by Religion, 2004

Religion	*Percentage*
Hindu	17.2
Christian	32.1
Muslims	8.0
Total	16.9

Source: Zachariah, K.C. and S. Irudaya Rajan (2004). "Gulf Emigration of Women in Kerala", *Samyukta*, Vol.4 (2).

TABLE 15.16

Educational Attainment of Female Emigrants, 2004

(per cent)

Less than primary	3.5
Primary, less than secondary	17.3
Secondary	34.3
Degree	44.9
Total	100

Source: Same as Table 15.15.

TABLE 15.17

Economic Sector of Activity of Female Emigrants

	Before Emigration		*After Emigration*	
	F	*T*	*F*	*T*
Government	3.6	1.5	5.2	3.6
Semi government	3.0	2.7	7.2	7.3
Private sector	13.3	9.1	28.4	35.9
Self employment	0.8	7.2	1.3	5.5
Unpaid family worker	0.3	0.8	0	0
Agricultural labourer	0.6	1.8	0	0.2
Non agricultural labourer	4.4	33.1	6.2	36.4
Job seekers	35.1	33.8	5.9	1.8
Job not required	1.1	0.4	1.8	0.4
Students	10.2	5.3	10.1	3.3
Home hold duties	27.3	4.1	33.8	5.2
Pensioners	0.3	0.1	0	0
Total	100	100	100	100

Source: Same as Table 15.15.

TABLE 15.18

Demographic and Health Status of Women

Indicators	*Kerala*	*India*
Life expectancy (females) 2001	75.9yrs	61.8yrs
*Infant mortality rate (2002)	10	63
*Maternal mortality rate (2002)	0.87	4.37
*Couple protection rate (2002)	66	52
Effective age at marriage of girls (yrs), 2001	22	19.5
Proportion of girls marrying after 21 years, 2001	63	25.9
Proportion of girls marrying between 18 and 20 years, 2001	32.3	53.4
Percentage of institutional deliveries	93.0	33.6
Total Fertility Rate	1.9	2.9
Sex ratio	1058	933

Source: *A Situational Analysis of Women in Kerala*, National Commission for Women, Directorate of Health Services, Thiruvananthapuram.

that for India as a whole but it is also about five years more than that of men in Kerala. Infant and maternal mortality figures in Kerala are much lower than those of all-India.

Underlying these achievements is the significantly higher age at marriage, particularly the percentage of girls marrying after 21 years of age. While these factors have contributed greatly to the demographic and development scenario in Kerala, sole emphasis on them tends to mask the fall outs of health transition in the state and particularly its adverse implications on women. These implications are particularly strong where reproductive health of women is concerned. Low and declining levels of fertility have brought women in the reproductive age under tremendous pressure in terms of decisions on child birth and prenatal care. It is not unlikely that this pressure is reflected in the rising level of caesarean-section deliveries in Kerala and its possible association with private sector institutions. It is common knowledge that contraception is almost entirely the women's terrain, reflected in the high levels of sterilisation of women. Health and demographic transitions have been achieved at the cost of intervention into women's bodies and lives in ways that require serious critical reflection and inquiry.

It is understood that the prevalence rates of severe mental disorders such as schizophrenia show no significant gender difference. However the prevalence of the common type conditions such as depression and anxiety is higher among women across socioeconomic levels and in diverse societies (Sonpar and Kapur, 2003). Research seems to indicate social (rather than entirely psychological) influences on common mental distress in women, in particular to domestic problems. There are clear indications to suggest that violence and mental distress are serious problems in Kerala, warranting social concern and intervention (Mohammed, *et al.*, 2002). Striking is the higher levels of stress among middle income groups of Syrian Christians and Nairs. Case studies suggest that women suffered from greater stress (Mohammed *et al.*, 2002). In a micro level study of 133 survivors of attempted suicides in 1994-95, more than half were women. In general the incidence of completed suicides is higher for men and attempted suicides higher for women (see Tables 15.19, 15.20). Further, the proportion of female suicides is lower in Kerala than in all-India. A major factor associated with suicide attempts by women is marital disharmony. It was found also that one-third of the women suffered from domestic violence. Men however related economic problems and family problems as the major factors. While harassment of women was not linked directly to dowry according to this study, an autopsy study conducted in one of the districts in Kerala revealed that more than one-third of the women had a dowry problem preceding suicide.

TABLE 15.19

The Suicide Scenario in Kerala: Incidence and Rate of Suicide by Years and Gender, 1995-2002

Year	*Rate of Suicide*		
	M	*F*	*Total*
1995	38.06	15.35	26.38
1996	36.35	16.95	26,38
1997	41.33	17.26	28.96
1998	42.84	17.45	29.79
1999	44.72	18.04	31.00
2000	42.72	16.46	29.22
2001	42.72	16.85	29.74

Source: *www.maithrikochi.org*

TABLE 15.20

Percentage Distribution of Female Suicides in Kerala (1996-2003) & India (1996-2001)

Year	*Percentage of Females*	
	Kerala	*India*
1996	33.0	41.97
1997	31.2	-
1998	27.2	41.09
1999	28.7	40.78
2000	31.9	39.19
2001	29.10	38.88
2002	26.96	-
2003	26.66	-

Source: Kerala - *Economic Review*, 2004, India - *Accidental Deaths and Suicides in India*, NCRB, 2001.

A study of cases brought before the Family Court in Thrissur, between 1995-98, indicate that petitions filed increased from 477 to 860, almost two-thirds of them filed by women for divorce and maintenance, induced by protracted marital disharmony. Through case studies, the author of that study suggested that women suffered from intense stress (James, 1999). Based on his experience with psychiatric patients in Trissur district, a psychiatrist asserted that the most common cause of stress among educated women is lack of employment and the roles they are expected to assume after marriage. There exist clear indications that violence and mental distress are growing to be serious problems in Kerala.

Violence against Women

Violence against women is clearly embedded within patriarchal structures. It is known that resistance to patriarchal norms and demands constitute the key trigger of such violence. The National Family Health Survey (NFHS-2) reveals that significant proportions of women justified wife-beating on some ground or another. In Kerala 70.2 per cent (69.4 for all-India) of women who had experienced violence at least once, agreed with at least one reason for wife beating as did 60.8 per cent (53.3 of all-India) of women who had never experienced violence. This section draws on an analysis of National Crime Records Bureau data on Crime Against Women (CAW).[7] The data at the state

7. A combination of state level (1995-97) and district level (1996) analyses highlighted both the usefulness and the limitations of the data (see Mukherjee *et al.*, 2001). A major irritant was the possibility of underreporting and the associated distortion of the data. Despite this Mukherjee *et al.*, (2001) derived robust patterns from the data. The relevance of the data, despite suspicion of underreporting was demonstrated through the contiguity of district which recorded the highest levels of crime. Also variation in the rates of crime against women across districts increased from districts with low rates of total crime to districts with higher total crime rates, producing a neat cone on the scatter diagram. If underreporting of crime against women was proportionately greater than other crimes it is more likely to create a positive skewness (Mukherjee *et al.*, 2001).

level for the period between 1995-2000, was analysed using moving averages.

The NCRB data on reported CAW fall into six categories—rape, kidnapping and abduction, dowry deaths, cruelty by husband and relatives, molestation and sexual harassment. Dowry deaths and cruelty at home are strongly associated with the domestic context as against rape, molestation and sexual harassment which involve different degrees of a genre of crime against women, not necessarily associated with the domestic context. Kidnapping and abduction are taken separately as those two categories present difficulties owing to the circumstances that motivate parents or guardians to file cases (see Mukherjee *et al.*, 2001). It is seen that in the ascending order of total CAW, Kerala ranks 24th i.e., if the states are organized into four groups based on ranks, Kerala comes among states/UTs with higher rates of CAW. In two categories—molestation and cruelty at home—Kerala ranks 29th in the group with the highest rates of CAW. Only in dowry deaths and kidnapping and abduction, does Kerala rank among states with lower rates of crime (Table 15.21).

TABLE 15.21

Ranks of States According to the Average Rate (1998-2000) of Crimes Committed Against Women (per lakh)

	Rape		*Kidnapping*		*Dowry & Abduction*		*Cruelty by Husband Deaths*		*Molestation and Relatives*		*Sexual Harassment*		*Total Crime Against Women*	
States	*Rate*	*Rank*	*Rate*	*Rank*	*Rate*	*Rank*	*Rate*	*Rank*	*Rate*	*Rank*	*Rate*	*Rank*	*Rate*	*Rank*
A&N Islands	1.33	15	0.6	9	0	1	0.97	10	4.47	26	0.43	20	9.4	13
Andhra Pradesh	1.2	11	0.93	12	0.63	24	6.37	28	4.2	22	2.27	30	17	28
Arunachal Pradesh	3.03	29	3.43	27	0	1	0.63	8	4.7	27	0.13	11	11.97	17
Assam	2.83	28	4.33	28	0.17	14	3.27	22	2.77	17	0.07	7	13.63	21
Bihar	1.53	18	0.93	12	1.07	30	1.47	14	0.5	3	0.1	9	6.8	8
Chandigarh	1.9	22	4.53	29	0.53	23	2.67	17	2.67	14	1.07	25	15.67	25
D& N Haveli	2.37	27	1.57	22	0.37	19	2.17	16	2.3	13	0.17	13	9.27	12
Daman & Diu	1.2	11	1.17	17	0	1	1.47	14	0	1	0.27	18	4.57	5
Delhi	3.17	30	7.3	32	0.93	29	0.77	9	4.4	23	1.1	26	18.27	29
Goa	1.2	11	0.57	8	0.13	13	0.97	10	1.47	8	0.5	21	6.67	7
Gujarat	0.73	5	2.17	26	0.2	15	7.8	30	2.27	12	0.3	19	13.6	20
Haryana	1.97	23	1.63	23	1.47	32	6.2	27	3	19	1.87	29	16.2	26
Himachal Pradesh	1.87	21	1.5	20	0.1	10	4	25	4.4	23	0.23	15	12.17	18
Jammu & Kashmir	1.8	20	5.7	31	0.1	10	0.37	6	5.13	28	3.57	32	16.73	27
Karnataka	0.53	4	0.6	9	0.4	20	3.03	20	2.83	18	0.23	15	10.97	16
Kerala	**1.63**	**19**	**0.37**	**3**	**0.1**	**10**	**7.33**	**29**	**5.3**	**29**	**0.23**	**15**	**15.2**	**24**
Lakshadweep	0.47	3	0	1	0	1	0.5	7	0.5	3	0	1	1.47	1
Madhya Pradesh	4.5	31	1.17	17	0.8	26	3.77	24	10.1	32	0.97	24	21.5	31
Maharashtra	1.4	16	0.8	11	0.43	22	7.93	31	3.17	21	0.93	23	15.13	23
Manipur	0.43	2	1.9	25	0	1	0.1	4	0.57	6	0	1	3.03	4
Meghalaya	1.43	17	0.53	7	0	1	0	1	0.5	3	0.17	13	2.73	3
Mizoram	7.63	32	0.23	2	0	1	0	1	7.07	31	0	1	15.03	22
Nagaland	0.77	7	0.47	4	0.03	9	0	1	0.2	2	0	1	1.5	2
Orissa	2.1	25	1.23	19	0.73	25	3	19	4.43	25	0.5	21	12.97	19
Pondicherry	0.37	1	0.47	4	0.27	16	0.33	5	2.67	14	1.67	28	10.07	14
Punjab	1.17	10	1.13	16	0.83	28	2.67	17	0.93	7	0.07	7	7.03	9
Rajastan	2.33	26	4.83	30	0.8	26	9.93	32	5.73	30	0.1	9	23.97	32
Sikkim	1.23	14	0.5	6	0	1	0.97	10	2.67	14	0.13	11	5.27	6
Tamil Nadu	0.73	5	1.5	20	0.3	17	1.03	13	3.07	20	2.8	31	20.4	30
Tripura	2.07	24	0.97	14	0.4	20	3.23	21	1.8	11	0	1	8.57	10
Uttar Pradesh	1.03	9	1.67	24	1.3	31	3.27	22	1.5	10	1.57	27	10.6	15
West Bengal	1	8	0.97	14.	0.33	18	4.9	26	1.47	8	0.03	6	8.83	11
Total (All India)	*1.57*		*1.6*		*0.7*		*4.43*		*3.27*		*0.93*		*13.8*	

Source: Compiled from various annual reports of Crimes in India. National Crime Records Bureau, Ministry of Home Affairs, Government of India.

TABLE 15.22

Moving Average of Rate of Crimes Against Women (per lakh)

	Rape	*Kidnapping & Abduction*	*Dowry Deaths*	*Cruelty by Husband and Relatives*	*Molestation*	*Sexual Harassment*	*Total*
Kerala							
1996	1.33	0.47	0.10	3.73	3.77	0.10	9.70
1997	1.67	0.47	0.10	5.13	4.77	0.20	12.50
1998	1.70	0.43	0.10	6.60	5.23	0.23	14.43
1999	1.63	0.37	0.10	7.33	5.30	0.23	15.20
2000	1.60	0.33	0.10	7.77	5.47	0.23	15.87
2001	1.63	0.30	0.10	8.00	5.77	0.23	16.57
2002	1.47	0.30	0.10	8.50	6.03	0.23	17.20
All India							
1996	1.57	1.57	0.60	3.67	3.13	0.57	12.23
1997	1.57	1.63	0.63	3.97	3.17	0.67	12.87
1998	1.57	1.63	0.67	4.17	3.23	0.77	13.33
1999	1.57	1.60	0.70	4.43	3.27	0.93	13.80
2000	1.60	1.50	0.70	4.60	3.30	0.97	13.97
2001	1.57	1.40	0.63	4.63	3.23	1.03	13.73
2002	1.53	1.30	0.60	4.67	3.17	1.07	13.43

Source: Crime in India 1995-2000, National Crime Records Bureau, Ministry of Home Affairs, Govt of India. Total includes crimes considered under the Dowry Prohibition Act, not shown here.

Table 15.22 shows that between 1995 and 2002 the rates of cruelty at home, molestation and sexual harassment rose sharply in Kerala. The high increase in the rate of reported sexual harassment was partly because it had been earlier reported to be nil. An analysis of two high-profile cases of sexual harassment recently revealed the strong disincentives (of time, resources, efforts and legal procedures) attached to reporting sexual harassment (Devika and Kodoth, 2002). In contrast, rape and dowry death, being more heinous, are more likely to be reported. Bihar which ranks 30 and 18 in dowry death and rape respectively, ranks lower (in the group with low rates of crime) in all other categories of crime against women. It may be reasonable to expect that states reporting high levels of dowry murder would also have high levels of cruelty at home. In fact the rate of cruelty at home is found to be consistently higher than the rate of dowry deaths in all states. However, Bihar, Uttar Pradesh, Delhi, and Punjab which are in the highest group of states in dowry death show significantly lower ranks for cruelty at home (see also Mukherjee, *et al.*, 2001).

During 1995-2002, the rate of dowry deaths in Kerala remained unchanged at a level significantly lower than for India as a whole. Kerala was for long considered free of this crime because of its matrilineal traditions and customary regulation of the practice of dowry among patrilineal groups. However the fact that dowry deaths are being reported consistently in the state is an indication of the significant shift that has come about in marriage practices in the state.

Kerala ranks among the highest group of states in the matter of cruelty at home and a continuous increase in the rates of cruelty at home has been reported between 1995 and 2002.[8] Women in Thiruvananthapuram reported similar levels of physical violence as women in Vellore and Lucknow (ranging between 21 and 26 per cent) according to a study of domestic violence undertaken between 1997 and 1999 in seven cities of India (INCLEN/ICRW, 2000). The study also revealed that more than two-thirds of the sample women in rural and a little lower proportion in the urban non-slum areas had experienced psychological violence. A more recent study of domestic violence in Thiruvananthapuram (rural and urban) found that overall 35.7 per cent of women reported experiencing

8. Several primary studies which deal with lifetime prevalence (while the crime statistics are based on reported violence from year to year) have also reported rapid increase in the number of cases of cruelty at home. It is also important to note that primary surveys probe closely respondents' experience of violence.

TABLE 15.23

Percentage Distribution by Sex of Operational Holdings and Area under Operational Holdings (in hectares) According to Size-class Groups in Kerala (1995-96)@

Size class	*Number of Operational Holdings*				*Area under Operational Holdings*			
	Male	*Female*	*Institution*	*Class (%)**	*Male*	*Female*	*Institution*	*Class (%)#*
0.5 to 1.0	75.29	23.75	0.96	93.96	77.68	21.16	1.16	53.24
1.0 to 2.0	83.42	15.03	1.55	4.16	83.55	14.88	1.58	20.44
2.0 to 4.0	84.87	12.86	2.26	1.52	84.40	13.32	2.27	14.24
4.0 to 10	82.54	12.30	5.16	0.31	82.14	12.19	5.67	6.07
Above 10	66.61	8.61	24.78	0.05	44.84	3.62	51.54	6.00
Total	75.79	23.18	1.03	100.00	78.14	17.16	4.70	100.00

Note: @ This table is based on provisional data from the agricultural census of 1995-96, * Percentage of the number of holdings in each size class to the total number of holdings, # Percentage of the area in each size class to the total area under operational holdings.

Source: Agricultural Census Division, Directorate of Economics and Statistics, Government of Kerala in Women in Kerala, 2001.

some form of physical violence at least once in their married life. The corresponding figure was considerably higher (64.9 per cent) for psychological violence (Panda, 2003).

The socioeconomic correlates of domestic violence investigated into by these studies are instructive. The INCLEN study revealed that gender gap in education and employment was significant in explaining violence. Violence was more frequent when the woman respondent was more educated (> 2 years) and had a better type of employment than of her husband. The unemployment status of the husband was significantly and positively associated with both measures of violence. These findings underline the importance of work status to male identity. Existing evidence for India and Kerala also points to the negative association between socioeconomic status and domestic violence (INCLEN/ICRW, 2000; Panda, 2003). In particular, Panda (2003) found that education status of men and women was negatively associated with lifetime prevalence of violence and that women engaged in irregular/casual employment were more likely to experience violence while regular employment was likely to reduce it. However as INCLEN/ICRW (2000) point out that it is entirely open to interpretation whether women of higher socioeconomic levels actually experience lower levels of violence or merely under-report violence. Ownership of property (land and house) by women was found to reduce both physical and psychological violence against women (Panda, 2003). The INCLEN study found that in male dissatisfaction with women, the major causes were, sharing of domestic responsibilities, disobedience, infidelity and alcoholism. Panda noted that 30 per cent of women who had arranged marriages cited dowry as a factor in violence. Clearly these pieces of evidence provide strong indications of patriarchal structures underlying violence against women.

Women's Property Rights

Customs that regulate women's property rights have strong implications for their ability to claim ownership and exercise control over property, irrespective of favourable laws (Agarwal, 1994, Jaisingh, 1997). Recent data on the extent of land held (operational holdings) by men and women in Kerala[9] drawn from the agricultural census of 1995-96 for Kerala, show wide disparity between men and women in the holding of operational units of land. Table 15.23 shows that women hold less than a third of the number and of the area of operational holdings held by men. As the size of holdings increases, women's share of the number of holdings and area declines. Disparity gets more pronounced in the case of area of holdings. In the above-10 hectares category, women hold less than 10 per cent of the number and less than five per cent of the area of operational holdings. Recent research based on primary data has documented that women are increasingly taking over responsibility for management and cultivation of land (as well as other family

9. The agricultural census takes the household (i.e., a commensal unit) the unit of enumeration. As members of a single household are not recognised as joint holders, individual holdings stand in for households. Further, operational holdings do not refer to title or ownership, as they include owned and leased-in-holdings.

responsibilities) in the context of diversification of household incomes and the shift of male members from agriculture to other occupations through migration or otherwise (Morrison, 1997; Arun, 1999). Significantly however, women actively involved in agriculture and animal husbandry continue to report themselves as housewives (Narayana, 2002a). In recent times this tendency has been associated strongly with the negative connotations that manual and other low status work carries (Osella and Osella, 2000).

What factors constrain women's title and access to, and control over, property? If practices that regulate inter-generational transfer of property are clearly important, so also is women's poor occupational profile in the state, which severely restricts their ability to acquire property. However existing gender-differentiated property rights are long-term outcomes of practices that endow and regulate title and access to property. There have been definitive indications over the last quarter of the 20th century that dowry is replacing inheritance rights as a mode of transfer of property to, or on account of, women. While women's bargaining position in their marital family could vary with the property they bring as dowry, even a large dowry is no guarantee of security. Upto at least the mid-1970s, women of the matrilineal groups used to inherit some property, though distinctions were drawn among different kinds of property (Gough, 1952; Fuller, 1976). A study of women's participation in the land market in a highland south Travancore village found that a much higher proportion of Nair women than men sold the land they inherited and that 'migration due to marriage' was the most important reason for the sales (Varghese, 1988). This indicates a higher turnover of immovable property inherited by women consequent on patriarchal marriage and residence with husband. Among the erstwhile matrilineal Izhavas of central Travancore, land was sold and the cash proceeds given to the husband, a form of dowry that is not usually under the control of the wife. Osella and Osella point out that many women no longer have land to pass on to their daughters and that the practice of mother-daughter inheritance is declining. In a survey of widows in selected areas of north and south India, Chen (2000) found that 67 per cent of the widows whom she surveyed in Kerala had inherited land from husbands as against only 27 per cent who had inherited land from parents. The anchoring of women's inheritance rights to marriage reflects their dependence status and vulnerability within marriage.

There is substantial evidence of the increasing practice of dowry payments at the time of marriage of girls across social and economic groups. The practice of giving *stridhanam* at the marriage of a girl had been customary among patrilineal communities—Christians, Muslims, Izhavas and Nambudiris—and among a few specific matrilineal groups—Tiyyas, Mappillas, and Izhavas. Importantly in the case of the latter, the dowry did not deprive women of their right to inherit property. Dowry as a highly 'competitive' market practice divested of its previous customary regulations, has been documented recently among the Christians (Viswanathan, 1999; Kurien, 1994). Among the matrilineal groups, over the past half a century, there has happened a broad shift towards dowry marriages (Osella and Osella, 2000; Puthenkalam, 1977). More importantly perhaps the notion of dowry itself has gained widespread acceptance in the state, across social and economic groups (Eapen and Kodoth, 2003; Lindberg, 2001).

Dowry includes a combination of cash, gold, land and consumer durables. Osella and Osella (2000) note that some notional distinction has been made for land and gold to remain in the bride's name and for cash and goods go to the husband and his family. In practice, however most women lost control over the entire dowry, which happens to be used to support the needs of the husband's family. Transfer of land at marriage is recorded in the community register of the Nair Service Society (NSS) and the Sree Narayana Dharma Paripalana Yogam (SNDP), in areas in which these organisations wield clout on their followers. (Osella and Osella, 2000). Efforts at regulation indicate that transfers on marriage are widely practised. Recently, Lindberg (2001) has documented the increasing prevalence and the steep escalation of dowry paid among cashew workers of different castes in Quilon district during the past half a century. For women, there are no guarantees that they will have title to or control over property transferred at marriage on their account, underlining their vulnerability in the marital conflict. Women's property rights hinge on a host of factors which are weak or absent in the framework of patriarchal marriage. The 'thinning' of women's inheritance rights over parental property and women's very low rates of participation in paid employment provide conditions that force women to conform to patriarchal gender codes and expose them to domestic violence when they do not meet patriarchal expectations.

BOX 15.1

Political Representation of Women

Levels of representation of Kerala women in the Lok Sabha have been consistently dismal. In the eight Lok Sabhas between 1957 and 1989, there was never more than one woman and, on four occasions there were no women at all (Table 15.24). In 1991 for the first time Kerala had two women in parliament. The number went down to one in 1999 and we currently have two women. This compares poorly with several states that trail behind Kerala on indicators of education or health. Nor is the picture substantially different in the state assembly. The number of women representatives peaked in 1996 with 13 members. In the previous assembly, we had eight women, constituting 5.7 per cent of total membership. The average proportion of women in the assembly since 1957 in Kerala, has been considerably low (Government of Kerala, 2001).

TABLE 15.24

Number of Women Representatives in Parliament and State Legislative Assembly

Year	*Parliament*	*Year*	*Kerala Assembly*
1957	0	1957	6
1962	0	1960	7
1967	1	1965	3
1971	1	1967	1
1977	0	1970	2
1980	1	1977	1
1984	0	1980	5
1989	1	1982	4
1991	2	1987	8
1996		1991	8
1999	1	1996	13
2004	2	2001	8

Source: Government of Kerala. *Women in Kerala,* 2001 Directorate of Economics and Statistics, Thiruvananthapuram.

Gender Budget Initiatives and Decentralised Planning

Gender budget work focuses on the impact of government budgets on women and men and different sub-groups within them. A distinct methodology has evolved to undertake such an analysis. An important component of the methodology is an understanding of the socio-economic situation of women and men and an examination of policies, in particular relating to women, to understand the extent to which they address 'gender gaps'. A gender disaggregated beneficiary incidence analysis and a gender disaggregated beneficiary assessment analysis also are undertaken to monitor the extent to which the distribution of budget resources flows to women and the programmes or services meet their needs.

Kerala's development policy continues to be embroiled in some servicing assumptions regarding gender roles in a patriarchal society that give primacy to women's domestic role and to 'outside' world activities of men. Women's economic vulnerability is associated with dowry related crime and domestic violence, growing areas of concern in the state which for long has been considered free of this crime. With a major shift in structures of governance towards decentralised functioning (following the 73rd and the 74th Indian Constitutional Amendments in the early 1990s) which mandated 33 per cent representation of women in local bodies, it is critical to understand to what extent the management of economic resources at a decentralised level with a feminised political leadership was able to throw up a gender-sensitive allocation of resources, and make women economically less vulnerable while making the environment amicable. In the 'People's Plan Campaign' coinciding with the state's 9th Plan (1997-2002) almost 30 per cent of the plan funds were devolved on the local bodies. A conscious attempt was made also to incorporate gender issues in the process of planning. The effort was sought to be strengthened through a Women Component Plan (WCP). The local bodies were mandated to set apart 10 per cent of the plan grant-in-aid for preparing projects that directly benefited women.

Gender based data[10] on flow of resources are not available except for allocation under *Kudumbasree*. An attempt was made therefore to examine the budgets of select *gram panchayats* (GP) for a gender analysis. Four GPs were selected in Thiruvanathapuram district keeping in mind their physical, political and gender-based characteristics. While the primary objective of the analysis was to squeeze out as much information as possible regarding gender differentiated flows of resources of each budgetary item, it was found impossible to do so from an appraisal of the *panchayat* records. Discussions with *panchayat* members and efforts to elicit information on the amounts flowing to women from all 'mainstream' expenditures indicated that in agriculture-related activities like vegetable growing,

10. While the amended Panchayat Act (1999) exhorts the local bodies to present an integrated budget including plan grant-in-aid, state and centrally sponsored schemes, own revenues, institutional finance and voluntary/beneficiary contributions, we found very little of this in practice in the 9th Plan.

animal husbandry and small scale industries, the beneficiaries were almost exclusively women. Similarly in the service sector, resource flows under major heads such as drinking water, sanitation, housing, welfare of SC/STs, benefited both men and women; roads and bridges dominated the infrastructure whose benefits for women were, if at all, only indirect. The WCP was meant to be for projects directly benefiting women. A four-pronged strategy to do a gender budget analysis of the select GPs was therefore adopted: (a) an analysis of sectoral allocations in the GP plan budget over the five year period 1997-02; (b) an examination of the type of projects included under the WCP; (c) a gender distribution of funding for a primary health centre in one of the *panchayats*; and (d) an assessment of its services to women, in particular in the transformation into a more women-friendly institution.

In respect of the shares of different sectors in total plan expenditure, the guidelines[11] seem to have been broadly adhered to—the productive sector, that is agriculture and industry—accounted for 30-40 per cent. However, after the first two years its share declined to between 20-25 per cent, in terms of actual expenditure. In the last two years of the Plan, there was a discernible slowing down of plan grant earmarked for local bodies. The shortfall was higher in the case of the productive sectors. The gender implications of such shifts in sectoral expenditures have not been, however, favourable to women; during the last five years, the *gram panchayats* did meet the 10 per cent target mandated for the WCP. Most of the activities were organised in self-help groups (SHGs). However, diversification of the projects undertaken towards unconventional areas for women was only marginally evident; the greater emphasis continued to be on garment-making and livestock/poultry/traditional industry based activities. Also, as was pointed out above, the expenditures in the service and infrastructure sectors which benefit both men and women, have continued to be large even while the share of the productive sector declined, particularly in the closing years of the plan. It is possible that amounts spent under the service/infrastructure sectors (for instance housing, sanitation, drinking water and roads[12]) with women beneficiaries, which should have remained in the general sector, were included as projects under the WCP to meet the 10 per cent target. On the average, 10 per cent of plan grant for WCP implied an amount varying from Rs. 5-10 lakhs per *panchayat*. Another tendency, though well-meaning, was the effort to build infrastructure like mini-industrial estates and buildings for business and industry, out of the WCP to encourage women's enterprises. However, such schemes out of such a small total amount not only left little resources for other projects, they also blocked funds for two to three years; gender disaggregated data on outpatients (by age) compiled for two years, 2001 and 2002, from the registers of the PHC studied, revealed that women beneficiaries exceeded men beneficiaries in all age groups; however the proportion of men to total patients was higher in the older age groups, suggesting that younger men use higher institutions of health care; and in respect of the transformatory potential of the PHC, the outcomes were disappointing: simple problems of women like the need for privacy, services of gynecologists, consultation timings to suit women's rhythm of household work and toilets as well as attitudes of doctors and staff toward beneficiaries, and involvement of women in the participatory process of strengthening the delivery services of the PHCs, continue to be given little attention. The fact that most of these changes have been suggested by women, some of whom have been very active in *panchayat* deliberations, and show tremendous awareness on health issues, proves that women's voice is still not fully heard.

Nonetheless, the strength of the WCP, in particular the SHGs, lies in the fact that a dense state-wide mobilisation of women exists, albeit only of women below the poverty line, which can be geared up to take on developmental activity at the local level. The enthusiasm with which these women come to *gram sabha*/development seminar meetings is proof of their desire to improve their living standard. The potential of decentralised governance including budget making, for redressing gender inequality is enormous. It needs to be deepened, bringing into it a gender analysis framework to change attitudes, embedded in extant institutions, which continue to disadvantage women.

Socioeconomic Conditions of Elderly Women

The ageing of population is seen as an obvious consequence of the process of demographic transition. The problems associated with an ageing population could be located in a developmental context i.e., in the institutions that have been shaped by this experience.

11. For rural local bodies the 9th Plan guidelines for allocation by sector were: agriculture, animal husbandry, minor irrigation etc.—40-50 per cent; service sector including education, health, sanitation, housing, drinking water, nutrition, etc.—30-40 per cent; infrastructure including roads, bridges, energy—10-30 per cent.

12. In the course of our discussions with women in a *panchayat* it was disclosed that at times roads too are put under the WCP.

Institutional factors include on the one hand the norm of a restricted definition of work as marketrelated productive activity and the association of ageing with 'non work' and dependency; on the other hand state and market failures to internalise the interests of a heterogenous aged population constitute another set of factors. The recent interest in the process of ageing in the developing world is attributed to the growing numbers of the elderly and to institutional failures for old age care. The uncertainties of the market, which are in the forefront of the process of globalisation in the developing world, have implications for the aged population in terms of increasing their vulnerability to poverty particularly in the absence of adequate social security. Notably Kerala is in the forefront of ageing in the Indian context, though there is considerable inter-district variation within the state (Table 15.25).

TABLE 15.25

District-wise Distribution of Elderly Population in Kerala, 2004

	M	*F*	*T*
Thiruvananthapuram	13.62	13.92	13.77
Kollam	13.21	12.27	12.73
Pathanamthitta	20.48	21.21	20.86
Alappuzha	14.29	15.60	14.97
Kottayam	17.30	19.34	18.32
Idukki	11.43	9.47	10.47
Ernakulam	15.01	16.31	15.67
Thrissur	12.25	13.89	13.11
Palakkad	12.57	14.27	13.47
Malappuram	9.64	9.58	9.61
Kozhikode	13.15	13.07	13.11
Wayanad	8.57	10.14	9.38
Kannur	12.06	13.60	12.87
Kasaragode	10.51	10.53	10.52
Kerala	**13.17**	**13.85**	**13.52**

Source: Irudaya Rajan, S. and Sabu Aliyar (2004). "Gender, Ageing and Social Security" in *Samyukta*, Vol. IV (2), July.

Women's life expectancy is higher than that of men; further, as men are usually older than the women they marry, there is a higher proportion of widows among the aged population (Table 15.27). Thus while 86 per cent of aged men are currently married 56 per cent of aged women are widows. It is expected then that most aged men live within a framework in which care is available to them from spouses, an advanage much less certain for women (Table 15.26). An important problem that arises in this context is the position of aged widows.

TABLE 15.26

Marital Status of the Elderly in Kerala, 2004

	M	*F*	*T*
Single	2.0	3.1	2.6
Married	85.9	39.4	61.2
Widowed	11.5	55.9	35.1
Divorced/seperated	0.4	1.4	1.0

Source: Same as Table 15.25.

TABLE 15.27

Percentage of Widows among 60+, 70+, 80+, 1991

	Kerala	*India*
60+	58.0	54.0
70+	60.5	67.2
80+	77.5	69.8

Source: Irudaya Rajan, S. (2004). *Chronic Poverty among Indian Elderly, CPRC-I I PA Working Paper* No. 17. Indian Institute of Public Administration, New Delhi, Chronic Poverty Research Centre.

These Tables show the increasing percentage of aged widows in successive age groups as well as the distinctly higher percentage of widows in Kerala than all-India. The proportion of fully dependent widows is much higher in Kerala than in all-India. More than half the aged widows in Kerala and all-India were fully dependent (Table 15.28). Notably a significantly higher proportion of aged women than aged men lived alone; while three quarters of the aged men lived with spouses and children, only half the aged women did so (Table 15.29). More importantly, only a very small percentage of aged women and widows reported themselves to be head of households as against a majority of aged men. More than 65 per cent of the aged men and women suffered from at least one chronic disease in rural India (Table 15.30). In this case also, the proportion of women was slightly higher than of men.

TABLE 15.28

Fully Dependent Elderly (females) by Place of Residence

(per cent)

	Kerala	*India*
R	57.7	58.2
U	66.9	64.2
T	61.4	60.6

Source: Same as Table 15.27.

TABLE 15.29

Distribution of Kerala Elderly by their Living Arrangements, 2004

Living Arrangement	*M*	*F*	*T*
Living alone	0.95	3.94	2.54
With spouse alone	10.56	5.07	7.65
With spouse, children& grand children	76.11	50.51	62.54
Without spouse but in the children, grand children.	11.42	38.47	25.76
Without spouse but with relatives other than children and grand children	0.79	1.87	1.36
With now relatives	0.17	0.15	0.16
Total	100	100	100

Source: Same as Table 15.27.

TABLE 15.30

Per cent of 60+ Males and Females having Chronic Diseases in Rural and Urban Areas in Kerala

(per cent)

Types of Disease	*Rural*		*Urban*	
	Male	*Female*	*Male*	*Female*
Cough	25.5	18.0	20.9	12.7
Piles	8.2	4.0	4.2	2.8
Problem of joints	47.1	56.5	31.1	42.1
High/low blood pressure	16.9	18.1	21.0	23.1
Heart disease	8.8	4.7	6.6	3.7
Urinary problem	4.3	2.7	3.9	2.2
Diabetes	8.7	7.7	9.7	9.0
Cancer	0.6	0.5	0.0	0.7
Any	67.9	69.7	60.0	62.5

Source: *Economic Review*, 2004.

The following are the issues for policy consideration.

A. General

- creation of an environment of respect for women.

B. Education

- Comprehensive gender audit of teaching practice and school environment.
- Gender sensitisation through programmes in school, on the basis of findings of gender audit.
- Introduction of demand-based vocational and educational training programmes for girls beyond the school level.

C. Work

- Respect for women's work.
- Recognition of the importance of paid employment for comprehensive social security for women.
- Recognition of the need to share domestic work between men and women.
- Incentives for women to seek work in unconventional areas.

D. Property Rights

- Incentives to increase property in women's names.
- Loans at low rates of interest to purchase land and house in women's names.
- Prioritisation of women, particularly women above 40 years and widows in government schemes for grants of land and house.

E. Marriage

- Questioning of the entrenched belief in marriage as the most preferred source of livelihood security for women.
- Guarantee of employment to women.
- Discussion-based campaign against the practice of dowry.

F. Prevention of Violence against women.

- Encouragement to women's organisations and voluntary groups working against violence.
- Heavy publicity campaigns on redressal mechanisms against violence against women.
- Assessment of the mechanisms in place for working against sexual harassment at the workplace.
- Sensitization of law and order enforcing agencies of the fact that all women have to be respected irrespective of their social status.

G. Governance

- Access to gender related data at disaggregated levels of the budgetary allocation under beneficiary schemes, women-specific programmes and mainstream expenditures which impact on women.

References

Agarwal, Bina (1994). *A Field of One's Own: Gender and Land Rights in South Asia.* Cambridge: Cambridge University Press.

Agnes, Flavia (1999). *Law and Gender Inequality: The Politics of Women's Rights in India.* New Delhi: OUP.

Arun, Shoba (1999). "Does Land Ownership make a Difference: Women's Roles in Agriculture in Kerala, India", in Caroline Sweetman (ed.), *Women, Land and Agriculture.* Oxford: Oxfam Publishing.

Chasin, Barbara H. (1990). "Land Reform and Women's Work in a Kerala Village", *Working Paper* No. 207. Women in International Development, Michigan State University.

Chen, Martha Alter (2000). *Perpetual Mourning: Widowhood in Rural India.* New Delhi: Oxford University Press.

Devika, J. and Praveena Kodoth (2002). "Sexual Violence and the Predicament of Feminist Politics in Kerala", *Economic and Political Weekly.*

Eapen, Mirudel (2001). "Women in Informal Sector in Kerala: Need for Re-examination", *Economic and Political Weekly,* June 30.

Eapen, Mridul and Praveena Kodoth (2003). "Family Structure, Women's Education and Work: Re-examining the 'High Status' of Women in Kerala", in Swapna Mukhopadyay and Ratna Surdarshan (eds.), *Tracking Gender Equity under the Economic Reforms.* New Delhi: Kali for Women.

Fuller, C. J. (1976). *The Nayars Today.* Cambridge: Cambridge University Press.

Franke, Richard W. and Barbara Chasin (1996). "Female Supported Households: A Continuing Agenda for the Kerala Model?", *Economic and Political Weekly,* Vol. 31 (10), pp.625-30.

Gough, Kathleen (1952). "Changing Kinship Usages in the Setting of Political and Economic Changes among the Nayars of Malabar", *Journal of the Royal Anthropological Institute,* Vol. 82: 71-88.

Government of Kerala (2001). *Women in Kerala (2001).* Trivandrum: Directorate of Economics and Statistics.

———. (1997). *Kerala Gazette Extraordinary,* Vol XLII(42), 9th October.

———. (1957). *Opinions on the Agrarian Relations Bill.* Trivandrum: Government Press.

Haggis, Jane (1998). "Good Wives and Mothers or Dedicated Workers? Contradictions of Domesticity in the Mission of Sisterhood' Travancore, South India", in Kalpana Ram and Margaret Holly (ed.), *Maternities and Modernities: Colonial and Postcolonial Experiences in Asia and the Pacific,* Cambridge: Cambridge University Press.

Heward, Christina and Sheila Bunwaree (eds.) (1999). *Gender, Education and Development: Beyond Access to Empowerment.* London: Zed Books.

Hirway and Mahadevia (1996). "Critique of Gender Development Index: Towards an Alternative", *Economic and Political Weekly,* Oct 26.

International Institute of Population Sciences (2000). *National Family Health Survey-2, 1998-1999.* Mumbai.

INCLEN/ICRW (2000). *Indiasafe: Studies of Abuse in the Family Environment in India – A Summary Report.* India: International Clinical Epidemiologists Network.

Irudaya Rajan, S . Mala Ramanathan and U S Mishra (1996). "Female Autonomy and Reproductive Behaviour in Kerala: New Evidence from the Recent Kerala Fertility Survey", in Roger Jeffrey and Alaka Basu (eds)., *Girl's Schooling, Women's Autonomy and Fertility Change in South Asia.* Chapter 11. New Delhi: Sage Publications.

Irudaya Rajan, S., U.S. Mishra and T.K. Vimala. (1996). "Choosing a Permanent Contraceptive: Does Son Preference Matter?", *Economic and Political Weekly,* Volume 31(29): 1980-84, July 20.

Jaisingh, Indira (1997). "Women's Inheritance Rights in Contemporary Jurisprudence", in Nitya Rao and Luise Rurup (eds.), *A Just Right: Women's Ownership of Natural Resources and Livelihood Security.* New Delhi: Friedrich Ebert Stiftung.

James, Lizzy (1999). "Family Counselling in Family Court: An Analysis of Psycho-Social Dynamics of Families of Litigants (Thrissur Family Court)", *Discussion Paper* No.13. Kerala Research Project for Local Level Development, Trivandrum.

Jeffrey, Roger and Alaka M. Basu (ed) (1996). *Girls Schooling, Women's Autonomy and Fertility Change in South Asia.* New Delhi: Sage.

Kodoth, Praveena (2004a). "'Gender, Property Rights and Responsibility for Farming in Kerala", *Economic and Political Weekly,* Vol 39(19).

Kodoth P. and M. Eapen (2005). "Looking beyond Gender Parity: Gender Inequities of some Dimensions of Well Being in Kerala", *Economic and Political Weekly,* Vol XI(30), July 23.

Kumar, Rachel (1992). "Women, Work and Development: Issues in Female Labour Force Participation in Kerala". Trivandrum: Centre for Development Studies. M. Phil Dissertation.

Kumar Shiva, A.K. (1996). "UNDP's Gender-Related Development Index", *Economic and Political Weekly,* April, 6.

Kurien, John (2000). "The Kerala Model: Its Central tendency and the Outlier", in Govindan Parayil (ed.), *Kerala: The Development Experience.* London: Zed Books.

Kurien, Prema A. (2002). *Kaleidoscopic Ethnicity: International Migration and the Reconstruction of Community Identities in India.* New Jersey: Rutgers University Press.

———. (1994). "Non Economic Bases of Economic Behaviour: The Consumption, Investment and Exchange Patterns of Three Emigrant Communities in Kerala", *Development and Change,* Vol . 25: 753-83.

Lakshmi Devi (2002). "Education, Employment and Job Preferences of Women in Kerala: A Micro Level Study", *Discussion Paper* No.42. Trivandrum: KRPLLD.

Lindberg, Anna (2001). *Experience and Identity,A Historical Account of Class, Caste, And gender among the Cashew Workers of Kerala, 1930-2000,* Department of History, Lund University.

Mehta, Asha (1996). "Recasting Indices for Developing Countries: A Gender Empowerment Measure", *Economic and Political Wekly,* October 26.

Mohamed E., S. Irudaya Rajan, K. Anil Kumar, P.M. Saidu Mohammed (2002). "Gender and Mental Health in Kerala", Unpublished Report. New Delhi: Institute of Social Sciences Trust.

Morrison, Barrie M. (1997). "The Embourgeoisement of the Kerala Farmer", *Modern Asian Studies,* Vol. 31(1): 61-85.

Mukherjee, Chandan, Preet Rustagi and N. Krishnaji (2001). "Crime Against Women in India", *Economic and Political Weekly,* Vol. 36(43).

Mukhopadyay Carol and Susan Seymour (eds.) (1994). *Women, Education and Family Structure in India.* Boulder: Westview Press.

Narayana D. (2002a). "Dairying in Malabar: A Venture of the Landowning based on Women's Work?", *Indian* Journal *of Agricultural Economics,* Vol. 57 (4), 698-713.

———. (2002b). "Persisting Deprivation in Kerala: Failure of Public Action or Lack of Diversified Growth", presented at the third annual symposium on *Poverty Research in Sri Lanka.* Colombo: Centre for Poverty Research. Aug 16-17.

National Crime Records Bureau (1996-2000). *Crime in India.* New Delhi: Government of India.

Nagaraj, K. (1999). "Labour Market Characteristics and Employment Generation Programmes in India", in Barbara Harriss-White and S. Subramanian (eds.), *Ill-fare in India.* New Delhi: Sage Publications.

NSSO (1990). "Results of the Fourth Quinquennial Survey on Employment and Unemployment (all-India) (July 1987-June 1988), 43rd Round *Sarvekshana.* Government of India.

———. (1996). *Participation of Women in Household Duties and Specified Activities,* 1993-94, Report No.416. 50th Round. Government of India.

———. (1997). *Employment and Unemployment in India, 1993-94,* 5th Quinquennial Round, Report No.409, 50th Round. Government of India.

———. (2001). *Employment and Unemployment Situation in India, 1999-00,* Part 1 and 2, 55th Round. Government of India.

———.(2001). *Participation of Women in Household Work and Specified Activities,* 1999-2000, Report No. 465. Government of India.

Osella, Filippo and Caroline Osella (2000). *Social Mobility in Kerala: Modernity and Identity in Conflict.* London: Pluto.

———. (1999). "From Transience to Immanence: Consumption, Life Cycle and Social Mobility in Kerala, South India", *Modern Asian Studies,* Vol. 33(4).

Panda, P.K. (2003). "Rights-based Strategies in the Prevention of Domestic Violence", *Working Paper* No.344. Trivandrum: Centre for Development Studies.

Parayil, Govindan (ed.) (2000). *Kerala: The Development Experience–Reflections on Sustainability and Replicability.* London: Zed Books.

Prabhu Seeta *et al.* (1996). "Gender-Related Development Index for Indian States: Methodological Issues", *Economic and Political Weekly*, October 26.

Puthenkalam, S.J. (1977). *Marriage and Family in Kerala.* Calgary: University of Alberta.

Ramachandran, V.K. (1997). "On Kerala's Development Achievements", in Jean Dreze and Amartya Sen (eds.) *Indian Development: Selected Regional Perspectives.* New Delhi: Oxford University Press. pp.205-356.

Saradamoni, K. (1999). *Matriliny Transformed: Family, Law and Ideology in Twentieth Century Travancore.* New Delhi: Sage Publications.

———. (1983). "Changing Land Relations and Women: A Case Study of Palghat District, Kerala", in Vina Mazumdar (ed.) *Women and Rural Transformation: Two Studies.* New Delhi: Concept.

———. (1980). *Emergence of a Slave Caste: Pulayas of Kerala.* New Delhi: People's Publishing House.

Sivanandan, P. (2003). *Village Restudy: Kadakkavoor.* Report prepared for the KRPLLD, Centre for Development Studies, Trivandrum.

Sonpar, S. and R.L. Kapur (2003). "Non-conventional Indicators of Gender Disparities under Structural Reforms", in S. Mukhopadhyay and R. Sudarshan (eds.) *op. cit.*

Srivastatva, N. (1999). "Striving for a Toehold: Women in the Organised Sector" in T.S. Papola and A.N. Sharma (eds.), *Gender and Employment in India.* New Delhi: Vikas Publishing House (P) Ltd.

Standing, G. (1999). "Global Feminisation through Flexible Labour-A Theme Revisited", *World Development*, Vol. 3.

Sundaram, K. (2001). "Employment-Unemployment Situation in India in Nineties: Some Results from the NSS 55th Round Survey, 1999-00", *Economic and Political Weekly*, March 17.

Unni, J. (2001). "Gender and Informality in Labour Market in South Asia", *Economic and Political Weekly*, June 30.

United Nations Development Programme (1975). *Human Development Report*, Delhi: Oxford University Press.

Varghese, T.A. (1988). "Commercial Cultivation and Land Market: Participation of Women in a Kerala Village", paper presented at a *Workshop on Women in Agriculture.* Trivandrum: Centre for Development Studies. February 15-17 .

Visaria, Leela (1996). "Regional Variations in Female Autonomy and Fertility and Contraception in India", in Jeffrey and Basu (ed.) *Girl's Schooling, Women's Autonomy and Fertility Change in South Asia.* New Delhi: Sage Publications.

Viswanathan, Susan (1999). *The Christians of Kerala: History, Belief and Ritual among the Yakoba.* Delhi: Oxford University Press.

Zachariah, K.C. and S. Irudaya Rajan (2004). "Gulf Emigration of Women in Kerala", *Samyukta*, Volume 4(2): 41-52.

Zachariah, K.C., E.T. Mathew and S. Irudaya Rajan (2000). *Dynamics of Migration in Kerala: Dimension, Differentials and Consequences.* Report of a Study. Trivandrum: Centre for Development Studies.

———. (2003). *Dynamics of Migration in Kerala: Determinants, Differentials and Consequences.* Hyderabad: Orient Longman Private Limited.

Chapter 16

Tourism

Introduction

Tourism today is an effective instrument for generating employment, earning foreign exchange, promoting cultural edifices and thereby facilitating the overall development of the localities involved. It is one of the world's largest and fastest growing industries. Statistically speaking, the activity of tourism accounts for 10.7 per cent of the global income, 12.8 per cent of the global exports, 8.2 per cent of global employment and 9.4 per cent of the global capital investment. The steady growth of tourism in recent decades has given it an important place in the economic planning schemes of every country having tourist potential, across the globe.

The statistics provided by the World Tourism Organization shows that the number of international tourists has shot up from 25 million in 1950 to 166 million in 1970, to 500 million in 1993 and to 700 million in 2002 at an average annual growth rate of 8 per cent. International tourism receipts (excluding spending on international transport) have registered an annual growth rate of 13 per cent, rising from US$ 2 billion (in 1950) to US$ 18 billion in 1970, to US$ 324 billion in 1993 and to US$ 474 billion in 2002. It should be noted that these growth rates are higher than the growth rates of exports of commercial services and merchandise.

However, tourism is highly vulnerable to disturbances, especially during periods of political unrest, terrorist menace, military conflicts and natural calamities. Global crises have devastating effects on the industry. The Gulf War is one instance, with the more recent ones being the SARS scare in Asia or terrorist attacks in the USA. Such incidents result in a massive fall in the tourist receipts of the concerned areas.

Currently, France, Spain and the United States register the largest international tourist arrival, with the United States in the lead. Asia also has emerged as a strong tourism force in recent years. International tourist arrivals have been growing at a rate of eight per cent in Asia; the strong trend of intra-regional tourism, however, is the major foster factor. As for outbound tourism, it is still concentrated in Europe, America and East Asia.

Tourism in India

With its wide range of climatic conditions, cultural edifices and historical monuments, India has a lot to offer to visitors of all profiles, ages and interests. The history of tourism in India dates far back to the ancient times. Foreigners have always been charmed by India.

India has been experiencing a downswing in terms of growth of tourist arrivals since 2001, after the World Trade Centre bombing (Table 16.1). The SARS scare in the Asian region has also contributed to this fall.

Tourism in Kerala

Tourism in Kerala has a long history. Travellers from the Far East as well as from West Asia and the Persian Gulf had trade and tourism links with Kerala for centuries. The name 'God's Own Country' has now become a well-identified tag of Kerala. Chosen by the National Geographic Travel as one of the 50 must-see destinations of a lifetime, hailed as one of the 10 paradises of the world and winner of a handful of other accolades, Kerala has made its way into possibly all available international tourist brochures.

Myths have it that Kerala was born when the sea god, Varuna, receded to give Parasurama, the sixth incarnation of Lord Vishnu, that much land that his

TABLE 16.1

Foreign Tourist Arrivals to India (1980-2002)

Year	*Number of Foreign Tourist Arrivals to India*	*Increase/ Decrease*	*Per cent of Variation Over PreviousYear*
1980	800150		
1981	853148	52998	6.62
1982	860178	7030	0.82
1983	884731	24553	2.85
1984	852503	-32228	-3.64
1985	836902	-15601	-1.83
1986	1079568	242666	28
1987	1163744	84176	7.8
1988	1239992	76248	6.55
1989	1337232	97240	7.84
1990	1329950	-7282	-0.54
1991	1236120	-93830	-7.06
1992	1434737	198617	16.07
1993	1442643	7906	0.55
1994	1886433	443790	30.76
1995	2123683	237250	12.58
1996	2287860	164177	7.73
1997	2374094	86234	3.77
1998	2358629	-15465	-0.65
1999	2481928	123299	5.23
2000	2649378	167450	6.75
2001	2537282	-112096	-4.23
2002	2361587	-175695	-6.92

Source: *www.indiastat.com*

FIGURE 16.1

Number of Foreign Tourist Arrivals to India

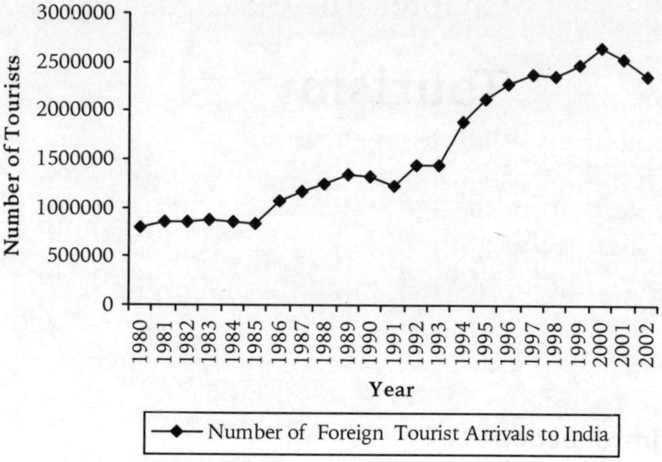

Source: Same as Table 16.1.

axe (*parasu*) thrown from Gokarna (a place of north Kasargod) would cover. Parasurana wanted calm and quiet, so the land was filled with lush vegetation and tranquil beaches; he was mighty, so the land held lofty mountains; he was beyond all prejudices of life, so the culture here embraces all religions and sects; and to mirror the salvation (*moksha*) that its founder had founded in this land, the people here uphold peace, harmony and tranquility.

One of the most alluring elegances of Kerala is its four month long monsoon season that drenches the whole of the state. Kerala's rivers, 44 in all being monsoon-fed, turn into rivulets during summer. Backwaters add to the charm of the region. The biggest among the backwaters in Kerala is the Vembanad Lake, with an area of 200 sq. km.

Kerala has over 25 per cent of India's 15,000 plant species. The lush vegetation and the fertile environment make it almost a herbarium of rare, medicinal and geographically specialised plants. Kerala also has an abundant wildlife population with over 100 species of mammals, 550 species of birds and 169 species of reptiles. Forests cover 29 per cent of the total area. Kerala has 3 national parks, 12 wildlife sanctuaries and 7 zoos. The total protected area comes to nearly 2,350 sq. km.

It is claimed that the quality of life of the Keralite society compares favourably with that of developed nations. Kerala holds the highest literacy rate in the country; it is the only state with a feminine sex ratio (1,058 females per 1,000 males in 2001), and the lowest infant mortality rate (10 per 1,000 live births). Kerala has many a tall tale of valour to tell; the sagas of its territory and lore of the glorious episodes of the reigns of several Dravidian rulers. The land has lured foreign traders by its rich spices and abundant hospitality from times of yore. Kerala prides over a long history of cultural and trade links with many ancient and foreign nation—the Phoenicians, the Arabs, the Chinese, the Portuguese, the Dutch and the English.

Tourists of all types have expressed fascination for the performing arts of Kerala, *Kathakali*, *Mohiniyattom*, *Oppana*, *Margamkali*, *Ottamthullal*, *Yakshaganam*, *Thiruvathirakali*, and *Chakyarkooth*, in addition to the manifold folk dances, tribal dances, folklores, religious festivals and rituals. The handicrafts of Kerala include artifacts carved out from coconut shell, ivory, horses and sandal woods. There exist also remarkable and fascinating pieces of artistic excellence that present marvels of Kerala's charms such as the snake boat and *Kathakali* faces, and Chinese fishing nets.

The traditional exotic cuisine of Kerala has tickled many gourmet taste buds, its seafood preparations, vegetable curries and meat delicacies, all spiced and flavoured. The cuisine of Kerala has been influenced by *Ayurvedic* principles to promote vigour and vitality to its consumers.

In fact *Ayurveda*, or the science of life, predominates in Kerala's health care traditions. Kerala's equable climate, wealth of medicinal plants and herbs, and the cool and comfortable monsoon seasons do facilitate the practising of *Ayurveda*.

Ayurveda, Backwaters, and Culture & Cuisine (ABC) are the major tourism products offered by the state; the beaches, the hill stations, the wildlife sanctuaries and the numerous cultural festivals add further taste to the products. The state is comprised of 14 districts, with every district with its own story to tell and its own special products to offer.

Though Kerala is a small state, its tourist attractions and destinations hold diversity unparalleled to those of any other destination in India. The region may be described in greater detail by looking at it in three parts–the southern, the central and the northern parts.

Southern Kerala

Beaches and backwaters are the major tourist attractions of this part of Kerala. It has some of the best beaches in India, with its backwaters flowing through thick-growing coconut groves. Thiruvanathapuram, the state capital, is the main city in this part; Kollam is a renowned trading centre; Pathanamthitta, is considered 'the Headquarters of Pilgrimage Tourism'; Alappuzha, is known as the 'Venice of the East'; and Kottayam, is farmed as 'Land of Letters, Latex and Lakes'. This region, which was earlier part of the princely state of Travancore, boasts of numerous palaces, museums and monuments, standing testimony to the valour and pride of its rich legacy. The historical monument at Punnapra in Alappuzha gives a glimpse of the region's recent turbulent past entwined with communist revolts.

The long coastline that borders this area is decked with famous beaches such as Kovalam, Shanghumugham, Varkala, Vizhinjam and Thangassery. Beach resorts have sprung up in many of these beaches, and *Ayurvedic* treatment is also being offered in them. Religious places of great renown—Sabarimala, Sri Padmanabhaswamy temple, Oachira, Vallikavu (the headquarters of *Mata Amritandamayi Math*), Vaikkom, and Erumeli—abound in this region. Religious congregations held in Maramon, Bharananganom and Arthungal attract large crowds of devotees and visitors.

Backwater cruises, either in *kettuvalloms* (i.e., houseboat) or traditional boats known as *vanchi* are one of the most exciting tour experiences in Kerala. The most popular of these cruises is the one on the Ashtamudi Lake on the Kollam-Alappuzha route. This boat ride gives vivid insights into the lives of the rural Keralite whose major vocations are toddy- tapping, coir-making, or fishing. These backwaters are also the venue for many famed boat races such as the *Uthrattathi* boat race and Nehru Trophy boat race. Sasthamkotta, the largest fresh water lake in Kerala has tourist cruises too. Kuttanad, 'the rice bowl of Kerala', is the only place in the world where farming is done below the sea level. Veli and Aakulam are reputed for their tourist parks and boating facilities; Kumarakom and Pathiramanal have island resorts with excellent hotel facilities and offer tours by land and lake. They have also excellent bird sanctuaries of international repute.

This region holds a number of wildlife sanctuaries of which the major ones are the Neyyar and the Peppara dams, the Thenmala ecotourism centre, and the Periyar wildlife sanctuary. Hill stations such as Ponmudi and Wagamon, waterfalls such as Palaruvi and Perumthenaruvi and water reservoirs such as at Konni and Pamba make this region a perfect tourist paradise.

Central Kerala

This region hosts Idukki, the spice land of Kerala; Kochi, the Queen of the Arabian sea and the commercial capital of the state; Thrissur, the cultural capital of the state; and Palakkad, the granary of Kerala.

Idukki is an assortment of all that nature has to offer to her lovers. A dozen looming peaks including Anamudi, the highest peak in Kerala, numerous rivers including Pamba, Manimala, Meenachil and Periyar, extensive plantations in Munnar, the Indo-Swiss cattle project at Mattupetty, sandalwood forests in Marayur, Thommankuthu waterfalls, Thekkadi wide life sanctuary, the Mullaperiyar dam and the extensive forest lands make Idukki the wild glory of Kerala.

The rest of the region tells us stories about its age-old relations with the outside world. Kochi and Kodungalloor in Thrissur district had been major ports of spice trade for several centuries in the ancient past. The trade with the Arabs, the Chinese, the Portuguese, the Dutch and the British had left indelible impressions on the culture and crafts of this region. The Chinese fishing nets, the Jewish Synagogue, the Dutch palace and several architecturally invaluable churches in Gothic style that adore many pilgrim centres in this region, are all remnants of a colourful and glorious past.

Thrissur is home to almost all the important cultural organisations of the state, the Kerala *Kalamandalam* being the most prominent among them. Guruvayoor, the place famed for the temple of Lord Krishna, is one sure destination on a pilgrimage itinerary. Kodungalloor, a port where St. Thomas landed in 52 A.D. to spread Christianity in these parts of the world, has some of the most beautiful and famous temples, churches and mosques. The Palakkad fort is a solid remnant of the turbulent history of the locality.

The Fort Kochi beach, the Cherai beach and the Chavakkad beach are sure tourist attractions. Other important tourist destinations are the Athirapally and the Vazhachal waterfalls, the Malampuzha dam and the gardens around it, the Peechi dam, the Silent Valley National Park, the Dhoni reserve forest and the Sholayar and Parambikulam wildlife sanctuary. Amusement parks built in recent years at Ernakulam, Athirapally, Vazhachal and Malampuzha are sure tourist attractions too.

Northern Kerala

This region of Kerala has remained subdued in the tourist agenda of the state for long. This area comprising Malappuram, Kozhikode, Wayanad, Kannur and Kasragod, has not received the attention it deserves. Malabar like the rest of Kerala has also fascinating beaches, backwaters, jungles, rivers, hills, forts, monuments, temples, mosques and churches.

Forts of Thalassery, Kannur and Pazhassi and the Arackal Palace are monuments with great historical significance and importance. It was in the Kappad beach near Kozhikode, that in 1498, Vasco Da Gama set foot in India. It was still further north, in Thalassery, that the German missionary Herman Gundert spent time in compiling the first Malayalam dictionary. Some of the beaches with great scenic beauty comprise Bekal, Payyambalam, Chavakkad, Kappad and Nattika which, if refurbished, would become favourite tourist destinations.

Malappuram, the house of the Kottakkal *Arya Vaidya Sala*, is the authentic repository of *Ayurveda* in Kerala. The district holds the largest concentration of aborigines. It has many interesting picnic places such as the Muthanga wildlife sanctuary, Pookot lake, Edakkal caves, Thusharagiri waterfalls and Thirunelly temple. Kannur, known as the city of looms and lores, and Kasargod give us glimpses of traditional rituals such as *Theyyam* and *Yakshagana*. The Muthappan temple and the Snake Park at Parassinikkadavu near Kannur have already developed into great centres of tourist attraction.

Kerala Tourism – Through The Years

The share of Kerala in the nation's tourist market has been increasing in recent decades (Table 16.2). In fact, Kerala is recognised to be the world's fastest growing tourist destination after Turkey; from 2.7per cent in 1980, the proportion of tourist arrivals in Kerala to the total number of tourists arrived in India has gone to 5.06 per cent in 1985, to 6.32 per cent in 1992, to 8.15 per cent in 1999 and to nearly 10 per cent in 2002. Kerala has always remained a stronghold in the tourist market. Even in the past two years when the tourism industry has been reeling all over the world, Kerala had only a marginal dip of 0.53 per cent; the fall for India during the period has been as high as 4.23 per cent. Besides, while the lean patch of India has been continuing in the case of foreign tourist arrivals (a decline of 6.92 per cent in 2002), Kerala registered a growth of 11.37 per cent.

This achievement may be attributed to the wide publicity that the state has gained over the past few years, especially with the National Geographic's declaring Kerala as one of the 10 paradises on earth and one of the 50 "Must See" destinations in a lifetime. Along with the National Geographic, several other international journals too spoke of Kerala as a must see destination. Publicity was also due to the high praise of illustrious tourists who visited Kerala. The Kerala government has taken elaborate measures for marketing the state "The God's Own Country", nationally as well as internationally.

In Kerala, tourism gained unprecedented importance during the last decade of the 20th century. Amidst unpredictable fluctuations in agricultural prices and the tendency for expatriate earnings to fall, tourism emerged as the major potential earner for the state economy. In fact the earnings from tourism came to Rs. 81.8 billion or 7 per cent of the Generalised System of Preferences (GSP) according to the results of the Transportation Security Administration (TSA) conducted by the World Travel and Tourism Council (WTTC) and Oakdale Educational Foundation (OEF). It was in the light of this potential that the WTTC made Kerala its

TABLE 16.2

Share of Kerala in Tourist Arrivals in India

Year	Number of Foreign Tourist Arrivals in Kerala	Increase/ Decrease	Per cent of Variation Over PreviousYear	Number of Foreign Tourist Arrivals in India	Increase/ Decrease	Per cent of Variation Over Previous Year	Per cent of Tourist Arrivals in Kerala	Per cent of Variation Over PreviousYear
1980	21604			800150			2.7	
1981	24315	2711	12.55	853148	52998	6.62	2.85	5.56
1982	24515	200	0.82	860178	7030	0.82	2.85	0
1983	25215	700	2.86	884731	24553	2.85	2.85	0
1984	24292	-923	-3.66	852503	-32228	-3.64	2.85	0
1985	42347	18055	74.32	836902	-15601	-1.83	5.06	77.54
1986	50841	8494	20.06	1079568	242666	28	4.71	-6.92
1987	51816	975	1.92	1163744	84176	7.8	4.45	-5.52
1988	52083	267	0.52	1239992	76248	6.55	4.2	-5.62
1989	62952	10869	20.87	1337232	97240	7.84	4.71	12.14
1990	66139	3187	5.06	1329950	-7282	-0.54	4.97	5.52
1991	69309	3170	4.79	1236120	-93830	-7.06	5.61	12.88
1992	90635	21326	30.77	1434737	198617	16.07	6.32	12.66
1993	95209	4574	5.05	1442643	7906	0.55	6.6	4.43
1994	104568	9359	9.83	1886433	443790	30.76	5.54	-16.06
1995	142972	38404	36.73	2123683	237250	12.58	6.73	21.48
1996	176855	33883	23.7	2287860	164177	7.73	7.73	14.86
1997	182427	5572	3.15	2374094	86234	3.77	7.68	-0.65
1998	189941	7514	4.12	2358629	-15465	-0.65	8.05	4.82
1999	202173	12232	6.44	2481928	123299	5.23	8.15	1.24
2000	209933	7760	3.84	2649378	167450	6.75	7.92	-2.82
2001	208830	-1103	-0.53	2537282	-112096	-4.23	8.23	3.91
2002	232564	23734	11.37	2361587	-175695	-6.92	9.85	19.68

Source: Compiled from various issues of the Annual Economic Reviews brought out by the Kerala State Planning Board and periodic issue of Statistics for Planning brought out by the Department of Economics and Statistics, Government of Kerala.

first partner state and then conducted the TSA for the state. Directly, tourism contributes Rs. 39.3 billion of GDP or 3.7 per cent of GSP and (378,584) or 3 per cent of the jobs (788,551 or 6.2 per cent of total employment). Exports services and merchandise are to the tune of Rs. 41.0 billion or 16.6 per cent of total exports. Capital investment in tourism is to the tune of Rs. 18.1 billion or 7.8 per cent of total investment. Government expenditure on tourism stands at Rs. 1.4 billion, i.e., one per cent of GDP.

As per WTTC's findings, by 2013 Kerala's travel and tourism is expected to achieve an annual growth rate of 11.4 per cent and earn as much as Rs. 569.3 billion. Receipts from the tourism industry, including the value of exports which visitors make form nearly 14 per cent of the value of total exports of the state. Tourism receipts have been on the increase for the state since the mid-1980s. It was in 1984 that the receipts from tourism hit a rock bottom level of Rs. 8.16 crore, a fall of 65.29 per cent over the previous year. Since then, the earnings have been increasing steadily; the growth rate was 111.28 per cent in 1992, the highest growth rate that fetched for the state, an amount of Rs. 59.75 crores.

FIGURE 16.2

Share of Kerala in the Indian Tourist Market (1980-2002)

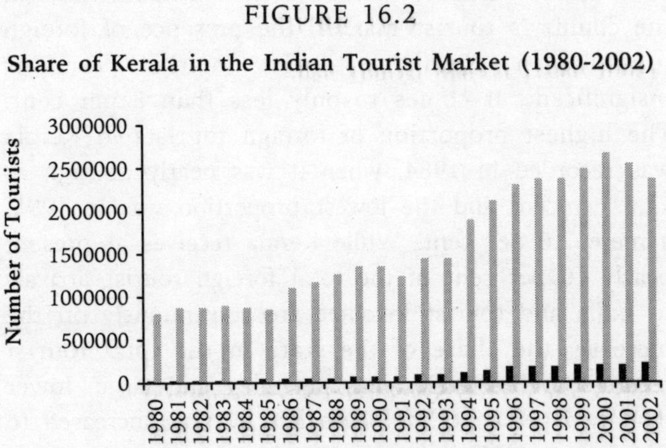

Source: Same as Table 16.2.

TABLE 16.3

Tourism Receipts

Year	*Rs. in Crores*	*Increase/Decrease*	*% Change*
1980	13.01		
1981	20.01	7	53.80%
1982	21.38	1.37	6.85%
1983	23.51	2.13	9.96%
1984	8.16	(-) 15.35	(-) 65.29%
1985	14.22	6.06	74.26%
1986	17.07	2.85	20.04%
1987	17.41	0.34	1.99%
1988	17.5	0.09	0.52%
1989	21.15	3.65	20.86%
1990	26.99	5.84	27.61%
1991	28.28	1.29	4.78%
1992	59.75	31.47	111.28%
1993	105.72	45.97	76.94%
1994	116.11	10.39	9.83%
1995	158.76	42.65	36.73%
1996	196.38	37.62	23.70%
1997	273.2	76.82	39.12%
1998	302.08	28.88	10.57%
1999	416.07	113.99	37.74%
2000	525.3	109.23	26.25%
2001	535	9.7	1.85%
2002	705.67	170.67	31.90%

Source: Same as Table 16.2.

and 35 per cent of the tourist flow to the country, respectively.

It is the tourists from Europe who account for a major portion of Kerala's foreign tourist arrivals. The tourists from the UK have always maintained a clear lead over tourists from other countries. They constituted nearly 16 per cent of the total foreign tourists in 1991, 19 per cent in 1994, 21 per cent in 2001 and slightly less 20 per cent in 2002. Tourists from the USA, France and the rest of Europe followed, in that order.

FIGURE 16.3

Tourism Receipts (1980-2002)

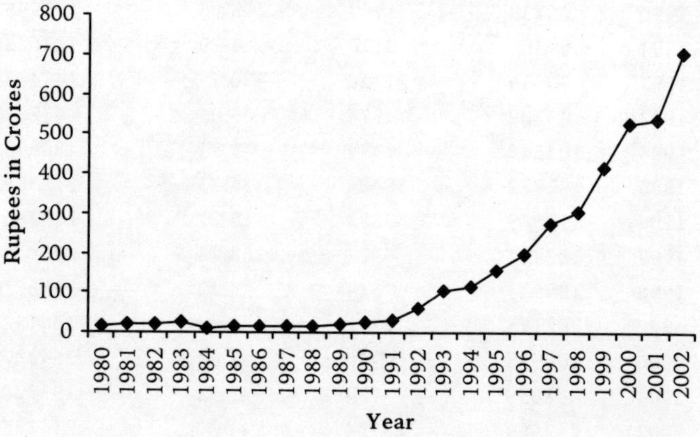

Source: Same as Table 16.2.

Receipts from tourism have been continuously on the increase from Rs. 105.72 crore in 1993 to Rs. 273.2 crore in 1997, to Rs. 416.07 crore in 1999 and Rs. 705.67 crore in 2002. The underlying annual growth rates were around 30 per cent.

In spite of the fact that Kerala has a major share in the country's tourist market, the presence of foreign tourists in Kerala's tourist market remains insignificant. It comes to only less than 8 per cent. The highest proportion of foreign tourists in Kerala was recorded in 1984, when it was nearly as high as 11.5 per cent and the lowest proportion was in 1995, a mere 2.6 per cent. While Kerala receives at present nearly 10 per cent of the total foreign tourist arrivals to India and tourist incomes are continuously on the increase; the share of the state in the total tourist receipts of the nation has been, by and large, lower than two per cent; the share has by now increased to five per cent. However, the tourism sector of Kerala is yet to catch up with other states such as Tamil Nadu and Andhra Pradesh, which receive around 30 per cent

Kerala has been unable to attract high-end tourists. Though foreign tourist arrivals are on the increase, the proportion of foreign tourists to total tourists to the state is very low, in the range of 3 per cent to 8 per cent. In 1995, foreign tourist arrivals in the state were 1,04,568 persons and domestic tourists 39,15,656 persons. In 1984, the proportion of foreign tourists to total tourists was around 11.5 per cent. Even in the year 1992 when there was a huge growth in receipts from tourism, the proportion of foreign tourists to total tourists was merely 6 per cent.

Tourism Experience of Kerala

A Kerala State Tourism Policy was formulated in 1995 with the objective of increasing foreign tourist arrivals to 5 lakh persons and that of domestic tourists to 50 lakh persons by the turn of the century. Though the target was met in the case of domestic tourists, in the case of foreign tourist arrivals, the target remains unattained; the number of foreign tourists to the state in 2000 were only 2,09,933 persons.

TABLE 16.4

Tourist Arrivals in Kerala: Total Number of Tourists over Years

Year	*Foreign Tourists*	*Domestic Tourists*	*Total Tourists*	*Increase/ Decrease*	*% Change Over Previous Year*
1980	12562	172832	185394		
1981	21604	194520	216124	30730	16.58
1982	24315	196120	220435	4311	1.99
1983	24515	201720	226235	5800	2.63
1984	25215	194336	219551	-6684	-2.95
1985	24292	338776	363068	143517	65.37
1986	42347	423756	466103	103035	28.38
1987	50841	510619	561460	95357	20.46
1988	51816	582050	633866	72406	12.9
1989	52083	634248	686331	52465	8.28
1990	62952	866525	929477	243146	35.43
1991	66139	948991	1015130	85653	9.22
1992	69309	994140	1063449	48319	4.76
1993	90635	1027236	1117871	54422	5.11
1994	95209	1284375	1379584	261713	23.41
1995	104568	3915656	4020224	2640640	191.41
1996	142972	4403002	4545974	525750	13.08
1997	176855	4953401	5130256	584282	12.85
1998	189941	4481714	4671655	-458601	-8.94
1999	202173	4888287	5090460	418805	8.96
2000	209933	5013221	5223154	132694	2.61
2001	208830	5239692	5448522	225368	4.31
2002	232564	5568256	5800820	352298	6.47

Source: Compiled from various issues of the Annual reports of the Tourism Department, Government of Kerala.

In fact, domestic tourists have remained the mainstay of Kerala tourism, with the proportion of domestic tourists to total tourists always hovering above 90 per cent, the only exception being experienced in the year 1984, even when it was around 88 per cent. In the year 1995, the total tourist flow increased by 191 per cent over the previous year, i.e., from 13,79,584 in 1994 to 40,20,224 in 1995.

Studies made by the Department of Tourism show that while domestic tourists spend around Rs. 682 per head, foreign tourists spend around Rs. 1,764 per head during their visits to Kerala; while domestic tourists stay on the average for 5-6 days, foreign tourists stay for 16 days. Domestic tourists are either pilgrimage tourists visiting temples at Guruvayoor or Sabarimala or persons coming to visit friends and relatives in the state, both not of a highly productive value to tourism coffers. It is foreign tourist arrivals which have

FIGURE 16.4

Foreign and Domestic Tourist Arrivals in Kerala

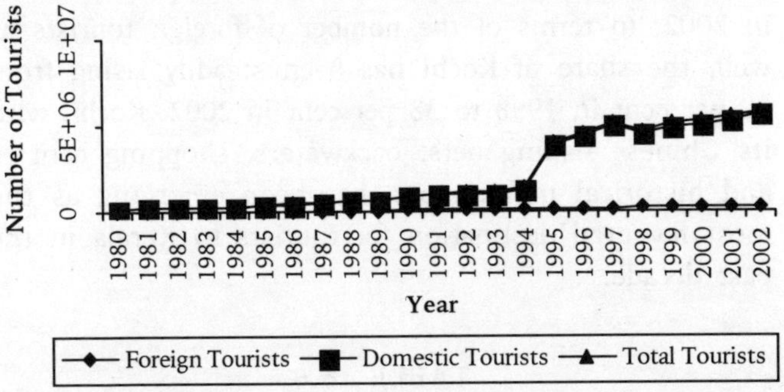

Source: Same as Table 16.4.

TABLE 16.5

Per Day Expenditure of Domestic and Foreign Tourists

Industry	*Per Day Expenditure of Domestic Tourists (Rs.)*	*Per Day Expenditure of Foreign Tourists (Rs.)*
Hotel	390	693
Food on Trip	38	80
Beverages	28	85
Local Transport	70	116
Health Rejuvenation	19	59
Entertainment	21	65
Communication	16	60
Personal Care	12	13
Shop – Handicraft	13	182
Shop – Textiles	7	82
Shop – Spices and Cashews	8	62
Shop – Leather and Rubber	6	43
Shop – Others	24	165
Miscellaneous	31	60
Total	682	1764

Source: Same as Table 16.4.

therefore to be promoted with special emphasis on quality tourism rather than quantity tourism. Foreign tourists also need to be attracted towards the handicrafts as well as the cultural and art forms of the state.

Of the 14 districts in the state, Thrissur, home to the famed Guruvayoor temple, had the highest number of domestic tourist arrivals, nearly 40 per cent of the total number of domestic tourists in 1996. But, since then, Guruvayoor has lost out its premier position to Kochi. While the arrivals in Kochi increased from 13 per cent in 1996 to 17 per cent in 2002, Thrissur's has gone down by 25 per cent during the same period.

Thiruvananthapuram used to receive the maximum number of foreign tourists; its share has been on the decline; it fell from 45 per cent in 1998 to 28 per cent in 2002. In terms of the number of foreign tourists as well, the share of Kochi has been steadily rising from 30 per cent in 1998 to 38 per cent in 2002. Kochi, with its Chinese fishing nets, backwaters, shopping centres and historical monuments, has been emerging as the most favoured destination for tourists to Kerala in the past decade.

TABLE 16.6

Average Duration of Stay of Tourists in Kerala

Place	*Domestic Tourists*	*Foreign Tourists*
Thiruvananthapuram	2.5	4.4
Kochi	2.5	4.6
Thekkady/Munnar	2.7	3.5
Kumarakom/Allappuzha	2.2	2.4
Guruvayoor	2.1	2.7
Total	6.5	14.1

Source: Same as Table 16.4.

FIGURE 16.5

District-wise Arrival of Domestic Tourists (1998-2002)

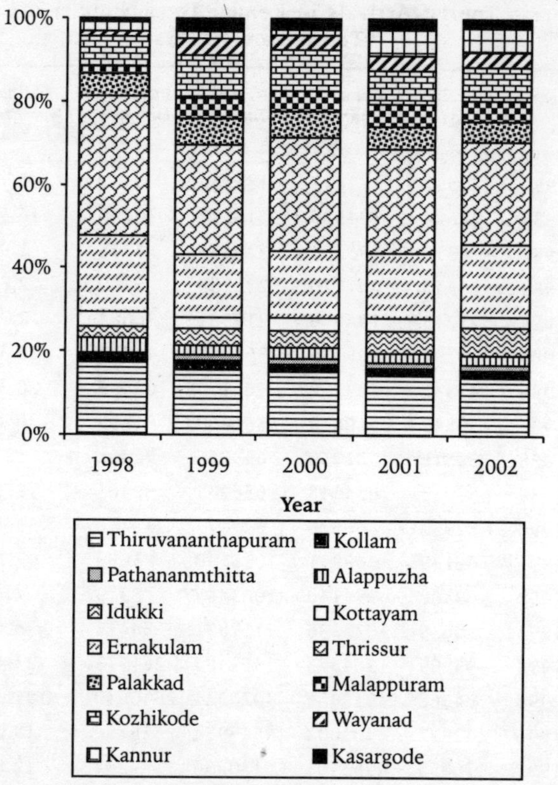

Source: Same as Table 16.4.

The distribution of tourists was favourable to the South and the Central regions. The decision-makers have by and large neglected the Northern region beyond Kozhikode in promoting tourism in the state. Given the fragile ecosystem of Kerala, a balanced development of tourist locations all over the state including the north is essential, particularly since the already famed destinations of Kovalam, Thekkady, Alappuzha, and Kochi are fast reaching saturation levels.

There seems to exist distinct off-seasons and active seasons in the case of foreign tourist arrivals. The period from October to March is the active season and that from April to September, the off-season. The seasonal distribution of the domestic tourists is fairly even all through the year. However, a mild increase in the fourth quarter of the year is noticed in recent years, probably because it happens to coincide with the Sabarimala pilgrimage season.

A major factor affecting tourist arrivals is the state of infrastructure of the state, i.e. accommodation facilities, road conditions, transportation facilities, power and water supply, public sanitation, etc. The state has been found wanting in many of them. The number of foreign tourists travelling by air have come down from 35 per cent in 1994 to 29 per cent in 2002, while that of tourists travelling by rail and road have

FIGURE 16.6

District-wise Arrival of Domestic Tourists (1998-2002)

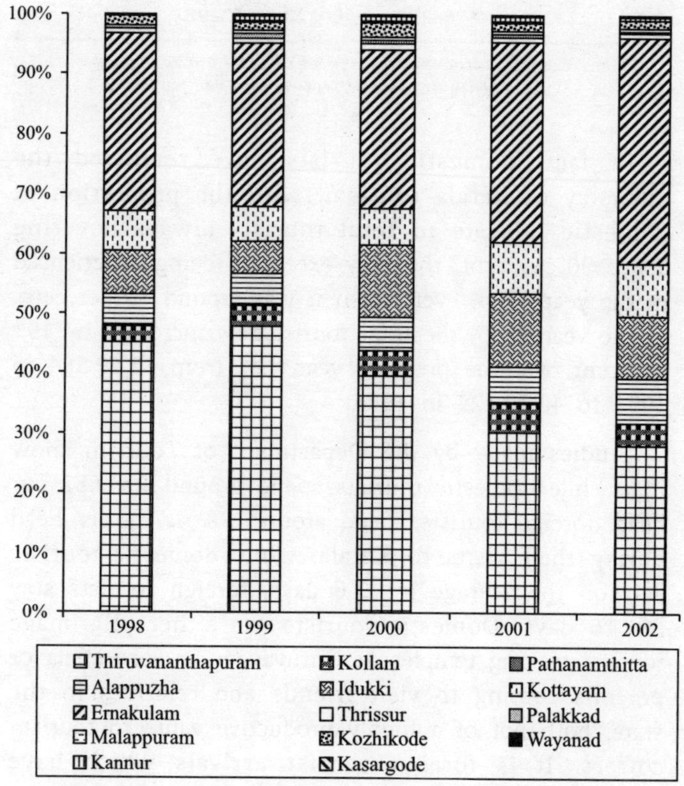

Source: Same as Table 16.4.

FIGURE 16.7

District-wise Arrival of Domestic Tourists (1998-2002)

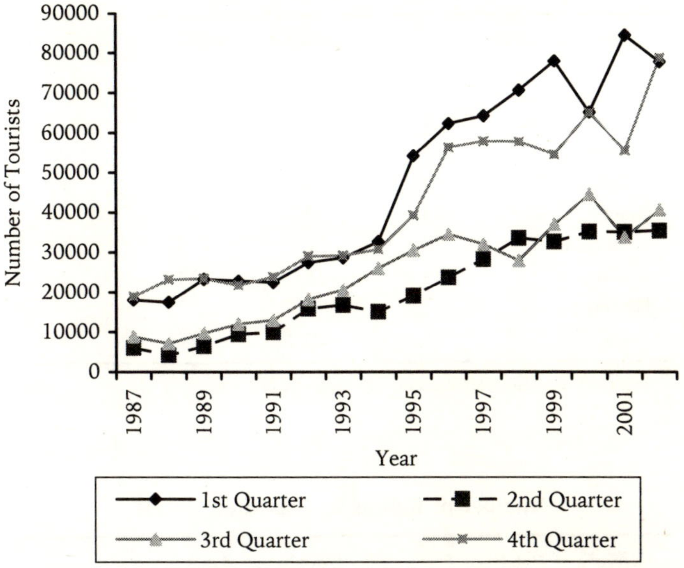

Source: Same as Table 16.4.

TABLE 16.7

District-wise Arrival of Domestic Tourists (1998-2002)

District	*1998*	*1999*	*2000*	*2001*	*2002*
Thiruvananthapuram	781477	755897	763345	749968	775225
Kollam	80279	110569	96103	90490	91331
Pathananmthitta	25470	76311	67041	72267	67514
Alappuzha	157573	111050	127719	121867	139305
Idukki	117267	185579	209639	278081	366861
Kottayam	166814	142143	140320	161828	160269
Ernakulam	802060	734837	810527	819442	961820
Thrissur	1506424	1285029	1376692	1317797	1369419
Palakkad	246576	301861	300888	274716	266438
Malappuram	78072	250326	241740	285326	272911
Kozhikode	325877	499062	496060	424531	442602
Wayanad	62974	190559	171040	170880	202291
Kannur	82160	96918	76565	326632	317879
Kasargode	48691	148146	135542	145867	134391
Total	4481714	4888287	5013221	5239692	5568256

Source: Same as Table 16.4.

gone up from 62 per cent to 65 per cent during the same period. There has occurred a gradual decrease over the years in the number of tourists travelling to the state by ship.

The opening of the Konkan railway has brought about a major reduction in the travel time from different parts of the country to Kerala and has boosted domestic travel. Since several roadways of the state as well as of the country are yet underdeveloped, tourists prefer in general railways to roadways.

TABLE 16.8

District-wise Break up of Foreign Tourist Arrivals

District	*1998*	*1999*	*2000*	*2001*	*2002*
Thiruvananthapuram	86035	96536	82803	63197	65240
Kollam	5068	7430	8997	9970	8478
Pathanamthitta	45	141	208	148	177
Alappuzha	9878	10478	12013	12871	17261
Idukki	13631	10719	24842	25385	24692
Kottayam	13006	11832	12876	17744	20488
Ernakulam	56199	55546	55819	69972	87357
Thrissur	1507	1634	2057	1950	1979
Palakkad	821	1512	1517	809	611
Malappuram	251	855	856	964	1048
Kozhikode	2944	2968	5159	3232	3076
Wayanad	98	449	561	630	563
Kannur	257	1271	1415	1197	1014
Kasargode	151	802	810	761	580
Total	189941	202173	209933	208830	232564

Source: Same as Table 16.4.

FIGURE 16.8

Quarterly Break up of Domestic Tourist Arrivals

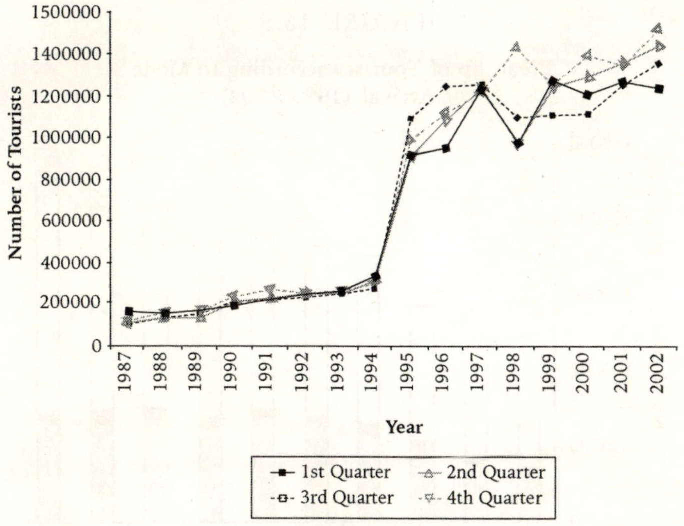

Source: Same as Table 16.4.

Accommodation facilities in Kerala have been increasing steadily over time albeit at a slow pace. Under the classified group of hotels, the number of 5-

star deluxe hotels have increased from 1 in 1999 to 2 in 2002, of 5-Star non-deluxe hotels from 4 to 5, of 4-Star hotels from 9 to 10, of 3-Star hotels from 24 to 60, and of 2-star hotels from 35 to 41; but the number of 1-Star hotels decreased from 24 to 21 and of heritage hotels grown from 7 to 9 in the same period. It is thus the 3-star category of hotels that has registered the highest rate of growth of more than 35 per cent, a fact which shows that it is the budget travellers who comprise the majority of the market. In the case of bed availability, the highest rate of growth was registered in the 5-star deluxe segment where an addition of just one hotel has brought about growth of 170 per cent, while those in the 5-star and the 1-star category have been showing decline. Kochi has the maximum concentration of both categories of 5-star hotels.

Tourism had remained gravely neglected in the state till the 1980's. It was in 1986 that tourism was first announced as an industry. But Kerala was the first state in the country to declare tourism an industry, the first to set up agencies for tourism development, the first to patent slogans, and the first to formulate a tourism policy. The state has also been winning national as well as international accolade for the developments it has made on the tourism front.

All this accolade may be attributed to the organisational set up under which development activities on tourism have been taking place in the state.

FIGURE 16.9

Break up of Tourists according to Mode of Arrival (1993-2002)

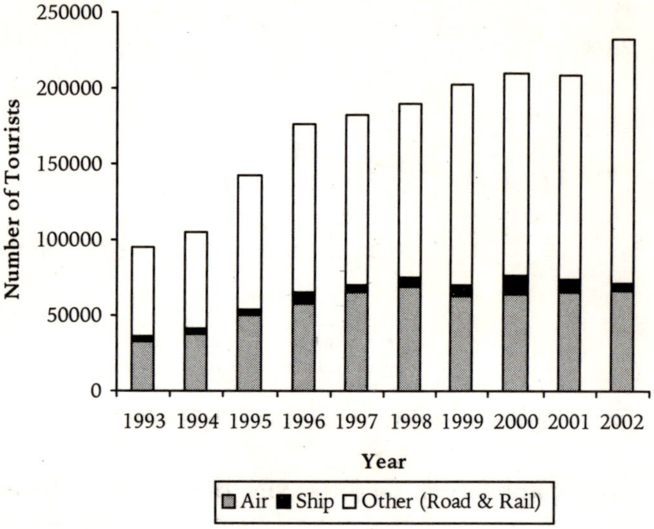

Source: Same as Table 16.9.

TABLE 16.9

Number of Classified Hotels

Category of Hotel	*Number of Hotels*			
	1999	*2000*	*2001*	*2002*
5 Star Deluxe	1	1	1	2
5 Star	4	6	6	5
4 Star	9	9	9	10
3 Star	24	39	46	60
2 Star	35	36	34	41
1 Star	24	24	24	21
Heritage	7	7	7	9
Total	104	122	127	148

Source: Tourism Department, Government of Kerala.

TABLE 16.10

Number of Rooms in Classified Hotels

Category of Hotel	*Number of Hotels*			
	1999	*2000*	*2001*	*2002*
5 Star Deluxe	93	93	93	247
5 Star	445	594	594	373
4 Star	571	571	571	544
3 Star	1010	1555	2094	2374
2 Star	938	919	848	1130
1 Star	740	728	728	681
Heritage	112	112	112	234
Total	3909	4572	5040	5583

Source: Same as Table 16.9.

TABLE 16.11

Number of Beds in Classified Hotels

Category of Hotel	*Number of Beds*			
	1999	*2000*	*2001*	*2002*
5 Star Deluxe	183	183	183	494
5 Star	843	1141	1141	752
4 Star	904	904	904	1108
3 Star	1872	2892	3867	4571
2 Star	1758	1740	1604	2219
1 Star	1312	1290	1290	1208
Heritage	290	290	290	423
Total	7162	8440	9279	10775

Source: Same as Table 16.9.

Tourism Institutions in the State

It is necessary that tourism destinations have adequate infrastructure, enough human resource support and an able agency to ensure development of the area. The quality of the organisation and the manpower involved in the process of tourism promotion are pivotal for the success of tourism marketing of a destination. From the point of view of effective organisation and efficient work force, Kerala is observed to be strong. Kerala has been able to develop a huge workforce committed to cater to the requirements of domestic and foreign tourists and an organisation committed to the development of tourism in the state. A summary view of the organisational support and the framework that has made Kerala tourism a global success is presented below.

Tourism Department

The state tourism department acts as the nodal agency for tourism development planning, publicity and marketing. This department had existed under the State Guest Department in the erstwhile Travancore state and under the Hospitality Organisation in the erstwhile Cochin state. These agencies had the duty of maintaining official buildings and palaces, and looking after royal guests. The State Guest Department had been functioning in Travancore since the 1930s. After the formation of the Kerala state, these two separate organisations were merged into one in 1958. It still handles the hospitality duties as well, along with tourism promotion. It was renamed in 1981, the Department of Tourism.

The Department of Tourism has three main functions.

- Hospitality management of the State government,
- Estate Office Duty, and
- Tourism Development.

It was in the 1980s that a major shift took place in emphasis from hospitality management to tourism development. The budget allocation for tourism development is done mainly under the following heads:

- Marketing & Promotion,
- Planning & Development and
- Support to other agencies.

The Department is the coordinator of these functions and a facilitator for other agencies. It is also involved in Human Resources Development, investment Promotion, Enactment of Legislative Measures, etc. It also endeavours to attract investors to less developed areas in the state.

FIGURE 16.10

Growth of Hotels

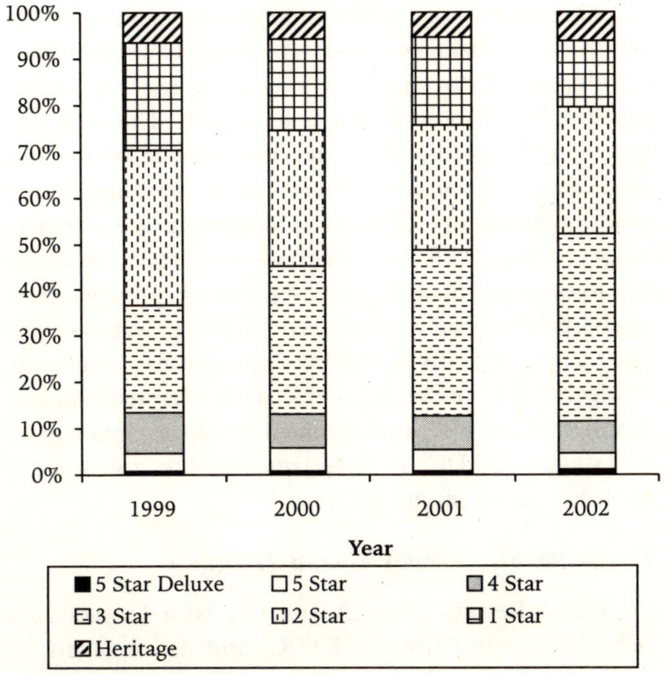

Source: Same as Table 16.9.

Kerala Tourism Development Corporation (KTDC)

The Kerala Tourism Development Corporation is involved in building the infrastructure needed for developing tourism in the state. It has more than 60 properties across the state that includes a range of luxury and budget hotels as well as *yatri nivases* and motels. It has the largest chain of hotels in the state. Almost all these exclusive properties are set in exotic theme locales across the state and all the properties have multi-cuisine restaurants, bars and coffee shops. The department also conducts tours to different tourist spots. During the initial years, it served also as the major instrument for direct government investment.

Bekal Resorts Development Corporation (BRDC)

Bekal, in Kasargod district, was identified as a potential locale for a beach resort destination, following a survey conducted by the Government of India, in 1990. In 1992, Bekal was declared a 'Special Tourism Area'. In 1995, the Bekal Resort Development Corporation (BRDC) was formed for the implementation of the Bekal Tourism Project. Six resort sites have been prepared on a 100 acre area, of which two have already been allotted to the Taj and the Oberoi groups. Detailed planning has been done with a view to avoiding disturbance to the eco-balance of the region, which makes Bekal the first site with such in-depth planning.

The main objective of BRDC is to elevate Bekal to a beach destination of international standard.

Other than the infrastructure development in Bekal, many other areas of tourist interest have also been developed in the vicinity, such as in the nearby beaches, an aqua park and a boat club. The area also has immense potential for the development of *Ayurvedic* medicinal centres, amusement parks, heritage homes, traditional crafts, etc. Besides identifying the potential resort sites, BRDC's persuasive role includes strengthening of the existing infrastructure, (i.e., roads, power supply, sanitation, lighting, water supply etc.), inviting investors and promoters, devising strategies for marketing Bekal as a planned tourism destination as well as coordination of development at all stages. BRDC is also responsible for speedy implementation of the project.

Tourist Resorts (Kerala) Limited (TRKL)

Tourist Resorts (Kerala) Ltd. has been formed as a subsidiary company of KTDC and is engaged in implementing projects such as investment in joint venture companies, promotion of land banks, etc. TRKL maintains a list of properties available for the tourism industry, and which facilitate investment by interested parties.

Recently, the State Government decided to merge the Bekal Resorts Development Corporation (BRDC) with the Tourist Resorts Kerala Ltd. (TRKL). While BRDC has an excellent resource base and skilled personnel, TRKL has excellent partnerships with the Taj and the Oberoi groups of hotels. The new Corporation will exist as a separate entity or as a subsidiary of KTDC.

District Tourism Promotion Councils

The District Tourism Promotion Councils were set up in every district to develop lesser known tourist centres.

Modified Tourism Policy in the State

Tourism is increasingly recognised as the backbone of the Kerala economy. The poor prospects of the manufacturing sector, the threats encountered by the agricultural and industrial sectors, and the poor prospects of growth of the expatriate receipts from Non Resident Keralites (NRKs) are making tourism an instrument of development of the state. Tourism also has made Kerala renowned all over the world as the 'God's Own Country'. Employment generated in tourism is estimated to be about seven lakh persons.

Tourism was recognised as an industry in the state in 1986. The first Tourism Policy of the State was announced in 1995. The main aim of the policy was to serve as a guiding force for making maximum use of Kerala's tourism potential and also to make it an ideal instrument for social and economic growth. The focus of the policy was on the development of the following four aspects:

- Infrastructure.
- Tourism products.
- Human resources, and
- Marketing.

Infrastructure Development

Large-scale investment in infrastructure is a pre-requisite for boosting tourist arrivals. A Tourism Investment Agency was proposed to be set up to ease off red-tapeism in the process of sanctioning investments, and, thus, to act as a bridge between potential investors and interested institutions.

Grihasthali, a programme to encourage people to convert traditional homes into heritage accommodations for tourists, was begun.

Another novel step was the 'Destination Kerala Programme' proposed for the wholesome development of select destinations in the state.

Tourist Centres Listed in the Destination Kerala Scheme

The following are the tourism centres listed in the Scheme.

Thiruvananthapuram city, Kovalam, Ponmudi, Varkala, Kollam, Palaruvi, Alappuzha, Kumarakom, Thekkady, Munnar, Kochi city, Kalady, Aluva, Guruvayoor, Malampuzha, Nelliyampathy, Nilambur, Parambikulam, Kozhikode city, Kappad, Kadalundi, Wayanad, Muzhappilangad and Bekal.

Special tourism schemes were declared for the promotion of areas with potential, such as the Kollam-Alappuzha waterways. A proposal was also made to start a helicopter service under the private sector or as a joint venture to inaccessible areas, given the undulating nature of the Kerala landscape. The emphasis on quality tourism more than quantity tourism calls for further investments in luxury coaches and revision of tax structure. A special backwater tourism plan was to be drawn up for implementation, so as to promote the backwaters in Kerala as a unique tourism product. Attempts to rope in foreign collaboration and assistance in tourism marketing were also to be considered.

Tourism Product Development

Concerted efforts are required for preserving as well as for reviving traditional handicrafts and art forms. A right balance has to be struck between local expertise and international tastes. Training programmes need to be initiated for craftsmen in designing, packaging, etc.

A self-employment scheme has been launched in the tourism sector in collaboration with the Kerala Financial Corporation. The government lays stress on creating employment through development of tourism. The Tourism Regulation Act is to be strictly enforced for ensuring the security of tourists. The Tourism Department protects historical monuments which are not yet under the custody of the Archaeological Survey of India or the Archeology Department of the state.

Human Resource Development

Tourism is an industry that involves intensive interpersonal relations which require services of a large number of trained personnel. Kerala Institute of Tourism and Travel Studies (KITTS) and Institute of Hotel Management and Catering Technology (IHMCT) are the two pioneer institutes in this field; there are also several institutes in the private sector. Special training programmes are organised in the tourism department for tourism entrepreneurs and officials as well as for all those who are in regular contact with tourists, such as cab drivers and traffic police personnel. These two pioneering institutions are playing a great role in developing quality manpower for the tourism sector. Both have designed tourism education and training programmes to cater to different strata in the tourism value chain that includes tour operators, hotel personnel, travel agents, cab drivers and boat drivers. These programmes include long duration courses for developing managerial talent as well as short duration courses to enhance skills of managers and ground staff. They also conduct tourism awareness schemes for the public to enable them to create good impressions among tourists, who would then carry with them pleasurable experiences and pleasant images about Kerala. The courses range from those on tourism-related business administration subjects to certificate courses for masseurs. KHIMS conducts courses in catering technology and applied nutrition and also specialises in Indian and Kerala special delicacies.

Market Development

The main objectives of tourism marketing are the promotion of tourist arrivals, both domestic and international, and increase of the time and money they spend within the state, while enabling them to have a close acquaintance with Kerala's life and culture.

The strategy, though focused on the largest source for the Kerala's tourism market *viz*, Western Europe, also addresses other economically strong countries with tourism potential. The promotion is done through participation in travel fairs, advertisements that make use of the electronic media, international seminars, and hospitality to travel writers and tour operators. Another very important function is the speedy dissemination of relevant information to tourists.

Tourism Vision 2025

The new tourism policy was announced in August 2002. The Tourism Vision 2025 "envisages development of Kerala as an up market, high quality tourist destination through optimal use of resources with focus on conserving and preserving heritage and environment." The government is withdrawing from making fresh investments and will only act as a catalyst. The slogan of the tourism vision is "Conserve Nature and Promote Tourism." The targets of the tourism vision are:

- To increase earnings from tourism at the rate of 10 per cent annually.
- To achieve an annual rate of growth of seven per cent in foreign tourist and nine per cent in domestic tourist arrivals.
- To create employment opportunities for 10,000 persons every year.
- To add the required number of hotel rooms in star categories of hotels every year.
- To innovate and promote at least one tourism product/destination every year.

The Action Plan of the Vision 2025 envisages short-term, medium-term and long-term programmes which have the following objectives:

- To elevate tourism as an economic and employment priority of the state.

- To pursue sustainable tourism development with focus on conservation and Preservation of heritage.
- To guarantee quality services in all sectors of tourism.
- To create and develop infrastructure through private sector participation.
- To continue to focus on Backwaters, *Ayurveda* and Ecotourism.
- To concentrate on basic infrastructure and new tourism products.
- To create sufficient quality human resources in the field of tourism within the state.
- To strengthen the institutional mechanism.
- To develop and promote handicrafts, souvenirs, artefacts and the shopping industry.
- To enact proper legislation to sustain the industry and to regulate tourism activities.
- To explore and develop new markets for Kerala tourism products at domestic and international levels.
- To conserve and preserve the cultural heritage of the state, and
- To ensure safety and security of tourists.

Preservation of the art, culture and heritage of the state is part of the policy objectives. Special tourism zones are identified and measures taken to preserve and conserve them.

Given the cost-effectiveness of medical treatment in India as compared to facilities abroad, the national focus on health tourism to lure foreign tourists, has also opened new vistas for Kerala. Though *Ayurveda* remains an USP for Kerala tourism, the presence of many super- specialty hospitals in the state also helps in attracting foreign visitors.

Ecotourism Initiatives in Kerala

The Western Ghats of Kerala with their tropical forest ecosystem provide a natural advantage for development of this segment of tourism. Ecotourism initiatives help accelerating growth of tourism in Kerala. The Western Ghats regions of Kerala are projected as an Ecotourism zone. Ecotourism projects the concept of sustainability in the tourism sector where there is a balance between nature and the people living around it. Kerala has 12 wildlife sanctuaries and two national parks. They form the basis for ecotourism planning. The biological diversity of the state is an added advantage. The water bodies formed within the forest areas provide scope for developing recreational facilities. Mountaineering, trekking and bird-watching programmes are planned around vast stretches of greenery of the Western Ghats. These destinations have a location advantage of being close to the sea and having well-developed road networks up to the forest area and well-trained forest staff with expert knowledge in wildlife and ecotourism.

A well-informed public and numerous conservation groups help in moderating the adverse impacts of ecotourism related development. The Thenmala Ecotourism Development Project covers the southern part of Kerala. The objectives of this project are to develop Thenmala and its surroundings into a major tourist destination and to promote ecotourism on the basis of sound principles of ecological sustainability. The vast stretches of greenery and biological diversity make Kerala a very good destination for eco-tourists.

Several measures to develop the tourism infrastructure including direct air connections from the major tourism markets to the three International Airports in the state are also being implemented. All major tourist roads are proposed to be developed on a BoT basis for which rationalisation of many existing laws is also required.

Attempts are also being made to market the products of the state at the national as well as the international levels. Steps in this direction are made by patenting such logos as 'God's Own country' as the baseline and logos as well as other products associated with Kerala Tourism such as 'Kerala Travel Mart', 'India International Boat Show', *'Nishagandhi Festival'* and 'Evergreen Kerala'. Kerala Tourism has become the first Tourism Board in India to get registered.

Kerala Tourism – A Pioneer

Kerala has been a pioneer among the states of the India in developing a model tourism package. Though it was a latecomer into tourism development, it has done more than any other state in India in building up a brand value for itself. It has learnt from the mistakes committed by others and has brought in several innovations which other states might like to emulate. The achievements of the state include the following:

- The first state to announce tourism as an industry.

- Focussed marketing of its strengths – ABC.
- WTTC's first partner state.
- Innovative programmes such as *Grihasthali* and Destination Kerala Programme.
- Patenting of products and logos such as 'Kerala Travel Mart' and 'God's own country'.
- First Tourism Board to get registered.
- Public and private sector partnership.
- Use of Electronic Media and Internet for publicity. First tourism body to launch a website; and
- Tourism policy announced as early as in 1995.

New Tourism Thrusts and Goals for Future

In its blueprint for new tourism, the WTTC provides a vision for all interested governments to develop their tourism potentials and opportunities. The development must be on the basis of clearly defined principles such as the ones mentioned below:

- The government must recognise Travel & Tourism as of top priority.
- A balance must be struck between economics on the one hand and people, culture and environment on the other;
- There must be a shared pursuit of long-term growth and prosperity.

The growth of tourism could be inhibited by local conditions of taxation, unhealthy attitudes of the local public towards visitors, poor infrastructure, lack of hygiene, etc. as well as by external factors such as political uncertainty, risk of terrorism, incidence of criminal acts and the high prevalence rates of epidemics. While solutions to the latter type of maladies exist at the national level, the solutions for the former have to be sought at the local levels themselves. Everyone involved in tourism related activities has to have a through understanding of the potentials of this sector and must take full responsibility for contributing towards the social goal.

For realising the full benefits of tourism development, cooperation and coordination between the private and the public sector mechanisms is essential. Such a movement will also help reducing the risks of external events.

The state government has been by and large successful in understanding the importance of the tourism sector to the state economy, but is yet to assign it top priority. Travel and tourism must be factored into all policies and decision-making. Structures and funding should be reorganised so that there will be effective planning and management. Leadership must contribute strategies that impact travel and tourism positively. Measures must be devised to reduce the negative impact of external factors on the industry. The government must encourage investment, facilitate innovation and job opportunities, and guarantee respect for the local environment, culture and well-being. Special care must be given for sustaining the natural assets as well as the cultural resources. The focus must be on long-term development with emphasis on infrastructure development.

The WTTC calls for policy recommendations to be taken up by the government in consultation with municipal authorities and the private sector, for sustainable development. Unplanned construction and overcrowding of beaches need to be curbed if they are not to lose their appeal. More agencies such as BRDC should be constituted for integrated development of tourist destinations. Such development agencies must draw up master plans for the areas using the help of experts and professionals such as architects and landscape artists. They must also look into the construction of essential infrastructure such as good approach roads, transport and accommodation facilities, power, water and sewage systems.

While the potential of the numerous water bodies of the state needs to be harnessed without leading to their over-exploitation, through the launching of luxury boats, cruise boats, house boats, yachts etc., extreme care should be taken to see that the fragile ecosystem is not disturbed with overcrowding. Transport must be so designed as to ensure that their varied features appeal to different pockets and tastes. Tie-up with neighbouring coastal countries may prove to be of help in bringing in more revenue if luxury cruise routes are mapped out and navigated. Introduction of water sports is also likely to be appealing to high-end tourists.

Kerala has been basking under the success of its *mantra* of ABC—*Ayurveda*, Backwaters and Culture and Cuisine. However, care must be taken to ensure that the pursuance of this *mantra* is not overdone. Government must see that *Ayurveda* practitioners have proper licences and that no illegal or anti-social activities are conducted in the name of *Ayurveda*. A list of all fairs and festivals would help tourists in planning their itinerary. Special thrust on the festivals during the off-season period would help tide over the off-season pall.

The total expenditure on tourism by the state as well as by the central government has been around a mere 1 per cent of GDP. The proportion is expected to grow merely by 0.1 per cent in the next 10 years. The rate of increase has to be enhanced.

Tourism Development Expenditures under Five Year Plans in Kerala

The following are the major heads of tourism expenditure in the Five Year Plans.

- Tourism Infrastructure.
- Tourist Accommodation.
- Tourist Transport Services.
- Promotion & Publicity of Tourism.
- Assistance to PSUs & Other Undertakings.
- Other Expenditure.
- Direction & Administration, and
- Training.

Plan allocation for Tourism has registered significant increase from Rs. 17.30 crore in 1995-96 to Rs. 80 crore during 2002-2003 (Table 16.12).

TABLE 16.12

State Plan Allocation

Year	*Allocation (in crores)*
1995-96	17.30
1996-97	29.20
1997-98	36.00
1998-99	37.20
1999-2000	36.00
2000-01	46.00
2001-02	40.00
2002-03	80.00

Source: Same as Table 16.2.

Central Financial Assistance for Promotion of Tourism in Kerala

It is not possible without adequate resources to build a site from scratch into a choice destination of global tourists. In such an endeavour, the cooperation of the central government in the form of investments and plan allocations is essential. The amounts received by Kerala by way of central assistance for tourism development are shown in Table 16.13.

TABLE 16.13

Central Financial Assistance

Year	*Rs in Crore*
1995-96	2.10
1996-97	2.36
1997-98	2.77
1998-99	6.99
1999-2000	9.30
2000-01	5.93
2001-02	4.39

Source: Same as Table 16.2.

During the period 1995-96 to 2001-02, central financial assistance to the tourism sector in Kerala increased from Rs. 2.10 crore to Rs. 4.39 crore, by more than 109 per cent. Necessarily, the public as well as the private investment in the sector needs to be increased. Special attention must be given also to improve the tourism transport facilities.

Proper training is required for the manpower of the industry. Institutes such as KIITS, KIHMS and IHMCT have to be developed into centres of excellence with special emphasis on tourism-related education.

Kerala also suffers from low air connectivity. Foreign airlines are constrained by seat capacity. A liberal airline policy is required for developing air access to the state. High levels of service taxes practised in the state as compared to those in other states, form another barrier to development of tourism. While taxes are 7.5 per cent for the non air-conditioned and 15 per cent for the air-conditioned rooms, sales tax is 9.2 per cent on food, 100 per cent on imported liquor and 10 per cent on locally manufactured alcoholic beverages. Such prohibitive tax rates need to be lowered appropriately for promotion of tourist arrivals.

The objectives outlined in the tourism vision for the state have included all the ingredients of proper development of the tourist industry. However, for the realization of all these goals, joint efforts by all stakeholders are required. All the impediments to development such as infrastructure hurdles, pollution, congestion and legislative hurdles need to be removed so that development would become a smooth process.

Conclusion

The problems that inhibit the growth of tourism in the state may be grouped into inadequacy of basic infrastructure and transport facilities. Particularly, airport facilities in the state have to be vastly improved.

The majority of the airlines in Europe and the USA are dynamically moving towards co-branding and marketing lesser-treaded destinations like Kerala in composite packages. So the marketers of Kerala tourism should look for wholesale deals than retail sales in which individual tourists book their destinations in Kerala. There should be an attempt to do corporate sales in the foreign countries and to link performance measures of employees with visits to Kerala like it is being done with Bahamas and Tobago Islands. There should be an attempt in Kerala to tie up with European airlines for promotion of foreign tourist arrivals in Kerala. Attempts are also essential to create facilities for the landing and the maintenance of chartered planes.

Though there has been an improvement in the bed capacity of the hotels, the investment patterns and the type of hotels that have come up do not serve to augment high value tourism in Kerala, undoubtedly in areas other than in the Central Kerala region. Kerala needs to think seriously about the possibility of increasing FDI flows into the development of quality hotels and catering facilities in Kerala. The hotel sector in Kerala suffers from seasonality factors and high labour turn over. There have not been enough attempts by hoteliers to build strong hotel brands in foreign countries. They have just piggybacked on the success of Kerala Tourism and made profits; but brand-building efforts are found missing from individual promotion campaigns. There is also need for establishment of independent and isolated hotel units rather than hotel complexes in Kerala, particularly in Central Kerala for providing privacy and exclusivity to tourists. The government should also monitor the reactions and impressions of tourists through a compulsory monitoring system so that the cases of tourist dissatisfaction and cases of theft and duping could be minimised in Kerala.

Special interest tourism is an emerging area of interest all the word over. Kerala has a huge potential to develop special interest tourism programmes related to ethnic biodiversity and flora and fauna trips. The land structure also supports the promotion of sports and adventure tourism. Specific routes could be planned for trekking trips through the Western Ghats and lush green tea and coffee gardens of Central Kerala. Initiatives along these lines have to be made in collaboration with local governments to make sure that proper equilibrium is maintained and that both the local governments and the tourism department gain from this process. The tourism department has to plan for quality manpower and for eliminating labour shortages that may arise in the future due to larger tourist inflows. The tourism industry should try to achieve sustainable development without disturbing its gifts of nature, the attraction of which brings the tourist to the state. Protection of such resources is possible by involving the common man in the tourist industry and making him aware of the value of tourism for the economic upliftment of Kerala. Development of cultural tourism will help in offering a long-term and sustainable growth path.

The path to success is graphically laid down in the tourism-planning document of the state. Growth should come through proper destination planning, marketing and promotion, development of new and special products with sustainable competitive advantage and development of the road and rail transport and the airline sectors. Special-event-marketing would also attract tourists to the state for which we have to showcase the centuries old practices and cultural heritage of the state. The promotion of ecotourism in Kerala and the showcasing of the conservation and ecological balance that Kerala has developed over the years has also to be diligently pursued.

Chapter 17

Local Self-government

Studies on 'Kerala Model of Development' generally attribute its successes to the legacy of 'public action' (Dreze and Sen, 1989). The history of democratisation of Kerala society and the role of 'public action' in it has been too well documented to require any discussion in detail here (Ramachadran, 1996). The recent experiments of democratic decentralisation in Kerala represent one of the latest episodes of this history of democratisation of Kerala society[1]. In essence, it is an attempt at deepening democracy in the state by augmenting the space for 'public action' and peoples' participation in governance in general and planning in particular.

The state government launched the people's campaign for decentralised planning in 1996 and declared that 35 to 40 per cent of the state's plan funds would be devolved in the form of grants-in-aid to the local self governments (LSGs) for formulating and implementing local development plans[2]. The local people and their self-governments were given the right to use the plan grant-in-aid, and additional resources mobilised locally, for formulating and implementing local development plans on their own. Since it was a pioneering initiative in the national history of planning in India, the process of local level planning initiated in Kerala did not have well-established models, or time-tested methodologies, to emulate. The state government, the LSGs and the volunteers at the local level had to learn almost everything related to participatory planning from below, by trail and error.

The apprehensions that the local communities and their governments would not be able to live up to the challenge of local level planning and development, administration were proved wrong by the experience of the state. The LSGs in Kerala were able to evolve a fairly elaborate methodology for participatory plan formulation and implementation for local level development. And they planned and implemented annual plans throughout the Ninth Plan period (1997-2002). Further, in spite of the change in government, the participatory approach to local level planning has been sustained and carried out into the Tenth Five-year Plan period.

The picture emerging from the experience of the participatory local level planning in Kerala is not one of unmixed success. The processes and outcomes of the experiment in terms of different indicators of analysis vary significantly across different tiers of local government, among local self-governments belonging to the same level/tier, and among regions. Similarly, the levels of performance have varied significantly across different components of the experiment. The LSGs in Kerala have become interesting sites for detailed studies on participatory local level planning. In this chapter, an attempt is made to draw lessons from the Kerala experiment, which will be of some use not only for the ongoing exercise within Kerala, but also for efforts at democratic decentralisation of governance and planning in other parts of the world.

A major hurdle that local level planning encounters in Kerala is the absence of reliable local level database. The statistical system of the state is tuned to the requirements of the centralised system of planning and

1. The new experiment of democratic decentralisation cannot be traced to the same kind of popular pressure from below as had been in the case of land reforms and other such progressive initiatives in the past. No major struggles or mobilisation campaigns of the people were waged to realise participatory decentralisation. But, it was for long a prominent slogan and electoral promise of almost every political party in the state, a fact which indirectly reflected the public opinion in favour of participatory decentralisation.

2. The state is administratively divided into 14 districts, 61 *taluka*, 152 blocks and 1452 revenue villages. Kerala has also 990 village *panchayats*, 152 block *panchayats* and 14 district *panchayats*, besides 53 town municipalities and 5 city corporations.

governance. It provides data on a large number of variables at the district, the state, and the national levels, but, hardly anything at levels below the district. Even though the state government has sought to overcome this limitation in different ways the problem of paucity of data continues to plague the process of planning from below. Obviously, local planning also encounters the problem of paucity of reliable data. For the present study, therefore, we have sought to supplement the data available from the State Planning Board, with data collected through a sample survey of 72 *gram panchayts.*[3]

Setting the Environment

Kerala has a fairly long-drawn-out legislative history in local self-governance. During the period since Independence, several attempts were made to put in place a genuine system of LSGs. None of these, however, could leave a lasting impact. It was the 73rd and the 74th amendments to the Constitution of India enacted in 1993 that revived the efforts at deepening democracy by strengthening *panchayat raj* and *Nagarapalika* institutions. These amendments accorded constitutional status to local self-governments of the country and made periodic elections to them mandatory.

The highlights of the 1993 constitutional amendments are the following:

- Reservation of seats to Scheduled Castes and Scheduled Tribes (SC and ST) according to their shares in the population; one-third of the reserved seats to be allotted to women belonging to SC and ST communities.
- Reservation of one-third of the general seats for women.
- Reservation to the posts of office-bearers for SC and ST communities and women.
- Provision for appointment of State Finance Commission every five years to make recommendations regarding devolution of financial resources.
- Provision for appointment of independent State Election Commission for overseeing election to local self-governments.

Even though the constitutional amendments were a landmark in the history of local self-governments and set the broad contours of a genuine democratic and equitable system of local governance, they left most of the details of the new system to be taken care of by the state governments concerned. The state governments were supposed to follow up the constitutional changes with appropriate state level legislation. Accordingly, Kerala Panchayat Raj Act, 1994 and Kerala Municipality Act, 1994 were enacted in the state. These acts marked a major step forward in the history of devolution of powers and responsibilities to the lower levels of governance in the State. An important change ushered in by the 1994 acts - besides the points highlighted in the discussion on the constitutional amendments—has been the detailed listing of functions, responsibilities and powers to be transferred to the LSGIs.

The 1994 Acts of Kerala had some important limitations too. They were drafted and enacted in a hurry to meet the deadlines stipulated by the Constitution. Further, they did not correctly anticipate the enormity of the extensive programme of participatory planning from below that would be started in 1996. In order to overcome these limitations and to suggest changes to be brought about in the Acts, the state government appointed a committee under the chairmanship of S.B. Sen in 1996 (Sen Committee). The Sen Committee submitted detailed recommendations for amending the 1994 Acts and also for empowering the local self-governments in the state to take up planning responsibilities. The 1999 amendment to the Acts were meant mainly to give more autonomy to the local bodies, by reducing the state's power to interfere and regulate, so that local bodies would get transformed into genuine local self-governments. For instance, the State Election Commission was accorded more autonomy by augmenting its powers to delimit wards/constituencies independently of the state government. Similarly, most of the provisions relating to state government's power of intervention in the affairs of the local bodies were done away with.

Another important contribution of the 1999 amendments was the strengthening of the *Grama Sabha* (local assembly of voters). This was done by assigning well-defined powers to *Grama Sabhas*. However, as the state government's powers to intervene and regulate local governments were drastically cut, there was need for alternative institutional mechanisms to deal with grievances against local self-governments. The 1999 amendment sought to fill in this gap by establishing

3. For the present study, extensive use has been made of the data obtained from a primary survey of 72 panchayats undertaken as part of a CDS study during 2002. For details of the sampling procedure see Chaudhuri Shubham, K.N. Harilal and Heller Patrick (2004). Does Decentralisation Make a Difference? A Study of the People's Campaign for Decentralised Planning in the Indian State of Kerala. Project Report, Centre for Development Studies, Thiruvananthapuram.

new independent institutions such as Tribunals and Ombudsman.

The development administration in the state until 1996 had been highly centralised with its characteristic top-down approach. It was the line departments, which formulated plan projects to be taken up in their respective jurisdictions. The State Planning Board used to make the state level plan by prioritising and integrating the plan proposals submitted by the line departments. Implementation of development projects used also to be the prerogative of the line departments. In most cases the people were not accorded any role even at the implementation stage. But in the case of some schemes, especially under the Rural Development Department, beneficiary committees of local people used to be constituted and their participation ensured. The alienation of the people from nation-building activities—from planning and implementation of development programmes—had many widely acknowledged adverse consequences. The development programmes tended to be insensitive to the felt needs as well as the development problems of the people; they failed to take into account local specificities; lack of vigilance from the part of people led to the spread of corruption; and upkeep and maintenance of assets was poor. Another important limitation of the centralised system was the so called departmentalism, a term used to represent lack of coordination and integration of activities of the line departments of the government. Each department worked in isolation, without taking into account the activities of other departments, resulting in duplication of activities, and contradictions and conflicts among departments.

The launching of a new plan—the Ninth Five-year Plan—provided an opportunity for a major shift from the above scenario. An overriding concern of the Ninth Five-year Plan of Kerala was the redressal of the development crisis of the state in its multifarious dimensions. Keeping this consideration in view, the ninth plan put forth a two-pronged strategy—the state-level plan to be implemented through the line departments of the government and the local-level plan to be formulated and implemented by the lSGs. The division of responsibilities and powers was based on the guiding principle that everything that can be done efficiently at the local level should be done so by maximising peoples' participation and that only the rest of the things should be taken up at the state level. The state level plan, therefore, was supposed to take up general development problems, requiring centralised planning, mobilization of resources and implementation of activities such as power generation, state highways and higher education. Local plans were supposed to address problems in which local specificities and direct participation of people are of prime importance.

According to the Kerala Acts of 1994 (as amended in 1999), lSGs belonging to higher tiers do not have any hierarchical control over lower tiers (see Chart 17.1). Village *panchayats* are not controlled by block *panchayats* and block *panchayats* are not under the supervision of district *panchayats*. In order to ensure coordination among the different lSGs in a district, the Acts provide for a District Planning Committee (DPC). DPC is empowered to make district perspective plan, besides co-ordinating plans prepared by rural as well as urban LSGIs.

The ninth five-year plan marked a major break also in the fiscal history of the country. The programme of democratic decentralization introduced dramatic changes in the financial profile of lSGs. Table 17.1 presents data on total plan grants made to LSGs between 1997 and 2001. Around 35 per cent of the state's plan budget was earmarked for local governments.

FIGURE 17.1

Kerala: Local Governance Structure

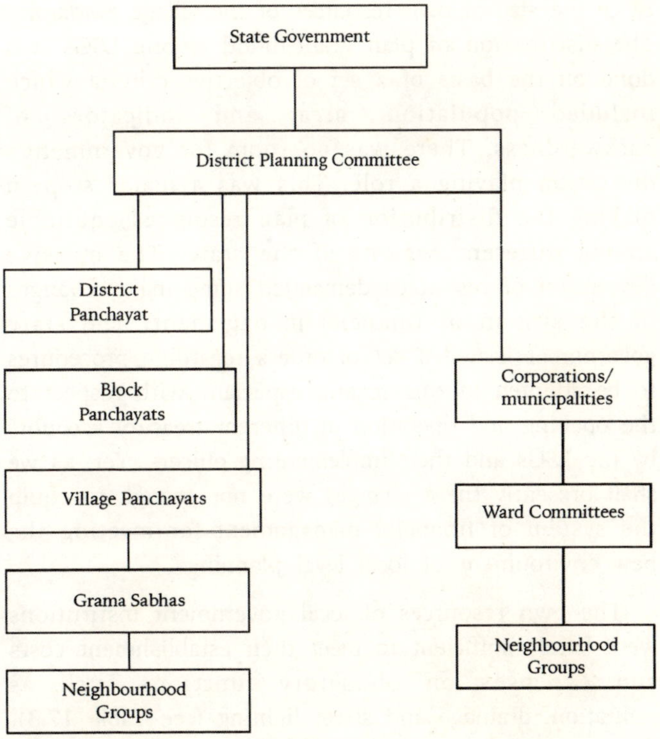

TABLE 17.1

Total Plan Grants to LSGs (Rs. Million)

Year	*State Plan Size*	*Village Panchayat*	*Block Panchayat*	*District Panchayat*	*Municipality*	*Corporation*	*LSGI Total*	*LSGI Share in State Plan Per cent*
1997-98	28550	5069	3872	1889	153	138	11120	38.95
1998-99	31000	6146	2325	1706	1017	585	11780	38.00
1999-00	32501	6393	2005	1697	895	443	11434	35.10
2000-01	35350	6364	1846	1667	980	567	11424	32.32

Source: Second State Finance Commission Report, Kerala, January 2001.

Interestingly enough, the LSGIs in Kerala had a high level of fiscal autonomy even prior to the launching of the decentralisation experiment in 1996. *Grama panchayats*, for instance, had been levying a variety of taxes including those on property, profession and entertainment, besides receiving revenue from certain important taxes levied by the state government such as basic tax (a general tax on land), surcharge on stamp duty and motor vehicles tax. What decentralisation did was to improve the degree of fiscal autonomy of local governments several fold. A comparison between the total own revenues of *grama panchayats* with the amounts of plan grant-in-aid allotted to them, as illustrated in Table 17.2, would give an idea about the impact that the people's plan campaign had on local finance. The plan grants-in-aid devolved were almost twice the size of own resources of the village *panchayats*. The distribution of plan grant-in-aid among LSGs was done on the basis of a set of objective criteria which included population, area, and indicators of backwardness. There was no room for government's discretion playing a role. This was a major step in making the distribution of plan resources equitable among different regions of the state. The massive devolution of resources demanded some major changes in the system of financial management. The state government issued a set of orders regarding procedures to be adopted in this regard, especially with respect to the opening and operation of different treasury accounts by the LSGs and their implementing officers. Yet, as we shall presently these changes were not enough to equip the system of financial management for meeting the new environment of local level planning.

The own resources of local government institutions were barely sufficient to meet their establishment costs and expenses on obligatory functions such as sanitation, drainage and street lighting (see Table 17.3). The surplus, if any, used to be spent mostly on village roads. This state of affairs explain the background of the lack of visibility of LSGs in the sphere of development planning and governance during the period prior to the decentralisation campaign. The plan grant-in-aid made a big difference not only because of its sheer size but also because it was earmarked entirely for development/plan expenditure.

The resources for local level plans under the people's planning campaign were not limited, however, to the plan grant-in-aid from the state government. LSGs were encouraged to mobilise additional resources so that the plan size could be enlarged.

An important limitation of the centralised system of planning was the absence of efforts to horizontally integrate development activities undertaken by various agencies including the line departments. A major reason for the absence of horizontal integration, and growth of departmentalism, was the absence of genuine democratic institutions of self-governance below the state level. The 73rd and the 74th constitutional amendments and the state level Acts filled this void by strengthening the institutions of local self-governance. The LSGs, however, had to be given various forms of support to be able to integrate development activities undertaken through various agencies. The preparatory steps in this regard included redeployment of a segment of government employees from line departments to the control of LSGs; making local officials of line departments accountable and answerable to LSGs; integration of all centrally sponsored and state sponsored programmes implemented at the local level with the development plans of LSGs, and establishing credit linkages between commercial banks and the local plans. The LSGs were to become in the process, the centralising and integrating interface between different development agencies.

TABLE 17.2

Own Revenue and Plan Grant-in-aid of Village Panchayats

(Rs. Million)

Item	*1993-94*	*1996-97*	*1997-98*	*1998-99*
Total own revenue	1180	2099	2414	2598
Plan grant-in-aid	-	1000	4205	5495

Notes: (i) in 1996-97 Plan grant-in-aid was called United Funds; (ii) Total own revenue includes receipts from own tax, assigned tax, shared tax and non-tax, and grants-in-aid (other than plan grant-in-aid) from state government.

Source: *Second State Finance Commission Report*, Kerala, January 2001.

TABLE 17.3

Expenditure Pattern of Gram Panchayats

(Rs. Million)

Items	*1993-94*	*1996-97*	*1998-99*
Establishment Costs			
Salaries	356 (44)	603 (43)	812 (50)
Office Expenses	40 (5)	72 (5)	117 (7)
Obligatory Duties			
Public Health/Sanitation	7 (1)	73 (5)	81 (5)
Water Supply/Drainage	17 (2)	64 (5)	59 (4)
Street Lighting	81 (10)	100 (7)	116 (7)
Development Works			
Roads	213 (26)	381 (28)	310 (19)
Buildings	26 (3)	23 (2)	34 (2)
Other Amenities	71 (9)	71 (5)	94 (6)
Total	811 (100)	1386 (100)	1623 (100)

Note: Expenditure under People's Campaign not included. Figure in bracket shows percentage.

Source: *Second State Finance Commission Report*, Kerala, January 2001.

For the vertical and horizontal integration of plans and projects prepared by LSGs at different levels in a district, institutional arrangements had to be put in place. The District Level Expert Committee (DLEC) and District Planning Committee (DPC) were expected to support the task of integration. The perspective plan of the district prepared by the DPC was conceived of as the guiding document for coordination and integration.

The local plans invariably involved development projects requiring considerable amounts of technical inputs at different stages starting from project formulation, to preparation of estimates, detailed drawings, implementation, supervision and measurement. The LSGs lacked sufficient technical staff to take care of all these tasks. It was therefore proposed to set up Voluntary Technical Corps (VTC) comprising technical personnel drawn from among retired government officials, teachers belonging to aided colleges, and employees of private sector companies who were competent and ready to offer their services on a voluntary basis. Later, Expert Committees were set up at block (BLEC), district (DLEC), municipality (MLEC) and state levels (SLEC) which included serving government officials and members of VTC. Expert Committees played an important role in technical vetting as well as technical supervision of the process of implementation.

Methodology of Participatory Planning

An important contribution of the Kerala experiment to local level planning is the methodology of participatory planning evolved through a process of learning by doing. It is one thing to theorise on the virtues of participatory planning and quite another to successfully experiment it on the ground. Planning is generally taken as a visionary expert's job. How can the process of planning be demystified? How are the local people going to plan on their own? An initial step in the process of making a local development plan would be to identify development problems/needs. Once the development problems are identified, the task is to search for solutions. Next in the sequence is the task of making viable project proposals. On account of scarcity of resources, it would not be possible to address all the development problems—or to take up all the project proposals—in an annual plan, or for that matter, even in a five-year plan. Prioritisation and selection, therefore, become important. An equally important task at this stage would be of integration. Before the plan is implemented, it has to be ensured that programmes are both vertically and horizontally integrated and made technically viable. The final stages are of implementation, maintenance and auditing. It needs to be emphasised here that the methodology has been evolving over time and continues to do so even now.

The identification of the needs of people and gaps in local development is achieved through discussions at '*grama sabhas*' in *panchayats* and `ward conventions' in municipalities. The average attendance in '*grama sabhas*' used to be low prior to the introduction of decentralised planning. To ensure maximum participation, especially of women and socially and economically backward sections, various propaganda methods are innovated by *panchayats*. Neighbourhood groups, formed for every 25 to 30 households, in many panchayats, also play a major role in the convening of *grama sabhas*. The role of *grama sabhas*, however, is not restricted to identification of development needs. *Grama sabha* meetings are convened to involve people in other aspects of planning including selection of beneficiaries and social auditing.

The key event of the second phase is the development seminar at the *panchayat* or municipal level. It is in the seminar that tentative solutions for various problems identified at *grama sabhas*/ward conventions are arrived at through discussions among people's representatives selected by the *grama sabhas*, members of *panchayat samithi*, local political leaders, key officials of the area and experts from the locality and outside. It is the task of the third phase of the campaign to convert solutions into project/scheme proposals in a format that could be included in the plan. The plan grant-in-aid and the estimates regarding local resources that could be mobilised set the resource limits (budget line) of the local plan. The draft local plan is prepared by selecting projects according to the availability of resources (budget line). The fifth phase is the preparation of plans at block and district level. As noted earlier, the block *panchayats* and the district *panchayats* lack administrative control over the village *panchayats*. As such they do not have any direct means of influencing village level plans. However, they are free to make their plans, taking the nature of village level plans into consideration. Incidentally, the District Planning Committee is supposed to take a lead role in ensuring the integration of plans prepared by all LSGs in the district.

Only a competent authority can guarantee the technical viability of a project. Similarly, an empowered and accountable agency is needed to sanction the estimated cost of the project. Expert committees comprising government officials and technically qualified volunteers are entrusted with the task of giving technical sanction. The expert committee vets each project before according sanction. In case of inadequacy, the expert committee gives detailed advice to LSGs to firm up the project proposal.

The final phase is implementation, monitoring and auditing. The mode of implementation differs according to the nature of the project. In the case of simple projects, implementation is done directly by the LSGs through their own implementing officers. In a large number of cases, works are assigned to the committees of beneficiaries. If beneficiary committees are not coming forward, the work would be contracted out. Regardless of the mode of implementation, transparency norms are insisted upon to encourage public involvement and vigilance. Monitoring committees are constituted for every project. In the case of individual beneficiary projects, beneficiaries are to be selected only through the *grama sabhas*. For auditing, apart from engaging government auditing agencies, reporting of accounts in the *grama sabhas* is mandatory.

The Outcome

The decentralised system of planning in the state has by now become institutionalised. The new system is well backed by constitutional amendments, state acts, approved rules and procedures, a wide variety of organisations, established conventions related to local level planning, and support of the people at large.

A methodology of planning from below has been evolved, field-tested and stabilised. All the LSGIs have been able to formulate and implement their development plans. The methodology, the central features of which have already been institutionalised, however, needs improvement on many counts. Several limitations associated with different phases of the planning process have come to notice to which we shall turn presently.

Measurement of the development impact of decentralisation is difficult, especially within a short time span. Methodologically, three problems present themselves. First, a major part of the available data is unreliable. Most attempts to measure the impact of decentralisation have examined the levels of public spending; but in the absence of established accounting practices, conclusions drawn on the basis solely of expenditure data would be unreliable. What is more, expenditure and outcome are hardly one and the same thing. Second, it is extremely difficult to develop a comparative frame to assess the differential impact of local government. The creation of local government introduces new accounting and record-gathering units, making 'before' and 'after' comparisons virtually impossible. Third, it is difficult to isolate the impact of local government given a range of other confounding variables. To what extent, for instance, could an increase in the quality of local schools be attributed directly to actions of the local government?

Participation

Nevertheless, democratic local governance should not be reduced to a mere means of achieving a few goals of economic development. Significantly enough, the approach, which emphasises participation as an end in itself, is gaining prominence and acceptance (Rehman and Mehman 1998; UNDP, 1993). Personal fulfilment is an integral aspect of human development and hence participation, which allows people to realise their full potential and to make their best contribution to society, and should be seen as an end in itself (UNDP, 1993). Another aspect worth mentioning here is the one related to the new discourse on development. Poverty is not just a lack of physical resources of development; it also implies, among other things, powerlessness or inability to exert influence upon the forces, which shape one's livelihood (Oakley, 1991). There is thus every reason to count participation as an outcome in itself. The great and enthusiastic participation of people in almost every single stage of the planning process has been thus the most important outcome of people's planning in Kerala.

From near invisibility, local people have moved to the centre stage of local level development initiatives. Data collected by the State Planning Board from all the 990 *panchayats* for the first two years of the campaign show that 10.3 per cent of the electorate participated in the first annual *Grama sabhas* in 1996 and 10.6 per cent in 1997. The social composition of the campaign improved drastically in the second year. If in the first year of the campaign SC/ST participation was well below the average for the general population, by the second year, they participated in higher proportions than non-SCs. Similarly, the participation rate of women also registered some improvement, with women constituting 40 per cent of all participants in 1997-98.

While *grama sabhas* serve important functions of communicating basic information and discussing and airing general demands, they do not directly make budgetary decisions. Development seminars and task forces are, on the other hand, deliberative bodies, which make concrete inputs into the planning and budgeting process. Because they are involved in substantive decisionmaking which requires intensive knowledge and skills, these bodies are likely to be influenced by powers that be and to discard and discourage participation of socially and economically weak sections. Indeed, this is what one study (Isaac and Franke, 2000) found in the case of women. In the first year of the campaign itself, women's representation progressively fell as the participatory process as a whole went ahead.

An overall picture of participation, based on data gathered from a sample of *panchayats* at the different levels of participation, is presented in Table 17.4. Overall participation, measured in terms of the participation rate (participants as a proportion of the relevant population), declined from 7.8 per cent in 1997 to 4.7 per cent in 1999. But, interestingly, the social composition of the participants appears to have stabilised.

TABLE 17.4

Social Composition of Participation in the Planning Process

Forum	*Participation Rate (% of Relevant Population)*		
	Overall	*Women*	*SC/ST*
1996 Planning *Grama Sabha*	7.6	4.2	4.4
1997 Planning *Grama Sabha*	7.8	4.3	11.7
1999 Planning *Grama Sabha*	4.7	3.8	5.9
1999 Budgeting *Grama Sabha*	5.3	4.6	6.1
1999 Development Seminar	0.8	0.6	1.1
1999 Taskforce General Body Meetings	0.4	0.2	0.5

Source: Sample Survey.

Data for 1999-00 suggest some improvement in the participation of disadvantaged groups. SC/STs had higher participation rates than the overall population had at all the three levels. In development seminars and task forces, women's participation was, however, much lower than even that of SC/STs.

The foregoing discussion suggests the following general trends:

- Participation differed across regions: there were pockets of low participation.
- Participation has been generally low in urban areas.
- Participation varied across different tasks and stages of the planning process. Participation was the highest in the process of selecting beneficiaries. It was generally low at the stages of implementation and monitoring.
- Persons who participated were not always keen in promoting the public good. Considerations of private benefits tended to dominate.
- The orientation of the process towards the socially and economically marginalised groups has tended to keep the well-off sections away.
- Despite formal participation, women, scheduled castes and scheduled tribes were not in a position to assert their views. Participation of the 'outlier' groups was in general of a nominal nature.

Resource Mobilisation and Expenditure

The resources for local level plans are not limited to the plan grant-in-aid from the state government. Decentralised participatory planning was expected to promote local level resource mobilisation. The additional sources to be tapped by village panchayats include 'own funds' (i.e., surplus from own revenue after discharging traditional functions), allocations of centrally and state-sponsored projects to be implemented in the village, loans from banks and cooperative societies, beneficiary contributions, and voluntary services. Table 17.5 shows a steady decline in the plan funds allotted to LSGs since 1997. Incidentally, the decline gets more pronounced when actual disbursements, which tended to fall steadily on account of fiscal crisis in the state, are considered.

TABLE 17.5

Financing Local Development Plans (per cent)

Item Heads	*1997-98*	*1998-99*	*1999-00*	*2000-01*
Total Plan Fund	77.14	70.90	66.25	65.57
General Fund	57.03	55.45	51.82	51.82
SCP Fund	18.96	13.94	12.94	12.25
TSP Fund	1.15	1.50	1.49	1.51
State Sponsored Schemes	3.14	3.28	4.11	5.53
Central Sponsored Schemes	1.67	2.89	3.23	4.45
Own Fund	5.26	6.90	7.78	11.31
Beneficiary Fund Collected by Panchayat	3.19	4.78	3.75	2.59
Bank Loan General Projects	0.49	0.35	2.58	0.00
Bank Loan Individual Projects	0.07	0.00	0.54	0.06
Cooperative Institutions	0.34	0.06	0.00	0.19
Voluntary Service	2.56	3.53	5.29	2.58
Donation (Purchase of materials)	0.09	0.06	0.04	0.07
Land	0.07	0.10	0.11	0.29
Beneficiary Contribution (as labour)	5.97	7.15	6.32	7.36
Total	100.00	100.00	100.00	100.00

Note: Number of sample *Panchayats* 65.

Source: *Sample Survey* - Panchayat Schedule I.

Financial dependence of local plans on plan grant-in-aid declined from around 77 per cent in 1997-98 to 65 per cent in 2000-01 (see Table 17.5). This trend, however, cannot be attributed to local resource mobilisation alone. The increase in the share of sources other than plan grant-in-aid has come partly from state and centrally sponsored schemes. Funds for the sponsored schemes are made available by either of the governments concerned. Over the years the *grama panchayats* appear to have put in more efforts to integrate sponsored programmes into their local development plans. There is evidence to show, however, that the panchayats have made some serious efforts to mobilise local resources especially from beneficiaries. Alternative definitions of local resource mobilisation are possible. Broadly speaking, local resource mobilisation amounted to 20 to 25 per cent of plan expenditure. The contribution of own funds has increased significantly. The increase in the share of own funds could also be seen as a reflection of higher levels of integration. *Panchayats* have succeeded in integrating some of the traditional development activities (which they used to undertake with own funds), with the local development plans formulated under the campaign. As the data on financial institutions show, village *panchayats* have not been able to ensure the credit link to local development plans. Financial institutions were, in general, reluctant to extend credit to beneficiaries of local development plans. Even though the contribution of voluntary services and contribution of beneficiaries have been substantial, the estimates made on their basis suffer from problems related to valuation made by investigators. The data on beneficiary funds collected by *panchayats* are more reliable. This item accounted for about 3.6 per cent of the total plan expenditure at the local level. Local resource mobilisation (of own funds and beneficiary funds) came to 8 per cent to 14 per cent of the total development outlays under local development plans.

The enthusiasm for additional resource mobilisation for local plans is not found in the collection of local taxes. On the contrary, available evidence supports the view that devolution of resources from higher tiers has dampened the enthusiasm for tax collection at the local level. As data presented in Table 17.6 show, the rate of growth of revenue from taxes levied by village panchayats has declined under the campaign (1996-97 to 1999-00) *vis-à-vis* that under the period immediately prior to it (1991-92 to 1996-97). The decline was quite sharp in the case of building tax and entertainment tax. However, revenue from profession tax grew more rapidly during the second half of the 1990s than during the first half.

Nevertheless, the decline in the rate of growth of revenue collected from taxes at the local level cannot be attributed exclusively to laxity on the part of village *panchayats*. In fact, a similar pattern of decline is noted in the tax revenue of the sate government as well. Further, as both the first and the second State Finance

TABLE 17.6

Growth in Revenue of Village Panchayats (%)

Item Heads	*1991-92–1996-97*	*1996-97–1999-2000*
Panchayat taxes and rates	22.90	8.01
Building tax	22.46	3.35
Entertainment tax	34.13	18.70
Profession tax	12.76	40.46
Realisation under spl. acts	18.22	26.65
Revenue derived from panchayat properties	21.76	45.93
Panchayat fees	85.41	-4.30
Government grants and contributions	73.24	-4.70
Miscellaneous revenue	9.50	129.14
Capital account receipts	97.71	20.98
Debt head account receipts	99.54	-8.86

Note: Number of sample *panchayats* 44.

Source: Sample Survey – Schedule II.

Commissions pointed out, the rates of local taxes have remained unchanged over a long period of time. One exception has been profession tax, revenue from which has been quite buoyant in recent years. Another reason for the decline in tax collection has been the shortage of staff. Those who were responsible for collection of local taxes had to be entrusted with several responsibilities related to the people's campaign. One would, therefore, require more in-depth studies to draw any firm conclusions in the matter.

The gap between plan grant-in–aid (allocation) on the one hand and its expenditure on the other has been increasing over the years, especially over the past three years. As Table 17.7 shows the proportion of grant spent has been as low as 44 per cent in 2002-03. This laxity is explained mainly in terms of the fiscal crisis of the state government and the consequent confusion and delay in the disbursement of the installments of grants to LSGs. If this trend is allowed to continue, it might endanger the very process of decentralised planning. A more disturbing aspect of local plan implementation has been the lower rates of expenditure of the plan grant made under the special component plans. In 2002-03, for instance, the proportion of SCP\TSP grant spent has been as low as around 35 per cent as against 48 per cent in the general category.

Prioritisation and Resource Allocation

The pattern of prioritisation in local plans may be studied in terms of the distribution of funds under plan grant-in-aid or the total plan outlay across sectors. However, the following analysis is made mainly in terms of the distribution of grant-in-aid. The data on the distribution of grant-in-aid across sectors for the local self governments in the state are given in Table 17.8.

Crop Husbandry (8.56%), Animal Husbandry (3.15 %), Soil and Water Conservation (2.71 %), Minor Irrigation (5.33 %), Industries (5.25 %), Education (4.02%), Public Health (2.65%), Drinking Water (6.16%), Sanitation (2.34 %), Housing (19.31 %), Women and Child Welfare (7.29%), Energy (2.12 %), Roads and Bridges (21.02%), and Public Buildings (3.48%), which together account for the lion's share of the grant-in-aid and constitute the leading sub-sectors of the local level plans. The rest of the sub-sectors put together account for only about seven per cent of the grant-in-aid.

TABLE 17.7

Expenditure of Plan Grant-in-aid

(per cent)

Local Government	*1997-98*	*2001-2002*				*2002-2003*				
	Total	*General*	*SCP*	*TSP*	*Total*	*General*	*EFC*	*SCP*	*TSP*	*Total*
Grama panchayats	95.92	68.27	46.27	45.94	63.25	48.06	32.59	36.32	29.16	44.56
Block panchayats	91.97	71.90	44.74	54.50	62.21	53.84	21.43	35.96	33.33	48.21
District panchayats	94.30	54.04	38.60	51.84	48.91	39.91	0.00	32.81	30.34	37.87
Municipality	97.49	64.46	35.54	25.00	59.80	54.40	36.05	23.46	25.00	46.98
Corporation	101.55	57.15	19.69	0.00	50.18	42.87	27.65	22.55	0.00	38.43
Total	95.70	65.84	42.59	49.57	59.93	48.10	32.62	34.37	30.19	44.17

Source: Economic Review various years. Kerala State Planning Board, Thiruvananthapuram.

TABLE 17.8

Sub-sector-wise Distribution of Plan Grant and Total Outlay

Sl.No	Item	Grant-in-aid (in per cent)				Total Outlay (in per cent)			
		1997	1998	1999	2002	1997	1998	1999	2002
1	Crop husbandry	10.25	9.51	7.59	8.56	15.94	10.35	7.11	9.43
2	Animal husbandry	7.57	6.76	3.85	3.15	10.04	6.94	3.69	4.52
3	Fisheries	1.06	1.32	0.84	0.96	1.55	1.45	0.99	1.41
4	Soil and water conservation	2.65	3.96	2.33	2.71	2.43	4.03	3.06	2.49
5	Minor irrigation &Flood control	7.41	10.07	7.02	5.33	5.67	7.48	6.17	4.02
6	Industry	4.81	8.46	6.52	5.25	6.19	7.62	5.48	5.16
7	Others	0.2	0.52	0.16	0.29	0.5	0.39	0.17	0.24
	Productive Sector Total	33.95	40.6	28.31	26.25	42.32	38.26	26.67	27.27
8	Education	4.52	3.19	2.96	4.02	3.4	2.6	2.21	3.77
9	Sports, youth welfare, art and culture	1.61	1.78	1.43	1.18	1.37	1.35	1.29	1.05
10	Health	2.54	2.06	1.81	2.65	1.98	1.83	1.67	2.24
11	Drinking water	7.79	5.02	7.43	6.16	5.61	3.79	4.51	6.56
12	Sanitation	5.14	4	2.85	2.34	5.37	4.73	3.76	3.29
13	Housing	15.15	14.61	24.84	19.31	12.46	14.92	29.02	17.54
14	Women and children welfare	1.01	2.85	3.45	7.29	0.82	1.92	2.1	6.16
15	Others	3.88	4.44	3.58	3.74	7.4	8.05	5.01	3.53
	Service Sector Total	41.64	37.95	48.35	46.69	38.41	39.19	49.57	44.14
16	Energy	3.04	2.68	2.37	2.12	3.04	2.44	1.55	1.58
17	Roads and bridges	19.8	16.71	18.28	21.02	13.8	16.76	18.34	21.93
18	Waiting sheds/Bus stands	0.36	0.38	0.28	0.37	0.57	0.68	0.46	0.64
19	Public buildings	1.12	1.43	2.27	3.48	1.75	2.3	3.24	4.39
20	Others	0.12	0.04	0.14	0.06	0.07	0.14	0.15	0.06
	Infrastructure Sector Total	24.44	21.24	23.34	27.05	19.23	22.32	23.74	28.6
	Grant Total	100	100	100	100	100	100	100	100

Source: Economic Review (various years), Kerala State Planning Board, Thiruvanathapuram.

The apprehension that the LSGs would not be earmarking enough resources for the productive sectors has been proved wrong by experience. On an average, the productive sectors received 30 per cent of the plan grant-in-aid. But, this was made possible mainly by the mandatory guidelines of the state government. Nevertheless, in spite of the guidelines and the awareness campaigns the importance accorded to the productive sectors has been on the decline. All the leading sub-sectors in the productive sector, *viz.*, crop husbandry, animal husbandry, fisheries, irrigation and industries have experienced steady decline in terms of allocation. What the productive sector lost was gained by the service and the infrastructure sectors. Housing, women and child welfare, roads and bridges, and public buildings are the sub-sectors, which gained the most. The above four sub-sectors together account for nearly 50 per cent of the plan allocation. Housing, roads and bridges take between them roughly about 40 per cent of the plan resources.

Development Impact

To address the question of the development impact of democratic decentralisation, a profile of the sample *panchayats* based on the opinion of our key respondents is presented below. The respondents of the CDS surveys were asked to assess the extent to which services (such as health care, education, roads) and development (such as housing for the poor, support of agriculture, efforts to improve income and employment) declined or improved with the campaign. On all questions, respondents indicated improvement (Table 17.9). For every category, a large majority of respondents felt there had been improvement (either 'some' or "significant"). In 5 of 13 categories, over 40% of respondents felt that there had been "significant" improvement. The

TABLE 17.9

Respondents' Perceptions of Change

	Fraction of Respondents Who Said:					*No. of Responses*
	Deteriorated		*Not changed*	*Improved*		
	Significantly	*To Some Extent*		*To Some Extent*	*Significantly*	
Primary health care	0.3	1.2	9.1	66.1	23.4	816
Childcare and child development	0.2	0.5	1.6	36.5	61.2	825
Primary education	0.1	0.7	16.8	60.9	21.5	806
Drinking water	0.0	1.4	8.2	48.1	42.3	813
Sanitation	0.3	0.4	9.3	48.5	41.7	811
Roads	0.2	0.2	3.1	34.1	62.3	827
Irrigation facilities	0.3	1.6	13.1	61.7	23.4	811
Housing for the poor	0.1	0.5	0.8	28.3	70.3	832
Assistance to poor	0.0	0.3	10.5	56.9	32.4	809
Support for agricultural cultivators	0.2	1.1	8.5	61.8	28.4	821
Income and employment creation	0.3	1.1	25.9	62.7	10.0	807
Income and employment for women	0.1	0.7	17.7	56.1	25.4	816
Income and employment for SCs or STs	0.3	0.6	21.1	56.9	21.2	807

Source: Sample Survey.

performance of *panchayats* was however not been uniform across the districts. The campaign's most marked successes were reportedly in building roads, housing for the poor and *anganawadis* (child services); in these activities almost two-thirds of the respondents felt the difference to be significant. In contrast, less than a fourth of the respondents felt that *panchayats* made a significant difference in the rate and pattern of economic development (employment, agricultural support and irrigation).

The evaluation of change may also be examined by types of respondents. Table 17.10 provides information on the proportion of respondents by category who reported improvement (either some or significant). For all questions, the majority in all the respondent categories felt improvement has taken place. Even a cursory glance at this Table indicates that there is not much difference of opinion across respondent categories at this level of aggregation of responses. This is true of all categories of politicians, government officials and civil society representatives. These findings have to be interpreted, however, with caution. Because most of the key respondents were involved in some capacity in the campaign, their perceptions might very much have been influenced by the campaign's self-publicity. For this reason, it is particularly instructive to note the response of opposition politicians who logically should be expected to be more skeptical of the campaign's impact. It is observed that the heads of the local branches of the opposition party had an overwhelmingly positive view of the campaign. Similarly, government officials, including those from line departments, have an overwhelmingly positive view. This evidence suggests that the general finding that the campaign led to improvement in development is robust.

One undisputed area of tangible gains has been infrastructure facilities. LSGIs have allocated around 25 per cent of the grant-in-aid to the infrastructure sector. Out of this around 20 per cent had gone for improving local connectivity—by improving the network of roads, culverts, bridges, etc. Other areas of improvement in the sector include public buildings (primary schools, public health centres, child development centres), street lighting, public comfort stations and waiting sheds.

Performance in the objective of improvement of the quality of services also has to be addressed adequately. As a part of the process of decentralisation, many local institutions providing services, (viz., schools, primary health centres, child development centres, social welfare centres) were transferred to LSGs. This gesture has by itself contributed in a significant way to improvement in the accountability of teachers, doctors, paramedical staff, social welfare workers etc. In addition, LSGs have formulated projects for improving the performance of

TABLE 17.10

Fraction of Respondents, by Category and Indicator, Who Felt Situation in Panchayat had Improved, Compared to before the Campaign

Category of Respondent	*Primary Health*	*Childcare*	*Primary Educ.*	*Drinking Water*	*Sanitation*
Panchayat member from ruling party or coalition	92.0	98.7	88.2	96.1	97.4
Panchayat member from opposition	85.9	95.4	73.4	87.3	89.1
Head of local branch of ruling party	87.7	95.4	87.7	92.3	92.4
Head of local branch of main opposition party	80.3	90.3	65.6	79.4	77.8
Panchayat secretary	95.3	98.5	85.7	95.3	95.3
Panchayat-level implementing officer (e.g. agricultural officer)	92.6	96.4	84.9	86.8	86.8
Other line department official	90.8	100.0	84.4	87.5	84.4
Civilian task force member	96.7	100.0	86.4	91.8	93.3
Representative of caste association or religious organisation	74.6	100.0	71.7	88.5	86.5
Representative of labour union or farmers' association	96.7	98.4	84.5	88.3	86.4
Representative of mass-based development organisation	92.4	96.9	84.9	92.4	92.4
Representative of women's group	90.3	100.0	87.3	93.8	95.2
Representative of SC or ST organisation	85.7	100.0	83.6	93.6	91.9

Category of Respondent	*Roads*	*Irrigation*	*Agricultural Support*	*Incomes & Job Creation*
Panchayat member from ruling party or coalition	98.7	94.7	92.1	83.8
Panchayat member from opposition	95.4	78.5	85.9	59.7
Head of local branch of ruling party	97.0	93.8	95.3	75.4
Head of local branch of main opposition party	87.1	71.0	79.4	52.4
Panchayat secretary	100.0	92.1	92.1	76.6
Panchayat-level implementing officer (e.g. agricultural officer)	100.0	89.7	90.0	70.9
Other line department official	95.4	82.0	92.1	77.1
Civilian task force member	96.8	77.8	90.3	80.0
Representative of caste association or religious organisation	92.7	84.6	85.2	59.6
Representative of labour union or farmers' association	96.8	88.3	87.3	70.5
Representative of mass-based development organisation	100.0	86.4	96.9	80.6
Representative of women's group	96.9	83.9	93.8	78.1
Representative of SC or ST organisation	95.2	81.4	90.2	76.3

Source: Sample Survey.

such institutions. Almost every LSG had projects for improving physical infrastructure. The concerned institutions were supported by constructing new buildings, renovating old ones, ensuring water supply, providing for latrines, urinals and drainage and supplying equipment. There were also meaningful interventions focused on quality of services. For instance, programmes for improving quality of teaching were undertaken almost in all panchayats in the state. The local public have acquired a sense of ownership of public institutions through the decentralisation campaign. Local plans on housing, sanitation, and women and child welfare, which together received nearly 30 per cent of the plan grant-in-aid, have tremendously aroused popular enthusiasm.

It is the productive sector that lagged behind the rest of the sectors in terms of investment efforts as well as of outcomes. The achievements in agriculture and industry leave much to be desired. This limitation of the decentralisation programme has unfavourable implications for generating sustainable employment and income opportunities. A related drawback of the decentralisation programme has been its failure to integrate the institution of the market into its framework. The local development interventions of the LSGs do not work in a vacuum. Almost all of their interventions have an interface with the market. For instance, production-oriented programmes cannot wish away the problem of marketing. The same is the case with programmes involving procurement of goods or services. Therefore, it is important that local development plans specify their strategy of dealing with the market. Marketing of agricultural output, particularly vegetables, have turned out to be a major problem, endangering even sustainability of many big projects in this sector. Duplication of project ideas, competition among LSGs, shortage of inputs, etc. are some of the widely reported problems. Clearly, industry is yet another weak link. Marketing problems and intense competition from big firms, especially multinationals, constrain local level initiatives in the industrial sector. It needs to be emphasised here that many aspects related to agriculture and industry, such as prices of inputs and outputs and the larger policy parameters, are beyond the control of LSGIs and local people. Individual success stories have emerged in the process of decentralised planning. Many LSGIs have emerged as models on account of their remarkable performance. Success stories of individual projects have been reported from many parts of the state. In fact, success stories have come up even from sectors, whose overall performance under the new system has been lacklustre. Many success stories were made because the new system provided local actors in them with the space required for trying out their ideas. They also signify the tremendous potential of the decentralised system of planning. In contrast, there were also stories of miserable failure, indicating loopholes and loose ends in the new system.

The wide variation in the performance of local plans across development sectors/issues demand problematisation of the architecture of decentralised planning. There are many aspects that lie beyond the control of local people and local governments. Many typical development issues such as poverty and unemployment belong to this category. In addressing such development issues, local self-governments cannot at all be left to fend for themselves. Similarly, there are development sectors in which actions of individual local self-governments would have far reaching implications for people not belonging to the locality. In short, the architecture of decentralised planning in the state has many design problems. The division of powers and responsibilities among different tiers of LSGs remain vague. There exists considerable amount of overlapping, duplication and waste. For instance, in the initial years, LSGIs at all levels competed among themselves for implementing vegetable cultivation programmes – resulting first in shortage of planting material and later in severe problems of marketing of the produce. The mechanisms meant for ensuring vertical and horizontal integration did not work in desired ways. The legacy of departmentalism and the influence of stereotype projects of line departments have tended to persist. The attempt to integrate the state and the centrally sponsored programmes with local development plans has not been quite successful either.

Technical know-how is a crucial input in planning. It is important at every stage of planning such as project design, execution, monitoring, accounting and auditing. The introduction of participatory planning opened up the possibility of using local knowledge of the people. But in many cases local knowledge had to be supplemented by knowledge from external sources. But, such technical help was not easily available. In some cases local people though aware of technological alternatives, such as watershed management and water harvesting, were not able to obtain services of experts capable of preparing programmes for the locality. In short the link between LSGs and the sources of technical expertise was rather weak (Nair, 2000). Further, the system followed for giving technical sanction has encountered much adverse criticism, for causing undue delays. The mechanism has been found particularly hostile to beneficiary committees.

Office management and record-keeping are in a bad shape in LSGs. Procedures related to financial management are another important weak link. The old system of keeping accounts and preparing budgets had to be changed. The new system would require concerted efforts, including detailed studies and training programmes, to evolve and establish procedures and practices that ensure transparency and people's control.

While decentralisation enthusiasts believe that it would help empower the hitherto marginalised sections, the skeptics fear that the process would help only the local elite. In this regard, the decentralisation programme in Kerala has taken a cautious approach; the issue of equity was not left to be settled completely at the local level. A part of the plan grant-in-aid was to be mandatorily used for formulating special component plans for scheduled castes, and another part for tribal sub-plans. Further, from the general component of the plan grant-in-aid, ten per cent was to be used exclusively for the women component plan. The special component plans for SC, ST and women have binding regulations that limit the autonomy of local self-governments. The regulations sought to ensure that the marginalised groups belonging to SC, ST and women, have control over decisions regarding the special component plans, with respect to prioritisation and selection of beneficiaries. For instance, in special component plans, housing, drinking water and sanitation received nearly 50 per cent of the allocation. The allocation is reflective of the special problems faced by the concerned sections of the population. Further, such schemes are little susceptible for corruption and leakage. However, widespread complaints have arisen on two counts. First, the gap between allocation and expenditure has been increasing in the case of the special component plans. Second, the special component plans were particularly weak in creating sustainable income/employment generating activities. Further, in the case of women component plans, many projects included were not helpful in empowering women.

The new experiment of decentralised planning initiated in 1996 had aroused big expectations among the people, but the developments at the national and international levels, were soon to belie the wild expectations. The global changes and the economic reforms introduced at the national level have had severe detrimental effects on the regional economy of Kerala. The fall in the prices of agricultural products has been a major blow for the state's agricultural sector. The industrial sector and the employment situation have also been badly affected. The gains of decentralised planning were no match to the losses emanating from the hostile external environment: at best they had only a cushioning effect. The changes in the external environment and their adverse impact on the regional economy were useful in conveying the message regarding the limits of local level participatory democracy.

Lessons of Democratic Decentralisation in Kerala

The Kerala experiment of democratic decentralisation was an attempt to augment the space for 'public action' by establishing a decentralised, participatory system of planning. The experiment has proved that the scope of 'public action' may be significantly increased through democratisation of the planning process with favourable effects on the quality of life of the people. The review of the outcome points out, however, several aspects of the process of participatory planning from below that need correction and improvement. An important lesson of the experiment is the light it throws on the 'limits' of local level participatory planning and governance.

The experiment in Kerala has been successful in demystifying planning. It has shown that LSGs and local communities are capable of undertaking planning and development governance on their own. It has evolved a detailed methodology of participatory planning from below and successfully formulated and implemented local development plans.

The Kerala experiment has also been able to institutionalise the new system of local level participatory planning. Mobilisation of people in the campaign mode during the initial years has helped in overcoming resistance against democratic decentralisation. The LSGI Acts of Kerala (as amended in 1999), the relevant rules, the related government orders, and the practices established over the past few years together provide the necessary institutional framework.

The decentralisation experiment marks a benchmark in the fiscal history of the state. The devolution of resources that it has facilitated has been spectacular. It has enhanced the command over resources of LSGs manifold. In addition to the plan grant-in-aid, the LSGs have also been mobilising resources locally on their own for their development plans. Nevertheless, there remain aspects of the resources scenario that need improvement. First, since 1997 a marked decline is noted in the proportion of plan funds allocated to the LSGs. Second, there have also been serious lapses on the part of the state government in the timely disbursement of the sanctioned funds to the LSGs. Third, the gap between budget allocation and expenditure of LSGs has been growing over time. Fourth, there has been a clear decline in efforts by LSGs for collecting local taxes.

The experiment has undoubtedly enthused people to participate in the process of planning and implementation. It has demonstrated that people would actively participate in development activities, if they are given genuine opportunities for participation. The experiment had demonstrably positive effects on social inclusion. The participation rates of SCs and STs have been higher than those of the general population. Participation rates of women have also been commendable. However, a disturbing aspect noticed has been the steady waning of participation rates since 1997. It is important to find out why the new experiment failed to sustain the initial levels of interest in participation among the local people.

The development impact of the experiment appears to have been in general favourable. This is particularly true of development activities in infrastructure and services. The Kerala experience ascertains most of the ideas regarding the virtues of participatory planning from below. It has improved the sensitivity of the system to the local specificities on the one hand, and the felt needs of the people, on the other. It has also added to the sense of involvement and ownership of the people and reduced corruption and leakage.

Its development impact has been relatively small in the productive sectors. Over the years under the new experiment, LSGs have been reducing the allocation of funds to the agricultural and the industrial sectors. The poor performance of the productive sectors has special implications for the ability of local plans to generate sustainable employment and income-earning opportunities.

The development activities of the LSGIs, especially in the productive sectors, will have to take marketing aspects into consideration. The institution of the market would need to be internalised in the process of local level planning.

The differences in the levels of performance of the new experiment across sectors call for a review of the architecture of decentralised governance and planning. The division of powers and responsibilities across different tiers of governance should be subjected to a rethink. Confusions on questions of responsibility and power should be minimised at all levels to avoid controversies, conflicts, duplication and waste as well as to improve performance. In the light of experience, it should be possible to develop a more efficient architecture of decentralised planning. Institutional arrangements and procedures for ensuring integration—vertical, and horizontal—should be improved.

LSGs should be provided with adequate technological support. Educational institutions and research centres should be entrusted with the responsibility of serving LSGs by providing ideas, undertaking studies, and giving practical guidelines on technological possibilities and alternatives.

The system of office management and accounting needs thorough strengthening and revision for meaningful housekeeping, review and auditing.

It is advisable to have top-down regulations for ensuring inclusion of the marginalised groups. Unequal local power relations left to themselves might otherwise work to the disadvantage of the marginalised sections. The issue of the growing gaps between allocation of plan grant-in-aid and expenditure under SCP and TSP, needs special scrutiny since it has serious equity implications.

Local people and their plans must recognise the limits of decentralised planning. There are many things, which lie beyond the control of LSGs and local populations. Such problems cannot be taken up and handled fully at the local level. For instance, poverty and unemployment are not problems which necessarily have local level origin. It is always better to confine the role of LSGs to matters predominantly within their control. Participatory planning at the local level should not be seen as a solution to all problems at the local level. In dealing with problems caused by external factors, LSGIs and local communities would need guidance and support from higher tiers of government. Similarly the involvement of higher tiers would be needed in the case of problems in which actions of individual LSGIs would have significant externalities.

References

Bandhopadyaya, D. (1997). "People's Participation in Planning: Kerala Experiment", *Economic and Political Weekly*, Sept. 27, pp.2450-54.

Chathukulam, Jos and M.S. John (2002). "Five Years of Participatory Planning in Kerala: Rhetoric and Reality", *Economic and Political Weekly*, Dec. 7.

Chaudhuri, Subhan, K.N. Harilal and Heller Patrick (2004). *Does Decentralization make a Difference?*, Project Report. Thiruvananthapuram: Centre for Development Studies.

Chattopadhyay, S. (2001). "Resource Mapping for Decentralised Planning: Lessons from Kerala:, Paper presented at the workshop on *Decentralisation in Kerala: An Assessment*, October 22-24. Thiruvananthapuram: KRPLLD, Centre for Development Studies.

Das, M K (2000). "Kerala's Decentralised Planning: Floundering Experiment", *Economic and Political Weekly*, Dec. 2, pp.4300-03.

Dreze, Jean and Amartya Sen (1989). *Hunger and Public Action*. Oxford: Clarendon Press.

———. (ed.) (1996). *Indian Development: Selected Regional Perspectives*. New Dehi: Oxford University Press.

Franke, Rechard and Barbara Chasin (1992). *Kerala: Development through Radical Reform*. New Delhi: Promilla Publishers.

———. (1997). "Power to the Malayalee People", *Economic and Political Weekly*, Vol.31(10).

George, K.K. (1993). *Limits to Kerala Model of Development: An Analysis of Fiscal Crisis and its Implications*. Thiruvananthapuram: Centre for Development Studies.

Government of Kerala (2000). *Economic Review 1999*. Thiruvananthapuram: State Planning Board.

———. (2002). *Economic Review 2001*. Thiruvananthapuram: Kerala State Planning Board.

———. (1997). *Final Report of the Committee on Decentralisation of Powers*. Thiruvananthapuram.

———. (2001). *White Paper on State Finances*. Thiruvananthapuram

Harilal, K.N. (2002). "Goods Producing Sectors and Local Level Participatory Planning: The Experience of Participatory Planning in Kerala", Paper presented in the International Seminar on *Income Generating Activities*. Kochi: Cochin University.

Harilal, K.N. and K.J. Joseph (2000). "Stagnation and Revival of Kerala Economy: An Open Economy Perspective", *Working Paper* 305. Thiruvananthapuram: Centre for Development Studies.

Harilal K.N. and Mariamma Sanu George (2000). "Prioritisation in Local Level Participatory Planning: The Kerala Experience", *mimeo*, paper presented in the International Conference on Kerala Studies. Thiruvananthapuram: Kerala State Planning Board.

Heller, Patrick (1996). "Social Capital as Product of Class Mobilisation and State Intervention: Industrial Workers in Kerala, India", *World Development*, Vol. 24(6).

Isaac, Thomas T.M. (2000). *People's Planning: Theory and Practice (Malayalam)*. Thiruvananthapuram: State Planning Board. pp.101.124.

Isaac, Thomas T.M. and K.N. Harilal (1997). "Planning for Empowerment: People's Campaign for Decentralised Planning in Kerala", *Economic and Political Weekly*, January, pp 53-58.

Isaac, Thomas,T.M. and Richard Franke (2000). *Local Democracy and Development: People's Campaign for Decentralised Planning in Kerala*. New Delhi: Left Word. pp.1-359.

Isaac, Thomas T.M. *et al.* (1995). *Kalliasseri Experiment in Local Level Planning*. Thiruvananthapuram: KRPLLD, Centre for Development Studies.

Kerala State Land Use Board (1997). *Resource Based Perspective Plan–2003 A.D.* Thiruvananthapuram: Government of Kerala.

Mohanakumar, S. (2002). From People's Plan to Plan Sans People, *Economic and Political Weekly*, Vol 37(16): 1492-97, April 20-26.

Nair, Gopinathan N.D. (2000). "People's Planning in Kerala: A Case Study of Two Village Panchayats, Kerala Research Programme on Local Level Development", *Discussion Paper* No. 16, Feb. Thiruvananthapuram: Centre for Developing Studies.

Oakley, Peter *et al.* (1991). *Projects with People: The Practice of Participation in Rural Development*. Geneva: International Labor Organization.

Panikar, P.G.K. and C.R. Soman (1984). *Health Status of Kerala*. Thiruvananthapuram: Centre for Developing Studies.

Pushparajan, K. (2002). *Niyamadhishtitha Panchayat Bharanam: Yanthravum Thanthravum* (Malayalam). Thiruvananthapuram: Thunchan Smaraka Samiti

Ramachandran V.K. (1996). "On Kerala's Development Achievements", in Jean Dreaze and Sen Amartya (ed.), *Indian Development: Regional Perspectives*. New Delhi: Oxford University Press.

Rehman, Kanta and M.M. Mehman (1998). *Participation in Rural Development*. Geneva: International Labour Office.

State Finance Commission (2001). *Second State Finance Commission Report*, Part-I. Thiruvananthapuram: Government of Kerala.

UNDP (1993). *Human Development Report 1993*. New York: Oxford University Press.

Zachariah K.C. *et al.*, (1994). *Demographic Transition in Kerala in the 1980s*. Thiruvananthapuram: Centre for Development Studies.

Chapter 18

Governance at the State Level

Governance is the process of decisionmaking and the process by which decisions are implemented. It constitutes the exercise of power by various levels of governments. It assures that corruption is minimised and the views of all section s of the citizenry are taken into account in decision-making over allotment of resources. During the past two decades, e-governance has been introduced in most countries of the world.

Kerala is among the front-runners in implementing e-governance in India. Introduction of e-governance and the use of computers in the government of Kerala may be traced back to the 1950s (Box 18.1). Data processing with the use of computers began in the mid-1970s. Surveys, College admissions processes, calculation of DA arrears of employers, consolidation of treasury accounts etc., began in the early 1980s. The departments of public works, finance, forest, agriculture, animal husbandry and collegiate education started using computers by the mid-1980s.

During the late 1980s and the early 1990s, the state witnessed a slow-down of computer-based activities. Except in a few areas like dairy cooperatives, no progress was made in e-governance. The spread of computers was stalled fearing loss of jobs and replacement of human beings by computers. In the late nineties, the perceptions were set right and e-governance efforts caught up in right earnest. Almost all government departments implemented e-governance projects.

Kerala's was the first state government in the country to come out with IT policies aimed at coordinating and accelerating the pace of IT and e-governance projects. In 1998, the policies were focused mainly on creation of IT infrastructure in data communication and IT education. In 2001, policies were broader and covered industries like Information Technology Enabled Services (ITES) and provided for liberalisation of labour laws. They also provided for the use of free software in e-governance.

BOX 18.1

History of Use of Computers in Kerala

"Arithma", a Czech-made electromechanical computer used in the 1950s by the Kerala University seems to have been the first computer in Kerala. In 1974, VSSC installed one of its IBM II generation 1620 card-based computers in the University of Kerala. Staffing support for operating the computer was provided by VSSC. In 1972, the state government set up the Kerala State Electronics Development Corporation of Kerala Limited (KELTRON), a pioneering initiative in the field of electronics in the state.

In 1976, a Data-Processing Centre under the Finance Department of the state government was established in association with the University of Kerala and the IBM 1620 supplied by VSSC was put to use. However, in 1977, the central government asked IBM to close down its operations in India, thus making it difficult to get accessories for the IBM 1620 computer. Subsequently, the Data-Processing Centre purchased III generation TDC-316 computer and the IBM 1620 was donated to the Science and Technology Museum.

The state has been making giant strides in the ICT infrastructure front also. In April 1997, Kerala became the first state to have public telephones in all its villages, accessible from any part of the world. In April 1998, Kottayam became the first district in India to complete computerisation of all the *taluk* offices connecting them with the District headquarters. In 2004, Palakkad Collectorate became the first fully computerised Collectorate in the country.

Kerala has made vast strides in IT-enabled services since the turn of the century. Many projects aimed at providing citizen-friendly services have been introduced. FRIENDS (Fast, Reliable, Instant, Efficient, Network for Disbursement of Services) was set up to offer an integrated point for utility payment such as electricity bills and water charges, property tax, professional tax, etc., SEVANA aimed at converting 400 rural libraries into IT dissemination centres and PEARL (Package For Effective Administration of Registration Laws) aimed at providing public interface for registration and information kiosks in every village panchayat ward for citizens to adopt the Internet revolution, are typical examples.

Realising the need for people's participation in e-governance, an innovative project for capacity building among citizens in IT-related areas called "Akshaya" was launched in Malappuram district to bring about universal e-literacy. Another venture has been that of the IT@School, which aims at introduction of computer training in government schools. The State Government has also initiated the 'Information Kerala' project for the deployment of technology at the grassroots level as a model for participatory governance through effective use of Information Technology. This project aims at modernisation and integration of government functions using IT by networking and computerising the 1214 local self-governing bodies to expedite transactions such as communication of the essence of certificates, issue of licences, tax collection, training and orientation of personnel at the village, district and state levels of governing bodies and setting up internet kiosks in sites accessible to the public, in every *panchayat* ward. All the 152 development blocks in the state are connected, a first-of-its-kind achievement in the country.

All treasuries/sub treasuries in the state are networked and the Secretariat Wide Area Network links the offices of the Ministers, Secretaries and departments.

Information Technology Policies

The potential of IT industry to generate opportunities of employment with exerting little pressure on land, environment and other resources, has been understood and appreciated by the people of Kerala. IT is seen not only as a tool for improving governance and creating jobs, but more significantly, as a means to enhance the standard of living of the people.

Kerala Information Technology Policy, 1998

The Kerala Information Technology Policy, 1998 sought application of Information Technology in all walks of life, enhancement of IT industry base and creation of robust State Information Infrastructure and Human Resource Development for Information Technology (Box 18.2). A high power committee was proposed, chaired by the Chief Minister, to co-ordinate and direct strategies to achieve use of IT in all sectors.

BOX 18.2

Mission Targets—IT Policy 1998

PC penetration of 10 per 1000 of the population by the year 2001.

All colleges to be hooked to internet by the year 2000 and all schools by 2002.

Internet kiosks in every *panchayat* ward.

Modernisation and integration of government functions using Information Technology.

The policy also sought to facilitate the creation of a sound IT production base through conscious efforts and policy initiatives comprising the following:

- Creation of IT-specific infrastructure in different parts of the State.
- Removal of hassles in the regulatory environment, making it pro-active and sensitive to the needs of the industry.
- Incentives and concessions for IT ventures.
- Special package for financing IT ventures.

The Policy further recommended the promotion of Kerala as a location for IT investments, through efforts like strengthening of Technopark, setting up Software Technology Parks & Software Complexes in major cities and formation of a venture capital fund to meet the financing requirements of the IT industry. It spelt out establishment of a sound State Information Infrastructure (SII) with a communication backbone, Network Operation Centres, Nodes, Access Networks and Data Warehouses as a high priority area (Box 18.3). It sought to harness the existing infrastructure and to develop and integrate it to create an Information Infrastructure that could effectively handle the traffic for several years.

BOX 18.3

Mission Targets for Information Infrastructure—IT Policy 1998

Connectivity at 2 MBPS to any user department in the three major cities of the state and at multiples of 64 KBPS in other parts of the state by the year 2000.

All district head quarters be provided with the connectivity of 622 MB capacity by 1999, all *taluk* head quarters by 2000 and all village offices by 2002. Concurrently, one SII node in each Block by 2000 and in each *Panchayat* by 2002.

Strengthening data warehousing for promoting trade, commerce and tourism and for enhancing delivery and transparency of Government services and empowerment of the people.

The IT Policy 1998 also addressed Human Resource Development problems for development of Information Technology. It proposed the following measures to ensure rapid capacity building in IT:

- Establishment of an Institute of Information Technology.
- Introducing Information Technology as a specialised branch of study.
- Development of Centres of Excellence in Information Technology.
- Creating a fund for upgradation of training/educational infrastructure, and
- Introduction of a system for accreditation.

Kerala Information Technology Policy 2001

Kerala is the first state to implement the core recommendations on labour regulatory framework for the IT industry made by the Planning Commission. Kerala's IT Industry Policy, 2001-2005 incorporates a regulatory framework for the IT industry wherein software companies would be deemed establishments under the Kerala Shops and Commercial Establishments Act, 1960. Kerala is the first State to permit three shift operations, women working in night shifts, and flexi-time working. IT industry has been deemed a Public Service Utility under the Industrial Disputes Act, 1943. The Policy also permits self-certification in respect of nine acts. It provides for part-time working and tele-working, both enabling ITES operations.

The IT Industry Incentive Scheme 2001-2003 encompasses a unique, comprehensive package of incentives and policies for IT products and Software and Information Technology Enabled Services (ITES) industry. The IT Industry Employment Promotion Scheme provides incentives for higher employment providers and the Pioneer Incentive Scheme provides for grants to companies (with permanent investment of Rs. 10 crores) for setting up business in fields like software development, IT-enabled services, hardware production, rural ICT connectivity provider, and also facilities for training 1000 candidates a year.

The Policy envisages a Private Parks Scheme, which facilitates and encourages creation of quality physical infrastructure by the private sector in the state. Provision for the creation of a new category called IT Industry with Floor Area Ratio (FAR) of 5 (as opposed to 1.5 earlier) for IT software units is made under State Building Rules (Kerala Building Rules, in this case) for the first time in India. It also provides for setting up of private parks that comply with set standards, along with the state-sponsored parks.

The IT policy 2001 also seeks to create a trained pool of manpower with skills and aptitudes appropriate to the ITES industry, through focused statewide HRD programmes. Bridge programmes for engineering graduates, Communicative English, Soft Skills, Accent Neutralisation, ITES sub-domain level training, etc., have been identified as thrust areas. These programmes are envisaged to be woven into mainstream collegiate education.

Infrastructure

The infrastructure facilities available for communication and ITES in Kerala are unmatched in the country. All the 988 Telephone Exchanges in Kerala are Digital. All the 14 District headquarters and 63 *Taluk* headquarters are networked. About 98 per cent of the Telephone Exchanges in the State are connected by Optical Fibre Cable (OFC) to the National Internet Backbone (NIB). All the 1468 village *panchayats* within three km. of a Digital Telephone Exchange are connected to the NIB over OFC. One of the two submarine cable landings in India is located in the state (15 GBps bandwidth supported 'SEA-ME-WE-3' and 'SAFE' cable landing). VSNL's primary international gateway in India which handles two-thirds of the country's data traffic is in Kochi. Kerala also boasts of the highest telephone density in the country; 10.98 per 100 persons, double the national average. The state also has the highest rural telephone density; 8.43 per 100, 8 times the national average. The state government has also set up two IT Parks: Technopark, Thiruvananthapuram and Infopark, Kochi.

BOX 18.4

Web Portal of GoK

The Web Service Division of C-DIT hosts the official web portal of Government of Kerala, which runs to over 20,000 web pages. Website of information and the public relations department of Kerala are also maintained by C-DIT. The web portal of the Government of Kerala, www.kerala.gov.in, provides information/links on various government authorities/services/agencies such as the following:

Details regarding the Governor, Chief Minister and other council of Ministers.

Email facilities to ministers and top officials of various government departments.

Details on various Government departments, District Offices, Judiciary, Local Self Government, etc.

Vital Statistics of the State including *panchayat*-level Statistics.

Formats of various application forms.

Results of various Examinations like SSLC, HSE, VHSE and Medical/Engineering entrance, etc.

Government Press Releases, Notifications, Orders, Tenders etc.

Details on Budget 2005-06, ADB Loan documents, MGP documents, Economic Reviews, etc.

Details on the Higher Education and General Education facilities/institutions available in the State.

Details on industrial promotion agencies in the State.

Kerala PSC rank lists/examination mark lists.

Details on the various social welfare schemes of the government.

Details on Human Rights Commissions, Legal Service Society, Women's Commission, Ombudsman, Lokayukta etc.

District hand books of Kottayam, Alappuzha, Palakkad, Kannur, Wayand and Kasaragod districts.

Agencies/Institutions in E-Governance

The Department of Information Technology, supported by a Mission group of Professionals, coordinates the implementation of the IT policy of the state and chalks out specific strategies for achieving the objectives. The major agencies/institutions involved in various e-governance activities in the state are:

- Kerala State IT-Mission.
- Centre for Development of Imaging Technology (C-DIT) (Boxes 18.4 & 18.5).
- Centre for Development of Advanced Computing (C-DAC) (Box 18.6).
- National Informatics Centre (NIC) - Kerala Unit (Box 18.7).
- Information Kerala Mission (IKM).
- Indian Institute of Information Technology and Management–Kerala (IIITMK).
- Kerala State Electronics Development Corporation (KELTRON) (Box 18.8).
- IT @ School (Boxes 18.9 and 18.10).

BOX 18.5

Features of WAN of Local Bodies in the State

The project aims to develop and deploy software developed in an Indian language to computerise and network the 1215 local government institutions including *panchayats*, Blocks, municipalities and corporations. It aims to develop innovative programmes for establishing ICT-based knowledge societies at the grassroots level under the leadership of Local Self Governments and a mechanism for regular monitoring of local body plan implementation and targets achievement, over the network. Initiatives include: *Samvedita* – a web portal of 1215 local bodies of Kerala under the URL www.localgovkerala.net, *Sanchita* – a repository of legislations, executive orders and promulgations on decentralisation, and *Swatantra* – urban local body information System on 53 municipalities and 5 Corporations in the State. Pilot implementation is in progress in five *Grama panchayats* and corporations.

BOX 18.6

State WAN

State WAN aims to provide a common IT infrastructure for the government for the e-governance initiatives. State WAN will have a state of the art data centre in Thiruvananthapuram and network centres at Thiruvananthapuram, Kochi and Kozhikode. The project aims at aggregating the free bandwidth provided to Government of Kerala at the three locations and making them available to government departments and organisations.

In the second phase, the backbone bandwidth would be made available at all district headquarters enabling departments to connect all their district level offices to their head office. In the third phase, the connectivity would be extended to the *taluk* level, where the next lower level of field offices of the departments is located. The Akshaya e-centres are also planned to be connected to the State Information Infrastructure.

Major E-governance Initiatives

The Government of Kerala has been giving a major thrust to e-governance projects during the past 4 to 5

BOX 18.7

E-Governance initiatives by NIC, Kerala State Unit

PEARL: Package for Effective Administration of Registration Laws

TRIM: Treasury Information System

ABACUS: Water Billing System for Kerala Water Authority

SSLC MIS &

HS EMS: SSLC &Higher Secondary Examination System (from issuing of hall tickets to printing of mark sheet for the entire state)

AIMS: Agricultural Information Management System

CALLS: Computer-aided Learners Licensing System

BOUGETTE: The Budget preparation software for Govt. of Kerala

TETRA–PDS: Targeted Efficient Transparent Ration Allocation & Public

Distribution System

THOZHIL: Employment Exchange Computerisation

SWIFT: A single window interface for taluks of Kerala

Smart Move: Transport Department Computerisation

TREND: An Online Transmission of Election Data and Result Display

NIC state unit has also introduced *DC-Suite*, a one point solution for the G2C functions of the collectorates and the Rural Soft, which monitors the implementation of SGRY schemes at the block level. The design, development and maintenance of official web sites of all districts in the state are also carried out by the state unit of NIC.

BOX 18.8

E-Sringhala

The e-chain kiosks are designed to provide information regarding schemes of various departments and facilities for down loading of applications for government support, incentives, subsidies, on-line submission of application forms, schemes for which separate notification is necessary, and government redressal modules for specific senior government functionaries. The kiosks have special module for counselling farmers on latest agricultural practices. They also provide updated information on census and electoral data. Schemes and application forms of the Industries, Civil Supplies, Motor Vehicles and Drugs Controller departments have been incorporated. On-line applications may be submitted for registration of SSI Units, besides sending representations and grievances to the Chief Minister and the other Ministers, Chief Secretary and District Collectors. The kiosks also provide discussion forums for the various interest groups.

BOX 18.9

IT @ School Project

Information Technology is introduced in high school education in the state for qualitative improvement of conventional teaching methods and learning systems, so that the core subjects would be easily understood by students. The project aims at imparting computer education to High School students and to equip teachers to use computer as an educational tool in classroom teaching. Out of the 2422 schools, computer labs have been set up in 2050 schools. Internet connection has been made available in 258 schools. Training of teachers is in progress.

BOX 18.10

Project *Siksha*

The Rs. 10 crore 'Project *Siksha*' of Microsoft and IT @ School envisages providing IT training to school teachers and students by setting up an IT academy in the state. A three-member expert committee has been appointed to take the final steps towards signing an MoU with Microsoft. As part of the project, Microsoft would provide scholarships to competent students and teachers. The IT academy will be housed in an area of 3000 sq ft. and will have facilities to impart training of international standards to teachers in the State on the advance courses of Microsoft.

years. These projects are implemented with a view to empowering the citizen in three major areas of interface with the government, *viz.*, Right for Entitlement, Right for Information and Right for Effecting Payments. The underlying yardstick in all the e-Governance initiatives of the Government of Kerala is the imparting of transparency and ensuring of speediness and correctness in various governmental activities/ procedures that have direct impact on the citizen. The following are certain other e-governance initiatives of the state.

Friends

It is a unique e-governance project taken up by the Government of Kerala, to take the benefits of Information Technology to the common man. It is a Single Window Scheme in which the consumer is given the option of paying for the common services rendered to him under a single roof. Functioning in all the district head quarters, the FRIENDS is a one-stop service centre in which payments of electricity bills, telephone bills, various taxes, water bills, examination fees, etc., may be made quickly. The computer-controlled queue management system of FRIENDS eliminates queue and reduces waiting time. The help desks also provide information on various government schemes and programmes and make available a variety of application forms.

The total collection through FRIENDS centre during 2001-02 was Rs. 52.39 crore and Rs.153 crore during 2002-03. It is reported that the overall satisfaction level of clients at FRIENDS is about 97 per cent, the average time saving about 43 minutes and cost savings of about Rs. 46 per transaction.

Akshaya

Akshaya constitutes the first step in taking Information Communication Technology to the masses of Kerala. Through *Akshaya* the government wanted to initiate a programme that would reach out even to the underprivileged citizen living in the remotest part of the State and make an impact on his life. Under this project, one person each in all the 65 lakh families in Kerala will be familiarised with the basic use of computer and empowered to access relevant e-content in the regional language. This involves setting up around 6500 information hubs called e-centres across Kerala. Each centre, run by private entrepreneurs, will cater to the requirements of around 1000 families and the programme would make available the power of networking and connectivity to the common man in the state.

The project piloted in the district of Malappuram is being replicated all over the state; Kerala would thus be made the first e-literate state in the country and a model in development for the whole world (Box 18.11).

Basic computer training has been provided to six lakh persons in Malappuram district, reaching out to 13 remote tribal colonies and 15 coastal villages in the district. A group of entrepreneurs has created a health profile for 30,000 persons in Cheakode panchayat. The project has brought in private sector investments of over Rs. 30 crore during the first phase (Box 18.12).

The wireless broadband connectivity infrastructure that is being established through project *Akshaya* supports several value-added services including an interface between the Government on the one part and Business and Citizens on the other on a single platform. Since the locations of the e-centres are strategically planned and spatially distributed to cater to the people in even the remotest part of the state, they form a powerful network to bring the full benefits of all e-governance initiatives of the state government to the common man. The *Akshaya* e-centres are being positioned as service delivery points for the citizens of the State (Box 18.13).

BOX 18.11

IT Majors Keen on Joint Ventures in *Akshaya*

With the success of *Akshaya*, IT majors are queuing up with partnership and investment proposals. Intel is on course to set up a hardware facility at the Kinfra Park in Kakkanchery. They have expressed interest in providing technical support to the *Akshaya* entrepreneurs in assembling personal computers and undertaking annual maintenance contracts. Intel would also support the *Akshaya* entrepreneurs to bring out joint venture brands of personal computers. The company will also develop special education content for children to be made available through *Akshaya* centres. Deliberations are on with Rediff and Sify to go for customised content with a special focus on Kerala. Yahoo is also keen to pitch in by providing exclusive e-mail space for the nearly five lakh neo e-literate families in Malappuram district. This will be executed by customising their e-mail and web chat facilities. With project *Akshaya* entering its second phase, 615 *Akshaya* entrepreneurs have been divided to form eight groups, and they would soon embark on income-generating activities

BOX 18.12

***Akshaya* Project Short-listed for Stockholm Challenge International IT Award**

The highly successful *Akshaya* computer literacy programme launched in Malappuram district of Kerala was short-listed for the prestigious Stockholm Challenge International IT Award. *Akshaya* was considered for the honour due to the phenomenal impact it made in the socioeconomic development of the district. *Akshaya* competed with 900 projects from 100 different countries before securing a place in the final list of potential award winners.

BOX 18.13

Haj Pilgrims Connected to Their Kith and Kin

Another milestone for the *Akshaya* e-literacy campaign is that the Haj pilgrims from the Malappuram district enjoyed the Internet Protocol based videophone facility made available through the *Akshaya* broadband network. This facility is available at the 615 *Akshaya* e-learning centres.

Phase II of Akshaya

Akshaya plans to develop during phase II, 620 centres in Malappuram to function as communication hubs, information kiosks, e-transaction centres, and training centres for various courses recognised by the government. The *Akshaya* centres are planned to take up services currently undertaken through FRIENDS counters such as tax payments and payments of government bills. The government also plans to take steps to cut down power tariffs to *Akshaya* centres.

Secretariat Wide Area Network

Secretariat Wide Area Network Project (SWAN) (networking Secretariat, Secretariat Annexe, *Vikas Bhavan* and Public Offices, and offices of Ministers, Secretaries to Government and 37 Departments in 6 blocks) is being set up in a phased manner. The current Secretariat Internet Communication System (SICS), which is internet based, supports the communication process between the secretariat and outside offices. About 500 computers work in the networked environment. In phases, the number of computers is planned to be enhanced to 3000.

Knowledge Bank Archival System (KBase)

In order to ensure timely access to critical information including laws and rules and sharing of information, knowledge and experience, a Knowledge Bank Archival System (KBase) is being implemented. This initiative is intended as a knowledge based decision-making system in the Secretariat, a comprehensive and computerised file flow system, a centralised repository of Acts and Rules and an appropriate mechanism for sharing of information among departments. The project is being implemented in three phases: (i) Implementation as a pilot project in the Health Department (ii) implementation in all other departments and finally (iii) easy access to the public on all general orders and Acts and Rules.

Call Centre Assistance for State Farmers- KISSAN

The government has opened call centres of farmers enabling dissemination of farm and agriculture-related information. The service is run on a 24 hours for 7 days (24x7) basis and called "KISSAN" (Karshaka Information Systems, Services and Networking). Farmers may seek information pertaining to a wide range of subjects like fertilisers, crops, market prices, pesticides and animal care, free of cost, round the clock. Queries made to the call centres are responded to in Malayalam

Enabling Malayalam for E-Governance (CliCK)

The CliCK project (Centre for Linguistic Computing, Keralam) aims to consolidate and coordinate efforts at integrating Malayalam with IT. Standardisation of keyboard, production of Unicode-supported Malayalam fonts and evolving a corpus of Malayalam are the major projects. At the product level, the idea is to produce linguistically and culturally customised software. Completed products include *Webdarshini* (Malayalam web browser), *Chitrakkudukka* (Clip art CD), *Aksharavidya* (Malayalam editor) and *Chitravidya*.

Initiatives in Various Government Departments

In addition, projects have been undertaken by individual government departments to improve delivery of services and citizen friendliness. Computerisation is underway in a majority of the state government departments.

The government has been making concerted efforts to improve the service delivery standards of its institutions and departments. Rapid progress has been achieved in e-governance and Kerala is at present one of the leading states in making available government services to citizens and utilisation of computers in government and quasi-government institutions. It is also true, however, that more concerted efforts are required to create an impact on the public. A central plan is required for organised growth of e-governance rather than ad hoc attempts of development, taken up due to special reasons, or availability of funds from funding agencies. A coordinated functioning of various agencies in the IT sector would enable effective reaching of IT services to the citizenry.

BOX 18.14

MGP Initiative

Modernising Government Programme aims to overhaul and improve its services to the people of the state. The thrust in MGP is to facilitate public servants and elected officials to serve the citizens of Kerala more effectively, efficiently and equitably and with greater accountability. MGP proposes a development approach for Kerala around five important themes - Minimum Needs Programme, Enabling Environment for Economic Growth, Fiscal Sustainability, Core Government Functions and Local Self Governments. One hundred initiatives covering a set of selected key results in each of the five themes is under implementation. The Service Delivery initiative and a majority of the other initiatives, especially those under Core Government Functions and Local Self Governments, are expected to improve delivery of services to the citizens, thereby increasing the citizen friendliness of governance.

Being a very literate state, law and order institutions in the state are always in the limelight and acts and omissions on their part are severely discussed in the media. The general feeling is that these institutions, especially those related to police, are not citizen-friendly. The government is in the process of modernising the police administration, as part of the comprehensive Modernising Government Programme (MGP), (Box 18.14) and creating a cadre of police force that is people-friendly, accessible and just.

Transparency of government functions and participation of people in governance have improved as a result of the institution of local governments and the decentralisation of functions and authority. The process of formulating development plans at the local level has ensured participation of all stakeholders through the *Grama sabhas*, thus improving transparency also.

Citizen-friendliness of the government administration is proposed to be improved significantly through the appropriate use of information technology. Access to information through internet and thereby more transparency, simplified systems and procedures and thereby faster services, lesser chances of mistakes and thereby increased efficiency, etc., are the expected outcomes of the use of information technology. FRIENDS centres in the state are cases in point. The *AKSHAYA* project is the first step in providing citizen-friendly services even to rural areas. The Online Banking for Treasury Savings Banks project could be trendsetters (Box 18.15). The government website provides information on the activities of the various government departments/institutions, though there is scope for improvement in the information provided in the website.

BOX 18.15

Online Banking for Treasury Savings Banks

Online banking for treasury savings banks is a project on the anvil. Initially, ATMs will be provided in three district treasuries - Thiruvananthapuram, Kochi and Kozhikode and later on will be expanded to the remaining 11 districts in the state. Once operational the online facility will allow the account holders of treasury banks to operate their accounts from anywhere in the state. Secondly, pensioners, who constitute a sizeable proportion of the population will also receive their monthly dues from anywhere in the state. Computerisation of 22 district treasuries has been completed; out of the 165 sub-treasuries, 102 have achieved full computerisation. The government plans to launch its on-line banking services shortly.

In Kerala, efforts are already on to make governance increasingly citizen-friendly through the Modernising Government Programme (MGP) and e-governance initiatives. The specific areas for improvement with regard to citizen friendliness are the following:

- Service Delivery: Benchmarking of the quality of services to be provided and the period within which such services can be delivered, need to be carried out by all government departments/ agencies/statutory bodies/local governments. The grievance redressal mechanism should be strengthened and held accountable so that common citizen will get to know the officials whom he/she should contact in case of grievance, and the time required to receive the grievance attended.
- Extended Services should be given for providing information to citizens and to strengthen Government-citizen interface. All concerned government officials should be trained in customer services and the resolution of public grievances.
- The system of ISO 9000 certification should be introduced for government offices in order to eliminate hassles likely to be faced by common citizens in getting things done.
- Priority areas of critical citizen concern need to be established through careful priority analyses.
- The Citizens' Charter should be dynamic with progressive, moving targets to be achieved.

Opportunities for good governance and provision of clean, transparent, efficient and hassle-free environment for the delivery of government services through utilisation of IT have to be tapped seriously. Simplification of procedures and improvement of processes are also of vital importance.

Efficiency Assessment

The assessment of results achieved in government may take a number of forms including feedbacks from citizens, reports of the Auditor General, feedbacks from the government sources, including Committees of the Legislature and the Cabinet, issues raised in the Legislative Assembly, and reviews of departmental plans with respect to performance measures and expected results. The state is yet to develop a system for feedback from citizens.

The efficiency of the performance of government is indicated in different ways through a number of publications (see Box 18.16). However, none of these provides an easy and simple indication of the overall efficiency that could be assimilated, understood and reacted upon by common citizenry. The contents of the administrative reports of the government departments are not tuned to discussing efficiency of actions either.

BOX 18.16

Publications That Throw Light on the Efficiency of Governance

Reports of the Comptroller and Auditor General of India on Kerala

Budget Documents of Government of Kerala

Annual Administrative Reports of Government Departments

Annual Reviews of PSUs in Kerala by Bureau of Public Enterprises

Evaluation Reports by Kerala State Planning Board

Economic Surveys—Government of India

Economic Reviews—Kerala State Planning Board

Reports of Central Finance Commission

Report of State Finance Commission

Subject Committee Reports of Kerala Legislative Assembly

Estimates Committee Reports of Kerala Legislative Assembly

An initiative under the Modernising Government Programme aims at establishing a Results-Based Management System (RBMS) for improving performance. Another initiative aims at designing a rational Performance Appraisal System for the officials transferred to the local governments.

A critical element to determine whether a department an organisational unit or an individual is achieving the desired results, is a performance measure (Figure 19.1) of governance.

Extracted from Measuring Performance in Government: A Discussion Paper (Internet)

The Performance Management System in government has to be an integrated one which provides the framework for implementing annual plans (Figure 19.2) and focuses on critical elements (Box 18.17). The performance measurement activities should ideally occur at the corporate, the departmental, the unit and the individual levels and the attributes of the performance measures and indicators should lend themselves to effective measurement of performance (Box 18.18).

FIGURE 18.1

Approach to Government

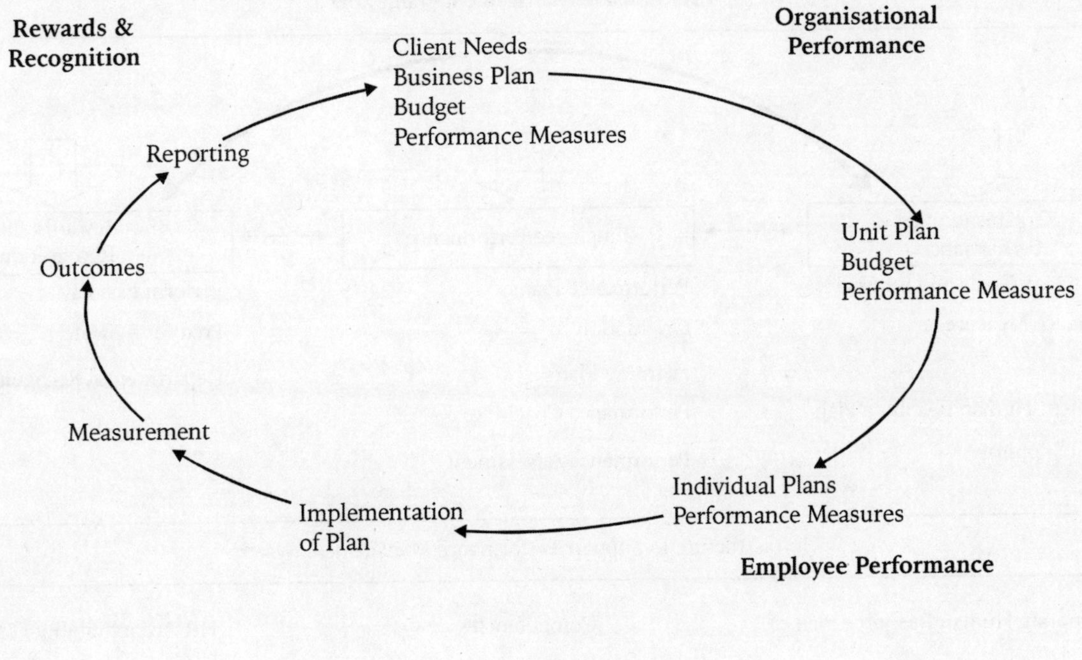

BOX 18.17

Elements of Performance Measurement

Measurement of Results: To focus on outcomes in addition to inputs and processes. Outcomes are the impact government outputs have on customers/clients.

Measurement of Efficiency and Effectiveness: The focus is on the management of resources and optimisation of resources to produce outputs at the lowest cost. Effectiveness is a measure of outcomes; it is a measure of quality as determined by the citizen as well as a measure of satisfaction and importance of government services, programmes, products and solutions for the citizen.

Measurement of Policy and Programme Outcomes: The focus is on measuring policy (broader social-economic impact) and programme (narrower targeted audience and impact) outcome of the actions.

Combination of Quantitative Measures with Qualitative Evaluation: Both quantitative and qualitative data have to be used to assess the degree of success **since** many results in government may not easily lend themselves to quantitative measurement for a variety of reasons.

BOX 18.18

Attributes of Performance Indicators

Performance indicators and measures should:

be driven by client/customer requirements and annual plans

be tied to critical success factors

facilitate measurement of results achieved and progress made in the implementation of plans

direct effort towards desired results

be few and critical to the organisation's success

consider financial, operational and client/customer measurements

allow for assignment of responsibility and accountability for monitoring, reporting and assessment of achievement

be observable and verifiable

FIGURE 18.2

Scheme of Financial Accountbility in State Government

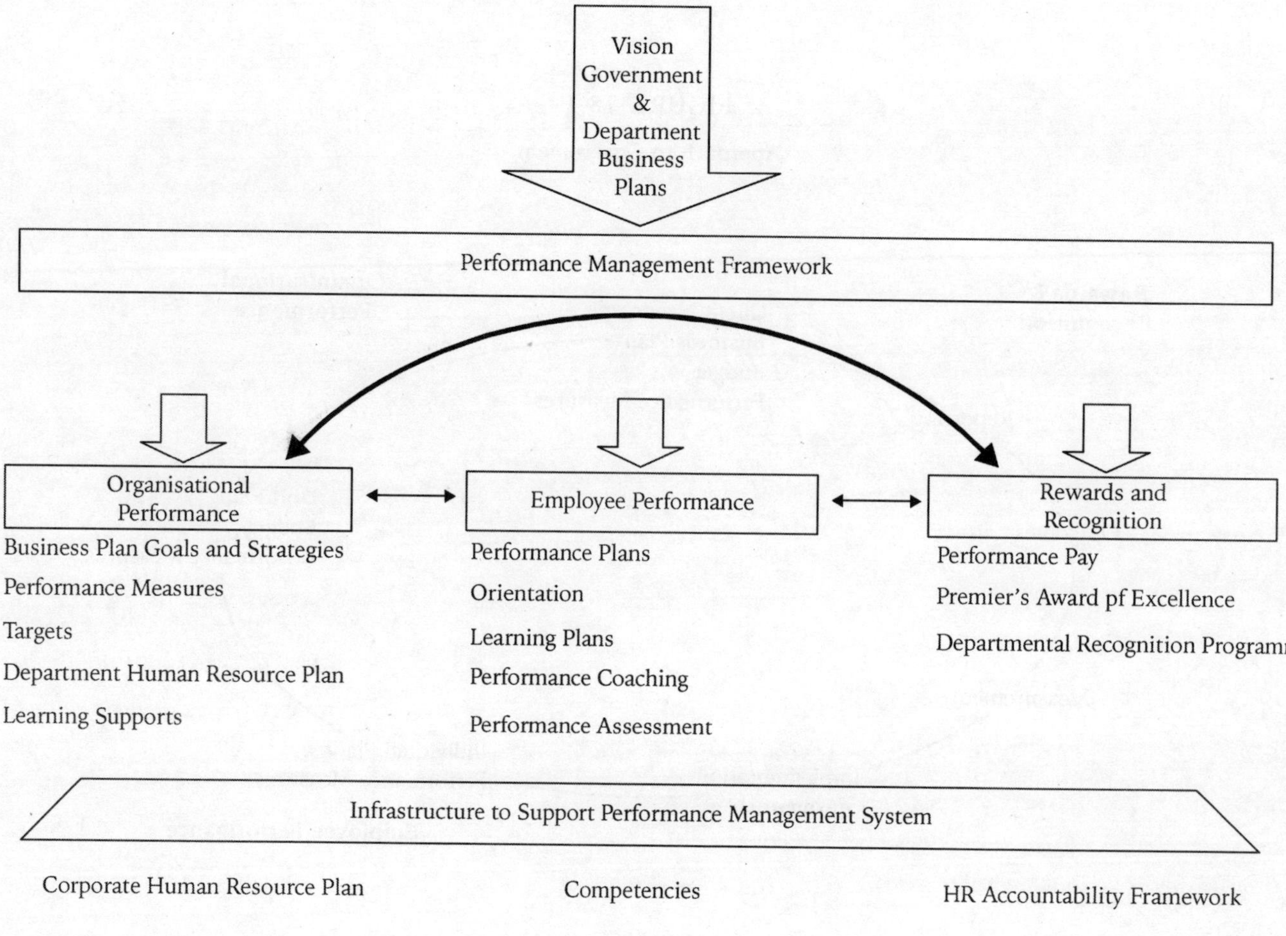

Concurrent Monitoring

Various governments with the help of appropriate agencies/institutions have successfully undertaken concurrent monitoring of the implementation of government programmes involving substantial fiscal outlay, in order to ensure effective implementation and ensuring of efficient achievement of the objectives. This is a mechanism to ensure good performance, through continuous evaluation and mid-term adjustments.

Feedback from Citizens

Correctives based on client feedback are essential for improved performance and increased efficiency and effectiveness. Effective systems for collating the citizen feedback on government performance and putting them to use are yet to be developed in the state. Regular as well as periodical interface with the citizenry will support the cause of improving efficiency in government services.

Performance and Reward

Several independent observers have made adverse comments on the poor performance orientation of civil services. Good performers are not rewarded, nor are bad performers punished in Kerala. The present system lacks objective measurement of performance of government employees. The reward system in the State government is allegedly designed for non-performance, status quo and risk avoidance. An appropriate reward system will be an effective motivational tool for good performers in government.

Way Forward

Time-tested methods to improve performance may be applied at the government level also to increase the efficiency of its actions. The state will have to focus on:

- Rational performance measurement system, benchmarking.
- Feedback from citizens.
- Redefining the functional roles of employees.
- Rationalisation and simplification of procedures.
- Modification of statutes.
- Effective utilisation of information technology.
- Reducing monotony of work.
- Improving the work environment.
- Rewards/Incentives for good performance.
- Delegation of powers and their effective exercise.
- Improving the quality of decision-making through appropriate management information system, and
- Training and retraining to enhance technical and software skills.

Grievance Redressal

Kerala has instituted formal systems of grievance redressal, like other states in the country have done. The Ahmednagar pattern of administrative reforms in district offices, the SPEED programme, the Mass Contact programme, *Adalats*, etc., are examples of initiatives in the state to speedy grievance redressal. The government also keeps on issuing instructions for timely settlement of public grievances.

The Kerala Environment

The Kerala society being highly literate and socially advanced, the awareness levels on the rights of citizens are very high. There also exist among the citizenry vague feelings of injustice and exaggerated notions of self-righteousness. Resultantly, governance in Kerala sounds near synonymous with grievance redressal and the time and effort spent on grievance redressal. Dishonesty in government and inefficiencies of governance too form major causes for public resentment and grievance.

Systems for Grievance Redressal

Human Rights Commission

As provided for in the Human Rights Act of 1993 enacted by the Indian Parliament, state level rules were framed in Kerala in 1998. The first Kerala State Human Rights Commission was constituted on 11th December 1998, for the protection of rights relating to life, liberty, equality and dignity of the individual, guaranteed by the constitution or embodied in the international covenants and enforceable by courts of law in the country.

The first five years of the commission succeeded to a certain extent in creating increased awareness of the protection of human rights. However, the impact has not been substantial, though there have been spurts of action. Many of the reports and recommendations of the commission are yet to be taken up seriously and the process of redressal has been slow, due to structural constraints in government as well as apathy of officials concerned.

Ombudsman for Local Self Governments

Ombudsman is a high-powered institution, consisting of a single member, vested with vast powers to check malfeasance in local self governments in the discharge of developmental functions. Instituted in May 2000, its activities include investigation and/or enquiry in respect of any action allegedly involving corruption or misadministration or irregularities in the discharge of administrative functions by Local Self Government Institutions or by employees or officials working under Local Self Government Institutions or by employees or officials working in offices or institutions transferred to Local Self Government Institution or by elected Members of the Local Self Government Institutions including their Presidents or Chairpersons and for the disposal of complaints relating to such actions in accordance with the provisions of the Kerala Panchayat Raj Act, 1994. Sittings of the Ombudsman (earlier they used to be held in Thiruvananthapuram only) are held in district headquarters.

The Ombudsman has issued important orders that have gone a long way in the grievance redressal process of the public and have had far-reaching significance in the Administration of local bodies. A significant provision in the system is that the cost of submission of a petition is as low as Rs. 10, a provision which makes it extremely citizen-friendly, especially in a period during which legal expenses are rapidly increasing.

Kerala Women's Commission

The Kerala Women's Commission has been constituted as a statutory organisation under state government, to improve the status of women in the state of Kerala and to inquire into unfair practices against women. The commission has three members and is headed by a Chairperson. It also undertakes promotional and educational research in order to suggest ways of ensuring due representation of women in all spheres, apart from conducting legal awareness programmes in different districts. It also runs a 'Short-Stay Home' for women. The commission provides counselling to couples who are willing to submit themselves for counselling. The commission also provides free legal service to clients who are below the poverty line.

The commission has been performing reasonably well in redressing grievances of women; petitions alleging criminal offences are sent to police stations for necessary action. In other cases summons are issued by the commission to the parties concerned to appear before it for hearing Serious allegations of unfair practices are enquired into by the Director of the Commission as envisaged under section 17(2) of the Act and appropriate further action taken. Nonetheless, the commission as an institution has not remained beyond reproach. Appointment of the Chairperson and other members of the commission has also become a political issue.

Lokayukta

The *Lokayukta* was set up in 1999 after cessation of the Kerala Public Men Corruption (Investigation and Inquiry) Commission. The *Lokayukta* has the power to conduct investigation into complaints against the Chief Minister, Ministers, MLAs, Government servants, Presidents, Vice-presidents or members of local self governments or Chairmen of statutory bodies including Corporations and cooperative societies. Besides, it may also inquire into complaints against Presidents, Secretaries, Treasurers or any other office-bearers of trade unions registered under the Indian Trade Unions Act 1926 and office-bearers of any political party.

The *Lokayukta* has wide powers, including the ordering for searches. It can direct police officers in the rank of Deputy Superintendent of Police to conduct searches or carry out inspections in any building and seize concealed property, documents, money, or other valuables. It can also award compensation if allegations are partially or wholly substantiated.

Once the *Lokayukta* is satisfied that the allegations levelled are wholly or partially sustainable, the findings, along with the recommendations and relevant documents, will be forwarded to the competent authority. The *Lokayukta* may also file interim reports recommending the granting of interim relief to complainants at the stage of preliminary verification or investigation, if it is felt that the complainant has suffered injustice or undue hardship as a consequence of the act mentioned in the complaint. The competent authority is under an obligation to intimate the action taken following the report of the *Lokayukta* within one month of the date of receipt of the interim report. The act also proposes a five year time bar from the date of action for filing complaints.

No complaint will be permitted to be withdrawn unless the *Lokayukta* is satisfied that the complaint was made under a bona fide mistake, or the grievance complained of has been adequately redressed. The complainants and public servants are free to engage lawyers for presenting their cases before the *Lokayukta*. With regard to false or maliciously made complaints, the rules allow the *Lokayukta* to accord sanction for prosecuting such complainants before a first class chief judicial magistrate court.

Sutarya Keralam

Sutarya Keralam is the latest initiative of the current government in the matter of grievance redressal. It envisages providing people an opportunity to put across their grievances directly to the attention of the Chief Minister. It is operated in association with *Akashvani* and *Doordarshan*; citizens may get in touch with the Chief Minister, on a weekly basis, for half an hour. The progress of actions on the grievances of the public is posted in the website of the state government. *Akshaya* centres are also envisaged as disseminators of information on progress of grievance redressal.

Administrative Reforms Committee (ARC) 1997

This high level committee appointed in 1997 had two predecessors, the first in 1958 and the second in 1965. The latest ARC had dealt with the question of grievances fairly exhaustively and its first report in a long series of fifteen publications was on *"Citizens Charter, Grievance Redressal, Transparency and Right to Information."* On the basis of its recommendation, the Kerala Legislative Assembly passed a bill for ensuring "Transparency and Right to Information."

The ARC 1997 gave several recommendations for grievance redressal and prepared a draft Citizens Charter for several government departments and public bodies that come into regular contact with the public. The Committee has discerned broadly two approaches on the part of the government in dealing with grievances: organising mass contact programmes and improvements in the internal mechanism for grievance redressal.

In order to focus reforms on the minimising of grievances, the committee has taken initiative to draft Citizens Charters for several departments and State Level Public Organisations such as Civil Supplies, Motor Vehicle Department, Water Authority, Electricity Board, KWA, KSEB, Municipalities and *Grama panchayats*. The committee had also endorsed the speedy decentralisation and democratisation of the administration by invigorating lower level elected bodies. The recommendations, though accepted in principle in 1998, remain mostly unimplemented. However, the new initiative under "Modernising Government Programme" (MGP) has been implementing most of these recommendations.

Accountability and Control of Malfeasance

Governmental accountability is an essential element of democracy; it is the duty of public officials to report their actions to citizens, and the right of the citizens to take action against officials whose conduct the citizens consider unsatisfactory. The issue of accountability in the state has been in the limelight after decentralisation, the local governments getting closer to the citizenry.

Governance at State Level: Kerala has a system of governance in tune with the Constitution of India. The Government functions through its legislative, executive and judicial set up. The Governor rules under advice from the Council of Ministers, headed by the Chief Minister and accountable to the Legislative Assembly (LA), elected by the people. The State Assembly has full legislative powers on all subjects under the purview of the State as per the Indian Constitution. The executive comprises 35 departments headed by Secretaries to the Government, the top layer of the state level bureaucracy positioned in the Government Secretariat, which is about 5000 strong. The High Court, which is the apex court in the state, along with the junior courts forms the judicial set up. The Auditor General's Office is responsible for the audit of accounts of the government departments/institutions/agencies.

Governance at Street level: A major part of governance is through primary level organisations, referred to as Street Level Public Organisations (SLPO), managed by the government directly or indirectly, and having direct contact with citizens, communities or organisations. The lower level governments are run by elected representatives of people and comprise *grama panchayats*, block *panchayats*, district *panchayats*, municipal councils and municipal corporations. The government has set eight statutory bodies as autonomous public enterprises in the areas of power, public transport, housing, water supply, warehousing, industrial infrastructure, industrial finance and village industries. There are about a hundred public enterprises, set up to serve specific public purposes, incorporated as public limited companies. Government managed/supervised bodies like Universities, Research Institutions, Commissions and others functioning as autonomous entities also exist.

System of Financial Accountability

The executive, legislative and judicial wings along with the auditor general form the total governing system at the state level. Accountability in terms of social and economic performance is sought to be ensured by the political right of the people to change the government or even the system of government, through the electoral process. Financial accountability is ensured by a closely knit system of budgeting, accounting, auditing and review as enshrined in the Constitution of India and developed over the past half a century of independence. The significant stages through which this system of accountability functions are shown in the following chart.

Annual Plan and Budget

The annual budget, prepared by the Finance Ministry of the State Government, based on the proposals put up by various government departments and within the constraints and parameters specified by the Central Government, is placed before the Legislative Assembly for deliberations and approval. The budget proposals of each department are subjected to detailed scrutiny by the Subject Committee of the legislature, presided over by the concerned Minister. The proposals are approved by the legislature based on the consensus recommendations of the Subject Committees after due deliberations. The annual budget of the Government for a year gets final approval on passing of the finance bill by the Legislature.

Audit

Accounts of all the field departments are prepared by the Chief Accounts and the Auditor General (C&AG)of the State under guidance from the Auditor General of India. Annual audit reports brought out by C&AG are

FIGURE 18.3

Legislative Assembly

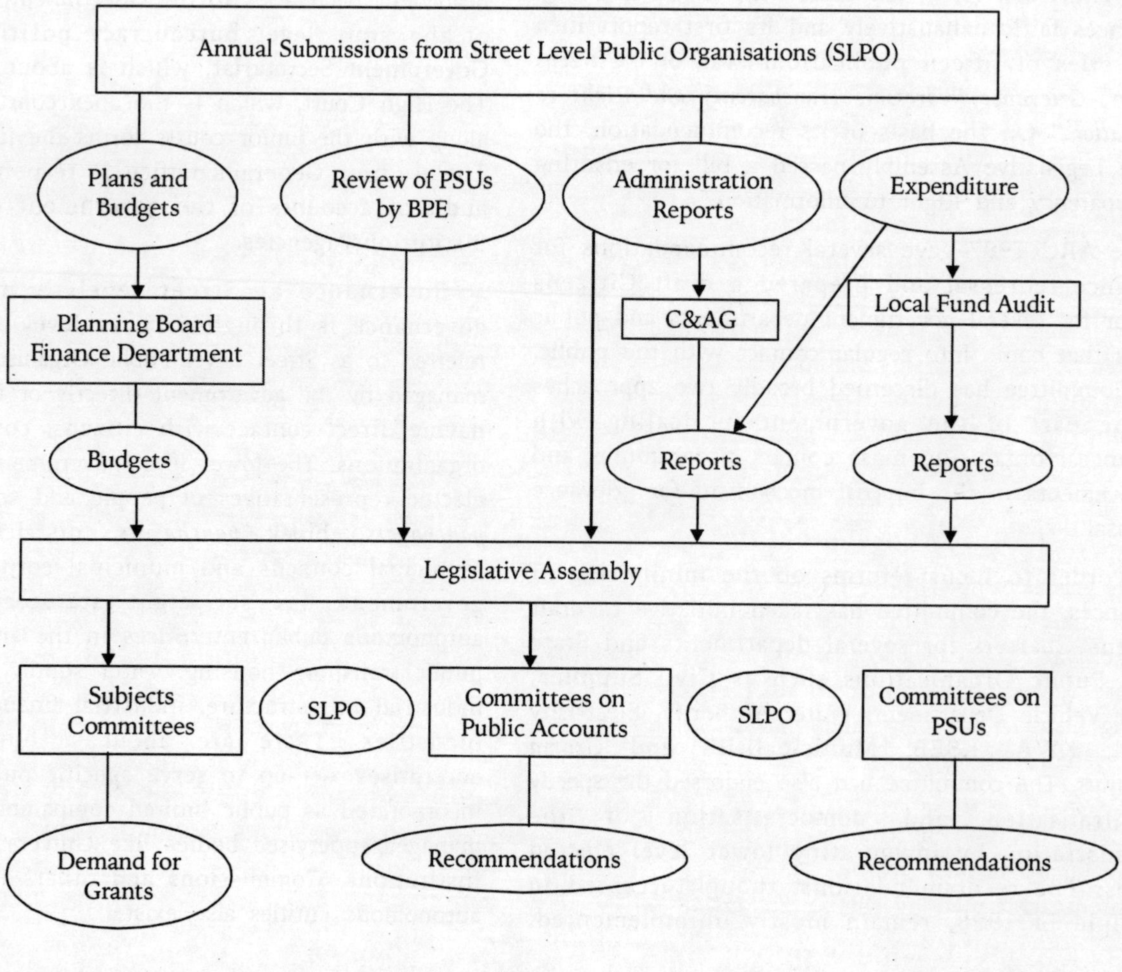

placed before the legislature and reviewed by its Committee on Public Accounts. Accounts of *Panchayats*, Municipalities, Corporations, and autonomous bodies like Universities are audited by the Department of Local Fund Audit and the summary of its major findings are placed as reports to the Legislatures; the Committee on Local Funds Audit of the Legislature reviews these findings and gives its recommendations. Accounts of Public Sector Enterprises are audited by Chartered Accountants in pursuance of the Companies Act and then subjected to concurrent audit by the Auditor General of India. Their reports and observations are reviewed by the Committee on Public Sector Undertakings for evolving policy corrections. The Bureau of Public Enterprises brings out an annual performance review of all public enterprises which is placed before the Legislative along with the budget documents.

Accountability Through Audit Agencies

Like in other states in India, the C & AG and the Local Fund Audit Department carry out audit of annual accounts and activities in government/government institutions in Kerala.

Audit Reports of C&AG

Annual reports of C&AG, submitted to the Governor of the State, with audit observations on matters arising from examination of Finance Accounts and Appropriation Accounts for the preceding year are also placed before the State Legislative. The audit observations are examined in detail by the Public Accounts Committee to recommend corrective actions by the Government. The C&AG takes up performance audit of individual departments and public undertakings every year, selected on a random basis and the audit findings are included in these annual reports. Reports containing the observations on statutory corporations, boards and government companies are placed before the Legislature Assembly separately as required by the law and relevant rules.

There has been a growing feeling that the enormous time and effort that go into preparation of such reports often go waste. The reports of the C&AG in recent years are replete with observations pointing towards declining financial propriety and financial accountability in the system of governance.

Local Fund Audit

The Local Fund Audit Department of the government (governed by the Kerala Local Funds Act 1994) is responsible for the audit of numerous organisations and local self governments. Inordinate delays in audit of accounts make it almost impossible to initiate corrective measures and punitive actions against the errants. The issue gets complicated by the delay in review of audit reports by the Committee of the Legislative formed for the purpose.

Accountability Through The Legislative Assembly

The Rules of Kerala Legislature provide for the Legislature to play a vital role in ensuring accountability in government. They provide for the constitution of committees of the elected members of the Legislative for specific purposes. These committees have the mandate to examine and review the activities and accounts of various government departments/ institutions /agencies. The important committees in charge of ensuring financial accountability include the Public Accounts Committee and the Public Undertakings Committee.

Committee on Public Accounts (PAC)

This eleven member committee whose members are selected from the non-minister members of the Legislature based on proportional representation, and headed by a senior representative of the major opposition party, is considered to be the most powerful committee of the Legislature. It is the watchdog of financial accountability in government/government institutions and any diversion of funds or misuse of funds for purposes other than that voted for by the Legislative is viewed seriously. The duties and responsibilities of the committee as detailed in article 242 of the Rules of Kerala Legislature include examining the accounts of the government and the audit reports of the C&AG/other auditors with a view to initiating corrective actions.

Delays are not uncommon in the functioning of the PAC. Excessive delays call into question the credibility of checks and balances, built into the system of democratic governance.

Public Undertakings Committee (PUC)

The PUC consists of 11 legislators selected for a two year term, beginning with the financial year. Its duties as defined in rules 247 and 248 of the Rules of Kerala Legislature enable it to examine whether the public undertakings listed in the fourth schedule as well as the companies in which the state government has a minimum stake of 51 per cent and the statutory

Corporations, function on sound commercial principles and in accordance with the laws of the land. As per rule 247 (d), the PUC could exercise the powers vested with the Estimates Committee and the Public Accounts Committee to the extent they relate to specific public undertakings.

Theoretically, PUC is the right mechanism for ensuring accountability, including financial accountability, of public undertakings and the mandate given to them through the above definitions sounds satisfactory. Nevertheless, most of the reports, brought out by PUC are on the pattern set by PAC and the focus of its attention has been on audit paragraphs and bureaucratic explanations with little attention given to vital questions of role clarity and organisational autonomy of public undertakings.

Reports of Committees of Kerala Legislative Assembly

Examination of the reports brought out by the numerous committees and placed before the Legislative Assembly reveal that their quality is, in general, poor. The reasons for the poor quality as summarised from discussions with the Speaker of the Kerala Legislative Assembly, a cross section of officials connected with the work of the Legislature (active as well as retired), members of SLA and Ministers (former as well as present) are presented in Box 18.19.

BOX 18.19

Financial Accountability: Role of State Legislative Assembly (SLA)

With regard to financial accountability in governance, the State Legislative Assembly (SLA) plays a crucial role. In theory and as provided in statutes, not even a Rupee should be spent by the government from the consolidated fund without the specific authorisation and approval by SLA. However, this constitutional commitment is honored more in form than in essence, despite the numerous checks and balances built into the system.

Performance and plans of each department or SLPO are considered and supposed to be debated in detail in the Subject Committees, before the requests for grants are conceded and placed before the full house for its consideration. Members of the Legislative Assembly have, apart from the benefit of direct feedback from citizens, the annual Administration Reports prepared by the various departments, audit reports from C & AG or Local Fund Audit Department and other review documents.

The reasons for the poor coverage and quality as well as the time lags in submission of reports were diagnosed as the following: (1) officials and employees were poorly equipped or trained in rendering professional help to the Legislature Committees compared to their counterparts in the Indian Parliament (2) members of SLA were not well informed about the obligations of the government to place Administration Reports before them and were not demanding on quality, content and timely delivery; (3) nurturing of own constituencies and activism in the open House being the first priorities, members of SLA are indifferent to the quality of collective work through committees.

Accountability Through Elected Local Bodies

Kerala has made significant progress in administrative and financial decentralisation since 1996. One-third of the Plan resources of the state, which are mostly borrowings, are earmarked for local governments at the three levels. The grant is practically untied and gives freedom to the local governments to plan and implement their development programmes. Apart from audit of annual accounts by the Local Fund Audit Department, the local bodies are also subjected to social audit and performance audit. A semi-structured social audit is conducted in *grama sabha* and ward *sabha*. Since the majority of the plan funds are devolved to local bodies, a special concurrent audit system has also been prescribed as a corrective mechanism to help local governments put their systems in order. The responsibilities of the performance audit authority are comprehensive and cover not only scrutiny of the financial statements of the local bodies but also functioning of *panchayat* offices including works undertaken, issues related to tax collection, resource mobilisation, debt position and timeliness of various reports including annual reports. Detailed procedure for performance audit has also been developed. However, experience does not vindicate the efforts made in developing exhaustive procedures for audit; accountability could not be ensured as envisaged, basically because performance of local bodies has remained lackadaisical.

Accountability Through Watchdogs

The audio-visual media, the social organisations, the public awareness organisations and the consumer organisations function as effective watchdogs in ensuring accountability in public life and in a government. Kerala being a highly literate society, readership/viewership of audio-visual media is very high. The state is ahead of the rest of the states in India in the number of printed periodicals, the number of copies printed and the per capita circulation of daily newspapers. Stiff competition prevails in the print media; investigating into official corruption or malfeasance is their most favoured pursuit, next only to perceptions on development.

The revelations in the media on impropriety of government actions and/or government employee actions are however short-lived. Social organisations, public awareness organisations and consumer organisations also wage lonely battles; they too have failed to create the expected impact.

Factors Promoting Accountability

Access to and Transparency of Information

Perhaps the most important factor ensuring accountability is the right of citizens to observe, understand and evaluate the conduct of public officials. Access to information deters official misconduct. According to James Madison, the fourth President of the USA, "A popular government without popular information or the means of acquiring it, is but a prologue to a farce or a tragedy or perhaps both." Accountability is assured only when the government, the political institutions and the community adequately recognise the relationship among democracy, accountability and access to information.

Transparency ensures "open government." There should be public access to government proceedings, government documents and information. Disclosure of financial dealings by government officials and civil servants in the executive, legislative and judicial branches of the government is another way to provide citizens information to judge the variety and appropriateness of official dealings. The provisions for open government may conflict with other values, especially those of personal privacy. Information policies of democratic societies should therefore be defined taking into consideration both the importance of access to government information and the protection of private, personal information. The state is yet to tap a major part of the enormous opportunities provided by information technology revolution in improving transparency of government actions and citizen's access to information. The Kerala Panchayati Raj Act of 1994 has a section on Right to Information. A bill on Transparency and Right to Information was passed by the State Legislature during the late 1990s. The state is currently in the process of instituting the necessary systems and structures for implementing the Central Act on Right to Information. Access to Information is expected to improve significantly in consequence.

Institutional and Individual Integrity

The laws and regulations of the land impose general procedural requirements on all the three agencies of democracy: the executive, the judiciary and the legislature. They are envisaged to ensure that the government actions are conducted in a fair and consistent manner and in the light of the public gaze. The key factor is that the activities of any government are carried out by individuals. Individual integrity thus has an important bearing on the performance of the government and its accountability.

Political Activities of Employees

Politics is strongly entwined with the psyche of the Kerala society and political activities of employees are very much a part of Government functioning. Employee organisations are often constrained to protect the interests of even erring employees. Political parties, Legislature and employee representatives often fail to exploit the immense potential of political activities to foster individual integrity, work ethics, honesty, dedication and commitment, all factors that affect accountability, among the employees.

Review of Performance

Performance review, both of the institutions and their employees, is yet another important factor to ensure accountability. Currently, all government departments/institutions/agencies are required to prepare annual administration reports to be made available for scrutiny. Administrative reports are found to lack reviews of the actual performance in terms of the utility of the actions to the public and their efficiency and effectiveness. Annual reports should provide the performance plans/goals to be achieved and evaluate the plans against actual results achieved. Similarly, performance appraisal reports of the employees do not actually reflect on accomplishments (work-related) of the employees concerned, either. Unless performance reports are viewed seriously and scrutinised effectively, it will be difficult to ensure accountability.

Nor does the state have a system of evaluating the various departments and the programmes they undertake. Such a system should be installed essentially to focus on delivery of services as well as programme outcomes and not merely on adherence to guidelines and procedures.

Skills, Work Ethics, Dedication and Commitment

Individual work skills as well as soft skills or behavioural aspects are important. A work force with dedication and commitment is critical to governance. Equally important is upgradation of work related skills of employees. The government has made serious efforts to address this issue through a training policy as part of the Modernising Government Programme to cover the entire government workforce; the potential for improving the work skills and soft skills of the workforce is considered high.

Public perception about the government is one of dishonesty of its employees in most of its activities. The potential of employee organisations to act as change agents is going waste. One of the effective ways to control malfeasance is to initiate internal cleaning by the work force themselves. The system of providing protection for "Whistle Blowers" in USA or "Bell Ringers" in Netherlands is worth exploring in the state.

Control of Malfeasance

Vigilance Setup in Kerala

The Vigilance and Anti Corruption Bureau, functioning as a separate department since 1964, is the main agency of the state to fight corruption. The Bureau is responsible for investigations/inquiries into allegations of malfeasance against government servants and public servants in public sector undertakings of the state government. It conducts vigilance enquiry, confidential verification and surprise checks with prior sanction of the government or as directed by it. This setup is headed by a senior IPS officer and has offices in all District headquarters and major departments and PSUs.

There are three special courts (Thiruvananthapuram, Kochi and Kozhikode) each headed by a Special Judge and Enquiry Commissioner to consider the cases and to file First Investigation Reports (FIRs). In addition, two Vigilance Tribunals function at Thiruvananthapuram and Kozhikode, set up according to the provisions of the Kerala Civil Services (Vigilance Tribunal) Act of 1960. They have been set up to enquire into complaints of malfeasance referred to them by the state government.

Conclusion

Most of the appropriate systems, procedures and institutions to ensure accountability and control of malfeasance in government are in place in Kerala. However, the effectiveness of these systems, procedures and institutions is often in doubt. The compounding effects of delays in initiation and completion of activities, delays in providing financial statements for audits, delays in audits, delays in review of audit observations and delays in corrective actions coupled with employee apathy have been defeating the efforts in ensuring government accountability and controlling malfeasance.

Accountability and efficiency in governance can hardly be improved by merely strengthening institutional mechanisms. The content and quality of work done by these institutional mechanisms in the executive, legislative and judicial set up needs significant improvement. In the absence of objective norms and standards, there have existed no dependable criteria for judging operational efficiency.

Active participation of the public is also essential. There is need for improved access to information, increased transparency in activities and alternate systems of review of performance. Mechanisms for continuous consultations with the public and other stake holders are indispensable for ensuring accountability and control of malfeasance in government. Strategic planning and evaluation of achievements/outcomes against the plans are also necessary. Performance audits and social audits at the local government level have to be improved. Effective mechanisms for identifying corrupt, inefficient officials of doubtful integrity, and initiating corrections, are to be developed; for this purpose, amendments to the concerned laws may be required. More efforts are required in the behavioural front also to take government employees into confidence.